THE GARDENER'S CATALOGUE 2

THE GARDENER'S CATALOGUE 2

THE GARDENER'S CATALOGUE 2

A
Complete Compendium
for
Indoor, Outdoor,
Hydroponic and
Greenhouse Gardeners

QUILL · New York · 1983

THE GARDENER'S CATALOGUE 2

The Gardener's Catalogue People

The Gardener's Catalogue 2 was produced under the editorship of Eunice Riedel and was designed by Blackbirch Graphics but owes its existence to the contributions of many people. We owe special thanks to writers Sara Pyle, whose dedication to the earth and its conservation kept us on the right ecological track; Mai Browne, for her generous and skilled aid, unfaltering perseverence, and wry humor; and Mark Smith, whose enthusiasm never waned and whose perspective gave added depth to the contents. Thanks also to our other writers—David Granger, Laurie Kalb, Bobbie Geary, and Leon Falk. We are also indebted to Marta Hallett, who greatly improved the clarity, readability, and accuracy of the manuscript; to Ande Dorman, our proofreader; to Edith Barry, who labored valiantly over the illustrations; to Nancy Paule, who filled in on so many jobs; to Jennifer Worden, for editorial assistance; and to John Patterson, whose unflappable style and good humor saw us through the hectic deadlines. Finally, all of us who have worked on this book owe a special debt of gratitude to Naomi Black, whose administrative skills kept us together, organized, and sustained.

Illustrations on pages 252–254 from the Christian Brothers Collection at the Wine Museum of San Francisco

Library of Congress Catalog Card Number:
ISBN 0-688-01238-8 (pbk.)

Printed in the United States of America

1 2 3 4 5 6 7 8 9 10

Design by Blackbirch Graphics, Bethlehem, Connecticut

Contents

Words to Know

air-layering A method of propagation, especially useful for plants with woody stems, whereby a cut is made in the stem, wrapped with moist moss, and enclosed in a moisture-proof piece of plastic until a rootball forms several months later. The new plant is severed just below the rootball and planted.

air plant Synonym for *epiphyte*.

annual Plant that must be resown every year.

anthracnose A fungus disease characterized by numerous reddish-brown circular spots on fruit and leaves of affected plants.

Bacillus thuringiensis (BT) A microbe disease available commercially for use to control insect pests.

bacterial blight A disease especially affecting legumes.

bacterial wilt A disease characterized by slow wilting of plants.

biennial Plant requiring two growing seasons to grow from seed to maturity, e.g., parsnip.

biological control A method of pest control based on maintaining a natural balance of forces in the garden, e.g., introducing ladybugs to eat harmful insects.

blackleg A fungus disease affecting cole crops.

black rot Bacterial or fungus disease characterized by blackened veins, stems, and/or leaves on plants.

blossom-end rot A disease caused by a lack of calcium and worsened by uneven soil moisture. It is characterized by large, dark, sunken spots at the blossom end of fruit.

blue mold A fungus disease limited to the Southeast and to south-central states; attacks spinach.

bonsai The technique of growing miniature trees in containers.

broadcast To scatter fertilizer or seeds evenly over a wide area.

broadleaf evergreen An evergreen group including rhododendron, palm, and laurel.

carbaryl A widely used insecticide, commonly marketed as Sevin, known to be toxic to bees and under study for toxic effects on animals and humans.

catch crop A cover crop sown specifically to absorb and store soil nutrients and reenrich the earth when plowed under.

chlorosis The yellowing of plant leaves because the soil contains too little available iron.

cloche A clear plastic "tent" to protect individual plants from harsh weather.

coldframe A small plant-growing structure, usually a sash-covered pit, frame, or box, placed directly on the ground and used to advance or extend the growing season of otherwise tender plants. It is good for rooting cuttings, hardening off transplants, and growing late-season flowers and vegetables.

cole crops Closely related vegetables in the brassica family, including cabbage, cauliflower, Brussels sprouts, broccoli, and kohlrabi; the cabbage family.

companion crop A particular crop grown near or within a row of another plant to discourage harmful insects, as when garlic is scattered among lettuce to deter aphids.

compost A nutrient-rich mixture of soil and decayed organic matter produced artificially by layering organic material, soil, manure or fertilizer and allowing it to decompose.

conifer Tree group characterized by needlelike or scale-like leaves. Most conifers are evergreen.

corm The swollen underground stem of a plant with a basal plate from which the roots grow.

cover crop A temporary crop such as winter rye or clover planted to protect ground from damage by winter winds and from spring rains that would carry off valuable topsoil. Cover crops are usually turned over to enrich the soil.

cultivar Synonym for *variety*.

crop rotation The practice of switching the location of crops in order to prevent injury from soil-borne diseases and the depletion of certain nutrients.

crown Where roots and stem join.

crown rot A fungus disease affecting houseplants, activated by overwatering or poorly drained soil.

cucurbit Vegetable crops identified by their prostrate, sprawling vines, including cucumbers, melons, squash, gourds, pumpkins.

cultivate The process of stirring the soil surface to increase soil aeration and water absorption and to prevent weeds.

damping off The most common soil-fungus disease, it attacks germinating seeds and seedlings; prevented by using a sterile growing medium and treating seeds with a fungicide.

dieback A dying back of the cane or shoot from the tip; caused by damage from frost or incorrect pruning.

disbudding Pinching off a bud.

division A method of propagation whereby plants that make clumps or multiple crowns are cut or pulled apart so that new sections have a bit of crown and some root.

drip irrigation Watering technique involving the use of plastic pipe or hose laid very near a row of plants that provides a continuous supply of moisture to the roots of crops, delivering the water to where it is of greatest use.

double digging Intensive-gardening technique according to which seed beds are cultivated to a depth of 13 to 18 inches.

early blight A fungus disease, prevalent in warm, moist regions, characterized by small irregular brown spots on leaves that expand into large spots with concentric rings; affected stems develop brown cankers at the soil line.

epiphyte A plant that grows nonparasitically on another plant, such as many bromeliads, ferns, and orchids.

exposure 1. The direction of the sun relative to plants. 2. The amount of natural light reaching plants.

flat Shallow container used for starting seeds.

foliar feeding A method of fertilizing house and garden plants by spraying their leaves with water-soluble plant food.

forcing Bringing plants, such as bulbs, to maturity out of their natural season.

fusarium wilt A fungus disease causing gradual yellowing and wilting of some crops, especially peas and tomatoes.

green manure A crop grown for the purpose of being plowed under to add specific nutrients to the soil, e.g., annual rye, sweet clover, vetch.

harden off To expose plants that have been started indoors to gradually more difficult conditions, usually in a coldframe opened for increasing periods each day.

hardpan A layer of dense, cementlike soil that prevents drainage and does not permit root penetration.

hardy Description of plants that can survive the cold temperatures of a particular region.

heel-in A method of storing a plant awaiting permanent planting by covering its roots with soil after setting it in a shallow trench.

herbicide Weedkiller.

hilling A growing method whereby soil is drawn up in a mound around the bottom of the plant vine as it grows.

hotbed A heated coldframe; a hotframe.

hot cap A plastic cover to protect individual plants from harsh weather.

hotframe A heated coldframe. Heat is provided by thermostatically controlled electric wires or naturally by setting the hotframe upon a pit of decomposing manure.

humus The dark, fibrous decayed vegetable matter that gives topsoil its spongelike quality of soaking up and storing nutrients and moisture.

hybrid A cross between two species.

hydroponics The practice of growing plants without soil, usually by employing an inert medium, such as perlite, for physical support and irrigating with a chemically balanced nutrient solution.

incurved Description of blossoms with close, regular petals that curve toward the center of the flower.

incurving Description of blossoms with loose, irregular petals that curve toward the center of the flower.

intercropping The practice of planting a fast-growing crop between or within rows of a slower-growing crop in order to make the most of available space.

interplanting Synonym for *intercropping*.

intensive gardening Technique of planting crops in broad raised beds prepared with generous amounts of organic and other nutrient materials so that plants can be spaced more closely than in row planting.

inorganic fertilizer Plant food derived from chemical or mineral sources.

late blight A fungus disease that may appear in cool, moist weather, it is characterized by water-soaked spots on leaves and fruit.

leaching The loss of nutrients from soil because of water draining through the ground.

leaf blight A fungus disease affecting carrots.

leafmold A crumbly, brown humus consisting of decayed leaves.

leaf spot A fungus disease on leaves, beginning as small spots with light centers and dark edges.

legumes Plants in the family *Leguminosae* that have the capacity to fix nitrogen in the soil. Legumes include peas, clover, beans, and vetch.

lethal yellowing A mycoplasmic disease attacking palm trees.

malathion A chemical insecticide for general use not to be applied within a week of harvest.

methoxychlor A chemical insecticide for general use not to be applied within two weeks of harvest.

mosaic viruses A group of diseases producing mottled, curled leaves, reduced yields, and stunted plants; e.g., tobacco mosaic.

midew A plant disease that appears as powdery white areas on the upper or lower surfaces of leaves.

mulch A soil covering of organic matter, plastic, or other material applied with the intention of controlling weeds, regulating soil temperature, conserving moisture, and reducing soil disease; organic mulches also decompose to enrich and/or condition the soil beneath.

nematodes Ectoparasitic organisms that feed on the outside surfaces of plant roots; chiefly a problem in southern gardens.

nitrogen fixation The conversion of free nitrogen to combined forms available as soil nutrients to plants, usually by planting legume crops and introducing an earthworm population.

offset A growth at the base of a mature plant that develops into a new crown. Offsets, or suckers, can be severed and rooted; however, they are often pinched because they sap energy from the parent plant.

organic fertilizer A plant food derived from plant or animal substances, such as manure, cottonseed meal, and compost, or from naturally occurring mineral sources, such as limestone.

organic gardening The production of crops without the use of inorganic fertilizers, herbicides, or pesticides.

organic matter The decomposed plant or animal residues in soil.

peat moss Partially carbonized and decomposed vegetable matter derived from bogs or marshes.

perlite Exploded white volcanic rock used as a soil amendment or, in hydroponics, as a neutral growth medium.

perennial Plant that comes up every spring for several seasons without replanting.

petiole Leaf stem.

pH A measurement of the relative alkalinity or acidity of a substance on a scale ranging from 0 (acid) to 14 (alkaline). Soil with a pH of 7.0 is considered neutral.

pinching Removing the growing point of a plant to prevent elongation and encourage extra bushiness.

pruning A plant-grooming method designed to improve the vigor and appearance of plants. It varies from pinching new growth to drastic cutting back of foliage.

pyrethrum A relatively safe organic insecticide spray effective against most fruit and vegetable pests.

raised beds Planting beds of soil worked to a depth of 20 to 24 inches, raised 4 to 5 inches above the ground, and bordered with walkways. Raised beds are fundamental to intensive gardening.

reflexed Description of petals that curve away from the center of the flower.

rhizoctonia disease A fungus disease affecting cole crops.

rhizome Similar to a tuber but more horizontal in shape, it has a tendency to sprout new shoots some distance from the parent plant (e.g., the bearded iris).

root tubers Tubers with no eyes and only a bud at the apex (e.g., dahlia tubers).

rot (root and stem) A fungus or bacterial disease.

rotenone An organic insecticide spray made of ground derris roots that discourages and controls most chewing and sucking insects.

rust A fungus disease characterized by red to black pustules on foliage and stems.

sash The transparent or translucent covering(s) of a hotframe or coldframe.

scale 1. A fungus of tubers that lives on in soil. 2. A sucking pest frequently found on houseplants such as ferns and container-grown citrus plants.

set Small dry plants, usually onions, grown the year before so they can be planted in spring.

sidedressing A method of fertilizing whereby a light application of organic or chemical fertilizer is spread along one or both sides of a row of crops.

smut A soil-dwelling fungus affecting sweet corn.

soilless culture Growing plants in an inert, nonorganic medium, as in hydroponics, and nourishing them with a chemical solution.

specimen plant A plant, unique in form, color, texture, or a combination of these elements, that can be used singly as a dramatic unit in itself or can be used as the focal point of an indoor grouping or an outdoor composition.

sphagnum A moss genus indigenous to moist, humid regions; sphagnum is used as a soil amendment in potting mixtures.

standard A plant trained to grow so that it resembles a small tree.

subsoil Tightly compacted, pale-colored layers of soil beneath the organically rich topsoil that are unsuited to growing plants.

succulent A plant, such as cactus, that stores water in its leaves, stem, or understock to carry it through periods of drought, which it would suffer in the wild.

sucker Synonym for *offset.*

systemic An insecticide to apply to the soil for absorption into the internal system of plants.

tender Description of plants that cannot survive the cold temperatures of a specific region. Tender vegetables must be planted in thoroughly warm soil.

terminal bud The end bud of a shoot that produces a hormone that keeps lateral buds from growing.

thinning The process of removing certain seedlings from an overcrowded row to provide sufficient room for remaining plants to grow.

top dressing A method of fertilizing whereby the upper two inches of soil in a pot is removed and replaced with an enriched soil mixture.

topsoil The upper layer of soil, usually containing enough humus and mineral material to support plant life.

transplanting Shifting of a plant from one soil or culture medium to another.

true leaves Leaves that develop on plants after the initial seedling leaves.

tuber A kind of swollen underground stem that can grow into a new plant.

vermiculite A growing medium consisting of water-absorbent micaceous flakes; excellent for seed-starting and to improving drainage in potting soil.

verticillium wilt A fungus disease.

1
Living With Plants

How to Use This Book

Anyone can have a garden.

What counts is not the amount of space you have—or even whether you own outdoor property—but proper planning.

To have a successful and beautiful garden, whether it is a miniature landscape in a saucer or complex plantings stretching over several acres, you need to know which plants to choose. You need to know what plants are available and what their growing requirements are. You need to know where to buy them.

But most of all, you need to analyze yourself and your lifestyle. How much time, money, and energy do you want to expend? Do you want carefree plants or do you enjoy fussing over delicate varieties? Do you want plants for decorative purposes, or to save your heating bills, or both? Do you want to grow vegetables because home-grown taste better or to cultivate orchids just for kicks? Until you are clear in your own mind about what you want, you cannot be a happy gardener.

We hope this book will help you to know what you want and will give you the information to make the garden of your dreams a reality.

During this century, revolutions in architecture and lifestyle have drastically altered our attitude toward plants.

Our homes, previously conceived as boxes to barricade us against the elements, and crammed with tiny rooms and dark hallways, are today open in plan. Interiors are spacious, with few or no walls and partitions. This allows for flexibility—the family can rearrange the interior to suit changing needs and interests.

Yet in an open plan temporary solutions must be devised for creating niches for privacy and for segregating quiet enclaves from busy traffic lanes and activity areas. Nothing seems quite so appropriate for such temporary barriers as plantts. Plants not only are flexible—capable of being shifted about as new needs arise—but are often the loveliest and cheapest solutions.

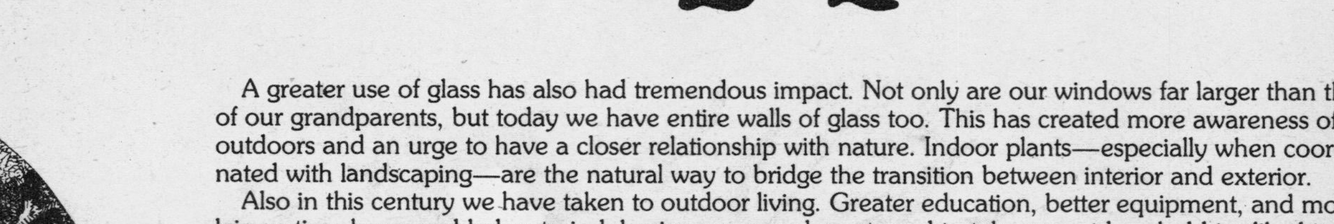

A greater use of glass has also had tremendous impact. Not only are our windows far larger than those of our grandparents, but today we have entire walls of glass too. This has created more awareness of the outdoors and an urge to have a closer relationship with nature. Indoor plants—especially when coordinated with landscaping—are the natural way to bridge the transition between interior and exterior.

Also in this century we have taken to outdoor living. Greater education, better equipment, and more leisure time have enabled us to indulge in year-round sports and to take up outdoor hobbies like bird-watching and wildflower identification. The family living area in the nineteenth century was largely restricted to the interior of the home and perhaps to a small porch. Only the wealthy, with extensive grounds on which to plant picnic lawns or construct teahouses, played outdoors. Today, convivial sitting terraces and barbecue pits are commonplace on even the smallest lots. Outdoor living areas in urban and suburban districts with limited land have heightened people's interest in plantings for creating a beautiful setting as well as for practical purposes such as screening for privacy and against sun, wind, noise, dust, and other annoyances.

All of these factors have combined to make us more knowledgeable about plants, more expert at exploiting their advantages, and more appreciative of their beauty. Though more than a third of the North American population gardens as a hobby, millions more cannot escape being gardeners to some degree, even if their interest is sometimes limited to finding plants requiring the least care for their indoor and outdoor needs.

To help you orient yourself in this vast new world of new plants, new plant uses, and new attitudes toward plants, in this section, "Living With Plants," we will discuss the general characteristics and features of plants, and how you can use them indoors or outdoors.

Sections 2 through 4 describe indoor plants and their care, including gardening under lights and specialties such as terrariums.

Due to the introduction of fluorescent light, container gardening, and many new hybrids adaptable to a wide range of conditions, many plants today are equally suitable for culture in the home or in the garden. Such plants vary from common begonias to exotic orchids and ferns to vegetables. These plants and their care, special cultivation techniques for greenhouses and soilless gardening, and a host of tips on how to propagate your plants and deal with problems such as insect pests are covered in Sections 5 through 8.

For outdoor gardeners, Sections 9 through 11 cover all aspects of flower gardening, lawn care, trees, shrubs, growing fruits and vegetables, and all the know-how you need on soil, fertilizer, and irrigation. Section 12 tells you how to landscape your grounds, and Section 13 details the types of specialty gardens you can design.

Finally, "The Gardener's World," Section 14, helps you bring the larger world into your home and garden. It describes ways to encourage animals and birds to visit your garden, details sources of information and aid, means for further study, and places to buy what you need.

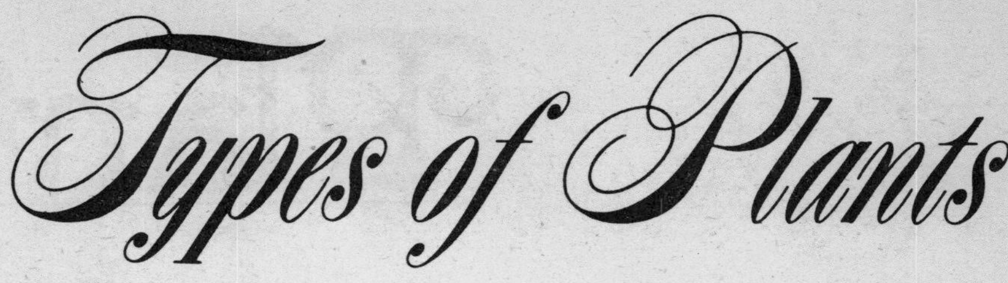

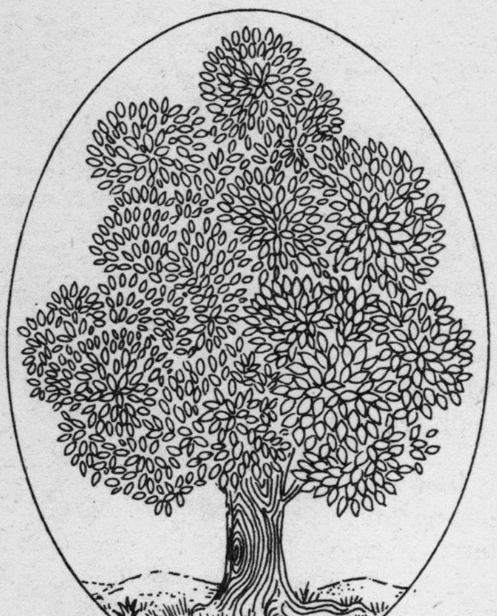

To distinguish basic plant types you need to know only three definitions:

1. *Deciduous*—from a Latin root meaning "to fall off"—refers to plants that drop their leaves in winter. With trees and large shrubs, this can be an advantage for homeowners in northern climates. Deciduous plantings provide shade in summer and then conveniently drop their leaves in colder weather to allow the sun to warm the house. When you are using plants for decorative effects either indoors or outdoors, however, a deciduous quality is not desirable. Indoors, you need a place to store unsightly plants during their dormant periods. Outdoors, a landscaping theme based totally on deciduous species will probably be unattractive in winter. Though a few trees have especially nice winter silhouettes, most shrubs do not, and landscape plans should include attention to year-round attractiveness by incorporating evergreens.

2. *Conifers*—are plants with needlelike or scalelike leaves and are usually evergreen (though a few exceptions, such as larch, are deciduous). Although conifers also drop their leaves, they do not do so all at once. The leaves are replaced gradually in cycles that may extend from two to ten years, so that the tree or shrub always looks green.

3. *Broad-leaf evergreens*—are plants that replace their leaves gradually the way conifers do and are therefore also always green. Unlike conifers, however, the leaves are not spiny but may be fleshy, glossy, or resembling those of deciduous plants. Most broad-leaf evergreens are tropical, and these are therefore the plants most popular for indoor culture. Species such as palms, magnolias, bougainvillea can be used outdoors in the South. Some, eucalyptus is an example, survive well in areas such as the West Coast where the ocean provides moderating temperatures. For cold climates the selection is more limited—holly, laurel, and a few others. Nevertheless, interest in landscaping for year-round attractiveness has created a demand for broad-leaf evergreens in northern climates, and research continues to produce hybrids with vastly expanded ranges.

WEEPING BEECH IN WINTER.

TREES

ROUND—GLOBE—SHAPED
Arnold Crabapple • Japanese Maple
Mulberry • Green Ash • Pistachio
Hawthorne Sycamore

FAN SHAPED—HORIZONTAL BRANCHING
Flowering Dogwood
Silk Tree • Redbud
Amur Maple

CONICAL TREE OR TRIANGLE
American Sweetgum
Pin Oak

Plant Form

The shape of a plant is a major consideration in your choice for either indoor or outdoor use. Though plants grow in many forms, in general they take the following four basic shapes:

1. *Vertical.* The most exaggerated forms of upright growth are found in columnar cacti (like the stately saguaro, some poplars, and cypress) that rise erect without side branches. Some cedars and conifers are also very erect, though in many cases the branches give them a pyramidal rather than ramrod-straight form. This is also true of American sweetgum. Sansevieria is a table-size plant with a vertical thrust. Some plants with small, thick, fleshy leaves—such as *Ficus nitidia*—if pruned of lower branches, can also give a fairly columnar impression.

Vertical plants convey a restless feeling and are good choices when you want drama and excitement. They provide height and accent for plant groupings. Used singly, a rigidly upright plant placed in a corner indoors or at a corner outdoors can soften a harsh architectural line.

2. *Rounded.* Again, cacti (such as the barrel cactus) are the most exaggerated form, but in fact most plants fall into this category. Plants such as begonias and African violets, many ferns, and some ivies that crowd close to the ground, give a decidedly globular effect. But most plants from succulents to Crotons to Aglaonema grow in more or less rounded shapes. Among trees, this form is found in some maples and cedars, and among shrubs, in aptly named snowballs.

These plants are not only the most numerous but have the most versatile uses. Used singly, they can make charming desk or table accessories indoors or fine single specimens in gardens and on lawns. In group plantings, they add mass. Their unobtrusive shapes also make them ideal for borders outdoors and for basic plant material indoors.

The only danger in rounded plants is that because they are most prevalent you may be tempted to choose all your plants of this form. The effect can be dull unless you introduce some accent of other shapes.

3. *Horizontal.* Plants with branches that spread laterally also have a dramatic element, but these are the most restful and serene forms. Dogwoods, for instance, bring forests and skyscrapers down to human size in rural and urban settings. Hawthorns, pin oaks, and other trees that branch horizontally are effective for landscaping low-lying modern homes. These spreading shapes are also good in grasslands and other environments without much upright growth, as they repeat the line of the horizon. Indoors, the low-lying spreading effect can be achieved with bromeliads, kentia palms, and some ferns.

4. *Drooping.* These are wonderful plants to use as intermediaries between other plant shapes. Their soft and subtle lines can be used in front of stiff, vertical plants to temper a transition to low-growing, rounded species. A weeping willow, for intance, can draw attention down from tall conifers to shrubs, or even be used to point to a garden accent such as a fountain. Any trailing plant such as the espiscias and many ferns can edge down large plant masses both indoors and outdoors. And all weeping and trailing plants can be used to soften hard edges in furnishings or architecture.

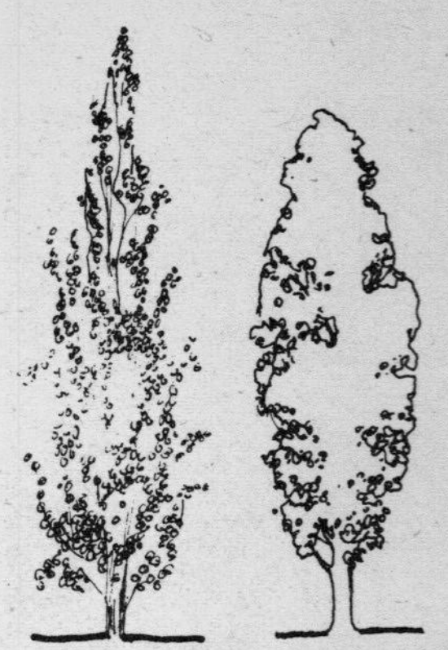

FASTIGIATE TREE OR COLUMNAR TREE
Dawyck Beech • Siberian Crabapple
English Oak • Poplar • Sargent Cherry
Sentry Ginkgo • Lombardy Poplar
Pyramidal European Birch
Linden

BROAD OVAL TREE
Bradford Pear
Sugar Maple • Labarnum
European Mountain Ash

SHRUBS

LOW 1½′–5′
February Daphne • Bush Cinquefoil
Anthony Waterer Spirea
Japanese Barberry

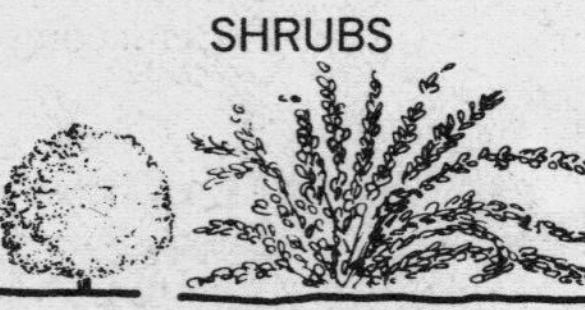

MEDIUM 5′–12′
Snowball • Forsythia • English Privet

TALL 12′–18′
Crapemyrtle • Spindle Tree
Russian Olive • Lilac

LOW, GROUND COVER OR VINES

Prostrate Pyracantha

Lantana

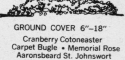

GROUND COVER 6″–18″
Cranberry Cotoneaster
Carpet Bugle • Memorial Rose
Aaronsbeard St. Johnswort

VINES
Wisteria • Passionflower • Bittersweet
Virginia Creeper • Clematis • Grapes

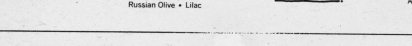

CONIFERS

BROADLEAF EVERGREENS

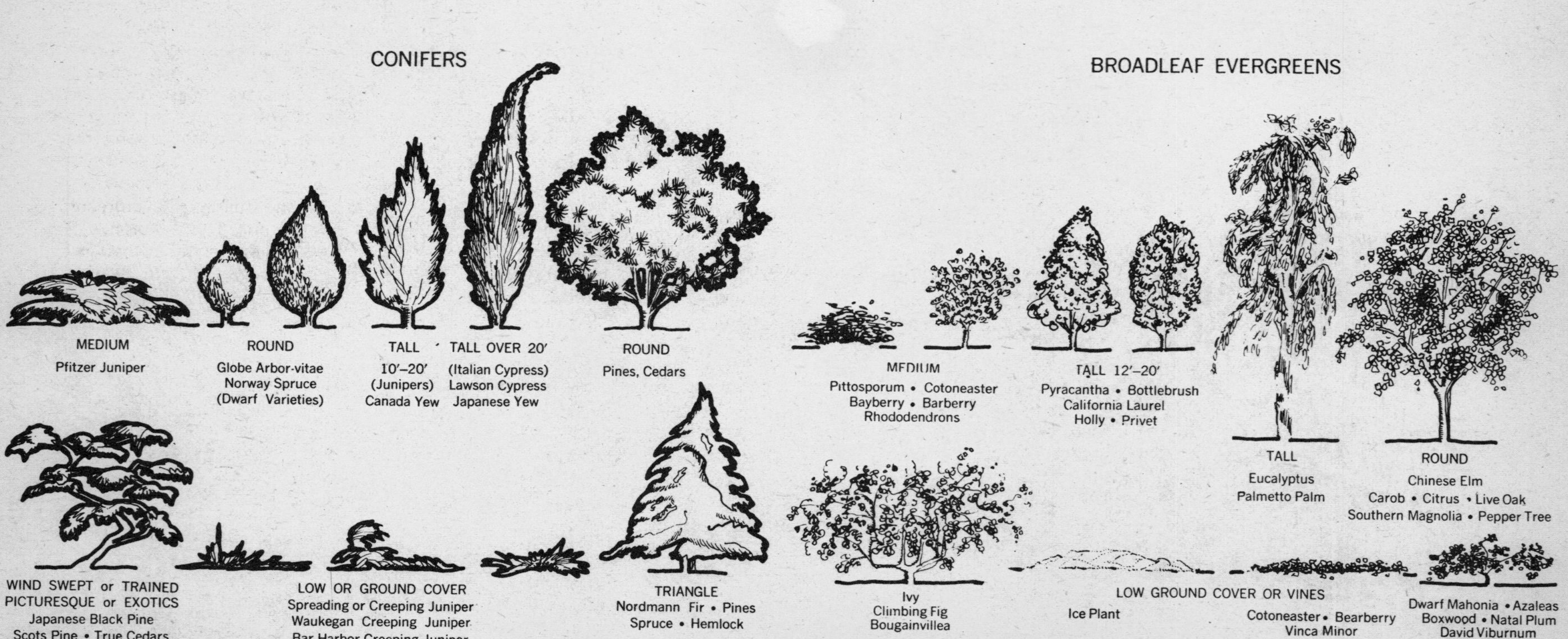

MEDIUM
Pfitzer Juniper

ROUND
Globe Arbor-vitae
Norway Spruce
(Dwarf Varieties)

TALL
10′–20′
(Junipers)
Canada Yew

TALL OVER 20′
(Italian Cypress)
Lawson Cypress
Japanese Yew

ROUND
Pines, Cedars

WIND SWEPT or TRAINED
PICTURESQUE or EXOTICS
Japanese Black Pine
Scots Pine • True Cedars
Eastern White Pine

LOW OR GROUND COVER
Spreading or Creeping Juniper
Waukegan Creeping Juniper
Bar Harbor Creeping Juniper

TRIANGLE
Nordmann Fir • Pines
Spruce • Hemlock

MEDIUM
Pittosporum • Cotoneaster
Bayberry • Barberry
Rhododendrons

TALL 12′–20′
Pyracantha • Bottlebrush
California Laurel
Holly • Privet

TALL
Eucalyptus
Palmetto Palm

ROUND
Chinese Elm
Carob • Citrus • Live Oak
Southern Magnolia • Pepper Tree

Ivy
Climbing Fig
Bougainvillea

LOW GROUND COVER OR VINES
Ice Plant

Cotoneaster • Bearberry
Vinca Minor

Dwarf Mahonia • Azaleas
Boxwood • Natal Plum
David Viburnum

Plant Height

All plants tend to grow more quickly in youth and to slow down in maturity. And the growth of any particular plant is influenced by the light and other environmental conditions you provide. Despite all this, some plants do grow faster and taller than others.

In general, pot-bound plants grow less slowly than those planted in a garden, and plants with runners or other root offshoots grow more quickly than those with single stems.

In many cases, the growth rate and height at maturity will be unimportant to you. You may not care about the size of your plants, or you may be willing to keep it within bounds by pinching back new growth or by pruning or even by drastically cutting it back.

But if you are buying a plant for a specific decorative purpose, and you want one of a particular height or shape, then you should look for a slow-grower. This will insure that the plant retains the characteristics you want for the longest possible time.

If you are planting seed, taking cuttings, or buying a young plant, you may prefer a species that has a fast growth habit so that you will be rewarded with a decent-height specimen before your patience frays.

Growth rates are usually not as important to indoor gardeners, because pot-binding and other conditions and care seldom allow plants to get out of bounds. But outdoor gardeners are frequently faced with the problem of a plant growing so rampantly as to become a garden nuisance. In general these are the ground hugging plants like violets, as well as the vines, but mints and many large bushy plants often spread sideways as well as grow taller than you've planned. It's good to learn in advance the problem plants of your area, so as to avoid them or to be alert to their dangers before they get out of hand.

Knowing the growth rate and the size of mature plants is especially vital in landscaping. Failure to consider the mature height of a small tree can result in planting it too close to the house or even in choosing the wrong species. A little evergreen planted in front of a window can shoot up to block the light and air from the interior of your home. Shrubs that grow too quickly to a mature height can ruin the scale of your landscape scheme while waiting for the slow growers to catch up. And if you have not considered the mature height of all your landscape plantings, your design can be totally out of scale within a few years. More specifics on landscaping problems are given in the landscaping section later in this book.

And for both indoor and outdoor gardeners, the mature height of plants is specified in subsequent sections on plant descriptions.

The largest indoor plants are treelike forms that range from three feet up to six or even eight feet. Some of these are plants that grow larger outdoors, but containing their roots inhibits their growth. Among these are most of the palms that can be cultivated indoors, schefflera, *Dracaena marginata* and *D. massangeana*, tree fern, tree cactus, false aralia, Norfolk Island pine, yucca, ming tree, several ficus (*F. benjamina, F. elastica, F. lyrata,* and *F. nitida*), and several philodendrons, such as saddle-leaf and split-leaf.

Most other indoor plants grow between one and three feet in height.

For plants under a foot high, you have ample choice among many cacti and succulents; the bromeliads, whose leaves tend to grow laterally rather than upright; a number of ferns such as the maidenhair and bird's nest; aphelandra, maranta, fittonia, pilea, tillandsia, georganthus, peperomia, gynura, rhoeo, plus several compact flowers such as African violets, geraniums, and begonias. Many vines or vinelike plants, such as zebrina, *Philodendron oxycardium,* tradescantia, hedera, syngonium, and others have long stems that trail but remain low in form.

Among outdoor plants, the large trees (over 35 feet) include most maples, oaks, lindens, the tulip tree, the London plane tree, eucalyptus, ginkgos, and the Pacific dogwood and *Magnolia heptapeta.*

Most magnolias and the flowering dogwood, however, are smaller. Most pines, most palms, most cedars, the Japanese maples, the fringe tree, hawthorns, silk tree, the serviceberries, and all the fruit trees are small or medium sized. Many of these, especially the fruit trees, evergreens, and those prized for decorative flowering qualities rather than for fruit, are also available in dwarf-size ranges.

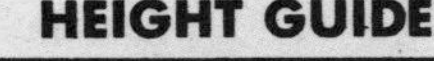

HEIGHT GUIDE

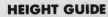

2–8″

Achillea
Aethionema
Ajuga
Antennaria
Anthemis
Arabis
Arenaria
Artemisia
Aubrieta
Campanula
Cerastium
Chrysanthemum
Chrysogonum
Convallaria
Dianthus
Draba
Euphorbia
Gaillardia
Geranium
Geum
Heather
Hypericum
Hylomecon
Iberis
Leontopodium
Lewisia
Linum
Lotus
Mazus
Myosotis
Nierembergia
Pachistima
Pachysandra
Phlox Subulata
Phlox Divaricata
Platycodon
Polygonum
Potentilla
Primula
Pycnanthemum
Scabiosa
Sedum
Sempervivum
Senecio
Silene
Stachys
Thymus
Tunica
Veronica
Vinca
Viola

9–18″

Acanthus
Alchemilla
Allium
Alyssum
Anchusa
Anemone
Aquilegia
Armeria
Aster
Astilbe
Bergenia
Caltha
Campanula
Carnation
Catananche
Chrysanthemum
Coreopsis
Corydalis
Dianthus
Dicentra
Erigeron
Euphorbia
Festuca
Filipendula
Geranium
Geum
Gypsophila
Heath
Heather
Helianthemum
Hypericum
Iberis
Incarvillea
Lamium
Lavandula
Leontopodium
Linum
Lychnis
Liriope
Lysimachia
Mertensia
Molinia
Nepeta
Oenothera
Penstemon
Platycodon
Phlox
Plumbago
Polemonium
Polygonum
Potentilla
Primula
Pulmonaria
Ranunculus
Ruta
Salvia
Santolina
Saxifraga
Scabiosa
Sedum
Statice
Stokesia
Symphytum
Teucrium
Thermopsis
Tradescantia
Veronica

19–36″

Achillea
Adenophora
Anemone
Anaphalis
Amsonia
Anthemis
Aquilegia
Artemisia
Asclepias
Aster
Bergenia
Campanula
Centaurea
Chrysanthemum
Clematis
Crocosmia
Delphinium
Dianthus
Dicentra
Dictamnus
Digitalis
Doronicum
Echinops
Erigeron
Eryngium
Eupatorium
Funkia
Gaura
Geum
Gillenia
Heathers
Heliopsis
Helleborus
Heuchera
Inula
Iris Siberica
Liatris
Ligularia
Lychnis
Lythrum
Malva
Monarda
Oenothera
Pardanthus
Penstemon
Pol
Peony
Phlox
Physostegia
Physalis
Poppy
Pyrethrum
Rudbeckia
Salvia
Santolina
Sedum
Solidag
Sidalc
Statice
Tellima
Thalictrum
Tritoma
Trollius
Valeriana
Veronica

36″ and over

Aconitum
Anchusa
Artemisia
Aster
Baptisia
Bocconia
Boltonia
Clematis
Delphinium
Digitalis
Filipendula
Gypsophila
Helenium
Helianthus
Hemerocallis
Hibiscus
Hollyhocks
Iris Spuria
Iris Japanese
Iris Marhigo
Lathyrus
Liatris
Lobelia
Lythrum
Miscanthus
Phlox
Rudbeckia
Salvia
Thermopsis
Verbascum
Yucca

The smallest outdoor plants include lichens, many mosses, and alpine species, as well as low-lying ground covers such as prostrate pyracantha and ice plants. Ground covers vary in height, however, and those with rough-textured foliage like the junipers can rise several inches off the ground. Cranberry cotoneasters and lantanas are similar. Some of the vines like wisteria, ivies, and bougainvillea, assume a number of heights because they are equally capable of creeping along the ground or climbing.

Scale

To look their best, your plants should be chosen of a proper height and width that will be in keeping with their surroundings.

If you are going to buy only one or two plants and have a choice of locations for them, scale may not matter too much. You can simply carry the pots around and try them out in different locations to see where they look best.

But if you are buying a plant for a specific location, then you should consider scale in advance of purchase. Otherwise you could end up with a three-foot plant that looked strong and dramatic in the nursery but that seems to shrink to insignificance when you place it next to a huge dresser or table. It is smart to measure in advance the exact area where the plant will go so as to judge the size that will look best. Unfortunately there is no exact rule you can use, but placing jars or other props of the approximate size in place may be an aid. The Greeks used a ratio called the Divine Proportion, and if you are good at mathematics you can figure your household furnishings and plantings this way, but a more informal approach—that looks right—is usually sufficient.

If, however, you intend to invest in a large arrangement, such as a room divider or to decorate your home extensively with plants, or to landscape a terrace or patio, then you would be wise to consider scale more seriously. In such circumstances, draw up a complete scale-model of your room or area on graph paper, as we suggest later in this book for landscaping. Outline the dimensions of the room or patio on the graph paper—say, letting every square on the paper equal one foot—and then fill in to exact measurement all the windows, doors, and your present furnishings. In the margins around the area outline, also indicate the exposure, amount of sun, and temperature ranges.

This sounds like a lot of bother, but it will be worth it in the long run. You will have a much clearer idea of the exact space the plants will occupy in relation to the area as a whole and to the existing furnishings, and you can then design the plantings to good scale.

The graph paper will of course give you only two dimensions—showing what space your plants would occupy if you were viewing them from above. It is a good idea to make three-dimensional sketches, showing how the plants would look if you were sitting beside them.

This planning will allow you to buy the exact number of plants of the proper dimensions for your needs. You can make as many mistakes in planning as you like and implement new ideas that may come as you work out the planting details. Discarding sketches is cheaper and less frustrating than discarding plants or being forced to live with mistakes made by not planning in advance.

In planning your grouping, take into account not only the full height of the plants you intend to buy but also their other features such as length and texture of leaves. The smaller your grouping, the smaller each individual plant should be. The plants should have fine textures that harmonize with each other. If you use color, it should be subdued and limited. The larger your grouping, the bolder you can be with leaf size, texture, and color. But before you invest, consider how the plants' forms and other characteristics will harmonize with your furnishings.

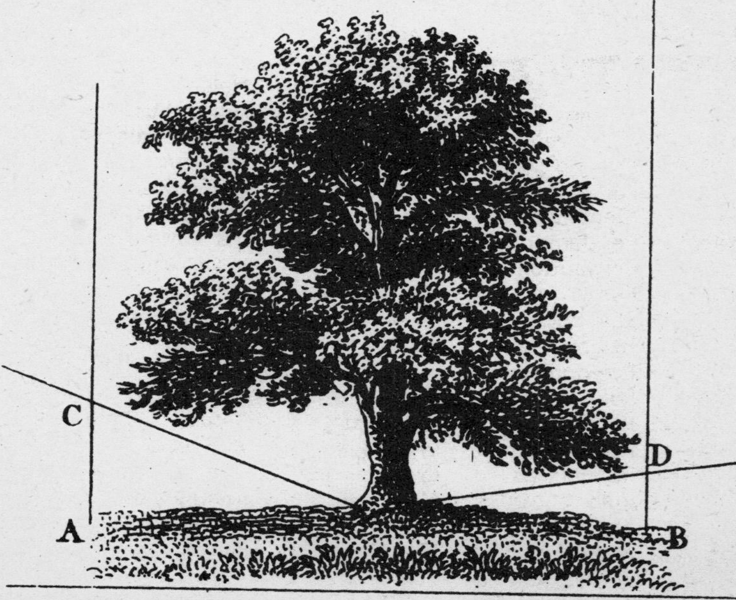

Though in some large trees the texture of bark can be prominent and important, in most plants the primary textural quality resides in the leaves. Foliage texture is complicated because it depends on many factors from the length and shape of the individual leaves to how they are spaced and their manner of hanging from the stems. Roughly, though, foliage can be classified as having coarse, intermediate, or fine texture.

Coarse texture is generally found in plants with large and widely spaced leaves. These leaves, as in banana trees or on spathiphyllum, often tend to be stiff as well. Leaves with prominent veins, such as dieffenbachia, or with hard precise edges such as ginkgo trees, also look coarse. Thus the foliage of pilea, though small and clustered, gives a rough-textured appearance due to deep crinkles, while the needles of pine trees are so dense and stiff that they too appear coarse.

Plants with coarse texture tend to give a feeling of strength—to such an extent that they can even be overpowering. They are not the sort of plants to place next to delicate figures, but they look well against leather furniture or stark white walls. Outdoors, a rough-textured tree or shrub can be used to define a corner or boundary and a grouping of such plants makes good background foliage against which to place a species with delicate leaves.

Coarse texture tends to decrease the apparent distance between the plant and yourself. That is, these plants tend to look closer than they are. Because the light does not bounce off them, they can look darker and more massive than they are. As a result, these plants, unless very small, can easily overwhelm finer-textured plants in a grouping. They are less successful in a limited space such as a windowsill than when they stand alone. They are also too strong for areas where you want to create a feeling of intimacy.

In a grouping, one or two rough-textured plants can be used as balance against a larger mass of plants with airy leaves. In a few cases, coarse plants can be used to hold down a composition; for example, a mass of pilea can be effective as an underplanting for kentia palms or other species with open, arching, fine-textured foliage. The pilea will add weight and darkness to balance the lightness above.

Leaf Texture

Intermediate texture, being a catch-all, into which most plants fall if their foliage is not especially coarse or fine, characterizes the plants you are apt to be using most. Being less distinctive, plants of intermediate texture would constitute the bulk of your garden and landscape plantings, with the roughly textured and finely textured plants used to achieve balance, accent, rhythm, or other special effects.

The larger your planting area the more textures you can combine, but in a confined space you will be more successful if your display textures are limited. Thus a composition of several plants with glossy, leathery leaves like ficus and succulents should be combined with only one other, well-chosen texture. While limiting yourself to a single texture can be dull, too many contrasts create a chaotic, restless grouping.

Outdoors, intermediate textures are good choices for middle-ground composition, where you want the eye attracted to foreground plantings and distant focal points. Intermediate textures between the two will allow the eye to skim easily over the middle ground.

Fine texture is found in plants with tiny, clustered leaves like the smaller ivies. Leaves with deeply indented margins or fernlike structure, or plants with very soft, folding foliage also look delicate. The effect is greater when the foliage grows from long, drooping stems as in weeping willows and the nephrolepis fern, because air currents riffling the leaves create movement as well as light plays. Leaves with light-green or whitish stripes, such as those of chlorophytum, or with lighter undersides such as those of elms, also catch light and appear to have delicate texture.

For small, intimate designs, either indoors or out, plants with fine texture are best. In compositions, they can be used as borders and underplantings to edge down more dramatic species. In cramped quarters, they are also good for hanging baskets. While opaque, heavy, fleshy leaves like donkey's tail can create a dramatic point of interest in a basket on an outdoor patio or in a large room, an airier feel is necessary in a small room or in a window display.

COLOR

Of all plant characteristics, color is perhaps the most prized and yet the most difficult to analyze and execute in interior and landscape design.

Color Variation

One reason is that color is not stable but changes according to the amount of light or shade hitting the plant. Warm colors—the reds, oranges, and yellows—tend to retain much of their full brightness and richness under cloudy skies or in shade. Yellows in particular are often enhanced by shade.

But the cool colors—blues, greens, and violets—are changed and dulled, sometimes to the point of almost disappearing, by shade. Flowers you buy in a sunny nursery or from the brilliant illustration in the seed packet

can look faded and be ineffective in your living room or garden.

White flowers can also often be misleading. Usually they are tinted with blue, pink, or some other color that can appear more or less prominent in different lights. An analysis of sun in your home or in your property can avoid disappointment.

Color Placement

Warm colors, in addition to being less modified by shade, are called advancing colors because they seem to leap out at you. The eye is immediately attracted to them. Red poppies across the garden will catch your attention faster than blue delphiniums at your feet.

In small and intimate areas, therefore, the cooler colors are more suitable. Paler shades of warm colors, such as pinks, can give a serene and pastoral effect, and an occasional bright yellow might be used as accent. But masses of red or orange flowers can seem garish in limited spaces.

For distant effects, warm colors are more appropriate. Zinnias, marigolds, or petunias can be used to carry the eye across the garden to a focal point at the far end. Red geraniums are also effective in windowboxes or urban streets, as they can be spotted at a distance.

With either distant or close plantings, however, color is usually not effective unless you have a large enough quantity in proportion to the area you are designing. Even on a windowsill, one African violet is not apt to be as attractive as two or three pots together. In larger areas, one potted or planted flower can look forlorn or even silly. For full effect, the mass of color has to be in good proportion to the scale of your indoor or outdoor garden. Indoors, small, low-lying plants like rhoeo and some geraniums can be effective on bookshelves or in crannies. For a floor planting such as a room divider, you would need several pots of taller plants such as begonias to achieve an attractive look. Outdoors, the number of plants must be chosen in scale to their height and width. One blue spruce could be sufficient contrast for a corner of a suburban plot, but you would need masses of asters or iris to give a similar effect on a far lower level in the same corner.

Color Clashes

Another major problem with color is that some colors clash with others. It is handy to have a color wheel or chart for making flower arrangements or designing color into your home or garden. The colors closest together on the color wheel are those most likely to clash, and using such colors together takes skill. Complimentary colors—those on opposite sides of the color wheel—are the easiest to combine to good effect. Examples would be a yellow flower contrasted with a blue-violet one, or a red flower set off against blue-green foliage.

Even if your color combinations are well chosen, though, flowers and foliage can seem inharmonious unless the amount of color is in keeping with the space.

Indoors, unless you have extra large rooms or a dashing modern decor of vigorous color, a preponderance of pastels and cool colors is best. Most rooms can't take more than one brilliantly colored plant. Yet even outdoors many gardens are ruined by an overabundance of color. In a small area, you are safest using only one color, achieving variation by contrasting it with its tints and shades. You could, for example, have a bromeliad with a red center on your patio table and set begonias with a similar red in the blossoms along the edge of the patio. You can also get good effect with a mass of one color contrasted with a small amount of its complement for accent. With a larger area, you could use three colors, provided one was dominant. On extensive property you can indulge in all colors of the rainbow, but when you get into more than three colors you run more danger of color clashes. To avoid this, you could tie the entire scheme together by using one color predominantly throughout the landscape. You could also shade a brilliant color off by using softer shades as a transition to a new color.

Foliage Color

Green presents special problems because it's easy to think all foliage will look well together. But a coarsely textured or furry leaf that absorbs

light will seem far darker and duller than a glossy leaf that mirrors the light. Finely textured foliage also has a richer color due to reflected sunlight.

Moreover, foliage varies from dark and deep green to light greens that appear silvery or ash-colored. In between are gray-greens and blue-greens. Even if you stuck to

evergreen, you could end up with an unattractive mishmash of color by buying several species.

Complicating the foliage problem is that so many plants have more than one green. Frequently leaves have undersides that are paler. Many leaves are marked with yellows and creams or with reds and purples, or may be entirely red or purple. These variegated foliages are exceedingly attractive if used with restraint—say one white-striped or red houseplant or one purple plum in your garden as an accent against a pure green background of even color. But several variegated foliages in an indoor display or landscape composition can look too busy. The larger the area you are working with, the more room you have for variation, but in small plant groupings an overabundance of different greens can be jarring rather than restful.

Color Permanence

A difficulty in including flowers in an indoor or outdoor grouping or landscape is that blossoms are transitory. Once the petals bloom and fade, the design you based on a color scheme is left with a gaping hole. This is more of a problem outdoors than indoors, but even indoors you may not want to keep replacing blooming plants unless you are a dedicated gardener and have a place to store plants during their dormant season. In general, it is better to create groupings or other large-scale plantings with more permanent characteristics for the basic design structure and to use flowering plants only for accent. You can do this and still get color by incorporating plants with color in the foliage. A few plants too, such as African violets and *Begonia semperflorens*, bloom on and off all year.

Often, at least outdoors, you do better to choose a plant for characteristics other than color and to take the color as a transitory bonus. Flowering plants frequently have foliage that is lovely in itself. But many trees, shrubs, and vines ideal for other purposes are handy for continuing color into fall and winter when other plants fade.

For autumn color, most oaks and maples turn red (except the Norway maple, which turns yellow), as will dogwoods (Cornus florida and Kousa), the sour gum or tupelo, and *Pistacia chinensis*, the sourwood. Bradford pear trees also turn red. *Nandina domestica*, heavenly bamboo, is scarlet in fall and winter, while *Prunus thundercloud* turns almost purple. Other purples are found in *Juniperus horizontalis "Plumosa"* and *"Douglasii." Euonymus alata* is a rosy shade, while *E. radicans colorata* is again purple. Barberries and some viburnums (*V. prunifolium, V. sieboldi*) are red. *Rosa rugosa* has an orange fall color, and *Cercidiphyllum japonicum* tends to orange too. *Ligustrum "Vicaryi"* has golden yellow foliage all year, while the fringe tree turns deep yellow. *Chionanthus virginicus* and *Fagus grandiflora* also turn yellow.

Many plants also develop beautifully colored fall berries and fruits that are long-lasting. Hawthorns are among these; *Crataegus phaenopyrum* has brilliant red fruit, while *C. lavallei*'s fruit may be red or orange. *Cydonia oblonga* has yellow fruit and *Diospyrus kaki* has especially large orange fruit. Yellow to orange fruits are found in *Eriobotrya japonica* and in *Pittosporum rhombifolium,* but the latter are more spectacular. *Sorbus aucuparia* has fruit that is orangey but tinged toward red.

Red berries develop on barberries (*Berberis mentorensis* and *B. thunbergi*) as well as on the bearberry cotoneaster. Brilliant blue berries appear in late summer on *Ampelopsis brevipedunculata*, while *Viburnum davidii*'s are almost turquoise in hue.

Succulents and Cactus

For foliage color alone, many of the succulents are spectacular. Lithops often have two-toned patterns with casts of blue, cream, gray, and even red. Sempervivums and aloes often have leaves edged with red, and some agave foliage is edged or streaked with white. Pachyphytums have dusty hues of bluish or gray tones, while pachyverias have deeper blues, grays, lavenders, and pinks. Cotyledon leaves are sometimes yellow, and the kalanchoes, which frequently have gray or blue leaves, sometimes boast red foliage. Crassula foliage is unusually shaped as well as varying from vivid red to delicate, variegated patterns.

A few cacti and succulents have flowers that resemble those of other plants. Lapidaria and fenestraria produce blooms of white or bright yellow that look much like daisies, and mamillopsis somewhat resemble waxed petunias. Most of these plants, however, have flowers quite unlike any others. Carallumas have five-pointed, fleshy blossoms in yellows and reds from spring to fall. Chamaecereus has neat little scarlet flowers in summer. Echeverias, which often have blue or other colorful foliage, bloom profusely and spectacularly from spring to fall, depending on the type, usually in shades of red. Edithcoleas are, unfortunately, hard to grow. Their flowers are unique—flat, star-shaped blossoms three or four inches across, yellowish or creamish in color and marked with brownish purples. Euphorbias are more dependable, and produce pretty small flowers in clusters at various times of year, depending on the type. Gymnocalycium flowers are delicate whites and pinks, and are formed of many waxy petals that recur most attractively. Hoya's star-shaped flowers are fragrant. Lobiria's huge blossoms appear in spring and summer and are elegant and brilliantly colored. Among the most dependable bloomers are mammillarias, with bell-shaped flowers between spring and fall in vivid as well as pastel colors.

COLEUS

Notocactus has summer blossoms that are large and clustered. Schlumbergera are so dependable they are usually cultivated especially for their brilliant red blooms, which appear in winter. Selenicereus has exotic-looking, waxy flowers as large as ten inches across. Finally, stapelia has unusual-looking star-shaped blossoms, but these have such a horrible odor you wouldn't want to cultivate them indoors.

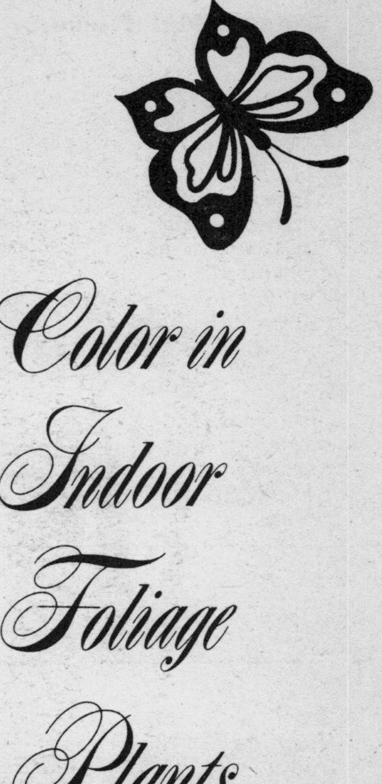

Color in Indoor Foliage Plants

A few plants grown primarily for their green foliage also provide color. Some varieties of anthurium have bright red, coral, pink, or white blossoms. Asparagus fern produces small white flowers followed by reddish berries. Aucuba develops long-lasting red or creamy berries. Dwarf citrus varieties bear miniature oranges and lemons. Cordyline foliage may be marked with pink or red, and its blossoms may be red, yellow or white. Pilea flowers with tiny red blooms. Plumbago usually produces manes of blue flowers in summer, though some varieties have white or red blooms. Spathiphyllum sometimes develops white flowers. Tradescantia may have leaves of red, purple, yellow, or cream, and the flowers are white or shades of purple.

Many foliage plants—such as ivies and peperomias—have green leaves striped or marked with white, yellow, or cream. Some hoffmannias have green leaves with brilliant red edgings, while cissus and some fittonia leaves have red veins. Some calathea foliage is striped or marked with red or white, while chlorophytum leaves may come in yellow and green or white and green. Codiaeum leaves can be red or yellow, and sometimes a combination of two or three colors. Coleus comes with foliage in reds, yellows, and pinks as well as green. Caladium leaves may be scarlet, white and pink, and other shades of red. And gynuria foliage is purple.

COLOR GUIDE TO INDOOR FLOWERING PLANTS

Red and Pink Flowers
acalypha
acanthus
allamanda
ardisia (berries)
beloperone
bougainvillea
calceolaria
capsicum (fruit)
carissa (berries)
clerodendrum
costus
euphorbia
fuchsia
grevillea
hibiscus
impatiens
manettia
nerium
passiflora
pentas
hibiscus
lantana

White Flowers
acanthus
arthropodium
bougainvillea
campanula
capsicum
carissa
costus
eugenia
fuchsia
hibiscus
hoya
impatiens
nerium
osmanthus
passiflora
pentas
primula
punica
rosa
ruellia
solanum (fruit)
strelitzia

Orange Flowers
costus
crossandra
impatiens
lantana
punica
solanum (fruit)

Yellow Flowers
allamanda
calceolaria
costus
eugenia
primula
rosa
ruellia
solanum

Blue Flowers
campanula
clerodendrum
eranthemum
exacum
fuchsia
passiflora

Lavender Flowers
acanthus
campanula
lantana
pentas

Purple Flowers
fuchsia

COLOR GUIDE TO GARDEN FLOWERS

Red
Achillea
Allium
Anemone
Armeria
Aster
Astilbe
Aubrieta
Bergenia
Carnation
Dianthus
Gaillardia
Geum
Heather
Helianthemum
Heuchera
Hibiscus
Hollyhock
Incarvillea
Iris
Lathyrus
Linum
Lychnis
Lythrum
Malva
Monarda
Penstemon
Peony
Phlox
Poppy
Polygonum
Primula
Pulmonaria
Pyrethrum
Rudbeckia
Sedum
Sempervivum
Symphytum
Teucrium
Thymus
Tradescantia
Tritoma
Viola

Pink
Aethionema
Ajuga
Anemone Japonica
Antennaria
Aquilegia
Arabis
Armeria
Aster
Astilbe
Aubrieta
Carnation
Chrysanthemum
Clematis
Dianthus
Dicentra
Dictamnus
Erigeron
Gaura
Geranium
Gillenia
Gypsophila
Heaths
Heather
Helleborus
Helianthemum
Heuchera
Hibiscus
Hollyhock
Iberis
Iris
Lamium
Lathyrus
Lavandula
Liatris
Lewisia
Lythrum
Monarda
Penstemon
Peony
Phlox
Physostegia
Platycodon
Polygonum
Poppy
Primula
Pyrethrum
Pulmonaria
Rudbeckia
Saponaria
Scabiosa
Sedum
Sidalcea
Stachys
Teucrium
Thymus
Tradescantia
Tunica
Valeriana
Verbascum
Veronica
Viola

Purple and Lavender
Ajuga
Allium
Anemone
Aster
Aubrieta
Campanula
Delphinium
Echinops
Funkia
Geranium
Heaths
Heather
Incarvillea
Iris
Lavandula
Liatris
Liriope
Lythrum
Nepeta
Penstemon
Platycodon
Poppy
Phlox
Salvia
Sidalcea
Statice
Thalictrum
Tradescantia
Veronica
Vinca
Viola

Orange
Asclepias
Crocosmia
Erigeron
Geum
Helenium
Heliopsis
Hemerocallis
Ligularia
Pardanthus
Penstemon
Poppy
Phlox
Physalis
Potentilla
Tritoma
Trollius

Blue
Aconitum
Adenophora
Ajuga
Amsonia
Anchusa
Aquilegia
Aster
Baptisia
Campanula
Catananche
Centaurea
Clematis
Delphinium
Eryngium
Erigeron
Eupatorium
Funkia
Geranium
Iris
Linum
Mazus
Mertensia
Monarda
Myosotis
Nepeta
Penstemon
Perovskia
Phlox
Platycodon
Plumbago
Polemonium
Pulmonaria
Salvia
Scabiosa
Statice
Stokesia
Tradescantia
Veronica
Vinca
Viola

White
Achillea
Aconitum
Ajuga
Anaphalis
Anthemis
Aquilegia
Arabis
Arenaria
Aster
Astilbe
Aubrieta
Bergenia
Bocconia
Boltonia
Carnation
Cerastium
Chrysanthemum
Convallaria
Clematis
Delphinium
Dianthus
Dictamnus
Digitalis
Euphoriba
Filipendula
Funkia
Gypsophila
Heaths
Heather
Helleborus
Helianthemum
Heuchera
Hibiscus
Hollyhock
Iberis
Iris
Lathyrus
Leontopodium
Liatris
Linum
Lychnis
Monarda
Nierembergia
Peony
Phlox
Pimelia
Physostegia
Platycodon
Poppy
Polygonatum
Potentilla
Pyrethrum
Rudbeckia
Scabiosa
Saxifrage
Sedum
Sidalcea
Silene
Stokesia
Thymus
Tritoma
Tradescantia
Verbascum
Veronica
Vinca
Viola
Yucca

White
American bugbane
Bearberry
Bishop's-cap
Black cohosh
Bloodroot
Boneset
Bowman's root
Bunchberry
Canada anemone
Canada mayflower
Canada violet
Common yarrow
Confederate violet
Creeping snowberry
Culver's root
Dutchman's-breeches
Dwarf ginseng
Early white snakeroot
False spikenard
Flat-topped aster
Frostflower aster
Galax
Ginseng
Golden seal
Goldthread
Grass of Parnassus
Hairy alumroot
Hepatica
Large white trillium
Mayapple
Mountain lady's-slipper
Musk mallow
Nodding mandarin
Nodding trillium
Ox-eye daisy
Ozark trillium
Painted trillium
Partridgeberry
Purple loosestrife
Pussytoes
Red baneberry
Rock geranium
Rue anemone
Seneca snakeroot
Shinleaf
Shooting star
Showy lady's-slipper
Small white lady's-slipper
Snow trillium
Spikenard
Spring beauty
Squirrel corn
Starflower
Star-flowered false
Solomon's seal
Star-of-Bethlehem
Sweet white violet
Tall meadow rue
Trailing arbutus
Twinflower
Twinleaf
Two-leaved toothwort
White baneberry
White mertensia
White phlox
White turtlehead
Wild calla
Wintergreen
Wood anemone
Woodland strawberry

Orange
Blackberry lily
Butterfly flower
Canada lily
Michigan lily
Tiger lily
Turk's-cap lily
Wild columbine
Wood lily

Pink to Red
Bearberry
Blazing star
Bowman's root
Cardinal flower
Common milkweed
False dragonhead
Fringed polygala
Jessie's red violet
Joe-pye
Kansas gayfeather
Mountain phlox
Musk mallow
Nodding wild onion
Oswego tea
Partridgeberry
Pink bleeding heart
Pink lady's-slipper
Pink skullcap
Prairie phlox
Prairie smoke
Prairie trillium
Purple corydalis
Purple trillium
Queen of the Prairie
Red turtlehead
Rose Mandarin
Rose trillium
Rose verbena
Rue anemone
Shooting star
Spotted cranesbill
Spring beauty
Swamp milkweed
Toadshade
Trailing arbutus
Twinflower
Two-leaved toothwort
Western bleeding heart
Wild ginger
Wine cups

Yellow
Barren strawberry
Blue cohosh
Bluebead lily
Canada goldenrod
Canada lily
Celandine poppy
Common cinquefoil
Common tansy
Cypress spurge
Downy yellow violet
Ginseng
Golden ragwort
Grass-leaved goldenrod
Hoary puccoon
Indian cucumber
Lady's mantle
Lakeside daisy
Large yellow lady's-slipper
Marsh marigold
Merrybells
Moneywort
Nodding mandarin
Ox-eye
Prairie goldenrod
Silverweed
Smooth yellow violet
Solomon's seal
Stoneroot
Swamp candles
Trout lily
Wild oats
Wild senna
Yellow stargrass
Yellow trillium

Aethionema
Alchemilla
Ajuga
Alyssum
Arabis
Arenaria
Armeria
Aubrieta
Baptisia
Dianthus Caesius
Festuca
Heath
Heather
Helleborus
Helianthemum
Heuchera
Iberis
Lewisia
Liriope
Linum Narbonense
Nepeta
Pachistima
Pachysandra
Phlox Subulata
Potentilla
Rosemarinus Officinalis
Sedum Acre
Sedum Alba
Sedum Album Magnificum
Sedum Bronze Carpet
Sedum Lydium
Sedum Reflexum
Sedum Spurium Dragons Blood
Sedum Sexangulare
Sedum Spurium Coccineum
Sempervivum
Senecio
Teucrium
Thymus
Tunica
Vinca
Yucca

Overcoming Winter Blahs

The days are long past when gardeners had to wait for spring to be surrounded by flowering plants. With today's artificial light gardens, wide choice of exotics, and hybrids developed for out-of-season bloom, it is possible to have flowers even in the dead of winter.

A number of flowering plants will provide blossoms on and off all year. Among these are beloperone, euphorbia, impatiens, osmanthus, and pentas.

Flowers that bloom specifically in winter include acalypha, with scarlet blossoms; and exacum, which has perfumed blue flowers from fall into late December or January. Ruellia produces showy blossoms from fall until spring; most are white, but you can get varieties in several shades of red. Although ardisia blooms earlier, it develops bright red berries that will last all winter. Capsicum, the red-pepper plant, blooms in spring, but in autumn it develops a red or yellow-and-red conical fruit that resembles a red pepper; these fruits last several months if you can keep the plant at a temperature of 55° to 60°. Solanum, the Jerusalem cherry, also produces a red or orange fruit that lasts several months. Primula, the primrose, delivers a profusion of white or red flowers from January until April or May and makes a good transition from winter-blooming plants to those that flower in spring. Flowering maple (Abutilon) is another good transition plant, blooming in February.

Eranthemum nervosum, blue sage, is a tiny plant you can easily fit into a corner of your home for bloom from fall into spring. In late fall, about October or November, the cinnamon orchid (Lycaste aromatica) blooms fragrantly, and this is also the time when the pomegranate (Punica) and shrimp plant (Beloperone) flower. Among succulents, the schlumbergeras and kalanchoes bloom profusely in winter.

Outdoors, apart from green-leaved evergreens, some of the blue-toned ones like blue spruce and blue cedar add cheerfulness to winter landscapes. Mountain laurel remains green, and the hollies remain shiny, throughout the winter. The leaves of some azaleas and leucothoes turn red in fall and then are retained until new growth begins in spring. Even deciduous plants that lose their leaves in fall can be attractive if their bare limbs or twigs are of attractive forms and vivid in tone—an example are the red branches of Cornus alba, a dogwood originally from the Far East.

Fragrance in Plants

HONEYSUCKLE.

With so many other characteristics to consider in buying plants, it is easy to overlook fragrance. But if perfume turns you on, you have an abundance of plants to choose from for both indoors and outdoors—from ground covers such as lily-of-the-valley to citrus trees.

Indoors, jasmine is always popular and is a good choice for living rooms. Several scented plants are popularly called jasmine. The true jasminum has enough perfume to permeate an entire room when it flowers—from February or March into November. Some jasminum are vines and some are shrubby, but all have dark-green, glossy leaves and bear white or yellow flowers. Most will grow up to around six feet, so need to be pruned; but they grow slowly. They like sun, but will thrive also in bright light, 50 percent humidity, and well-drained potting soil kept evenly moist. They grow well at over 55° but dislike heat and are best kept under 65°. These are easily propagated from cuttings.

Star jasmine (trachelospermum) is another vine with shiny, dark-green leaves and is named for its star-shaped white or yellow flowers. It needs pinching back and does well in a hanging basket with lots of sun and evenly moist potting soil. It prefers cool temperatures (50° to 60°) and can be propagated by cuttings.

Madagascar jasmine (*Stephanotis floribunda*) has handsome leathery leaves and bears waxy white flowers from about April to the end of August. This is again a vine—it grows nicely on a trellis—easily propagated by cuttings. It needs sun and frequent misting. Water it about three times a week in summer, but after flowering it should be allowed to rest for six weeks or so with less watering.

Also frequently called jasmine are the jessamines. Murraea, or orange jessamine, is an evergreen shrub with shiny foliage. In summer and fall it bears clusters of white flowers that smell like orange, and these are followed by long-lasting red berries. It likes lots of sun and water, temperatures below 70° but above 55°. You can propagate this handsome plant by cuttings.

—WHITE LILY. MADONNA LILY.
LILIUM CANDIDUM.

Cestrum is a bright-green shrub that needs pruning, especially if you keep it indoors. *C. parqui*, willow-leaved jessamine, grows up to three feet tall and bears whitish flowers. More popular is *C. nocturnum*, the night jessamine, which can grow up to six feet tall and can be grown indoors or outdoors. Its star-shaped, heavily scented, white blossoms open in the evenings. Both bloom on-and-off all year, like sun, 50 percent humidity, soil kept evenly moist, and will thrive at temperatures from the 50s to the 70s.

Clerodendrum (glory bower) and the wax plant (hoya) have heavy scents. Other indoor plants you might try include ardisia, carissa, osmanthus, rosa, and *Solanum jasminoides*. Exacum, a lightly scented violet, might be appropriate for a baby's room. All of these are described in the houseplant section. Some of the lightly perfumed orchids are nice for bedrooms—such as bifrenaria or coelogyne. Brassavola is so strong it will spread its fragrance throughout an entire room. Hyacinths, lilies, and other bulbs also provide scents.

In the kitchen, some cooks enjoy having scented geraniums. These come in several varieties that smell like apples, lemons, nutmegs, and other spices. Here it is not the flowers that exude scent, though—you must pick and crush the leaves. The same is true for many of the herbs—marjoram, sage, lavender, various mints, and others—described farther along in this book.

Gardenias, ginger lilies, regal lilies, day lilies, roses, honeysuckles, carnations, and citrus trees are all adaptable to container gardening and all provide scent.

Your Child and Plants

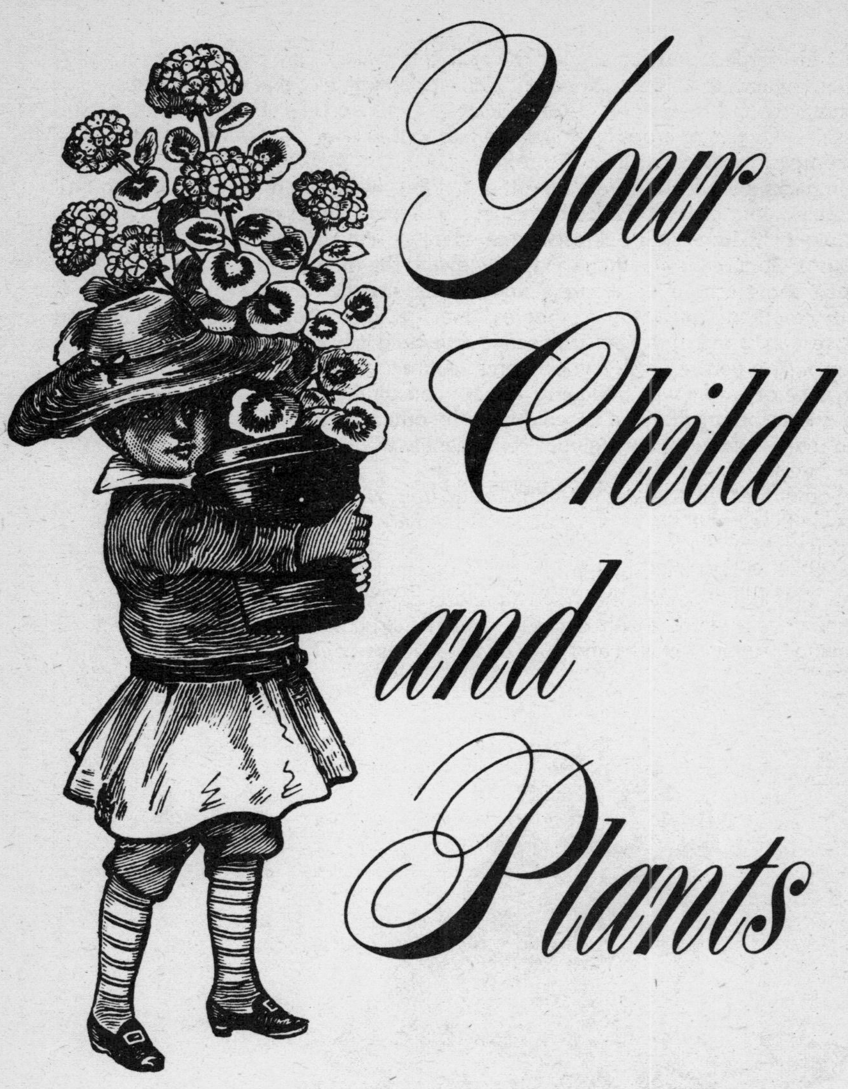

Common at this age are accidents while the child is exploring. Indoor plants the child can reach by standing on tiptoe, or by climbing onto a chair or other height, should be in shatterproof containers rather than in clay or ceramic pots that can inflict cuts when broken. Large plants on the floor or ground should be in tubs heavy enough so that the toddler cannot topple the whole thing by yanking on or hanging from the stalks. Any plants in containers on the floors indoors, or on porches or patios, though, are apt to suffer as your child learns to run and engage in active play with other children—a stage that will last for several years. During these years it will be easier to limit fragile plants to your bedroom or other protected area, and to leave only the hardier species in areas where the children will brush against or bang into them. If you have plant groupings, you can protect the more fragile plants by keeping them behind a barrier of sturdier types. Even a "fence" of thorny or spiky plants that children will learn to avoid is a possibility once your youngster is steady on its feet.

At this stage, too, some children develop passing fears. Especially in a child's bedroom, you may want to avoid plants that tower above the child and prove intimidating. Plants with large leaves, or those with strange shapes like the staghorn-fern, can be misread as monster images. Children may also be frightened even by small plants if a light is placed in such a way that the leaves cast weird shadows.

Despite these problems, this is also the age when your child can begin to develop a love for foilage and flowers. At about the same time children learn to be gentle with animals, they can learn to use a soft touch with plants too. This is especially true once the child is able to understand that a plant is a living thing like a human, requiring similar needs of food, water, light, and sleep. Drawing such comparisons will go a long way toward solving the problem of protecting the plants from children. Pointing out anything unusual about a plant, such as the furry brown rhizomes of davallia and polypodium ferns, which resemble a rabbit's foot, will also help a child develop affection for plants.

If a toddler shows an interest in your indoor plants, you can encourage the child to water or groom one of the hardier plants while you are caring for the others. Beyond the toddler stage, some children will take an interest in a plant of their own, at least temporarily. This is especially true if you select a plant about to undergo a rapid change—a bulb about to bloom or one of the projects in the "Fun with Leftovers" section (page 79) that will grow quickly. If the child soon loses interest, it is better to introduce another plant at a later date than to try to force renewed interest in the present project.

Outdoors, too, you can encourage a love of nature if you remain alert to flowers, fallen leaves, acorns, or other—often very ordinary—things your young child notices, and you comment. Children will sometimes respond with interest if you point things out yourself, especially if you choose some of the more colorful plants and those at or below the child's eye level.

Infants

For your baby's room, plants that please you will do nicely. But you're unlikely to find huge, overpowering plants, or thorny and spiny ones, appropriate. More likely you'll prefer soft-leaved begonias, feathery palms, light ferns, or masses of tiny flowers like star-of-Bethlehem. You might also like accents of color, as from flowering bulbs.

Place some of the colorful plants on windowsills or tables, so your baby can enjoy them from the crib. Or hang one or more baskets with trailing vines or flowers from the ceiling above the crib, so they'll move slightly in a breeze and amuse the baby learning to focus.

Once your baby learns to crawl, you'll have to start taking precautions in the living room, the baby's room, or wherever else you set your baby on the floor. Any pots on the floor should be large and sturdy enough so that they cannot be toppled with that determined, vise-like grip exploring children develop. Trailing plants dangling from tables and windowsills are an invitation to grab on and pull, and must be eliminated.

Since at this age everything goes into the mouth, you'd naturally have removed any species that are internally poisonous (see "Poisonous Plants," page 128). But you're not likely to be pleased with the result on either the child or the plant if the baby insists on ingesting a lot of leaves of even a *non*poisonous plant. So if you can't keep a constant eye out, any plant reachable by a crawler must be placed higher up. Spiny cactus and any plants with thorns or spikes must also be placed out of your baby's reach. Even the pebbles in a pebble tray might look good to eat. And of course many babies develop a fondness for soil. Depending on how active your baby is, how much supervision you can give, and your baby's prediliction for soil, flowers, and vegetation, you may have to remove all floor pots from the crawling area.

Toddlers and Preschoolers

Once your child can stand, you'll have to start taking additional precautions with house plants—not only in the child's room but throughout the home.

Some children continue to display a fondness for eating leaves, flowers, and soil, but by now most also discover the new trick of digging, and some may try copying your watering and plant grooming techniques. To save plants you especially value, you may temporarily have to resort to high shelves, hanging baskets, or locked rooms until your child learns to treat plants with respect.

Schoolchildren

By now your child should have an understanding of plants so that you should not have to worry about harm *from* plants and you should have to worry far less about harm *to* plants. Still, it's not fair to either children or plants to place fragile varieties in areas where children are active. Rubber plants, many philodendron, ivies, and other hardy types are good choices for the child's room, the family room, or other areas where the child should not feel inhibited.

During these years, children develop a fascination with growing things, sometimes fostered by school lessons and projects. You can suggest they watch their own indoor plants grow by planting seeds or bulbs, or by propogating from leaf cuttings or offset (see Propagation). While older children show more patience, younger ones should be given quick-growing plants so their interest won't wane.

In the garden, you can suggest the child might like a little plot to care for. Guard against the child's exuberant plans for a large plot that will prove discouraging, and insist upon a size appropriate to the child's abilities. Again, be sure to select flowers or crops least likely to fail, so that your child develops a sense of accomplishment rather than failure.

In parks, woods, marshes, and other outdoor walks, be ready to follow up on anything your children notice before trying to point things out yourself. While younger children often will respond favorably to the commonplaces like dandelions, during this age they will move toward the more bizarre—Indian pipe, mushrooms, lichens, miniature alpine flowers, strange cactus, burls on trees, gypsy moth infestations and other leaf damage, and so forth. If you have nothing interesting to say, don't be surprised if your child is bored by your inane comments. Arm yourself with a good home nature library. You can bone up in advance of a walk with intriguing facts, or consult the books later to answer questions that might have arisen during the outing. If you carry field guides, you can make a game of having your child identify wildflowers, trees, or shrubs on your walks.

Sometimes children are more interested in moving targets, so one way of drawing their attention to vegetation is to remark on the insects and birds you see. If your child hears an oriole, you can point out that this bird prefers oaks. If you see a Pine White butterfly, you can note it alights on pine and fir trees. Strange-looking beetles that have a preference for black locust, cottonwood, or apple trees give you an opportunity to share field-guide identification that will expand both your child's and your own horizons about the ecology.

To develop self-confidence in your child, choose projects that are least likely to fail. If you are going to give your child a plant to care for, avoid chancy ones like African violets and stick to those like aspidistra, which are apt to thrive even if the child is careless in watering and grooming. Later, if the child still has an interest, you can encourage more demanding projects. Once a child has had success with a hardy plant, he or she may be willing to devote more time and care to a new plant. But if the earlier plant has died, a child can become too sad and guilt-ridden to want another. Good indoor plants for a child to begin on are the Lazy Gardener's specials.

If you are going to suggest your child watch a plant grow, by propagating, choose leaf cuttings from the more foolproof varieties like begonia or peperomia, or from a succulent like echeveria. Herbs like chives, that children can chop into their food, also are likely to be hits.

Children at this age are more interested in the process than in the finished product, so fast-growing beans, or a carrot in water where they can watch roots emerge, are more enticing projects than slower-growing seeds and cuttings that might eventually produce a more attractive house plant.

For older children with more patience and a better sense of time, a flowering bulb, a small orange tree, that will produce a fruit, or a pepper plant that produces peppers, can be satisfactory. Older children also are often intrigued by unusual plants—like the carniverous ones or those grown in terrariums. An occasional child will become engrossed in propagation, hybridization, and other projects.

If you are inventive and knowledgable, you might think up learning projects that will seem like games. Your child might enjoy comparing different types of soil from sand to loam, not only as to color, feel, and other observable aspects but also with a soil-testing kit. Some children can get totally involved in projects such as measuring the width, depth, and velocity of a stream and inventorying the plants along the banks. Others might be more turned on by watching insects pollinate. Often small beginnings like this can lead your child on to greater involvement on his or her own.

Teenagers

If you have not been successful in encouraging a love of nature in your child before this, you will have a harder time now. A few teenagers will have developed a burning passion for roses or succulents or hybridization that they will continue, or may have become interested in a serious study of entymology or ornithology as a result of an interest in plants. But the average adolescent will have passed the stage of being intrigued by watching plants grow from seeds or cuttings, and is not likely to want to spend time in the garden. Many become obsessed with decorating their rooms, however, and some might be amenable to keeping plants that match the colors of the school flag, that have some other unique quality, or that enhance the decor. They might also favor a few large plants to screen a pile of dirty laundry or other mess.

Using Plants Indoors

Plants are often the cheapest and prettiest way to solve a host of decorating problems. They can be used instead of curtains to screen windows or to make a window the focal point of your room. They can be used to cheer up the bathroom, make a skylight entertaining, give an inviting look to your door, brighten ugly corners, partition conversational groupings or areas for privacy, or hide a messy work area.

With fluorescent tubing, you can grow foliage plants and even flowers under tables, in unused fireplaces, on corner shelving, even in drawers. Small and inexpensive pumps are now also available that enable you to have dainty sprinklers or miniature waterfalls among your plants. If tastefully designed, these water systems can supply moisture to the air. While they will benefit most plants, they will also allow you to grow humidity-loving species for which your home might otherwise be too dry.

There is no limit to what you can do with plants indoors, and a few avid gardeners have been known to turn entire apartments into gardens complete with goldfish pools and fern grottoes. Even if you don't intend to go that far, below are a few suggestions to get you started.

Room Divider Plants make wonderful room dividers. One possibility is to work from the top down by inserting a row of hooks in the ceiling and suspending hanging baskets from them. Vary the height of the baskets, with some down near floor level, others high, and some in between. If all of your baskets are the same, you'll achieve a formal effect; for more informality, use different types of baskets. You need not use real baskets, of course. It's easy to drill holes in plastic boxes and globes and to insert cords for hanging. For the least maintenance, choose easy-care plants or even suspend a series of terrariums that take care of themselves once you get them balanced.

Another possibility is to work from the ground up, by setting your plants on the floor. Here it's sensible to make a pebble tray to stand them on. You can line the sides of the pebble tray with painted bricks, tiles, or other materials to delineate it clearly and prevent people from tripping into the plants. Where you are starting at ground level, you can use plants that grow three to six feet high—palms, ficus, dracaenas. A formal arrangement could be made by using several specimens of the same type, such as a row of *Ficus nitida*, or you could use a row of several palms of differing types. You could also combine one or two of these tree-size plants with medium-sized varieties, setting some on stools, upturned pots, or other supports to achieve an attractive arrangement at different levels.

Another way to make a room divider is to combine the above two methods by standing some of your plants at floor level and hanging a couple of others that will trail down to meet them.

You could also use a piece of furniture as the basis for the room divider—a sofa, a fold-up desk, a table, or a cabinet. One treelike plant could be put beside the piece of furniture on the side that extends into the room. If you are using a desk or cabinet, small plants could be placed on top, and in any event a basket or two could be suspended from the ceiling. If the bark or the furniture is ugly, place a couple of large plants with full, spreading foliage, like schlefflera so that they cover the bark. If you are using a table that is open underneath, you can install fluorescent tubes on the underside to create a light garden.

You could also put plants at varying heights on painted or decorated boxes, plastic cubes, pedestals, or other forms of support placed in a row. With this type of arrangement three or four plants with wide, arching leaves—like spathiphyllum, *Phoenix roebelenii*, bromeliads, or succulents—could do the trick.

Room dividers are often in places where they get little light, so choose plants that tolerate poor light. Tougher plants are sensible if people will be brushing the divider, and since you will be incorporating a number of plants you will most likely want to select easy-care species. If you want to have flowering plants, you could attach vertical fluorescent tubes to the wall along one side of the divider or horizontal tubes to the ceiling above hanging baskets.

Ceilings If you have an ugly ceiling, or an unfinished one, or one with stains, cracks, or other problems, you could mask it with plants. One way would be to place tension rods across the room at the marred area, and either suspend baskets from the rod or train a full-leaved vine across it. You could even put in enough parallel rods to hide an entire ceiling this way, especially in a small room like a pantry. For small areas of stain or other marring, you could use a full plant, such as a Boston fern, suspended from a basket near the ceiling or from a wall bracket below the stain. With unfinished ceilings you could simply install series of hooks in the crossbeams from which to hang plants. Most ceilings receive dim light, so your plants should be chosen accordingly. On an old porch, however, you could suspend baskets of brilliant blooms at eye level so people don't notice the ceiling.

Walls Wall decoration with plants can vary from one sedate specimen set on a wall bracket to an entire wall landscaped its length and height. If you are satisfied with one or two plants, you could hang them, set them on pedestals, or put them on a wall shelf. For a few more plants, you could install a planter at any level from the ground up to about waist-height and fill it with a number of plants, including some that climb a trellis or log support. A trellis is not really impractical indoors, because many of the vines that can be trained to them—such as ivies and *Philodendron oxycardium*—grow well in containers and in less than ideal light. Indoor gardeners have been known to construct entire arbors, sometimes with the help of artificial light, on indoor trellises. They can be used around doorways, dining tables, windows, and even beds (in fact, they are nice additions to loft beds and double-decker beds).

If you intend to decorate a large area such as an entire wall, it is sensible to make your design on paper first. It is easier to make changes on paper rather than to lug heavy pots around and install hooks and wall brackets in what you later decide were the wrong places. Your design need not be all plants; it could incorporate furnishings or be used to display a collection of sculpture or other prized possessions. You might

profit from reading the elements of design in the landscaping section, because it is easy to become overenthused and incorporate too many disparate species, colors, and details when you are working with a large area. For a formal, peaceful effect, use widely spaced plants. For a lush, tropical effect, mass them closer together at heights from the floor to the ceiling. Any supports you use for background plants can be masked by plants in the foreground. Plants of similar heights usually do not look attractive in a large display, and you will probably design a more handsome landscape by working from treelike plants in the background, through medium-size plants, to rambling groundcovers in the foreground.

Large-scale plant decoration is usually most attractive if you limit the number of species and concentrate your attention on achieving good scale and a balanced, unified design. Your basic plants—those that do not require a great deal of maintenance—are wise unless you want to spend a great deal of time caring for your landscape. Dieffenbachias, for instance, range in size from a few inches to several feet tall, have cheerful light-green foliage, and do not demand high humidity levels. Philodendrons also come in many forms—some very dramatic—and are among the most inexpensive plants. The dracaenas and ficus varieties also give you a wide range of size and leaf structure in easy-care plants. A garden based on palms is another possibility, and a fern garden is feasible if you can supply adequate humidity. With these types of foliage plants to supply your basic mass, you could incorporate a bit of color with begonias or other sure-fire flowers.

Entries and Hallways Doorways can be made to seem more welcoming if flanked with plants. Often this is a routine part of landscaping the street side of a home, so that arrangements flanking residential entries are commonplace. But plantings can be equally nice at side and back entrances, where they are less common. Best of all they can solve many indoor problems, though they are seldom used this way. A long, dark hallway that terminates at a door can be made more cheerful if the door is flanked with attractive plants that make it seem important. In some old-fashioned homes, extra wide hallways lined with doors can look monotonous, yet these areas are hard to decorate without interfering with traffic patterns. Plants placed at every other doorway, or between doorways, can create interest and variety.

Usually doors are flanked with tall, treelike plants in pots on the floor or ground. If you have lots of room beside the door, and can place the containers sufficiently off to the side so that people passing through the door will not brush the foliage, you could use schefflera, areca palm, ming tree, or other varieties with full and spreading foliage. If space is limited, as in a narrow hallway, you will need to use a plant that grows vertically, like bamboo, or a plant such as *Ficus nitida* that can be trained free of lower branches so that the foliage is above the heads of people passing through the door. If you have almost no space, you could train a vine up poles flanking the door, and even join the vine ends above the doorway to form an arch.

If you don't want a treelike plant, smaller plants will sometimes be attractive. This depends on the size of the plant in proportion to the height of the door. A wide doorway might look well with kentia palms or with a group of two or three low plants on either side. Small plants can also be raised on pedestals to make them seem in good scale with their surroundings.

Another possibility is to use hanging baskets high on either side of the doorway, with long trailers cascading toward the ground. Episcias, ferns with extra-long fronds such as *Polypodium subauriculatum*, donkey's tail, and others with long stems could work.

With careful choice of plants, it is even possible to use an upright floor plant and a hanging basket on either side of a doorway, arranged so that the leaves almost touch.

Since doors are symmetrical, it is usually best to be rather formal and place identical plants at each side of the door. The formality of the plant should also be in keeping with the formality of the interior decor or architecture.

In some situations it is possible to use an asymmetrical planting arrangement. This is harder to create than a symmetrical design, as it requires careful balance. Outdoors, depending on the roof line and other architectural elements, a small, spreading tree—such as a dogwood or fringe tree—might be planted so as to arch above the doorway. Where the arch of the tree ends, hanging plants, or potted plants or shrubs at ground level, or lush clambering vines, or a combination, would have to be added as balance.

In some modern interiors, especially those with curving and free-form walls and staircases, asymmetrical plantings can also work if the architectural balance is mirrored in the plants.

Many older homes and apartments open into small foyers. These are difficult to decorate as they frequently have several doors, yet are dark and cramped. A small table with a careful arrangement of a piece of sculpture and a handsome plant is frequently a good solution. As this area receives considerable traffic, a tough plant such as philodendron is a wise choice. Even if a stem is damaged others will regrow. A hanging basket or plant on a wall bracket is another solution.

In modern, open-plan homes, the door sometimes opens to too ample an area, leaving guests momentarily confused as to which way to go. Here containers that will indicate direction—say toward a conversational grouping—is a welcoming gesture. Two or three container plantings perpendicular to the door and coming up to knee-height—though they may be taller—is usually sufficient to steer a new arrival right or left.

Some homes have ugly halls that end at a blank wall or turn a corner, or pieces of blank wall in confined areas where decoration is difficult. These are good places for specimen plants. Vertical varieties, such as sansevieria, and hanging baskets can be used where floor space is limited. With more room, globular cacti or rounded, busy plants like a compact begonia might be suitable. A good-size, nicely arching dieffenbachia or spathiphyllum or a bromeliad are other choices. On staircases that twist past little windows, you might have room for flowering plants.

Living Room What type of plant is appropriate depends to some extent on your furnishings—whether you have a traditional, formal style or a modern, relaxed style or some variation in between. A single, upright-growing orchid, a bush pilea, a compact pteris, or a well-formed aphelandra would go well on tables, bookshelves, or as specimens on pedestals. For free-standing decorative effects, a manicured ficus or kentia palm in a handsome floor container would be a suitable choice. The foliage color and texture should be chosen to go well with the finishes on the furniture. Fleshy and glossy leaves often go well with marble, for instance, while leaves that are too dark a green will often not contrast sufficiently with dark woods and leathers.

If your style is more casual, you can use any of the above plants plus those of more extravagant form. *Dracaena marginata*, twisted euphorbias, spiny yuccas, or strap-leaved bromeliads can stand alone for dramatic focal points in your room. For soft elegance, a feathery, horizontally branching davallia fern can be beautiful.

How tough your plants should be will depend on how much hard wear your living room gets. If you do much entertaining, you will probably not want a palm or other large plant with easily damaged foliage out in the open. Such plants should be put in corners or behind chairs or other furnishings. On tables, where people might be reaching for drinks, canapes, or ashtrays, plants that are not easily bruised—such as philodendrons, dieffenbachia, or ficus—are a good idea. Small, delicate plants like African violets are best on windowsills, in bookshelf light gardens, or in other sheltered places.

In a household that includes children and large dogs, these precautions may not be sufficient. To prevent plants from being toppled, you will probably want to avoid putting them on pedestals and small tables. You can achieve stable, table-level plantings by installing planters behind couches or other immobile pieces of furniture. You may want many of your plants hung high in baskets or trailing down from high shelves and wall brackets, especially if they are delicate or flowering varieties. Treelike forms in tubs will get less abuse if they grow vertically, like bamboo, rather than overhang traffic or activity areas. If your living room opens directly onto the outdoors, where children are apt to be running in and out, you will need plants that tolerate drafts.

Dining Room or Alcove With a full-size dining room, which often tends to be sparsely furnished with rather massive pieces, your concern may be brightening corners and softening rectangular edges. Large plants will be necessary if you have heavy furniture, but you will want something relaxed too. Tall treelike plants like calamondin orange, ficus, schefflera, or ming trees might be good solutions. Hanging baskets of large ferns could also work well. You won't, however, want bizarre-shaped plants or varieties that are so colorful or dramatic they detract from the food and conversation.

In a dining alcove, your main concerns may be providing screening from the kitchen or other activity area and making a more intimate enclosure. Large plants will not give a feeling of intimacy, and you are better off with medium-sized, fine-textured plants such as begonias or coleus or, again, ferns. These could be put in eye-level planters or hanging baskets, or you could design a combination of both for floor-to-ceiling enclosure. If you have active children, however, plants at their level would have to be tougher—philodendrons, dracaenas, and other hardy types.

For centerpieces, low-growing ivies, maidenhair fern, bird's nest fern, small flowering plants like rhoeo or begonias, or small foliage plants with variegated leaves can be attractive. The main requirement is that they be low enough so people don't have to crane their necks to see each other and that they be serene rather than disturbing.

Bedrooms Since bedrooms are usually sanctuaries, you will want restful plants here. In addition, unless you use your bedroom a good deal during the day, you will probably want a low-maintenance place so you won't have to keep running in to look after them. And you will want plants that look well under artificial light and that will cast soft shadows.

This means you will probably not want plants that are of dramatic shape such as euphorbias, or spiny ones like cacti, and perhaps not even plants that grow too rigidly upright like sansevieria or have stiff leaves like bromeliads.

Your choices will probably run to feathery, airy ferns or one of the softer palms like *Phoenix roebelenii*, if you want a large plant. For table-size plants, delicate crassulas with tiny leaves, or plants with soft or furry foliage like tolmiea, begonias or African violets might be appropriate. Small orchids might be nice too.

For a cheerful sight in the morning, you might consider bulbs or a hanging basket of light and clean-looking cholorphytum.

Teenagers, however, might prefer something flashier, like a carnivorous plant.

If you live in a cold climate and like the bedroom window open at night, choose varieties that can withstand coolness and that don't react adversely to sudden temperature changes.

Kitchen Because the kitchen tends to be humid, especially over the sink, it is a good place for humidity-loving plants like ferns and tradescantia. But the most sensible things to grow are herbs. These can be put in pots on counter tops, and installing artificial light under the cabinets will provide them with light. If your counter space is at a premium, they can be put on a kitchen window sill or on glass shelving installed across the windows, or planted in hanging baskets that can be placed in wasted space such as over the refrigerator. If your kitchen is too small for the herbs you want to grow, and you cannot spare a closet shelf for a light garden, you could grow small pots on a tray elsewhere in the house and carry it into the kitchen only when you are likely to use the plants. Or you can keep them in a planter on wheels that can be trundled about. The section on herbs later in this book provides herb-growing tips.

Kitchens, if you have or can provide enough light, are also a good place for edible flowers, such as nasturtiums you might add to salad.

Some older kitchens have wasted space between the cabinets and the ceiling where low-growing plants can be installed with artificial light. Aluminum foil will not be seen, so can be laid around the plants to enhance reflection of light. In more modern kitchens there is sometimes a clerestory near which baskets can be hung. Put these baskets on pulleys for easier maintenance.

Bathroom Since bathrooms tend to be humid, they are a good place for humidity-loving plants such as ferns, dracaenas, and tradescantia.

If your bathroom window faces south, you could grow flowering

plants—and even match the color scheme of your towels or tile with appropriately colored blooms.

If your bathroom has no window or gets poor light, you could turn it into an indoor light garden by installing fluorescent light to be kept on sixteen hours a day.

With either a south window or fluorescent lights, however, you may not have luck with flowering plants if the bathroom is used during the night. All plants need rest, and turning on the light for even a few minutes can disrupt their period of darkness sufficiently to prevent their blooming. In addition, plants like a lower temperature at night, so it's not a good idea to try to grow any but hardy foliage plants if you keep your bathroom warm at night.

Where can you put plants in your bathroom? If you have a large bathroom with plenty of floor space, you can put large specimen plants such as dracaenas, palms, and ferns on the floor.

Most bathrooms today are small, though, so at best you might have room for a columnar plant such as a tall *Ficus nitida* or *Dracaena marginata* in a corner. If you have a free-standing sink, you can fill the ugly, wasted space under it with plants, and install fluorescent tubes either between the sink and the plants or against the wall behind the plants. If you have an unattractive standing pipe, you could train a climbing plant such as philodendron around it. Some modern tubs have wide enough rims to hold potted plants, and you could use medium-sized, humidity-loving plants such as dieffenbachia.

A toilet tank, the top of a projecting medicine cabinet, or a vanity top (where the mirror would add reflected light) are also good places for plants. Here you would probably want small species such as African violets, tradescantia, ivies, smaller ferns like maidenhair, or perhaps orchids.

Hanging baskets can be hung from the ceiling, especially in corners, and even above a bathtub/shower if placed high enough so they are not sprayed with hot water. You can also install glass shelving or wall brackets high on the walls, again especially in corners. Trailing and cascading plants that like a moist atmosphere—cissus, hoya, chlorophytu, or asparagus fern—would be good choices.

The bathroom is also a good place for a terrarium.

Windowless Rooms You may have a windowless cubicle of an office, or your home may contain cubbyholes such as a dressing room, a butler's pantry, or some strange corner resulting from inferior architecture or remodeling.

Overhead fluorescent light and the tricks for increasing light reflection described in the sections on indoor lighting will enable you to grow many plants tolerant of dim light, including aspidistra, aglaonema, philodendrons, and some ferns and dracaenas. Such areas, though, can be made home for even sun-loving flowering plants if you install the higher levels of fluorescent light described in the section on gardening under lights. Lights around a dressing-room mirror, for instance, can be used to grow African violets. Pantry and office shelves can be outfitted with vertical or horizontal fluorescent tubes for growing a variety of herbs, vegetables, or foliage and flowering plants.

Conservatory During the Victorian era, many homes incorporated an unheated, light-filled area for plants. Sometimes this was a proper conservatory, but in more modest homes garden rooms or glassed-in porches functioned as special plant rooms where morning coffee, lunch, or tea could be served when the sun was up. It was also the place where gardening tools and equipment could be stored, and a work area for repotting and grooming could be provided and camouflaged. This type of unheated or lightly heated plant room allows you to grow plants that like lower temperatures than most of your rooms provide. It is also handy if you are growing a lot of indoor plants and need an area to store those that become unsightly during dormancy periods. In a plant room you can hide the less attractive plants among evergreen types and store bulbs during the winter. If you have been using containers outdoors to landscape a terrace, swimming pool, or other area in summer, a plant room is handy too; your less hardy outdoor plants can be brought indoors for the winter.

Your home may have a porch or terrace you can enclose for this purpose, perhaps with glass panels that can be removed in spring. In a modern house, you may have an atrium. In an older house you may have unheated pantries or storage rooms. And if you have a zonal heating system or are closing off some of your rooms during winter to save heating bills, you may have several rooms you can convert to conservatories. In cities, balconies or parts of roof and townhouse gardens are possible places for conservatories.

Basements Basements and cellars were once used only for storing certain fruits and vegetables and perhaps some flower bulbs. But today basements are frequently nicely finished living areas where the addition of fluorescent tubes can create indoor gardens.

Unfinished cellars are generally too unattractive (and often too space-cramped) for much living use, but they are usually warm enough to provide more than storage space for gardeners. Plants that are unattractive in their dormant stages can be moved there, and with fluorescent light installations (and perhaps small space heaters) cellars are a good place to start seeds and cuttings. In fact, any plant processes and stages too unattractive for display can be cheerfully delegated to this area of the home.

Decorative Flower Stand for Parlor, Window, or in front of Looking Glass.

Increasing Apparent Size

When your curtains, glass doors, or glass walls are lined with drapes, blinds, curtains, or other materials, these create a barrier that stops the eye. The effect is to make the room seem smaller. For a large room in a cold climate, you might desire such a barrier, as the room will seem warmer and cozier.

But if you have a small room, you can increase its apparent size by not stopping the eye at the building openings. You can do this by planting identical—or nearly identical—plants inside and outside the glass. This coaxes the eye to travel right past the glass into a larger vista, and the room seems larger. You might want this effect year-round in some milder climates. In a cold climate you might wish to use drapes or other barriers during the winter months and remove them during warmer seasons.

The most forceful way to carry the eye outdoors is to use identical plantings and other materials at ground level—i.e., when you have a full-length glass wall or door. Some modern architects, for example, have designed homes in which rocks, flagstones, and other pavings plus plantings, are duplicated on either side of glass walls and extend somewhat into the interior of the house and into the landscape. You can achieve this type of transition by placing containers of indoor/outdoor plants such as ivies or dwarf cypresses on either side of the glass. Using identical containers, and choosing plants of similar size and form for placement at the glass, will enhance the effect. Though evergreen plants are useful if you want to create a permanent, year-round arrangement, you could vary the plantings seasonally. You might use evergreens in winter and geraniums in summer, for example. Incorporating color is also possible if you choose hollies or other plants with long-lasting berries, or citrus varieties with long-lasting fruits.

Although identical plants are foolproof, you can be more subtle by matching indoor and outdoor plants that are not the same but that strongly resemble each other in foliage color and texture or in other important characteristics. If you had juniper or pine outdoors, you might use Norfolk Island pine indoors. A brilliant red bromeliad indoors might be matched with a similar red of geranium or begonia outside.

This type of bridging is easiest when the glass comes down to ground level, but it will also work at glass doors set in frames or in ordinary windows—provided the indoor and outdoor plantings are matched at appropriate heights. Say you wanted to create a transition from a city apartment to a balcony separated by a door of small panes that had two feet of wooden frame at the bottom. In this case you would need to match plants of about a three-foot height at the door and probably graduate plants to taller heights the farther they stood from the glass. With a windowsill at hip or waist level, you would need to match the shrubbery just beyond it. Vines such as lantana that can survive your indoor and outdoor conditions could be used to edge one side of a window or trained around the entire window, both inside and outside. Windowboxes with compatible plantings can also be

used on either side of the glass to carry the eye onto other plantings beyond the window sills.

This technique is especially handy for modern homes on small plots and for city apartments with tiny balconies and terraces. It is also useful for townhouses that open onto small patios and yards.

A related technique, using mirrors, is also useful when you are at a disadvantage due to limited indoor space.

Although mirrors are expensive, they are a good investment for cramped quarters as they greatly increase the apparent size of your rooms. Lining the walls of entries, hallways, and rooms with mirrored panels stretching from floor to ceiling makes these appear to double in size. Such walls will also double the brightening effect of any artificial lights you install for growing plants. A spare closet with the door removed can be lined with mirrored panels on all three sides and on the ceiling, and with fluorescent light made into an endlessly reflecting indoor garden. If the mirrors are lining only one wall, even just a few plants will seem like a lush display, and depth can be added with plants of graduated height or with the judicious interjection of a flowering variety or one with colored foliage. In any of these cases, plants can be incorporated into the design in such a way as to hide the fixtures for lighting or the installation of mirrors.

A Moveable Feast

Plants grown in indoor or outdoor containers need not be permanently placed in one location. A large planter on wheels in which you grow flowers in a sunny window or on a terrace can be rolled into the living room or dining room when you are entertaining. Inconspicuous hooks for hanging baskets can be installed in a dark corner of, say, a dining room so that a basket of cascading blossoms can be hung there during a festive dinner and carried back to its growing location afterward. Small pots that are no trouble to carry can be moved from good light to dim light for dining table centerpieces or living room or bedroom decoration during hours you are using these rooms.

Large foliage plants in rolling tubs can be used for impromptu screening. If you are entertaining children and adults in a living room or family room, or on an outdoor terrace or patio, a temporary row of large plants can give privacy to each group. Unsightly messes due to relandscaping or redecorating or some other project, or an on-and-off problem such as the kids' toys in the family room, can also be hidden behind a temporary plant barrier. A guest overnighting on a convertible sofa in the living room, or an adult sharing a child's bedroom for the night, can be given privacy by wheeling a screen of plants into place.

For outdoor gardeners plagued by shade, a couple of tubs on casters, moved along a terrace or path to take advantage of sun, can be a way to grow varieties requiring good sun.

Urban Apartments

Your inner-city apartments may have only one exposure, which will limit the type of plants you can grow. In addition, whatever the exposure, your windows will undoubtedly provide less light than you would get in a suburban or rural location. Ventilation is also apt to be a problem in city apartments, and city rooms are usually warmer and drier than those in less urban settings.

If you do not want to fuss over plants, look for those varieties that withstand high temperatures, low humidity, medium or dim light, and that do not require abundant fresh air.

Soot and dust can also be a problem, so for the easiest care avoid plants with hairy or other highly textured leaves, or with intricate or small foliage structure. The larger and smoother the leaf, the easier it will be to wipe the grime off and keep the pores clear.

If you are willing to go out of your way a bit for plants, you can improve light by installing artificial light gardens. Ventilation can be improved with fans. For the problem of dry air, you can install a humidifier. You can also buy little water-circulating devices that provide small fountains and waterfalls to increase humidity levels in a plant grouping.

Where space is a problem, choose floor and pot plants with vertical form, use hanging baskets, or grow trailing plants in pots that can be set on high shelves or brackets and that allow the foliage to cascade down. Placing mirrors behind your plants will make it seem as though you have twice as many plants as you do.

With a small apartment you can often make a better display if you choose one good window at which to create a bank of plants rather than try to scatter plants here and there around the rooms. A concentration will help maintain humidity, is easier to care for, and can take advantage of your best possible light.

If you have a balcony, it can be screened with a trellis from an adjoining one, or even screened on both sides from neighbors. You'll find helpful hints in later sections on roof gardens and container gardens.

If you are lucky enough to have a ground-floor yard, you can turn it into a greenhouse with plastic roofing materials or shield it with vine-covered trellises overhead for privacy. Most city yards get little or no sun, so you will have to concentrate on shade-loving species. Nevertheless, you have handsome choices in trees with such shade-loving varieties as oriental dogwood (*Cornus kousa*), with lovely white flowers and bright red fruit, and some crab apples. Caladiums and impatiens are among flowers that thrive in shade. Soil will likely be more of a problem, since city yard soil is likely to be mixed with debris in addition to being poor in quality and probably compacted. If the effort and cost of revitalizing the soil are too much, you can still have an attractive garden by growing all your plants in containers.

Large picture windows can be flanked with handsome ming trees or large palms instead of with drapes. Depending on how nice a view you have, you may want to keep the

glass area clear and put any plants beneath or to the sides of the sills. If privacy is your need, you can easily screen a window with hanging baskets staggered at several levels, either informally or in a geometric pattern, or by using vines and sill pots.

Office Plants

Plants for your office can run the gamut from gardenias or cactus in sunny windows to aspidistra and others that thrive in dim light if you have a windowless office. You would therefore choose office plants as you would any indoor plants, using the descriptions given under "Indoor Foliage and Flowering Plants" and the guidelines offered under "Indoor Plant Lore" and "Indoor Gardening Under Lights."

But a few extra considerations may be in order when you are considering purchase of an office plant:

Probably, your desk is very large and you also have file cabinets and other massive furnishings. If so, large specimens would be in better scale with their surrounding than small plants.

In addition, your office is likely to be impersonal and utilitarian, with steel, glass, perhaps marble, and other hard materials. Plants with soft foliage and delicate form are apt to look incongruous, and you will probably do better with plants that have bold shapes and large leaves. Rubber trees, philodendrons, and ficus will probably be appropriate.

If your office color scheme is dark, you may want light-colored foliage or a flowering plant with yellow or orange blooms. With an office done in light shades or in bright colors, in contrast, dark-green foliage might be better.

Time can be a factor if you have a busy job, one in which you must travel, or one in which you cannot be certain of being able to care for your plants on a daily basis. If so, choose varieties that can take a bit of neglect, such as the tough foliage plants or, for color, the bromeliads.

Even if you can attend to your plants weekdays, however, the major worry with office plants is what will happen to them over weekends and holidays.

Although you will have chosen your plants for the light conditions of your office, these can change on weekends. In a sunny or bright-light exposure, cleaning people may be instructed to close blinds or drapes over weekends, and if you cannot contravene these orders you may have to forego some flowering plants. In any case, the artificial lights will be off for the weekends, afflicting especially those plants grown in windowless cubicles. This should be no problem if you stick with aglaonema, dracaenas, philodendrons, or others tolerant of dim light. But if your plants appear to suffer, you might place them near a sunny window for the weekend or give them extra light on Mondays to revive them.

If your office gets sun, your plants will dry out quickly over weekends, and flowering plants especially may suffer. Keeping them on pebble trays that you fill on Fridays, or using automatic wick-watering systems or other subirrigation devices, can conquer this problem.

Also on weekends, the heat and air conditioning are turned off. You probably won't have to worry about the heat being turned off in winter because heated buildings retain residual warmth for a long time. If there is danger of the building going too cold, maintenance heat is usually provided to keep water lines open. Most buildings will therefore not cool down enough to bother most plants. In fact, many plants will enjoy a little coolness, and the lowered temperatures will mean they will not suffer for lack of water.

Lack of air conditioning can be more serious, as the temperature will rise and dry out the plants. Water your plants thoroughly before leaving on Friday. If you are not using a pebble tray or self-watering devices, leave a pan of water next to the plant so the water will evaporate and raise the humidity level. If your plants are scattered about, it will also help to put them together for the weekend. If you have a humidifier, leave it on while you are gone. (Unless your office is very modern, the humidity is probably too low anyway; if you cannot convince your firm to provide a humidifier, you might invest in one for your own health as well as for that of your plants.) For really severe humidity problems, you might consider a terrarium instead of plants in open pots.

Using Plants in Windows

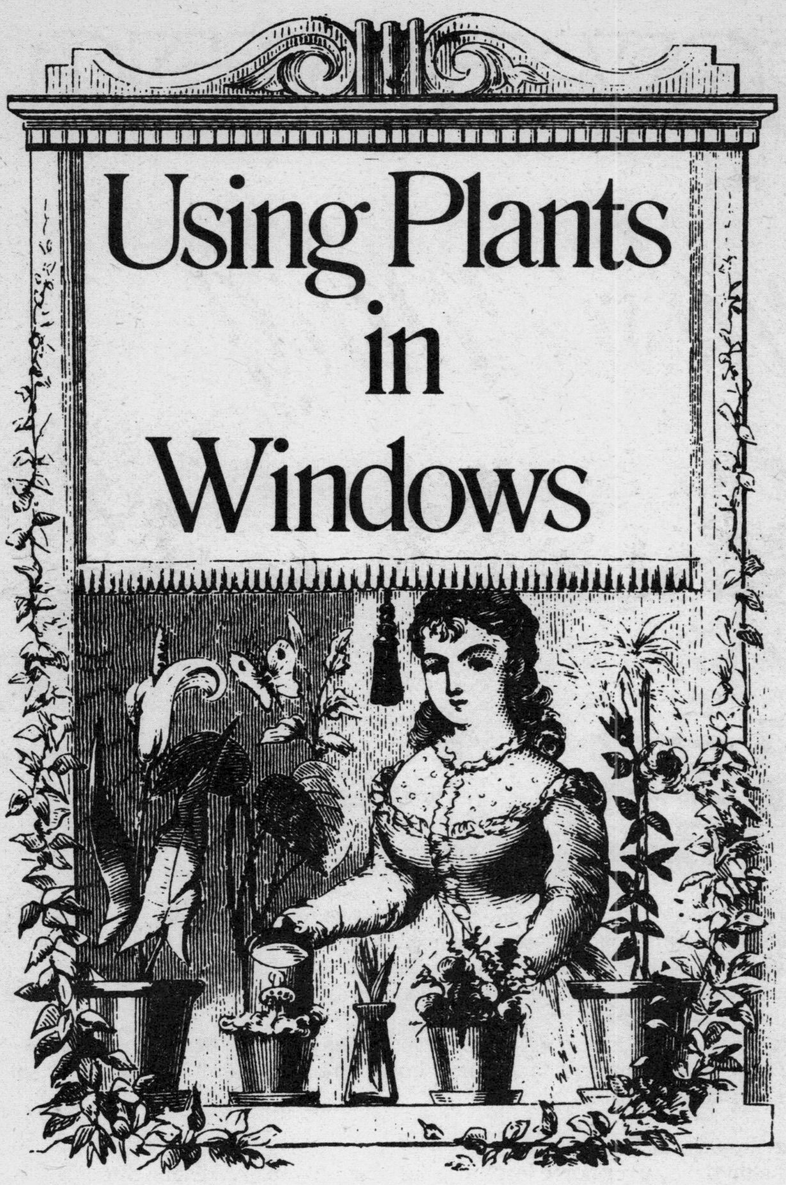

Windows are an obvious place for plants, and in addition to using the sills, you can increase the shelf area by installing one or two glass shelves, or even shelving the full window height. You can also hang plants at various levels in the window from holders inserted at the top or from brackets attached to the sides of the window frame. Ivies and other climbers can be trained to cover the entire window frame.

If you need the light from the window, you will want to use only open, airy plants like young ferns that will not cause too much obstruction. In colder climates, blocking most exposures is not sensible except perhaps in summer. In winter you would want to move obstructing plants so your rooms can have the full benefit of the sun, but plants that do well in your sunny windows in summer are not going to prosper if you move them to northern exposures in winter. In some hot climates, where you would be covering your windows with drapes or shading them with awnings to block light, plants offer an alternative that is often more attractive. In a hot and humid climate, where you do not want sun but do want all the air you can get, an open window screened with lantanas, cascading petunias, and other trailers can be an attractive solution. In a hot and arid climate, you might want to block sun from the south or east more effectively with fleshy-leaved hanging succulents like donkey's tail.

Light requirements are explained in the sections "Indoor Plant Lore" and "Indoor Gardening Under Lights," and for additional plant suggestions see the listings of indoor foliage and flowering plants in Section 2 as well as the indoor/outdoor specialties described in Section 5.

North Window

While you may be able to keep a flowering plant alive in a north window, it will not blossom under these light conditions. You might do well with a flowering plant such as an African violet if you kept it at a northern exposure only during the summer, but for a full and long bloom you would have to move it to more natural or artificial light the rest of the year. For north windows, therefore, the foliage plants are best. Plants whose requirements do not exceed the limits of subdued daylight will thrive at northern exposures.

Many ivies will do well.

Among the ferns, you are best off with nephrolepis or the davallias.

Bromeliads, except for tillandsia, may thrive, and you might especially try nidularium and vriesia (the flaming-sword plant).

The dracaenas do splendidly, and you can choose among marginata, sanderiana, massangeana, Warneckii, and others.

Among palms, the kentia palm (howea) is a good choice, or you might pick the chamaedoreas.

Rex begonias also do with little light.

Other good bets for a north window are:

- Aglaonema (Chinese evergreen)
- Araucaria (Norfolk Island pine)
- Aspidistra (cast-iron plant)
- Dieffenbachia (dumbcane)
- Ficus elastica (rubber plant)
- Hoffmania
- Maranta
- Peperomia
- Philodendron
- Pleomele
- Sansevieria (snake-plant)
- Schefflera (umbrella plant)
- Scindapsus (Pothos)
- Spathiphyllum
- Syngonium (arrowhead)
- Zebrina (wandering jew, spiderwort)

WINDOW WITH BRACKET AND SHELF.

East or West Windows

Plants that are adaptable to north light—such as ivies, dracaenas, peperomias, philodendron, and wandering jew—will also do well in eastern exposures. In addition, with an eastern or western exposure you have a wider choice of ferns as well as flowering plants such as African violets, gloxinias, and other gesneriads. Caladium, fatshedera, serissa, aphelandra, hoya (wax plant), maranta, and pandanus (screw-pine) are other possibilities. Plants with colorful foliage such as coleus do well, and you can grow exotica such as orchids and bromeliads. For larger varieties, palms are a good choice. Many cacti and succulents can be grown in east and west windows. Finally, potted dwarf citrus trees and even some vegetables can be grown in this light.

South Window

Southern exposures provide more light than other windows, and here you do well with almost any of the flowering plants. All of the flowering bulbs—tulips, narcissus, amaryllis, hyacinths, Calla lily, Easter lily, and others—like good sun at least until the buds take on color. Then they can be moved to locations with less light.

Flowering plants that enjoy good sun all year include:

- Azalea
- Begonia
- Cyclamen
- Gardenia
- Oxalis
- Roses

In fact, only a few flowering plants, and several foliage varieties, whose leaves are susceptible to burn (as mentioned in their descriptions elsewhere) cannot be grown in southern exposures.

Many of the more brightly colored foliage plants enjoy a great deal of light:

- Coleus
- Crotons
- Gynura
- Poinsetta

Cacti and succulents thrive with sun, and most of the citrus and vegetable plants grow in south windows.

ENERGY-SAVING Landscaping

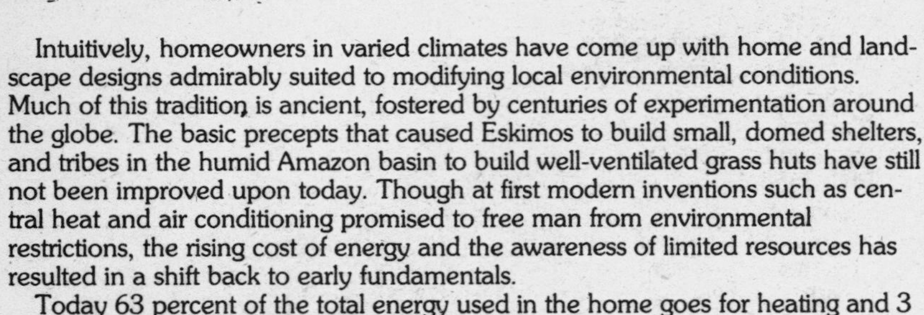

Intuitively, homeowners in varied climates have come up with home and landscape designs admirably suited to modifying local environmental conditions. Much of this tradition is ancient, fostered by centuries of experimentation around the globe. The basic precepts that caused Eskimos to build small, domed shelters, and tribes in the humid Amazon basin to build well-ventilated grass huts have still not been improved upon today. Though at first modern inventions such as central heat and air conditioning promised to free man from environmental restrictions, the rising cost of energy and the awareness of limited resources has resulted in a shift back to early fundamentals.

Today 63 percent of the total energy used in the home goes for heating and 3 percent for air conditioning. Modern research has shown that proper landscaping can reduce heating bills by as much as 15 percent, while air conditioning costs may be cut 50 percent or more. If you live in a cold climate, where your energy costs 90 percent of your total cost, mostly into heating, your savings through landscaping could be even more significant. And if you live in a warm climate where you spend a great deal on air conditioning, landscaping against sun and heat can add up to substantial savings. In any area, proper landscaping can make your home more comfortable on a year-round basis.

The aesthetics and practical aspects of landscape design will be covered later in this book, but this section will concentrate on the practical ways in which using plants can help you solve a wide range of problems due to the elements.

To take full advantage of using plants to save on your energy bills in either hot or cold climates, it helps to understand the three major ways in which your house gains or loses heat.

Air Infiltration

This is the passage of outside air into the house through open doors or windows (or the cracks around them when they are closed), through porous materials used in construction, and through any extra openings such as clerestories or chimneys.

One of the two major ways outside air is forced into your house is by wind. When wind seeps into your house from one side, it forces an equal amount of air out of your home through openings on the opposite side. The greater the wind velocity, of course, the more hot or cold air it pumps through the house to increase your fuel bills.

In a cold climate, and in most warm areas where you are using an air conditioner, you would therefore want your home to be as impermeable as possible to wind, especially on the side hit by the prevailing winds. You would want as few doors, windows, and other openings as possible on that exposure. You would want good insulation. And you would want tree barriers to reduce the force of the wind before it hit your home.

The other method of air infiltration is due to the fact that warm air rises. Warm air seeping out of any cracks or other openings near the top of your house is replaced by cooler air sucked in through lower openings. This type of air circulation, called the "chimney effect," is less affected by wind, but increases as the difference in temperature between inside and outside air increases.

For the average home, from 20 percent to 33 percent of the heat loss in winter is by air infiltration. Wind on cold days can cause up to a 50 percent loss of heat. Statistics for air conditioned homes are similar.

Windbreaks can significantly reduce air infiltration, and your savings will depend on how much of your heat or cool air loss is due to wind and how much to the chimney effect.

Conduction

A home also gains or loses heat when there is a difference in temperature between its inner surfaces and its exterior surfaces. The materials of which the house is built transfer heat to each other by conduction in an attempt to equalize the temperature.

Materials that are very good at conduction include metal and glass, while still air is one of the poorest conductors of all. For this reason, double-pane or storm windows—and double doors—that trap a layer of air between them are effective in preventing heat loss or gain by the house. Insulating materials also work on the principle of being constructed to trap air.

Controlling the difference in temperature between the air inside and outside your home is one of the best ways to reduce conduction. Lowering your thermostat works because it decreases this difference.

Outside, allowing the sun to shine as much as possible on a heated home in winter and shading the air-conditioned house as much as possible in summer are the best ways to increase the temperature of exterior surfaces to make them closer to those inside. The best way to do this is with landscaping that shades or opens the house to the sun in the proper seasons. Vines and other plantings against house walls can also serve as insulation, as they create a wall of still air between themselves and the house's outer wall. A trellis is especially effective.

But the effect is lessened if there is wind, and so again landscaping to include a windbreak is sensible.

Heat conduction is responsible for from 33 percent to 50 percent of the total heat losses and gains from the average home. In some cases it is more important than air infiltration.

One-Way Solar Radiation

The third way your home loses or gains heat is by solar radiation through windows or other glazed surfaces.

When sunlight hits a single pane of glass at a perpendicular angle, up to 90 percent of the solar radiation will be transmitted into the home. Sunlight will be increasingly reflected by the glass as the sunlight departs from the perpendicular.

This is essentially a one-way process. Radiation from the sun is short wave and easily passes through glass. But radiation from a home's interior is long wave and is not well transmitted through glass. Any solar radiation you get is therefore going to stay inside.

Moreover, reflected radiation from the sun can bounce at you from any reflective surface, such as shiny pavings, the surface of still water, and even glossy plant leaves.

In cold weather, you want as much of this solar radiation as possible, so ideally you want your windows to be fully exposed to the sun all day long, even when the sun is at a low angle. Evergreen plantings too close to the house can interfere with winter sun, and deciduous trees that drop their leaves in fall are therefore preferable.

In warm weather, you naturally want as little solar radiation as possible—especially at noon—and your landscaping should therefore be geared to preventing the sun from reaching any window surfaces.

Regional Variations

Landscaping cannot solve all energy problems, and sometimes the goals conflict. You will save most on your energy bills if you concentrate your landscaping goals on the method of heat loss or gain that is most crucial in your region.

In cooler, northern climates, most energy is consumed by winter heating. Control of cold-air infiltration is therefore paramount.

In hotter, southern locations, shade to control heat conduction and air conditioning is most important. If your home is air conditioned so that its temperature is frequently 20° or 30° cooler than the outside air, hot-air infiltration is also vital.

In temperate climates, you should concentrate on year-round energy conservation, giving equal consideration to problems in each season. In your subsequent landscaping, give highest priority to the problems that are affecting your fuel bills most.

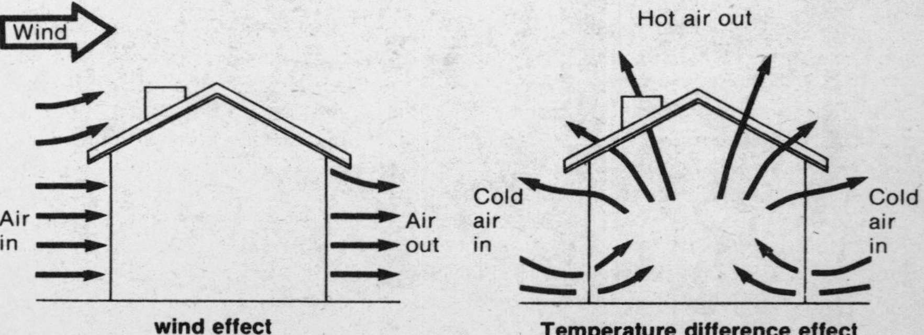

wind effect

Temperature difference effect

CONTROLLING SUN

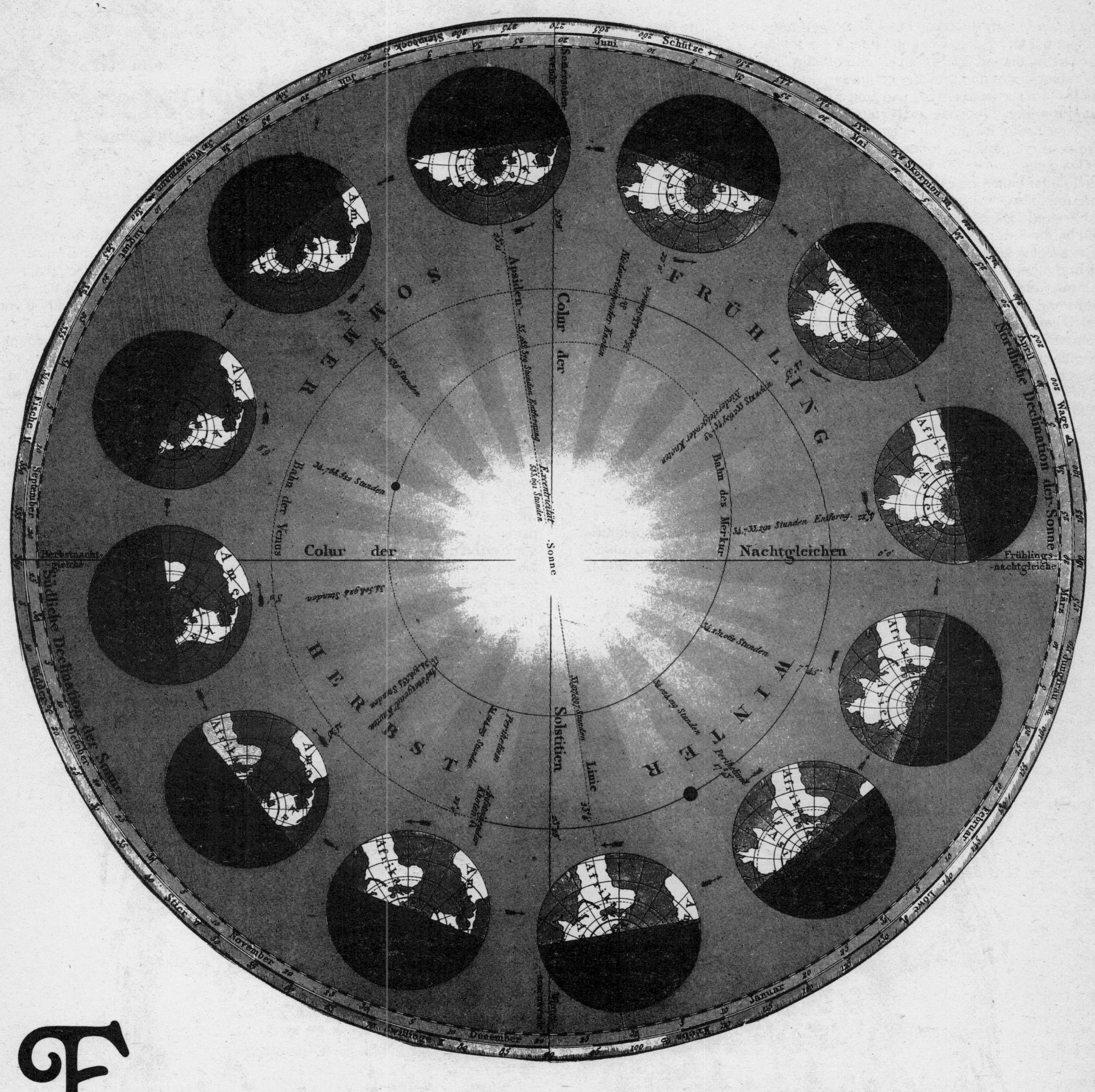

For saving on fuel bills in either hot or cold climates, controlling sun takes priority. In the South, where the sun often sizzles, up to 75% of the energy needed to air-condition a house can be saved simply by shading the roof with the right tree (or trees).

Where shading the entire roof is impossible, you can still save a lot of energy by shading as little as 20% of the roof. Closing drapes on the sunny side of the house, and using plantings that shade windows and house walls with further reduce air conditioning bills. Even without air conditioning, a house in a warm climate is far more comfortable with shade. Properly shaded, the exterior of a house can lower the interior temperature by as much as 20 degrees.

Shading the roof in a northern climate can have the reverse effect of what occurs in the South. It could *increase* your heating needs by as much as 12%. Here, opening the house to as much winter sun as possible is advantageous. Indoors, this means closing drapes at night to reduce heat loss; during the day, opening the drapes will enable your house to better absorb solar energy. Plantings around the house should not block the sun in winter. By planting a natural windbreak, you can substantially reduce the chilling effects of wind velocity and save another 10% to 15% on your heating bill.

The cost of providing shade is often much less than for landscaping against the wind. While a windscreen usually requires a number of large trees, screening from sun on many properties can be effective with only one large tree. On smaller lots, small trees often are preferable aesthetically and practically. Additional screening, as with vines on overhead trellises, also is inexpensive. Sun screening is therefore almost always cost effective.

Why Trees Are Best

Though you can get shade in other ways, such as with wooden canopies or roof overhangs, vegetation is superior. Overhangs and canopies provide summer protection against the sun, but they can limit the amount of sunlight your house will get in winter. In addition, they deprive the area under them of rainfall, which

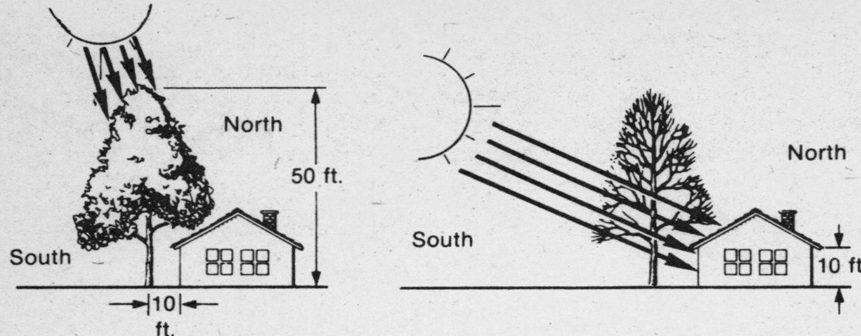

limits the types of plants you can grow to drought-resistant varieties—unless you want to spend a lot of time watering under these shelters.

While it's true that artificial canopies and other manmade structures block sun, vegetation blocks sun *and* provides coolness.

About 90% of the solar energy reaching a tree is absorbed by the topmost leaf canopy. This energy raises the temperature of the foliage. Just as a radiator or stove radiates heat outward, the treetop radiates its solar heat outward. Heat therefore does not penetrate to the base of the tree, which is why it's always cool under a leafy canopy.

Trees do a far better job of reducing the air temperature under them than either an umbrella or canopy covering the same area. This is because a tree has a depth of layered foliage. Heat not absorbed by the topmost leaves can still be deflected by the lower layers. Trees have five to seven times as much absorbing surface as a single-layer sun shield such as an umbrella or canopy.

Trees and other plants also cool the air through their process of transpiration. During transpiration, plants move moisture from the soil through their roots, up their stems and stalks, to evaporate from their leaf surfaces. Every gram of water evaporated carries away into the atmosphere 580 calories of heat.

The air temperature near plants subsequently is several degrees cooler than in an area without plants; and if you are simultaneously getting shade from these plants, the temperature difference can be considerable.

USDA Forest Service researchers calculate that transpiration from a single city tree may produce 600,000 BTUs per day for cooling. This is equivalent to five average-size room air conditioners running twenty hours a day.

Trees have another advantage over manmade canopies. As the sun goes down and solar radiation is lost, most exposed surfaces cool rapidly. The leaf canopy, however, now does its work in reverse. It acts like a blanket to keep the warm air from floating upward. Nighttime temperatures under trees are therefore higher than in adjacent open spaces.

In extremely hot conditions, especially in humid areas where high temperatures persist past nightfall, heat retention can be a disadvantage. In virtually any other situation, though, outdoor living areas placed under trees will remain comfortable longer as the nighttime temperature falls.

The blanket effect of tree canopies provides a bonus for gardeners in that the frost-free period is longer under trees than in open parts of the garden.

VILLERÉ'S MANSION.

Sun Movement

To say that vegetation for shading should be put between your house (or any other area you want to shade) and the sun—or that plantings to maximize sunlight should not be placed in the sun's path—sounds obvious. In fact, plantings to provide maximum shade or sun are not so simple to design. The sun's angles change seasonally, daily, and hourly, all of which is further complicated by your latitutde.

The sun's duration is affected by latitude. In the Florida keys you can count on twelve hours of sun during summer; even at winter solstice you will have ten hours. As you move north, the seasonal difference is more marked, so that at summer solstice the sun shines for sixteen hours and at winter solstice only six hours. Still farther now, this phenomenon results in the midnight sun at the Arctic Circle (23½ degrees latitude), and a sun that never drops below the horizon from late March to late September at the North Pole.

The two major factors involved in controlling sun are the vertical and horizontal angles at which the sun reaches you. The verticle angle of the sun influences chiefly the height of your plantings; the horizontal angle influences mainly the width of your planting. Together, they should determine the location of your plantings and the type of vegetation you choose.

Vertical Angles How high the sun rises in the sky depends on the latitude where you live. The sun rises highest at the equator, and its height diminishes the farther north you go. In southerly climates your landscape should account for an overhead sun—and the fact the sun will be overhead for a much longer period than in more northerly latitudes.

The sun is always highest at noon, but in the far north its angle is considerably lower. In the Florida Keys, the summer sun at noon could make an angle of, say, 85 degrees with respect to your home. Around the Winnipeg, Canada, area, the angle might be only about 60 degrees to 62 degrees. In designing plantings, you therefore have to consider lower angles and longer shadows the farther north you are.

The height of the sun, however, is not the same year round. It varies seasonally, being highest at the summer solstice (June 22) and lowest at the winter solstice (December 22). These changes are radical. Using our example of the Florida Keys, the summer sun that was coming at you at noon from an 87 degree angle at the summer solstice will have dropped to a 40 degree angle during the winter solstice. Around Winnipeg the 60 degree angle of the summer sun will have shrunk to 16 degrees ot 17 degrees at winter solstice. In any area, therefore, lower angles and longer shadows become most pronounced as winter approaches. During spring and fall, people in the Florida Keys will be experiencing sun at angles similar to those Winnipeg residents have in mid-winter.

Of course, the height of the noonday sun is not the sole consideration, since the sun's angles will be changing through each individual day as well, increasing during the morning hours and decreasing during the afternoon.

These angles influence the vertical height of plantings you should design to block or encourage sun. In a hot climate, you will want shade as directly overhead as possible—not only to shade outdoor living areas but for the roof as well.

Sunrise at 7 A.M. and sunset at 5 P.M. is the norm for the winter solstice from a latitude of 25 degrees in the Florida Keys to a latitutde of 30 degrees, which covers roughly Houston, New Orleans, and St. Augustine. In the rest of the United States and in southern Canadian cities such as Toronto and Montreal, sunshine at the winter solstice lasts from 8 A.M. to 4 P.M.. At 50 degrees latitude, just north of Winnipeg, sunrise is at 9 A.M. and sunset is at 3 P.M..
At the summer solstice, the Florida Keys have sunlight from 6 A.M. to 6 P.M., a pattern that continues to about 30 degrees latitude. Sunrise at 5 A.M. and sunset at 7 P.M. holds true for the rest of the United States and Canada up to the 50th parallel. There the summer day begins at 4 A.M. and sunset is at 8 P.M., and the day lengthens as you go farther north.

The above times do not take into account daylight saving time when, though the duration of sun will not change, the time of sunrise and sunset must be corrected.

No neat and easy rules are possible for calculating the angles of the sun. The general principles are easy enough: directly overhead, the sun will cast shadow only directly under a tree; when the sun comes in at lower angles during the morning or afternoon, the shadows it casts from the same tree will be shortest as the sun approaches its noonday height, and longest the lower it is in the sky. Thus the winter sun at the 50th parallel casts the longest shadows of all.

An accurate, scientific analysis of sun angles requires tables of data and trigonometry. You might safe yourself some time by consulting *Landscape Design That Saves Energy* by Anne Simon Moffat and Marc Schiler (William Morrow & Co., Inc., 1981), which provides such tables as well as formulas for computation.

Horizontal Angles How high the sun rises is only part of the problem in obtaining maximum sun or shade. The sun also shifts its direction from east to west throughout the year. Though we are taught that the sun rises in the east and sets in the west, it actually rises due east and sets due west only in spring and fall. As it rises to its maximum height in summer, dawn breaks in the northeast and sunset is in the northwest. The low winter sun rises in the southeast and sets in the southwest.

These angles, called the bearing angles of the sun, are pretty much the same for all latitudes. The only difference is time of day. Since the sun rises earlier in winter in the South, it will be rising a few degrees more to the southeast than in the north, where the sun will be a bit farther southwest by the time it rises. Likewise, winter sunsets will be farther southwest in the South since the sun sets later than in the north.

These east/west shifts in the sun affect the horizontal design of your landscape plantings.

Measuring Sun

Unlike the wind, which can create annoying landscape dilemmas due to sudden changes in frequency, direction, and force, the sun is reliable. Wherever you live, the sun's duration, angles, and strength, though they change hourly and seasonally, are predictable.

You can easily get the duration of your sunlight by consulting the times of sunrise and sunset in a local newspaper or in almanacs and other readily available reference works. During spring and fall, sunrise at about 7 A.M. and sunset at about 5 P.M. is standard for the spring and fall equinox throughout the United States and the most heavily inhabited areas of Canada. What changes most is the duration of sun in winter and summer.

For a rougher estimate, you simply make observations on your property and record them for reference. Try this on a sheet of graph paper where you can outline your property to scale—say each square on the graph paper equaling a foot of your property.

You will not have to record all sun data—just the angles you need for the specific landscaping purpose you have in mind.

For example, if you live in the north and want optimum sun on your southern exposure, or you live in the south and want minimal sun from that direction, take note of where the sun first hits your property in the morning and at what point it last touches your property in the evening. You probably won't have to get up at dawn to do this either, because unless you live in a flat area like the Plains or facing a seacoast, the sun will probably enter and leave your property for a shorter period than it actually shines over your region. Mark the boundaries of the sun's horizontal path on your graph paper and use that as a basis for planning openings—or screenings—along the southern exposure of your property.

Even more important is to note how high the sun ascends and the length of the shadows it casts. If you are trying to block the sun, you will need plantings that will be high enough to screen the sun at its height. If you are trying to catch as much sun as you can, you will need plantings low enough not to obstruct the sun's lowest angle. Vertical height will be easiest to figure if you already have trees or high shrubs on your property. By observing your tallest tree in relation to the sun at noon, you can determine the height new plantings would need to be to screen the sun. Also measure the shadows at various times of day to get an idea of how far they cast; this is handy if you want to plant a tree to shade your house or an outdoor living area, but you're unsure about how far away to plant it. If

your property has been stripped of high vegetation, you can try to extrapolate from the way your house casts shadows, or you can simply plant a couple of poles on your property to use as guidelines.

In a cold climate, knowing where the winter sun crosses your southern exposure may be sufficient. In temperate climates, you may need winter and summer observations on the south to fulfill your varying seasonal goals. Unless you require morning sun from the east, or the setting sun bounces unpleasantly off your terrace or swimming pool, your eastern and western plantings probably will not be a major consideration. Only in hot climates are you likely to need sun calculations on three, or even four, exposures and for all seasons.

Types of Vegetation

Where you require year-round shade, heavy reliance on broadleaf evergreens is a good solution. For high shading above, large spreading trees such as live oaks and magnolias are appropriate selections. These can be combined with smaller evergreens such as camellias, junipers, and hollies. In arid areas, you'll want to concentrate on drought-resistant species such as desert gum and desert willow, Arizona cypress, and yucca. Palms are adaptable in arid as well as moist climates.

In temperate climates, summer shade must be balanced against the need for winter sunshine. Here deciduous vegetation will provide shade in summer and allow the sun to shine through after leaf drop in autumn.

HANCOCK'S HOUSE, BOSTON.

In truly cold climates, where summer heat never becomes oppressive, you want an absence of high vegetation—at least on the southern exposure.

In selecting deciduous shade trees that will lose their leaves in fall, you may want one that has an unusual and attractive bark to give interest to the winter landscape. Cherries, birches, and beeches are among these. Some of the nicest are:

The paperbark maple, *Acer griseum,* which has peeling, cinnamon-colored bark, or the striped maple *(A. pennsylvanicum),* which has a trunk striped green and white.

Chinese paper birch, *Betula albo-sinensis,* has bright orange bark that peels latitudinally.

American hornbeam, *Carpinus caroliniana,* has an interesting gray trunk that appears to have muscles.

Russian olive, *Elaeagnus angustifola,* has brown bark that shreds off longitudinally.

Amur cork tree, *Phellodendron amurense,* has bark that resembles cork.

Finally, *Prunus serrula* is a cherry tree with brilliant, glossy red bark.

Tree Form All plants provide shade, but the type of shade you need will determine the form of the trees and shrubs that will be most effective.

Normally you would not choose trees or bushes of columnar or vertical structure when you want heavy shade. For overhead sun they are virtually useless, and against vertical sun these cast very narrow strips of shadow that lift all too quickly with the sun's movement. When the sun is low, a vertical tree will cast a far longer shadow, and if the shadow width doesn't matter, you might find this tree shape useful.

In a few instances, though, columnar form is useful. A row of trees or tall shrubs of vertical growth habit would be practical for shading a narrow driveway where you don't want foliage overhanging the drive. In arid areas where your choice of leafy trees is restricted, large columnar cacti might be arranged in a staggered formation so that the shading limitations would be overcome by having the group as a whole compose an effective shield against the sun. Another idea is to position columnar shrubs and trees so that they catch and funnel air flow to create breezes.

Conical and triangular forms—such as are found in some firs and spruces, in pin oaks and sweetgums—are handy when you want shade directly in front of the tree, and where it does not matter whether there is shade in the area shadowed by the tapering top of the tree. Such trees, if they have heavy growth at the bottom, make good windbreaks while still allowing the sun to reach around the tapered tops.

If the lower branches begin a good distance above the ground and are widespreading, triangular trees can shade overhead sun, though not as ideally as other types of trees. Conical forms are most useful against sun angling in from the side if the tree's shape and placement can be adjusted to the sun's path.

For heavy shade purpose, trees of globular or rounded forms are the best choice. These offer the fullest protection from the sun's east/west movement. If chosen of a height adequate to block the sun at its summer zenith, globular trees form excellent overhead sunscreens in temperate climates. Used in combination with other plantings, they help form the more extensive screening desirable in hot climates.

Because the globular form has many variations, however, not all rounded trees are adaptable to every purpose. When the sun reaches you from a low angle, you'll want a species that begins to branch close to the ground; some cedars, for example. A tree with a long, bare trunk and a high canopy—like some pines—permits a low sun to angle in beneath the foliage. the tree will not block the sun at all. But if you want a view beneath the foliage or shadows cast at a greater distance, a high-canopied tree might be the solution.

The denser the canopy, and the more layers it has, the more shade you'll get. The dense canopies of oaks and maples are excellent for controlling strong sun from the south. Such trees screen as much as 90% of the sunlight. Where you want to shade an area from sun that is not as strong, such as morning sun from the east, a lighter, looser leaf canopy may be sufficient. In this case, a tree such as the honey locust would do nicely; it will screen about 50% of the sunlight.

Trees that branch laterally are frequently the best choice for areas with high heat and humidity. Live oaks, for instance, are basically a rounded form, but the horizontal branching habit gives the foliage the overall shape of an egg lying on its side. These trees provide shade at exceptional distances from the trunk. Also, because the branching begins high up, the large shadowed area beneath the foliage is open to wind currents.

Arching foliage, such as palm trees, is also a good solution for hot climates where you welcome breezes.

Trees that spread their canopies horizontally are useful for shading outdoor living areas. Planting them to one side of a terrace or barbecue pit and will provide the designed shade on these areas. Good choices include the coral tree, golden-rain tree, Jerusalem thorn, silk tree, or Texas umbrella tree.

Tree Height Consider the mature height of the tree, as well as how quickly it grows.

A slow-growing tree may remain an acceptable height throughout your lifetime, or for as long as you intend to reside on your property. The tulip tree, for example, grows fairly quickly but does not mature for more than a hundred years, so if you plant a young one it may not grow disproportionately tall for your purposes. Other slow-growers among the large trees are most of the oaks, European mountain ash, ginkgo, shagbark hickory, and European beech. Carob trees, Japanese black pine, and Libocedrus decurrens are among the low-growing evergreens.

Faster growing trees are those you would choose if you want a tree to reach maturity quickly. (These might be avoided if you don't want your trees reaching mature heights while you own your property.) Most maples are fast-growers, as are katsura, platanus (including eastern sycamore, California plane, and London plane), most elms, black locust, Arizona ash, European larch, European white bark, and of course poplars. Most fruit trees are fast-growers too. Among evergreens, eucalyptus, some pines, white fir, silk oak, selected varieties of cedar and cypress, Norway spruce, and a few specialties such as the Brazilian pepper tree also grow quickly.

Among the taller shade trees, those that offer the least problems and the least maintenance include:

European beech *(Fagus sylvatica)*
Sugar maple *(Acer saccharum)*
Litteleaf linden *(Tilia cordata)*
Red maple *(Acer rubrum)*
Northern red oak *(Quercus borealis)*
Tuliptree *(Liriodendron tulipfera)*
Pin oak *(Quercus palustris)*
White oak *(Quercus alba)*
Cucumbertree *(Magnolia acuminata)*

On a small lot, however, these may grow too large and out of scale in relation to your house and other plantings. With one-story homes, rambling ranch-style houses, and some split-levels, the smaller shade trees look better. Among the hardies of these are:

Trident maple *(Acer buergerianum)*
Hornbeam maple *(Acer carpinifolium)*
Fullmoon maple *(Acer japonicum)*
Manchurian maple *(Acer mandshuricum)*
Nikko maple *(Acer nikoense)*
European hornbeam *(Carpinus betulus 'Globosa')*
American hornbeam *(Carpinus caroliniana)*
Eastern redburd *(Cercis canadensis)*
Flowering dogwood *(Cornus florida)*
Russian-olive *(Elaeagnus angustifolia)*
Balkan ash *(Fraxinus holotricha)*
Flowering ash *(Fraxinus ornus)*
Golden-rain-tree *(Koelreuteria paniculata)*
Summer magnolia *(x Magnolia soulangeana)*
Sourwood *(Oxydendrum arboreum)*
Chinese elm *(Ulmus parvifolia)*

Leaf Texture Because leaves use solar radiation to evaporate water from their surfaces, trees that provide the most coolness are those with the most leaf surface. Trees with thousands of tiny leaves provide better protection than those with a few large leaves like banana trees.

Coarse leaf surfaces absorb solar radiation better than do smooth, reflective surfaces. And of course dark leaf colors will absorb more of the sun's heat than will lighter shades.

Shiny or glossy leaf surfaces actually reflect some light and heat. Under very hot climate conditions you might prefer to avoid shiny species that grow low to the ground. Shiny surfaces on high-canopied trees such as magnolias would, naturally, radiate the heat way above you, to your benefit. But groundcovers or low bushes with glossy leaves should not be placed so that they radiate into your house or garden.

In cold climates, conversely, you would welcome any reflection, however weak, of solar radiation. Any hard surfaces should be left unshaded, and low plants with glossy leaves might be planted near the house.

Tree Life While investigating trees for landscaping purposes, take into account their life expectancy. Most of the common large shade trees such as oaks, American beech, maples, conifers, live oaks, magnolias, and other live at least seventy-five to a hundred years or more. Some live several centuries, given the right conditions. Arbor vitae, mimosa, and other smaller trees have far shorter life-spans—often no more than fifty years. Many of the small, decorative trees and dwarf varieties can grow old and deteriorate in your lifetime, requiring replacement or substitution. Replacing these small trees is not expensive or troublesome, so you may not mind it. But if you are planning for the long range, and designing basic elements you don't ever want to change, the life expectancy of trees is important.

Welcoming Sun

In any region cold enough to produce significant heating bills, welcoming sun takes precedence over plantings for summer shade.

You should calculate the sun's path across the southern exposure of your property from the time you normally turn the heat on in fall until you turn it off in the spring. For the coldest regions, where you may need heat as early as September and as late as May, you must calculate the sun's path and altitude from the spring equinox through winter to the fall equinox. This means you should consider not only the sun that comes to you from due east, but also the entire southern swath from southeast to southwest. You're especially lucky if your home has wide boundaries on the south and if your home is oriented so that most windows face south. When buying a new home, these are advantages to look for.

Plantings from the southeast to southwest should be low enough so that the winter sun—which may have an altitude angle at 20 degrees or less—will not be obstructed. Even though the sun is weaker on the east and west, you will still want the sun to strike these walls to reduce heat loss through conduction. Unobstructed windows that will catch the sun's radiant energy are also important. Trees should be placed far enough from the house so that they do not shade the roof. Since sun at low angles may cast shadows three or four times the height of the tree, a fifty foot tree may have to be placed two hundred feet away from the house. If for aesthetic or other reasons you do not want trees on the south, east, or west, choose vertical forms that will cast the narrowest shade, and deciduous types that will drop their leaves in fall.

Consider the sun's lowest angles when selecting plants. A moderate-size evergreen bush planted on a Winnipeg property in spring, when the sun's altitude angle might be 40 degrees at midday, might seem at a proper height all through summer as the sun rises higher and even into fall when the sun drops to angles similar to those at planting time. But in winter, as the sun approaches lowest angles, the bush could block sun entirely.

A major complication for people in the North is that protection from wind also is essential. Where, as is common, the wind comes from north or west, windbreaks will not interfere with your sun control. Only when the wind comes from the south or east will you have to balance the relative merits of your plantings for sun and wind. You may be able to design the windscreen at a far enough distance from the house so that it won't cast shadows. Since windbreaks should be perpendicular to the wind, they may angle out in a way that won't appreciably interfere with sun.

In more temperate climates, balancing summer shade with winter sunshine poses more of a problem. Here the solution is to rely heavily on deciduous trees that will shade in summer, but allow sun to filter through in winter. Yet even deciduous trees without leaves can block 20% or more of the sun. To keep trees on the southern exposure from shading your home in midwinter they should be planted at a distance from the house of slightly more than twice their mature height if you live between the 38th and 42nd parallels. As you go farther north and get sun at lower angles, increase the distance to three and eventually four times the tree's height. As you go south, decrease the distance.

To block a hot morning sun in summer, but retain the benefit of morning sun in winter, requires only a calculation of the sun's angles. In summer the sun rises in the northeast, while in winter it rises in the southeast. Careful placement of trees or shrubs can be designed so as to block the sun's summer path but to leave the winter path exposed. Similarly, a setting sun can be blocked in summer with vegetation in its path to the northwest, and openness can be provided on the southwest where the sun sets in winter.

Screening Sun

Although the hottest sun comes at midday and requires overhead screening (see below), most of the sun will be coming onto your property at angles that vary hourly. Where you require maximum sun protection, your plantings should cover the full height and breadth of possible sun penetration. And if you need year-round protection you will want evergreen species. In more temperate regions, most of your shade plantings should be deciduous and calculated to give you sun in winter. Also, your plantings need not screen you as extensively as in the south, because early morning and late afternoon sun may not be as bothersome.

In all climates, the area that should get priority is the southern exposure. Here you will want trees to shade the house, and probably additional trees to shade outdoor living areas. Trees on the south should be those with dense canopies, preferably dark foliage, and preferably of globular or spreading form.

For shading the house, trees with overhanging foliage are better than those with trim canopy shapes. To screen the house they must be considerably higher than your roof, because the sun at its height will cause the tree's shadow to angle downward. Shade therefore drops off quickly at a sharp angle and doesn't extend very far. In southern latitudes it is difficult to shade the roof completely with trees to the south, and overhead screening is necessary too. Where the summer sun at noon makes an angle of less than 80 degrees—that is, in latitudes north of 35 degrees—you may be able to protect most of the roof by choosing tall tree varieties and planting them as close as possible to the house. A distance no more than six or eight feet is best. The farther north you are, the greater the distance can be. Depending on the size and structure of your house, you may need several such trees.

Trees used to shade the roof will not necessarily shade all of your southern wall. This additional shading can be accomplished with lower vegetation at heights and locations calculated to block the ascending and descending sun. In hot climates, where cool air currents are welcome, large, heavy-canopied trees (like magnolias) that provide extensive shade and cool the air before it reaches the house are ideal if you have property that is spacious enough. On smaller properties, groups of small decorative species and fruit trees, plus arbors, can accomplish similar ends.

Groundcovers help reduce the amount of reflected light onto outdoor living areas and windows.

House walls facing east or west should also be protected in temperate climates during summer and for longer periods or year-round in hot climates. Because the sun comes to these surfaces at lower angles than on the south, your plantings need not be so high.

In temperate climates, plantings on the west may be evergreen since the winter sun here is not as important, but vegetation on the east should be deciduous.

East of the house, plantings need not be as heavy as on the south side, and dogwoods, fruit trees, and others with delicate branching structure are good choices. Open foliage is especially desirable if you get your summer breezes from the east. In the Southwest, low vegetation like honey mesquite or cacti and succulents of moderate height can do the trick. Since plants of moderate and short height do not cast long shadows, they must be planted close to building walls to be effective. If, like some cacti, they are of vertical form and cast narrow shadows, they should be grouped or arranged in staggered plantings so that their total shade area can be extended.

West of the house, shading is less important in temperate zones but is necessary in southern regions, and especially in the West. Since the sun sets at low angles, vegetation here should provide good protection where the sun makes angles of below 60 degrees with the horizon. Low-growing palms and other trees and bushes with foliage of good screening quality are possible choices here. Again, low-growing vegetation must be planted close to the house if it is to shade the walls.

Screening Overhead Sun

Screening sun from above is essential for keeping homes in hot climates cool and for reducing air-conditioning bills, and is also beneficial in summer in temperate climates.

In temperate climates screening is a little easier because even the hottest summer sun comes in at an angle. In latitudes of 40 degrees to 45 degrees, for instance, the sun's altitude angle will vary from about 70 degrees to 74 degrees at noon in summer. Trees higher than the roof, planted close to the south side of the house—say, six to eight feet away—may give almost full protection. Deciduous species are necessary so the trees won't block the sun in winter.

Farther south screening is more difficult because the sun's height increases. At latitudes of 25 degrees to 30 degrees the sun is almost directly overhead in summer—with altitude angles at noon of 80 degrees to 85 degrees or more. Even in spring and fall the angles extend to 60 degrees and in winter do not drop much below 40 degrees. Screening from the south may therefore be insufficient to protect the entire roof, and you will want trees that overhang the entire house. Probably, too, you will want sun protection year-round, and evergreens will be your choice.

The ideal tree should have a high trunk bare of branches, with a draping canopy starting high enough to clear the roof. Many palms fit this description. Such trees take up little room at ground level and can be planted all around the perimeter of the house and/or in courtyards or atriums. Bare trunks also allow for the circulation of breezes. Unless your circumstances allow you to nestle your home in a grove, the mature height of the trees you select should not be too much higher than your roof. Otherwise they may grow so tall that they will provide proper shade only at noon, allowing heat to pour in under them as the sun slants in the morning and afternoon.

Trees protecting the roof do not, however, provide complete protection. Often you must screen the southern wall of your house and any outdoor living areas as well. Arbors and trellises are a good solution. Just as a trellis will insulate a wall in the North against wind and cold, so in the South a trellis will insulate your house from wind-blown heat and from solar radiation, thus redressing loss of coolness from conduction. Trellises are especially effective if constructed as extensions to the roof on the southern exposure. In temperate zones the trellis vines should be deciduous, and in hot climates the vines should be evergreens. Freestanding arbors and trellises can be constructed elsewhere on the grounds to provide a cooling effect from vines as well as shade.

Angled trellises and roof overhangs in temperate climates should be calculated to tilt so that they protect from the summer sun coming in high but will not block the lower winter sun. Where you want year-round screening in the south, the tilt will have to protect against sun at only a 40 degree angle altitude in winter.

Evergreen plants suitable for trellises include ivies and flowering varieties such as clematis. Bougainvillea is a favorite due to its showy blossoms. Also popular are fragrant flowering varieties because the scent is enhanced in arbors and trellis-surrounded enclaves; honeysuckle and star jasmine are among these.

Undesirable Shade Trees

The American elm *(Ulmus americana)* has an attractive form with many branches radiating at angles from the main stem, and a handsomely draped, open canopy. If you've got lots of land you could risk an elm. But this tree is susceptible to Dutch elm disease and is therefore a poor choice when you are planting only a few trees, particularly if each is going to be important to you. Thornless honey locust is attacked by the mimosa webworm.

Ginkgo trees have elegantly shaped leaves and attractive, unique forms. These do well in cities and the male tree is often recommended for urban landscaping. The female tree, unfortunately, produces unpleasant, messy fruit. Similarly undesirable fruit is characteristic of white mulberry *(Morus alba)*. Ailanthus altissima, euphemistically named tree-of-heaven, is the tough tree that grows even in Brooklyn, but its fruit has a repulsive stench.

Horse chestnuts, sweetgum, hickories, even oaks and crabapples, produce fruit that some people find a nuisance, especially on small properties. If you don't have them near lawn, or don't mind the fruit, however, these are good shade trees.

Poplars, willows, red maple, and silver maple are among trees with strong shallow root systems that clog sewers and heave sidewalks. They are thus undesirable near new homes, sidewalks, and paved areas, but can be used if you plant them on lawns or other areas where they cannot cause damage.

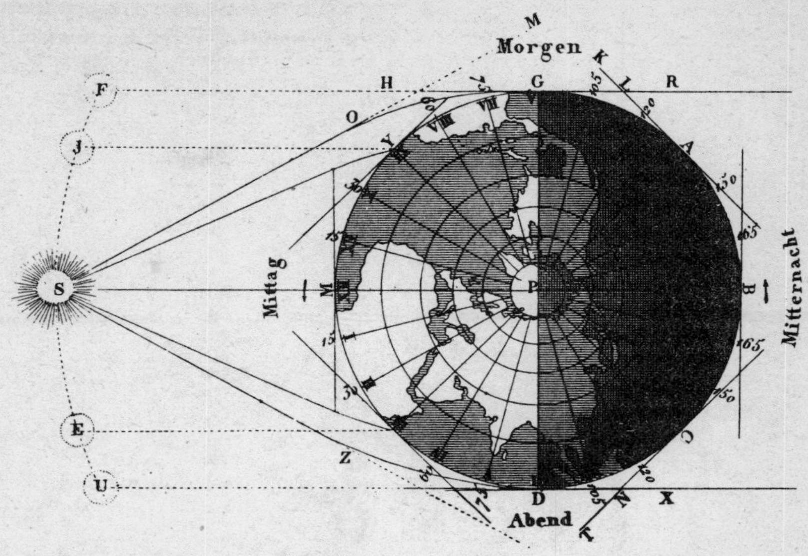

Siberian elm (Ulmus pumila) and silver maple are among those trees having an especially brittle wood and v-shaped crotches that do not allow much branch movement. They are therefore subject to storm damage.

In any particular region there are additional trees that are susceptible to local pests, that for one reason or another do not thrive, or that are subject to disease in certain climates. Seek the advice of local nurseries and government agricultural experts to avoid the wrong trees and select hardier varieties.

Trouble Free Trees

Among trees that seem remarkably free of pests and diseases are:
American hornbeam *(Carpinus caroliniana)*
Katsura tree *(Cereidiphyllum japonica)*
Cornelian-cherry *(Cornus mas)*
Golden-rain-tree *(Koelreuteria paniculata)*
Scotch laburnum *(Laburnum alpinum)*
Sweetgum *(Liquidambar styracifula)*
Hophornbeam *(Ostrya virginiana)*
Amur corktree *(Phellodendron amurense)*
Japanese pagodatree *(Sophora japonica)*
American yellowwood *(Cladrastis lutea)*
Maidenhair tree, male *(Gingko biloba)*

For your particular area there will be other trouble-free trees that you can learn about from nursery or government forestry experts.

MACARTÉ'S, JACKSON'S HEADQUARTERS.

Outdoor Living Areas

Patios, terraces, and other areas with stone surfaces, paving, or reflective materials radiate heat and sunlight toward the house. In an air-conditioned house this can increase energy bills, and raise the temperature of the garden or outdoor living area. To keep the house and outdoor living areas cooler, in warm climates reflective surfaces should be kept to a minimum and shaded with tall plantings. Where possible, replace reflective surfaces altogether with groundcovers or lawns.

Where glaring surfaces are off your property but radiate hat and light onto it, you can use plants of a proper height to screen the glare.

Swimming Pools A wide apron of concrete or other solid surface reduces the amount of dirt and plant debris that would otherwise collect in a swimming pool. The apron can be handsomely landscaped with container flowers like petunias and geraniums as well as with dwarf fruit trees.

In colder climates, the pool-heating bill can run high, so you will want your pool to catch as much sunlight as possible. The smartest landscaping would be to have low shrubs edging the pool apron, and to avoid overhanging trees. Also smart would be to make these shrubs evergreens with needle-like leaves. Such leaves are shed gradually at different times of year and therefore never form a hugh accumulation at any one time; and being heavy, they drop to the ground beneath the plants. Poor plant choices near a swimming pool are deciduous ones that drop their leaves all at once, especially when the leaves are light and easily carried into the pool by the wind. In the vicinity of the pool avoid, by all means, any plants that drop messy fruit directly into the pool, or that can roll there along the apron or be carried there by the wind.

In warmer climates where pool temperatures can rise unpleasantly, you will naturally want shading at the pool. You can block some sun with plantings at a distance from the apron, but this will not solve the problem of overhead sun. Again, deciduous trees and those with messy fruit are a poor choice; you should probably go with evergreens, especially broadleaf evergreens. Some ferns are tall enough to overhang the pool. Palms are feasible if you take care to knock off the fruit before it hits bathers. Look for species of plants with large leaves, as these are easier to clear up than tiny leaves.

Swimming pools, like all large bodies of water, produce glare. In hot areas, proper shading can reduce glare. On level land, however, glare can be directed toward the house where the sun is at a low angle and creeps in under the shade trees. Screening with plants of moderate size can avoid this.

Shade Trees for Poor Soil

In cities and other selected areas, the soil may be too dry and sterile for many shade trees.

One possibility is the Dahurian birch *(Betula davurica),* which survives even on gravelly sites. It has curling, reddish brown bark, and its foliage turns a pretty yellow in autumn.

The Japanese pagodatree *(Sophora japonica)* is also attractive. In late summer it blossoms with pyramidal clusters of yellow, pealike flowers.

The California black oak *(Quercus kelloggii),* and *Q. acutissima,* the sawtooth oak, are also tolerant of poor soil. *Fraxinus pennsylvanica,* the seedless green ash, and *F. velutina,* velvet ash, also provide excellent shade under adverse conditions.

Two other handsome choices are *Koelreuteria paniculata,* the golden-rain tree, and *Sassafras albidum,* the sassafras.

Shade Trees for Wet Soils

In areas where the soil tends to retain water, some of the more common shade trees will not thrive. Species naturally adapted to wet soils include:

Red maple *(Acer rubrum)*
Sweetgum *(Liquidambar styraciflur)*
Sweetbay *(Magnolia virginiana)*
Black tupelo *(Nyssa sylvatica)*
Swamp white oak *(Quercus bicolor)*

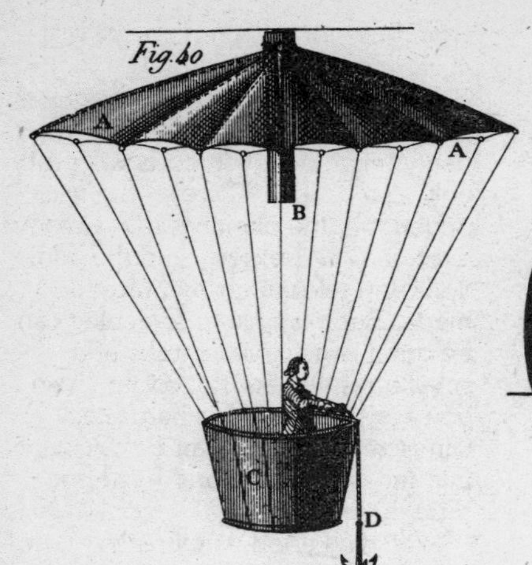

Controlling Wind

Wind—in all its variations from zephyrs to hurricanes—is a major factor in your heating and air-conditioning bills as well as in your general comfort.

Outside air is forced, or drawn, into the interior of your home by pressure differences caused largely by wind. In a hot climate you will usually welcome whatever breezes can be coaxed into your garden and home, and your plantings will therefore be arranged to funnel the wind onto your property.

In the north, where bitterly cold winter winds will be your major concern, you will want plantings to form a windbreak that will keep wind from reaching your property—or at least to reach it at reduced velocity.

Plantings calculated to deflect wind have other uses as well. You can use vegetable to reduce soil erosion caused by wind and to prevent snow from piling up in your driveway. In arid areas, such as the Southwest, where blowing sand can cut seedlings off at ground level and hot winds will evaporate your soil moisture, windbreaks can make the gardening season more pleasant, reduce plant loss, and reduce watering. In coastal areas, where breezes may be mild but annoyingly persistent, wind barriers can make your outdoor living areas more enjoyable.

Windbreaks serve double duty, too. Since they must be high, they provide excellent visual screening. If you are unfortunate enough to have a beautiful view in the direction of your prevailing wind, you would not want to cut it off by planting a windbreak. In this instance you would be limited to planting vegetation to enframe and enhance the view; some of these trees and shrubs might deflect a bit of wind, but it is unlikely you could design a windproof barrier that was effective and retained the view as well. Most homeowners won't have this problem and will welcome whatever visual screening they can get. Since windbreaks must be placed at some distance from the house, they will help to enclose a garden area for privacy.

If you like birds and animals, you'll find your windbreak will also work to encourage them. Because windbreaks must be thick, they afford good protective cover for wildlife. In choosing trees for your windbreak, you can select varieties favored by the birds you most want to encourage.

Finally, vegetation placed to screen wind can also be used to prevent snow and sand from drifting where you do not want it.

Even if you do not intend to plant a windbreak, learning the principles involved can be profitable. Your property may have plants so carelessly placed as to create undesirable wind effects. Since wind picks up velocity above and on either side of a windbreak, plantings that are too low or too narrow may be creating unnecessary turbulence on your land. Since an effective windbreak should be dense throughout, you may have a partial windbreak that is encouraging wind velocity in the wrong places. High-crowned trees placed upwind and not protected with lower plantings can be deflecting wind downward onto your land. Plant groupings on the upwind side may be funneling wind and increasing its speed in open spaces between them. Some of these conditions can be corrected by filling in open space with additional plantings, while others may require removing poorly placed plants.

How Windbreaks Work

Because trees and large shrubs block or deflect air currents, they affect the course, direction, and velocity of the wind. Properly placed, they can moderate wind-chill factors and decrease the amount of heat you must use. But the effectiveness of plantings on wind force depends on their height, width, foliage, density, and other variables.

The direction from which you get the wind is called the "upwind" or "windward" direction and the direction toward which the wind goes is called the "downwind" or "leeward" side. Windbreaks create a slight drop in wind velocity on their upwind side, but the greatest benefit in tempering the wind occurs on the downwind side. On the downwind side a windscreen gives maximum effect for a distance of three to five times its height. Lesser but still significant reductions in wind velocity continue for more than double that distance, the effect gradually diminishing.

In other words, a 15-foot windscreen will give you maximum protection to leeward for 45 to 75 feet—where your house should be—but will continue to be effective for more than 75 feet beyond your home. A windbreak at one end of your property is therefore capable of moderating the wind over your entire plot if your lot runs 150 to 200 feet deep. As the trees grow to maturity, their effect will carry correspondingly farther.

This is a very impressive benefit. Of course, trees are not the only form of windbreak. You could also use a solid fence or wall. But vegetation has decided advantages over fencing as a wind screen.

For one thing, walls and fences of adequate height to function as windbreakers are expensive. In most circumstances, too, they are inappropriate and ugly. Most important of all, though, solid barriers do not provide as large an area of protection as do permeable barriers. Solid, stone walls or wooden fences do stop the wind effectively on the upwind side, but due to the pressure systems created in the process, the wind quickly resumes its speed on the downwind side. You would therefore receive wind protection only if the wall or fence were built smack up against the windward side of your house. Solid barriers are, therefore, practical against wind only in special circumstances where no other choice is possible.

An easy way to understand why vegetation makes a windbreak far superior to a solid barrier is to examine the way snow or sand piles up around various types of fencing. At concrete or other solid barriers, snow or sand piles up high on both upwind and downwind sides. This is because a solid barrier stops the wind at the upwind side and forces it up over the top. But due to the pressures created, the wind hardly changes speed as it resumes its path on the downwind side.

Side view

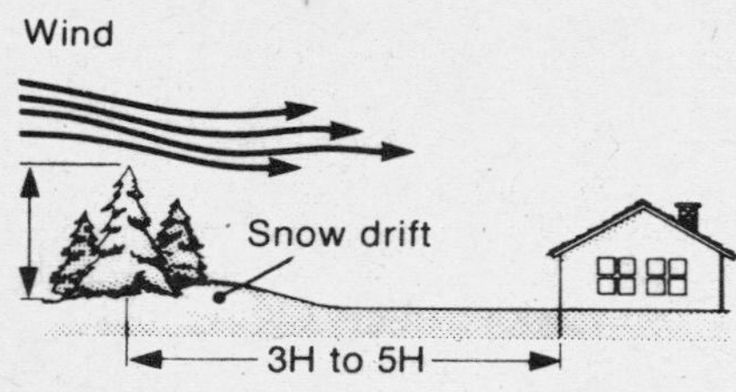

In contrast, fencing made especially for snow and sand is constructed of narrow vertical slats held apart with wire so that the space between the slats allows for passage of air. When the wind hits this type of fencing, only part of the wind is deflected over the top of the fence. The rest passes between the slats and loses speed. This creates less pressure variation between the upwind and downwind sides of the fencing. As a result, the snow or sand does not pile up as high but is spread farther—especially on the downwind side where the reduced wind velocity carries it long distances.

Windbreaks of vegetation work the same way, because like slatted fencing they allow passage of air. When the wind hits a windbreak, the part of the air that is deflected up over the trees hardly changes speed. For that reason, the windbreak should be high enough to allow this air to pass over the roof of your house.

The part of the air passing through the trees loses a great deal of speed. How much speed is lost depends on the density of the vegetation, but the greatest reduction is made at first impact. Wind approaching a forest, for example, drops velocity as soon as it hits the trees. As the wind continues to travel through the forest, however, it will keep most of the remaining speed. Planting acres of trees between yourself and the wind is therefore not going to be any more effective—if at all—than planting a few well chosen species in the proper positions.

Assessing Wind

To construct a windbreak or a wind funnel, you must know with certainty the direction from which you get the wind—i.e., the upwind or windward direction.

You cannot use your area's generally prevailing wind direction as a guide. If you live in the East, for example, you would expect to get winter winds from the west. Yet if your property is in a depression or on a slope, or in a mountainous area, your wind might reach you from another direction. Surrounding forests or large stands of vegetation planted by others could also affect your wind. Neighboring structures, the position of your own home, and other factors could mean your miniclimate with regard to wind is quite different from the generally prevailing wind direction of your region. To determine your upwinds accurately, you cannot go by what others in your locality say about the wind. You have to make your own observation of how the wind passes over your particular property.

Very likely, too, the winds at your home will vary in direction and velocity from season to season. You will want to make an accurate assessment of these seasonal variations before deciding where to construct the windbreak or whether you want one at all.

Top view

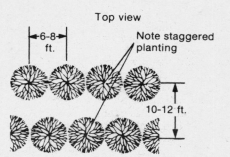

6-8 ft.
Note staggered planting
10-12 ft.

Windbreaks are therefore nothing to jump into precipitously, and you should give yourself ample time to fully assess how the wind blows on your property.

You can do this by hoisting small flags, or strands of woolen yarn at strategic heights and distances around your property. In a snowy area or at the seashore you can also note how the snow or sand is blown.

Costs

To reduce soil erosion, plantings need be only at ground level, and most of the creepers and vines you would use for this purpose are relatively inexpensive.

To provide wind screening against moderate velocities and at human-head height or lower, costs will probably also be low. The expense will depend on the plantings that already exist on your property and the additions and relocations that must be made. But this type of screening can be done largely with shrubs and small trees that are not costly. Even if you are starting with a bare site, windscreening trees can be calculated into the overall cost and need not raise the budget.

Providing good windbreaks to protect your home from heat loss, however, requires tall trees that will run into more initial investment—an ivestment not repaid until they reach effective heights. The fast-growing softwoods are more easily damaged by strong wind, and may break under snow accumulations. Before investing in these, check to be sure they can withstand the wind conditions on your property. The sturdier hardwoods are often slower growers. If existing trees on your property are properly placed and need only be supplemented, your costs will naturally be lower. But if you are on land that was formerly agricultural or that has been stripped by a developer, you have to start from scratch.

To save initial costs, you can buy young trees and plant them yourself. You can do this by hand if the trees are small enough. In some areas you can rent tree-planting machines. The cost of planting your windbreaks is low. These will not, however, provide much protection until they reach the taller heights—about fifteen feet for the average one-story house. This can take several years, the time depending on whether the trees you buy are fast-growing or slow-growing.

Planting more mature trees costs more. The trees themselves are higher priced, and you will probably need to pay for professional installation. Though these costs are reflected more quicklly in your energy bills, you may not want to invest this much.

A compromise is to plant temporary, fast-growing species at the same time you plant your permanent trees. You need space for this, as temporary trees should be planted in one or two rows at least fifteen feet upwind of your permanent windbreak. Fast-growing deciduous trees (such as poplars) or evergreens (such as pine) should be chosen. In addition to providing a faster windscreen for your home, they will protect the young trees in your permanent windbreak. The temporary trees should be removed before they retard the growth of your permanent species.

The final cost of a windbreak therefore involves a bit of figuring. You have to juggle factors such as how long you intend to live on your particular property, how fast your trees will grow, the cost of installation, and the savings on your energy bills in the short and long runs.

Savings In an area with high winds such as the Great Plains, windbreaks can reduce heating bills by 25 percent. In the more northerly areas, the savings could be more—on the order of 30 percent.

Where winds are less severe, such as in forested temperate areas, savings can vary from between 3 percent and 15 percent.

But your savings depend on how carefully your windbreak is planned. In one Pennsylvania home studied by the government, a windbreak consisting of a single row of white pine reduced the heating bills by 11 percent. The study revealed, however, that the cold winds on this property blew against the windbreak only 65 percent of the time. Had extra plantings been made to reduce wind from other directions, the fuel bill savings could have been 17 percent.

In another study, deciduous trees had been planted close to the home to provide summer shade and in addition cut winter wind velocity by 40 percent. The heating bills were reduced by only 8 percent, however. The reason was that the trees were so close to the home that the branches, even without leaves, had effectively blocked much of the winter sun.

Because windbreaks are rarer in warm climates, less information has been gathered on the effects of windbreaks on air-conditioning bills. Some evidence exists, though, that windbreaks could increase cooling bills if they prevented air currents from carrying heat away from unshaded surfaces. In a well-shaded home, good savings might result if the reduced wind cut the rate of hot-air infiltration into a home that uses an air conditioner.

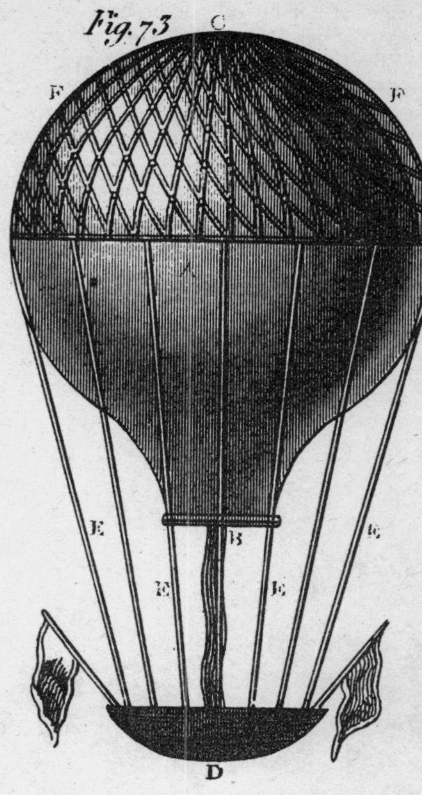

How to Make a Windbreak

1. Windbreaks should be located *upwind* from the home and perpendicular to the prevailing wind.

Any alteration in this 90-degree angle will reduce the effectiveness of your wind-resistant plantings.

A double row of maple trees about forty-feet high, planted perpendicular to the prevailing wind direction, will reduce wind speed downwind by 50 percent.

However, if the wind does not hit the trees at a 90-degree angle, wind speed would not decrease as much. Wind hitting trees at an acute angle would mostly sweep right past them, scarcely reducing the wind speed. The effectiveness of your plantings therefore depends on how accurately you assess the direction of the wind and how closely to a perpendicular angle you place your plantings.

Where wind is variable, you may want windbreaks in more than one position.

2. The *height* of an effective windbreak depends on the height of your roof. For a single-story house, trees will usually be effective once they reach a fifteen-foot height. Though the trees will continue to grow to their mature height, the added height will not give you much more benefit in your heating bills (you will, however, get more shade, which could cut down your air-conditioning bills). For taller homes, the trees would have to grow correspondingly higher before becoming fully effective.

But a windbreak is fully effective only if the wind is barricaded the full length from the ground up to the treetops. If you are using black or red spruce, douglas fir, or other trees whose forms offer foliage their full length, then you need no other plantings. Evergreens, such as many pines, where lower branches are bare, sparsely needled, or nonexistent require smaller species planted with them, preferably on both windward and leeward sides. Most of the deciduous trees require this type of underplanting too.

3. The *distance* of the windbreak from your home depends on the effective height of the trees you intend to use. The optimum distance for a windbreak is one to three times the height of the trees *once they have grown to an effective height.* Roughly, this usually means a distance of about forty to fifty feet from a single-story home.

That is, if you are planting four-foot trees, you do not figure the distance from their height at planting time but from the height at which they will become effective. If the effective height is *H*, and you plant the trees at 3H, then they will still be in the recommended 1H to 3H zone when they have reached maturity. For example, say you are planting maples that will reach forty feet at maturity but that will attain effective heights at fifteen feet. Planting them at 3H would mean a distance of forty-five feet at their forty-foot maturity, they would be slightly over the 1H minimum distance of forty feet.

At maturity, these same trees would still be effective if they were as far as 120 feet from the house. But planting trees at distances calculated at their mature heights means you have to wait many years to derive any benefit from the windscreen.

These distances are optimum and you can be somewhat flexible. The 1H to 3H guide is for maximum protection. In fact, your protection with dense foliage will still be excellent up to at least 5H. When you are using trees with looser and more open foliage, their wind-resistant effect carries even farther so they can be placed at greater distances.

In determining height and distance for a windscreen, however, your sunlight requirements must be taken into account. In a northern climate, for instance you don't want the windscreen to cut off the winter sun that will help to warm your home—a possible danger if you are trying to barricade yourself against a wind from the south or east and plant the trees too close to the house.

4. An optimum *width* of the planting is achieved if you can extend the windbreak fifty feet beyond the house and/or garden boundaries you are trying to protect.

This assumes you have a lot of space, but it is the optimum amount and you can do with less. In most cases, where you will be protecting against cold wind, you will not be using your garden in winter; the windbreak would therefore be protecting only the house.

Getting enough breadth in a windbreak becomes a problem chiefly where you are trying to protect a garden from hot and disruptive wind in spring or summer, as you might in the Southwest. On a small lot, where the garden covers most of your property, a windbreak may not be a good idea if you cannot achieve a full width. Too narrow a windbreak would mean you would be subjected to increased wind velocity at either side of the planting, which could be worse than having no windbreak.

5. The optimum *depth* for a windbreak is three to five rows of trees.

If you have limited space, however, even a single row is worth planting, because you will be using shrubs and other lower-growing plants to complete the barrier. A single row of trees is especially effective if you choose dense conifers such as spruce trees.

The rows of trees should be planted ten to twelve feet apart.

Within each row, the trees should be planted six feet apart if you are going to have one, two, or three

rows. If you are using four or more rows, plant the trees eight feet apart.

Trees in each row should be staggered. That is, once you have planted the first row, plant the trees in the second row so that they are between the trees in the first row rather than aligned with them. This is not only necessary for effective protection, but creates a more aesthetic, natural-looking planting.

If you are using three or more rows, the central or core row or rows should consist of the fastest growing and tallest trees. The outside rows—on both upwind and downwind sides—should consist of denser and lower varieties of trees.

6. Optimum *density* for windbreaks varies, depending on wind velocity in your area and other factors.

A windbreak of dense evergreens, such as spruces, can cut wind velocities up to 80 percent and give year-round protection. Speed reductions by dense deciduous trees can be up to 60 percent when they are in full leaf, but drop to half or less of this efficiency when they lose their leaves in winter.

Density varies from species to species, however, depending on size and form of leaf and the form of branching and of the entire tree. Pines are not as dense as spruces. Maples cut wind velocity only about 50 percent, and trees of more open form, like poplars, only 40 percent. For most purposes, windscreens are best composed of a few compatible species that include evergreens and deciduous types.

These figures do not, however, mean that everyone should plant dense spruce barriers. This type of planting is most appropriate the farther north you go, and especially if your wind comes from only one direction and is chiefly a strong and cold wind. In a cold northern climate, cutting off such wind is rightfully the main concern.

In more temperate climates, wind velocity may also be tempered, and cutting the speed by 50 percent may be sufficient. This is especially true when year-round climate is considered. If your summer breezes come from the same direction as an occasional biting winter storm, you might prefer to take the brunt of the storm rather than construct a windbreak that would make your garden unbearably hot in summer. You will also want all the sunlight you can get in winter, and deciduous trees might therefore be a better choice than evergreens. In general, in temperate zones the decisions are less clear and you have to balance off the advantages of windbreaks from cold wind against the welcome winds of summer and your sun requirements.

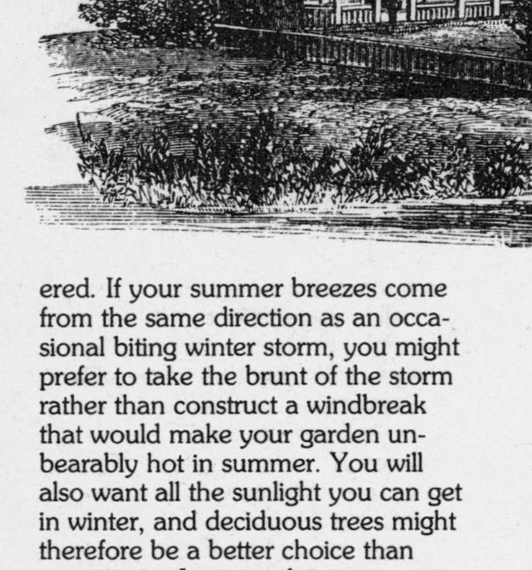

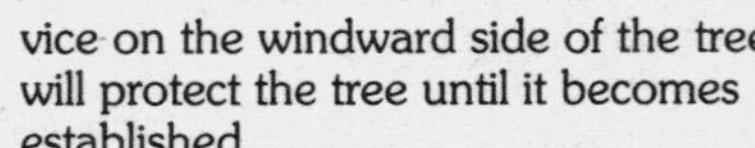

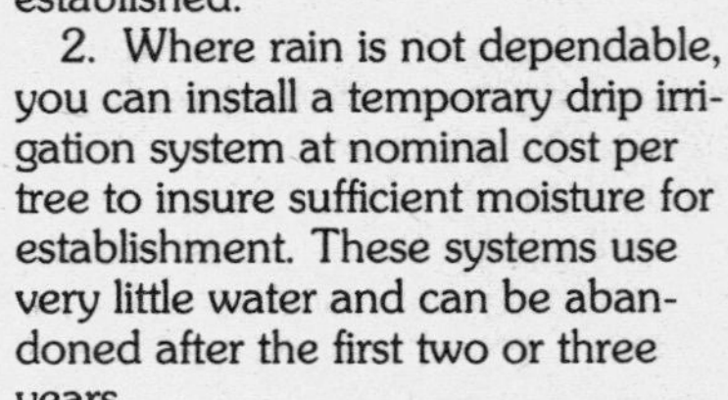

In general, as you go farther south, screening from sun takes increasing precedence over screening from wind, and the wind is to be encouraged rather than barred. Only where hot and unpleasant winds arise in spring or summer is windscreening a major concern, and here you may again want a good density, especially if the wind carries sand.

Tips on Windbreaks

1. In areas with high wind, young trees may need protection—especially since you are placing them precisely where the wind does its worst. Hammering into the ground a cedar shingle or other protective device on the windward side of the tree will protect the tree until it becomes established.

2. Where rain is not dependable, you can install a temporary drip irrigation system at nominal cost per tree to insure sufficient moisture for establishment. These systems use very little water and can be abandoned after the first two or three years.

3. Free help with planning windbreaks is available from forestry agencies and conservation districts as well as from some conservation groups. In some areas, you may be able to buy trees at moderate cost through the government agencies.

Wind Funnels

Wind funnels are plantings calculated to trap the wind and steer it straight toward your house and garden. They are useful only in hot, humid areas; in a few situations in hot and arid climates where refreshing breezes are available from a particular location; and in temperate zones where summertime temperatures can be oppressive yet prevailing breezes do not originate from the same direction as winter winds.

Ideally, for a funnel you want a wide space open to the prevailing breezes but vegetation that will concentrate and narrow the wind as it approaches the house. Thus the plantings should be in a V-shape, with the open end of the V farthest from the house and the narrowest end closest to the center of your property. This should make the wind velocity increase and provide the benefits of a bit of wind-chill factor, provided the vegetation flanking the V is high enough.

Wind funnels are most effective on large properties where you can control plantings for a considerable distance. On small plots they can be impossible to achieve unless neighboring buildings and plantings fit into your plan. Usually the best you can do is rather negative—being sure that no large shrubs or trees interfere with a desirable breeze.

One trick, discovered long ago on humid southern plantations, is to orient an avenue of overhanging shade trees or arbors toward the prevailing breezes. The overhanging vegetation will cool any air currents passing under it. Thus, if you create V-shaped plantings under a vine-hung trellis or arbor, or within the shade of large, leafy trees, hot air will lose a good deal of its unpleasant quality before reaching you.

In hot and arid areas, hot winds can sometimes be funneled through shaded trellises or archways or other architectural openings into a cooler interior courtyard that contains a fountain to add moisture to the air. This was a principle invented in the Middle East. It was carried to Spain by the Moors and then to North America by the Spanish. For doorways, the Moors built a series of archways, solid at the bottom and decorated at the top with intricate openwork designs. Cooler air passed through the lower archways, but the hotter air rose to the ceiling. There it was filtered through the openwork designs that cooled it before it reached the interior courtyard, where fountains added humidity. Though modern Southwestern homes do not usually involve such intricate designs, they often do incorporate thick walls and shaded, arched entries leading to cool courtyards. Wind funneling toward such openings can therefore be effective in reducing heat, especially if the air currents first pass through an avenue of palms or other shading.

Controlling Erosion

Erosion, the wearing away of topsoil, is a problem anywhere that plant cover has been removed, because plants are the major way soil is held in place. Developers are responsible for the widespread erosion problems in suburbs, due to their habit of stripping trees and other vegetation before building. When the rich topsoil washes away or is blown away, the more compacted, less fertile subsoil is exposed. Many plants cannot survive at all, and others will be stunted and weak.

Most erosion problems are due to wind and rain, and are exacerbated on slopes. Even on level land, bare spots worn into a lawn by active children or by disease can be enlarged and deepened by wind and rain. Bare soil on a slope can be blown away by the wind, but running water wears the land even faster and is more damaging. During a single downpour, the rain quickly seeks a slight depression for the runoff, and the little gully created by the end of the storm will be quickly found and enlarged by succeeding storms. Eventually cascades of mud will carry off surrounding plants, deepening and widening the eroded area.

Yet all of these problems can be prevented by vegetation. Trees and other plants with underground root networks act as deep barriers against the action of running water. But if erosion has progressed far enough, most species will not survive until the soil has been built up. In this case, grasses and other low-growing groundcovers can be used to tie down the soil. These are the fastest and cheapest devices for reclaiming a badly eroded area. At first, newly planted vegetation will simply hold the soil in place with roots and will reduce the damaging impact of wind and rain on the soil surface. Leaves, branches, and grasses soften the impact of rain, so that it hits the ground with diminished strength. Leaves and grasses also reduce wind velocity and therefore its power to carry off soil. Eventually, even on badly eroded land, the plants will rebuild the soil so that it contains a high level of organic material. Because this type of earth, unlike sand and compacted soil, absorbs and holds water, runoff is greatly reduced.

Timber land that has been swept by a forest fire.
There is no cover to prevent erosion.

Erosion along seacoasts is affected by wind and by ocean waves that are less subject to human control. Attempts to modify wave action by building jetties or breakwaters have proved self-defeating, as these could not contain the ocean but simply changed the pattern of erosion, often making it worse. Destruction of seashore vegetation by overrunning of dunes and by home-building can, however, be remedied. Planting of sea oats and other species tie down sand just as vegetation holds soil in place; the above ground portion of the plants moderates the force of the wind and water, while the root systems exert a stabilizing influence below. Eventually, the bare sand will build up to support complex communities of seashore plantings such as can be seen in the rare oceanfront preserves where vegetation has survived due to the protective state of federal legislation.

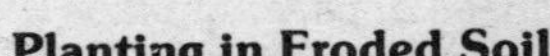

Planting in Eroded Soil

In considering plants for erosion control it is a good idea to know the exact nature of your soil by having a soil test done. Eroded soils are apt to lack the nutrients necessary to establish a good cover.

Sheep destroy forest cover and are thus often factors in soil depletion.

You may have to buy fertilizer before planting the groundcover species you want. Sometimes you find plants that will help enrich the soil. For example, for soils lacking nitrogen, you can install nitrogen-fixing trees or shrubs that will grow in infertile soil with little maintenance. These plants have bacteria and tiny fungi attached to their roots that take nitrogen from the air and convert it to a form the plant can use. Once these plants have supplied nitrogen to the soil, weeds will invade to protect the bare earth under the trees and shrubs. Two nitrogen-fixing plants are Cardinal autumn-olive and Arnot bristly locust.

Once you have seeded or planted in eroded soil, you must protect the bed until the plants establish themselves. Especially on slopes, the wind and rain blow away the seeds or uproot the plantings. Applying mulch over the seedbed, and tying it down so it will not wash or blow away, will prevent this. Even on flat ground the mulch provides the coolness and moisture that encourages sprouting and early growth.

Straw is an excellent mulch. Use a maximum of 70 to 90 pounds for every 1000 square feet. With too heavy a cover the new plants may have to fight to get through or may not emerge. Hay, excelsior, glass fiber, and other materials may be used in place of straw as mulch. To keep the mulch in place, cover it with one of the nets made of paper or other material that can be stretched across the planting bed and pinned down at the edges. Some heavy jute nettings, or mats of glass or wood fibers, are sold that can be put against the bare soil after seeding; these do not require mulch.

Temporary Covers

If your permanent choice of plant is going to take time to establish, you might want to protect the soil in the meantime with a temporary cover. Short-lived, fast-growing perennial grasses and legumes are good solutions. If you have a seasonal need, you will find winter annual and summer growers good.

When you are ready to plant your permanent cover, the temporary cover can be mowed for grown-in-place mulch and seeded over, or it can be worked into the soil when you prepare the final seed- or plant-bed with spade or tiller.

Good temporary species include annual or perennial ryegrass, sudangrass, rye, field bromegrass, redtop, and Korean lespedeza.

Grasses to Use

Grasses are the most versatile and valuable plants for badly eroded areas. Varieties are available that tolerate excessive heat and excessive cold, and that will grow in wet, dry, acid, alkaline, sandy, clayey, rich, or infertile soil. Bunchy grasses are long-lived and require little maintenance; these can be used on cuts and fills such as along the roadside of your property. Sod-farming grasses, such as Kentucky bluegrass used for lawns, have fibrous root systems and dense surface growth. Many of these provide wear-resistant cover, but if an area is not going to be walked on leafier groundcovers can be used.

Kentucky bluegrass comes in many varieties adaptable to a wide range of conditions. In cooler climates it is often combined with creeping forms of red fescue for greater strength. Kentucky 31 withstands drought and wear, is tolerant of poorly drained soil, and takes heavy runoff surface wear. Reed canarygrass survives in wet soils and is therefore often used to prevent erosion along the banks of streams or ditches.

In hotter and drier areas, Bermudagrass varieties resist the scouring effect of running water and human wear. In dryland areas of the West, where there is little rainfall, buffalograss, sideoats grama, and blue grama are useful. With more moisture, western wheatgrass is a good sod-farmer for slopes and waterways. For tough sites, two drought-resistant sod-formers are Sodar streambank wheatgrass and Critana thickspike wheatgrass. Sodar requires almost no maintenance and is so wear-resistant it can be used in parking lots and playgrounds.

In the more humid areas of the Southeast, bahiagrasses and brunswickgrasses are good choices for lawns, banks, and recreational use. Wilmington bahiagrass is resistant to the chinch bug.

In the Great Plains, native grasses such as big, little, and sand bluesteim; indiangrass; and switchgrass predominate in soil conservation. Though each variety has a narrow range of adaptation, several types are suitable in any one locality. A few introduced species, such as smooth bromegrass, are also used.

For sandy areas, there are native species such as switchgrass and coastal panicgrass as well as introduced species such as weeping lovegrass from South Africa.

Groundcovers to Use

If you have bare soil you are anxious to cover quickly, you may be tempted by fast-growing English ivy or the kudzu vine. Though these provide beautiful, dense growth, they grow so quickly—both along the ground as well as climbing trees, fences, and other barriers in their path—that they require constant pruning. Kudzu, once recommended by U.S. agricultural experts, has, in fact, become known as the vine that ate the South and can be found strangling shrubs and trees along country roads and busy highways.

You'll be better off with species that stay in bounds with a minimum of maintenance. Periwinkle and pachysandra are handsome, dense, and shade tolerant—and require a minimum of maintenance.

In California and other areas of the Southwest where fire is a problem during hot, dry summer spells, the iceplant is a good choice due to its fire-retardant qualities. It has dense, attractive growth that will keep the soil from washing away in rain, but it is a succulent with fleshy leaves that will slow the spread and lower the intensity of wildfires. If not too badly damaged, its roots will continue to protect the soil after a fire while the leaves regrow. In areas where fire is a hazard, plants with inflammable oils should be avoided, and if you want to avoid groundcovers altogether you can protect the soil surface by landscaping with widely spaced cacti and succulents separated by earth covered with crushed stone or gravel. This type of covering will reduce weeds and help conserve moisture.

—DOUBLE PERIWINKL]

Crownvetch, a legume, has pink flowers in addition to dense top and root growth, and it grows well on slopes. It is widely used, so varieties adaptable to many geographic areas have been developed. Dwarf Japanese fleeceflower is also attractive and provides color with its bright red fruiting stalks. Both of these spread by shoots from underground stems. They are good for winter protection on slopes because the stems mat down to form a mulch.

Woody and evergreen herbaceous plants that are suitable for slopes and rock gardens are the spreading forms of juniper and other needled evergreens as well as leafy plants like cotoneasters. Some of the junipers are bluish, and the rockspray cotoneaster, which has shiny, flat-growing foliage, produces bright red berries.

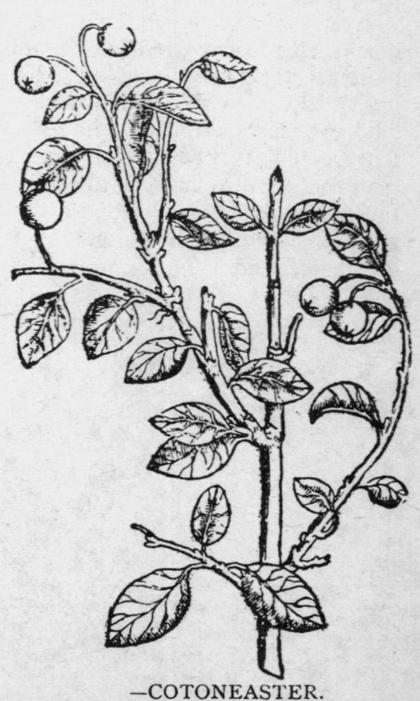

—COTONEASTER.
COTONEASTER VULGARIS.

The most important function plants perform for humans is converting the carbon dioxide we exhale into the oxygen we need to survive. For this reason alone, increasing plantings in urban areas where carbon dioxide levels are highest would go a long way toward making our air healthier.

Yet supplying us with oxygen is only the beginning of the aid plants can give us in our efforts to have healthier air.

Plants as Detectives

Plants are pollution detectives. Many sensitive species show visible effects from air pollutants long before any effects are noticeable in humans.

Trying to grow a garden in smoke and smog is not a new endeavor. In seventeenth century England, people labored valiantly to create private pieces of beauty in coal towns such as Leeds that stank of sulfur fumes. Many people gave up trying to grow plants. Writers of the time already lamented urban development that tempted many of the wealthy to sell their garden acreage for home plots. The diminution of greenery in cities became so commonplace that new cities in the New World were laid out—with a few notable exceptions such as Savannah—with no thought at all to gardens or green public areas. Thomas Fairchild, an important eighteenth century horticulturist, published *The City Gardener* in 1772, which in eight volumes attempted to instruct Londoners on plants suitable to the urban environment of the time. Among Fairchild's recommendations were pears, figs, plane trees, grape vines, lilac, and lily of the valley.

By the nineteenth century, people had noticed that conifers such as pines, spruces, and firs did not survive in the vicinity of industries like smelters that spewed out sulfur dioxide. Evergreen leaves and needles are especially affected because they live longer than the leaves of deciduous trees. Since the leaves of deciduous trees are renewed annually, these plants take longer to show the effects of pollution.

Because plants are such good detectives, West Germany requires plantings of sensitive species around certain industrial sites. The overemission of toxicants can be seen quickly on the vegetation, eliminating the need for costly monitoring with instruments. The health of vegetation in your area can likewise tell you a lot about the air quality.

White pine is one species especially sensitive to pollution. During periods when air stagnates, even those trees in rural areas can be damaged by polluted air reaching them from far-off urban and industrial centers. People in rural areas are therefore not immune to pollution produced elsewhere.

REDUCING AIR POLLUTION

—HAWTHORN.

Yuca (yucca)

—LILAC.

Pollution Effects

The major air pollutant in North America is ozone, closely followed by PAN (peroxyacetyl nitrate). Both are photochemical oxidants formed by sunlight acting on the end products of fuel combustion. Most of our ozone and PAN comes from car and truck exhausts.

Ozone damage can be seen in both deciduous and evergreen plants. Broad-leaved plants develop many small, irregular lesions—called fleck or stipple—on the upper leaf surfaces. The leaf veins remain green until an advanced state of injury, when the whole leaf may turn yellow. When leaves grow upright—as in grasses—the lesions develop on both sides of the leaf. On pine trees, ozone causes yellowing (chlorosis) of the foliage, and the tips of the needles die. This is most noticeable on the lower leaves.

PAN affects young leaves especially, and makes the leaves look silvered, glazed, or bronzed—especially on the lower leaf surface. The injury may affect the whole leaf or may appear in transverse bands. The damage you see is evidence that the leaf tissue has collapsed.

Sulfur dioxide is another common pollutant. It results from smelting ores and from burning fuels (such as coal and crude oil) that contain sulfur. Sulfur dioxide causes the leaf surfaces between the veins to have white, gray, or creamy blotches. The blotches show through on both sides of the leaf. Small veins may lose color, but larger ones remain green. On grasses and other plants with parallel veins, the leaves will be streaked and the tips dry and hard and brown.

Nitrogen dioxide comes chiefly from motor vehicle exhausts and may stunt plant growth and cause premature aging. In low concentrations it does not mark the leaves. In high concentrations leaf markings may develop that look like those produced by sulfur dioxide.

Laboratory experiments have shown that citrus yields can be halved by polluted air, and that many vegetables (potatoes, onions, radishes, beans) double in size when grown in unpolluted air. Seedlings are also stunted by pollution.

Another experimental finding is that plants grown in dry air and dry soil are less sensitive to pollution than the same plants grown in moister air and soil. Except in the Los Angeles basin, where high pollution levels occur year-round, pollution is generally highest from June to September—unfortunately, the time when plants are undergoing the most growth.

Pollution, by injuring the leaves and reducing the vitality of trees, can make them more susceptible to insect and disease attack and lower their resistance to environmental stress such as drought.

Plants Trap Dust

Apart from cleaning the air of toxic substances we cannot see, plants catch and hold the heavier dirt particles that settle as dust, soot, and cinders. The foliage of leafy species catches most of the dirty material, and hairy-leaved species are most effective of all. Small leaves catch more than large leaves. In nature these airborne particles are then washed down to the soil by rain.

Though this means that periodically the leaves of houseplants must be sponged, and that urban trees in dirty areas must be hosed down, the dust trapped by plants reduces the amount we breath in. Studies have shown that the air in tree-lined streets may have only a tenth of the dust content carried by the air on a street without trees.

Trees and shrubs can be planted to act as dust screens between streets and apartment buildings in cities, between a home and a dirt road in the country, or between residential areas and highways in urban areas.

Pollution-Resistant Plants

Those plant species that survive pollution do so because they are able to absorb toxic substances. These are therefore desirable species to have around in highly polluted areas, as they can significantly reduce the amount of pollution humans would otherwise be exposed to.

Plant leaves are covered with tiny stomata or microscopic pores. Each square inch of leaf surface contains several thousand of these pores. When these pores are open (in light), they absorb pollutants such as fluorides. Experiments have shown that 50 percent or more of pollutants can be removed from air in their vicinity by the leaves of trees and smaller plants.

Though we usually think of pollution control by visible plants, the soil around plants contains a great number of microscopic plant species in symbiotic relationships with the plants we see. When air permeates the soil, these invisible plants are efficient at removing carbon monoxide, hydrocarbons, and other pollutants from it. Other microorganisms degrade many toxic chemicals, such as sulfur dioxide and nitrogen dioxide, that enter the soil. Plants therefore fight pollution in inivisible as well as visible ways.

Each species varies in how much pollution it can absorb before injury occurs. European linden is more tolerant of ozone than is white ash, for instance. One of the most tolerant of all is ailanthus, the so-called Chinese tree-of-heaven that grows like a weed in city alleys and abandoned lots. Unfortunately, unless you are in a desperate situation, this is not a desirable tree as it produces a fruit with an unpleasant stench. Far more appealing choices are Norway maple, honeylocust, the attractive ginkgo, Austrian and Scotch pines, the London plane tree, and the Washington hawthorn.

The evidence on shade trees such as oaks and maples, and on the smaller decorative flowering trees like cherry, magnolia, and flowering crabapples is less clear. They may be pollution-resistant in one area yet not in another.

Shrubs resistant to pollution include lilac, Japanese barberry, Van Hout spirea, forsythia, snowberry, and privet. Yucca also seems to thrive. Camellias are among resistant flowering plants. Cotoneaster, acacia, pittosporum, and viburnum are other possibilities.

With pollution levels increasing, much research is being done in this field with an eye to developing resistant varieties. Some species such as mints and alpine plants seem especially sensitive, but with other species resistance seems to vary from plant to plant. Breeders are attempting to isolate the factors involved in popular plants such as rhododendron so as to produce more resistant strains. Thus far a number of food plants (such as potatoes) have been isolated as having resistant qualities, and you should look for these if you are in a highly polluted area.

Overcoming Salt Pollution

—WHITE-FLOWERED OLEANDER.

Salts, which occur naturally in soil and water, supply plants with mineral nutrients essential to their growth. Too much salt, however, damages plants. Because plants normally absorb salts through their roots, most drainage occurs when the soil salinity rises. Many plants, though, also will absorb salt through their leaves, and these plants can be injured when sprayed with salty water.

Normally, oversalinity in soil or water is a problem only on seacoasts, where planting salt-tolerant species is the solution. But today, two factors are making salt pollution a widespread danger away from ocean environments—de-icing with salt and irrigation.

De-Icing with Salt

In northern climates where sidewalks, streets, and highways are de-iced with salt, some of the damage to trees and shrubs is caused by melting snow and ice sprayed onto the foliage by traffic. Woody trees, shrubs, and vines are most affected. These will show burns at the leaf tips or along the leaf margins, and burning may be followed by dieback of stems and eventual death of the plants.

In addition, salted water draining off sidewalks and traffic arteries into soil can raise the soil salinity so high that most sidewalk shade trees and other common roadside plantings cannot survive. The only solution here is to design drainage systems that will carry the brine solutions away from the plants. If enough of the water cannot be carried away, then you will have to use only salt-tolerant species for plantings.

Irrigation

The second and larger danger today comes from irrigation. Salts in the soil are usually leached out by rain, and oversalinity of soil is therefore less of a problem in humid areas than in subhumid and arid regions. Plants that are irrigated—whether they are potted indoor plants you water and fertilize by hand or areas of crops watered with complex automatic irrigation systems—absorb only the water and the few minerals they need through their roots. They leave the rest of the salts behind in the soil. The only way to remove these salts i by leaching—that is, soaking the soil with more water than the plants can use. If this excess water can drain away below the roots, it will carry with it the excess salts. This is easy enough to do with a houseplant; you immerse the pot in a sink or bucket of water every couple of months to clear out the unwanted salts. On a larger scale, leaching is so difficult that many irrigated areas have been "salted out." Salting out occurs not only because flushing the minerals from large tracks of land is difficult, but also because leaching drives the minerals into nearby waterways. Thus the rivers that supply the water for irrigation are themselves too salty, vastly complicating the problem.

The symptom of salt injury in plants due to overly saline soil is stunted growth. Leaves, stems, flowers, and fruit are smaller than normal, and their size decreases as the level of salinity increases.

Leaching with a six-inch depth of water will reduce the salinity of the top foot of soil by fifty percent and will be sufficient for small plants and those with shallow root systems. For larger plants and deeper root systems, or to reduce the salinity by 80 percent in the top foot of soil, you will need to leach with a twelve-inch depth of water. Leaching is not workable, however, unless your subsoil as well as your topsoil drainage is good. If your soil problem is severe, you will have to obtain expert advice and perhaps use chemical additives to reclaim the soil.

—ROSEMARY.

Salt-Tolerant Plants

Seawater has a salt content of 3.5 percent, and concentrated brine a salt content of 35 percent. In contrast, salt-tolerant plants accept a salt content of only slightly over 1 percent. Moderately tolerant plants will be adversely affected by a salt content above 0.5 percent. Sensitive species, such as African violets, strawberries, and roses, will not tolerate over 0.2 percent.

Most nonwoody flowering plants are moderately salt tolerant. Most shrubs are also moderately salt tolerant. The most sensitive include groundcover such as Algerian ivy, flowering plants such as roses, fruits such as pineapple and guava, and some holly. But bougainvillea, oleander, dodonea, bottle brush, natal plum, and rosemary are moderately tolerant. Bermudagrass tolerates salt very well.

Among trees, the most salt-tolerant are the mangroves and tamarisks. Black locust and honey locust are also tolerant. Moderately tolerant trees include white oak, red oak, spreading junier, arborvitae, ponderosa pine, and eastern red cedar. Salt-sensitive trees include confiers such as blue spruce, white pine, and Douglas fir.

REDUCING NOISE

Because woods tend to be quiet, many people mistakenly assume that vegetation is exceedingly effective at noise abatement. But if you've ever heard a chainsaw or an ear-piercing bird call in the woods, you've probably realized that vegetation is not all *that* effective.

Often woods are quiet because traffic and industry may be nonexistent or distant. Also, you may be distracted by close sounds such as bees buzzing or leaves rustling—a psychological stance that helps you blank out other noises. In addition, the sound of wind through vegetation surrounding you can be so loud that it effectively covers any more distant noises.

The truth is that while vegetation is somewhat effective in noise abatement—noise does not bounce back as it does off a hard surface—the amount of planting necessary for a perceptible reduction of noise is not practical for the average homeowner. You may succeed in screening a bit of noise with planting on an average home plot, but you will do best at significant noise reduction if the project is a community—rather than an individual—effort.

One reason is that the most effective screening involves planting trees and shrubs close to the source of the noise—the highway or the noise-making business—rather than at your property. To obtain plantings next to a highway you are going to have to round up community members to lobby (and perhaps harrass) the proper authorities. To obtain plantings next to a factory or machine shop you are going to have to negotiate with the owner. You may have more success with a large firm eager to keep the community's good will than with a one-person operation not dependent on you for income, but in either case, rights-of-way, land-use requirements, and other practical factors could make the project impossible. This is because effective plantings require considerable depth—a minimum of twenty feet—that may be difficult or impossible to achieve.

Finally, if your noise problem is from above treetop level—as from planes or an elevated highway—plantings will not be effective.

Nonetheless, below are some guidelines for noise-reducing plantings that might be attempted by community groups. If your property is large enough, you might be able to implement these ideas on your own land. If you are buying a new home, these guidelines may be of aid in choosing your plot. And if you have an average piece of land, you may be able to include at least a few of these ideas in your landscape scheme to screen out some noise.

For small properties with noise problems the best solution might be to build a wall—of stone, concrete, rammed earth, or some other solid substance—between you and the source of the noise and use plants to pretty it up or disguise it completely.

How Sound is Measured

Sound is measured in decibels, named for Alexander Graham Bell. A zero-decibel level corresponds to the threshold of hearing, and one decibel is the smallest change in loudness that most people can easily detect. The highest level of sound humans can tolerate is about 120 decibels; above that, sound becomes painful.

Since people differ in their perception of sound, to get an idea of what levels are comfortable for you, here are some comparisons:

10 decibels	a whisper
20 decibels	quiet conversation; a library
30–40 decibels	normal conversation; light traffic
50 decibels	loud conversation; a manual typewriter
70 decibels	normal traffic; a quiet train
80 decibels	subways; blaring rock music
90 decibels	heavy traffic; thunder
100 decibels	a jet plane taking off

For most people, an outdoor noise level of 55 to 60 decibels is comfortable during the day, and 50 to 57 during the evening.

How to Reduce Noise

1. To reduce noise from moderate-speed car traffic in an urban area, plant a 20- to 50-foot wide belt of dense trees and shrubs. The edge of the belt should be within 20 to 50 feet of the center of the nearest traffic lane.

Use shrubs 6 to 8 feet tall next to the traffic lane, with backup rows of trees 15 to 30 feet tall.

2. To reduce noise from high-speed car and truck traffic, plant a 65- to 100-foot wide belt of dense trees and shrubs. The edge of the belt should be within 50 to 80 feet of the center of the nearest traffic lane.

Use shrubs 6 to 8 feet tall next to the traffic lane, with backup rows of taller shrubs and of trees at least 45 feet tall.

3. The above plantings should reduce noise 5 to 10 decibels, an appreciable difference. Such plantings would be even more effective if the ground surfaces between the source of noise and your property were soft rather than hard—the softer the better. There should therefore be a minimum of pavement and gravel. The most effective sound absorbers are tall grasses, but garden plants and even low groundcovers will help too.

4. If you are protecting yourself from a factory or other noise source, rather than from a highway, the plantings should be as close as possible to the source of the noise. A distance of 100 feet or more from the offending noise and from your property is desirable. Shorter distances will mean less sound reduction.

5. The planted belt should be approximately twice as long as the distance from the noise source to your property for maximum effect.

6. Before the trees have grown, a solid wall can be erected as close as possible to the noise source. This can be taken down when the trees reach 15 or 20 feet in height.

7. Trees and shrubs should be densely planted—give them the minimum distance allowable for the particular species. The object is to form a continuous barrier that is as dense as possible.

8. Tall trees with dense foliage are best. Choose evergreens or deciduous varieties that retain their leaves most of the year to avoid increased noise after leaves fall. It is also best to choose trees that have uniform foliage most of their length. If this is impossible, combine them with smaller trees or tall shrubs so that you have dense foliage mass from the ground to the treetops. If you cannot plant tall trees, use a combination of small trees, shrubs, and tall grasses or other soft groundcovers.

9. Be sure the plantings are healthy. Trees and shrubs in poor condition will be too straggly to provide the mass necessary to muffle noise.

Controlling Rain and Humidity

The use of vegetation for controlling rain and humidity is usually overlooked because the other uses of plants—such as shade—seem so much more important. But in regions of high rain or low humidity, these aspects take on more importance.

If your land is at all subject to erosion, because you are in a development stripped of vegetation or on former agricultural land, trees and large shrubs can be helpful. Trees have a great deal more surface on which to hold water—more than you would think from the ground space they take up—due to the many layers in the leaf canopy. Most trees will intercept some 15 to 20 percent of the rain falling on them and hold this on their leaves. This is not only 15 to 20 percent less water than might otherwise be eroding your land, but it also provides some humidity to the air—which is especially welcomed in dry areas such as the Southwest. Shrubs will do the same, with effects in proportion to their size.

Because snow piles up on tree branches, and particularly on the heavy branches of evergreens, they are, in effect, water reservoirs. Trees are often planted in watershed areas to shade the snow on the ground. This retards spring melting of snow, helping to prevent floods and runoffs. Trees will have the same effect in your garden.

During the process of transportation, plants evaporate moisture from their leaf surfaces. This has a cooling effect and also increases the humidity. For indoor use, plants therefore create a healthier environment, especially in areas where heating units and air conditioners do not provide enough moisture for optimum human needs. This quality of plants is also advantageous in dry climates.

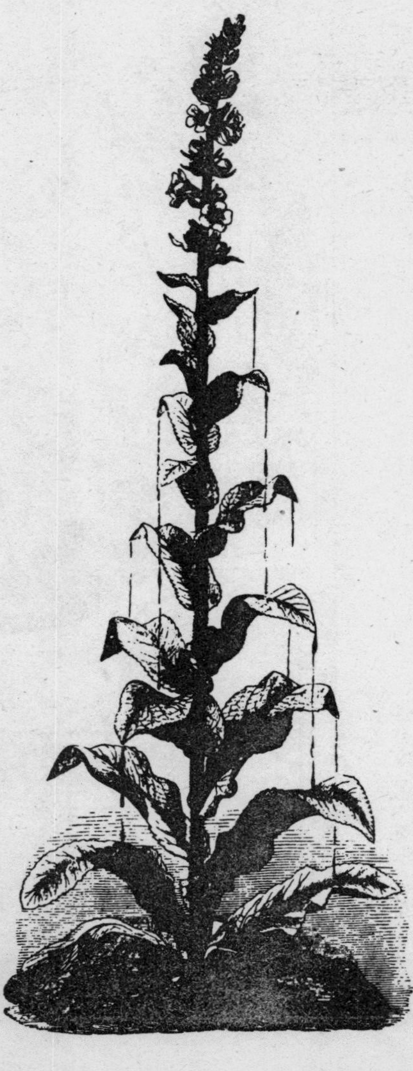

Fig. 14.—Irrigation of Rain-water.

Climate and Miniclimate

No climate chart is going to be an accurate barometer of your local environmental conditions, because any attempt to carve up the North American continent into convenient segments is going to result in many exceptions to the rule. The Southwest, for instance, is a convenient way of categorizing the general climate from Texas across New Mexico and Arizona to southern California, yet some of the Southwest's climate characteristics can be found as far north as central Utah.

If you live in the Southwest, you know that, in general, you will be subject to low rainfall, extremely low relative humidity, (as low as 4%), and high solar radiation with many sunny days. Yet this is not the whole picture because the number of frost-free days you have in your garden can range from 365 if you are below sea level to less than 60 if your land is above 8,500 feet.

Wherever you live, statistics for your area will include similar extremes that have been averaged out and may be totally inapplicable to your locale. Your particular area is going to have idiosyncracies that distinguish it from the overall data on temperatures and other climatic factors in your region. If you live in a mountainous area, for example, the wind may be funneled quite differently across your land from the generally prevailing pattern.

Some measurements may not apply to your area because they are taken at an official climatological station that differs in some important respect from your own locality. New York City residents, for instance, are frequently given their city's temperature from a recorder in Central Park. The recorder is set on a hill and surrounded by greenery, giving readings different from those one would get on treeless city streets.

When you are moving to a new area, it pays to notice the plants on land around you. Those that appear to thrive, as well as those that do poorly, can be a tipoff to soil and other variations in the locality. It is also worthwhile consulting local nurserymen, avid gardeners who are long-time residents, and government agricultural experts before investing in plants. From experience they can suggest varieties of plants that are especially suitable and warn against local pecularities of pest infestation or soil conditions.

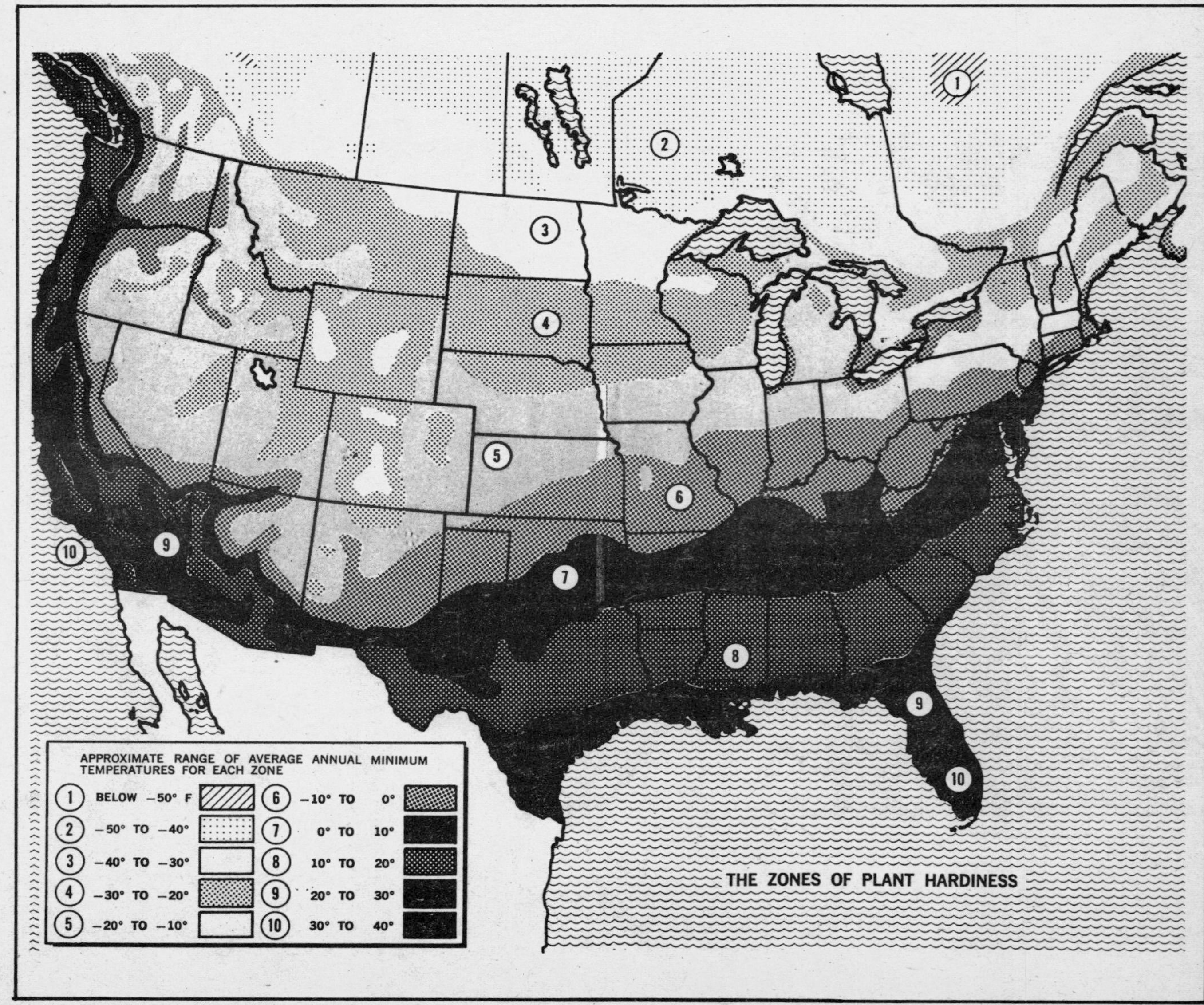

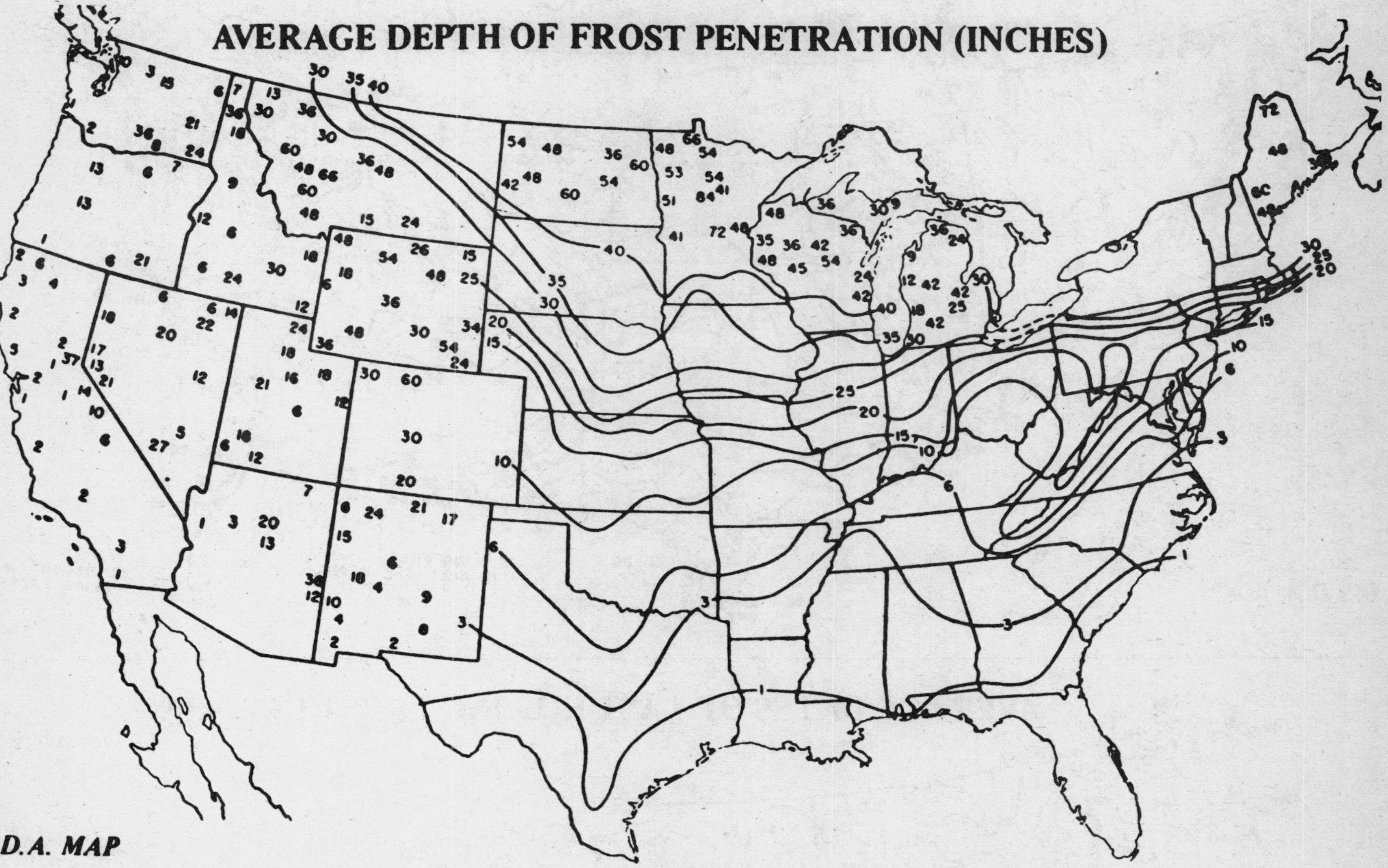

AVERAGE DEPTH OF FROST PENETRATION (INCHES)

U.S.D.A. MAP

Miniclimate

Still, your own land is a world unto itself. Your plot's climate may vary from that of folks a few miles away. And if your land is on a stream and your neighbor's is up the hill, subtle but significant differences could dictate what plants you should grow and how your home can be most intelligently landscaped.

Elevation can be especially critical. If you are on a slope, you are going to have drier soil than if you were on a bottom. Slopes are therefore an advantage in areas with heavy rainfall and less desirable for arid area plantings.

Since warm air rises, a slope can also make a difference in your growing season. If you are on a bottom, the cold air will settle there and give you a shorter frost-free season. Higher up on a slope, your garden will benefit from warmer air and you will have a longer growing season.

The smaller your plot, the more important the finer gradations of climate will be. On a small plot, the house takes on enormous significance. The style of the house will of course influence the style of the landscaping. More than that, though, the house will help to determine your miniclimate.

A three-story Victorian house will throw more shades across your grounds than will a low-lying ranch-style home. In either case, the house may be so situated as to cut off appreciable sun from your garden. If your home is painted white or constructed of light-colored material, it will have greater reflective quality than a house with a dark-colored exterior. A south-facing wall exposed to the sun will therefore throw more light and heat onto your grounds. In a northern climate this might be desirable, but the slight elevation in temperature is something you might want to avoid in a southern climate by screening southern exposures with plantings.

Analyzing your miniclimate is essential for successful garden or landscaping plans. An analysis enables you to predict the ease or difficulty of establishing and maintaining particular plants. You are not totally at the mercy of your miniclimate, but a crucial decision in gardening is whether to accommodate yourself to your land or whether to modify the land to accommodate your desires.

Going along with the land, and choosing only those plantings that thrive, is the easiest and least costly decision. It is the only sensible decision if you are highly mobile and move frequently.

On the other hand, modifying the miniclimate can be the sensible decision if you plan to occupy the same home for a number of years. Proper plantings can cut down your heating and air conditioning bills and make your grounds more pleasant for family enjoyment. Even site changes can be profitable on a long-term basis. If you're high on a slope and want to increase your flower or vegetable growing area, you can terrace the grounds, if you're on a bottom and want to lengthen your growing season you can plant hedgerows and other barriers that will trap warm air and keep it from rising out of your garden.

AVERAGE DATES OF FIRST KILLING FROST IN FALL

KILLING FROST LIABLE ANNUALLY

KILLING FROST LIABLE IN HALF THE YEARS

NO RECORD OF KILLING FROST

U.S.D.A. MAP

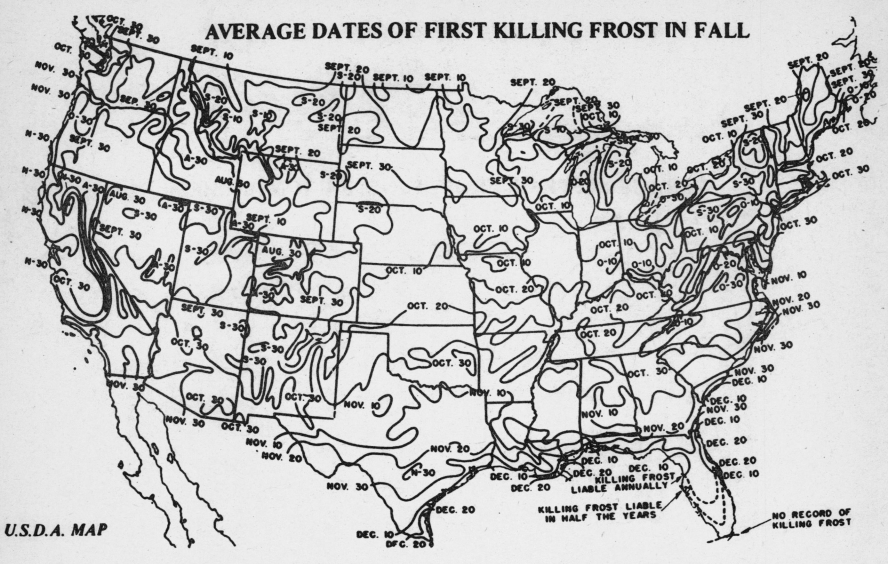

AVERAGE DATES OF LAST KILLING FROST IN SPRING

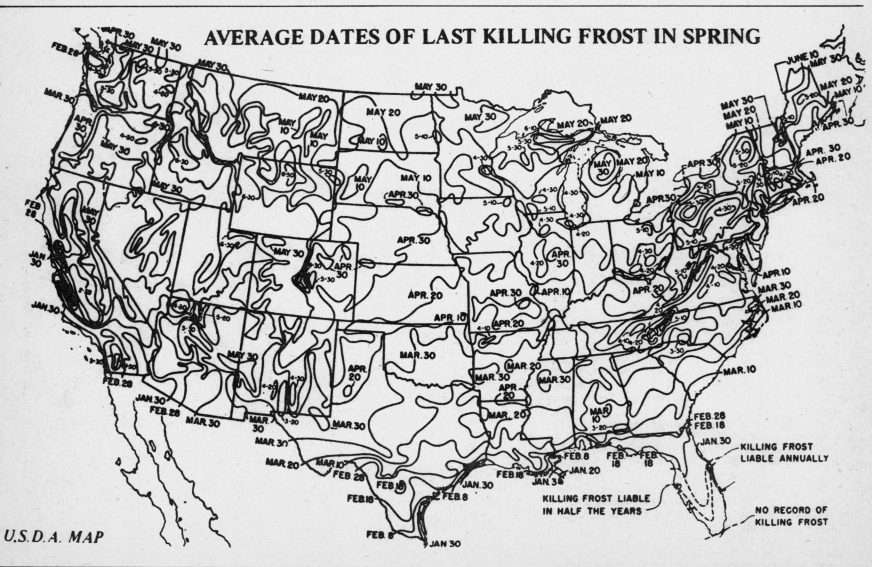

KILLING FROST LIABLE ANNUALLY

KILLING FROST LIABLE IN HALF THE YEARS

NO RECORD OF KILLING FROST

U.S.D.A. MAP

2

Indoor Foliage and Flowers

Indoor Foliage Plants

Abutilon.

Abutilon
flowering-maple
Temperature: 45–55°F
Humidity: 50%
Light: full sun
Description: The green or variegated leaves of this shrub look rather like maple leaves, but from spring to late summer various varieties blossom with delicate bell-like flowers in reds or yellows. A small plant can be grown in a pot or hanging basket, but even in a pot abutilons can grow three feet high.
Culture: Use regular potting soil, and water when the soil is dry to the touch. Keep in full sun, and provide fertilizer. Abutilon tends to get leggy, so pinch new growth to get a full plant. You can start new plants from cuttings taken in the spring.

Aglaonema
Chinese-evergreen
Temperature: 60–70°F
Humidity: 50%
Light: subdued daylight
Description: These attractive foliage plants grow under forest canopies in the tropics and are therefore very adaptable to adverse light conditions. Most species have dark-green leaves and grow up to 2 or 3 feet high. The most popular is *A. modestum*, with oblong, waxy leaves, growing upright form canelike stems, and tapering to a thin point. Leaves of some of the other species are variegated, with splashes of silver, yellow, or cream. Under optimal conditions, your plant may produce a white flower resembling a calla lily.

Culture: This plant will grow under bright light, in shade, or under artificial light. It's a good choice for a north window.

A good soil mix would be equal parts loam, peat moss, and sand. Keep the soil moist but not water-logged—let the soil become dry to the touch before you water again. Chinese-evergreen grows well in water, too, and a glass container will show off the attractive roots.

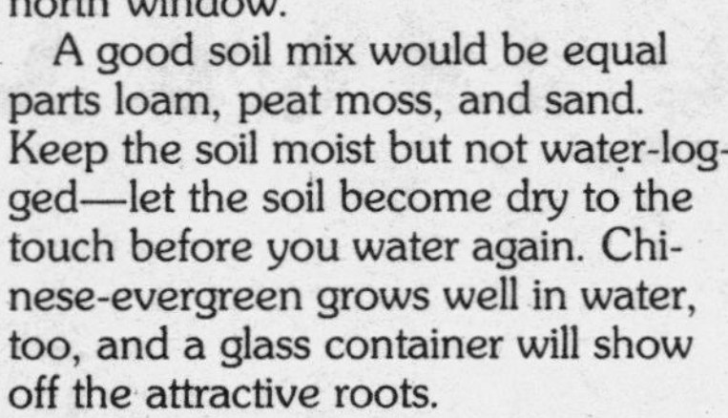

Special features: This plant adapts so well that it is good for beginners or people who don't want to fuss over their plants. Apart from watering, you only have to sponge the leaves from time to time to keep them dust-free.

Chinese-evergreen does have a tendency to get leggy, though, and you may want occasionally to cut off leaves to keep the plant at its most attractive. Such cuttings are very easy to propagate, so you can get several new plants from your original. One way to start a new plant is to cut the stem—with a diagonal cut—two inches below the leaf, and root it in a small vase of water. You can also start new plants by cutting stems into two- or three-inch pieces and setting them in moist sand or soil.

—Design for Plant Stand.

Decorative Flower Stand for Parlor, Window, or in front of Looking Glass.

Anthurium
flamingo-flower
Temperature: 65–75°F
Humidity: 80%
Light: indirect sunlight
Description: These handsome plants, from the jungles of Central and South America, require that you provide the warmth and humidity of their tropical origins. But some varieties will reward you with exceptionally beautiful foliage and others produce unusual, long-lasting blooms.

Of those grown for foliage, *A. crystalinum* has large, elliptical, velvety-green leaves beautifully marked with silver along the veins. Although the flowers are inconspicuous, the large foliage makes a full and dramatic plant a bit over a foot high. A similar species is *A. forgetti*, with leaves that are oval in shape.

Varieties grown for their flowers tend to have shield-shaped leaves tapering to a point and to be glossy rather than velvety. But it is the brilliantly colored flowers, looking like patent leather, that are spectacular. Most popular are *A. scherzerianum*, with bright-red blooms, and *A. andreanum*, with flowers in red, white, coral, or pink.
Culture: Pot in humus soil with drainage. A mixture of half regular potting soil and half sphagnum moss *or* firbark *or* osmunda fiber is good. Keep the soil moist at all times. To provide the high humidity you'll need a pebble tray and frequent misting. The plants should be kept warm; don't let the temperature fall below 60°F at night. Anthuriums do not like direct sun, but will grow well in indirect sun or subdued daylight and other shaded locations.
Special requirements: Anthuriums produce aerial roots below the base of each leaf. Wrap these aerial roots in sphagnum moss, and keep the moss damp.

Aphelandra
zebra-plant
Temperature: 55–75°F
Humidity: 40–50%
Light: indirect sunlight

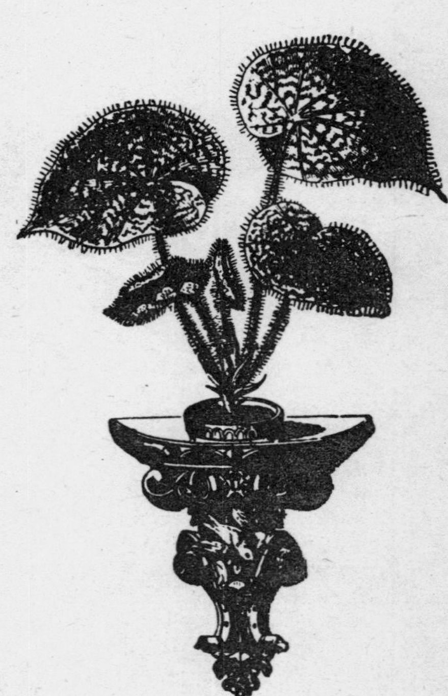

Description: Aphelandra has elliptical, shiny leaves prettily veined with white. One of the showiest of the hardier indoor plants, it grows to about a foot and a half tall. The most popular species, *A. squarrosa louisae*, produces a spike of waxy yellow flowers; other varieties have orange flowers.
Culture: This plant needs a rich humus soil and likes to be kept moist. Water frequently or keep it on a pebble tray and mist daily. If leaves begin to wilt, or edges turn brown, increase the amount of water and/or misting. It grows best in indirect sunlight but tolerates dim light. In winter and with too much sun, the plant tends to get leggy and needs pinching back. If it becomes ugly-looking, take tip cuttings and root new plants in moist soil.

Araucaria
Norfolk Island Pine
Temperature: 50–70°F
Humidity: 50%
Light: indirect sunlight
Description: This little evergreen from the South Pacific (off the east coast of Australia) is especially pleasing for its formality—the needled branches grow in symmetrical tiers. In its native habitat it grows over 200 feet tall, but it grows well in a pot, too. It produces a new tier of branches annually, and makes a miniature Christmas tree two to four feet high.
Culture: This evergreen prefers cooler temperatures, so if you have it in a room over 60°, you will have to provide more humidity. Keeping it on a pebble tray will help, but even then you may have to mist it daily. Plant it in a well-drained pot in a mixture of equal parts loam, sand, and peat moss. Water thoroughly—immersing the pot in a pail once a week is the easiest way—and then let the soil dry out before watering again. Norfolk Island Pine prefers indirect sunlight, such as filtered sun from an east or west window (if the needles begin to yellow, it may be getting too much sun), but it will also grow in north light.

Norfolk Island Pine needs repotting only when the roots have jammed the pot, which will be about every two or three years. If the tree grows too tall, you can air-layer the top (see propagation).

Asparagus:
asparagus-fern, emerald feather
Temperature: 55–75°F
Humidity: 50%
Light: indirect sunlight
Description: These vining plants, which may grow from three to six feet, are popular for their feathery foliage—an effect created by their clusters of tiny leaves spread along thin stems. The foliage is lime-green, and the small whitish flowers are followed by red or purple berries. Asparagus fern is especially graceful in hanging baskets, but it may also be used as a specimen plant on a table or pedestal. *A. plumosus* has the darkest foliage, and *A. asparagoides* is popular for flower arrangements; but *A. sprengeri* is most common as a house plant.
Culture: Plant in a mixture of equal parts loam, peat moss, and either sand or perlite. Soak the soil and then allow it to dry to the touch before watering again. This plant tolerates a range of temperatures but prefers 60° to 68°. The bright light of an east or west window is ideal, but it will even grow in a north window. Asparagus-fern propagates easily from seed if you allow the berries to dry, extract the seeds and sow them.

Aspidistra
cast-iron-plant
Temperature: 50–70°F
Humidity: 70%
Light: subdued daylight
Description: Due to easy maintenance and its tolerance of adverse conditions, aspidistra has long been a household favorite. It was so common in Victorian times that it became almost synonymous with a middle-class lifestyle. Its dark green, arching foliage grows to about two-feet long. Sometimes it produces sprays of dark purple flowers near the soil. *A. variegata* has foliage striped with white.

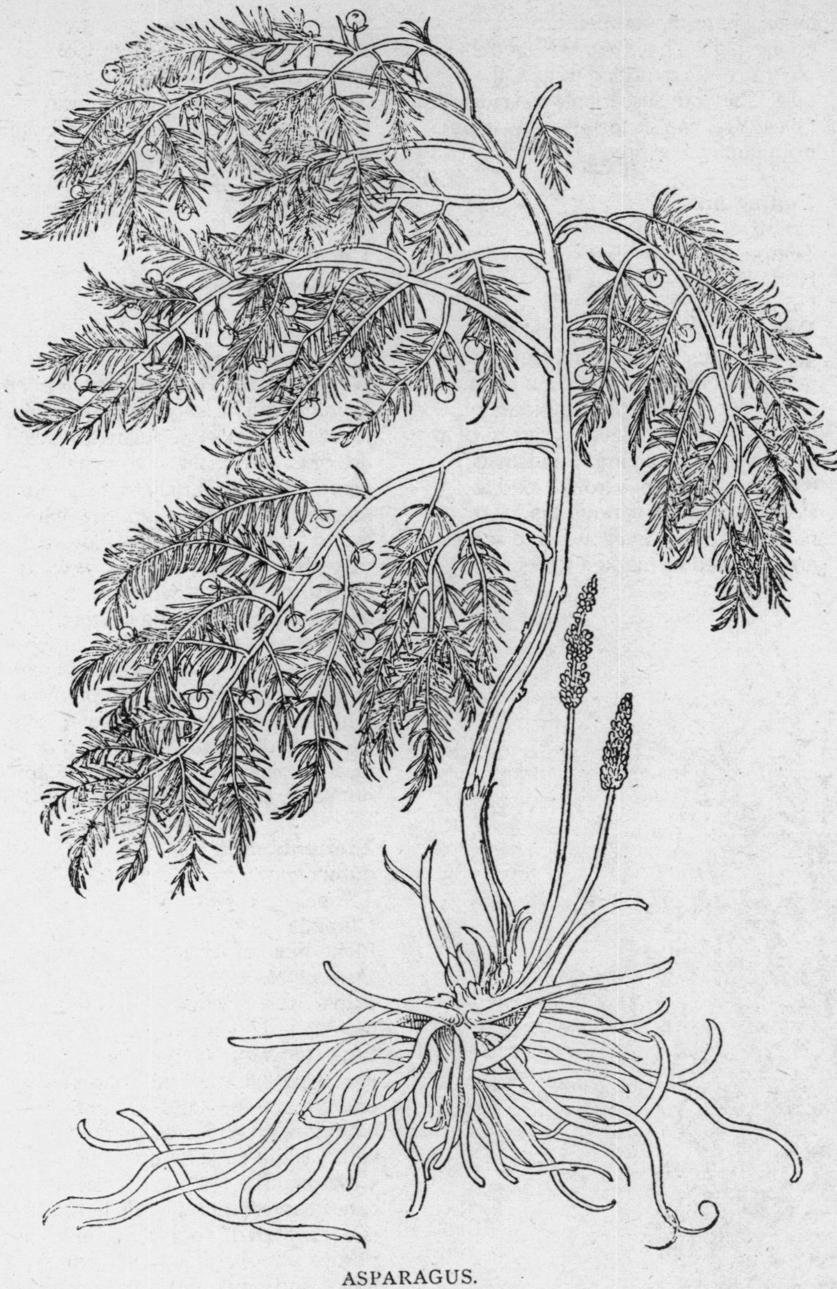
ASPARAGUS.

These plants tend to be spindly, so you may want to plant two or three to a pot for an attractive display.
Culture: Aspidistra is called the cast-iron-plant because it tolerates heat, dust, darkness, and even lack of watering. For best health, though, plant it in potting soil and rewater when the soil becomes dry to the touch. Grow it in shade, under artificial light, or in subdued daylight.

Aucuba
gold-dust-tree
Temperature: 50–75°F
Humidity: 50%
Light: indirect sunlight
Description: This Japanese evergreen has large, shiny green leaves that appear to be sprinkled with gold dust. It usually grows to a medium size plant, but might go as high as four or five feet. Berries may be red or creamy.
Culture: Plant in a mixture of equal parts loam, peat moss, and sand. Let the soil dry between waterings. Although it likes good light, it also tolerates shade. As it grows, prune it to get the shape you want.

Bambusa
bamboo
Temperature: 50–70°F
Humidity: 50% or more
Light: full sun or indirect sunlight
Description: These treelike feathery plants are elegant in tubs and will grow indoors to ceiling height. You can buy small varieties that will grow only three to four feet tall, such as *B. nana*, but most reach heights well over six feet. They make excellent framings for entries or barriers for walkways.
Culture: Plant in regular potting soil and keep soil evenly moist by rewatering when the soil feels dry to the touch. These plants like plenty of air circulation around them. They tend to overspread, so divide the clumps in spring to repot as new plants.

Caladium
Temperature: 60–70°F
Humidity: 60–70%
Light: indirect sunlight
Description: The large colorful leaves make these tuber plants popular for borders and as accents in groupings, as well as singly for decorative effects. Many varieties are available, some with leaves up to two feet long. The thin, arrow-shaped or heart-shaped leaves may be crimson, rose, scarlet, white and pink, white and green, and other combinations. Often the foliage is marbled or spotted, and the veins may be in contrasting color.
Culture: Caladium grows best in indirect sun and humus soil, to which you may want to add some charcoal and sand for drainage. Watering is a bit tricky because, while these plants like plenty of water when they are growing vigorously, they rot easily if you overwater.
Special requirements: Start the tubers in spring in the shade, in warmth (75°), and water sparingly. Once the plants are started, water generously through the summer. In fall, gradually lengthen the periods between waterings until the leaves die down and the plant becomes dormant. When growth has completely stopped in late fall, remove the tubers from the soil, let them dry out, and store them in a cool place (about 60°) in clean dry sand or wrapped in paper over the winter. In spring, repot them and resume watering.

Calathea
Temperature: 60–80°F
Humidity: 75–80%
Light: indirect sunlight
Description: These Brazilian plants grow one to four feet high and are so handsome that new varieties have become available as their popularity has increased. The leaves, which grow upright from rigid canes, are a shiny green striped or marked with lighter or darker greens, reds, or whites.
Culture: Calathea is rather particular about its needs. It likes a rich humus soil, kept constantly moist, and should be kept on a pebble tray and misted to keep its atmosphere humid. While they grow in shade, bright light or indirect sunlight is best.

Chlorophytum
spider-plant
Temperature: 55–75°F
Humidity: 50%
Light: indirect sunlight
Description: Its long, slender leaves, fresh green color, and tolerance of neglect make the spider-plant a household favorite. There are all-green and yellow-and-green varieties, but the most popular has the grass-like leaves striped with white, which gives the plant an especially light air. Mature plants bear plantlets and tiny, white star-shaped flowers. The plantlet emerges on a long, slender stem, and when it has produced a half a dozen leaves you can cut the stem and root the plantlet in soil or water. The flowers give way to leaf clusters.
Culture: Pot in a mixture of equal parts loam, peat moss, and sand, and let the soil dry out between waterings. This plant does well in indirect sun and under artificial light.

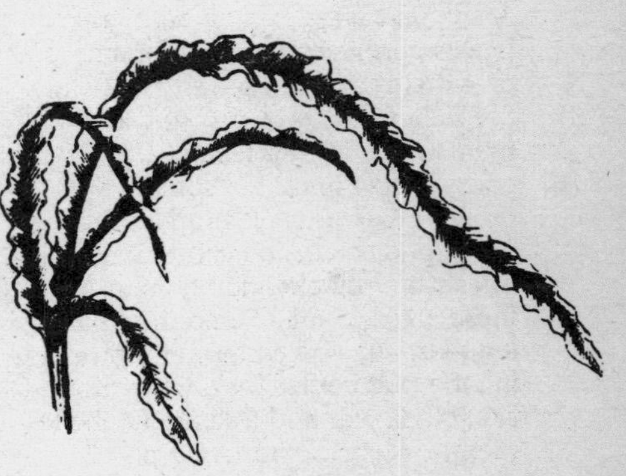

Cissus
Temperature: 50–75°F
Humidity: variable
Light: subdued sunlight
Description: These fast-growing climbers and trailers have holly-shaped leaves in rich greens that vary from light to brownish tones. *C. rhombifolia*, grape ivy, is most common. It has shiny, three-lobed leaves

that turn darker green and fuzzy underneath as the plant matures. *C. antarctica* has brown-veined oval leaves in dark green, and the leaves of *C. discolor* have red veins. All are good for hanging baskets as well as pots.
Culture: These vines like rich soil, so pot them with extra peat moss, and add sand for proper drainage. Water heavily, and wait until the soil is dry to the touch before watering again. Wash the foliage from time to time. If your cissus is kept at the upper temperature range, it will probably do best with some misting too. While these vines do best in subdued sunlight, they are tolerant of sun and will also grow in dim light. You can root cuttings in water, though they root more slowly than other plants.

GREEN-LEAVED BAMBOO.

Citrus
orange, lemon, lime trees
Temperature: 55–60°F
Humidity: 70%
Light: subdued daylight
Description: The dwarf and semi-dwarf citrus trees sold for home use are especially attractive indoor plants. They have small, shiny, dark-green leaves and their spreading branches give the trees attractive shapes. They are rather slow growers, so will remain at two to four feet a considerable time, but some will grow as high as six feet under the right conditions. You can buy these trees with fruit already on them; these are decorative, and the fruit is long-lasting. You can also try producing the fruit yourself. Varieties most likely to flower and fruit are Otaheite orange, Meyer lemon, and ponderosa lemon. After the tree has flowered you must pollinate the blossoms with a paintbrush to get fruit. Since these are small trees, the fruit is also dwarf size but can be used for marmalades and preserves.
Culture: Plant in regular potting soil. Keep the soil moist while the trees are in bloom or have fruit, and let the soil dry out between waterings the rest of the time. These trees like to be on the cool side, so do best on enclosed terraces, porches, or other areas where the temperatures don't go too high. They may need a pebble tray and/or misting to look their best. They are susceptible to spider mites. You can propagate new trees from cuttings or seeds.

Codiaeum
croton
Temperature: 60–75°F
Humidity: 65–70%
Light: full sun
Description: These tropical evergreen shrubs with colorful leaves can grow over three feet tall, and so may stand alone as decorative pieces or may be used to relieve the green of a foliage-plant grouping. The leaves, with varying shapes from broad to slender, come in various shades of reds, greens, and yellows, and some are speckled or marked with two or three colors. Several varieties are available.
Culture: Crotons do best with sun a couple of hours a day and bright light the rest of the time. Plant in potting soil and keep the soil moist while the plant is growing vigorously. In winter it will rest and require less watering. To keep the humidity high, use a pebble tray and mist frequently.
Special requirements: These plants are sometimes susceptible to red-spider mites. As crotons grow old, the lower leaves drop off, leaving the trunk bare. If the plant begins to look unattractive, you can start a new plant by air-layering the top.

Coleus
Temperature: 55–65°F
Humidity: 70%
Light: full sun
Description: Their colorful foliage has made these plants so popular that many varieties are available—you can get plants with leaf combinations of reds and greens, yellows and greens, yellows and reds, pinks and reds, and others. They are easy to grow and will reach 1½ feet in height in homes and offices, but will grow larger in greenhouses.
Culture: Pot in regular potting soil and keep the soil moist by watering every couple of days. If the leaves show signs of wilting, you are probably not watering enough. Coleus likes full sun, or at least bright light. You can root cuttings in water or moist sand. For a well-rounded plant, pinch back new growth to induce branching. Coleus is susceptible to mealy bugs.

Cordyline
Hawaiian ti plant
Temperature: 55–75°F
Humidity: 70%
Light: indirect sunlight
Description: These attractive plants from Hawaii have graceful, palmlike leaves. The most popular varieties are of *C. terminalis*, with metallic-green foliage that may be edged or marked with pink or red; the "Firebrand" has a red rosette. Flowers may also be red, or yellow or white.
Culture: Ti plants will grow in regular potting soil, or even in water. If you have them in soil, keep it moist but not soggy. In winter, keep them at the lower end of the temperature range and give them less water. They like bright light, such as filtered or diffused sunlight. They also like high humidity, so mist frequently.

Dieffenbachia
dumbcane
Temperature: 60–75°F
Humidity: 50%
Light: indirect sunlight
Description: Spectacular little plants that seldom grow over three feet high, dieffenbachia is noted for thick stems topped with large, oval leaves prettily spattered with yellow and creamy markings. *D. amoena*, with dark green leaves marked with white, is the most hardy.
Culture: The roots and base of the canes can rot quickly if dieffenbachia is overwatered. Therefore plant it in a porous soil of equal parts loam, peat moss, and sand, and after watering let the soil dry out a few days before watering again. If you're not watering enough, the leaves will start to droop, and this may happen especially in summer. Misting the leaves in between watering times will keep them fresh. As the plant grows, the lower leaves turn yellow and should be removed. If the stem looks too bare, you can cut off the top of the plant on the diagonal and root it in sand or water, but keep the lower cane—it will eventually sprout lateral shoots. Spring is the best time for this. Dieffenbachia does best in indirect sun but will also tolerate light shade.
Caution: The sap of dieffenbachia is toxic in open cuts and will cause numbness on the tongue. Therefore, take care in removing leaves and cutting the cane. And do not keep this plant in the house if you have young children who might be tempted to nibble the leaves.

Dizygotheca
false aralia
Temperature: 55–75°F
Humidity: 70%
Light: indirect sunlight
Description: These graceful tree-like plants grow quickly to over five feet in height. *D. elegantissima* has long, narrow, dark-green leaves that are notched their full length and that arch like palm fronds. The leaves of *D. veitchii* have red veins.
Culture: Pot in soil of equal parts loam, sand, and peat moss. Keep the soil evenly moist but not soggy. Though false aralia tolerates high temperatures, it likes humidity, and you'll have to add moisture to its atmosphere in proportion to its warmth. Keep it on a pebble tray and mist it daily.

This plant can get leggy, so you might want to pot several together and to prune the stem tips to prevent the foliage from thinning at the bottom. If the plant grows too tall and/or leggy, you can propagate new plants by air-layering the top or taking cuttings. You can also cut the original stem back to four to six inches from the soil to regrow leaves. These propagation processes should be done in spring.

Dracaena
cornplant
Temperature: 60–70°F
Humidity: 50%
Light: indirect sunlight
Description: Dracaenas, African plants that do well under less than optimal conditions, are possibly the most attractive of the hardy indoor plants. As a result, several species have become enormously popular for indoor decorative effects. These tend to be large plants, growing up to five or even six feet high, but they grow slowly. A small dracaena will therefore remain of a size suitable for table display for several years, and if you want a treelike size it is best to buy one of approximately the size you need for your decor. Although all dracaenas are foliage plants with spear-shaped leaves, green and yellow leaf bandings as well as varying leaf widths make the various species look totally unrelated.

D. deremensis "Warneckii" has spear-shaped leaves that grow up to two feet long and layer down over each other to create a compact yet airy effect. The leaves are gray-green, with green center stripes. This is an especially good choice for locations without much light.

D. fragans has broad green leaves streaked with yellow that taper to a point. In older plants the leaves can grow up to three feet long.

D. godseffiana is especially hardy. Its dark-green leaves, spotted with creamy yellow, grow about six inches long.

D. marginata has a long, slim trunk that terminates in an exuberant arching spray of slender dark-green leaves, edged with red, 15 to 18 inches long. The effect is that of a little palm tree. *D. marginata* is especially attractive if you plant several, of different heights, in a large floor pot. The trunks tend to grow fairly straight at first, but in larger plants the trunks develop twists and bends. As a result, this dracaena is especially adaptable to groupings or to special designs.

D. massangeana has broad deep-green leaves banded with lighter green and yellowish tones. The leaves arch away from the plant and droop down in a graceful, airy layering effect. This dracaena also resembles a small tree, because the leaves drop from a rosette atop a straight, thin trunk. Used singly it can be very dramatic, and it is also adaptable as a background tree for a grouping with smaller plants.

D. sanderiana has slender, twisting green leaves with white edgings that grow up to nine or ten inches long. The leaves form at widely spaced intervals from a chunky main stalk—a light and dainty plant. This one also does well on little light, and can be grown in water.

Culture: Dracaenas should be kept away from heating vents but otherwise will thrive in average home or office temperatures. Keep them out of direct sun; though they do best in good light, *D. sanderiana* and *Warneckii* can do well with little light. Keep the soil moist but not soggy, rewatering when the soil feels dry to the touch. You can pot them in commercial potting soil, but add sand or perlite for good drainage. Dracaenas need some humidity, so it is best to keep them on a pebble tray. If the leaves start to get dry and brown at the tips, they are not getting enough moisture and you will have to mist them—perhaps on a daily basis. If the leaves start to get spotty, too much humidity is accumulating. Dracaenas, incidentally, are fairly easy to propagate from stem cuttings.

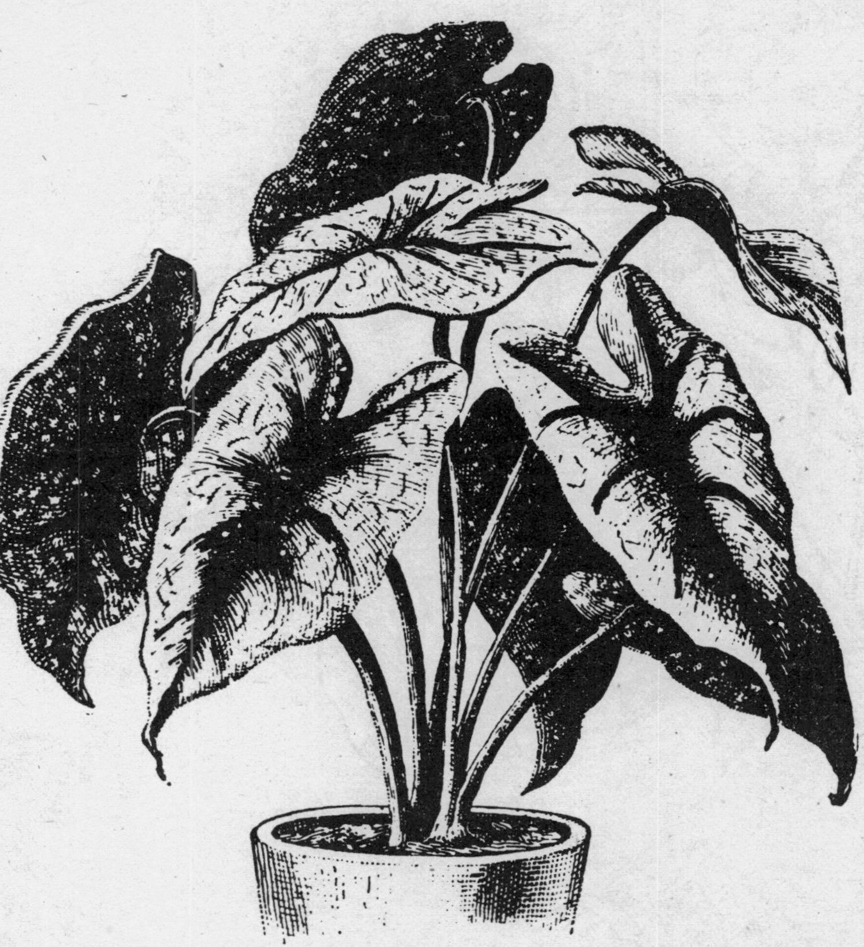

FANCY-LEAVED CALADIUM.

Fatshedera
tree-ivy
Temperature: 55–75°F
Humidity: 50%
Light: indirect sun

Description: These evergreen shrubs look like ivy and are a cross between Irish and Japanese ivies. They have lustrous, dark-green, five-lobed leaves that are leathery-looking. The leaves of *F. variegata* are edged in white. They will grow three feet tall, but you'll probably have to stake the main stem.

Culture: Pot in regular potting soil, and water when the soil becomes dry to the touch. Though these do best in good light and a humidity of 70°, they will survive in rooms with 50% humidity and with less light.

Fatsia
maple-leaf
Temperature: 55–75°F
Humidity: 50%
Light: indirect sunlight

Description: These decorative foliage plants are very hardy and withstand untoward conditions. They have shiny, leathery, green leaves that may grow more than a foot in width and that resemble huge, maple leaves. These plants grow four to five feet tall, but you can keep them to table size by pruning them back. *F. japonica* has all-green leaves, while *F. variegata* has green leaves edged with white.

Culture: Pot in regular potting soil and keep the soil moist but not soggy. These will grow in good light but also in shaded indoor areas away from light sources.

Ficus
rubber-plant, fig plants
Temperature: 60–75°F
Humidity: 70%
Light: diffused sun

Description: Ficus are not only adaptable to a wide range of environmental conditions but come in such a variety of shapes that the species show little superficial relation to each other. Hence, they are versatile and you can use several types in your home without becoming bored with them. They range from small trees to sturdy, leathery plants with large, glossy leaves to creepers with tiny leaves. What most species share in common (with many humans) is a dislike of drafts!

F. benjamina, "weeping fig," is named for small (two-inch), vivid-green, oval leaves that drop like teardrops from branches off the main stem. A tree-like plant with an airy feel, it can grow five feet or higher. You can let it grow more or less naturally, with branches all the way up the stalk that give it a bushy appearance, or you can lop off lower branches to produce a straight trunk with a bowl of leaves at the top.

F. carica, the common fig, doesn't grow quite as high, has larger leaves that are deeply lobed, and loses foliage in winter.

F. diversifolia, "mistletoe fig," grows about three feet high. It has broad leaves and bears yellow fruit.

F. elastica, the "rubber-plant," has broad, leathery dark-green leaves that grow almost a foot long. It is an especially rugged plant that will do well in almost any light and will grow to three or four feet. The leaves branch upward at an angle off the main stalk, so it's a sturdy-looking plant that can stand singly as an ornament. It's too massive to be put with delicate plants or objets d'art.

F. lyrata (pandurata), the "fiddle-leaf" fig, grows up to about five feet and is also highly decorative. Its thick, glossy leaves are fiddle-shaded and wavy and can grow to well over a foot long and almost a foot wide.

F. pumila, "creeping fig," has small (one-inch) leaves. This creeping plant forms a mat of clinging stems and is therefore often used to cover masonry walls or to cover the soil in planters containing taller plants.

F. nitida, "Indian laurel," has three-inch long glossy oval leaves that are rather tightly packed along the branches, giving it a neat, contained appearance. This is a sedate tree that will grow a good four-feet high and has a rich green tone. Its attraction is its clean lines rather than the feathery feel of palms and other tall plants.

Culture: Pot in a well-drained mixture of equal parts loam, peat moss,

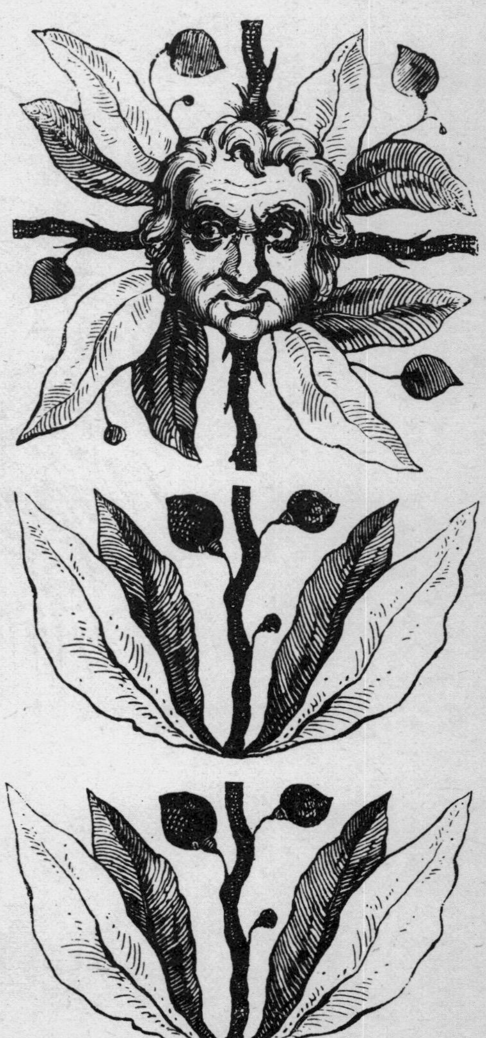

CITRUS AURANTIUM.

and sand. Especially with larger plants, it is best to set the pot in a bucket of water so that the moisture penetrates the roots, and then not water again until the soil has thoroughly dried. Though these plants do best in moist, warm atmospheres, they are adaptable and can be grown in sun or shade.

The main peculiarity is that these plants don't like being moved, being chilled, or being in drafts—and their leaves may drop off. If the leaves drop, you can air-layer the top. You can also propagate new plants from leaf cuttings.

Sponge the leaves to remove dust every two or three weeks.

Fittonia
mosaic plant
Temperature: 60–80°F
Humidity: 50%
Light: subdued daylight
Description: This creeper comes from under the canopies of South American forests and is therefore used to shade. Its four-inch-long, oval leaves are green with silvery veins—though one variety (F. verschaffeltii) has red veins. This can be used as a table plant, for dish gardens, or to cover soil in planters under larger plants.
Culture: Plant in regular potting soil and let the soil dry to the touch between waterings. These are easy to propagate from stem cuttings.

Georgenanthus
seersucker plant
Temperature: 55–75°F
Humidity: 50%
Light: indirect sunlight

Grass growing in Pine Cones.

COLEUS

Description: This low-growing, suckering plant is named for its fleshy, quilted leaves. Leaf tops are a dark green, banded with gray, while the undersides are red. This plant is good for tabletops as it has a compact form.
Culture: Plant in regular potting soil and keep the soil evenly moist but

–*Ficus* with girdle-like clasping roots, at Darjeeling in the Sikkim Himalayas. (From a photograph.)

not soggy. The seersucker plant does well in dry rooms.

Gynura
velvet-plant, purple-passion-plant
Temperature: 65–70°F
Humidity: 40–60%
Light: full or partial sun
Description: Gynura grows well over two feet tall, and has large, ragged-edged leaves of purple foliage. Tiny purple hairs cover the leaves and stem, catching the light and giving the plant a velvety texture. This is a striking plant either alone or as an accent in groupings. The vine form grows stems two feet long. Both produce tiny orange flowers.
Culture: While gynura will not die in dim light, it requires direct or partial sun to bring out the color. Pot in a soil mixture of equal parts loam, peat moss, and sand, and water frequently to keep the soil moist or grow it in water. Humidity is important for maintaining good color, so keep in a pebble tray and mist frequently.

Since gynura has a tendency to get leggy, pinch back the stems to force branching. It is easy to propagate stem cuttings in water; so if the plant becomes unnattractive, root some stems and pot them beside the original plant to achieve a fuller look.

Hedera
ivy
Temperature: 50–60°F
Humidity: 30–70%
Light: indirect sunlight
Description: These climbing and trailing plants are so hardy they are extremely popular and come in many varieties. Most common are the three-lobed type, with all-green leaves, but ivies are available with variegated leaves tinged with creamy and yellowish tones, with five-pointed and other leaf shapes, and with miniature leaves. These last can

HEDERA HELIX.

be especially attractive for home use, either by themselves or to cover the soil of planters. All can be used in baskets, on trellises, and on topiary forms.
Culture: Plant in regular potting soil. After watering, let the soil dry to the touch before watering again. Though ivies will grow in sun, they do best in bright light. They tolerate a wide range of humidity, but are less tolerant of heat—they do best in coolish rooms. Ivies may be susceptible to aphids and spider mites, so wash the foliage occasionally in soapy water. Begin training ivy when it is small by pinching back new growth to produce lateral shoots. If it becomes straggly, you can propagate by taking cuttings.

Hoffmannia
Temperature: 50–75°F
Humidity: 50%
Light: subdued daylight
Description: These are handsome Mexican plants prized for their multicolored foliage. The leaves have a velvety texture and colors range from deep brownish greens to brilliant-red edgings. Depending on the variety, they will grow from one to four feet high.
Culture: Plant in regular potting mix and keep soil evenly moist. Any sort of bright light suits these plants, but not direct sun. They can be propagated by cuttings.

Maranta
prayer-plant
Temperature: 60–80°F
Humidity: 50% or more
Light: subdued daylight
Description: Called prayer-plant because the leaves are horizontal in good light but fold over and become vertical at night or in dim light (a unique invention to force leaf moisture to the roots), *Maranta leuconeura kerchoveana* is attractive and easy to grow. It has oval leaves about six inches long, with gray-green on top, purplish on the underside, and shiny veins. It will grow a little over a foot high and turns darker with age.

Culture: Maranta is not too particular about light and will grow in diffused sun, at north windows, and elsewhere where the light is not the best. Plant in regular potting soil, which should be kept moist. The roots can rot, however, so don't allow water to stand on the crowns, and water less when the plant is resting (late fall). You can propagate easily by cutting off leaves to pot.

Monstera
Swiss-cheese plant, split-leaf philodendron
Temperature: 55–75°F
Humidity: 50%
Light: indirect sunlight
Description: Monstera belongs to the same family as philodendron, and *M. deliciosa* is often called split-leaf or windowleaf philodendron. Like philodendron, these are climbing plants with glossy, showy leaves, but monstera leaves are huge. *M. delicios*'s leaves grow up to three feet long and may have such deep indentations that they resemble large hands with fingers; some leaves, for some unknown reason, do not develop splits.
Culture: See philodendron. Monstera like bright light but not direct sun and will grow in shade. It prefers moist soil and will thrive in water. Leaves should be washed once a month to remove dust and keep them looking glossy. *M. deliciosa* needs a support (it can climb over five feet high) and pinching back.

Pandanus
screwpine
Temperature: 60–75°F
Humidity: 50%
Light: indirect sunlight
Description: The common name comes from the way the long, arching leaves, shaped like sword blades, are arranged spirally along the trunk. The leaves are about three inches wide at the base but taper to sharp points, and vary in color from dark to light green and cream. These plants grow over three feet tall and some varieties may reach a couple of feet higher. As the plant grows, new shoots will develop below the main rosette.
Culture: Pot in regular potting mixture and allow the soil to dry moderately between waterings. Grow in bright light. These plants prefer warmth and react adversely if you subject them to rapid temperature changes.

Peperomia
Temperature: 55–75°F
Humidity: 50%
Light: indirect sunlight
Culture: Peperomias are among the most colorful and attractive foliage plants. Their low, bushy feel make them excellent table plants; trailing varieties are nice in hanging baskets; and small varieties may be used in terrariums. Those with strikingly marked leaves make good contrast

—Maranta fasciata.

with green foliage plants. The upright peperomias—such as *P. metallica* with brown leaves striped with light green, or *P. ornata* with dark-green leaves striped with deep red—don't grow over a foot high. These have rounded, smooth-edged leaves on short stems that produce a full-looking plant. *P. sandersi*, watermelon peperomia, has heart-shaped leaves in deep green marked with silver bands—coloring similar to a watermelon. Trailing varieties include *P. obtusifolia*, which has fleshy oval leaves marked in yellow and green.
Culture: Though peperomias tolerate dim light, they grow best in bright light, such as indirect or filtered sunlight. They are not too particular about soil, so ordinary potting soil will do. The main thing to watch for is that they will rot if overwatered; therefore let the soil dry out to the touch between waterings.

Philodendron
Temperature: 60–75°F
Humidity: 50%
Light: indirect sunlight
Description: Philodendrons grow so well in the environment found in most modern homes and offices that they are among the most popular house plants. By nature, philodendron is a climbing plant, though it also trails, so for most species you need to supply a support—such as a piece of bark inserted into the pot, or a small trellis. These are tropical plants with large, leathery leaves. Some species have smooth-edged leaves, but others have leaves with deep indentations. Many types of philodendron are readily available, and you have a choice of species with huge leaves for dramatic effects, of small glossy-leafed varieties for a desk or table, or of fast-growing vines to be trained to cover an entire wall. Among the most common are:

Maranta (Calathea) Massangeana.

P. andreanum is a vine with dark-green, heart-shaped leaves that have lighter green veins. The leaves grow as large as ten inches long, and if kept pinched back, produce a nice table-top plant two or three feet high.

P. bipinnatifidum, "twice-cut" philodendron, has 8-inch leaves that are so deeply notched as to be almost star-shaped. This species does not need a support and is a slow grower, which makes it a good tabletop plant.

P. cannifolium has large, dark, glossy, spear-shaped leaves. Because this species is not a vine but grows from rosettes, it produces its large leaves on very short stems and makes a nice, full plant.

P. dubium, cut-leaf philodendron, is named for its deeply indented leaves, which are much like those of *P. bipinnatifidum* but only half the size. A slow grower, this species requires less pinching back to keep under control.

P. oxycardum is the most common philodendron, found not only in homes but ubiquitous in lobby groupings and plantings outside large residential and commercial buildings. It's a tough vine, with small heart-shaped leaves, and very adaptable. You can pinch it back to make it a dense tabletop plant, train it on a piece of bark, or let it trail over the edges of desks, balconies, or bookcases. Using wire, string, or other supports, you can train it to frame a window or mirror. Because it grows quickly, it's a favorite for covering trellises or even entire walls. You don't even need soil—it will grow in water or moss.

P. panduraeforme, fiddle-leaf philodendron, is named for its olive-green leaves in an irregular shape, which more or less resembles a fiddle. These are medium-sized plants that can be used on a table or on the floor.

P. pertusum, "split-leaf" philodendron, is actually a juvenile form of *Monstera*, which see.

P. selloum, "saddle leaf," one of the more dramatic species, has leaves that are almost solid when the plant is small. As it grows larger, the plant produces notched leaves more than a foot long and a foot wide. It is also called finger-leaf philodendron because the deep notches create finger-like forms. This species is especially resistant to cold, withstanding temperatures in the 40s. Because it is not a vine but grows from rosettes, it makes a full, massive plant.

P. squamiferum doesn't look much like other philodendron. It's far more delicate, with small, dagger-shaped leaves covered with red hairs.

P. wendlandii is again not a vine but produces narrow leaves a foot or more long from rosettes and makes a full and attractive plant without pinching back. It is tolerant to extremes of temperature and humidity.

Culture: Philodendron are easy to grow. You can plant them in regular potting soil, but adding peat moss and perlite, vermiculite, or sand will help them thrive. *P. oxycardum* can also be grown in water. Keep the soil moist. Because the leaves of this plant are showy, some people wax the leaves. However, you can achieve the same glossy effect by washing the leaves once a month with soap and water (don't let the soapy water get into the soil, though). If the atmosphere is too dry, you might want to mist occasionally.

Philodendron came originally from tropical forest floors and therefore do not like direct sun, but they will grow in most other shaded and subdued light conditions.

Because most philodendron are vines, which in nature grow by means of aerial roots along the trunks of trees, your only problem will be pinching back new growth to make an attractive house plant. If you allow the vines to keep growing, they will produce long stringy stems with small, immature leaves. Pinching back new growth will give you larger leaves and a more bushy, massive plant.

Those with rosettes (*P. bipinnatifidum*, *selloum*, and *wendlandii*) do not require a support. For the other, vine-like species, you will need a trellis, piece of bark, or other support in the pot for the plant to cling to, though some—like *P. oxycardum*—can also be allowed to trail.

Philodendron are also easy to propagate. Any leaves or new growth you remove can be stuck in water or moist sand to start a new plant.

Pilea
aluminum plant
Temperature: 55–75°F
Humidity: 50%
Light: indirect sunlight
Description: These are a group of small foliage plants with colorful leaves ranging from light green to brown in color. They produce clusters of tiny flowers, usually red. Due to their small size, these are good choices to cover the soil of large tubs or planters, or for use with medium size plants. The most popular is *P. cadierei*, the aluminum plant, with fleshy, puckered, light-green leaves marked with silver and bearing red flowers; it comes in a dwarf variety. Also popular is *P. microphylla*, another dwarf, with fernlike foliage; it is called the artillery plant because the flowers discharge a cloud of pollen when shaken. *P. nummulariaefolia*, creeping Charlie, is a trailing plant with quilted bright-green leaves and red flowers; this one is nice for hanging baskets.
Culture: Pot in humus soil, which should be kept moist except when the plants are resting. Though they should grow well in most rooms, watch for signs you might have to provide humidity through misting. Trailing varieties may require pinching back to promote branching.

Pittosporum
mock orange
Temperature: 50–75°F
Humidity: 50%
Light: indirect sunlight
Description: This highly decorative evergreen, which will grow over three feet tall, has thick, glossy leaves that grow in whorls like petals on a flower. Rather elegant, it has a full, rounded look and can stand alone as a table or floor plant. You can train it to be a miniature tree, too. In spring it *sometimes* produces tiny white flowers that smell orangey. *P. Tobira* has all-green leaves; a *variegatum* form has green-and-cream leaves.
Culture: Pot in a mixture of equal parts potting soil, humus, and sand. Water well, then allow soil to dry to the touch before watering again; err on the side of watering too little rather than too much. Although it prefers bright light, it also tolerates shade. It can be propagated through seeds or cuttings.

Plumbago
leadwort
Temperature: 50–70°F
Humidity: 70%
Light: full sun
Description: *P. capensis*, a bushy trailing plant, which can be supported in an upright position or allowed to trail, produces masses of two-inch azure-blue flowers all summer. Less common varieties produce white or red blooms.
Culture: Pot in regular potting soil, keep in full sun, and water well from spring to fall; in winter, when it is dormant, water sparingly. It may need misting in hot weather. You can propagate leadwort by cuttings.

Podocarpus
Southern yew
Temperature: 55–75°F
Humidity: 50%
Light: indirect sunlight
Description: *P. macrophylla* is an evergreen tree with needlelike leaves up to three inches long. It can grow to a high of fifty feet in the wild but that is more likely to stay within five or six feet in your home or office. If it grows too tall, shear the top. *S. nagi* is a related shrub that has an attractive spread. Both have a deep-green color.
Culture: Pot in regular potting mix and let the soil dry between waterings. This plant grows well in shade and at the cooler end of the temperature range.

Polyscias
Temperature: 55–75°F
Humidity: 50%
Light: subdued daylight
Description: These compact plants are attractive for terrariums and dish gardens when young but will grow into table plants as they mature. The small shiny leaves can be leathery or fine, and may be all green or have light or dark edgings.
Culture: Pot in regular potting soil and keep the soil moist but not soggy. These can be propagated by cuttings.

Rhoeo
Moses-in-the-cradle
Temperature: 55–75°F
Humidity: 70%
Light: indirect sunlight
Description: These attractive little table plants have stiff, waxy, arching leaves shaped like slender lances. These fleshy leaves are dark green on top and glossy purple on the underside. The plant's common name comes from the boat-shaped bracts that bear tiny white flowers when the plant blooms.
Culture: Pot in regular soil mixture and keep the soil moist. Locate in bright light. Humidity is important, and rhoeo requires either a pebble tray and/or frequent misting.

Sansevieria
snake-plant
Temperature: 55–75°F
Humidity: 50%
Light: full sun to subdued daylight
Description: One of the toughest plants around, the snake-plant thrives under adverse conditions and with little care. The most popular species have thick-fleshed leaves with pointed tips. These include *S. laurentii*, with yellow bands on the leaves, and *S. zeylanica*, with bands of light green and cream, which grow over two feet high. Leaves on some plants can reach a length of four feet. Other species, with creeping rootstock, grow in dense, circular clusters.
Culture: Pot in a mixture of equal parts loam, peat moss, and sand. If you allow the soil to dry moderately between waterings, but keep it moist, the plant will continue to grow; with less water it will do well but grow slowly. Snake-plants thrive in any light intensity, but they need sun to bloom (they produce pinkish flowers). Leaves should be sponged every couple of weeks.

Schefflera
umbrella-tree
Temperature: 55–75°F
Humidity: 50%-70%
Light: indirect sunlight
Description: *Schefflera actinophylla* is a hardy choice if you want a tree—it grows to about five feet tall. Attractive, deep-green, compound leaves are slender, with prominent veins. They radiate out from the stalks like little umbrellas. A mature plant has a full, bushy look that makes it a good background tree in groupings; it can also stand alone to fill up an empty corner.
Culture: Although schefflera does not like sun, it grows best in bright light, as from a shaded window. Pot in regular potting soil, but add some sand and ensure good drainage. Submerge the pot in a bucket of water and allow the soil to dry before rewatering. It will do best if you keep it on a pebble tray and mist it daily. If leaves begin to drop, you are probably watering too frequently or the soil has insufficient drainage.

Spathiphyllum
Temperature: 55–75°F
Humidity: 50%
Light: subdued daylight
Description: Huge, thin, glossy leaves on short stems make these graceful, arching plants of table size that will stand alone as decorative pieces. These are South American imports. Their white, wafer-thin flowers, on fragile stems, resemble anthuriums.
Culture: Plant in regular potting soil, and keep it moist all the time. Except in winter, when you can water less frequently, the soil should be kept wet. These will grow in bright locations with indirect sun, in areas without direct sun, and will tolerate low light.

Syngonium
arrowhead
Temperature: 55–75°F
Humidity: 50%
Light: indirect sunlight
Description: These little pot plants with all-green or variegated foliage have heart-shaped or arrow-shaped leaves. Smaller varieties, such as *S.*

TRADESCANTIA VIRGINICA.

wendlendii, a white-veined creeper, are good in terrariums. Other varieties have leaves up to six inches long. These are fast growers and make pot plants two feet tall or higher on a pole or totem for support.

Culture: Plant in regular potting soil and keep the soil moist (these will also grow in water). Though they grow best in good light, they tolerate shade too. You can propagate these by cuttings, and in fact they grow so quickly you may have to prune them occasionally to keep them in bounds.

Tradescantia
spiderwort, inchplant, wandering jew
Temperature: 55–75°F
Humidity: 70%
Light: indirect sunlight

Description: These fast-growing trailing plants with tiny leaves come in a variety of foliage colors and are easy to grow. Leaves may be combinations of light or dark green, red, purple, gold, and creamy, and the flowers may be white or shades of purple. The common names vary, and all may be called wandering jew (see also Zebrina). They are especially nice in hanging baskets.

Culture: Pot in regular potting soil (these plants also grow in water), and keep the soil moist by watering generously. In winter, water less frequently. These plants will grow in shade, but the foliage does best under bright or indirect sunlight (not in direct sun—some are susceptible to sunburn).

Because this plant grows so fast, it can look stringy. To keep it full, pinch back new growth regularly. It is easy to propagate, and you can cut off two or three inches of new growth to root in water or moist soil.

Zebrina
wandering jew, spiderwort
Temperature: 55–75°F
Humidity: 70%
Light: indirect sunlight

Description: These fast-growing trailers are so similar to tradescantia that they are difficult to tell apart, and all varieties are known as wandering jew. They have tiny, purplish leaves marked with cream or silver, and bear tiny purple flowers. Zebrina may be used in terrariums.

Culture: See tradescantia.

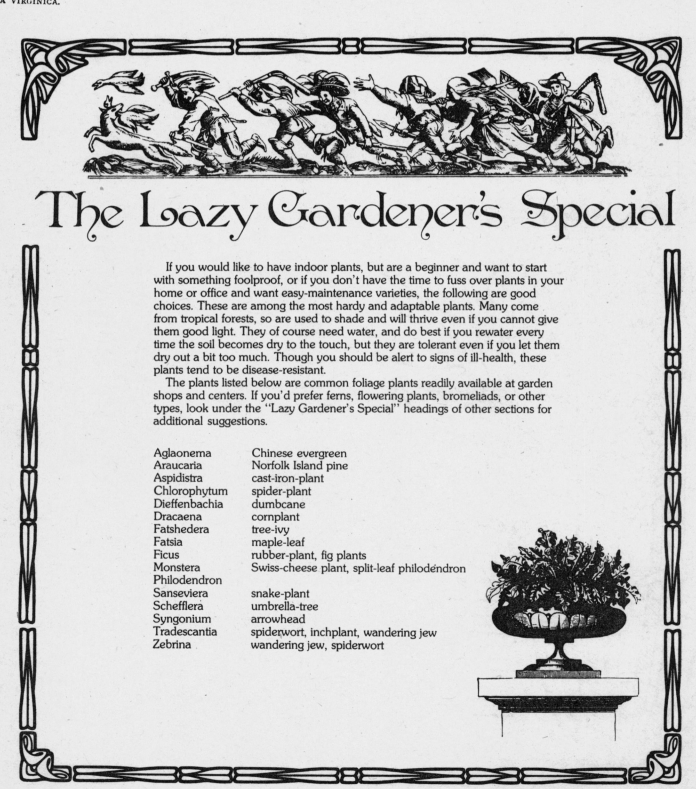

The Lazy Gardener's Special

If you would like to have indoor plants, but are a beginner and want to start with something foolproof, or if you don't have the time to fuss over plants in your home or office and want easy-maintenance varieties, the following are good choices. These are among the most hardy and adaptable plants. Many come from tropical forests, so are used to shade and will thrive even if you cannot give them good light. They of course need water, and do best if you rewater every time the soil becomes dry to the touch, but they are tolerant even if you let them dry out a bit too much. Though you should be alert to signs of ill-health, these plants tend to be disease-resistant.

The plants listed below are common foliage plants readily available at garden shops and centers. If you'd prefer ferns, flowering plants, bromeliads, or other types, look under the "Lazy Gardener's Special" headings of other sections for additional suggestions.

Aglaonema	Chinese evergreen
Araucaria	Norfolk Island pine
Aspidistra	cast-iron-plant
Chlorophytum	spider-plant
Dieffenbachia	dumbcane
Dracaena	cornplant
Fatshedera	tree-ivy
Fatsia	maple-leaf
Ficus	rubber-plant, fig plants
Monstera	Swiss-cheese plant, split-leaf philodendron
Philodendron	
Sanseviera	snake-plant
Schefflera	umbrella-tree
Syngonium	arrowhead
Tradescantia	spiderwort, inchplant, wandering jew
Zebrina	wandering jew, spiderwort

Indoor Flowering Plants

In general, the indoor flowering plants require a bit more care than do the hardier foliage varieties. Often they need more sun, higher humidity, and more grooming. Some also tend to be more susceptible to plant pests.

Despite all this, nothing is quite so rewarding to the indoor gardener as a plant in full bloom. By choosing those that bloom at different seasons, or those that flower virtually all year, you can have blossoms even in winter.

Described below are many plants that produce profuse or exotic flowers, or that have long-lasting fruits and berries, and that are especially suitable for the indoor gardener.

But some flowering plants, such as African violets and other gesneriads, are so popular and come in such variety that they are described in more detailed sections to follow.

In addition, some of the special plants described under "Indoor/Outdoor Plants"—such as the bulbs, orchids, begonias, cacti, bromeliads, herbs, and others—also produce flowers. Forget-me-nots, pansies, marigold, petunias, and other outdoor garden plants are also sometimes successfully potted indoors.

Finally, if you want color rather than blossoms *per se*, you might look over "Indoor Foliage Plants." Some of these have brilliantly colored leaves.

Acalypha
a—chenille—plant
Temperature: 65–75°
Humidity: 60%
Light: indirect sunlight
Description: This attractive tropical shrub grows over two feet high, and some varieties are grown for their foliage alone. *A. hispida*, however, produces brilliant-red blossoms on long drooping stems from late fall into spring.

Culture: Grow in a mixture of equal parts garden soil, peat moss, and sand, or pot in peat moss alone. The soil must be kept evenly moist, so to keep the plant from wilting you will have to water more heavily in warm weather than in winter. It tolerates full sun in winter, but should have indirect sunlight or subdued daylight the rest of the year. Propagate by cuttings.

Acanthus
architectural plant, Grecian urn
Temperature: 50–70°
Humidity: 50%
Light: indirect sunlight or subdued daylight
Description: These compact plants have decorative, glossy-green foliage, and in summer they produce a spike of white, pink, or lavender flowers. Acanthus grows well over two feet, so it is suitable for a floor plant.
Culture: Plant in regular potting soil, which should be kept moist during growth and barely moist during the rest period after flowering. During active growth, acanthus can be kept in indirect sun, but it survives well in subdued light. During the rest period it should be kept in subdued light. You may propagate acanthus by seed or by rhizome division in spring.

Allamanda
Temperature: 55–70°
Humidity: 50%
Light: full sun
Description: These evergreen climbers and shrubs have waxy leaves and golden or brilliant-red

flowers in spring and summer. If you prune it, to keep it within bounds, you can keep it in a pot or window box, but it will grow large enough for tubs.
Culture: Plant in a regular potting mix and keep soil evenly moist during growth. In winter it will become dormant and you should water sparingly. Prune it back in spring. Spring cuttings (take at least two joints) can be propagated easily if kept in shade in vermiculite at a warm temperature until rooted.

Ardisia
coralberry
Temperature: 50–65°
Humidity: 60%
Light: indirect sunlight
Description: This compact little tree with glossy, holly-like leaves will give you color in midwinter. The fragrant flowers are followed by red berries that will last from about November through late spring. The green and red colors make it a popular Christmas plant, and a mature plant may grow over two feet high.
Culture: Plant in a mix of equal parts garden soil, peat moss, and sand, and keep the soil barely moist. Coralberry likes humidity, so keep on a pebble tray and/or mist frequently. In fall or winter it can be kept in a sunny window, but it does not like the full summer sun. It is best propagated from cuttings.

Arthropodium
Temperature: 50–75°
Humidity: 50%
Light: full sun

Acanthus ſativus.
Garden Beares-breech.

Acanthus ſyl. aculeatus.
Prickley Beares-breech.

Description: This pot plant with light-green foliage will grow over two-feet high. It's handy because it produces clusters of small white flowers in early spring, when your other plants may not yet be in bloom.
Culture: Plant in regular potting mix. Water generously during periods of growth, and keep soil lightly moist after flowering. Propagate by division.

Beloperone
shrimp plant
Temperature: 55–75°
Humidity: 50%
Light: full sun
Description: These fast-growing pot plants have deep-green leaves and provide year-round color on beautiful red bracts, which look like shrimp (a delight to children). The white flowers are so tiny they are hard to see. Plants grow quickly to three or four feet, so keep them the size you want by pruning frequently.
Culture: Plant in a mixture of one part garden soil and two parts peat moss. Water well, and then let the soil dry out before watering again. Keep in a sunny place with good ventilation. Propagate by tip cuttings, which produce blooms within a year.

Bougainvillea
Temperature: 50–65°
Humidity: 50%
Light: full sun
Description: This fast-growing vine with spectacular blooms grows huge outdoors, but can be kept within bounds indoors if you cut the plant back each spring or prune it when it gets too big. The flowers are striking, often brilliant red, but some varieties produce multicolor, white, or softer shades of bloom. The flowering period varies, but is usually about six months, and some hybrids bloom all year.
Culture: Plant in a mix of equal parts garden soil, peat moss, and sand. Soil should be kept evenly moist, which means the plants need more water during vigorous growth. When they are resting, you can keep the soil somewhat dry. Feed the plants every two or three weeks. You can propagate from seed or from tip cuttings.

Calceolaria
lady's pocket book
Temperature: 45–60°
Humidity: 50%
Light: subdued daylight
Description: These extremely colorful plants are named for their round, pouch-like flowers that resemble old-fashioned purses. Flowers are usually bright yellow or bright red, and may be spotted. Hybrids with double pouches are also available. Lady's pocketbook is an annual that you buy ready to flower in spring. After the plant has bloomed, you must discard it. You can also grow your own plant from seed. *C. herbeohybrida* and *C. multiflora* grow a foot-and-a-half to two feet tall, but dwarf varieties that grow eight or nine inches high are more compact and appealing.
Culture: If you are buying a plant ready to bloom, keep it in subdued daylight or shade and at a cool temperature with good air circulation. Keep the soil evenly moist but do not overwater.

If you are growing plants from seed, you can sow these in August or September to have flowers around May. Artificial light in winter (an extra five hours a day) will make the plants bloom about two months earlier. The miniscule seeds should be spread over the planting medium, covered with grass, and kept in dim light until they germinate. Then transplant them to three-inch pots. In spring, transplant to five-inch pots.

Campanula trachelium

Campanula
star of Bethlehem, bellflower, falling star

Temperature: 50–60°
Humidity: 50%
Light: indirect sunlight in summer; full sun rest of year
Description: Excellent choices for hanging baskets, these trailers provide bloom from summer to early winter. The trailing stems grow almost two feet long and are covered with masses of star-shaped flowers in white, blue, or lavender.
Culture: Plant in regular potting soil, and allow soil to become dry to the touch between waterings from spring until growth slows in late fall. These plants like to be well ventilated, so be sure they get good air circulation. Although they do not like the full force of the summer sun, they appreciate sunlight the rest of the year. While plants are in active growth, use a water-soluble fertilizer according to directions on the package. To keep the stems from getting too straggly, and to produce more compact bloom, pinch back during early spring. Picking off flowers as they fade also helps promote good bloom.

In late fall or winter, when growth slows, cut the stems off to within five or six inches of the soil. Keep the soil on the dry side, stop fertilizing, and keep the plants in a cool (down to 45° is okay) place. When the plants start to regrow in spring, repot them, and resume regular watering and fertilizing.

Campanula can be propagated from cuttings taken in spring or from seeds.

Capsicum
red-pepper plant
Temperature: 55–60°
Humidity: 50%
Light: full sun
Description: Although this is an annual that must be discarded or restarted from seed each spring, it provides excellent color from fall into winter. It's a bushy plant with green foliage that flowers in spring; most varieties have white blossoms. In autumn it produces a conical fruit that will last several months. The fruit resembles red peppers in shape and may be red or yellow and red.
Culture: Plant in regular potting mix and keep soil evenly moist. Give full sun. Unless the room temperature is on the cool side, however, the fruits will drop off.

Carissa
natal-plum
Temperature: 55–65°
Humidity: 50%
Light: full sun
Description: These compact little shrubs with glossy green foliage grow to about two feet tall. They produce scented white flowers followed by long-lasting red berries.
Culture: Use regular potting mix and keep soil evenly moist during growth; water sparingly during rest. Natal-plum will not flower unless you mist regularly to keep its humidity high. Give it good ventilation, too. Propagate by cuttings.

Clerodendrum
glory-bower
Temperature: 50–70°
Humidity: 50%
Light: full sun except in summer
Description: These easy-to-grow vines have handsome green foliage and produce spectacular blooms that are usually scented. For fragrance, choose *C. bungei* or *C. fragrans pleniflorum* (called cashmere bouquet). Both flower in early fall with red blooms. Other varieties flower in spring or summer and offer blue, and white-and-red blooms. These are adaptable to hanging baskets as well as for pots.
Culture: Plant in a mix of equal parts garden loam, peat moss, and sand. Keep the soil evenly moist during flowering and growth, and after flowers have faded keep on the dry side until growth resumes in spring. Don't worry if the plants drop a few leaves during the rest period. These do not tolerate full sun in summer, so give them filtered or indirect sun, but they do like sun in spring and autumn. Feed during growth.

Costus
Temperature: 55–75°
Humidity: 50% or more
Light: full sun
Description: These South American plants grow at least three feet tall, and sometimes more. They have shiny green leaves and large, extraordinary flowers in brilliant hues of red, orange, yellow, or white. They bloom from spring or summer into fall.
Culture: Plant in regular potting mix and keep the soil evenly moist during

vigorous growth. In spring you can propagate them by dividing the clumps and repotting.

Crossandra
Temperature: 55–70°
Humidity: 70%
Light: full sun
Description: This evergreen has large, glossy, dark-green leaves with a waxy texture and produces bright-salmon flowers almost all year. It will grow to about two-and-a-half feet tall.
Culture: Plant in mixture of three parts humus and one part sand, and keep the soil moist. Keep in the sun on a pebble tray, and mist the plants to maintain high humidity. It flowers best at the higher temperature ranges. You can propagate crossandra by rooting tip cuttings or by sowing seed at any time of year.

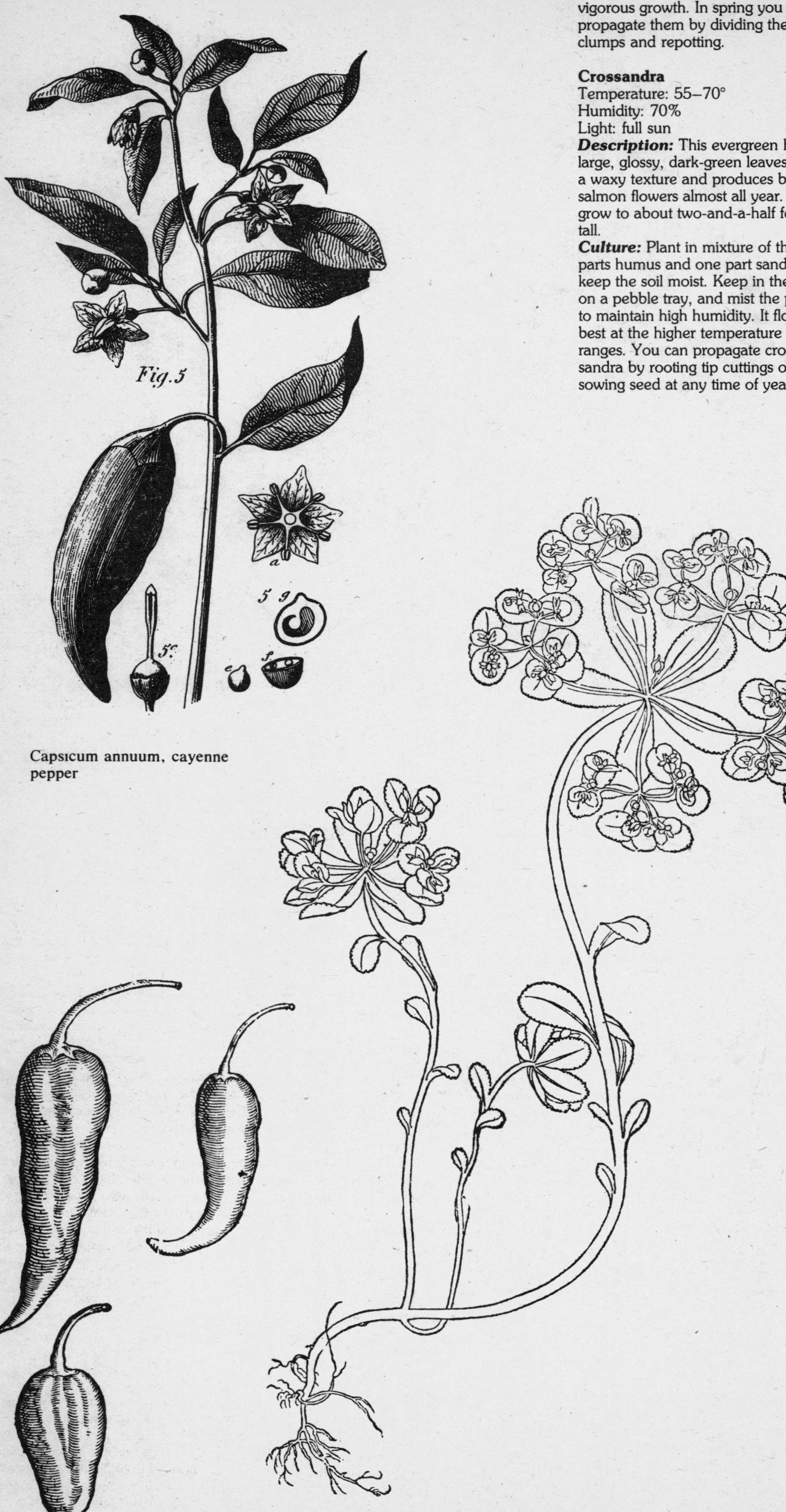

Capsicum annuum, cayenne pepper

—SUN SPURGE.
EUPHORBIA HELIOSCOPIA.

Eranthemum
blue sage
Temperature: 50–75°
Humidity: 50%
Light: full sun
Description: This is a good choice if you want winter bloom. The plant will grow two feet or more. Foliage is a shiny green. Flowers are small and blue.
Culture: Plant in regular potting mix and keep soil evenly moist, but not soggy. If leaves begin to drop off, you are probably overwatering. Mist to keep up the humidity. Root cuttings may be propagated in spring.

Eugenia
rose-apple, Surinam cherry
Temperature: 50–65°
Humidity: 50%
Light: full sun
Description: These little trees are handsome all year round. With pruning, they will grow to about three feet indoors. They have shiny green foliage. *E. jambos*, the rose-apple, produces yellow flowers. The delicate white flowers of *E. uniflora*, the Surinam cherry tree, are followed by long-lasting red berries.
Culture: Plant in regular potting mix and keep soil evenly moist during vigorous growth. When plants rest, water more sparingly. You can propagate from cuttings.

Euphorbia
crown-of-thorns
Temperature: 50–75°
Humidity: 50%
Light: full sun
Description: Euphorbias are related to poinsettias (see page 170), but while poinsettias are grown for their decorative colored leaves, other euphorbias have green leaves and are grown for their flowers. *E. splendens*, the crown-of-thorns, has small green leaves, an abundance of long spines, and produces brilliant-red flowers most of the year. Because this is a climbing plant, you can train the stems onto supports to get the shape you want. This and other euphorbias will grow up to two feet, but dwarfs also are available.
Culture: Plant in a mix that is at least one-quarter sand, because euphorbias come from arid areas and like their soil moist but not soggy. They are resistant to most pests but susceptible to drafts. Some leaves drop in fall and winter, but new ones will regrow in spring. You can propagate euphorbias by taking cuttings.

Exacum
German violet
Temperature: 50–65°
Humidity: 50%
Light: full sun
Description: This is a nice little pot plant if you want winter bloom. The perfumed blue flowers emerge in fall and continue until late winter. The glossy green foliage forms a compact plant that grows over a foot tall.
Culture: Plant in regular potting mix and keep soil evenly moist. You can propagate by seed.

Fuchsia
lady's eardrops
Temperature: 50–65°
Humidity: 70%
Light: subdued daylight
Description: These plants are popular for their brilliantly colored, bell-shaped, drooping flowers. Purple is the most common color, but single and double blooms now are available

in a wide range of colors—blue, white, and several shades of red. Trailing varieties are best for hanging baskets, but upright plants can be grown in pots and will reach two to three feet in height.
Culture: Plant in regular potting soil or in a mix with a bit more humus added, but be sure there is good drainage. Keep the soil moist, especially during vigorous summer growth. Keep in bright light or filtered sun, but not in full sun. These will grow best if you can keep them at about 60°, and mist them to maintain humidity; high nighttime temperatures and insufficient light will inhibit flowering. Feed every two weeks during spring and summer. In winter, while they are dormant, cut back on watering and keep the plants cool.

To encourage branching and a nicely shaped plant, pinch back new growth in spring. You can train upright varieties into tree shapes by rubbing off side shoots until the main stem reaches the height you want, and then pinching the tops to encourage branching.

Fuschia may be propagated by seed or by cuttings.
Special requirements: These plants are susceptible to a number of pests, such as white flies, so be on the alert. They may also develop fungus diseases if good air circulation is not provided.

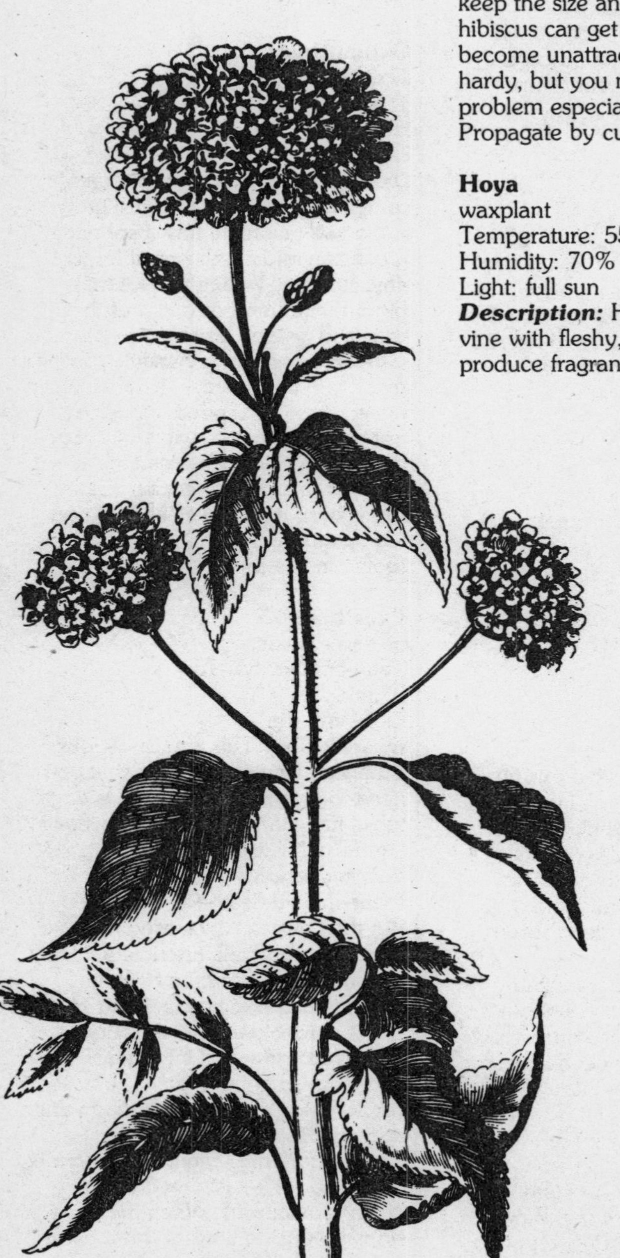

Scarlet Lantana

Grevillea
silk oak
Temperature: 55–75°
Humidity: 50%
Light: full sun
Description: These small trees, that will grow quickly to four or five feet, are attractive and easy to grow. They have green foliage and produce red or red and yellow flowers.
Culture: Plant in regular potting mix and keep soil evenly moist. These are hardy plants, not too fussy about temperature or humidity, and you will probably not have to worry about pests or disease. You can propagate them from seed.

Hibiscus
Temperature: 55–75°
Humidity: 50%
Light: full sun
Description: These treelike plants will grow (quickly) up to four feet and are so popular that a number of varieties are available. Some have green leaves, others variegated foliage. Flowers, which bloom on and off all year, may be single or double, and range from golden yellow to brilliant red to white and to pastels.
Culture: Plant in regular potting mix, give abundant water, and maintain humidity with a pebble tray and misting. To get enough water to the roots, it's a good idea to stand the pots in a bucket of water once every few weeks. In spring, prune them to keep the size and shape you want, as hibiscus can get out of bounds and become unattractive. These are fairly hardy, but you may have a pest problem especially with red spider. Propagate by cuttings.

Hoya
waxplant
Temperature: 55–75°
Humidity: 70%
Light: full sun
Description: Hoya is an attractive vine with fleshy, shiny leaves that produce fragrant flowers when mature (which is about four-years old.) Flowers of most varieties are white with reddish centers and grow in clusters. These vines can be grown in hanging baskets or on a trellis or other support.
Culture: Pot in regular potting mix and keep soil evenly moist. In winter, when hoya is dormant, you can keep the soil drier. As a foliage plant, hoya will survive in subdued daylight, but to flower it needs sun. It likes high humidity, so a pebble tray and frequent mistings are good ideas. When the foliage has faded, don't remove the old stems, as they will reflower in spring. These plants can be propagated by cuttings in spring.

SINGLE FUCHSIA.

Impatiens
Temperature: 50–65°
Humidity: 70%
Light: full sun
Description: Impatiens, available in trailing varieties for baskets as well as uprights that will grow up to two feet tall and dwarfs for pots, provide almost continuous bloom during the year. Flowers tend to be various shades of red or orange but may also be white. Usually the foliage is green, but some plants have red stems and leaves.
Culture: Plant in regular potting soil and keep evenly moist but not soggy. Grow in a sunny window or other bright light and keep them warm. Leaf drop indicates they are not warm enough. They like good air circulation around them. Fertilize every two weeks when they are in bloom. Pinch off the tips to make the plants branch.

If grown from seed, keep the propagating box warm (about 70°). You will get the first blooms three or four months later. You can also propagate from cuttings.

Lantana
Temperature: 50–75°
Humidity: 70%
Light: full sun
Description: Lantana flowers all year, both indoors and outdoors. *L. camara*, often used as a bedding plant outdoors, can be kept in pots or baskets indoors. Its flowers are generally orange, but yellow and other colors are available. *L. montevidensis*, trailer with lavender flowers, is especially pretty in hanging baskets.
Culture: Plant in regular potting mix or in one with a bit of extra sand for good drainage. Water thoroughly and let the soil become dry to the

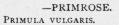

—PRIMROSE.
PRIMULA VULGARIS.

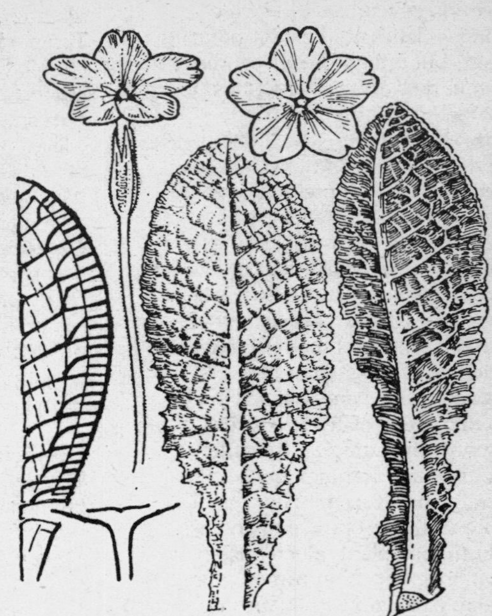

—DETAILS OF PRIMROSE.

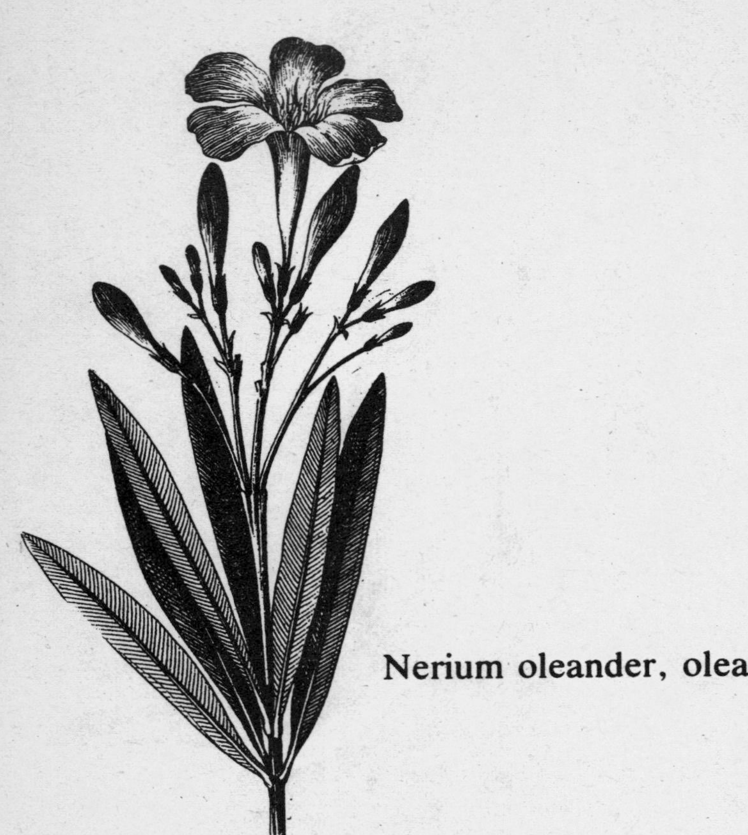

Nerium oleander, oleander

touch before watering again. During vigorous summer growth, keep the soil moist; in winter, you can cut the plant back and keep the soil drier. To be attractive, these plants need to be trained to a nice shape by cutting back. Bloom is best if the plant is kept at about 60° or 65° and humidity is maintained. You can propagate by cuttings any time of year or from seed sown in spring.

Manettia
Mexican firecracker
Temperature: 55–75°
Humidity: 50%
Light: full sun
Description: These fast-growing vines can be kept in a pot or trained onto a trellis or around a window. Almost all year you'll be rewarded with red flowers tipped with yellow.
Culture: Grow in regular potting mix. Water well and then let the soil dry out before watering again. Keep the humidity up by misting, and be sure these plants get ventilation. If your vine is in a pot, prune it frequently to keep it bushy. It is easy to propagate by cuttings.

Nerium
oleander
Temperature: 55–75°
Humidity: 70%
Light: full sun
Description: Oleander blooms profusely in early summer and into the fall. Blossoms may be single or double and in white or shades of pink, salmon, and red. It can grow up to five feet and can be trained into a tree if you remove the side shoots as it grows.
Culture: Pot in regular soil mixture and keep the soil moist throughout the blooming period. Grow in full sun. Once the flowers fade, decrease the amount of water gradually. Then prune the plant and store it over the winter in a light but cool place; if you water only once a month or so, oleander can withstand cold temperatures just above freezing. When growth starts again in spring, repot and resume plentiful watering. Oleander can be propagated from seeds or from new tip growth in spring.

Caution: All parts of oleander are poisonous when eaten. One leaf is enough to kill an adult. Don't keep oleander in the house if you have small children. Avoid handling fresh or dry leaves or inhaling the smoke from burning plants.

Osmanthus
sweet olive
Temperature: 55–75°
Humidity: 50%
Light: indirect sun
Description: This decorative and compact pot plant, which will grow up to two feet high, has crisp, dark-green leaves. But it's prized for its tiny, four-petal white flowers that bloom on and off throughout the year and give off a rich perfume.
Culture: Grow in rectangular potting mix, and keep soil evenly moist but not soggy. It likes good ventilation. Although it can take winter sun, osmanthus should be shaded in summer, and in indirect or diffused sun is best. It does well at the lower temperature ranges. Cuttings may be rooted in summer.

Passiflora
passion-flower
Temperature: 55–75°
Humidity: 70%
Light: full sun
Description: This attractive South American vine is so prolific that you need to give it lots of room—a large tub is fine—and to prune it severely annually. It is also spectacular in hanging baskets. The leaves are spear-shaped, leathery, and green. But the flowers, which are produced in summer and fall, are unique. They vary from white to blue to pink to bright red, and the central part of each round blossom is surrounded by a circular fringe. Unfortunately the blossoms do not last, so it is best to cut them the morning they open and use them as cut flowers.
Culture: Plant in regular potting mix and keep soil moist. Feed when growth is vigorous. When the plant stops producing flowers, cut it back to the level of the soil, decrease water, and let the plant rest over the winter. Passiflora may be propagated from seeds or cuttings in early spring.

Pentas
Egyptian star flower
Temperature: 55–75°
Humidity: 50% or more
Light: full sun
Description: These medium-sized plants, growing to about two feet high, have light-green pointed leaves but are popular chiefly for their flowers. Large rounded umbels, each composed of dozens of tiny star-shaped flowers, give effective bloom on and off most of the year. Flowers may be white, pink, light red, or lavender, and are favorites in flower arrangements as they are long-lasting.
Culture: Plant in regular potting mix and keep soil evenly moist. To create high humidity, a pebble tray and misting help. Propagate by cuttings.

Primula
primrose
Temperature: 45–55°
Humidity: 50% or more
Light: indirect sunlight
Description: These popular gift plants that grow about two feet high provide a profusion of bloom during winter (January to April or May). *P. malcoides* is called "baby" or "fairy" primrose for its tiny flowers. These blooms range from white through shades of red and are produced almost continuously along long stems. *P. obconica* is called "poison" primrose because its foliage irritates some skins. It produces flowers in large clusters that range from white to purplish-reds.
Culture: Pot in regular potting soil and keep the soil evenly moist at all times. The plants will wilt and the leaves turn yellow if the soil dries out. Keep plants in a cool location and out of direct sun. Groom the plant to remove fading flowers. Primulas may be propagated from seed in summer or from young shoots that appear beside the main stem.

Caution: Some primula foliage, especially that of *P. obconica*, gives some people a rash similar to that of poison ivy. Keep plants away from children and use gloves or extra care, especially when transplanting.

Punica
pomegranate
Temperature: 55–75°
Humidity: 50%
Light: full sun
Description: These plants, no more than a foot high, resemble little trees and are therefore often used in bonsai or dish landscapes. The tiny green leaves are shiny, and the red or orange flowers are usually followed by red fruit.
Culture: Plant in regular potting mix and allow soil to dry out between waterings. These plants do not like to be overwatered. They do, however, like humidity, so are best kept on a pebble tray and misted. In winter, the leaves drop off but new ones will grow in spring. You can propagate by seed.

Rosa
rose
Temperature: 50–60°
Humidity: 60%–70%
Light: full sun
Description: A number of miniature rose varieties—plants only three to ten inches high that will produce beautiful blooms—have been developed especially for indoor gardeners. Flower colors vary from white to various shades of reds, all small versions of roses grown outdoors.
Culture: Plant in a mix of equal parts garden soil and peat moss or shredded sphagnum moss. Keep the soil evenly moist, mist daily, and feed every two weeks during the spring and summer growing period. When plants become dormant in fall, prune them and store them in a frostfree but cool (about 40°) place. In January, begin forcing by watering and bringing them into higher temperature. Propagation is from seed or from spring cuttings.

Indoor roses are susceptible to mildew as well as to pests such as aphids and red spider.

Ruellia
Temperature: 55–75°
Humidity: 50%
Light: full sun
Description: These delicate plants, which may grow two to three feet high or be used in hanging baskets, have dark-green leaves and will produce showy flowers from fall to spring. Blossoms may be white, but most varieties are in hues of red.
Culture: Grow in regular potting mix, and allow soil to dry thoroughly between waterings. These plants are not too fussy about temperature and humidity, but they react badly to overwatering. Propagate from cuttings.

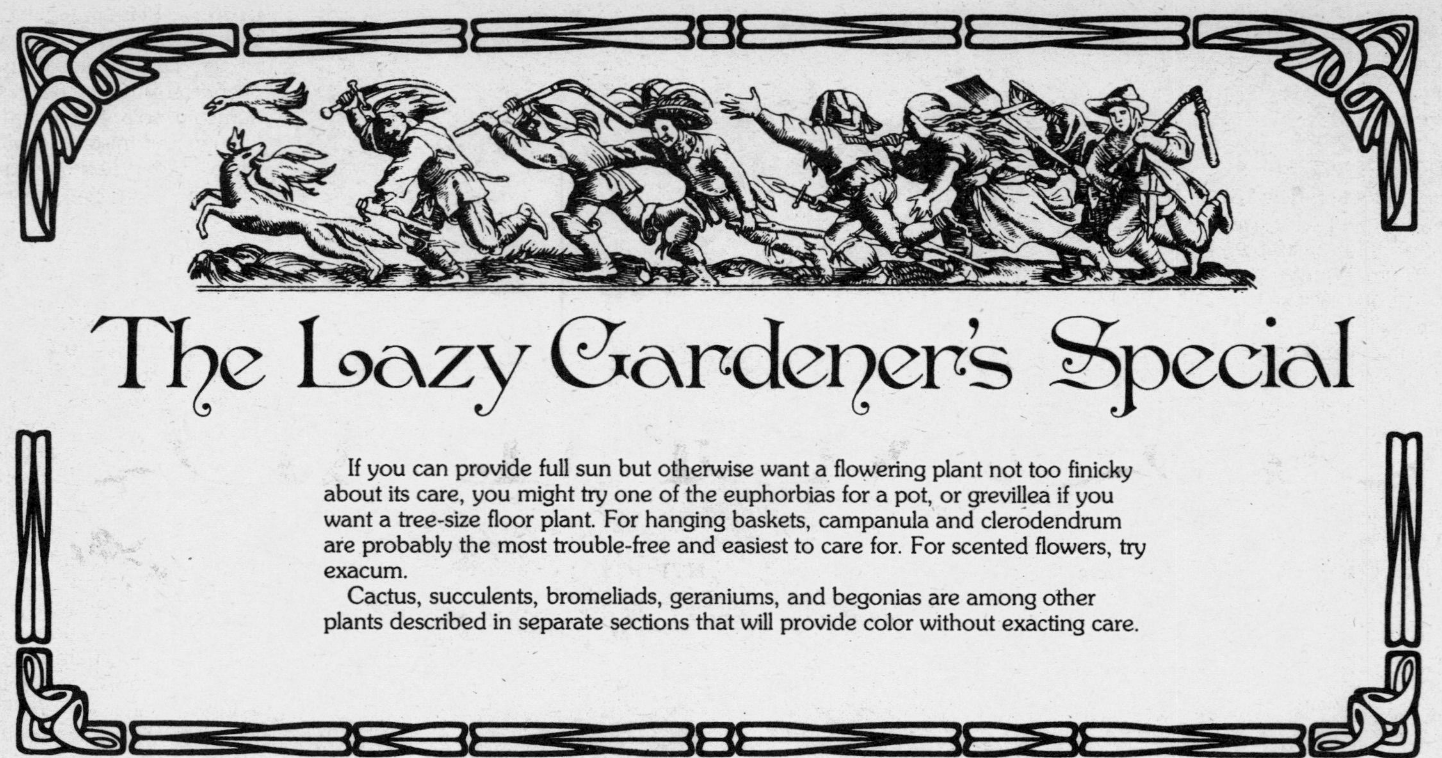

The Lazy Gardener's Special

If you can provide full sun but otherwise want a flowering plant not too finicky about its care, you might try one of the euphorbias for a pot, or grevillea if you want a tree-size floor plant. For hanging baskets, campanula and clerodendrum are probably the most trouble-free and easiest to care for. For scented flowers, try exacum.

Cactus, succulents, bromeliads, geraniums, and begonias are among other plants described in separate sections that will provide color without exacting care.

Solanum
Jerusalem cherry
Temperature: 50–60°
Humidity: 70%
Light: full sun
Description: *S. pseudo-capsicum* is a South American shrub that will grow about three feet high and produce white flowers followed by cherry-sized, long-lasting, orange or scarlet fruit. It is best to discard the plant after a year, because plants more than a year old do not produce much fruit, but if you want to save the plant, repot it in late spring and prune it to about nine inches from the soil. A related plant, *S. jasminoides*, is a climber that produces perfumed, star-shaped white flowers.
Culture: Plant in regular soil mix, and allow the soil to dry between waterings. Keep the humidity high or the plant may drop its leaves and develop bare stems. In winter the plant will survive at about 50° if you keep the soil fairly dry. Propagating from seeds is probably a better idea than trying to keep this plant from year to year.
Caution: Avoid handling the fruit, and don't keep this plant if you have small children, because the fruit causes a skin rash in some people.

Strelitzia
bird-of-paradise
Temperature: 55–75°
Humidity: 50% or more
Light: full sun
Description: Increasingly popular for their long-lasting bloom, which can give an exotic touch to a flower arrangement, these are tropical plants with long, thin, banana-like green leaves up to three feet long, and thick stalks. Their glory, however, is the flower, which is produced when the plant is mature and which looks somewhat like a brilliant multicolored bird. The exterior petals are bright orange and the lip is deep blue.
Culture: Plant in humus soil and keep soil evenly moist. Place in a sunny spot and use a pebble tray and/or misting to provide humidity. These can be propagated by seed or by dividing the tubers.

Flowering Plants for Poor Light

Most flowering plants require full sun in order to bloom. If you cannot provide long hours of direct sunlight for your plants, you might try acanthus or calceolaria. These should grow in light from a north window or in other strong light. Fuchsia also does not like full sun and prefers sun filtered through a curtain or other strong light.

GESNERIADS

Gesneriads are tropical plants—many come from Central and South America—that reward you with spectacular and brilliantly colored blooms. Some will bloom for months, and by staggering their planting times and/or selecting a variety of different gesneriads, you can have flowers all year. In addition, these plants often have velvety and richly colored foliage, so they are decorative even when not in bloom.

Most popular of the gesneriads are the saintpaulias (African violets), described below, which have tiny flowers. Probably next in line are sinningia (gloxinias), which have large, velvety blooms. These are described below, along with other favorites.

Gesneriads can live comfortably in your home if you provide sufficient light (natural or artificial) and humidity. They range from compact plants that are nice in pots, either alone as specimen plants or in groupings, to trailers that are stunning in hanging baskets.

One consideration in choosing which to buy is that gesneriads have three different growth systems. Some have fibrous roots like those of most other plants. These, which include air plants, grow all year without a rest period. African violets are an example. Other gesneriads grow from tubers. Still others grow from scaly rhizomes, which are thick roots so scaly they resemble pine cones. The tubers and rhizomes need a rest period after the plants have bloomed; you must dry them out, store them, and then repot them for new growth. Here's how they stack up:

scaly rhizomes
achimenes
kohlerias
smithianthas

tubers
rechsteinerias
sinningias

fibrous roots
aeschynanthus
columneas
episcias
hypocyrtas
streptocarpus

Altogether there are more than forty genera of gesneriads, many of which are air plants (epiphytes), with countless species. In addition, new varieties are continually being hybridized. Only the most common forms are described below. To keep up to date with new developments, you may want to join the American Gloxinia and Gesneriad Society.

ACHIMENES is called the magic flower or the rainbow flower because the blooms, shaped like those of petunias, come in virtually every color of the rainbow. The leaves are finely cut, glossy, and tinted red or green. These offer exceptionally fine display, and by staggering the times you plant the rhizomes you can have flowers all summer long.

Largest of the achimenes, growing over two feet high, are *A. grandiflora*, with purple blooms that fade into white at the base, and *A. pedunculata*, with orange flowers. Other varieties, with purple, orange, red, pink, and yellow blooms, make nice upright pot plants about a foot and a half tall. Beautiful cascading varieties, including the brilliant red-and-orange *A.* "Vivid," are exceptional choices for hanging baskets.

AESCHYNANTHUS is a fibrous-rooted air plant known as the lipstick vine for its trailing habit and brilliant red blooms. Some varieties have yellow, orange, or multicolored flowers, however. These bloom in summer and are more shade-loving than other gesneriads. The evergreen leaves are dark green with a waxy look.

COLUMNEA are fibrous-rooted air plants that are quite popular and widely available. Beginners will probably find the newer hybrids easiest to grow. Most of these are trailing plants, good for hanging baskets, with tiny leaves and large red or orange blooms. But upright plants, with leaves six-inches long and three-inch blossoms, are also available; some grow as high as three feet.

EPISCIA are air plants with such brilliantly colored flowers that they are commonly called flame violet or peacock plant. The tubular flowers, often in flaming reds or oranges but also white and lavender, bloom in spring and summer. The foliage is especially attractive, often exotically patterned in metallic colors—silver, copper, or even red. These are fibrous-rooted vines with runners like those of strawberry plants, which are attractive for hanging baskets.

HYPOCYRTA are trailing air plants with small oval leaves and bulb-shaped blossoms in dazzling reds and oranges. Some of these have erratic blooming seasons. The dark-green foliage may be pruned after flowers have faded to induce branching, and *H. strigillosa* has such stiff stems that you can grow it as an upright plant.

KOHLERIA gives you a lot for your money. The leaves are large, soft, and attractive, making a compact pot plant, though *K. amabilis* may be grown in baskets, too. Trumpet-shaped flowers, each dangling from its individual stem, are pretty shades of lavenders, pinks, and other colors, and in several varieties are spotted. Blooming periods are long; depending on the variety, you can have blossoms spring through fall. *K. lindeniana*'s blossoms are scented. This is a small plant, under a foot in height; other types range up to two feet. In addition to all this, the rhizome grows quickly, so that you can separate it to make several new plants or plant the individual scales like seeds to multiply your original plant many times over.

RECHSTEINERIA is closely related to the sinningias, and in fact, the two have been crossed to produce a hybrid called "gloxineras." Rechsteinerias are especially handsome and exotic. The leaves tend to be large, dark-green, and soft—some are covered with fine hairs—and make a perfect background for the startingly brilliant flowers in bold reds. These are all upright pot plants, usually one to two feet tall, though dwarfs are available too. Like gloxinias, they must be rested three or four months after blooming ceases, and then repotted when new growth begins.

SINNINGIA, or more accurately *S. speciosa*, is the dramatic and popular gloxinia from Brazil. Many loyal fans rate gloxinias above other gesneriads and, in fact, over other flowering indoor plants. The leaves are dark, velvety, green, and so large (four to ten inches in various plants) and soft they drape gracefully. The flower stems are so short they are hidden in the foliage, so the dozen or more flowers seem to pop right out of their

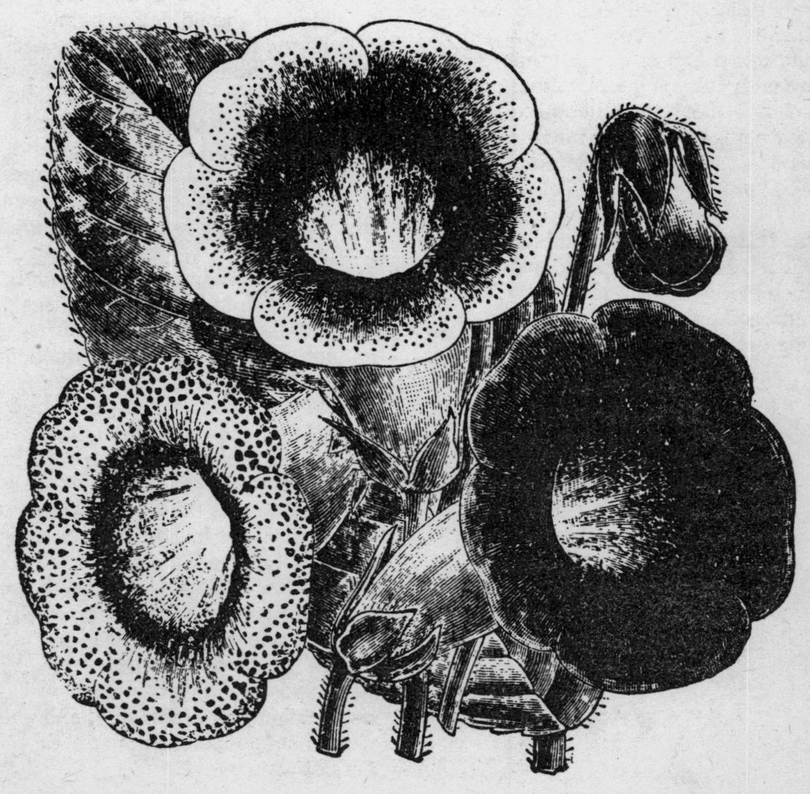

background. So many hybrids are available that you can choose blossoms of solid color, of speckled or banded patterns, or of contrasting color. *S. barbata*'s flowers are white with red streaks. In addition to large, trumpet-shaped flowers, you can get

doubles (hybrids with two rows of petals) and slipper varieties with small, nodding blooms. Though gloxinias were originally dormant in winter, today you can buy hybrids for bloom most any time.

Also interesting is *S. pusilla*, which bears delicate lavender flowers and which is so small, you can grow it in a jar, under a glass or in a terrarium. This is so charming a plant that other miniatures have been hybridized. Their names tend to be rather romantic—"Wood Nymph" and "Doll Baby" are examples.

SMITHIANTHA are called temple bells for their bell-shaped flowers, which bloom in fall and winter. These branch off a stalk that rises above huge velvety leaves. The foliage is

soft and often covered with thin hairs. Many hybrids are available, so you can get flowers in bold reds or oranges—often spotted—or in pastel shades. These are tall plants, growing a foot and a half to two and a half feet high.

STREPTOCARPUS, the cape primrose, has many varieties and species with dark-green leaves and trumpet-shaped blossoms that have especially narrow throats and expanded frilled edges. Colors range from white and pinks to red and purple. *S. grandis* is a strange form, which produces only one leaf—but it can grow two or three feet long. *S. zaxorum* is a trailing plant. Most common are the *S. rexii* hybrids, with large blooms in pleasant proportion to the leaf lengths.

Culture

Temperature. Gesneriads do well at normal room temperatures of 65° to 75° during the day and even up to 80°. But being tropical plants, they cannot tolerate cold. The temperature at night should not go below 60°. If you keep them on windowsills, take precautions against cold drafts in winter and don't let them touch cold windowpanes. If your windows get very cold at night, you could insert a piece of cardboard, some newspaper, or another insulating barrier between the plants and the windowpanes until morning.

Humidity. Gesneriads like high humidity—60% to 80%—so chances are your rooms will not be moist enough, especially not when the heat is on in winter. Keeping them on a pebble tray—especially if you group several together—is a good idea. Misting them once or twice a day also helps. However, like African violets, other gesneriads develop spots on the leaves if the foliage receives water that is not at room temperature. Since water cools as it is sprayed, use water hot enough to be at room temperature when it hits the leaves. Except for the fibrous-rooted gesneriads though, your plants will be dormant part of the year, and you won't have to worry about the dryness of winter.

Light. Gesneriads do best in indirect sunlight. In winter, when the sun is weak, they will benefit from a southern exposure, but in summer use a sheer curtain to shield them from full sun or keep them in east or west windows. Gesneriad leaves should grow out nearly horizontal to the main

stem and be rather compact. If your plants are growing tall and spindly, they are not getting enough light. If the leaves are turning yellow and hugging the pot, they are getting too much light. Turn the pots, a quarter turn each day in the same direction, daily. Gesneriads may be grown under artificial light, and some suppliers sell light stands especially for them (though these stands are not always most attractive for display). You will probably need three fluorescent tubes placed about a foot above the pots and turned on about fourteen or fifteen hours a day.

Soil. Gesneriads prefer a loose, well-drained soil. You can buy a ready-made mixture prepared for African violets, or, if yours is an air plant, one for epiphytes. If you mix your own, use equal part loam, peat moss, and leaf mold, with enough sand for good drainage—all ingredients sterilized, of course.

Potting. Plants should be potted between December and March. Squatty flower pots about five inches in diameter are good for new plants. Cover the bottom with pebbles and then pour in the soil, but do not press it down. Place the tuber (round side down) or rhizome in the pot and cover with about another inch of soil. Water until water runs out of the bottom of the pot, and place in good light.

Watering. Water thoroughly—with *lukewarm* water—and then do not rewater until the topsoil is dry to the touch. Never let the soil become thoroughly dry, however, because the plant will become dormant. During vigorous growth, gesneriads rquire lots of water. Many growers prefer to water from the bottom of the pot, because gesneriads react badly to water standing on their leaves.

Gesneriads with fibrous roots, which grow all year without a rest period, like the soil to be kept evenly moist at all times.

Those with scaly rhizomes or tubers, however, need a rest period after blooming. When the flowers have died, let the soil dry out gradually.

Fertilizer. Most of the fertilizers on the market are too strong for most gesneriads. Buy a soluble mix especially prepared for African violets and add a quarter teaspoon to a gallon of water; use this diluted mix for watering the gesneriads. Once a month flush the pots by watering heavily with plain lukewarm water to prevent undissolved fertilizer minerals from building up on the soil.

Troubleshooting. Gesneriads are not especially susceptible to pests. Most common is bud blast, where the buds dry out, turn brown, fail to open into flowers, or drop off. This is usually caused by insufficient humidity, overwatering, or too much fertilizer, though insects and air pollution are other causes. Crown rot can also result from overwatering.

The most common pest is the cyclamen mite, but aphids, spider mites, mealybugs, whitefly, and root nematodes also attack.

Special requirements. Fibrous-rooted gesneriads generally grow all year, though you can decrease water and fertilizer somewhat when the growth seems less vigorous. Usually this will happen in winter, but the species vary.

Gesneriads growing from tubers, however, have a clearly defined life cycle. When you first plant these, water sparingly until growth shows above the ground. Most should be planted between January and March, though some hybrids can be started in fall. If you have several, you can stagger the planting times so that flowering will also be staggered and longer lasting. A five-inch or six-inch pot is usually sufficient, and you should place the tuber close to the surface with the rounded side down.

You can cover the top of the pot with paper or plastic to keep the soil warm (about 60° is good), but remove the covering once growth appears. If more than one sprout pops up, break off the weaker ones so the most robust one can mature. Then water regularly and begin fertilizing, and the plant will grow quickly. Within three or four months you should have flowers.

AN IDYL OF SPRING
THE PULSE OF THE GROW-
-ING EARTH BEATS FAST
SHY CREATURES CREEP FROM
THEIR WINTRY HOME
FOR LO! THE WINTER IS OVER
AND PAST
AND THE SINGING BIRDS HAVE COME
THE SPRING IS HERE WITH HER MASQUE
OF FLOWERS AND LOVE IS ABROAD IN HER
LEAFY BOWERS

After the plants have finished blooming, decrease the water and fertilizer gradually. Techsteinerias can be left in pots and stored in a cool place (about 55°) in dim light for three or four months, until new growth appears. Then they should be repotted and put back into light and watered. Once sinningias have finished blooming, cut off the stem, leaving only the lowest two good leaves. Water for another three or four weeks, because sometimes new growth will appear and the plant will initiate a second cycle of bloom. If no new growth appears, though, stop watering and let the plant wither. Store the pot in dim light at 50° to 60° temperature and water about once a month. Gloxinias vary in their periods of dormancy—some will rest six weeks, some a couple of months. Don't try to force your plant into activity by watering, or you are likely to rot the tuber. Wait until it produces a new sprout of its own accord. Then repot it in fresh soil, and you'll probably need a pot a size larger than before.

Gesneriads growing from scaly rhizomes should be treated pretty much like the tuberous ones. Again you can plant between January and May, staggering the plantings of several rhizomes to assure consecutive, long-lasting blooming. In this case, though, it is best to plant about an inch deep in damp sphagnum moss or vermiculite in a shallow bulb dish, and to transplant to five-inch pots once the growth is a few inches high. Trailing varieties can be transplanted to hanging baskets. Be especially careful to keep the soil evenly moist, as these rhizomous plants tend to go dormant quickly in dry soil.

If you have started smithiantha in March, they should bloom from November into spring. Achimenes and kohleria will bloom in six to eight weeks and continue to flower through the summer. Once the flowers have died, taper off your watering and fertilizing, and let the plant wither. Some growers store the rhizomes in their pots, others remove them to dry sand or vermiculite for storage. In either case, they should be stored in dim light at a temperature of about 50° until spring, when you can repot them and return them to good light.

All of the gesneriads benefit from a bit of grooming, such as picking off dying blossoms and leaves.

Propagation. Gesneriads grow easily from seeds planted in a covered box with sphagnum moss or vermiculite kept damp but not soggy or wet. Gloxinia seeds are so tiny that to sow them evenly you have to put them in a folded piece of paper; move the paper across the moss, tapping it with your other hand so only a few seeds fall out. Do not bury gloxinia seeds. Keep out of sunlight in a warm place until sprouts appear. Then begin fertilizing (see above).

When the plants have four leaves, transplant them to a covered box with starting medium, planting them an inch apart. After a week, raise the box cover or elastic covering a bit, and increase the height daily for another week before removing it entirely. When the leaves reach out to touch each other, transplant to two and a half-inch pots of African violet soil. Handle gently, or the sprout will detach from its tuber. You can transplant them to permanent four-inch pots once they are about five inches high. They won't bloom before four months, and perhaps not for double that time.

Tuberous gesneriads also can be propagated by planting the extra shoots that appear. For the original plant, you want to preserve only the most vigorous sprout. But the others can be pulled off the tuber once they are about two inches high, and planted in a rooting medium. Some of the other gesneriads, such as the episcias, produce offshoots that you can propagate.

Most gesneriads can easily be propagated by leaf cuttings. For fibrous-rooted varieties, stem cuttings are the best method.

Gesneriads with scaly rhizomes can be multiplied by dividing the rhizome, or by planting single scales as you would seed.

Suppliers of Gesneriads

The African Violet Co.
100 Floral Ave.
Greenwood, SC 29647

Annalee Violetry
29-50 214th Place
Bayside, NY 11360

L. Easterbrook Greenhouses
10 Craig St.
Butler, OH 44822

Fischer Greenhouses
Oak Ave.
Linwood, NJ 08221

Harborcrest Nurseries
4634 W. Saanich Rd.
Victoria, B.C.
Canada V82 3G8

Klinkel's African Violets
1553 Harding
Enumclaw, WA 98022

Engardt's Violet House
7457 Schuler Drive
Omaha, NE 68114

Lyndon Lyon
14 Mutchler St.
Dolgeville, NY 13329

Julius Roehrs Co.
R D 2 Box 144
Farmingdale, NJ 07727

Tinari Greenhouses
2325 Valley Rd.
Huntington Valley, PA 19006

Tropical Paradise Greenhouses
8825 West 79th St.
Overland Park, KS 66204

Volman Brothers Greenhouses
2714 Minert St.
Dallas, TX 75219

African Violets

In 1890, Baron Walter von Saint Paul, a district commissioner in the colonial administration of Tanganyika (now Tanzania) sent to Europe some seeds from an interesting flowering plant he discovered while on an expedition into the mountains. Two years later, the genus Saintpaulia was named for the young baron and saintpaulias, or African violets, were on their way to becoming a popular plant throughout western Europe. By the 1920s, seeds of British and German hybrid saintpaulias had traveled to North America, and American hybridizers were beginning to develop their own strains of African violets. The real boom in African violets began shortly after World War II when fluorescent lighting attracted great numbers of people to the pleasures and possibilities of indoor gardening.

Today, there are thousands of varieties of African violets, thanks to a combination of planned hybridization and spontaneous mutation, the latter occurring during the process of rooting selected leaves to reproduce particular plants.

The colors of saintpaulia flowers range from actual violet to pure white, with all shades of blue, pink, red, and lavender in between. Blossoms may be single, double, or semi-double and of many different sizes. Miniature and trailing African violets also exist. The many varieties vary in how velvety the foliage is and in slight differences in leaf shape and coloration.

Although of African lineage, saintpaulias are not violets at all. They belong to the gesneriad family (Gesnericea), which includes other popular flowering house plants like gloxinias. When they were first imported, African violets were considered exotic and difficult to grow, and later they acquired a certain mystique perpetrated by their enthusiastic devotees. But the truth is that thousands of cultivars are available, and new and hardier varieties are constantly being developed. Though African violets do need some care and attention, they are now easy to live with if you follow a few simple rules for their environmental needs—which are luckily closely allied with conditions in the average home.

Buying an African violet

Helen Van Pelt Wilson, whose writings have done much to spread the popularity of African violets, recommends that home gardeners purchase smaller plants. Her reasoning? They acclimate more quickly than large ones to home conditions, which are bound to be different from those at the grower's greenhouse or at the plant shop. If you buy well-started greenhouse plants, Ms. Wilson suggests letting them spend several weeks in their original pots before shifting them to a larger one.

If you are a novice, start your collection with a plant that has plain leaves because these are easier to grow than those with curly foliage.

Plants with double, rather than single, blossoms have longer-lasting flowers.

Avoid supermarket saintpaulias. Have you wondered why those little African violets from the supermarket or five-and-ten don't live when you

get them home? Often those plants are potted in a soil mix with almost no nutrients and may need careful watering and extra mild fertilizing—or even transplanting—to start them out in a home environment. Sometimes, too, their roots are very underdeveloped. Buy saintpaulias only from specialists and reliable garden centers.

Culture

Temperature. Saintpaulias do best when the temperature is between 70° and 80° during the day and 65° to 70° at night. They do not bloom well at higher temperatures, and their growth is slowed if they are kept too cool.

Though they like good air circulation, avoid drafts. If you have them in a window, move the pots away from the cold panes on wintery nights. Or you can protect them from the panes by placing newspaper or another barrier between the plants and the glass.

Humidity. Keep the humidity at 40% to 50% or a bit higher. If your home or office does not have this, use a pebble tray. The higher the temperature, the more humidity the plants will need. If your plants are not getting enough air moisture, the leaves may curl and flower buds may drop off before blooming.

You can mist African violets, but not while they are in a draft or exposed to direct sunlight. In addition, light-colored spots will develop on leaves wetted with water that is cooler or warmer than the air. When top-watering or misting, therefore, be sure to use room-temperature water. Water from a mister cools as it is sprayed, so one good trick is to fill the mister with hottish water that will be tepid by the time it reaches the leaves.

Light. Proper light is essential, and indirect sunlight is best. Light from an east or west window is good, and so is some mild sun from a southern exposure in late autumn and winter; but shield your saintpaulias with a curtain or other screening device from the full rays of the sun from spring through early fall.

If you are growing your African violets under artificial light, use the fluorescent tubes for twelve to fourteen hours a day. Usually eight to twelve inches from the light source is a good distance for young plants, with up to sixteen inches away for mature plants. In a display of several varieties with light- and dark-colored flowers, set the lighter blossoms under the ends of the fluorescent tubes because they require less light.

If your plants have flat rosettes with good bloom, they are getting proper light. Excess sun will cause spotting, loss of color, and brittle foliage. Too little light will result in elongated stems and will reduce or eliminate blooming.

Soil. Soil mixtures especially prepared for African violets are available commercially, and these are usually your best bet. Some of them, however, are not porous enough and will become waterlogged. Many growers prefer to mix their own for which there are dozens of recipes. One is equal parts African violet soil, perlite, and vermiculite, with horticultural charcoal and a teaspoon of lime optional but sensible additions. You can also use regular potting mix with equal amounts of organic matter such as peat moss or compost and sand or perlite for drainage. If you are mixing your own soil, be sure it is sterilized—or you may face crown rot or other problems.

Potting. The leaf stems (petioles) may rot if they lie on the wet rim of a clay flower pot. To protect the lower stems, some gardeners use a plastic pot or cover clay pot rims with paraffin or aluminum foil. Plastic pots are preferred under artificial light. The pot should be up to a third the size of the plant's diameter to promote flowering. The fit should be slightly tight, without strangling the pot's inhabitant.

How often should pots be changed? Saintpaulias grow slowly and probably will not need a new pot more than once a year.

The ancestors of our saintpaulias grew on the mountain ranges of Tanzania and Kenya in humus (formed from the fallen leaves of overhead trees) mixed with topsoil. In their natural state, their roots spread out rather than reached downward. Therefore, in captivity African violets do well in shallow containers, e.g., short pots or even bulb dishes.

Watering. Overwatering is the greatest source of trouble in growing African violets, and hundreds of articles and a great deal of space in books on houseplants are devoted to this subject. Since different surroundings affect various plants differently, there is no fixed rule to follow. Keep the soil moist but not soggy. Every couple of days, you need to check each plant to see whether the soil looks dry. African violets are somewhat succulent and are unlikely to want water more than twice a week, even under lights.

When you water saintpaulias, use *lukewarm* water, due to the leaf spotting problems described above under "Humidity." If you water from the top, don't let water stand on the leaves. Remove excess water from the pot saucer once the soil has absorbed as much moisture as it can hold. Many saintpaulia fanciers prefer subirrigation (see "Watering Indoor Plants" on page 86–87), or, even better, to alternate top and bottom watering. Alternating the two methods assures that moisture will reach all roots, and also flushes out the accumulation of undiluted mineral slats left over from fertilizers you have been adding to the water.

Fertilizer. Growers specializing in African violets usually feed their plants highly dilute solutions of fertilizer at every watering. There is a very good reason for this practice; high concentrations of fertilizer tend to destroy the delicate leaf stems and distort leaves.

What kind of fertilizer? Any water-soluble fertilizer will do. Peters' African Violet Special 12-36-14 is a popular constant-feed preparation when diluted with one-quarter teaspoon per gallon of water. Helen Van Pelt Wilson, in her *African-Violet Book*, suggests using several different fertilizers in rotation because each has a different chemical formulation.

Pests. To avoid contaminating your old plants, isolate newly acquired saintpaulias for two to three months, until you are sure they are healthy and free of insects. African violets are usually kept pest-free by washing the leaves regularly in soapy water at room temperature. Blot off the excess water and let the leaves dry thoroughly in a shady place before returning the plants to strong light. These precautions are necessary due to the tendency of the leaves to spot (see "Humidity," above).

Signs of trouble may be the following: If the center foliage turns gray and hard, you may have mites, which are one of the most common problems. Mites can also cause the stems to look dry, stunted, and twisted. Streaked leaves and flowers, and other blossoming problems such as blasted buds and flowers dropping off, are often caused by thrips. Sometimes mealybugs can also be a problem. Crown rot can be prevented by not overwatering, and mildew can be avoided by providing good air circulation.

Special requirements. To look their best, African violets need some hands-on care as they grow. If you want a symmetrical plant, unless the plant is directly under lights, you must remember to give it a quarter turn (in the same direction!) each week. But even if you don't care about raising aesthetic masterpieces, you will have more robust specimens if you remove spent flowers with small sharp scissors (never pull them off) and pick off suckers, or offsets (little green growths among the foliage stems that look like tiny leaves). If suckers are allowed to elongate, they will ruin your plants' looks and probably prevent further blooming.

If you've neglected your plant and now have a specimen with a long neck because the lower leaves have died off, it is time to make a move. You have two courses of action. The first, and simpler, is merely to shift the stalky plant to a larger pot and bury its neck down below the soil. The second remedy entails cutting off the top of the plant and rerooting it. If you decide to do that, it may be necessary to remove some of the older outer leaves. (But don't chuck them out—see "Propagation," below). Leave one and a half inches of the old stem, scrape it clear of strings, and dust it with Fermate. Then root it in moist sphagnum moss in a drinking glass—the plant's foliage can rest undamaged on the rounded rim of the glass until a good new root system develops and the rehabilitated plant is ready to be potted in soil.

Propagation. Leaf cuttings placed in water, moist vermiculite or sand, or a commercial rooting medium will produce roots in about two weeks. You can also propagate from offset shoots or seeds.

1

Violet colour'd African

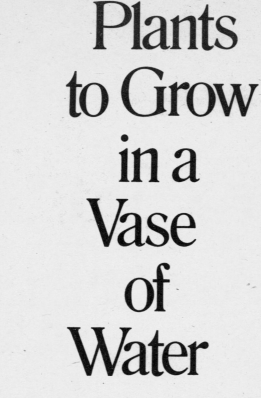

Plants to Grow in a Vase of Water

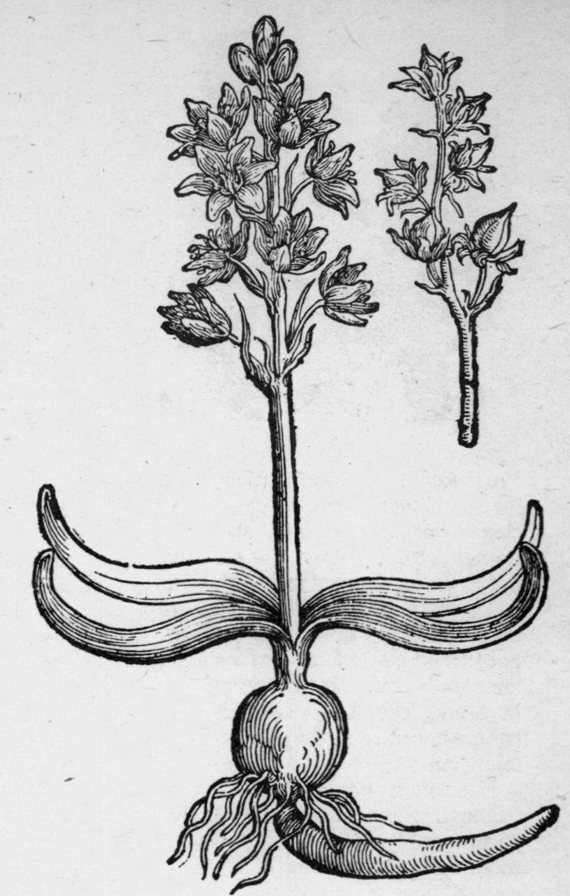

If you would like houseplants but don't want to be bothered with soil and pots, a number of species will grow quite satisfactorily for long periods in a vase with ordinary tap water.

Putting a few pieces of horticultural charcoal into the vase will keep the water from souring. If your container has a wide neck, you can hold plants upright with styrofoam.

Growing plants in a pottery vase or other opaque container that does not transmit light will inhibit the growth of algae in the water. But if you like to see the root system as well as the foliage, you may prefer a transparent vase. If algae forms, wipe it gently off the larger roots, clean the container thoroughly, and fill it with fresh water at regular intervals.

Among the foliage plants that will grow in water are:

Aglaonema
Coleus
Cordyline
Dracaena sanderiana
Gynura
Ivy
Monstera
Philodendron, especially P. oxycardum
Sansevieria
Scinadapsus
Syngonium
Tradescantia
Zebrina

Hawaiian tree ferns also grow in water.

Phial

If you prefer flowering plants, some bulbs may be grown in water, and in fact this is a way of forcing early bloom.

Dutch hyacinths are so often grown in water that a special hyacinth glass is available for this purpose.

French-Roman hyacinths and narcissus can also be grown in water, but the difficulty here is that the bulbs are so small, a suitable container is hard to find. Bulbs must have water at the base to root, but if the neck of the bulb is covered with water the bulb will rot. You might find a suitable bud vase. Most folks, however, prefer to plant several bulbs together in a shallow dish filled with pebbles, pearl chips, or vermiculite. In addition to holding the bulbs erect and the necks out of water, this provides a more impressive display of several bulbs flowering at once.

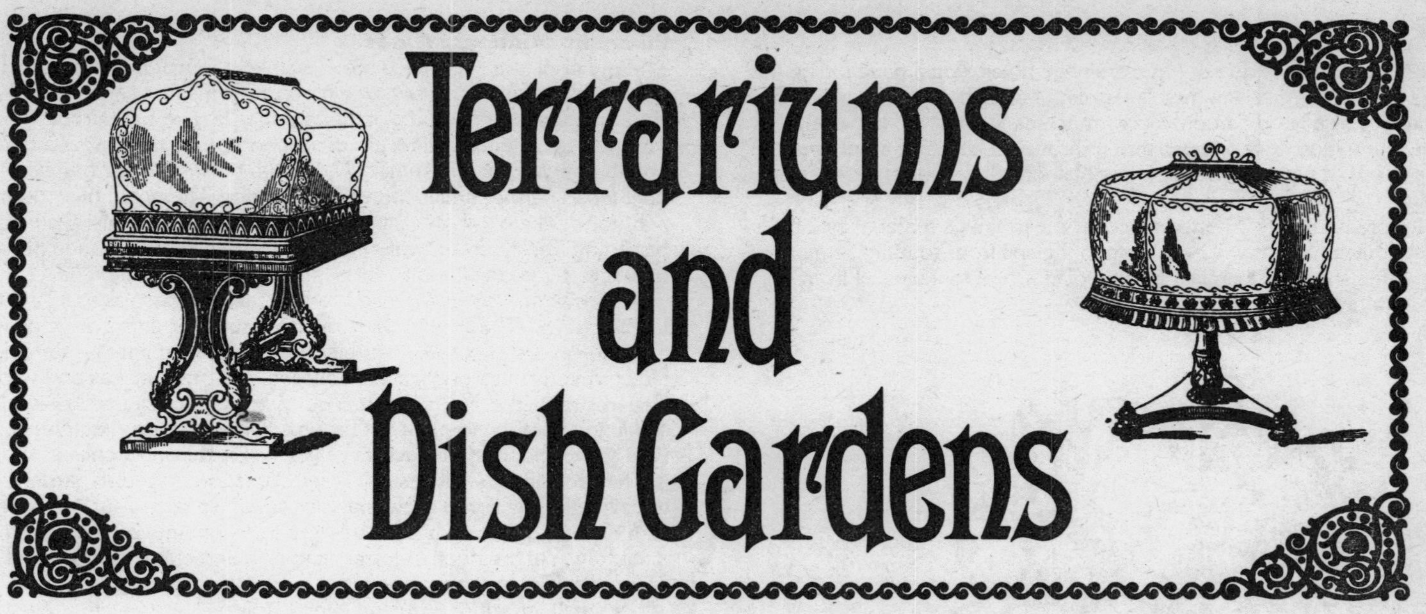

Terrariums and Dish Gardens

Terrariums and dish gardens are versatile miniature landscapes. If you live in a northerly climate you can have an arid, Southwestern landscape of cacti. If you live in a mild climate you can raise alpine plants from northerly regions that can be a refreshing change from your area's vegetation. You can raise exotic foreign plants, give a living landscape as a gift to a friend or invalid, or create a little fantasy for yourself if you live in an ugly urban area without much greenery.

The difference between terrariums and dish gardens is that terrariums are glass-enclosed and dish gardens are open. The terrarium eventually becomes moisture-balanced—that is, the enclosure allows moisture to go through cycles of condensation so that you no longer have to water the plants. A dish garden requires watering.

For a terrarium you can use a brandy snifter, a fishbowl, an aquarium, a plastic or glass globe, a bottle—any container clear enough to admit good light that you can cover with glass or plastic. A bottle with a small neck, however, will require infinite patience and an extra-long pair of tweezers with which to lower the plants. Bottle gardens require such skill and patience that they are not the best for beginners. A wide-mouth container is easier to plant.

For a dish garden you can use any sort of bowl, baking dish, or shallow ceramic tray. You could also use wood, metal, or even plastic containers. The only requirement for containers is that they be deep enough to hold two to four inches of soil.

Garden centers sell miniature tools for constructing miniature landscapes—tiny shovels on long handles, long tweezers, pruners, and other implements to help you place your soil and plants properly. These are handy if you are using containers with small openings or are attempting to achieve fine effects. If you have a wide-mouth container, you can use kitchen spoons (ice cream spoons are good), forks, and ordinary tweezers. You can elongate the tweezers, if necessary, by tying sticks to them. A small paintbrush is also handy.

Most miniature landscapes are designed for table tops or shelves where they can be examined minutely. If you do use globes or round fishbowls with lips, however, you can also suspend a terrarium from the ceiling or from wall brackets. You could even use several such terrariums the same way you would hanging plants—suspended at various levels to create a room divider or suspended over a table as a decoration that leaves the surface free for use. A few people create large-scale landscapes in huge aquariums. Terrariums and dish gardens may be grown under artificial light, too. You might even fashion a terrarium into a lamp base.

Plants advertised by nurseries are called miniatures if they grow up to five inches, and dwarf if they grow up to eight inches. Avoid fast-growing species, as they will rapidly develop out of scale and ruin your design.

Terrariums and dish gardens can be broadly categorized as woodland, tropical, or desert, depending on the type of soil and plants. You can also create miniature rock gardens, herb gardens, and rose gardens, or even a bog garden with carnivorous plants. Some gardeners add small lizards or other amphibians—transforming the terrarium to a *vivarium*—but this becomes more complex because the animals' needs must be met as well, and they must be fed.

Miniature Landscape Design

If you are a beginner, you will probably find working on a larger scale a bit easier.

Before you begin, it is best to make a sketch of your landscape on paper, noting where you will put each plant, especially if you will be using several plants. Flat soil is not as appealing as creating little hills and valleys, so take levels of ground surface into account. You can also use stones, bark, or even small personal belongings in the landscape. Children often like to include miniature plastic animals or dolls in their landscapes.

A major consideration is scale. The plants should be in attractive proportion to each other, the container, and any other elements you will include.

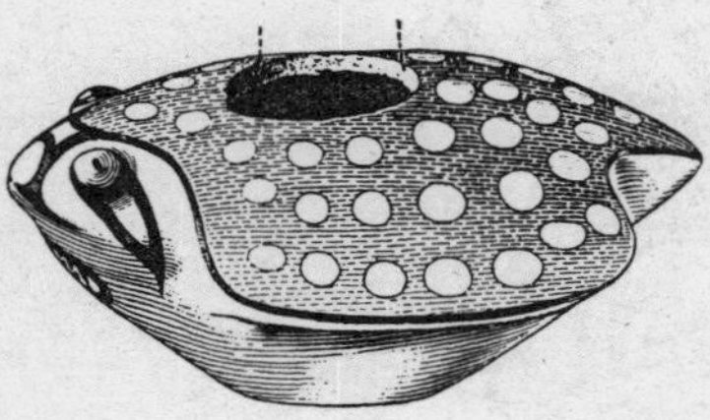

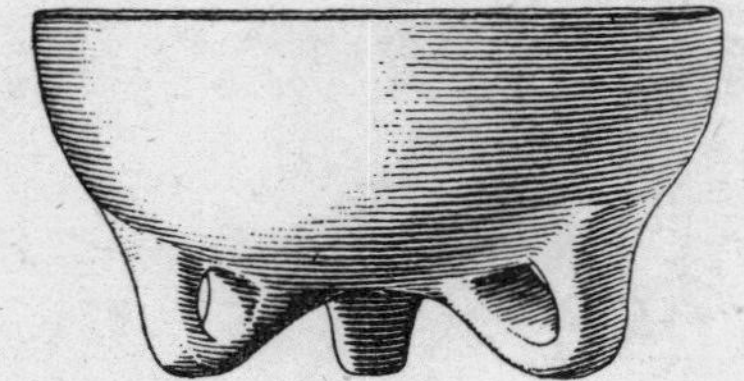

Don't have any plant so large it overpowers all the others.

Another consideration is that you choose compatible plants—you cannot mix cacti with mosses, for example. Your miniature landscape should contain plants with roughly the same requirements for temperature, humidity, light, soil, and water. Humidity-loving plants do best in terrariums, while open dishes are fine for cacti. You can, however, grow cacti in a terrarium if you are careful not to overwater, and you can grow humidity-loving plants in dish gardens by misting frequently.

If your miniature garden is to be viewed from all sides, place taller plants in the central portion of the design and smaller ones around them, with mosses or creepers along the edges. If the landscape is to be seen from one side only, then the tallest plants should go at the back, with smaller ones in front and to the sides.

Your design can be formal or informal (for oriental designs, see "Bonsai"). It need not be elaborate. One plant and a couple of stones in balance and to good scale is more attractive than a large grouping arranged without much thought. If you want a more elaborate landscape, you can use plants with single, sturdy stems for trees. Combine these with plants that branch nicely and are slightly lower. Complete the design with tiny ground covers.

Planting

Because most dish gardens do not have drainage holes, you'll have to line the bottom of the container with a one-inch layer of gravel, pebbles, or finely broken pieces of crockery. For a large garden, use as much as two inches. If the terrarium opening is small, you may have to pour this in through a kitchen funnel or a funnel you make out of paper. Shaking the container will distribute the drainage material evenly.

For a terrarium requiring high humidity, cover the drainage material with a thin layer of crushed charcoal. This will help to keep the soil from souring. Some gardeners use a thin sheet of fiberglass instead of charcoal to keep soil from sifting down to the drainage materials.

Next add one to three inches of a sterilized soil mix, the amount depending on the size of the container. Use whatever soil mixture is appropriate for the type of plants you will be growing.

Mound the soil to a slope at one end of the landscape, or create little hills and valleys.

Then begin to add the plants. It is easier if you start with the dominant plant and work your way down to the smallest. That way, if your design is not coming out as well as you had hoped when you outlined it on paper, you can make adjustments in proportion to the dominant plant as you go along. If the plants are too tiny to handle with your fingers, or must be lowered beneath a rim, use tweezers. Use the tip end of a pencil to dig a hole for small roots and the eraser end to tamp the plant into place after planting.

Creating an effective design is exacting work, and you may not like what you've done and have to start over several times.

Once you are satisfied, clear any soil from the foliage with a small, dry paintbrush. Then spray the plants and soil lightly with water.

Care

A dish garden of cacti can be placed immediately in a sunny location, and a dish garden of other plants in light appropriate to them.

Terrariums, however, should be covered with a lid, a sheet of glass, or a piece of plastic film. Place terrariums where they get bright light, but not in sun. Sun will cause the air to heat up to too high a temperature and kill the plants.

After one night, check your terrarium to see if the soil is dry, and give it additional water if necessary. But if drops of water have collected on the inside surface of the glass, you have given it too much water. In that case, leave the cover off for a day to let the soil dry out. Keep checking the terrarium until you get a good balance—a thin film of vapor forming overnight on the inside surface of the glass indicates perfect conditions. Once balanced, the terrarium will need very little care. You may not have to water it for months.

Terrariums are not totally airtight, and some air seeps in and out around the lid. But to insure a change of air, you might remove the cover (for only a few minutes) once every week or two.

The humid conditions of terrariums are perfect breeding grounds for certain diseases and pests. These can be largely avoided if you use sterilized soil and healthy plants. For the first few weeks after planting, however, keep an eye out for signs of trouble. Once the terrarium is properly established, turn your dish garden or terrarium from time to time, as you would a pot, so all the plants receive equal light and grow uniformly. If a plant gets too big, cut it back with a thin, sharp, artist's knife.

Overwatering is the chief danger. Water only enough to keep the soil moist, not so much that the water rises above the level of the drainage material. With small gardens, watering with a syringe or even an eyedropper may help.

Plants for Miniature Gardens

Many cacti and succulents are available in miniature and dwarf forms for dish gardens. Mammillarias have nice globular forms that can be used as a dominant plant in a landscape. Also globular are the deep-green *Parodia aureispina* (Tom Thumb cactus) and *Echinocereus melanocentrus*, the gray *Rebutia Kupperiana*, and the bright green *R. miniscula*, all with brilliant red or orange blooms. *Echinopsis kermesiana* is round and has ribs. These can be combined with upright forms like old-man cactus for effective arrangements. *Opuntia mammillata* has a tiny treelike form, while *O. microdasys* has oval-shaped pods that look like they are covered with polkadots.

Adromischus maculatus also has flat leaves. Crassulas and kalanchoe have treelike forms. The echeverias grow from rosettes, some more compact than others, and can be effectively combined with plants of a more upright nature. Haworthia, with striped leaves, does well in terrariums, as do the other fleshy-leaved succulents. Many dwarf sedums are especially dainty—such as *Sedum stahli*, the coral-bead plant. Other possibilities include *Aloe brevifolia*, *Agave filifera compacta*, gasteria, gymnocalyciums, and living stones.

The cacti and succulents are especially favored for dish gardens. They are equally effective if you grow only one type to a dish—such as a treelike crassula with a stone or two or a tiny sculpture for company, or echeverias overspreading a flat tray. Yet their varied forms, textures, and colors can be used for dramatic group displays too.

For small terrariums you can choose foliage plants such as dwarf dracaenas, dwarf palms, and dwarf ferns (adiantum is especially dainty). Peperomias are excellent. Maranta, coleus croton, ivies (including the attractive grape ivy), zebra plants, philodendron, aglaonema, polystichum, zebrina, pileas, some ficus, and miniature hollies are other choices. The date palm, *Phoenix roebelenii*, comes in tiny sizes for terrariums too. Various small varieties of euonymus are also popular. For larger terrariums you might consider dieffenbachia, aspidistra, and spathiphyllum too.

Miniature African violets do well in terrariums, and of other gesneriads the tiny sinningias are particularly attractive. Small azaleas and small-leaved and trailing begonias, as well as columneas are choices if you want color.

Small orchids (coelogynes, masdevallia, and broughtonia, for example) are attractive in terrariums, as are many bromeliads—cryptanthus, dyckia, neoregelia, and tillandsia. Even the exotic carnivorous plants like Venus Fly Trap can go in your terrarium.

Tiny ground covers include baby's tears (Helxine), and several pileas, all of which like semi-shade.

Acorus, called miniature flagplant or sweet-flag, are little grasslike plants that grow in tufts up to about nine inches tall. They are not especially attractive if grown by themselves. They are, however, nice in bonsai as base plantings under specimen plants as well as in terrariums. They like filtered or diffused sun.

Selaginella are tiny fernlike plants that are very attractive ground covers in terrariums and dish gardens too. They like shade and high humidity, but avoid getting water on the leaves, as they can rot. *S. lepidophylla* is the so-called resurrection plant that turns brown and dead-looking when dry but comes alive to a bright green shade when watered. *S. kraussiana*, called by common names like trailing Irish moss and cushion moss, are an excellent bet; these are small creepers with teeny bright-green leaves. Another small variety is *S. willdenorii*, with a bluish cast to the leaves. You can propagate these easily by cuttings.

Saxifraga, strawberry geranium, is named for little leaves that resemble those of geraniums but are the color of strawberries. These trailers may be grown in small pots or hanging baskets, and they are ideal for adding color to a terrarium or dish garden. They are not too particular about temperature but they do like bright light. You can propagate them from the runners.

Sources

Christen Inc.
59 Branch St.
St. Louis, Missouri 63147

IMS Corp.
P.O. Box 3399
Albuquerque, N.M.

Union Products
511 Lancaster St.
Leominster, Mass. 01453

Peter Pauls Nursery
Canadaigua, N.Y. 14424

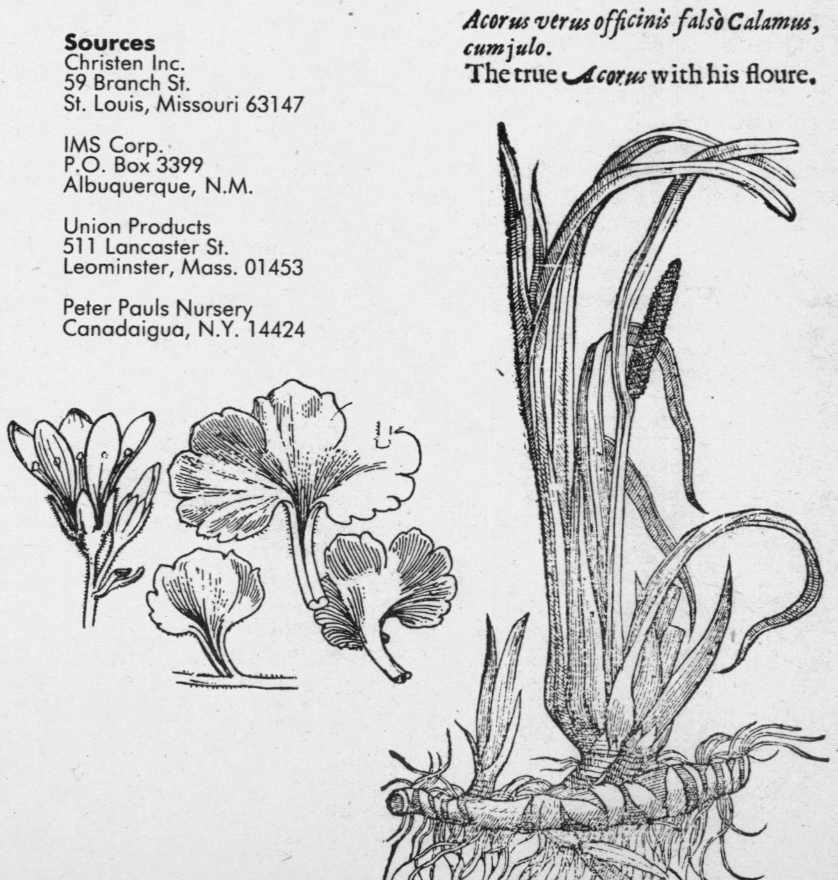

Acorus verus officinis falsò Calamus, cum julo.
The true *Acorus* with his floure.

Fun with Leftovers

Avocado

The central pit in an avocado pear is actually a huge seed that can produce an attractive, leafy tree as tall as your ceiling. To begin, remove the pit from either a Florida or California avocado, wash it, peel off the brown skin covering it, and dry it off gently. Then stick 3 or 4 wooden toothpicks at regular intervals around the pit about a third of the way up from the base. (Usually, you know which end of the pit is the base because it's wider; if you have trouble because your pit is oval-shaped, look for the end with a dimple.) Now, set the pit in a glass of room-temperature water. About a half inch of the pit's base should be submerged.

Suspended flat end down in water and kept in a dimly lit, warm location, the avocado pit will produce roots after a few weeks. While waiting for this first sign of life, be sure to maintain the water level—and keep the faith. After roots appear, eventually, too, the top of the pit will begin to split. Little by little, over a period of just days or several weeks, the pit will separate and exhibit the beginnings of a stem growing between the two halves.

When the first tiny green leaves appear at the tip of the stem, gather your courage and clip them off. This seemingly cruel procedure stimulates the root system, which at this point in the avocado's development is more important than foliage. When the stem begins to grow again, allow it to reach a height of 6 or 7 inches before cutting it back, this time leaving 3 or 4 inches. (If you do not cut the little

avocado back, you will end up with a spindly weedlike plant instead of a beautiful, lush tree.) Within 2 or 3 more weeks, but no later, the plant will be ready for potting in soil. By then, the root system should be flourishing, and the stem ought to be growing taller again.

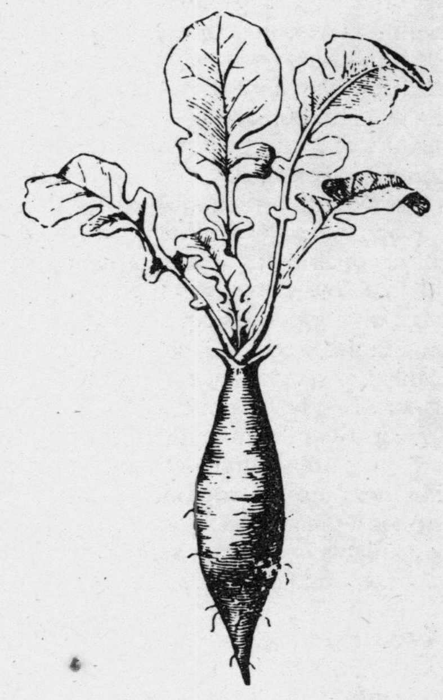

Pot up the avocado plant in a well-drained terra-cotta flowerpot—not a small one, but a pot measuring 8½ to 10½ inches. Use a mixture of 1 part sand or perlite to 2 parts soil, enriched by humus if available. Line the bottom of the pot with broken crockery and fill with the soil mixture. When you plant the pit, leave the upper half exposed. Water the potted avocado with room-temperature water, and keep it in a sunny place.

Avocados like moist soil and humidity. Apply water as often as necessary to keep the plant from drying out. Be sure to water thoroughly so that some water drains into the underdish, which, if lined with pebbles, will catch and hold the excess while providing a moist atmosphere.

Let the plant reach a height of 6 inches and then pinch the topmost pair of leaves. Pinch new growth frequently and move the growing tree into a larger pot whenever its roots become cramped. With care and patience, you can grow a large tree.

When the avocado reaches a height of 1½ feet, it will need support from a stake. Fasten the stem to a dowel with string or to a tomato stake that you have inserted about an inch from the pit. As the plant becomes a tree, it will probably continue to require support from taller dowels or a length of bamboo. If the tree gets too tall, cut off the top half inch of the main stem to encourage the appearance of a new stem at the base of the plant. Apply liquid fertilizer every 3 or 4 weeks.

Bean

You can plant fresh beans that you have removed from the pod, or you can use dried black beans, kidney beans, limas, pinto beans, navy beans, or even less common types like mung beans. Fresh beans can be planted as they are, whereas dried beans should be soaked overnight in water before planted to give them a better start. The soaking makes beans sprout more quickly.

Plant the bean in a light growing mixture such as equal parts soil, peat moss, and sand or perlite, and keep the soil moist. Within 1 or 2 weeks, a tiny plant will appear with the first set of leaves. Now put the bean plant in a sunny window, water it regularly, and watch it take off. In 2 or 3 weeks, your plant should develop a tendril that soon turns into a vine that wants to climb toward the sun. A vine calls for a bean pole, and the best kind is a straight, but knobby, stick or a rough, but skinny, stake. Place the bean pole in the center of the pot and tie the bean plant to it with twine or strips from old nylon stockings. In about 60 days after the seed was sown, your bean plant may begin to bloom. Flowers are a sign that the plant is mature and ready to develop beans. Pick the first crop before they are large. Then flowers, followed by beans, will keep coming.

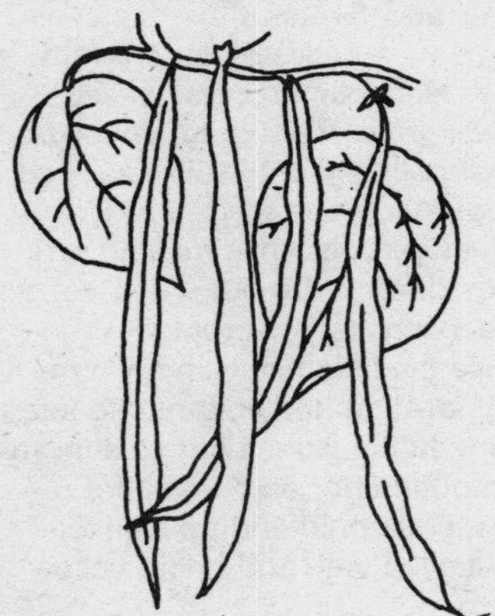

Carrot

Slice off all but the upper 2 inches of a fat carrot and trim away leaves from the top. Prepare its growing medium by lining a shallow bowl with 1½–2 inches of pebbles or clean gravel. Nestle the cut-off carrot top among the stones or gravel and add water to the dish so that it just covers the growing medium. New, curly sprouts should appear within 2 or 3 days and growth may continue for up to 4 weeks. Keep the carrot plant in a bright window.

Beet, parsnip, rutabaga, and turnip tops will also grow in a pebble-filled bowl.

Coffee

Unroasted coffee beans produce attractive trees with shining, bright green leaves. To germinate, soak the beans overnight before planting. You can sow them in a mixture of sand and peat moss or in moistened vermiculite and then transplant the coffee plant when it has its second set of leaves. Coffee trees grow to a height of 8 feet over a period of several years. They like bright light, warmth, and well-drained soil—equal parts soil, sand, and peat moss. If leaves start turning brown and crinkly around the edges, the pot is too small or the plant is being overwatered.

Citrus Fruit

Orange, grapefruit, lemon, and kumquat seeds produce attractive houseplants. Plant fresh seeds or keep seeds moist in layers of wet paper toweling until you are ready to plant them. Old, dried-out seeds will not germinate, but fresh seeds, which are naturally wet, should be dried off with paper toweling before they are planted.

Place the seeds, a few per container, in a mixture of 1 part perlite or sand, 1 part moistened peat moss, and 2 parts soil. Plant several seeds because only a few will germinate. Cover with a half inch of the growing medium and move the container to a dim, warm, draft-free spot. Remember to keep the seeds moist.

When seedlings are about 1 inch tall, place them where they receive indirect light. When they are several inches tall, move into direct light. Thin out the seedlings by gently removing those that can be lifted out and replanted in their own little pots.

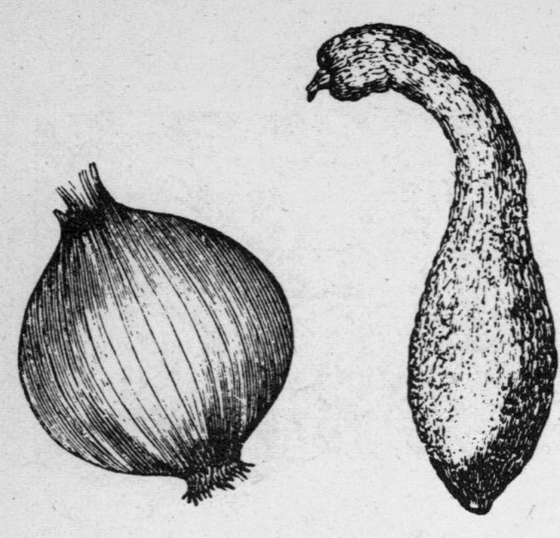

Grass
Indoor grass plants don't last as long as the usual run of houseplants, yet it's fun to grow tall green shoots, especially during the gray winter months. Grass plants are also an excellent source of chlorophyll and roughage for pet cats who, almost without exception, love chomping away at home-grown greenery. Lawn grasses and cereal seeds like alfalfa take 25 to 35 hours to begin vigorous sprouting. Cereal seeds for sprouting are available in small amounts at health food stores.

Method 1. Enclose a wet sponge sprinkled with grass seeds in a clear plastic bag or on a plate under an inverted glass casserole dish. After the seeds sprout, put the sponge in a saucer in the open air where it gets good light. Keep enough water in the saucer to prevent the sponge from drying out.

Method 2. Fill a flowerpot with lots of crocking in the bottom and then add a mixture of 1 part potting soil (humus-enriched, if you can find humus or have some from your outdoor garden) and 1 part sand. Fill the pot to within 1 inch of the top. Moisten the growing mixture with water and sprinkle the seed over it. Add a thin layer of soil and place the pot in a dimly lit spot. Until the seeds germinate, keep the soil moist by gently dribbling water on its surface or, better yet, spray the seed bed with a plant sprayer. When sprouts appear, move the pot to a bright spot and water gently so as not to dislodge the tiny roots. In another day or two, the sprouts will be strong enough to withstand direct sunlight. Keep the soil moist but not soaking.

Herbs
Some herbs, like parsley, take a couple of weeks to sprout, while coriander, dill, and fennel seeds sprout within a week. Some other "easy" herbs to try are anise, catnip (for your cat), chives, mint, and sage. To ensure success, where you want only one plant, plant a few seeds. Plant them in moistened vermiculite, a Jiffy-7 pellet, or in a soil mix of equal parts soil, sand, and peat moss. (Moisten the peat moss before mixing it.)

Keep the growing medium moist until a couple of plants appear. Then trim away the weaker ones. When the remaining plants have a second set of leaves, if they were germinated in vermiculite or a Jiffy-7 pellet, transplant them into a flowerpot.

Mango
Getting the mango to seed takes a bit of patience. First, remove the slippery inner husk from the mango, wash it, and use a stiff brush to remove pulp from it. Then set it aside to dry for a couple of days. When the husk is dry, open it carefully by making a small cut with a scissors and pulling it apart. Remove the seed and soak it for 24 hours before planting it horizontally in a mixture of soil and perlite or sand and peat moss. Cover the seed with a half inch of soil, and place the container in a warm place. Don't overwater or the roots will rot.

A sprout should appear in 2 to 3 weeks. Move to a draft-free, warm, sunny location and keep the soil moist. A potted mango is unlikely to bear fruit, but its foliage alone makes a nice plant.

—POMEGRANATE.

Melon and Squash
The many varieties of melons and squash all contain scores of seeds that will grow. Plant them directly in a small pot filled with soil, one seed per pot. Allow the seeds a few days to develop roots while making sure the soil doesn't dry out. Then transfer the seedlings to flowerpots.

Place the little plants in a warm, sunny location and continue to keep the soil damp. By adding a dilute solution of fertilizer each week for 6 weeks, you could end up with a large-leaved vine and bright yellow flowers.

Miscellaneous Fruits
Seeds from fruits that grow in zones where winters are cold—apples, cherries, peaches, pears, and plums—need to undergo a cold process before they can be sprouted. First, refrigerate the seeds for 6 to 8 weeks in a closed plastic bag containing damp peat moss. Then plant each seed in its own Jiffy-7 pellet that is kept wet, but not soaking. Transfer plants to a regular pot when their roots fill the pellet. For every dozen seeds that you attempt to sprout, you will be fortunate to succeed with 1 or 2.

Onion
If you've ever left an onion bulb too long in the bottom of the kitchen closet, you've noticed a sprout growing out of the top. Garlic and shallot bulbs, also members of the onion family, grow the same way. When roots and tops develop, you can set onions, or a mixture of onions, shallots, and garlic, in a bulb dish with gravel or pebbles. Add some plant fertilizer once a month.

Papaya
The black seeds that fill the inside of a fresh papaya are protectively enclosed in a gelatinous substance known as aril. This must be removed before planting. To do so, roll the seeds in a sheet of paper toweling or newspaper. A second preplanting step to prevent damping off is to soak the seeds in a fungicide (available at plant and garden supply stores). Plant the seeds, several to the pot, in clay pots with a lot of crocking over the bottom drainage holes. Use a soil mixture of 1 part peat moss and 1 part perlite or sand. Cover seeds with a half inch of the soil mixture.

Place the pot in a plastic bag with a couple of air holes in it, and put the pot in a consistently warm place (*e.g.*, on a food warmer set at low, or on a radiator covered with a folded blanket or several layers of newspaper). In a few weeks, seedlings appear. Keep them in indirect light until they are several inches tall, then thin them out, leaving only the strongest plant in each pot. Grow papaya plants in a warm, sunny window, and keep the soil moist.

Peanuts
Peanuts, which are not true nuts, grow into lively, leafy plants with yellow flowers. To sprout, place one *unroasted*, unprocessed peanut in its own Jiffy-7 pellet and water daily until the roots fill the pellet. Then, for each seedling, fill a flowerpot with soil, add sand or perlite to assist drainage, and plant the Jiffy-7 pellet, making sure the rim is slightly below the soil surface. Keep peanut plants moist.

Pomegranate
Like papaya seeds, pomegranate seeds are covered with a pulp called aril that needs to be removed before planting: Rub the seeds with newspaper or roll them in paper toweling. Plant seeds a half inch down in a mixture of 1 part soil and 1 part perlite or sand. Cover with a plastic bag to retain moisture. Left in a warm place, the seeds ought to germinate within a month to 6 weeks. This time is greatly shortened if the seeds have bottom heat (from a radiator topped with a blanket or layers of newspaper or a food warmer). Thin out pots after sprouts appear, leaving only the hardiest seedlings. Grow pomegranates in a warm, bright spot. Fertilize biweekly during summer months. By growing several pomegranate plants together, you can make a bushy-looking plant with delicate, narrow leaves.

Peas
Fresh peas from the pod are really seeds and can be planted. Dried peas need to soak 8 hours before planting. They like a mixture of equal parts moistened peat moss, perlite or sand, and soil.

Potato
Method 1. Using toothpicks, suspend the lower end of a potato in a glass or jar of water and place it in a location *away* from sunlight. When roots appear, move the potato to better light and wait for stems and leaves to grow out of the eyes. Keep up the water level during sprouting.

Method 2. Leave a potato in a dark place until the eyes produce little buds. Then cut off a fairly thick slice with 2 or more buds and let it dry for 24 hours. Plant the piece of potato in a well-drained flowerpot about 3 inches below the soil surface. Keep the soil moist and be sure the pot is in a sunny spot when a plant begins to peak out of the dirt. By the time this new plant has reached a height of 1 foot, new potatoes will be forming within its root system. These little potatoes are edible. Fertilize the plant with fish emulsion.

Sweet Potato
A relative of the morning glory, a sweet potato will sprout into attractive vines that can be trained to climb along a vertical cord. Using toothpicks, suspend the narrow end of a sweet potato in a glass or jar of water large enough to accommodate the root system that will eventually grow. Place potato plus glass in a warm, dark place. Maintain the original water level and within a few days roots will begin to show. When, in about 10 days, stems appear, move the plant to a sunny window. Before long, the stems become vines with pale-green scalloped leaves that can be trained around a small trellis or grown up and around a window frame.

For a longer-lasting plant, you can also pot up the sweet potato vines in potting soil improved with about a third part sand to assist drainage. The lifespan of a sweet potato plant ranges from 6 months to 2 years. If you have trouble rooting a sweet potato from the supermarket, try an organically grown one from the health food store. Commercial sweet potatoes often undergo a process known as kiln-drying that is meant to prevent sprouting.

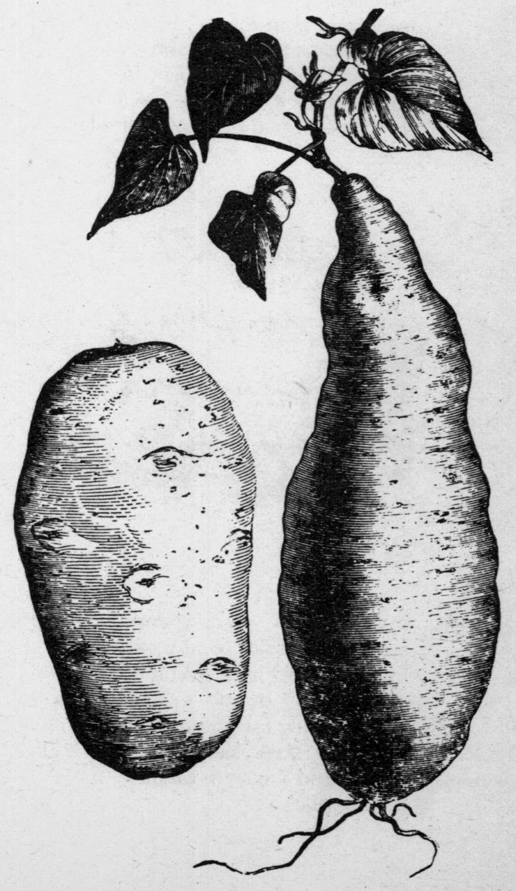

3

Indoor Plant Lore

How To Buy A Plant

Before you buy a plant, you should analyze why you want it, how much attention you are willing to lavish on it, and whether you are going to adjust to it or it will have to adjust to you. Otherwise, you are apt to end up with a plant inappropriate to your needs.

Environment

The first factors to consider are the light, temperature, and humidity conditions under which you live. If you don't want to make any changes in your environment, then you should choose plant species able to survive in your home or office as it is. Environmental requirements for indoor plants are given under the plant descriptions so that you can choose suitable types. Without making changes, you will find an abundant variety of foliage plants, and if you can provide sun you will also be able to choose among flowering plants.

If you are willing to make changes such as lowering your home's temperature, providing more humidity to your air, or supplementing your natural light with artificial light, then you will greatly increase your choice of plants to grow. Again, checking the plant requirements will enable you to decide which adjustments you want to make. It isn't wise, however, to become overenthused and decide to change everything to accommodate the widest variety of plant types. Any one change, such as humidity, will widen your prospects sufficiently to increase your choices.

Care

If you would like a plant, but don't want to spend much time on it, then you should choose easy-care varieties. These are listed in the Lazy Gardener's Special sections of the following pages.

You might also want easy-care plants if you intend to buy an entire plant grouping—such as to use for a room divider—where delicate plants would be impractical.

Use

If you are buying a plant for decoration, then you should look for an attractive, well-shaped plant of the size and texture you need. When it gets too tall or if it develops unattractive growth, you can discard it and buy another.

If you are buying a plant for its flowers, get one about to bloom and discard it once its flowering is over.

If you enjoy watching plants grow, however, buy young ones two or three inches tall. These are a lot cheaper than mature plants. Moreover, a young plant will adapt more readily to conditions in your home than will a mature plant.

Tips on Buying House Plants

1. Buy during their growth season.
2. Look for signs of leaf buds on foliage plants and flower buds on flowering plants.
3. Don't buy plants that show
   - spindly growth
   - yellowing leaves
   - unnatural blotches or speckles
   - wilted leaves
   - leaves that have been artificially waxed
4. Check for insects by looking on the underside of the leaves and in the joints of the leaves, stems, and branches.
5. Buy plants from reputable garden centers and other reliable sources. This is especially important for expensive and exotic species, where you want a firm that will stand behind what it sells and perhaps advise you on care of the plant you buy. But even with more ordinary species, you are apt to get a healthier plant from a shop where the entire collection looks fresh and well-cared for than from a variety shop or supermarket where the plants are neglected.

Bringing Home a New Plant

Often the plant you buy has been grown under ideal, or close to ideal conditions in a greenhouse. Your new plant is going to have to adjust to conditions in your home or office. Even if you have chosen your plant well, with an eye to a species that can accommodate itself to the environment you provide, the move is probably going to result in some shock to the plant.

If you live in a cold climate, don't buy plants in winter, as even a short exposure to cold temperature on the way home can be detrimental or even fatal.

Give the plant all the help you can by placing it in proper light, supplying sufficient water, and keeping it out of drafts from air conditioners, heating systems, or other sources. The humidity is especially apt to be less than what the plant was accustomed to, so misting may help.

Many new plants will react to a change in environment by dropping a few leaves. If it is a healthy plant this is inconsequential and the plant should start new growth in about three or four weeks.

If you have other plants, do not put your new plant among them until you are sure it is healthy and pest-free. Isolate the new plant for at least three weeks to a month if it is hardy. African violets and others susceptible to pests should be isolated for two months.

LIGHT

Light is the single most important factor in your selection of houseplants. Moreover, natural light is the factor over which you have the least control. Before you buy a plant, you should therefore consider the amount of light you have available.

No matter what your light conditions are, though, you will find a wide choice of plants adaptable to your home, factory, workshop, or office by consulting the light requirements given under the descriptions of the indoor plants described in this book.

You also have some flexibility. Normal overhead fluorescent light in a room without windows is sufficient for growing many low-light-tolerant plants. Even if your light is poor, you can adjust many foilage plants to the light levels your room offers—see "Growing Plants in Dim Light" on the following page.

Another alternative is to supplement the natural light you have with fluorescent light, or to grow plants entirely under artificial light by providing enough flourescent light to satisfy their needs. Even plants requiring full sun will blossom under artificial light of sufficient duration and intensity. See "Indoor Gardening Under Lights" for details.

If you want only a few plants for decorative purposes, and especially if you are going to stick to the hardy foliage varieties, you'll be safe enough taking a guess at what your light is and buying the appropriate plants. An easy do-it-yourself test is to hold a piece of paper up to your light source in the area where you want to place a plant. If the paper throws a sharp-edged shadow, you have bright light; if you can hardly see the shadow, you have dim light. You can do the same test by holding your hand up against the light.

Key to Light

Full Sun: This is direct sunlight unbroken by curtains, frosted glass, or other filtering material. South windows have full sun for the longest period of the day. Many flowering plants require this type of exposure, but some plants scorch if they receive the sun's rays directly.

Indirect Sunlight: This is sunlight diffused through a lightweight curtain. It emanates from an east or west window where the sun would shine through for only short periods each day and at low angles. A variety of foliage and flowering plants can be grown in this light.

Subdued Daylight: This is daylight with no direct sun. You would get this type of light through a north window. An east window blocked by exterior foliage or tall buildings, however, could also result in only this light intensity. Ferns and shade-tolerant plants will do well in this light.

Dim Light: This is the type of light you would have in the interior of rooms, away from windows, or in rooms without windows. Only shade-loving plants or especially adaptable and hardy species survive in this type of light.

Tips on Light

1. Turn your plant pots a quarter turn each day or two—always in the same direction—to insure that all parts of the plant receive an equal amount of light. Otherwise, the growth is apt to be lopsided. Plants placed to the sides of windows, so that they get strong light from only one direction, are especially likely to have uneven growth unless turned.
2. Plants you keep in poor light will do better if you keep their air temperature at the lowest end of their temperature range.
3. Because sun will dry out your soil and plants, plants in south windows need the most watering.
4. Your plants receive full light only if they are directly in front of the window. If you place your plants to one side of your window, they will be getting only half the exposure or less.
5. Light from southern windows will keep its strengths about three feet into your room. East and west window light, however, decreases more rapidly within that same distance, and the weak light of northern windows drops off to a third of its intensity within three feet.
6. Though your plants will grow best if you provide them with the amount of light favoring optimal growth, many—especially the hardier foliage plants—will survive on less light. They will require less food and water, however, and will grow slowly.

Tips on Increasing Light

1. ***Mirrors:*** Place your plants against mirrors so that they will have the light bounced back at them. Mirrors make your rooms seem larger, too.

   If your plants are in a recessed area, such as one shelf of your bookcase, lining the inside walls with mirrored panels will not only reflect the light but make your collection look larger than it is.

   If your plants are in a planter whose sides are out of view—such as up near the ceiling of your kitchen—lining the inside of the planter with aluminum foil will help reflect the light.

   Mirror panels are cheaper than full-size mirrors, and by judicious placement of plants you can pretty well hide the seams between panels if you cover large areas.

2. ***White Paint:*** If the walls in your home or office are painted white, they will reflect more light than will dark walls.

   If your plants are in a recessed area, such as a shelf in your bookcase, a shelf in a closet, or niches on staircases, painting the inside surfaces of the recess in white will aid reflection.

   If you own your own home, painting roof overhangs white will reflect more light into your room.

3. ***Window Screens:*** Depending on the type of screen you use, screens can reduce light by well over 25% and up to 40%. Try to avoid screens on windows where you keep sun-loving and light-loving plants.

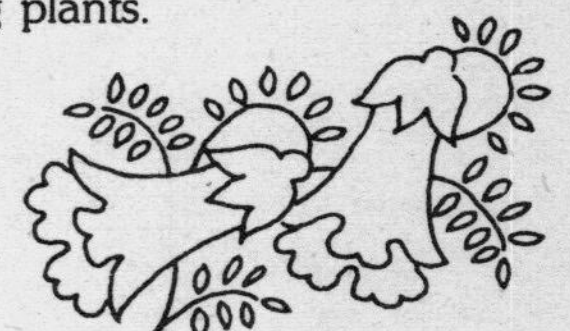

4. ***Skylights and Clerestories:*** If you have a skylight, you can place plants directly under it. You can also install small window boxes inside the skylight and grow plants that will trail down. Or you can suspend hanging baskets from the rim of the skylight. If you stagger the height of the baskets dangling from the skylight, you won't block the light. If you have no skylight, you might consider installing one.

   Clerestories are also perfect places for plants if you install long, thin window boxes their length. Depending on the construction, placing the boxes under the clerestory should not block the light. Again, trailing varieties of plants are best. You could also put hanging baskets at the ends of a clerestory.

5. ***Hanging Baskets:*** Trailing plants in hanging containers allow you to take advantage of natural light sources such as tiny windows in stairwells or full-size windows in cramped quarters where there is no room for floor or table pots.

6. ***Pebble Trays:*** Use bright, white pebbles or white marble chips in your pebble tray to reflect light upward. If the pebble tray is above eye level so its inside rim is hidden, you can line it with aluminum foil.

GROWING PLANTS IN DIM LIGHT

Plants that will grow in poor light, provided you do not overwater them and that you use a third or less fertilizer than is recommended in plant-food packages, include Chinese evergreen (aglaonema), spathiphyllum (peace lily), and parlor palm (*chamedorea elegans*). You may also have luck with aspidestra, many dracaenas, syngonium, and some ferns (such as bird's nest, holly, and mother ferns). All of these will take a certain amount of neglect too.

But many of the hardier foliage plants, though they may prefer more light, can be gradually acclimated to the low light levels provided by the ordinary ceiling fluorescent lighting fixtures in your office, factory, or home, even if you have no windows or other light.

If the ceiling of your room has two 40-watt fluorescent tubes, this will be sufficient light, provided you can place the plants close enough to the tubes.

Most species will do best if you can place them three feet under the lighting fixture. This would mean placing them on high furnishings such as the tops of the shelf units or file cabinets.

However, anthurium hybrids, bromeliads, peperomia, and sciudapsus can be placed up to 4½ feet from the fluorescent tubes. Depending on the height of your ceiling, this could mean keeping them on desk or table tops. And aglaonema, dieffenbachia, dracaena (*D. marginata, D. sanderiana, D. surwlosa,* and *D. fragrans*), and philodendron will tolerate the light as much as 5½ feet above them.

If you can place your plants on high shelves or on brackets closer than three feet to the light, you could also grow fatshedera, ficus (*F. elastica* or *F. pandurata*), hedera, maranta, and schefflera. You could also use hanging baskets with chlorophytum, cissus, hoya, or other trailing plants.

While you might be able to grow some of these plants under regular incandescent bulbs, or reflector floods used for spot-lighting, this type of light gives off a great deal of heat. Chances are the heat generated in an attempt to provide sufficient light would make the air too hot to keep the plants in good shape.

Acclimating Plants

The acclimating process will take up to three months, during which time you will gradually reduce the water, fertilizer, and if possible, the temperature.

1. ***Watering:*** Begin by giving normal amounts of water—that is, soaking the soil and letting it dry out before watering again. Then begin to water it only every third day, even if the soil is dry; then reduce the length of time between waterings gradually to every fourth, fifth, and sixth day, and so on.

Depending on the plant and the temperature and humidity conditions, you may eventually adjust the plant to watering only every twelfth or sixteenth day, or even longer periods. During this process, it is handy to keep track on a calendar of when you last watered the plant. That way you won't overwater it due to forgetting the changing intervals.

While you are adjusting the plant to dry-soil conditions, a few of the oldest leaves may drop off. You need not worry about this, as this is part of the plant's adjustment.

Your eventual aim is to *water the plant only often enough to prevent wilting.* Do not, however, let the foliage wilt at any time.

2. ***Fertilizer:*** As you reduce the amount of water, also reduce the amount of fertilizer you give the plant. Instructions on plant-food packages assume a plant will be growing vigorously, but under dry-soil conditions your plant will be growing slowly. As a result, use only a third as much fertilizer as the plant-food package recommends.

3. ***Temperature:*** While the species recommended for dry-soil, low-light acclimation will usually survive temperatures over 70°, the closer to 60° you can keep their air temperature the better they will do. Since warm air rises to the top of the room, it may be a problem to keep their temperature low in a heated room in winter unless you have a good air-circulation system or normally keep your room on the chilly side.

4. ***Misting:*** If possible, add additional moisture to the air around the plants by misting—or using a pebble tray or keeping open pans of water near them.

5. ***Potting:*** If you double-pot the plants, it will be easier to control soil moisture than if you use a single pot that exposes more air to the soil.

Most of the plants recommended for indoor gardeners come from tropical areas of the Americas, Africa, or the Far East and will do well at normal room temperatures—a range of 55° to 75°. Even when the original plants came from high elevations, or otherwise were used to coolness, horticultural research has developed varieties especially suited to home or office culture.

The temperature ranges preferred by each plant are given under the descriptions of all indoor plants in this book. Night temperatures are especially important. Plants manufacture food during daylight hours, but they circulate and assimilate it at night. During the absorption process they prefer a lower temperature. If you turn down your heat at night—so that the temperature drops 10°—you will therefore have healthier plants.

Key to Temperature

Warm: Daytime temperatures above 70° and night temperatures in the 60°s are most common in human indoor environments. This range suits the majority of foliage plants as well as the gerneriads. Many flowering plants, however, will not bloom well or at all unless you can reduce their night temperatures to 55° or 60°.

Moderate: Temperatures between 60° and 70° in the day and as low as 50° at night suit the overwhelming majority of foliage and flowering plants. Many palms, ferns, evergreens such as araucaria, and many flowering plants such as begonias, though they may survive at higher temperatures, will look their best in this moderate range.

Cool: Temperatures from 55° to 60° in the day and down to 45° at night are favored by many ferns, ivies, and spring-flowering bulbs. Primula, cyclamen, abutilon, and others will also do best at these cool temperatures. Evergreens such as pittosporum and podocarpus, and some flowers such as camellias, can take temperatures down to 40°.

Tips on Temperature

1. Though many plants adapt to a wide range of temperatures, none like their temperature switched suddenly. Some react badly to variables of only a few degrees. If you have been keeping a plant in a warm environment and want to relocate it to a cooler room, or vice versa, do so gradually over a period of weeks.
2. On winter nights, excessively cold air may seep in around windows in northern climates. Protect your plants by moving them back and insulating them by putting newspaper or another barrier between the plants and the window panes. Do not let the leaves touch the panes.
3. Browning leaf edges may indicate a plant is too cold.
4. Some plants go into dormant periods, usually in winter, when they require cooler temperatures than at other times of year. See individual plant descriptions for instructions.

Watering

Unfortunately, although overwatering is the most common cause of houseplant failure, no hard and fast rule governs proper watering. Your particular plant, your area's climate, the amount of sun your plant gets, its humidity, even the type of pot—all these and other factors affect the amount of water your plant needs. *The closest one can come to a general rule is that a plant's soil should be thoroughly soaked and then allowed to dry to the touch before watering again.* This rule applies to most of the more common fibrous-rooted houseplants. You can test for dryness by pressing the soil with your fingertips. Or you can take a pinch of soil between your fingers to see if it powders, in which case it is too dry. Usually this means watering about three times a week—more if the plant begins to wilt.

But there are many exceptions to this rule. Bog plants don't like their soil drying out at all, and cacti can survive long periods of drought. Some plants should be watered well during periods of active growth and then kept dry during their dormancy period. Plants with wiry roots, often thick and matted, need good air circulation at their roots and prefer drier soil.

In the following pages, watering procedures have been given for all plants, but here are some general rules for gauging proper watering for your particular plants and their environment:

1. When a plant is in vigorous growth—producing flowers or new leaves—it requires more water than when it is resting.
2. Plants with hairy, thorny, or waxy leaves need more water than do plants with thin leaves.
3. Soil in porous pots, such as clay, dries out faster in hot or breezy weather, and so plants in these pots need more watering. Plants in plastic pots, which do not allow water to evaporate through the walls, need less water. Plants in double pots (see "How to Pot a Plant") also require less water.
4. Plants in a south window or other bright light will need more water than those in shadier locations. (When plants that are in sun wilt, it's probably an indication that they are not getting enough water.)
5. If you live in an area of high humidity, your plants will need less watering than if you live in an arid area. Plants draw water through their roots and then transpire it through their leaves, a process enhanced when the air is dry. When the air is already heavy with moisture, plants transpire less and therefore draw less water up through their roots. Even if your area is not especially humid, your plants could require less water during spells of cloudy or rainy weather or during humid spells.

6. If you live in a cool area, your plants will require less water than plants grown in hot, dry climates.
7. Except for aquatic and bog plants, most plants do not tolerate soil so wet it cuts off air from the roots. To prevent root rot, use the proper soil mix for your particular plant and put pebbles or other drainage materials in the bottom of the pot so excess water can drain out. Don't let plants stand in water after the soil has taken up what it can hold.
8. Few plants can go completely dry. Even those in periods of winter rest should usually be watered every three or four weeks.
9. Watch your plants for signs of ill health. If the leaves drop off, lose their normal color, or become spotted, you may be overwatering. If the leaves turn brown, you may be watering too little.
10. If in doubt, you are generally safest watering too little rather than too much.
11. Any potable water is safe for watering plants *except* for water that has water softeners added. Water softeners have a high sodium content that destroys soil structure.
12. Plants absorb water in relation to their root size. Seedlings and plants with young, undeveloped root systems should therefore receive small, frequent watering.

How to Water:
Water thoroughly, not in dribs and drabs. When you water, the soil should be soaked thoroughly—until it can absorb no additional moisture.

You can do this from the top or from the bottom, or with a wick system.

Top watering: Fill the pot to the rim and wait until the soil absorbs the water. Repeat until water drains from the hole in the bottom of the pot.
Bottom watering: You can do this by putting water in the saucer under the pot; repeat until moisture reaches the top of the soil. This is easy with tiny pots, but it can take a long time with larger pots.

Large plants in tubs, or those with heavy root systems, may not get sufficient water to their root systems with top watering. You can set these in a sink or bucket with water reaching to the rim of the pot. It can take an hour or more for air bubbles to stop breaking on the soil surface and for the water to penetrate the soil. (This system works only if you use clay or other porous pots.) Many plants that you normally water from the top benefit from a full soaking by bottom watering every once in a while. This is especially true when they are in periods of vigorous growth.

HOMEMADE Wick-Watering Systems

1. When you pot the plant, run the wick through the pot's drainage hole, leaving a tail long enough to reach the water reservoir or wet sand.

   The wick may be cotton, fiberglass, or spun glass, all available at garden centers, but you can also use coarse rope, a tight roll of burlap, or even ordinary string. If you use string, you may have to use more than one ply—a four-inch pot might require three ply or four ply.

   Perishable wicks—such as of cotton or rope—will have to be replaced from time to time as they rot. Glass or fiberglass wicks are therefore best for slow-growing plants that will not need frequent repotting.

   At least two inches of the wick—a longer length with large pots—should be left inside the pot. It should be long enough so that you can flatten it out on the bottom of the pot. Do not use any pebbles or shards in the bottom of the pot. Pack the soil around the wick to hold it in place, then add the plant and remaining soil.

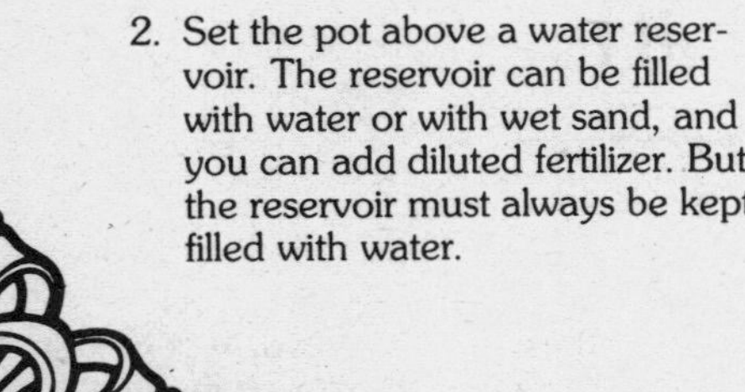

2. Set the pot above a water reservoir. The reservoir can be filled with water or with wet sand, and you can add diluted fertilizer. But the reservoir must always be kept filled with water.

   For one pot, a water reservoir should be low and sturdy enough not to tip over, which means it should be slightly wider than the pot. If you're lucky, you might find attractive open-mouthed pottery with an inner lip of exact dimensions to hold the pot above the water level. If not, you can use covered plastic containers, such as those made to hold leftovers; cut a hole in the center of the plastic lid for the wick, and a larger one toward one side for watering, and then place the pot on the lid.

   If you are using wet sand instead of simply water, you can put the pot in a deep saucer or cup filled with sand and bury the wick in the bottom. The pot bottom should be wider than the cup bottom so that the pot doesn't sit in the water. Or else the pot should have an ample supply of pebbles or other drainage materials so that the excess water can drain back out into the saucer. In this case, the wick will have to be inserted high enough in the pot to reach the soil above the pebbles.

   With several plants you have more options. Your reservoir can be baking trays of metal or glass, or a shallow pottery dish, or large, shallow plastic containers filled with water or wet sand. The most convenient shapes would be long, rectangular containers to support the pots above the reservoir. Place strips of wood—redwood slats would be attractive—across the containers, leaving enough space between the slats for the wicks. Place the pots so that their drainage holes (and wicks) are di-

rectly above the space between the slats and bury the wicks in the sand or dangle them into the water. Leaving one slat free at the end of the tray will enable you to fill the reservoir with water without removing any plants, or arrange the plants so that only one has to be lifted when you are resupplying the water.

   For large plant groupings, such as in bay windows or ground-level room dividers, you can use a series of containers or build in a reservoir suited to your dimensions. In this case, you can use a criss-cross of slatting that will support all the plants yet leave spaces large enough for you to pour water through.

3. Water the plant or plants from the top to start capillary action. From then on, if you keep the reservoir filled, the wick will soak up water as the plant needs it.

Wick system: Subirrigation by means of a wick system is often preferred by indoor gardeners with many plants, as it saves carrying a lot of pots to the sink. It is also a handy system if you cannot attend to your plants daily. For water-loving plants, it is an efficient way of insuring proper root moisture. And it is preferred by owners of hairy-leaved and other plants that dislike moisture on their leaves—such as gloxinias, African violets, and some geraniums.

You can buy individual wick-fed flower pots and elaborate systems for several plants, but it is easy to make your own. The principle is simply to run a wick through the drainage hole of the pot to a water supply below the pot. The water supply may be water alone or wet sand. You can then keep the water reservoir filled and let the wick take care of supplying moisture to the soil. To start capillary action after you have set the wick up, however, you first have to water from the top.

Tips on Watering:

1. Water at room temperature is best. A few plants, such as African violets *insist* on room-temperature water.

2. It is best to water in the morning, when plants are becoming active and can make most of water and minerals.

3. If your water is chlorinated, some plants (some ferns, for instance) may be sensitive. Let the water sit for twenty-four hours to evaporate the chlorine.

4. It's a good idea, especially if you are feeding plants, to alternate top and bottom waterings. If you water only from the bottom, minerals can accumulate on the top of the soil, and you can wash these out by watering from the top every third or fourth watering.

5. If you repot a plant, water may not penetrate the root ball if it is dense. Use a knitting needle or other sharp implement to poke a few holes in the root ball so that water can be channeled to the roots.

6. If you have many plants, try to group them according to their watering needs so you don't get confused about the individual requirements of your many plants, and to make things easier on yourself.

Humidity

Most indoor plants prefer a relative humidity of about 50%, and many of the plants listed on the following pages have a humidity specification of 50%. However, most of these plants will grow well at humidity levels down to 40%. The hardier species such as philodendron will grow at only 30%.

Does your home or office provide these levels? Unless you have a humidity gauge you cannot know, but it's a good idea to get one since these levels are healthy for humans as well as plants. If you live or work in a modern building, it probably has an automatic humidifying system that provides these levels. In older buildings, though, especially those heated with steam heat, humidity could be half this amount. Some air conditioners also dry out the air.

For some plants listed on the following pages, humidity specifications are higher—up to 70% or more.

If you want to grow high-humidity plants, or to provide optimum air moisture for medium-humidity plants, here are a number of measures you can take to increase the humidity:

1. You can buy a portable humidifier for use during dry periods or for year-round use, helpful to yourself as well as your plants if your home's humidity levels are too low. If you have a special area where you want to put high-humidity plants, you can buy a humidifier just for this area.
2. If you have radiators, put pans of water on them or under them.
3. Cluster your plants. Each will benefit from the moisture others give off. Just don't cluster them near radiators or hot-air vents.
4. Keep plants in the most humid areas of your home—usually the bathroom or kitchen (especially above the kitchen sink).
5. Best of all, provide a pebble tray—see instructions on this page.
6. And by all means mist your plants—daily if you can, and more often in hot weather or when the heat is on. See "Misting," below.
7. If you want humidity-loving plants without providing extra humidity to your rooms, consider a terrarium.

Misting

Misting is applying a spray of water to your plant's foliage.

Misters are available in garden centers or variety stores, but you can also recycle a spray bottle of any sort—such as the ones window cleaners come in. For small plants you can use a perfume atomizer.

With the exception of a few hairy-leaved plants such as African violets that react badly to moisture on their leaves, virtually every houseplant will benefit from misting. Misting does not replace watering, since it provides moisture to the air surrounding the plants rather than to the roots, but it is invaluable for maintaining a good level of relative humidity for your plants. Misting is especially important during hot spells, or for year-round use if your plants need more humidity than your home or office provides.

The best time to mist is in the morning, when plants become active, and you can spray (or spray again) at noon in midsummer when the sun is hot. But don't spray at night, because plants go into a rest period then. Excess moisture on their leaves when they are resting can lead to disease. If your household temperature goes up at night in winter due to the heating system, you can spray the soil around the plants or the air near them, but avoid getting moisture on the leaves.

How To Make A Pebble Tray

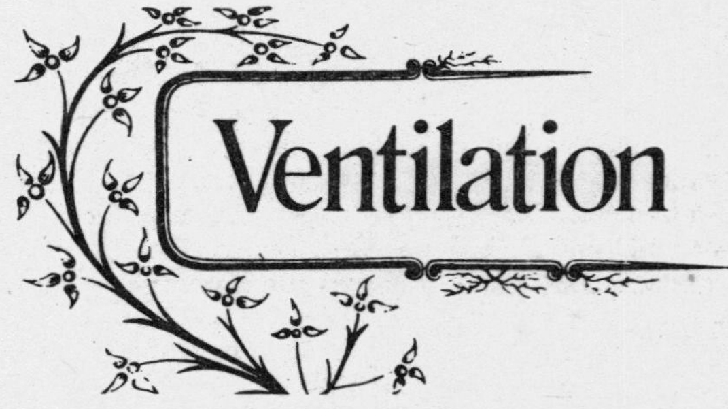

A pebble tray is simply a shallow, waterproof container filled with round pebbles on which you stand your plant pots. You then fill the container with water until it reaches just below the pebbles. The idea is to have the water evaporate to provide humidity surrounding your plants, yet to have the pots above water so the roots do not become waterlogged and rot.

A cheap way of making a pebble tray is to use any shallow container, such as a glass baking dish. If you have window groupings, a series of such dishes—two or three inches deep—should suffice. If you don't like the looks of glass, you can often find attractive shallow containers in pottery shops, some intended as fish or meat servers and some intended as plant pebble trays.

If you have a large plant grouping however, such as a room divider with large flower pots, you may want to construct—or have constructed—a specially-fitted pebble tray three or four inches deep. On an elaborate scale, this could be done with tile, calked to prevent leaks. Cheaper models can be constructed with wood frames and lined with heavy plastic.

Ventilation

Virtually all plants suffer from stuffy air and may develop mildew or other problems if not properly ventilated. The danger lies in the fact plants transpire—that is, lose water vapor through small pores on their leaves. In an unventilated room, this water vapor condenses on the leaf surfaces, and forms a film of moisture ideal for incubating a number of disease-producing organisms. Trouble from stale air is especially likely to occur if you try to keep plants cooped up to maintain high humidity levels.

Consider, too, that plants usually do not like drafts, and a few sensitive types will drop their leaves if air of a slightly different temperature hits them.

For hardy plants, such as many foliage plants, air from open windows can be beneficial. For more sensitive plants, which are apt to include many indoor flowering variaties, keep open windows at a distance from the plants—even a window in the next room—to prevent drafts from hitting the plants. Don't place plants where cold air from air conditioners or hot air from heating vents will reach them. Humidifiers, on the other hand, usually have small fans that will stir the air while keeping it moist.

In contained areas, such as small, windowless bathrooms, small rotary fans can be used to circulate the air.

If your home is heated with gas, or if you have plants in a kitchen with a gas stove, watch out for escaping gas. Plants are sensitive to gas fumes and other air pollutants.

Fertilizing

Most household plants require fertilizer, and you will find a variety of plant foods available in variety stores and garden centers. Fish emulsion is a safe, organic plant food suitable for most houseplants, but you'll also find a number of chemical fertilizers in granular form that you mix with water before applying to the soil. Some fertilizers come in liquid or tablet form. Follow the manufacturer's directions *exactly*—too much fertilizer can kill your plants. The water-soluble varieties are the fastest acting and generally also the most expensive.

Some plants are especially sensitive to fertilizer and you'll find preparations especially for these. Plant foods sold for African violets, for example, can be used on any gesneriads.

If you are using fertilizer in the water you feed your plant, all of the minerals may not dissolve, especially if you are subirrigating. These minerals can accumulate on the soil surface and pot rim. It's a good idea—especially with sensitive plants such as gesneriads—to flush the pot once every month or two by pouring a quart of lukewarm, clear water through the soil. Also remove and replace the white-encrusted upper layer of soil.

Many commercial crops and other plants are fed by spraying the leaves with water containing fertilizer, and a few gardeners apply fertilizer this way to indoor plants too. It is not necessary, however, and not the method usually recommended. If you are going to apply fertilizer to leaves of indoor plants, do not do so to any plant with hairy leaves (such as African violets and some begonias).

Rules for Fertilizer Use:

1. *Never fertilize when the soil is dry.* This can burn your plant's roots and leaf edges.
2. Fertilizer, like water, should be given early in the day so the plant can make the most use of it.
3. New plants in fresh soil will not require fertilizer for several weeks.
4. Air plants such as bromeliads and orchids do not require fertilizer at all.
5. Do not fertilize a plant that is not producing new leaves and buds.
6. Do not feed a plant that appears to be in ill health or that appears leggy.

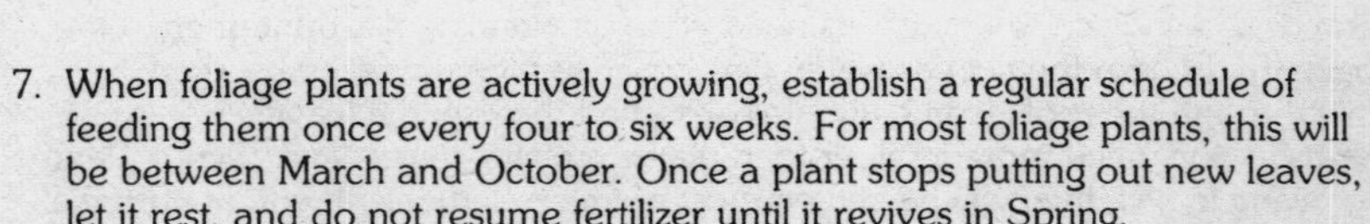

7. When foliage plants are actively growing, establish a regular schedule of feeding them once every four to six weeks. For most foliage plants, this will be between March and October. Once a plant stops putting out new leaves, let it rest, and do not resume fertilizer until it revives in Spring.
8. Flowering plants require more fertilizer during their active growth than do foliage plants. Once buds have formed, feed the plant every two weeks and continue to feed as long as blooming lasts.
9. Do not feed flowering plants after they have bloomed. Remove the flower stalk and give the plant a chance to rest for four to six weeks.
10. In general, the broader a plant's leaf, the more fertilizer it needs.
11. If in doubt, feed your plant too little rather than too much.

Fertilizer formulas

The formulas for fertilizers are indicated on the package with numbers such as 5-10-5 (a common garden formula), 20-20-20, or 8-12-4. These figures stand for the ratio of, respectively, nitrogen, phosphorous, and potassium (soluable potash). In other words, an 8-12-4 mixture would have eight parts nitrogen to twelve parts phosphorous to 4 parts potassium. Many also contain magnesium, iron, and other minor elements.

Nitrogen, sometimes called the growth element, stimulates the growth of foliage, stems, and fruit. It also gives foliage a dark green color. Pale, yellowish leaves and stunted growth may indicate nitrogen deficiency. Usually it is the older leaves that begin to fade and yellow first. Too much nitrogen causes overgrowth of foliage and reduces flower development. Nitrogen is available in humus, leafmold, compost, manure, or in synthetic form.

Phosphorous encourages early root formation, stem growth, and blooming. A deficiency results in slow growth and stunting, and the leaves may turn too dark or too blue a green. Adding bone meal to soil increases the phosphorous level.

Potassium makes a plant strong and vigorous, and increases resistance to certain diseases. Spindly plants may indicate a deficiency. In severe deficiency, the tips of the lower leaves will burn, and then the leaf margins, and finally the burn will progress upward in the plant. Commercial potash, bought separately rather than in a formula, is often wood ashes (you can use ashes from your fireplace).

If you have the proper soil mixture and use commercial fertilizers as directed, you should have no problem with mineral deficiencies.

Fertilizer problems

If you seem to be doing everything right but you're still having trouble with your plants, it could be the fertilizer.

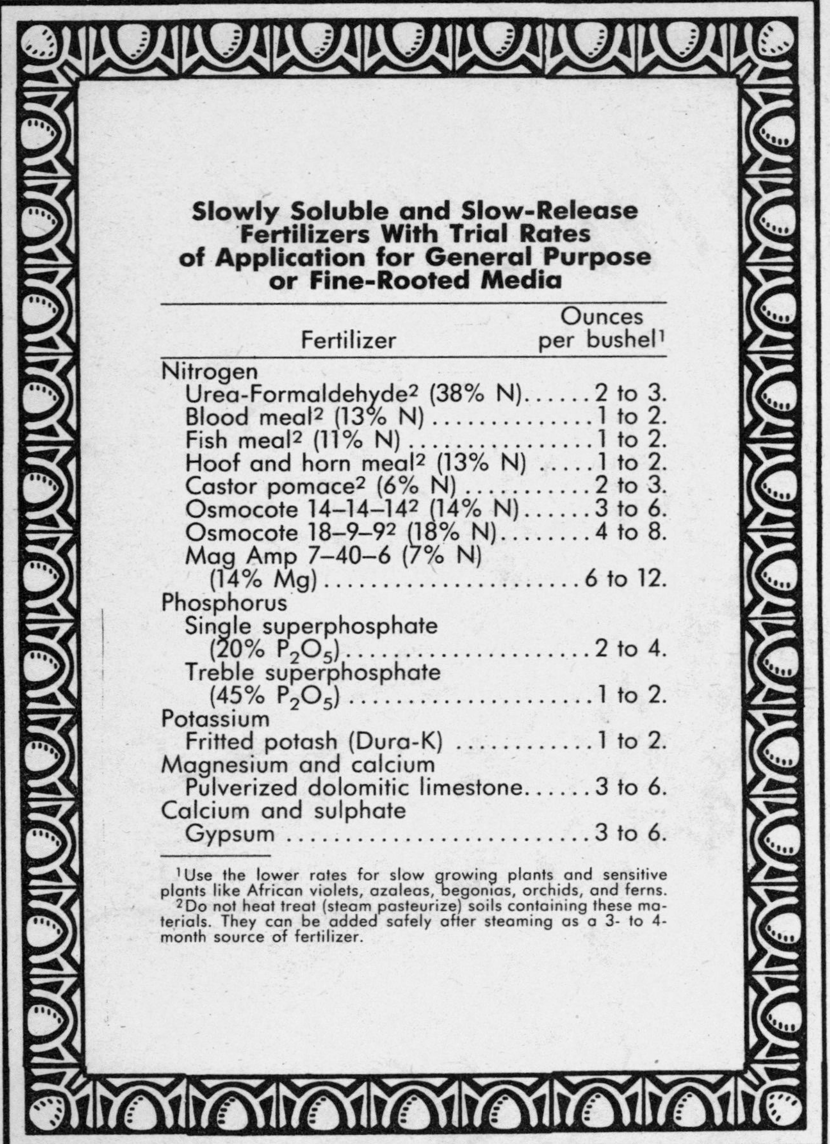

Slowly Soluble and Slow-Release Fertilizers With Trial Rates of Application for General Purpose or Fine-Rooted Media

Fertilizer	Ounces per bushel[1]
Nitrogen	
Urea-Formaldehyde[2] (38% N)	2 to 3.
Blood meal[2] (13% N)	1 to 2.
Fish meal[2] (11% N)	1 to 2.
Hoof and horn meal[2] (13% N)	1 to 2.
Castor pomace[2] (6% N)	2 to 3.
Osmocote 14–14–14[2] (14% N)	3 to 6.
Osmocote 18–9–9[2] (18% N)	4 to 8.
Mag Amp 7–40–6 (7% N) (14% Mg)	6 to 12.
Phosphorus	
Single superphosphate (20% P_2O_5)	2 to 4.
Treble superphosphate (45% P_2O_5)	1 to 2.
Potassium	
Fritted potash (Dura-K)	1 to 2.
Magnesium and calcium	
Pulverized dolomitic limestone	3 to 6.
Calcium and sulphate	
Gypsum	3 to 6.

[1]Use the lower rates for slow growing plants and sensitive plants like African violets, azaleas, begonias, orchids, and ferns.
[2]Do not heat treat (steam pasteurize) soils containing these materials. They can be added safely after steaming as a 3- to 4-month source of fertilizer.

To grow, plants need a total of 16 elements (if you want to know what they are, see below). They get two of these (carbon and oxygen) from the air as carbon dioxide, which is why plants need good air circulation around them. One of these (hydrogen) they get as water. The other 13 elements are absorbed mainly through the roots (some are also absorbed through the leaves).

Plants in pots need more fertilizer than plants growing in gardens. If your plants are growing in soil, they will be getting most of these elements. If you are using a soilless medium, however, you will have to use fertilizer more frequently.

The amount of fertilizer a plant needs also depends on the type of plant:

—Plants requiring less fertilizer are those that are small (including seedlings) and slow-growing, and/or that have fine roots.

—Plants requiring more fertilizer are those that are large, rapidly growing, and/or have coarse roots.

Plants vary from species to species in their exact requirements for nutrients, and the soil mix you are using plus other factors in the environment determine their fertilizer needs. Any one of these factors could mean your plant food is not doing the trick.

The fertilizer formula you're using may have been a 5-10-5 or a 10-10-10, and by switching to a different formula you may see improved results.

Plants use more nitrogen and potassium than they do the other elements, so these need to be replaced more frequently. If you have been using a 5-10-10 fertilizer and your plant is showing little or no sign of growth, you might try a 10-10-10, or if that fails to work, go up even to 20-10-10. On the other hand, if your plant seems to be growing *too* fast, you can slow its growth by switching to a plant food with less nitrogen.

If you have been using organic or completely inorganic fertilizer, this might be the problem. These—often touted as being more natural—can be dangerous unless you know what you are about, especially for plants in containers. Many organic fertilizers vary greatly in their chemical composition from batch to batch and from year to year, and unless you can make a chemical analysis you won't know what's in yours. Also, even if it works on one of your plants, it may not be working on the others. Root loss can result from excess fertilizer. If you want to experiment with your own fertilizer, you can get advice from government agricultural experts. It will probably be easier, however, to switch to commercially packaged plant foods. Organic fertilizers have decided advantages when you are raising crops to eat, but for ornamental plants you need not be so fussy about their digestive systems.

Commercially packaged fertilizers vary not only in proportion of ingredients but also in strength and method of application. A slow-release type might best be applied by mixing a tablespoon into the soil once every three months. One intended to be used every time you water your plants might call for a teaspoon to a gallon of water. It is therefore important to read the manufacturer's instructions and follow them exactly. If you are having problems with your plants, the fault may not be with the formula, rather that you are applying the fertilizer incorrectly.

Fertilizers for Advanced Students

The 16 elements needed for plant growth are carbon (C), hydrogen (H), oxygen (O), phosphorus (P), potassium (K), nitrogen (N), sulfur (S), calcium (Ca), iron (Fe), magnesium (Mg), chlorine (Cl), molybdenum (Mo), boron (B), copper (Cu), manganese (Mn), and zinc (Zn). If you want to memorize these elements, here's an easy way. Learn this sentence:

The Mob comes in to see Cl. Hopkins, cafe manager.

MoB CuMn Zn C Cl HOPKNS CaFe Mg.

Since carbon dioxide is supplied by the air and hydrogen by the water, a plant that is being properly watered and getting good air circulation and the proper fertilizer formula for nitrogen, phosphorus, and potassium, may be deficient in one of the remaining elements. Phosphorus, sulfur, and calcium usually are applied prior to planting as 20 percent (single) superphosphate ($CaH_4(PO_4)$ and $CaSO_4$), calcium and sulfur as gypsum ($CaSO_4$), calcium as pulverized limestone ($CaCO_3$), and calcium and magnesium as dolomitic limestone ($CaMgCO_3$).

Iron, chlorine, molybdenum, boron, copper, manganese, and zinc are present in sufficient quantities in most soils to supply the needs of a container-grown plant for several months. However, the soilless media do require applications of these elements. Some of these elements are added as impurities in low analysis complete fertilizers such as 5-10-5 or 10-10-10. Some must be added as separate fertilizers.

Containers

Pots

These are the most common and versatile containers for plants. The traditional pot is made of red, unglazed clay and has a drainage hole. It is available in garden centers in sizes ranging from two inches to 24 inches in diameter.

The advantage of unglazed clay is that it is porous. It allows air to get to the plant roots and water to evaporate from the soil. In fact, unglazed clay pots have been used to hold drinking water in Mediterranean countries for centuries, because evaporation keeps the water fresh and amazingly cool without benefit of refrigeration. With a clay pot you are providing similar freshness to your plant's soil, especially important if you live in a hot or humid area, and the porosity insures that excess water will also be evaporated so that your plant's roots never become waterlogged.

One disadvantage of a clay pot, though, is that it discolors. In addition, while it can look attractive in certain settings such as patios, it is often inappropriate for indoor decors. To correct both of these features, you can hide it in a basket or in a larger container that will be more attractive in your home. Clay pots also shatter easily, so are less desirable if you have children or pets (especially cats, which like to walk among your plants). Shattering is often no great calamity for a small pot, but many gardeners prefer something safer for tree-size plants. Some gardeners also object to clay because its porosity means the plant will need more watering.

Plastic pots are the most popular today, and they may be the only type you'll find if you go to a variety store or supermarket rather than to a garden center. Plastic pots come in the same sizes as clay pots, are cheaper, easier to clean, and do not discolor or break as easily. Also, they are available in a variety of colors, which might suit your decorative purpose. Many people find them ugly, though, and they have a tendency to topple if you put large plants in them.

Their chief disadvantage is that they are not porous. Water evaporates only through the surface of the soil and your plant can easily become waterlogged. You therefore have to be very careful in watering, giving less than to similar plants in clay pots. More drainage material in the bottom of the pot, to drain off excess water, will also help. You might also try a lighter soil. However, a wide variety of plants are grown successfully in plastic pots and if you want to use them you may encounter problems only with those plants that are extra-fussy about not having wet feet.

The lightness of a plastic pot as against clay or pottery vessels may also be a consideration if you plan to move your plants around a lot or if you keep them on overhead locations so that you must lift them down to water them.

A variety of decorative glazed pots are also available. Garden centers do not always have the most attractive varieties, but you can often find handsome ones in department stores, gift shops, and especially from local potters. For decorative effects these are unsurpassed. You can get square, round, columnar, bulbous, and other shapes, low oval dishes, squat circular dishes, and endless other varieties in a wide range of colors. Fiberglass containers also come in handsome shapes, colors, and a variety of finish textures.

Any of these will have the same water problems that plastic pots have, *if* they have drainage holes. If they don't have drainage holes you will be excluding oxygen from the roots as well as compounding the water-logging problem. In some of the above containers you might be able to drill holes in the bottom, or you might be able to put clay pots inside. If not, at least use a thick layer of fine gravel at the bottom and be careful not to overwater. You will probably be most successful if you choose water-loving plants, too. These precautions also apply if you recycle old jars, cups, glass or ceramic cookware, or other household equipment for your plants.

Special vases and pans for bulbs are also available, but with these you don't have to worry about drainage.

Though this sounds pretentious, in choosing a planter you should consider—apart from the plant's needs—the elements of style outlined in "Living with Plants" and the landscaping sections. Attention to design elements will do much to help make the most effective use of plants in and around your home. Obviously a casual hanging basket on your patio made of rude rope will look fine, but would be distinctly odd in a Regency-style dining room. A little plateful of mosses would be neat in a cove, such as a stairwell or small study, but would look ridiculous in a huge, baronial or barnlike room. For these you need huge containers with dramatic plantings.

Color is also a factor. You don't want the planter to compete with the vibrant color of your fuschias, so in this case a drab color in a planter is best. But if you have foliage plants without color in a modern setting where doors, carpets, or other features are emphasized in brilliant color, you might want your plant pots to be equally vibrant in color, with the foliage providing the serene, mellowing effect.

A lot depends on the plant too. A spiny cactus is just not going to look right in the wonderful planter you found delicately painted with lords and ladies dancing. A more forthright peasant style, such as a Mexican pot originating from similar human conditions under which the plant evolved, would be far more appropriate.

If you buy clay, plastic, or other pots intended for plants—that is, with drainage holes—you should also get a saucer intended to catch extra water. Some leave a protective coating or may be made of nonporous material, but some will mar fine furniture. Saucers from broken teacups and other odd pieces of household crockery do just as well or better. If you buy a square or other oddly-shaped container without a saucer, you may have difficulty finding a saucer to go with it. Saucers are no problem if you keep your plants on pebble trays.

Making Your Own Containers

There's no reason you have to be limited by the plant containers available on the market. If you are handy and want unusual containers, you can construct them yourself.

Sometimes you can find hollowed-out rocks and driftwood that could be used as containers, or you could construct a container from lightweight featherock or other materials available at building suppliers, craft and hobby shops, brickyards, lumberyards, and plastic suppliers. Plastic

suppliers have square cylinders, domes, and other attractive shapes, as well as sheeting of many weights and colors that is easy to cut to size and glue together.

If you are using pots, the container and its materials need not even be waterproof or require a drainage hole. You could, for example, use wood paneling, fabrics, floor tiles, or other materials to cover shoeboxes or other cardboard boxes of a large enough size so you can hide your pot and saucer inside.

Window Boxes, Planters and Tubs

You can buy outdoor planters especially made for windows, terraces, roof gardens and other uses. They are made of wood, concrete, fiberglass, asbestos-concrete, metal, and other materials. Indoor planters also are available, with or without lights, and the most common size is 36 inches long and 10 inches wide. Those with lights can be installed as room dividers and for other areas, but those without lights can be used only at windows or window-walls.

You can also construct your own custom-sized planters of wood, plastic, or building materials such as brick or tile.

The chief problems wth any planter are water and drainage. Ready-made wooden planters may come with galvanized pans that fit inside, or with plastic pans. If not, or if you make your own, you will have to provide waterproofing (sheets of heavy-duty plastic will do if properly installed). This is true even if you are installing the planter out of doors. Unless you are placing it in an area with sufficient drainage and a waterproof surface, the flooring, roofing, or other material beneath it could rot.

Many gardeners find it far more convenient not to put their soil and plants directly into the planter. It is hard to keep the soil from becoming soggy and sour (light watering, a layer of drainage material, and charcoal mixed with the soil will help prevent these problems). Instead, they pot their plants in individual clay pots and put them on pebble trays laid down in the bottom of the planter. If you want to make the plants look as though they were

planted in the soil, you can surround the pots and cover them up to the rims with coarse sphagnum moss or one of the artificial soils (see double potting, below). Individual pots make it easier to remove a plant that looks ill or is not thriving in a particular location, and to switch your plants around if you don't like the arrangement, or their blooming period ends, or just for variety.

Large wooden tubs made for tree-sized plants also require a waterproof pan inside. Redwood is especially attractive and lasts for years without preservatives, but other woods need to be treated. Copper napthenate is a wood-treatment that will not harm plants or animals. Today most tubs are made of plastic. You can also use

plastic garbage cans or laundry baskets, foot tubs, pickle barrels, and exotic or antique vessels of suitable size.

A second major problem with planters is weight. From time to time news stories are published of a roof caving in under the overenthusiastic efforts of a gardener. But porches, balconies, and interior plantings of any large size should be preceded by an evaluation of structural strength and the amount of weight that will be involved in your garden. Many gardeners prefer to avoid such problems by using the lightweight artificial soil mixtures rather than soil, which is extremely heavy.

The lightweight artificial soils are also an advantage if you will be moving your tubs and planters about. It may be necessary, for instance, to bring a dwarf fruit tree in a tub into a more protected area for the winter. A big plant in a large tub may require a commercial dolly. It is therefore easier to have all tubs and planters on casters. If you cannot attach the casters to the planter itself, as you frequently cannot, you can make a plywood base on which to mount the casters. If you cut the plywood slightly smaller than the bottom of the tub or planter, and paint the edges the same color as the planter, it won't even show. Four casters should be enough for a tub, but larger planters may require six or eight.

Light weight can also be a problem. Tall treelike plants in plastic or other light pots may tip over. Their weight, especially those with heavy foliage on top, such as some ficus, must be properly counterbalanced with a pot that is heavier than the crown. You can test this easily by pulling first on a few leaves on the crown. Some plants you buy already potted will tip over at the lightest pressure. If you have only adults in your home and don't give wild parties, a tipping or a moderate tug on the leaves may be all right. But if you have active children apt to bound into plants, or you are using the plant in an area such as an office with public traffic, you will want a heavy base—obtained with pot as well as soil choice—to prevent accidents.

If you are putting several types of plants together in a large planter, try to choose species needing similar care. Otherwise you will go crazy trying to remember what each needs and fulfilling all their requirements adequately. For large planters, in fact, you might consider easy-care varieties so that if your enthusiasm for plant care wanes with time and you neglect them somewhat they are apt to survive anyway.

How Large a Pot?

The most pressing question to new plant owners is frequently what size pot to buy. Most new gardeners, in fact, buy pots that are too large in the belief this will help thir plant grow better. The opposite is true. A potted plant with a lot of new soil will put all its energies into sending roots out in all directions, even at the expense of the part you see above the soil. Indeed, if you have a sickly looking plant, you might try putting it in a smaller pot; often this perks it up immediately.

And if you are uncertain what size pot to buy, even after reading the explanation below, opt for the smaller

size. If it really is too small, in a few weeks the plant will let you know this by sending roots through the drainage hole. In that case, you can simply repot it in a container with a diameter one-inch wider and no damage will have been done. This is preferable to allowing the plant to develop a weak, dangling root system, a problem much harder to remedy.

A plant in an excessively large container is in for a lot of trouble. This could happen if you were trying to space a few plants widely apart in a large windowbox or other large planter. If the roots are not draining all the soil from the water, the soil remains too wet and becomes sour. This results in root rot. In addition sour soil allows toxic elements to build up that are also harmful to plants.

The answer to the question of what size pot to use is that the size of the pot should be in pleasing proportion to the amount of plant you see above the soil.

In general, this means that *the diameter of the pot should be one third the height of the plant.* This is, however, only an average rule, because much depends on the size and shape of the plant. It works well for upright plants with fairly bushy leaves such as Chinese evergreen, schefflera, or philodendrons.

Some plants look better if the pot's diameter is *less* than a third of their height. If your plant is the type that rises on a tall stalk lacking lower leaves, so that the foliage spreads out at the top, the plant will often look better balanced if the pot's diameter is only a quarter of its height. *Dieffenbachia maculata, Dracaena marginata,* and *Ficus elastica* are plants for which this might be true. Tall-growing plants with feathery leaves that have an airy look—such as false aralia and some ferns—may look overpowered in large pots. You might want a diameter only a fourth to a fifth of its height.

Some plants look better in pots whose diameter is *more* than a third of their height or equal to their height. This is true of plants that lie low to the soil. The lush, crouched growth of African violets is one example. The leaves hug the edges of the pot rim, giving a pleasing effect, even though the pot's diameter might be equal to the plant's height. The same would be true of spreading begonias, low-growing succulents, and many bromeliads with stiff, spearlike leaves that jut out horizontally across the pot.

Another example are the cactus plants that grow in round ball shapes, such as barrel cactus. These would look ridiculously top heavy in pots with diameter's a third of their height. For these, the pot's diameter should allow an inch of space around the cactus. In other words, a cactus with a five-inch diameter would look best in a seven-inch diameter pot, and a cactus ten inches in diameter would use a twelve-inch diameter pot.

Some of the plants with unusual leaves (such as the spring euphorbias, some orchids, some bromeliads) or without leaves (such as columnar cacti) look best in pots whose diameters are about half their height.

Trailing and hanging plants are the hardest to judge pot size for, and no rules can be made. In general, the pot should look full and be pretty much obscured by foliage. With creeping plants, you can pinch back new growth to get a full effect over the top of the pot before you allow stems to grow beyond it. Many of these are such fast growers, though, that even if you buy too large a pot your plant will soon fill it anyway.

One time you need not worry about pot size being too big is when you are growing plants from seed. In this case, though, as explained in the section "Propagation," you are providing special conditions for optimum root development.

See "Indoor/Outdoor Plant Lore" for more on container gardening and hanging baskets.

SOIL.

If you buy a plant from a caring garden center it will usually be potted in the proper soil mixture, and in a pot large enough to allow for new root growth so that you will not have to repot it for awhile. (If you are buying an expensive plant, you should insist on this.) But plants you buy in supermarkets or variety stores, or that you may be given as gifts, may not have the proper soil and may already be outgrowing their pots.

In any case, at some point your plant will need transplanting, and you will have to deal with the soil.

If you don't want to learn about soil, you need not. You can buy prepackaged, sterilized, regular potting mixtures that are adequate for the most common varieties of houseplants. The principal types of mixes are listed below (see "Common Soil Mixtures") and in the descriptions of indoor plants we have indicated the type of soil each needs. And even if you are growing something a little special—say, African violets, orchids, or cacti—you can find potting soils especially mixed for a number of specialty plants at garden centers.

Most gardeners, though, become intrigued with plant growth and develop enough affection for their plant to want to be fully informed of its requirements. In addition, few indoor gardeners stop with one plant. You may start with this idea, but pretty soon you are apt to succumb to the temptation to add another and then another, until you have a half dozen or more. Once you have a collection, you may find buying the prepackaged mixes rather expensive and find it cheaper to mix your own soils. You may also develop enough expertise—especially if your collection consists chiefly of one particular type of plant—to want soils custom-mixed to your particular circumstances.

For all such indoor gardeners, here is the basic know-how:

Soil Consistency

Soil should be firm enough to anchor the roots and support the top growth but not be so hard and compact that air and water cannot reach the roots of your plant. Yet a plant derives nutrients from the soil, and the richest soils are high in organic matter that is rather compacted. As a result, most soil mixtures try to balance organic matter with drainage materials. The perfect balance differs with the plant variety, but you need a soil that will allow enough drainage so that the plant's roots will not become waterlogged and rot, yet one that doesn't have so much drainage material that the water will pour right through, and leave the roots dehydrated.

For most plants, the right mix should be loose ("friable"). A good way to test your mix is to moisten it and crush it in your hand. It should fall apart in your palm when you open your fingers. If it remains balled-up, you need more perlite, vermiculite, or sand.

Don't make the mistake of thinking a very rich soil is a kindness to your plant because it will provide more nutrients. Plants that do not naturally grow in rich soil can be overstimulated to produce long, spindly, unattractive growth.

Common Soil Mixtures

REGULAR POTTING MIXTURE: This is the most common type of soil mixture, suitable for the widest variety of plant types, and there are as many recipes as there are avid indoor gardeners.

The most common recipe is that recommended by the U.S. Department of Agriculture. It consists of equal parts garden soil (loam) and organic matter (peat moss or shredded sphagnum moss), to which you add a level teaspoon of 20% superphosphate (available at garden centers) to every quart of mixture.

Most private gardeners seem to prefer a mixture of equal parts garden loam, organic matter such as peat moss or leafmold, and sand. University agricultural divisions often offer soil mixtures appropriate for their areas.

For dry plants such as cacti, the sand content should be closer to a half than to a third of the soil mix. For moisture-loving plants, some gardeners increase the amount of peat moss a bit.

HUMUS is a dense, absorbent mixture of pure sphagnum moss, firbark, or osmunda fiber. It is suitable only for water-loving plants such as ferns and some orchids. Humus is high in nitrogen.

HUMUS SOIL, a mixture of three parts humus to one part sand, is a dense, rich mix with more drainage than humus alone. It is suitable for water-loving plants that are nevertheless particular about having their roots airy and dry. Examples are most orchids and bromeliads.

Artificial Soil

The New York State College of Agriculture at Cornell University has developed soilless, artificial growing mediums known as Cornell mixes. These contain no loam. They consist of such ingredients as volcanic materials like perlite and vermiculite, ground dolomitic limestone, sphagnum moss, firbark, and various other nutrients. Cornell mixes are available for special purposes, such as the Cornell Epiphytic Mix for air plants such as bromeliads, as well as for general use (Cornell Foliage Plant Mix). Since artificial soils contain fewer nutrients, ground limestone and other fertilizing material is usually part of the recipe.

These mixes are popular for propagation, and because they are light they are also handy for large plants growing in tubs that you want to be able to move about.

Soil Ingredients

POTTING SOIL, GARDEN SOIL, GARDEN LOAM, OR LOAM—under whatever name you see it by—is a dense black soil that provides body and absorbency to most potting mixtures. It holds water close to the roots and also provides nutrients. Used alone, however, it is too dense and heavy for most plants. If you are going to use soil from your garden or elsewhere for indoor plants, it is essential that you sterilize it first (see "How to Sterilize Soil").

PEAT MOSS consists of partially organic matter. Found in temperate zone swamps and bogs, it is formed by the decay of aquatic and semiaquatic plants such as reeds and mosses, and it has a high acidity and is rich in nitrogen. Since most tropical plants used indoors like a pH of about 5.5 to 6.5 (7.0 means the alkalinity and acidity are in balance), peat moss (or leafmold) is often added to soils to prevent them from being too alkaline. (Testing the pH of indoor plant soils is not necessary if you use recommended soil mixtures, but if you are finicky or especially interested in this aspect you can buy a soil-testing kit at garden centers.) Peat moss is spongey and therefore

provides two advantages: It allows air to get to the plant's roots by preventing the sol from forming a hard mass, and it absorbs and retains moisture (up to twenty times its weight) to prevent the soil from drying out. Being common for commercial and home gardening purposes, peat moss is readily available in sizes from home-size packets to farm-size loads.

Acid-loving plants often do well in a soil mix that contains up to 50% peat moss. These include azaleas and rhododendrons, dogwood, magnolia, heather, mountain holly, primrose, phlox, trailing arbutus, lady slipper, painted trillium, lily of the valley, some lilies, iris, some begonias, wild indigo, marsh marigolds, gentian, raspberries, and blackberries. The leaves of these plants may yellow if the soil becomes too alkaline, because these plants cannot absorb iron chelates unless the soil is acid. If your plant shows such deficiency, you can buy iron chelates in soluble form; follow the package directions.

Sphagnum moss is an ingredient of peat moss. It consists of gray mosses that give excellent drainage and are slow to decompose. It, too, is readily available in various grades from finely milled to coarse.

LEAFMOLD, as its name implies, is a crumbly, brown humus consisting of decayed leaves. It is typical of the rich soils found on forest floors.

OSMUNDA is a genus of ferns, and osmunda fiber is made by chopping up the roots of these ferns. It is a rich, absorbent organic material that can be added to soil mixes in place of peat moss. More commonly, however, it is used alone as the soil for bromeliads and orchids. It is available in several grades at nurseries.

FIRBARK, also used for orchids and bromeliads, is made by steaming the bark of evergreens. It is sold in packets at garden centers, and like osmunda comes in several grades, according to how finely it is screened. Among the barks used are Douglas Fir, white or red fir, or redwood.

SAND available at nurseries is a coarse type, called builder's sand, added to soil mixes to provide drainage. While perlite and vermiculite also are used to loosen and aerate the soil for most types of indoor plants, sand is almost always preferred for cacti and succulents. Some gardeners prefer sand over perlite and vermiculite for most uses.

PERLITE is a white volcanic substance used to lighten soil so that air and water can reach plant roots. Its main function is to create porous soil conditions, and it does not absorb moisture.

VERMICULITE, an expanded form of mica, is also popular for creating a loose soil that will enable air and water to reach plant roots. Unlike sand or perlite, however, it soaks up and retains water. It is therefore commonly used for propagating seeds and cuttings. Since vermiculite is sold commercially for many uses, and some mixtures may be toxic and not sterile for plants, be sure you buy a horticultural type.

CHARCOAL, also called activated charcoal and horticultural charcoal, is frequently sprinkled into soil to keep it fresh. It is used especially for plants requiring a great deal of water, and should be used if you are growing plants in water alone. The higher the organic content of soil, the more likely it is to sour, and charcoal is therefore especially important in soils with a great deal of peat moss, leafmold, or humus.

BONE MEAL is used like charcoal to keep moist soils from becoming sour and encouraging root rot. It is also rich in phosphorus.

Other ingredients gardeners may add to soil include sawdust, wood ashes (for potash), compost or manure (both organic materials high in nitrogen), and pulverized dolomitic limestone (for magnesium and calcium).

Alkalinity and Acidity of the Soil

The alkalinity and acidity of soil are measured on a pH scale that runs from 0 to 14, with 7 being neutral. At 7 the alkalinity and acidity are balanced. Measurements above 7 to 14 indicate the degree of alkalinity, while measurements below 7 to 0 indicate the degree of acidity.

Houseplants generally like their soil with a tinge of acidity—a pH of about 6.5. Most foliage plants, cacti, bulbs, and ferns fall into this category and find ranges of 6.2 to 6.8 acceptable. Some flowering plants, such as azaleas, camellias, begonias, geraniums, and gardenias, prefer a little more acid, and a few plants like a minor degree (7.5 to 8) of alkalinity.

Usually, if you have used the soil mixture recommended for your

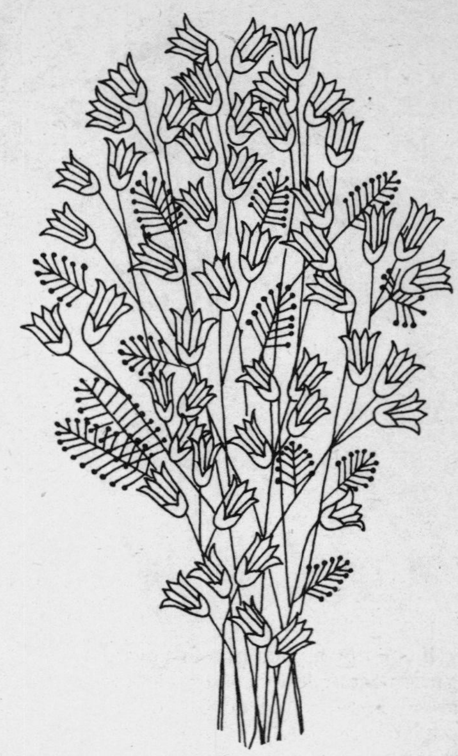

plant, you will not have to worry about the pH of your soil. Most soil mixes include peat moss for acidity, and if you are growing an acid-loving plant you can add a bit more peat moss.

If, however, you are growing large numbers of plants and want the pH of your soil mixture tested, you can mail a soil sample to your state's Department of Agriculture experimental station. They will test your soil without charge. To correct acid soil, you add a small amount of ground limestone (about 2 teaspoons to every quart of soil); and to correct alkaline soil, you add a small amount of sulphur (about a teaspoon to a quart). However, you should get expert advice before attempting to put additives in your soil, and in most cases a slight rebalancing of the amount of garden loam, peat moss, and sand in your mix will correct the situation.

How To Sterilize Soil

Prepackaged soil that you buy in supermarkets or garden centers is already sterilized. If you want to pot your plants in soil from your garden or elsewhere, however, you will have to sterilize the soil to kill off any pests (including eggs and larvae too small to see), bacteria, weed seeds, and harmful fungi.

Place the soil in a shallow baking pan and add one cup of water for each gallon of soil. Bake the soil in the oven at 200° for two hours.

Cool the soil at least twenty-four hours before using.

Sterilization is also necessary for sand, gravel, or other ingredients you add to the soil that you do not buy in prepackaged form. Sand and gravel may be sterilized by putting them in a pan of water on the stovetop. Bring the water to a boil and boil about three minutes.

How To Pot A Plant

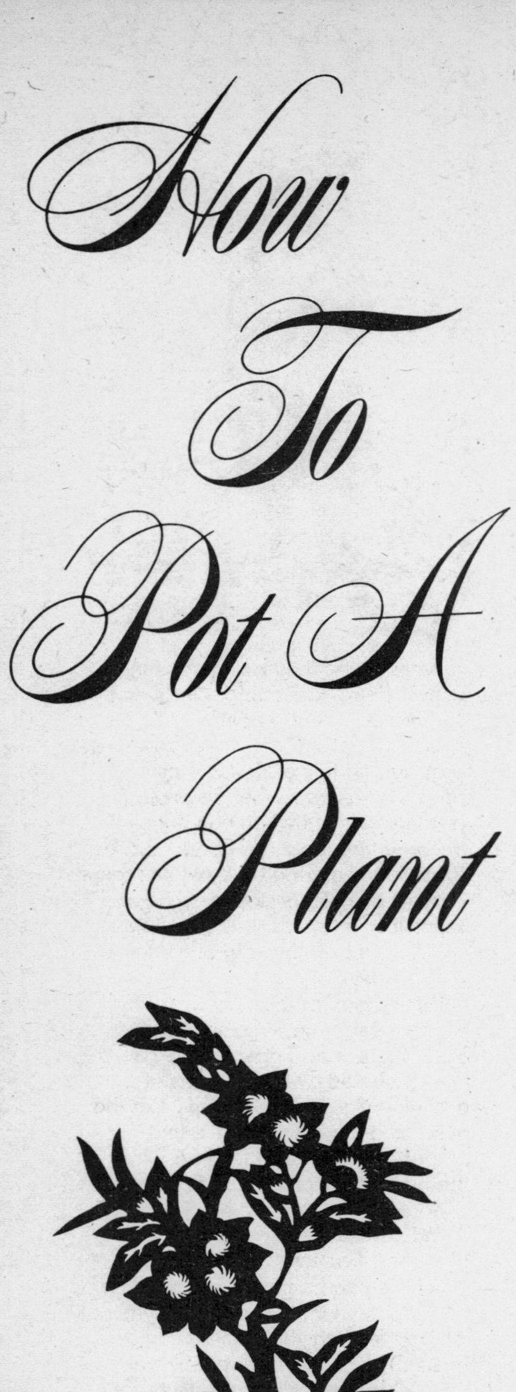

1. Use a clean container.
   New clay pots and certain types of pottery are apt to contain toxic materials used in their manufacture. Soaking them in clear water overnight will remove these.
   In addition, any porous pot should be soaked overnight in water before use or reuse—otherwise it will immediately draw moisture from the soil when you put the plant in it.
   Used clay pots or porous pottery vessels should be soaked in a mixture of ammonia or bleach and water, and then scrubbed with a stiff brush or steel wool pads, rinsed thoroughly, and then soaked overnight in clear water.
   Used plastic and nonporous vessels should be scrubbed with strong detergent, using a stiff brush, and rinsed thoroughly.
2. Over the drainage hole place an arched piece of broken pottery or a large pebble to keep soil in but allow water to seep out.
3. Add a layer of gravel, perlite, porous pebbles, crushed brick, or bits of broken pots. For a six-inch pot you need an inch of this drainage material. Drainage material is especially vital if you are using plastic pots and you can increase it to an inch and a half. For containers without drainage holes, use two or three inches.
   You may also add pieces of horticultural charcoal to this drainage material.
   Some gardeners like to add a thin layer of peat moss or sphagnum moss to keep the soil from draining down, but this is not necessary for many soils and is done only when you are using soil with a high sand or other grainy content.

4. Pour about an inch and a half of soil into the pot, and then hold the plant in the pot to see if you need more. The depth is determined by the plant's root ball. When potted, the plant should sit so that the top level of the soil is an inch below the pot rim.
5. Holding the plant in the center of the pot, use a spoon or small trowel to sift sand around the roots and then up to within an inch of the pot rim. If you rap the pot sharply against a hard surface a couple of times as you work, this should settle the soil. You can also tamp the soil lightly against the roots, but don't mash it in.
   If you are potting a cactus or other spiny plant, wear gloves. If you don't have gloves, you can hold the plant within a wad of folded newspaper. It also helps to put the soil in the pot with a long-handled wooden spoon, a ladle, a folded piece of paper, or any other device that will keep your hand away from thorns and spines.
6. Once the pot is filled, firm the top of the soil with your fingers and test to see if it is properly planted by lifting the plant by the stem. If the plant doesn't pull out of the pot, you have the roots firmly in place.

7. Water the soil thoroughly (best done by placing it in a sink or pan of water until the moisture reaches the surface of the pot) and put the plant in a light, but not sunny, place for several days so it can get accustomed to your home's environment. If it is a sun-loving plant, you may then move it into the sun.
   After potting in new soil, a plant will be getting sufficient nutrient, so you can wait two or three weeks before fertilized.

Double Potting

You can reduce the frequency of watering for container plants by double-potting. Here you take a container larger than your clay pots and fill it with peat moss. You bury the pots in the peat moss so they are covered up to their rims. Then you do not water the pots themselves but the peat moss. The porosity of clay pots enables the pot soil to draw water from the peat as needed. This method is handy for planters, windowboxes, and other large containers. You must, however, use porous clay pots—it will not work with plastic, glazed, or painted pots.

Repotting

Your plant will tell you when it needs a new and larger pot. Usually you will see white roots poking out of the drainage hole, but sometimes you will see them on the surface of the soil.

How long before this happens varies. Without fertilizer, plants in pots deplete the soil nutrients faster, and send out roots in an effort to look for more. So if you are giving your plants plant food, it will be longer between repottings. Some naturally slow-growing cacti live happily several years without repotting, while fast-growing vines may outgrow their pots within a year. Plants in large containers (fourteen inches or more in diameter) often grow satisfactorily for five years or more in the same pot, which is lucky since they can be hard to unpot. You can avoid repotting them if you replace the top three to five inches of soil every year or two. Since young plants are more active growers, they will need repotting more often than mature species.

If you're having doubts about whether your plant needs repotting, take it out of the pot and examine it. If the roots have formed a complete network following the shape of the pot, it is time to repot. If you don't see such a network the plant doesn't need repotting.

The best time to repot a plant is in spring or fall. In spring, the vigor of the growing cycle will be starting up and will help the plant recover from the shock of being transplanted. In summer, plants have the extra stress of heat to deal with so you don't want to exhaust them further. In fall, they have time to recover before their dormant period begins. Winter is a bad time, for plants usually have their slowest activity then and recuperation will take longer. Flowering plants are best repotted after the flowers have faded.

To repot a plant, choose a time when the soil is moist. Put your hand over the soil so the plant stalk is between your fingers. Then turn the pot upside down and rap it on the sides and bottom. The whole plant will fall into your hand.

Dislodge as much of the old soil as you can from between the roots, being careful not to damage the roots. Examine the roots for any sign of insects or root rot. Even if you've never seen root rot, you can tell unhealthy roots—cut away any slimy or unhealthy looking portions of the root system.

Repot the plant in a container only one-inch in diameter larger than the previous container.

The plant may show signs of decreased vigor after repotting, but this disappears quickly.

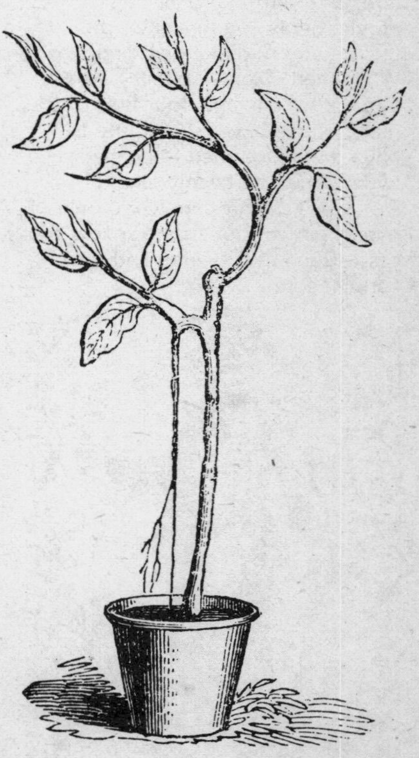

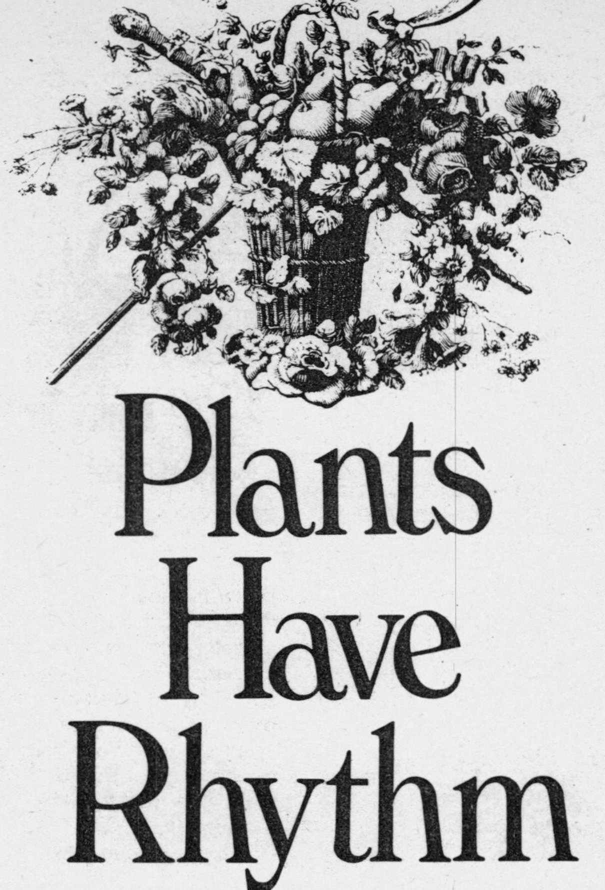

Plants Have Rhythm

All plants have daily biological rhythms, and to have your plants grow at their best most of them need alternating periods of light and darkness. They need a period of rest on both a daily and a seasonal basis.

Light and Dark

If you tried to grow a tomato plant under continual light, the plant would weigh less than normal, would develop small, brittle, yellowed leaves, and would be marred by dark patches of dead tissue.

Experimenters, in fact, discovered that trying to grow tomato plants on schedules such as six hours of light followed by six hours of darkness, or of twenty-four hours of light followed by twenty-four hours of darkness, also produced damaged plants. It seems the tomato plant has a decided bias in favor of twelve hours of light alternating with twelve hours of darkness.

Scientists have found that this urge is so strong in plants that rhythmic phenomena are not limited to a plant as a whole. They have been detected also in detached leaves, strips of leaf tissue, and even in single cells.

While the optimum amount of light is important to plant growth, it appears that even more crucial is that light and dark periods be synchronized with the plant's internal rhythm. Though by use of artificial light you can extend a plant's day longer than would be normal in nature, in order to fulfill its light requirements you must also provide the amount of darkness it prefers. While many plants operate, like the tomato, on a twenty-four-hour clock, many others have been found to have rhythm attuned to between twenty-one and twenty-eight hours. And these rhythms apply not only to overall growth but also to special processes such as flowering and seed germination.

Some of the variation in preferred night length has to do with the latitude where the plant originated. Many tropical houseplants, for example, come from areas near the equator, where day and night are each consistently twelve hours long. As you go north from the equator, the days are longer in summer and shorter in winter. Temperate zone plants are therefore more used to accommodation. Orchids and other tropical plants retain their native growth cycles related to rainy and dry periods even when brought into temperate climates.

Plants can be very particular about their darkness. Researchers trying to figure out how long a day was favored by flowering plants were surprised to discover the plants didn't care so much about the days. More critical to flowering plants was the length of darkness. In general, they want *total*, uninterrupted darkness. Some are such sticklers that if you turn on a light in their dark room, even for only a few minutes, they will refuse to bloom. This is true even if the darkness is interrupted by low-intensity indirect light from another room. Though some flowering plants are fussier than others, for best results you should try to provide complete, uninterrupted darkness.

Temperature

A second major discovery was that when plants go into darkness they also like a temperature change.

For a great many plants, the temperature should be lower at night. To a number of evergreens, the night temperature is paramount, though, and they tolerate a variety of daytime temperatures. Potatoes produce tubers only in climates where their night temperatures fall to 50° to 60°. Tomatoes also like cool nights. And many fruits—including plums, apples, and strawberries—will flower better, produce better quality, and even taste better when grown in climates that have cool nights. You can therefore get a more delicious strawberry from mountainous West Virginia than you can from flatlands offering less temperature variation between days and nights.

But cool nights are not enjoyed by *all* plants. Zinnias and African violets are among the contrary-minded plants that prefer their nights warmer.

And many species, including many hardy foliage varieties, don't seem to care too much one way or the other.

So while as a gardener it is important to know your plant's daytime needs, an understanding of its nighttime preferences is essential too. Though all plants need rest, in situations where temperature and darkness are particularly important we have tried to note the plant's requirements in the descriptions in this book.

Requirements for daylight and dark, and for temperature change, are of particular interest to indoor and greenhouse gardeners, who can to some extent control conditions under which their plants grow. But rhythm is important also for outdoor gardeners, especially those who like to import non-native species. It can explain mystifying failures with some imprinted plants and can provide guidelines for puchases of new, nonnative species.

Seasonal Rhythms

Season rhythms in plants are most striking in northern climates, where numerous deciduous trees and shrubs develop brilliant foliage before dropping their leaves. Seasonal rhythm is also apparent if you grow bulbs or annuals that simply go to sleep on you when their growth period ends.

But rest is not so apparent in evergreens or in tropical plants cultured indoors. Often seasonal changes are scarcely perceptible unless you are alert to the possibility.

Plants from northern latitudes experience dramatic changes in the length of daylight between the longer summer days and the shorter winter days. Simultaneously they experience a wide fluctuation in temperature. Usually, too, the rainfall varies seasonally. Such plants cannot survive unless they can predict in advance the radical changes in their environment and prepare for them. In spring and summer they grow vigorously and flower. In fall they produce seeds or other ways of reproducing again when conditions become favorable. Trees and shrubs form overwintering buds, while many herbaceous plants stop growing and reproduce as seeds, bulbs, or tubers. Many count on the cold of winter to repress development.

While none of this is news to the outdoor gardener, who simply goes along, indoor and greenhouse gardeners should watch for signs of declining vigor in their plants. Let the plant lead the way. Reduce the amount of water and fertilizer when the plant stops producing new leaves or shoots, or when the blooms start to fade and are not replaced by new blossoms. For some indoor plants, which demand a period of complete rest, we have indicated where watering and feeding should cease altogether. Bulbs, for instance, remain dormant for months. But other plants are more subtle in their seasonal changes and therefore require more subtle care—just slight decreases in water or feeding rather than cessation.

Most of your plants will have their dormant period in winter. This is true of most of the summer-flowering plants. But a few will surprise you—ruellia becomes dormant in late summer to early fall and then revives in late fall just when you think it should be going dormant. Some geraniums go dormant in summer too. African violets bloom all year.

The best time to repot plants, top them, or do other extensive grooming is just after dormancy, when new growth begins to appear. Water or fertilizer should be increased or restarted at this time too.

Grooming

Your plants will stay healthier and look their best if you establish a regular schedule—say, once a week or once a month—for grooming.

1. Remove all wilted or withered leaves, stems, and flowers with sharp scissors or a sharp knife.
2. Check the foliage color and texture for wilting, yellowing, or other signs of trouble. Examine the stems (especially where they branch or join larger stalks) and leaves (especially the underside) for signs of illness or pests.
3. Consider how the plant is growing. If it's getting leggy, pinch out new growth to encourage branching and a more compact shape.
4. Wash the plant (in a sink is best) with lukewarm, soapy water, using a soft sponge. Clean both sides of the leaves, as well as stems and buds. Rinse with clear water and allow the leaves to dry before returning the plant to its place. The only plants that should not be washed are those with hairy leaves, such as African violets and some begonias.
5. If the soil is compacted, loosen the surface soil with a fork, being careful not to injure the roots.

Going on Vacation

If you must leave your plants for a long time, you will have to get a friend to water them (professional plant sitters are available in many areas) or board them at a local nursery or greenhouse.

For a vacation of ten days to two weeks, however, you can usually take measures to keep your plants moist enough to survive your absence.

Cactus, succulents, and other water-conserving plants such as many bromeliads are acustomed to drought and can be safely left without worry.

Plants requiring water can be heavily watered before departure.

Some can then be placed in plastic bags. Close the bags with the ties provided to make a tight seal. Or cover large ones with plastic sheeting tied with string around the tub. Even if these are sun-loving plants, leave them in a good light but not in the sun. While this may work for many hardy plants, more delicate varieties may react adversely.

A solution more adaptable to a wider variety of plants is to install a wick system. If you already have a wick-feeding system for your plants, filling the reservoir should be adequate for your absence. Unless your plants are types that require continual moisture, a little drying out toward the end of your stay should not bother them. If you don't have a wick system, you can buy glass wicks and set up a temporary system using jars as reservoirs.

Handiest of all are glass tubes made especially for vacationing indoor gardeners. These are narrow at one end, which you insert into the soil, and are open at the opposite end; you fill them with water and they release water automatically as the soil dries. If you water your plants thoroughly before leaving, and then insert one of these tubes into the pot, you can vacation without qualms. Should you fear an especially thirsty or large plant will not survive your absence, you can insert two or three of these glass tubes into the pot. Stocking up in advance with enough glass tubes to take care of your plant collection, of whatever size, is reassuring and allows you to make last-minute plans without feeling that your plants' needs are inhibiting your activities.

If your plants love humidity, or if you habitually mist them to certain humidity requirements, you might also want to stand open containers of water around them while you are gone. You might even drape a cape of plastic wrap around the plants and the open water containers to keep the evaporation near the plants rather than dissipating quickly into the room.

TOOLS

For indoor gardening you need very little equipment, and what you need can be recycled from regular household equipment.

1. *A watering can.* If you have only a couple of plants, especially large floor-size ones, you can use old jars or pitchers for watering. If you have many grouped small plants, however, a watering can with a long, thin spout will enable you to reach through and around foliage to get the water into the pots without slopping it all over. A long, thin spout is particularly handy for hairy-leaved plants that do not like water on their leaves.

   The old-fashioned watering can, with a broad spout that issues a strong, wide spray, is not handy for indoor gardening unless you have large groupings, such as a room divider, on a pebble tray. Also, if you have atrium, terrace, porch, or plant room arrangements with plants on waterproof bases for runoff, so that nothing will be damaged by excess water, the old-fashioned can could be handier than the thin-spouted type.

   If you are going to buy a watering can, choose an attractive one that you can leave out as a decorative part of your plant display. If you buy an ugly one, you'll have to hide it in a closet between use.
2. *A mister*—see "Misting," on page 88.
3. *A fork* for turning the soil. You can use an old table fork or buy a miniature rake in a plant shop.
4. If you are going to repot, you will need pots or other containers, pebbles or other drainage materials, and soil.
5. If you are going to use a pebble tray, see "How to Make a Pebble Tray" on page 88.

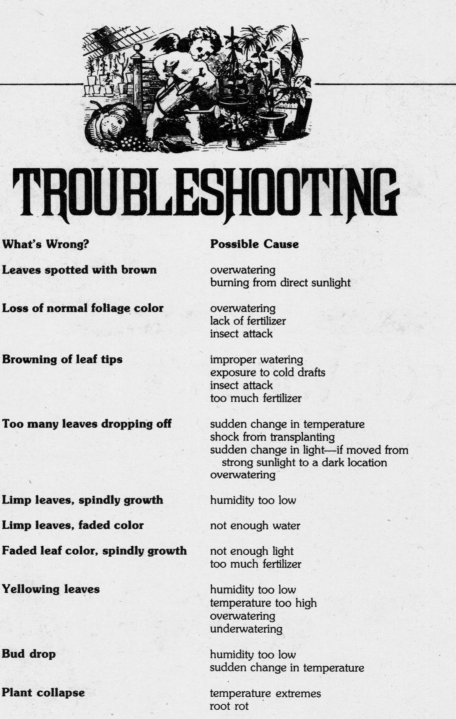

TROUBLESHOOTING

What's Wrong?	Possible Cause
Leaves spotted with brown	overwatering burning from direct sunlight
Loss of normal foliage color	overwatering lack of fertilizer insect attack
Browning of leaf tips	improper watering exposure to cold drafts insect attack too much fertilizer
Too many leaves dropping off	sudden change in temperature shock from transplanting sudden change in light—if moved from strong sunlight to a dark location overwatering
Limp leaves, spindly growth	humidity too low
Limp leaves, faded color	not enough water
Faded leaf color, spindly growth	not enough light too much fertilizer
Yellowing leaves	humidity too low temperature too high overwatering underwatering
Bud drop	humidity too low sudden change in temperature
Plant collapse	temperature extremes root rot

All of the above are conditions cuased by improper plant care and can therefore be avoided. Insect infestations, however, can occur even under the most devoted care. Remedies for these are given on page 157.

Plants are also occasionally subject to disease. The most common of these is mildew, which may come on especially in damp weather, and especially to plants you keep in high humidity. The leaves begin to acquire a white coating. You can dust them with sulfur or spray them with a sulfur solution to eliminate this. Some commercial preparations are available too.

Less common are viruses and bacterial diseases that can result in strange splotches on foliage, flowers, or stems, or in gray mold on foliage and flowers. Commercial preparations are available, but unless it is an especially rare or cherished plant it's easier simply to discard it.

4

Indoor Gardening Under Lights

Indoor Light Gardening

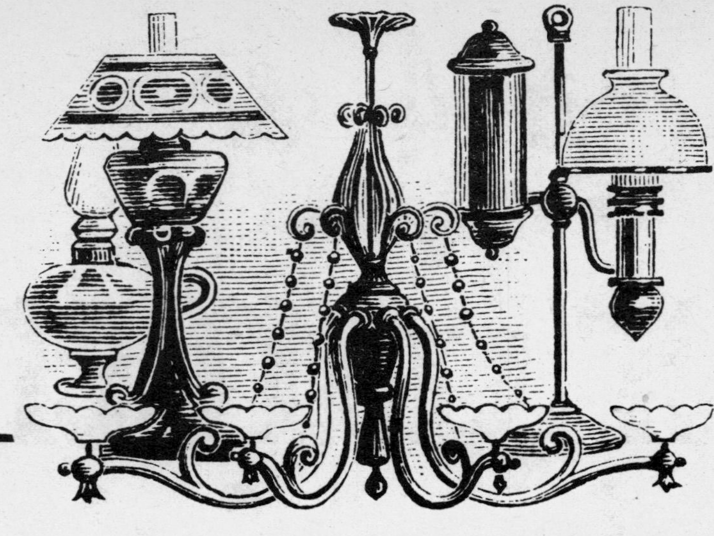

With the advent of fluorescent light, you are no longer restricted to growing only those plants suitable to the natural light you have available.

In a typical home light garden, that is, under a 2-tube 24-inch or 48-inch fluorescent fixture, you can grow herbs for the kitchen, compact foliage plants, and many flowering plants such as begonias, African violets, impatiens, and oxalis. If you have the discipline necessary to provide your plants with a consistently humid environment, you can raise more unusual and challenging varieties, such as orchids, anthuriums, gardenias, and many ferns. Indoor light gardens are also the perfect settings for producing stocky plants from seed to transplant into outdoor flower and vegetable gardens.

In terms of duration and intensity, artificial light can give an indoor garden the equivalent of a summer's day worth of light all year round. You can therefore even have flowers in the dead of winter. You can also force bulbs and stimulate cuttings to throw out roots. You will, in general, have more light control than you can achieve with outdoor plants.

Learning to use fluorescent light enables you to make more versatile and imaginative use of plants in decorating your home. Plants need no longer be bunched at the windows but can be put anywhere you want them. Artificial light will convert your darkest corner into the perfect location for sun-loving plants.

You will grow plants more successfully under artificial light if you first learn a bit about light in relation to plants. If you are not interested in these technicalities, you can skip down to the section on fluorescent lighting.

Why Plants Need Light

Plants need light because without light there is no chlorophyll, the green coloring matter in leaves and stems that corresponds to blood in an animal. Plants also need exposure to light in order to absorb carbon dioxide from the air and to feed by drawing up water and other nutrients from the soil with their roots.

Scientists have demonstrated that these vital functions are best performed when plants are exposed to light of a certain hue, or wavelength.

For example, chlorophyll is formed better under red light than blue. Light from both ends of the spectrum is best for the absorption of carbon dioxide and the production of sugar and starch. Stems grow well under red light, not blue.

Natural sunlight consists of many hues or wavelengths of light, and outdoor plants apparently pick the light they need to carry out certain processes. In indoor gardens lighted artificially, it is up to the gardener to provide his or her plants with conditions favoring optimal growth. Some plants will stay alive if they receive enough light from an ordinary light bulb, but, depending on the type, they may not flourish.

Incandescent light is yellowish because it emits more energy in the yellow and red regions of the spectrum. For optimum plant growth you need a more balanced light, available in ordinary fluorescent tubes and in fluorescent lights especially designed for indoor gardens.

In fact, artificial light not only frees you from restrictions imposed by the natural light available in your rooms and allows you to grow a more interesting variety of plants, but your plants will probably be larger, healthier, and more attractive than those grown in natural light. This is because with artificial light you can fine-tune the precise amount of light each plant needs.

How Much Light Are You Getting?

The intensity of light is measured in food-candles. (One foot-candle is equivalent to the amount of light a candle in the dark will throw one foot away.)

The amount of light you receive through a particular window varies with the direction the window faces. If you have an unobscructed south window, you might get as much as 8000 foot-candles, while an unobstructed east or west window could measure less than half of that and a north window less than 500 foot-candles.

Few windows, however, are unobstructed. In urban areas, tall neighboring buildings could reduce the light considerably, and in more rural settings foliage is apt to intervene. Foot-candle readings can be reduced up to 50%. Outdoor awnings and overhangs, indoor curtains, smog, air pollution, even the number of cloudy days you have in your area are among the many influences on the amount of light your room actually receives. An obstructed east or west window in one setting might yield only the same amount of light that an unobstructed north window might give you elsewhere.

The size of the window also makes a difference. A glass wall facing north could throw more light into a room than a small window facing south. The situation is further complicated if your room has windows with more than one exposure.

Latitude and seasons are additional variables. In some areas, a reading taken at noon in summer could give you 3000 foot-candles or more than a reading taken in winter. If your window is obstructed by foliage, on the other hand, you could get a higher reading in winter, once the leaves have fallen. Depending on the angle of light, a room could get more light in winter when the sun is low.

With all of these variables, it is difficult to know exactly how much light you are really getting at your windows, and the difficulties increase the farther you move away from your windows into the interior of your rooms.

How to Measure Light

The only way to measure your light accurately is to buy or borrow a foot-candle light meter. Such light meters are not too expensive, but unless you are going to continue to use it, try to borrow one from a local garden club or a gardening addict or a friendly physicist specializing in photometry.

If you cannot get a foot-candle meter, you can make do with a photographic lightmeter, but it is not as accurate and it's complicated to convert the measurement. If you set the ASA exposure index at 75, the lens opening at *f*/8, and use a 1/60th of a second exposure time, you'll get the rough equivalent of 1000 foot-candles. For 2000 foot-candles, use half the ASA exposure, one *f*-stop less, or half the exposure time. For only 500 foot-candles, you can either double the ASA index or exposure time, or use one *f*-stop larger.

When you measure the amount of natural light you have available, you'll probably need to take several readings. This will not be necessary if you are going to put plants in a windowless office lighted entirely by artificial means. But in rooms that get some natural light, the amount of that light will vary during the day. If you get sun, it is especially important to note how far it penetrates into the room, for how long, and at what angles. You can then avoid burning the foliage or shade-loving plants by keeping them out of the sun's path.

It is a good idea to take readings several days running, even for a week, so that you can average out daily variations. And don't take readings if you happen to be having an unusually rainy period or other unique weather situation that would distort the amount of light you usually get.

Also take into account seasonal variation. If you live in a northerly latitude and set minimal artificial light standards based on summer readings, the light may be insufficient in winter.

After you have bought your artificial lights and installed them, it is a good idea to take readings again. That way you can be reassured that your plants are getting the amount of light you intended.

Light Intensity

FULL SUN and bright light conditions will give you readings between 4000 and 8000 foot-candles.

You can expect the higher readings near the glass at an unobstructed south-facing window during sunlight in summer. In winter the reading could be toward the lower end of this range. If your southern exposure is obstructed by vegetation, buildings, or awnings, your readings could be considerably lower. A south window usually gets three to four hours of sun a day.

This high intensity does not penetrate far into a room—depending on how large your window is, you will probably get this high a reading only about three feet into the room. Plants placed farther than this into the room, or placed at the sides of the window, could receive 1000 foot-candles or less.

If you are using artificial lights for plants requiring bright light, providing 1000 to 2000 foot-candles of light (or less—perhaps down to 500 foot-candles) over a 14-hour or 16-hour day should do the trick. Plants grown with 2500 to 3000 foot-candles above them respond much like plants grown outdoors. But if you try to achieve levels above this, the lamps

tend to produce extreme heat and rapid drying of plants and soil, so longer light exposure at more moderate intensity will produce a more attractively shaped plant.

INDIRECT SUNLIGHT refers to filtered or diffused light and can vary between 1000 and 3500 foot-candles. This intensity is sometimes called high light or good light.

You will get this kind of light from an unobstructed east-facing or west-facing window in summer. Winter readings would be less. You could also get this amount of light from a south window covered with a light-weight curtain or shaded with blinds. A plant placed five or ten feet inside an unobstructed south window, or to the sides of the window, would also get light intensity in this range.

If you keep artificial lights on for about sixteen hours, providing 200 to 1000 foot-candles, you would be duplicating indirect sunlight conditions.

This amount of light will be enough for most flowering plants and vegetables, for orchids, and for African violets and begonias. Plants that will thrive at 500 to 1000 foot-candles include Norfolk Island pine, citrus, coleus, and caladium.

SUBDUED DAYLIGHT—sometimes called medium light—is for plants that require no sun but like light in about the 200 to 500 foot-candle range.

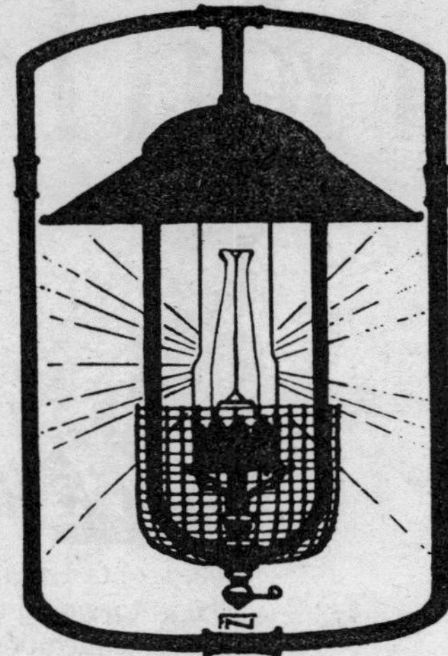

You would get this type of light intensity from east or west windows with thin curtains or where their light is partially obstructed by vegetation or buildings. Light from a southern window could also be reduced to these amounts eight or ten feet into the interior of a room. If you put plants about four or five feet into a room with east-facing or west-facing windows, or to either side of such windows, they would also get light in these ranges. North-facing windows, if they get the fullest amount of available light, will also yield this intensity.

Such light intensity is easy to duplicate with artificial light, either by supplementing the daytime light or by lengthening the photoperiod.

Foliage plants such as schlefflera, dumb cane, and rubber plants will thrive at this light level.

DIM LIGHTS are low light levels that fall below 200 foot-candles.

While a plant placed in a north window might get 150 foot-candles, if the light is in any way obstructed or if the plants are placed to the sides of, or at a four- or five-foot distance from the window, you might get readings of only 75 foot-candles. Plants you place in the interiors of rooms—say ten feet away from east or west windows or twenty feet away from southern exposures—could also be getting only 100 to 75 foot-candles.

A few of the most tolerant species—such as aspidistra—will survive at light levels down to about 20 foot-candles (what you might get from a reading lamp). Other plants that normally prefer higher levels can be gradually accustomed to less light—see "Growing Plants in Dim Light." Most plants categorized as growing under dim light, however, prefer 75 to 100 foot-candles.

Pothos, English ivy, and many ferns will thrive at 50 to 200 foot-candles.

Light Duration

Luckily for gardeners, the intensity of the light is not as important to plants as the total number of foot-candles they are exposed to in a day. And plants do not distinguish between natural and artificial light. You can therefore supplement your natural light with artificial light.

One way to do this is to supplement the light your plant receives during the day. If you have a north window that does not provide sufficient light for a given plant, for example, you can add artificial lights to increase the amount of light the plant is getting.

More common is to increase the photoperiod—or the plant's day—by giving the plant artificial light before and/or after the natural daylight it gets. If your plant is getting some natural light from a north or west window, for instance, but this light is insufficient for its needs, you can add artificial light before dawn or after sunset. By figuring the amount of natural light it gets, you can add an appropriate number of hours of artificial light and bring it up to the total number of foot-candles it prefers.

And, of course, you can grow plants totally in artificial light—in dark corners, in closets, even under your bed—if you provide the proper amount of total foot-candles.

Artificial light need not be the same *intensity* as natural light—so long as the *duration* of light is sufficient to supply the plant's total foot-candles needs. For example, if a plant needs 12,000 foot-candles of light in a day, it will not insist on getting this by experiencing eight hours of sun and other bright light that averages out to this amount. It will be just as happy getting twelve hours of 1000 foot-candles.

Nonetheless, plants do have limits. The light you provide must to some extent approximate the rhythms of nature. Plants need hours in light to absorb food and then hours in darkness to circulate this food. So if a plant requires 6000 foot-candles of light, you can't force it to accept this total in a hour or to stay awake twenty-four hours to absorb it at only 250 foot-candles an hour. You have to reach a compromise. The most usual compromise acceptable to plants is to spread the light over a twelve to sixteen hour period, and in a few cases to eighteen hours.

Some plants—chrysanthemums, gardenias, kalenchoes, Christmas begonias, and poinsettia for example—are classified as *short-day* plants. These need only ten to thirteen hours of artificial light a day to bloom but like a rather long night.

At the opposite extreme are *long-day* plants—many annuals grown for spring flowering, dahlias, calceolaria, coreopsis, nasturtiums, and others—that require fourteen to eighteen hours of light to bloom, and therefore will make do with a shorter night.

The *intermediate* plants—roses, carnations, gesneriads, coleus, begonias, and geraniums—are those that are apt to flower at any season of the year. These will blossom in varying degrees of abundance whether they are exposed to 12, 14, 16, or 18 hours of light a day. African violets and other gesneriads do well with 14 to 16 hours of light.

When You Buy Light

Light intensity requirements vary from plant to plant. If you are growing plants under artificial light, you can easily figure (with the help of the light manufacturer) the intensity from the number of lamp watts per square foot of growing area.

Many houseplants, especially foliage plants, are considered *low-energy* growing plants. This means they require only about 15 lamp watts per square foot of growing area. Lights 12 to 15 inches above the plant tops should be sufficient.

High-energy growing plants, in constrast, require 20 lamp watts or more per square foot of growing area. This includes many flowering plants such as roses, carnations, and chrysanthemums, as well as many vegetable crops such as beans and tomtoes. Again, the light source should be 12 to 15 inches above the plant tops.

For germinating seeds and rooting cuttings, you will need 10 lamp watts per square foot of growing area. Here, however, the light should be no more than 6 to 8 inches above the soil or planting medium.

When you buy artificial light dispensers, such as Gro-Lux, Plant-Gro or other brands, the manufacturer specifies the wattage and will also give you tips on what plants to grow.

If you want to get technical about it, however, lamp manufacturers rate their lamps in lumens. If you divide the lumens by the input wattage of the lamp, you have a measure of the lamp's efficiency in terms of lumens per watt. Light striking leaves is measured in lumens per square foot or foot-candles.

Often these values are given in metric units. Under the metric system, light intensity is measured in lux (lx) or kilolux (klx). One lux is equivalent to a lumen per square meter. To convert foot-candles to lux, multiply by 10.764. Thus, 1,000 foot-candles equals 10,764 or 10.764 kilolux.

Types of Lamps

If you are going to buy a light, you have a choice of fluorescent, incandescent, and high-intensity discharge (HID) lamps. Fluorescent lights are by far the best for indoor light gardens.

High-intensity discharge lamps include mercury, sodium, xenon, and metal halide lamps. Perhaps in the future they will gain more widespread acceptance for horticultural use. They are very efficient, have a long life, and give a good spectral quality. However, the temperature of the bulbs is high, so you have to keep them at a greater distance from the plants. Fluorescent lamps, being cooler, can be installed in nooks and crannies in close proximity to your plants. Another disadvantage is that HID lamps tend to be expensive and require special equipment and knowledge for proper installation and use.

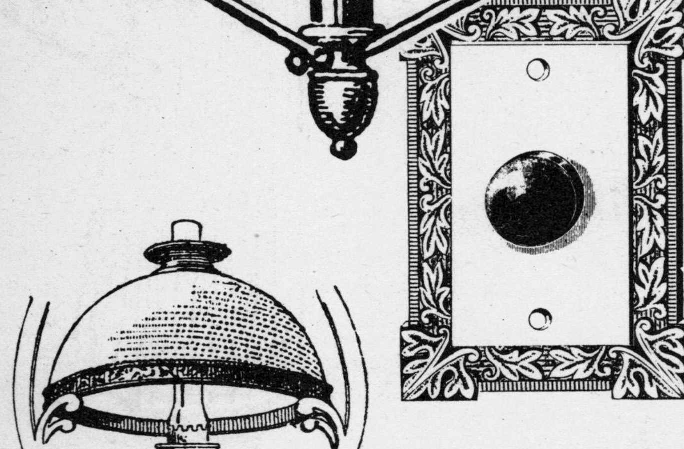

Incandescent lamps are inexpensive and easy to install. However, they have a low efficiency and emit most energy in the red region of the spectrum. Fluorescents are preferred for their wider spectral qualities. Incandescent bulbs also have a short operating life (only about a thousand hours) so will burn out quickly if you keep them on long enough daily to satisfy plant needs. Worst of all, incandescent bulbs are hot. They will dry out the plant and soil, and eat up the moisture in the air that most plants need. This heat, if the lamps are placed close enough to the plants to provide proper light, can burn foliage. Due to these facts you are restricted in the types of plants you can grow under incandescent light, and these lamps do not provide sufficient intensity for flowering plants. Nonetheless, incandescents do have some uses for the indoor gardener.

Incandescent Light The light you read by can serve the double purpose of revitalizing a plant that isn't receiving quite enough light over at the window. A 60- to 150-watt bulb shone on a light-starved plant for six to eight hours every evening can be a stylish as well as practical solution to a horticultural dilemma. Any ordinary table lamp will do the trick as long as you place your plant within the circle of the lamp's brightest light. But feel the leaves to be sure they are not becoming warm.

Incandescent light, per watt of energy required, is far less efficient than fluorescent light. And less efficient means more expensive. Incandescent bulbs are best used to supplement natural light, particularly around large indoor specimens, and to illustrate your favorite plants at night.

If a table lamp or other incandescent fixture is your plant's only source of light, you'll need to burn the light about 16 hours per day. (To ensure a uniform photoperiod, use an automatic timer.) Even then, you can grow only plants tolerant of dim light conditions because incandescents deliver only about 15 ot 20 foot-candles. For a low-light plant receiving some natural light during the day, six hours of additional illumination in the evening will promote new growth.

If you use a flood light either singly or in combination with other lights on a track, remember to place it as much as two to three feet away from the leaves. You can judge the correct distance by feeling the plant. When the leaves are warm to the touch, the light is too close.

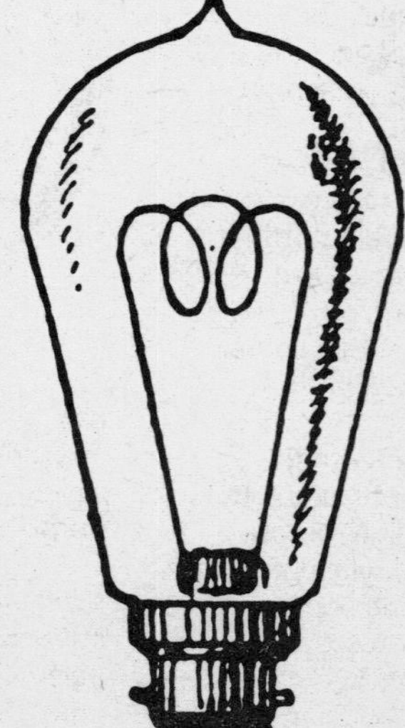

Like fluorescents, incandescent bulbs lose power as they age, and they should be replaced about halfway through their life span (about a thousand hours). Since they dry out the air in the room, you'll have to provide the moist atmosphere most plants need to thrive. To keep moisture levels up, consider investing in a cool-vapor room humidifier.

Incandescents are becoming more expensive as fossil fuels become rarer. Mercury-vapor reflector bulbs, which cost more up front, actually last twelve times longer than ordinary light bulbs. Their efficiency is also a big plus—a 175-watt mercury-vapor bulb produces as much usable light as 400 watts of incandescent lighting.

Because incandescents supply the far-red light that may be low in fluorescents, some gardeners like to use an incandescent lamp in combination with narrow-spectrum fluorescent tubes.

Fluorescent Lights Fluorescent lights are the least expensive and most widely used form of artificial light for gardening. They are widely available and easy to install, and have an average life of 7500 to 12,000 hours.

These lamps are available in a wide range of colors, and any type of fluorescent light pleasant to the eye enables plants to grow. Standard cool white light is suitable for most foliage plants, but flowering plants will not set buds and bloom. Flowering varieties require light energy from both the blue and red ends of the spectrum for buds to set, and an equal combination of cool white and warm white tubes provides verdant foliage and natural-looking color while being easy on the eyes. Special "growth" tubes are marketed specifically for horticultural purposes. These cost more than ordinary fluorescents, but provide a wider spectrum of color. Examples are the Gro-Lux lamps manufactured by Sylvania, and the Vita-Lite offered by Duro-Lite. General Electric, Westinghouse, and Verilux are other manufacturers.

Illumination in foot-candles at various distances from two or four 40-watt standard cool-white fluorescent lamps:

Distance from lamps (inches)	Two lamps (Used 200 hours)	Four lamps mounted 2 inches apart: Used 200 hours	Four lamps mounted 2 inches apart: New lamps
	Ft.c	Ft.c	Ft.c
1	1,100	1,600	1,800
2	860	1,400	1,600
3	680	1,300	1,400
4	570	1,100	1,300
5	500	940	1,150
6	420	820	1,000
7	360	720	900
8	330	660	830
9	300	600	780
10	280	560	720
11	260	510	660
12	240	480	600
18	130	320	420
24	100	190	260

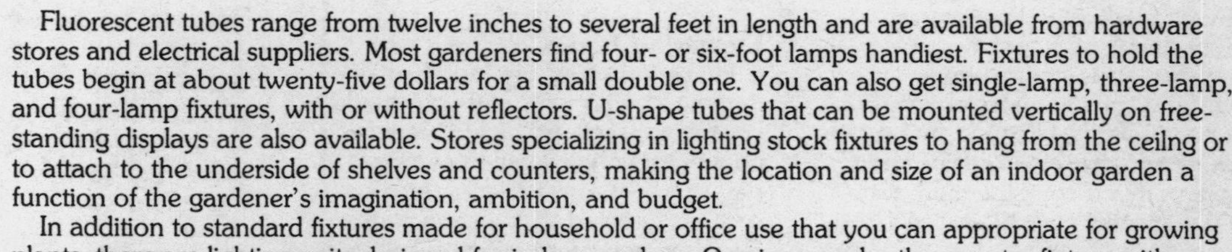

Fluorescent tubes range from twelve inches to several feet in length and are available from hardware stores and electrical suppliers. Most gardeners find four- or six-foot lamps handiest. Fixtures to hold the tubes begin at about twenty-five dollars for a small double one. You can also get single-lamp, three-lamp, and four-lamp fixtures, with or without reflectors. U-shape tubes that can be mounted vertically on free-standing displays are also available. Stores specializing in lighting stock fixtures to hang from the ceilng or to attach to the underside of shelves and counters, making the location and size of an indoor garden a function of the gardener's imagination, ambition, and budget.

In addition to standard fixtures made for household or office use that you can appropriate for growing plants, there are lighting units designed for indoor gardens. One is an under-the-counter fixture with a reflector for directing the light, a growth-light tube, and an electric plug. Tabletop units consisting of an adjustable fixture on legs are also practical, the size depending on the type and size of display desired. You can also get light-garden carts on wheels to move from one location to another. Self-contained units that include built-in waterproof trays for pebbles or wet sand are also available. Seed companies, such as Park, Harris, and Burpee, offer a selection of fixtures in their mail-order catalogues.

Fluorescent lamps are manufactured in different energy levels. This level is based on the electrical current used and is called "loading." For example, a standard 48-inch fluorescent tube comes with three levels of loading: light loading, also known as the 40-watt lamp; medium loading, or a high-output lamp; and heavy loading, known as the 1500-milliampere (MA) lamp. These lamps are not interchangeable, and each requires a different types of lamp holder and ballast (electric current controller).

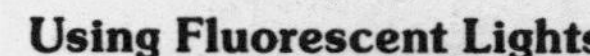

Using Fluorescent Lights

For growing most house plants, your lamps should probably provide 1500 to 2000 foot-candles. You can get this within a foot of 1500-MA lamps. If you are using 40-watt lamps, you would need to have the tubes about six inches apart and place the plants quite close to the tubes to obtain the same amount of foot-candles.

In general, flowering plants and vegetables need more light than do foliage plants. For plants requiring less light, or for combining natural and artificial light, see the discussion of light intensities, above. For light requirements of seeds and cuttings, see "Propagation" on page 132.

For the most part, lighting units should be switched on for fourteen to sixteen hours per day. (More specific information for special varieties is given below.) Rather than rely on memory, attach a 24-hour automatic timer and set it to go on at 6 A.M. and off at 8 or 10 P.M. If you don't have a timer, and forget to turn the plant lights off at night, your flowering plants may fail to bloom.

How far should plants be from the light source? In general, about six to ten inches, but again more details are given below. Having reflective surfaces, such as white walls or mirrors, around your light garden will help you achieve more uniform lighting.

If your plants are becoming leggy, they are too far from the light source or the lamps are becoming dim with age.

If your plant leaves curl, the foliage is too close to the fluorescent tube.

Plants to Grow Under Lights

The intensity of the light level you establish will limit the types of plants you can keep under a fluorescent unit. This is true whether you are using overhead or vertical tubes.

If you want to grow sun-loving plants in the same location, those needing the least light should be placed at either end of the overhead tubes or farthest away from a vertical source of light.

If all your plants need the same light intensity, you won't be able to grow plants of different heights together under an overhead fixture. If you do want to mix tall and tiny plants together in one display, you would have to set the small ones on inverted pots or other pedestals. Vertical fixtures are another solution.

Tall plants are difficult to grow under overhead fluorescent fixtures, because they tend to get too much light on top. This leads to huge crowns and spindly undergrowth. For such plants, vertical fixtures are best.

You cannot get blooms from short-day plants if you combine them with long-day plants in a light garden timed for only eight hours of darkness. Short-day, long-night flowering plants need their own, specially timed garden.

Foliage Plants

Most of the common foliage plants—such as peperomia, philodendron, and ivies—require 14 to 16 hours of fluorescent light a day. They will flourish between six and twelve inches from the tubes. Many of these can also be grown under incandescent light, but they should be 18 to 24 inches away from the light bulbs.

Fern foliage is susceptible to burn and should be a good eight to twelve inches from the light source.

Most kitchen herbs should be placed about Six inches from the light.

Flowering Plants

Flowering plants are more variable in their requirements and you should consult the section "Light Duration," above, for an explanation of long-day and short-day varieties. Also see sections devoted to flowering plants for additional information on culture.

Many flowering plants will bloom if you give them light 14 or 15 hours a day and place them six to ten inches away from the light source. But you may have to experiment a bit to achieve the perfect distance and light duration. Most orchids, for instance, will thrive on only 14 hours of light. Depending on the type, they should be put between four and eight inches from the light. Cacti and succulents generally like a bit more light—say 15 ot 16 hours—and they like to be closer to the light. Six inches away is good for many, but opuntia, golden barrel, and others like to be only four inches away.

Vegetables

You can grow salad crops, tomatoes, and dwarf varieties of a number of vegetables in indoor light gardens. In general, they require about 14 to 16 hours of light a day and can be placed a foot or so away from the light source, but for complete success you should get more specific instructions on the variety you plan to grow.

Tips for Light Gardeners

1. It is convenient to put your plant's fluorescent lights on a switch separate from that of your regular lights. That way you won't waste electricity if you are not using the room.

2. An automatic timer is so handy most indoor gardeners find it indispensable. It will turn your plant lights on and off as required, even if you are away. It also saves you having to remember to turn them on and off when you are home.

3. Where possible, to save electricity, locate your light garden so that it can also take advantage of natural light.

4. A disadvantage of fluorescent lights is that their light becomes dimmer as they age. The life of the lamp may be up to 12,000 hours, but by the time it has been used 8000 hours it may be giving only half its original light.

One way to overcome this is to move plants closer to the fluorescent tubes as the tubes age.

Another way is to replace the tubes. For standard lamps of 400-500 milliamperes (MA), this will be within one or two years of 15 hours of daily operation. For 1500-MA lamps, which provide extra intense light, yearly replacement is recommended.

If you have a number of fluorescent plant displays, or a great many tubes, you could sequentially replace some of the tubes on a fixed schedule.

5. Although fluorescent tubes generate less heat than other types of lamps, they do generate some (especially at the ballast). If your rooms are warm to begin with, you may not be able to grow plants that prefer cool conditions.

6. With artificial lighting, your plants will be getting optimum light. They will probably therefore need more water than those grown in natural light.

7. Heat from artificial light can create problems with providing sufficient humidity. Using pebble trays, buying a humidifier, or other measures to increase air moisture may be necessary.

8. Though light gardens are handy for brightening dark corners, be wary of lack of ventilation in such corners. Plants requiring good air circulation may not thrive.

9. If possible, save on electric bills by using your lights for more than one purpose. Fluorescent light for plants may be enough to light a room for most uses. An incandescent lamp you read by can be used simultaneously to provide light for a plant.

10. Artificial light does not fall the same way natural light does. Therefore, reflective surfaces all around your plants, or as much as you can achieve, are important to insure even light distribution. The use of mirrors, white-painted walls, and other reflective devices, useful for all indoor plants, are even more important for those grown under artificial light.

SUPPLIERS

Garden supply centers and lighting stores sell plant lights manufactured by General Electric, Westinghouse, Verilux, and Duro-Lite. The stores in your area may have what you require. If not, these concerns supply indoor lighting equipment:

Floralite Company, 4124 Oakwood Rd., Oak Creek, WI 53154
The Green House, 9515 Flower Street, Bellflower, CA 90706
Indoor Gardening Supplies, Box 40567, Detroit, MI 48240
Shoplite Company, 566 Franklin Ave., Nutley, NJ 07110
Marko, 94 Porete Ave., North Arlington, NJ 07032 (waterproof garden trays for wall mountings: wall-mounting fixtures with Para-Wedge louver shielding that concentrates light on plants and eliminates glare)
Plant-Lite Furniture Inc., 2195 Elizabeth Ave., Rahway, NJ 07065 (several models of elegant electrified plant stands, in contemporary, traditional, early American, and Danish modern design)
Earthway Products, Inc., Dept 9 HPLR, Box 547, Maple St., Bristol, IN 46507

For More Information

The Complete Book of Houseplants under Lights by Charles Marden Fitch (New York: Hawthorne Books, 1975).

Plants Are a Turn-On

Developed in the 1970s by Dr. Bing Chiang and Dr. Alfred Hoyte at Howard University, Viva Switch enables you to light up a room by touching the leaves of a plant. It consists of a small black box with a socket that you plug into the wall and a wire tipped with metal probes that you insert into the soil of a plant. When you touch the plant you conduct electromagnetic waves from the air through your body. These waves continue to flow through the plant fluids to the probes and on to the switchbox. The three integrated circuits in the switchbox analyze the signal and, according to the number of touches, a light plugged into the switch box turns on or off. Viva Switch, P.O. Box 552, Beltsville, MD 20705.

5
Indoor/Outdoor Plants

Succulents and Cactus

Succulents and cacti are fascinating plants whose one common characteristic—the ability to store water and nutrition in their leaves and stems—has allowed them to propagate in a wide range of climates around the world and take an incredible variety of shapes and forms. Because they survive long droughts, they are hardy—perfect for busy households—and seem to thrive on lack of water and care. Most succulents have a thick, tough skin that makes them invulnerable to insects. Some skins are covered with fine hairs, some with long dangerous spines; others are waxy. Leaves, or in the case of many cacti, ribs, usually have a symmetrical form that lends itself to beautiful intricate patterns. Many species have all-green leaves, though these greens go anywhere from a light gray-green to a deep dark green. Other species have leaves brightly marked with crimson, yellow, or pink. Succulent flowers come in many sizes and colors, from minuscule to brilliant orchidlike individuals reaching diameters of more than twelve inches. Certain succulents have flowers with very dry petals (like rice paper) that last for months.

Strictly speaking, there is no *difference* between succulents and cacti. Succulents exist in some thirty different plant families—the cactus family being only one. Although most cacti have spines and most other succulents don't, there are exceptions, such as the agave and aloe families of spiny succulents. Cactus is always succulent, but succulent doesn't always mean cactus.

Succulents exist in deserts the world over, but can also be found growing in high mountains with cold seasonal changes, hanging from tall trees in rain forests, and living near lakes and seashores in semiarid regions. The cactus family lives in the Americas, as well as in the West Indies, subarctic regions of Canada, Chile, and Patagonia. The broadest range of cacti exists in Mexico, but they thrive from the deserts of the Southwest to the high plains of Argentina, Peru, and Bolivia.

Succulents make excellent house plants. Nearly all species can be grown outside year-round in warmer climates such as southern California or Florida. But no matter where you live, the following list includes several succulents and cacti you can grow with great success.

—SUCCOTRINE ALOE.

ABROMEITIELLA have thick, spiny green leaves that grow in dense clumps 3 to 4 feet in diameter—making it an almost exclusively outdoor plant. Two-inch-long green or yellow cylindrical flowers appear at the ends of leaf clusters in summer. With a temperature range of 25° to 95°, this plant prefers direct sunlight and requires little water.

ACANTHOCALYCIUM is a small plant perfectly suited to potting either indoors or out. At maturity reaching a diameter of 4 to 5 inches and a height of 8 inches, this prominently ribbed Argentine cactus has a pretty blue-green skin with thick, dark needles 1½ inches long. White, pink, or yellow funnel-shaped flowers are often more than 2 inches in size and appear in summer. Keep fairly dry in winter; water occasionally in summer. *A. glaucum* is so-named for its glaucous-blue skin color, and is beautiful even when not blooming. *A. violaceum* (violet sea urchin) is known for its unusual purple flowers.

AOENIUM include some of the most varied species of all succulents. Some are dense ground cover with rosettes packed together tightly. Others grow into large bushes with tall stems topped with individual broad rosettes. Colors range from lime green to jade green fringed in maroon to a solid wine. Flowers are small, but beautiful for their number and the drama with which they appear—usually as bright yellow bunches at the ends of protruding stems. Easy to grow, they do well in an average gritty soil, but need regular watering and a mixture of direct sunlight and shade. *A. arboreum* grows into rather a large bush with 16-inch rosettes reaching 3 feet in height; it is best for the garden, but its long-stemmed flower, when cut, will last for up to 3 weeks. *A. lindleyi* and *A. tabuliforme* are lower-growing and bloom in summer, while *A. haworthii* flowers in spring.

—AMERICAN ALOE

AGAVE come in much variety of size, shape, and color. At maturity growing anywhere from 3 inches to 8 feet, some are fine indoor plants, while others are striking garden specimens. They usually are a full plant with short stems and thick triangular leaves that often have sharp spines. The color range includes gray-green, blue, and dark green, line-marked with white or yellow. An excellent beginner's plant, agave needs plenty of water and liberal fertilization in growing season. White or yellow flowers appear only once in the life cycle. *A. americana marginata* rosettes reach 5 feet in diameter and are deep green, edged with bright yellow. *A. victoriae-reginae* is a compact 10-inch avocado-green rosette, perfect for indoors.

ALOE are also diverse. Foliage is often comprised of soft but thick triangular leaves, sometimes spotted and sharply spined. They range from dish gardens miniatures to specimens for big tubs. Miniature columnar flowers 1- to 1¼-inch long are lifted above rosettes by stems. Colors are pale green to white and yellow. Generally, they grow easily with good drainage and sandy soil, and regular watering, but overwatering is fatal. Light requirements vary with species, so check your plant's needs when you buy it. *A. barbadensis* have green leaves whose juice soothes minor burns. *A. ferox* is popular for its spear-shaped green leaves fringed with red. *A. brevifolia* is smaller, stemless, good indoors.

APOROCACTUS send out many long tendrils that hang to lengths up to 6 feet and turn from green to brown as they mature. They make excellent hanging plants, requiring a rich soil and partial shade. Red to pink cone-shaped flowers are 2 to 3 inches and appear along the entire length of hanging tendrils. Frost is fatal.

ARIOCARPUS is a stout-looking plant, orbicular in shape, with jagged though nearly spineless leaves. Its diameter ranges from 6 to 10 inches. This stubborn cactus loves cramped quarters, sandy soil, scant water. Beautiful pink, purple, and yellow flowers appear from 1½ to 3 inches in autumn. *A. fissuratus* show magenta flowers, while *A. retusus* and *A. trignonus* (the biggest species) have white, rose, or cream blooms.

ASTROPHYTUM are bulbous, globular cacti that grow anywhere from 6 inches to 3 feet high and are most commonly spineless. Often looking like a bald head with protuberant ribs, this pulpy plant usually has gray-green skin. One- to four-inch yellow flowers come out on top of the plant in spring. The plants grow best in sandy soil kept fairly dry. *A. myriostigma* (bishop's cap) is especially interesting and good indoors.

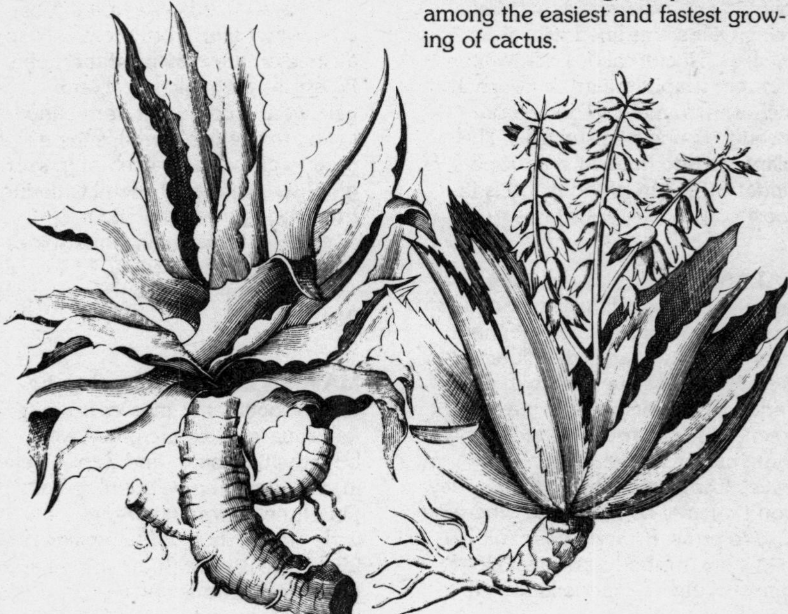

BEAUCARNEA are among the largest succulents, reaching 20 feet at maturity. They are not unlike weeping willow trees in appearance, except for their trunk bases, which eventually become huge tubers. Long, chalky-green leaves dangle from the high stooping limbs. Flowers are insignificant and only appear after several years. Despite their possible size, they make good houseplants when given plenty of room for their branches. They need rich soil, regular watering, undersized pots.

BORZICACTUS grow in multi-columnar form to a height of 3 feet, and look something like miniature waxy-green organ pipes. Spines and flowers vary greatly according to species. *B. trollii* (Old-man-of-the-mountains) is covered with long thin spines that give the appearance of bushy gray hair. Hardy plants, these require little water and sandy soil.

BOWEIA roots are made up of potatolike bulbs that rest on top of the soil and reach a length of 6 inches. Out of these bulbs grow thin brown branching stems that turn into a tangle of green hairlike tentacles. This African tropical needs water and fertilizer during growing season, but rests in winter. White one-inch blooms are abundant in fall. A good indoor plant, it will climb, so needs to be staked.

CEPHALOCEREUS stand in groups of columns 8 to 10 inches in diameter and reach heights of up to 10 feet. Yellow fuzz and thick spines run along the edges of the deeply ribbed, chalky-green bodies. Small, red to white cone-shaped flowers are produced on column tops, but don't appear until the plant is 15 to 20 years old. Flowers are nocturnal. This South American cactus has a temperature range of 35° to 100° and makes a good windowsill specimen while young.

CEREUS are deeply ribbed, knotty, columnar plants that branch out and up to 20 feet. Their hard, thick skin comes in a variety of hues between blue, green, and gray. Sharp one-inch spines radiate from each nodule. Six- to eight-inch white trumpet-shaped flowers are borne along the lengths of the columns. Blooms are nocturnal and appear in summer. The size can be controlled by undersized potting. With rich soil and moderate watering, this plant is among the easiest and fastest growing of cactus.

CEROPEGIA have many long thin leaf-covered stems that either hang or climb to more than 10 feet. Small heart-shaped leaves are usually silver-green and seem to be lightly powdered. Requiring a rich soil and slightly more water than most succulents, ceropegia make excellent hanging plants, indoor or out. Small black flowers appear in summer, spring, and fall.

CHAMAECEREUS. Imagine masses of stubby fingers cramped together, delicately ribbed and spined, that can become 6 inches long and a half inch in diameter. Long-lasting daisylike flowers are usually brilliant red and come out in summer. Shallow dishes and scant water are best.

CISSUS are mainly comprised of a disproportionately large caudex at their base, which looks like a huge gray yam. Gnarled stems grow out of the tops of these tubers and then branch into jagged-edged triangular leaves. *C. caudexes* can grow more than 10 feet, but usually stay under 24 inches. Bunches of small yellow flowers appear at stem ends in summer. *C. bainesii* (African tree grape) is particularly interesting, with hairy leaves.

CLEISTOCACTUS grow in groups of thin tubular stems that are approximately 3 inches in diameter and usually 2 to 3 feet high. Yellow spines that thickly cover the many-ribbed columns range from delicate and furry to sharp and needlelike. Bottoms of the columns are dark brown while the middles are green and tops yellow. Three- to four-inch cylindrical flowers are borne along the upper lengths of the columns in summer, and bloom in magenta, orange, and red. Cleistocactus grow well in pots and offer an interesting vertical dimension to the indoor garden. They prefer direct sun and scant watering.

COCHEMIEA are individual columnar cacti, commonly 2 to 5 inches in diameter and sometimes up to 6 feet. The avocado-green skin has lumpy tubercles that radiate thin, sharp spines. The upper halves of the columns bear brilliant red tubular flowers in spring and summer.

CORYPHANTHA are usually small globular or pear-shaped cacti, but size and shape vary greatly. They can grow as individuals and in clusters. The dull green skin is covered with variously sized nodules, at the tips of which radiate dark brown spines. Beautiful large flowers, from spring through summer, range from yellow to purple, white to pink. They make excellent windowsill or outdoor specimens, preferring direct sun.

CATYLEDON grow with great diversity of size and shape. Generally they have very fat succulent leaves in tight clusters and short scaly gray stems. Leaves range in color from apple-green tipped with maroon spots to glaucous-blue and gray, and are often covered with velvety hairs. Long brittle stalks extending above leaf clusters bear orange funnelform blooms in spring and summer. Rich soil and bright light bring out colors best.

CRASSULA are perhaps best known for the species commonly called "jade plant." But they come in myriad form, most of which offer beautiful and interesting patterned designs. Crassula plants usually have big thick succulent leaves that lie closely together and give a symmetrical appearance. The stems, covered with leaves, are most often unseen. Leaves are waxy and thick, and range from forest green to pale green and cream with a red rim. Red, yellow, and orange flowers appear on stalks that rise above the plant during spring and summer. Crassula are rugged, able to tolerate considerable lack of light and water. *C. argentea* (jade tree, baby jade) is the most popular, very easy to grow. *C. lycopodioides* (rattail crassula) is a mossy variety that likes to hang. *C. teres* (rattlesnake) is an almost sculptural specimen.

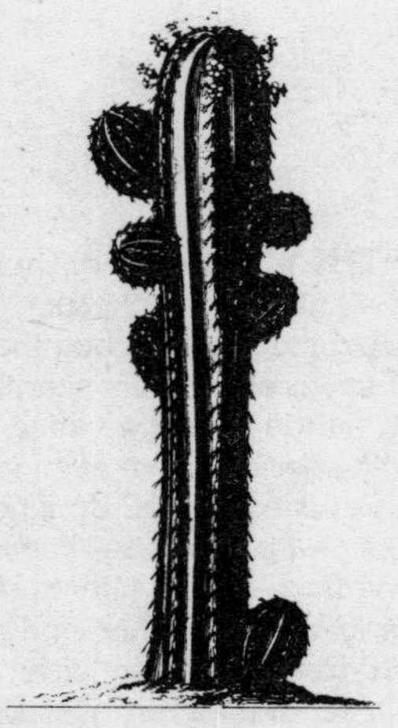

CYCAS often look much like stunted palm trees, except for their long spearlike leaves. Short, dark-brown trunks have a scaly appearance. They vary in size, but are usually about 2 feet wide and 3 feet high. Leaves range from chalky green to avocado green. Rather than flower, this plant bears a yellow cone. Equally good indoors and out. *C. revoluta* (sago palm) is a good bonsai specimen.

DIPLOCYATHA grow in clusters of knotty, fingerlike stems that seldom exceed 3 inches in length. This South African native is equipped with small spines, and its skin hue ranges between blue and green. Its menacing appearance is mitigated by the beautiful summer blooming of a bright cream-and-wine star-shaped flower. Diplocyatha thrive in an especially lean, gritty soil, seldom require watering, love neglect, and make good windowsill specimens.

DUOLEYA. Large symmetrical rosettes, either individual or in clumps, stand atop thick scaly stems. Rosettes reach a diameter of up to 1½ feet. Stiff, lance-shaped leaves are silver-gray and light green, and seem to be lightly powdered. Small star-shaped flowers from early spring to summer range from white to yellow to orange.

DYCKIA are stemless succulents whose long bowing leaves radiate from a central clump to give a fountainlike appearance. Leaves are usually barbed with long soft spines, light green to maroon, but often covered with a glaucous powder that makes them a silvery blue-green. In spring, slender stalks bloom with clusters of red, orange, and yellow flowers. Not recommended for indoors.

ECHEVERIA has a common element in the rosette form, but some have tightly clustered teardrop-shaped leaves that are fat and succulent; other leaves are thin and broad, with strangely irregular lines. The stems are usually short, so that rosettes grow close to the ground. Velvety hairs that cover some species lend a luminosity to the color range, which includes pink, silver-blue, apple green tinged with blood color, and maroon. Red, pink, or orange flowers appear in fall, spring, or summer. Echeverias like rich soil and generous watering. *E. agavoides* have pulpy green leaves fringed with red. *E. "Black Prince"* is a hybrid with maroon leaves. *E. elegans* (Mexican gem) has opalescent green leaves and yellow-tipped rose flowers.

ECHINOCACTUS, "barrel cactus," a rugged native of Texas and Mexico, is either stoutly cylindrical or pumpkin-shaped. Globes may reach 3 feet in diameter. Apple-green skin has ribs lined with dangerous yellow spines. Rose to yellowish funnelform flowers come out in summer. Put them in bright light and dry soil out between waterings.

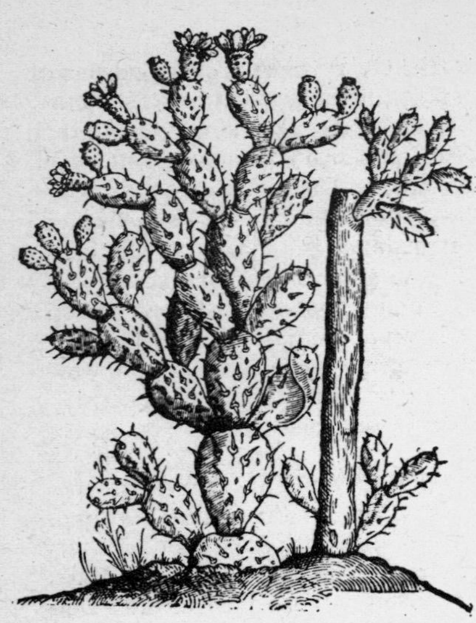

ECHIOCEREUS grow in clumps of small (2″ to 4″ thick) tubular stems that go to heights of 2 feet. The dark-green skin is finely ribbed and has bright-white bristles, but spine patterns vary with species. Bell-shaped summer flowers range from 1 to 5 inches, and deep violet to pink and yellow. Let their sandy soil get dry between waterings, and give them plenty of light.

ECHINOPSIS, "sea urchin cactus," are plump columnars that grow in clusters of 4 to 16 inches. Bodies are green with white and yellow bristles. Eight-inch trumpet-shaped flowers, borne in summer, are long-lasting. Blooms come in pink and white. Easy to grow. Give bright light, scant water, and a cramped pot.

EPITHELANTHA grow in clusters of what look like finely bristled mushrooms. They rarely go beyond a height of 4 inches. The light-green bodies combine with bright-white spines to give a velvety white appearance. Tiny white and rose flowers sprinkle the tops of stems from spring through fall. They like sun, but cannot stand full sun always. They are good dish plants for windows.

ESCOBARIA are thick, clustered columns with white and yellow spines. Their ribbed and often hairy-topped columns reach 8 feet. Horn-shaped flowers appear in white and pink through spring and summer. These are best grown outdoors, preferring direct sun, very gritty soil, and very scant water.

ESPOSTOA are clustered tubular cacti to 18 feet. The branching stems are covered with yellow spines and are an overall yellow-green color. Two-inch trumpet-shaped blooms are nocturnal and white. This plant does best outdoors, but will grow in pots.

FEROCACTUS. Like its big brother the barrel cactus, orbicular in shape, this cactus has a diameter of 8 inches. Each solitary globe has 10 to 20 ribs armed with spiderlike spines, which range widely in length (½″ to 2″) and color (white, yellow, and red). Yellow and magenta flowers go to 3 inches, and appear in summer only after the plant is several years old. This slow-grower does especially well in pots or dishes. *F. latispinus* (devil's tongue) has red spines and flowers. *F. wislizenii* (fishhook cactus) has orange flowers and long, hooked spines.

FRAILEA grow in clusters or orbicular stems; these clusters reach an equal diameter and height of 2 feet. The lime-green bodies are ribbed with stellar spine clusters ranging from light brown to yellow. The shy flower is only coaxed out by the hottest sun, and even then it rarely opens. A good window specimen; needs good sun and scant water.

GASTERIA. The stemless rosettes are made up of pulpy triangular leaves and grow in clumps low to the ground. The leaves are mottled green with white markings, and grow 1½ inches wide and 18 inches long. A tall drooping stem above the plant yields arching tubular flowers 1 inch to 2 inches long. Blooms are brick- to blood-colored and appear in summer. Like the ox's tongue these plants are commonly named after, gasteria like shade and plenty of water.

GYMNOCALYCIUM grows in an orbicular column to approximately 12 inches. Yellow spine clusters emerge from tubercles that cover the plant. The older, bottom part of the plant is brown, while the upper half is apple green. Small white, pink, and magenta blooms pop up in spring and summer and are long-lasting. Spare, gritty soil suits this cactus. Dry out between waterings. *G. denudatum* (spider cactus) has light pink and white flowers.

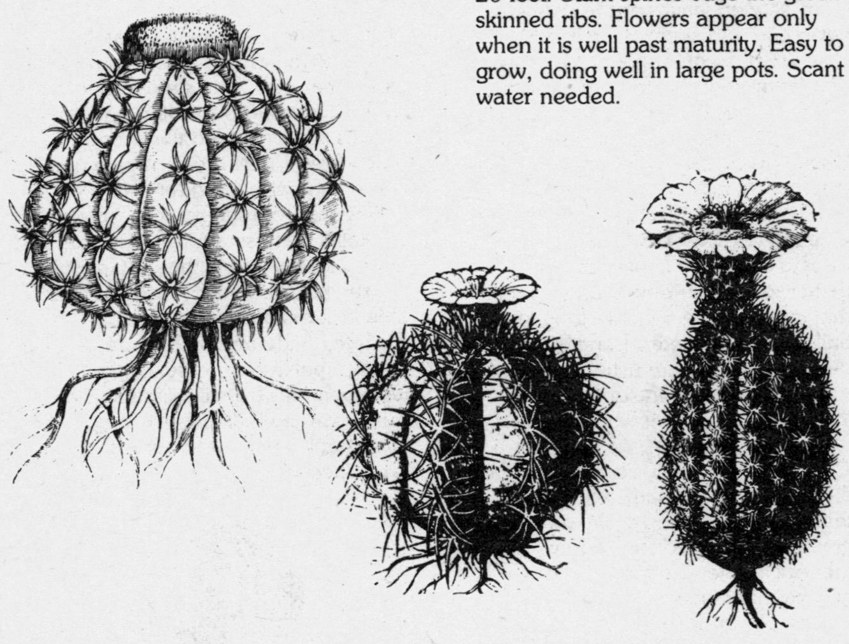

HAWORTHIA, often a very short-stemmed plant, have thick, succulent-leafed rosettes that hug the ground. Leaves are usually sharply triangular, although shape varies greatly with species, some even looking like clusters of stacked dominoes. Leaf colors and patterns are beautiful, ranging from bone white, to deep greens, gray, maroon, blue, and purple-brown. Relatively insignificant flowers cluster at the ends of stalks and bloom intermittently the year round. Generally easy to grow, especially in shade, they need more water in summer than the rest of the year. Foliage that dies as the plant matures should be stripped away. Excellent windowsill and bonsai specimens. *H. attenuata* have dark-green leaves with white markings. *H. limifolia* (fairy's washboard) are green with brown ribs. *H. truncata* look like stacks of slate-colored dominoes.

HOYA grows as a twining ivy, into small shrubs. The green leaves are waxy and teardrop-shaped. Wonderful symmetrical clusters of small, starlike blooms are white, yellow, red, or violet with brown markings. Flowers must remain on plant in order to reproduce themselves. Moderately rich soil and plenty of shade suit Hoya. *H. bella* is an ideal hanging plant.

HYLOCEREUS are either a high-climbing or low-hanging vinelike cacti, with stems lined with short prickles. Nocturnal flowers, white trumpet-shaped beauties, reach 15 inches in diameter. They bloom through spring and summer. This plant loves to hang in shady spots. *H. undatus* (queen of the night) is the most common species.

KALANCHOE stems are thick and branch crookedly into big triangular leaves that look like lifted elephant ears. The leaves are often fluted at the edges and have velvety hairs. Varied leaf colors include gray, green, blue, bronze, and red. Flowers come out on thin stalks above the leaves from spring through fall. They won't tolerate cold, but are otherwise easy to grow. *K. beharensis* (old man's hat) embody essential elements of the kalanchoe kind.

LEMAIREOCEREUS are a deeply ribbed columnar cacti that grow in clusters or individually to heights of 20 feet. Stark spines edge the green-skinned ribs. Flowers appear only when it is well past maturity. Easy to grow, doing well in large pots. Scant water needed.

LEUCHTENBERGIA grow in clusters of spiny orbs to approximately 2 feet. Young plants are apple green, turning browner with age. Three or four years of growth are required before yellow horn-shaped flowers are produced. They like a dry, hot culture, and are a good specimen for medium-sized pots.

LOBIVIA is a small orbicular cactus that grows either individually or in low clumps. The green body is finely ribbed with soft starlike prickles. Brilliant flowers that resemble a cross between a daisy and a chrysanthemum. Blossom colors range within a spectrum of pinks, yellows, peaches, and creams. Gritty, dry soil is best.

MAMMILLARIA are usually either globular or columnar, but great diversity abounds in the species' varying colors, sizes, and habits of growth. Some are tall slender columns that grow in tightly packed groups to 7 and 8 feet. Others are small (3″) globes that crawl low to the ground in great numbers. The southwestern United States and Mexico host huge camps of these spiny devils. Mammillaria flowers are produced in a way dissimilar from most other cacti. Blooms appear between the tubercles, rather than from them, and form a circle on the crowns of the stems. Blossoms are pink, white, and yellow, and come out from early spring to late fall. Perhaps the easiest cacti to grow, these do best in spare, gritty soil with fairly liberal watering from spring through early fall. *M. compressa* have small white spines and are a smaller variety. *M. zeilmanniana* (rose pincushion) have purple flowers.

MAMMILLOPSIS. Small globes cluster together in masses up to 6 feet square. Orbs are green with bright-white spines and 2 to 3 inches in diameter. The beautiful red and pink funnelform flowers are 2 inches wide—very showy. Mammillopsis love crowds of each other, make good potted house plants. *M. senilis* have yellow and orange flowers.

MELOCACTUS are a beautiful melon-shaped cactus that can reach 18 inches in diameter and 3 feet in height. Protruberant ribs are finely shaped and dotted with spiderlike spine clusters. A crown of soft, furry spines sits atop the stem and is usually pink. The white, pink, or red flowers are borne from the cephalium in spring and summer. Put this plant in a shallow dish with very loose, gritty soil. Water less in summer and winter. *M. intortus* (turk's cap cactus) grows to 3 feet. *M. matanzanus* is a miniature, reaching 4 inches.

MYRTILLOCACTUS are comprised of branching oblong columns 8 to 12 inches in diameter that can reach a height of 20 feet. The pulpy, apple green bodies have vertical rows of softly rising tubercles. Stout black spines are spread out. The crowns wear nimbuses of small white flowers in spring and summer. A fine grower indoor or out.

NOTOCACTUS are orbicular while young, but become columnar with age, finally reaching a height up to 12 inches. Bristles on the green body are usually many and small, rendering a furry appearance. Other species have thick yellow spines. Red and yellow flowers, produced at the tops of columns in summer, measure 1 to 3 inches in diameter. Notocactus are excellent for beginners. They like shallow dishes and do well indoors.

OPUNTIA are usually comprised of flat oval succulent pads, approximately 1-inch thick and up to 12 inches in diameter, that joint and branch crookedly into large tangled patches 4 to 5 feet high and more than 100 feet square. The paddlelike green pads are dotted with tufts of small furry spines. Some species have long thin stems to 4 feet, others are orbicular. Large funnelform flowers appear around edges of pads.

This rugged cactus withstands cold and is best for landscape; it won't bloom indoors. *O. basilaris* (beaver tail) is the most common species, with red flowers.

PACHYPHYTUM is made of many tightly packed plump succulent leaves that are almost exactly the size and shape of babies' toes. These baby-toe leaves take form in dainty little rosettes atop short stems. Skin colors are a beautiful mix of hues—blue, gray, pink, and green at once. Small bellform flowers in spring and summer. Optimal leaf colors are brought out by bright light, but not constant sun. They are beautiful hanging specimens. *P. "Blue Haze"* is a hybrid of bluish hues.

PACHYPODIUM. Stout tuberous stems branch up like extremely fat fingers. They are covered with thick thorns, and from their tips soft green leaves sprout. Leaf clusters look like small Japanese fans, and are deciduous. Two-inch spring blooms appear on the extremities of this Madagascaran-Angolan curiosity. They should not be watered once the leaves fall off—through winter. *P. windsorii* is best for bonsai. *P. lealii* is bigger, with stark spines and white flowers.

PARODIA is a small globular cactus that grows individually to heights of 10 inches. It becomes more cylindrical with age, its yellow-greenish body reaching only 3 inches in diameter. Symmetrically placed tubercles sprout yellow spines. Flowers appear on plant's crown in spring and summer. Requires a rich soil, good drainage, and regular watering year-round.

PELECYPHORA are small pale-green globes that grow solitarily in tight clusters. Maximum height is usually about 3 inches, while globe diameter ranges between one-half inch and 2 inches. Strange tubercles look like dill seeds lying in fine symmetrical formation. Very fine white spines cover the tubercles. Pelecyphora bear short tubular blooms around their crown, pink to purple, that remain from early spring through summer. Suited to window and bonsai gardens, these require gritty soil and scant water. *P. aselliformis* (hatchet cactus) are a larger species, reaching 4 inches high. *P. strobiliformis* go to only 1½ inches high and have red blooms.

PORTULACARIA becomes a thick bush, having a brownish-red trunk and stems. The small leaves are a green-and-white variegation. Older specimens show clusters of light rose-colored blooms. Easy to cultivate; do well in small pots in shade. *P. afra* (elephant bush) is the bigger variety.

REBUTIA grow in bulbous clusters of tiny globes that are approximately the size of marbles. They are either a whitish green or dark green, and have many minuscule tubercles and white prickles. Big beautiful daisylike flowers appear in abundance through summer, ranging from yellow to pink and purple. Perfect for the smallest windowsill garden; excellent for beginners. Keep in well-drained gritty soil and filtered sun. *R. deminuta* have orange-red flowers. *R. miniscula* (red crown) have magenta blooms.

RHIPSALIS have long, spindly tubular stems that branch out and joint to give the appearance of emaciated, bony hands, and that either climb or dangle to lengths of 3 feet. The stems are apple green and spineless. Flowers vary greatly in size, shape, and color, depending on species. Some are small, insignificant clusters, while others are large trumpet-shaped solitaires of white and red. Rhipsalis are tropical cacti, needing a rich soil and plenty of water. They require less water in winter. *R. burchelli* (mistletoe cactus) have rose-colored berries. *R. capilliformis* have cream-colored blooms. *R. paradoxa* have white flowers and red berries.

SCHLUMBERGERA are comprised of many flat, oblong leaflike pads about 2 inches long and 1 inch wide, usually deep green with waxy skin. Drooping stems radiate from a central point at the base, giving a fountainlike appearance. Bellform and brilliant red blooms appear in great numbers in winter. They are another tropical cacti, requiring rich soil and more water in winter than summer. They grow best in hanging pots, and do well indoors. *S. bridgesii* (Christmas cactus) is the most popular species, and perhaps the prettiest. *S. truncata* is similar to *S. bridgesii.*

SEDUM. The numerous species are incredibly diverse. Generally, they have small rosettes formed by clusters of tiny, plump, succulent leaves like babies' toes. Leaf colors range from green to bright oranes and yellows, the vividness depending on the amount of sun they get. Sedums yield tiny flower bunches on the ends of short stems. They are white, yellow, rose, and red. They are among the easiest succulents to grow, requiring plenty of water. *S. morganianum* (donkey's tail) is the best known variety, a hanging and hardy plant. *S. oxypetalum* is a shrub to 5 feet tall. *S. rubrotinctum* has green foliage that turns red in sun.

SELENICEREUS have tough hanging or climbing stems a half inch to 1½ inches thick that can grow to 12 feet. Stems are green while young and turn purple with age. They have aerial roots. Beautiful flowers can reach a diameter of 10 inches, and are borne the lengths of the stems in summer. They are nocturnal. These tropical cacti require plenty of water and make wonderful hanging specimens. *S. grandiflorus* (queen of the night) have ribbed stems and white flowers. *S. pteranthus* (princess of the night) have scented blooms.

SEMPERVIVUM are nearly stemless rosettes which cluster to form a beautifully patterned ground cover. Rosette leaves are sharply teardrop-shaped, with small pointed tips, usually deep green with red to maroon edges; but the red tinting depends on the amount of sun they get. Rosettes, rarely bigger than 3 inches in diameter, are covered with soft fuzz. Though flowers vary widely, they are usually small and appear on long stalks above the rosettes. Easy to grow, and one of the few succulents that are very winter hardy, they do well outdoors in cold climates. *S. arachnoideum* (cobweb houseleek) have smaller rosettes with red flowers. *S. tectorum* have bigger green rosettes with red-tipped leaves.

SENECIO is a many-specied genus, with long-stemmed and short-stemmed succulent rosette clusters that climb or creep; long, stringy stems that hang to great lengths; even big bushes. Leaves can be teardrop-shaped and fat, or flat or spherical, and may be a shiny dark green or a powdery gray-blue. The small flowers that cluster at stems' ends in summer—never exceeding 1-inch wide on any species—are white, yellow, or red. *S. rowleyanus* (string of pearls) looks just as its common name suggests—all green, however.

SETIECHINOPSIS grows in groups of fat fingerlike cylinders to heights of 6 inches. It is a deep green-brown, with many short fine prickles. Two-inch white flowers are produced in spring and summer. Do well in pots with scant water and gritty soil.

STAPELIA are best known for their strange flowers, which look very much like starfish in size (to 5" across), shape, and often in color. To attract the flies that pollinate them, the flowers give off a nasty carion odor, which usually makes them unwanted houseguests. The leafless stems are approximately 1-inch wide, and grow in clusters to 2 feet. They are persnickety growers, requiring a very gritty, loose soil, and careful watering attention. *S. hirsuta* (hairy toad plant) have yellow or brownish-violet blooms.

SULCOREBUTIA are similar to rebutia. Bulbous globes made up of many small spiny orbs, they rarely grow beyond 3 inches high or wide. Large (2") trumpet-shaped flowers, very delicate, range in color from a yellow-brown to red and bright orange. Easy to grow; perfect for the window garden.

THELOCACTUS are deeply tubercled orbs and columns that grow to 1 inch high. Stout needlelike spines arm this gray-green-bodied Mexican desert dweller. Daisylike flowers on the crown in spring range from pink to yellow. Pot in a very gritty soil, dry out between waterings.

TILLANDSIA. The long, thick triangular leaves of this tropical American epiphyte form large individual rosettes. These leaves can grow quite long (3'), and curl back from the stem with a seemingly wicked coquettishness. Foliage is usually a light, steel gray color with a silvery powder. A stalk produces groups of small flowers in a rainbow assortment of colors. Mount on a piece of wood or bark, and mist. They are slow growers. *T. ionantha* have smaller rosettes with green outer leaves and red inner leaves. *T. usneoides* (Spanish moss) are silvery gray with many-branching vines.

TRICHOCEREUS is a branching tubular cactus that can stand in reserved columnar form or creep to lengths of 30 feet and more. It is a deeply ribbed, dark-green specimen with sturdy spines, able to withstand 120°F to 25°F. Beautiful white flowers reach 8 inches in diameter. Good for landscape. *T. pachanoi* are erect. *T. spachianus* are lower and branching.

TURBINICARPUS, small disk-shaped cacti, grow in tiny clusters and have dark green bodies with irregularly placed tubercles. Spines are light brown, and some become long and hairlike with age. Flowers, large and daisylike, appear in late summer. These do best in small pots or dishes, and make ideal windowsill specimens.

Succulent and Cactus Favorites

Epiphylum: The huge, beautiful flowers of epiphylum, "orchid cactus," have made it the most popular genus of the cactus family. More than 3000 hybrids exist, with flowers of almost every color of the rainbow, up to 8 inches across. In their native habitat of the Central American tropics, their stems can grow up to 200 feet long. These flat stems, with scalloped edges and varying from light to dark green, give a waterfall effect in hanging baskets. Epiphylum are easy to grow; give filtered light, porous soil, a seemingly undersized pot, cool nights (about 50°F), and keep soil barely moist during winter rest. Plenty of sun and light aid flower production. These are good indoors or out.

Flowering stones: Native to the hottest, driest parts of South and East Africa, these plants have reduced their leaf area to an absolute minimum—flat, pulpy lobes that store water to survive long droughts. To disguise themselves from thirsty animals, they imitate the smooth, rounded stones among which they live. Among more than 20 diverse genera, *Conophytum* are first-class stone mimes; colors range from dark browns with marbling to light green, and the separation between the bulbous lobes is an almost indistinguishable cleft or dimple. *Lapidaria* are light green, seldom over an inch, and look like stones until they produce bright yellow, daisylike flowers in winter. *Lithops* are short, oval-topped columns that cluster as thick ground cover and range from gray to brown-pink; winter flowers are white to yellow. Pot in a mix of half sand and half soil, keep well drained, and don't water in cold or cloudy weather or in winter. They love to be cramped in small pots or dishes, prefer temperatures above 50° F, and thrive indoors or out.

Euphorbia has more than 1000 species so diverse that generalizations are impossible. Though they are not cacti, some look like cacti, with large spines; others have weird sculptural forms. *E. obesa* are brown, dry globes the size of basketballs, and *E. pulcherrima* is the Christmas poinsettia. Easy to grow, euphorbias live for years indoors or outdoors with little attention. Give them porous soil kept moderately moist all year, bright light or sun.

Sedum medium teretifolium.
Small Prickmadam.

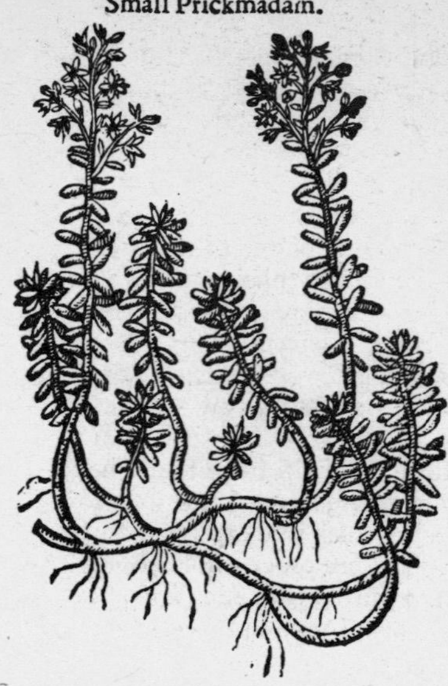

Ice plants stay low to the ground, creeping with soft finger-like succulent leaves that form small rosettes. Especially on slopes, they make good ground cover, and their fire-retardant quality makes them useful in arid areas where bush fires are a hazard. As a bonus, each rosette sports a bright flower in summer and spring; banks of blooming plants can sometimes be seen from miles away.

Most ice plants are native to coastal areas with moderate climates. When drought occurs, the plant gets its moisture from the sea air. Ice plants, however, will grow in most climates except those that are extremely hot or cold. Watering is necessary when an ice plant is grown in inland regions. Soil is almost never a problem; ice plants grow in almost anything but heavy clay. Most are best outdoors. The best for erosion control are: *Carpobrotus chilensis* (sea fig) and *C. edulis* (Hottentot fig) are best for gradual slopes; yellow and purple flowers. *Delosperma "Alba"* (white trailing ice plant) is good for flat expanses or steep slopes. Small white flowers. *Drosanthemum floribundum* and *D. hispidum* have smaller leaves that cling to the steepest cliffsides. Pink and purple flowers in spring and summer. *Lampranthus aurantiacus* (bushy ice plant)—grows in higher clumps, is best as a sidewalk border or on gradual slopes. *L. spectabilis* (trailing ice plant)—provides a thick ground cover, but is less attractive than other ice plants when not blooming. *Malephora crocea* (Croceum ice plant) and *M. luteola* (yellow trailing ice plant)—provide thick ground cover, with handsome appearance while not in bloom. *M. crocea* are better on slopes.

Sedum minus paluſtre.
Small water Sengreene.

Sedum maius arboreſcens.
Tree Houſleeke.

Sedum Portlandicum.
Portland Sengreene.

Culture

Temperature: The extreme temperature range of the group as a whole goes from 20°F to 120°F. No single species, however, has this range. As a general rule, succulents will grow well between 80°F and 40°F. With the exception of some the more exotic genera—such as edithcolea, melocactus, and pachypodium—most will survive down to 35°F.

Light: Most succulents require varying degrees of bright light or sun. Although most survive without full light, light deprivation often prevents flowering and/or fullest possible foliage coloration. Indoor succulents thrive under 2 to 4 flourescent bulbs 1½ to 2½ feet above the plant. Keep the lights on 4 to 5 hours a day.

Humidity: Many varieties will survive in anything from 35% to 75% humidity, while some of the tropical kinds need 60% and above. For tropical kinds indoors, misting helps; outdoors, keep them predominantly in shade.

Soil: Succulents and cacti usually grow best in a soil of 50% regular potting mix and 50% sand. The tropical varieties require a richer soil with humus, while many desert cacti thrive in a very lean, gritty soil of mostly sand, gypsum, and clay.

Watering: With all but tropical succulents and cacti, let the soil dry out between waterings. Most succulents, however, will tolerate some, if not constant, overwatering. Tropical succulents, and generally those with thinner leaves, require an evenly moist soil.

Troubleshooting: The worst thing for succulents is overpampering—overwatering, wiping or washing of leaves, excessive moving, etc. Simply follow the right recipe for your plant, and otherwise leave it alone. Only a few of the more delicate varieties are susceptible to insects such as aphids and mealybugs. Bugs stay deep between the leaves where they can't be seen. Look on the undersides of leaves, or watch for discolored blotches, or a generally unhealthy appearance of leaf or stem. Succulents and cacti are also sometimes susceptible to generally untreatable fungal and viral diseases. These are evidenced by dry blotches on leaves or scaling stems, and a general moribundity of leaves and rosette clusters. Cut away dead or dying leaves.

Propagation: Most succulents will propagate easily with cuttings.

Sources

Abbey Garden
176 Toro Canyon Rd.
Carpinteria, CA 93103

Arthur Eames Allgrove
No. Wilmington, MA 01887

Beahm's Epiphyllum Gardens
2686 Paloma St.
Pasadena, CA 91107

Cactus Gem Nursery
10092 Mann Drive
Cupertino, CA 95014

Cactus by Mueller
104011 Rosedale Hwy
Bakersfield, CA 93308

Desert Dan's
Nursery Seed Company
Minitola, NJ 08341

Desert Plant Company
Box 880
Marfa, TX 79843

Grigsby Cactus Gardens
2354 Bella Vista Drive
Vista, CA 92083

Grote's Cactus Gardens
13555 So. Leland Rd.
Oregon City, OR 97045

Ben Haines
1902 Lane
Topeka, KS 66604

Helen's Cactus
2205 Mirasol
Brownsville, TX 78520

Henrietta's Nursery
1345 North Brawley
Fresno, CA 93711

Intermountain Cactus
1478 North 750 East
Kaysville, UT 84037

Jessup's Cactus Nursery
P.O. Box 327
Aromas, CA 95004

K & L Cactus Nursery
1217 Stockton Blvd.
Galt, CA 95632

Kirkpatrick's Rare & Unusual Cactus
27785 De Anza St.
Barlow, CA 93211

Linda Goodman's Sun Plants
P.O. Box 20014
Riverside, CA 92516

MacPherson Gardens
2920 Starr Ave.
Oregon, OH 43616

Merry Gardens
Camden, ME 04843

Modlin's Cactus Gardens
2416 El Corto
Vista, CA 93083

Oakhill Gardens
Rt. 3, Box 87
Dallas, OR 97338

Rainbow Gardens
Box 721-Hi2i
La Habra, CA 90631

Scott's Valley Cactus
5311 Scotts Valley Drive
Scotts Valley, CA 95066

Ed Storms, Lithops
4233 Pershing
Fort Worth, TX 76107

Sturtevant's Cactus and Succulent Nursery
Arlington, OR 97812

The Succulent Safari
4793 State Rt. 82
Mantua, OH 44255

Walter's Exotic Plant House
RD 3, Box 30
Catskill, NY 12414

BROMELIADS

Bromeliads are fascinating plants—mostly from tropical America—that are cultivated as ornamentals because they require very little care and provide beautiful, long-lasting color. They are exotic-looking plants. The foliage is tough (too tough for most insects, so bromeliads are almost pest-free). Leaves, which may be spear-shaped or strap-like, jut up or out stiffly. A few species have all-green leaves, but often the foliage is striped or marked, and sometimes it is brightly colored. Flowers vary but are unusually showy. Some have stiff, waxy petals; some have a rounded brush-like effect. Other bromeliads have tiny, inconspicuous flowers on vivid bracts, or rigid, brilliant flower spikes that rise a foot or more above the plant. Flower spikes and berries often last for months.

Most bromeliads are air plants (epiphytes), so-called because in nature they do not root in soil but depend on larger plants and trees for support. Bromeliads are not, however, parasites, because they do not live off their host plants but manufacture their own food the way other green plants do, through photosynthesis. Since air plants do not root in the earth, their main problem is water—they cannot obtain moisture from the soil as other plants do. Most grow from rosettes that have developed "vases," or pockets in the foliage that retain water between rainfalls. As a result, they are often called "living vase" plants. Some species can go for long periods in drought, and though they dry up and look dead, they recuperate quickly with new rain. For bromeliads in your home to look their best, therefore, the main attention you have to give is to keep their vases filled with water. Because they do not root in soil, you don't have to worry about providing fertilizer or commercial nutriment, and because their leaves are too tough for bugs, you never have to wash or spray your bromeliads against insects. Many bromeliads can be planted outdoors in warmer climates such as in Florida or California.

Bromeliads come in wonderful variety. Some tiny species are excellent for terrariums or dish gardens. Larger types may be used singly in pots as table decorations or focal points elsewhere, or arranged in planters with other plants. And some grow large enough for tubs.

The bromeliad everyone knows is the pineapple, Ananas. The commercially grown variety has spiked green leaves, and you can grow this from the tops of fruits you buy in the grocery (see "Fun with Leftovers" on page 79). Other types of pineapple, with orange and reddish foliage, are available from garden suppliers. In summer these develop white or red bracts. Though these all like the bright light and the "vase" watering of other bromeliads, they should be potted in sandy soil.

More common than pineapple as household plants are the following bromeliads:

AECHMEA have glossy, stiff leaves of brilliant, variegated color. Most grow close to two feet, but *A. ramosa* spreads more than three feet. The long flower spikes bear tiny flowers hidden in the bracts, and the colorful berries last for months. Those that bloom in winter include *A. racinae*, with yellow, black, and red flowers, and *A. "Maginali,"* with beautiful red flowers followed by deep-blue berries. Spring bloomers include *A. fasciata*, with pink and blue flowers, while *A. ramosa* blooms in summer with red bracts and yellow flowers. *A. pubescens*, which blooms in the fall, has creamy-colored flowers followed by white berries.

BILLBERGIA have multihued green leaves, and various varieties produce one to three foot plants. These also have tiny flowers, which may be blue or in shades of red, and the bracts vary from rosy to brilliant red. Most bloom in summer, but *B. nutans* ("queen's tears"), a common variety from Brazil with blue-edged green petals and bright-red bracts, blooms in winter.

BROMELIA is one of the most compelling air plants. It has dark-green leaves, but it's called the volcano plant because the center turns brilliant red in bloom. The smallest variety grows at least two feet across, while the largest is well over four feet across, so these are not plants for small rooms. Also, their stiff spines require that you wear gloves or handle gingerly. These enjoy full sun, but also do well in lesser light.

CATOPSIS grows in soil (equal parts humus and potting soil) and sun, and produces spikes of yellow or yellow-and-white flowers.

CRYPTANTHUS, the starplants, have small, flattened rosettes, seldom growing more than a foot, and are therefore popular for dish gardens. All types bear fleshy white flowers, and species variation is in the beautifully colored leaves. These grow in rosettes, are often striped or marked, and vary from metallic browns to greens—often marked with silver. The leaves are stiff, with prickly margins. *C. bromeloides tricolor*, the rainbow-plant, has green, white, and red foliage. *C. zonatus* has long, crinkly, striped leaves.

DYCKIA, earth-star, has silver and green fleshy rosettes, often with prickles. These grow a foot or more, and produce orange or yellow flowers. *D. frigida* has leaves two feet long and two inches wide, but varieties with small (six-inch) leaves are available. These do well outdoors.

GUZMANIA rosettes, which can bear red or green foliage, are small and therefore favored for terrariums and dish gardens. They can, however, grow to about two feet. *G. berteroniana* has yellow flowers in spring, *G. zahnii* (red and white) and *G. lingulata* (orange-red) flower in summer, and others flower in fall. Bracts last three or four months.

HOHENBERGIA, from Jamica, has such tough, spiny leaves that you do best to wear gloves when handling this plant. These are large plants, their rosettes spreading 4 feet across, and their spikes of lavender flowers riding three feet or higher. They like full sun and will do well outdoors, too.

NEOREGLIA comes in foliage of varied color—dark-green, creamy, or striped, and *N. spectabilis* is called "painted fingernail" because the thin green leaves have bright-red tips. Although flowers are small, the rosettes, which can have three-foot spreads, turn red in the center when the plant blooms. *N. carolinae* blooms in the winter, other varieties in the summer, and blooms last several months.

PORTEA, when it blooms in summer or fall, has appealing flowers of pink and green. The dark-green rosette grows three feet across.

TILLANDSIA, with slender spear-like leaves that resemble palm foliage, usually has reddish or purplish flowers, but some plants bloom in orange or white. Smaller varieties, such as *T. ionanthe* which blooms in summer, are popular for terrariums and dish gardens. Larger species, such as the fall-blooming *T. cyanea*, have more than two-foot spreads. You can also choose between drooping or stiffly erect varieties. Unlike other bromeliads that do well in dimmer light, tillandsia requires full sun.

VRIESIA rosettes are leafy and softer looking than the foliage of most bromeliads. Leaves vary from light green to dark green, and some varieties have leaves banded with brownish markings. These plants are called "flaming sword" because they produce spectacular yellow, red, and orange spikes that rise a foot or more above the plant and last for several months. With *V. malzinei* you'll get a one-foot plant, while other species will grow up to two feet or more.

Culture

Temperature: Bromeliads grow in temperatures of 55° to 75° and are therefore suitable for most homes and offices. But they are mostly tropical so do not do well in cold. Avoid cold drafts from open windows in winter or air conditioners in summer, and do not let them go below 50° at night.

Humidity: Most bromeliads will live in the 40% to 50% humidity found in most homes and offices, but since these plants originated in moist tropical forests they prefer higher humidity. They do best on pebble trays, with frequent misting to create a moister atmosphere.

Light: Most of the bromeliads will grow in shade, but they do best in bright light and various degrees of sun, especially if you want them to bloom nicely. Exceptions are tillandsia, which thrives only in full sun, and bromelia and hohenbergia, which also enjoy sun. Those with stiff leaves need more light than those with soft leaves, such as guzmanias and vriesias. If you grow bromeliads under artificial light, use four fluorescent tubes and keep them on about fifteen hours a day. The stiff-leafed-varieties should be no farther than two feet from the lights.

Soil: Pot bromeliads in humus—pure sphagnum moss, firbark, or osmunda fiber. Cornell has a special mix for bromeliads—Cornell Epiphytic Mix. An exception is vriesia, which should be potted with a mixture of equal parts humus and potting soil.

Watering: Keep the "vase"—the center of the rosette of leaves—full of water. The humus should be kept damp but not soggy. Occasionally sponge or spray dust off the foliage. These plants are almost pest-free, and any scale they develop usually comes off with a good washing.

Propagation: After bromeliads have bloomed, they eventually die. However, after the flowering you'll find offshoots appearing at the base of the plant. You can cut these off when they are two or three inches long and plant them in moist vermiculite to produce new plants. Keep these in a shaded and warm (over 75°) location for the first few weeks.

Suppliers

BENNETT'S BROMELIADS & BONSAI
Box 1532
Winter Park, Florida 32789
Send stamped envelope.

CORNELISON'S BROMELIAD NURSERY
225 San Bernardino St.
North Fort Myers, Florida 33903
Send stamped envelope.

FUCHSIA LAND
4629 Centinela
Los Angeles, Calif. 90066

JENKINS NURSERY
Box 702
320 E. 33rd Ave.
Covington, Louisiana 70433

MARZ BROMELIADS
10782 Citrus Dr.
Moorpark, Calif. 93021

PLAZA NURSERY & FLOWER SHOP
7430 Crescent Ave.
Buena Park, Calif. 90620

SEABORN DEL RIOS NURSERY
Rt. 3, Box 455
Escondido, Calif. 92025

WILLIFORD'S NURSERY
Box 511, Rt. 3
Smithfield, North Carolina 27577

ORCHIDS

Although orchids are often believed to be parasites, none are true parasites, and most grow in soil (are terrestrial) or are air plants (epiphytic). Orchids from tropical and subtropical forests are mainly air plants. But the greatest number of genera are the terrestrial orchids that grow in the temperate zone; 150 genera are native to North America.

Although the flowers range from cascades of tiny blooms to solitary blossoms, each orchid bloom usually has only three petals. Even more unusual, each flower usually also has three petal-like sepals—one of which, prominent and lip-shaped (called a labellum) secretes nectar to attract pollinating insects. The lip is often showy, and varies enormously from orchid to orchid, accommodating the local insects. One orchid in Africa, for example, has a foot-long labellum perfectly suited to the local moth with a foot-long tongue that pollinates it.

The epiphytic orchids—or air plants—attach themselves to forks or on broad, flat surfaces of trees to feed on decaying dead leaves and other accumulating organic matter. Air plants have a stem swollen at the base, called a pseudobulb, where food and moisture are stored. This fills during heavy rains, and then feeds the plant cells during drought. Epiphytic orchids usually have pendulous aerial roots to draw moisture from the air. Terrestrial orchids grow in soil like most other plants, and have underground roots.

Acineta are air plants with broad green leaves that produce a wealth of two- to three-inch blossoms in spring or summer. The flowers, which grow on long, graceful stems, are yellow with red markings.

Aerides have leathery, deep-green leaves. For about a month in summer they reward you with a profusion of fragrant blossoms borne on pendent stems that grow one to two feet long. Several varieties are available, with colors that include pink, red, purple, and white, and a few are spotted with contrasting color.

Angraecum are air plants with leathery leaves that come in miniature varieties of a couple of inches to plants of two or three feet. Generally winter-blooming, they have white, fragrant flowers.

Ansellia are air plants that bear a profusion of red and yellow flowers. These are large, up to four feet, and have light-green leaves.

Ascocentrum are air plants available in miniature as well as in varieties that grow over a foot. The dark-green foliage is leathery, and the blossoms, which usually arrive in spring, are masses of small flowers shaded from orange to bright red.

Bifrenaria are South American air plants with leaves over a foot long, and the racemes of large flowers in spring may be white and red or pink and red. *B. atropurpurea* has fragrant blooms.

Brassavola are small, some only six inches high, but produce large, scented white flowers. *B. nodosa* are especially fragrant. The blooming period varies.

Broughtonia are air plants of only a few inches that are popularly grown under glass. They have dark-green leathery leaves and bloom in winter with racemes of flowers in shades varying from rose to scarlet.

Cattleya are the lavender orchids popular for corsages. They have pseudobulbs, grow one to two feet high, and may bloom in spring or fall. They are rather hardy and come in an extraordinary number of hybrids.

Coelogyne are available in many varieties. These air plants generally grow well over a foot high, though miniatures are popular for growing under glass. Generally they bloom in winter or early spring, and are among the showiest orchids. *C. cristata* produces a dozen or more snow-white blossoms, each three inches across and fragrant. Other varieties bear cascades of one-inch flowers. The blossoms may be white or whitish, sometimes with orange, yellow, or brown accents. Though these are easy to grow, and may even bloom twice a year, each variety requires slightly different care for blooming; consult your gardening center or the Orchid Society for details.

Cypripedium (also called papiopedium) are the native orchids called lady-slipper or moccasin-flower, and are mostly terrestrial. Rather hardy, these come in a variety of delicately tinted and marked blooms in reds, greens, yellows, whites, and combination. Flowers usually grow singly, may be as much as six inches across, and usually bloom in spring and summer. The plants themselves grow more or less a foot tall and, since they come from forest floors, prefer shade.

Dendrobium are among the easiest orchids to grow indoors, outdoors, or in greenhouses. They range from miniatures only two inches tall to plants two to three feet high. Some are evergreens, some are scented. Often the flowers are yellow, though lavender, white, and other colors are available, and the blossoms may come in cascades of dozens of blooms or may be single flowers from one to three inches across.

Epidendrum are air plants that may have pseudobulbs or cane stems. Their flowers—red, pink, orange, white, brown—are produced in spring, summer, or fall, and last well over a month. These come in miniatures no more than two inches tall, but most grow two to three feet, and one (*E. o'brienianum*) is a giant that may reach over five or six feet in height. Most of these will produce dozens of flowers from one to three inches across.

Gongora have two-foot long light-green leaves and pendent stems of yellow, apricot, or purple flowers in summer.

Laelia are air plants with pseudobulbs and leathery leaves. The flowers, which are various shades of pink-to-red, may be four inches across. These orchids grow up to three feet, but dwarfs are available. Some of the many varieties bloom in fall and winter.

Lycaste may be terrestrials or air plants and grow almost two feet tall. *L. aromatica* produces several golden-yellow flowers that have a scent akin to cinnamon. Other varieties have huge white flowers or smaller, pale-green blooms spotted with red. Some flower in winter, others in spring.

Masdevallia may be air or terrestrial plants and have leathery leaves. Usually they bloom in winter, and the flowers may be various shades of red, from pinkish to purplish, yellow and red, or stark white. Some varieties will grow over a foot tall, but dwarf varieties may be used in terrariums. While these like high humidity (80%), they are less fussy about light and can be grown in north windows and subdued daylight.

Miltonia are air plants that grow one to almost two feet tall. Flowers last four weeks or more. These are often called pansy orchids because the multicolored blooms resemble pansies—combinations of yellow with purple, or yellow and red. These like high humidity (up to 80%). Blooming season varies with the type.

Odontoglossum are air plants. Because they come from high altitudes in the Andes mountains, they can withstand cold better than other orchids. They do well in cool plant rooms or glassed-in porches where temperatures may fall into the mid-forties, and also in air-conditioned rooms. Dwarfs are available, but most grow a bit over a foot tall with leaves up to a foot long. Depending on the variety, these bloom in all four seasons, and as the flowers open in turn, you can have flowers for weeks. Blooms come in many colors, but many of the flowers have combinations of browns with yellow, light green, or red on long scapes. *O. pulchellum*, a dwarf variety, has tiny, fragrant white flowers, while *O. grande*, called the tiger orchid, has blooms five or six inches across.

Oncidium are air plants that grow from either pseudobulbs or canes. These grow one to two feet high and have sprays of tiny blossoms or large solitary flowers. Usually the flowers are a brilliant yellow and may be combined with shades of brown. Most of these bloom in winter or spring.

Rynchostylis are air plants that bear dozens of small, scented, rosy or pinkish tinted flowers on long scapes that are commonly called foxtails. These grow over two feet tall, and have dark-green leathery leaves. They flower in summer.

Stanhopea are air plants with psuedobulbs that grow two to three feet tall and have leaves of almost equal length. In summer they bear several fragrant, showy flowers. Though short-lived, the blooms are large—perhaps six or eight inches across—and usually yellow or white with purple spots.

Vanda are air plants that grow over two feet. They have fleshy leaves and flower at various seasons. The clusters of fragile-looking blossoms may be blue or in combinations of yellows, browns, and other colors.

Zygopetalum are air plants that may or may not have pseudobulbs. Leaves tend to be rather large, up to twenty inches long or more in many types. *Z. garrianum*, from Ecuador, has large, solitary flowers in shades of violet; *Z. intermedium*, from Brazil, has green petals spotted and striped with reddish and purplish tones, and the flowers grow in racemes. Several varieties have flowers with chocolate-brown markings.

Culture

Buying orchids. Buy mature plants that already have buds. Your nurseryman will supply you with specific instructions on requirements for the variety you buy.

Temperature. Most orchids do well in the 55° to 75° range, but the coelogynes, some dendrobiums, laelias, lycastes, masdevallias, miltonias, and odontoglossums prefer the lower end of this range. To bloom they like the temperature to drop at least 10° at night. These will thrive in temperatures down to 50° in the day and a degree or two under this at night. Epidendrums, some dendrobiums, gongoras, rhynchostylis, stanhopeas, and randas do well up to 80° in the day and down to 55° at night. None can survive freezing temperatures.

Humidity. Orchids like a high humidity (at least 50% but up to 70%); keep them on a pebble tray and mist frequently. This is especially true of evergreen dendrobiums, masdevallias, miltonias, stanhopeas, and randas, and others that like warmth. However, some orchid fanciers report good results at 50% humidity. Start with that, and increase it as necessary.

Light: Orchid species with pseudobulbs (such as laelias) generally like sun, but most other varieties prefer indirect sunlight. Exceptions are the coelogynes, which prefer bright light to sun, and the masdevallias and paphiopedilums, which prefer shade. Many orchids rest for a month or two or after blooming or both, and can do with less light at this time.

Orchids that do best under artificial light include the smaller cattleyas, cypripediums, miltonias, and oncidiums. Most growers prefer alternating cool white and warm white tubes, one to eight inches above the leaves, timed from 6 A.M. to at least 6 P.M. Depending on the variety, you may have to provide an additional two to four hours of light. Four 40-watt tubes, each four-feet long, will be the minimum you need if your orchids are in a windowless bathroom or dark basement.

Soil. The air-plant orchids require a rich soil, and most growers today prefer firbark. This is light material that allows for circulation around the roots and comes in several grades from coarse to fine. You can also use osmunda fiber or commercially mixed orchid mix. Terrestrial orchids should be planted in regular potting mix, or in a mix of two-thirds humus and one-third soil.

Watering. Both air-plant and terrestrial orchids should be watered about once a week, when the soil is almost dry to the touch. Do not let them stand in water, however, or the roots will rot. In summer, you might have to water them daily or every three or four days. In winter, when the plants rest, water only every ten days or so. Some varieties, such as lycastes, like to go completely dry for about six weeks. Terrestrial orchids also vary their water needs seasonally, and you may have to water every other day or so to keep up with them in growth periods. A few varieties, like gongora and brassavola and odontoglossums, seem to require less water than most. Those with pseudobulbs and aerial roots can store water and obtain it from the air, so you can let these dry out somewhat.

Fertilizer. Orchids of the air plant type planted in osmunda require little feeding, but as firbark contains no nitrogen, you should add a fertilizer formula of 30-10-10 (a teaspoon to a gallon of water) every two or three weeks during vigorous growth (and half this amount in winter). You can also buy commercially prepared orchid food that comes with its own instructions. Terrestrial orchids should be fed as other types of soil-growing plants.

Pests. Orchids of the air-plant type, grown indoors, are remarkably free of diseases and pests. If flowers develop gray mold, remove them and cut down on watering and humidity. If you have good air circulation and don't keep the soil too soggy, you should have healthy plants. Orchids are sensitive to pesticides, and if a problem should develop, consult an authority such as the Orchid Society rather than spraying your plants.

Terrestrial orchids, if grown or kept temporarily outdoors, could pick up pests from surrounding vegetation. Check them for pests before returning them indoors.

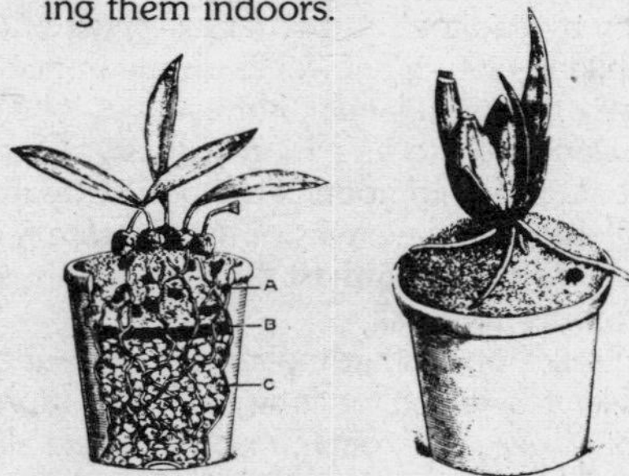

Propagation. Commercial growers propagate orchids from seed, but this takes experience and a lot of patience—some will not bloom for years. You can propagate pseudobulbs by division; terrestrial orchids with more than one growth, like cypripediums, can also be divided. Some orchids, such as evergreen dendrobiums, produce plantlets that can be removed and repotted.

Further Information. For further information, consult the American Orchid Society, 84 Sherman Street, Cambridge, MA 02140.

Suppliers

Alberts & Merkel Bros. Inc.
2210 South Federal Hwy
Boynton Beach, FL 33435

Armacost & Royston
P.O. Box 385, 3376 Foothill Rd.
Carpinteria, CA 93013

M.J. Bates Orchids
7911 U.S. 301
Ellenton, FL 33532

The Beall Company
The Beall Rd.
P.O. Box 467
Washon Island, WA 98070

Fennel Orchid Co., Inc.
The Orchid Jungle
26715 S.W. 157th Ave.
Homestead, FL 33031

Fox Orchids, Inc.
6615 West Markham
Little Rock, AK 72205

Great Lakes Orchids, Inc.
P.O. Box 114
Monroe, MI 48161

Greenbreier Orchids
4711 Palm Beach Blvd.
Fort Myers, FL 33905

Hardy & Fouguette Orchids
9443 E. Heaney Circle
Santee, CA 92071

J & L Orchids
20 Sherwood Rd.
Easton, CT 06612

Kraus Family Orchids
West Boxford, MA 01885

Ann Mann's Orchids
Rt. 3, Box 202
Orlando, FL 32811

Rod McClellan Co.
1450 El Camino Real
South San Francisco, CA 94080

Orchid Gardens
6700 Splithand Rd.
Grand Rapids, MN 55744

Orchids by Hauserman
P.O. Box 363, Dept. A
Elmhurst, IL 60126

Sea Breeze Orchids
P.O. Box 1416
Bayville, NY 11709

Seagulls Landing Orchids
P.O. Box 388
Glen Head, NY 11545

Fred Stewart Orchids
1212 East Las Tunas Drive
San Gabriel, CA 91778

Sunshine Gardens
70 willard St.
Garfield, NJ 07026

Yamamato Dendrobiums Hawaii
P.O. Box 235
Mountainview, HW 96771

Zuma Canyon Orchids, Inc.
5949 Bonsall Drive
Malibu, CA 90265

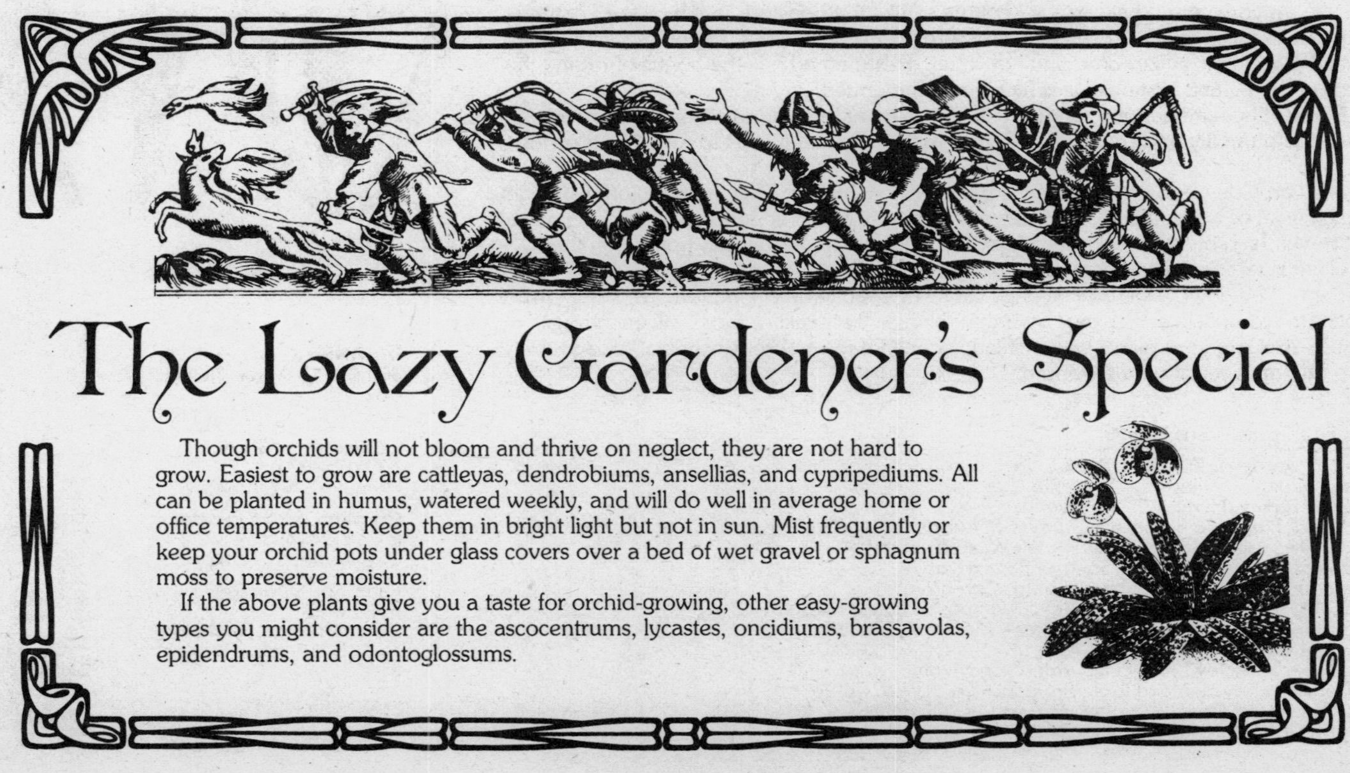

The Lazy Gardener's Special

Though orchids will not bloom and thrive on neglect, they are not hard to grow. Easiest to grow are cattleyas, dendrobiums, ansellias, and cypripediums. All can be planted in humus, watered weekly, and will do well in average home or office temperatures. Keep them in bright light but not in sun. Mist frequently or keep your orchid pots under glass covers over a bed of wet gravel or sphagnum moss to preserve moisture.

If the above plants give you a taste for orchid-growing, other easy-growing types you might consider are the ascocentrums, lycastes, oncidiums, brassavolas, epidendrums, and odontoglossums.

Carnivorous Plants

Beautiful, intriguing, and deadly, carnivorous plants have more personality than some people. Growing in boglands where the soil is poor in nitrogen, carnivorous plants must extract this nutrient from the bodies of animals. They feed on insects, reptiles, and sometimes small mammals attracted to their alluring scents and brightly colored leaves and flowers. The prey are ensnared by ingenious built-in traps, then drowned and digested by the plants' fluids.

Consider growing these natural insecticides to help keep your home free of bugs. The Venus flytrap devours hundreds of ants a day. Sundews love mosquitoes. Pitcher plants may be the solution to your cockroach problem!

The more than 450 species of carnivorous vegetation grow in many parts of the world, from Australia to the American southeast. They vary greatly in size, shape, color, trap design, and prey. Many species can be grown in the home, outdoors, and in greenhouses if provided with abundant water, light, and humidity. The following is a description of the three most cultivated kinds of plant predators, but the general instructions on how to grow them apply to many other species as well.

Venus flytrap (*Dionaea muscipula*). Its animal-like movement makes the Venus flytrap an object of fascination. Indigenous to Wilmington, North Carolina, this "green pet" can grow to about a foot high. Its stem supports a cluster of white flowers during the spring. At the bottom is a tuft of lobe-like leaves that are hinged at the center. The inside surface of each lobe has three trigger hairs, and the edges are fringed with sharp bristles. When an insect lands on one of these sensitive hairs the leaves quickly snap shut, imprisoning it. The trap then fills with digestive juice which breaks down the soft parts of the insect. After the Venus flytrap has assimilated the food (it takes four to twenty days, depending on the meal), the trap opens and the leaf is in position for another victim. When a leaf has caught several insects it withers and dies. A new trap replaces it.

Venus flytraps are available in bulb form or as young plants. They also can be propagated by seed or leaf cuttings.

Sundew (*drosera*). It is not difficult to see why mosquitoes and other insects are drawn to the drosera. The clear fluid on its leaves, glistening in the sunlight, gives it a jewel-like appearance. The sundew relies on its brilliance and sweet smell to lure prey. Once an insect lands on the leaves it becomes stuck. Struggling to escape only stimulates the plant's glands to produce more adhesive. Tentacles fold in around the creature and hold it. The fluid suffocates the bug. Within hours it is digested by the sundew's juices.

Most American species are about four inches long, but the leaves of the *Drosera regiae* of South Africa can reach two feet and capture small mammals. One of the hardiest plant predators, it is commended for home growing. It self-fertilizes and can also reproduce asexually.

Pitcher plant (*sarracenia*). The pitcher plant relies on neither movement nor adhesive to capture its prey. Instead it uses its unique, trumpet-shaped leaves, which function as deadly tunnel-traps and as vessels for digestive fluid. Lured by a sweet odor, a bee, cockroach, or other insect alights inside the mouth of the brightly colored "pitcher." Hairs lining the inner surface bend upward so the insect can't crawl out. It can't fly out because of the curvy lid. The victim is forced farther and farther down by glassy hairs and the slippery surface. Finally it falls into the pool below and is disintegrated by the plant's enzymes. Some of the larger species have been known to devour giant rats!

The leaves of the different pitcher plants are strikingly beautiful. Some are white with green and red veins, some yellow-green with yellow flowers, or green mottled with red.

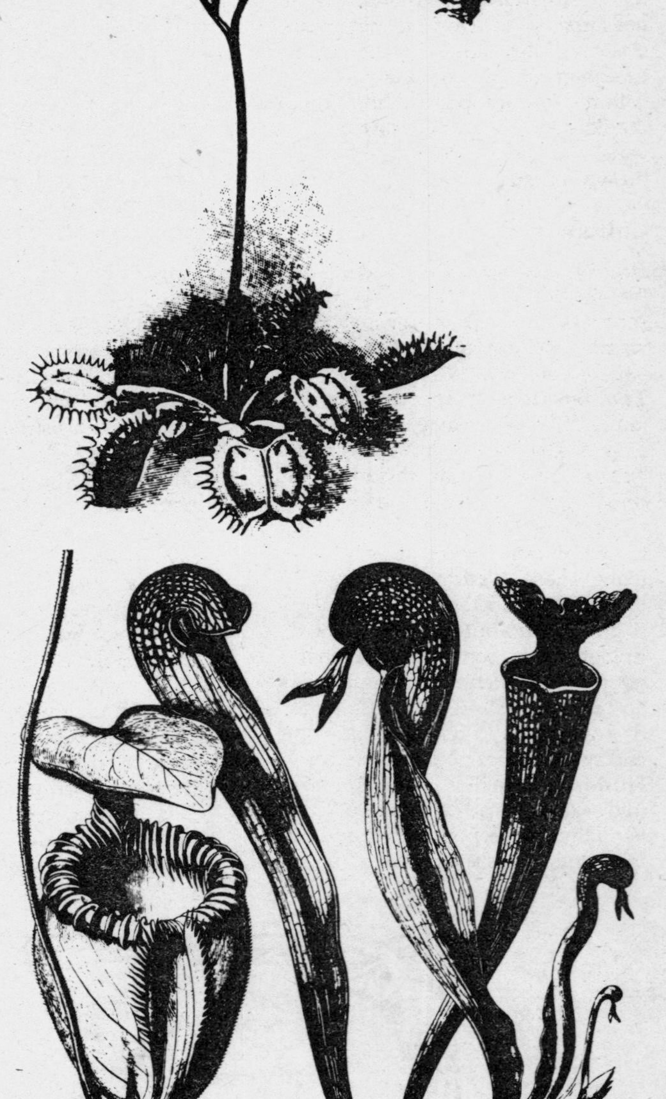

Most carnivorous plants require the same basic conditions: a steady diet of insects, and plenty of water, light and humidity.

Feeding: Care is minimal. Your house or apartment probably has an ample supply of bugs to satisfy the plants' needs. If they seem undernourished you can try feeding them a small piece of hamburger or cooked egg white, but no more often than every six weeks. If they are overfed they may die prematurely.

Soil: The medium should be acidic. Live sphagnum moss is the medium most similar to the plants' natural environment. They will also grow in dried sphagnum moss, which is easier to find. Dried moss requires replacement more frequently than live.

Light: Carnivores should be placed in direct light, so keep them near a window. If your home is dark, you can grow the plants successfully under artificial lights. The Venus flytrap may still need sunlight occasionally. Do not light the plants constantly; they need rest for several hours each night.

Water and humidity: Carnivores should always be kept moist, like the boglands in which they naturally thrive. Daily watering is essential if you're growing them in a regular drainage pot. Expert growers recommend placing the potted plants in a saucer or tray full of water. This method has the bonus of raising the humidity, which is vital to the plants. Misting also is highly recommended.

Temperature: 80° is a healthy temperature. Growth will be slower at lower temperatures. Too-high temperatures will lower the humidity and cause dryness and wilting. Be careful not to turn on air conditioners too high.

Terrariums: Terrariums provide good environments for carnivorous plants. They admit a lot of sunlight while maintaining a high level of humidity. It isn't necessary to buy specially designed terrariums. You can use any clear container with high or inward-sloping sides. Don't let terrariums get too hot. Open them occasionally if the sunlight is raising the temperature too high.

How to plant terrariums: Lay down a shallow layer of gravel or pearlite on the bottom. This will ensure drainage. Place an inch or two of acid soil or peat over that. Nonsterilized soil or moss will encourage insects to lay eggs, thus supplying your plants with a steady supply of food. A few inches of sphagnum moss should make up the top layer of your terrarium.

Where You Can See Carnivorous Plants:

Brooklyn Botanical Gardens, Brooklyn, New York.
California State University, Fullerton, California.
California State University, Humboldt, California.
Columbia Zoological Park and Botanical Garden, Riverbanks Park Commission, Columbia, South Carolina.
Cranberry Glades, Monogahela National Forest, West Virginia.
Longwood Botanical Gardens, Kennett Square, Pennsylvania.
Los Angeles State and County Aboretum, Arcadia, California.
Missouri Botanical Gardens, 2315 Tower Grove Avenue, St. Louis, Missouri.
Montreal Botanic Garden, 4101 Sherbrooke Street, Montreal, Quebec.
New York Botanical Garden, Bronx, New York.
Phipps Conservatory, Schenley Park, Pittsburgh, Pennsylvania.
San Francisco Conservatory, Golden Gate Park, San Francisco, California.
University of California Botanical Gardens, Berkeley, California.
University of North Carolina at Chapel Hill, North Carolina.

Suppliers

Armstrong Associates Inc.
Box 127
Basking Ridge, NJ 07920

Carnivorous Gardens
P.O. Box 331
Hamilton, NY 13346

Carolina Exotic Gardens
P.O. Box 1492
Greenville, SC 27834

Peter Pauls Nurseries
Building 2
Canandaigua, NY 14424

WID
Box 303H
Grant, FL 32949

Herbs & Spices

Agrimonie.

Cammomill.

Anise.

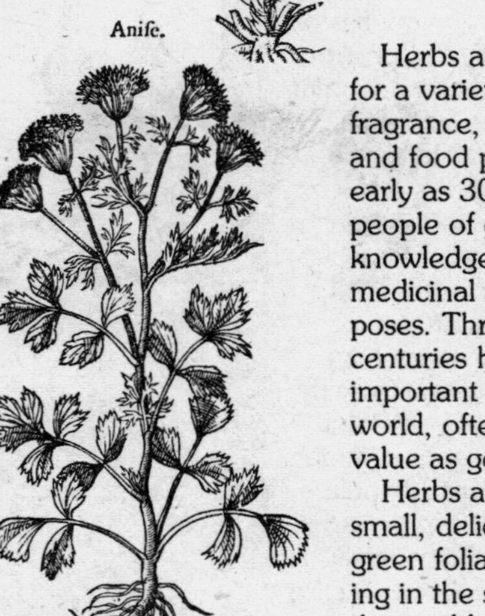

Herbs and spices have been used for a variety of purposes—flavoring, fragrance, cosmetics, medicines, dyes and food preservatives. In China as early as 3000 B.C., herbalists were people of great and mysterious knowledge who prescribed herbs for medicinal as well as spiritual purposes. Throughout the ensuing centuries herbs and spices became important items of trade around the world, often with the same intrinsic value as gold and silver.

Herbs and spices are generally small, delicate plants with soft, deep-green foliage, most varieties originating in the subtropical regions around the world—mainly Asia and the Mediterranean. Indoors or out, they grow best in medium-rich soil, require average watering with good drainage, and at least six hours of sun a day. Bugs are seldom a problem, since most herbs and spices are stoutly resistant to insects.

Great Basill.

Agrimony. Called cocklebur and church steeples, this perennial grows to three feet. Its leaves cluster thickly, and smell like apricots. Minuscule yellow blossoms show atop long, thin stems in summer. Flowers later become hook-like seed pods. Keep soil dry between infrequent waterings. It is happiest outdoors in full sun, but will adapt to partial shade. Propagation by seed is easiest, but cuttings work, too. Dried leaves are used for apricot fragrance.

The Bay tree.

Anise. This plant is perhaps best known as the central ingredient in the French liqueur anis, or anisette, having a powerful licorice flavor. Leaves in triplet clusters grow along the stems which reach twenty-four inches. Anise is a slow-growing annual that does well outdoors in warmer climates. In cool climates, grow in a pot indoors, then move outdoors as temperatures warm. It does best in full sun, in semi-rich soil kept well drained.

Basil. This native of the African tropics grows as a small bush to two feet high, and has velvety green, creased leaves. Keep stem ends pinched for fullness. Grow in or out of doors, in full sun, though it adapts to partial shade. It needs rich soil kept slightly moist. Propagate by seed.

Garden Burnet.

Bay. When dried, leaves have a sweet flavor that integrates well with many foods. The plant is a perennial shrub, that will grow into a small tree if given the right conditions. Yellow flowers with black berries are produced in summer and spring. Grow in any well drained soil. Let soil dry out between waterings. Bay does best in seemingly undersized pots, and requires direct sun in summer and coolness in winter. Propagation is difficult, so buy bay from nurseries.

Bergamot. This perennial has at least three common names—bee balm, Oswego tea, and horsemint. Its leaves were used as a tea substitute by the American patriots during the famous Boston Tea Party boycott. These days it is still used as tea, though more so as a mint fragrance. The plant is shrublike, grows to three feet, and produces bright red flowers. It likes a fairly cool winter, and needs to be pruned almost to the ground in fall. It requires full sun (it tolerates little shade) and a moderately moist, humus-rich soil. Definitely an outdoor plant.

Burnet. The round, prickly leaves of this stout perennial grow in clustered rosettes low to the ground. Flower stems rising two feet above the plant bear strange-looking pink blooms in summer. Give full sun, and just about any well-drained soil; let dry out between waterings. Often planted outdoors as a ground cover, it can be grown indoors if you keep the shoot ends pinched. Propagate either by seed or cuttings.

Caper Bush. This annual herb is known for its pickled flower buds. The plant is equipped with thorns, and most often has a weedy, straggling appearance. It may be grown outdoors in warm regions, but otherwise requires a greenhouse. It does best in a spare, gritty soil allowed to dry between waterings. Propagate by seed.

Caraway. Umbrella-shaped clusters of tiny white flowers shade the angular, branching stems of this interesting biennial. They grow to fifteen inches the first year, and to two feet the second year. Seeds have a licorice flavor. Caraway prefers full sun, and grows in most any soil with occasional watering. Its long roots do not transplant well. Propagate by seed or cutting.

Catnip. The chopped, dried leaves are used as a stuffing for cat toys, but also make a nice minty tea. This perennial grows to three feet. Randomly branching stems are covered by heart-shaped green leaves with toothed edges. Thornlike flowers appear white and purple in summer. Not entirely unweedlike, catnip grows in practically any soil and light conditions, so long as it is kept moist. Keep it trimmed back. Protect seedlings from felines, whose curiosity will kill not the cat, but the catnip. Propagate by division, seed or cuttings.

Chamomile. The deep-green lacy foliage if this plant grows at heights of three to twelve inches, and spreads to cover vast fields. Yellow and white daisy-like flowers sit atop the delicate branching stems in summer and spring. A delicious tea of the Europeans is made from dried chamomile petals. Grow as a ground cover or a garden border row. Start by seed or small plants. For contained rows, bury header boards six inches deep. Propagate by seed or division in spring.

Round leafed Capers.

Chervil. Fernlike, lacy green foliage reaches heights of two feet. Chopped dried leaves have a flavor best described as half parsley and half anise. The foliage turns a peculiar shade of pink in the fall. Small white blooms cluster in summer. Grow in or out-of-doors, and give it slightly more shade than sun. Plant seedlings in a rich soil kept moderately moist.

Chinese Chives. Seed pods radiate from stem tips to form small globes on this two-foot-high perennial. These are more powerful than common chives. Grow in a contained area outside, in full sun or partial shade. Propagate by seed or division.

Chives. Very easy to grow year round, chives are perennials that grow as soft, thin green stems up to ten inches high. Grow indoors or outdoors. They are bug resistant. Clip stems down to the base as needed. Chives prefer a rich soil kept fairly moist, and full sun. Propagate by division or seed.

Caruwaies.

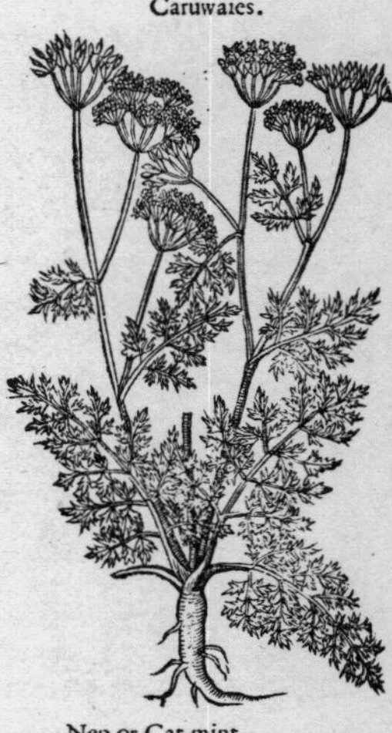

Comfrey. Otherwise known as blackwort and knit-bone, this perennial produces a large furry green leaf that makes a subtle tea. The plant grows to three feet, and bears yellow purple, blue, or white funnel-form blooms throughout much of the year. Keep stem ends pinched to encourage fullness of leaves. Grow outdoors in full sun and a rich, moist soil. Propagate by root divisions or cuttings.

Nep or Cat-mint.

Coriander. The whole seed is usually referred to as coriander, while the ground form may be known as cilantro and the cut leaves as Chinese parsley. It is a fast-growing annual that reaches heights of thirty inches and has elliptical green leaves with toothed edges. Light pink feathery flowers crown the branching stems. Coriander grows well in or out-of-doors, but prefers full sunlight. Plant in moderately rich soil, and propagate by seed.

Cumin. This plant is smaller than, but otherwise similar to, the caraway plant. Cumin is grown for its small epitical seeds, which have a pungent flavor similar to that of caraway. Parasol-shaped clusters of tiny white flowers with seed pods sit atop delicate stems at heights up to six inches. Maturation to seeding requires at least three months of warm weather. So, if you live in a cool climate, start in pots indoors. Let soil approach dryness between watering. Propagate by seed.

Cheruill.

Dandelion. Every part of the plant—roots, stem, and flower—is edible; dried roots and stems are usually used in beverages. Most varieties grow at heights between four and ten inches. Some of hybrid species have better tasting leaves than the wild kinds. If planted outdoors, confine them in boxed-off plots. Any soil and

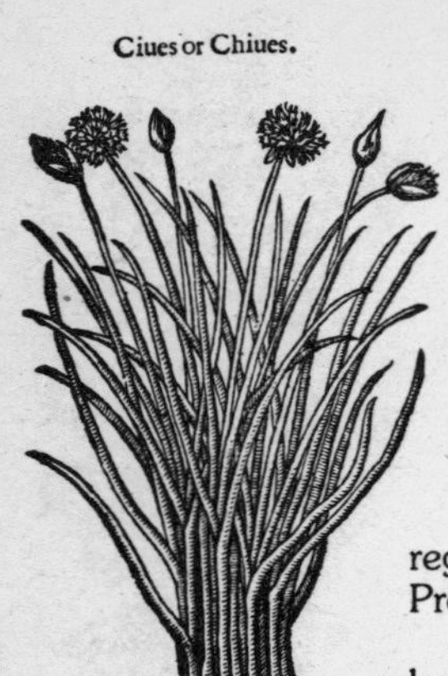
Ciues or Chiues.

Dandelion.

Dill.

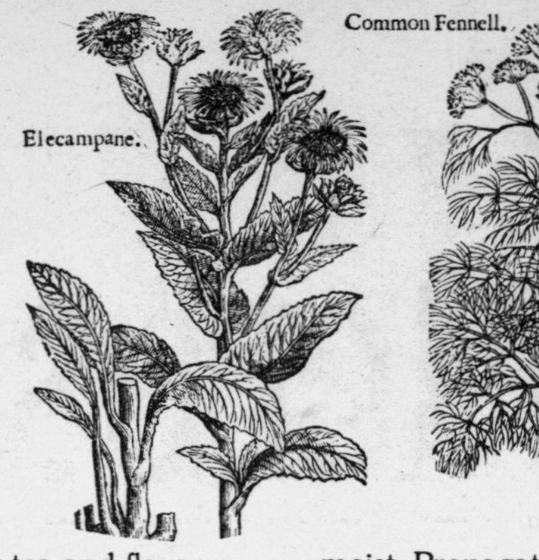
Elecampane.

Common Fennell.

Garlicke.

Coriander.

Comfrey

Cumin.

Dittanie of Candie.

regular watering suits dandelions. Propagate by seed.

Dill. Thin pulpy green stems branch up to heights of two to four feet. Perched atop are umbrella-shaped clusters of tiny yellow flowers. Grow in any well-drained soil. Full sun is essential; or fluorescent lights indoors. Propagate by seed.

Dittany of Crete. Velvety white hairs cover the roundish leaves of this perennial that grows a foot high. The plant spreads, and produces many small rose-colored blooms. Dried leaves taste vaguely similar to marjoram. Plant in full sun and allow its soil to dry out a little between watering. Propagate by root division, stem cuttings, or seeds.

Elecampane. A four- to six-foot bushy perennial, this bears large heliotrope-like blooms of bright yellow. Delicate, fingerlike green leaves reach lengths up to eighteen inches. Dried roots are used in liqueurs, as well as for dyes. Grow out of doors in full sun and an average soil kept moist.

Fennel, Sweet. This fernlike perennial grows to five feet. Soft pulpy stems branch into a lacy deep-green foliage. The ground, dried leaves and whole dried seeds have a sweet licorice flavor. Almost strictly an outdoor plant, it needs full sun and a fairly lean, sandy soil that approaches dryness between waterings. Do not attempt to transplant. Propagate by seed.

Fennel Flower. Sometimes called black cumin or love-in-a-mist, fennel flower looks very much like sweet fennel—with feathery deep-green foliage and stems to approximately five feet. However, the two fennels are not related. Fennel flower bears small azure or white flowers in summer, followed by seed pods. Seeds have a nice spicy flavor not unlike nutmeg. Grow outdoors in full sun and any ordinary soil. If planting for seeds, plant generously, since each plant produces few seeds. Propagate by seed.

Garlic. Garlic bulbs send up long, thin green stems up to two feet high. At maturity, the stems yield white and purple flowers. The bulbs of this perennial multiply during the season, finally appearing as clusters of small cloves or bulblets. Plant in full sun and rich soil. Propagate simply by dividing bulbs.

Ginger. This fine garden plant has long, delicate green leaves that grow in clusters on columns rising above the plant. In its natural habitat of tropical Asia, the leaves turn brown around the edges, at which point the roots are dug up and used as spice. Ginger can be grown in or out of doors. If you live in a cooler than subtropical climate, pot indoors until summer. It loves sun, rich, moist soil, and high humidity. Propagate by root cuttings.

Horehound. Horehound has furry stems and leaves, and yields clusters of small white flowers in spring and summer. Dried leaves make a slightly bitter tea and flavor candies. Best outdoors in sunlight and a lean, sandy soil kept fairly dry between infrequent waterings. Propagate by seed.

Horseradish. The bulbous roots of this tough perennial are usually used in a pureed form. The two-foot plant bears clusters of tiny white flowers. Usually an outdoor plant, horseradish produces higher quality roots when planted in contained clumps of loose, rich soil. Otherwise it grows very weedily. Soil must be kept moist throughout the year. Fuller roots are the result of delaying the harvest until late October or November. Propagate by root offshots.

Hyssop. The dried leaves of this densely foliated perennial shrub were once a major ingredient in sachets and potpourris. White, pink, or azure blooms appear in spring and summer. Grow outdoors in full sun and a slightly alkaline soil kept dry between waterings. Propagate by root cuttings, stem division, or seed.

Lavender. When in bloom, the wonderful fragrance of this perennial can be smelled at a distance of many yards. The lacy plant grows from two to four feet, and has small, dryish green leaves. Light to deep purple flowers in spring and summer. This winter-hardy plant needs full sun and dry soil. It can be grown indoors or out, but blooms better outside. Propagate by stem cuttings or seed.

Leek. This annual grows best in full sunlight and a rich soil kept fairly moist. The leaves taste far better if the plant is liberally fertilized. Plant leeks six to eight inches deep, on loose mounds ten inches above normal ground level. Propagate from seeds or by division.

Lemon Balm. This low-growing perennial has green oval leaves on vine-like creeping stems. The mint look-alike has a tendency to clump, and can sometimes reach thirty inches high. The crushed, dried leaves are used for tea and as a substitute for lemon peel. Tiny rosetted clusters of white flowers appear in summer. Give it full sun or bright light and a lean, dry soil indoors or out. Propagate by seed or stem division.

Lemon Verbena. The chopped, dried leaves make a lemon-flavored tea or a culinary spice. Sometimes grows taller than ten feet. Depending on the species, the pale green leaves will fall off in fall or not. Unless you live in a warm climate, plant in pots indoors, then move outdoors in summer. It requires full sun and average garden soil kept fairly dry. Propagate by young stem cuttings.

Marjoram. This somewhat bushy, low-growing ground cover has variegated green oval leaves. Dense white to deep violet flowers appear in summer. Grow indoors or out, in full sunlight with partial shade and a lean, alkaline soil. Keep soil evenly moist. Propagate by seed or stem cuttings.

Mint. There are many varieties of mint, which vary greatly in flavor but hardly at all in looks. Generally, mint is a low-growing, bushy perennial that spreads quickly. Delicately ribbed deep-green oval leaves are attached at right angles to thin reaching stems. Depending on the species, mint grows to heights from one to three feet. Orange bergamot mint (*Menthe piperata var. citrata*) have more roundish leaves with a delicate white fuzz and purple edges; violet and white blooms appear in summer. Pennyroyal (*M. pulegium*), popular especially for sachets and potpourris, has six- to twelve-inch flower stalks that range from violet-azure to a rose color. Spearmint (*M. spicata*) is frequently used in mint jelly. Mints require about 50% shade and rich soil kept lightly moist. Mint grows well indoors or out. Contain creeping stems if grown outdoors. Propagate by root cuttings or stem division.

Oregano. Delicate small leaves are attached to clumping feathery stems that grow in a bush-like form. The perennial has tiny pink flowers, and its stems get woody with age. Grow in a fairly dry soil and full sunlight. It will do well indoors under artificial light. Propagate from root cuttings, stem division, and by seed.

Orris. Widely known to herbalists for its sweetly-scented roots, an ingredient in sachets and potpourris as a scent preservative, this has long spear-like leaves and large cream-colored flowers streaked with purple and yellow. It grows to two feet, and is a spring bloomer. Give full sun and average soil kept slightly moist but well-drained. To propagate, dig up old bulbs and replant.

Parsley. This biennial grows to twenty inches and has soft pulpy stems. Seeds must be soaked an entire day before planting. Grow in partial shade, in a rich soil kept moderately moist. Propagate from seed.

Peppers. More commonly referred to as chili peppers (to distinguish them from the black and white table peppers of the Far East), these are red or green in color, and grow as hollow pulpy pods. Depending on the species, they range from sweet to very hot. The following are hot: Jalapeno chili, Hungarian Wax, Red chili, and Cayenne chili. String mature chilis on a wire or string to dry, then chop finely or grind them into powder. Temperatures between 75° and 85°F are required to set chili blossoms, but temperatures above 90°F or below 60° will make them fall off. Start in pots indoors until weather is warm. They like a slightly rich soil kept evenly moist through the flowering period. They are an attractive indoor plant. Propagation by seed requires soaking.

Rocket. The young leaves of this weed-like annual can be substituted for horseradish. The low-growing shrub bears clusters of dainty white,

Horehound.

Hyssope with blew floures.

Lauander.

Leeke.

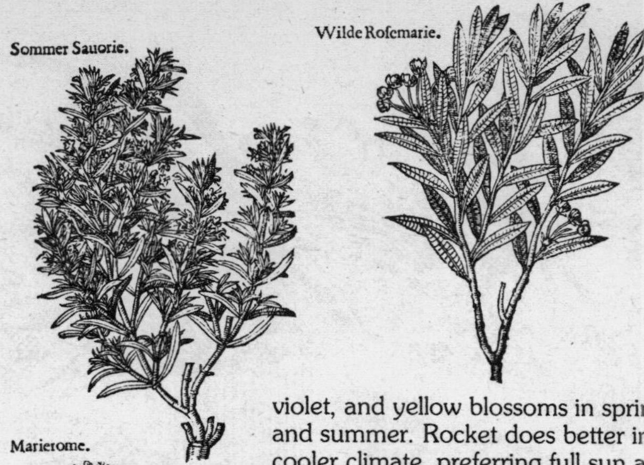

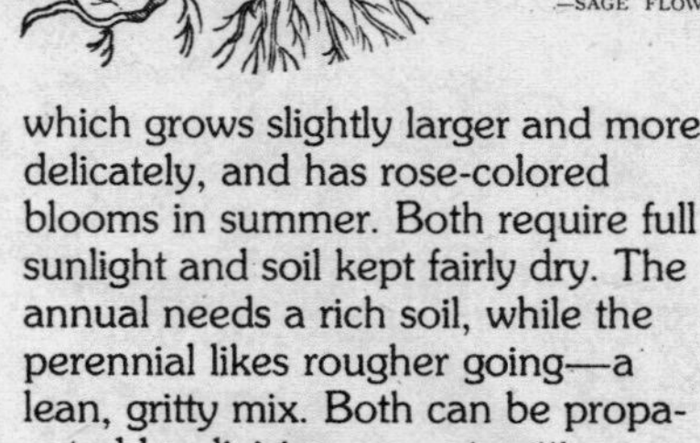

Marierome.

violet, and yellow blossoms in spring and summer. Rocket does better in a cooler climate, preferring full sun and average garden soil. Propagate by seed.

Rosemary. Thin armlike stems covered with tiny dull-green leaves reach heights of two to six feet. It is a perennial, and an evergreen if grown in warm climates. Violet and azure flowers appear throughout spring and summer. The dried leaves and flowers of rosemary are a familiar kitchen spice. Grow indoors in fairly sizable containers. Move outdoors in summer. Rosemary needs full sun and dry soil between waterings. Propagate by cuttings of half-mature woody branches, or by seed.

Safflower. Otherwise called American or false saffron, this annual spice is used as a saffron substitute, but more often for dyes. Prickly leaves on thin stems grow from one to two feet high. The yellow-orange flowers look much like thistles, and are dried to produce the deep-orange powder. Give sunny warmth and a light, gritty soil kept fairly dry. Propagate by seed or cuttings.

Saffron. This low-growing annual has grassy leaves which sprout from bulbous bases and reach eighteen inches high. Slightly thicker flower stems are only three to four inches high and are crowned with tiny violet blooms. The spice, made from the orange flower stigmas, is tedious to harvest. To cultivate your own spice, you must plant a whole field. Plant saffron bulbs at the end of summer in a rich soil kept lightly moist. Bulbs multiply and are thus self-propagating. Divide every two or three years for best results.

Sage. This sturdy perennial is used for tea, fragrance, and dyes. The plant grows as a small thick bush with tough powdery green leaves of an elliptical shape. Purple and azure blooms are produced in spring. Pineapple sage (*S. elegans*) is a good indoor specimen, having extremely aromatic leaves and magenta blooms in summer. Golden sage (s.o. var. 'Golden Sage') also does well indoors. Sage thrives in full sun and a spare, gritty soil kept fairly moist. Propagate by seed or stem cuttings.

Santolina. Called lavender cotton, santolina has many tiny gray leaves on creeping stems. At some distance, the plant appears as a patch of gray wool, and makes an excellent ground cover. In summer, small round yellow flowers appear. *S. chamaecyparissus* is the slow-growing variety, with yellow blooms. *S. virens* grows more quickly and has green foliage with scarlet flowers. Plant in any average garden soil, in full sun. Keep soil on the dry side. Propagate by stem cuttings.

Savory. Feathery leaves thickly cover delicate stems that curve out and up to sixteen inches. Especially hardy, "winter savory," the perennial variety, can stand temperatures down to 10°F. Summer savory is an annual which grows slightly larger and more delicately, and has rose-colored blooms in summer. Both require full sunlight and soil kept fairly dry. The annual needs a rich soil, while the perennial likes rougher going—a lean, gritty mix. Both can be propagated by division or root cuttings.

Sesame. This tropical annual, occasionally called benne, grows two feet tall and has thin delicate green leaves up to five inches in length. Its tiny dry seeds have a nutty flavor. White funnelform blooms appear in summer. To grow sesame for the seeds, plant many, since each seed pod yields only a tablespoon of seeds. Grow in full sunlight and well-drained but regularly watered soil. In most areas, you need a greenhouse, since it requires 120 days of very warm weather to bloom.

Shisho. This annual native of Asia is also known as purple perilla and summer coleus. Pulpy purple stems branch into many thin leaves covered with white fuzz on top and violet fuzz on their undersides. Popular with the Japanese as a culinary herb, shisho has a flavor very much like cinnamon. Two to four feet tall at maturity, the plant bears pink flowers in clusters. Shisho grows best in full sun with partial shade, and an average soil kept moderately moist. Propagate by stem or root cuttings.

Sweet Cicely. This perennial grows two to three feet, with flowing delicate fronds very like fern. Stems and leaves are deep green. Every part of sweet cicely is edible, and has a distinct licorice flavor. Small clusters of white blooms appear in spring, succeeded by tiny black berries. Grow in a rich acidic soil and partial shade. Deep roots require deep planting. Cicely can be grown indoors, but does better outdoors, especially needing cool winters. Propagate from cuttings of root eyes.

Tarragon. This perennial has small, long thin leaves that grow about the tangled weak stems in a random, disheveled fashion. Yellow-green flowers appear through summer. The plant does not bear seeds, and spreads by rhizomes. Grow indoors or out, in any average garden soil. It needs bright light and some shade. Propagate by root division or cuttings.

Thyme. The many varieties of thyme all have brittle woody stems that curve up erectly from their base clump and are dotted with small, round dry leaves. The most common, *T. vulgaris*, is a perennial about a foot high with frail violet blooms. *T. x citriodorus*, lemon thyme, has leaves faintly variegated with yellow and a strong lemon scent. Silver thyme (*T. x c. var. 'Argentus'*) is more delicate, with smaller silvery leaves. All thymes are easy growers indoors or out, happiest in a lean, porous soil and full sunlight. Regular trimming keeps plants from getting woody. Propagate by root or stem divisions.

Sources

Catnip Acres Farm
Christian St.
Oxford, CT 06483

Comstock, Ferre & Co.
263 Main St.
Wethersfield, CT 06109
(free illustrated catalog)

Country Herbs
Box 357
Stockbridge, MA 01262

Glie Farms
2828 Bathgate Ave.
Bronx, NY 10457

The Herb Patch
3726 Thomasville Rd.
Tallahassee, FL 32312

Howe Hill Herbs and Merry Gardens
Camden, ME 04843

Leader Nurseries
7206 Belvedere Rd.
West Palm Beach, FL 33411

George W. Park Seed Co.
610 Cokesbury Rd.
Greenwood, SC 26947
(Catalog free)

Rutland of Kentucky
P.O. Box 16
Washington, KY 41096

The Sandy Marsh Herb Nursery
Rt. 2 Surret Cove Rd.
Leicester, NC 28748

Stillridge Herb Farm
1037 Rt. 99
Woodstock, MD 21163

Sunnybrook Farms
9448 Mayfield Rd.
P.O. Box 6
Chesterland, OH 44026

Tillotson's Roses
802 Brown's Valley Rd.
Watsonville, CA 95076

Well Sweep Herb Farm
Mount Bethel Rd.
Port Murray, NJ 06865

Herbal Outlets

Aphrodisia
28 Carmine St.
NY, NY 10014

Borchelt Herb Gardens
474 Carriage Shop Road
East Falmouth, MA 02536

W. Atlee Burpee
300 Park Ave.
Warminster, PA 18974

Caswell-Massey Co. Ltd
320 W. 13th St. (catalog)
518 Lexington Ave.
NY, NY 10017 (store)

Gardens of the Blue Ridge
Rt. 221
Pineola, NC 28662

Greene Herb Gardens
Greene, RI 02872

Hickory Hollow
Rt. 1, Box 52
Peterstown, WV 24963

Hilltop Herb Farm
Box 1734
Cleveland, TX 77327

Indiana Botanic Gardens, Inc.
P.O. Box 5
Hammond, IN 46325

Joseph J. Kern Rose Nursery
Box 33
Mentor, OH 44060

Kiel Pharmacy, Inc.
109 Third Ave.
NY, NY 10003

Logee's Greenhouses
55 North St.
Danielson, CT 06239

Nature's Herb Co.
281 Ellis St.
San Francisco, CA 94102

Nichols Garden Nursery
1190 Pacific North Hwy
Albany, OR 97321

Meadowbrook Herbs & Things
Whispering Pines Rd.
Wyoming, RI 02898

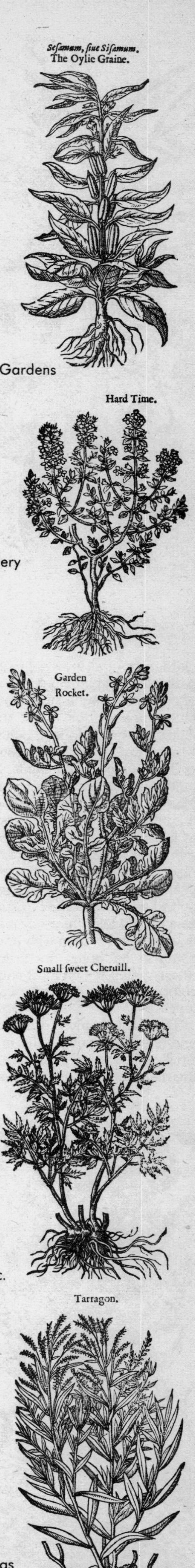

Gardeners of all levels of experience, particularly beginning gardeners, often harbor vague suspicions that bulbs are somehow exotic and very difficult to grow. In fact, quite the reverse is true. As well as creating some of the most beautiful plants, flowering bulbs are among the easiest to grow. Many types do as well indoors as they do out, and the many varieties include such a diversity of flowering schedules that you can be assured of plants in bloom almost the entire year. Over the last twenty years hybridists have worked to successfully develop more new kinds of flowering bulbs than with any other plant, so that bulbs now include unquestionably the greatest variety of colors and color patterns of all flower types.

There is little mystery about bulbs and how they grow. Bulbs are like small storehouses. Each one contains the makings of all the various parts of the mature plant—roots, leaves and flowers. They grow in a very defined cycle, as follows: blooming, foliage growth; and rest period, when they are dormant. When you buy bulbs from a nursery they are in their dormant stage, ready to be planted. Once in the ground, feed them with water and nutrients and they will grow to produce one or more flowers. During second stage, foliage growth, the plant collects as much energy and nutrients as possible from the soil and air, in preparation for the winter dormancy period. When you grow bulb plants, never cut off the foliage before it is completely dead, because when the plant starts to turn brown it is a sign that the energy gathered in its leaves and stems is slowly being sent for storage to the bulb. If you cut the plant's half-dead foliage, you are robbing it of its energy supply for next year's flower.

"Bulbs" is a blanket term which actually includes bulbs, tubers, corms, and rhizomes. For our purpose the differences between these are small, as they all share the same growth habits and culture requirements. There is, however, one general categorical distinction—between *hardy* bulbs and *tender* bulbs.

Hardy bulbs are those that necessitate a cold period to complete their natural growth cycle. These are most often spring bloomers, planted between October and November. Without the cold temperatures of winter they simply won't grow. However, they can be "tricked" into blooming indoors during wintertime by a technique known as "forcing."

A forced bulb is one whose natural cycle has been started early by some means of artificial cooling, in a refrigerator, for example, or a cool garage. After a period of six to eight weeks in this cold storage, their roots have developed and the plants are ready to bloom. Some of the most beautiful bulbs are hardy, such as tulips and daffodils, and can be forced into blooming indoors during the middle of winter.

Tender bulbs are those that cannot tolerate the cold temperatures of winter. Although some can remain in the ground in milder climates, most tender bulbs need to be removed from the earth and stored during the winter months. Subsequently, tender bulbs are usually planted in the spring and bloom from mid-summer through late fall. The main advantage of tender bulbs is that they need no period of special or artificial climatic preparation so can be planted and started growing immediately. However, the growth habits of tender bulbs vary. Some will flower nearly all year long, while others require dormant periods. Special requirements will be listed with specific varieties.

Culture
Neither tender nor hardy bulbs are very particular about their soil, and they both do well in the same simple mixture: two parts garden soil, one part fine clean sand, and one part peat moss. Because bulbs store their own supplies of nutrients, they do not require fertilizer when first planted. However, some bone meal added to the soil mixture will help the plant. The soil should be filtered through a ½-inch wire screen to eliminate clumps. Make sure that the soil is loose enough to drain well, yet of a makeup that is moisture retentive. Bulbs will usually do as well in soils other than the one suggested here, but whatever the soil, it must be both well-draining and moisture-retentive. Flowering bulbs will not grow in clay, or in soil that is too sandy.

When potting bulbs, or when planting in the ground, put gravel at the bottom level to insure good drainage. Then cover the gravel with a layer of the soil mixture and set the bulb in place, top up. The bulb should always sit firmly on the bed of soil. If the hole in which the bulb sits is not level, allowing a pocket of air beneath the bulb, the bulb may rot. Once in place, cover the bulb to the required depth and water thoroughly. After this initial watering, water sparingly until growth is well under way. Then begin a regular watering schedule. Indoor bulbs should be removed from sunlight after the flowers have opened, to insure longer-lasting blooms.

EARLY ROMAN HYACINTHS
WHITE-YELLOW-PINK-BLUE

After the bulb has finished flowering, remember not to disturb it until all the foliage has turned brown. Then, with hardy bulbs, cut back the foliage to about five inches above the ground. Hardy bulbs can remain in the ground. Tender bulbs must be gently removed from the soil before the first frost. Cut their dead foliage back to about two inches, clean the bulb by careful wiping, and store in a cool (60 to 65°F), dry place through the winter. If you live in a temperate climate, tender bulbs can stay in the ground year-round. One important note: once a hardy bulb has been forced, it is not repeatedly forceable. You must remove it from its pot to a permanent place in your garden. It may not bloom the first year in the garden, but thereafter it should bloom and grow well.

Bulbs of the best quality are not inexpensive. But, it is better to buy a few good bulbs than many poor ones, because one good bulb will produce more and better flowers than a few bad ones. Usually a good variety of bulbs is available at your local nursery. Also, a multitude of varieties is available through mail order catalogs. Bulbs usually become available about the time they should be planted. So, if you select and plant an assortment of bulbs, both hardy and tender, as they become available, you will have beautiful flowers all year. Choose from the following list the bulbs you want to grow. Unless otherwise indicated, all bulbs need full sunlight.

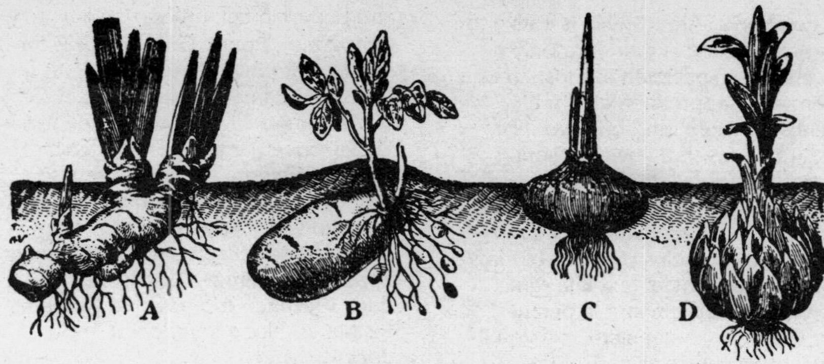

Tiges souterraines.

A. Rhizome (*Iris*). — B. Tubercule (*Pomme de terre*). — C. Bulbe tuniqué (*Oignon*). — D. Bulbe écailleux (*Lis blanc*).

DOUBLE NARCISSUS.

Acidanthera. Popularly called Abyssinian sword lily, this corm reaches three feet in height and yields three-inch lilylike flowers atop long slender stems in summer. Plant the corms in spring, three to four inches deep. Dig them up after they fade and store them through winter. *A. bicolor* is cream-colored with brown variegations. *A. hybrida tubergemii* has large white flowers that have a sweet scent.

Agapanthus. Amid the long, sweeping triangular leaves, large erect flower stems rise to five feet. Known as lily-of-the-Nile, this has globe-shaped flowers in summer. Plant in full sun in the spring. *A. africanus*, the most popular, has large clusters of beautiful blue blooms. *A. orientalis* has blue and white flowers.

Allium. There are many varieties of "flowering onion." Most send long stems to as high as five feet, and all have spectacular globular flower clusters. Plant in early spring, after the danger of frost is gone. Blooms from late spring through summer. *A. azureum* has dark blue flowers. *A. christophii* has purple and blue blooms. *A. moly* (lily leek) yields yellow stellar blooms in July. *A. neapolitanum* (Naples lily) has white flowers.

Alstroemeria. "Peruvian lily" prefers shade to sun. Long grasslike leaves surround flower stems that reach up to three feet in height. Plant dormant bulbs in a slightly richer than the usual soil in early spring. Starlike blooms of red, yellow, and violet appear in summer and are long-lasting cut flowers.

Amaryllis belladonna. Plant the bella donna lily very early in the year for early spring flowers, or force indoors in winter. Almost any soil will suit this bulb, which grows quickly to its maximum height of two feet. The red and pink trumpet-shaped flowers grow in groups of five or six atop the stems. When you plant *Belladonna*, allow its upper tip to just peek out of the ground.

Anemone. Low-growing bulbs, anemones produces charming one- to two-inch blooms in great profusion, in a wide range of colors and petal forms. Some have only four or five broad petals that form a round bloom, while others have many pointed petals. Growing to one foot high and thriving in partial shade, these make excellent border specimens. *A. blanda* (Greek anemone) has pointy petals of dark blue, and is particularly good for cool climates. *A. coronaria* is the poppy-bloomed type, and has three-inch flowers in lavender, vermilion, pink, or white.

Babiani stricta. With the strange common name baboonroot, this low-growing bulb is perfect for covering large areas with vivid color. It grows to twelve inches, and has stems topped with starlike flowers in blue and white. Plant in early spring so it will bloom during spring and summer. These are tender bulbs, and must be removed and stored in cold-winter areas.

Bessera elegans. This delicate plant grows to three feet high, and is formed by slender stems crowned with radiating flower-fingers that bear dangling red or red-and-white blooms in summer. Otherwise known as coral drops, this plant looks its best when grown in profuse groups. If your winters don't dip below freezing, besseras can remain in the ground. Otherwise, they must be dug up and stored.

Bletilla hyacinthina. "Chinese ground orchid" is one of the more difficult bulbs to grow. Its broad, lance-shaped leaves and crooked flower stems reach twelve inches in height and require shade. Flowers are a lovely violet color and appear in summer.

Brodiaea. The tiny lilylike flowers are produced in globe-shaped clusters at the tops of the three-foot stems. The foliage is grassy and the flowers may be either purple or white. Plant corms in a slightly sandy soil, and water them less often than other bulbous plants. They bloom very early in spring. *B. elegans* has all purple flowers, while *B. hyacinthina* comes in white and purple.

Bulbocodium vernum. Sometimes known as spring meadow saffron, this early-bloomer grows to only six inches and is subsequently, after flowering, an excellent ground cover. The charming tiny flowers, a beautiful rose color, appear even before the foliage. This hardy bulb should be planted in early fall. Although it can be forced, it looks best in the outdoor garden.

Calochortus. "Mariposa lily" grows to two feet high and produces many delicate, tiny flowers. It prefers a slightly sandy soil and fairly scant watering. A hardy bulb, it should be planted late in fall, but before the frosts. *C. albus* has tiny white flowers. *C. pulchellus* (golden lantern) has yellowish flowers, and *C. venustus* comes in lavender.

Camissia. The lovely twisting foliage and delicate star-shaped flowers grow hand-in-hand to three feet high. Plant the hardy bulb in fall, about three inches deep. This fairly late-bloomer is a good addition to a predominently early-blooming garden. Flowers show in various shades of blue.

Canna hybrida. Along the tops of their five-foot stems, the four- and five-inch flowers appear in clusters in summer and fall. They range from white to pink, red and scarlet. They require more water than most bulbs, and are fairly hardy, necessitating removal and storage only in harsh, cold climates.

Chionodoxa sardensis. "Glory-of-snow" grows a foot high in early spring and has many dainty, star-shaped blooms of blue and white. It does best in cold climates. Plant in fall.

Chlidanthus fragrans. Chlidanthus looks very much looke the Chionodoxa, growing to one foot high, with clusters of star-shaped blooms. But, *Chlidanthus* is a tender bulb that needs to be removed from outside in all but the mildest of climates. Plant bulbs two inches deep in spring, after the threat of freezing temperatures is over. *Chlidanthus* requires plenty of sun to do its best. Flowers are bright yellow and bloom in summer.

Clivia. Many interesting and beautiful color combinations adorn the flower, which grows on stems to thirty-six inches and is called the kafir lily. Clivia seem to thrive in relatively poor soil, and need to be dried out between waterings. Plant in fall for spring flowers. *C. miniata* is a bright orange color. *C. nobilis* is perhaps more interesting, with red-and-yellow flowers that are fringed in green. Zimmerman and Belgian hybrids also include some beautiful varieties.

Colchicum. "Autumn crocus" is always a satisfying member of the garden. The graceful stems are delicately crowned with funnelform blooms in fall that reach one foot high. Plant them in August and let them grace your garden for years, without special care. *C. autumnale* has pale pink-and-white flowers, while *C. speciosum* blooms in pink, violet, and white.

Convallaria majalis. Lily-of-the-valley has striking, broad green leaves at its base and slender flower stalks that grow to twelve inches high. Tiny, fragrant, bell-shaped flowers dangle from the stems in spring. Once these get established, they demand almost no attention. Put them in a shady spot and keep their soil evenly moist. Flowers are white.

Crinum. The three-foot stalks sprout spectacular funnelform clusters of white or pink flowers in summer. This does well in pots outdoors, and requires at least four hours of full sun a day. This tender bulb should be dug up in cold areas. Give lots of water. *C. asiaticum* are most common, with white flowers.

Crocosmia. Looking very like the exotic *Bletilla hyacintha*, with crooked but graceful flower stems, *Crocosmia* is much easier to grow, and reaches three feet high. The bright orange, orchidlike blooms are borne in summer. Also known as montbretia, this plant is long-lasting when cut. It is a tender bulb, so lift it before the frosts and store through winter.

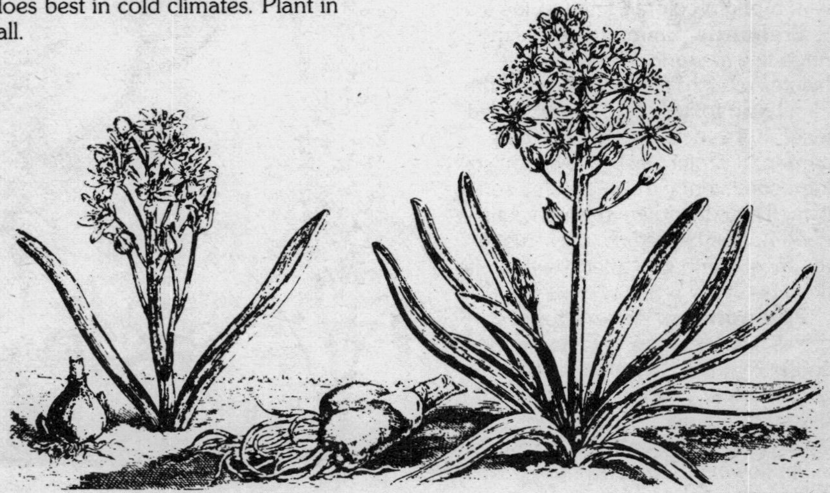

42.—SCILLA. Flowers, blue. C. v. d. P. (*Liliaceæ.*)

THE PLANT NOVELTY OF THE AGE.

Crocus. The beautiful lobe-petaled flowers are one of the first harbingers of spring, often even pushing through a shallow layer of snow in an effort to bloom. They grow to a height of six inches and cover large areas. Plant the bulbs in late fall. *C. chrysanthus* (golden crocus) has vivid orange and yellow flowers, while *C. vernus* (common crocus) blooms in either white or purple.

Cyclamen. This summer- and fall-blooming plant is somewhat difficult to establish, but once so it will spread consistently and produce many attractive blooms. Cyclamens generally do well in a bright spot with some shade, such as under a lacy tree. These plants grow to one foot high and have dark-green mottled foliage. *C. coum* has violet blooms with red markings. *C. persicum* (florists' cyclamen) has larger flowers in white and purple.

Dahlia. Dahlias come in practically every color, and in many interesting shapes. They grow to an average of two feet high on slender stems. Dahlias are one of the most popular bulbs because it is so beautiful yet easy to grow. It better when given regular feedings.

Eranthis. The dainty one- to two-inch flowers stand atop one-foot stems and are interestingly backed by jagged-edged green leaves. Plant in fall for masses of very early spring blooms. *E. cilicia* has yellow flowers with a bright-colored tinge to the leaf.

Eremurus. Eremurus grows in huge flower-studded columns to heights of eight feet and is called the Himilayan foxtail lily. Tall spires add a colorful verical dimension to the garden. It prefers a slightly sandy soil kept consistently moist and full sunlight. They die down in winter, but need not be moved. *E. robustus* is the most common variety, with white flowers.

Erythronium. Adder's tongue grows twelve inches high and prefers cooler climates. Plant in late summer or fall for early spring blooms. *E. albidum* has either solid green or variegated leaves and white, rose, or violet flowers. *E. americanum* has yellow blooms, and *E. origonum* white.

Eucharis. Amazon lily is native to the tropics, and is therefore only a greenhouse specimen in most areas. It grows to approximately thirty inches in height, and has two-inch, white blooms that flower in spring, summer, and fall. It also grows well indoors and loves to be crowded. Let it dry out between waterings. Frequent misting helps produce blooms.

Eucomis. Imagine a tall, slim, flower-studded pineapple perched on the top of a slender stem and you'll have an accurate picture of the eucomis. Thus its common name, pineapple lily. The stalk grows to two feet and is covered with light-green funnelform flowers in summer. This half-hardy plant needs protection, such as a tarp covering, in cold winters. Plant in fall.

Freesia. Freesias have one of the most beautiful and interesting flowering formations of all bulbous plants. Unfortunately, it is fairly difficult to grow in the average garden, as easily drained soil that is kept evenly moist and constantly cool temperatures are requirements. The plant reaches twelve inches high, and its white, red, or orange flowers open in winter and spring.

Fritillaria. Preferring shade to sun, fritillaria grow to three feet high and come in several interestingly colored varieties. Also, the different flower forms of *Fritillaria*, commonly called fritillary, are most unusual. These hardy bulbs should be planted in fall or summer for spring blooms. Once established, they reproduce year after year.

Galanthus. Snowdrop is a dainty plant very similar in look and growth habits to the crocus. Grasslike stems and nodding blooms quickly grow to their maximum height of ten inches, usually during earliest spring. Like the crocus, snowdrop is often first seen amid a light layer of spring now. Plant in a shady spot in the early fall, and leave undisturbed indefinitely.

Galtonia. Known as giant summer hyacinth, this summer bloomer grows as a flower-studded column to four feet. The fragrant white flowers are long-lasting when cut. Plant bulbs eight inches deep in spring and dig them up before the first frost in fall.

Gladiolus. Gladiolus is a spectacular plant—their four-foot stems covered with large lilylike blooms. Plant corms six inches deep in spring and dig up in fall, unless you live in a temperate climate. *G. hybridus* is the most common variety, and comes in every color imaginable.

Gloriosa. This climbing vine can thickly cover large walls and fences with vivid color. The vines grow to more than five feet in length and are covered with beautiful, delicate foliage. Masses of red or orange flowers appear in summer. An excellent indoor specimen too, plant in January for March blooms (indoors) or outdoors in March or April for summer flowers.

Haemanthus. A fine indoor specimen, haemanthus is very sensitive to cold. It is known as blood lily for its deep-crimson blooms—spectacular atop three-foot stems. Plant this tender bulb in late spring, when cold has gone. *H. coccineus* has salmon-colored flowers early in fall. Grow *H. multiflorus* for the blood-red flowers.

Hippeastrum. These beautiful flowers, called amaryllis, are disproportionately large in comparison to the two-foot-high plant. Some varieties have flowers measuring eight inches in diameter. Bulbs are available that produce flowers in many shades of red, rose and white, and that bloom in winter, spring, and summer. Amaryllis prefers partial shade and a fairly rich soil.

Hyacinthus. Hyacinths grow as columnar stems studded with many different shapes, sizes, and flower forms. Plant in the fall and leave undisturbed in your garden for years. *H. o. albulus* is thick with rose, azure, or white flowers in summer.

Hymenocallis. The elaborate flowers of this three-foot, summer-bloomer are common to Japanese-flower-arrangement specialists. They grow atop long, thin leafless stems and give an almost wicked appearance; hence, their common name, spider lily. This tender bulb must be dug up in fall.

Iris. Iris is available in myriad sizes, flower forms, and colors. Generally, blooms are delicate, exotic-looking arrangements of a few oval petals that stand on eighteen-inch stems. It prefers a bright spot with partial shade. Plant in fall for spring and summer blooms. This hardy bulb can stay in the ground through winter. *I. reticulata* is a many-specied variety with azure to purple flowers. *I. xiphium* (Spanish iris) comes in white, yellow, orange, or blue.

Ixia. Called corn lily, the clustering flowers of this corm perch around the tops of thirty-inch stalks amid long, lance-shaped green leaves. The flower's color ranges from rose to yellow, orange and crimson. Plant in fall for spring and summer flowers.

Lachenalia. A beautiful specimen for borders, "cape cowslip" is one foot high and grows easily in most climates. Plant in fall for spring flowers and do not disturb thereafter. *L. bulbifera* has deep-green, grasslike leaves that are sometimes marked with spots, and its large flowers are yellow, red, or lavender.

Lapeirousia. This charming little plant grows a foot high and has quaint rows of tiny funnelform blooms on thin, bent stems. It looks lovely in clumps as a border specimen, or as a specimen in a rock garden. Flowers are a deep-maroon color and appear in spring and summer. In very cold winter regions, dig up and store the bulbs.

Leucojum. "Snowflake" is a delicate but hardy bulb similar in looks and growth habit to the crocus. Snowflake grows to eighteen inches and has white, oval petals that nod in groups atop the stems. It is very easy to grow and lasts for years, in the ground, without special care. Plant in fall for spring and summer blooms.

DAHLIA.

Lilium. To describe the beauty of lilies, it need only be said that this is the bulbous plant to which at least thirty percent of all bulbous plants are compared. These plants are extremely graceful, and come in a multitude of sizes, growth habits, shapes, and colors. Generally, they grow as long, sparsely-leaved stems topped with either individual flowers or clusters of many nodding blooms. The foliage is light- to dark-green. Lilies love to grow in groups in the garden, and prefer bright sun with good drainage soil. They are hardy bulbs, and require frequent watering during the growing season. *L. candidum* (Madonna lily) has three-inch-long white flowers edged with lavender. They bloom in summer. *L. regale* are all-white. *L. longifolium* is the Easter lily.

Lycoris. Golden spider lilly, a lovely summer- and fall-blooming plant, grows to two feet. Sitting atop the slender stalks are clusters of four-to-eight, large, lilylike flowers, with long curling pistils. It is a tender bulb and must be lifted. *L. aurea* has gold or yellow blooms, while *L. radiata* varies from a light-rose color to red.

GLADIOLUS.

Moraea. The three-petaled yellow flower is borne in summer. It sits at the top of a two-foot grasslike stem set amid grasslike foliage. Moraea look its best in groups, adding a delicate patch of color variation to the garden. Plant bulbs in spring and watch them increase in number year after year. *M. bicolor* has a fragrant yellow flower with a deep-brown spot in the middle. *M. iridioides* (butterfly iris) has white blooms with yellow or dark spots.

Muscari. "Grape hyacinth" are interesting little plants with purple-and-blue cob-shaped flower clusters atop eighteen-inch stems. They are easy to grow, blooming in spring, year after year. *M. armeniacum* is the most commonly grown variety.

Narcissus. Alternatively, and perhaps better-known as daffodils, these are ubiquitous. Wide hybridization has created an incredible variety of flower shapes and colors. Perhaps the most beautiful is the narcissus trumpet, with a one-and-one-half-inch-long trumpet flower that extends from a star-shaped cluster of petals. Most varieties grow to two feet and prefer a bright spot with partial shade. They bloom in spring year after year, and need occasional compost feedings.

Nerine. The long, thin petals form wide curling stars each of which clusters in sixes or eights at the stem's apex, some eighteen inches high. The straplike leaves are twelve inches long and a deep-green color that goes beautifully with the pale-pink flowers. Nerine blooms in summer and fall, and likes frequent watering.

Ornithagalum. Known as star-of-Bethlehem, this two-foot-high plant produces masses of lovely, star-shaped blooms, during summer. They are long-lasting as cut flowers. *O. arabicum* has white flowers with black centers. *O. thrysoides* (chincherinchee) has white or yellow flowers. *O. umbellatum* (star-of-Bethlehem) is white with green stripes.

Oxalis. A low-growing delight often called wood-sorrel, this dainy plant has some varieties that bloom year-round, others that bloom in winter, spring, or summer specifically. The cheerful cloverlike flowers come in yellow, white, rose, red, and purple. They are very easy to grow: simply plant them in any garden soil and let them do their thing.

Polyanthes. This unusual and attractive plant sends up flower spires to a height of three feet. The cone-shaped clusters are made of pointy water-lilylike flowers of a snow-white color. Polyanthes can be kept in bloom almost year-round by a successive planting schedule. In winter, however, it must be dug up and stored.

Puschkinia. Excellent as a border specimen, this plant grows to only twelve inches but offers almost a solid blanket of color. Also called striped squill, the one-inch blooms are light-blue or white with a dark-blue stripe. Puschkinia grows better in cool climates. Plant bulbs in fall for summer blooms, and let them remain in the ground undisturbed thereafter.

Ranunculus. Looking like wide, thick-petaled roses, ranunculus, otherwise known as buttercups, are amazingly varied in color, and stand atop pulpy stems that are twelve to eighteen inches high. Ranunculus needs an especially loose, well-draining soil that is kept evenly moist. Plant in early spring for spring and summer blooms. Lift bulbs in winter.

Scilla. The charming miniature flowers cluster around the one-foot stems and give the nodding belllike impression that their common name—bluebells—implies. Easy to grow, they produce masses of flowers in spring. *S. hispanica* flowers are usually blue, but may be rose, lavender, white, or a cream color. *S. nutans* (English bluebell) has the same colors as *S. hispanica. S. sibirica*'s flower is always blue.

Sparaxis. The star-shaped flower is commonly called harlequin flower for its masklike, high-contrast colors. The plant grows to two feet, and does well when cut. In warm climates, plant outdoors in fall for spring blooms. Flowers are bright red, blue, or yellow.

Sprekelia. With flowers looking very like the French *fleur de lis* emblem, this specimen, strangely, has the common name of Aztec lily. The spectacular crimson flowers stand atop four-foot stems and appear in summer and fall. Sprekelia does well indoors and as cut flowers. Outside it must be dug up in winter.

Sternbergia. This quaint plant bears much similarity to the crocus, both in look and growth habit, except that the star-shaped flowers of sternbergia appear in fall rather than spring. The blooms are usually gold-colored, and perch atop the twelve-inch, grasslike stems. A very hardy bulb, sternbergia tolerates winter temperatures to five degrees below zero.

Tigridia. "Shellflower" has bright-red flowers that survive for only a single day. However, each flower stem produces many successive blooms for a period of four weeks during every summer. The three-petaled flowers are borne at the tops of three-foot stems. Plant in a warm soil for best results. Also, you must unearth and store in winter if temperatures in your area dip below 10°F.

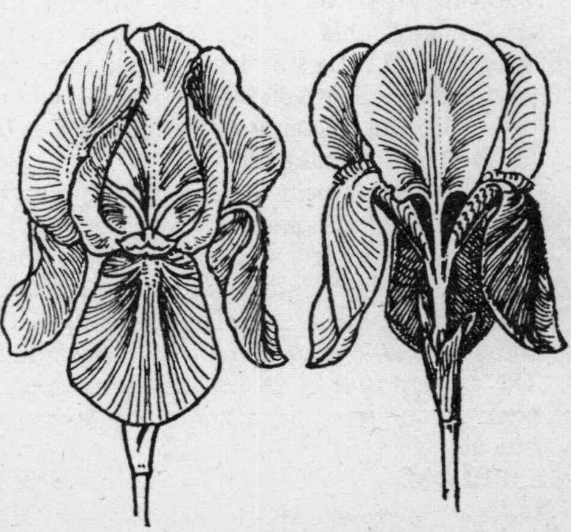
PURPLE IRIS.

Tritonia. The delicate, crooked stems are quaintly dotted with beautiful gladiolalike flowers. The plant grows to three feet and flowers appear in a variety of colors in summer. This is a good cutting flower, and hardy to 10°F. It requires frequent watering.

Tropaeolum. Widely known as nasturtium, this dainty plant is formed by thin, curling vines that creep to cover walls and trellises. The pansylike flowers have a wide range of vivid colors, and are hard to beat for simple beauty. Plant nasturtium in any garden soil, keeping lightly watered. The plants prefer cool weather and bloom in summer and fall. *T. majus* has red flowers. *T. peregrinum* has yellow blooms, while *T. polyphyllum* has smaller blooms in bright-orange.

Tulbaghia. Globe-shaped clusters of violet flowers stand atop eighteen-inch stems. Commonly called society garlic, this summer-bloomer is tender and should be dug up in the fall.

Tulipa. The variety of tulip sizes and especially colors is staggering—all colors of the rainbow and intricate patterns. Choose both early and late-blooming kinds, so you'll have flowers for several weeks. Tulips require cool temperatures early in their seasons. If you live in a cool climate, plant bulbs between October and November. If your winters are relatively warm, store the bulbs in the refrigerator for six weeks before planting.

Vallota. Well-known as scarborough lily, the beautiful scarlet flowers of this plant are yielded on the apex of their thirty-inch stems during summer and fall. Plant in a shady spot, during summer, with its top just peeping above ground level. It is a good idea to grow these in pots outdoors, and take them indoors when the cold weather arrives.

Watsonia. The slender spires stand to heights of four feet and are symmetrically lined with delicate, star-shaped blooms in summer. The flowers are approximately two to three inches across, in red and rose-colors. When grown in temperate climates, watsonia can stay in the ground year-round.

Zantedeschia. The exotic-looking flowers have a waxy, almost plastic texture, and make spectacular cut specimens. Their trumpet-shaped individual blooms appear atop thirty- to forty-inch stems. Also, green, lance-shaped leaves are abundant. Commonly known as calla lily, the plant blooms in spring and summer, and its bulbs must be lifted in winter.

DOUBLE MIXED TULIPS.

Zephyranthus. "Rain lilies" are charming plants that grow a foot tall and spread to cover vast fields. Lovely pink flowers are produced *en masse* in summer and fall. Plant in the fall and give plenty of water during the growing season.

Sources

Berkery Inc.
P.O. Box 67
Staten Island, NY 10314

Borbeleta Gardens
10078 154th Ave.
Elk River, MN 55330

Breck's Reservation Center
6523 N. Galena Rd.
Peoria, IL 61632

W. Atlee Burpee Co.
300 Park Ave.
Warminster, PA 18974

Carroll Gardens
P.O. Box 310
Westminster, MD 21157

The Daffodil Mart
North, VA 23128

deJager Bulbs, Inc.
188 Asbury St.
South Hamilton, MA 01982

Doornbosch Bulb Co.
1320 South St.
Hackensack, NJ 07601

Howard B. French
Rt. 100
Pittsfield, VT 05762

Russell Graham
4030 Eagle Crest Rd. N.W.
Salem, OR 97304

Jackson & Perkins
Medford, OR 97501

Quality Dutch Bulbs, Inc.
50 Lake Drive
Hillsdale, NJ 07642

Rex Bulb Farms
Box 145
Newberg, OR 97132

John Scheepers, Inc.
63 Wall St.
NY, NY 10005

Spaulding Bulb Farm
1811 Howey Rd.
Sebring, FL 33870

Van Bourgondian Bros.
Dept. 305-202 P.O. Bx.A
Rt. 109
Babylon, NY 11702

Sven Van Zonneveld Co.
c/o Mrs. C. Bishop
810 Cassel RD
Collegeville, PA 19426

Wyatt-Quarles Seed Co.
331 S. Wilmington St.
P.O. Box 2131
Raleigh, NC 27602

FERNS

Ferns are among the oldest living plant forms, and during the Carboniferous era ancestors of modern ferns constituted the dominant vegetation on the earth. Ancient forms varied from miniatures to huge treelike varieties, and even today some species grow thirty to forty feet tall in tropical areas. Fern fanciers often cultivate exotically named types, such as adder's-tongue fern (*ophioglossum*) or rattlesnake fern (*botrychium*), which are among the most primitive forms. Some ferns are air plants, others such as *marsilia* and *salvinia* are aquatic.

True ferns (those of the polypody family) usually have traingular fronds subdivided into many leaflets (pinnas). Those that grow fairly upright are good for pot plants. Those with drooping or trailing fronds are appropriate for hanging baskets. The crested ferns are so named because the fronds fork at the tips, creating several crests that flutter in breezes above the sturdier remainder of the frond.

For indoor use, greenhouses, and gardens in warm climates, many tropical ferns are available commercially. For outdoor use, imports from England, Japan, and other parts of the temperate world can be grown in colder climates into Canada. Many ferns, such as adiantum (the maidenhair) are suitable for both indoor and outdoor use.

Hundreds of ferns native to North America are adapted to every region. Ferns are surprisingly hardy and often thrive in climates remote from their native territory. Several southern shield ferns (*dryopteris*), for example, which grow wild in Louisiana and other southern states, do well in latitudes above 40 degrees even without mulching. Others will overwinter in areas colder than their native habitat if they are mulched. Wild ferns are usually easy to transplant if you are careful how you handle their roots. Of all plants, ferns have among the most sensitive roots. In transplanting from the wild, dig well around the plant so as to lift out the entire root system with as little disturbance as possible. Also be sure that you don't cover the crown with soil, because this is where new growth originates. Transplanting can be done from spring to fall, but avoid the heat of summer, which is a stressful time for many ferns. Water generously after transplanting to establish the root system quickly.

Many ferns are evergreens. Sometimes the fertile fronds will turn brown after releasing spores but the sterile fronds will continue to be green. This will make the plant look somewhat frowsy for a while until new growth starts in spring.

Indoors your ferns will do best if you keep them out of drafts and can provide temperatures that drop to at least 60° at night. Many, including pterias, require high humidity to thrive; if you cannot provide high humidity, stick to less demanding varieties.

For outdoor gardeners, ferns are an excellent solution for garden areas without much sun, since most of them come from forest floors and require shade. They also provide a subtle background to flowering plants such as lily-of-the-valley, trilliums, and foxglove, which also enjoy shade. Small ones make good groundcovers, and treelike forms can be used as specimens to provide garden accent.

Readers interested in ferns might consider joining the American Fern Society (Address: c/o Dr. Judith Skog, Department of Biology, George Mason University, Fairfax, VA 22030). The society maintains a spore bank of more than a thousand species available to members at moderate cost.

ADIANTUM (maidenhair fern) has sprays of tiny, light-green leaves, sometimes compared to coins, carried on long, thin, black stems that are almost invisible. The effect is lacy, almost shimmering. Adiantum is good for hanging baskets. The fronds are delicate and may turn brown at the tips if they hang on furniture; stand pots on an inverted pot or other pedestal to keep the fronds free. Many varieties are tropical, but *A. pedantum*, a native species, and the imported *A. venustum*, or Himalayan maidenhair, withstand northern winters. The latter is especially handsome, with full, feathery fronds six to eight inches long that arch outward. It spreads well, too. All adiantums like humidity and well-drained soil.

ASPLENIUM are dainy. *A. nidus* (bird's-nest fern) has shiny, bright green, wafer-thin leaves growing from rosettes that resemble a bird's nest. *A. bulbiferum* (mother fern) has black stems and darker leaves and is nice in hanging baskets. Keep these well watered, but they are tolerant of dry air. *A. platyneuron*—spleenwort—has narrow, upright, single-pinnated fronds with rigid black stems. Wild varieties of asplenium are easily transplanted.

ATHYRIUM includes *A. niponicum* (Japanese painted fern), a hardy species with spectacular colored fronds—dark red along the veins and light to dark green along the margins. It's easy to grow indoors if well ventilated and if temperatures do not got over 70°, and outdoors it survives as far north as Canada. *A. Filix-femina*, lady fern, has a wide range in the wild in temperate climates, withstands northern winters, and is easily transplanted.

BLECHNUM (tree fern) has dark-green leaves and comes in varieties suitable for pots or growing up to four feet tall in floor planters. Fronds grow to two feet. *B. spicant*, deer fern, is an evergreen that is easy to grow. These ferns do not require as much humidity as most other types.

CIBOTIUM *schiedei* (Mexican tree-fern) is a slow grower that reaches to twelve feet outdoors but only around three indoors. It has a sturdy build. Pale-green, graceful fronds that arc and droop can grow to three-feet. If you give it support, you can even grow it in water. It likes the higher temperature range, and in soil doesn't need as much watering as many other ferns.

CRYTOMIUM (holly fern) has glossy, leathery leaves of a deep-green color like holly. It is especially adaptable to household conditions and dish gardens. Common in North America, this fern is one of the easiest to transplant to home gardens from the wild.

CYATHEA *arborea* (tree-fern), a leathery, tree-size fern that grows three to five feet, has lemony tinted, green fronds. It likes the higher temperature range, moist soil, and subdued daylight.

CYSTOPTERIS, bladder fern, is noted for two especially popular varieties. *C. bulbifera* (bulblet bladder fern) has elongated, lance-shaped, twice-pinnate fronds with large, fleshy bulbs on the underside. The bulbs are buds that fall off, root, and form new bladder fern. The fronds are delicate and feathery, tapering from a broad base to narrow tip. Cystopteris likes moisture and are often found clinging to wet rocks near waterfalls from Tennessee to Canada. Its budding habit insures a plentiful supply of new plants. *C. fragilis* (fragile bladder fern) has small, lance-shaped fronds, pinnated two or three times, and toothed. It is one of the first ferns to appear in the spring, along streams and in rock crevices from Georgia to Newfoundland. Like the bulblet, it is an excellent choice for rock gardens and bog gardens.

DAVALLIA (rabbit's-foot or squirrel-foot fern) is named for its fuzzy, brown rhizomes. One of the best ferns for indoor culture, these have exuberant lacy fronds. Several varieties are available, and they look best in hanging baskets or on pedestals. These plants like to be misted.

DRYOPTERIS is a large group of ferns that includes many evergreens. *D. Braunii*, Braun's Holly Fern, is an evergreen shield fern with thick, twice-pinnated fronds. This large, hardy fern is found in deep-wooded, mountainous areas from Pennsylvania to Canada. It transplants well and adds a rich deep green to the garden year round. *D. cristata*, the crested shield fern, has lance-shaped, twice-pinnated, fork-tipped fronds. The forking or cresting gives this fern a feathery, lustrous appearance. The sterile fronds are generally shorter than the fertile fronds and are evergreen, lasting through the winter after the fertile fronds have released their spores and have turned brown. The plant is found in swampy areas from Kentucky to Newfoundland. Many cultivars of the shield ferns are commercially available, as their elegance makes them a favorite with fern fanciers. They require constantly damp soil and deep shade to grow best.

A real beauty is the colorful Japanese shield fern, *D. erythrosora*, also called autumn fern. Its fiddleheads are bronze colored; mature fronds are dark green, and the sori on the undersides are bright pink. Fronds may grow as long as three feet. This variety is excellent for adding splashes of color to the typically all-green fern garden, and it grows well throughout temperate regions.

MATTEUCCIA *struthiopteris*, ostrich fern, is named for its plumelike fronds. It has a vaselike crown. A North American native, it withstands cold weather.

NEPHROLEPIS (Boston fern or sword fern) is a fast-growing indoor favorite with drooping, sword-shaped fronds. Named Boston fern because it was discovered in a shipment of tropical ferns in Boston, it is one of the hardiest ferns. It does best in bright light. In winter it may tolerate some sun, but requires shade in summer. Nephrolepis is available in dwarf form as well as in varieties with fronds three to five feet long and with ruffled leaves.

OPHIOGLOSSUM *vulgatum*, adder's tongue, has small, leaflike fronds. The sterile portion of the frond is an ovate leaf, while the fertile portion is a tall, slender spike that resembles the adder's tongue for which the plant is named. This one proliferates from root buds and spreads rapidly. It grows from the southern United States through Canada in moist fields. The simplicity of the leaflike spiked frond makes a nice contrast among more crested and feathery ferns. However, it is small and should be planted where it will not be overshadowed by large, showier plants. Adder's tongue was once a great favorite in folk medicine for the cure of snake bites.

OSMUNDA includes *O. regalis*, the royal fern, has twice-pinnate fronds with finely toothed margins that grow up to six feet long. *O. cinnamomea*, cinnamon fern, has broad, lance-shaped, single-pinnated fronds which grow in a tall, graceful crown of sterile green fronds around tall, erect, cinnamon-brown fertile fronds. The fertile fronds appear first in spring and their fiddleheads are covered with a soft wooly wrapping which remains as a tuft of rusty wool at the base of the plant. The cinnamon fern, found in swampy areas from Florida to Nova Scotia, is a deep green during the summer and turns bright yellow in the fall. It needs plenty of water.

PELLAEA (button fern or cliff-brake fern) is easy to grow. These have round, unfern-like leaves. This plant grows from rhizomes, and spreads quickly. It is popular for indoor culture and attractive in hanging baskets.

PHYLLITIS *scolopendrium* (hart's tongue), named for its tongue-like fronds, is a crested fern that grows wild in England. Its dark-green, strap-shaped leaves have forked tips. Indoors it grows about two feet tall, and larger outdoors. It does best if the temperature doesn't go above 70°, and with mulching can overwinter in many shady temperate-zone gardens.

PLATYCERIUM (staghorn fern), an indoor favorite, is a strange-looking air plant with enormous, leathery, forked fronds that resemble antlers. Its dramatic form is less evident in group plantings; to show it off, set it on a large piece of furniture, mount it on cork or redwood, or put it in a hanging basket or in a pot fastened to a wall bracket. Grow it in humus, with charcoal added, kept constantly moist; and mist it daily. It needs strong light but not sun. The most impressive is *P. grande*, with fronds five feet long, but varieties with fronds half that size are also available. This fern develops flat fronds that turn brown; these are not dying—they assist the plan to collect moisture.

POLYPODIUM (polypody) is a large group named for thick brownish rhizomes, sometimes called hare's foot. The fronds vary from bright green to gray green and are dramatic rather than feathery. These plants can be used in pots or hanging baskets, and they require moist soil, misting, and bright light. They often temporarily react badly to transplanting but soon recover.

POLYSTICHUM has several popular names, such as leather fern and Christmas fern. Foliage varies from stiff and thick, upright fronds to light, feathery leaves. Dwarf varieties are adaptable for terrariums, while plants two feet or so in height are attractive in pots. *P. acrostichoides*, Christmas fern, is a good one for your garden. It has lance-shaped, leathery, once-pinnated, evergreen fronds. Found in rocky woods from Florida to Canada, this is an excellent winter fern because of its deep-green, highly polished sheen. Attractive in the spring as well because of the contrast between the delicate, pale green unrolling fiddleheads and the darker, leathery mature fronds of the older plants. *P. setiform*, also hardy for cold climates, is a soft, leathery shield fern.

PTERIDIUM *aquilinum*, bracken or brake fern, is a large, coarse, twice-pinnate fern. It grows vigorously in dry, wide-open spaces. The most widely distributed of all the ferns, it occurs in one form or another in all parts of the world. It is believed to be the "fearn" of the early Saxons that lent its name to many English towns and villages. Bracken fern was also a staple of medieval medicine and magic, as effective for curing head colds as for chasing witches away. Bracken is a delicate light-green in the spring and becomes darker through the summer. Hardiest of the ferns, it can be useful as a foundation or border plant under trees and alongside walls and pathways, though it requires containment (bricks or other edging strips) due to its unruly growth habit. A "dry" fern, it requires some sun to grow well.

PTERIS (brake fern or sword-brake) is good for table pots because most varieties grow only one or two feet high. Fronds are light green, sometimes silvery. These grow rapidly, and may need repotting annually.

Culture

Temperature: Most ferns like the 55 to 75°F range; nephrolepis and platycerium do well up to 80°. Most will do well at 50° or a few degrees below, but don't change their temperature quickly; acclimatize them gradually to lower temperatures. A nighttime drop of at least five degrees is important for good growth. Outdoors, if you are not using a native fern from your area, you may have to experiment to see which will survive your winter conditions. Mulching with several inches of pine needles or a foot of deciduous leaves enables many ferns to survive cold conditions.

Light: Ferns do best in strong light, such as subdued daylight. In southern-facing windows, they should be placed at some distance away from the direct light. They can tolerate a few hours of direct sun, but indirect, filtered sunlight is preferable.

Humidity: Humidity is the most important part of fern culture. Dry air is usually the cause of failure indoors. Crytomiums and blechnum tolerate low humidity, but for others you can't go wrong by using a pebble tray—though this is not essential—and daily misting will probably be necessary.

Watering: Fern roots must be kept well watered. Even if you keep the soil moist to the touch by watering from the top, moisture may not be penetrating the entire root system. Soak a pot-bound fern once a week for half an hour in a pail of water. At the same time, don't overwater and provide good drainage. Outdoors, be alert to watering needs during hot, dry spells. A covering of wood chips on the soil will help retain moisture. Ferns rest part of the year, and during this period you can reduce the amount of water.

Soil: Ferns need a rich humusy soil, but their dense root systems require that the soil be loose. The best mixture is humus, to which sand has been added for drainage. Coarse sand is best, but sponge rock or shredded firbark also can be used in container gardening. Sprinkling in a bit of charcoal will keep the soil from becoming sour. Outdoors, if you garden soil is not especially rich, add compost to the hole before sitting in a fern.

Fertilizing: Fertilizer will enhance the color of ferns. Provide fertilizer once a month during the months when they are growing most vigorously.

Pest Control: Mealybugs and scale insects are the most troublesome to ferns. Some ferns have delicate foliage, so remove any pests on the fronds with a spray of tepid water and a cotton swab, rather than using commercial sprays.

Propagation: Ferns may be propagated in several different ways depending on their individual growth habits: nephrolepis by division; davallias by cutting and rooting rhizomes; staghorns by removing and rooting the suckers; and the mother fern by cutting and potting the plantlets that grow on the fronds.

Sources

Alberts & Merkel Brothers Inc.
Post Office Box 537
Boynton Beach, FL 33435

Boldue's Greenhill Nursery
2131 Vallejo Street
St. Helena, CA 94574
(exotic ferns)

Mrs. E. Reed Brelsfoit
1816 Cherry Street
Jacksonville, FL 32205

Edelweiss Gardens
Robbinsville, NJ 08691
(exotic ferns)

Fancy Fronds
1911 4th Avenue West
Seattle, WA 98119
(hardy and exotic ferns)

Fern Hill Farm
Rt. 3, Box 191
Greenville, AL 36037

Fronds, Inc.
P. O. Box 20026
Cincinnati, OH 45220
(hardy and exotic ferns)

Gardens of the Blue Ridge
Rt. 221
Pineola, NC 28662

Henderson's Botanical Gardens
Rt. 6
Greensburg, IN 47240

Illini Gardens
P. O. Box 125
Oakford, IL 62673

Leatherman's Gardens
2637 N. Lee Avenue
South El Monte, CA 91733

Leslie's Wild Flower Nursery
30 Summer Street
Methuen, MA 01844
(hardy ferns and wildflowers)

Logee's Greenhouses
55 North St.
Danielson, CT 06239

Merry Gardens
Camden, ME 04843

Orchid Gardens
6700 Splithand Rd.
Grand Rapids, MN 55744

Ritchey's Rock Garden Ferns
1014 S. E. Fern St.
Grants Pass, OR 97526

Roehr's Exotic Nurseries
Rutherford, New Jersey 07070
(exotic ferns)

Frances M. Sinclair
RFD #2 Newfields Rd.
Exeter, NH 03833

Siskiyou Rare Plant Nursery
2825 Cummings Road
Medford, OR 97501

Sky-Cleft Gardens
Camp Street Extension
Barre, VT 05641

Sperka's Woodland Acres Nursery
Route 2
Grivitz, WI 54114

Talnadge's Fern Gardens
354 "G" St.
Chula Vista, CA 92010

The Three Laurels
Madison County
Marshall, NC 28753

Van Bourgonhan Bros.
Box A
Babylon, NY 11702

Varga's Nursery
2631 Pickerton Rd.
Warrington, PA 18976

Wake Robin Farm
Route 1, Box 33
Home, PA 15747
(hardy ferns and wildflowers)

The Wild Garden
Box 487
Bothall, WA 98011

Thomas M. Wood
Constantia, NY 13044

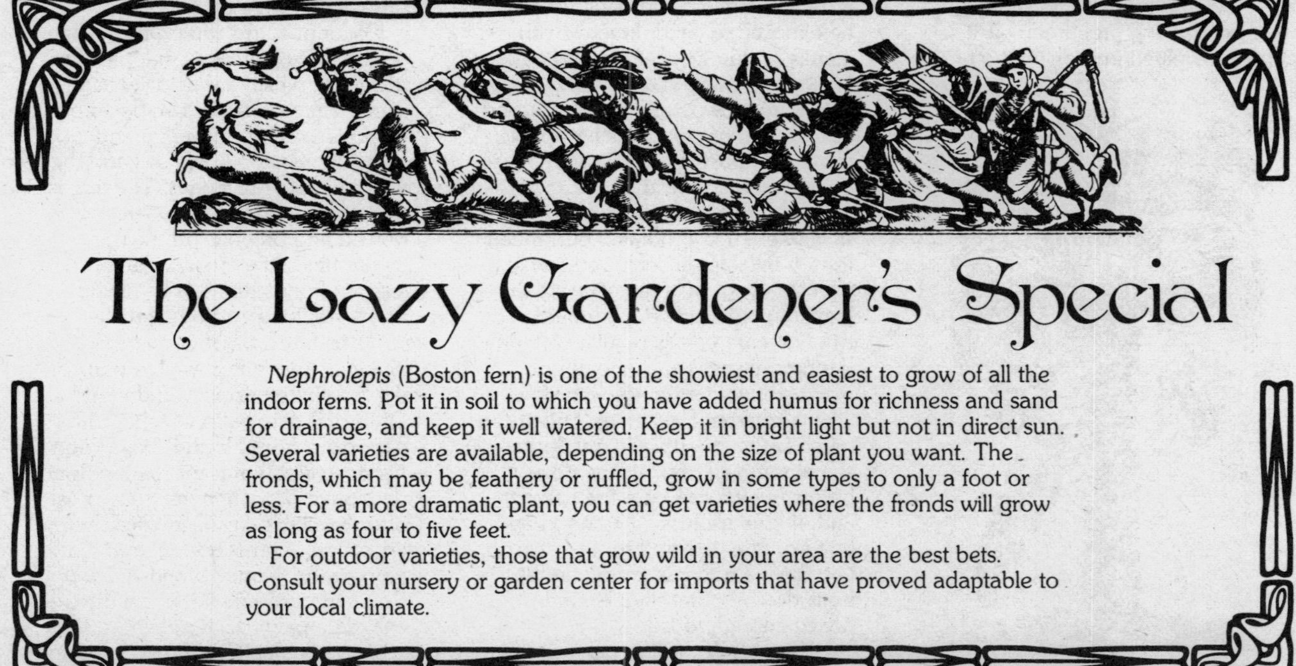

The Lazy Gardener's Special

Nephrolepis (Boston fern) is one of the showiest and easiest to grow of all the indoor ferns. Pot it in soil to which you have added humus for richness and sand for drainage, and keep it well watered. Keep it in bright light but not in direct sun. Several varieties are available, depending on the size of plant you want. The fronds, which may be feathery or ruffled, grow in some types to only a foot or less. For a more dramatic plant, you can get varieties where the fronds will grow as long as four to five feet.

For outdoor varieties, those that grow wild in your area are the best bets. Consult your nursery or garden center for imports that have proved adaptable to your local climate.

After perhaps 120 million years of evolution, palms do not look all that different from their primordial prototypes; 4000 species are found in all the warmer places in the world. They are most common in the tropical Americas, Southeast Asia, and the Pacific Islands.

Nine genera native to North America are found in Florida and the southeastern Coastal Plain, except for California washingtonia, which is native to the Southwest. Date palms and coconut palms are among scores of imported palms that adapt well to cultivation in North America. While these two were introduced primarily for economic reasons, other palms have been brought here for their beauty. Among these are the manila palm (*Veitchia merilli*), which resembles a small royal palm and is used to line avenues.

Palms belong to a botanical subdivision known as monocotelydons and are more closely related to orchids, grasses, lilies, and irises than to pines and hardwoods. Palm trunks do not have a layer of bark; instead, they are covered with a sort of rind, like that of bamboo trees. Nor do their trunks produce branches or attain an extra ring of wood each year; their growth takes place at the very top of the tree. A thickening trunk, as occurs with a few species, results from enlargement of the original cells, not from the addition of new cells. Palms characteristically produce a few large feathery or fan-shaped evergreen leaves that appear one at a time and cluster at the stem (trunk) tip. When young, leaves are erect and swordlike in the center of the tree's crown.

Although most palm trees have single trunks, several species have multiple trunks. These can be handsome additions to a landscape where they have room to stand out from other foliage.

Landscaping with Palms

When choosing palm trees for your property, consider the shape, maximum size, and rate of growth of each specimen. Before buying a tree, try to see a mature version, for, in a few years, its proportional scale to buildings and other trees may change drastically. These are six of the best palm collections: Fairchild Tropical Garden, Miami; Federal Experiment Station, Mayaguez, Puerto Rico; Foster Botanical Garden, Honolulu; Huntington Botanical Gardens, San Marino, California; Los Angeles State and County Arboretum, Arcadia, California; U.S. Introduction Station, Miami.

Also consider in advance the tree's hardiness and its humidity, soil, and sun requirements. Although tropical palms will not survive frost, you might be able to find a tree imported from a cooler habitat. Palms are famous as tropical sun-lovers, yet they grow as far north as Ireland and Scotland and a few, such as *Geonoma*, *Chamaedorea*, and *Rhapis*, prefer shade. The saw palmetto withstands temperatures as low as 10°F, but since it does not transplant well, except in containers, it is rarely seen in northerly locations.

Planting Palms

Palm trees can be planted at any time of the year, but the best time is the beginning of the spring growing season. Most palms are adaptable in new environments as long as they have fertile, moist, well-drained soil.

If you live in an area where palm trees can grow, your soil is likely to be somewhat porous and sandy, and your preplanting preparation will consist mainly in improving the undersoil and topsoil. Begin by ascertaining that your soil has no mineral deficiencies and make any necessary corrections.

—DATE PALM.

Start preparing the ground by digging a hole much larger than the rather small root ball of the tree. Mix the backfill with generous amounts of humus-forming material, such as compost, dampened peat moss, leafmold, and grass clippings, and put most of the soil back into the hole. Ideally, you will have given yourself several weeks of lead time in order to give the bacteria in the organic filling a chance to bring the soil to a richer state.

Place the root ball in the pit and cover it with humus-rich topsoil that has been mixed with slow-acting fertilizer. Don't be alarmed by a surprisingly small root ball on a nursery specimen. Usually nothing is wrong with the tree. Once planted, palms sprout roots directly from the underground portion of the trunk. Sometimes, roots even grow above ground level. Before transplanting a large tree to your home, however, ask the nursery to prune off some of the older green leaves (unless you intend to grow the palm in a container). This measure prevents excessive transpiration en route that would weaken the root system.

When the new palm is in the ground, water it thoroughly. If it will be exposed to wind, brace it with planks or guy wires. Palm trees like relatively moist soil at all times (that's why they grow near springs in desert oases), and organic mulch of peat moss, compost, or other material will help preserve moisture.

Care. In nature, palms grow very slowly, but if you obtain your tree(s) from a reliable nursery, you can expect steady growth almost from the beginning of its life in your garden. Routine care entails regular watering during dry spells and one, if not more, annual fertilizings with slow-acting fertilizer. Palms don't need much pruning—usually only occasional removal of unsightly dead leaves (which can be a fire hazard) and, if you are fussy, cutting away dried out flowers and fruit clusters. If you have a coconut palm, cut the fruits down before they become heavy enough to fall.

Palmettos do best in rich soil but adapt readily to less-than-ideal conditions. The cabbage palmetto even tolerates poor, sandy soil. You can start your own palmettos easily by sowing fresh seed in a growing medium that is half peat moss and half sand.

"Hardy" Palm Trees for Gardens

Acromia totai
Allagoptera campestris
Arecastrum romanzoffianum
Butia capitata
Caryota urens
Chamaedorea cataractarum
C. costaricana
Chamaerops humilis
Erythea armata
E. brandegii
E. edulis
E. elegans
Jubaea chilensis
Livistonia australis
L. chinensis
L. mariae
Phoenix canariensis
P. dactylifera
P. reclinata
P. robelinii
P. sylvestris
Rhapis excelsa
R. humilis
Rhapophyllum hystrix
Rhapostylis sapida
Sabal causiarum
S. etonia
S. minor
S. palmetto
S. texana
Seronoa repens
Thrinax microcarpa
Thachycarpus caepitosus
T. fortunei
Trithrinax acanthocoma
T. brasiliensis
Washingtonia filifera
W. robusta

Cherry palms grow to a maximum of 26 feet, although the usual height is 10 to 15 feet. The Florida cherry palm (*Pseudophoenix sargentii*), also known as the buccaneer palm, is found in the upper Florida Keys as well as in several Caribbean countries.

The **coconut palm** genus apparently contains a single species, *Cocos nucifera*. No one knows for sure where it originated, although the islands of the Indian Ocean are a likely area. In the United States, coconut palms occur naturally along the coast of southern Florida and in the Keys. Southern Californians who try to grow them have no luck.

Coconut palms top 65 feet. They are the only palm tree that produces coconuts, which are actually large seeds. Ripe coconuts can be sprouted if planted broadside up and showing just above the soil and then watered every few days. The tree is distinguished by its often leaning or bowed and bulbous trunk. The crown has stiffly arched feather-shaped fronds that can be as much as 18 feet long and 6 feet wide.

Date palms, native to tropical Africa and Asia, adapt well to parts of the Southwest, Texas, and Florida. Of the 18 date palm varieties, the date palm from North Africa (*Phoenix dactylifera*) and the Canary Island date palm (*P. canariensis*) are most often available from American nurseries. The latter is a stock tree that tends to be planted along avenues. You can occasionally obtain the Senegal date palm (*P. reclinata*), a fast-growing, multiple-stemmed tree, and the pygmy date palm (*P. roebelenii*), a small palm with shiny dark green leaves that grows to 11½ feet at maturity.

Date palms are best grown from suckers rather than as transplants. Individual date palms survive in southern Florida, but to bear fruit this tree needs the long, hot summers of southern Arizona and California. Still, some Florida trees produce good-quality fruit, especially if the dates are picked when underripe and carefully cured.

While some palms produce male and female flowers, or single flowers that are bisexual, individual date palms produce only female or male flowers; only female trees whose flowers are pollinated bear fruit. If you have a female tree near a male counterpart, you can hope for a substantial annual yield of dates. Cultivated date palms bear up to 220 pounds of dates each year.

Pygmy date palms (*P. roebelinii*) are popular in yards and as container trees. Native to Vietnam and Burma, they can grow more than 11 feet high outdoors. Under ideal conditions, their rough trunks (sometimes multiple trunks) attain a thickness of 6 feet in diameter. Their long cascading leaves bow over toward the ground. Pygmy date palms can be grown slowly from seeds, which remain viable for 2 to 3 months and take about 5 weeks to germinate.

Canary Island date palms (*P. canariensis*), with their long (15 feet), featherlike leaves, are wind-resistant, drought-resistant, and salt-tolerant—in short, trees that withstand just about everything southern Florida weather has to offer. Unlike some other date palms, though, they do not sucker and must be grown from seed. They produce edible but mediocre fruit.

The cliff date palm (*P. rupicola*) is a rare, graceful form with a slender trunk and feather-shaped, bright-green drooping fronds that can be as long as 10 feet when the tree attains a maximum height of 25 feet.

The **Everglades palm** (*A. wrightii*) is a native of Florida's southern tip. The sole species in the genus *Acoelorrhaphe*, it is a clump-forming, salt-tolerant tree originating in swampy areas. Nevertheless, it survives with rich soil in slightly drier situations. Its interesting shape makes it an effective addition to a landscape, provided you have room to accommodate its propensity to spread. But this tree is hard to get. Removing Everglades palms from their natural habitat is restricted by law. However, they can be grown (slowly) from seed.

Fan-leaved **palmetto palms**, of which there are 20 species, belong to the genus *Sabal*. Native to the Western Hemisphere, they occur along the southern Coastal Plain and in Florida. Of the 6 species native to North America, three are trees and three are shrubs. All have solitary, usually stout trunks crowned with a dense thicket of fan-shaped leaves, but the trunks of some palmettos are underground.

The cabbage palmetto (*S. palmetto*), the state tree of Florida, occurs naturally as far north as southeastern North Carolina. Its native habitats are seacoast woodlands, marshes, and the sandy soils along the coast, but cabbage palmettos can do well in a variety of soils. Because cabbage palmettos are shade-tolerant, they are used for coastal and inland landscaping and make an excellent avenue tree.

The bush palmetto (*S. minor*) is the hardiest palmetto and likes wet ground. In its eastern range, it rarely has an above-ground trunk, and is usually a bush 6 to 10 feet high with a rounded crown of fan-shaped leaves. In its western range, which extends to southeastern Texas and up the Mississippi Valley to southeastern Arkansas, it may grow into a small tree. Its normal habitats are sandy soils and alluvial soils of floodplains. In early summer, flowers appear; in October or November, it produces numerous globe-shaped fruit.

Texas palmetto (*S. texana*) originates in the area around the mouth of the Rio Grande. The stout, erect trunk is crowned with fan-shaped leaves. This tree can attain a height of 60 feet. It does well in southern Texas. As it ages, it sheds its old leaf bases, called "boots," leaving a fairly smooth trunk.

Royal palms are medium-sized to tall branchless trees with smooth, light gray, columnar trunks that sometimes bulge at or above the middle. The broad crown of featherlike leaves is large and spreading. These are the palms most frequently planted along streets and used for landscaping public buildings and large houses. The genus *Roystonea*, named after an American general, contains about 16 species, of which one, the Florida royal palm (*R. elata*) is native to southern Florida. Also encountered in southern Florida are the native species, which still grows wild in Everglades National Park, and the Cuban royal palm (*R. regia*).

Some royal palms grow as high as 132 feet. All require rich soil and full sunlight.

A purely American tree, the **saw palmetto** (*Serenoa repens*) is the sole member of its genus and not the most noble of palms. It grows throughout the southeastern Coastal Plain. Much of the scrub land in Florida is forested with saw palmettos. Although its trunks are given to horizontal creeping, some trunks grow vertically to a height of 20 feet or more. The leaves of this tree are fan-shaped; its fruit and terminal bud are edible (removing the terminal bud, however, kills the tree). White-tailed deer and raccoon feed on its fruit. Saw palmettos are hard to work with; generally, they resist transplanting from the wild unless you grow them in a container.

Thatch palm native to North America are the Florida thatch palm (*Thrinax floridana*) and the brittle thatch palm (*T. microcarpa*). Both are small, slender trees with fan-shaped leaves and long, slender, often drooping, leaf stalks that split to form a forked base. The Florida thatch palm grows wild in hammocks and along shorelines and is salt-tolerant. Sometimes attaining a height of 30 feet, it has a thick trunk that remains tough until the tree is old. Its leaves are distinguished by a yellowish green underside. Brittle thatch palms grow slightly taller, and the undersides of their leaves are silvery white. Both grow in sandy pineland soil and in the dry coral soil of the Florida Keys. They produce fragrant white blossoms.

Coccothrinax is a small tropical palm genus with only one American member, the silver thatch palm or Florida Silverpalm (*C. argentea*). All palms of this group tolerate partial shade and grow in limestone soils. The undersides of their fan-shaped leaves are silvery white, like brittle thatch palms, but the leaf stalks are not split. Although the tallest Florida Silverpalm may exceed 30 feet in height, most specimens are under that. It has a straight, columnar trunk topped with a rounded crown of leaves up to 2 feet in diameter. Its fleshy edible fruits are bright purple berrylike globes that turn almost black as they mature.

One species of **washingtonia palms**, which occur only in the Western Hemisphere, is native to the Southwest. California washingtonia (*Washingtonia filifera*) is a tall, erect tree distinguished by enormous fan-shaped fronds with blades up to 6 feet across. New light green leaves spring from the top of the tree on stout, spiny stems. Their many-folded blades often split to or below the middle; their edges carry threadlike color, and remain for years, forming a brown skirt around the trunk and below the crown. California washingtonia grow in desert, tropical, and subtropical climates. Large stands are found near Palm Springs, California, yet they also grow well in southern Florida's humid climate.

Attractive ornamental trees, washingtonia palms flower in midsummer, producing branching clusters of fragrant yellow blossoms. The persistant dried leaves provide a nesting site for birds and small animals.

Occasionally, American nurseries stock a Mexican washingtonia, *W. robusta*. The fan-shaped leaves of this palm are not so deeply split and they lack the fibery strings at the ends.

Indoor Palms

Palms grown indoors are usually imports from tropical areas—seedlings and saplings of species that may grow to something like sixty-foot heights in the wild but that grow slowly enough in tubs to be useful indoors for a number of years.

In nature, some palms, such as phoenix, grow singly, and these are best if you want a specimen to stand alone. Because most palms naturally grow in clusters of their own kind or in combination with other types of trees and shrubs, they look attractive in plant groupings or planted several to a pot.

Beaucarnea, the pony-tail palm or elephant's foot, has a trunk shaped like a thermometer, with a bulb at the ground that tapers to a thin stem. The foliage grows in sprays of slender leaves resembling a pony tail. It grows five feet or higher.

Caryota—fishtail palm—are imports from Asia and the Pacific. *C. mitis* has glossy-green fronds four feet long. *C. plumosa* is especially feathery. Its tall stems look best if several are planted together.

Chamaedorea, from Central and South America, is available in several varieties. *C. elegans*, the parlor palm, has long feathery fronds, each growing from a single stem; plant several stems together. *C. erumpens*, the bamboo palm, can stand singly; its stem clusters are topped with short fronds. It will grow over six feet tall. *C. humilis*, the fan palm, is smaller, with stiff, fan-shaped leaves in olive green.

Chrysalidocarpus, butterfly palm, has slender creamy stems and feathery, light green leaves that shine. It grows over five feet tall.

Cycas, sago palm or fern palm, grow five to six feet tall but are slow growers. These have sturdy trunks. The leathery, dark green fronds arch upward and are especially tough.

Howeia, the kentia palm, has arching, feathery leaves that give an umbrella effect. As these grow to over four or five feet, they can be used to overhang chairs and other furnishings or to give height to group plantings. These are among the prettiest and most versatile of all palms for indoor use.

Livistona, the Chinese fan, has, as its name implies, fan-shaped leaves. It has a sturdy trunk and can stand alone to fill up empty areas of large rooms. It will grow over eight feet tall indoors.

Phoenix, the date palm, is especially adaptable and grows to about six feet in a pot, but dwarf varieties are available. It has arching, dark green foliage. One dwarf, *P. roebelenii*, makes a delicate table plant, and you can get it extra tiny for bonsai and dish gardens.

Rhapis, the lady palm, has fronds on tall stems that are best planted several to a pot. Fan-shaped, leathery leaves are about a foot wide.

Veitchia, Christmas palm, has a thin trunk topped with light-green, arching fronds. This one grows over five feet and can stand alone.

Indoor palms need bright light, without direct sun, but most are also tolerant of dim light and will do well in shaded areas. They prefer temperatures in the 55 to 75°F range, and a relative humidity of about 50%.

Pot palms in regular potting mix, and keep the soil evenly moist. They do not like soggy soil. During the active growing season, usually spring through fall, palms need frequent watering. In winter, let the soil dry to the touch before watering again.

Palm fronds are sensitive. If you have an active household, place the palms in corners where they will not be brushed too often. Exposed fronds are apt to split and look straggly. Browning and drying of tips, however, are signs the palm is not getting enough humidity, and regular misting will take care of the problem.

To keep indoor palms from growing too rapidly, plant them in pots smaller than you might think they need—containers only five or six inches in diameter are sufficient for mature specimens. Do not repot for several years, when the roots have thoroughly crowded the pot.

The best proof that begonias are miracle plants is that you find them blooming in the filthiest urban centers. On city window-sills and around the bases of trees in heavily trafficked inner-city streets, they thrive despite soot and pollution—and often under the care of people who know little about plants. So if you are a beginning gardener, or too busy to devote time to delicate vegetation, and you want a plant that is about as close to indestructible as a plant can get, consider begonias. You can grow them indoors, outdoors, or in greenhouses.

But you will face a bewildering array. Thousands of varieties—mostly from tropical America but also from Africa and Asia—are available. They differ in height and shape. One type (rex begonias) is grown for its decorative foliage, but most others are grown for their flowers—though the colors and season of bloom vary enormously.

Begonias are usually classified by their root systems, which indicate the care they should be given, and which are of three types:

1. ***Rhizomatous.*** These begonias grow from rhizomes and are dormant in winter. They include the rex plants cultivated for beautiful foliage, as well as flowering species.
2. ***Fibrous-rooted.*** These are year-round begonias with underground root systems like those of most other plants. Included are the semperflorens, angelwings, and hirsute (hairy-leaved) varieties, all with smallish but profuse and reliable flowers. These are the easiest to grow, and are the choice for indoor gardeners.
3. ***Tuberous.*** These begonias grow from tubers that must be dried out and repotted annually. Nevertheless, the flowers are larger and more interesting than those of fibrous-rooted begonias. Most of them bloom in summer, but winter-flowering ones are also available. These begonias require more care, and are favorites with greenhouse and outdoor gardeners.

Below are more detailed descriptions of these three types as well as instructions for care.

Rhizomatous Begonias

These begonias grow from rhizomes—thick, gnarled root systems that don't stay under the soil but protrude onto the surface.

Rex begonias are beloved for their beautiful foliage. Many have colorful leaves, usually in reds that are shaded from crimson to dark wine colors, though a few have green leaves. In most cases, though leaf shapes vary, the foliage is large and soft and drapes gracefully to make a compact plant. This draping is especially attractive because most varieties have foliage that is streaked, spotted, banded, edged, or otherwise marked with contrasting color. Examples are deep-red leaves edged with silver, light-green leaves banded with darker green, or brilliant red leaves dotted with silver. Some of the smaller varieties, good for indoor use, grow eight inches to a foot high, but most grow up to two feet tall.

Flowering varieties have leaves that vary from light green to purplish in color; that may be round, star-shaped, or formed like maple leaves; and that may have twisted or ruffled edges. The flowers are usually pink, often on spikes that tower above the leaves, but sometimes they are white. Most of these plants will grow to a foot and a half, but miniatures down to only eight-inch heights are available.

While sun will cause the colors in the foliage to fade and the leaves to burn, rex can be easily grown in problem light locations. North windows, shaded porches, or dappled-light areas of the garden are good spots for these. In northern climates, indoor rhizomatous begonias can be moved outdoors in summer.

In winter these begonias often become dormant. Some drop their leaves and appear dead. Water them sparingly and they will revive in early spring.

Fibrous-rooted Begonias

Fibrous-rooted begonias are the most popular because they are attractive year-round and are among the hardiest. These are also among the best for indoor use.

Semperflorens—wax begonias—are ubiquitous. Their advantage is that, as their Latin name *B. semperflorens* implies, they bloom almost all year. They are also fairly tolerant of neglect. The leaves tend to be small and shiny, and vary from light to dark green, with the darker shades more common. The small but plentiful flowers may be single, double, or semidouble, and are usually white, scarlet, or pink. These are excellent for window boxes and pots, as they seldom reach a foot in height, and miniatures about six inches tall are available. In gardens they are popular bedding plants. These can get leggy, though, so to have compact plants pinch back new growth. If you fail to do this, and your begonia gets straggly and unattractive, you can take cuttings to start new plants.

Angelwings are so named for their wing-shaped leaves. Foliage may be lobed, pointed, or arrow-shape, and is usually a shiny green. Some varieties have leaves marked with silver. These begonias flower profusely, mostly in shades of pink or red, but some varieties yield white blossoms. Angelwings tend to sprawl, so are excellent for hanging baskets. But this means they can also get out of bounds, and you can find yourself with an unattractive plant sprawling three or four feet long. You should prune angelwings to keep them the shape you want.

Hirsute or hairy-leaved begonias have furry green leaves in round, tapering, or other shapes. The many tiny flowers are usually in shades of red or pink, or may be white. These grow somewhat over two feet tall and are especially adaptable to indoor use.

Tuberous Begonias

These begonias are more demanding than the rhizomatous or fibrous-rooted plants, since the tubers must be dried out and repotted annually. In addition, unless you grow them under fluorescent light, you may have difficulty getting them to bloom indoors. Nevertheless, the tubers produce flowers that are larger and more spectacular than those of other begonias.

The summer-flowering varieties, which include pendant plants that are great for hanging baskets, have crisp green foliage and blossom from late June to November. The flowers may be white, in pastel shades such as pink, or in brilliant scarlet, orange, or yellow. Some may have double blossoms or frilled edges, and many

resemble other flowers such as roses or camellias. To create more compact plant forms, pinch out young shoots early in the spring to encourage new growth. If you can stand it, you can also pinch out the first flower buds that appear; this delays flowering, but it allows your plant to build a better root system and produce finer blooms later on.

Tubers, which should be plump, are usually planted in March. Plant them two inches apart in seed trays or small pots, with the hollow side up, in a mixture of peat moss and sand. The tubers should be covered with another quarter-inch of the growing medium. Cover the trays or pots with polythene and put them in a warm place where the temperature will not fall below 60°, though higher temperatures are fine too. As soon as shoots appear, remove the cover, and water generously so the soil doesn't dry out. You can also give plant food. It will take some five or six weeks (a little less for the pendant types) from planting for the shoots to reach a height of two inches—at which time they are ready for transplanting. Plant each tuber in an individual pot in a light porous soil mixture (see "soil," below) and keep well watered on a windowsill or other well-lighted place. You may prefer bottom watering, as the tubers can rot if water collects in the hollow end.

If you have a greenhouse, your begonias will not need transplanting again. But if you want to put your plants in windowboxes, in hanging baskets, or in the garden, wait until May, when the plants are about three-inches high. For windowboxes, plant them six inches apart. For hanging baskets, plant two or three tubers in a five-inch pot. For the garden, wait until frost danger has passed and plant the begonias ten inches apart. A location where they will get three or four hours of sun is ideal. Water generously, especially on hot days. Give plant food about once every three weeks. Your begonias will flower continuously for four or five months.

In a greenhouse or warm climate they may cease blooming toward the end of summer. You can stop fertilizing, and reduce the water so that they stay fairly dry, for about three weeks to encourage new growth. This will keep them in another flowering period through fall.

When the plants start to die in the fall, stop watering and let them dry out. Remove them from the soil, wash and dry them, and clear off roots and dead leaves. Store the tubers in dry peat moss or dry sand at a temperature of 45° to 50° until spring, when you can restart them.

The winter-blooming begonias—cheimanthas and hiemalis—flower from November through March. Cheimanthas blossoms range from white to shades of pink and red. Hiemalis has larger flowers, which may be pink, orange, apricot, or other colors. These are not the easiest to grow. They need 50° humidity or more, are sensitive to drafts, and like their soil moist but not soggy. Yet hiemalis in particular is subject to mildew and root rot. They need bright light, and temperatures of about 60° to 65° when they are in bloom. When the flowers fade, you have to cut the plants back, water sparingly, and keep them cool (50° to 55°). Cheimanthas will produce new shoots. With hiemalis you can repot the same tuber each year in the spring.

Culture

Temperature: For most begonias, temperatures of 65° to 75° are ideal.

Rhizomatous begonias need the most warmth and should not go below 65° at night.

Fibrous-rooted begonias will adapt to temperatures down to 55° at night, provided you do not switch them from warmer temperatures suddenly.

Tuberous begonias will do well down to 60° at night, and the winter-flowering hiemalis and cheimantha tolerate 55° at night.

All begonias, while adaptable to wide temperature ranges, react badly to sudden environmental changes. If you are going to move them to locations with more or less light or warmth than they have been accustomed to, you will have to acclimatize them gradually or they may protest by dropping their leaves. Begonias also resent drafts, and angelwings especially will react by defoliating.

Humidity: Being tropical plants, begonias thrive in humid atmospheres. Indoors, if you keep them on pebble trays and provide a relative humidity of 60% or 70%, or even higher in a greenhouse, they will do well. *B. rex* is especially sensitive, preferring about 60%. But if you cannot keep these levels, most varieties will be fine at 50%. Hirsute begonias and *B. semperflorens* do not seem to mind drier air.

Light: In general, begonias do not tolerate a great deal of direct sun and are therefore classified as shade plants. Geographic area makes a difference, however. In areas such as the Southwest, with strong light, begonias should be placed in shaded or dappled-sun areas. In northern climates, on the other hand, many will benefit from some sun. This is especially true in urban areas, where large buildings, air pollution, and other factors filter or reduce the amount of sun plants really get. The type of begonia you grow also makes a difference. The colored foliage of *B. rex* and the hairy-leaved begonias do best with shade outdoors and subdued daylight indoors, while the summer-flowering tuberous begonias will do well where they get three or four hours of sun a day. Hirsute types need winter sun for blooming. Angelwings don't like noonday sun, but morning or afternoon sun will help you get colorful cascades of blooms. *B. semperflorens* also flower best with some full sun, and should have at least diffused sun.

If you are growing begonias under artificial light, most will do well if you set your timer to allow sixteen to eighteen hours of fluorescent light (cool white or warm white) a day. Rhizomatous begonias, however, need fifteen hours of darkness in winter to bloom; reduce this gradually over a month's time to thirteen or twelve hours to simulate spring and induce the plants to flower. If you are using two tubes, the tops of mature plants should be six to ten inches below the tubes, but young seedlings and cuttings should be only two inches away from the tubes.

Soil: Most begonias are susceptible to root rot, so avoid keeping their feet too wet by providing drainy soil.

Outdoors they should be grown in loamy soil with good drainage.

Indoors, plant them in a mix of three parts humus to one part coarse sand, or in a mix of half garden loam, a quarter humus, and a quarter sand. In general, the *B. rex* varieties need the most humus, and *B. semperflorens* need the least.

The gnarled roots of the rhizomatous begonias like to push out onto the surface. Don't try to cover the rhizomes with soil—they like the air.

Potting: Fibrous-rooted begonias such as *B. semperflorens* should be planted in regular pots indoors or in the garden, but the angelwings look best in hanging baskets.

Tuberous begonias are popular for garden borders and for window boxes. Pendant types are best in hanging baskets.

Rhizomatous begonias need room for their rhizomes to spread out, so these should be planted in low, broad pots or in bulb pans.

Watering: While begonias are susceptible to root rot if overwated, their roots will shrivel if they are underwatered.

Keep the soil of rhizomatous begonias evenly moist, but let the soil dry out between waterings. In winter, when they go dormant, water sparingly until they revive in spring.

Fibrous-rooted begonias vary somewhat in their watering needs. Angelwings like their soil evenly moist. Hirsute begonias, on the other hand, do not tolerate overwatering,

nor will the wax begonias *(B. semperflorens)*. Keep these drier, soaking them and then allowing the soil to dry out thoroughly between watering.

Watering needs for tuberous begonias vary seasonally. When the tubers are first planted, you should water sparingly, but once the shoots develop you should not let the soil dry out. They should be watered generously while they are blooming, especially if the weather is hot. When they begin to lose bloom, keep them on the dry side again, as this will begin a new growth cycle. When they bloom again resume generous watering. Then, in the fall, when the plants start dying, let them dry out completely.

Fertilizer: When begonias are growing vigorously, give them a commercial water-soluble plant food every two or three weeks, following instructions on the package. Don't feed begonias, however, when they have ceased to flower and seem to be resting or about to go dormant. Also don't fertilize immediately after repotting.

If in doubt, it's better to feed the plants too little than to overfertilize.

Troubleshooting: In general, begonias are fairly free of diseases and pests. Any pests they do get can usually be eliminated by clean running water. If not, following the directions for ridding plants of aphids, mealy bugs, and other pests on page 157.

If the leaves of an older plant lose color, it may be potbound and need replanting.

If the leaves yellow and drop off, you are probably overwatering. If the plant wilts suddenly, you have probably underwatered.

If the leaves turn brown at the tops or develop brown patches, your begonias may be getting too much sun and/or not enough humidity.

If the flower buds or leaves suddenly fall off, insufficient humidity may be the answer. However, some begonias are more sensitive than others to temperature changes or to altered environmental conditions that result from being moved to a new location. Angelwings are especially sensitive, and a draft can make all their leaves drop off suddenly.

When begonias don't get enough light, they can become leggy and unattractive, and they will bloom poorly or not at all.

Older plants, grown under artificial light, will sometimes develop top-heavy leaves that must be pruned to allow sufficient light to reach the lower parts of the plant.

Luckily, whatever happens to your begonia, you need not despair. You can take cuttings from any that have grown unattractive, too high for their location, or are otherwise not doing well. Cuttings are easy to propagate, so you can start all over again with new plants. If a fibrous-rooted type, such as the angelwings, loses its leaves, you can simply cut the plant off close to the pot and new shoots will develop.

Special Requirements: Begonias will do best if you keep them well-groomed by removing flowers and leaves as they wilt.

Propagation: Fibrous-rooted begonias can be propagated from seeds. If you sow seeds in June, the plant should flower by mid-winter. To have plants for transplanting in May, start seeds in January. More popular are stem cuttings, which you can root in water or damp vermiculite and then pot. Rhizomatous begonias can be propagated by cutting the rhizomes into pieces, but the preferred method is to root leaf cuttings in damp (not wet) vermiculite.

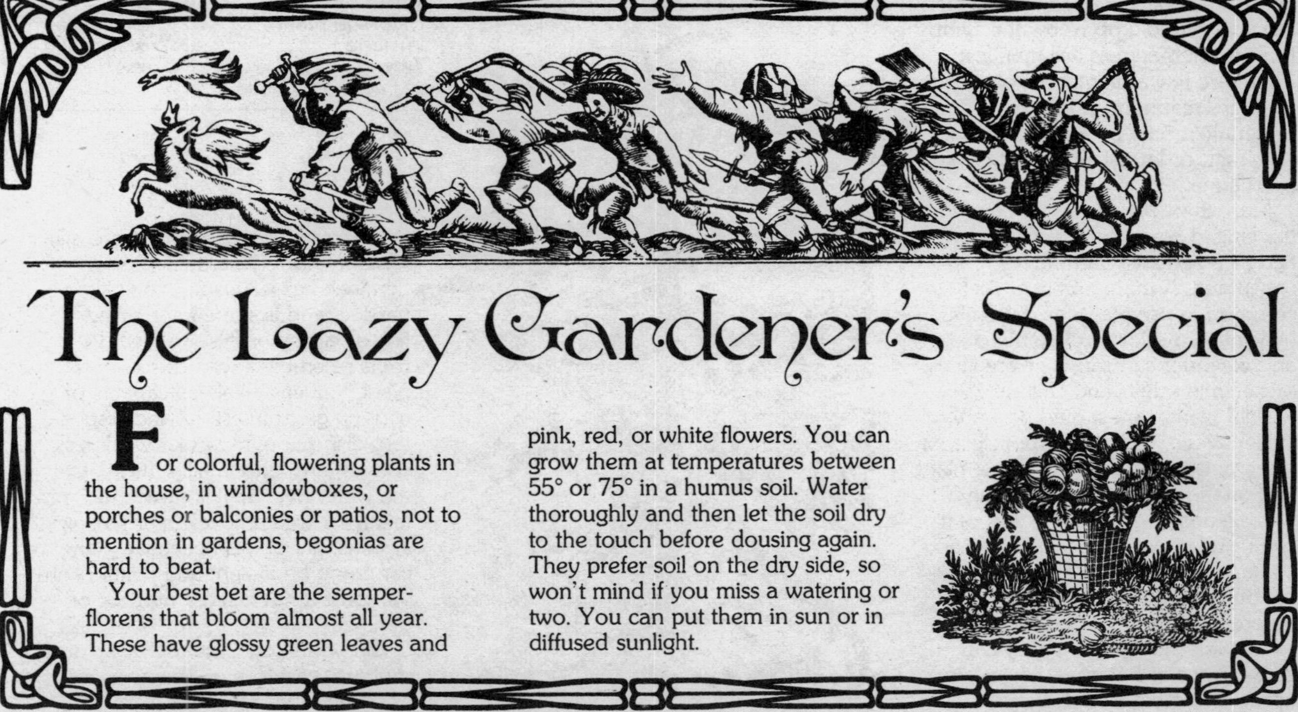

The Lazy Gardener's Special

For colorful, flowering plants in the house, in windowboxes, or porches or balconies or patios, not to mention in gardens, begonias are hard to beat.

Your best bet are the semperflorens that bloom almost all year. These have glossy green leaves and pink, red, or white flowers. You can grow them at temperatures between 55° or 75° in a humus soil. Water thoroughly and then let the soil dry to the touch before dousing again. They prefer soil on the dry side, so won't mind if you miss a watering or two. You can put them in sun or in diffused sunlight.

Poison Hemlock.

Poisonous Plants

The incidence of plant poisonings increased threefold during the 1970's and is likely to rise as the back-to-nature explosion continues. Plants are the second highest cause of poisoning in children under age five. Anyone can understand the attraction that brightly colored flowers, berries, and foliage have for children. Kids are undiscriminating as to what they put into their mouths, so it is best to keep plants out of their reach. Extra caution is required when they are playing outdoors. A guide to poisonous plants should be a standard reference in every home where plants, children, and pets live together.

Poisoning by plants is difficult to diagnose—it may be confused as poisoning by some other agents, like paint, insecticides, or contaminated water. So catalog the potentially dangerous materials your child or pet is likely to get hold of. Know the symptoms these materials will manifest. There are few antidotes for plant poisoning. Treatment should be undertaken only by a physician, veterinarian, or knowledgeable first-aid practitioner.

More than 700 plants that grow in the United States have been identified as potentially harmful if consumed. A mere nibble of such common house plants as daffodils, hyacinths, mistletoe, dieffenbachia, and oleander can cause severe illness or death in adults and children.

Wild plants you should be wary of: jimson weed, which is responsible for more poisonings than any other plant and often found in backyards and waste lands. Ingesting any part of it can result in delirium, incoherence, coma, and death; the innocent-looking buttercup holds juices that can severely injure the digestive system; swallowing lilies-of-the-valley can cause irregular heartbeat, digestive upset, and mental confusion.

—DEADLY NIGHTSHADE.
ATROPA BELLADONNA.

Hyoscyamus Niger.
Blacke Henbane.

POISONOUS PLANTS

Common Name	Botanical Name	Poisonous Part
Apricot	Prunus armeniaca	Stem, bark, seed pits
Azalea	Rhododendron occidentale	All parts
Baneberry	Actaea spicata	Berries, roots, foliage
Belladonna	Atropa belladonna	All parts
Bird of Paradise	Strelitzia regirae	Fruit, seeds
Black cherry	Prunus serotina	Leaves, seed pits, stems, bark
Black locust	Robinia pseudoacacia	Bark, foliage, sprouts
Boston ivy	Parthenocissus quinquefolia	All parts
Bunchberry	Lantana	All parts
Buttercups	Ranunculus	All parts
Caladium	Caladium	All parts
Castor bean	Ricinus communis	Seeds, if chewed
Choke cherry	Prunus virginiana	Leaves, seed pits, stems, bark
Christmas rose	Helleborus niger	Root
Creeping Charlie	Glecoma hederacae	All parts
Crows		Bulb
Daffodil	Narcissus	Bulbs
Daphne	Daphne mezereum	Berries, bark, leaves
Deadly nightshade	Solanum nigrum	All parts
Dumbcane	Dieffenbachia	All parts
Emerald duke	Philodendron hastatum	All parts
Foxglove	Digitalis purpura	Leaves, seeds, flowers
Glacier Ivy	Hedera glacier	Leaves, berries
Golden-chain	Laburnum anagyroides	Seed capsules
Heartleaf	Philodendron cordatum	All parts
Hemlock false parsley snakeroot	Conium maculatum	All parts; root and root stalk—especially poisonous
Henbane	Hyoscyamus niger	Juice
Hens-and-chicks	Lantana	All parts
Hyacinth	Hyacinthus orientalis	Bulb, leaves, flowers
Hydrangea	Hydrangea macrophylla	Leaves, buds
Iris		Underground stems
Ivy, English	Hedera helix	Leaves, berries
Jack-in-the-pulpit	Arisaema triphyllum	All parts
Jerusalem cherry	Solanum pseudocapsicum	All parts, unripe fruit
Jessamine	Cestrum	Berries
Jimson weed, Angel's trumpet	Datura stramonium	All parts
Jonquil	Narcissus	Bulbs
Lady's-slipper	Cypripedium	May cause slight skin rash
Larkspur	Delphinium	Young plants, seeds
Laurel	Kalmia	All parts
Lily-of-the-valley	Convallaria majalis	All parts
Lords-and-ladies	Arum maculatum	All parts
Majesty	Philodendron hastatum	All parts
Mandrake	Podophyllum peltatum	Roots, foliage, unripe fruit
Marble queen	Scindapsus aureus	All parts
Mayapple	Podophyllum peltatum	Foliage, fruit roots
Mistletoe	Phoradendron flavescens	Berries
Monkshood	Acontium napellus	All parts
Morning glory	Ipomoea violaces	Seeds
Nephthytis, Arrowhead vine	Syngonium podophyllum albolineatum	All parts
Nightshade	Atropa belladonna	All parts
Oaks	Quercus	Foliage, acorns
Oleander	Nerium oleander	All parts including dried leaves
Parlor Ivy	Philodendron cordatum	All parts
Poinsettia	Euphorbia pulcherrima	Leaves, flowers
Pokeweed, Inkberry	Phytolacca americana	All parts, roots, foliage
Pothos	Scindapsus aureus	All parts
Primula	Primula obconica	All parts
Red princess	Philodendron hastatum	All parts
Red sage	Lantana camara	Green berries
Rhododendron	Rhododendron	All parts
Rhubarb	Rheum raponticum	Leaves
Saddeleaf	Philodendron selloum	All parts
Split-leaf philodendron	Monstera deliciosa	All parts
Star-of-Bethlehem	Campanula	Bulb
Sweet pea	Lathyrus odoratus	Seeds, pods
Tulip	Tulipa	Bulbs
Umbrella plant	Cyperus alterrifolius	All parts
Wisteria	Wisteria	Seeds, pods
Yew	Taxus	Needles, bark, seeds

Some poisonous plants are easily mistaken for edible ones. Poison hemlock has leaves that look like parsley, and is sometimes called fool's parsley or false parsley. Its roots resemble a wild carrot. This plant contains alkaloids capable of causing gastrointestinal and respiratory disruption, muscular weakness, convulsions, and fatality. Its relative, the water hemlock, is sometimes mistaken for wild artichokes or parsnips. A small bite of this deceptive plant can bring on violent and painful convulsions. It has killed a number of people.

Did you know that apples, spinach, rhubarb, cashews, cabbage, as well as many other common fruits and vegetables, have poisonous aspects? The pits and seeds of apples (as well as plums, peaches, pears, and apricots) contain cyanide; rhubarb leaves are filled with oxalic acid which, when eaten in large amounts, can cause convulsions, coma, and death; spinach also contains oxalic acid, but is not harmful if eaten in normal amounts. The shell of the cashew is a relative of poison ivy and can cause blisters. Excessive cabbage consumption can result in goiter—the glycosides in it may prevent the thyroid gland from storing iodine.

We have listed here the most common of poison plants. Hundreds more are listed John M. Kingsbury's guide, *Deadly Harvest* (Holt, Rinehart & Winston).

6

Indoor/Outdoor Plant Lore

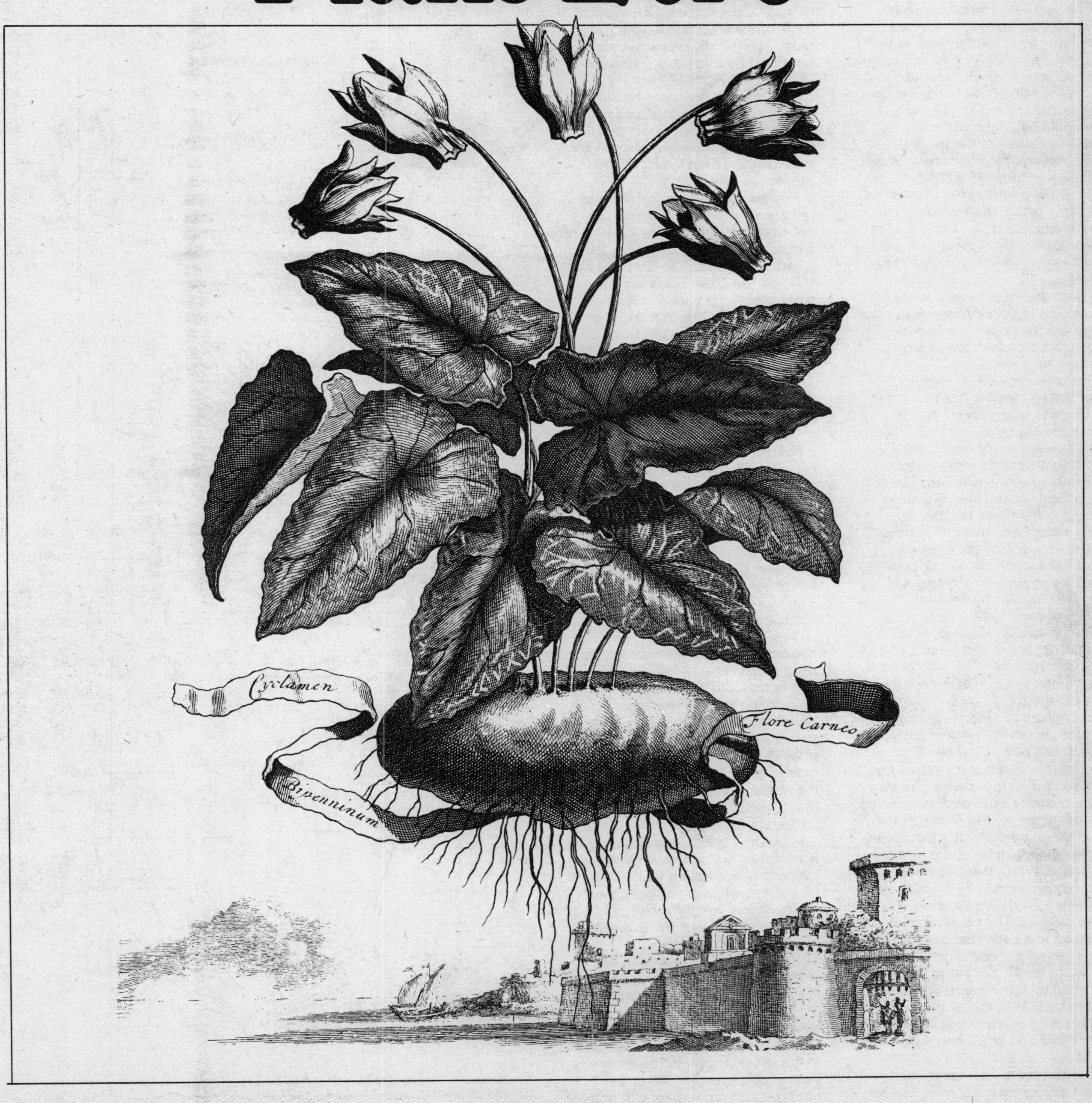

Sex in Plants

Flowers are reproductive organs—about the prettiest, best smelling, and most colorful reproductive organs nature has invented.

The petals usually surround the female organ (the pistil), that will eventually produce the seed, as well as the male organs (the stamens), but the two seldom meet. Self-pollination within the same flower—except for a few species especially adapted for it—would be a form of inbreeding that would weaken the species.

To prevent this, plants have elaborate devices to avoid self-pollination. If the pistils and stamens are within the same petals, they will often mature at different times. But often the male and female organs are in separate flowers—or even in separate plants.

Given this inconvenient setup, plants had to develop ingenious ways of getting the pollen from a male organ to a female organ so fertilization can take place.

Trees and grasses, though they bear flowers, tend to blossom rather inconspicuously. This is because they are pollinated by the wind. In trees, the stamens usually tower above the petals to expose themselves and wave about so the wind can carry off the pollen. Grasses, being close to the ground and less buffeted by wind, often eject their pollen forcefully from a special sac to give it a good head start. The female organs also project above the petals, and frequently have downy or other coverings capable of snaring pollen (which is usually sticky) from the wind. Corn is one of the rare vegetables pollinated by wind—the pollen falls by gravity or breezes from the tassel at the top.

But wind pollination is so chancy that the stamens must produce vast amounts of pollen—whose lifetime may be less than two hours—to ensure survival of the species. Trees produce such clouds of dustlike pollen (often yellow) that it carpets the ground around them. It is the wind-borne pollen of trees and grasses, including ragweed, that is the bane of hayfever sufferers.

Plants with showy flowers are more efficient. They produce and waste far less pollen because they use more select pollen carriers than the wind. Mostly the transport is provided by flying insects with hairy bodies such as bees, but plants also use crawling and hopping insects and even raindrops, birds, bats, and snails.

The shapes, colors, scents, and nectar-producing qualities of flowers are intricately linked with their pollinators. Some plants are rather rigid in their choice of pollen carrier. Certain edible varieties of figs, for instance, are pollinated only by the fig wasp. And yucca produces a large stalk of white or lavender blooms that are pollinated only by the yucca moth.

Other plants are more flexible, but you can often tell the type of pollinator by the shape, color, and amount of scent in the flowers. Flowers that have shallow, flat petals, with exposed reproductive organs, may be pollinated by butterflies. Blossoms with funnel-like shapes and recessed organs may be pollinated by hummingbirds or insects with long nectar-sucking tubes. Intricately formed flowers are pollinated by insects able to fly or crawl in to the hidden reproductive organs.

Hummingbirds favor orange and red tubular flowers that usually do not attract insects, and the coloring of particular species in butterflies often is coordinated with the blossoms they choose. The Great Swallowtail butterfly, which has blue-green wings, often alights on lavender and bluish flowers, while white butterflies may camouflage themselves while feeding by selecting flowers with white petals.

Plants pollinated by nocturnal moths, such as evening primrose and honeysuckle, often have a heavy fragrance but light rather than deep or brilliant colors in their petals.

Bees pollinate a wide variety of plants from red clover to orchids, and two plants demonstrate the enormous complexities in flower construction that insure the insect services both male and female organs yet never pollinates within the same flower.

In mountain laurel, the bee first meets and brushes against the pistil, or female organ, depositing pollen it has carried from its previous visit to another laurel bush. But as the bee digs further into the nectar, it runs into a trap set by the stamens, or male organs, carrying pollen. The stamens are bent and held firmly in place like springs by notches in the petals. As the bee probes deeper into the nectar, it triggers the release of the stamens. The stamen shoots up, showering the underside of the bee with pollen it will carry to the next laurel bush. Some bees carry the pollen on brushy hairs on their abdomens, while others clean themselves off and comb the pollen into a special pollen basket that is usually located on the hind leg.

The ladyslipper has its own devices. Its charm, to a bee, is a nectar-filled pouch. But the ladyslipper is so constructed that once the bee has entered it cannot back out. Moreover, the inviting opening leads it straight to the female organ. While the bee is busy ingesting nectar, the pollen it has brought from its prior visit to another ladyslipper is scraped off by the pistil. Then, to get out of the flower after it has drunk its fill, the bee has to move forward. There the stamens lie in wait in its path to dump another load of pollen on it—to be carried to yet another ladyslipper.

Bees are especially good pollinators. While they may visit a number of plant species in their lifetimes, they restrict themselves to a single species on each foraging trip.

In addition to decorative shrubs and plants, insects also pollinate fruits such as berries, peaches, apples, melons, plums, mangos, apples, apricots, nectarines, tangerines, and some pears. They also pollinate almond and macadamia trees, and many vegetables, including squash, eggplant, peppers, and lima beans. Bees visiting an apple tree for only one day may produce a well-shaped fruit. But with other plants, such as cucumber, you would need bee activity for three or four weeks.

A few plants without seeds (parthenocarpic) produce fruit without pollination. Examples are some varieties of figs, pears, and cucumbers; seedless oranges and seedless grapes; and pineapples and bananas.

A chief reason pesticides are to be avoided is that they kill pollinating insects in addition to pests. Without insects, you must pollinate your plants by transferring the pollen yourself (usually done with a paintbrush).

IMPERFECT FLOWER

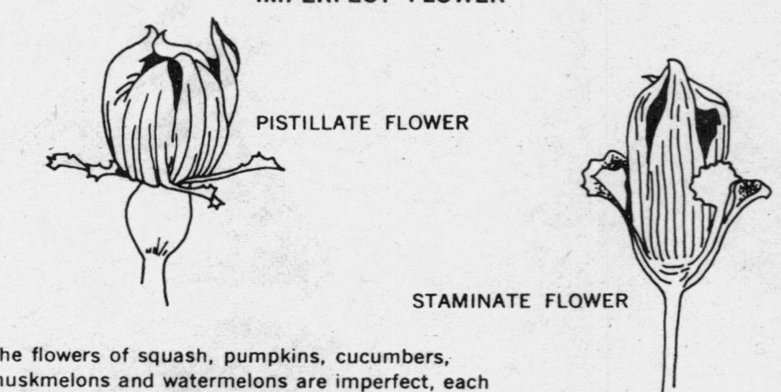

The flowers of squash, pumpkins, cucumbers, muskmelons and watermelons are imperfect, each flower having only one type of sex organ.

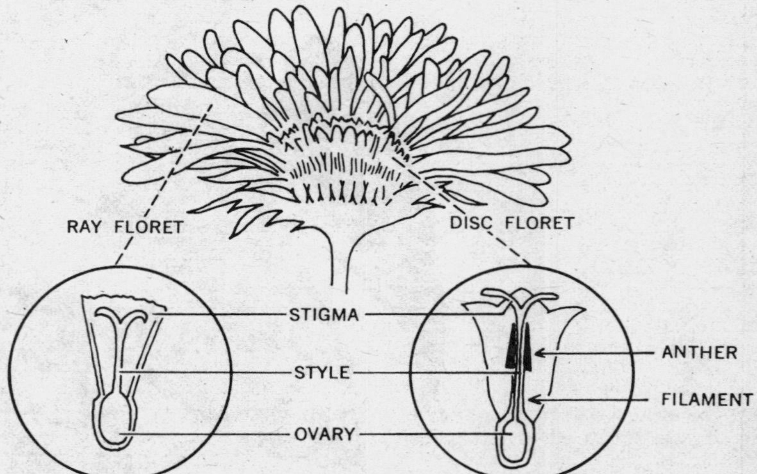

Cross section of chrysanthemum. Flowers, such as chrysanthemums, zinnias, marigolds, and daisies are made up of clusters of florets.

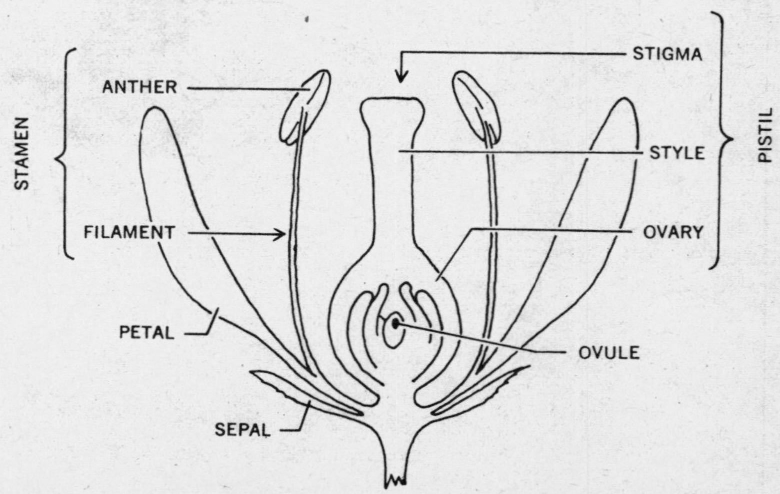

Parts of a flower. The flower shown here is a perfect flower; that is, it has male and female reproductive organs. The stamen is the male organ and the pistil is the female organ.

Hybrids

Growing plants from seed is not always possible or desirable. In the case of hybrids, seeds often will produce offspring that inherit only some of the parental qualities. The object of hybridization is to cross two related plants (related by genera or species) to produce a better plant. Say you have a rose with a flaming color that is susceptible to disease and another with weak color that is disease-resistant. Your object would be to produce a rose that had the beautiful color and was also disease-resistant. This is not an easy process, since you can easily get a rose with weak color and a propensity for disease. But as our knowledge of genetics has increased, and it is improving rapidly today, plant breeders are getting better and better results.

An enormous number of plants on the market today are hybrids. The number of hybrids available varies with the type of plant and its popularity.

One factor is growth cycle. It is easier and faster for plant breeders to perform experiments with fast-growing than with slow-growing plants. Trees, for instance, have such long growth cycles that it takes years to evaluate seedling populations and mature growth characteristics. You will therefore find fewer hybrid trees. Though some research has been done on shade trees such as maples, most tree hybrids are usually of the smaller varieties with attractive blooms that are popular for decorative purposes—such as magnolias, ornamental pears, and crabapple. Breeders have worked on developing such characteristics as lusher bloom and longer flowering periods, as well as resistance to disease and expansion of the climate ranges within which the trees will survive. In addition, with increased urbanization resulting in less spacious personal property, the development of dwarf varieties of decorative trees such as magnolias has received a lot of attention. Crabapples and dogwoods suitable for growing in pots on terraces, rooftops, and other limited urban areas are also widely researched.

The other type of tree for which many hybrids are available are those producing fruit. Here some of the research is also directed at expanding ranges and resistance to disease, but crop yield, attractiveness of fruit, and development of new fruits (such as the tangelo, created by crossing a tangerine and a grapefruit) are paramount breeder concerns. As with ornamental trees, much research effort is expended in developing dwarf fruit trees suitable for home gardeners.

Commercial exploitation is another factor determining how much research is expended on a plant, and this is true even though the government, rather than private enterprise, does much of the research. Experimentation is therefore extensive on crops such as wheat and corn, which are of economic importance. Much of this study does, however, eventually benefit home gardeners because techniques for breeding disease-resistant, hardier, or more food-productive plants can be applied to a wide variety of vegetables and fruits of more interest to them.

Yet a large amount of plant breeding has concentrated on the plants most popular with home gardeners. To some extent this is because home gardeners constitute a significant market and there is money to be made by pleasing them. In addition, most of the home-garden plants have short life cycles, making experiments rewarding for professionals and amateurs alike. Thus industrial and government research is supplemented by discoveries made by individual hobbyists and by private societies devoted to specific plants.

This is not a new phenomenon. John Bartram (1699–1777) was a farmer without formal schooling, yet his contribution to North American horticulture in collecting native species and exchanging plants with collectors abroad was invaluable. George R. Hall was a nineteenth-century physician who resided for many years in the Far East and introduced many Japanese plants—including dwarf Japanese yew and star magnolia—and other oriental varieties to the New World. Camellias are Asian plants introduced here chiefly by Southern planters who enjoyed their scent in the humid, warm air. Their interest was put on a more formal basis when fanciers formed the American Camellia Society. Today many hybrid camellias are available, bred for qualities such as color and scent, and much work is being done on breeding them to withstand colder temperatures.

No flowering plant has been more hybridized than the ever-popular rose. In one five-year period in the 1960s, for example, when 53 new varieties of gladiolus and 40 new azaleas were introduced, 232 new roses were established; this constituted roughly a third of all new

plant patents issued during that period. One reason, perhaps, is that roses are susceptible to disease such as canker, black spot, and mildew that are annoying and disheartening to their fanciers, who hope for more disease-resistant strains. Another reason is that the beauty and long life of the cut flowers make roses popular even among nongardening folk, creating a far greater interest in roses than in many other plants.

Increased fascination with landscaping is another trend that has influened hybridization. Today people want more plants and want them to be more attractive. But because they want more plants, they want each plant to be easier to care for and freer of pests and disease problems. Much research is therefore now going into developing better varieties of basic landscaping material such as azaleas and rhododendrons. Both plants are subject to wilt, and rhododendron especially to root rot, so some studies are focused on resistance to disease. Azaleas better able to withstanding heat and cold, and rhododendrons adaptable to drier soils, are increasing the areas in which these plants may be grown. More dwarfs are now available for people with limited space. And even improvement in flower color is a subject of study.

Hybridization is a desirable activity that makes plants more adaptable, useful, and beautiful for larger numbers of people. The disadvantage for those eager to propagate new plants from seed is that some hybrids are sterile and others produce seed that will not create a duplicate of the parent plant. The seed of a plant bred for a specific characteristic such as cold hardiness may produce a young plant that is not as cold-tolerant. For this reason, your hybrids are often best propagated by cuttings or other vegetative propagation methods.

Propagation

Propagation refers to the reproduction and multiplication of plants.

In nature, most plants are propagated by seed which, given the proper germinating conditions, will produce a new plant.

For home gardeners seed propagation is the cheapest way of obtaining a lot of new plants. The cost of a packet of seeds is nothing compared to buying young or mature plants. For indoor gardeners, however, seeds remain only a hobby or a fun project, because seed propagation produces far more plants than you can use. Indoor gardeners are apt to limit their seed experiments to an occasional avocado pit.

For outdoor gardeners it is a different story. The flower gardener who wants a long border of geraniums along the driveway or who wants to have masses of impatiens in a corner will find a significant cost savings in germinating seeds rather than in buying bedding plants. For food gardeners, too, planting from seed is far cheaper than buying started plantlets.

Propagating from seed is not, however, possible for all varieties of plants you may wish to grow. Some exotic plants do not produce vital seed. This is especially true of hybrids, which are sometimes sterile. Other hybrids, though they produce ample seed, do not always breed true. That is, the plants you get from their seed will not always resemble the parent plant. Seeds of red delicious apples, for instance, are unlikely to produce fruit remotely resembling the original.

In addition, some gardeners do not like starting plants from seed because it takes so long to get a decent-sized plant.

Luckily for the impatient, there are other methods of propagation. These methods are called vegetative propagation and involve growing a new plant from a piece—a leaf or a piece of root—of the parent plant. These methods work because plants are capable of regeneration. Just as a salamander is able to regenerate a lost leg or tail from the remaining stump, plants are able to recreate themselves entirely from the smallest sliver. With hybrids vegetative propagation assures that the new plant will resemble the parent.

Vegetative propagation occurs in nature. Some plants, especially trailing varieties such as strawberries, multiply by extending runners along the soil. These take root to produce new plants. Other plants, such as some lillies, produce bulblets that become new plants.

Over the centuries gardeners learned to take advantage of plantlets and other offshoots that could be removed from a parent plant to make new plants. And eventually they learned to multiply plants with a number of methods from stem cuttings to layerings.

Vegetative propagation methods produce plants much faster than do seeds and is especially appropriate if you want to produce only a couple of new plants rather than a great quantity.

An advantage of learning propagation if you have an outdoor garden is that it gives you something to do in winter when you would otherwise be idle. Many seeds can be started in January and be ready to plant outdoors once the weather warms up sufficiently. You can also chop up and propagate unattractive houseplants and have good-size plants for spring planting outdoors.

Cuttings

Cuttings can be made from virtually any part of the plant—leaves or portions of leaves, stems, and roots—but some parts propagate more easily than others, depending on the type of plant.

However, while cuttings from stems have to generate new roots, and cuttings from roots have to generate new shoots, cuttings from leaves have to generate both new shoots *and* new roots. As a result, leaf cuttings are used only for a few easily propagated plants such as African violets, begonias, peperomia, gloxinia, sansevieria, and tropical plants with thick leaves. Leaf cuttings from many plants, especially woody species, will readily form roots but may not develop new shoots.

Root cuttings can be used for poppies and a few other plants with suckers, but propagation of roots is usually through division (see below).

The method that works best on the widest variety of plants is to propagate by stem cuttings. The easiest stems to propagate are those whose tissues are soft and succulent. This includes herbaceous annuals and perennials. Softwood cuttings, a bit more woody, are usually taken during the first six weeks of the growing season. If you have never propagated stem cuttings, start with geraniums, chrysanthemums, carnations, begonias, and other of these easy-to-propagate varieties.

Semiripe cuttings, made about mid to late summer, mean the plant tissue has become harder and less succulent.

Hardest of all to propagate are hardwood cuttings, also called mature or dormant cuttings. These are made from stems taken after growth has stopped in fall. The stems are harder and less yielding, require more time to root, and need more heat. Hardwood cuttings of deciduous plants will, of course, contain no leaves; only narrow-leaved and broad-leaved evergreens will still have leaves.

Apart from the above, some plants are simply more amenable to stem cutting than others. Even closely related species can vary enormously. Rhododendrons with red flowers, for instance, are more difficult to root than those with white or pink flowers. The upright junipers are hard to root, while spreading varieties root easily.

Succulents and cactus are so easy to propagate that you can get carried away and end up with a houseful of plants. But since many species are now becoming rare or endangered, the ease with which they propagate means you can obtain plants by getting cuttings from friends or by contacting other fanciers through a garden society. Cactus and succulents can be propagated by leaf cuttings, stem cuttings, offsets, and division. In fact, you can take an older plant that has grown too big or unattractive, and make a couple of dozen new plants of it by chopping it to pieces in the proper places. And if the plant has a main stalk, as does echeveria, you can save this too; little rosettes or other new growth will appear, and you can remove these and pot them individually.

Stem Cuttings: These are cuttings made with a piece of stem plus two or three leaves (or needles in the case of some evergreens). It is best to take these cuttings early in the day, when the leaves are crisp.

Using a sharp knife, razor, or pruning shears, cut off a piece of stem at a 45° angle, just below a leaf node—the slight swelling on the stem from which leaves grow. For herbaceous cuttings, the stem should be three or four inches long; for other types of plants, cut them six to eight inches long. Remove any foliage on the lower two inches, as well as any flowers or buds anywhere above.

If you cannot plant them right away, you will have to keep the cuttings from drying out. You can place them in plastic bags or in a vase of water in the shade. If the planting delay will be several hours, put the cuttings in plastic bags in the refrigerator.

Many cuttings—especially of herbaceous and softwood—will root within one to three weeks. Semiripe cuttings can take an additional three to six weeks, though. Hardwood cuttings of narrow-leaved and broad-leaved evergreens can take two to six months to root.

On cactus, the cutting should be made from the stem tip. With succulents you can also use any section of stem that contains leaf nodes. Cut the stems into segments, each with two or three leaves. Unlike most other plants, however, cactus and succulent cuttings should not be planted immediately. Let them dry out for three or four days first.

Leaf Cuttings: Leaf cuttings can be propagated in two ways. You can cut off a leaf on its stalk (which may be from a half-inch to an inch long) and plant it in the medium precisely as with a stem cutting. The stalk should be firmed into the medium, and the leaf should project above. African violets can be propagated in this way, and new growth will appear at the base of the parent leaf in a few weeks. Wait until there is a cluster of new plantlets before you cut off the parent leaf and plant the offspring. Many begonias, peperomias, gloxinias, and streptocarpus can be similarly propagated.

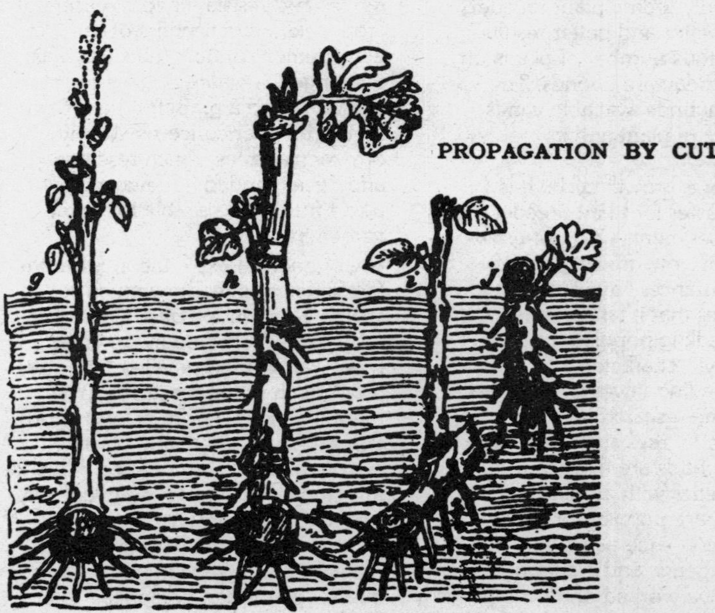

PROPAGATION BY CUTTINGS.

The second method is used with large, prominently veined leaves such as are found in Rex and rhizomatous begonias and gesneriads such as gloxinias. Here you slash through veins and then lay the leaf flat on the rooting medium, holding it in place with toothpicks or pebbles so that the cut veins are held in tight contact with the rooting medium. New plants will grow at the cuts. Begonias are especially fun to propagate with leaves because you have several choices. You can plant the stem end of a cut leaf, a method best for small-leaved begonias. For large-leaved varieties you can cut the stem off by slashing a circle around it that will intercept the leaf veins; you can then plant the remaining leaf into the rooting medium by cupping it so it enters the medium yet remains erect. Plantlets should appear in four to six weeks; when they have sufficient roots, you can separate and transplant them.

Other plants that are fun to propagate this way are cactus and succulents. With these plants you can cut any long leaves into sections of three-inch lengths, provided you take care to remember which end is up (the section farthest from the main stem is up, and the section nearest the main stem should be planted). You can thus chop up one plant to create a dozen or more. As with stem cuttings, dry the leaves out for about four days before you pot them. It is handy to dry them on paper on which you can write where the top ends are, to prevent forgetting and then planting them upside down. Gasteria, agave, sansevieria, and any other long-leaved varieties can be treated this way.

With shorter-leaved types, such as kalanchoe, you can cut the leaf off at the stalk, being careful to include the bud at the base of the stalk. After you dry this out and pot it, new plants will emerge (in two to three months) and you can later cut the original leaf off. The small leaves of many varieties, such as crassula and echeveria, will frequently form roots if you put the stem ends into small containers of water containing a few charcoal chips and keep them cool and shaded. Ice plants can be chopped into tiny bits with a dicing knife, sprinkled on soil, and then covered lightly with more soil and kept moist.

Leaf cuttings usually develop roots in about three weeks, but it may be another three or four weeks before shoots develop.

PROPAGATION OF GRAPE VINE BY EYES.

Root Cuttings: Any plant with suckers (such as staghorn fern) may be propagated by root cuttings. You do this in fall or winter when the plant is dormant.

Take the plant out of its pot or the ground and cut the roots into pieces two to four inches long. Use the larger roots—those about the thickness of a lead pencil. So that you don't become confused about which end is up and plant the roots upside down, it's handy to cut the end closest to the crown (the top) on the diagonal and to cut the other end (the bottom) straight across.

Plant the cuttings in a rooting medium to a depth of two to three inches. You can plant them in flats for greenhouse propagation and then transfer them outdoors in the spring. If you're going to propagate them outdoors in temperate zones you should mulch them over the winter and transplant them following the first growing season.

Many orchids, bromeliads, succulents, and gesneriads, among others, develop various types of offsets at the base. When these are easy to handle—say over two inches—you can cut them off and root them like stem cuttings.

Some plants produce runners, little plantlets sent out on long stems to reconnaisance the surrounding territory with an eye to taking root. Episcia, Boston fern, and chlorophytum are examples. These are easy to snip off and pot.

When to Make Cuttings

Cuttings should generally be made when the plant is in vigorous growth, but it is hard to set rules to cover all plants.

With some plants, such as chrysanthemums, geraniums, and other easy-to-root varieties, the timing is unimportant. Cuttings taken in winter may take a little longer to root, but cuttings can be rooted any time there is new growth.

Many ornamental shrubs such as California privet and forsythia can be propagated at several times of year—in early summer as softwood cuttings, in mid to late summer as semiripe cuttings, or in winter as hardwood cuttings.

But some plants are fussy about when their cuttings are made. Rhododendrons and azaleas can be propagated as softwood cuttings after bloom or as semiripe cuttings in September—yet they may not root if you take the cuttings a week to ten days too early or too late. Holly roots are best if you take cuttings in late summer or early fall. Narrow-leaved evergreens do best if you take them in late fall after they have been subjected to a couple of frosts. Cactus and succulent cuttings should be taken when the plants emerge from dormancy during the warmer months (usually in May or June).

HOW TO PROPAGATE HOUSEPLANTS

SCIENTIFIC NAME	**COMMON NAME**	**HOW TO PROPAGATE**
Abutilon spp.	flowering maple	stem tip cuttings, seeds
Acorus gramineus variegatus		division
Adiantum spp.	maiden-hair fern	division, spores
Aechmea spp.	airpine	offsets, suckers
Aeonium spp.		leaf cuttings, offsets
Agapanthus spp.		seeds, division
Aglaonema modestum	Chinese evergreen	stem tip cuttings, air layer
Aloe Variegata	Kanniedood aloe	ofsets
Amaryllis spp.		seeds (slow), bulbs
Anthericum spp.		offsets
Anthurium spp.		division
Araucaria excelsa	Norfolk Island pine	stem tip cuttings, shoot cuttings
Ardisia crenata	coral berry	step tip cuttings, seeds
Asparagus plumosus	asparagus fern	seeds, division
Asparagus sprengeri		seeds, division
Aspidistra elatior	cast-iron plant	division
Asplenium nidus	birds-nest fern	spores
Azalea spp.		stem tip cuttings, seeds
Begonia rex		stem tip cuttings, leaf cuttings
Begonia semperflorens		stem tip cuttings, seeds
Beloperone guttata	shrimp plant	stem tip cuttings
Billbergia spp.		division
Caladium bicolor		bulbs
Calathea sanderiana	Sanders calathea	division
Camellia japonica		stem tip cuttings
Capsicum frutescens var. conoides	tabasco redpepper	seeds
Ceropegia woodi	rosary vine	stem tip cuttings, aerial tubers
Chlorophytum capense	spider plant	offsets, runners
Cissus antarctica	kangaroo vine	stem tip cuttings
Clivia miniata	Kafir-lily	division
Coleus spp.		stem tip cuttings
Crassula arborescens	jade plant	stem tip cuttings, leaf cuttings
Cryptanthus sonatus var. zebrinus		offsets
Cyanotis somaliensis	pussy ears	stem tip cuttings
Cyclamen persicum	florists' cyclamen	seeds
Cyperus alternifolius	umbrella plant	leaf cuttings, division
Dieffenbachia spp.	dumb ane	stem tip cuttings, air layer
Dracaena fragrans		air layer
Dracaena godseffiana		stem tip cuttings, air layer
Echeveria spp.		leaf cuttings, offsets
Epiphyllum spp.		stem tip cuttings
Episcia cupreata		leaf cuttings, runners
Euphorbia pulcherrima	poinsettia	stem tip cuttings
Euphorbia splendens	crown-of-thorns	stem tip cuttings
Fatshedera lizei		stem tip cuttings
Ficus elastica	rubber plant	leaf cuttings, air layer
Ficus lyrata	fiddle-leaf fig	stem tip cuttings, air layer
Ficus pumila	climbing fig	stem tip cuttings
Ficus radicans var. variegata	variegated rooting fig	stem tip cuttings
Fittonia verschaffelti	tall fittonia	stem tip cuttings
Fuchsia spp.		stem tip cuttings
Gardenia spp.		stem tip cuttings
Gasteria hybrida		offsets
Gynura aurantiaca	velvet plant	stem tip cuttings
Haworthia spp.		offsets
Hedera helix	English ivy	stem tip cuttings
Helxine soleiroli	baby's tears	division
Hoya carnosa	wax plant	stem tip cuttings
Impatiens sultani	touch-me-not	stem tip cuttings
Kalanchoe blossfeldiana		leaf cuttings, seeds
Kalanchoe	daigremontana	
small plants form on leaves		
Kalanchoe pinnata	air plant	small plants form on leaves
Kalanchoe tomentosa		leaf cuttings
Lachenalia tricolor	Cape cowslip	offsets
Lantana spp.		stem tip cuttings
Malpighia coccigers		stem tip cuttings
Mammillaria microcarpa	fish-hook mammillaria	seeds, offsets
Maranta Leuconeura var. kerchoveana	prayer plant	stem tip cuttings, division
Monstera deliciosa	ceriman	stem tip cuttings, air layer
Neomarica gracilis	apostle plant	division, new plants from flower shoots
Nephrolepis exaltata var. bostoniensis	Boston fern	division, offsets, runners
Notacactus leninghausi		seeds, offsets
Oxalis rubra		division
Pandanus veitchi	screw-pine	stem tip cuttings, offsets, suckers
Pelargonium hortorum	zonal or fish geranium	stem tip cuttings
Pelagonium peltatum	ivy-leaved geranium	stem tip cuttings
Peperomia obtusifolia		stem tip cuttings, leaf cuttings
Peperomia sandersi var. argyreia		leaf cuttings, division
Primula malacoides	fairy primrose	seeds
Saintpaulia ionantha	African-violet	leaf cuttings, division
Sansevieria zeylanica	snake plant	leaf cuttings, division
Saxifraga sarmentosa	strawberry-geranium	division, runners
Schlumbergera bridgesi	Christmas cactus	stem tip cuttings
Scindapsus aureus	Solomon Island ivy-arum	stem tip cuttings
Selaginella uncinata	blue selaginella	stem tip cuttings
Sempervivum spp.	house-leek	offsets
Senecio cruentus	cineraria	seeds
Sinningia speciosa	gloxina	leaf cuttings, seeds
Solanum pseudo-capsicum	Jerusalem cherry	seeds
Stapelia grandiflora	carrion flower	seeds, division
Syngonium podophyllum		stem tip cuttings
Tolmiea menziesi	pick-a-back-plant	leaf cuttings, offsets
Tradescantia spp.	wandering jew	stem tip cuttings
Veltheimia viridifolia		bulbs
Zantedeschia elliottiana	golden calla	seeds, division, bulbs

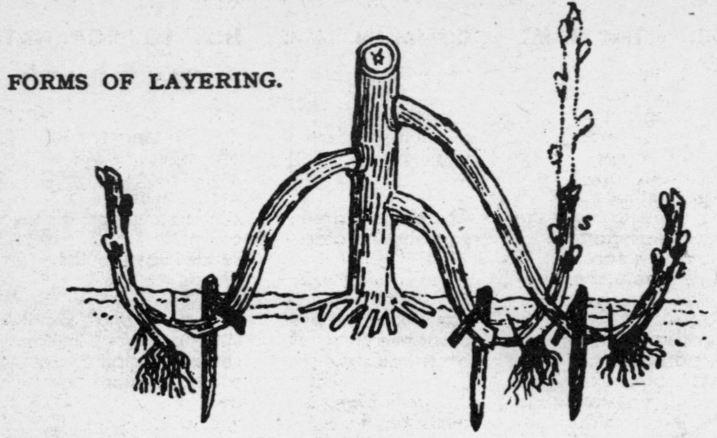
FORMS OF LAYERING.

Which Plant to Select

Select a plant that is growing vigorously and is healthy.

Do not take cuttings from plants that seem to be diseased or that are wilting.

If you have been fertilizing a plant you want to propagate, stop feeding it for a few weeks before taking cuttings.

Cuttings are best taken from youthful or middle-aged plants. Very young plants may be too weak, and old ones may be slow or hard to root.

If the soil of the parent plant is dry, water the plant thoroughly, soaking the soil, a day or so before taking the cuttings.

If you are taking cuttings from seedling trees not more than four or five years old, these will be easy to root. But as trees become older, success in rooting rapidly diminishes. Cuttings from many trees that have reached the flowering stage may be difficult to root, and you do best to root from sucker stems arising at or near the soil line or from the roots.

Container

To root cuttings successfully, you need plenty of warmth and humidity. Professionals use controlled-growth chambers where all environmental elements can be monitored and controlled. What you want for home use is the closest approximation to this you can achieve.

Greenhouse gardeners use "flats," long, shallow, wooden trays that they cover with sheets of plastic. An advantage is that the bottom of the flat is open, allowing water to drain so that overwatering cannot occur.

For your own use you can use any baking dish, casserole, or other container with a cover. You could also use open dishes, trays, or jars that you cover with plastic. Or an aquarium. Since none of these have drainage openings, however, you must take care not to overwater.

The best solution may be a clay pot that you enclose in a plastic bag. Tie the bag tightly at the top to prevent water from evaporating. Another good solution is to put an empty clay pot, with its drainage hole plugged, into the center of a larger container filled with sand or other rooting medium, and to enclose the whole thing in a plastic bag. If you plant the cuttings in the rooting medium and fill the center pot with water, the clay center pot will release water into the rooting medium as needed.

Cactus and succulents, being arid-area plants, do not require this high a humidity and can be propagated in ordinary, uncovered dishes, boxes, or pots. A container that will hold four or five inches of soil is ideal.

Soil

The most important rule is that the medium must be sterile. A good general-purpose medium is two parts perlite and one part peat moss.

Many gardeners, however, have their own pet medium in which to root cuttings. Some prefer to use vermiculite, perlite, sand, or crushed granite alone or to mix one of these with peat moss or sphagnum moss.

Mixtures containing peat moss are especially good for rooting acid loving plants like azaleas, primrose, trailing arbutus, rhododendron, columbine, blueberries, and blackberries.

For woody plants, like gardenia and citrus, a mix of half sand and half peat moss is good.

For cactus and succulents, the mix should be drier. Three parts sand to one part loam is a good proportion.

For most cuttings, the rooting medium should be four to six inches deep.

Plants can even be rooted in water. Philodendron, geranium, begonia, ivy, African violets, succulents and cactus, or any of the plants that will grow in water (see list on page 76) can be rooted this way. Some large plants, like pussy willow and forsythia, are also easily rooted in water. A problem with this system is that while stem cuttings are easy to prop up in a vase, you may have trouble keeping leaves upright. One solution is to cover the vase with plastic and then punch holes in the plastic; you can suspend the leaf so its stem reaches the water and the leaf remains in the air.

Some gardeners do not like to root in water, however, because such roots are frequently brittle. They may break off later, when you try to plant them in soil. In addition, unless the water has enough oxygen, many plants will rot instead of root. Adding a few charcoal chips to the water will help keep it fresh.

Steps in Propagating Cuttings

1. Take the cutting as indicated under the various types.

2. Dust the cut section in a root-inducing chemical compound available in garden centers. This is a powder containing acids that stimulate root growth as well as fungicides to prevent disease from entering the vulnerable cut surfaces. This is not necessary if the rooting medium is sterile, but most gardeners do it as a precaution.

3. Insert the cutting into the growing medium to about a third of its length. This will usually be to a depth of about two inches. You can first use a pencil or a nail to make a hole in the medium. Once you have the cutting in place, press the medium firmly against the cutting with your fingers to insure the medium is in contact with the cutting.

4. Water the growing medium thoroughly, and check to be sure the cutting is firmly set.

5. Since a plant takes in water through its roots and loses it through its leaves, your rootless cutting is going to have a tough time obtaining water. What it gets will be only through the cut you've made, so you must be careful to keep the medium moist. But don't let the medium become soggy or the plant will not have sufficient air to develop a root system, and rot may set in.

6. A major cause of cutting failure is insufficient humidity. Be sure your cuttings are in a covered dish or insulated with plastic—lift the cover an hour or so a day to ventilate. Believe it or not, 100% humidity is ideal.

7. Cuttings must be kept warm—at about 75° to 80°—so set them above heating units or provide some other form of heat for them if your home doesn't automatically provide these levels. Some varieties will prosper nonetheless if you cannot provide quite so much heat—say only 65° to 70°—so long as the humidity remains high. It's also best if the night temperature drops 5° to 10°. Your basement may provide these conditions best.

8. Cuttings like bright light and, in general, the brighter the light the faster the roots will form. But indirect sunlight is better than full sun, since sun will dry the cuttings out too much. At least avoid direct sun for two weeks after planting, and thereafter avoid mid-morning to mid-afternoon sun. If you are propagating under artificial lights, the cutting tray should be placed about six inches below the lights and you should provide light for 14 to 16 hours a day. Three to four weeks for rooting is average under artificial light.

9. Once plants have rooted, they should be transplanted, though it's hard to pinpoint the exact time you should do this. In general, you should pot your cuttings when they have ten to fifteen roots one or two inches long. Ideally, the roots should have formed all around the stem, not just on one side. The new shoots on top will probably be at least a half-inch long. While you want a good root system before transplanting, you also don't want to delay too long because the rooting medium may not provide sufficient nutrients. Transfer the plants to small pots—2½ to 3 inches—with the proper soil for the variety of plant. From there on, follow the culture instructions given for various plants on the following pages.

Note: For cactus and succulents, the method is somewhat different. After taking the cutting, let it dry out in the air about four days. Then pot it in a sandy mix. Don't push them in deep—just enough so they are in contact with the soil. Keep the soil just barely moist but don't let it dry out, and keep the pots in shade. With succulents particularly, you can tell when they are well rooted because they will plump up. You can then pot them individually.

Tips on Cuttings: 1. To avoid disease entering the cut surfaces, keep your work area clean. Tools should be sterilized, if possible, by dipping them in alcohol or laundry bleach between cuttings. If you are using a knife or razor blade you can run it through a match flame.

2. The planting medium should be sterile.

3. Coat all cut surfaces with a rooting hormone powder containing a fungicide as a preventive against disease.

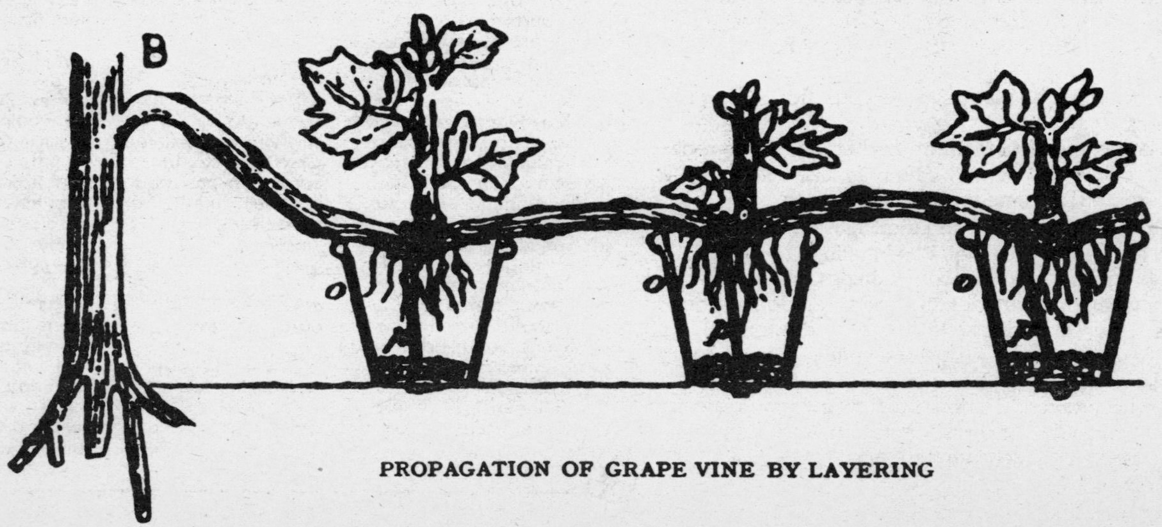

PROPAGATION OF GRAPE VINE BY LAYERING

4. Keep the rooting medium moist but not soggy, keep the temperature and humidity high, and keep cuttings out of direct sun.
5. If you're making a lot of cuttings from several plants, label each cutting if you think you will mix them up.

Division

Any plant that grows in clumps with numerous shoots or that has multiple crowns can be propagated by division. This is a fast, easy method, since all you have to do is pull the plant apart. Just be sure each section has some crown and some root.

Some plants divide easily in your hand. For tougher plants you will have to use a sharp knife, pruning shears, or even a spade—but the implement should be sterilized first. Also, dust all cut surfaces with a fungicide or sulfur to prevent disease.

From a multiple-crowned African violet you may be able to get a dozen or so new plants. This method also works for some ferns, orchids, ginger, chrysanthemums, calatheas, and others.

Early flowering woody plants and herbaceous perennials with multiple crowns can be divided after the plant has become dormant in late summer or early fall. Woody plants and perennials that bloom in mid to late summer are divided in early spring before the buds begin to swell.

However, you will not want to divide perennials that require several years after planting to flower more than every few years. Iris rhizomes, for example, should be divided in mid-July once every three or four years. Cut the rhizomes into sections, so each section has a visible growth above, and immediately replant. Plants that are rampant growers you may want to divide every year or two.

Dahlia tubers and peony roots should be divided so each root piece has a bud (eye) on the stem piece at the top of the root. Dahlia may be divided in early spring just prior to planting, but peonies should be divided only every six or seven years. Some ferns and other rhizomatous plants can also be divided that way.

Bulbs, corms, and similar plants that are not hardy enough to overwinter in the ground should be handled like dahlia. But hardy bulbs such as daffodils, narcissus, tulips, and lilies can be divided in summer after the tops have died down. Dig them up, clean them, let them dry out, and then cut in half. You can replant them in late summer or early fall.

Division is a major way of multiplying plants for food gardens. Tubers such as potatoes, bulbs such as onions, and tuberous roots such as those of the sweet potato may all be divided.

Cactus and succulents with multiple crowns usually have to be severed with a knife, and if the plants have thorns you'll have to wear gloves.

Orchids with pseudobulbs can be divided when the front eye swells and new roots begin to appear.

LAYERING FRUIT STOCKS, SHOWING NOTCHES.

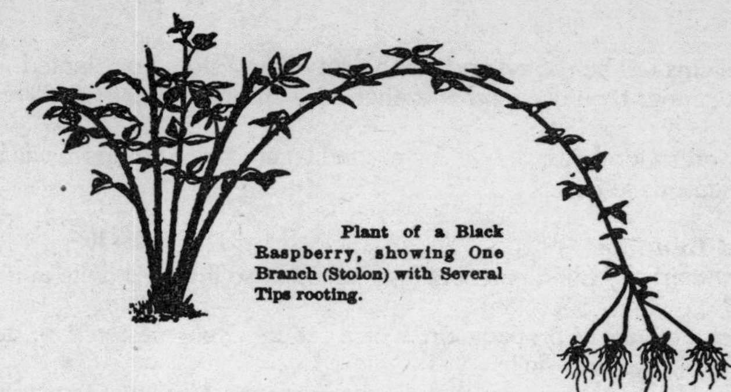

Plant of a Black Raspberry, showing One Branch (Stolon) with Several Tips rooting.

Layering

Layering is really just another method of propagation by stem cutting. The difference is that in stem cuttings you remove the stem to root it in soil. With air layering you allow the stem to develop a good root system before you remove it from the parent plant. The advantage of layering is that the parent plant continues to supply water and nutrients to the new plant.

Air Layering, also called pot and Chinese layering, may be used on indoor and outdoor plants.

For indoor plants it is especially popular for the woody tropical varieties such as dracaena, rubber plant, croton, pandanus, aralias, and dieffenbachia. Sometimes these plants grow ungainly as they age, losing their lower leaves so that you are left with heavy foliage on a long, bare stalk. Air layering allows you to preserve the plant by rerooting it at the bottom of the foliage and then discarding the bare stem.

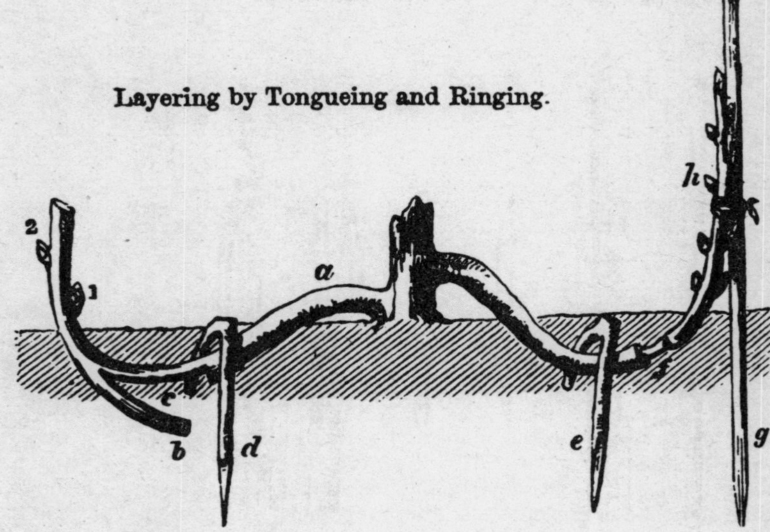

Layering by Tongueing and Ringing.

With a sharp knife, make a diagonal, upward cut through to the center of the stem, but don't cut so far that you detach it. You may split the stem an inch or two upward from the point your knife entered, or cut downward to make a notch an inch or two long. Dust the inside of the cut with a rooting hormone; this is available in powder form at garden supply centers. To keep the cut open, insert a sterile pebble or stick. Press a wad of moist sphagnum moss between the cut surfaces and wrap more moss around the stem for about two inches above and below the cut. Then bandage the wound tightly with plastic wrap. The plastic should cover all the moss. You want a tight seal, so fold the edges of the plastic wrap several times and then bind the plastic firmly to the stem with waterproof tape. If you get a good seal, the sphagnum moss will remain moist more than a year.

You may not have to wait this long, however, though you will have to wait at least six to nine months. You will see the roots in the moss ball through the plastic wrap. Leave the plant in a shaded location during this time. When it looks as though a good root system has formed, remove the plastic and moss. Cut the rest of the stem from the parent plant by slicing below the root ball, and pot the new plant.

If you cut the stem of the parent plant back to two inches from the soil, it may produce new shoots, giving you two new plants.

Air layering can also be done on many woody trees and shrubs outdoors, so long as you protect the plant from excessive heat buildup from the sun.

Simple layering is useful for some outdoor plants. Here you bend a branch to the ground before growth commences in the spring. Bury a 5-inch to 10-inch portion at the center of the stem in the soil, but leave several inches of the tip exposed to the air to form new leaves. You'll have to anchor the stem firmly in the ground so it doesn't pull out. Also, stake the exposed tip in an upright position.

Dusting the stem with a root-inducing powder also helps. To improve rooting, you may also make a diagonal cut about a third of the way through the stem, remove a ring of bark from around the stem, or cut a notch on the lower part of the stem. When well rooted, divide the new plant from the parent and plant it.

Tip layering is done by placing the tip of a branch into one or two inches of soil and anchoring it securely. Again you divide and plant when well rooted. Black raspberries, blackberries, and *Forsythia suspensa* are easily propagated this way.

Mound layering, or stooling, starts during the plant's dormant season. Cut it back severely, almost to the soil. As soon as new shoots appear in spring, cover the bases of the stems with soil. As growth continues, keep mounding the soil over the stems until you have six to eight inches of stem covered with soil. Never cover the stem tip.

By fall the stems will be rooted and can be cut off and stored or planted.

Gooseberry, currant, quince, and hydrangea are among plants that will root the first year.

Magnolias and rhododendrons can be mound layered too, but these will take two growing seasons to root.

Grafting and Budding

Grafting is the art of joining parts of plants together so they will unite and continue their growth as one plant.

Unlike other methods of propagation, which can be easily mastered by novice gardeners, grafting requires skill.

The chief problems involved are that the two parts must be fitted together exactly and that the plants must be related. The bottom section of the graft—usually a trunk and root system of one plant or tree—is called the rootstock or *stock*. The section to be fitted on it—usually a smaller branch—is called the *scion*. Unless the stock and scion are closely related—the closer the better—they will not have enough affinity to grow together as one. Success depends on uniting the cambium layer of stock and scion. The cambium is a thin layer of reproductive tissue between the bark and the wood of a stem, and it regulates the growth cycles that you can see as tree rings in sawed tree trunks. Since this is the active growth section of the plant, it is the most critical section to unite in grafting. Yet since the cambium is very thin, it is no easy feat to unite the stock and scion successfully. It is usually also helpful if the stock is in growth and the scion dormant.

Grafting is often quite technical and best left to professionals. Sometimes it also requires special equipment and facilities to control temperature and other factors. However, some techniques have been in use since at least Roman times, and can be more easily mastered. These are the ones described below.

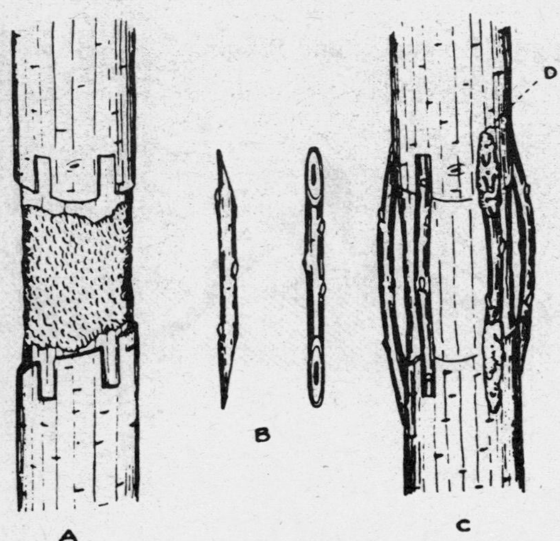

Bridge Grafting. a. Injured trunk showing ragged edges of bark trimmed and the rectangular sections of bark removed. b. Two views of a scion cut properly. c. Scions in place and nailed. Note the bow of the scions and the exposed wood under the scions is painted. d. The scions waxed properly.

The most common reason for grafting is to perpetuate a plant that cannot be reproduced with cuttings or other easy methods of propagation. An example of this is budding or bud grafting, which can be used to propagate hybrid plants such as roses and fruit trees.

Some grafting is done to obtain a new form of plant not found in nature. The grafting of one shape of cactus or a cactus of a distinct shape is an illustration.

Another reason for grafting is to create a better plant. Say you want to grow a tree in a climate that is not suitable for it, you could graft it as a scion on the rootstock of a tree perfectly adapted to the climate. Or say you have a tree susceptible to disease; you might want to graft it as a scion onto the stock of a tree that is especially disease-resistant.

Grafting of fruit trees is commonly done to increase their productivity.

The bridge graft: This is used to repair badly damaged bark on a tree. Sometimes bark is nibbled by mice or porcupines. Damage also can be by humans—running your lawnmower into a tree or hitting a tree repeatedly with a child's swing.

Here what you want to do is graft a piece of living tissue over the wound so that the tree will continue to live and grow. Any large amount of bark damage will prevent the tree from carrying the food its leaves manufacture to the roots.

The best time to do this type of graft is in early spring, just as the buds are beginning to break. Several weeks before grafting, gather shoots one-fourth to one-half inch in diameter from the tree. You need enough shoots to set every 2 or 3 inches across the injured area, and they should be long enough to extend above and below the wounded area. These shoots will be your scions.

When you cut the shoots, mark the tops with red paint or by some other means so that you know which is the top end (the part farthest from the trunk). If you place them upside down on the tree, they will have trouble transporting the tree's food in the right direction. Store them in the refrigerator until time to use. This will keep them dormant.

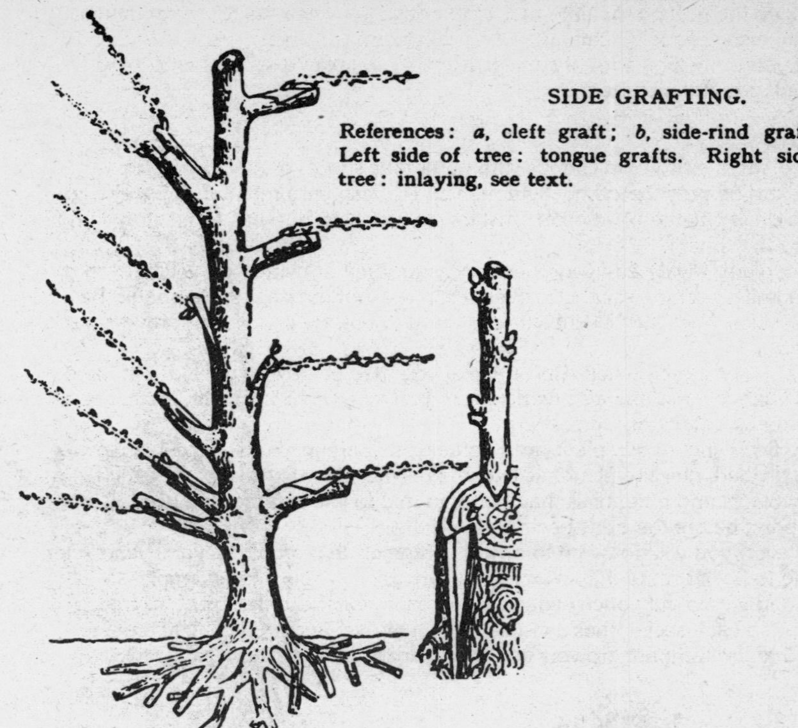

SIDE GRAFTING.

References: *a*, cleft graft; *b*, side-rind grafting. Left side of tree: tongue grafts. Right side of tree: inlaying, see text.

Then the ends of the scions should be cut on the diagonal, as illustrated. Remove the damaged tissue around the edges of the wound. Cut out rectangular sections of bark every two to three inches apart where you are going to plant the scions (see illustration), so that their ends will be touching live tissue above and below the wound. Place the scions on the tree and nail them to the trunk with small flat-headed wire nails. Be sure the scions are all right-side up before you nail them.

Then cover the entire area with grafting wax. This will prevent drying out and disease.

Keep an eye on the shoots, and if they develop buds, cut these off.

Within a few years the scions will enlarge and completely cover the wounded area.

The cleft graft: You can use this to graft additional branches on your fruit tree, or to add branches that will give you more than one variety of fruit from the same tree. You can also use it to insert a male branch in a female holly tree to insure pollination.

Cleft grafts can be done at any time the trees are dormant, but are best done just before buds begin to swell in the spring.

Cut off a branch not over 4 inches in diameter, and split the stub vertically for a distance of 2 to 3 inches. You can do this by using a mallet to pound a heavy knife or wedge into the stub. If a knife is used, a screwdriver or wedge should be inserted to hold the split open.

Insert two shoots (scions) 3 to 4 inches long with a gently sloping cut on the basal 2 inches of the shoot into opposite sides of the split. The outer edge of the shoot should match the outer edge of the branch so that a union can be formed.

After you have inserted the shoots, remove the screwdriver or wedge so the shoots will be firmly held in place. Cover the top of the stub and the union between stub and shoots with grafting wax.

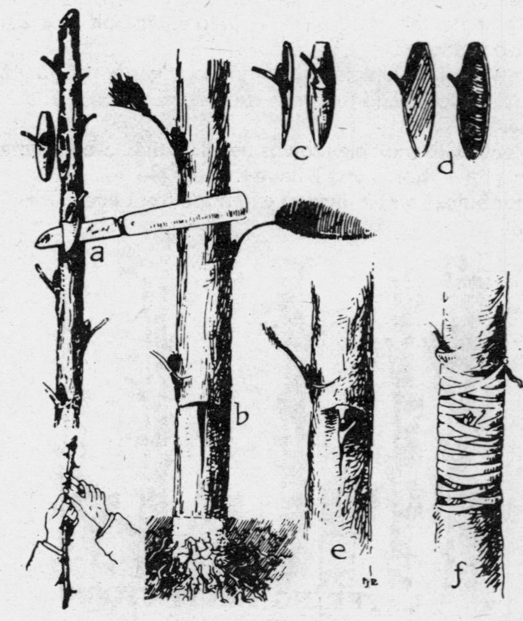

Budding or bud grafting, using the T-bud or shield bud technique.

a. Bud-stick. Proper method of holding knife and cutting bud is shown in lower left-hand corner.

b. T-cut on stock.

c. Side and front view of a "bud."

d. Inside view of bud with and without wood.

e. Stock with bud inserted.

f. Bud in place and tied with rubber band.

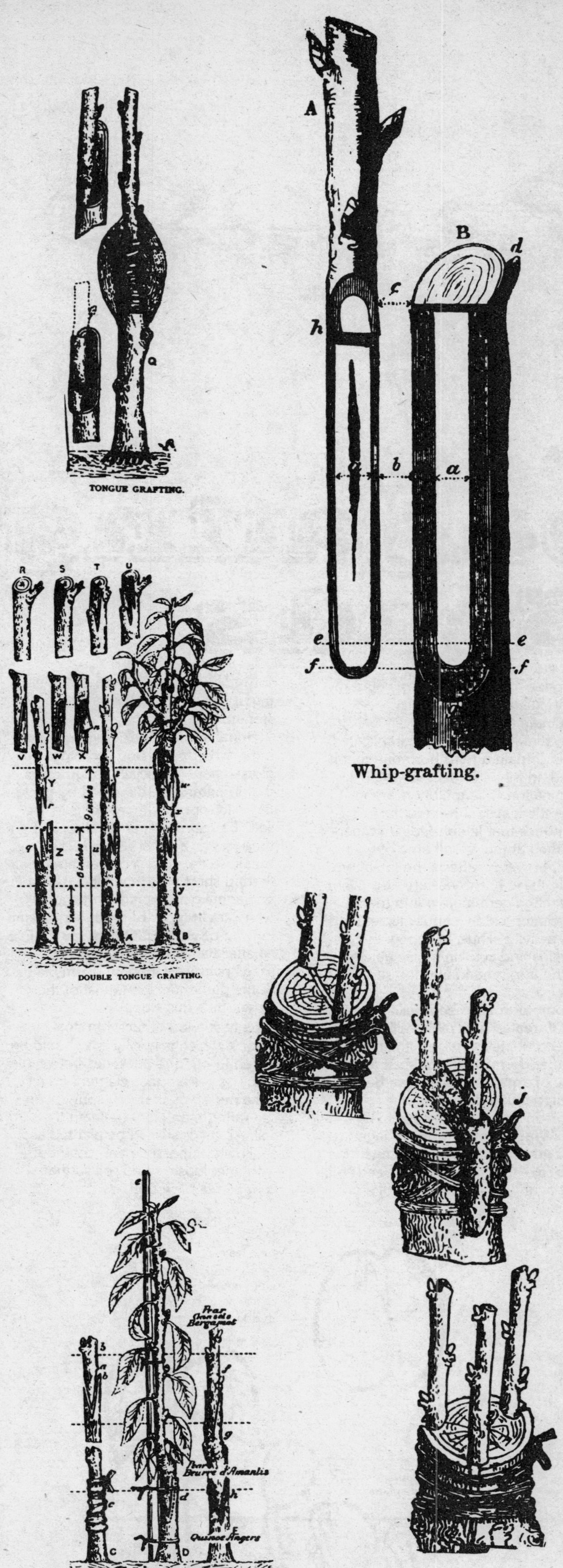

TONGUE GRAFTING.

Whip-grafting.

DOUBLE TONGUE GRAFTING.

WEDGE GRAFTING.

Budding: Budding or bud grafting is popularly used to propagate a wide variety of ornamentals that, due to being hybrids or for other reasons, are difficult to propagate by cuttings. It is especially popular with growers of roses and fruit trees.

Bud grafting consists of inserting a single bud of the rose or fruit variety you want into the bark of a seedling or other stock. The technique is shown on the accompanying illustration.

Budding should be done when the bark is easily separated from the wood. The bud is inserted between the bark and the wood. Most budding is done in the fall since there is more time for the union to form before new shoot growth starts the following spring.

Cactus graftings: Grafting is especially popular with cactus growers because you can combine two totally different plants to create a form not found in nature. Only members of the cactus and euphorbia families may be grafted, however, not all succulents.

The chief object in grafting is to make an attractive new plant, and this means paying attention to scale and proportion, to textures that will go well together, and to forms that will retain a pleasing shape as they grow. Many cactus fanciers, however, do it just for the fun of creating weird-looking plants and don't care if the results are ugly. The types of cactus chosen for stock are generally those with tall straight growth, like cereus, and scions are often round, chubby forms like cephclocereus, but you can also use more leaf-like forms such as epiphyllum.

The method of graft you use depends on the form. The easiest method is a flat graft, which is best for rounded shapes. Here you slice off the top of plant that is to be the rootstock by cutting straight across with a sterilized knife. Trim off the rim so no dead tissue will enter the graft. Because the cut surface must be kept sterile and moist to avoid rot and assure good adherence, it's a good idea to then cut a very thin slice on stock section but leave it temporarily in place to keep the surface you are going to use moist and clean. Instead you can cover the cactus with a moist, sterile pad. Then you slice off the bottom of another cactus, to use the top as a scion. Slice this also straight across, trim the rim, and mount this head on your first cactus, after removing the slice or sterile pad.

Press the scion on the stock, and hold the pieces in place with string or rubber bands. You can also use cactus spines to hold the pieces together, and these will dissolve later. You can use toothpicks too, but these have to be removed and will leave scars.

Keep the plant in the shade for a couple of days to let it rest, and then return to the sun.

The graft will succeed only if the inner growth rings of the top and bottom pieces match each other perfectly. This means the growth rings must have identical diameters.

In the side graft, which may be necessary if you are going to mount a rounded head as a scion on a stock with a straight form such as cereus, you make your slices on the diagonal instead of straight across.

For the third method, the cleft graft, you make a V-shaped cut on the stock plant. Then you've got to cut the scion so that it has a V-shaped bottom that will fit exactly into the stock's cuts—not at all easy to do. This method is necessary only when you are trying to make grafts with flat leaves like epiphyllum.

Cactus grafting should be done only when the plants are growing and have lots of sap growing (May or June to September or October).

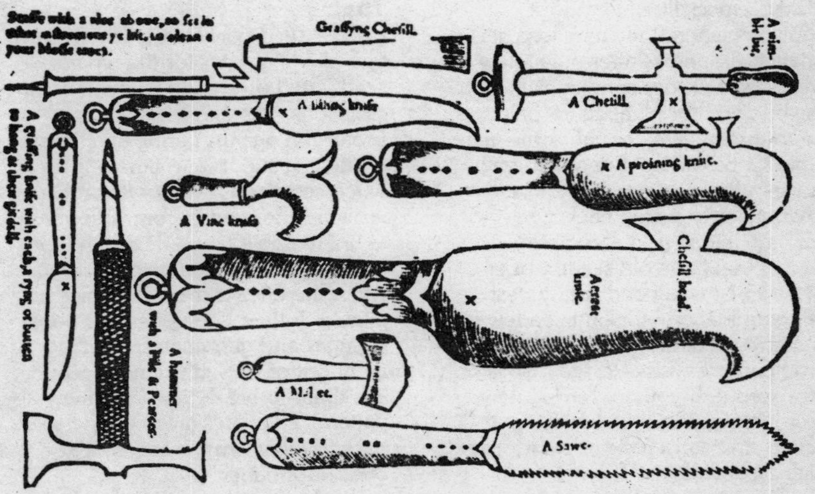

TOOLS USED IN GRAFTING.

Propagating from Seeds

Growing plants from seeds is inexpensive and reliable. Seeds available today are the product of intensive research that insures the resulting plants will be as disease-free as possible, will provide the most spectacular blooms or best vegetables, and will be free of contamination by the seeds of weeds and other undesirable plants. Often, too, researchers have developed seeds that are capable of germinating over a wide range of climatic conditions. Plants from seeds may therefore be more reliable and robust than those you produce through vegetative reproduction.

Because seeds are subject to government regulations, their packaging contains useful information, such as the percentage of seeds you can expect will actually germinate, the percentage of weed or other seeds. As a result, you often are better off buying commercial seed than using your own, which are not subject to such strict supervision and safeguards. As mentioned under "Hybrids," above, seeds from hybrids are especially unreliable, and for hybrids you should use cuttings or other methods of propagation.

In addition, seeds deteriorate quickly, especially under moist conditions where they may lose germinating properties after only a few weeks. Even in dry conditions they may be good for planting for only one to three years, though some vegetable seeds will last twice that long. You should therefore look for seeds in hermetically sealed packages, and keep any leftovers in a cool, dry place. If you have old seeds you are not sure of, it is a good idea to test their germination by planting a few in a suitable medium—even between damp paper towels—to see if 50% or more sprout. If you are buying new seed, look for the best quality, in packets that conserve freshness, from reliable sources.

Looking through illustrated seed catalogs makes many gardeners go bonkers. It's easy to envision masses of stupefyingly beautiful flowers and huge, luscious vegetables. The tendency is to over-order. Try to keep your dreams in check and order only what you will really use.

The size of seed varies radically. The seed can be a fistful—avocado and mango are examples. You can hold these—one at a time—in your hand, and such seeds therefore tend to be special. You nurture each as an individual and mourn if it fails to grow properly. Midway on the scale are plants such as marigold. These are visible, distinct seeds you may not hold quite so much in esteem. Nevertheless, you can still count the number of successes or failures you have. But when you get down to seeds such as primula or begonia, your whole outlook changes. Here you are not dealing with specific seeds, for they are too fine to be identifiable, but rather whether or not the *process* of propagation works. Logically, perhaps, it doesn't make too much sense—a seed is a seed. But, in fact, you will find yourself emotionally much more involved with some seeds than others.

Timing

Each seed packet you buy will give you planting dates for the type of seed, and you should follow these instructions. Seeds have built-in protection against germinating and producing shoots at a time of year when conditions are not favorable for growth. The seed becomes dormant at unfavorable times. Through a process not entirely understood, it senses when the environment becomes hospitable. It then undergoes hormonal changes and germinates. Planting them out of season will not encourage them to break this dormancy pattern. The dates given on the seed packets tell when the seeds will be out of dormancy.

Seeds germinate with the aid of two plant hormones—gibberellins and cytokinins. The absence of one or both of these hormones would result in failure of the seed to germinate.

To make things more complicated, seeds contain a third hormone that is called an inhibitor because it blocks germination. The inhibitors are important because these are the hormones that keep seeds from germinating at the wrong time of year. Cold, however, affects the inhibitors. While these hormones are effective in preventing germination into the fall and winter, cold weather decreases their activity. Thus, in spring, the gibberellins and cytokinins are able to get the upper hand and the seed germinates.

Some dormant seeds will germinate if treated with gibberellins alone or in combination with cytokinins.

Other dormant seeds, such as those of apple and pear, can be germinated if you duplicate the conditions they would have in nature. Wrap them in moist sphagnum moss and store them in a refrigerator at 35° to 40° for the winter. Seeds of grasses and grains can be broken of dormancy by only five days of chilling at 50° or by prolonged dry storage.

Some seeds—including geranium, okra, sweet-peas, and morning glory—have especially tough coats that in nature are dissolved by bacteria, acid, or other ingredients in the soil. To speed up germination, rub these seeds against sandpaper to break up the coat. You can also soak them a short time in sulphuric acid, and some gardeners report success with certain types of seeds by soaking in wine or vinegar. Others say it's just as effective to soak tough-coated seeds overnight in plain warm water. Some gardeners treat most of their large seeds this way.

Light is another factor in dormancy, which is why seeds should be stored in opaque packages between use. Light is a major element in germinating seeds that you sprinkle on soil rather than plant beneath the soil. All seeds should be planted as shallowly as possible and covered with fine, loose, sifted soil so that light can get through.

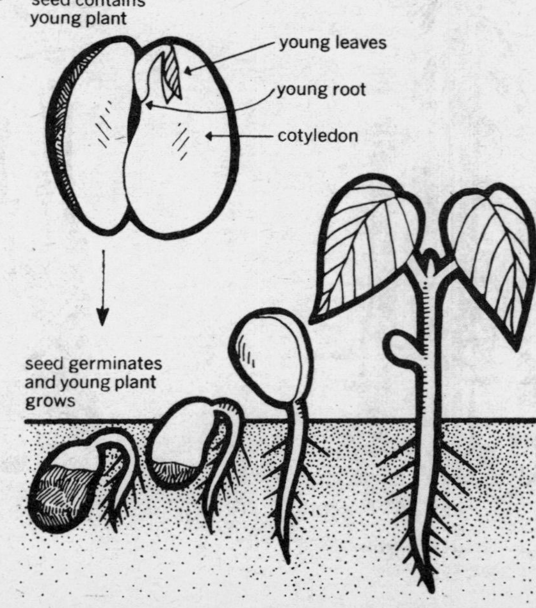

Vegetables are divided into categories according to the temperatures they enjoy. Cool-season vegetables are those that are least susceptible to injury from frost. Even in northern regions with severe climate, some vegetables—asparagus, horseradish, parsnip, Jerusalem artichoke, and rhubarb among them—are so hardy they can be left in the ground over winter. These are perennials that, though they produce seeds annually, will continue to regenerate each spring. Others, such as cabbage, beets, and carrots are biennials, while peas are annuals. Also among the cool-season vegetables are broad beans; members of the cabbage family such as broccoli, Brussels sprouts, and cauliflower; celery and endive; leafy plants such as some lettuce, cress, and spinach; onions, parsnips, radish, rutabagas, and turnip; leeks and parsley.

Cool-season vegetables also usually require high temperatures for germination—above 70° for the cabbage family and 75° to 80° for onions, for example—but you can set the seedlings out quite early, as soon as the ground can be worked. Some will grow at temperatures as low as 50°, some require 55°. If you have limited space for germination, you may prefer to buy these seedlings at garden centers, and save your indoor space for vegetables that require more pampering. Many varieties of tomatoes and peppers, for instance, need temperatures of about 60° to grow, while eggplant and others demand at least 65°.

The same is true of flowers. Tougher flowering plants—asters, celosia, marigolds, nasturtiums, and zinnias—can be planted outdoors as soon as the ground is warm enough for working. If your indoor space is limited, therefore, you will want to germinate the impatiens, begonias, coleus, and others instead. Many of these annuals can be started in January or February to have them ready for outdoor use when the weather warms up.

If you are going to germinate many seeds, either of flowers or vegetables or both, check the germination time and outdoor growing temperatures in advance. You can then calculate how long your flats will be in use for the earlier plants. If you have started annuals in, say, February, and transferred them to pots, you can reuse your flats for vegetables, many of which require only six weeks or so from sowing to outdoor planting.

Precaution

The chief reason seedlings fail is damp-off, a fungus disease. Spores of this fungus are present in most soils but may be fairly harmless under normal outdoor garden conditions. The fungus thrives, however, in warm, moist conditions—the exact environment you are trying to get for your seeds.

Your best defense is operating-room cleanliness. Use only sterile soil. Sterilize all your tools. Use propagating containers that are as clean as possible, preferably also sterilized. And keep your hands clean.

Containers

You can sow seeds in anything from eggshells to professional seed flats. Your choice of container depends mostly on how many seeds you are planting, though the size of the seed can also be a factor.

If you are planting many seeds, the flats are an aid. These are shallow, rectangular wooden boxes large enough for you to plant several rows of seeds. These are handiest for outdoor gardeners starting numerous seeds indoors.

If you are starting fewer seeds for greenhouse or for outdoor or indoor use, flats probably will be too big. You can buy a number of rigid containers made of peatmoss that vary in size from trays to individual pots, ranging from ¾ inches to several inches high; or strips of tiny trays joined together; or even pellets and cupcake-like containers of various sizes. The advantage of these, apart from their size range, is that you can avoid transplanting. Put these peatmoss containers directly in the ground, and the growing roots will eventually force them apart and make them disintegrate. Some gardeners swear by peatmoss containers while others fail to see much advantage, especially if they are dealing with large numbers of small seeds or are sprouting only a few seeds for indoor use.

You can also use baking dishes, casseroles, regular clay pots, or any other container that seems suitable for the number and size of seed you will need. Pots with drainage holes should have broken crockery at the bottom to prevent soil from washing out, and containers without drainage holes should have pebbles or sand in the bottom to allow excess water to drain from the soil.

Some people like to use covered clear-plastic boxes. Holes can be drilled (or, with some, burned, with careful match applications, but this is a less certain procedure) in the bottom for drainage. This can then be bottom-watered to get the soil moist. The procedure is especially good for fine seed such as that of gesneriads or primula, where you will probably be germinating limited quantities of seed.

Soil

To avoid fungus disease, most gardeners use sterile artificial soils such as perlite or vermiculite for seeds they are starting indoors. You can also buy commercially prepared propagating mix that is sterile.

If you want to mix your own, a good soilless mix would be equal parts perlite, peat moss, and ground sphagnum moss. Some gardeners use milled sphagnum moss alone.

If, despite the risks, you want a soil mixture, a good proportion would be equal amounts of loam, peatmoss or leaf-mold, and sand. You will, however, have to sterilize it. And you may also want to use a fungicide in the water you use to moisten the mixture.

What you need in soil is that it be moisture-retentive, that it be loose enough to allow oxygen and light to reach the roots, and that it be loose enough so that seedlings can be removed easily, without damaging the roots, when it comes time to transplant.

If your plants are for your outdoor flower or food garden, you will often be starting seeds indoors with one of the above mixes.

If you are going to plant seeds in deep pots, adding a little charcoal to the bottom of the pot will keep the soil from souring.

If you are going to sow seeds outdoors, then follow our pointers in the section on soil. The soil should be loosened before planting to allow the roots to develop easily, and a conditioner-like peatmoss should be added. For seeds, it is a good idea to have the top inch of soil very rich in humus.

Preparation for Sowing

If you are using flats, spread the bottom with coarse sand for drainage, then fill to within a half-inch or a quarter-inch of the top with your propagating medium. Place the flat in a sink or other large container with water, and leave it until the water has soaked to the top of the soil.

You can do the same with any container that, like a flat, has bottom drainage. If your container has no drainage, you should add water a bit at a time to be sure you get even moisture without having the soil sopping.

The reason that you do not fill the container all the way to the top is that you want to add a fine, sifted medium around the seeds themselves. This will insure light and air for germination.

If you are sowing outdoors, water the ground well beforehand. The soil should be moist but not soggy.

Because light and oxygen are important to germination, the right amount of water is important. While the seeds need moisture, you don't want their soil so dense that they will not get air and light.

TIME TO SOW SEEDS AND TO TRANSPLANT ANNUALS TO HAVE PLANTS READY TO SET IN THE GARDEN THE LAST WEEK IN MAY

Plant	*Sow seed in*	*Transplant seedlings in:*
Ageratum	March, third week	April, third week
Amaranthus	April, third week	May, first week
Anagallis	April, first week	April, fourth week
Babysbreath	April, third week	May, first week
Balsam	April, second week	May, first week
Bachelor's button	April, third week	May, first week
Calendula	April, third week	May, first week
California poppy	April, third week	May, first week
Calliopsis	April, first week	April, third week
Candytuft	April, third week	May, first week
China aster	April, second week	April, fourth week
Chrysanthemum	April, third week	May, first week
Clarkia	April, fourth week	May, second week
Cleome	April, third week	May, second week
Cockscomb	April, second week	April, fourth week
Cosmos	April, fourth week	May, second week
Cynoglossum	April, first week	April, fourth week
Dahlia	March, first week	March, fourth week
Dianthus	April, first week	April, fourth week
Dimorphotheca	April, first week	April, fourth week
Gaillardia	April, third week	May, first week
Godetia	April, second week	Aprii, fourth week
Gomphrena	April, third week	May, second week
Hunnemannia	April, first week	April, fourth week
Kochia	April, second week	May, first week
Larkspur	April, first week	April, fourth week
Lavatera	April, second week	May, first week
Lobelia	March, third week	April, third week
Marigold	April, second week	April, fourth week
Mignonette	April, third week	May, first week
Mimulus	April, third week	May, first week
Morning glory	April, third week	May, first week
Nasturtium	April, third week	May, first week
Nicotiana	April, second week	May, first week
Nierembergia	March, third week	April, first week
Nigella	April, first week	April, third week
Petunia	March, third week	April, first week
Phlox	April, second week	April, fourth week
Poppy	April, fourth week	May, second week
Salpiglossis	April, first week	April, third week
Salvia	April, first week	May, first week
Scabiosa	April, third week	May, second week
Schizanthus	April, third week	May, first week
Snapdragon	March, second week	April, first week
Statice	April, first week	April, third week
Straw flower	April, first week	April, third week
Sunflower	May, first week	May, second week
Sweet alyssum	April, second week	April, third week
Verbena	March, second week	April, second week
Vinca	April, first week	April, third week
Zinnia	April, fourth week	May, second week

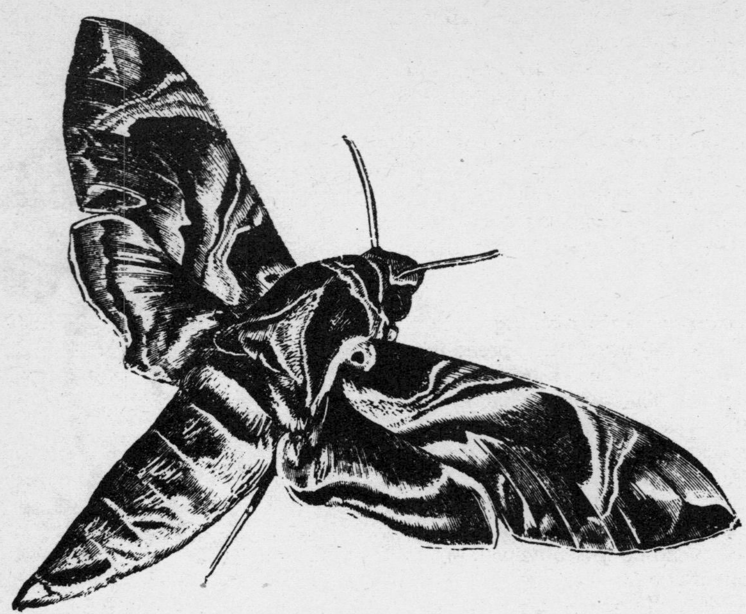

Sowing Seeds

Seeds should be planted as shallowly as possible, because light and air are important to germination. But how deeply you plant them depends on the size of the seed. The general rule is to plant them to a depth of twice their thickness, at most, but at least to a depth of their thickness.

1. Large seeds can be placed, one by one by hand, in the growing medium and then covered with additional medium sifted through a sieve. Often you will be planting these singly in small pots. For slightly smaller seeds, such as nasturtiums, you may want to plant several to a larger pot.

If seeds are smaller yet, you probably will be planting them in rows. You can mark off the rows with a ruler or trowel—making the rows about two inches apart—and then sow the seeds in these rows. Sift a fine layer of your medium over them. For cactus, cover with crushed limestone.

Some plants have very fine seed that you cannot handle. Begonias, crassula, primula, snapdragons, impatiens, petunias, coleus, and gesneriads are among them. Put the seeds on a folded piece of paper and sprinkle them over the entire surface of the medium by tapping the paper lightly. Mixing the seeds with sand also will help you get even distribution. The more evenly you can distribute the seed, the easier it will be to transplant the seedlings later. Such seeds do not need to be covered with additional soil but you can pat them into place.

If you don't like dealing with fine seed, you can buy what are called "pelleted" versions. These are seeds coated with plant food and, usually, fungicide, and the coating makes them larger and easier to handle.

2. In sowing, the most important point is to be sure the seed is in contact with the soil. This sounds simplistic, but in fact seeds are often so small that in sowing you can easily leave gaps between them and the soil. Tamping the soil with your fingers will help avoid this. If the soil is properly moist, tamping should do the trick.

If you are planting outdoors, you can drill a shallow hole for each seed and wrap the seed in a little damp soil before you drop it in. Then plug the hole with a little bit more moist soil.

3. Seeds that are easy to germinate, such as those of bromeliads, can be placed between moist paper towels to sprout before being transferred to the growing medium.

4. If you are sowing more than one kind of seed, label the containers, preferably with waterproof marking crayons. If you are using flats with different plants in each row, label each row. It is easy to forget what you've planted, and seedlings look remarkably alike when they first emerge from the soil. You may also want to add special care instructions on each label. For outdoor gardeners, a variety of durable plastic and metal label holders are available, but for short-term use you can improvise with wooden tongue depressors, color-coded plastic swizzle sticks for which you keep the information on cards indoors, or any other waterproof surface that can be inserted into soil and won't blow away in the wind.

5. After you have sown the seeds and covered them with sifted soil, mist the soil. Use a fine hand sprayer or mister so that you do not disturb the seeds. Even if you have not covered the seed with soil, as with the fine seed of impatiens, for instance, misting will help them adhere to the growing medium.

If you are planting outdoors, spray the top of the soil lightly with a hose.

6. Cover the seed containers to preserve humidity and even temperature. If you are using a plastic box or other covered container, you can use the lid. Most gardeners use plastic. For pots and small trays or baking dishes, you can use plastic bags. Even large flats can be put in plastic bags, though sheets of plastic that you can fold under the flat's edges will be cheaper if you have a lot of flats. If you are using an aquarium or flats, you could also cover these with glass.

Light

Seeds should be kept in good light, but out of direct sunlight, if you are germinating them indoors. In greenhouses, if shade cannot be provided, use translucent rather than clear plastic to cover your flats. Or, if you are using glass or clear plastic for covering, spread a sheet of newspaper over the top.

If you are germinating seed under artificial light, the soil should be kept about six inches from the light source, and the lights should be run between 14 and 16 hours a day. A minimum of 1000 foot-candles of cool white fluorescent light is required for most seeds, and you should start this as soon as the seeds are sown. Before the seedlings emerge, you can, in fact, run the lights 24 hours and the new sprouts will not mind this for a week or two after they push through the soil. As they grow, however, they will demand a rest period in darkness and you should set your timer to give them at least eight hours of night. Some leafy vegetables, such as spinach and Chinese cabbage, will go to seed if grown in more than 15 hours of light.

Temperature

Temperature is the most critical factor in germination, and temperature optimums of many ornamental plants as well as vegetables are very high—86° during the day and 75° at night.

Nevertheless, many seeds of ornamentals and other plants will germinate at lower temperatures. So-called cool-season vegetables such as carrots will germinate at 50° to 60°. Often the temperature will determine germination time rather than lead to germination failure. Some sweet corn, for instance, will germinate in two or three days at 80° but will germinate also at 50° if you give it ten days. Begonias like 70° but are easily germinated, with more time, at 15° to even 20° below this.

If you are propagating plants from your own seed, and are not sure of temperature requirements, you are probably safe keeping the daytime temperature at 70° to 75°, with a 10° drop at night. If you are buying seed, however, the seed company can provide guidance on which leafy vegetables will sprout at these temperatures; eggplant, onion, pepper, and tomato may require 75° or above, and begonias, 85°. With continued advances in plant development, more leeway is possible, and rules are hard to set because some seeds have been developed to germinate at widely ranging climate conditions.

Cactus and succulents do best at 78°.

Development of a Bean

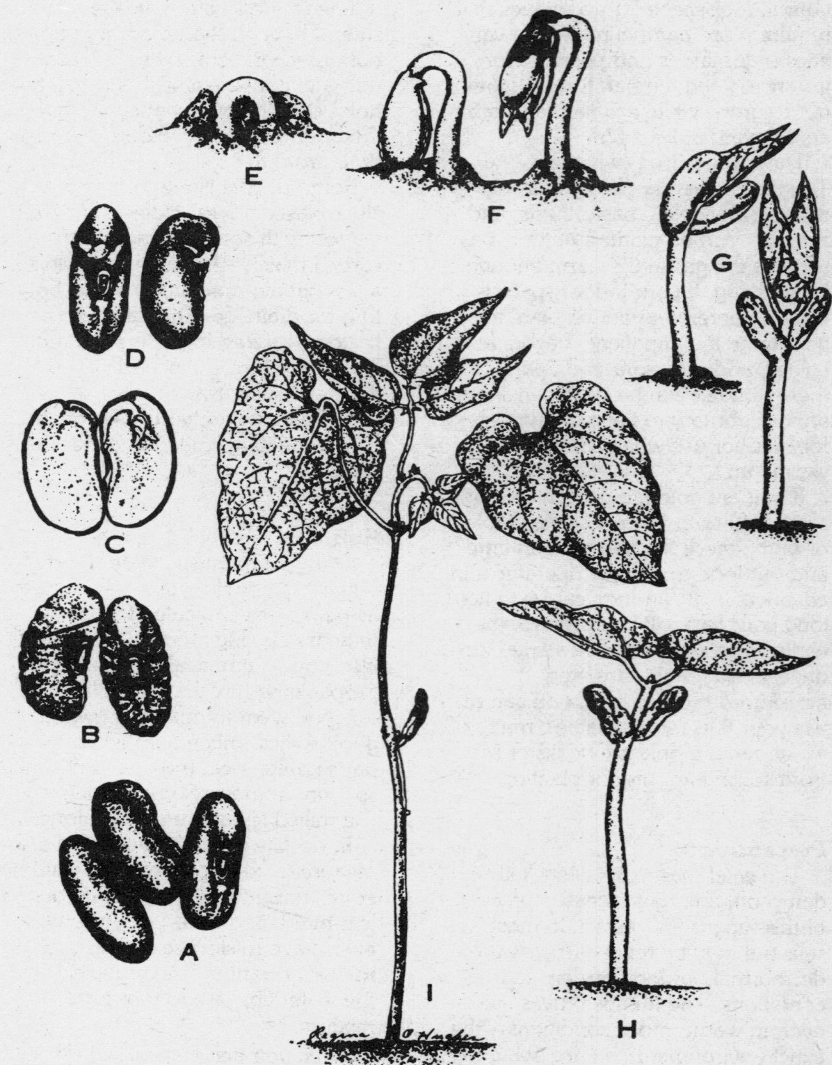

A, dry seeds of beans; **B**, the seeds have imbibed water, the seedcoats are winkled; **C**, the seed opened to show the embryo; **D**, the radicle appears; **E**, the seekling is pushing up through the soil; **F**, the seedlings are up, part of the seedcoat still adheres to the one on the right; **G**, the seedlings are straightening up, the primary leaves are unfolding, and the seedling on the right shows how the two leavs are fitted together; **H**, the primary leaves are open and the stem has elongated; **I**, the trifoliate leaves have appeared.

If you are planting seed outdoors, you must wait until the soil has warmed to the temperature required by your seeds. This means you have to predict the weather in your area, and be more accurate in proportion to the more northerly latitude you live on. If you find this difficult to do, you are in plentiful company. In fact, it is why many gardeners prefer to start as many seeds as possible indoors, where temperature can be controlled. Before setting young plants outdoors, you should gradually reduce their indoor temperature to harden them to conditions they will experience outside.

Providing such high temperature ranges, even indoors in heated human habitations, may be difficult. Many people, especially today as fuel bills soar, are setting their thermostats lower and lower.

If you are germinating only a few seeds, you can set them in the vicinity of heating devices or on top of any heat-giving appliances you may have (such as the top of an electric refrigerator). The top of radiators, however, would probably be *too* hot as well as too dry.

If you are germinating many seeds, you probably will want a soil-heating cable or other device such as a heated propagating mat. With a greenhouse, you may want to install heaters in any case, some of which can be diverted to seed propagation as needed.

A circulating fan can help you achieve even temperatures throughout the day and night.

Care of Seedlings

Inspect the seedlings daily, removing the cover while you do so to give them fresh air. Otherwise, the covering will sweat. As soon as the seedlings emerge, remove the cover. Most of the seedlings will sprout at about the same time, and if you have sown a lot of seed you don't have to wait for them all to come up before removing the cover.

With gesneriads and other plants, you may keep the cover on until the plants have four leaves, but the cover should be lifted each day—or the bag opened more and more—to provide ventilation. Over a two-week period, gradually increase the length of time you lift the cover, until you remove it altogether.

Most seedlings will emerge within one to two weeks, but the time can vary enormously. Your cabbage may poke up in only four days, begonia in a week, while celery may take ten to twenty days. A few cactus require almost a year.

Light: Once the seedlings come up, you can remove them to brighter light and eventually to sun (if they are sun-loving plants), provided you do so gradually. Seedlings are delicate and will not survive abrupt changes in light and temperature.

If you are growing your plants under artificial light, beyond the seedling stage they will require 1500 to 2000 foot-candles. You can get this about 12 inches from 1500-MA lamps or about one inch from new 40-watt lamps spaced six inches apart.

Unless you buy growth lamps or combine warm and cool fluorescents to supply the red and far-red light that is low in cool fluorescents, your plants will benefit if you give them about 20% additional energy from incandescent lamps. For optimum growth, 2000 to 2500 foot-candles is the minimum, but some plants like more.

Your steup should therefore include at least 50 watts per square foot of cool white fluorescent light, 10 watts per square foot of incandescent light—or a combination of warm and cool light fluorescents—reflectors around the planters, and a timer to insure the young plants get at least eight hours of darkness at night.

Watering: If you have watered the soil properly at time of sowing, the seedlings should not need watering again until sprouts push through the soil.

The soil should not be allowed to dry out, however, and if you have not watered your indoor container soil properly you may have to mist or bottom water the pots.

Outdoors, rewatering should not be necessary unless the seeds are taking three weeks or more to germinate or you have sown in the baking sun. Water lightly if necessary, with a spray, but do not let the soil become soggy and cut the air from the seeds.

Once the sprouts emerge, however, they will require regular watering. For indoor plants, this will be the amount of water recommended for each species, and those in sun will require more water than those in less light. The soil should be kept evenly moist even for dry-area plants like cactus and succulents.

If you have sown outdoors, give the soil a good soaking as soon as the sprouts appear, and continue to soak the soil thoroughly less often rather than sprinkling the top more frequently. You want your plants to develop deep rooting, and if you water only the surface of the soil they will develop shallow roots.

Fertilizer: Do not give plant food to seeds. All the nourishment they need is contained within the seed.

Once the sprouts have pushed through the soil surface, however, you should begin to feed them. This is especially true if you are using one of the sterile planting mediums, as these contain almost no nutrients. You can start with a weak fertilizer solution and bring it up to full strength gradually.

Ventilation: Plants need carbon dioxide to grow, and this is especially

Annuals that often self-sow and that can be planted directly in the garden in fall

Calendula
Calliopsis
Centaurea cyanus (Bachelor's Button)
Cleome (Spider Flower)
Cosmos
Cynoglossum
Dianthus
Eschscholzia (California poppy)
Gaillardia
Iberis (Candytuft)
Larkspur
Lathyrus (Sweet pea)
Lobularia (Sweet alyssum)
Nicotiana
Nigella
Poppies
Salvia farinacea (Mealy cup sage)
Snapdragon

important in the life of young plants. The air normally contains only 300 to 350 parts per million of carbon dioxide, which is considerably below optimum level for plant growth (which is closer to 1000 parts per million). Outdoors you don't have to worry about this, because air currents will keep resupplying carbon dioxide to your plants.

In your home, the carbon dioxide level may be higher than outdoors (perhaps double) due to the exhalation by humans, but it will still not be sufficient. If there is no air movement around your plants, they will quickly deplete the carbon dioxide in the air around their foliage. While you don't want your plants to be in drafts, some form of air circulation should be provided. This is especially true since you are apt to be keeping the unsightly flats or containers in your basement or a stuffy, hidden corner. A small household fan or a humidifier should work wonders. Leafy plants like lettuce, grown in laboratory conditions with insufficient carbon dioxide, grew only half as large as plants with optimum carbon dioxide levels, so attention to air circulation will make an enormous difference in the size of food plants and in the attractiveness of ornamental plants.

Transplanting: Where seeds are large enough to be sown at carefully spaced intervals, you will have separate sprouts with distinct root systems easy to transplant. But where you have sown very fine seed such as begonia, you will get bunched seedlings more difficult to separate and transplant.

When do you transplant? When the plants develop one or two sets of true leaves, say some gardeners, and this is the minimum. Others prefer to wait until the plant has three sets of leaves. The difference often has to do with the size of the original seed. The smaller the seed and the more closely it was sown, the more entangled the roots of individual plants are going to become with time. It is wise, though you may have to steel yourself, to watch as the seedlings emerge and eliminate the weaklings so that the more vigorous plants have a better chance. If the seedlings are close together, don't try to pull the weaklings out by the roots or you could damage the roots of better plants; cut the weaker ones off close to the soil with scissors or shears.

The chief danger in transplanting is that you can damage the delicate root system of a new plant. For this reason, it's best to wait until the plant has developed good roots, as evidenced by leaves, but not to wait beyond the third set of leaves when the roots will be spreading out widely and be difficult to extract from the soil without damage. A plastic fork or wooden tongue depresser or other lightweight tool helps avoid damage. And handle the plants as gently as possible.

Shock also accompanies transplant. To reduce this, don't water (or feed) the plant several days before transplanting. When you are about to transplant, water the plants thoroughly. This will make the soil adhere to the roots, so you can lift the ball out without damaging any root ends.

To transplant seedlings, prepare a two-inch or three-inch pot with the usual drainage material in the bottom. But in this case, fill the pot with soil and then make a hole into which you can lower the seedling. The hole should be large enough so that you do not have to bend the roots. Also, don't try to brush the rooting medium from the roots. Lower the seedling, being careful not to bury any of the leaves. Rap the pot to settle the soil and then press the soil down around the roots.

Transplants should be allowed to rest in bright light for several days with plastic wrapped around them to retain humidity. Once they look pert—as though they have caught into their new medium and are beginning to grow—you can remove the plastic and gradually accustom them to sun. You should also start plant food at this time.

If you are going to be using the plants indoors, you probably will have to repot them again when they are four to five inches tall.

For outdoor plants germinated indoors in trays or flats, some gardeners now transfer them to peat pots of two or three inches that can be kept on wooden, plastic, or metal trays. (You can use ordinary baking trays). This allows you to shift groups of plants gradually into stronger light and cooler air before placing them outdoors. A sun porch makes a good intermediate area to toughten them up on cool nights. The peat pots later can be planted directly into the ground outside, where they will eventually disintegrate. If you don't use peat pots, you will have to transplant them again, this time directly into the ground, after a few weeks of conditioning in individual pots. Trays of clay pots are heavier to carry about.

If some seedlings are leggy, you can cut the tops back with scissors. They will regrow in a week or two.

Perennials that grow easily from seed[3]

Achillea
Aethionema
Ajuga
Alyssum
Althaea
Anchusa
Anthemis
Arabis
Armeria
Artemisia
Aquilegia
Asphodelus
Aster
Asclepias
Aubrieta
Bellis
Boltonia
Campanula
Centaurea
Cerastium
Chelone
Chrysanthemum
Coreopsis
Delphinium
Dianthus
Digitalis
Doronicum
Echinops
Epilobium
Erigeron
Erinus
Eryngium
Eupatorium
Euphorbia
Gaillardia
Geum
Gypsophila
Helenium
Helianthus
Heliopsis
Hesperis
Hibiscus
Hypericum
Iberis
Incarvillea
Inula
Kniphofia
Lamium
Lathyrus
Lavandula
Liatris
Limonium
Linaria
Linum
Lobelia
Lotus
Lupinus
Lynchnis
Lysimachia
Lythrum
Maclaeya
Malva
Mentha
Mimulus
Myosotis
Nepeta
Oenothera
Onopordum
Papaver
Penstemon
Polemonium
Polygonum
Potentilla
Pyrethrum
Physostegia
Platycodon
Primula (common species)
Rudbeckia
Salvia
Saponaria
Scabiosa
Sedum (common species)
Sidalcea
Stokesia
Tradescantia
Tunica
Valeriana
Verbascum
Veronica
Viola (common species)
Sempervivum
Silene
Solidago
Stachys
Teucrium
Thymus
Trifolium
Yucca

[3]Applies to the more common cultivated species and assumes fresh seed.

SOURCES FOR SEEDS

Abbott & Cobb
4744-46 Frankford Avenue
Philadelphia, Pennsylvania 19124

Adams County Nursery
Aspers, Pennsylvania 17304

Alexanders Nurseries
1225 Wareham St.
Middleboro, Massachusetts
02346 (blueberries)

Applewood Seed Co.
P.O. Box 4000
Golden, Colorado 80401

Asgrow Seed Company
Box 725
Orange, Connecticut 06477

George J. Ball, Inc.
P.O. Box 335
West Chicago, Illinois 60185

Vernon Barnes & Son Nursery
P.O. Box 250L
McMinnville, Tennessee 37110

Breck's
200 Breck Building
Boston, Massachusetts 02210

Burgess Plant & Seed Company
P.O. Box 218
Galesburg, Michigan 49053

W. Atlee Burpee
6350 Rutland Ave.
Riverside, California 92505

Burrell Seed Growers Company
Rocky Ford, Colorado 81067

Charter Seed Company
P.O. Box Y
Twin Falls, Idaho 83301

Comstock, Ferre & Co.
263 Main Street
Wethersfield, Connecticut 06109

DeGiorgi Company, Inc.
1141 Third St.
Council Bluffs, Iowa 51501

Dessert Seed Company
P.O. Box 181
El Centro, California 92243

Farmer Seed & Nursery Company
Faribault, Minnesota 55021

Ferry-Morse Seed Company
P.O. Box 153
Buffalo, New York 14225

Henry Field Seed & Nursery Company
Shenandoah, Iowa 51602

H. G. German Seed Company
Smethport, Pennsylvania 16749

Germania Seed Company
5952 N. Milwaukee Avenue
Chicago, Illinois 60646

W. R. Grace Co. (Rudy-Patrick Seed)
1212 W. 8th Street
Kansas City, Missouri 64106

Grand Rapids Growers, Inc.
401-433 Ionia Ave., S.W.
Grand Rapids, Michigan 49502

Gurney's Seed & Nursery
Yankton, South Dakota 57059

Joseph Harris Company, Inc.
Moreton Farms
Rochester, New York 14624

H. G. Hastings Company
Box 4247
Atlanta, Georgia 30302

Herbst Brothers Seedsmen, Inc.
1000 N. Main Street
Brewster, New York 10509

Hollar & Company, Inc.
P.O. Box 106
Rocky Ford, Colorado 81067

Holmes Seed Co.
P.O. Box 9087, 2125 46th St., N.W.
Canton, Ohio 44709

J. W. Jung's Seeds Company
Randolph, Wisconsin 53956

Kelly Brothers Nurseries Inc.
Dansville, New York 14437

Keystone
P.O. Box 1438
Hollister, California 95023

Letherman Seed Company
501 McKinley Ave., N.W.
Canton, Ohio 44707

Makielski Berry Farm & Nursery
7130 Platt Rd.
Ypsilanti, Michigan 48197

Earl May Seed & Nursery Co.
Shenandoah, Iowa 51603

McFayden Specialty Division
McKenzie Seeds
P.O. Box 1600
Brandon, Manitoba, Canada

Merrimack Farmer's Exchange
Concord, New Hampshire 03301

Niagara Seeds
Niagara Chemical Division, FMC
Corp.
Middleport, New York 14105

Northrup King Co.
1500 Jackson St.
Minneapolis, Minnesota 55413

L. L. Olds Seed Company
P.O. Box 1069
Madison, Wisconsin 53701

George W. Park Seed Co.
P.O. Box 31
Greenwood, South Carolina 29647

W. H. Perron & Co., Ltd.
515 Labelle Blvd.
Chomeday, Port Quebec, Canada

Pieters-Wheeler Seed Company
P.O. Box 217
Gilroy, California 95020

Pinetree Seed Co.
P.O. Box 1399
Portland, Maine 04104

Porter & Son
Stephenville, Texas 76401

Reed Brothers
Cortland, New York 13045

Martin Rispens & Son Seed Store
3332 Ridge Road
Lansing, Illinois 60438

Clyde Robin Seed Co.
P.O. Box 2855
Castro Valley, California 94546

Rogers Brothers Seed Company
Box 2188
Idaho Falls, Idaho 83401

Savage Farms Nurseries
P.O. Box 125 SF-1
McMinnville, Tennessee 37110

Seedway, Inc.
Hall, New York 14463

R. H. Shumway Seedsman
P.O. Box 777
628 Cedar St.
Rockford, Illinois 61101

Standard Seed Company
Kansas City, Missouri 64120

Stokes Seeds, inc.
P.O. Box 548
Buffalo, New York 14240

George Taits & Sons, Inc.
900 Tidewater Drive
Norfolk, Virginia 23504

Otis S. Twilley
P.O. Box 1817
Salisbury, Maryland 21801

Western Nurseries, Inc.
East Main St., Rt. 135
Hopkinton, Massachusetts 01748

Willhite Seed Co.
Poolville, Texas 76076

Woodside Seed Growers
200 S. Main, P.O. Box C
Rocky Ford, Colorado 81067

Wyatt-Quarles
Bx 2131
Raleigh, North Carolina 27602

The Lazy Gardener's Special

In garden supply shops you can buy seed-starting kits that contain everything you will need to propagate seeds. Such kits include a container, propagating medium, a soil-heating cable, plastic covering, and even implements such as waterproof marking crayons. You also get a booklet of instructions.

GOOD BUGS

Certain bugs cause no damage to either man or plants and are, in fact, beneficial. These are bugs that feed on the larvae and adults of destructive insects. They can thus be good friends, helping you to keep your plants healthy without your having to resort to insecticides. At the very least, you'll therefore want to learn to recognize the beneficial insects to avoid destroying them.

You may want to go further. Many gardeners who do not have beneficial insects or who wish to increase their supply, order good bugs by mail. The praying mantis, ladybugs, and certain wasps are among the insects you may order by mail—and details are given below.

The following are the most common of the good bugs distributed throughout North America.

Antlion *doodlebug*
This insect gets its name because the larvae are fond of ants, though they also feed on other insects.

Doodlebugs (the larval stage) live at the bottom of cone-shaped pits that they make in the sand to trap ants and other insects. They are therefore found mostly in arid areas of the South and Southwest. Some species do not build pits but conceal themselves in sand or debris until prey happens by. These bugs are about a half inch long, with short legs and rough brown bodies from which bristles protrude. Their oversized heads have sickle-shaped jaws.

Aphid Lion *lacewing*
As its name implies, the aphid lion feeds on aphids. It also, while in the larval stage, eats mealy bugs, scales, thrips, mites, and other soft-bodied insects.

The adult is a fragile-looking insect with oblong, lacey wings that are green and crisscrossed with veins so they are patterned like gauze. It has prominent yellow eyes on either side of the head and two slender, hairlike antennae about the same length as its wings. It deposits eggs singly on plant stalks.

The larval stage is about a third of an inch long and chunky in the middle, tapering to a sharp point at the tail. At the head end, the body tapers more gradually to a squared-off head with prominent, dark eyes on top. It may be yellowish or tannish, or mottled red or brown. Prominent hairs project here and there along the body. It has large, sickle-shaped jaws.

Other net-veined insects—so-called because all have transparent wings crisscrossed by veins—include other types of lacewings, the mantidflies, the antlions, and owlflies. All help to control destructive insects.

Assassin Bug
The assassin bug is one of the gardener's best friends, as it feeds on a wide range of immature, destructive insects. It is named for the way it stabs its victims.

The adult is one-half to three-quarters of an inch long and light brown. It looks a bit like a stretched-out bee-

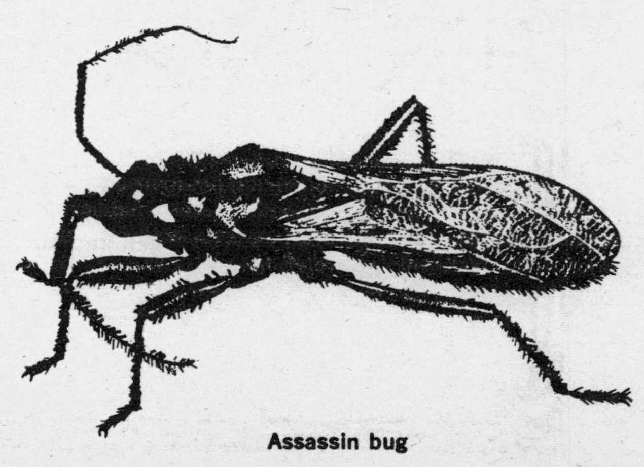

Assassin bug

tle, but acts more like a praying mantis. On its long legs it walks slowly and clumsily along plant stalks. To capture and grasp prey, it holds its forelegs in a prayerlike position. Once prey is captured, the assassin bug sucks out the body fluids.

Damsel Bug
Damsel bugs feed on aphids, fleahoppers, and the small larvae of other insects.

Damels look a lot like assassin bugs but are a bit smaller—less than half an inch long—and pale gray rather than brown in color. Like assassin bugs they use their forelegs to capture prey and suck out the body juices.

Ground Beetle
Both adults and larvae of ground beetles, of which there is over 3000 species in North America, feed on caterpillars and other insects. Some species eat slugs and snails as well.

Adults have elongated oval bodies, usually dull black or brown, but some species are shiny and brightly colored. During the day, they hide on the ground under logs, stones, or loose debris and run rapidly on their long legs if disturbed. They feed at night.

The larvae have flat, slender bodies that taper at the tail end, which terminates in two spines or bristles.

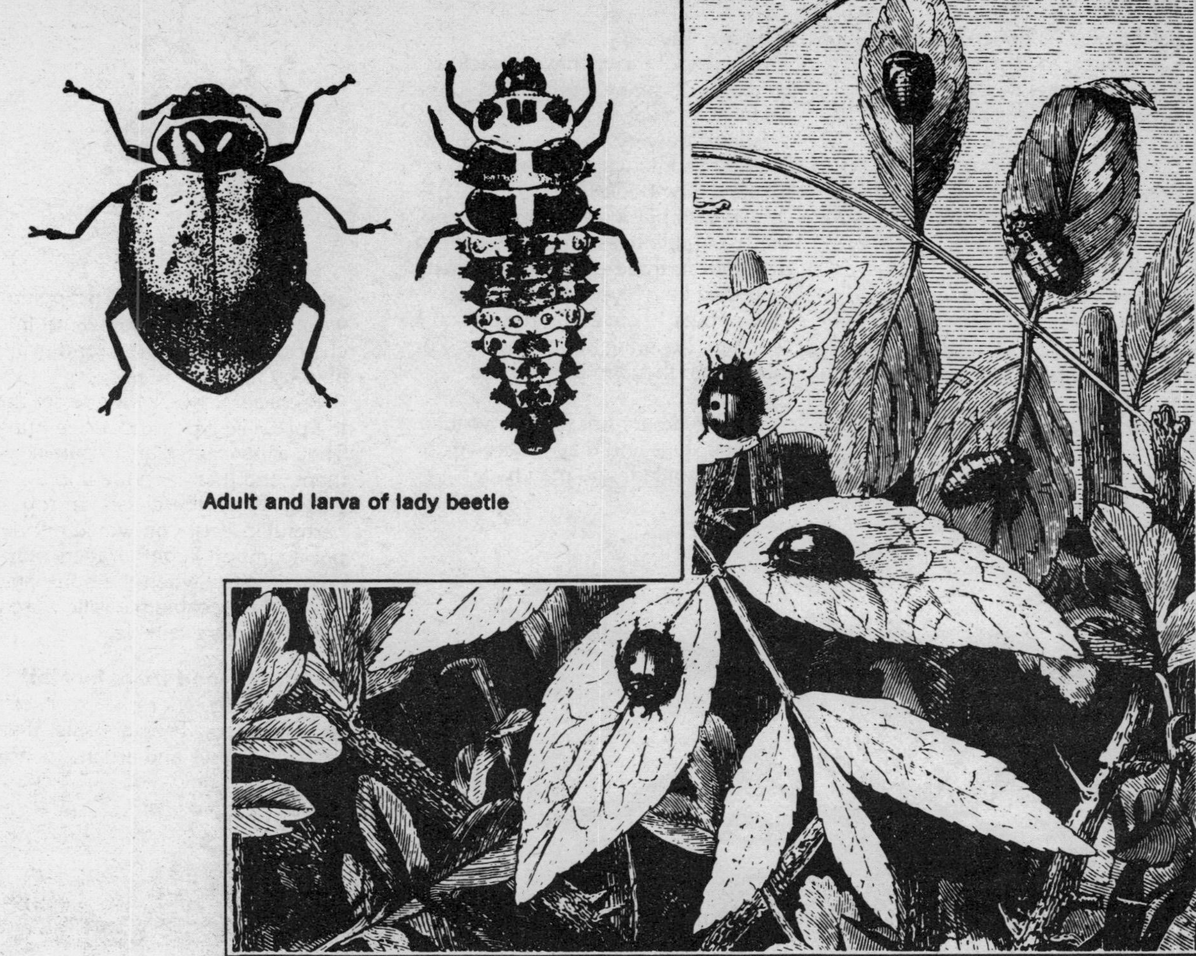

Adult and larva of lady beetle

Minute pirate bug

Ladybug Beetle
Ladybug beetles or lady beetles are called ladybird beetles in Britain. They were so named because, during a plague of pests during the Middle Ages, they saved the European grapevines by ridding them of destructive insects. The religious folk of the time in gratitude dedicated them to the Virgin or "our Lady." Ladybugs live on aphids—their favorite food—as well as on spider mites, scales, mealy bugs, and other soft-bodied plant-feeding insects.

Adults have oval bodies, and the many species vary in color from bright red to orange to yellow. Some have black spots, but not all. Some are black with red or yellow markings. All, however, are shiny and about a quarter to a fifth of an inch long.

The larvae are carrot-shaped, tapering at the tail, and up to a quarter-inch long. They have a warty or bumpy look, and may be bright blue, orange, or gray, with black and creamy-colored bands and markings.

Mail-order ladybugs are shipped in containers filled with straw or excelsior. They should be placed gently, near the plants you wish to protect, in the evening after the garden has been watered. With enough food, ladybugs will remain in a garden permanently. To mate and deposit eggs, they must remain at least 2 days.

Minute Pirate Bug
Both adults and larvae feed on small insects such as mites. They also feed on eggs and larvae of many destructive insects.

Adults of the minute pirate bug, of which there are several species, have oval, flat bodies somewhat like beetles. They are only a sixteenth of an inch long. Most species are black, marked with white spots or streaks.

The nymphs, which are found on flowers and under loose bark, look like adults but are yellowish-brown.

Mites
At least 30,000 species of mites have been identified, and the Audubon Society estimates that at least a million more remain to be identified. Although some mites are the bane of gardeners—the spider mite is an example—many species are parasites of destructive insects. Velvet mites, for example, are parasites of many insects (as well as scorpions) and are so tenacious they will cling to a host's wing even in flight. Velvet mites are easy to identify—they are bright red with dense, velvety hair.

The larvae of mites have six legs, but after the first molt they grow two additional legs. Adults thus resemble spiders in having eight legs; but unlike spiders, mites have oval bodies that are not separated into a cephalothorax and abdomen. Predaceous mites feed on spider mites, cyclamen mites, aphids, and thrips, as well as on the larvae and eggs of many kinds of insects.

Praying Mantis
Young mantids feed on aphids and other small insects. Older mantids devour many kinds of larger insects, including caterpillars and flies. The praying mantis is not a native mantid. It was accidentally introduced from Europe in nursery stock in 1899. Because it devours gypsy moth caterpillars, it was hoped the praying mantis would make a dent in the gypsy moth population. Unfortunately, however, mantids are so cannibalistic that they spend a good deal of time eating each other. The praying mantis has not increased in large enough numbers to affect the gypsy moth population. Despite this, they are well worth having in your garden.

There are about 20 species of mantids, but most are so slender and light green that they are easily missed on plant stalks. The thin wings of the praying mantis are green, with brown front edges, and when the mantid is at rest the wings fold over the long, thin abdomen. The thorax (section between the head and the abdomen) is slender and wedge-shaped. Mantids have movable heads. The legs are very long and thin, and the enlarged front legs have spines for grasping prey. Adults range from two and a half to five inches in length.

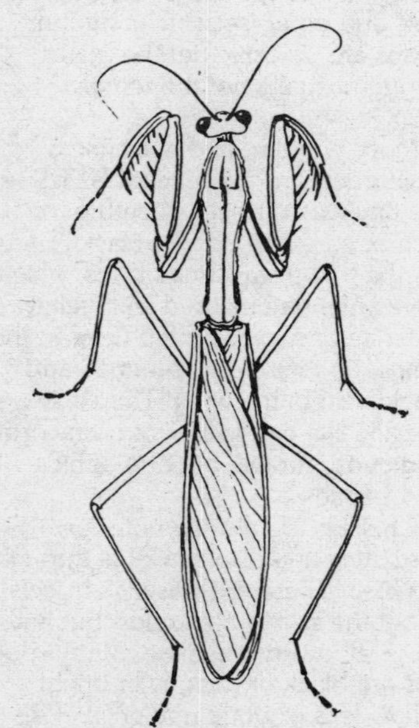

Praying mantid

In the fall, adult females lay eggs in masses on shrubs or tall grasses and cover them with a frothy fluid that hardens. When the young mantids hatch in spring, they resemble adults except that they lack wings.

The praying mantis is easy to introduce into pest-infested areas. Four egg cases take care of ¼ acre without trees or shrubbery. To protect trees and shrubs, tie one egg case to each. They will also protect greenhouses. Once they have been introduced, praying mantises will remain. They can be ordered through the mail during their dormant period, approximately November 1 to mid-May.

Spiders
North America has more than 3,000 species of spiders, all of which have eight legs and seven segments to each leg. Unlike mites and other members of the arachnids, though, spiders have a head segment and abdomen clearly separated by a thin "waist." Most species also have eight eyes.

Spiders are beneficial to gardeners. Unfortunately, however, many people don't like spiders and some are even afraid of them. This is not very rational because spiders seldom bite people and their venom is almost always harmless. The rabid wolf spider, for instance, despite its frightening name is harmless to people. One with venom strong enough to be poisonous to humans is rare and localized (the violin spider of the Southwest), and the bite is not fatal though it takes time to heal. The most feared, the black widow, is a shy creature that normally hides rather than bite. Only the female is poisonous, and she rarely leaves her web, which is funnel-shaped and built in secluded places. She is black with a red hourglass marking on her round abdomen. Yet even the black widow is unlikely to bite unless you disturb her egg mass, which is a pale-brown, pear-shaped sac a third to a half inch wide. If you live in areas where these few poisonous exceptions exist, it pays to learn to identify them so that you can be on friendly terms with all the other spiders in your vicinity.

Since the main food of spiders is insects, they are one of your best insurances against having to use pesticides. They are, moreover, fascinating. Trapdoor spiders dig burrows in the ground that they cover with silk that will vibrate when prey approaches, and they have relatives with a fancier variation, a

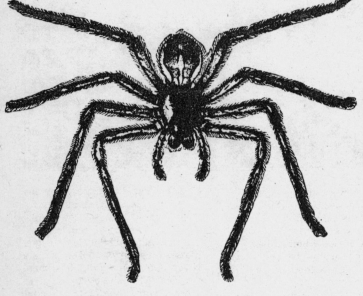

Syrphid Fly
The larvae of this fly have voracious appetites for many insects, and a single larva can eat an aphid a minute.

Adults are very pretty—they mimic bees and some wasps with their bright yellow bodies edged and striped with black. In movement, too, they resemble bees. They range from a quarter to three-eighths of an inch long, and have eyes so large that they appear to cover the head. You'll see them hovering about flowers. For this reason they are often called hover flies.

The larvae are not so pretty—they look like slugs and may be brown, gray, or mottled, and may have stripes.

scale and mealy bugs. Trichogramma wasps are the most popular of the chalcids with gardeners, and available by mail.

Predaceous wasps are larger than the parasitic types and active hunters. They sting caterpillars to paralyze them, and then feed them to their young. While these also destroy harmful insects, you would not purposely import large numbers onto your property when the nonstinging or more peaceable parasitic wasps are so readily available.

Ordering Good Bugs by Mail
It is easy to order friendly insects from suppliers. They are safer than chemical sprays and are inexpensive. All you need to do is follow directions and time the distribution when it is likely to do the most good. For instance, trichogramma wasps should be released in late May or early June to do their best against pests.

When sending your initial query to an insectary, indicate the size of your property to avoid ordering too many rapacious insects.

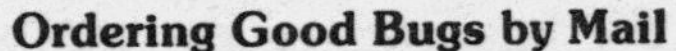

folding trapdoor. Spitting spiders, which cover their prey with a sticky secretion, really do spit—a distance of about three-quarters of an inch. Others are distinguished by the types of webs they construct—orbs, sheet-webs, or other shapes attractive in the garden, especially when they glisten with dew. One (the bola spider) does not spin a web but lassos it with a silken line. Jumping spiders also do not use webs—they simply leap on their victims and then spin out some silk for immoblizing it. Whatever method they use, to catch their prey, spiders are invaluable, free, and interesting helpers in ridding your plants of insects, millipedes, and other unwelcome intruders.

Large web-spinning spiders entrap and kill large flying and crawling insects. The small hunting and jumping spiders kill and eat flies, beetles, caterpillars, aphids, and leafhoppers.

Wasps
Wasps vary widely in size, color, and body structure, but they are of two types—parasitic and predaceous. In the parasitic type, adults usually drink only nectar—it is the larvae that eat voraciously. Many wasps are also valuable as pollinators of crops and plants.

Parasitic wasps are tiny, and their game is to lay eggs in the bodies of insects. As the larvae develop, they use the host for food and eventually kill it. Among their favorite foods are caterpillars of hornworm moths, gypsy moths, and other moths, though some species prefer beetles, flies, and other isects. Ichneumon wasps are parasitic but the males (though usually not the females) sting.

More popular, and available by mail order, are the braconids. These are tiny wasps one-sixteenth of an inch or so—and usually black. They can be told from ichneumons, which have antennae marked with yellow or white or two recurrent veins in the wings, by their dark antennae and single vein in the wing. They especially like caterpillars of hornworm and gypsy moths, but also aphids and beetles.

Chalcids are also favorites with gardeners and also available through the mail. These are wasplike insects about the size of braconids, but have short, elbowed antennae. Many species are black or dark, with bright yellow legs or body markings. If disturbed, some species jump away, while others curl up and pretend to be dead. Chalcids eat other wasps, flies, and the larvae and pupae of

Sources

Bio-Control Co.
Rt. 2, Box 2397
Auburn, CA 95603

California Bug Company
Rt. 2
Auburn, CA 95603

Eastern Biological Control Co.
Rt. 5, Box 379
Jackson, NJ 08527

Ecological Insect Services
15075 W. California Ave.
Kerman, CA 93630

Gothard, Inc.
P.O. Box 370
Canutillo, TX 79835

Lakeland Nurseries
Hanover, PA 17331

Mellinger's
2310 W. South Range
North Lima, OH 44452

Mincemoyers Nursery
RD 5, Box 379
New Prospect Rd.
Jackson, NJ 08527

Rincon Vitova Insectaries, Inc.
Box 95
Oak View, CA 93022

Shoor's Sierra Bug Co.
Box 114
Rough and Ready, CA 95975

West Coast Ladybug Sales
Rt. 1, Box 93-A
Biggs, CA 95917

World Garden Products
2 First St. East
Norwalk, CT 06855

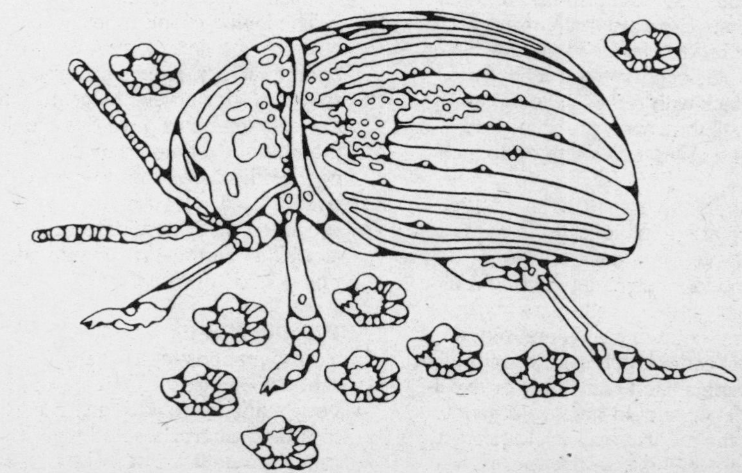

BEES

What would the earth be like without bees? It is impossible to imagine such a world, for bees, and especially honey bees, are among nature's most important agents of pollination. In the course of gathering nectar and pollen, the honey bee pollinates from 50 to 90 different crops grown throughout the United States, as well as perhaps 1800 other types of plants. Wind takes care of pollinating crops of the grass family, such as corn and wheat, but most flowering plants depend upon insects, and honey bees account for 80 percent of insect pollination. Indeed, some plants, such as cantaloupes and cucumbers, depend almost entirely on bee pollination.

In seeking food from blossoms, bees inadvertently pollinate fruits, vegetables, nuts, and forage and legume crops. They also pollinate many range plants, medicinal herbs, ornamentals, spices, and forest trees. In 1977, it was estimated that honey bees pollinated more than $1 billion worth of agricultural crops in the United States. And that's not counting their benefit to the millions of home gardeners, many of whom have little appreciation of the contribution bees make to flower beds, vegetable patches, and fruit trees.

American Bees

More than 5000 species of bees, most of them indigenous, live on the North American continent. The honey bee, *Apis millifera*, which has become the most important species for agriculture, was originally an import. The first recorded arrival of honey bees was in 1621 in the colony of Virginia, although the Vikings or Celts could have introduced honey bees on their voyages to North America during the 10th century, and the early Spanish and French missionaries may have carried honey bees to Central America, as much as for a source of wax for liturgical candles as for honey.

During the 19th century, the honey bee kept up with westward migration across the continent. As people and farming moved west, so did the bee. Extensive beekeeping in the 1800s made possible the development of the fruit industry in Oregon, Washington, and California.

As the 20th century draws to a close, the importance of bees in agriculture is increasing. They take the place of native pollinating insects that have been decimated by the widespread use of pesticides and intensive cultivation of the land.

Several strains of bees were imported after the first English bees. German black bees were the largest group of honey bees brought in during the 18th century, and in the mid-19th century Italian bees arrived. These Italian bees, which were to be followed by bees from Egypt, Greece, and Eastern Europe, combine a gentle disposition with high production of honey. They quickly became, and remained, the most popular variety among beekeepers in the United States.

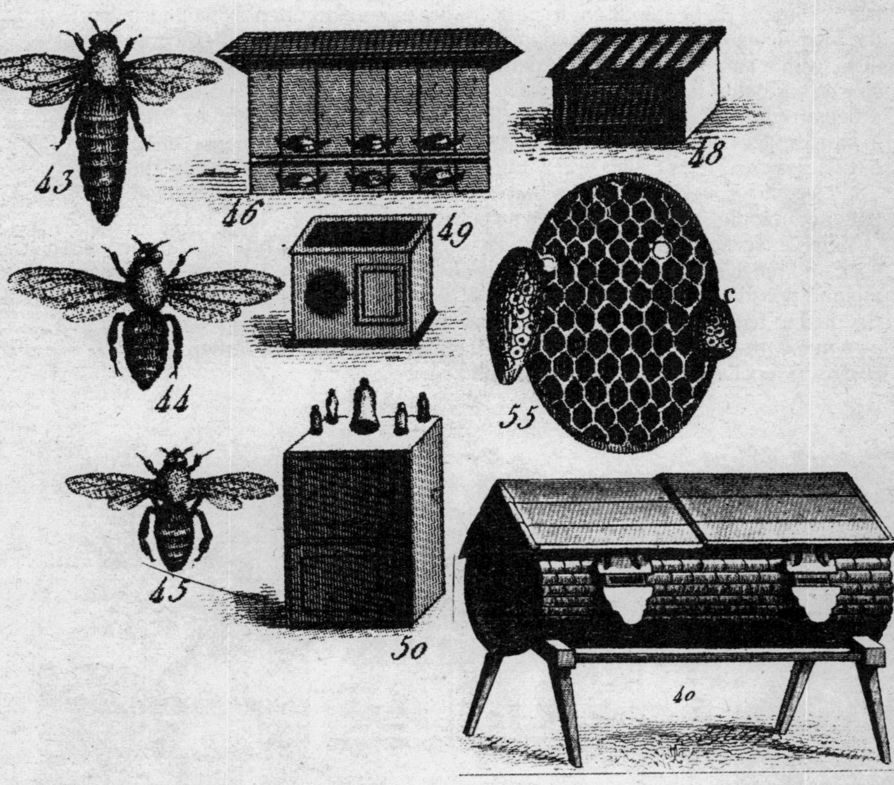

The Bee Colony

Most bees are actually solitary insects. Except at mating time, the female lives alone with her brood in a nest that she has constructed by herself. Those bees who visit the backyards of gardeners are generally bumblebees and the more advanced honey bees, both types that live in colonies under a complex social system of queens, workers, and drones. The well-organized life in the beehive is considered the highest development of the division of labor found in nonhuman animal society.

The Queen. Every colony of bees has one queen who lives from 3 to 5 years and dedicates her entire existence to reproduction. During her life, she may lay as many as 2000 eggs per day at the height of her activity. The only time she emerges from the hive is during her mating flight, which takes place from 4 to 10 days after she has hatched from the pupal stage and has killed other potential queens by stinging them before they crawl out of their cocoons. After mating on the wing with as many as 10 drones, the new queen returns to the hive and begins to lay eggs within 2 days. She has received a supply of sperm sufficient to fertilize the thousands of eggs she will lay during her reign as queen.

Both queen bees and worker bees develop from fertilized eggs. Those destined to become queens are deposited by a queen bee or by workers in specially large cells. After about 3 days, queen and worker larvae hatch from the eggs and remain in the larval stage for 9 days. During this period, both future queens and workers are fed over 10,000 times, or an average of 1300 times a day per individual. The queen larvae consumes a never-ending supply of royal jelly, a rich food secreted by the worker bees who act as royal nurses, whereas worker larvae eat beebread, a mixture of honey and pollen. Royal jelly causes larvae to develop into sexually complete, or queen, bees. The ordinary diet of honey and pollen produces sexually undeveloped worker bees.

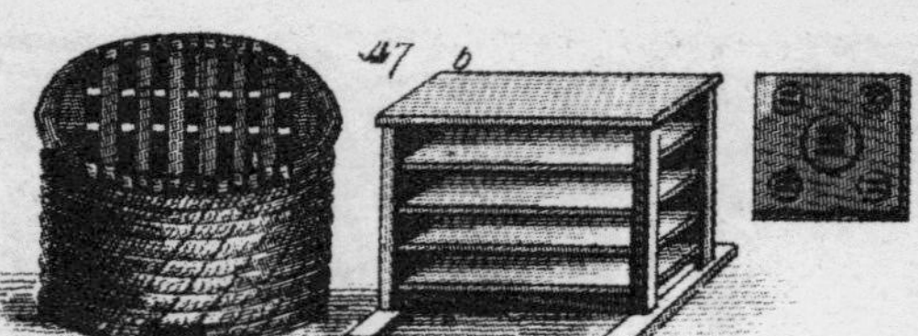

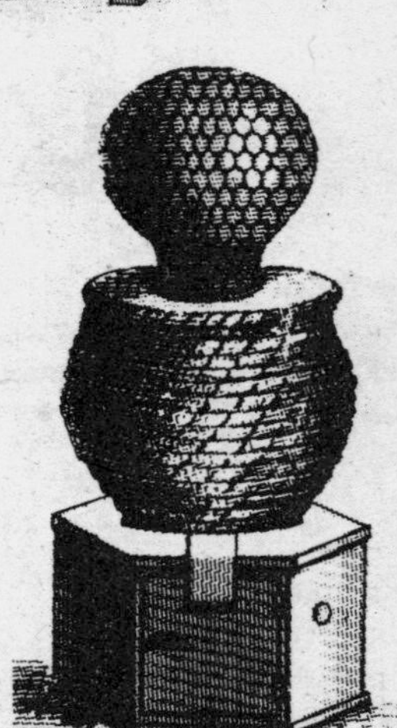

At the end of the larval stage, both worker and queen brood cells are capped, and the larvae spin cocoons and enter the pupal stage. For queens, this lasts 4 days, while worker pupae take 9 days to mature.

Drones. Drones are hatched from unfertilized eggs in spring. Their primary task in life is to mate with a new queen, and those who succeed die shortly thereafter. Remaining drones have nothing much to do but hang around the hive and generate heat. Having no stingers for self-protection and no instinctive program for food gathering, they depend on workers for protection and for a share of plant nectar and pollen gathered in the fields. This arrangement is all very well during the warm weather while the nectar flow is abundant. When in autumn the nectar flow ceases, however, worker bees stop feeding the lazy, helpless drones, bite their wings off, and push them out of the hive.

Workers. The bees who do the work of the colony—and of nature—are worker bees. They are sexually incomplete females who look to the queen bee to lay all the eggs for the colony.

Although their sexual apparatus is underdeveloped, workers have other sophisticated organs that equip them to perform the many and often difficult tasks of the hive. Their heads are more triangular than the queen's, and their compound eyes, with a large number of independently functioning lenses, are more widely spaced for better navigation. Specially positioned wings enable worker bees to move around with great agility inside flowers to collect nectar, and to maneuver in small spaces inside the hive. Their mouth parts consist of a tongue enclosed in a tube designed for sucking honey into a special storage sac within the abdomen. Their legs are covered with hairs that collect pollen, and their hind legs have flattened middle sections that serve as pollen baskets.

When a worker bee emerges from its pupal cocoon, it spends the day cleaning itself and receiving food from other bees. It then spends the next few days cleaning and polishing empty brood cells, after which it becomes a "nurse" bee devoted to feeding developing larvae and the queen. During the 2-week period as a nurse, the worker develops 4 sets of wax glands on its abdomen, and it begins to receive nectar from the foraging bees.

Inside its body, the worker converts the simple sugar (sucrose) of nectar into more complex sugars (dextrose and levulose) and regurgitates these sugars as honey, which is stored in combs inside the hive. A thimbleful of honey represents a bee's visit to between 60,000 and 90,000 flowers. Wax secreted by the abdominal glands is a by-product of the bee's digestion of carbohydrates. As bees age, these glands degenerate.

After stints as cleaners and nurses, young worker bees go out into the field as scouts and collectors. Scouts seek out nectar and pollen on forays that can extend 3 or 4 miles away from the hive.

During winter, workers eat the stored honey in order to maintain body heat. Activity within the hive, which is tightly insulated, keeps the colony warm. The brood (eggs, larvae, and pupae) requires a constant 88–89°F (31°C), and bees maintain this temperature even in frigid weather by clustering in 2 layers around the brood chamber.

When the weather is hot, a portion of the colony's worker contingent hovers about the hive, fanning it with their wings, while others fetch water to the hive.

The food supply and living space within the hive determine the size of a bee colony. Should a hive become overcrowded, scout bees go out in search of a good place for a new hive, nurse bees construct new queen cells, and a large number of drones are produced from unfertilized eggs. When the queen brood cells are capped, the old queen, in the company of older workers and some drones, leave the hive in a swarm and head for their new home. It is not long before a new queen takes over the hive and begins to repopulate it.

Bee Communication

Effective communication among bees makes possible the complex social life of a typical colony. Like some other insects, bees rely heavily on stimuli such as smell, hearing, and touch to orient themselves within the life of the hive as well as the outside world. They also have a remarkable series of dances that communicate very precise information such as the direction and distance from the hive and the quality of a food source.

When scout bees return from a reconnaissance trip, they let the collector bees know what they have discovered from the angle of their movements relative to the sun. Once the collector bees are in the general area of the food source, their acute olfactory sense enables them to zero in on it. Other bee dances include an alarm dance, a cleaning dance, a dance for joy, and even one used when a worker needs a massage.

Bee Plants

Bees exhibit distinct preferences for certain plants. In gardens planted with several varieties of trees, flowers and/or vegetables, they return again and again to plants they especially like, ignoring others completely. Witness the fact that clover and alfalfa honey are widely available in the stores whereas gladiola honey, for example, is not. Bees visit garden flowers, but they love all clovers, alfalfa, most fruit trees, and milkweeds. These and the following so-called bee plants can be planted specificially to attract bees to a garden:

bluecurls
buttonbush
buckwheat
Cleone surrulata (Rocky Mountain bee plant; stinking clover)
eucalyptus
mesquite
orange trees
sage
thyme
tulip trees
wisteria
shrubs in the *vitex* family

A supplier of bee plants:

Forestfarm
990 Tetheraha
Williams, OR 97544

Beekeeping
Human beings have eaten honey since prehistoric times and kept bees for many thousands of years. As long ago as 2600 B.C., the ancient Egyptians knew how to smoke bees out of their hives, extract honeycomb, and store honey in sealed jars. Indeed, fresh honey from the hive is perhaps the closest substance to ambrosia, the legendary food of the gods.

In recent years, a growing number of Americans and Canadians have rediscovered the virtues of unrefined honey along with the unhealthful effects of refined sugar. Supporting this revival is a growth in beekeeping not only as a business but also as a hobby.

To get started as a beekeeper, all you need in addition to some knowledge of the habits of honey bees is a suitable location and the basic supplies. The first attribute of a good location for a beehive is a place where people are unlikely to get stung. In warm climates, hives also need some shade so as not to overheat, and in areas with freezing winters hives need a sunny location that is nevertheless protected from the prevailing winds during the cold season. In all geographic regions, bees require a nearby supply of fresh water and a good source of food and pollen, that is, flowering plants and trees that produce nectar, the raw material of honey as well what bees mainly eat, and pollen, which, combined with nectar, is formed into beebread.

Major nectar sources in the United States are:

alfalfa	locust
aster	mesquite
buckwheat	palmetto
catclaw	tulip tree
citrus fruit	tupelo
clover	sage
cotton	sourwood
fireweed	star thistle
goldenrod	sweetclover
holly	sumac
horsemint	willow

An average colony uses about a hundred pounds of pollen each year. Among the many wild flowers, ornamentals, weeds, shrubs, and trees that provide pollen, some especially good sources are:

aster	maple
clover	wild mustard
dandelion	poplar
fruit blossoms	ragweed
goldenrod	willow

Equipment. To start a hive on your property should cost under $100. The essential equipment includes a *hive* with movable frames. During this century, the handwoven skep has been replaced by scientifically designed factory-made hives fitted with movable frames. You will also need *gloves* to protect your hands, a *veil* to protect your face; a *hive tool* to pry frames apart to examine the hive or harvest the honey; and a *smoker* to blow smoke into the hive to pacify the bees while you work with them.

The planning for a new hive should begin before spring arrives. Springtime is when flowers and trees are in bloom, so your equipment should be ready for stocking with bees before them. To start a colony in the empty hive, you can purchase 2 or 3 pounds of bees from another beekeeper or a commercial supplier. Be certain your bees have a certificate of inspection indicating that they are free of disease.

If you start beekeeping in spring, the new colony will quickly obtain the nectar and pollen they need to survive. Until they have their own food supply, however, they will need a substitute diet, usually a syrup of sugar and water that the beekeeper places in a special *feeder* at the entrance of the hive.

Care. A healthy bee colony gets bigger, and when it hasn't enough room for expansion of the brood section, a large number of bees will leave with the queen in search of a new home. Such an exodus can weaken the remaining colony and ought to be avoided by adding extra boxes of combs (supers) to the hive, or onto the supers already in place.

Bees need honey to make it through the winter, and you should only harvest your colony's surplus. A hive is prepared for winter with about 90 pounds of honey, or approximately 15 to 20 frames.

Before disturbing the hive, direct smoke into it to calm down the bees. You will learn the correct amount with practice.

Diseases of bees are a growing concern because bees are essential to the prosperity of agriculture in North America. It is illegal to buy or sell bee colonies and equipment not certified free of disease. The USDA assists beekeepers in the identification and control of diseases found in bee colonies. For specific information, contact your local county agricultural agent or one of the USDA research laboratories:

Bee Research Laboratory
2000 East Allen Road
Tucson, AZ 85719

Bee Breeding & Stock Center Laboratory
R.R. 3, Box 82-B
Ben Hur Road
Baton Rouge, LA 70808

Bioenvironmental Bee Laboratory
Bldg. 476, BARC-East
Beltsville, MD 29705

Honey & Maple Research Eastern Regional Research Center
600 East Mermaid Lane
Philadelphia, PA 19118

Wild Bee Biology & Systematics Laboratory
U.M.C. 53, Room 261
Utah State University
Logan, UT 84322

North Central States Bee Research Laboratory
Russell Laboratories, Rm. 436
University of Wisconsin
Madison, WI 53706

Pesticides/Bee Diseases Laboratory
University Station
P.O. Box 3168
Laramie, WY 82071

One of the worst threats to the health of a bee colony is the wax moth whose larvae eat combs. To prevent wax moths from laying eggs inside the hive, bees fill cracks and crevices of the hive with a sticky resin known as propolis, fetched from trees in the worker bees' pollen baskets.

Bad Bugs

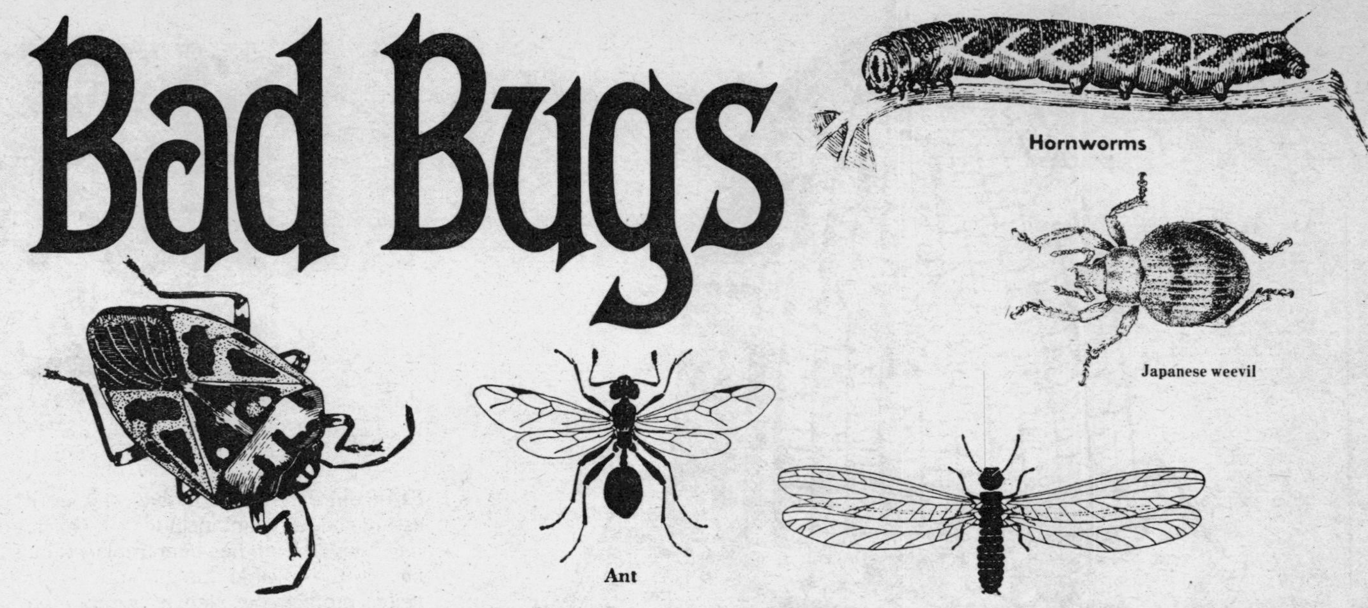

Insects harmful to plants fall into several categories. Sucking insects attach themselves to leaves, stems, roots, or flowers to suck out the juices, leaving the tissue damaged or dead. These tend to be the worst pests, as they are frequent carriers of viruses and other plant diseases. Chewing insects, like caterpillars, simply take bites out of foliage. Finally, some insects do their dirty work underground, feeding on root systems, where you cannot see them.

Pests so enrage gardeners that the earliest plant manuals include suggestions for stamping them out. Gardeners once put smoldering pots about to smoke out insects, though one early horticulturist advised it was more satisfying to pluck each one by hand and squash it underfoot. Handpicking is still an excellent way of dealing with many pests.

Worms that attack foliage are seldom a problem except on food plants. Often carbaryl is effective, but foods are the last place you want to use a pesticide. In most cases you can handpick enough cutworms and other worms to keep the damage under control. Hornworms that attack tomatoes and lilac can be handpicked or controlled with Bt. For wireworms, which live in the soil and attack roots, stems, and tubers, prevent infestation by not planting in infested soil, or treat soil with diazinon a week or more before planting. Loopers are small worms that crawl by doubling up, or looping. They are usually light green and feed on the underside of leaves, making ragged holes. Control with Bt or malathion sprayed on the underside of the leaves.

Ants of certain species harvest and dig up newly planted seeds or seedlings. A few eat leaves—these species live mostly in the South and Southwest. But the chief damage comes from species that are fond of honeydew—a sweet secretion produced by aphids and related sucking insects. Ants dig tunnels to plant roots and then carry aphids there to create a sort of cafeteria where they can come to eat at will. The activity of ants plus aphids presents a double threat. If the ants are present along with aphids, mealybugs, or scale, treat the latter problem first. Depriving ants of their food supply may make them move elsewhere. If they do not, locate the ant nests. Malathion, diazinon, chlorpyrifos, and propexur are recommended by the USDA for indoor and outdoor use against ants; carbaryl only for outdoor use. But do not use any of these on food plants or fruit trees; treat only the soil.

Where you have ants attracted to tree sap, clean out the area of the wound, removing ants and damaged wood with stiff brushes and other tools until you are down to sound, hard wood. Then coat the edges of the wound—and about an inch into the cavity—with shellac. Paint the remaining interior of the cavity with coal-tar creosote.

Aphids, or plant lice, are sucking insects that feed on stems, leaves, and flowers. They are found throughout all of North America. Aphids are often only 1/16 of an inch long, though the giant willow aphid grows up to a quarter of an inch. Usually they are light green, but they may also be dark green, brown, black, red, gray, pink, blue, or lavender. Aphids have tiny heads with long antennae and soft, pear-shaped bodies with long legs. Some have wings, others are wingless. Some, such as rosy apple aphids or root aphids, appear to be dusted with a whitish powder. From the anus aphids secrete a sticky liquid called honeydew which attracts many other insects, and some ant species milk aphids to obtain this secretion.

Except for a few species, such as rose aphids that may remain on rose bushes all year, most aphids migrate from the plants they hatched on to a different type of plant during the summer. In fall, they migrate back to their original tree or bush. Most aphids lay eggs on the woody stems of shrubs or tree branches in autumn; some use rose bushes. Aphids cluster along stems and on the underside of leaves—a colony may cover a stem entirely. They weaken plants, causing stunted growth. Leaves become thick and curl, turn yellow, and die. Honeydew makes the leaves sticky and slimy, and provides an excellent base for the growth of sooty mold. Aphids also transmit diseases. Wash houseplants with soapy water. In the garden, encourage ladybugs and other aphid-eaters. Spray trees and shrubs with soapy water under high pressure—unless, of course, larvae of lady beetles or other aphid-eaters also are on the trees and shrubs. With vegetables, remove and destroy damaged plants early in the season; apply malathion or diazinon to any crops listed on the label, but not to food crops not specified on the label.

Beetles and Weevils. Beetles are the largest order (Coleoptera) in the animal kingdom, with more than 30,000 species in North America alone. They include beneficial insects like ladybugs, fun ones like whirligigs and lightning bugs, and many destructive species that include weevils and chafers (see also "Borers," and "Japanese Beetle," below).

Weevils, a type of beetle, come in two major categories. The primitive type is a beetle with an elongated body that bores into rotting wood. They invade trees that are already dying. Thus, if you keep your trees in good condition and remove dead branches, these weevils will be no problem. More troublesome are the snout beetles and weevils of the family Curculionidae with 2500 species in North America. The females bore into seeds, fruits, and stems to lay eggs, and the developing C-shaped larvae do the rest of the damage. All of these have hard and elongated bodies, and frequently large snouts.

Some beetles can be controlled by handpicking adults and crushing the egg masses. This is true of the Colorado potato beetle, which despite its name is widespread and attacks many plants other than potatoes, agave and yucca billbugs, and the rhubarb curculio. Malathion works on a wide variety of beetles (asparagus, Fuller rose, Mexican bean, striped cucumber beetles; cowpea curculio; pea and rose weevils).

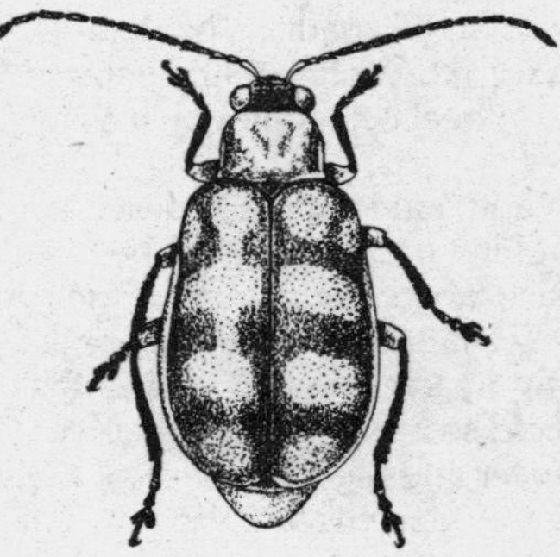
Banded cucumber beetle.

Pepper Weevil

Squash Vine Borer

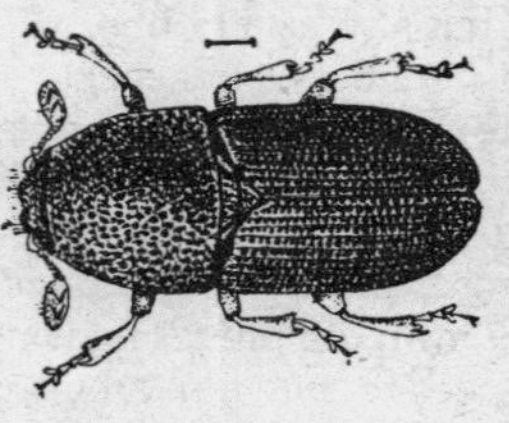
Shot-hole borer (Adult)

Borers are usually cylindrical beetles about a half-inch long that bore into twigs, branches, and under bark, where they and their larvae feed. The name is also applied, however, to the larvae of moths that bore into branches, to weevils, and to various other boring insects. While this is a large group of pests, each species generally restricts its activities to specific plants. Your best defense is a healthy tree. Many borers (such as the shothole borer that makes a tree-trunk look peppered with birdshot) attack young trees and trees with wounds, pruning scars, or dead and dying branches where the boring is easy.

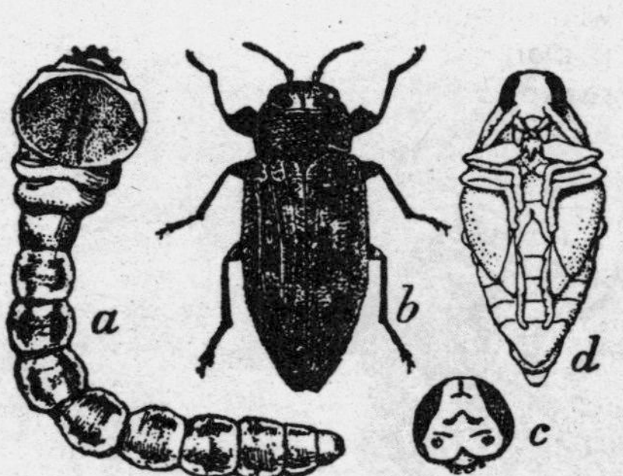

—Flat-headed Apple-borer.

Some borers, such as the dogwood twig borer, can be eliminated simply by pruning out infested branches. With sugar maple, linden, and poplar borers, you can probe the tunnels with wires to kill the grubs. Then place a small quantity of nail polish remover containing ethyl acetate in the hole and plug the hole with moist soil or putty; this will kill the remaining borers. For squash vine borers, stalkborers, and others that attack soft stems, split the stem with a razor blade, puncture the worm, and bind up the stem.

Flowering fruit trees (peach, cherry, nectarine) are attacked by the peachtree borer, a moth whose larvae feed on trunk tissue, usually just below soil level; you may notice gum oozing from entry holes farther up the trunk. The similar lesser peachtree borer enters through tree wounds. Before planting trees, dip their roots in an endosulfan concentrate in water. On established trees, apply endosulfan to the trunks—especially near the soil line—in early July and repeat three weeks later.

Rhododendron borers can be probed out with wire; then inject a few drops of carbon tetrachloride into the tunnel, and seal it for a day or two; then clean out the tunnel and paint it with tree-wound dressing. Most other borers of woody shrubs and trees require potent pesticides such as lindane.

Cankerworms are of two species—the spring and the fall cankerworm. Adults are brown moths with striped wings. The larvae, brown or green looping worms, feed on leaves and may defoliate plants. Apply Bt when caterpillars are first noticed in the spring. To avoid a recurrence, prevent the females from climbing the tree to lay eggs—in late fall and again in spring (during the

Sweetpotato Weevil

Flea beetle that causes damage to many garden plants is not much larger than a flea and jumps like one when disturbed.

Blister Beetles

Rhubarb Curculio

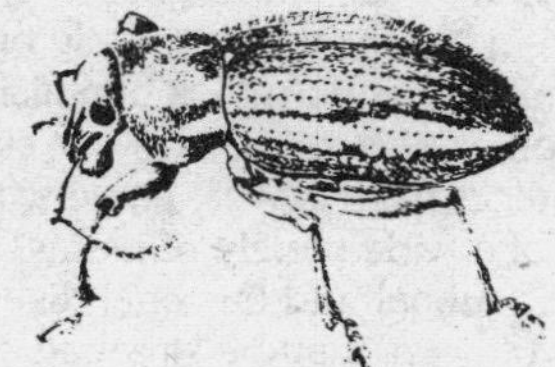

White-Fringed Beetles

first warm weather in February or March) girdle the tree with a band of sticky material such as tanglefoot. Place the girdle two to four feet above the ground.

Casebearers and Bagworms are names that cover several species of small gray moths. Casebearers have fringed wings while bagworms have clear wings. Casebearers are found throughout North America, while bagworms are usually found east of the Rocky Mountains. The larvae are brown. Bagworms grow up to 1½ inches and are found in leaves in conspicuous, spindle-shaped cases or bags. Casebearers are ⅜ of an inch long and are found in brown or gray cases that are cigar-shiped. Both larvae eat leaves and make small holes in buds. In winter, handpick any bags that can be easily reached and destroy them. In spring, use Bt or malathion.

Cyclamen Mites, too small to be seen by the naked eye, feed by sucking plant juices. Mites go for young leaves, young stem ends, buds, and flowers, and are troublesome only on houseplants and in greenhouses. Leaves of infested plants are twisted, curled, and brittle. Buds may be deformed and fail to open. Flowers are deformed, often streaked. Blackening of injured leaves, buds, and flowers is common. Trim off badly injured plant parts where practical. Immerse infested plant, pot and all, for 15 minutes in water kept at 110°F.

Gypsy Moths have now invaded 23 states and Canada. Eggs deposited in July hatch the following April or May. The larvae are dark, with yellow stripes down the back; stiff brown hairs project from their sides; their backs have two neat rows of five pairs of blue dots followed by six pairs of red dots. They dangle from silken threads that are blown by wind to nearby eating sites. Once they have consumed deciduous leaves in an area, they move on to evergreens. In all, they eat more than 500 species of trees, plus associated undergrowth. The caterpillars are active April through early June. Many evergreens cannot survive defoliation. Most deciduous trees will regrow new leaves in midsummer, but are left weakened and may succumb to repeated defoliation in the second or third years.

Before the caterpillars hatch, remove the egg masses on your land. Once eggs hatch, Bt is effective. Broad-spectrum chemical sprays (acephate, phosmet, methozychlor, and carbaryl) are more dangerous and more likely to kill the gypsy moth's natural predators. ACECAP 97, an acephate implant available in packages of ten, protects large trees high up to their crowns. Insert the implants in ⅜-inch holes drilled at 4-inch intervals around the base of a tree. In June, when caterpillars are too large to be affected by BT, many can be trapped. Wrap a 1-foot-wide strip of burlap around tree trunks at 4 or 5 feet above the ground. Tie with twine and allow the top half of the burlap to flop over. Caterpillars coming down the tree will snuggle under the fold. Each afternoon, remove the burlap and shake the caterpillars into a container of detergent and water, rubbing alcohol, charcoal lighter, or alcohol.

If you have trees that have survived one attack of gypsy moths, strengthen them for a possible new infestation:

1. Fertilize them in early spring and again in July by spreading well-rooted manure or compost around the root area. 2. Water during rainless periods. 3. Prune trees and remove dead and damaged branches in autumn and winter to decrease the trees' moisture needs.

Here are the steps in control:

1. Feed wild birds from fall through early spring to keep birds in your yard. Some 45 species of native birds, including warblers, cuckoos, chickadees, and crows eat gypsy moth larvae.
2. Spray with Bt at 10- to 14-day intervals from April through early June while caterpillars are *under* one inch in length. Use a sprayer powerful enough to reach treetops. Timing is important—by July the caterpillars pupate and spraying is useless.
3. In June, apply burlap traps.
4. During autumn, winter, and early spring, scrape the fawn-colored egg masses from tree trunks into a coffee can. Dump into a mixture of detergent and water to kill the eggs. Use gloves to avoid getting a skin rash, and look everywhere—under rocks and crevices, on the sides of your house, and on garden furniture.

False Spider Mites are mites rather than spiders that infest greenhouses and house plants. These flat, oval, dark-red mites are too tiny to be easily seen. Adults, or the bright-red eggs and young, are mostly on the underside of leaves, usually along the veins or any leaf irregularity. They cause finely stippled brown or bronze areas, especially along the veins. Edges of leaves may die, leaves may lose color and drop off. Use a soapy spray.

Fungus Gnats are a problem only indoors and in greenhouses. Adults (delicate, gray, flylike insects) swarm around light but do not damage plants. The whitish immature maggot lives in soil and damages roots. Plants will seem off color, may not grow vigorously, and may drop leaves. Avoid overwatering. The maggots soon grow to adults and pose no further problem.

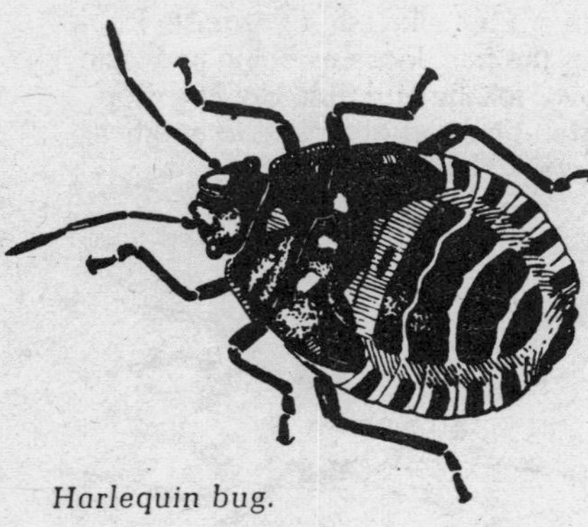

Harlequin bug.

Harlequin Bug is shield-shaped and black, with markings in brilliant yellow or red. Handpick adults and crush the egg masses.

Japanese Beetle is most prevalent in the East and Midwest. Adults are shiny green, oval-shaped, with reddish brown outer wings and white heads. Larvae are white with brown heads. Larvae feed on roots; adults skeletonize leaves, which turn brown and die. These beetles attack trees, decorative shrubs, and food crops. Protect small trees and shrubs by covering them with plastic or cloth netting as soon as beetles appear. Place plastic on the ground under large trees and then shake the branches to dislodge the beetles. Do this early in the morning when the temperature is low and the beetles are sluggish. Shake the beetles into a bucket of water with a little kerosene floating on the surface. See also "Traps and Tricks," below.

Lacebugs, distributed throughout North America, are named for the pretty, lacey wings on the adult. There are many species. Nymphs and adults suck sap from the underside of leaves, causing the upper surfaces to have a gray, stippled appearance. The underside of leaves are discolored with excrement and cast-off skin. Use malathion.

Leafhoppers are jumping, wedge-shaped insects that attack trees, flowers, shrubs, grasses, and food crops. Over 2500 species live in North America, but each species feeds on a specific plant trap. They secrete honeydew that attracts ants, flies, and wasps. The young frequently crawl sidewise like crabs. They look a bit like miniature grasshoppers. Leaves wilt, curl, crinkle, and become discolored. Growth is stunted and plants may die. Many leafhoppers spread disease. Malathion is effective.

Leafminers is a name covering several species of small moths, beetles, and flies distributed throughout North America. They are named for the tunnels—or mines—they build in plant tissue. The larvae are tiny, segmented worms. Leaves are deformed and develop dead areas. Leafminers attack trees, shrubs, and food plants. Pick damaged leaves from plants. Rake up fallen leaves and dispose of them. For severe infestation use diazinon.

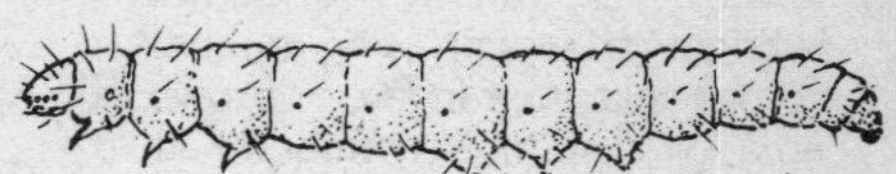

Azalea leafminer

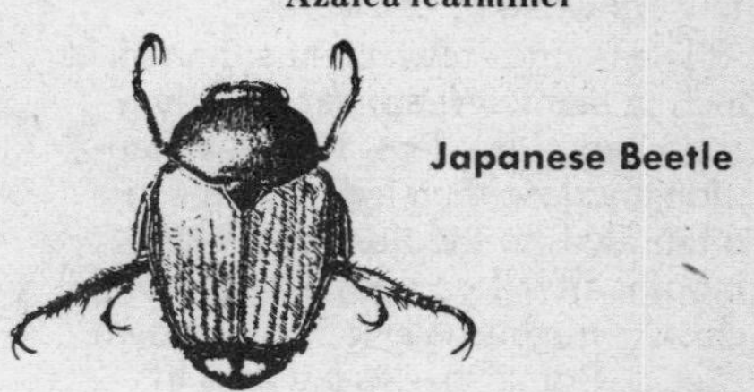

Japanese Beetle

Lygus Bugs are flat, oval, and mottled with white, yellow, and black splotches. Though widespread, they are seldom seen because on approach they fly or move to the opposite side of a stem. Adults and nymphs suck juices from pods, stems, and blossoms. To prevent overwintering, clean up and destroy trash in the fall. Apply dimethoate or carbaryl.

Lygus Bugs

Mealybugs look white and cottony because their bodies are coated with a white, powdery wax; the egg mass is covered with fuzzy white filaments. They have soft, oval bodies, about a quarter-inch long. They rest or crawl along stems (especially where stems and leaves join) or leaves (especially along veins on the undersurface). The young have flat, oval bodies, and are light yellow. Sucking by mealybugs on roots, stems, and leaves weakens plants and dwarfs their growth, sometimes killing them. Those that attack roots cause the plants to wilt between waterings. Some mealybugs excrete honeydew on which sooty black mold develops. Indoors, mealybugs are easily controlled by washing the plant or swabbing the bugs with alcohol. Outdoors, be alert to the young crawlers that emerge in spring and spray them hard with soapy water. If that doesn't work, use malathion.

Sawflies usually lay eggs in plants, so that the larvae can feed either inside the stems or leaves or on the outside of the foliage. The most troublesome are the ash sawflies, found mostly in the eastern and central parts of North America. The rusty willow sawfly is limited to California. Related species are the western willow sawfly (from Canada to Washington and Colorado) and the elm sawfly (widely distributed in Canada and the northern United States). Several sawflies specialize in evergreens. For most sawflies, apply carbaryl while larvae are young and before they can defoliate the tree. No registered chemicals are known to work against the elm sawfly. For spruce sawflies or the European pine sawfly use malathion (except on white pine).

Scales are so named for their soft, waxy scales or heavier wax armor. They occur throughout North America. In the South, one species that feeds on grass sap forms wax cysts on the roots called "ground pearls," which are sometimes used for jewelry. The Cottonly Cushion Scale is bright red when young and becomes yellow, orangey, or brown as an adult. The more common native species are brown or gray, though a few are white or black.

The young crawlers (less than 1/8 inch in diameter) appear in early spring and have legs. Females then molt and lose their legs and attach themselves to the host plant with mouthparts. If you don't look too closely, they usually look like brown specks. Some species lay eggs in a whitish sac that can be mistaken for mealybugs. Scale may be found on leaves and stems which may be discolored. Sucking causes stunted growth. Many species secrete honeydew that makes leaves look shiny, attracts ants, and provides a base for sooty mold to develop.

It is imperative to catch the young crawlers in spring while they are still soft-bodied and moving about. At this stage they can be scraped off twigs and crushed. They are easily knocked off with toothpicks or alcohol swabs or baths of soapy water. Once scales develop their shells, however, they blend so well in to plant stems and bark that they are hard to see, especially since they remain motionless at this stage. They also cling stubbornly. Washing, even with insecticides, is no longer so effective, and you may have to discard the plant. Outdoors, dormant oil spray used in fall or early spring may smother them. Otherwise you will have to resort to malathion or other sprays.

Sowbugs and Pillbugs are found in areas with high humidity. Active mostly at night, during daylight they hide in loose soil or other cover. When discovered, sowbugs scurry for cover but pillbugs roll up in a ball and play dead. Sowbugs and pillbugs have oval, segmented bodies, in varying shades of gray and brown. Although they usually feed on decaying organic matter, they sometimes eat roots and tender plant parts. They are especially damaging to bedding plants and seedlings. Finding and eliminating their hiding places is the best course. Otherwise spray malathion on the soil surface.

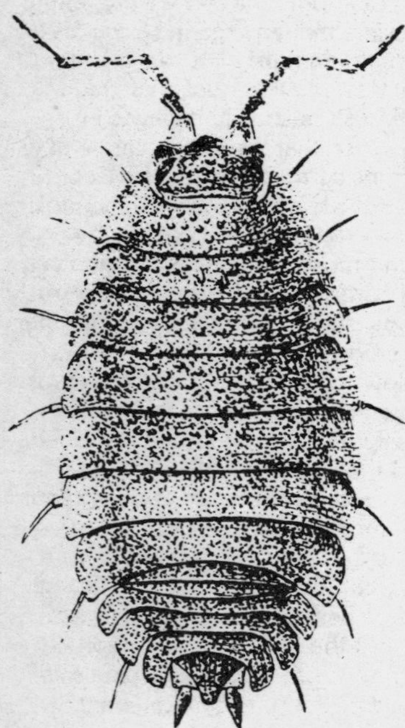

Sowbug

Spider Mites, also called Red Spiders, are common in flower and vegetable gardens and on trees. They like warm, dry air; as cool weather approaches they begin to die outdoors, so they invade greenhouses and indoor plants. They like cactus and other plants that are kept dry. Eggs, laid on twigs and buds in fall, hatch in spring. The young drain juices from tender foliage and flower buds, and also introduce diseases. Spider mites are barely visible. They have flattish, oval bodies and may be greenish, yellowish, or reddish. Look for the frail, loose webbing they spin over foliage and fruit. Spiders drop from one part of a plant to another on silk filaments.

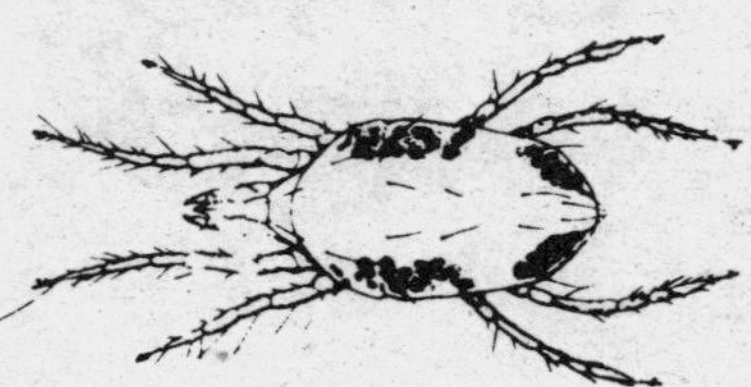

Spider Mites

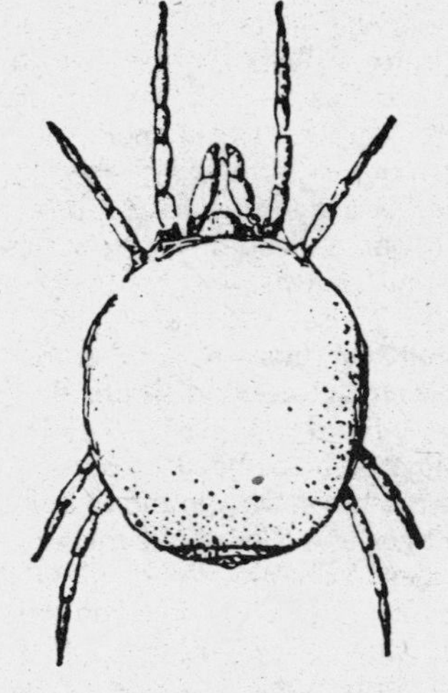

Red spiders do not like humidity, and misting indoor plants or keeping them on pebble trays helps to discourage them. They usually first attach to the undersurfaces of leaves, and the top surfaces develop whitish or yellowish speckled areas. As time goes on, the leaves will yellow or bronze and may die and/or fall off. Heavily infested plants become stunted and may die. Flowers may be faded, fruits and vegetables may be stunted. A forceful spray of soapy water will break up the webbing and dislodge spider mites, but be sure to spray the underside of the leaves. If this and other nontoxic methods fail to work, you may have to spray with malathion or dicofol. (Some commercially prepared spider mite sprays contain sulfur; do not use these on vegetables or fruits.)

Springtails are minute, wingless insects, named for a special organ on the abdomen that snaps and tosses the insect into the air. Most species eat leaf litter on forest floors or decaying plants on beaches. Some species, however, invade the soil in flowerpots and greenhouses. Pouring hot water (90°F) over the soil of potted plants forces springtails into the saucer, which you can then empty.

Stink Bugs, named for the foulsmelling fluid they discharge when disturbed, perform a good function by sucking juices from many caterpillars and beetle larvae. Some species, however, suck the juices from a wide variety of flowers, foliage, and fruit. These bugs are shield-shaped. The green bug attacks vegetables and fruit trees; brown or black ones attack vegetables. Because stink bugs are fond of weeds, keep your garden weed-free. Only pesticides such as barbaryl and naled seem effective.

Tent Caterpillars and Webworms are names covering a number of white to brown moths that lay eggs in filmy, tent-like webbing in trees throughout North America. The eastern tent caterpillar is dark, with a dotted white stripe down its back. The tent is usually found in the crotches of tree limbs in early spring. The fall webworm is spotted with black and orange. Its tent is constructed at the ends of branches in summer and fall. Larvae feed so voraciously they can totally defoliate trees.

The egg masses of the eastern tent caterpillar have a firm, shiny brown covering that makes them look like twig enlargements. The larvae develop in these masses but do not hatch until spring. Egg masses can be removed and destroyed before then. Once the worms have hatched, remove them, webbing and all, by winding the filaments on the end of a pole or brush and then killing the caterpillars. For tent caterpillars apply malathion and for webworm apply methoxychlor when webs are first noticed.

Other webworms are moths whose larvae tie together the foliage of plants with silken threads to construct a shelter in which to dine. These have limited distribution and are partial to particular plants. Use diazinon on webs of mimosa and barberry webworms, and malathion for cabbage webworm.

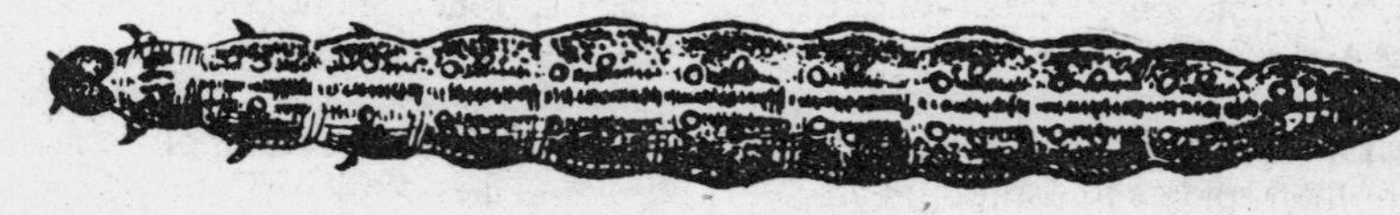

Beet Webworm

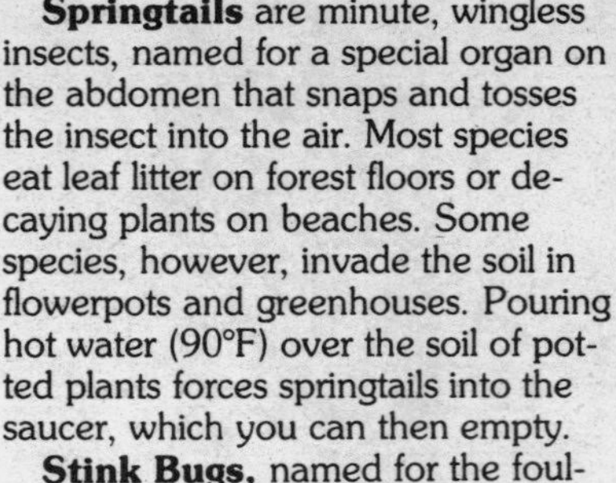

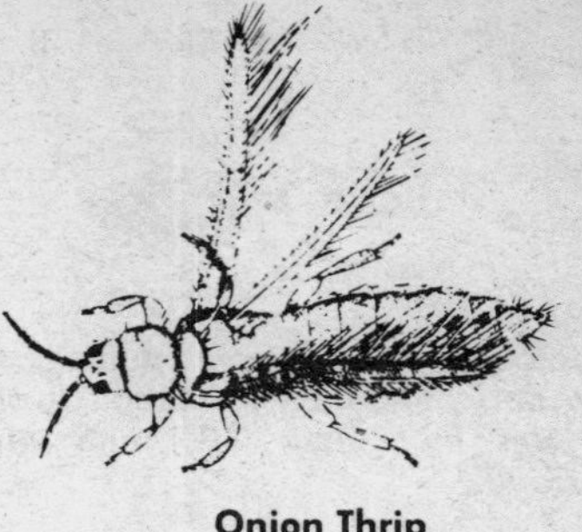

Onion Thrip

Thrips. At least 600 species are known in North America. Only one, the bonded-wing thrip, is beneficial; it eats aphids and mites. The rest suck plant juices from leaves, flowers, and stems of a wide variety of plants, and transmit fungal and bacterial diseases. Flowers may be streaked or deformed, or the petals may be flecked. Buds may turn brown and die. Injured areas are irregular, may look silvery, and are speckled with tiny black dots of excrement. Foliage may blotch or drop.

Hot, dry weather encourages outbreaks, and thrips hibernate in winter. Barely visible to the naked eye, thrips are slender and needlelike, and range from yellow, orange, and black to combinations of yellow and orange. Most have wings but some do not. When disturbed, the adults fly or leap away or run rapidly around on the plant, seeming like tiny, moving specks. You can identify them best by shaking the flower or leaf over a piece of paper. Watch for them once warm weather sets in, usually by May if not before, and try to catch them early with soapy water spraying. Your best defense is to buy ladybugs and other good bugs. As a last resort, try malathion or diazinon.

Whiteflies are tiny mothlike insects that take flight in a cloud when disturbed. They look like minute snowflakes or bits of white ash as they swirl about. Whiteflies are tropical and cannot survive frost, so they invade houseplants and greenhouse plants in fall. Those found in gardens of the North have usually come from indoor plants, so inspect plants before planting them in the garden. The young are immobile, attached to leaves, usually on the undersurfaces; they are pale green to yellow to whitish, oval in outline, and found in large clusters. Adults and young feed on leaves and suck out the juices; leaves pale and yellow, eventually die or drop off. Whiteflies secrete sticky honeydew on leaves, which encourages sooty mold fungus. On indoor plants concentrate soapy water spray on the underside of the leaves; repeat treatment several times. Outdoor infestations will die off when frost sets in. Food crops may require spraying with malathion. See also "Traps and Tricks."

Whitemarked Tussock Moth, widely distributed, is least troublesome in the South. Adult moths are gray. Larvae are hairy, striped yellow and black, with two bright red spots on the back near the hind end, and four tufts of short, white erect hairs on the back. Larvae skeletonize leaves. Apply carbaryl when the larvae appear in spring; repeat treatment for later broods.

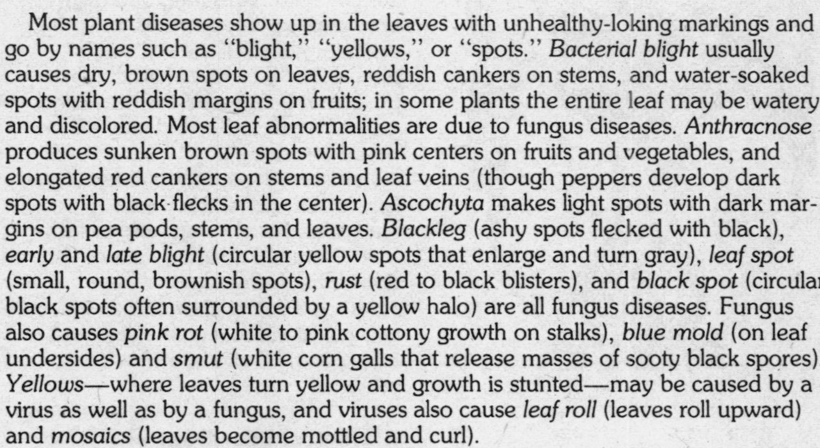

Plant Diseases

Most plant diseases show up in the leaves with unhealthy-loking markings and go by names such as "blight," "yellows," or "spots." *Bacterial blight* usually causes dry, brown spots on leaves, reddish cankers on stems, and water-soaked spots with reddish margins on fruits; in some plants the entire leaf may be watery and discolored. Most leaf abnormalities are due to fungus diseases. *Anthracnose* produces sunken brown spots with pink centers on fruits and vegetables, and elongated red cankers on stems and leaf veins (though peppers develop dark spots with black flecks in the center). *Ascochyta* makes light spots with dark margins on pea pods, stems, and leaves. *Blackleg* (ashy spots flecked with black), *early* and *late blight* (circular yellow spots that enlarge and turn gray), *leaf spot* (small, round, brownish spots), *rust* (red to black blisters), and *black spot* (circular black spots often surrounded by a yellow halo) are all fungus diseases. Fungus also causes *pink rot* (white to pink cottony growth on stalks), *blue mold* (on leaf undersides) and *smut* (white corn galls that release masses of sooty black spores). *Yellows*—where leaves turn yellow and growth is stunted—may be caused by a virus as well as by a fungus, and viruses also cause *leaf roll* (leaves roll upward) and *mosaics* (leaves become mottled and curl).

A second major sign of plant ill-health is wilting. *Wilts* caused by fungus may be rapid—such as in crown rot that affects container plants, which suddenly collapse. With *bacterial wilt*, the plant is apt to droop more slowly. But these are not iron-clad rules. *Fusarium wilt*, a fungus, causes gradual (often a shoot at a time) yellowing and wilting of crops such as peas and tomatoes. *Verticillum wilt*, again a fungus that afflicts tomatoes, comes on faster, appearing on all branches at the same time. Sprays and dusts are not effective.

Decaying vegetation turns dark, and diseases resulting in decay are usually called "rots." *Black rot*, caused by bacteria, produces blackened veins (stems look black inside if you cut them open, and may eventually turn black outside too); leaves frequently yellow and die. When black rot is caused by a fungus, the leaves again turn black. *Root rot*, a fungus afflicting trees, shrubs, flowers, and vegetables, yellows plants and makes them look sickly; stems may be discolored. Rhizoctonia fungus disease turns the stems of seedlings dark and shrunken above the soil—an injury called "wire stem." *Blossom-end rot* is bacterial and causes dark, sunken, leathery spots at the blossom end of vine fruits and vegetables. Though the last often occurs in hot, dry weather that dries out the soil too quickly and may be corrected by adding calcium to the soil, most rots are fatal.

Three of the most bothersome plant diseases are:

1. *Damping-Off Disease:* This fungus affects plants grown from seed. It causes seeds to rot and seedlings to collapse and die. The disease is carried in soil, and the temperature and moisture conditions necessary for germination are exactly those best suited to the fungus. Even if you can save some seedlings it is not always worth the effort, because the survivors are usually weak and spindly and never become vigorous garden plants.

Damping-off can be prevented if you use sterile soil, sterile containers, and sterile implements for starting seeds. Coat seeds with captan or another fungicide dust before planting; tear off the corner of the seed packet, pour in as much fungicide dust as will fit on the tip of a small penknife blade, fold the torn cover of the packet, and then shake the seeds to coat them.

2. *Mildew:* Common on many indoor and outdoor ornamentals and on many vegetables, powdery mildew is a powdery white growth that appears on the *upper* leaf surfaces. On flowering plants it stunts blossoms. Quick temperature changes and periods of extended dampness often bring on powdery mildew. Dusting leaves with sulfur usually clears it up. Downy mildew produces a downy growth on the *undersides* of leaves and on the stems. Leaves dry, curl, turn yellow, shrivel, and die. Apply an organic fungicide.

3. *Nematodes:* Also called root knot, root nematodes are extoparasitic organisms that feed on plant roots, destroying some and producing large knots or swelling on others. Nematodes are chiefly a problem south of 40 degrees latitude. Apart from distorted and crinkled leaves or shoots, or discoloration between the leaf veins, the plant wilts easily in hot, dry weather and may die. Indoor plants should not sit in water. Outdoors, establishing a garden can destroy the natural control agents for nematodes. Rotate susceptible crops with resistant crops (radishes, onions, corn, and mustard and turnip greens). In flower gardens, plant marigolds, as these flowers are not susceptible. Soil with good organic content controls nematodes, as it supports their parasites and predators and generates chemicals toxic to nematodes. Nematocides may work on indoor plants (otherwise discard the plants), but outdoors they work best if you use them in addition to crop rotation and soil improvement.

Preventing Disease

Organic fungicides, safe to use and effective on many diseases, include captan, ferbam, maneb, zineb, and ziram—each available under a variety of trade names. Fixed copper compounds are also available, but these require careful handling and are not suitable for many types of plants (follow label instructions carefully). But since fungicides are useless against many yellows, rots, and other diseases, prevention is vital.

1. Viral diseases are usually transmitted by insects—especially aphids, but also leafhoppers, beetles, and others—so prevention and control means controlling insect pests.

2. Viral, bacterial, and fungus diseases are frequently carried on seed. Buy varieties resistant to diseases prevalent in your area.

3. Bacteria are carried on human hands and spread more rapidly on wet foliage. Be sure your hands are clean and avoid working with plants when they are wet. Smokers can transmit tobacco mosaic virus to tomato plants by hand.

4. Disease is encouraged by lack of sun and air, so keep plants separated and ventilated, and be sure overhanging foliage does not shade underplantings.

5. Root diseases can frequently be prevented by well-drained soil and by not allowing indoor plants to stand in water.

6. Leaf diseases can frequently be prevented by keeping leaves dry. Indoors, bottom-water susceptible plants. Outdoors, water plants (such as roses susceptible to black spot) in the morning so the sun can dry the foliage.

7. Many diseases are carried in the soil or on the refuse of diseased plants. Indoors, use sterilized soil. Outdoors, rotate susceptible plants with nonsusceptible plants, so that diseases will not be carried over from year to year. Rotation disrupts the life cycle of diseases, causing the organisms to decline. If you have had a disease problem, dig out all traces of the plants involved and burn them—viruses and bacteria can overwinter on tiny pieces of old plants you leave in the soil. Prune promptly all diseased branches on trees or shrubs. And don't put any diseased plant parts into your compost.

8. Virus and other diseases may be carried on perennial weeds, so keep your garden weed-free.

9. Companion planting is a boon. The acid in the roots of plants such as tomato and garlic, for example, act as a natural fungicide against diseases such as black spot.

Natural Pest Control

What are garden pests? They can be

1. bacteria, viruses, and other types of microorganisms
2. insects
3. weeds
4. mollusks (e.g., snails, slugs)
5. fungi
6. nematodes
7. birds and animals

On a large scale, outbreaks of pests can be caused by catastrophic natural events such as earthquakes and floods. Very often, however, human beings have been responsible for important pest problems. Some outbreaks happen when somebody has introduced a pest into a favorable environment without importing its natural predators. The gypsy moth infestation began about a hundred years ago with a few caterpillars from France. In 1916, the first Japanese beetles infested a mere square acre in New Jersey.

A second kind of human-based pest buildup occurs with monoculture, that is, the growth of a single crop in abundance, so that the insects to which the particular plant is susceptible are able to multiply beyond their natural numbers.

A third common cause of pest outbreaks is and has been the unthinking belief that environmental manipulation by humans is "progress." This is the perspective of pesticide users. Disturbing the earth's natural balance, by deforestation and other physical interventions or applying pesticides injudiciously, kills the natural enemies of targeted pests and adversely affects beneficial organisms. Some insects, after constant exposure, have become resistant to pesticides. In California's citrus groves, for example, there was a resurgence of cottonycushion scale after its natural enemies were suppressed by the application of chemicals.

Although man has changed the earth's environment permanently, within specific regions there is usually what can be loosely termed a "natural balance" among pests, the plants they eat or destroy, and the biological agents that regulate the effects of pests. Modern pest control, emphasizing the avoidance of pesticides, is in many ways a return to traditional horticultural practices. It consists of attempting to provide plants with a healthy soil and to attract or retain natural allies in the battle against pests.

Nasturtium Petreum. Stone Cresses.

Tanacetum inodorum maius. Great vnsauorie Tansie.

"GREAT MOUNTAIN GARLIC."

Think Twice About Pesticides

Because they can actually be counterproductive as well as harmful, chemical pesticides are the last step in a well-thought-out program designed to control pests. Not all insects are garden pests, and when you spot some bugs on your plants, don't reach for a pesticide. An overquick reaction could even harm your garden by killing ladybugs and other beneficial insects that are already doing a lot to keep your garden pests under control.

Step one in dealing with possible pests is research—knowing the good bugs from the bad bugs. Many basic gardening books identify important garden pests; a classic work is Cynthia Wescott's *The Gardener's Bug Book* (New York: Doubleday).

In the long run, even if individual gardeners and farmers use only small amounts, these millions and millions of "small amounts" are added to the environment where they did not exist before. Thanks to DDT, for example, the American Bald Eagle became an endangered species, without ever being directly sprayed.

The mere fact that anyone can purchase pesticides does not mean that they are safe either for the environment or the person who applies them. Since safe alternatives to chemical pest control do exist, these are definitely worth your consideration.

Reasons to avoid pesticide use:

1. Recent evidence indicates that pesticides contaminating the environment accumulate every year.
2. Many destructive insects have become resistant to chemicals.
3. Chemical pest control is expensive. Chemicals must be used year after year, usually in increasing amounts.
4. Chemicals destroy insects—such as bees—that carry on pollination of the plants that insecticides are supposed to protect.
5. Pesticides kill parasites and predators—such as wasps and the praying mantis—that naturally control populations of destructive insects. Often, the damage resulting from such upsets may far outweigh the benefit gained by the chemical control of the original pest.

Grow Strong Plants

An effective pest-control strategy begins with good soil, optimally a loamy porous soil (see "Soil" under Outdoor Plant Lore). If your garden soil is not a good medium for growing, or if it is too acid or too alkaline for the varieties you have planted, spend some time analyzing what is lacking and make the necessary improvements to be sure you are providing the proper conditions for healthy, pest-resistant plants.

Conditioning the soil. Add humus and compost to give your soil a rich organic composition that naturally nourishes plants.

Soil solarization. Use sun power to rid your garden plot of disease-producing fungi while significantly reducing nematodes and weeds. Sun can accomplish all this by, in effect, pasteurizing soil to a depth of 12 to 18 inches.

1. Begin by soaking the plot with water. Water enhances the soil's heat conductivity.
2. Cover the plot with sheets of *clear* polyethylene plastic and bury the edges in a trench dug around the garden.
3. Leave the plastic in place for 3 to 4 weeks during the summer months when the sun is at its hottest. The soil will heat to 140°F, which is sufficient to kill pathogenic organisms without harming beneficial soil microorganisms.

Plow. Turning up the garden soil early in autumn (during bird migration) exposes beetle grubs to predatory birds. If the soil can be turned 2 or 3 times before the first frost, so much the better. When the ground freezes, the cold may kill exposed insect eggs.

Fertilizer. Stock up on natural fertilizers that enrich the soil with nitrogen, phosphorous, and potash. See "Natural Fertilizers" under Outdoor Plant Lore.

Mulch. Protect your garden in winter against alternating thawing and freezing, frigid winds, and soil erosion.

Biological Pest Control

Biological pest control is a term for a broad spectrum of activities to outsmart and destroy garden pests without employing potentially harmful poisons. Basically, it is the introduction of predators, parasites, and pathogens to reduce the number of pests. Biological control sometimes occurs naturally, without human intervention. A famous incidence was the arrival of California seagulls in Utah in time to save the Mormon's harvest by consuming grasshoppers. The first recorded instance of human intervention dates from 1762, when someone had the genius to save the crops on the Isle of Mauritius from a plague of red locusts by importing from India their natural predators, myna birds.

Advantages of biological controls are:

1. No further expense after the initial costs of the importation and distribution of the predator, parasites, or pathogens.
2. The prevailing natural balance of potential pests to the area is preserved.
3. Pests do not develop resistance to biological controls.
4. They pose no danger to the health of human beings and other animals.
5. Biological controls cause no harm to the well-being and health of the plants they protect.

Natural Allies and Their Enemies

Birds eat several times their weight in insects each day, and although they do damage fruit and berries they are generally far more helpful than harmful. Different trees, shrubs, and vines attract different kinds of birds. See "Attracting Birds" later on in this book.

Insects. Of the million or so species of insects inhabiting the earth, the majority are actually beneficial or innocuous. Many parasitic insects, such as wasps, help gardens flourish. They lay eggs near or in a host insect, and their hatched larvae feed on the tissue of the host. Other insects that are helpful to gardeners are the predators. Among these are the

ladybugs and the praying mantis. Parasitic and predatory insects are, in fact, so beneficial that you can buy the good guys through the mail to help rid your garden of the bad guys. For details, see "Good Bugs."

"Germ" Warfare. One of the first insect-killing pathogens available to home gardeners is *Bacillus thurigiensis*, which is toxic to larvae of many kinds of moths, butterflies, tomato hornworms, and many other leaf-eating insects, including caterpillars. Marketed under the brand names of Dipel, Biotrol, and Thuricide, *B. thurigiensis*, or Bt, is harmless to humans, animals, and beneficial insects. Applied as a spray as soon as larvae appear in spring, this pathogen works within 24 hours. Bt is sold at garden supply centers and by seed supply concerns.

If you have a plague of grasshoppers, modern science has a possible answer to your problem—*Nosema locustae*, a parasitic protozoa that attacks grasshoppers and is also transferred to grasshopper eggs.

Another recently developed pathogen is *milky spore disease*. It is sold under an apt trade name, Doom, as well as by other labels. Its primary use to home gardeners is control of Japanese beetles. Spread on lawns and fields, milky spore disease attacks the grubs of the beetle. If you have already resorted to an insecticide against Japanese beetles, however, don't bother with this agent. For the disease to spread, a substantial grub population is necessary, and drastically reducing their numbers with chemicals is counterproductive when you wish to use this natural method.

Milky spore disease is available from some of the major seed supply companies, garden supply centers, or by mailorder.

Sources

B. thuringiensis
International Mineral & Chemical Corp.
Crop Aid Products Dept.
5401 Old Orchard Rd.
Skokie, IL 60076

Thompson-Hayward Chemical Co.
Box 2383
Kansas City, KS 66110

Grasshopper Spore
Geo. W. Park Seed Co., Inc.
Hwy. 254 N
Greenwood, SC 29647

Reuter Laboratories
2400 James Madison Hwy.
Haymarket, VA 22069

Milky Spore Disease
Fairfax Biological Laboratory
Clinton Corners, NY 12514

Reptiles. The presence of a lizard, land turtle, or snake in your garden is a good omen for your end-of-season harvest. Lizards are especially useful garden predators in areas with a warm climate, and land turtles eat grubs, worms, snails, slugs, caterpillars, millipedes, and insect larvae. Garden snakes dine on all sorts of insects.

Amphibians. Frogs, toads, and salamanders are all insectivorous. They don't disturb gardens, yet they consume large quantities of plant-killing insects. During a 3-month period, one toad can consume up to 10,000 insects, 16% of which are likely to be cutworms. They also love flies, squash bugs, caterpillars, moths, ants, spiders, rose beetles, wasps, and yellow jackets.

Nematodes. These tiny wormlike creatures are usually listed on every gardener's Most Unwanted List, yet one crop protector is the caterpillar nematode, *Neoaplectana carpocapsae.* It is effective against soil insects such as click beetles, root beetles, and weevils; pests occurring on the soil surface such as cutworms and armyworms; and against above-ground bugs, too, if placed in close contact with the tissue of the plants you wish to protect. Caterpillar nematodes kill gypsy moth larvae and adults. One quart of this critter protects a 50-square-foot garden for about $5.

Source

The Nematode Farm, Inc.
2617 San Pablo Ave.
Berkeley, CA 94702

Homemade Strategies

For a truly healthy garden, you may wish to implement some additional techniques to enhance the effectiveness of the biological pest controls that fit into your approach to gardening. Besides providing and maintaining the right soil, you can adapt the technique of interplanting, or companion planting, use lures, repellents, or traps, or mix up your own biodegradable nontoxic bug sprays and weedkilllers.

Companion planting. Each spring, flats of marigolds abound at garden supply centers for a very good reason apart from their aesthetic appeal as a flower. Marigolds are among the many plants that bestow protection on other flowers and vegetables by repelling insects. Scientists have discovered that marigolds work to control nematode infestations, too, and commercial growers in The Netherlands, Zimbabwe, Ceylon, and India have planted these bright flowers on a field-wide scale for that purpose. Other anti-insect plants are asters, chrysanthemums, nasturtiums, and cosmos.

Plants that repel pests tend to have a common characteristic—a potent scent and a sharp taste; but it is believed that the strong smell is what insects dislike. Among the most aromatic of plants are herbs, and devoting a corner of a small garden to herbs might keep it almost pest-free (while the flowers attract bees). In a fairly large garden, planting herbs beside susceptible crops repells enemies.

Nicotine Sulfate: Nicotine sulphate, which is available at garden centers, kills caterpillars but not ladybugs.

GARDEN COMPANIONS

Plant	Grown near	Helps control
Asters	most plants	most insects
Beans	potatoes	Colorado potato beetles, Mexican bean beetle
Castor beans	vine crops	most insects
Dill	tomatoes	tomato hornworms
Garlic and chives	a. the base of rosebushes	aphids, mildew, blackspot
	b. lettuce, peas	aphids
	c. red raspberry	Japanese beetles (the following summer by preventing the grubs from hatching), aphids
Geraniums	rose bushes, grapevines	Japanese beetles
Herbs (in general)	flowers, vegetables	most insects (rosemary, thyme, sage, peppermint, catnip, hemp, mint, and summer savory drive away white cabbage butterflies)
Hyssop	cabbage	cabbage butterflies
Marigolds	most plants	Mexican bean beetles, nematodes, most insects
Nasturtiums	flowers, vegetables, fruit trees	aphids, cucumber beetles, squash bugs, and others
Oregano	cucumbers	most insects
Parsley	rosebushes	rose beetles
Radishes	cucumber	cucumber beetles
Rue	tomatoes	most insects
Tansy	a. cabbage	cabbageworms, cutworms
	b. black rasberry	ants, aphids, beetles
Tomatoes	asparagus	asparagus beetles
Soy beans	a. corn	chinch bugs, Japanese beetles
	b. snapbeans, polebeans (as a border)	beetles
Wild marjoram	cucumbers	most insects
White geraniums	corn	Japanese beetles
Zinnias	flowers, vegetables	Japanese beetles

Botanical Repellents

These are sprays derived from botanical sources that contain no persistent poisons and are not harmful to the soil or human beings. They are biodegradable and do not harm the purity of ground water. Still, it is wise not to use these on vegetables and fruits.

Botanical	Use against	Toxic to
Nicotine sulfate	aphids, white flies, leafhoppers, and others	mammals, but dissipates quickly
Pyrethrum	aphids, whitefly, leafhoppers, thrips	fish
Quassia	slugs, thrips, aphids	
Rotenone	aphids, flys, spittle bugs, spider mites, harlequin bugs, pea weevils	fish, nesting birds
Ryania	Japanese beetles, elmleaf beetle, cabbage looper, squash bug, corn borer	
Sabadilla	squash bugs, stink bugs	

A Few Facts about Carbaryl

Carbaryl, widely marketed under the trade name of Sevin, has been placed on a HEW list of pesticides that are "considered a potential hazard to man." Even when used with the utmost care, carbaryl:

—kills many of the predators and parasites that are enemies of harmful insects, eventually resulting in a greater plague; kills bees; kills water insects that fish eat and contaminates water supplies; kills insects that birds eat; kills insects and microorganisms that help break down dead leaves and other litter on forest floors, making fertile soil, and may cause birth defects in animals.

Nicotine fumigants are especially good for use in greenhouses. They are available by mail from California Spray Chemical Corp., Richmond, CA 94800, and Fuller Systems, 226 Washington St., Wobun, MA 01801. Tobacco dust can be applied directly to plants. It is available from Quaker Lane Products, Box 1000, Pittstown, NJ 08867.

Quassia: Quassia is the ground-up wood of a South American tree. Soak 1 ounce of quassia in a half gal-

Toll-free Pesticide Hotline

The Environmental Protection Agency Office of Pesticide Programs has established a toll-free service supplying general, technical, or emergency information on pesticides. Names, addresses, and telephone numbers of persons working in pest control are also available.

The numbers are 1-800-531-7790 (except Texas) and 1-800-292-7764 (Texas only). Written queries can be addressed to Texas Pest Hazard Assessment Project, Drawer 2031, San Beneto, TX 78586.

lon of water for 3 days. Strain, mix in 1 ounce of soft soap, and spray. Quassia is available from George W. Parks Seed Co., Greenwood, SC 29646; Meer Corporation, 318 W. 46 St., New York, NY 10036; and Desert Herb Tea Co., 736 Darling St., Ogden, UT 84400.

Pyrethrum: Made from dried pyrethrum flowers. If you cannot find dried pyrethrum flowers in your garden store, you can grow them and then grind the flowers yourself. Ground flowers can be dusted on infested plants or used to brew up a spray. (Steep 1 heaping teaspoon in a quart of hot water for 3 hours, add ½ ounce soft soap, and spray.) Pyrethrum lasts for about 12 hours. To locate a source of dried flowers, contact the Pyrethrum Institute, 744 Broad St., Newark, NJ 07102. Seeds are available from seed companies.

Rotenone (also Derris): Made from the roots of a South American plant, rotenone helps do away with sucking and chewing insects but is harmful to nesting birds, fish, bees, ladybug larvae, and other beneficial insects. Potent for about 48 hours, rotenone is available in garden supply stores.

Nontoxic Homemade Sprays and Powders

1. *Water.* A. Use an ordinary plant sprayer or pressure tank to produce a forceful, but meager, stream of water directed at foliage. B. Dip small plants in water that is 120°F for 30 seconds. Kills aphids.
2. *Water + detergent.* A 1% to 2% solution of Ivory Liquid works well if sprayed on houseplants and leafy vegetables such as lettuce. Repeat applications every few days. For scale: mix ¼ teaspoon olive oil, 2 tablespoons baking soda, and 1 teaspoon Ivory Liquid with 1 gallon water.
3. *Water + salt.* 1 tablespoon salt dissolved in 2 gallons of water makes a spray to kill cabbageworms without harming cabbages. 1 ounce of salt dissolved in 1 gallon of water makes an antispider-mite spray.
4. *Water + vinegar.* Spray a mixture of 1 tablespoon of vinegar to 2 quarts of water to remove mold on plant soil.
5. In a blender, blend slices of raw onion with equal amounts of water and spray against spider mites and aphids.
6. Grind hot pepper pods and add to an equal amount of water. Add a little liquid detergent or shaved soap to make the mixture slick. Spray against ants, caterpillars, cabbageworms, and tomato worms.
7. Dust foliage and vegetables with ground dry hot pepper or cayenne pepper to deter insects.
8. *Water + cayenne pepper.* Spray against flea beetles and caterpillars.
9. In a blender, blend together 2 tablespoons of hot red peppers, 3 large onions, 1 whole garlic bulb. Mix with 1 quart of water to which 1 tablespoon of soap has been added. Makes an all-purpose spray for azaleas, beans, roses, chrysanthemums, and other plants. Respray after a rainfall.
10. *Rhubarb.* Boil rhubarb leaves in water, cool, and strain out the liquid. Spray roses to protect them against blackspot and greenfly.
11. *Tomato leaves.* Soak macerated leaves in water overnight. Strain, and use spray against aphids on rosebushes.
12. *Tea grounds.* Work old tea leaves into the soil around radishes to keep them wormfree.
13. *Buttermilk + flour.* Mix 2 tablespoons of buttermilk with 1 cup of flour and dilute with a gallon of water. Spray infested plants.
14. *Chive tea.* Pour boiling water over chopped chives (the same proportions as for regular tea). Let steep for 15 minutes and use as general spray.
15. *Bug juice.* Gather specimens of the destructive insect, put in blender, and grind them up with 2 cups of water. Strain and spray the infested plants.

Traps and Tricks

Aphids: Mulch strips of aluminum foil distributed through a flowerbed or vegetable patch reflects the sun's ultraviolet light and confuses flying aphids. See also whiteflies, below.

Corn Earworms: Black light protects corn from corn earworm moths. Mount a standard 15-watt fluorescent black-light fixture (with a hood to keep off rain) atop an eight-foot pole. Mount a pan of water under the light. The device will attract moths at night and cause them to drown.

Gypsy Moth: Commercial traps are impregnated with a synthetic pheromone to attract male moths and prevent their mating. Some also contain a sweet, fragrant food called PEP. Only mildly effective.

Japanese Beetles: Cover an open can or small jar of grape juice with a piece of wire screening and set it in the center of a pan nor tray of water. The beetles try to get to the juice and drown in the water; dump them out and reuse the grape juice. Commercial beetle traps are also available.

Slugs and Snails:

1. Bury a shallow saucer or tin can up to its rim and fill evey night with beer or a mixture of yeast and water. Remove dead slugs in the morning. 2. Slugs are attracted to banana peels, to overturned halves of oranges and grapefruits, and to slices of potatoes. 3. Hydrated lime, sawdust, or wood ashes scattered about the garden can dehydrate shell-less slugs. 4. Slugs do not like the splinters in old wood such as railroad ties. If you have a barricade of splintery wood somewhere in your garden, you'll often find slugs clustered there and can destroy them. 5. Slugs and snails crawl under wood as light dawns, so you can collect quite a few simply by laying down pieces of bark or other wood.

Whiteflies: Paint a 1′ × 1′ square board with a deep orange-yellow paint (scientists used Rost-Oleum 659). When dry, coat the board with heavy motor oil (SAE 90) and hang it from wires within a few feet of the plants. When the board is coated with white flies, wash it and reapply the motor oil. Commercially made "Stiky Strips" are coated on both sides with a sticky yellow substance. Hang these near indoor or outdoor plants or attach them to metal stakes inserted into the soil. They attract aphids as well as adult whiteflies. Suppliers include Herbst Brothers Seedmen, Inc., 1000 North Main Street, Brewster, NY 10509, and Olson Products, P. O. Box 1043, Medina, OH 44258.

Sources

Agrilite Systems, Inc.
404 Barringer Bldg.
Columbia, SC 29201

D-vac Co.
Box 2095
Riverside, CA 92506

Electro-Lite Dist. Co.
Dept. 3B
12507-11 Ave. N.
Minneapolis, MN 55427

E. C. Geiger
Box 285
Harleysville, PA 19438
(Sticky strips)

IMS Corp.
Box 3399
Albuquerque, NM 87110

Insect-O-Light Co.
1925 Queen City Ave.
Cincinnati, OH 45214

Mellinger's
2310 W. So. Range
North Lima, OH 44452

Tanglefoot Co.
314 Straight Ave. S.W.
Grand Rapids, MI 49500

Phytotoxicity

Plant damage resulting from exposure to pesticides is called "phytotoxicity." The labels on pesticide containers sometimes tell what plants not to spray. Prepare your plants for treatment by watering them thoroughly, preferably a day beforehand. Wilted plants are easily damaged by sprays. The foliage should be dry, and the humidity ought to be low enough to allow the plants to dry off reasonably soon after being sprayed. Spray in the morning, especially indoors. Spray only until the mixture begins to run off the leaves.

Phytotoxicity of Various Pesticides

Pesticide	Dangerous Uses
carbaryl (Sevin)	Do not use on Boston ivy, Virginia creeper, schefflera, English ivy, Boston fern, peperomia. Damage may occur on tender foliage when prolonged mist, rain, or high humidity follows spraying.
demeton (Systox)	May damage azalea, holly, mountain ash. Repeated applications may injure birch.
diazinon	May injure Rose of Sharon. Do not use on gardenia, hibiscus, poinsettia, pilea, African violet, stephanotis
dimethoate (Cygon)	Use only on arborvitae, birch, boxwood, camellias, cedar, euonymus, hemlock, juniper, oak, pine, rose.
dormant oil	Do not use on blue spruce, birch, beech, Douglas fir, Japanese maple, hickory, walnut, butternut.
dormant oil + ethion	Do not use on Douglas fir, blue spruce, beech, sugar and Japanese maple, hickory, walnut, butternut.
endosulfan (Thiodan)	Do not use on birch. May injure roses.
endosulfan + ethion	May injure American redbud and Anderson yew.
ethion	May cause needle drop on Anderson yew.
lindane	Do not apply when plants are wet.
malathion	Injury may occur on certain ferns, small-leaf spirea, white pine, maple, crassula, canaerti, hickory, viburnum, African violet, gloxinia, anthurium, aralia, asparagus fern, ficus, peperomia, pilea, schefflera.
Meta-Systox R	May damage Douglas fir, azalea, elm, holly, viburnum, wisteria, chamaecyparis, yew, begonia, geranium.
Morestan (an acaracide)	May injure ornamentals, including roses, especially in hot weather.
Nicotine	May injure aster, crassula, gladiolus, kalanchoe, fern, gardenia, lily, and some chrysanthemum varieties.

Tips for Pesticide Safety

1. Read the label thoroughly and follow directions and cautions precisely.
2. Measure accurately.
3. Make indoor applications in a well-ventilated spot. Outdoor applications should be made on windless days.
4. Prevent skin exposure to the pesticide by wearing suitable protective clothing.
5. Avoid inhaling fumes.
6. Don't mix pesticides near wells, cisterns, ponds, or streams where there is a chance that spills or overflows will get into the water supply.
7. Wash hands thoroughly after use.
8. If an antidote is prescribed, keep it on hand and understand its use.
9. Clean all equipment after the application.
10. Store pesticides under lock and key.
11. Take the same precautions when handling for disposal as would be taken for spraying. If local ordinances permit, burn paper containers. Rinse glass and metal containers at least twice and empty rinse water into the sprayer.
12. Use the right chemical for the right problem and the right time. Do not, for example, use an insecticide on a fungus.
13. Do not use toxic pesticides if your pets like to munch on your plants.

Prevention

1. Examine any new plants, even cut flowers, that you bring into your home to be sure they are free of pests.
2. If you have more than one plant, isolate any new ones for at least a month (some gardeners prefer to isolate new plants up to three months). During this time you can watch the new plant for any sign of disease or pests.
3. Use sterilized soil for potting. Soil—or soil ingredients such as sand—can contain fungi, larvae, and other pests. Soil you buy prepackaged is sterilized. If you are obtaining soil from your garden or elsewhere, sterilize it before use.
4. Many indoor insects will be repelled if you keep a pot of parsley or a scented herb such as mint among your plants and bruise the leaves from time to time to release the fragrance.

What to Do:

1. Washing: Wash your plants in soapy water. Use two teaspoons of a mild detergent to a gallon of water. Using a soft cloth, sponge, or brush, wipe all leaf surfaces gently, as well as stems and stalks. With small plants and trailing plants, you can turn the pot upside down in your hand and immerse all the foliage in a pail of soapy water. Rinse the plant with clear water and let the foliage dry before replacing it in the sun or bright light.
2. Handpicking: Aphids, mealyworms, and other pests can be picked off with tweezers or toothpicks. Caterpillars can be picked off by hand and destroyed. Slugs, snails, and cutworms hide in daylight; locate them when they emerge to feed at night.
   Small, hand-held vacuum cleaners are sometimes effective for catching flying insects, such as clouds of adult whiteflies.
3. Alcohol: Mealybugs and aphids may be removed by dipping a cotton swab in alcohol.
4. Nontoxic pesticides: Use one of the recipes for "Nontoxic Homemade Sprays and Powders."
5. Commercial pesticides: If, as a last resort, you are going to buy one of these, you will find a number of ready-to-use sprays in pressurized cans with pushbutton spray tops. These are available in hardware stores and gardening centers. Read the label carefully to be sure the spray is one that can be used on indoor plants. The wrong spray can burn your plants and even kill them. Most of the sprays contain rotenone and other botanical repellents. These are the least harmful of the pesticides, but they should not be used if you have small children or animals that enjoy nibbling on plants. Be sure to follow instructions on the container carefully and to wash your hands after applying. Store the containers out of reach of children and pets.

REPELLING ANIMALS

A seventeenth-century text for English gardeners took quite an angry view about animal garden invaders and averred that in addition to a strong fence and a slingshot for small birds like blackbirds, ". . . you must have a fayre and swift greyhound, a stone-bowe, gunne, and if needs require, an apply with an hooke for a Deere, and a Hare-pipe for a hare . . .". English gardeners also employed professional molecatchers who were paid by the dozen for the adult moles (half price for a dozen young ones) they caught. To catch your own moles, it was suggested you flood their holes and try to catch them as they emerged. Or, if you stuffed the tunnel entrances with garlic or leeks, the smell would cause the moles to move elsewhere. Finally, you could chop red herring into tiny bits and burn this mess on the molehills, creating a foul odor sure to drive the moles a good distance from your territory.

Today, gardeners are apt to be a bit more tolerant of wild animal visitors. Even moles, who do indeed tunnel up lawns, are now known to do good by breaking up the soil and by consuming countless tons of garden insects every year. And even where animals do cause a problem, today's gardeners are more apt to look for repellents than to reach for guns and slingshots.

A do-it-yourself repellent against hungry small animals is a spicy spray—one of the recipes for nontoxic homemade sprays and powders—heavily laced with red pepper. This should keep cats and rabbits from nibbling tender sprouts, but you must respray after every rainfall. Several commercial sprays are available to deter small animals like rabbits from evergreen foliage and dogs and cats from other garden areas. Various sprays, pellets, and attachments are sold in garden supply centers and through seed catalogs.

Squirrels can be discouraged from eating crowns and tulip bulbs by burying the bulb under a three- to five-inch mulch of leaves.

Cats and dogs can sometimes be deterred by scattering dried blood along the edges of vegetable gardens and flower beds.

For deer, you need high fencing—at least eight-feet high—to get truly effective prevention. Deer are less likely to trample a garden patch protected with these two repellents: (1) small bags or panty hose hung from trees containing a mixture of equal parts bloodmeal and bonemeal or containing unwashed human hair; (2) ropes or heavy cloth strips soaked with creosote and hung around the borders of the garden.

Sources

"Big Game Repellent"
McLaughlin, Gormely, King Co.
8810 10th Ave.
Minneapolis, MN 55427

"Hot Sauce"
Miller Chemical Corp.
Hanover, PA 17331

"Mountain Lion Deer Repellent"
National Scent Co.
Box 7
Garden Grove, CA 92640

PRUNING

Pruning is a grooming method that keeps plants healthy and looking their best. You can pinch back flowering plants to encourage larger blossoms, foliage plants to create a fuller, more compact form, and fruit trees to produce better fruit. Pruning hedges makes them thick. Old and diseased shrubs and trees are frequently pruned to give them new life.

Pruning can vary from mild to drastic. In the latter category are old privet hedges that can be cut to within a half-foot to a foot of the soil to allow new and sturdier shoots to rejuvenate the hedge. In the wild, natural pruning occurs when wind or gravity removes dead and dying branches from a tree. With pruning, you try to carry out this process more intelligently. How much you prune depends on whether you are simply grooming a plant to keep it in shape, or trying to recondition or revive one that has gotten out of shape, or whether you are giving temporary emergency care to a tree or shrub severely damaged by lightning or ice. A few types of pruning, such as to develop standards and espaliers, are for purely decorative purposes.

Most plants are healthier if groomed on a regular basis, and early pruning can save a plant from having to be discarded later. Although pruning gives you control over the shape of a plant, don't try to re-form a plant by pruning. Pruning can make a bushy plant bushier, but it won't turn a plant of vertical growth habit into a spreading form.

To understand pruning, you first have to realize that all new plant growth comes from buds. Buds contain the rudiments of branches, leaves, and flowers—giving you control over all three—*provided* you learn where and how the buds occur on each particular plant.

A tree, which has its buds above the trunk, grows only from its upper reaches. Though the trunk broadens with age, don't expect a branch four feet off the ground to rise higher as the tree grows. A branch four feet off the ground in a sapling will still be four feet above the soil when the tree has matured. You can control tree growth—but only at a height.

Bushes and flowers, in contrast, have buds quite close to the ground, enabling you to control their growth from wherever the buds occur. Every plant is different, and so you have to learn the budding habit of each species to become master of their growth rate and form. Weigela, for instance, produces new growth right at soil level, so you can cut the entire plant off to the ground and it will regrow. Many viburnums produce buds a foot or more above the soil. You can prune these back only to their lowest buds, but not to the ground.

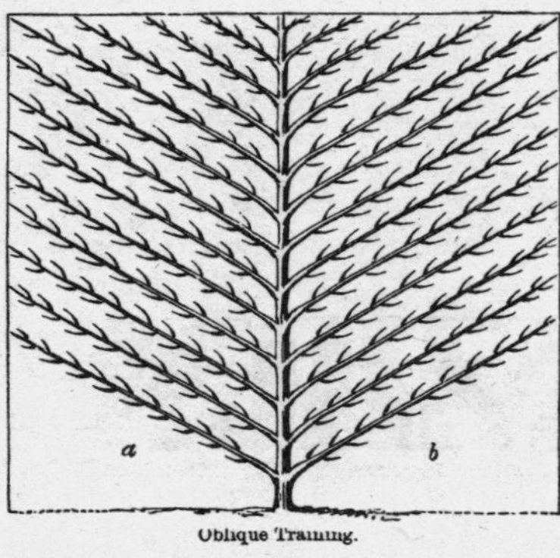

Oblique Training.

The object of most pruning is to cut *above* a bud, because the plant will usually then expand that bud to replace the part you have cut off. You can thus increase the flower and fruit yield, or control the amount and direction of growth, by manipulating a plant's buds.

But buds do have certain innate characteristics that limit your mastery. For one thing, buds branch in only one direction—the direction toward which they point. Plants have two major types of buds: terminal and axillary.

Terminal buds occur at the end of a stem and their function is to extend the length of that stem. You can therefore limit the size of stems by removing terminal buds. Where the terminal bud points upward you can limit upright growth, and where it points laterally you can limit lateral spread.

Axillary buds occur at the angle where leaf and stem meet. The function of these buds is to produce side or lateral branches. By clipping off the stem above an axillary bud, you force a plant to branch in the direction you want. Pruning thus allows you to control shape, as well as height or size.

But a complication arises because some buds produce growth inhibitors that prevent buds beneath them from breaking. To a large extent, you can guess at the existence of these growth inhibitors from the shape of a plant.

One of the most extreme forms of growth inhibition occurs in tropical plants. The terminal buds of palms, for example, release such strong growth inhibitors that no buds below them can break. Thus palms have long trunks with high canopies but no side branches. Removing the terminal bud from such a plant can cause it to die, because buds below the leader may never open.

The more common pattern in temperate zone plants (especially those of globular form) is to have weak growth inhibitors. Eliminating a terminal bud in such plants induces buds below it to open. Often these buds are so hidden in bark or other plant tissue that you cannot see them, and they don't begin to swell until the terminal is gone. Holly is a good illustration. No matter where you trim it, hidden buds will send out new shoots within a few eeks. Though other globular-shaped plants may not react so promptly or break out so profusely, with most—such as maples—you can be assured of several new shoots after pruning. In fact, globular forms can produce so many new shoots after pruning that they can become topheavy or otherwise unattractive. With these, you are better off drop-pruning, in the case of trees, and thinning, in the case of smaller plants.

Evergreens have their own peculiar growth patterns and stand midway between these two extremes. Evergreen trees of conical shape such as some spruces tend toward the tropical pattern. Buds near the top of a spruce are inhibited by the leader, and the farther down the tree a bud occurs the less it is inhibited. Thus the conical shape is achieved by lower branches growing more freely than those above.

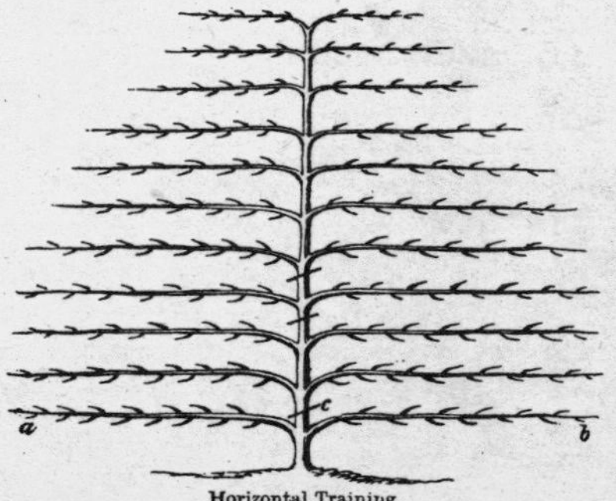

Horizontal Training.

Removing the terminal shoot of an upright needle evergreen may make the tree lose its upright growth and branch laterally. Should this happen accidentally, as in a storm, you can often trick the tree into accepting a new leader. Remove all the vertical growth on the stem down to a dense growth. Here, select a strong lateral shoot and stake it—with a piece of wood tied on with cloth—into an upright position. In a couple of years it will convince itself and its surrounding branches that it is the leader! You can encourage this misconception by removing any lateral branches just under it.

Except by accident, however, you would not normally remove the terminal shoot of a needle evergreen. Instead, you can control growth by shortening it. With a sharp knife, you can trim off about half of the new growth before the needles have hardened. Leave the central "candle" (new growth distinguished by a lighter, fresher color) a bit longer than those surrounding it. If you cut below new growth, however, no buds will break. Similarly, old branches you remove from conifers will not cause buds below them to break, and so any pruning gaps you leave will be permanent.

Pruning Methods

Pinching: Pinching, the simplest and most useful method of pruning, is a technique every gardener should learn. Pinching means removing terminal shoots of soft-stemmed plants. Because pinching is done at an early stage of development, when the plant tissue is tender, you need no tools. You simply pinch the bud—which may be hidden amid a cluster of new leaves—between your thumb and forefinger and pull it out. Pinching flower buds on annuals such as snapdragons will increase the number of blossoms. Pinching new shoots on foliage plants such as philodendron and ivies will cause them to branch more fully into compact shapes. To control axillary buds, simply rub them off with your thumb as soon as they appear.

Since pinching is done on fast-growing young tissue that heals quickly, this method does not produce scars. If you wait until stems become hard and woody, you will need pruning tools and a method that will probably produce a scar. By pinching, you save yourself a great deal of work in future months and years.

Thinning: Another easy method of pruning is thinning, simply removing a small young shoot—finger-length or longer—from beneath a cluster of branchy ends.

Spreading junipers and other evergreen and deciduous shrubs that are cut back to restrict their growth will form new branches beneath each cut. Thus they run the danger of becoming too dense and thick unless you remove some of these new shoots.

Many plants also develop root sprouts or suckers that may eventually give a plant an unattractive, even lopsided, shape. These should be thinned out at their source below soil level. Deciduous shrubs should be thinned of old stems before these develop gnarled mature bark. Such stems should be cut to the ground so light can penetrate the younger stems.

Thinning also can develop beautiful shapes in evergreens, flowering ornamentals, and other specimens. By removing distracting branches, you shape a tree to a dramatic form that emphasizes its basic growth habit.

Cutting Back: When a plant or tree has been neglected, has overgrown or become diseased, it must be rejuvenated.

1. Cut out all dead and diseased wood.
2. Cut all stems back to about one-third their length—or at least to the healthy growth—to just above a bud, to allow new growth to sprout. A few shrubs, including privet, can be cut right to the soil level; so can ivies, honeysuckle, wisteria, and other climbing plants. Thin shrubs of any shoots that are touching and could inhibit each other's growth. On a tree, cut out any branches that rub against or interfere with each other by drop-pruning.
3. Remove sucker growth.

Though the plant may look worse after this treatment, with care and feeding, time will heal its wounds. As the plant begins to recover, resume pinching. Watch the young shoots as they grow, thinning them to get the shape you want.

Spreading evergreens, including yews and arborvitaes, can be severely cut back, provided you do not cut beyond green foliage. Evergreens of upright growth habit, however, cannot replace lost lower limbs and do not regrow if cut back from the top; a regular pruning program is the only answer for these, and if they have been neglected beyond repair they must be replaced.

Sylvan Inarching.

Time, however, is the enemy when a tree or shrub has been damaged by an extraordinary circumstance such as wind, rain—or even a car accident. Forget cosmetic appearance and take quick action. Damaged branches should be cut off at the crotch, and wounds dressed. Split trunks must be bolted back together. Ragged bark areas must be cleaned and sealed. Holes may have to be filled with mortar. The key is to decide on a remedy and quickly effect it. Your action here is decided by the damage rather than by the optimum pruning methods, and you can only hope for the best.

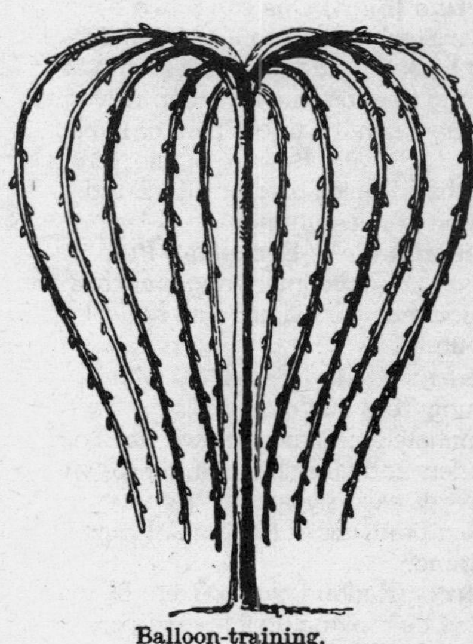
Balloon-training.

Drop-pruning: Drop-pruning is used when branches get too long or too heavy—as happens in windy areas where trees grow lopsided against the wind and are in danger of tipping over. Drop-pruning is also used when tree crowns become so thick that they prevent the rest of the tree—or its underplanting—from receiving light. Drop-pruning is effective because it thins out old growth while discouraging new growth. When a branch is simply cut back, buds form just below the cut and bush out. By drop-pruning—or removing an entire limb or branch at its source—few buds, if any, will break.

Looking at a tree, you see that where a pair of branches join a limb a "crotch" is formed. Follow the branches out from the crotches to see where limbs look too heavy or where they are feeding branches into an already crowded area of the canopy. By drop-pruning you take such limbs out entirely, or remove some of their branches or both.

Starting from the top of the tree and the outside of selected limbs, cut off one of the two branches at an outer or inner crotch. The deeper into the tree you cut and the farther down the crotch, the larger the opening you'll make in the tree canopy. This procedure will enable you to remove a good deal of the bulk of the tree without substantially altering its shape. Avoid leaving a stub. Angle the cut on the limb being removed so that it equals the angle of the limb that is to remain. For large shade trees it is generally best to call in a professional, as special equipment is required.

The Gardner

Root-pruning: Drop-pruning and pinching remove excess growth; root-pruning prevents the development of such growth. This method can encourage the creation of a thicker, stronger root system when readying a plant for transplantation, and it can control top growth. Root pruning is, however, a sophisticated technique. Young trees are root-pruned by digging them up in autumn before the leaves fall off, cropping the oldest roots, and removing any roots growing straight down. Small roots and branchy roots should not be disturbed. Replant the tree quickly and add rich soil and organic matter to the earth around the tree. Stake the tree to keep it from toppling over.

Trench-pruning: Older, larger trees can be root-pruned without removing them from the ground. Use a fork to dig a trench around half of the tree, at a distance from the tree qual to two-thirds the length of the lowest branches. Leave the small roots uncovered alone, but cut the old roots without branches. Pack rich soil around the uncovered roots. Next year do the other half of the tree.

When to Prune

Indoor tropical plants, plants growing in warm climates, and plants that grow quickly may be pruned at any time of year and may require pruning throughout the year.

Evergreens should generally be pruned as soon as new growth starts in spring, and pruning can continue into fall. To keep your needle trees small, cut as much as half of the candle. Spreading evergreens—such as arborvitae, yew, and juniper—may be generously pruned while in vigorous growth, and entire branches near the base can be removed.

Shade trees can be pruned throughout the year with the exception of late winter, as many have a tendency to bleed if cut at this time. Many small trees like magnolia and dogwood bleed into early spring. Shape your tree in the winter, and repair storm injuries at this time. When new growth begins in the spring, dead wood will show up. This should be removed. In the summer remove a few lower branches from young trees so that clear, tall trunks can develop. Rootwork can be done in the fall. Cut off any roots that appear to be strangling the tree at the trunk.

Fruit trees may be pruned and thinned, and any water sprouts can be removed from their trunks, during winter dormancy. In winter, too, you can prune branches on most flowering trees.

On mature shrubs, remove the oldest canes in winter. Once they have flowered, other canes may be removed. In spring and early summer you can stop-back young wood to encourage branching. In fall, remove basal suckers.

All perennials can use regular pruning. Early bloomers should have their stalks clipped off to a low point on the stem when you begin to see branching. This generally results in a second crop of blossoms. Perennials which blossom later should be pinched before the stems are hard and spindly. This causes lower plants that will not need to be staked. Always remove dead flowers before seed is formed on perennials.

As a general rule, winter pruning accelerates spring growth, while summer pruning inhibits growth. This is because removal of old wood in winter makes room for new spring growth. Summer clipping and pinching reduces the number of food-producing leaves, thus inhibiting the plant's ability to grow.

Tools

For pruning houseplants you usually need only a sharp knife or a pair of sharp scissors. For pruning larger, outdoor plants, you will probably need one or more secateurs (also called clippers and hand pruners). They are somewhat like scissors except that they have a spring that provides tension (which is often adjustable) and strength. They come in several sizes suitable for plants from miniature roses up to large, tough rhododendrons. Special shears are made for hedges; these have longer, serrated blades. For cutting tough, woody stems that are more than a half inch in diameter, you may want a lopper. Loppers have small shearing blades and very long handles, enabling you to exert more force with less effort. A pruning knife is favored by professionals because it makes a cleaner cut than you get with pruning shears. You have to practice a bit to use it well, however. Folding varieties that you can put in your pockets are handy.

To prune large shrubs and trees you may want pruning saws, available in lightweight models with

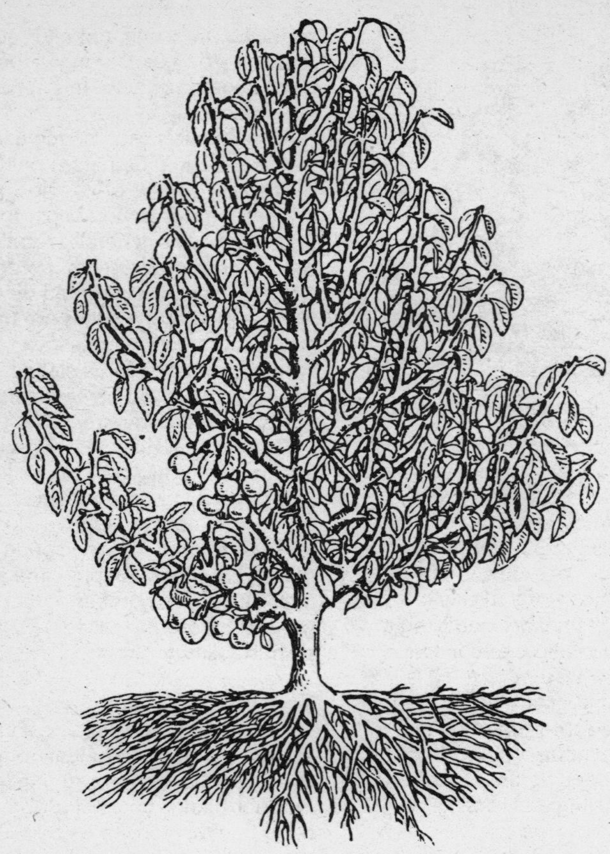

GOOD AND BAD PRUNING.
Right: branches crowded and roots coarse; *left:* fewer branches and more fibrous roots.

blades that run a little over or under a foot in length. (Curved blades are easier to manage than straight blades when you have to reach into shrubbery.) These come with several types of serrated edges, and you can also get folding models. Saws are better than shears for branches larger than an inch and a half in diameter.

For pruning brambles on large trees you may want a sturdy, heavy-duty saw with a straight rather than a curved blade. If you will be pruning trees from ground level, you may also want an extension pole adaptable to your shears or saw.

When you buy heavy-duty tools, look for good grips (often made of durable plastic) and, in loppers and heavy shears, also for shock absorbers. In the long run it pays to buy top quality. Invest in fine tools one at a time rather than buy shoddy models with poor shearing quality or handles that bend out of shape. Be sure your tools are always sharp so you do not leave ragged edges after pruning.

Tips on Pruning

1. Remove any broken or diseased branch immediately, even if this occurs at a time of year when you would not normally prune the plant.
2. If a plant seems sickly or appears not to be growing well, prune it drastically. You won't make it worse, and you may revive it.
3. If two tree branches are rubbing together, cut off the weaker branch—otherwise bark wounds will result.
4. Large cuts—say, those an inch or so in diameter or larger—should be sealed with tree-wound dressing (available in nurseries and garden centers in aerosol cans as well as in paste form). Large cuts may not heal quickly; you may have to reseal them annually in spring several years running.
5. If you keep an eye on your plants, pinching and doing small pruning jobs as little problems crop up, you'll save yourself a tougher pruning months or years ahead.
6. Always prune above a bud.
7. Slant your pruning cut away from the bud, and make as clean a cut as possible with sharp-edged tools. Do not leave ragged edges where disease or decay can creep in.

Pruning Trees

Abies (Fir) Do not prune except to remove injured or diseased branches. Prune only in very cold weather and use very sharp tools. To limit growth, remove the tip bud and pinch off the buds for a foot or so down the limb that is to be stunted. Thin areas can be filled in by removing end buds from the branches around the gap. This will stimulate growth below and around the open area.
Acer (Maple) Until the trunk reaches a two-inch diameter, about a third of yearly growth should be cut off around the sides of the tree in winter. Young trees should be protected from sunscald by wrapping the trunks during the winter after pruning. Older maples need almost no pruning except drop-pruning for shaping or letting in more light.
Aesculus (Horse-Chestnut, Buckeye) As weak crotches commonly occur, young trees should be pruned to create a single ladder. When a terminal bud is lost, the two lateral buds form equal branches. Cut back one. The unpruned branch will then dominate. Prune in late winter or early spring.
Albizzia (Japanese Silk Tree) Young trees must be protected from the cold by wrapping. In colder climates, older trees need only be pruned in the spring to cut out injured and weak wood. In warmer climates, this tree needs only a bit of drop-pruning every few weeks to thin out the top.
Araucaria (Monkey-Puzzle Tree, Norfolk Island Pine) The monkey-puzzle tree should not be pruned except for occasional pinching in spring to shorten new growth; cut off limbs that drag on the ground. Seal cuts. Norfolk island pine can be controlled simply by pinching back new growth in spring.
Betula (Birch) One can ruin a birch by excessive pruning. Only slightly cut back top side branches to grow a young tree to a single leader. Never prune when the tree is bare or it may bleed to death. Beware of thin, tender bark, which blackens if scarred. Prune in mid-summer.
Bumelia (False-Buckthorn) Prune only to remove interfering branches or for shape, in winter, and seal all wounds.
Cedrus (Cedar) Be patient with young trees that grow indiscriminately. In time they will develop leaders and take shape. If the crown spreads excessively later, remove lower branches at the trunk. Prune in summer.
Cercis (Redbud, Judas-Tree) Leave these trees alone until they require removal of dead wood in winter. Multiple-trunked trees are the most attractive.
Cornus (Dogwood) The large, tree-sized dogwoods need little pruning. Their beauty depends on allowing them to take their own shape. Simply thin to enhance natural patterns. Early in spring, remove weak inner limbs and any dead wood. Remove interfering limbs or overhanging branches while the tree is in full flower. Seal all cuts.
Crategus (Hawthorn) Patience is the key. Though young trees are tall and thin, they spread as they age (much like humans). Only drop-prune, but beware that a stubbed-off branch grows switches that will detract from its appearance.
Cupressus (Cypress) Exotic forms should be cared for by a professional. The Italian variety should be sheared when young to thicken it. Leave older trees alone.
Diospyros (Persimmon, Kaki, Date-Plum) These can be grown as tall, thin trees or small, gnarled, fruit-bearing trees. For a columnar tree, encourage the terminal shoot of a young tree by trimming back side shoots halfway up. To get the shorter tree, allow it to grow to about ten feet then remove the leader, and clip back side branches. Prune in winter.
Fagus (Beech) As beechwood is rather brittle, rid the tree of weak crotches by cutting half of the crotch back to the limb. Always remove sprung branches. Remove interfering and rubbing branches. With weeping species show off the silvery trunk by thinning out branches. Prune in late winter or very early in spring.
Fraxinus (Ash) With a young tree, develop a well-defined leader and prune in early winter for sturdy branching by forming a kind of scaffolding of side branches with wide crotches. Older trees can be strengthened by drop-pruning to remove excess growth at the ends of branches.
Ginkgo (Maidenhair-Tree) Leave it alone. Pruning can only hurt, as it is very slow to heal. Time will make it beautiful.
Halesia (Silverbell-Tree) Only thin terminal wood in spring to show off individual branches.
Humenosporum (Sweetshade) Pinching is continuously necessary to achieve a good specimen.
Jacaranda (Acutifola) With saplings, cut off young branches in spring until the tree reaches a height of at least eight feet. Drop-prune young trees to develop a round head. Older trees require little pruning.
Juniperus (Juniper, Red-Cedar) First decide how you want your juniper to look, then prune young trees. Old junipers should not be touched. To shorten a branch, follow it back to a wispy shoot running parallel to the branch, and cut just above this shoot. In one year the shoot will have grown to replace the old branch. In this way you can shape your tree. Do such pruning in spring and summer.

Kalopanax Leave young trees alone. When they develop a trunk of three to four inches pinch off small growth from the larger branches so that they will not be covered up. Older trees should be drop-pruned occasionally to thin the top. Prune in summer.
Koelreuteria (Goldenrain Tree) This tree is most attractive with three or four trunks. Protect the leader by pinching off side shoots below the main stalk. Let this tree take its own form. Remove only crossing branches and those that crowd. Always prune to a crotch. Summer pruning.
Laburnum (Goldenchain-Tree) Encourage these to grow upward by rubbing off the outside buds on branches. In summer pinch off new shoots growing to the side. Prune old trees only in emergencies. These trees have weak root systems and must be staked.
Larix (Larch) Prune in late winter and in spring. In winter, prune young trees to obtain a single trunk. In spring, prune older trees of dead twigs. Be careful not to damage the short, needle-bearing young branches when you cut back long, terminal growth to control horizontal spreading.
Liriodendron (Tulip-Tree, Tulip-Poplar) In well-fertilized, damp

ground this tree needs no pruning. It is delicate and does not heal well if damaged. When a branch is scarred or broken, seal the opening immediately. If pruning is necessary—when side branches begin to compete with the leader—prune offending side branches. In case of winterburn, cut out dry bark to the live bark and paint exposed wood with tree-wound dressing. Prune in early summer.

Magnolia These do not heal well, so only pinch young growth in summer. Some, especially deciduous varieties, respond well to wrapping branches; this spreads the crown and shapes with never a cut or a pinch.

Malus (Crabapple) On young trees remove only weak inner shoots and branches that crowd—in summer. Always cut at the crotch. To keep old trees from losing shape, almost half of the branches next to the trunk can be removed; the rest can be thinned. Press all cuts.

Morus (Mulberry) Weeping trees are not pruned except for occasional thinning in the summer. In a young shade tree, develop the leader by removing side shoots to three feet below the tip. Multiple-trunked trees should be pruned to leave plenty of room between branches.

Nothofagus (Antarctic-Beech) In the north this is a deciduous hardwood; in the south, an evergreen. Small trees are pruned to a single leader. When the trunk reaches a diameter of three to four inches remove poorly shaped branches. Older trees require little pruning. Prune in winter.

Olea (Olive) As a shade tree almost no pruning is necessary. Remove lower limbs in young trees to allow for clearance. Clear crowded and weak branches in spring. Suckers—which appear on the main limbs, around the base, and at the base of the crown—must be eliminated quickly.

Ostyra (Hop-Hornbeam, Ironwood) Need very little pruning. Prune young trees in winter to remove shoots that threaten the leader. If trees are to grown with multiple trunks, thin out branches as they age so that the trunks may be seen.

Oxydendrum (Sorrel-Tree, Sourwood) A complement for azaleas and rhododendrons. Leave this tree alone except to shape for character. Do any pruning in summer.

Paulownia (Empress-Tree) Prune heavily when young to encourage a single leader and to discourage basal shoots and side branches. In early spring clear injured branches. In summer pinch all side shoots until the tree has attained the shape you desire.

Phellodendron (Cork-Tree) Prune seedlings to a single trunk. Until the tree attains a trunk diameter of two inches rub off side buds, and clip off any shoots. Then let side branches grow, but shorten those near the leader. Prune in summer.

Pinus (Pine) Rigid shaping can be foregone unless you want an ornamental tree. Cut candles before they harden on the side branches of young trees to half their size to discourage bushing. As the tree ages, thin a bit to expose the trunk. To limit height, cut the candle at the free tip and the branch ends. Do all this in spring.

Platanus (Sycamore, Plane-Tree) Until the tree reaches about six feet, remove all side shoots, and head-back side branches to encourage the leader. Old trees require only minimal pruning.

Populus (Poplar, Aspen, Cottonwood) While the poplar is young cut new growth in spring around the base back to half its length; poplars look best when branching starts at ground level. Protect the leader on young aspens; drop-prune to thin branches, and seal all wounds. Remove side branches from the whips of young cottonwoods until they reach a height of eight feet; allow branches below the leader, but cut them back to half for one season; remove side shoots from the leader for the following three seasons.

Pseudotsuga (Douglas-Fir) In late spring prune to encourage a conical shape. From two feet on reduce new growth on branch ends by half. Do the same for side growth.

Quercus (Oak) Shorten side branches on saplings in summer to encourage the leader. Lower branches should be removed to leave a clean trunk. As V-crotches develop in young trees, remove one branch to assure a strong leader. Old trees need virtually no pruning.

Salix (Willow) Cut back newly planted whips almost to the ground to strengthen the root system. Encourage the leader by limiting competing growth, but train the tree to a single stem until it is about one inch thick. At this point, well-spaced side growth may be allowed, but limited. Water-sprouts and weak branches should be removed from older trees in winter.

Sassafras Young trees should not be touched. Older trees may have their crown raised by sawing off lower branches. Do not trench-prune (these sprout too freely when damaged). Young root sprouts may be pulled in the soft ground of spring.

Sciadopitys (Umbrella-Pine) In summer remove side branches that may compete with leader on new trees. Needs very little pruning.

Sequoia (Redwood) Encourage seedlings to form a single leader in summer. Once this is formed, and a dense body has developed, leave the tree alone.

Sorbus (Mountain-Ash, Service-Tree, Whitebeam) Discourage all growth threatening a single leader until the tree is at least twelve feet tall. Lightly cut back side growth and some trunk growth, leaving the wide-crotched branches. In trees not grown for shade, like the mountain-ash, thin branches enough to show the trunk, using drop-pruning. Pruning should be done in winter.

Taxodium (Bald-Cypress, Pond-Cypress) Cut off secondary leaders as they sprout on the trunk in spring to train the young tree to a single trunk. Young plants can be sheared and pruned; older trees not not be pruned.

Thuja (Arborvitae) The ideal should have only one trunk, so encourage the leader by removing all side branches. Cut back in spring or summer. If the plant comes as a bunch of equal-sized leaders, let it grow naturally. Never cut back branches beyond where there is greenery, or you'll create a bare spot that cannot be remedied.

Tilia (Basswood, Linden, Lime) Only cut side branches back halfway on young lindens to develop a firm leader. In the first few years, keep branches stripped up to the first third of the tree. Remove weak crotches and thin the top by drop-pruning. Prune in summer or winter.

Tipuana (Tipu-Tree) Until the young tree reaches at least five feet remove all side branches in winter. After this, thin lower branches to achieve a parasol shape. The tree should be rather dense and should grow straight.

Tsuga (Hemlock) Cut out all leaders but the most prominent in spring or early summer. Though the tree may appear a little scrawny, it will heal after about five years. Don't prune older trees.

Ulmus (Elm) Prune the leaders straight. Once it has reached about fifteen feet, only trim overly long side branches. Drop-prune about every decade to keep limbs from splitting from excess weight. Keep the tree free from weak, injured, or dead wood. Prune in summer.

Zelkova From the time the seedlings are above ground until they are shoulder high, prune them to one shoot. As it grows, keep cutting back to a single leader; eventually it will grow into a large tree which needs little pruning. Prune in summer.

Zizyphus (Jujube) Until the young tree has reached five feet, prune to a single leader every summer. At this point, side branches may be allowed to grow, but not too long. Retard their development by pinching buds. Don't shear these trees; encourage them to grow upward for as long as possible. After this, just thin to highlight the shape of individual branches.

Pruning Shrubs

Abelia (Bush-Arbutus) This dense plant has excellent foliage throughout most of the summer. Rejuvenate every two or three years in early spring. In cold areas for the first couple years pour a solution of potassium sulphate (one-half cup to three gallons of water) around the base in September to harden immature wood.

Amelanchier (Shadblow, Serviceberry) In early spring thin out and selectively pinch terminal buds and vigorous, unbranched shoots.

Agrifolium.
The Holly

Azalea (Evergreen, Deciduous Evergreen) Prune as little as possible. To keep plants in control, clip new shoots that break out just below the old flowerheads. Deciduous: Maintenance prune by cutting out old flower stems. Azaleas throw out long, unbranched canes; early in summer pinch these back to various heights while they are soft. Watch for another set of these in midsummer and nip these back close to the ground to get branches.

Berberis (Barberry) Prune these—both hedges and individual plants—according to their normal growth patterns. Every third year prune deciduous barberries through winter, removing some of the old wood. On evergreen varieties, thin out old and weak canes just before the buds break. Through summer pinch out new shoots at the base of the plant. Very old plants can be rejuvenated by pruning.

Calluna (Heather) In well-drained, sandy soil, you never have to prune. Beware of all-green branches. Cut these as soon as you see them. In general, prune as the plant seems to dictate: if it is high, cut it back enough to keep it dense and neat; if it is small, unambitious, leave it alone.

Caryopteris (Bluebeard, Blue-Spirea) Rejuvenate every year in early spring. In the South, cut only about a third back. In colder climates, cut to the ground. Do not prune or pinch during the summer as this will reduce fall flowers.

Cestrum (Jessamine) Get rid of the copious suckers at the base constantly. To control this plant, grow it against a wall or twine it around a support. Pinch terminal shoots to encourage branching. After bloom, cut each branch back two or three leaf stubs.

Chaenomeles (Japanese and Flowering Quince) Young bushes require only cutting out weak canes to let in light and air. Prune like lilac after flowering or in early spring. Old shrubs need to be rejuvenated every five years. Prune cautiously to avoid destroying shape. Thin out in winter because it tends to develop a thick, unattractive center.

Chionanthus (Fringe-Tree, Old Man's Beard) Good city plant. Grow as a shrub or small tree with several trunks. Single-trunk trees are susceptible to borers. Cut off spent flowers on the male; leave berries for birds in early winter, then clean up. Not much pruning necessary. If a tree, maintain a natural shape by pruning in spring like dogwood. If a multi-stemmed shrub, thin by removing old or unwanted stems to the ground.

Cornus Prune Gray Dogwood in late fall and early spring; remove terminal shoots for shaping; use renewal pruning if necessary. The Redosier Dogwood shrub is valued for its winter color; remove dark stem to the ground every spring to preserve the bright-colored stem. If plant becomes too large, pinch off some of the new terminal growth. Prune Yellowtwig Redosier in the same manner.

Cotoneaster Prune deciduous kinds in the winter, taking out crowded growth. Cut back old, overgrown branches back to a crotch. Prune evergreen kinds in spring. If a plant is crowded, take out old growth, and cut back some to last year's growth for shaping purposes.

Deutzia Transplants easily. Rejuvenate when needed. After flowers have faded, cut the oldest canes to the ground; cut back some of the other canes to new growth. Pinch off buds of new shoots at the base to stimulate branching.
Euonymus (Burning-Bush, Spindletree, Wahoo) With deciduous varieties, take out the awkward branches and insect-infested canes in early spring. Rejuvenate by cutting back in early spring. Cut out root suckers. Prune evergreens as they need it from early spring into summer. Rejuvenate when they become old and woody. Shear hedges when they look ragged. If hedge looks dried out, feed and water well for a season, then cut back to 6- to 12-inch stubs. Groundcovers can be sheared close to the ground if they become diseased.
Exochorda (Pearl-Bush) Require little care. Remove dead flowers. Rejuvenate every four years. Pinch basal sprouts and cut out any basal suckers.
Forsythia The perfect shrub for beginners, it is almost indestructible. Prune in late spring after flowering by cutting a few of the old canes to the ground. Pinch back new shoots that pop out low on the plant. To rejuvenate, cut the plant to about a foot, selecting five canes for survival. Remove the rest at ground level. By fall they will have grown two feet, and will bloom by spring.
Fothergilla Requires virtually no pruning. Every three years remove old canes to relieve overcrowding
Hamamelis (Witch-Hazel) Light maintenance pruning. Thin some of the oldest canes in winter. Root-prune before transplanting. Prune as you would flowering trees in early spring.
Hibiscus (Mallow, Rose-of-Sharon, Althea) Prune off woody branches to the ground during winter. Thin crowding by cutting to a crotch. Prune Rose-Mallow in the fall. Lay the cut stalks over the crown and cover with peat; uncover in spring, and after the shoots have grown to three feet, pull out the weak ones.
Hypericum (St.-John's-Wort) Rejuvenate every other spring after flowering. Encourage basal shoots.
Ilex (Holly) English holly does not develop a leader for several years. Do not prune young plants without leaders except to clean them up. Prune anytime. Cuts may be made anywhere. Prune Chinese holly and American holly in the same manner. To restrict size, cut back new growth severely.

Juniperus (Red Cedar, Juniper) Trim upright junipers and red cedar as little as possible—only enough to maintain the size and shape you want. Prune Pfitzer junipers in summer as freely and as often as you wish. The rapid-growing, spreading junipers are hard to prune because of their creeping growth habit; to control these, prune severely and often in summer. If you let them get out of hand, you'll have to reach deep into the plant later to remove entire branches. To create dense groundcover, cut back spreading types halfway through each year's growth for the first few years. Older junipers need little care aside from removal of dead branches.
Kerria (Japonica, Japanese kerria) In late spring, prune two-year-old wood to the ground. Remove some new wood to improve flower visibility. After flowers fade, cut weak canes to the ground.

Kolkwitzia (Beauty-bush) Cut old, large limbs to the ground. Prune hard and regularly in the spring. It won't be easy to remove canes as they grow very close together, but do so faithfully. Do not touch the top.

A grove of white pine, thinned and pruned.

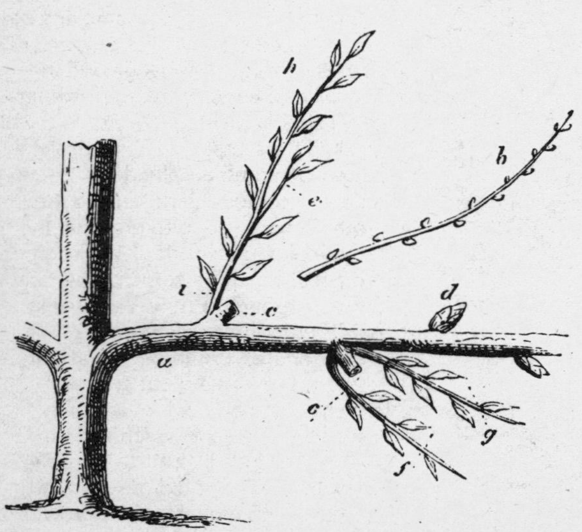
Pruning Horizontally Trained Pear Trees.

Lespedeza (Bush-Clover) Remove dead wood and thin out overcrowding; otherwise, respect its natural form.
Ligustrom (Privet) Pinch to shape throughout summer. If using as a hedge, shear to avoid a ragged look and shape so that light reaches all parts of the plant.
Lonicera (Honeysuckle) Do not try to limit the bush. In early spring, cut new shoots to half their length to cause density. Cut off only the oldest wood every four or five years. With vines, training is more important than pruning, but those that grow indiscriminately must be trimmed constantly. In winter remove ugly or diseased wood, and pinch off terminal shoots to bring about branching. May be trimmed in early spring.
Myrica (Bayberry, Sweet-Gale) Recovers rapidly from all types of pruning. Low kinds need only maintenance. Prune taller varieties to trees of several stems with small clusters of leaves at intervals along the trunk. Limit sweet-gale growth by cutting out suckers.
Nerium (Oleander) At the end of the growing season, severely cut back the previous year's growth. When new shoots have developed several leaves, pinch them to stimulate branching. In warmer climates, cut off the older canes at the ground every eight years to renew the plant.
Osmanthus (Holly-Olive) Pinch out new growth on new plants to encourage a defined leader. In spring, cut back the previous year's growth at least a third to insure an even appearance. Shear hedges once in early spring and perhaps twice through the summer.
Parthenocissus (Virginia-Creeper, Boston-Ivy) Pruned freely and keep under severe control. Do not allow it to attach to screens or woodwork as it leaves indelible marks. Old vines that have been cut back do not always grow back strongly; consider starting a new vine instead.
Philadelphus (Mock-Orange) For coronarius and virginalis and the shorter types, only thin out canes around the base every four or five years. Pinch out tips of new shoots around the base after they reach about six inches. Prune after flowering in early spring.
Physocarpus (Ninebark) If your plant looks good, don't worry. If it looks bad, remove a third of the old wood every third year, thin inside twigs, and cause branching of basal shoots. Prune in summer.
Rhamnus (Buckthorn) Discourage overzealous shrubs by drop-pruning. Only rarely remove old basal canes. In hedges, cut back one in spring just before new growth begins, and shear twice during the summer.
Rhododendron In late spring pinch new shoots to form a sprig with just three leaves to stimulate branching. Do not prune after the middle of summer. Renovate old plants (preceded by at least a year of heavy mulching and watering).
Rhodotypos (Jetbead) These plants tend to be thin around the base, so manure them and pinch out the tips of basal shoots. Generally thin. Only maintenance prune the top. Prune after flowering.
Rus (Sumac) Prune in early spring only to remove limbs that unbalance the plant or to weed out weakness. Cut out root sprouts.
Ribes (Currant) Prune to be open and airy, and to be composed of equal parts one, two, and three-year-old canes. Cut any canes older than three years. Seek out young plants that can be trimmed to three wide-spread stems. Keep side branches short and remove crowded and weak ones. Prune in late spring after new wood has matured; but for rejuvenation, prune in early spring.

Ribes vulgaris fructu rubro.
Red Currans.

Sarcococca (Sweet-Box) As canes begin to look bad, prune to the ground. To keep within bounds, root-prune.
Sheperdia (Buffalo-Berry) This shrub needs little more than maintenance pruning. In warmer climates, cut out blight each spring. Encourage branching.
Spirea The varieties with arching branches or that are upright need little pruning. These spring-bloomers should be pruned as the flowers fade. Do not shear off tops, as this creates a plant with a green tuft on top and a stemmy, dead base. Summer-flowering kinds should be pruned heavily in spring, cutting back to two or three buds to encourage growth on new wood.
Stephandra These are valued for their arching form, which can be destroyed by excessive pruning. Maintenance prune with discretion.
Symphoricarpos (Snowberry, Waxberry, Buck-Brush) Do not shear tops. Maintenance prune to remove old canes. In varieties that spread by long runners, pull the runners up to prevent having a yard full of these prolific plants. Prune in early spring.
Syringa (Lilac) On new plants, only pinch off shoots that pop out below a graft. Leave them alone for at least four years. Until the plant is about eight years old, exercise restraint, cutting only the oldest canes out at the ground. Then prune with severity, leaving no old canes and only half of the young, healthy canes. If this is done in summer, the bush will look pretty bad but will come around next spring. Prune after flowering.

Standards

Standards are plants trained to grow so that they resemble small trees. Some may be tiny, such as miniatures used in Bonsai, but you can also grow them two to four feet tall or higher.

Some nurseries sell ready-made standards, but you can start your own from a well-rooted cutting. This method can take several years with a slow-growing plant, so you may prefer to select a young plant that already has a nice upright stalk. Remove the lower side shoots, and keep removing these as new ones appear, so that you develop a trunk-like stalk and a canopy of foliage at the top. During this process, stake the stalk in order to develop a straight trunk. Staking must be done while the plant is young; once the stalk grows twisted it is almost impossible to straighten out.

Standards need not be foliage plants, although *Ficus diversifolia*, *F. nitida*, palms, podocarpus, bamboo, dracaenas, and others train well. Many flowering plants can be trained to standards also. Among the most popular are several types of geraniums, azaleas, acacias, oleanders, chrysanthemums, lantanas, camellias, and fuchsias. Roses also can be trained. Some succulents, such as crassula and kalanchoe, train well, too. Among the herbs, you can make little trees of rosemary, salvia, and others. If you want a really tiny tree, try one of the ivies with miniature leaves. Citrus trees and avocado plants are other possibilities.

Standards can be grown in any container of suitable size, though since they are special plants you'll likely want a somewhat fancy container.

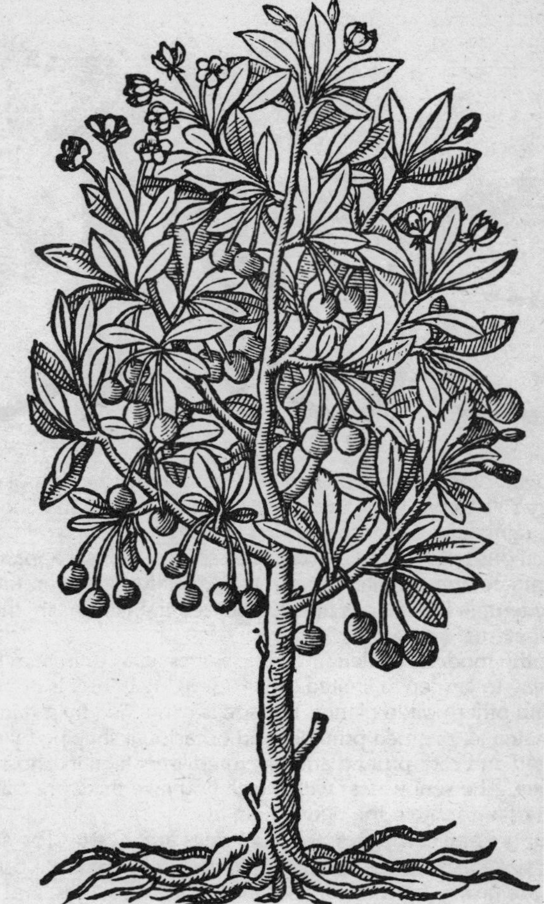

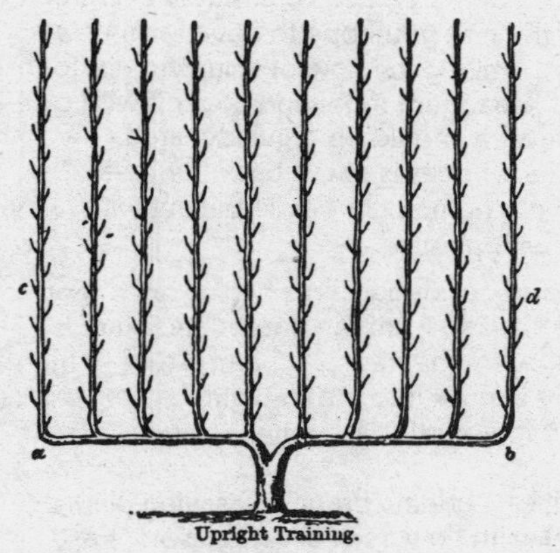

Upright Training.

Espaliers

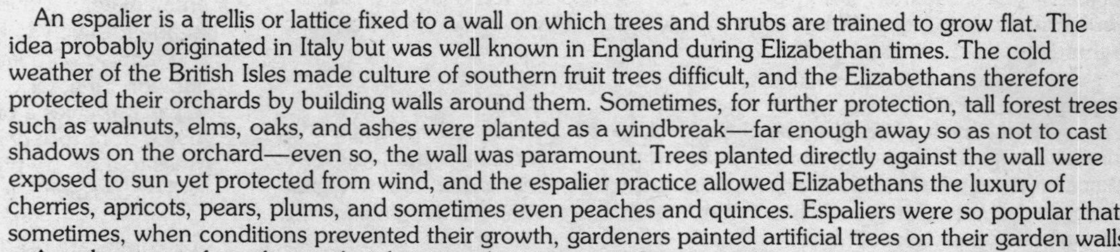

An espalier is a trellis or lattice fixed to a wall on which trees and shrubs are trained to grow flat. The idea probably originated in Italy but was well known in England during Elizabethan times. The cold weather of the British Isles made culture of southern fruit trees difficult, and the Elizabethans therefore protected their orchards by building walls around them. Sometimes, for further protection, tall forest trees such as walnuts, elms, oaks, and ashes were planted as a windbreak—far enough away so as not to cast shadows on the orchard—even so, the wall was paramount. Trees planted directly against the wall were exposed to sun yet protected from wind, and the espalier practice allowed Elizabethans the luxury of cherries, apricots, pears, plums, and sometimes even peaches and quinces. Espaliers were so popular that sometimes, when conditions prevented their growth, gardeners painted artificial trees on their garden walls.

An advantage of espaliers is that, because the trees grow flat against the wall, they are space-saving. In Elizabethan times, walls were costly, and espaliers made it possible for the interior of the orchard to be used for cultivating currants, berries, and flowers. Today's gardeners value this same space-saving technique.

Finally, espaliers can be ornamental. In training the tree or shrub flat against the trellis, it's practical as well as pretty to force the lateral branches into symmetrical patterns.

Chandelier-training, with Branches Oblique.

Trellises may be of wire, wood, metal, or a firm plastic. In hot climates, though, material (such as metal) that conducts heat is not desirable. Place the trellis against a garden or building wall—the espalier can be used to decorate an unattractive side of the garage, a tool building, or your home—so that there is at least a half-foot of space for air circulation between the wall and the trellis.

At the base of the trellis, in the center, plant a *young* specimen of the tree or shrub you want to train. As lateral branches emerge, train them to the sides of the trellis. The most usual design is symmetrical—with growth pattern matched exactly on either side of the trunk. You can produce a moderately formal tree by allowing the branches to grow at acute angles from the trunk, but the most formal arrangement is to train the branches so that they make 90° angles. In this case, the lowest two branches would leave the trunk at a sharp 90° angle and be trained horizontally to either edge of the trellis, at which point they would form a frame within which one or more upper pairs of branches would follow the same pattern. Asymmetrical designs also are possible, but require more thought to achieve a pleasing balance. Trees may also be trained along the edges of open crosshatch lattices.

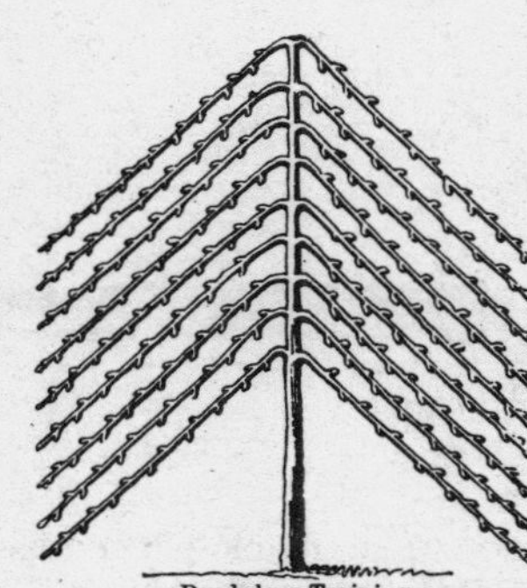

Pendulous Training.

The trick with espaliers is to retain only a few branches that are well separated from each other. In a small tree, two sets of branches separated by about a foot of space between them may be sufficient. Too many matching sets of branches will detract from the formality you are trying to achieve and will produce a tree that looks much like any other. When several lateral branches emerge close together, you must be ruthless in eliminating most of them. This is best done in the fall after the leaves have fallen. You can then cut back the lateral branches and terminal shoots to a bud. How far back you should cut depends on how quickly the tree has been growing. If growth has been very rapid you may want to pinch the plant back during the growing season, and to prune more than half of a shoot in the fall. With evergreens (such as yews) start pruning early in spring; then continue to remove branches and to check the growth of terminal shoots to avoid overgrowth and loss of symmetry.

In the spring, the lateral branches of shrubs and trees should be pinched back as soon as four leaves have formed, and terminal shoot growth should also be checked.

The slower growing plants are easier to control and require less work. Rapid growers like lilac and honeysuckle are difficult to manage. One popular choice is ceanothus, of which there are numerous hybrids. Most do well in California and the Southwest, but hardier varieties are available for northern climates. These produce showy small flowers—blue or white—in dense racemes that are especially effective on espaliers.

Dwarf fruit trees also are adaptable to trellis growth, and here you must thin out the spurs or fruit to discourage too much clustered growth. Flowering quince has been a favored espalier tree since Elizabethan times.

Some viburnums are good choices because they provide white or pinkish flowers followed by fall color and long-lasting fruit. The fragrant varieties are especially popular. Cotoneasters and pyracanthas offer similar advantages of flowers followed by long-lived fruit for extended attractiveness. Shrubs such as these should be pruned during the early growing season to make the flowers and fruit prominent.

Vase with Dwarf Stem.

BONSAI

As with other aspects of Japanese gardening, the bonsai gardener plays a secondary role to nature. The object is to create a tree that looks natural in all ways, but in miniature. Everything about the tree is kept in scale. Religious and mythic associations help to make these trees special. Bonsai apparently originated in eleventh-century China, appearing as miniature trees on the sides of mountains in tiny temple landscapes that symbolized the Horai-san, the sacred Taoist mountain of eternal youth.

For the modern gardener, bonsai serves as a contrast to full-scale gardening, or as a way to garden in limited space. Growing bonsai is not much different from growing other potted plants. The size is controlled by a minimal amount of soil, fast drainage, planned pruning, and occasional shaping by wiring. Bonsai are also repotted and root-pruned and given fertilizers high in phosphorus and low in nitrogen. The seriousness with which you take the work can range from the casualness of a hobby to the rigors of an art.

Four general categories of bonsai trees are by size. The smallest, usually from finger-size to six inches, is called *Mame*. These are the most difficult to maintain. They are grown from either seedlings or from cuttings, and may be grown into full-sized bonsai. *Ko* range from seven to eleven inches and can be kept at this height for years. Medium-sized plants—in the 12- to 24-inch range—are called *Chui*. The average *Dai* is 33 inches or slightly less, but these may range from two to three feet.

Buying

Avoid plants with unhealthy branches. Look for trees with good spacing, uniquely shaped branches, and needles or leaves of a good size. Symmetry is not essential. Trees with branches growing from the trunk at diverse angles may grow into bonsai of rare character. Choose hardy and fast-growing plants (junipers and pines are easy to work with).

When buying from a general nursery, you can choose from four stages of development. 1) Liner plants, developed from seeds or cuttings, are least expensive. Seedlings generally have stronger root systems than cuttings. Liner plants are particularly suited to *Mame* bonsai. 2) Container plants are sold in tin or plastic cans. Because of their shallow root systems they can often be set directly into bonsai containers. These are suited to *Ko* bonsai. 3) Bare-root plants have been heavily pruned and are sold, without soil, during the plant's dormant season. Because they have been heavily pruned, these plants are excellent for grafting. 4) Balled-and-burlapped plants are very good for beginners because the entire plant, including the root systems, is intact.

Though bonsai grown from seed take more time, they are healthier, with better root systems. Seedlings can be developed into excellent *Mame*. Often the only way to obtain a rare species is by importing the seeds. The easiest plants to raise from seed are birch, beech, fir, gingko, yew, spruce, pomegranate, pine, hornbeam, larch, sweetgum, and maple. Cuttings take much less time than seeds but may not develop spreading root systems.

Your First Bonsai

Formulate a mental picture of the tree you would like to create. Then examine the plant you have bought to see which limbs are important to the tree and to your design. Develop a sense of the natural structure of the tree. Then begin shaping by removing unimportant branches to show off the trunk. Also remove crossing or weak branches. To determine the importance of a branch, block it with your hand to see how the tree looks without it. Bend branches to experiment with styling. Try to create interesting groupings of odd numbers of branches; such clusters are traditionally made up of 3, 5, or 7 branches.

Classical proportioning of trees is done in thirds. The lower third is cleared to show the trunk's relationship to the ground and ground cover. The middle third is dominated by branches emphasizing and complementing the trunk. And the top is made up of young branches tapering to a tip.

When you have finished styling above the soil level, remove the plant from its container and root-prune. Root-pruning encourages growth, keeps the plant healthy, and keeps the roots and the top in proportion. It can be done by the beginner with very little risk to the plant. Remove soil only from the roots you will cut. These will be the larger ones, growing straight down. Slice across the bottom, parallel to the ground. Then trim off uneven or unhealthy roots that remain. Aim for a flat base to encourage a spreading root system.

Plant your tree in a bonsai container with at least one drain hole and with the bottom quarter taken up with gravel. Prune it in the early spring, just as the sap is beginning to flow and your plant reaches its peak of strength. Fast growers should be pruned earlier than slow ones. Most flowering trees must not be pruned until after they bloom or you will destroy this year's bloom which lies dormant in leaf axils. Layering and grafting are techniques for further shaping your plant.

Layering. Layering will develop a second set of roots in a thriving plant. Softwoods are the best specimens for ground-layering: Bend a healthy branch to the ground and make a small cut on its underside. Keep this cut open by inserting a stone or other handy object. Remove the leaves from the area above the cut and bury the stripped section of the branch four inches under the soil. Support the leafy end by staking it. Keep the soil moist. In as little as six weeks softwoods may root.

Air layering is another technique. A tree with a trunk of up to two inches can be air layered but an inch and a half is considered prime. To air-layer evergreens, use thin copper wire to tie off the part of the tree you hope to have form new roots. The wire should act as a tourniquet, limiting the flow of nourishment to this section. Wrap the girdled area with moist sphagnum moss and cover it with plastic. The moss must be kept damp and the area should be regularly aired.

The first phase when air-layering deciduous trees is to cut back the bark through the cambium layer in a ring around the branch. Girdle the cut with twine. Cover the wound with moss and wrap it with plastic.

The second phase for both evergreen and deciduous trees begins once roots develop. At this time cut the girdled section away from the parent and plant it immediately, without removing the moss. Keep the new plant damp and in the shade for two weeks. Thereafter gradually expose it to the sunlight.

Plants easy to layer are beech, birch, crape-myrtle, crypomeria, camellia, juniper, pine, willow, and spruce.

Grafting gives a broad range of possibilities—adding branches, saving plants dying from root damage, producing a tree with flowers of several colors. Easy trees to graft are pine, holly, maple, or gingko.

The basic graft is created by slicing the rooted plant (the stock) and inserting a *scion* (or child) into the cut. The parts then grow together, retaining individuality. Top grafts are used to create new branch structure. Side grafts are used to fill an empty space. Grafts are usually made just as sap has begun to flow in the spring. Use strong tips, two to three inches in length. In all grafts, smooth cut edges to minimize the risk of disease and rot.

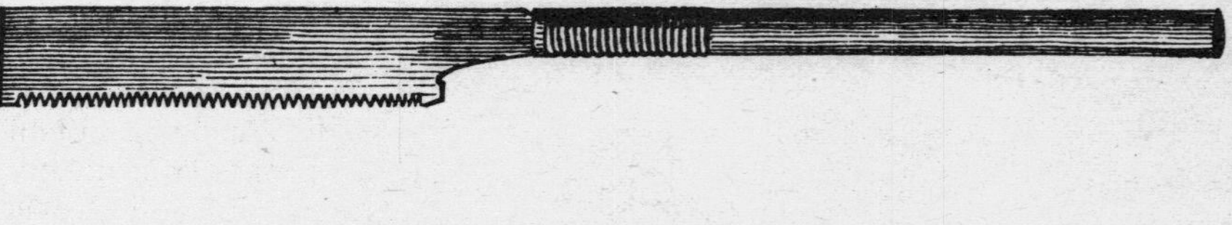

For top-grafting, trim the scion to a very thin paper. Place this as far as possible into the puncture. Be careful not to damage the bark. If the stock trunk is more than one inch thick, make a ½ inch cut between the wood and cambium layers. If the stock is less than an inch thick, make a one-inch wedge cut through the center and parallel to the trunk. Put the scion on the edge, at the cambium layer.

Side-grafting is similar to top-grafting, except that it is merged lower on the trunk, and the cut made in the scion is diagonal. The cut in the stock should be one to two inches long and made into the cambium layer but not deeper, and as close to ground level as possible. Cut the scion to approximate the angle of natural growth from the trunk.

In either top or side grafting, wrap the stock firmly to hold the parts together. Thread or vinyl tape will do, but rubber does not leave marks. Cover all exposed areas with a protective tree-wound dressing. For the first year keep the grafted stock in a training bed, then transfer it to a pot. Remove the wrappings after a year.

Wiring and Training Bonsai

Once your tree is pruned to the design you want, use wire to develop good form and to correct any branch defects. During the plant's dormant season, wrap one end of a wire around part of the tree, and secure the other end to the ground or another part of the tree. Bend the wired branch, and growth follows. After a certain amount of time the new shape becomes permanent.

Some general rules: Wire branches on conifers down, deciduous trees horizontally. To make a tree appear aged, prune it to have soft edges, pinch off buds and shoots, and then wire the branch tips downward. To create the impression of youth, leave the terminal growth alone and wire the tips upward.

Use copper wire. The right weight is the lightest wire that will control the branch you are training. But most trees require three gauges of wire. Use thinner wire while the tree is growing, and thicker wire during the dormant season. Wrap the wire in spirals in the direction the branch is to take, and on one-inch centers. After the wire is attached, form the new shapes by feel. Work slowly and patiently.

When wiring is finished, allow the tree to recover. Set it in a shady place, water frequently, and mist the leaves for several days. Fertilize to increase the sap flow and strengthen the tree, making it less liable to shock and more pliable. For abrupt changes in style, work in stages. Limit the tree's water supply for a couple of days after wiring, especially with stiff, woody trees. Do not repot the plant in the near future. Check the wires frequently. Trees grow quickly. Loose wires will soon become tight. If trees are unattended the bark may overgrow the wires and removing them will leave scars.

—CAMELLIA JAPONICA. OLIVE.

Wiring is not favored by all experts. Weighting or roping achieve similar results. To shape by weighting, attach weights (fishing sinkers) to alter the growth of a branch. Using rope instead of wire to tie branches to other branches or to the container produces effects comparable to wiring. These methods are not as foolproof as wiring, but may soothe the purist's conscience.

Controlling Growth: The most effective way of controlling growth is also the most simple. Use your fingers to punch buds and shoots. Occasionally strip some leaves. Without control, strength goes to the upper parts of a plant. This causes the remainder of the plant to weaken. Pinching the outward growth halts the sap flow and reroutes it to strengthen the lower regions. Generally the earlier pinching begins in the life of a plant, and the more severe it is, the slower the tree grows and the smaller it stays. Pinching varies according to species. Here is a general guide:

To keep candles in the upper branches of pines short, nip off the largest candle; or, if the candles form a group, remove the center one. Later, if necessary, take out some of the others. If growth is too rapid, pinch off a half of every candle. For juniper, spruce, and yew, trim from early spring through summer. Nip all new growth of over half an inch. Buds develop as balls. When they begin to elongate, pinch them, leaving 3 to 5 whorls. This may be necessary daily at the height of the growing season. For Sargent's juniper and cypress, nip new buds, but not so severely as to mar the spring foliage. Do not trim recently transplanted wild plants. Pinching brings about rapid new growth, and a transplanted tree should be allowed to rest for a full year.

Trident maple, oak, and zelkova should be trimmed early; continue trimming into fall as necessary. In early spring, cut back new growth to two sets of new leaves. Pinch buds that appear late. Dense trees should be nipped when shoots grow to one inch in length. The Japanese maple is unusual among maples; it is touchy. Pinch young maples often, but pinch older maples only once, early in the season. Pinch beeches and elms often. Shape hornbeams with shears. For fruit and flowering trees, wait until the blooming has finished. Pinch when buds and shoots are clearly visible but still tender. When suckers appear, remove them immediately.

Apart from pinching, here are two other methods for controlling the basic appearance of your tree. To restrict leaf size, force a second growth by stripping the tree, pulling off every other leaf, or cutting leaves in half. The second growth will be smaller.

To increase trunk or limb size, force the amount of nourishment passing through the trunk to increase by allowing the outer growth to expand. When the trunk or limb has thickened to your specifications, thin the unsightly, dense foliage that has resulted. Another method for achieving a similar end is to transplant the tree from the container to open ground for a year. Then repot it in the original container.

Plants To Use

Flowering Almond: Very durable deciduous shrub. Blooms from white to pink. Excellent foliage in the fall.
Arborvitae: Sturdy evergreen. Needs some protection from the sun or it may scorch. Keep moist.
Ash: Deciduous. Produces white blooms in May; bright leaves in the fall.
Azalea: The Satsuki and Kurume varieties are especially good for bonsai. Durable. Both evergreen and deciduous varieties.
Barberry: Evergreen. Particularly well-scaled. The deciduous varieties have berries which vary in color from yellow to dark red.
Beech: Spectacular in the fall. Beautiful buds in spring. The sieboldi is the most popular.
Birch: Very durable except in extreme cold. Good either individually or in groves. Tough as bonsai, but great, interesting bark.
Boxwood: Good in sun and some shade. These slow-growing plants come in several varieties. The Japanese are particularly suited to *Mame.* The Korean and English varieties make better, larger bonsai.
Camellia: Durable plant in cold. Sasanqua makes an interesting shade plant and a good bonsai.
Cedar: Durable in cold. Great for bonsai, with gnarled branches. Trains well.
Flowering Cherry: The general symbol of Japan, the flowering cherry is a hardy plant with spectacular blooms.
Cotoneaster: Evergreen with small pink and white blooms.
Flowering Crabapple: A sturdy and important bonsai plant, but prone to insects.
Crape-Myrtle: Needs lots of sun and winter protection. Prone to mildew in summer. Good for bonsai, with small leaves and good scale.
Cypress: Hinoki and Sawara are popular, with good reason. Monterey and Bald have potential.
Gardenia: The miniature is best for bonsai. Take care to avoid sudden temperature shifts.
Gingko: Dress all wounds on this tree. Grow the male, as the female's fruit is smelly. Deciduous.
Hawthorn: This slow-growing tree looks good in any garden.
Hemlock: Choose the Western. It has nice needles and is well spaced.
Holly: Deciduous except for Japanese, Perny, and Yaupon. Must have both sexes for fruit.
Hornbeam: Laxiflora has small leaves suited to bonsai. American is nice. Water with care in summer to avoid root damage.
Jasmine: All forms are popular for scented white and pink flowers. Most are not hardy.
Juniper: These are sturdy and about the easiest trees to grow and shape for bonsai.
Sweetgum: (Liquidambar): Good in cold. Valued for its bark. Medium rate of growth.
Maple: Important species in bonsai. For serious gardeners Trident and Japanese are necessary.
Oak: Hardy. Usually deciduous. Good branches and fall foliage.
Olive: Interesting trunks. Good in cold.
Pine: Very popular species in its endless variety. Red pine is the most difficult.
Pistachio: Do not grow in cold climates. Great fall color.
Flowering Plum: Protect in winter. This deciduous tree is valued for its trunk and dainty leaves.
Pyracantha. Firethorn: Easy-to-grow evergreen. Keep in the sun. Fruit production can be increased by pruning.
Flowering Quince: Prune off blooms to prevent weakening of plant. Keep in sun.
Redbud: Not often grown as bonsai, but makes an interesting specimen. Sturdy. Deciduous.
Rhododendron: Tough evergreen. Good possibilities. Varieties have varying leaf sizes.
Rosemary: Great trunk, bark, and leaves. Evergreen.
Spruce: This sturdy conifer is very popular.
Strawberry-tree: Protect in winter. Great leaves and flowers.
Tamarisk: Keep all varieties in the shade in summer. Generally sturdy with beautiful leaves. Deciduous.
Viburnum: Both deciduous and evergreen. Berries follow May blooming. Good leaves.
Willow: Deciduous. May grow too fast for bonsai. Needs a great deal of water.
Wisteria: The Chinese is usually chosen. This vine can be used effectively. Interesting trunks.
Yew: This sturdy evergreen is very popular. The female is best for bonsai.
Zelkova: Good for any collection. Elegant, erect. Good bark and fall color. Succulents, especially crassula species, are also adaptable to bonsai.

Container Gardening

Container gardening is nothing more than growing a plant in a container. It can mean one plant on a desk or table, a collection of pots attractively arranged on your patio, or an entirely landscaped roof garden. It thus applies to both indoor and outdoor gardening—and in fact to plants you may keep indoors in the winter and outdoors in warm weather. Also included in container gardening are miniature landscapes in dish gardens and terrariums. And while most container gardens consist of ornamental plants, you can create money-saving food gardens in containers too.

Many urban dwellers turn to container gardening as the simplest way to have a garden in the city. But suburbanites with outdoor ground often find containers useful. Portable tubs and other containers can be a boon where the garden is too shaded, or the soil too acid or alkaline or arid for certain plants you want to grow. Best of all, if you move frequently, your container garden can move along with you.

For information on containers, potting, care of indoor plants, and a full listing of indoor foliage and flowering plants, see our sections on indoor gardening. If your container is to be outdoors, see relevant sections of our chapters on outdoor gardening.

Plants for Container Gardening

For the most part, the plants you use in containers are the same ones you would normally grow elsewhere.

For indoor containers, any of the plants we have recommended for indoor gardeners may be used if your temperature, humidity, and light conditions meet their needs. Many of these indoor plants also can be grown outdoors all or most of the year in mild climates, or in summer in moderate climates.

For outdoor containers, consult the various sections in this book on outdoor plants—not only flowering plants, but also trees, shrubs, groundcovers, vegetables, and fruits. Except for trees, where you must set limits and choose only dwarf and small varieties, most outdoor plants can be grown in a container. In fact, an advantage of container gardening is that it allows you to expand your horticultural horizons. If your garden soil or other outdoor growing conditions are not appropriate for certain plants you would like to grow, containers often provide a solution. If your garden soil is not acid, but you'd like to have azaleas, heather, or blackberries, you can grow these in containers. If your climate is too cold for cactus, an indoor pot will allow you to enjoy one.

Restrictions on container gardening are, in fact, surprisingly few. One, as in the trees mentioned above, is size. Shade trees such as oak are out of the question, and if you want a living area around such a tree it makes more sense to install a deck or other living space around an already mature tree than to try to plant one in a tub on your patio. City-dwellers may be tempted to try more trees than country dwellers, and for their special conditions small ones such as the Oriental dogwood, which withstands shade nicely, could be excellent choices. But in addition to trees, you probably won't want to pot any giant shrubs, such as large varieties of rhododendron. With the increasing popularity of container gardening, though, more and more of the larger plants are being developed in dwarf forms of pot or tub culture.

Many groundcovers and trailing plants can be grown, either by themselves in pots, to provide a green base by being planted with taller pots, or in hanging baskets to trail from above.

Most annual and perennial flowering plants are also suitable for container culture. Some wildflowers and other types of plants that have deeply penetrating roots are exceptions; they may not like the confines of a pot. But mosses and other water-loving plants make nice miniature landscapes, as do the cacti and succulents.

Herb gardens—a mixture of several herbs in planters or hanging baskets—are handy in or near the kitchen.

Many vegetables can be grown in containers. Radishes, lettuce, and root vegetables are cool-season types that can be grown in sun or shade, in pots, window boxes or in larger areas. For most vegetables, you need containers of four-gallon capacity or larger to keep the soil from drying out too fast and requiring too much watering. Tomatoes can be planted, two large vines per container, in 20- to 30-gallon plastic garbage cans. But miniature varieties of tomatoes, cucumbers, and other vegetables are available that can be grown in window boxes that provide about 1½ cubic feet of soil for each plant. Spring and fall crops are usually most successful in cities, as rain and cooler weather reduce the stress in plants.

Miniature varieties of many fruits, such as melons, are also available. In addition, strawberries and other rambling berries may be grown in small containers. Some bush fruits can also be grown, but these, like berry and fruit trees, do best in sturdy containers to support the weight of their root balls. Half-barrels of 20-gallon capacity work well.

Fruit trees, however, pose a problem. In areas where winters are very cold, the pressures caused by freezing and thawing can destroy the large containers necessary to support trees. In such climates you should buy true dwarfs and put them in containers that can be taken to an unheated shelter during winter.

If you want a fruit tree in a northern city, you might do best with dwarf crabapples (beautiful spring flowers, edible though tiny apples, and nice fall color). Though it blossoms best in sun, it will flower in shade too.

Depending on the type of plant you want to grow, consult the special sections of this book for soil, watering, temperature, and other specifications for successful growth.

Problems of Container Gardening

1. Once you have filled a large planter, it may be too heavy to move. Be sure to figure out in advance where it should go, and move it to its location before filling it.
2. With large containers, it is often difficult to tell if you are giving enough water to get to the plant roots or if it is all being absorbed by the top of the soil. Double-watering is helpful. That is, you water thoroughly, until the plants look well watered. Then return in half an hour to do it again—often the soil will absorb the second watering as well, because it has taken time for the first water to seep through the soil.
3. With large containers, you may find watering a chore. If so, you can buy irrigation pipe systems for use with containers, complete with timeclocks. These water your plants automatically and are handy too when weekend trips and vacations keep you away from your plants.

4. Be wary of watering plants with a hose that has been lying in the sun. It may contain water so hot it will scald your plants.
5. You can't count on rain to cut down much on watering if your plants are in outdoor containers unless you live in an especially rainy area. If you had a geranium in a six-inch pot, you would need 1⅓ inches of rain a day to water it properly—*if* all the rain went into the pot. Unfortunately, most of it would run off the leaves and onto the ground.
6. For trees and shrubs grown in containers, the U.S. Department of Agriculture recommends the following fertilizer recipe:
   - 6 parts hoof and horn meal or bloodmeal
   - 1 part ammonium nitrate
   - 1 part treble superphosphate
   - 1 part sulfate of potash
   - 6 parts gypsum

   These ingredients are available at garden centers.

   Apply this mixture once a month during the early part of the growing season. Use one level teaspoon for a plant in a 4½-inch pot, 2 teaspoons for 6-inch pots, and 3 teaspoons for a 7-inch pot. Narrow-leaved plants require less plant food than do broad-leaved plants.

   Do not apply fertilizer in summer, because it encourages soft growth in late fall and the tree or bush may not survive the winter.

   If your plant has not been especially vigorous, however, you might want to resume fertilizer in winter. The plant is dormant then, but the roots will store the nutrients and use them in the spring.
7. If you live in an area with a cold climate, it is a good idea to line the inside of large outdoor planters with styrofoam sheets. This will protect them against the effects of freezing and thawing.

Problems of Urban Gardeners 1. If you have a roof garden, or a balcony or terrace several stories up, you may have a problem with wind. To avoid losing plants and injuring people below, avoid small pots. Use planting boxes, as explained above, for any small pots you want to have outdoors. Depending on how much wind you get, you may be able to shield some smaller pots from the wind by placing them on the lee side of a planter from the prevailing wind direction. Fencing is another possibility. To avoid damage to tree-size plants, anchor or chain them so they will not topple. It also helps if their containers are broad and sturdy rather than tall and slim.

2. Sun may be a problem, especially on roof gardens where wind prevents installation of awnings or other canopies. You may be able to grow only sun-loving plants. Lack of sun afflicts some ground-level gardens, where only shade-loving plants will thrive.
3. Watering may be hard to do for a roof garden or balcony where you have many plants, and it's a consideration you should give some thought to before investing in a lot of plants. Your work will be eased if you can use a hose, but that may mean running extra plumbing lines or draping the hose through other rooms from the kitchen or bathroom. If you are going to be carrying water from these last two rooms, consider the time and likely damage to the landscape between them and your plants. Another reason for keeping small pots in planters rather than setting them outdoors, incidentally, is that they will dry out less rapidly in planters.

CONTAINER PLANT SUGGESTIONS FOR VARIOUS CONDITIONS

Plants for Low Temperature (50°–60°F at Night)

Australian laurel	Cyclamen	Miniature holly
Azalea	Easter lily	Mother-of-thousands
Babytears	English ivy cultivars	Oxalis
Black pepper	Fatshedera	Primrose
Boxwood	Flowering maple	Sensitive plant
Bromeliads	Fuchsia	Spindle tree
Calceolaria	Geraniums	Vinca
Camellia	German ivy	White calla lily
Christmas begonia	Honeysuckle	
Cineraria	Jerusalem-cherry	
Citrus	Kalanchoe	

Plants for Medium Temperature (60°–65° F. at Night)

Achimenes	Crown of thorns	Poinsettia
Amaryllis	Easter lily	Rose
Ardisia	English ivy cultivars	Shrimp plant
Avocado	Gardenia	Silk-oak
Bromeliads	Grape ivy	Ti plant
Browallia	Hibiscus	Tuberous begonia
Chenille plant	Hydrangea	Velvet plant
Christmas cactus	Norfolk Island pine	Wax begonia
Chrysanthemum	Palms	Wax plant
Citrus	Peperomia	Yellow calla lily
Copperleaf	Pilea	

Plants for High Temperature (65°–75° F. at Night)

African violet	Chinese evergreen	Philodendron
Aphelandra	Croton	Scindapsus (Pothos)
Arrowhead	Dracaena	Seersucker plant
Australian umbrella tree	Episcia	Snake plant
Banded maranta	Figs	Spathyphyllum
Cacti and succulents	Gloxinia	Veitch screwpine
Caladium	Golddust plant	

Plants That Will Withstand Abuse

Arrowhead	Grape ivy	Spathyphyllum
Australian umbrella tree	Heartleaf philodendron	Trileaf Wonder
Cast-iron plant	India-rubber plant	Tuftroot *(D. amoena)*
Chinese evergreen	Jade plant	Veitch screwpine
Crown of thorns	Ovalleaf peperomia	Zebra plant
Devil's ivy	Pleomele	
Fiddle-leaf fig	Snake plant	

Plants for Extremely Dry Conditions

Bromeliads	Ovalleaf peperomia	Wandering-Jew
Cacti	Snake plant	
Crown of thorns	Scindapsus (Pothos)	

Vines and Trailing Plants for Totem Poles

Arrowhead	Grape ivy	Scindapsus (Pothos)
Black pepper	Kangaroo vine	Syngonium
Creeping fig	Pellionia	Wax plant
English ivy cultivars	Philodendrons	

Suggestions for Large-Tubbed Specimens

Australian umbrella tree	Fiddle-leaf fig	Philodendrons
Dracaenas	India-rubber plant and cultivars	Silk-oak
False-aralia		Tuftroot
Fatshedera	Palms	Veitch screwpine

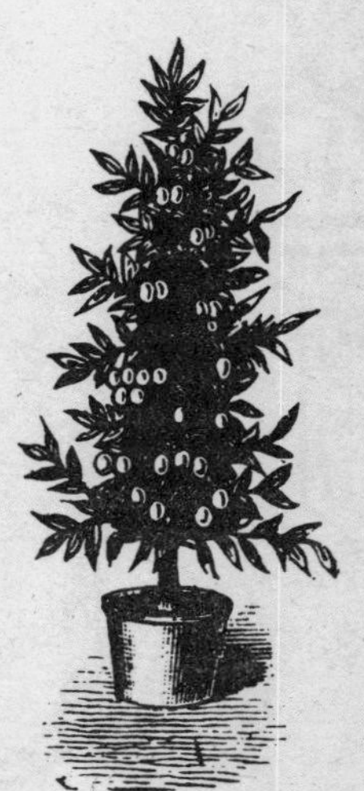

Hanging Baskets

Most indoor and outdoor gardeners eventually get themselves one or more hanging baskets. They serve such a multitude of purposes, it is hard to avoid them.

Hanging baskets can be used to screen windows or to provide a floor-to-ceiling room divider when placed above plants on the floor. They can provide an easy way to attractiveness in corners, or above furniture, or in other hard-to-decorate areas. If you are cramped for space, they allow you to have plants without losing an inch of floor space; this makes them especially handy in small rooms like bathrooms or for decorating narrow porches without losing outdoor living area. Because they can be hung at any level, hanging baskets, hung at different heights, can create unusual decorative effects from stairwells to skylights. Outdoors, hung from trees, as well as indoors, they can be important design elements, directing the eye from one group of plantings to another, providing color accents, or making a transition between decorative elements.

If your hanging basket is to be placed above eye level, you should consider the *underside* of the foliage and the way the blooms hang. Long, pendant or cascading blossoms of tiny size will be more visible than stupendous blooms up near your ceiling. With a basket placed at eye level or below, the topside foliage and blooms are most important.

The height at which you put your basket should also determine the type of plant growth you want. With a very high basket, you will want foliage that drops heavily and dramatically like *Sedum morganianum* or long stems with more grace like many ivies. At eye level or below, however, you may be more pleased with a plant that has more branching.

Basket plants have several things going for them—good air circulation and usually lack of accumulating water, for example—so are often easier to grow well than those in standing pots.

A basket need not contain only one plant. In those above eye level you could plant two or even three varieties that have dangling stems and like the same soil and other conditions. In baskets to be placed at eye level or below, you could plant an accent plant in the center and a trailing plant around it.

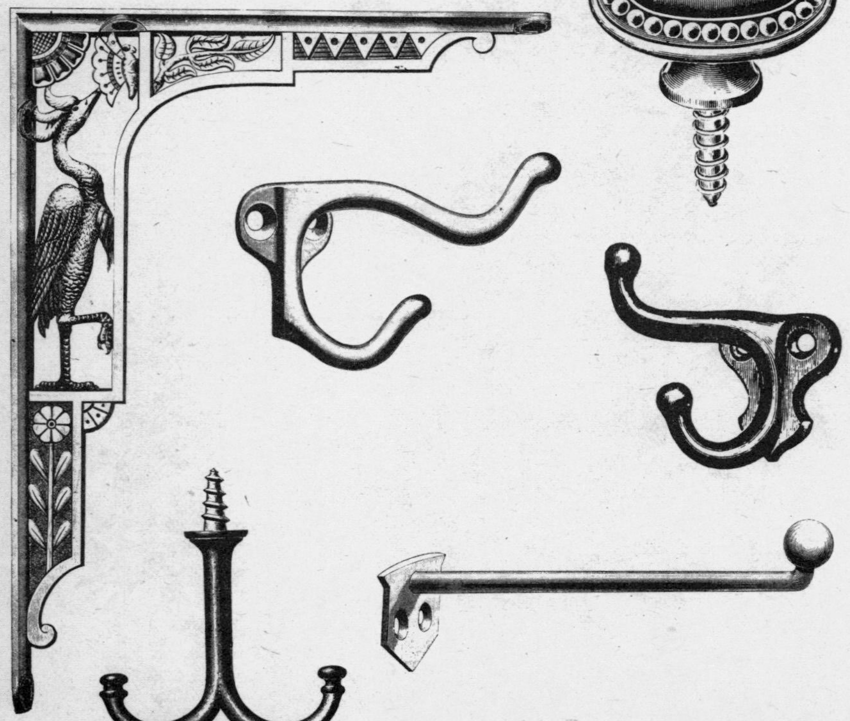

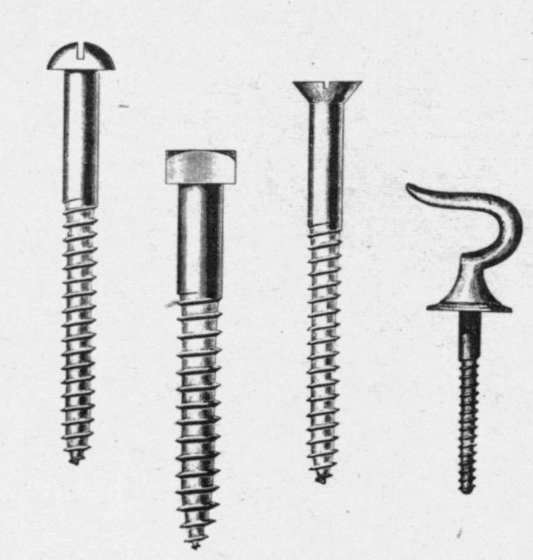

Containers

Containers for hanging are sometimes made of basketry, but the term "hanging basket" covers a wide range of materials, and most are usually not baskets.

One consideration in choosing a container is whether you want to place a drip pan on the floor to catch overflow each time you water yor plant. This can be avoided by purchasing a container with a saucer attached to the bottom. Some baskets come with internal containers. In many cases, you will be hanging your basket over others anyway—over a room divider or over plants in a windowsill—and perhaps over a pebble tray, so dripping will not inconvenience you.

You should also consider the weight of the container filled with soil and the sturdiness of the surface from which you intend to hang it.

Another consideration in choosing a container is the style of the container and the style of your room. Obviously you do not want gold-braided hanging ropes if your decor is informal, nor do you want rough rope if your decorating style is formal. Since many hanging plants cover their containers almost entirely, it is often what you hang it from, rather than the container itself, that is important.

Your choice of container varies enormously, as a wide variety is available in catalogs and from nurseries and garden centers, as well as from private potters and other sources. You can get the regular day pots, often with a saucer attached, to be hung by wires. These would be appropriate in an informal landscape or if you have a greenhouse. Wooden baskets—those of redwood are especially long lasting—are appropriate if you are choosing a plant with light green leaves or white or yellow flowers; they can be less appealing, though, if you have reddish flowers. Today plastic, either solid or woven, is popular, and even if the container is ugly it won't matter if you buy a plant that obscures it. Many gardeners prefer open-work wire baskets. These are among the most inexpensive, and you can line them with sphagnum moss to absorb the moisture. Ceramic containers also are available, and these are apt to be heavy.

The type of plant also will have a bearing on the container. Hanging plants are frequently subject to more air flow than your other plants, and this air will evaporate the water more quickly. You might therefore prefer to keep moisture-loving plants in plastic, metal (not open-work metal), or other less porous containers. Wire, wood, and latticed plastic containers are better for plants that are sensitive to wet feet.

Most baskets come with the wire or cord for hanging, but you have to buy something to hang it from. Usually you will be hanging it from the ceiling, so check your ceiling in advance. Some office ceilings are not true ceilings but subceilings of flimsy acoustrine materials that are not strong enough to hold a basket once it is filled with soil. If your ceiling is sturdy, buy eyebolts or other hardware devices strong enough not to pull out.

You may want to hang your basket from a wall bracket, and in this case be sure the bracket is long enough so that the plant will not touch the wall (or windowpanes). Leaves that touch hard wall surfaces will suffer damage, and cold window panes are especially lethal. The longer your backet is, the sturdier it will have to be at its contact point with the wall or window frame. You should check out in advance the area where you are going to hang a plant from a wall bracket. Some window frames are too narrow to hold a large bracket.

Planting a Basket

1. Line the basket with sphagnum moss that you have soaked in water and press this firmly in a layer against the sides of the basket.

2. Add the soil mixture that is recommended for the plant you've chosen and fill the basket to within an inch of the rim with this mixture.

3. In a small basket, don't plant more than three young plants, widely spaced. Trailing plants, in general, tend to be fast growers and can soon overwhelm a basket. In a larger basket you might risk four widely spaced plants along the perimeter, and either a nontrailing type in the center or a trailing plant you can pinch back to provide full growth, over the top of the container. For plants above eye level, trailing stems alone provide the desired effects; only those at or below eye level need full growth on the top of the container.

Plants to Use

If you are going to hang your basket in a shady location, ferns are good. Among the best are varieties of adiantum, asplenium, davallia, pellaea, and platycerium. Chlorophytum (the spider plant) has very thin, trailing leaves that are also good in baskets. Some of the tougher indoor plants, like philodendrons, aspidistra, and wandering jew (zebrina and tradescantia) provide more choices, as do various types of ivies.

Other foliage plants for baskets include cissus, peperomia, dieffenbachia, and pilea, as well as vines like aeschynanthus.

Should you have a sunny location and want a flowering basket, the lantanas are especially appealing, with lavender, orange, and yellow blooms. Also stunning are the fuchsias. Among the begonias, the angelwings and the pendant tuberous begonias are the best. Many gesneriads are splendid, including achimenes, aeschynanthus, columneas, episcias, hypocyrtas, and kohlerias.

Other flowers you might consider include impatiens, hoya, campanula (star of Bethlehem), clerodendrum (glory bower), and ruellia.

Honeysuckle and asparagus fern are also possibilities.

Because cactus plants are so stiff, they are not good for hanging baskets. Many, too, have low forms best appreciated from above. Only schlumbergera and Christmas cactus have basket possibilities. Succulents, on the other hand often have trailing and drooping forms that make distinctive basket displays quite unlike any other hanging plants. Some aeoniums and crassulas grow in stiff rosettes that have possibilities, and *Oscularia deltoides*, with plump gray leaves and lavender blooms, also can be trained to elegant form. But the most spectacular are the sedums. *S. sieboldi*, with small, round leaves and huge blossom clusters is a favorite, but *S. morganianum* (donkey's tail) may be the most appealing of all. Its tiny, plump leaves are densely packed on stems that will dangle four to six feet below the bakset. Others you may want to try are *Senecio rowleyanus* (string-of-beads), *Ceropegia woodii* (the rosary vine), and epiphyllums.

For an unusual, formal effect, baskets can be planted with species appropriate for topiary use; the foliage can then be sheared to globe or other geometric shapes.

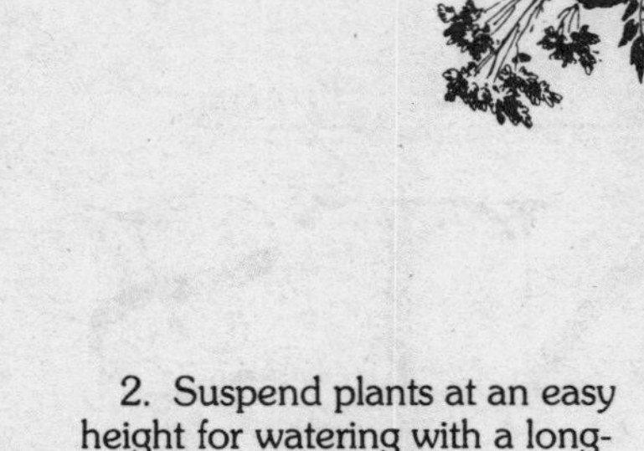

Tips for Hanging Baskets

1. Just as pots should be rotated a quarter turn in the same direction each day to assure the light hits all sides of the plant evenly, most hanging baskets should also be rotated. Unless the light is coming from above (as from a skylight), your plant will grow lopsided if you don't turn it frequently.

2. Suspend plants at an easy height for watering with a long-spouted watering can.

3. If your basket is hanging too high to be easily reached, it helps to hang it from a pulley so you can lower it for care.

4. When plants are above eye level, you may not be able to tell when they need water. If you have lined the basket with sphagnum moss, you can afford to overwater because the moss will absorb the excess moisture.

5. One advantage of hanging baskets is that, unless you place them in stuffy corners, they often get better air circulation than do table and ground-level plants. But beware of drafts to plants susceptible to temperature changes.

6. Depending on your lighting system and the height of your baskets, you may want to spotlight basket plants. If your night lighting is below the level of the plants, the hanging baskets can look forbidding and gloomy and may even cast spooky shadows. Spotlighting them will avoid this. However, incadescent bulbs may be too hot; you can buy cool-beam spotlights to avoid leaf scorching and other problems.

The Lazy Gardener's Special

If you want a foliage plant, philodendron is one of the hardiest, though chlorophytum, wandering jew, and many ferns are also easy to care for.

For a flowering plant, you will probably do best with campanula or clerodendrum.

How to Prolong the Life of GIFT PLANTS

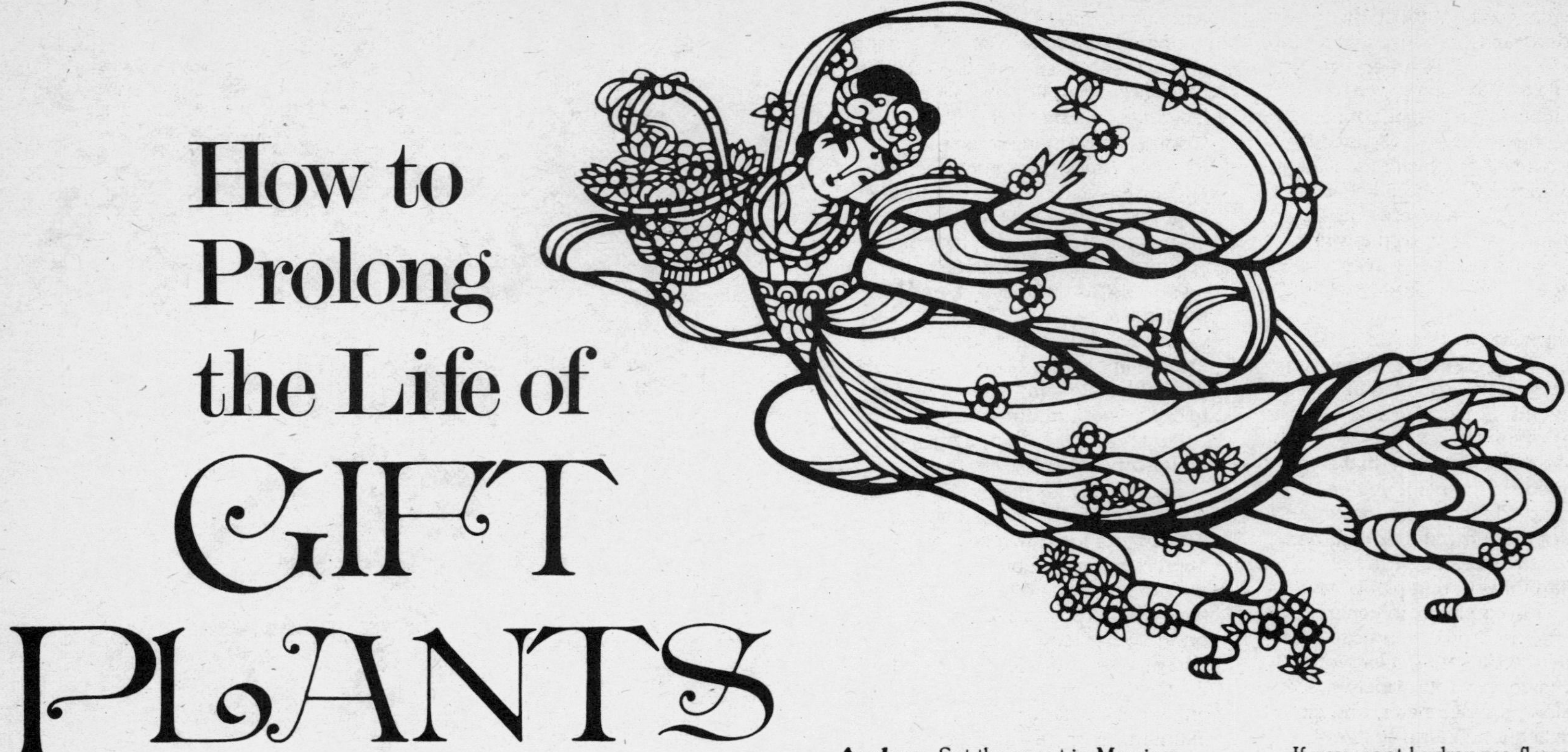

Indoors

Flowering plants from a florist have usually been adapted to greenhouse conditions that you cannot duplicate in your home. With a few exceptions, they will not thrive after their blooms have faded and are best discarded. Here's how to keep them blooming longest:

Azaleas: If you keep azaleas in diffused sunlight (sunlight filtered through a thin curtain or shade), in temperatures of 55° to 60°, and water them frequently, they should remain in bloom from midwinter until about May.

Chrysanthemums: To keep chrysanthemums blooming, place them in full sun where the temperature will remain between 60° to 70°. Water frequently so soil remains moist.

Cinerarias: These plants bloom from midwinter to about May. Place them in full sun, keep the temperature about 50° to 60°, and water frequently to keep soil moist.

Cyclamen: If you keep these at a room temperature of about 70°, the flowers will die after about two weeks. To make the flowers last longer you'll have to find a spot where the temperature will be closer to 50°. The flower shoots and bases of the plant are subject to rot, so be sure the pots are well drained and don't let water stand in the crown of the plant.

Easter lily: These will last several weeks if you saturate the root ball once a day, keep them in moderate light (not full sun), and keep the temperature (even at night) above 55°.

Hydrangeas: Keep these in moderate light and be sure the soil is moist.

Poinsettia: Put these in full sun in a South window for best color, and keep the soil moist. If you keep the plant at a room temperature of 70°, it should stay red for about three weeks. If you can keep the plant at lower temperatures (55° to 60°) the red poinsettias can last up to six weeks and the white up to eight weeks.

Primula: Keep these in full sunlight and keep soil moist.

Senecio: Place in a bright light but not in sun and water heavily. Blooms should last two or three weeks at normal room temperatures up to 70°F, but if you can keep the plant at lower temperatures (60° or even 50°) the flowers will last longer.

Outdoors

Some gift plants can be preserved if you have an outdoor garden. Some of the chrysanthemums are examples, though not all, and you will have to inquire of the florist who delivered it. Those that can usually be set out are:

Azaleas. Set them out in May in a mixture of half acid soil and half peat moss. Prune them lightly in late May or early June.

Before the first frost, repot them and move them to a frost-free coldframe. Unless you give them a period of chilling, they may not bloom again, or may do so irregularly.

Bring them indoors in November and keep them in indirect sunlight at a daytime temperature of 50° to 60° and a nighttime temperature of 40° to 45°. Water frequently, and sponge dust off the leaves from time to time. They should bloom six to ten weeks after you've brought them indoors.

Hydrangeas. After the plant has bloomed, cut it back to several internodes and repot it in regular potting soil.

In summer, place the plant in moderate shade outdoors and water frequently. When it becomes dormant, move it to a frost-free coldframe to prevent the flower buds from being killed by frost.

In January, bring the plant indoors and repot it. Grow for several weeks at 55° and then raise the temperature to 60° to 65°. The plants should bloom about three months after you have brought them indoors.

If you want hydrangea flowers to be blue, water the plant with a solution of one pound of aluminum sulfate in five gallons of water. Drench the soil thoroughly, and fertilize the plant lightly.

If you want pink blossoms, use a high-phosphate fertilizer (such as 15-30-15) in the water you use for watering.

Poinsettia. After the bracts have fallen, should be placed in subdued daylight at a daytime temperature of 50° to 60° (40° to 45° at night). Water sparingly. The plant will become dormant.

In April or May, cut the plant down to within six inches of the pot. Repot it in regular potting mix. Water frequently to keep the soil evenly moist. New shoots will begin to emerge. Cut these off when they are large enough to handle and root them. When they root, pot them in regular potting mix.

Before the first frost move all the plants—the original and the rooted cuttings—indoors to a sunny window. Starting the first of October, keep them at a nighttime temperature of 60° and protect them from artificial light at night. The plants should be brightly colored by Christmas.

How to Cut Garden Flowers
When you bring garden flowers into the house with the intention of keeping them fresh for several days, the time of day they are gathered is important. You have two choices: early morning and evening. The end of the day is actually better because that is when the food supply that has built up in the flowers during the day is at its peak.

Flowers last longest when cut just on the verge of maturity, that is, in the advanced-bud or early-bloom stage. Those that are cut while the buds are new produce blooms that do not last, and completely mature flowers have a short life span away from the garden.

Flowers should be cut from the plant, not ripped away. To do so, use a sharp knife or a pair of garden shears that makes a good clean cut. Stems cut just above a node will benefit the plant that remains. Also, the less handling the better, and the less time the severed stems are exposed to the air, the longer the flowers will last. Many gardeners plunge the stems of the flowers they are cutting right into a container of water the moment they are cut.

Conditioning
Optimally, fresh cut flowers meant to stay alive should undergo a process of conditioning before being placed on display. This is accomplished by leaving the container of flowers in a cool, dark room for at least eight hours or overnight. They should be away from sunlight, heating sources, and drafts, yet the air in the room should circulate freely. If your storage place is too dry, spray the room with a fine mist from your plant sprayer. This creates a kind of artificial dew that will settle on the flowers and leaves, inhibiting moisture loss.

Working with Flowers
Handle flowers gently, by their stems, and lay them down with great care. At the work table as you prepare to place flowers in a vase, align the individual flowers so that their heads extend over the edge of the table while you recut the stems in order to increase their ability to take up water. This recutting should be done with a sharp knife, not scissors, and the cut should be made at a slant about an inch above the end. Woody stems should be split four inches or more from the bottoms. Flowers with hollow stems should be recut under water to prevent air from interfering with their absorption of water.

Next, remove any bottom foliage as well as all foliage not necessary for decoration, and arrange the flowers in a vase of fresh tepid water to which has been added one of the commercially available nutrients for cut flowers or use the homemade recipe below. (When using such a nutrient, follow package directions religiously—a too-strong solution will finish off your bouquet in short order.) Aspirin, despite folk wisdom in its favor, does nothing to preserve flowers.

Once in a vase, cut flowers continue to need a bit of care to remain fresh. In the first place, they will not do well when set directly in sunlight or near working heaters. Secondly, the same water after several days may be full of bacteria, so fresh water on a daily basis will keep your flowers hardy longer. When changing water, if you take a few additional minutes to recut the ends of each flower stalk, the life of your bouquet will be further lengthened.

Factors that Affect Longevity
Good air circulation in the room where flower arrangements are kept is not only desirable but also necessary. The foliage and flowers of cut flowers give off minute amounts of ethylene gas, the same gas that produce distributors use to ripen fruit artificially. An airy, but not drafty, atmosphere dispells any ethylene.

Hot, dry air makes cut flowers work harder. It causes them to give off a lot of water through their petals and leaves and, to compensate, draw up more water through their stems. Flower arrangements that must endure high heat and low humidity will last longer when allowed to recuperate in a cooler room or if placed on the floor during the night.

The container influences the life span of cut flowers. Containers made of materials that rust should be avoided. Vases should be washed thoroughly after use.

Home refrigeration is harmful to cut flowers.

Charcoal in the flower container helps to keep the water sweet. The charcoal sold in bags in garden-supply stores is already clean. Wash off dust and loose fragments from charcoal chunks meant for barbecues. Don't use any barbecue charcoal impregnated with lighting fluid.

Special Care Techniques
Branches. Split long stem end three to four inches and short stems one to two inches. Discard flowers and foliage that will be in water (including the water in the conditioning container), and provide conditioning if the branches are freshly cut. This technique applies to crab apple, wisteria, flowering quince, forsythia, lilac, and perennial chrysanthemums.
Forcing branches to flower. You can have an indoor taste of the coming season by forcing cuttings from spring-blooming bushes to flower indoors. Take the cuttings six to eight weeks before outdoor flowering. Split the ends of the branches three to four inches and place them in containers of cool water with a few pieces of charcoal in it. Change the water every five to eight days, cutting off an inch of each branch end with each change. Place the arrangement away from direct sunlight until flowers appear, at which time direct sunlight will help produce bright, true colors. Spray the arrangement daily with a fine mist. (To hasten flowering, place the cuttings in very warm water once a day and allow the water to cool. To slow the blooming process down, keep the arrangement in a dimly lit spot.)

Bulbs (general). When cutting flowers from bulbs in the garden, leave as much foliage as possible on the bulb. The foliage serves to manufacture nourishment in the bulb for the coming year's blooms. Condition the flowers with cold water, and before arranging the flowers cut the stems diagonally with a sharp knife. Unless you need the thick white section at the base of the stem for height in your bouquet, remove it. If you keep it, make a vertical cut through its entire length.
Hairy stems. Heliotrope, calendulas, and some varieties of geraniums should be conditioned in very warm water, 80-100°F.
Hollow stems. When cutting hollyhocks and hollow-stemmed dahlias and campanulas, place the stems in water only as warm as body temperature. After allowing the water to cool, add cold water and give the bouquet the necessary conditioning before arranging them in a vase.
Stems with milky, yellow, or colorless fluid. If left untreated, the stems will clog with liquid and be unable to draw up nourishment. To keep water uptake working, special preconditioning is necessary. Split the stems 1 to 1½ inches and hold the split ends of each in a candle flame for 15 seconds. If you need to recut, the newly split ends will require the same searing treatment.
Store-bought flowers. These flowers have already been conditioned but will benefit from two to three hours of reconditioning in order to regain moisture lost while the stems were exposed to the air. Before the conditioning, however, remove any damaged flowers and foliage and cut the stem ends at a slant with a sharp knife.

Recipe for Making Cut Flowers Last

Combine one quart of water with:
1 teaspoon of vinegar
2 tablespoons of sugar

Preserving Flowers

Preserving the beauty of flowers goes back at least to the Egyptians, who kept pots of flower petals around their homes for fragrance. Europeans of the Middle Ages carried small cloth pouches of flower petals—to press to their noses and mouths when passing through malodorous parts of town. In the 1800s and 1900s, dried flowers were preserved whole and in bouquets for ornament. Today, chemicals have vastly improved the quality and longevity of preserved flowers.

There are three standard methods of drying flowers: hanging, pressing, and with desiccants (or drying agents). The method you choose depends on the flower, and how you plan to use the finished product.

Flowers should be cut in late morning or early afternoon, when blooms are fully opened and all dew has dried. Young, half-open blooms usually work better, since they tend to open fully as they dry. Avoid damaged or diseased plants. Strip all leaves and foliage from the stems.

Hang-drying. Tie bunches of flowers together at the stem bases with string, wire, or rubber bands, and hang them upside down in a dry (preferably dark) place. Suspend individually from rafters, or in groups of three to four from coat hangers. Flower bunches should not touch each other. Normally flowers will dry within ten days to two weeks. If the weather is humid, a small fan helps speed up the process.

Hang-dried flowers can retain their color and form for up to, and sometimes more than, a year. Tie them in simple bouquets with pretty ribbon, or make elaborate vase arrangements.

Although nearly all flowers can be successfully hang-dried, those especially adapted to hang drying are known as everlasting flowers, or simply, everlastings. These have dry flower petals while living, so that wilting is kept to a minimum when they are dried. Everlastings are usually small and give arrangements a lacy look. Everlastings include strawflowers, statice, globe amaranth, thistle, and rodanthe.

Drying Flowers with Desiccants. Desiccants are dry granular substances that slowly absorb the moisture from flowers to the point of total dehydration. Desiccants are the most effective means of drying flowers, since they allow flowers to retain most of their natural color and form. Common, easy-to-use desiccants are sand, silica gel, and borax.

Silica gel is the best desiccant. It looks like fine white sand, but contains blue grains that turn pink as the silica absorbs moisture. Silica gel can be dried out in a low oven and reused over and over. Just remember to store it in airtight containers when not in use, since it absorbs the air's moisture. If you use sand, it should be clean and fine; coarse or pebbly sand will damage flowers; dirty sand will render flowers dirty. Borax is as good a desiccant as sand but cannot be reused; mix two parts borax with ten parts common cornmeal.

A large, flat box is the best container for desiccant flower drying. It must be long enough for the flower and its stem, and deep enough for a base and a top layer of desiccant. A shoebox is fine for small flowers. On a one- to two-inch layer of desiccant, arrange your flowers so that blooms are not touching. Then cover them with desiccant. Place the box in a warm dry area. Cover the box tightly if you use silica gel. After about ten days, your flowers should be crisp or slightly brittle. Carefully remove one flower at a time and dust it off with a soft paintbrush.

Certain flowers dry better with their blossoms face up—camellias, columbines, pansies, peonies, irises, daffodils, tulips, and roses. Cut the stem to within one or two inches of the bloom. Place stems straight into the desiccant, so that the flower rests on the surface. Then sprinkle desiccant lightly over the flowers, making sure that it gets between each and every petal, until the flower is covered. With some heavy-headed flowers (tulip, calendula, and rose), florist's wire must be substituted for the stem before drying.

Flowers with dense, heavy petals dry better when placed in the desiccant face down—dahlias, zinnias, daisies, calendulas, rudbeckias, and hydrangeas. If long stems are desired, a deep box is necessary. Place flower face down on desiccant base and sprinkle with desiccant until flower and stem are covered.

Flowering herbs make excellent additions to dried flower collections. Many of them have a lacy appearance, to complement heavier dried flowers in mixed arrangements, and some retain fragrance. Herbs are best dried by the desiccant method.

Pressed Flowers. Press flowers as soon as possible after picking. Place them in a phone book or magazine until you can transfer them to a flower press. Actually, you can press flowers in a book or magazine, but the most effective way is a sandwich arrangement of wooden boards, corrugated cardboard, blotting paper and newspaper. You can buy flower presses. To make your own, you need two 12″ × 15″ × ¾″ pieces of plywood, two or four pieces of corrugated cardboard, two or four pieces of blotting paper, and some newspaper.

Place one of the plywood boards on a table. On top of the board put a piece of cardboard, then a piece of blotting paper, followed by a piece of newspaper. On this base, carefully arrange the flowers. Bend or shape flowers into artistic forms, or however you wish them to appear when dry. Then repeat the process in reverse order, putting newspaper, blotter, cardboard, and plywood on top of the flowers. Pressure must be applied, either by C-clamps, rope tied around boards, long bolts or simply heavy weights like bricks or books. Place the press in a warm, dry, preferably dark location for about ten days. Once dried, flowers can be stored in books, envelopes, between newspaper, or framed. Colors will remain more vivid if flowers are kept away from direct sunlight.

Potpourris

Potpourris are containers—pots, jars, vases—filled with dried flower petals, herbs and spices, scented oils, and scent fixatives. They give off a pleasant natural fragrance in rooms and closets. Nearly any flower will do. Dry the petals on a piece of cardboard in a dark place until they are crackly, or about ten days. Then combine dried petals with other potpourri ingredients (as shown in recipes below) in a tightly sealed plastic bag for four to five weeks, giving bag a daily shaking. Transfer the mixture to a decorative jar or vase. Seal potpourri containers when not in use. If potpourris begin to lose their scent, add a few drops of scented oil and perhaps some more fixative.

Rose Potpourris
5 cups dried rose petals
2½ cups dried rose leaves
⅜ cup orrisroot powder
1½ tablespoons ground cloves
2 drops oil of roses

Lavender Potpourris
4 cups dried lavender flowers
2 tablespoons dried lemon peel
4 tablespoons dried rosemary
8 tablespoons orrisroot powder
1 teaspoon benzoic acid powder
10 drops oil of lavender

Mixed-Flower Potpourris
2 cups dried rose petals
2 cups dried zinnia petals
2 teaspoons dried lemon peel
4 drops oil of potpourris

Sachets

Sachets are small cloth pouches filled with aromatic flower petals, herbs, and spices. They are commonly tucked into dresser drawers and closets, under bed pillows, and into suitcases, purses, or linen cupboards. Sewn into fine casings, sachets make excellent gifts.

When following sachet recipes (below), make sure all ingredients are equally crushed to a small size. Toss or stir ingredients until thoroughly mixed.

Rose Sachet
3 cups dried rose petals
½ cup dried rose leaves
2 cups vetiver or 3 ounces orrisroot
4 tablespoons sandalwood

Rose-Lavender Sachet
2 cups dried rose petals
4 tablespoons lavender petals
½ teaspoon dried lemon peel
10 cloves (crushed)

Flowering Herb Sachet
4 tablespoons dried lavender petals
2 tablespoons dried marjoram leaves or petals
2 tablespoons dried orange mint leaves
4 tablespoons dried rose petals
1 tablespoon dried rosemary flowers
1 tablespoon thyme petals and/or leaves
4 tablespoons vetiver or orrisroot

Insect Repellent Sachet
4 tablespoons dried santolina flowers
2 tablespoons wormwood petals
2 tablespoons pyrethrum
4 tablespoons tansy
4 tablespoons pennyroyal flowers
4 tablespoons dried lavender petals
2 tablespoons clary sage flowers

Pomanders

A pomander is either an orange, lemon, lime, or apple that has been studded with cloves and dried. Pomanders originated in much the same way as sachets, during the Middle Ages as means of masking bad odors and preventing diseases. They were worn on a string around the neck. These days, pomanders are placed in kitchens, bathrooms, cupboards, closets, and drawers for their attractive scent, as well as for their powers as insect repellents.

Choose a fresh, healthy lime, lemon, orange, or apple (apples are less desirable). Press dried cloves into the fruit one-quarter inch from center of clove to center of clove. Cloves should not be touching one another, nor should they be pressed in so close together that the fruit skin splits. Hang pomanders in a warm, dry place until all the fruit's moisture has evaporated. It will be about three-quarters its normal size, and the cloves will be closely crowded together. You can then dust the pomander with orrisroot powder and add some essential oil for heightened fragrance.

Rose Beads

Rose beads are made by stewing fresh rose petals into a thick mush that can be formed into beads. Start with five cups of fresh rose petals in an iron saucepan. Barely cover petals with water and boil uncovered for two hours, stirring occasionally. Let cool. Repeat until mixture is thick enough to be kneaded into small beads about ⅜″ in diameter. Pierce beads with pin or needle when they are not yet completely dry. Then string on wire or heavy thread and suspend until completely dry. Twist beads on wire once a day while drying so they don't stick. Heighten fragrance by storing beads in a tightly sealed jar with a cotton ball dipped in rose water. Finished beads can be strung intermittently with ceramic beads or by themselves.

7

Greenhouse Gardening

Greenhouse Beginnings

The first glimmering of greenhouse culture in England and France seems to have originated with a yearning for oranges. Records from 1561 reveal that oranges, lemons, and possibly pomegranates were imported to England from France for year-round culture. The French seller instructed that in warm weather the trees be grown outdoors, and then they should be potted and brought indoors for shelter in winter. Mansions began to incorporate an "orange court" or "orangerie," a long hall lined with large windows where citrus trees were kept in winter, warmed with stoves and pans of charcoal.

One gardening manual printed in 1660—*Garden of Eden* by Sir Hugh Platt—suggested that citrus trees be planted outdoors against a concave-shaped wall, lined with lead or tin for reflection, and warmed by fires. Platt also suggested growing delicate plants indoors in winter, forcing carnations and other flowers into early bloom by keeping them near household fires, and even that "brewers, diers, soap boilers or refiners of sugar, who have continual fire," might convey the "heat of steam" of their fires into an adjoining room to culture fruit trees in winter.

Greenhouse gardening did not come into vogue in England, however, until the eighteenth century, and then the impetus was provided by foreign travel. Englishmen were then venturing to America, the Far East, the Near East, and other areas where they encountered exotic new plants in areas with climate more temperate than back home. The desire to grow these new-found treasures in their own gardens led the English to extraordinary measures to provide the proper temperature.

One nobleman, who wanted to force grapes, trained the vines to walls then built ovens behind the walls. He kept these ovens going from January until the weather warmed up to a temperature the grapes could tolerate. In addition, while the grapes were in danger from frost, he is said to have protected the vines "with glasses."

Another Englishman invented a different device for grapes. He also trained them to a wall, but his wall was hollow. Within the wall were stoves, openings through which to shovel coals, and chimneys.

Still another inventor forced apricots and cherries by nailing the trees to a screen of boards. The trees faced south and were protected with glass. Behind the boards he provided a hot bed.

When one gardener raised a pineapple, which he presented to Charles II, his countrymen went crazy to duplicate his feat. After fifty years of trial and error with early greenhouse techniques, three books devoted entirely to instructions on cultivating pineapples were published in the late eighteenth century.

But it was really vegetables that provided the greatest motivation for greenhouses. Out-of-season southern vegetables, desired especially for festive occasions, had to be imported and were expensive. By 1717 a treatise on forcing melons and cucumbers, by using various glasses and frames, was published. One gardener managed to force cucumbers in winter in 1721, and presented two of them to George I on New Year's Day. Large estates began to force salad greens, melons, asparagus, cauliflower, herbs, and berries. Greenhouse nurserymen came into being to grow such crops, as well as fruit, on a commercial basis. Apparently these growers were not always successful, for one clergyman complained that many nurserymen cheated and sold inferior fruit or substituted a "dry, inspid" nectarine when he had ordered a pear.

Occasionally decorative plants were also cultured in makeshift greenhouses. In 1729, one man with an aloe that had grown twenty feet high—"the like whereof has never been seen in England before"—was undeterred by the approach of winter. He built a huge structure of wood and glass around it that could be raised higher, if necessary, to accommodate the "unexpected growth of this famous plant." Inside he arranged a store with pipes that would conduct heat all around the plant. Unfortunately, despite all this energy and good will, the aloe died.

By 1748, however, homemade greenhouses were popular in London. The usual technique was to make a mound of soil in which to put the plants. The mound was sloped toward the sun and surrounded by frames on which glass could be laid. The frames were then covered with matting and four inches of straw that could be removed when the sun was high. Among the vegetables grown this way were cauliflower, asparagus, radishes, and salad greens.

Hobby Greenhouses

What Kind of Greenhouse?
When it comes to choosing the right type of greenhouse, even people with money to burn and acres of property need to spend some time and thought before making a decision. Even when money and space are unlimited, a scaled-down version of the Crystal Palace may not be an appropriate structure for you.
Prefab or one of a kind? A custom-designed and custom-built greenhouse is the most expensive way to go. If you are a skilled carpenter or are willing to hire one, you probably can find a suitable greenhouse plan for free or for a few dollars by writing to the agricultural engineering department of an agricultural college or to one of the sources listed below. This is a less expensive way of extending your garden, but you are usually limited to a structure made of wood. To be sure that you have picked the right design, read up on the subject and, if possible, consult with a greenhouse manufacturer.

When selecting wood for the frame of your greenhouse, be on the safe side and avoid lumber treated with preservatives such as creosote and pentachlorophenol as well as arsenical preparations marketed under the trade names of Osmose, Greensalt, Koppers, Celcure, and Wolman. According to the Environmental Protection Agency, working with wood treated with these substances is dangerous. In addition, creosote and pentachlorophenol (usually called "penta") give off fumes for many years.

Prefabricated greenhouses, which come in many sizes and shapes, are engineered to grow plants, and they are less expensive than custom-designed structures. Greenhouse kits, however, can be nerve-wracking to assemble, and you may still have to do the glazing on your own. Prefabricated greenhouses also need foundations, so make room in your budget and schedule for this important extra.

Some kits are advertised as complete packages including ventilating and heating equipment. Resist the temptation to buy blindly until you have determined that you are actually saving money. No-frills kits are the least expensive, but they can turn out to be budget-busters by the time you buy needed accessories.
Size. When it comes to "druthers," most greenhouse gardeners wish they had more room. Larger greenhouses, though initially more costly, are more economical to operate because they cost less per square foot. The biggest equipment expenses you face are ventilating and heating systems, and this cost is not that much greater in larger greenhouses.

Large attached greenhouses become, in effect, an extra room, and many people use them as extra living space as well as for growing plants. Even unheated, attached greenhouses act as buffers between cold outdoor temperatures and heated interiors. (At night, heat loss can be prevented with curtains.) Larger greenhouses can actually conserve a significant amount of heat, particularly when designed as solar collectors. Because they are energy savers, solar greenhouses earn tax credit with the IRS.
Coverings. Until the introduction of plastic and fiberglass following World War II, glass was the only material that could transmit and contain solar heat inside a greenhouse. Glass is long-lasting, transparent, scratch-resistant, and inexpensive. Glass tends to lose heat easily at night through leaks and through the glass itself, which is a good heat conductor, but double glazing can take care of that problem. Thermopane glass is a fairly expensive double-glazing system. A cheaper way to reduce winter heat loss by a minimum of 20% is to "glaze" the inside of a greenhouse by stapling polyethelene film to the wooden frames.

One of the problems in using glass is its breakability, but this is only a consideration if you live in an area where there are violent hail storms. Breakage can be prevented by covering the greenhouse with wire mesh of the proper gauge. Another disadvantage of glass is the difficulty unskilled people have in working with it.

Other coverings for greenhouses are clear, rigid plastics, fiberglass, and plastic film.

Clear, rigid plastic generally transmits 80% of solar radiation compared to glass, which transmits 90%. Rigid plastics are more expensive than glass and, as anyone who has eyeglasses with plastic lenses knows, they scratch easily. They are very strong, however, and can bend.

Fiberglass differs from glass and rigid plastic in that it is translucent, although it diffuses more light and transmits as much or more solar radiation than glass. Your plants will do well enclosed in a fiberglass-covered greenhouse, but you may regret the feeling of being cut off visually from the outdoors. Fiberglass is easier to work with than plastic and glass and comes in corrugated and flat sheets.

Plastic films are easy to use. To fasten them to a wooden frame, all you need is a staple gun. If your frame is metal, you can purchase systems of affixing plastic films to them. Not all plastic films are the same, though. For example, polyethelene is only good for temporary greenhouses. Vinyl film, which lends itself to heat sealing, can be used in double layers.

If the idea of having a greenhouse appeals to you, study advertisements in gardening publications and write for catalogs from several suppliers. Think hard about the type of covering you buy. If you live in a cold climate, remember that single-pane glass is the least heat-efficient and needs the addition of polyethelene inside to keep heat inside. Double-layered polyethelene coverings tend to be the least expensive covering initially.

Hot greenhouses are rare not only because of high fuel prices, but also because their usefulness is limited to propagating and growing tropical plants. If you have a warm or cool greenhouse, you can easily have the benefits of a hothouse by installing a heated propagating case for starting seedlings.

If you are torn between a cool greenhouse for forcing bulbs and a warm one for growing orchids, conquer the dilemma by installing a glass partition and heating a part of the structure for tropical and flowering varieties.

If you must install a heater, look for a thermostatically controlled system of greenhouse heating that is clean and inexpensive. Soil-warming cables and propagating mats are practical ways of warming seed flats. By covering flats with a plastic sheet, you create a minihothouse within your greenhouse.

During the first winter, use minimum-maximum thermometer in different places around the greenhouse, and soil thermometers to keep watch on the temperature situation. Undoubtedly, you will discover cool spots and need either to rearrange your plants or redirect the heat. If you live in snow country, a temperature alarm set at the lowest safe temperature will warm you before your plants freeze.

Shade. Keeping plants from cooking under the summer sun can be a problem. The natural way of shading greenhouses is to plant deciduous trees in the way of the sun or to train vines up a trellis outside the greenhouse. You can also paint the greenhouse covering with special shading compounds or install blinds that can be rolled up and down as necessary.

Ventilation. Plants need circulating air as well as air of a certain temperature, and modern greenhouses are constructed to meet those needs. An inexpensive method of ventilating a greenhouse is a wall-mounted exhaust fan. Many prefabricated models are equipped with louvered doors for horizontal ventilation. The windows can be opened and closed with a thermostatically controlled electric motor. (Without a screen door, louvers admit insects along with the cool air. In winter, although closed as tightly as possible, they let in some cold air.)

Most free-standing structures have roof vents, which are really windows that open along the central ridge of the greenhouse. These cool by convection—hot air rises and moves out the vents. These also operate automatically with thermostatic controls. Manual ventilation is impossible and impractical during spring and fall when the outside temperature can fluctuate from hour to hour.

Humidity and watering systems. Greenhouse humidity should be maintained between 50 and 70%. The best way to maintain this level of humidity is to buy a greenhouse humidifier and connect it to a humidistat (a device to measure humidity) to govern it automatically. Manual humidifying is done by wetting down the walkways.

Watering. Watering your plants is another way to increase humidity. If you use a fine-spray watering can or hose, some of the small droplets will get into the air. The plants themselves also will exude moisture through transpiration. (Wet foliage in a greenhouse creates conditions for disease transmission.)

Greenhouse plant populations invariably multiply to overflowing, and pretty soon watering can become an enormous chore. To cut down on this work, many gardeners rely on automatic watering systems. Wick watering is the least complicated and least expensive method of automatic watering. Automated watering systems also are available.

Free-standing greenhouses. The essential feature of a free-standing greenhouse is its independence from other buildings. Beyond that, its design can vary from the rectangular glass-to-ground shed containing benches of plants to a lightweight, mobile quonset model that arches on aluminum ribs over a planting area in the ground.

Moveable greenhouses are the exception. Most greenhouses are permanent or semipermanent structures that require ventilating and heating systems. With the development of plastic films to replace glass as greenhouse covers, it is no longer necessary to hire an architect and spend a fortune to have a greenhouse.

Lean-to greenhouses. There are several advantages to an attached lean-to greenhouse. It enables you to have your garden right in the house. Because you only have to erect three walls, it is easier to install or build. As a permanent part of the house, it has a supply of electricity, water, and heat. With an outside door as well a a door to the house, an attached greenhouse is an extension of both house and garden.

Climate Control in Greenhouses

After selecting the type of greenhouse appropriate to your needs, it is time to think of some technical aspects of operating it: temperature, heat, ventilation, shade, light, water. By reading up on what it takes to have a successful greenhouse garden, you will be able to pick the right equipment from the slew of accessories that your greenhouse manufacturer will surely attempt to sell you. Accessories and equipment for climate control and watering can end up costing more than the structure itself.

Hot, warm, or cool? Plants vary greatly in their temperature needs. Many large botanical gardens have two greenhouses with noticeably different climates; for instance, warm and humid for tropical plants, cool and on the dry side for cacti. Hobby greenhouses are usually operated in one of three general ranges:

Cool greenhouse: 40–50°F
Warm greenhouse: 55–60°F
Hot greenhouse: 65–70°F

A cool greenhouse is heated only to prevent frost damage. It is well suited to growing most vegetables and houseplants, forcing spring bulbs, and wintering over cacti and other plants requiring a cool winter dormancy period to flower in spring or summer.

A warm greenhouse, which stays around 50°F, is heated more often than a cool greenhouse and can be expensive to operate. It provides a warm winter environment for most plants, including tomatoes and flowering varieties like geraniums and orchids.

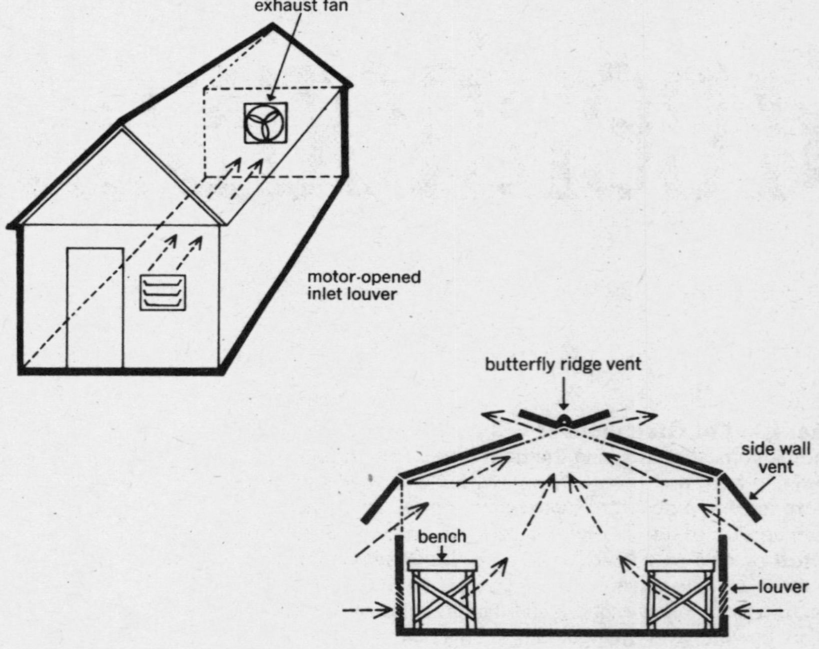

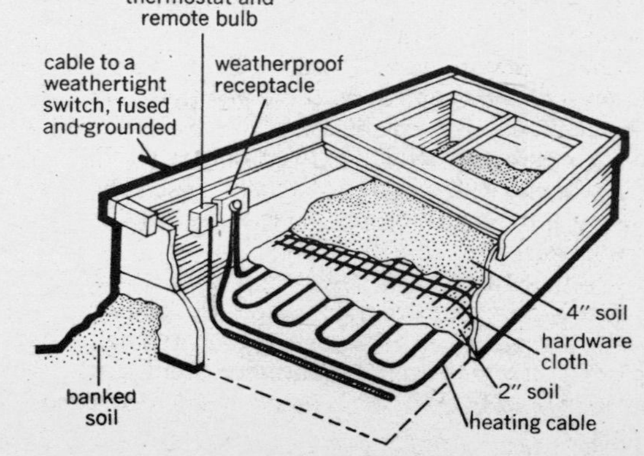

Choosing a Site

Orientation. Whether you want to build an attached lean-to greenhouse, or a free-standing greenhouse, you will want to situate your greenhouse where it will receive the maximum amount of light. With a free-standing, glass-to-ground structure, you are ahead of the game because light pours in from all sides. Still, orientation is of some importance. In northern latitudes especially, an east-west orientation results in higher overall temperature and light levels than does a north-south orientation.

Lean-to greenhouses do best with a south or southeast exposure; southwest exposure gets so much afternoon sun that they overheat. If you have only the possibility of a northern exposure, however, you can still grow many beautiful foliage plants as well as orchids, tuberous begonias, African violets, and other gesneriads.

Free-standing solar greenhouses depend on the sun for heat as well as illumination. They can be used throughout severe winters when they have a due-south exposure or an exposure slightly west of south (better for starting seedlings in spring), along with double glazing, sufficient insulation, and a solar-heat storage system.

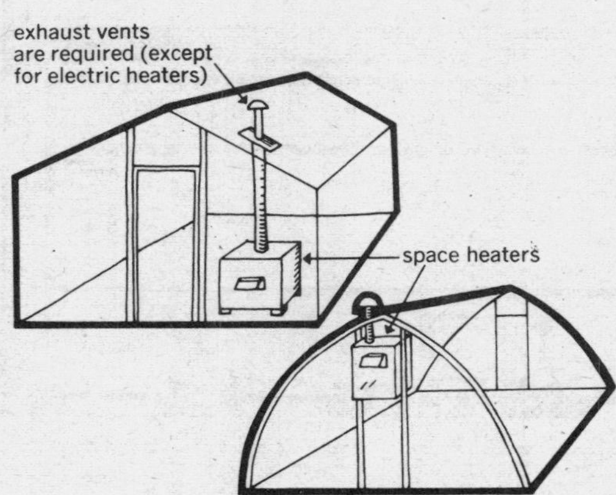

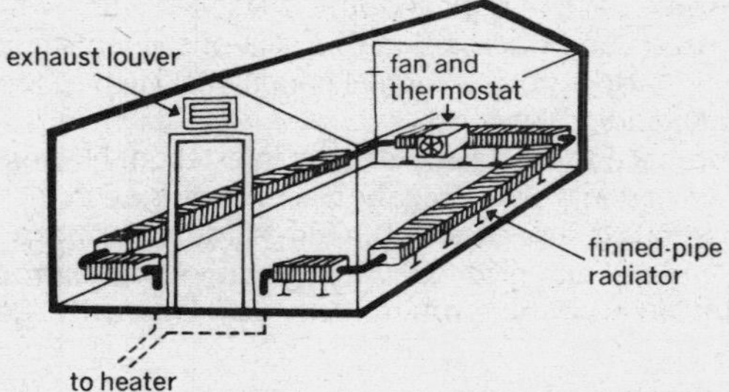

Some heating systems for greenhouses.

—Interior of Fernery.

Protection. In summer, most greenhouses benefit from partial shading to prevent overheating. Excellent for this purpose are deciduous trees, which obligingly shed their leaves just when extra light is wanted. When choosing a greenhouse sight, the potential absence of sun in winter is an important factor. Be sure that there are no fences, buildings, or evergreens closely to the south, lest they cast shadows when the sun is low on the horizon.

During the cold months, freestanding greenhouses also need protection from frigid winds, unless you are prepared to double your heating bills or abandon the greenhouse until spring. The best windbreaks—hedges and trees—let the wind through after absorbing its force.

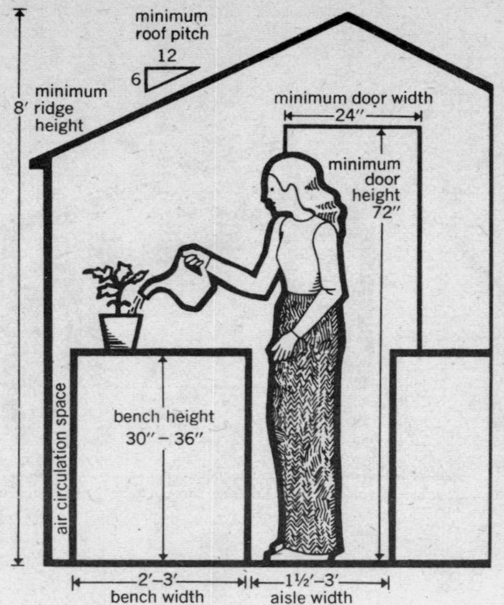

Drainage and water. Drainage of rainwater and groundwater is an important consideration when you are building a greenhouse. Even if you have the foresight to collect rainwater in a barrel (it's better for plants than chlorinated city water), you will also need a supply of water nearby. Don't set the greenhouse up at the bottom of a slope so that it gets a good sloshing during every heavy rainfall.

Greenhouse Horticulture

Soil. The ideal greenhouse soil contains one-fourth organic matter by volume. There are several very practical reasons for a high organic content. Because greenhouse soils are watered with a hose, unless they are of light texture, they tend to compact and restrict the amount of oxygen available to the roots of the plants you are growing. Lots of organic material helps soils resist compacting while increasing their water-holding capacity. Organic content in soil, as it decays, also creates conditions that provide nutrients to plants. And the dark, rich color warms up easily in sunlight.

Ordinary unimproved garden soil may not be suitable for your greenhouse any more than it is the best medium for an outdoor garden. It is unusual to find the necessary amount of organic matter in soil dug up from the backyard.

Keeping it fertile. Start with a good soil mixture. Greenhouse soils are usually combinations of organic matter (peat moss, compost, leafmold), field soil, and sand (perlite and vermiculite are also good). As with garden soil, the heavier the soil, the more organic matter should be added. Keep in mind that greenhouse soil should be lighter than garden soil.

If your base soil contains a lot of clay, mix in two parts organic matter and two parts sand for every one part soil. Mix soil that is already on the sandy side with an equal part of organic material. A loam that could do with better drainage should be mixed with one part organic matter and one part sand.

Greenhouse plants need periodic fertilizing. Beds on the ground can be improved with a green manure and fresh organic matter that is turned under. Water-soluble chemical fertilizers, fish emulsion, liquid seaweed, and manure tea also help keep up nutrient levels.

Soil pasteurization. Pasteurized soil is not always necessary. Any batch of soil from the garden, however, should go back to the garden after a year's service. Annual soil changes prevent soil diseases and fertilizer salts from building up. If you do plant seedlings in garden soil, protect them from damping-off fungus by treating the soil with Captan, an organic fungicide.

The best soil for growing seedlings is one that is as free as possible from pathogenic bacteria and insects. Pasteurization destroys most harmful organisms while leaving beneficial bacteria alive. You can buy pasteurized soil—it's incorrectly called "sterile soil" (sterilization kills even the good bacteria)—or you can prepare your own in small batches in the oven. To make pasteurized soil, spread three or four inches of soil in a baking pan or on a cookie sheet, cover it with foil, and "cook" it until the oven temperature reaches 180°F. Then turn the oven off and wait thirty minutes.

Border culture and crop rotation. Greenhouse gardeners often grow plants with extensive root systems directly in the ground. Known as "border culture," this is an excellent way to have fresh tomatoes, melons, and eggplants out of season if you have a warm greenhouse. As in an outdoor garden, however, in-

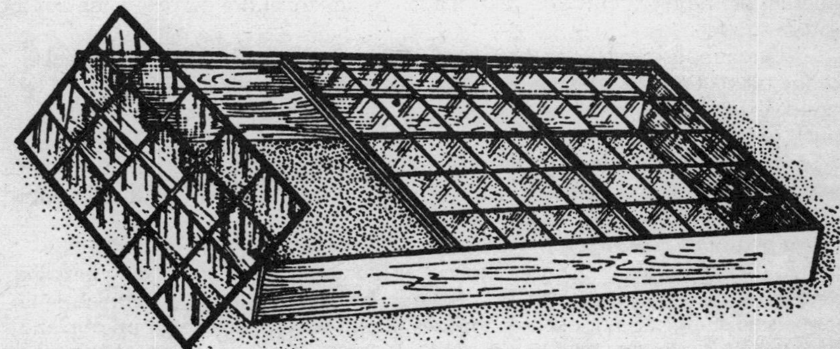

This shows the construction of an outdoor cold frame. A hotbed is built in the same way, except that for the hotbed a pit and manure are required.

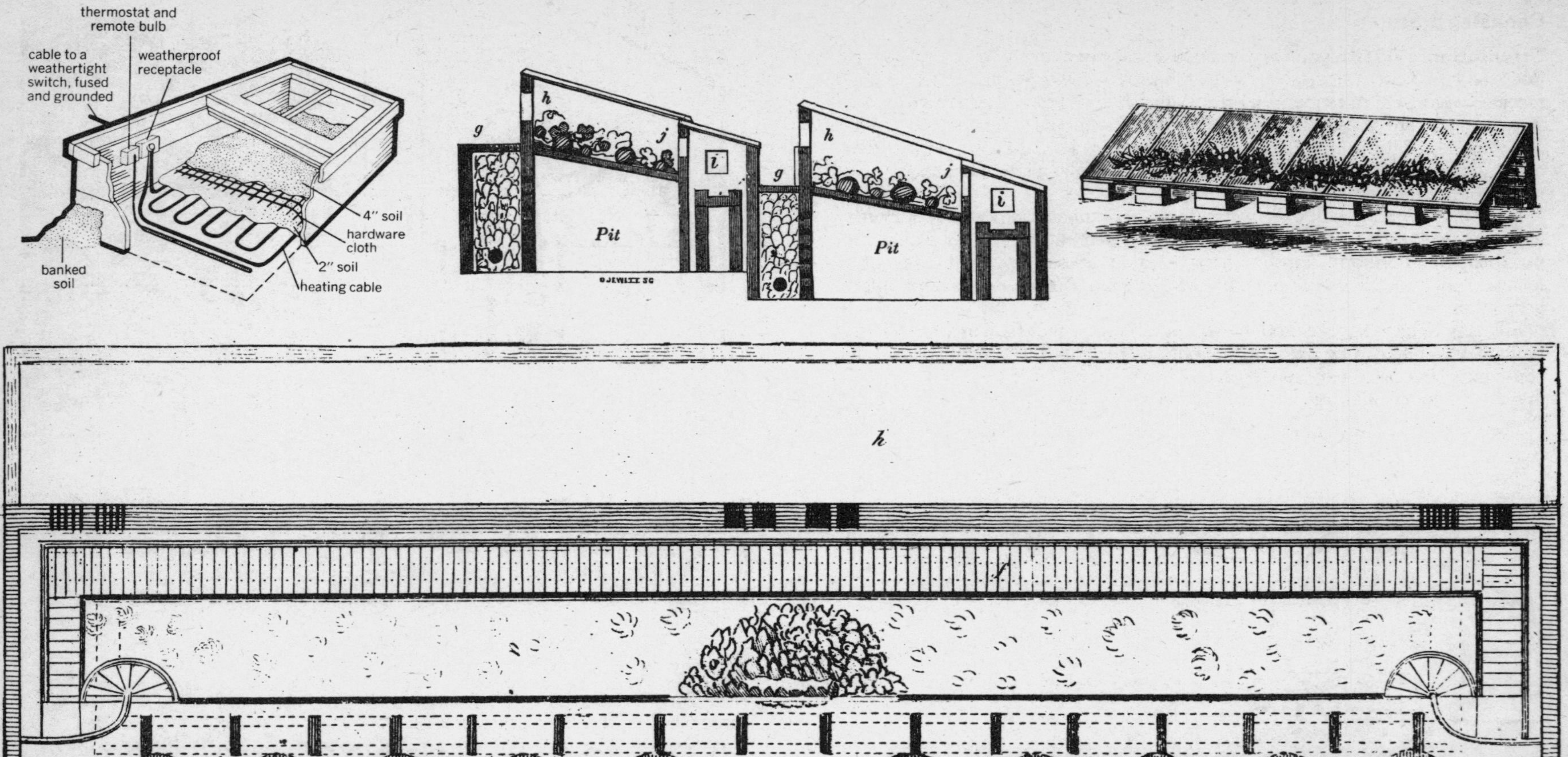

sects and disease spores build up when the same plants are grown in the same soil. A soil change would seem to be the solution, yet the roots of these large vegetables grow down very deeply and soil renewal is impractical in most instances.

Crop rotation of related plants on a three- or four-year schedule keeps soil-borne diseases and pests to a minimum as long as the border soil is maintained in good condition and kept fertile—just as in an outdoor garden. Container gardening and hydroponic culture are supplementary means of inhibiting pests and diseases.

Staging. Growing plants in raised beds, called "staging" or benches, is not only physically comfortable, but it enables you to have control over soil conditions and drainage. Staging can be arranged in many ways so you can also use your growing area most effectively. Air at waist height is warmer than at ground level and circulates better.

Benches for staging should be constructed of a durable wood that tolerates moisture. Redwood, cedar, and cypress are excellent materials. Staging with slatted beds is best for holding potted plants because they allow water to drain straight down while permitting air to circulate freely among the plant collection. Solid-bed staging, which is really a wooden container on legs, is filled with soil so that plants can be grown without pots. This type of staging is useful when you are raising many plants with the same cultural requirements. Since water is not meant to drain through, the space underneath can be used for storage.

When your greenhouse is an integral part of your living space, nothing but waist-level benches is visually boring. To add more plants and make the greenhouse more attractive, you can build extra shelves above the staging, hang basket plants from the ceiling, and introduce a few tall-growing or bush container plants as a note of contrast.

Soil testing. You can make an educated guess about the acidity or alkalinity of your garden soil based on where you live. If your area is arid or semiarid, the soil is probably alkaline; if you live in a region with over thirty inches of rainfall, your soil is likely to be on the acid side.

Knowing precisely the relative acidity or alkalinity of soil, i.e., its pH rating, helps you to provide the right conditions for your plants. Different plants have different pH requirements and cannot absorb nutrients from the soil when it is too acid or too alkaline.

Test greenhouse soil with a home soil testing kit. If the pH reading is too acid for the plants you are growing, add lime to make it more alkaline. Similarly, reduce excess alkalinity by adding sulphur. The soil testing kit will tell you how much of what to add to the soil.

Some elaborate soil testing kits also enable you to determine amounts of nitrogen, phosphorus, and potassium in your soil, but it is simpler to send soil samples to your state agricultural extension service.

Good growing conditions. Whatever you can grow in the house or in the garden you can grow in the greenhouse, as long as you create the right growing conditions. Healthy vegetables, houseplants, bulbs, vines, trees, perennials, and annuals all can grow in most greenhouses. If you have a diverse group of plants, there will be sunlovers, heat-lovers, shade-lovers, and cold-sensitive plants, all needing amounts of light and heat. Fortunately, though, no greenhouse provides completely uniform environment (unless you go to some lengths to impose one). For example, toward the apex of the greenhouse, sun- and warmth-loving plants find light and heat; closer to the sides, sun-loving plants that like cool nights do well.

A word on pests and disease. When a greenhouse is stocked with healthy plants, the appearance of insects and disease signals a lack of soil fertility, poor sanitation practices, and/or improper environmental conditions, such as too little or too much water, humidity, and/or light.

Prevention is the best approach to insect and disease infestation. Neatness and cleanliness are even more important in the greenhouse than outside in the garden because the smallest bit of debris can serve as a breeding ground for pests. Clean the glass frequently inside and out and give the whole greenhouse a thorough cleaning annually. Pots should always be scrubbed after use. Otherwise, general garden hygiene applies:

1. Do not work with wet plants.
2. No smoking in or around the greenhouse.
3. Wash hands after touching diseased or infested plants.
4. Check new plants carefully and isolate any possible problem plants.
5. Inspect all plants frequently.

Good ventilation is another way to keep plants healthy. Fresh air keeps moisture levels down and provides the circulating air plants like. Throughout the year, open vents for at least a half hour every afternoon.

Chemical pesticide sprays were invented for use on crops in large open areas, not in greenhouses, which are small, enclosed areas. Rich fertile soil, window screens, biological insect control, natural "organic" remedies, and companion planting are far safer ways to keep harmful insects out of under-glass gardens.

Applying a spray is not always the answer to bugs, even when the spray under consideration is nontoxic. For example, whiteflies often prey on magnesium- and phosphorous-deficient plants, and simply killing them off does nothing for the soil deficiency.

Solar Greenhouses

Like conventional greenhouses, solar greenhouses can be free-standing or attached to the house, and most of them provide an environment that makes year-round planting possible, even in northern climates.

The outstanding feature of solar greenhouses is the technology used to establish the right climate for plants during cold weather. For the most part, so-called solar greenhouses operate on heat and light received from the sun and rely little, if at all, on supplementary fossil-fuel heating. They are designed to collect and store heat from the sun during the day and maintain a certain temperature range during the night.

The type of collection-storage-insulation system in a solar greenhouse depends on climate, size, orientation toward the sun, and the gardener's financial resources. A greenhouse in Minnesota or New England needs a more elaborate heat collection-storage system than does a greenhouse in New Mexico or Arizona (which is one reason for the popularity of solar greenhouses in the Southwest).

Heat can be collected and stored in pools of water, water containers, rock walls, and storage beds made of rocks. Some solar greenhouses are erected over pits in the ground to take advantage of the earth's fairly constant temperature.

Solar greenhouses cost much less to heat than conventional greenhouses. Any extra expenses incurred during construction are soon offset by savings in heating equipment and fuel bills. Despite the fact that they represent an avant-garde mode of gardening, solar greenhouses are fairly simple to construct and do not require the installation of complicated high-tech equipment.

For More Information

"Building a Solar-Heated Pit Greenhouse." Country Way Bulletin, Garden Way Publishing, Charlotte, VT 05445.

Building and Using Our Sun-Heated Greenhouse, by Helen and Scott Nearing. Garden Way Publishing, Charlotte, VT 05445.

Build Your Own Greenhouse, by Charles C. Neal. Chilton.

The Complete Greenhouse Book: Building and Using Greenhouses from Cold Frames to Solar Structures, by Peter Clegg and Derry Watkins. Garden Way Publishing, Charlotte, VT 05445.

Correspondence Aid No. 34-134. U.S. Department of Agriculture, Washington, D.C. 20250 (a list of sources of greenhouse information).

"The Garden Way Solar Room," by Robert Holdridge and Doug Taff, designers. Garden Way Publishing, Charlotte, VT 05445.

Gardening Under Glass, by Jerome A. Eaton. Macmillan.

Green House Grow How, by John H. Pierce. Plants Alive Books, 5509 1st Ave. South, Seattle, WA 98108.

Greenhouse Handbook. Brooklyn Botanic Gardens, 1000 Washington Ave., Brooklyn, NY 11225.

The Solar Greenhouse Book, edited by James McCullagh. Rodale Press.

The Survival Greenhouse: An Ecosystem Approach to Home Food Production, by J. B. DeKorne. Walden Foundation, Box 5, El Rito, NM 87530.

Your Homemade Greenhouse and How to Build It, by Jack Kramer. Simon and Schuster.

Greenhouse Plans

"Build a Greenhouse This Weekend." Filon Corp., 12333 S. Van Ness Ave., Hawthorne, CA 90250.

"The Cornell 21 Plastic Greenhouse." Dept. of Vegetable Crops, Cornell University, Ithaca, NY 14850.

Extension Agricultural Engineering, Pennsylvania State University, University Park, PA 16802.

"A Gothic Greenhouse for Town and Country" (Publication 487). Extension Division, Virginia Polytechnic Institute and State University, Blacksburg, VA 24061.

"How to Build a Plastic Crop Shelter or Greenhouse" (Catalog no. A53-1337). Information Division, Dept. of Agriculture, Ottawa, Ontario K1A OC7.

"Plastic Covered Greenhouse" (Building plan no. 73). Oregon State University, Corvallis, OR 97330.

"Slant-Leg Rigid-Frame Plastic Greenhouse" (Plan 139). Agricultural Engineering Dept., Rutgers University, New Brunswick, NJ 08903.

Greenhouse Manufacturers

Ames Greenhouses, Inc.
R.R. 2
Ames, IA 50010

Aluminum Greenhouses
14605 Lorain Ave.
Cleveland, OH 44111

Canadian Greenhouses
Box 5000
Durham Rd.
Beamsville, Ontario LOR 1B0

Casaplanta
16129 Runnymede St.
Van Nuys, CA 91406

Country Hills Greenhouses
Rt. 2
Corning, OH 43730

Eden Aluminum Co.
5462 W. Broadway
Cedarhurst, NY 11516

Emerson Industries, Inc.
132 Adams Ave.
Hemstead, NY 11550

Enclosures, Inc.
80 Main St.
Moreland, GA 30259

English Aluminum Greenhouses
1201 Deerford Rd.
Willowdale, Ontario M2J 3J3

Environment
Box 7855
Austin, TX 78712

Foray Corp.
Box 1026
Kent, WA 98103

Four Seasons Greenhouses
910 Rt. 110
Farmingdale, NY 11735

Gothic Arch Greenhouses
Box 1564
Mobile, AL 36601

Greenhouse Sales
Box 42
Neche, ND 58265

Greenhouse Specialties
9849 Kimker Lane
St. Louis, MO 63127

Hansen Weather Port
313 N. Taylor
Gunnison, CO 81230

Janco Greenhouses
10686 Tucker St.
Beltsville, MD 20705

Lexington Gardens
500 Middletown Ave.
North Haven, CT 06473

Little Earth Construction
418 Montezuma
Box 2842
Santa Fe, NM 87501

Lord & Burnham
Irvington, NY 10533
or
Des Plaines, IL 60018

Lyndon Lyon Greenhouses, Inc.
14 Mutchler St.
Dolgeville, NY 13329

McGregor Greenhouses
1195 Thompson Ave.
Santa Cruz, CA 95063

Mesker's, Inc.
634 Rivervale Rd.
Rivervale, NJ 07675

Pacific Coast Greenhouse Mfg. Co.
430 Burlingame Ave.
Redwood City, CA 94063

Provider Greenhouses
Box 49708
Los Angeles, CA 90049

Redfern's Prefab Greenhouses
55 Mt. Hermon Rd.
Scotts Valley, CA 95060

Redwood Domes
Box 666
Aptos, CA 95003

Santa Barbara Greenhouses
390 S. Dawson Dr.
Camarillo, CA 93010

Texas Greenhouse Co.
Box 11219
Fort Worth, TX 76110

Turner Greenhouses
Rt. 117
Goldsboro, NC 27530

W. Atlee Burpee Co.
50026 Burpee Bldg.
Warminster, PA 18974

Water Works Gardenhouses
Box 905
El Cerrito, CA 94530

Solar Greenhouses (Designs and Prefabricated Units)

The Solar Room
Box 1377
Taos, NM 87571

Solar Technology Corp.
2160 Clay St.
Denver, CO 80211

Stearns Greenhouses
98 Taylor St.
Neponset, MA 02122

Sturdi-Built Manufacturing Co.
11304 S.W. Boones Ferry Rd.
Portland, OR 97219

Sunglo Greenhouses
4441 26th Ave. W.
Seattle, WA 98199

Greenhouse Suppliers and Accessories

Bramen Co., Inc.
Box 70
Salem, MA 01970
(solar-powered vent openers for coldframes and greenhouses)

Charlie's Greenhouse Supply
12815-T Northeast 124th St.
Kirkland, WA 98033

Dahlen Products, Inc.
201 Serlake Dr.
Knoxville, TN 37922

Humex Ltd.
2241 Dunwin Dr.
Mississauga, Ontario L5L 1A3

Kee Klamps, Inc.
79 Benbro Dr.
Buffalo, NY 14266
(Bench frames)

Redfern's Prefab Greenhouse Manufacturing Co.
3482 Scotts Valley Dr.
Santa Cruz, VA 95060

Shoplite Co., Inc.
650 Franklin Ave.
Nutley, NJ 07110

Sturdi-Built Manufacturing Co.
11304 Southwest Boones Ferry Rd.
Portland, OR 97219

Taydo Enterprises
1311 Elkhorn Crescent
Prince George, B.C.
Canada R2M 6L9

Texas Greenhouse Co.
2717 Saint Louis Ave.
Fort Worth, TX 76110

Turner Greenhouses
Turner Equipment Co.
P.O. Box 1260
Goldsboro, NC 27530

Walter F. Nicke
P.O. Box 667H
Hudson, NY 12534

Yonah Manufacturing Co.
P.O. Box 280
Cornelia, GA 30531

Ormson's Conservatory.

Gray's Conservatory.

Small-Scale Garden Extenders

Coldframes and Hotframes
A coldframe is a wooden or masonry box with a removable blass lid, called a "sash." The sash looks like—and often is—a recycled window or storm window. Some new coldframes are covered with plastic film or sheets of fiberglass.

With the top on, coldframes are low-lying greenhouses. You can set plants directly in the bed area inside the coldframe or grow plants in flats or pots. Warmed by the sun, they are useful for hardening off seedlings and forcing early crops in spring and, when planted with cold-hardy salad greens, for prolonging the gardening season several weeks past the first severe frost.

During the day, as does a greenhouse, a coldframe heats up to a temperature above that of the surrounding air. To prevent overheating, the sash is opened on warm days. The wider the sash is opened, the cooler the interior. At night, the coldframe is closed. In an ordinary coldframe, the earth itself acts as a solar collector (although not in extremely cold weather) and, if the outside temperature does not drop too sharply overnight, the interior of the coldframe stays warm until morning, particularly if it is almost airtight.

On very cold nights, you can keep plants from freezing to death by covering the coldframe with a blanket. Should your crop actually freeze, it can usually be revived. Just spray the plants with *cold* water and cover the coldframe with a light-blocking dark blanket for a couple of hours.

A hotframe is nothing more than a heated coldframe. Solar coldframes, which are specially insulated and contain heat collectors, are a new twist on the old idea of using nature to provide warmth to plants. Many ordinary coldframes can be improved by using solar heating techniques. To get more out of your coldframe, both before and after the normal growing season in your area, first check to see that it is as airtight as it can be. Then, insulate the north, east, and west sides with polystyrene foam and perhaps surround it on those three sides with bales of hay. For a heat-collection system, fill plastic jugs with black-dyed water, line the jugs up in front of the south side, and stack them along the inner sides of the coldframe, under the sash.

To make an old-fashioned, non-electric hotframe, you must create a bed of composted manure that supplies heat as it decomposes further. Start by mixing fresh manure with a third part straw, water the mixture, and allow it to decompose for four days. Turn the mixture and wait another four days, then dig out two feet of soil under the coldframe and fill the hole with the decomposing manure. Be sure the manure is packed down fairly firmly. Leave the sash open until fumes dissipate and the temperature inside the manure bed is about 95°F. Then cover the decomposing organic matter with a six-inch layer of good loam and plant seeds for an early-season crop. The carbon dioxide given off by the manure bed is excellent for young plants.

You can also supply bottom heat to a hotframe by running electrical coils under the soil. In northern areas of the United States, twelve to sixteen watts of heating cables per square foot of bed is needed. In the South, ten watts per square foot should suffice. By insulating the sides and covering the hotframe at night, operation costs can be kept to a minimum.

Climate control. Too much or too little heat in a coldframe spells doom for the plants inside. During the day, the temperature must not go over 100°F. Cool-season crops (cabbage, lettuce, cauliflower) like a daytime temperature of 60 to 65°F and about five to ten degrees less at night. True to their tropical origins, warm-season crops such as melons, tomatoes, eggplant, and peppers need a daytime temperature of 65 to 75°F, with a five- to ten-degree nighttime drop.

With a lot of luck and obsessive vigilance, you may succed in maintaining the right temperature inside your coldframe or hotframe. It is easier to let an automatic, solar-powered vent opener do the work. These are available from greenhouse equipment companies.

Size. Most coldframes measure in multiples of three by four feet or three by six feet. The height of the frame can be twelve inches in front (south side) and eighteen inches in back (north side). The higher the front wall, the longer its shadow. This size affords plenty of room for the young seedlings that will fill a large home garden.

Cloches
If a coldframe is a minigreenhouse, a cloche, or hot cap, as a cloche is often called, is a mini-minigreenhouse. Developed first in France, bell-shaped cloches began as devices to protect individual plants from moderate frost. Originally made of glass, cloches are now more commonly made of molded fiberglass that stands on its own or of polyethelene film stretched over a curved metal framework. Cloches have also evolved from single-plant protectors to soft plastic tunnels that arch over a whole row of plants.

Cloches, or hot caps, are useful to protect seedlings from slight frost (above 20°F) during spring. Because cloches are uninsulated, they cannot help when the frost is severe. In regions where winters are not too cold, cold-hardy vegetables such as lettuce, parsley, and spinach can grow outdoors during all or most of the cold season in tunnel-shaped cloches.

Cloches are available from seed companies and large garden supply centers, but you can easily rig your own by using plastic bags and coat hangers.

A new garden aid on the market since 1980 is the "Guard 'N Grow" minigreenhouse that works on the same principle as a cloche but it collects solar heat. It is a little house-shaped cloche made of polypropylene that can be folded up and put away after use. Individual units can be set up end-to-end to protect a row of plants. Write to Guard 'N Gro, St. James, NY 11780 for details.

For More Information
"Building and Using a Cold Frame." Garden Way Publishing, Charlotte, VT 05445.

The Solar Growing Frame. Rodale Press Plan Books, 33 E. Minor St., Emmaus, PA 18049.

8

Hydroponic Gardening

Gardening Without Soil

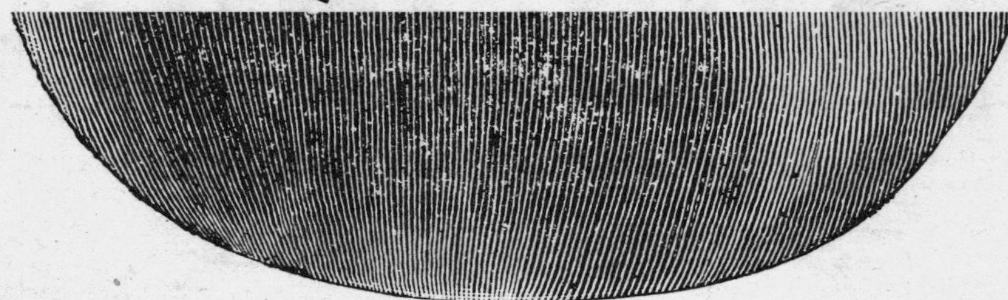

Do you like gardening but lack the time or even the space for a garden? Do you silently yearn for a tender, flavorful tomato in midwinter when tomatoes are faded and gritty? For many people, hydroponics is the answer to these and other unrequited yearnings.

Hydroponics, or the practice of soilless gardening, can be carried on indoors under lights, on apartment building rooftops and balconies, in greenhouses, and outdoors. Depending on your ambition and budget, you can establish anything from a small, portable herb and vegetable garden to a large-scale "farm." Hydroponic gardens supply crews of offshore drilling rigs and atomic submarines with fresh produce and enable farmers in desert regions throughout the world to grow nutritious green food.

What is Hydroponics?
In conventional agriculture, soil provides physical support for plants and also acts as a source of mineral salts that nourish plants. When water is added to soil, which is partly organic substance, it dissolves the mineral salts that are essential food for all growing things.

In hydroponic gardening, an inert aggregate, or growing medium, takes the place of soil. Usually, the aggregate consists of pH neutral gravel, perlite, vermiculite, haydite, or sand, but small stones, lava stones, broken tile, and even mixtures containing sawdust work, too. The function of the aggregate is to support the plants while permitting aeration of the roots. Because these growing mediums do not contain the same reserve of mineral salts that moistened soil releases to plants, in hydroponic gardening the natural nutrients plants need are premixed into the water and then added.

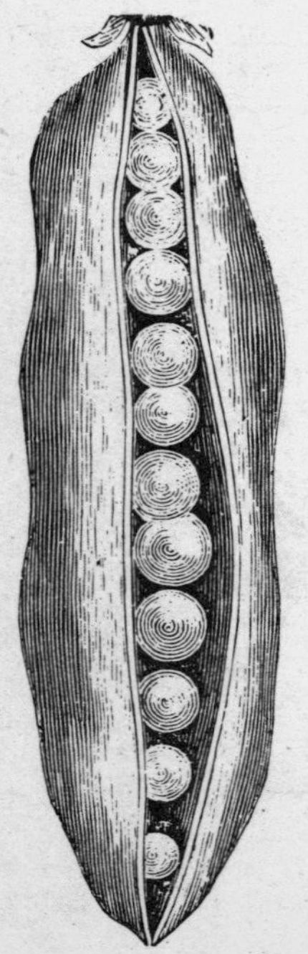

Because you are able to provide everything your plants need, you can achieve more consistent results with a hydroponic garden than with a plot of dirt. You can also raise more plants in a small space and achieve a higher yield than in the same size soil garden. For example, a 3 x 12 hydroponic bed can produce about as much as a 12 x 22 soil garden. And with hydroponics, there is no weeding, cultivating, digging, or even daily watering involved.

Nevertheless, hydroponic gardening is not magic. Like every other horticultural method, it provides plants with 3 key elements—nitrogen, phosphorus, and potassium—as well as essential trace elements (micronutrients)—boron, calcium, chlorine, copper, iron, manganese, magnesium, molybdenum, sulphur, and zinc. Of the many hydroponic techniques, all deal in the placement of nutrients in intimate contact with plant roots.

Hydroponic units relieve the gardener of the problems stemming from changing weather conditions as well as eliminating soil-borne diseases and pests. Units are manufactured in many sizes and for a variety of purposes. You can grow high-quality, farm-fresh vegetables year round right in your apartment, greenhouse, rooftop, or yard, feeding a single individual or many people, at a relatively low cost, and faster than if you were using soil.

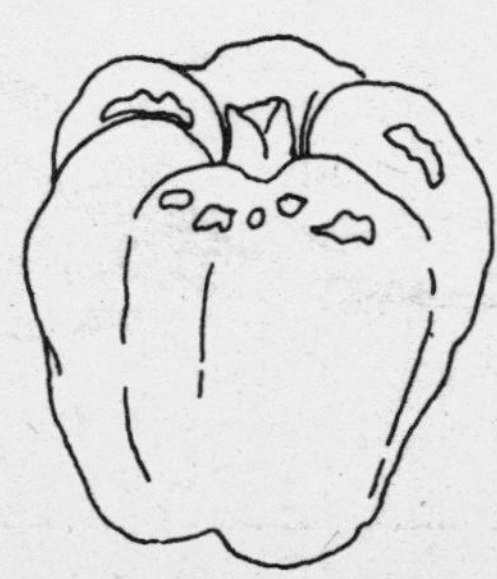

In addition to its appeal to our fascination with technology and gadgetry, hydroponics is also a workable alternative for the gardener who is interested in doing as little as possible to harm the environment. On the whole, hydroponically grown vegetables come to the table with a far lower expenditure of fossil fuel than store-bought, agribusiness-produced food. Also, since hydroponic systems are self-contained, they neither add chemical fertilizers to the local water supply nor deplete precious topsoil.

A Quick History
Until the 1930s, the closest amateur gardeners had come to controlling the growth of plants was the greenhouse. Then, in 1936, W. F. Gericke, a scientist at the University of California, succeeded in growing 25-foot-high tomato vines in vats of water mixed with a nutrient solution. Dr. Gericke dubbed his growing method "hydroponics." The North American public was amazed. The press touted the new soilless growing method as heralding an agricultural revolution. But soon widespread popular interest in hydroponics waned, and amateur gardeners turned from dreams of horticultural glory back to the familiar timeless struggle of soil gardening. During World War II and in the years that followed the war, scientists improved upon the original Gericke technique, developing large-scale hydroponic greenhouses suitable for raising crops to feed large numbers of people. Gradually, interest in the reliability of soilless culture spread to commercial growers throughout the world. In the 1970s, manufacturers began to market hydroponic units tailored to private gardeners, and hydroponics returned to the North American consciousness, now as a sophisticated yet easy-to-learn method of growing flowers, vegetables, and herbs.

Methods of Hydroponic Gardening
Today, there are several kinds of hydroponic systems, from containers costing under twenty dollars to huge commercial greenhouses, to experimental methods like aeroponics, whereby exposed plant roots receive nutrients from the constant application of fine mist sprays. Generally, beginners in the field are attracted to simple systems that can be set up indoors, on a patio, or in the yard. Many home hydroponic units are movable so that the gardener can take of advantage of natural light during the summer growing season and then move the operation indoors under artificial lights when the weather gets cold.

Among the simplest commercially available units are the *wick system* and the *continuous-flow system.*

The Wick System. One of the easiest hydroponic methods, the wick system involves no pumping or automation. It consists of an aggregate-filled growing container set within a second outer container that holds a nutrient solution—or it can be a standard-looking flowerpot with a built-in reservoir. Special wicks immersed in the nutrient solution run up through drainage holes in the bottom of the growing container into the growing medium, usually perlite. To operate the system, you begin by adding tap water to the growing container until the growing medium is thoroughly wet. Allow the excess water to drain out, then dissolve the dry nutrient in water, usually at the rate of 1 teaspoon per gallon, pour the solution into the reservoir container, and set the growing container in place.

Seeds can be started right in the aggregate or in Jiffy-7 pots that you set into the growing medium. After the seeds germinate and produce two-inch-high plants, the nutrient solution is changed, and from then on it ought to be changed every week. At all times, you must maintain the same water level in the growing medium by watering with regular tap water. After about six weeks, the growing container requires flushing out with tap water to remove accumulated salts, and every week or so you will need to check the pH level (see below).

Continuous-flow systems. With this method, you do not need plumbing of any kind, and a 110v wall outlet will put you in business. Nutrients and water are pumped automatically from a self-contained reservoir into an elevated growing bed filled with an inert aggregate, usually gravel. An electric pump floods the growth medium with nu-

trient solution, which then drains back down to the reservoir. In some types, the process is repeated twice a day in winter and four times a day in summer; in others, the circulating pump can be run continuously.

Some continuous-flow systems feature growth containers that are tube-shaped. These have openings in which aggregate-filled flowerpots are set, and the roots of plants grow down through the pots into the nutrient solution. Another type consists of an aggregate-filled planter with a built-in nutrient reservoir, timer, and circulation pump. Except in models with special seed starters, seeds should be germinated outside the unit. If you use Jiffy-7 pots, you can transplant the seedlings and pots directly into the hydroponic growth medium.

Even with this more complex hydroponic system, care is minimal. The nutrient reservoir needs a change of water every three to six weeks (depending on manufacturer's instructions and the type of crop), evaporated water should be replaced as needed, and the manufacturer's recommended pH level should be maintained (see below). Used solution makes a good fertilizer for your soil garden, so nothing need be wasted. Otherwise, all you must do is the normal planting, pruning, and harvesting of your crop.

Care of Your Hydroponic Garden

Water. Ordinary tap water is fine, provided it is not too hard or has not passed through a water softener. Most community water supplies are slightly alkaline. If your local water contains chlorine, you can evaporate that chemical by letting the water for your hydroponic system stand in an open container for two days.

Light. The minimum requirement for growing a hydroponic crop indoors is 1000 foot-candles, especially if you want to produce vegetables or blooms. Unless you have exceptionally strong natural light, you'll need artificial light to provide your plants with the energy they need to grow inside. A combination of a broad-spectrum fluorescent tube with a regular cool white or warm white tube turned on for sixteen to eighteen hours daily will enable you to raise both flowers and foliage plants.

Several suppliers offer adjustable light units on legs that fit over hydroponic growing containers. While convenient, these fixtures are fairly expensive.

The Right pH. When you get into hydroponics, you run smack into the mysteries of pH rating. Simply put, this is an assessment of the relative acidity or alkalinity of any water-soluble or wet material. A pH reading becomes important to hydroponic gardeners because a nutrient solution that is too acid or too alkaline causes the precipitation of the dissolved nutrients into unusable salts.

The pH scale runs from 0 to 14. Readings below seven indicate a predominance of acid ions and levels above seven mean that alkaline ions are more numerous. Plants do best between pH 6 and pH 7, and in hydroponics, the optimal pH reading for a solution that feeds vegetables is from 6 to 6.5.

By following directions when mixing up a new batch of nutrient, you ought to arrive at the proper pH level. After several days of use, though, the nutrient becomes alkaline, and when left unchecked it will harm your plants.

To correct the pH, you can take a reading with nitrazine paper, available at pharmacies, the pH test kit you use for your swimming pool, or a pH tester for gardeners. In most instances, you will discover a high pH, which you can adjust by adding a teaspoon of distilled white vinegar per gallon of water to the nutrient solution.

Temperature. Plants thrive when the temperature averages between 70° and 75°F. They like nights to be slightly cooler and days to be warmer. To approximate such conditions indoors, certain measures can be taken. In winter, hydroponic units should be away from heaters and cold drafts, and delicate plants should not be grown at floor level. In buildings with air conditioning, hydroponically grown plants can survive only if the air conditioning runs all day and all night or is turned on only at night. By turning off the cool air at night, you signal your plants to begin producing energy, which is what they do in the presence of both heat *and* light. Since they cannot manufacture energy without light, they will die in the attempt.

If you have a portable unit and an outdoor location, your indoor hydroponic vegetable patch can be converted to an outdoor crop that outproduces by far any plot of soil of comparable size. In addition, the growing season of a soilless garden is considerably longer. About a month before the last frost in your area, you can begin to acclimate your hydroponic unit to outside conditions by setting it in a sunny, protected location, beginning with an hour's exposure and lengthening the exposure until the plants can handle a full day and a full night outdoors.

Daily checks. Every hydroponic unit should be checked daily. The first place to look is the plants, which, if something has gone wrong, will show visible symptoms almost immediately. Look also at the growth medium to see that drainage is working, and check all automatic parts if you have a continuous-flow system. Remove all dust and dirt as well as dead and dying organic matter that attracts insects.

Nutrient Solutions

Beginning hydroponics gardeners usually order premixed nutrient preparations from the supplier of their equipment. With commercial nutrient mixes, all you have to do is add a small amount of water, stir, and apply to your unit.

If you have storage space and intend to go in for hydroponics on a fairly large scale, you can save money by making your own nutrient mixes according to one of the formulas recommended in one of the several books on the subject of hydroponics. Many suppliers sell a selection of fertilizer salts in large quantities.

In addition to the major elements (nitrogen, calcium, potassium, phosphorus, sulphur, magnesium, and iron), plants need trace elements to flourish. Again, you can also mix your own trace-element additive solutions from mineral salts that you purchase separately. Choose your formula by reading up on the subject.

Recently, some Montreal rooftop gardeners developed a formula that, when applied to a peat-perlite-sand aggregate, produces one-third higher yields of tomatoes than soil culture. The formula consists of one teaspoon of bloodmeal to one and a half teaspoons each of liquid seaweed and fish emulsion per gallon of water. Most gardeners find it difficult to formulate their own organic formulas. Sharing experiences with other hydroponics gardeners is therefore a good idea.

What Plants to Grow?

Nearly any plant that can fit into a hydroponic unit can be raised by soilless culture. Houseplants, many flowering annuals, herbs, and a wide variety of vegetables respond well to hydroponic methods as long as they are grown in an environment with their preferred levels of light, humidity, and warmth, as well as in the correct aggregate and with the right mixture of nutrients.

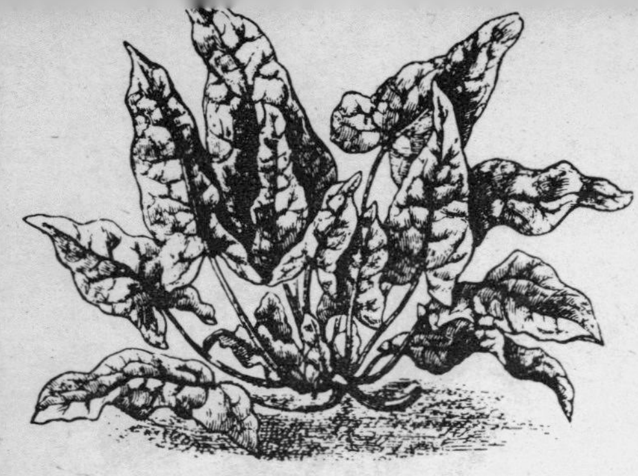

Vegetables. Most vegetables will grow in a hydroponic garden, but not all like the same growing medium, light levels, and nutrient solutions. For instance, sweet potatoes do best in a sand culture, and peas, spinach, and broccoli appreciate a well-aerated medium such as perlite. And celery requires a nutrient solution with sodium and chlorine, whereas leeks like nitrogen, potash, and goodly amounts of potassium.

When you grow several vegetable varieties with different requirements, you need more than one hydroponic unit as well as to formulate your own nutrient solutions. Before planting, take the time to read about hydroponic vegetable gardens in order to determine the kinds of crop you want.

One way to mix varieties is to practice the intercropping of tall and short plants. For example, tomatoes, which thrive in hydroponic culture, can provide shade for lettuce or cucumbers.

Herbs. Once you've used fresh herbs in your cooking, you miss their fragrance and flavor whenever you are forced to go back to using dried, store-bought herbs. In a soilless garden, you can easily grow many herbs, among them chives, tarragon, basil, dill, rosemary, oregano, and sage. Interplanted with a vegetable crop, they help to repel insects.

Foliage and flowering plants. Like certain vegetables, many kinds of nonfood plants cannot be grown in the same container with other plants because they have special requirements. Hydroponics cannot work miracles, and mixing plants with different needs for growth inevitably results in the predominance of the plants that your environment favors—and the disappearance of species unsuited to those same conditions. It should come as no surprise, however, that ferns and aloes do not grow well in the same pot for long.

Growing Plants from Seeds

Basically, hydroponics is the art of improving upon nature to ensure consistent horticultural results, and when it comes to starting plants from seeds, soilless gardening has several points in its favor:

1. The growing medium is free of soil-borne diseases and has a light texture for essential aeration.
2. Damping-off, the most common cause of failure with seeds, is impossible in a hydroponic growth bed.
3. The gardener can supply the right amount of nutrients to the young plants.

Hydroponics can be depended upon for a high rate of germination. The following steps outline the planting process as adapted to a hydroponic unit:

Step 1. Soak seeds overnight in water to hasten germination.

Step 2. Tuck seed a half-inch down into the growing medium in parallel rows. The aggregate should be lightly moistened with plain water. Cover the unit with dark plastic. It is all right to plant seeds closer together than the directions on the seed packets say because the roots of individual seedlings will not be competing for nourishment. How close you plant the seeds should be determined not by the roots but by how much space the eventual aboveground seedlings will need to spread out their leaves.

Step 3. Keep the unit covered with dark plastic until germination takes place. Different plants germinate at different rates.

Step 4. Where seedlings appear, remove the covering over that area of the planter. Remove the entire covering when all plant varieties have sprouted.

Transplanting

Except for some flowering houseplants, plants of any size that have been transplanted into a hydroponic garden do not go into shock the way they do when replanted in soil. The only precaution you need to take is to keep the root system intact.

A seedling being transferred from a growing medium such as vermiculite or perlite and planted from another soilless garden can be replanted right into a hole that has been prepared for it in the aggregate of your hydroponic planter. There is no need to wash the roots or remove any vermiculite or perlite that may be entangled among the roots. To transplant a seedling or plant that has been growing in soil, you will need to wash the roots gently under cold running water to clean away all dirt. When the last vestige of dirt is removed, if possible spread out the roots before placing the plant into the hydroponic growing medium.

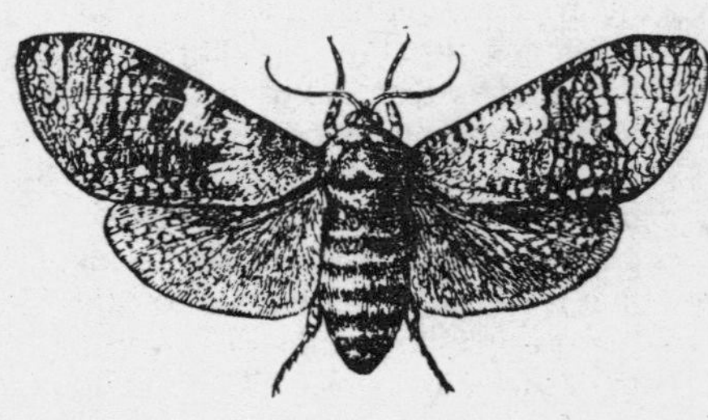

Pollination

Outdoors, the main agents of pollination are insects, especially bees and butterflies. Wind also commonly helps. Indoor vegetable gardens or balcony gardens in the middle of large cities, having no insects and possibly no breezes to carry on pollination, often require human intervention before fruit will form. This can be done by touching the male flower with the tip of a cotton swab or a delicate paintbrush and then lightly touching the female flower. To ensure success, choose a humid day and repeat the procedure for a couple of days thereafter.

Some flowering vegetables are hermaphroditic, that is, their flowers contain both male and female parts. These include tomatoes, beans, peas, eggplant, and peppers.

To Buy or To Build?

Hydroponics includes many methods of soilless culture, from a single container filled with aggregate to large greenhouse and outdoor setups, and gardeners at all levels of expertise can choose to construct their own units, or purchase some or all of the equipment they need from manufacturers. Two good texts for do-it-yourselfers are:

Hydroponics: Growing without Soil, by Dudley Harris (North Pomfret: David and Charles, 1975)

Home Hydroponics . . . And How to Do It! by Lem Jones (Paradise Valley: Beardsley Publishing Co., 1975)

Choosing Ready-made Kits and Equipment. Suppliers all over the country offer complete kits and components that can fit into or improve homemade hydroponic systems. You can purchase a simple unit with all the accessories for a tiny apartment or complete greenhouses.

The simplest unit, a wick system, which is really a modified flowerpot, should run under twenty dollars. Nutrient mix, aggregate, and pH tester are extra. If you decide to begin hydroponic gardening with a small single-unit kit, complete with nutrients, pH tester, aggregate, pumps, and fluorescent lights, your initial outlay can reach as much as two hundred dollars. Even though you can look forward to a yield of up to six times that of a soil garden, you will want to comparison shop before spending anything. Here are some tips on how to get the most for your money:

1. Decide what your hopes and needs are.
2. Learn enough about hydroponics to approach the subject intelligently. Don't rely on the suppliers for your education.
3. Try to examine a hydroponic system first hand.
4. Send for the catalogs of several suppliers.
5. Compare prices and materials.
6. Compare guarantees.

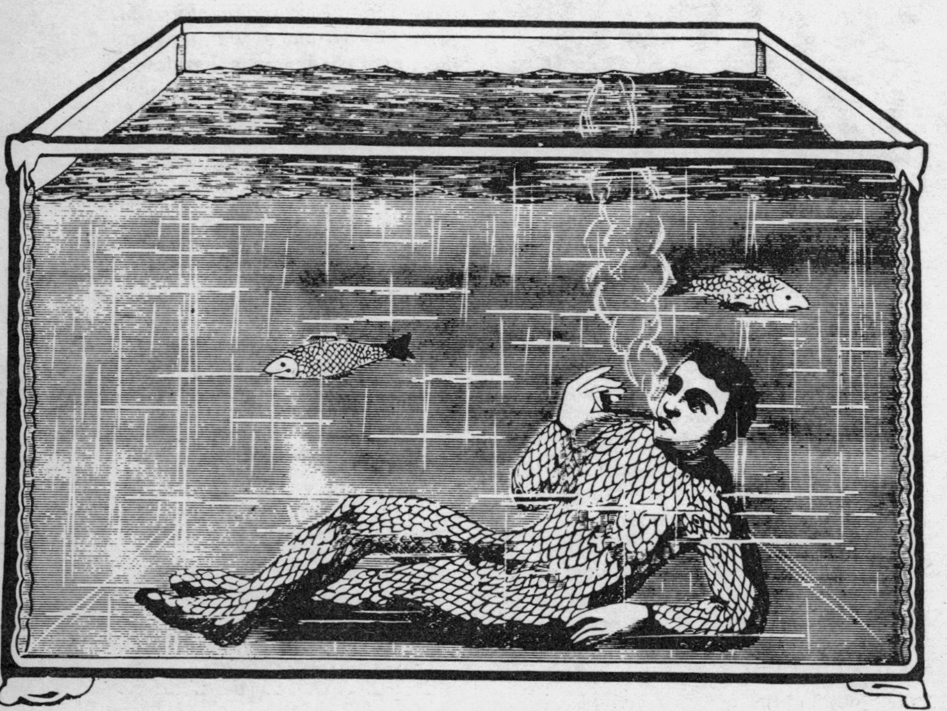

A Beginner's Library

Raymond Bridwell, *Hydroponic Gardening* (Santa Barbara: Woodbridge Press, 1974).

Alexandra and John Dickerman, *Discovering Hydroponic Gardening* (Santa Barbara: Woodbridge Press, 1975).

James Sholto Douglas, *Beginners' Guide to Hydroponics* (New York: Drake Publishers, 1973) and *Hydroponics: The Bengal System* (New York: Oxford University Press, 1977).

Carleton Ellis and Miller W. Swaney, *Soilless Growth of Plants* (New York: Reinhold Publishing Corp., 1947). Out-of-print pioneering work on a wide range of topics.

Richard E. Nicholls, *Beginning Hydroponics* (Philadelphia: Running Press, 1977).

Charles E. Sherman and Hap Brenizer, *Hydro-Story* (Occidental, CA: Nolo Press, 1976).

Equipment and Supplies

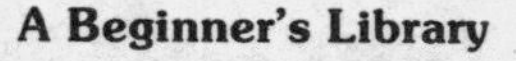

Manufacturers

Aqua-Ponics, 17221 E. 17 St., Santa Anna, CA 92701

City Green Hydroponics Corporation, 598 Bell Rd., Newark, NY 14513

Eco Enterprises, 2821 N.E. 55 St., Seattle, WA 98105

Environmental Dynamics, 12615 S. La Cadena Dr., Colton, CA 92324

I. Hochhauser, 395 South End Ave., Apt. 9M, NY, NY 10280

The Hydroponic Garden, 1117 Howard St., Omaha, NB 68102

Hydroponics Industries, 95 Rio Grande Blvd., Denver, CO 80223

Hydroponics of Nevada, 1513 Pacific St., Las Vegas, NE 89104

Pacific Aqua Culture, 3A Gate 5 Rd., Sausalito, CA 94965

Plantworks of Southeastern Connecticut, 95 Pennsylvania Ave., Niantic, CT 06357

Hydroponic Associations

The Hydroponic Association of America, P.O. Box 6067, Concord, CA 94524

International Working Group on Soilless Culture, P.O. Box 52, Waginen, The Netherlands

9

Outdoor Foliage and Flowers

A SHORT HISTORY OF *Gardens*

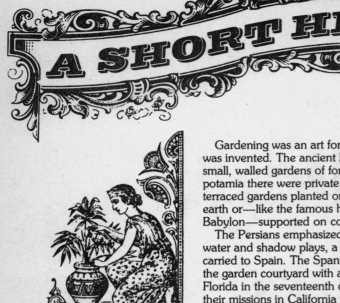

Gardening was an art form even before writing was invented. The ancient Egyptians enjoyed small, walled gardens of formal design. In Mesopotamia there were private parks as well as terraced gardens planted on artificial mounds of earth or—like the famous hanging gardens of Babylon—supported on columns.

The Persians emphasized decorative uses of water and shadow plays, a tradition the Moors carried to Spain. The Spanish, in turn, brought the garden courtyard with a fountain or pool to Florida in the seventeenth century, as well as to their missions in California and the Southwest—which also benefited from Aztec gardening techniques.

From the East, Buddhists spread the idea of planting sacred groves, and of enhancing a natural environment with plants especially selected for color and fragrance.

Yet it was centuries before all of these traditions came together in North America to create the rich heritage of varied gardens we enjoy today.

For the most part, North America inherited European gardening concepts that had culminated in the so-called English garden. The European tradition had begun in the classical world, where the Greeks frequently built their temples in groves of trees. Perhaps some plants were grown in Greek residential courtyards, but for the most park Greeks seem to have bought flowers from vendors who brought them into town from their countryside farms and who sold them door to door or in the marketplace. These flowers were used to decorate homes as well as temples at festival times.

Under the Romans, formal gardens—with a great many fountains and huge collections of statuary—were designed by architects whose chief intent was to set off their monumental public buildings and temples.

As power centers developed farther north, in less hospitable climates, there was a lull in horticultural development. Christianity did spawn monasteries throughout Europe, however, where monks cultivated utilitarian plots to provide food and crops of economic importance to support themselves and their dependents. Often, too, medicinal herbs, fragrant herbs, and food flavorings were grown in the cloister. The great castle estates also developed gardens similar to those of the monasteries—utilitarian and dull rather than ornamental.

During the Crusades, the techniques, ideas, and even plants of the Near East were brought back to Europe. But during the Dark Ages, gardening was hampered because most of the population lived in walled and guarded enclaves. Though farm laborers left their walled cities to cultivate food crops in the vicinity, this was not a time for pleasure gardening.

With the end of the Middle Ages, a more peaceable, pastoral lifestyle developed, beginning with the fifteenth-century Renaissance in Italy. The rich, the titled, and the princes of the church built country villas that included elaborate gardens. The gardens were generally laid out in geometric designs, often with terraces and staircases, and always with water displays and loads of statuary. Plants were secondary in this scheme of things. Trees, bushes, and hedges were clipped into formal shapes to enhance the architectural features, which were considered the focal points of the gardens. Nevertheless, some architects did defy convention and introduced some curvilinear garden designs.

France soon followed Italy's example—especially after Charles VIII imported a Neopolitan gardener to set the style. When Versailles was built (begun about 1662), more than twenty years was devoted to laying out its gardens—which were then copied from England to Spain. Yet even then gardens were the works of architects. They were formal, with axes that focused on features such as staircases. They were loaded with statuary, and much of the planting was topiary. They had garden structures, wooded areas, and terraces. But still plants were secondary to architectural aims.

England, where warfare continued into the sixteenth century, started with a pattern of small gardens enclosed by walls—a pattern colonists to the New World were to take along. But in the Tudor period, the great manor houses developed more extensive gardens. These were still formal, in geometric patterns, with lots of topiary and statuary. The royal garden of Henry VIII, for example, had thirty-eight stone statues of kings and queens, sixteen sundials, and an uncounted number of statues of lions and other animals plus statues of dragons, unicorns, and other mythical beasts. During the time of William and Mary, the Dutch influence introduced bulbs and other plants—but greatly exaggerated topiary too.

Finally, in the mid-eighteenth century, there was a rebellion—personified by the artist and architect William Kent. Kent wanted gardens to look more natural, so he converted the standard use of water in canals, marble basins, and fountains to pools and streams. He also descarded topiary and other clipped plants in favor of more natural forms. In fact, when he worked on Kensington Gardens, he went overboard and put in dead trees so the gardens would look more natural!

Kent was followed by other architects who did away with geometric paths, axes, avenues of trees, and other formal features. Even the terraces, gazebos, and other overlooks were done away with. In their place, grazing cattle and even fake ruins were introduced for a more "natural" look. This rage spread all over the continent, and beyond, and gave the "English garden" its lasting fame.

Though the mid-nineteenth century saw a revival of formal gardens—including grotesque topiary and too much sculpture and other garden accessories—this was the era of British exploration. Adventurers were going to the American tropics, to Africa, even eventually to the Arctic.

They brought back exotic plants from all over the world, wrote books (often inaccurate) on how to preserve them, and started fads for exotic plants. The rock garden constructed at Kew Gardens with alpine plants in the late nineteenth century was one influence. Greenhouse gardening also became a fad after the English learned of tropical plants from Africa and the Americas.

Meanwhile, in North America, a number of gardening traditions were developing independent of Europe. The "English garden" was best duplicated on the plantations of the South, where slave labor made extensive horticultural plantings possible. Many plants and cuttings were, in fact, imported from England. By the early eighteenth century magnificent showplaces such as Middleton Gardens were developed. Yet even Middleton, with its pools reflecting the river, its overlooks and secluded enclaves, included purely American aspects.

Elsewhere, though, and even in many parts of the South, such extravagance was unthinkable. Though some settlers brought with them decorative plants, such as Dutch bulbs, most had to concentrate their efforts on food production. Even where people tried to make their gardens attractive, such as in the dooryard gardens of New England or the courtyard mission gardens of the Southwest, most of the plants were utilitarian—medicinal and culinary herbs.

In addition, though many immigrants brought seeds and cuttings from their home countries, many of their imported plants did not survive. This did not matter, because from the Indians they learned of a wealth of new plants unknown in Europe. Some of these, such as tobacco, they adopted as economic crops. Others, such as corn and squash, they learned to eat. And still others they grew for purely decorative purposes.

So from the start, New World gardens were different from those in Europe. Rather than concentrating on theories of garden design, as Europeans did, North Americans became fascinated by plants themselves. Founding fathers of the United States such as Thomas Jefferson became enthusiastic naturalists, and interest in horticulture extended from admirers of arctic vegetation in Canada to champions of cacti and succulents in Texas. In the 1700s, the Philadelphia farmer, John Bartram, planted a botanical garden (called Bartram's Gardens today) to introduce into cultivation many native species. Thus, though garden design in America tended to follow the formal European patterns, the emphasis was less architectural and more horticultural. Moreover, even when European garden patterns were translated here, the native vegetation created totally different effects. Direct copying of a European idea such as a drive lined with trees, for example, defies comparison when the European version might be a stand of columnar poplars while the North American version might be wide-spreading live oaks garlanded with Spanish moss.

Other influences that have made North American gardens different from those of Europe include the more casual lifestyle here; the fact more people could own their own land, and larger parcels of land, than in Europe; and the fact that gardens here were initially carved out of wilderness. All of this has contributed to gardens that are far less formal and sedate. Our gardens are more expansive, more natural, than those of Europe.

Today's gardener in the United States and Canada is thus the inheritor of a tradition that goes back centuries, a tradition enhanced by plants and horticultural concepts from around the globe and enriched by the possibilities in native vegetation. Our gardens can therefore be more varied than ever before in history, and our opportunities for drawing pleasure from the soil are unrivaled.

Lawns

Nothing appears simpler or more common than the grasses that cover so much of the great outdoors. Grasses provide the rolling lawns we all enjoy, our athletic fields, golf links and parks, but they also make an important contribution to our ecology. By preventing wind and water erosion, grasses control pollution. They supply vital organic matter to the soil, and enrich the atmosphere with oxygen through photosynthesis.

But for all their ubiquity and apparent simplicity, planting and maintaining a grass lawn can be worrisome to the homeowner.

A lawn is not difficult to grow and maintain if you follow a few simple rules. The selection of seed or mixtures should correspond to the region and location of the lawn. Turfgrasses depend in large part on climatic conditions because their growth cycles vary with temperature (Fig. 1). Cool-season grasses grow best in the North and warm-season grasses in the South.

Preparing a good seedbed is important to a good lawn. Nearly all the grasses require an area that should first be plowed, disk turned, or rototilled to loosen the subsoil.

The addition of lime is generally required for soil east of the Mississippi River. When there is uncertainty about the need for lime, the soil should be tested. An average of 50 to 80 pounds of ground limestone should be applied per 1,000 square feet every five to six years. It should be incorporated into the soil, along with 30 to 40 pounds of phosphorus 0-20-0, per 1,000 square feet. For established lawns, lime can be applied on the surface.

LAWN GRASSES: PLANTING TIME, PROPAGATION, FERTILIZATION, AND MOWING HEIGHT

Season (Cool/Warm)	Grass	Best Planting Time	Seed (lbs. per 1,000 sq. ft.)	Sod (sq. ft.)[1]	Fertilizer (lbs. of nitrogen 1,000 sq. ft.)	Height of mowing (in.)
W	Bahia	Spring	2–3	—	4	2
C	Bentgrass, Colonial	Fall	1–2	—	4–6	½–1
W	Bermuda (hulled)	Spring	1–1½	5–10	5–10	¾–1
W	Blue grama	Spring	1–1½	—	2	1–2
W	Buffalo (treated)	Spring	½–1½	25–30	2	1–2
W	Carpet	Spring	3–4	8–10	2–3	2–2½
W	Centipede	Spring	¼–½	8–10	2–3	1–1½
C	Crested wheat	Fall	1–2	—	0–1	2
C	Ky. bluegrass	Fall	1½–2	—	3–6	1½–2
C	Red fescue	Fall	3–4	—	2–3	1½–2
C	Rough bluegrass	Fall	1½–2	—	2–4	1½–2
C	Ryegrass	Fall	3–4	—	3–4	1½–2
W	St. Augustine	Spring	None	8–10	4–5	2–2½
C	Tall fescue	Fall	5–6	—	3–5	2
W	Zoysia	Spring	None	8–10	4–6	¾–1½

[1]Needed to sprig 1,000 sq. ft.
[2]Seldom required on most soils.

Chart 1

Fertilization should proceed according to the needs of the lawn grass species or mixture in the lawn (Chart 1). A complete fertilizer contains nitrogen, phosphorus, and potash. The content analyses displayed on the bag are always listed in this order. For example, a 10-6-4 fertilizer containers 10 percent nitrogen, 6 percent phosphorus, and 4 percent potash. When applying a fertilizer containing 10 percent nitrogen, 10 pounds per 1,000 square feet would be appropriate but when applying a 20-10-10 fertilizer, 5 pounds per 1,000 square feet would be right.

Overstimulating lawns with nitrogen fertilizer can cause problems. A more succulent grass grows quickly and will require frequent mowing. It may also be more readily infected by fungus disease. Too much nitrogen added to the soil will also cause shallow rooting.

Fertilizer is seldom necessary on Western soils where blue grama and buffalograsses are used for turf.

Grass seed should be planted (Fig. 2) evenly over the seed bed with a spreader or by hand. If applied by hand, mix it with sand or soil to provide bulk. Half of the seed should be sown in one direction and the other half at a right angle to the first seeding. Lightly rake the seed into the soil to a depth of a quarter of an inch.

Scatter weed-free straw, hay, pine needles, or other mulch material over the seeded area. Mulch reduces erosion and provides shade and favorable moisture conditions for the emerging seedlings. One 60- to 80-pound bale of mulch is about enough per 1,000 square feet. About half of the soil should be visible after the mulch is laid.

Water the area lightly two or three times daily until the seedlings become established. Mulching materials need not be removed if they are used in moderate amounts.

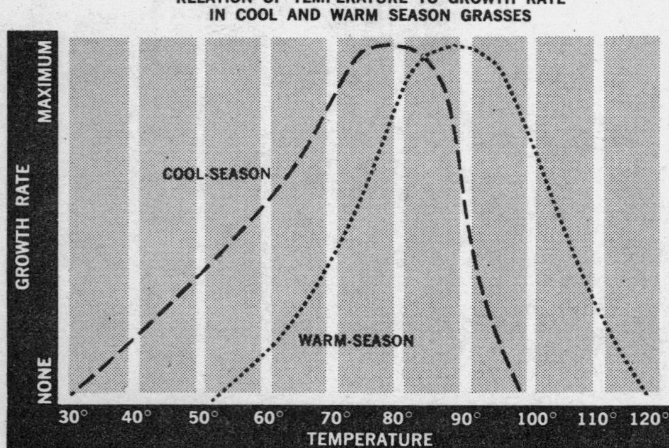

Fig.1

New lawns also can be established by laying down sod pieces, sprigs which are individual plants or runners, or plugs, which are round cores of grass and soil. Most southern grasses such as bermudagrass, St. Augustinegrass, and zoysia are established from sprigs or pieces of sod. These can be planted at 1-foot intervals. However, the closer together the sprigs, plugs, or sod pieces are planted, the more rapidly the lawn will become established.

Cool-season grasses such as Kentucky bluegrass, red fescue, Colonial bentgrass, crested wheatgrass, ryegrass, rough bluegrass, and tall fescue make their best growth in the fall and spring. Warm-season grasses such as bermuda, bahia, blue grama, buffalo, carpet, St. Augustine, centipede, and zoysia are planted in the spring and grow best during the summer months. The planting times, propagation, fertilization and mowing height appropriate to each of the grasses mentioned are contained in Chart 1.

Cool-Season, Northern Grasses

Colonial bentgrass (*Agrostis tenuis*) is a fine-textured grass with a few creeping stems and underground rootstocks (rhizomes). It forms a dense turf when heavily seeded and closely mowed. Colonial bentgrass is used for high-quality lawns in many of the New England States and west of the Cascade Mountains in Washington and Oregon (regions 1 and 6 on the map in Figure 2).

Colonial bentgrass requires fertile soil and frequent fertilizing. It must be watered during dry periods and it is susceptible to a wide variety of diseases.

Two strains of Colonial bentgrass are generally planted for lawns, Astoria and Highland.

Crested wheatgrass (*Agropyron cristatum*), a seeded bunchgrass, will thrive in most of the soils of the northern Great Plains and intermountain areas (regions 4 and 5). It is recommended for dry, cool areas where irrigation water is not available.

Crested wheatgrass withstands long, dry periods and heavy wear if not mowed too closely. It grows mostly in the fall and spring and becomes dormant during hot summer months.

Kentucky bluegrass (*Poa pratensis*) is a hardy, long-lived, perennial, sod-forming grass that spreads by underground rootstocks. Propagated by seed, it is one of the most widely used lawn grasses. Kentucky bluegrass is well adapted to regions 1 and 6, and grows in regions 4 and 5 if irrigated.

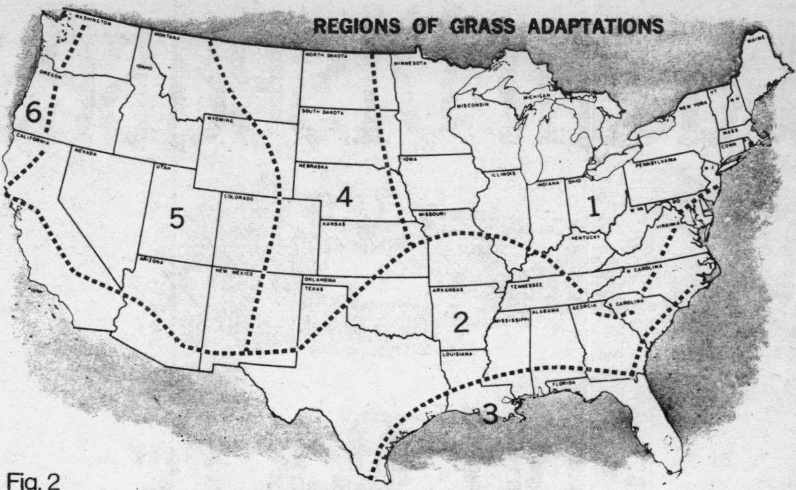

Fig. 2

CLIMATIC REGIONS, IN WHICH THE FOLLOWING GRASSES ARE SUITABLE FOR LAWNS:

1. Kentucky bluegrass, red fescue, and Colonial bentgrass. Tall fescue, bermuda, and zoysiagrasses in the southern part.

2. Bermuda and zoysiagrasses. Centipede, carpet, and St. Augustinegrasses in the southern part; tall fescue and Kentucky bluegrass in some northern areas.

3. St. Augustine, bermuda, zoysia, carpet, and bahiagrasses.

4. Nonirrigated areas: Crested wheat, buffalo, and blue gramagrasses. Irrigated areas: Kentucky bluegrass and red fescue.

5. Nonirrigated areas: Crested wheatgrass. Irrigated areas: Kentucky bluegrass and red fescue.

6. Colonial bent, Kentucky bluegrass, and red fescue.

Kentucky bluegrass will not grow well on poorly drained sites or in acid soils (below pH 6.0). Soil testing will indicate whether the lawn area has an acid or alkaline pH. A pH reading of 4 shows high acidity, while a pH reading of 7 is neutral. Merion was one of the first improved varieties of Kentucky grass to be released but others such as Fylking, Pennstar, Windsor, Prato, Sodco, and Park are also available.

Red fescue (*Festuca rubra*) and *Chewings fescue* (*Festuca rubra var. commutata*) rate next to Kentucky bluegrass in importance for northern humid regions. Red fescue will spread slowly from underground rootstocks. Chewings fescue is an upright, bunch-type grass.

Both fescues are established by seeding, and both are used extensively in mixtures with Kentucky bluegrass. They grow well in medium-shaded areas and on poor, droughty soils.

Improved varieties of red fescue are Pennlawn, Illahee, Golfrood, and Ruby. Jamestown is the only available improved strain of Chewings fescue.

Rough bluegrass (*Poa trivialis*) is a shade-tolerant perennial that is useful for lawns only in the North. It is established by seeding. Rough bluegrass grows best in moist sites. It is seriously injured by hot, dry weather.

The leaves of Rough bluegrass are similar in texture to Kentucky bluegrass, but more shiny. Stems and leaves lie flat and are a lighter green than most Kentucky bluegrasses.

Italian or annual ryegrass (*Lolium multiflorum*) and the ***perennial ryegrass*** (*Lolium perenne*) are propagated by seed. Much ryegrass lawn seed is a mixture of both annual and perennial ryegrasses.

Commercial lawn seed mixtures often contain too much ryegrass; the ryegrass competes with the slower growing Kentucky bluegrass and red fescue. For a late spring seeding and for seeding sloping areas, it is advisable to include some ryegrass for green color and erosion prevention.

Perennial ryegrass varieties include Pennfine, NK-100, Pelo, Manhattan, and Norlea. Varieties of annual ryegrass include Astor, Gulf, Magnolia, and Tifton 1.

Tall fescue (*Festuca arundinacea*) is a tall-growing, perennial bunchgrass that has coarse, dense, basal leaves and a strong fibrous root system. It is vigorous, grows well on both wet and dry sites, but does best on heavy soils.

Because of their wear-resistant qualities, two varieties of tall fescue, Kentucky 31 and Alta, are seeded in lawns, play areas, athletic fields, airfields, and other areas where a rugged turf rather than a fine-textured turf is needed.

Kentucky 31 tall fescue forms a tough, durable turf throughout much of the transition zone where neither cool-season grasses nor warm-season grasses are especially well adapted. Tall fescue is seldom seriously injured by insects or diseases.

When seeded at heavy rates, tall fescue produces finer leaves—the plants do not clump as readily—and a quite respectable lawn results.

Warm-Season, Southern Grasses

Bahiagrass (*Paspalum notatum*) is a low-growing perennial that spreads slowly by short, stout underground rootstocks. It grows best in the South Central Plains, where it is established by seeding. Several varieties are adapted to sandy soils from central North Carolina to eastern Texas. This grass is primarily for pastures and roadsides but the varieties Paraguay and Pensacola are used for lawns.

Bermudagrass (*Cynodon spp.*) is adapted to regions 2 and 3, where many varieties are sold. Each variety generally is for a specific use.

Common bermudagrass is coarse textured and propagated from seed. Other varieties are established from cuttings because the seed is sterile or nearly so.

Bermudagrass grows on a wide range of soils, from heavy clays to deep sands, provided they are fertile. A high tolerance to saline conditions enables the grass to grow satisfactorily on both acid and alkaline soils. It persists on relatively infertile soils yet high nitrogen fertilizing is required for good-quality turf. While rated drought tolerant in humid regions, the lawn still needs regular watering.

Bermudagrasses tend not to like shade, but there are slight differences among varieties.

The species will grow vigorously, spreading by runners and underground rootstocks. It often becomes a pest in flowerbeds and other cultivated areas. Once established, it is hard to eradicate.

This grass turns brown following the first frost and does not become green again until warm weather returns in the spring. Despite these shortcomings, bermudagrass is one of the most widely used turfgrasses.

Varieties of bermudagrass that exhibit high-quality lawns such as golf course greens, tees, and fairways are Tifgreen, Tiffine, Tifway, Bayshore, and Tifdwarf.

The grass requires frequent, heavy applications of nitrogen fertilizer in water soluble form. Dethatching once or twice a year to remove dead runners, roots, and leaves that accumulate will promote even growth.

Blue gramagrass (*Bouteloua gracilis*) is a low-growing, perennial bunchgrass adapted to parts of the Great Plains. As a turfgrass it is limited to cool, dry sites where there is little or no irrigation available.

This grass is highly drought resistant and is established from seed. It becomes semidormant and turns brown during excessively dry periods.

Buffalograss (*Buchloe dactyloides*) is a fine-leaved, warm-season, sodforming perennial that spreads by runners. It grows on the Great Plains from western Minnesota to central Montana, south to northwestern Iowa, Texas, and Arizona. It is drought resistant, tolerant of alkaline soils, and adapted to clay soils. Buffalograss can be established from sod pieces or by seeding.

Carpetgrass (*Axonopus affinis*) is a rapid spreading, perennial grass. It spreads by runners and produces a dense, compact turf when mowed, but is coarse textured. It can be established by seed or sodding. Carpetgrass is most abundant in lowland areas from coastal North Carolina to Florida and westward to Texas. It grows best in moist, sandy loam soils or those having a relatively high content of moisture throughout the year. It sometimes invades infertile, upland sites but does not grow well in dry soils or in regions where there is little rainfall.

Carpetgrass produces tall seedheads that are difficult to mow and make the lawn look ragged. Mowing frequently with a rotary mower is recommended. No improved varieties are available.

Centipedegrass (*Eremochloa ophiuroides*) will spread rapidly from short, creeping runners that form plants at each node or joint. What results is a dense, weedfree turf. The grass usually is planted vegetatively, but seed is available.

Centipedegrass is considered the best low-maintenance grass for the South. It has survived winter conditions as far North as northern Alabama and central areas of North Carolina.

Lawns of this type require less mowing, less watering, and less fertilizing than other southern grasses. Applications of iron compounds correct yellowing.

Centipedegrass should not be planted on farm lawns as it may escape and contaminate cropland. Common centipedegrass is most extensively planted. Oklawn is a variety selected for tolerance to drought and high temperature; it grows in shade as well as in full sunlight.

WASHINGTON'S HEADQUARTERS AT MORRISTOWN IN 1850.

St. Augustinegrass (*Stenotaphrum secundatum*) is the best shade-tolerant grass for the South. A creeping perennial, it spreads by long runners that produce short, leafy branches. The grass is restricted to the Gulf Coast States and milder parts of California. It is established vegetatively, and grows best in soils of high fertility. This grass can withstand salt water spray.

St. Augustinegrass is susceptible to chinch bug injury and to brown patch disease. Varieties available for lawns are Bitter Blue and Floratine.

Zoysiagrasses (*Zoysia japonica, Z. matrella, Z. tenuifolia*). Three species of zoysia are recognized and used for turf. They are distinguished primarily on the basis of size, vigor, and winter hardiness.

Common zoysia (*Z. japonica*), also known as Japanese lawngrass, has a coarse leaf that can be propagated vegetatively or from seed. Meyer zoysia, a selection from common zoysia, is intermediate in leaf width between common and Zoysia matrella. It is well adapted to the mid-Atlantic area. Meyer zoysia is more desirable for home lawns because of its finer textured leaves. This grass must be propagated vegetatively by sprigs, sod pieces, or plugs.

Although Meyer zoysia survives in soils of low fertility, it performs best when given liberal applications of complete fertilizers high in nitrogen. Meyer zoysia is relatively drought tolerant in humid regions. It is highly resistant to wear and withstands close clipping.

Emerald zoysia is a hybrid variety superior to Meyer zoysia in the South. The grass is fine leaved, dense growing, and dark green.

Manilagrass (*Z. matrella*) has about the same leaf texture as emerald but is a lighter green. Manilagrass is adapted to the South. It produces a dense carpetlike turf that resists weeds and wears well. Manilagrass is sensitive to highly acid soil so it responds well to liberal applications of nitrogen fertilizer. A lawn is established by sprigging or spot sodding.

Mascarenegrass (*Z. tenuifolia*) is a stoloniferous grass that is the least winter hardy of the zoysiagrasses. It is adapted to a very few locations in Florida and California. It ultimately becomes sod bound and humps up.

All zoysiagrasses turn offcolor during cool weather and become brown with the first killing frost. Zoysias do not become green until the warm weather in spring.

Maintenance

Once your lawn is established a few additional points must be remembered in order to maintain healthy, thriving grass:

Established lawns should not be watered frequently or lightly. When the lawn shows need for water by slight wilting and footprinting, the soil should be watered deeply to at least 6 inches and not watered again until the symptoms reappear.

Lawns should be mowed at the recommended height for the dominant species in the lawn (Chart 1). Mowing frequencies will vary depending on the grass species. Bermudagrass and bentgrasses require more frequent mowing than do most upright-growing grasses.

Where shade is a problem, shade-tolerant grasses should be planted. It is also helpful to remove the lower branches of trees.

Established lawns are kept vibrant by periodic, spot replanting. If the lawn has thinned out so only half of the perennial grasses remain, it can be restored without plowing and reseeding the entire area.

For the cool-season grasses, rake dead areas to remove the thatch and loosen the soil. The seed must come in contact with the soil in order to germinate.

After seeding, raking, and mulching, spread fertilizer over the lawn at recommended rates. Water the newly seeded areas two or three times daily. Continue to mow the lawn at the recommended height for the species.

Late August and September are the best times for renovating cool-season lawns, although seeding bare areas in early spring is frequently successful.

Southern, warm-season grasses that spread by runners (stolons) may be sprigged or sodded into dead areas without much soil preparation. Make a slit in the soil with a spade, insert the sprig, and firm the soil around it. More soil can be stripped with a spade and sod pieces laid and firmed into the soil the same way as with sprigs. Water the replanted area and apply fertilizer over the entire lawn. Continue to mow as usual.

Lawn Diseases

and Pests

Lawn and turf grasses are naturally hardy and abundant but they are also subject to disease and vulnerable to injury. Lawns can be made unsightly or be entirely destroyed by a number of factors including grass disease, infestation by insects or weeds, contamination by natural or manmade substances that result in smog, ozone or unfavorable water quality, and the damage caused by overuse and traffic wear.

Early recognition of specific diseases or infestations and the signs of contamination or overuse is most helpful in isolating the problem and its remedy.

Some problems can be prevented before they begin by the selection of grasses adapted to the soil, climatic, and light conditions under which they will be grown, and by the proper preparation and fertilization of seedbeds.

Other problems can be eliminated in their early stages by careful maintenance of the lawn on a daily basis. Grasses should not be cut too closely. Most varieties come with a specific recommended mowing length. For example, upright-growing grasses such as Kentucky bluegrass and red fescue are at their best height at 1¾ to 2 inches while creeping grasses such as bentgrass and zoysia can be cut at ½ inch or less. Grasses cut too closely or too frequently can be injured and develop a condition that looks like disease.

Grass should always be cut before it gets too tall, with not more than one-half of the leaf surface removed at one time. It's best to mow the lawn frequently enough in the fall to prevent the accumulation of a thick mat of grass before the snow falls. Such mats under wet snow are susceptible to mold growth. Clippings need not be removed unless the lawn is heavily fertilized, or during periods when the grass is growing rapidly.

Frequent light watering induces shallow rooting in grasses, leaving them vulnerable to injury during periods of severe drought. A lawn should not be watered until the grass begins to wilt, at which time the soil should be soaked to a depth of 6 inches or more. Watering should be done early enough in the day so that the grass leaves will dry out before night. If they remain moist too long, grass leaves become susceptible to fungus diseases.

Most established problems can be readily corrected by applying commercially available fungicides for specific disease conditions, pesticides for insect infestation, and herbicides for destructive weeds.

Problems caused by contamination can be corrected by removing or reducing the source of the contamination once it has been identified. When lawn injury is due to continuous exposure to smog, ozone, or overly clorinated water, the introduction of more resistant grasses may help to combat the problem. The wear of overuse can be corrected by restricting traffic until the lawn has recovered and, preferably when possible, by rerouting the traffic to adjacent paved or graveled areas.

Fungi cause most of the serious and widespread diseases of lawn grasses. They occur in the form of microscopically small filaments, or threads. The mass of threads, which sometimes have a cobwebby appearance, are called mycelium. Many fungi reproduce by means of microscopic fruiting structures called spores. These spores are most noticeable when grasses infected with rust or smut fungi are being mowed, and the spores are released like dust into the air.

Only those fungi that get their nutrients from a living host are true disease organisms. Such organisms cause Helminthosporium leafspot, fading-out, brown patch, rust, grease spot, dollar spot, stripe smut, and snow mold as they feed and thrive on the lawn grasses.

Fungi Diseases

Helminthosporium leafspot and foot rot. This disease, which gets its name from the Helminthosporium fungi that cause it, is one of the most widely distributed and destructive grass diseases. Kentucky bluegrass is one of the species most susceptible to the disease.

The principal fungus causing leafspot in Kentucky bluegrass also causes a foot rot condition known as going-out or melting-out. This is likely to occur mainly during cool, moist weather of spring and fall, but it may develop throughout the summer. Pure stands of Kentucky bluegrass favor development of the disease; mixtures of several recommended species usually retard the disease's onset, because most mixtures contain naturally resistant species.

Damage is most conspicuous in the leaves. However, the fungus responsible for the disease also causes a sheath rot or foot rot. This produces reddish-brown to purplish-black spots on leaves and stems of Kentucky bluegrass. Leaves shrivel and the stems, crowns, rhizomes, and roots discolor and rot. Leafspots and foot rots produced on other grasses by

different species of Helminthosporium resemble those on Kentucky bluegrass. Dead grass in attacked areas often is attributed to drought injury. Weeds and crabgrass usually invade these areas.

In Kentucky bluegrass lawns, leafspot can be controlled by growing less susceptible varieties such as Fylking, Merion, Pennstar, and Windsor. Some leafspotting may occur, but these varieties are more resistant than ordinary Kentucky bluegrass and are seldom killed during the destructive foot rot stage.

Following these management practices will reduce damage: Mow upright-growing grasses to a height of 1¾ to 2 inches rather than ½ to 1 inch; apply enough fertilizer to keep grass healthy and thriving; avoid overstimulation with nitrogen, particularly in the spring; and remove clippings, especially on lawns receiving heavy fertilization.

Fungicides that control Helminthosporium leafspot are listed in Chart 1.

Brown Patch. The fungus responsible for brown patch attacks practically all species of grasses, but is most serious on bentgrasses, fescues, Kentucky bluegrass, ryegrass, centipedegrass, and St. Augustinegrass. Brown patch is one of the most prevalent lawn grass diseases in the hot, humid regions of the United States. It occurs during warm, wet weather. Brown patch is most damaging following excessive application of nitrogen fertilizer. This promotes a lush growth of grass that is readily attacked. The disease spreads by fungus threads, or mycelium. New infections can start from mycelium carried on shoes, mowing equipment, or grass clippings.

Brown patch is characterized by irregular circular areas on the lawn, a few inches to several feet in diameter with a brownish discoloration. In bentgrasses a narrow, dark, smoke-colored ring borders the diseased area. This disappears when the weather becomes cool or dry. Sometimes only the leaves are affected and the turf recovers in two or three weeks. However, if the disease is severe and weather conditions remain favorable for its development, brown patch attacks the crowns and kills the grass. The dead grass generally remains erect and does not lie flat like grass killed by grease spot, a Pythium disease. The fungus threads, or mycelium, are frequently observed as filmy, white tufts early in the morning while the grass is still wet with dew. As the leaves dry, the fungus threads shrivel and disappear, leaving only dead and dying leaves. After several weeks, new grass grows back into the affected area.

Management practices that help in controlling brown patch are: Avoid excessive applications of nitrogen fertilizer; water lawns early in the day to give grass leaves time to dry out before night. Remove clippings if excessive. When treating brown patch with a recommended fungicide (see Chart 1), water the lawn 48 hours before the treatment and again at weekly intervals each time the treatment is repeated.

Rust. Rust fungi attack many lawn grasses. The disease usually occurs in late summer and remains until frost. Heavy dew favors its development.

Rust damage is more severe on Merion Kentucky bluegrass and zoysia than on other grasses. Meyer and Emerald zoysias are particularly susceptible to rust infection.

Rust appears on Merion Kentucky bluegrass from Rhode Island to California and from Canada to Oklahoma. The fungus seems to attack Merion wherever it is grown.

Some Kentucky bluegrass varieties resist rust infection entirely. Common Kentucky bluegrass is less susceptible to rust than Merion. However, it is vulnerable to the more destructive Helminthosporium leafspot.

Symptoms of the disease are yellow-orange or red-brown powdery pustules that develop on leaves and stems. Rub a cloth across affected leaves, and you'll see rust-colored spores that produce a yellowish or orange stain.

Lawns containing pure stands of Merion Kentucky bluegrass are especially susceptible to attack by rust fungi. Damage is less severe if the grass is mixed with common Kentucky bluegrass or with red fescue. Recommended mixtures are 50-percent Merion and 50-percent common Kentucky bluegrass; 50-percent Merion Kentucky bluegrass and 50-percent red fescue; or 50-percent Merion, 25-percent common Kentucky bluegrass, and 25-percent red fescue.

The Kentucky bluegrass varieties, Fylking, Pennstar, and Kenblue are more rust-resistant than Merion.

Those procedures recommended for the control of Helminthosporium leafspot and brown patch also will help prevent or control the development of rust in Kentucky bluegrass lawns.

Several chemicals (see Chart 1) control rust on Merion Kentucky bluegrass and other grasses. Chemicals do not completely eradicate rust or prevent the infection of future growth. Repeated applications may be necessary to keep rust under control, especially on Merion Kentucky bluegrass.

Pythium Diseases. The two most destructive lawn diseases caused by Pythium fungi are grease spot and cottony blight. Grease spot occurs in many parts of the country on a wide range of grasses; cottony blight occurs mainly on ryegrass in the South.

Pythium diseases thrive in humid areas and may be more widespread than is generally realized. The fungi are destructive at 70°F, and above, especially in poorly drained soils. These diseases are most common on newly established turf, but if conditions are favorable, they occur on grass regardless of age.

Diseased areas vary from a few inches to several feet in diameter and they sometimes occur in streaks as though the fungus had spread from mowing or from water flow following heavy rains. Injury is most perceptible in the early morning as a circular spot or a group of spots about 2 inches in diameter surrounded by blackened grass blades that are intertwined with the fungus threads. Diseased leaves become water soaked, mat together, and appear slimy. The darkened grass blades soon wither and turn reddish brown, particularly if the weather is sunny and windy. Grass is usually killed in 24 hours and lies flat on the ground rather than remaining upright like grass affected by the brown patch disease. New grass does not grow back into the diseased area.

The most important management practice is the avoidance of watering routines that keep foliage and ground wet for long periods, particularly during warm weather. Seeding should be delayed until fall because cool, dry weather generally checks the disease.

Chemicals give best results if used when the disease first appears.

Dollar Spot. Dollar spot, also known as small brown patch, occurs on many species of grass. The disease is particularly destructive in bentgrasses. It is most prevalent in the humid northern areas of the United States but occurs also in states farther south.

Dollar spot is most destructive during cool, wet weather. It generally attacks in May and June, stops during July and August, and starts again in September and October. The disease may occur in any turf regardless of management or soil fertility, but damage usually is greatest if there is a deficiency of nitrogen.

The disease is characterized by development of bleached spots the size of a silver dollar. Affected grass is killed, and the turf is left pitted. Sometimes the diseased areas merge and form large, irregular patches. At first, spots of diseased grass are dark and somewhat water soaked, then they turn brown and ultimately bleach nearly white. If the fungus is growing actively, a fine, white, cobwebby mycelium can be seen when dew is still on the grass. Sometimes only the uppermost grass blades are affected and light-colored blotches envelop them.

MANSION AT MOUNT VERNON.

Turf recovers quickly if treated with fungicides in the early stages of a disease attack. If the disease is left untreated it may take many weeks for new grass to fill in dead areas.

The best control of the disease is the use of chemicals suggested in Chart 1.

Stripe Smut. Stripe smut fungus attacks several lawn grases but it is most prevalent on Merion Kentucky bluegrass, principally in the northern half of the United States.

Smut spores in contaminated soil germinate and produce infection threads that invade grass seedlings and young tillers. Since the fungus grows systematically, infected plants remain diseased until they die.

Narrow gray or black stripes that may be continuous or discontinuous develop lengthwise in leaf blades. The gray stripes are unruptured smut sites called sori. The black streaks result when smut sori rupture and liberate a mass of black, powdery spores. Following rupture of the sori, diseased leaves wither, curl, shred from the tip downward, and die.

Diseased Kentucky bluegrass plants occur singly, or in spots from a few inches to a foot or more in diameter. Infected plants often are pale green to slightly yellowed. They also are shorter than neighboring healthy plants and may be obscured by them.

Stripe smut is most apparent on leaves during cool weather in spring and fall. Diseased plants are difficult to find during hot, dry weather because many infected plants die. Smutted plants also are difficult to find shortly after mowing due to their slower growth.

Fungicides are available for treating dollar spot. Smut damage is less severe if Merion Kentucky bluegrass is mixed with common Kentucky bluegrass, or if smut-tolerant varieties like Fylking, Kenblue, Park, or Pennstar are grown.

Powdery Mildew. In recent years, powdery mildew has become an increasingly prevalent fungus disease of Merion Kentucky bluegrass and other Kentucky bluegrasses. Powdery mildew also infects red fescue, bermuda and other grasses used for lawns. High amounts of nitrogen fertilizer produce an ideal environment for this mildew fungus.

The disease generally is more damaging to grasses in shaded and protected areas (on north and east sides of buildings), although it also occurs in severe form among Merion grasses during late fall and early spring. Because the fungus significantly reduces the growth of leaves, roots, and rhizomes, it is an important cause of turf deterioration in shaded areas. Many plants may be weakened, die from drought, or be winter-killed because of this deterioration.

Powdery mildew appears first as small superficial patches of white to light-gray fungus growth on leaves and sheaths. These patches enlarge rapidly and become powdery as spores are produced. The older, lower leaves often are completely covered by mildew. Leaf tissue under mildew becomes yellowed soon after infection and later turns tan or brown and is killed. Severely infected leaves gradually dry up and die.

This hardy fungus survives the winter as a mass of thread-like filaments on the live leaves of Kentucky bluegrass. Numerous spores are produced on these filaments in the spring. Spores are carried by the wind and initiate new infections during cool (optimum 65°F.), humid weather. With favorable temperature and high atmospheric humidity, the host tissue dies and the spores are carried to other grasses in neighboring turf areas to produce new infections and start the cycle once again.

Kentucky bluegrass varieties differ in their susceptibility to powdery mildew. Merion remains very susceptible while other varieties exhibit varying degrees of resistance.

To reduce turf shading and improve air circulation be sure to prune or remove trees and shrubs that shade or border turf areas. Keep the lawn vigorous but avoid overstimulation with nitrogen fertilizer. Water during dry periods to maintain adequate moisture in the soil. Where possible, mow at the recommended height and, when the disease is present, collect all clippings.

In the spring or early fall, when powdery mildew becomes evident, one or more applications of a fungicide at seven to ten day intervals should control the disease. Recommended fungicides for the control of powdery mildew are listed in Chart 1.

Fusarium Blight. Fusarium blight affects Kentucky bluegrass, bentgrass, red fescue, and many other grasses. The fungi that cause Fusarium blight survive the winter months in infected grass roots, crowns, and in thatch covering the lower portion of grass plants. The pathogens are widespread and occur on blighted turf wherever turf grasses are grown.

Bentgrasses are the most susceptible species, followed by Kentucky bluegrass and red frescue. The disease also occurs in Merion and Windsor Kentucky bluegrass, but other varieties vary in susceptibility at different temperatures.

The severity of the disease varies directly with light intensity, and areas that receive direct sunlight are the most severely infected. Infection of the leaves usually occurs when air temperatures are 70°F. to 90°F. and conditions of high humidity prevail. When temperatures fall below 70°F. and there is an absence of rainfall or humidity, the disease ceases to be active.

At first, diseased areas are light green but within 36 to 48 hours the areas fade to tan then to a light straw color. The diseased areas vary in size from a few inches to 2 or more feet in diameter. Dead areas may be circular, crescent shaped, streaked, or in circles with a patch of green grass in the central portion. The latter forms a distinctive "frog's eye" symptom pattern. Extensive damage occurs when diseased areas are numerous and coalesce.

Individual plants are killed when the crown tissues are destroyed. Irregular-shaped dark-green blotches form on the leaves. These blotches

rapidly fade to a dish-brown hue, and finally become dull tan.

The fungi that cause Fusarium blight grow in a layer of thatch on the soil surface. To control this disease, remove most of the thatch layer with a rake or lawnmower. A nitrogen imbalance in the soil causes the thatch on which the fungi feed to accumulate more rapidly.

To effectively control Fusarium blight, a preventive fungicide spray combined with thatch control is essential. Do not spray when night temperatures fall below 70°F. Spraying should be continued at 7 to 10 day intervals as long as daytime temperatures are 75°F. or above, and conditions of high humidity prevail.

Fungicides that will help control Fusarium blight are listed in Chart 1.

Red Thread. Red thread especially affects bentgrasses, red fescue, and Kentucky bluegrasses in the Northeastern states and in the Pacific Coast states of Washington and Oregon. In these regions, red thread occurs primarily in the early spring and fall during cool wet weather. This fungus disease also has been reported on bermudagrass lawns in Mississippi during December.

When the grass is growing rapidly, nitrogen fertilization is a quick and effective means of controlling the disease. However, the fungus again becomes destructive when grass growth slows down. Therefore, fungicidal eradication is necessary for satisfactory disease control.

The pathogen survives unfavorable conditions by lingering as fragments of dried fungal tissues and as dormant mycelium in the residues of the diseased plants. These fragments may be carried by the wind, or mechanically on mowers or similar machines.

Red thread attacks the leaves and leaf sheaths. These parts later become tan colored as the tissue dries out. The leaves may be completely covered by a pink, gelatinous growth of the fungus. As this growth spreads, it infects plant after plant.

In its final stages, the disease is characterized by reddish fungus threads at the leaf terminals. Diseased areas are usually 2 to 30 inches in diameter and irregular in shape.

Red thread is capable of growing over a wide range of temperatures: from slightly above 32°F. to about 86°F. The most favorable temperature range for growth lies between 60°F. and 70°F.

Red thread is serious only when cool temperatures slow grass growth or when the turf is underfertilized with nitrogen. Fungicides to control red thread are listed in Chart 1.

Copper Spot. Copper spot can cause a serious disease problem on bentgrasses. It is most damaging in the coastal states but is found throughout the United States.

The pathogen lodges in the debris of the previous season's growth. The disease occurs in warm, wet weather; active growth of the organism begins when air temperatures range from 68°F. to 75°F. When the weather is warm and humid secondary spores are produced and new lesions are formed.

The spores, spread by means of splashing water, germinate rapidly and new leaf infections take place within 24 hours. Outbreaks of copper spot may occur in epidemic proportions within a few days.

From a distance, copper spot looks like salmon-pink or copper-colored turf. The spots range from 1 to 3 inches in diameter. Unlike areas infected by dollar spot, areas affected by copper spot are not definite in outline. Wet weather increases the intensity of coloration.

Copper spot can be controlled by the use of fungicides. Apply preventive fungicidal applications at 10-day intervals when the daytime air temperatures stabilize at 70°F. to 75°F. Make curative applications at 4 to 5-day intervals until recovery is effected.

Ophiobolus Patch. Ophiobolus patch is the third most important fungus disease in the Pacific Northwest. It occurs west of the Cascades in Oregon, Washington, and British Columbia. The disease is especially common to bentgrass lawns.

The growth of the disease is stimulated by cool, wet weather. However, symptoms become most noticeable during midsummer under drier growing conditions. Ophiobolus patch usually appears as a thinning or drying of the grass in doughnut-shaped rings or larger areas. Both shoots and roots of the grass are severely attacked. Affected areas do not recover for several months.

The doughnut-shaped rings range from several inches to several feet in diameter. The injured areas are light brown in color becoming dull gray in winter. The centers of the rings are invaded by weeds and annual bluegrass.

Ophiobolus patch is first seen as depressed circular patches of blighted turfgrass, a few inches in diameter. The affected areas may increase to several feet in diameter and coalesce so that they become large, irregular-shaped patches. Coloring ranges from light straw to bronze. The centers of the patches often fill in with resistant species creating a "frog's eye" symptom pattern.

Ophiobolus patch is difficult to control with fungicides. However, the use of ammonium sulfate fertilizer as a source of nitrogen has proven effective.

Apply ammonium sulfate four times a year in March, May, June, and early September. Apply 7½ pounds of the product as it comes from the bag per 1,000 square feet for each application. Turf must be thoroughly watered after each application of fertilizer.

To balance applications of ammonium sulfate apply 0-20-20 (0-P-K) fertilizer twice a year in early spring and early fall. Use 7 pounds of fertilizer per 1,000 square feet for each application. After the disease has disappeared use a 12-4-8 fertilizer for normal lawn fertilization.

Snow Molds: Fusarium Patch and Typhula Blight. These diseases are especially severe on bentgrasses, but they also occur on other lawn grasses. Snow mold, or winter scald, is caused by several different fungi. It is most severe when snow covers grass for long periods, and is particularly difficult to control if the grass is green and growing actively when covered by lasting snow. Fusarium patch, also known as pink snow mold, can occur during the growing season when humidity is high and daily temperatures fall below 65°F. Any condition that keeps

GUIDE FOR SELECTING FUNGICIDES

Application Per 1,000 sq ft

Disease and Casual Organism	Fungicides	Ounces of Formulation	Table-spoons	Directions
Brown Patch *Rhizoctonia solani*	Cleary's 3336® WP 50% Daconil 2787® WP 75% Dyrene® WP 50% Fore® WP 80% Fungo 50® WP 80% Mertect 140–F® liquid Tersan 1991® WP 50% Tersan LSR® WP 80%	2 4 4–6 4 2 2 2 6	11 22 19–28 14 11 4 11 4–5	Disease can appear from June to August. Treat your lawn every 7–10 days until the disease has been controlled.
Copper Spot *Gloeocercospora sorghi*	See Dollar Spot (*Sclerotinia*)			
Dollar Spot *Sclerotinia homeocarpa*	Acti-dione-Thiram® WP Cleary's 3336R® WP 50% Daconil 2787® WP 75% Dyrene® WP 50% Tersan 1991® WP 50% Fore® WP 80% Fungo 50® WP 50% Mertect 140–F® liquid	2–4 2 2–4 4–6 2 6–8 1 2	11–22 11 11–22 19–28 11 14–21 6 4	Disease can appear from June to October. Treat your lawn at 7–10 day intervals until the disease has been controlled.
Fairy Rings Mushrooms *Psalliota campestris* *Marasmius* *Lepiota*	Captan WP 50% Dowfume MC–2	4–5	15–20	Disease can appear throughout the growing season. Pour double or triple strength concentrate of captan into 1-inch holes punches 4–6 inches deep and 6–8 inches apart both inside and outside the affected area. Alternative method: Fumigate infected area with Dowfume MC–2® (1 lb/100 sq ft) and reseed or resod. Recommended largely for gold courses, parks, and other large turf areas.
Fusarium Blight *Fusarium roseum*	Cleary's 3336® WP 50% Fungo 50® WP 50% Tersan 1991® WP 50%	4–8 4–8 2	11–22 19–38 33	Treat at first appearance of disease and repeat 7–10 days later. Water thoroughly to wet into soil.
Grease Spot and Cottony Blight *Pythium*	Tersan SP® WP 65% Dexon® WP 70% Fore® WP 80% Koban® WP 65% Zineb WP 75%	4 2 8 4 2	5–6 14 28 17 13–27	Disease can appear from July to September and in fall and winter during warm, humid periods in the South. Treat your lawn every 5–14 days until the disease has been controlled.
Helminthosporium diseases Leafspot (Blight, Going-out, Melting-out) *Helminthosporium* spp.	Acti-dione-Thiram® WP Captan WP 50% Cleary's 3336® WP 50% Daconil 2787 ® WP 75% Dyrene® WP 50% Fore® WP 80% Tersan LSR® WP 80% Zineb WP 75%	4 4–6 2 4 4–6 4 3–4 2	22 15–23 11 22 19–28 14 4–5 13–27	Disease can appear from April to August, depending on kind of grass and species of fungus. Treat your lawn every 7–10 days three times consecutively or until the disease has been controlled.
Powdery Mildew *Erysiphe graminis*	Acti-dione Thiram® Acti-dione TGF® WP Tersan 1991® WP 50%	4 1–2 2	22 6 11	July–September 7–10 days 7–14 days
Red Thread *Corticum fuciforme*	Acti-dione-Thiram® WP Cleary's 3336® WP 50% Fore® WP 80% Fungo 50® WP 50% Tersan LSR® WP 80%	4 2 4–6 2 6	22 11 14–21 11 4–5	May, June, and August, every 10–14 days.
Rust *Puccinia*	Acti-dione-Thiram® WP Daconil 2787® WP 75% Dyrene® WP 50% Fore® WP 80% Tersan LSR® WP 80% Zineb WP 75%	4 4 4–6 4 3–4 2	22 22 19–28 14 4–5 13–27	Disease can appear from June to September. Treat your lawn every 7–14 days until rust disappears.
Slime Molds *Physarum cinereum*	Fore® WP 80% Zineb WP 75%	6–8 2	21–28 13–27	Disease can appear throughout the growing season and can be controlled without fungicides.
Snow Molds Fusarium Patch *Fusarium nivale*	Tersan 1991® WP 50% Mertect 140–F® liquid Fore® WP 80% Fungo 50® WP 50%	2 2 6–8 2	11 2 21–28 11	Disease can appear from fall to spring. Treat your lawn at intervals of 2–6 weeks as needed.
Typhula Blight *Typhula itoana*	Tersan SP® WP 65% Dyrene WP 50%	6–8 2–3	5–6 19–28	Disease can appear from fall to spring. Treat your lawn at intervals of 2–6 weeks as needed.
Stripe Smut *Ustilago striiformis*	Fungo 50® WP 50% Tersan 1991® WP 50%	4–8 6	19–38 33	One application in October or early spring before grass growth begins. Water thoroughly to wet into soil.

CAUTION: Do not graze treated areas or feed clippings to livestock.
The directions given in the above table may not be complete enough. Be sure to read and follow the manufacturer's directions on the label for all fungicide applications.

Chart 2

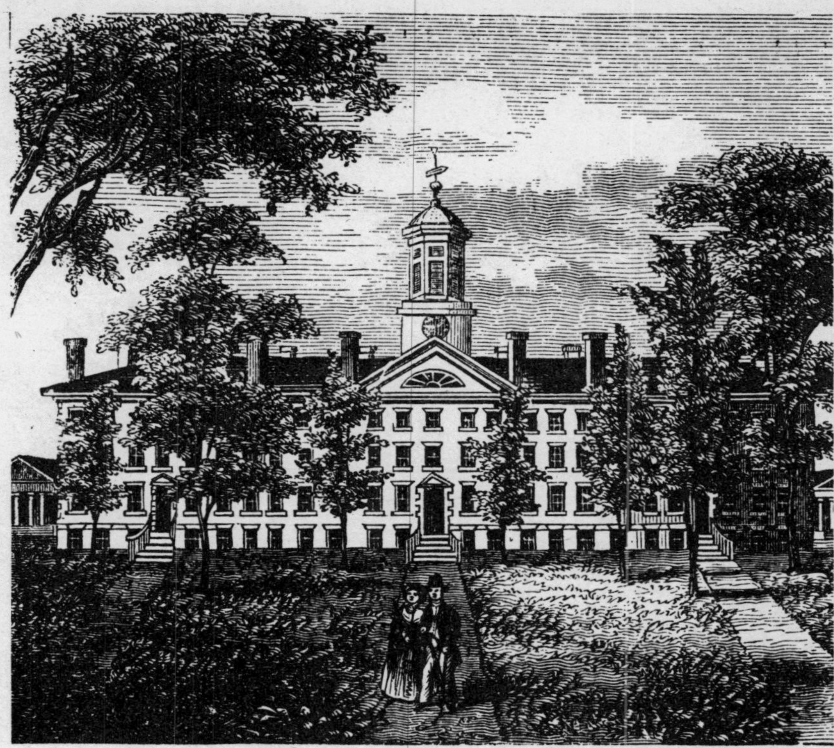

NASSAU HALL, PRINCETON COLLEGE.

THE STATE-HOUSE AT ANNAPOLIS.

the turf excessively wet, such as poor surface drainage, favors these diseases.

Snow mold symptoms appear first as white cottony growth on the leaves. As the leaves die they turn light brown and cling together. Diseased areas are usually 1 to 12 inches or more in diameter and discolored dirty white, gray, or slightly pink. Fusarium patch is characterized by development of irregular pale yellow areas from several inches to several feet in diameter. Later, affected areas become whitish gray. Sometimes the edge of an affected area has a faint pinkish color.

Typhula blight is particularly active under snow cover and is usually conspicuous at the first spring thaw. At first, the disease appears as light-yellow discolored grass areas 1 or 2 inches in diameter. Leaves of the infected plants change their discolored appearance to a grayish white. As the areas enlarge, a halo of grayish-white mycelial growth up to 1 inch in diameter develops. Affected areas may measure up to 1 or 2 feet, but under optimum conditions the diseased grass may coalesce into larger areas.

Initial disease development does not occur unless there is snow cover on unfrozen ground. When the ground is frozen, parasitic activity of the fungus essentially ceases. The disease is most active with the advent of cool air temperatures and humid conditions in the spring.

Fork and Rake

Proper management in the fall is especially important since the condition of the turf as it goes into winter determines whether the snow mold fungus can easily get established. Do not apply high nitrogen fertilizers late in the fall because that might stimulate growth and result in an actively growing turf when snow covers the ground. Keep the lawn cut in the fall to prevent a mat of grass from developing. Apply lime if soil tests indicate a need for it.

Mushrooms and Slime Molds. Some fungi such as mushrooms and slime molds are not true disease organisms. They do not attack lawn grasses directly but they are unsightly and the fruiting bodies of the mushrooms and dusty mass of slime molds occur repeatedly.

Mushrooms that grow individually or in clumps usually develop from buried organic matter such as pieces of construction lumber, logs, or tree stumps. They can be eliminated by digging up the pieces of buried wood. If this is impractical, drench the soil with captan. The simplest way to drench is to punch holes 6 to 8 inches apart and 6 to 8 inches deep in the ground within and surrounding the infected area. Use an iron rod or pipe for punching the holes, then pour a solution of captan down the holes.

Another group of fungi produces mushroom-like fruiting bodies in circles or arcs of dark-green grass surrounded by light-colored or dead grass. This condition is known as fairy rings. The fungi that cause fairy rings spread outward from an initial point of infection at the rate of 6 to 24 inches annually. Fairy rings are usually more noticeable in large lawns and seldom occur in lawns that are adequately fertilized and maintained.

For best control, fumigate the affected area with methyl bromide. As an alternate method, punch holes around the outside of the ring and throughout the affected area, then pour a solution of captan into the holes.

A group of fungi known as slime molds often cover grass with a dusty, bluish-gray, black, or yellow mass. Slime molds are not parasitic on grass, but they are unsightly. They feed on dead organic matter. The most damage they do to grass plants is to shade and discolor blades. Slime molds occur during wet weather, and will disappear rapidly as soon as it becomes dry. The large masses can be readily broken up by sweeping with a broom or by spraying with a strong steam of water. During prolonged damp weather slime molds can be especially annoying and it may be desirable to apply a turf fungicide listed in Chart 1 to affected areas.

Insects

About 60 species of insects injure lawn grasses by feeding on roots, stems, and leaves. This insect feeding weakens plants, causing patches of grass to turn yellow or brown and die. A few insects damage lawns by their burrowing or nesting habits.

It is virtually impossible to predict insect infestations, as populations fluctuate seasonally and locally depending upon climate, prevalence of natural enemies, abundance of food plants, and other factors. Fortunately only a few species are sufficiently abundant in any one year or any one place to justify control measures. Lawns should be examined frequently to detect insect infestation so that it can be properly treated before serious damage occurs.

Grubs are the most destructive soil inhabiting pests. They are the larvae of several species of beetles but are similar in appearance. Whitish, soft bodied, usually with brown heads, grubs are generally found in a curled position. These pests feed on the roots an inch or two below the surface, often destroying the turf.

The grubs hatch from eggs. They usually spend about 10 months in the soil, although some species require two to three years to reach maturity and emerge as adults. Birds, skunks, and moles feed on the grubs, often disturbing the lawn as they search for them. Adult beetles of most species feed on the leaves of trees and shrubs and do not damage lawns.

White grubs are the most widely distributed in the United States. They are the larvae of the familiar yellow-brown to blackish May beetles or June bugs that are attracted to lights.

Grubs of Japanese beetles are very damaging in some Eastern areas. The adults are shiny metallic green with coppery-brown wing covers and six patches of white hairs along the sides and back of the body. The beetles are active during the day and feed on many flowers and fruits.

Grubs of the Asiatic garden beetle, masked chafers, European chafer, and the Oriental beetles are other important species that damage lawns.

Billbugs are hard-shelled beetles 1/5 to 3/4-inch long with a long snout. The larvae are legless, as much as 5/8-inch long, white with a reddish or yellowish-brown head. The adults burrow in the grass stems near the soil surface and the larvae feed upon the roots, often cutting them off so the grass can be easily pulled out.

Since 1960, billbugs have been destructive to lawns. One species called the hunting billbug has severely damaged zoysiagrass lawns in the East.

Mole crickets, especially in the Southwest, often damage lawns by feeding on the grass roots. Their burrowing also uproots plants and allows the soil to dry out. Newly seeded lawns may be severely damaged. Adult mole crickets are about 1½ inches long, velvety brown with large, shovel-shaped front feet well suited for digging.

Several species of *ants* and a few species of *bees and wasps* have nest-building habits that sometimes will damage lawns. They mound up the soil around their nests and smother the grass.

Caterpillars of several species damage lawns. Sod webworms are the most troublesome. These are the larvae of small, whitish or grayish moths called lawn months that are seen flying over the grass on early spring evenings. They are easily recognized by their habit of folding their wings closely around their bodies when at rest. Several varieties exist in all parts of the United States. Sod webworms may have several generations per year depending on the species and location.

Larvae are about ¾-inch long when mature, and brown spotted. They feed on grass leaves and are most active at night. Damage is first noticed as irregular brown spots and later as patches of uneven growth.

The fall armyworm is commonly found on lawns. This insect overwinters only in the extreme South and migrates north as the season advances. When fully grown, the caterpillars are about 1½ inches long and vary from green to almost black. They feed on leaves and during outbreaks may devour the grass to the ground. The adults are ash-gray moths with mottled forewings. When the wings are opened they measure about 1½ inches across. The insect produces several generations per year on the southern part of its range.

The armyworm is somewhat similar to the fall armyworm in size and appearance but much less common in lawns. Moths of this species are brown with a small white spot near the center of each front wing. There are usually three generations per year.

Chinch bugs are the most important sap-sucking pests of grasses, particularly in the East and the South. The hairy chinch bug is common in lawns in the Northeast and the southern chinch bug is a major pest, especially of St. Augustinegrass, in Florida and along the Gulf Coast.

The adults are about ⅙-inch long and black with white wings folded over their backs. The nymphs are bright red when very small but turn gray as they grow older. They have a white band across their backs.

Both the nymphs and the adults suck plant juices, causing the grass to turn yellow in irregular patches. If feeding continues, the grass turns brown and dies. The hairy chinch bug has two to three generations per year and the southern chinch bug three to five.

Scale insects also suck plant juices. Some species attack the roots while others damage the aboveground parts. Newly born scales, called crawlers, are active and move about over the plant. In a few days they settle down, insert their mouthparts into the plant, lose their legs, and begin an attached existence. The Rhodesgrass scale, bermudagrass scale, and ground pearls are common species.

Leafhoppers are small wedge-shaped insects about ⅕-inch long, ranging from yellow to green and gray. Both nymphs and adults retard grass growth by sucking sap from the leaves and stems. Injury appears as whitened areas often mistaken for drought or disease damage.

The damage that insects cause to lawns can be reduced by following recommended cultural and maintenance practices. A healthy, vigorous turf can support greater insect populations without serious harm better than one in poor condition.

Biological control of insect pests helps to reduce damage. Birds seek out and destroy many insects in lawns. Insect parasites, predators, and diseases reduce populations but their impact on lawn insects has not been thoroughly studied. None of the grass varieties commonly used for lawns is resistant to insects. When lawn insects become too numerous they can be controlled with insecticides.

Weeds

Crabgrass (*Digitaria ischaemum and D. sanguinalis*), chickweed, annual bluegrass (*Poa annua*), dandelion, and to some extent white clover are weeds that can destroy turf cover when they develop vigorously or cause unsightly contrasts.

Some weeds render sports turf unusable. These include goosegrass, the sedges (*Carex spp.*) and white clover. White clover also can attract bees to home lawn sites.

While control of turf weeds varies with the species involved, the single, most often used and most effective weed control method is growing a dense and persistent cover of turfgrasses. Hand-weeding and the use of herbicides are increased in effectiveness when a good turf cover is growing.

Once weeds have invaded a turfgrass area, avoid management practices that will encourage their growth. For example, a good technique for the control of crabgrass in Kentucky bluegrass turf involves shading-out the weed seedlings before they have become established. Generous fertilization of the lawn in late summer and early fall, and allowing the grass to grow to 3 or 4 inches before mowing the following spring will result in a dense canopy of grass that will prevent the crabgrass seedlings from germinating. Once the crabgrass is under control, the mowing height can be lowered to approximately 1½ to 2 inches.

Proper choice of herbicides and observance of instruction for their use will help to control most common weeds. The herbicide 2,4-D has been used for 25 years. Low volatility forms of this herbicide are available, which reduce the possibility of damaging adjacent desirable plants. Combinations of herbicides will control most broadleaved weeds although damage can be done to some trees and shrubs if the chemicals are applied carelessly or at excessive rates. Chemical formulations vary with manufacturers. Follow directions and observe all precautions on the label.

Hazards

Lawn grasses tolerate a wide assortment of natural and manmade contamination hazards. Surprisingly few of these prevent grass growth, but they often do make growing good turf more difficult.

Annual bluegrass was found sensitive to California smog 20 years ago. Annual bluegrass and bentgrass have shown injury from ozone while red fescue and bentgrass are sensitive to sulfur dioxide. Red fescue is intolerant of industrial fumes in some parts of New Jersey. Selecting less sensitive or more resistant grasses in areas where such conditions exist is the only real remedy for avoiding the problem.

Grass tolerates a wide range of water quality. Water with heavy metals and/or high salt content can cause serious trouble, but is seldom encountered. Some water additives such as chlorine can be harmful but such injury is observed infrequently. Few soils fail to grow grass if the soil acidity is properly adjusted and management practices are favorable.

Concentrated inorganic fertilizers, if applied too heavily, burn grass in 2 or 3 days. Burned areas may occur in spots or streaks or the entire lawn may be damaged. To prevent injury, apply the fertilizer evenly in recommended amounts when the grass is dry, then water immediately. If burning occurs, water generously to wash off excess fertilizer and reduce injury.

Hydrated lime burns grass if it is applied unevenly and in large amounts. Ground agricultural limestone is safer and is usually recommended for lawns.

Wear

A key consideration in reducing traffic and wear problems of turf is to restrict traffic in order to give the grass time to establish a hardy cover and to allow it to reseed and strengthen when it is showing signs of wear and thinning.

Seedling turf must be protected from traffic for several mowings and even then only a limited traffic should be permitted during the first year. With very weak grass growth, where stand failure could result from various causes, use of the turf should be avoided to increase its chance for survival.

Keeping off turf at times when grass may be unusually susceptible to injury can provide more total use of the turf throughout the rest of the year. When the weather is hot and dry, traffic on the cool-climate grasses is very damaging. Conversely, the warm-weather grasses, bermudagrass and zoysia, are more intolerant of traffic in winter.

Where a choice of grass exists, use the most wear-tolerant species. In warm, sunny, subtropical areas such as the southern United States or in tropical areas, bermudagrass is excellent for the heavy wear areas. In the northern United States and similar cool, temperate areas, Kentucky bluegrass is most desirable because of its vigor. Grasses such as tall fescue, zoysia, and ryegrass have tougher leaves, and they may be the best grass where local conditions permit.

A very wet turf can be destroyed within a short time and the soil may become severely compacted. Saturated soils pack easily and bake hard when dry, especially where traffic is heavy. The soil may become packed so hard that water will not penetrate the surface. Grass then thins out and bare spots result. To correct this condition, loosen or perforate the soil with a tined fork or aerifying implement and, if necessary, fertilize and reseed the lawn.

The Lazy Gardener's Special
Ground Covers

Ground covers—which include any low-growing plants such as most vines, prostrate forms of conifers, broad- and narrow-leafed evergreens, and some annual and perennial herbaceous plants—are ideal for lazy gardeners and a solution to many lawn problems.

They can cover bare spots in the yard, prevent soil erosion, regulate foot traffic, tie together unrelated plants into an attractive composition, serve as a fire-retarding screen in arid regions, filter out dust particles from the air, and hide litter that may blow into the yard. Ground covers can be used in areas where no other kind of plant or artificial cover can be used—steeply sloping banks, inner courtyards, rock gardens, and areas of dense shade.

Establishing ground covers takes time. Regardless of the site selected, the soil must be modified to support root growth. Once established, though, ground covers require little maintenance.

Planting: Prepare the soil by digging to a depth of at least six inches. Spread two to three inches of organic material such as peat, well-rotted manure, or leafmold over the ground and spade it into the soil. Also add any fertilizer.

On uneven ground where the entire area cannot be worked, dig individual planting holes. Dig these deep enough so that they can be filled partially with soil mixed with organic material before setting out the plants. Use topsoil for the rest of the refill. Low banks two to three feet high can be planted without any additional preparation, but steep slopes should have retaining walls. Sloping areas are usually dry, so select plants that tolerate periodic drought. Large, vigorous plants, such as junipers or cotoneasters, are good choices for slopes.

Although ground covers can be planted any time during the growing season, early spring establishes plants during a long growing period before winter. Space the plants so they will spread to cover the site as quickly as possible. Small plants like bugleweed may be placed as close as four to six inches apart. Large plants, such as juniper or cotoneaster, should be set apart as much as four feet. Closer planting will cover the ground quicker, but the cost of additional plants may be prohibitive.

Maintenance: Fertilize the plants during the winter and again in early spring. To avoid burning the foliage, scatter a pelleted form of commercial fertilizer over the planting when the foliage is dry.

Because ground covers are slow to cover bare ground, weeds are likely to sprout, especially during the first year. Most weeds can be controlled with a mulch of wood chips, straw, or other organic refuse. Mulch will also retain the soil's moisture. If weeds break through the mulch, remove them by hand. Do not dig around the plants. Digging breaks the surface roots and promotes germination of weed seeds. It is also a good idea to keep the growing areas carefully defined, for appearance and to keep the plants within bounds.

Do not rely on summer rainfall to adequately water ground cover. Water throughout the growing season, particularly during dry weather, allowing the water to penetrate deeply into the soil. Water again when soil is dry to the touch and the tips of the plants wilt slightly at midday. One inch of water every ten to fourteen days is usually satisfactory for rapid establishment. In winter, water thoroughly when the weather is dry and the temperature is above freezing.

In cold climates with no permanent snow cover, plantings in direct sunlight may need protection to prevent the thawing of plant tissues. Also, direct sunlight can cause permanent damage. Plants can be protected by layering conifer branches or burlap over the beds. If the plants heave out of the soil in cold weather, push them back immediately. Do not wait until spring.

Ground covers will show winter injury as do other plants. Evergreens, for example, may suffer windburn during an extremely dry winter; shear them or prune damaged branches in early spring. Juniper may be so badly winter-damaged that soil areas become bare; replant bare areas rather than wait until old plants fill the gaps. Winter damage can be reduced by covering the plants with an anti-transpirant spray, which decreases moisture loss. Plants should also be sprayed when they are being transplanted.

Evergreens: Myrtle or periwinkle (*Vinca minor*) is creeping and vinelike with bright-blue spring flowers. An excellent choice for both full sun and shade, it forms dense mats; yet early bulbs such as grape hyacinths will thrive when interplanted with myrtle, if they are fertilized every year. *Bowlesii* is a superior form with larger flowers, but is slower to establish. White and purple and some double forms are available. Japanese spurge (*Pachysandra terminalis*) is one of the most common and satisfactory ground covers. It grows six to ten inches tall, has inconspicuous white flower spikes in early spring, prefers shade and acid soil, and spreads by underground runner. English ivy (*Hedera heliz*) grows especially well in shaded areas but tends to burn in winter sun. Baltica, an excellent small-leafed form, maintains its color throughout the year and is a controlled grower as well.

Ferns: Hay-scented fern (*Dennstaedtia punctilobula*) is yellow-green, turning to a light rust-color in the fall. In the sun, or when it is dried, it gives off an aroma of hay. It is a rampant grower to a height of two feet in somewhat damp, open shade. It is deciduous and sheds its leaves in late fall. Toothed or common wood fern (*Dryopteris spinulosa*) does best in moist, slightly acid soil in open shade. It stays green much of the winter. Cinnamon fern (*Osmunda cinnamomea*), the showiest fiddlehead, provides an attractive background to daylilies and other flowering perennials. It grows to three feet and is deciduous.

Royal fern (*Osmunda regalis*), lovely and graceful for sloping banks and paths, is especially attractive interplanted with Japanese iris. It grows best (to four feet) in a damp, highly acid location, and is deciduous. Christmas fern (*Polystichum acrostichoides*) looks especially good at the edge of woodland or when interplanted with narcissus. It grows to two feet and is almost evergreen. New York fern (*Thelypterisis noveboracensis*) is a yellow-green to medium-green fern—a nice contrast when planted alongside darker green ferns. It needs a rich, moist, slightly acid loam, spreads rapidly, and is deciduous.

Flowering Ground Covers: Barrenwort (*Epimedium spp.*) is a perennial with heart-shaped leaves. It grows six to twelve inches, depending on the form selected, and is covered in May and June with delicate yellow, white, pink, or red flowers. It thrives in partial shade or sun. Lily-of-the-valley (*Convallaria majalis*), a perennial, has fragrant, white, bell-shaped flowers that appear in spring. It grows to six to ten inches and likes partial shade and rich, moist, organic soil. Leadwort (*Plumbago larpentiae*) is a late-spring, spreading perennial that is covered with bright blue flowers from July to November. It grows to a height of eight inches and will accommodate either sun or semishade. Forget-me-not (*Myosotis scorpiodes, M. palustris*) has a light-green foliage with blue flowers in spring. Easy to grow from seed, it does best in light and open shade.

Shade Ground Covers: Sweet woodruff (*Asperula odorata*), a pretty, eight-inch-high perennial with small white flowers in May, spreads rapidly. Its leaves are used in May wine. Galax (*Galax aphylla*) is a ten-inch-high evergreen with bronze-colored, heart-shaped leaves and spikes of white flowers in June. It spreads slowly but is a vigorous, hardy shade ground cover. Wintercreeper (*Euonymus fortunei, E. radicans*), a hardy evergreen that quickly covers large areas with shiny foliage, grows best in moist, acid soils.

Full-Sun Ground Covers: Bearberry cotoneaster (*Cotoneaster dammeri*) is a prostrate evergreen with rooting stems that bear white flowers followed by bright-red berries that last into winter. It grows from six inches to three feet. Wild Scotch heather (*Calluna vulgaris*) is a long-blooming, low, bushy plant with rosy-lavender flowers from July to September. All heathers are evergreen. Sargent juniper (*Juniperus chinensis sargentii*) is a low-spreading evergreen that has excellent winter color. The plant will grow downward and is excellent for sloping areas. It may grow to a height of three feet and requires trimming. Forsythia (*Forsythia spp.*) roots easily and grows rapidly. It bears a profusion of small yellow flowers in spring and maintains a full, light-green foliage throughout summer. It grows to two feet and requires trimming.

Seashore Ground Covers: Bearberry (*Arctostaphylos uvursi*) is a dense, creeping evergreen that will cover large areas. Its small leathery leaves and white spring flower bells are followed by red berries that last all winter. It is an excellent hardy shrub in stony, sandy, or acid soils. Ground-broom (*Cytisus decumbens*), an evergreen with an abundance of bright-blue flowers in April and May, is low-growing and spreads easily in sandy soil. Box sand-myrtle (*Leiophyllum buxifolium*) grows into two-foot evergreen mounds that spread slowly over sandy areas. The mounds are covered with fluffy white flowers during June. Dwarf rugosa rose (*Rosa rugosa repens alba*) forms a hardy carpet on sandy, sunny banks. Its white June flowers are followed by red seed hips. It is very tolerant of salt spray.

Vines are found in most major plant groups, including bamboos and palms, which are generally thought of as having only upright growth. They occur even among ferns and lilies, and the night-blooming cereus is a cactus example.

Defining a vine is not easy, because no two vines seem to have exactly the same characteristics. In fact, many vines, finding no support, are content to trail along the ground while others grow upward. This kind of variation creates complications in categorization.

Most vines, however, prefer to attach themselves to a support and to keep moving upward. They do this in various ways. Honeysuckle and others prefer to twine around a slender support like a pole. The gloriosa lily is among those that use hook-shaped leaves to climb. Some, like English ivy, put out aerial roots or tendrils to cling to supports.

All vines grow quickly. Given unlimited room and optimal growth conditions, they spread quickly. Given less than optimal conditions, if, for example, confined by a trellis or other support, they need pruning to stay attractive and within bounds.

VINES

Allamanda cathartica trumpet vine
Light: Full sun is vital
Water: Moderate
Bloom: Brilliant yellow flowers in spring

This evergreen does not tolerate temperature extremes; has ovate leaves that are long in proportion to their width; and arresting tubular blossoms.

Akebia quinata five-leaved akebia
Light: Sun
Water: Moderate
Bloom: Purple flowers in spring

A delicate vine with tiny leaves and tiny flowers that tend to droop from thin stems.

Ampelopsis brevipedunculata porcelain ampelopsis
Light: Sun or shade
Water: Abundant
Bloom: Blue berries in autumn

This vine will accommodate itself to most soil conditions. The leaves are very attractive—with five broad lobes looking almost like a spread-out, flat hand, and somewhat fuzzy.

Antigonon leptopus coral vine
Light: Sun
Water: Moderate
Bloom: Rose blossoms summer through fall

This heat-loving plant does not do well in northern climates and dies back in winter. The leaves are spear-shaped, and the May flowers grow from short, separated stems, giving them a degree of formality.

Bignonia capreolata trumpet vine
Light: Sun
Water: Moderate
Bloom: Large, brilliant flowers all summer

This is an especially popular vine, because it spreads rapidly with little care. Also, the tiny, spear-shaped leaves are overwhelmed by the showy blossoms. They enjoy well-drained soil and tolerate heat.

FOUR GOOD CLEMATISES.

Calonyction aculeatum moonflower
Light: Sun
Water: Abundant
Bloom: Large, white flowers all summer

Moonflowers like rich soil. They have heart-shaped leaves tapering to a tip, but these are overshadowed by the large, open blossoms.

Celastrus scandens American bittersweet
Light: Sun
Water: Moderate
Bloom: Small, yellow flowers in fall followed by orange fruit

Celastrus has oval leaves so small they are not much bigger than its berries. Unlike some vines, it doesn't like to trail and requires support on a trellis wall.

Clematis Virgin's bower
Light: Sun
Water: Moderate
Bloom: Red, white, or blue flowers in spring and summer

Exceptionally popular and easy-to-grow if given rich, well-drained soil, clematis has attractive, dark-green leaves. Several varieties are available—some with flat, pointy petals; some fragrant; some with curled petals.

Doxantha unguis-cati trumpet vine
Light: Sun or bright light
Water: Abundant
Bloom: Yellow flowers in spring

Glossy, spear-shaped leaves are handsome, but the two-inch-long, funnel-shaped flowers with wide mouths are the main attraction.

Gelsemium sempervivens Carolina yellow jasmine
Light: Sun or bright light
Water: Abundant water (important)
Bloom: Fragrant yellow flowers in summer

This evergreen has stiff, glossy, lancelike leaves and funnel-shaped flowers that broaden at the mouth.

Ipomoea purpurea morning glory
Light: Sun
Water: Light
Bloom: Blue, pink, cream-colored flowers in summer

The heart-shaped leaves are of such light texture and undistinguished color that they fail to make much of an impression. The trumpet-shaped flowers, so delicate they seem about to drop (and, indeed, only last a day), are, however, very pretty against a green background. Morning glories grow like weeds with little care, but must be restarted annually.

Jasminum officinale jasmine
Light: Bright to semi-shade
Water: Moderate
Bloom: Small, scented white flowers in summer and fall

Jasmine, a semi-evergreen tolerant of many types of soil, likes support. It has spear-shaped, stiff leaves. The multiple flowers petals are rather flat and open.

Mandevilla suaveolens Chilean jasmine
Light: Sun
Water: Abundant
Bloom: Scented cream-colored or pinkish flowers in summer

This plant prefers rich soil. The leaves are heart-shaped and the long flower petals fold back, somewhat like those of iris.

Passiflora caerulea passionflower
Light: Sun
Water: Abundant
Bloom: Huge, spectacular flowers in summer

Passiflora is not too particular about soil, but it does appreciate sun. The four-inch flowers are solitary and unique—each consists of widely spaced petals surrounding a rich-colored center. This is one of the most serene and dignified flowers. Blossoms are followed by orange fruit.

Phaseolus scarlet runner bean
Light: Sun
Water: Moderate
Bloom: Brilliant red or white flowers in summer

This is a rather charming plant with smallish, pointed leaves and even smaller flowers.

Plumbago
Light: Sun
Water: Abundant
Bloom: Blue or white flowers from summer into fall.

The blossoms of plumbago emerge from stiff, short stalks and face in all directions.

Quamoclit starglory
Light: Sun
Water: Abundant
Bloom: Large red flowers in summer

This handsome vine can grow to twenty feet. Excellent for the trellis, fence, or walls.

Thunbergia black-eyed Susan
Light: Sun
Water: Abundant
Bloom: Yellow or orange flowers in summer and fall

Growing to ten feet, these annuals add colorful cover to trellises and trees. Thunbergia is somewhat intolerant of excessive heat.

Vitis coignetiae
Light: Sun
Water: Abundant
Bloom: Red foliage in fall

This fast-grower can reach forty feet, so use it only where there is plenty of space.

Wisteria floribunda Japanese wisteria
Light: Sun
Water: Abundant
Bloom: Fragrant lavender flowers in spring

This deciduous vine owes its popularity to its spectacular spring flowers. It needs a trellis or some kind of support.

Trees and Shrubs

Don't look for an Eleventh Commandment to tell you when to bring home a new shrub or tree, either from a nursery or from the woods. Your climate and the kind of plant you are dealing with determine the best time of year in every instance.

Most experts prefer to transplant when the soil is warm, when root growth will start immediately. In most areas, this occurs in late spring and late summer to early autumn. Spring is considered better for a tree or tall shrub that will be exposed to strong wind because the plant has a chance to establish itself in its new location. During the summer, evergreen roots grow little, if at all.

Deciduous species, if a generalization is possible, should be transplanted in spring, fall, and, in areas where the ground is not frozen deep below the surface, winter. The roots of deciduous plants continue to grow even after leaves have fallen; and in many areas those planted in autumn, given enough rainfall or watering, make significant root growth into, and sometimes through, the winter season.

To learn what timing works best in your area, check with the nursery from which you are buying. It may also be useful to take notice of when the local parks department puts in its new trees and other plantings.

Buying Trees and Shrubs

Sometimes it is hard to buy the tree or shrub you want, either because local nurseries cannot keep up with the demand or because it is rare in your area, although well suited in every way to climate and soil conditions. When you are bent on having a particular species, try shopping by mail through reputable dealers. A good nursery catalog will tell you the size of the specimen when shipped, as well as its ultimate size; growing conditions, disease-resistance, attractiveness to birds, and ability to tolerate air pollution.

Whenever possible though, it is best to buy at large nurseries that carry several specimens of the shrub or tree you want. If you know what to look for, you can compare quality and price (and judge whether a low price is a bargain or a method of unloading inferior plants).

Look at the Roots: A balled-and-burlapped tree or shrub should have a tight soil ball, which indicates a substantial root system. To judge the soil ball, grasp the trunk and move it gently from side to side. If the soil ball stays firm, there are enough roots.

Many plants are sold in containers. Discount any with roots poking through the soil surface. If possible, lift the plant you like out of its container to see whether it has an attractive network of evenly distributed white or beige roots firmly holding the soil. Don't buy any plants with loose soil or dark-colored roots.

Bare-rooted trees should have thick roots that radiate in all directions and on several planes. A shallow-rooted plant or one with short roots on one side is of lesser quality.

Check Out the Shape: Stand back from a group of trees or shrubs that interest you. Eliminate specimens that are not symmetrical. Young evergreens, in particular, should look like short versions of the mature tree. Don't expect one with a poor shape to recover.

Look, too, at the proportion of the rootball to top growth. A huge root system beneath minimal top growth could indicate stunted growth; a top-heavy tree or bush supported by a relatively small root system will require drastic pruning prior to planting. A small root system is not able to absorb all the water and nutrients that an overabundant top growth needs to survive.

Next, take a close look at the specimens that have passed muster so far. Evergreens should be bushy without brown or yellowed areas. Conifers should have short spaces between branches. New growth at the tips of branches should be unbroken. A healthy deciduous plant, if in leaf, has no discolored or wilted leaves. Twigs may be broken here or there, but all branches should be sturdy and intact. Look at the tree trunk for signs of splitting or sunburn.

Soil Tips

Most plants do well in soil with a pH range of 5.5 to 7.0, so make any correction necessary after doing a soil test. Some acid-loving species (preferring a pH of 5.0 to 6.0) are azalea, silverbell (*Halesia*), sourwood (*Oxydendrum*), rhododendron, yellowood (*Cladrastis*), hemlock, pine, spruce, laurel, and Franklin-tree (*Franklinia*).

Extreme changes in soil temperature affect trees as well as other forms of plant life. Cold soil retards or prevents roots from absorbing water and minerals. This threatens the well-being of shrubs and trees if the air temperature unexpectedly heats up. The warm air causes the leaves to dispose of excess water but deprives the roots of their share. In autumn, soil warmth and moisture can be conserved by applying a mulch (see "The Magic of Mulch" on page 224); in spring, remove mulch material to allow the sun to warm the soil.

Make It Better: Good soil has a high proportion of organic matter, is fertile, well-aerated, and well-draining. To improve the soil when you dig a hole for a new shrub or tree—and virtually all soil can use some improvement—mix the backfill with a generous amount of organic matter. As you dig the hole, separate the subsoil from the topsoil. Subsoil requires the most improvement, and you might replace it altogether with rich topsoil. Otherwise enhance it with well-rotted manure (*fresh* manure burns roots), peat moss, or other conditioners. Peat moss has a pH of 3.0 to 4.5 and provides an easy means of achieving optimum soil conditions for rhododendrons and other acid-loving plants. Sedge peat, less acid (pH 4.5 to 6.8) than peat moss and with a lesser water-holding capacity, nevertheless contains nitrogen and is an excellent conditioner for backfill.

If the soil is shallow, the subsoil will need to be aerated. For soil that drains poorly or is too heavy, you may need to hire a professional to install agricultural tiles that will assist drainage. In the Southwest, try to obtain treated ground redwood to use instead of peat moss; it lasts longer, does a better job of opening up heavy adobe soil, and helps acidify the alkaline soil, creating favorable conditions for evergreens. Mix one part ground redwood for every two parts planting soil.

Transplanting

Balled-and-burlapped shrubs and small trees are ready to go home with you and be transplanted with the best chance of success. They pose few problems. Trees or shrubs you are transplanting within your own garden or from the wild are a bit more difficult to transplant successfully.

Take the utmost care to dig well around the roots. Transplants can suffer shock, and damage to their root systems can ruin their chances of future normal growth. Unless you know what you are doing, start small, for the larger the shrub or tree, the more complex the transplanting operation. Immediately wrap the root ball in wet burlap to protect the tiny root hairs from injury and from drying out. Never lift an evergreen by its trunk; this shakes the root-ball and separates roots from air-protective soil. Lift the tree by the root-ball or, if it is too heavy, carry it in a sling fashioned from a tarpaulin.

Into the Ground: Preparing the site is *the* essential step in preparing a tree or shrub for survival. Ineptly planted, it will have several strikes against it, no matter what you do later.

The hole you dig should be large enough to accommodate the full root system of bare-root plants and two feet wider than the root-ball of balled-and-burlapped trees. With the exception of some palm trees, the new tree or shrub should be set at the same depth as it was originally, or slightly higher. Pine, spruce, hemlock, flowering dogwood, and American beech are trees sure to die if planted too deep. Add and remove soil until you have the right depth. For a tree or shrub to adjust comfortably to its new location, the soil in the hole should be moist, not soaking wet. Add more peat moss if you've mistakenly overwatered it.

With a bare-root shrub or tree, notice the root crown from which the roots grow downward and outward. Make a mound of soil at the bottom of the hole and place the root crown in it. With the roots spread over and down the sides of such a mound, it is easy to place soil around the roots without leaving air pockets. When the roots are covered and the hole refilled, tamp the soil down, forming a slight concavity in the ground around the stalk or trunk; this will catch and hold water. If you live in a northern area, fill this shallow basin with soil before the winter freeze.

After setting a balled-and-burlapped plant at the correct level, remove the cord tying the burlap, and, at the very least, loosen the burlap and leave the sides in the earth to rot away. If you can get the burlap off, so much the better—but be careful not to injure the root ball. Next, fill the hole half-way with the improved backfill or new topsoil and tamp it down firmly. Add water to eliminate air pockets, allow the water to seep away, and fill the rest of the hole with soil.

Support and Protection: Newly-planted trees and large shrubs require artificial support until their root systems spread out enough to anchor them firmly in the earth. One or two poles or stakes six to eight feet long should be driven two or more feet into the ground at a distance of six to twelve inches from a tree trunk. Use proportionately smaller sizes and lesser distances for shrubs. To prevent the bark from being cut, fasten the trunk to the pole(s) with wire enclosed in a section of garden hose.

Before you stand back to admire your handiwork, thoroughly water the earth to settle the soil around the roots. Then, to prevent sunscald, wrap the trunk of deciduous trees with burlap strips (available at garden centers and nurseries). Start wrapping just below the first branches and work your way down to the ground. Tie the tree-wrapping with stout cord, knotting it about every eighteen inches. Keep the wrapping on for one or two years.

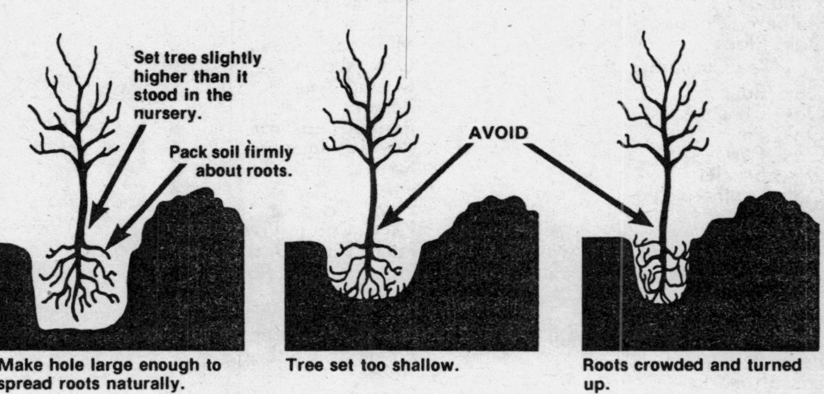
Set tree slightly higher than it stood in the nursery.
Pack soil firmly about roots.
AVOID
Make hole large enough to spread roots naturally.
Tree set too shallow.
Roots crowded and turned up.

After-Care

The soil in which a newly planted tree or shrub has been set must be moist enough to supply the plant with all the water it needs. Too much water, however, can do harm by displacing needed oxygen in the soil and creating conditions that foster the growth of root-damaging funguses. Evergreens, which are usually planted in warm weather, continue to give off water through transpiration. They require moist soil year-round. During a dry autumn or in an arid or semi-arid region, it may be necessary to give evergreens extra water. Planted in the fall, deciduous trees can usually last through the winter on soil moisture from a thorough watering that follows planting. Because they drop their foliage, they lose less moisture than do evergreens. For the first two springs after planting, watering new trees can be very helpful, if not essential, to their survival. With deciduous trees, time waterings to coincide with the appearance of new foliage. To make certain the water gets into the root balls, use a long, thin object and make one or two holes in the soil around the root balls.

In addition to making sure the roots receive enough (but not too much) moisture, new trees may need pruning of lower branches or undesirable crotches. Every once in a while, check to see that whatever stakes or guys you've used to steady young trees are still doing their jobs.

Feeding Even when trees and shrubs are growing on open lawns, they may not be getting all the moisture they need for good growth. The heavy sod, thickly interwoven with grass roots, uses much of the available water and food that would otherwise feed them. Lawns also inhibit soil aeration. Roots partially covered by concrete often do not absorb the water they require, and if trees are situated near buildings or underground drainpipes, their root systems may be unnaturally confined.

In a natural environment, no one comes around to remove the fallen leaves and other organic material that will decay to form a new supply of humus. When you gather up lawn clippings and autumn leaves, even if only to toss them into a compost heap, you are taking away an important source of nourishment from your plants. Sooner or later, undernourishment will result in a decline in vigor, and plants may fall prey to fungus and insect attact.

Properly measured and timed applications of fertilizer improve the condition and appearance of plants and gives them better resistance to attacks by parasites. Yet fertilization is not a cure. It can do nothing to alleviate diseases after the fact.

Also, not all plants respond to fertilizers in the same way. Basswood, elm, oak, and walnut respond slowly, whereas crabapple and American beech are so sensitive to fertilizer that they should receive half the dosage given to most other trees. Young shrubs and trees, for which rapid growth is desired, ought to have more food than older trees.

Commercial arborists and scientists agree that whatever fertilizer is used, it should contain the three most important elements in plant nutrition: nitrogen, phosphorus, and potassium. And that is where agreement begins and ends.

Nitrogen is a subject of controversy among tree experts. Some believe that applying only inorganic nitrogen sources (such as calcium nitrate and ammonium sulfate) is just as effective as applying organic nitrogen sources (such as dried blood, tankage, and cottonseed meal). Until recently, gardeners have given trees the usual 5-10-5 garden fertilizer, but new findings show that shade trees need a higher proportion of nitrogen (e.g., 10-6-4 or 10-8-6). Many gardeners also prefer a 10-10-5 formula for flowering shrubs. Soil pH is another factor to consider. Trees prefer a slightly acid soil. When you use a chemical fertilizer that leaves an alkaline residue, you alter the pH and affect the rate of mineral absorption by the roots. If you have any doubts about whether a particular fertilizer can affect soil pH, check with a local nursery or the Cooperative Extension.

A good rule of thumb to follow for fertilizers is to use slightly less than directions recommend. Even organic fertilizers and manure should not be overapplied. Fertilizers, especially those with a lot of nitrogen in them, stimulate abundant vegetation. Excessive use of artificial feeding can "force" trees and shrubs to grow more rapidly than is actually healthy.

Deciduous trees should get enough fertilizer to achieve the desired results yet not so much as to damage the roots. Use two to four pounds for each inch in diameter the tree trunk measures. For example, a tree with an eighteen-inch diameter should receive thirty-six to seventy-two pounds of commercial fertilizer. Small trees need proportionately less feeding so cut the above amount in half and give one to two pounds per inch in diameter of their trunks.

Evergreens, especially when small, may be easily injured by chemical fertilizers. Small, narrow-leaved evergreens respond better to organic fertilizers such as cottonseed oil, dried blood, or tankage. During spring apply about five pounds to every one hundred square feet of bed area and then water the ground. You can use commercial fertilizer without fear of harming large, narrow-leaved evergreens. For a lone tree, apply about two pounds of fertilizer for each inch in diameter the trunk measures. From two to four pounds of fertilizer for each one hundred square feet of bed area should suffice for a group of trees.

Broad-leaved evergreens such as rhododendron, azalea, and laurel thrive in acid soil, and fertilizers that tend to neutralize or sweeten the soil hurt these shrubs. Lime, wood ashes, or manure are out of the question. When planting them, incorporate a large amount of humus in the backfill. Then, use an acid mulch, such as rotted oak-leaf mold, acid peat moss, or humus. If you notice yellowing or poor growth on a broad-leaved evergreen, check the soil pH. If your soil is lacking, provide extra nitrogen by applying five pounds per one hundred square feet of bed area of dried blood or cottonseed meal. If your soil is very alkaline, maintaining an acid soil is inevitably a losing battle. A better garden will result from planting trees and shrubs that naturally thrive in alkaline soil.

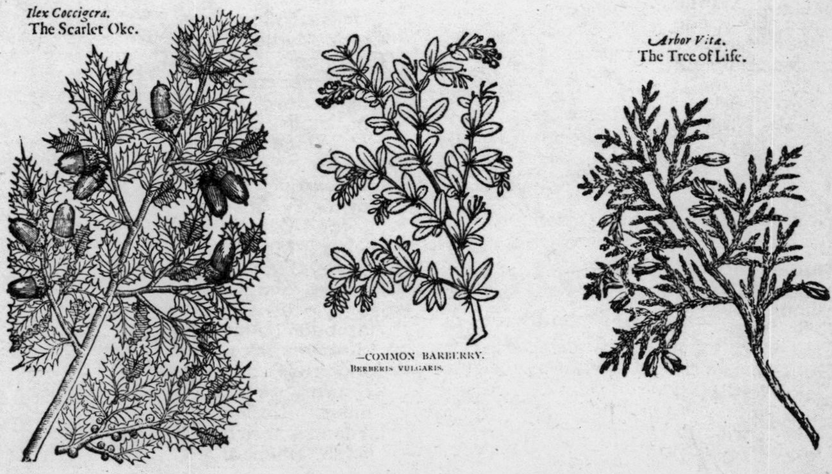
Ilex Coccigera.
The Scarlet Oke.
—COMMON BARBERRY.
BERBERIS VULGARIS.
Arbor Vita.
The Tree of Life.

HARDINESS REGIONS FOR TREES

Region 1

Evergreens, broadleaf
- Holly, American
- Magnolia, Southern

Evergreens, needle leaf and scale leaf
- Arborvitae, Eastern
- Arborvitae, Japanese
- Cedar, Deodar
- Cedar, Eastern Red
- Cedar of Lebanon
- Cryptomeria
- Fir, White
- Hemlock, Canadian
- Juniper
  (*See* Cedar, Eastern Red)
- Lawson False Cypress
- Pine, Eastern White
- Pine, Red
- Spruce, Colorado Blue
- Spruce, White

Deciduous
- Ash, Green
- Ash, White
- Aspen, Quaking
- Baldcypress
- Beech, American
- Beech, European
- Birch, Cutleaf European
- Birch, Paper
- Birch, White
- Buckeye
- Buckeye, Red
  (*See* Horsechestnut, Red)
- Catalpa, Northern
- Catalpa, Southern
- Cork Tree, Amur
- Cucumber Tree
- Elm, American
- Elm, English
- Elm, European Field
- Elm, Scotch
- Gingko
- Goldenrain Tree
- Hackberry, Eastern
- Hickory, Bitternut
- Hickory, Mockernut
- Hickory, Pignut
- Hickory, Shagbark
- Honeylocust, Thornless
- Hornbeam, American
- Hornbeam, European
- Hornbeam, Hop
- Horsechestnut
- Horsechestnut, Red
- Horsechestnut, Ruby
  (*See* Horsechestnut, Red)
- Japanese Pagoda Tree
- Kalopanax
- Katsura
- Kentucky Coffeetree
- Larch, European
- Linden, American
- Linden, Littleleaf
- Linden, Silver
- Locust, Black
- London Plane
- Magnolia, Cucumber
  (*See* Cucumber Tree)
- Magnolia, Sweetbay
- Maple, Norway
- Maple, Red
- Maple, Sugar
- Maple, Sycamore
- Mimosa
- Oak, Black
- Oak, Bur
- Oak, Chestnut
- Oak, Northern Red
- Oak, Pin
- Oak, Scarlet
- Oak, Shingle
- Oak, Turkey
- Oak, White
- Oak, Willow
- Oak, Yellow
- Pear, Bradford
- Pignut (*See* Hickory, Pignut)
- Sassafras
- Silverbell
- Sourgum
- Sweetgum
- Sycamore
- Tamarack
- Tulip Poplar
- Willow, Weeping
- Yellowwood
- Zelkova

Region 2

Evergreens, broadleaf
- Camphor Tree
- Holly, American
- Holly, Chinese
- Holly, English
- Laurelcherry
- Magnolia, Southern
- Oak, Laurel
- Oak, Live
- Wax Myrtle

Evergreens, needle leaf and scale leaf
- Arborvitae, Eastern
- Arborvitae, Oriental
- Cedar, Atlas
- Cedar, Deodar
- Cedar, Eastern Red
- Cedar, Incense
- Cedar of Lebanon
- Cryptomeria
- Hemlock, Carolina
- Pine, Eastern White
- Pine, Loblolly
- Pine, Longleaf
- Pine, Shortleaf
- Pine, Slash
- Spruce, Colorado Blue
- Spruce, Red

Deciduous
- Ash, White
- Baldcypress
- Beech, American
- Beech, European
- Birch, Cutleaf European
- Buckeye
- Catalpa, Northern
- Catalpa, Southern
- Cherry, Black
- Chinaberry
- Chinese Tallow Tree
- Crape Myrtle
- Cucumber Tree
- Elm, American
- Elm, Cedar
- Elm, English
- Elm, Winged
- Gingko
- Goldenrain Tree
- Hackberry, Eastern
- Hickory, Bitternut
- Hickory, Mockernut
- Hickory, Pignut
- Hickory, Shagbark
- Honeylocust, Thornless
- Hornbeam, American
- Hornbeam, Hop
- Japanese Pagoda Tree
- Katsura
- Kentucky Coffeetree
- Linden, American
- Linden, Littleleaf
- London Plane
- Magnolia, Cucumber
- Magnolia, Sweetbay
- Maple, Norway
- Maple, Red
- Maple, Silver
- Maple, Sycamore
- Mimosa
- Mulberry, Paper
- Oak, Black
  (*See* Cucumber Tree)
- Oak, Bur
- Oak, Chestnut
- Oak, Pin
- Oak, Post
- Oak, Scarlet
- Oak, Southern Red
- Oak, Water
- Oak, White
- Oak, Willow
- Pear, Bradford
- Pecan
- Persimmon
- Pignut (*See* Hickory, Pignut)
- Redbud, Eastern
- Sassafras
- Silverbell
- Sourgum
- Sourwood
- Sweetgum
- Sycamore
- Tulip Poplar
- Umbrella Tree (*See* Chinaberry)
- Yellowwood

Palms
- Palmetto, Cabbage

Region 3

Evergreens, broadleaf
- African Tuliptree
- Bell Flambeau (*See* African Tuliptree)
- Brazilian Pepper
- Cajeput
- Cocoplum
- Fig, Fiddle Leaf
- Fig, India Laurel
- Fig, Lofty
- Geiger Tree
- Holly, American
- Holly, Chinese
- Indian Rubber Tree
- Jacaranda
- Laurelcherry
- Magnolia, Southern
- Mahogany, Swamp
  (*See* Mahogany, West Indies)
- Mahogany, West Indies
- Oak, Laurel
- Oak, Live
- Oxhorn Bucida
- Pigeon Plum
- Silk Oak
- Silver Trumpet
- Wax Myrtle

Evergreens, needle leaf and scale leaf
- Pine, Longleaf
- Pine, Slash
- Pine, Spruce

Deciduous
- Baldcypress
- Bo Tree
- Crape Myrtle
- Cucumber Tree
- Fig, Benjamin
- Goldenrain Tree
- Linden, American
- Magnolia, Cucumber (*See* Cucumber Tree)
- Maple, Red
- Mimosa
- Mimosa, Lebbek
- Oak, Water
- Orchid Tree
- Pecan
- Redbud, Eastern
- Royal Poinciana
- Sweetgum

Palms
- Palm, Coconut
- Palm, Cuban Royal
- Palm, Fishtail
- Palm, Florida Royal
- Palm, Manilla
- Palm, Mexican Fan (*See* Palm, Washington)
- Palm, Washington
- Palmetto, Cabbage

Leafless
- Beefwood (*See* Casuarina)
- Beefwood, Horsetail (*See* Casuarina)
- Casuarina
- Cunningham Beefwood
- Scaly Bark Beefwood

Region 4

Evergreens, broadleaf
- None

Evergreens, needle leaf and scale leaf
- Arborvitae, Eastern
- Arborvitae, Oriental
- Cedar, Eastern Red
- Cedar, Incense
- Douglas Fir
- Hemlock, Canadian
- Juniper (*See* Cedar, Eastern Red)
- Juniper, Rocky Mountain
- Pine, Austrian
- Pine, Ponderosa
- Pine, Scotch
- Spruce, Colorado Blue
- Spruce, White

Deciduous
- Ash, Black
- Ash, Green
- Ash, White
- Birch, Cutleaf European
- Birch, Paper
- Birch, White
- Catalpa, Northern
- Cherry, Black
- Cottonwood, Plains
- Elm, American
- Elm, Siberian
- Hackberry, Eastern
- Hackberry, Western
- Honeylocust, Thornless
- Katsura
- Larch, Siberian
- Linden, American
- Linden, Littleleaf
- Maple, Silver
- Oak, Bur

Oak, Northern Red
Oak, Pin
Oak, Scarlet
Poplar, Plains (*See* Cottonwood, Plains)
Sugarberry (*See* Hackberry, Western)
Zelkova

Region 5

Evergreens, broadleaf
Oak, Live
Evergreens, needle leaf and scale leaf
Arborvitae, Oriental
Cedar, Atlas
Cedar, Eastern Red
Cryptomeria
Cypress, Arizona
Juniper (*See* Cedar Eastern Red)
Juniper, Rocky Mountain
Pine, Austrian
Pine, Loblolly
Pine, Ponderosa
Spruce, Colorado Blue
Deciduous
Ash, Green
Baldcypress
Beech, European
Buckeye
Catalpa, Northern
Catalpa, Southern
Chinaberry
Desert Willow
Elm, American
Elm, Chinese
Elm, English
Elm, European Field
Elm, Siberian
Goldenrain Tree
Hackberry, Eastern
Hackberry, Western
Honeylocust, Thornless
Huisache
Japanese Pagoda Tree
Katsura
Kentucky Coffeetree
Maple, Silver
Maple, Sycamore
Mesquite
Mulberry, Paper
Mulberry, Russian
Oak, Bur
Oak, Chestnut
Oak, Pin
Oak, Post
Oak, Shumard (*See* Oak Texas)
Oak, Scarlet
Oak, Spanish
Oak, Texas
Oak, Yellow
Pecan
Pistache, Chinese
Redbud, Eastern
Retama
Sassafras
Soapberry, Western
Sugarberry (*See* Hackberry, Western)
Sycamore
Umbrella Tree (*See* Chinaberry)
Zelkova
Palms
Palm, Mexican Fan
(*See* Palm, Washington)
Palm, Washington

Region 6

Evergreens, broadleaf
Olive, Common
Olive, Russian
Evergreens, needle leaf and scale leaf
Arborvitae, Giant
Arborvitae, Oriental
Cedar, Atlas
Cedar, Eastern Red
Cedar, Incense
Douglas Fir
Fir, White
Juniper, (*See* Cedar, Eastern Red)
Juniper, Rocky Mountain
Pine, Austrian
Pine, Ponderosa
Spruce, Colorado Blue
Deciduous
Ash, Arizona (*See* Ash, Modesto)
Ash, European
Ash, Green
Ash, Modesto
Beech, European
Buckeye
Buckeye, Red (*See* Horsechestnut, Red)
Catalpa, Northern
Cottonwood, Plains
Elm, American
Elm, Chinese
Elm, European Field
Elm, Siberian
Ginkgo
Goldenrain Tree
Hackberry, Eastern
Honeylocust, Thornless
Horsechestnut
Horsechestnut, Red
Horsechestnut, Ruby
(*See* Horsechestnut, Red)
Japanese Pagoda Tree
Katsura
Kentucky Coffeetree
Linden, American
Linden, Littleleaf
London Plane
Maple, Bigleaf
Maple, Norway
Maple, Sugar
Mulberry, Russian
Oak, Bur
Oak, Northern Red
Oak, Pin
Oak, White
Poplar, Plains (*See* Cottonwood, Plains)
Sweetgum
Zelkova

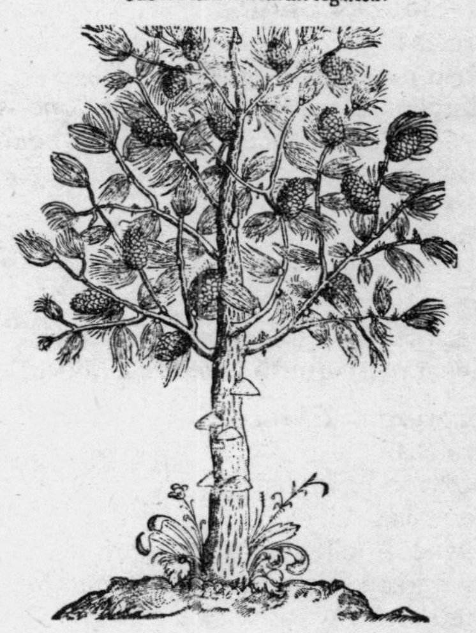
Larix cum Agarico suo.
The Larch tree with his Agarick.

Region 7

Evergreens, broadleaf
Carob
Eucalyptus
Gum (*See* Eucalyptus)
Olive, Common
Olive, Russian
Palo Verde, Blue
Evergreens, needle leaf and scale leaf
Cedar, Atlas
Cedar, Deodar
Cedar, Eastern Red
Cypress, Arizona
Cypress, Italian
Douglas Fir
Fir, Silver
Juniper (*See* Cedar, Eastern Red)
Juniper, Rocky Mountain
Pine, Aleppo
Pine, Austrian
Pine, Canary Island
Deciduous
Acacia, Baileys
Ailanthus
Ash, Arizona (*See* Ash, Modesto)
Ash, Green
Ash, Modesto
Baileys Wattle (*See* Acacia, Baileys)
Chinaberry
Cottonwood, Fremont
Cottonwood, Plains
Desert Willow
Elm, Chinese
Elm, Siberian
Ginkgo
Goldenrain Tree
Hackberry, Eastern
Hackberry, Western
Honeylocust, Thornless
Huisache
Linden, Littleleaf
Locust, Black
London Plane
Maple, Silver
Mesquite
Mulberry, Russian
Oak, Pin
Oak, Southern Red
Pecan
Pistache, Chinese
Poplar, Bolleana
Poplar, Carolina
Poplar, Plains (*See* Cottonwood, Plains)
Sugarberry (*See* Hackberry, Western)
Sweetgum
Tree of Heaven (*See* Ailanthus)
Umbrella Tree (*See* Chinaberry)
Wattle, Sydney
Palms
Palm, Canary Date

Region 8

Evergreens, broadleaf
Cajeput
Camphor Tree
Carob
Cherry, Australian Brush
Coral Tree
Eucalyptus
Fig, India Laurel
Fig, Moreton Bay
Gum (*See* Eucalyptus)
Jacaranda
Laurel, California
Laurelcherry
Laurel, Grecian
Magnolia, Southern
Oak, Canyon Live
Oak, Coast Live
Oak, Holly
Oak, Live
Palo Verde, Blue
Tanoak
Evergreens, needle leaf and scale leaf
Arborvitae, Oriental
Cedar, Atlas
Cedar, Deodar
Cedar, Incense
Cedar of Lebanon
Cryptomeria
Cypress, Arizona
Lawson False Cypress
Norfolk Island Pine
Pine, Aleppo
Pine, Canary Island
Spruce, Colorado Blue
Deciduous
Ash, Arizona (*See* Ash, Modesto)
Ash, Modesto
Chinaberry
Chinese Lantern Tree
Cottonwood, Fremont
Desert Willow
Elm, American
Elm, Chinese
Elm, Siberian
Ginkgo
Goldenrain Tree
Hackberry, Eastern
Honeylocust, Thornless
Japanese Pagoda Tree
Locust, Black
London Plane
Maple, Bigleaf
Maple, Norway
Maple, Red
Mimosa
Mulberry, Russian
Oak, Bur
Oak, English
Oak, Northern Red
Oak, Pin
Oak, Scarlet
Oak, Valley
Orchid Tree
Pistache, Chinese
Sweetgum
Tulip Poplar
Umbrella Tree (*See* Chinaberry)
Palms
Palm, Canary Date
Palm, Mexican Fan
(*See* Palm, Washington)
Palm, Washington
Leafless
Beefwood (*See* Casuarina)
Beefwood, Horsetail (*See* Casurina)
Casurina

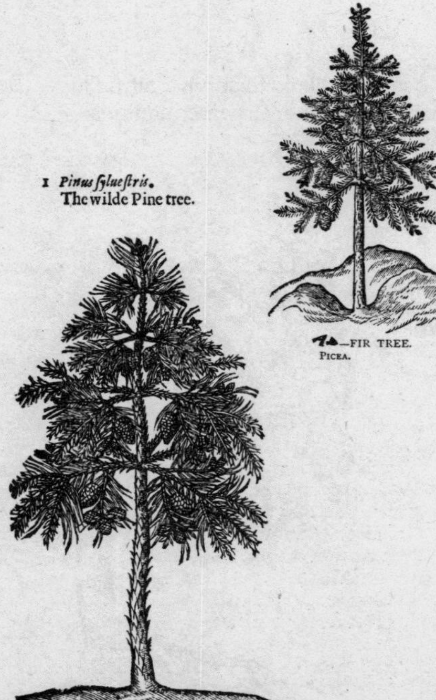
1 *Pinus syluestris.*
The wilde Pine tree.

74.—FIR TREE.
PICEA.

Morus.
The Mulberrie tree.

Cedrus Libani.
The great Cedar tree of Libanus.

Region 9

Evergreens, broadleaf
Holly, English
Madrone
Magnolia, Southern
Tanoak
Evergreens, needle leaf and scale leaf
Arborvitae, Giant
Arborvitae, Oriental
Cedar, Atlas
Cedar, Deodar
Cedar, Incense
Cryptomeria
Lawson False Cypress
Pine, Austrian
Pine, Ponderosa
Spruce, Colorado Blue
Deciduous
Ash, European
Ash, Green
Ash, White
Beech, European
Birch, White
Buckeye, Red (*See* Horsechestnut, Red)
Cork Tree, Amur
Dogwood, Pacific
Elm, American
Elm, Chinese
Elm, English
Elm, Scotch
Elm, Siberian
Ginkgo
Golden Chain Tree
Goldenrain Tree
Honeylocust, Thornless
Hornbeam, American
Horsechestnut
Horsechestnut, Red
Horsechestnut, Ruby
(*See* Horsechestnut, Red)
Japanese Pagoda Tree
Kentucky Coffeetree
Linden, American
Linden, Littleleaf
London Plane
Maple, Bigleaf
Maple, Norway
Maple, Red
Maple, Sugar
Mimosa
Oak, Northern Red
Oak, Oregon White
Oak, Pin
Oak, Scarlet
Oak, White
Silverbell
Sourwood
Sweetgum
Tulip Poplar
Yellowwood

When to Fertilize Early spring and late fall are the best seasons for fertilizing trees. Summer applications, contrary to what one might expect, provide few benefits. They stimulate the production of soft, succulent tissues that are susceptible to winter cold because they do not harden properly. If a tree is literally starving, feed it during any season.

Make fall applications when you are certain top growth has ended for the year. Some end-of-season feeding reaches roots and some will be available to increase tree growth in spring. Roots continue to grow even though trees have lost their leaves, so you are not wasting fertilizer by using it at this time of year.

Exact springtime feeding also depends on local climatic conditions. Try to apply fertilizer as soon as possible after the ground thaws. Later applications are less effective in terms of stimulating root and top growth.

Methods of Fertilizing Since your aim is to get fertilizer to the roots, you need to know the location of the feeding roots, that is, the hairlike roots capable of absorbing nutrition. In shrubs they are close to the stalks. But feeding roots of trees are not near the trunk but are located in a band just beyond the spread of the outermost branches—beyond the so-called drip line of a tree. How far from the trunk this circular band of feeding roots is and how wide an area it takes up varies greatly from tree to tree. It also depends on the kind of soil in which a tree is planted.

If you must guess where the band of feeding roots is, at least make an intelligent guess. Starting at the drip line of a tree, feeding roots extend outward about as many feet as the diameter of the tree measures at one foot above ground. Having determined the probable location of the feeding roots, that is where you will apply the fertilizer. If you've opted to use a dry commercial fertilizer, do not apply it within one foot of the tree trunk, because it can injure the trunk base and root collar.

Broadcasting is a good method to use sparingly, and only with shallow-rooted shrubs and small trees. When all the nutrients are near the soil surface, hungry roots turn upward. So if you keep applying fertilizer to the ground surface, your trees will develop shallow root systems, and heaven help them if a drought strikes your area. For the broadcast method to work at all, hoe the fertilizer into the soil or water the ground thoroughly so that the food *enters* the soil.

Punch Method involves using a soil auger or crowbar to circle a plant with holes over the area where the feeding roots are. For trees, make the holes eighteen inches deep and two feet apart and slant them inward, toward the tree. Then distribute the proper amount of dry fertilizer evenly among the holes and fill them with organic material, such as compost, peat moss, or topsoil. Tamp down the top of the hole by stepping on it. This method is appropriate for large trees because it places the fertilizer *below* the topsoil, down in the root area. During rainless periods, however, the dry fertilizer remains in the holes.

Foliar Feeding is so effective that lumber companies hope to devise practical methods to spray entire forests with soluble fertilizer. The ability of plants to absorb nutrients through their leaves varies. Some species have leaves that are simply better suited to the task. Healthier plants, as a general rule, can absorb more than less vigorous plants. The time of day and the weather also have an effect. The rate of absorption is faster during daylight hours, and spraying before noon or after 4 P.M. is more effective than when the sun is highest. High humidity also favors nutrient absorption through leaves. Foliage-nutrient sprays are particularly effective when rainfall is scant and tree roots are not able to absorb much nourishment from the soil. Not all water-soluble fertilizers are safe to spray on leaves. Check the directions on the package.

Ready-Made Feeding Methods are for gardeners who favor the TV-dinner approach to tree care. Most nurseries stock Jobe's Tree Food Spike, a water-soluble 16-8-8 fertilizer contained in a plastic cup that you can drive into the ground area of the feeding roots with an ordinary hammer. If the spikes are placed at a depth of eighteen inches, fertilizer rapidly leaches into the root zone.

Eeasy Grow Packets consist of heat-sealed, polyethylene-paper laminated envelopes containing a slow-acting, water-soluble 16-8-16 fertilizer. Each packet is pierced with tiny holes. To "apply" Eeasy Grow, set a packet near the feeding roots of a newly planted tree. Vapor from the soil will eventually enter the packet and dissolve small amounts of fertilizer that flows into the soil. During cold weather, no fertilizer is released. Eeasy Grow Packets are available at tree nurseries or from their manufacturer, Specialty Fertilizer Co., Box 355, Suffern, NY 10901.

Greenery in the City

The following trees and shrubs are among those most likely to survive air pollution, poor soil, lack of soil moisture and aeration, and other urban conditions:

Deciduous Trees

crab apple (*Malus*)
European hackberry (*Celtis australis*)
European white birch (*Betula pendula*)
fig (*Ficus carica*)
flowering dogwood (*Cornus florida*)
ginko (*Ginko biloba*)
green ash (*Fraxinus pennsylvanica lanceolata*)
hawthorn (*Crataegus*)
honey locust (*Gleditsa triacanthos*)
Japanese cherry tree (*Prunus*)
Japanese maple (*Acer palmatum*)
littleleaf European linden (*Tilia cordata*)
live oak (*Quercus virginiana*)
London planetree (*Platanus acerifolia*)
Magnolia soulangea
ornamental peartree (*Pyrus*)
pin oak (*Quercus palustris*)
pomegranate (*Punica granatum*)
Russian olive (*Elaeagnus angustifolia*)
sourwood (*Oxydendrum arboreum*)
tree of heaven (*Ailanthus altissima*)

Betula.
The Birch tree.

—SYCAMORE.

willow oak (*Quercus phellos*)
willow (*Salix*)

Evergreen Trees

Austrian pine (*Pinus nigra*)
bull bay (*Magnolia grandiflora*)
Ficus retusa
holly, American and English (*Ilex*)
laurel (*Laurus nobilis*)
live oaks (*Quercus*)
pineapple guava (*Feijoa sellowiana*)

Salix.
The common Willow.

—MAPLE.

Deciduous Shrubs

azaleas
bush honeysuckle (*Lonicera*)
Carolina allspice (*Calycanthus floridus*)
five-leaf aralia (*Acanthopanax sieboldianus*)
flowering quince (*Chaenomeles lagenaria*)
forsythia
hydrangea
rose of sharon (*Hibiscus syriacus*)
roses
star magnolia (*Magnolia stellata*)
sweet pepperbush (*Clethra alnifolia*)

—SPRUCE.

Evergreen Shrubs

azaleas
boxwood (*Buxus*)
camellias
Chinese holly (*Ilex cornuta*)
evergreen euonymus (*Euonymus japonica*)
firethorn (*Pyracantha*)
Japanese holly (*Ilex crenata*)
mock orange (*Philadelphus*)
oleander (*Nerium*)
pittosporum
privets (*Ligustrum*)
rhododendron
viburnum
yew (*Taxus*)

Laureola cum fructu.
Laurell with his fruit.

What's Wrong?

If you have chosen a vigorous, disease-resistant specimen, planted it in rich, organic soil, kept the soil moist, and generally tended to its needs, you have already done a great deal to prolong the lives of your trees and shrubs.

Poor growth and death of plants are sometimes the result of parasitic agents, yet these are far less likely to attack healthy trees and shrubs than weaker ones. Before you resort to spraying with a dangerous insecticide or fungicide, try to diagnose the problem.

First, look around your neighborhood. Do other plants of the same species seem to have the same problem that's plaguing yours? If so, perhaps a neighbor can enlighten you. If not, contact a tree expert, your agricultural experimental station, or a knowledgeable person connected with the Department of Plant Pathology at a nearby university. If, from your description, the expert does not immediately know what is wrong, you may be asked to send a specimen. Be sure to find out what facts ought to accompany the specimen.

Some tree troubles stump even experts who know what clues to look for. If you are totally mystified, ask how to proceed. An excellent questionnaire is included in *Tree Maintenance* (Oxford University Press), by P. O. Pirone, formerly a plant pathologist at the New York Botanical Garden.

Environmental Damage Conditions in the immediate environment can also be harmful—winter weather, lightening, hail, drought, and sudden spring or fall frosts. To care for trees injured by weather or by lightening, proceed with caution when pruning and repairing. Professional advice may help you save a valuable tree.

Nearby building or excavating may affect soil and water balances or disturb roots, especially of trees. Frequently, building on a wooded lot can cause several of the nicest trees to die mysteriously. Consulting an arborist before construction or excavation will probably enable you to avoid such injury.

Air pollution, smog, and smoke, are increasingly common causes of injury and death in plants. Unless caused by a leaking gas main or another specific situation, this type of damage usually varies from season to season and is often connected to the weather, including wind. Air pollution is ordinarily most severe in spring and autumn. Plant resistant varieties and avoid using high-nitrogen fertilizers or overwatering.

Chlorosis When leaves uniformly turn a sickly yellow (from a reduction in the normal amount of chlorophyll), suspect a case of chlorosis. In gardenias and pin oaks, chlorosis is usually caused by a lack of iron; in many others—catalpa; cottonwood; red, silver, and sugar maple; boxelder; and white oak—iron deficiency is a suspected cause. For a fairly small plant, crumble an old, rusty soap pad over the root area. For others, use water-soluble iron chelate as a foliar spray dissolved in water or as a dry powder sprinkled on the soil. This replaces application of iron sulfate and iron ammonium citrate, chemicals that organic gardeners are loathe to use.

Glauconite, or greensand, is an organic source of iron but, like iron chelate, may be only a temporary remedy. Iron deficiencies often occur in soil that is too alkaline. Adding humus to the soil around the affected tree or shrub restores proper acidity while making the soil more fertile.

Girdling Roots When planting shade trees, it is vital that the hole be large enough to accommodate the spreading roots. When holes are undersized, roots wind themselves around the base and begin to cut into the trunk of the tree, strangling the life out of it. Root girdling frequently damages city trees that have been planted in a hole surrounded by hard subsoil and potted trees that have outgrown their container.

The primary symptom of girdling roots is the slow death of a portion of the tree. Each year, more and more branches die until half are dead. Examine the surface of the soil near the trunk—or dig down a bit beneath the surface—to find the girdling roots. Cut the root or roots from the tree by jamming them with a crowbar. Severed girdling roots can remain in the ground to die because they no longer can hurt the tree.

TRUNK ROT

Winterizing Trees and Shrubs

Low temperatures can hurt even the hardiest trees and shrubs. Sudden spring freezes, especially combined with a late snowstorm, can kill tender twigs on deciduous trees and shrubs and cause defoliation of conifers. Early autumn cold waves are also lethal because plants are not yet in a dormancy stage, where they are able to withstand frost. Even during winter dormancy, certain weather conditions can spell doom. Surprisingly, the worst winters for many species in northern areas are years with less-than-normal snow or when the cold season is punctuated with a series of unexpected warm periods.

Snow on the ground acts as a protective winter mulch that maintains a constant ground temperature despite fluctuations in the air temperature. Sudden thaws followed by rapid freezing can kill shrubs and cause frost cracks in unprotected tree trunks. Frost cracks are long, vertical fissures that usually occur on the south and west sides of trees. Although frost cracks close with the advent of warm weather, they reopen during successive winters, making trees susceptible to wood-decay fungus. If a cavity becomes large, it will require the ministrations of a tree surgeon.

Unfortunately, evergreens are also susceptible to injury in freezing weather. Holly, pine, spruce, fir, laurel, and rhododendron may not escape damage by widely fluctuating temperatures, severe winter cold, and spring freeze—any of which occurring after they have begun to grow again. Since evergreens continue to lose water in winter, those that grow in a sunny and/or windy location risk drying out if their roots are unable to absorb water to compensate for the moisture loss. Browning edges of leaves are a symptom of cold-weather damage on rhododendrons and other broad-leaved evergreens. Damage to pines and other narrow-leaved evergreens is manifested by brown needles and highly brittle twigs.

Winter drying of evergreen trees and shrubs, including boxwoods and rhododendrons, can be prevented or attenuated by spraying them with Wilt-Pruf NFC, a liquid plastic that slows the rate of transpiration. The spray is also useful for coating the leaves and stems of a variety of other trees and shrubs planted in autumn.

Though it looks lovely when it mantles vegetation, consider snow winter enemy number one and shake it off of trees, hedges, and shrubs as soon as possible. Even staked, braced, and covered shrubs can be bent out of shape under the extra weight of snow. Moreover, snow allowed to melt slightly, on branches, and then subjected to air temperature dips, turns to ice—and real trouble begins! For most species suffering damage from dessication or ice, wait until spring to begin pruning.

Preparation for Winter. Nothing you can do in the way of preparing your trees and shrubs for winter can beat planting them in well-drained soil. Roots are more apt to freeze in poorly drained soil, and indeed a tree in poorly drained soil is more likely to suffer frost cracks. Plants also need fertile soil and periodic feedings to stimulate root growth. Good soil aeration, essential if roots are to grow deeply, also reduces the chances of winter injury. No protection is certain for trees and shrubs exposed to extreme cold. Native varieties, adapted to the weather in their area, have the best chance of lasting through most winters without much attention. Nevertheless, you can help these and other trees and shrubs do more than just survive. And whatever you do to protect fragile plants will surely pay off the next spring.

Planting. Late fall and early winter are good times to plant new trees and shrubs, but only hardy varieties. Leave those in the northern limits of their growing range for spring planting. If you do plant a variety that is not hardy in the northern limits of its range, wrap it with burlap or heavy paper.

Feedings and Pruning. Special fall care for all trees and shrubs consists of feeding and pruning. If you lack the time or ambition for both, feeding them is essential, whereas pruning, which should be done lightly, can be put off until a mild winter's day. Don't bother pruning trees and shrubs that suffer considerable dieback in winter. These would include any trees that are completely hardy when grown in a milder climate than in your area.

Winter Mulches. If you live where snow stays on the ground all winter, your trees and shrubs are protected by snow. If snow is not reliable, mulch any trees and shrubs not hardy and/or not native to your region. Other than the season of application—after the ground freezes but *before* the first snowfall—a winter mulch differs from a summer mulch only in that it should be thicker.

Mulch around newly planted trees and shrubs (as well as bulbs, perennials, and herbs). Fruit trees especially appreciate mulch, and broad-leaved evergreens, such as rhododendron and laurel, can use a water supply throughout winter. Heavy mulches of salt hay, straw, oakleaf mold, or acid peat moss prevent deep-frost freezing of the soil, enabling roots to remain active.

Don't apply winter mulches too early in the fall. Give the ground a chance to freeze a bit. Otherwise, mice and other rodents may set up winter quarters in your mulch and cause damage to plants underneath. Keep the mulch on past danger of frost. If tender shoots have begun to sprout under mulches, remove the mulches in stages. Like summer mulches, winter mulches can be left on the ground to enrich the soil, or can be collected and stored for reuse.

Hedge Care. In winter, evergreen hedges, like evergreen trees, continue to give off water they cannot replace because the ground is frozen solid. The results of winter transpiration show in May or June, when hedges inexplicably turn brown. Spray them with Wilf-Pruf NFC. Low hedges may instead be covered with boughs of evergreens. This also prevents breakage from snow and ice and guards evergreen leaves against windburn.

Hedges along driveways and sidewalks or otherwise exposed to cold winter winds may be frozen and pushed over by snow and wind. For tall hedges, snow fences or a series of stakes connected with taut, horizontal wires make good supports; a row of chicken wire alongside low hedges does a good job. Fall is also the time to cut back older branches on many types of deciduous hedges to improve their appearance and encourage new growth during spring. Not every kind of hedge, however, should be pruned in autumn. Prune tender ones in spring.

Protecting against Snow and Ice. Snow and ice slide off roofs and land good and hard on whatever is beneath, often decorative shrubs or hedges. Snowdrifts may also cover bushes and hedges. Protect trees and shrubs from snapping under heavy loads of snow by bracing them with stakes on two or more sides and tying them with twine. Braces keep shrubs from bending over when covered with snow. A particularly tender shrub or small tree can also be covered by a little rectangular plywood roof nailed to the tops of four stout stakes.

Coverings. Evergreens whose hardiness is borderline, often boxwoods and camellias, and other small trees and shrubs are often encased in burlap coverings or sacks to prevent drying caused by rapid moisture loss. Small specimens can be protected with inverted bushel baskets. If the bushes or trees are evergreen, however, make some holes in baskets to admit light. Some borderline deciduous trees and shrubs also benefit by wrapping during severe cold. This is more difficult with large trees (though if they lasted this long, they are probably planted where they are protected from frigid winds), but most trees from a warmer climate don't grow tall in the North. Examples of unrealiably hardy trees are figs and blue hydrangeas. Burlap coverings are most effective when backed by thick ground mulches.

PERENNIALS

Perennials are plants that die down to the ground each winter and—given the proper conditions—renew themselves in spring for at least three seasons.

Unlike annuals, perennials are particular about their soil. Prepare the soil to a depth of 18 inches, incorporating organic mater. At the last spading before planting, add 1½ lbs of 5-10-5 fertilizer per 100 feet. Drainage is important; bedding up the soil to create raised beds is a good idea; in heavy soil you may have to install drain tiles. When watering, saturate the soil and then do not rewater until the soil is dry to the touch and the tips of the plants wilt slightly at midday. Especially when plants are in bloom, try to water the soil rather than the flowers, which will rot if they catch and hold water. Mulch in summer to retain moisture, hold down weeds, and prevent soil from splashing the flowers. Mulch in winter to protect new plantings and less hardy varieties.

Buying bedding plants is usually the best way to start a perennial garden if you are a beginner, but propagating from seed is cheaper. Many perennials do not grow true to type from seed, so you should buy new seed or divide old plants. Start seed indoors no later than eight weeks before the last killing frost.

Perennials are top-heavy and require staking. Stake plants when you first set them out with twigs, dowels, bamboo, or plastic stakes that will be six to twelve inches shorter than the height of the grown plant. Don't tie the stems directly to the stake—make a loop around the plant and another around the stake.

Never allow perennials to remain in the same garden spot for more than three years, because roots at the center of the clump die and flowers will be sparse. Divide the clump by selecting the most vigorous three to five side shoots.

To maintain vigorous growth, remove mature flowers. Do not let perennials go to seed, as this promotes the growth of side shoots. In fall, remove dead foliage and stems.

ACHILLEA Yarrow
Height: Two feet
Use: Borders
Light: Sun

Plant seed in late fall or early spring to achieve a bloom that will last from June to September. Plants should be spaced three to six inches apart. Seed takes from one to two weeks to germinate. While it is in process of germination, water by gently misting. Blooms are white, yellow, or red.

ALYSSUM Golddust
Height: Nine to twelve inches
Use: Edging and rock gardens
Light: Full sun

Very good in dry or sandy soil. Bloom in early spring. Seed should be planted in early spring. Space plants twenty-four inches apart. Seed germinates in three to four weeks.

ANCHUSA Alkanet
Height: Four to five feet
Use: Borders and backgrounds
Light: Light shade

Refrigerate seed for three days before sowing. Seed can be planted from April to September. Space twenty-four inches apart. Germination in three to four weeks. Produces blue flowers.

ANEMONE Windflower
Height: Twelve inches
Use: Borders, rock gardens, planters

Anemone blooms in May and June. Plant in early spring or late fall, in full sun. Tuberous-rooted anemones should be planted in September in well-drained soil. Protect in winter by covering with straw. Seed germinates in four days. Space three to four feet apart. These come in many dramatic colors.

ANTHEMIS Golden Daisy
Height: Two feet
Use: Borders
Light: Full sun

This plant grows best in dry or sandy soil. Start plants indoors for eight weeks before planting outdoors, unless you delay until outside soil has fully warmed up. Space twenty-four inches apart. Germination in three to four weeks. Resistent to most insects.

AQUILEGIA Columbine
Height: Twelve to eighteen inches
Use: Rock gardens, borders
Light: Sun (Will tolerate shade)

Wide range of flower colors. Plant seed any time from April to September. Germination is irregular.

ARABIS Rockcress
Height: Eight to twelve inches
Use: Edging and rock gardens
Light: Mild shade

Blooms in early spring. Plant seed in well-drained soil in a shady area. Space twelve inches apart. Seed germinates in five days.

ARMERIA Sea Pink
Height: Eighteen to twenty-four inches
Use: Rock gardens, edging, borders
Light: Sun

Bloom comes in May in June. Plant in dry, sandy soil any time between spring and September. Space twelve inches apart. Shade the seedbed until plants are hardy. Germinates in ten days.

ARTEMSIA Wormwood, Dusty Miller
Height: Two feet
Use: Borders, rock gardens
Light: Full sun

Blooms in late summer. Grows in almost any soil. Space nine to twelve inches apart. Plant seed from May to August.

ASTER
Height: One to five feet
Use: Rock gardens, borders
Light: Sun

Plant seed in early spring. The plant will germinate in two to three weeks. Blooms in June. Space plants three feet apart. There are many species. One will be found to fit most any garden need. Plant in a moist, loamy soil.

ASTILBE
Height: One to three feet
Use: Borders
Light: Full sun

This plant blooms in stupendous masses of color in summer. Plant seed in early spring in rich soil, and space twenty-four inches apart. Germinates in two to three weeks.

AUBRIETA Rainbow Rockcress
Height: Six inches
Use: Borders and often used along dry walls
Light: Light shade

This dwarf, spreading plant blooms in April and May. Plant seed from Spring to September. Space twelve inches apart. Shade plants in summer. Divide plants in late summer.

CANDYTUFT
Height: Twelve inches
Use: Edging, ground cover, rock gardens
Light: Full sun

Plant seed in early spring or late fall in a sunny spot. Germinates in twenty days. Blooms in late spring. Remove flowers as they begin to fade to encourage branching.

CAMPANULA Bellflower
Height: Two feet
Use: Various
Light: Shade

There are many Campanulas, but generally these flowers will grow well in the proper conditions, which include shade, moist soil, and good drainage. There are many colors, but blue predominates.

CENTAUREA Cornflower
Height: Two feet
Use: Borders
Light: Full sun

Seed planted from June to September germinates in three to four weeks. Flowers through the summer. Space twelve inches apart.

CERASTIUM Snow-in-Summer
Height: Six inches
Use: Ground cover, rock gardens
Light: Full sun

This plant will form a sort of creeping mat that blooms in May and June. Grows well in dry soil, but be careful that it does not do so well that it overwhelms other plants in your garden. Space eighteen inches apart. Germinates in two to four weeks.

COLUMBINE (AQUILEGIA)
Height: To thirty inches
Use: Borders
Light: Full sun

Blooms in late spring and early summer. Needs rich, well-drained soil. Plant seed any time from spring to fall. Space at least one foot apart. Also grow as a biennial.

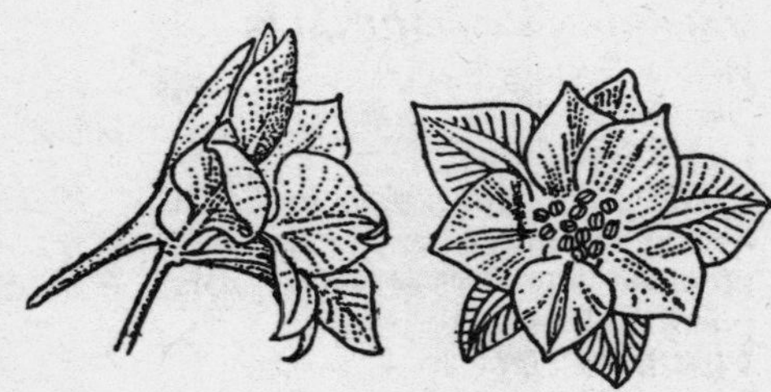

—LARKSPUR FLOWERS.

BELLIS PERENNIS English Daisy
Height: Six inches
Use: Beds, borders, rock gardens
Light: Sun

Most will bloom all summer. Needs lots of water. Moist, well-drained soil. Plant six inches apart.

DELPHINIUM
Height: To 6 feet
Use: Background
Light: Sun

This brilliant, blue bloom adds much to any garden. Plant seed from spring to September in well-drained, rich soil. Space two feet apart. Get rid of old foliage to avoid mildew. Stake plants to avoid wind damage.

DIANTHUS
Height: Twelve inches
Use: Borders, rock gardens, edging
Light: Full sun

These plants need rich, loamy soil and an even water supply. Grow in groups, spaced twelve inches apart. Long blooming season, beginning in May.

DICENTRA Bleeding Heart
Height: Two to three feet
Use: Borders, in front of shrubbery, planters
Light: Shade

Plant seed in late autumn. Space twelve to eighteen inches apart. Germinates in fifty days. Grow these to fill empty shady places in your garden. Charming but not spectacular.

DIGITALIS Foxglove
Height: Four to six feet
Use: Borders, background
Light: Sun

Good for tall masses of color. Need moist soil. Select strains that bear flowers at right angles to the stem. Space one foot apart.

ECHINACEA PURPUREA
Cornflower
Height: To four feet
Use: Various
Light: Sun

Reddish-purple flowers become gray-green at tips and have an orange center. Will tolerate some shade. Good addition to any garden, but don't overwater.

Bellis maior.
Thegreat Daisie.

EUPATORIUM COELESTINUM
Mistflower
Height: Three feet
Use: Border
Light: Bright sunlight

These should be grown in well-drained soil. Bloom through summer. Heart-shaped leaves, blue flowers. Water moderately. Space twelve inches apart when planting.

EUPHORBIA Spurge
Height: One and one-half feet
Use: Rock gardens, borders, ground cover
Light: Full sun

Relative of the poinsettia. Has colored bracts that appear to be yellow flowers. Grow in well-drained soil.

GAILLARDIA GRANDIFLORA
Blanket Flower
Height: Twelve to thirty inches
Use: Borders
Light: Full sun

Easy to grow from seed, which can be planted in early spring or late summer. These plants do not tolerate heavy soils, and the soil must be very well drained. Space plants twenty inches apart.

GENTIANA ASCLEPIADEA
Gentian
Height: To one foot
Use: Borders
Light: Full sun

If you have an acid soil, grow this plant. Beautiful blue flowers. Need an evenly moist soil. Space one foot apart. Grows in clumps.

GERANIUM GRANDIFLORUM
Cranesbill
Height: To twenty inches
Use: Border
Light: Full sun

Thrive in just about any soil, and require very little care.

GEUM
Height: Two feet
Use: Borders, rock gardens
Light: Bright sun

Plants need exceptional drainage. Rid the plant of faded blossoms to extend the blooming period. Most bloom in June and July. Space about eighteen inches apart. Hardy in winter if protected.

GYSOPHILA Baby's Breath
Height: To two feet
Use: Borders, background for more stunning plants
Light: Full sun

Grow in neutral soil. Plant has tiny, subtle flowers. Long blooming period. Space plants at least two feet apart.

Anemone Bulbocastani radice.
Chestnut Winde-floure.

HELENIUM AUTUMNALE Helen Flower
Height: Four feet
Use: Background, general garden
Light: Sun

Grow in any soil provided there is enough moisture. Pinch out tips of stalks early in summer to help prolong flowering.

HELIANTHUS Sunflower
Height: To five feet
Use: Background
Light: Sun

This plant blooms in summer, and is a better addition to the garden than most people think. Rapid growth, so dig up and divide every other spring.

DELPHINIUM

HELIOPSIS SCABRA
Height: To three feet
Use: General garden
Light: Sun

Long blooming season, through summer and into fall. Do well in any soil with lots of water. Profuse bloom. Space about three feet apart.

HELIOTROPUM
Height: Four feet
Use: Bedding
Light: Shade

Easy to grow, but do not overwater. Very little watering necessary. Accents the other plants in any garden well.

HELLEBORUS Christmas Rose
Height: Sixteen inches
Use: Specimen plants, borders
Light: Shade

These plants bloom any time, and the flowers last for quite a while. Needs a shady, moist place and a slightly alkaline soil. Space twenty-four inches apart.

HEMEROCALLIS Day Lily
Height: Three feet
Use: Among shrubbery, borders
Light: Bright sunlight

These plants are not easy to grow, though they are beautiful in bunches. They need perfect drainage, and take time to become established. Space twenty-four inches apart. Beautiful but difficult.

HEUCHERA SANGUINEA
Coralbells
Height: To three feet
Use: Borders, rock gardens, paths
Light: Sun/shade

Needs a rich, rapidly draining soil to thrive. Attractive in clumps. Plant in early spring or late fall. Divide every three years. Produces dozens of pink flowers on thin stems.

HIBISCUS
Height: Three to eight feet
Use: Beds or as backgrounds
Light: Sun

Enormous flowers. Grow in sun and in rich soil kept moist but not wet. Space two feet apart. Flowers from July to September.

CAMPANULA.

HYPERICUM MOSERIANUM
Saint-John's-Wort
Height: To thirty inches
Use: Border
Light: Bright sunlight

Grows in almost soil. Beautiful cup-shaped gold flowers make this a desirable plant for any garden. At the end of each season, cut the stems to the ground to encourage future growth.

KNIPHOFIA ALOOIDES Red-Hot Poker
Height: To nine feet
Use: Background
Light: Sun

Notable for its long, greenish leaves with flowers that change form coral-red to orange to yellow. Almost unaffected by insects.

LATHYRUS Everlasting Pea
Height: To eight feet
Use: Various
Light: Sun

Tough to establish, but pretty plants that do well in a loamy soil. These plants bloom in summer and need only moderate watering.

LIATRIS Gayfeather
Height: Five feet
Use: Background
Light: Full sun
These plants need well-drained soil; preferably loamy. Quite self-sufficient. Lavender and white flowers bloom from summer into early fall. If grown in clumps, creates a burst of color.

LIMONIUM Sea Lavender
Height: Two feet
Use: Seaside planting
Light: Sun
Resistant to salt spray. Delicate plants with lavender flowers. Must have well-drained soil.

LYCHNIS Maltese Cross
Height: To three feet
Use: General garden plant
Light: Sun
Requires excellent drainage and a great deal of sun. Adds a great deal of color. Plant two feet apart.

LYTHRUM SALICARA Purple Loosestrife
Height: To five feet
Use: Borders, bursts of color
Light: Sun
This very popular perennial grows best in a spot that is constantly moist. Its red-purple flowers bloom in July and August.

MECONOPSIS BETONICIFOLIA Blue Poppy
Height: To five feet
Use: Various
Light: Shade/bright sun
These plants thrive in a slightly acid soil, some shade, and general coolness. They require excellent drainage. These delicate plants produce sky-blue to lavender flowers.

MONARDA DIDYMA Bee Balm
Height: Three feet
Use: Borders, masses of color
Light: Full sun
This plant is easy to grow and produces bright scarlet flowers. Remove faded flowers to extend blooming. Blooming can last all summer. Space plants twelve to eighteen inches apart.

NEPETA MUSSINI Catmint
Height: To one foot
Use: Edging
Light: Full sun
This plant will grow in just about any well-drained soil. It has silver-gray leaves and lavender flowers. Perfect for edging.

Pæonia Byzantina.
Turkish Peionie.

When—

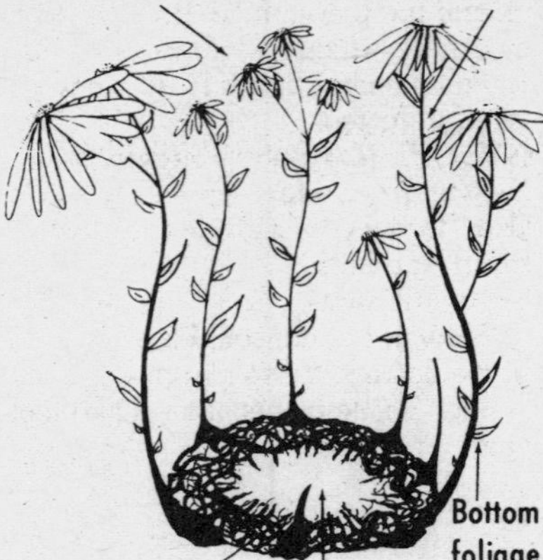

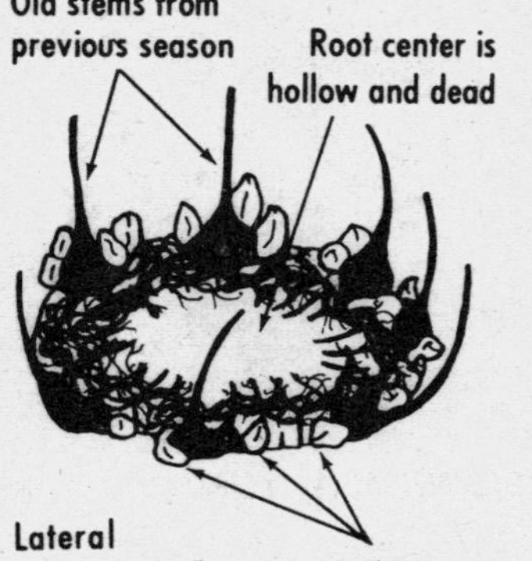

How—

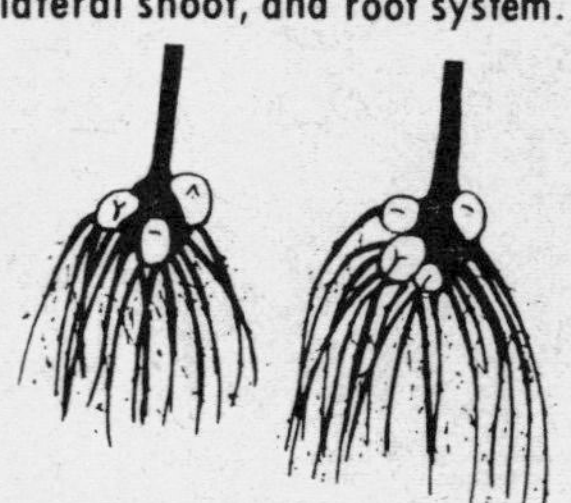

Lift plant. Wash most of soil from root system. Select divisions.
Pull or cut apart separate divisions.
Each division contains old stem, vegetative lateral shoot, and root system.
Plant divisions that have several vegetative lateral shoots and vigorous root systems.

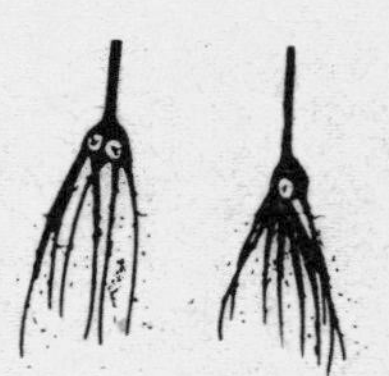

PAEONIA Chinese Peony
Height: Two to four feet
Use: Beds, borders
Light: Sun
These beautiful plants like well-drained soil and should be planted in a cool place. Blooms in late spring and early summer. Very good plant for any garden.

PHLOX
Height: To three feet
Use: Many, depending on species
Light: Sun
These plants are usually grown for masses of flowers of brilliant color. Most species require little attention. Great for gardens as they are versatile and easy to grow.

PHYSOTEGIA VIRGINIANA False Dragonhead
Height: To four feet
Use: Background
Light: Sun/shade
Easy to grow. Purple flowers and dark-green leaves are a striking combination. Will grow almost anywhere in almost any soil.

PLATYCODON Chinese Bellflower, Balloonflower
Height: Two to three feet
Use: General
Light: Full sun
Not essential to your garden, but a pretty group of flowers. Since they are easy to grow, you might try them. Space plants twelve inches apart.

PRIMULA Primrose
Height: One to two feet
Use: Many and varied
Light: Bright/shade
These are among the easiest plants to grow provided they get enough water (they require a lot). Primrose can be planted in rock gardens, by itself, or in a dozen ways. Likes a slightly acid soil.

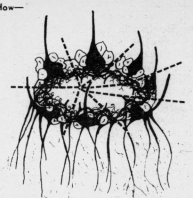

PULMONARIA ANGUSTIFOLIA Lungwort
Height: To two feet
Use: Border, edging
Light: Bright sun/shade
This plants like some shade and a lot of water. Its blue flowers have a long season.

ROMNEYA California Tree Poppy
Height: To eight feet
Use: Individual garden plant
Light: Sun
These plants require excellent drainage. One flower follows another, establishing a long season. Grow these by themselves rather than among other plants.

SCUTELLARIA BAICALENSIS Skullcap
Height: Two feet
Use: Rock gardens, front of flower gardens
Light: Sun
These plants produce blue or purple flowers and need well-drained soil. Easy to grow.

SIDALCEA Prairie Mallow, Miniature Hollyhock
Height: To four feet
Use: Groups
Light: Sun
These plants spread rapidly and require a great deal of water, good drainage, and lots of sun. Pretty pink to red flowers.

SOLIDAGO Goldenrod
Height: Three feet
Use: Background, borders
Light: Full sun
Though these are not usually found in gardens, they serve to set off other, more brilliantly colored plants. They will grow in any soil and need a good deal of water.

STOKESIA LAEVIS Cornflower Aster
Height: To eighteen inches
Use: Borders
Light: Sun
These plants make an excellent addition to any garden. Blue flowers and a long blooming season. They need excellent drainage and loamy soil.

THALICTRUM Meadow Rue
Height: To four feet
Use: Beds and backgrounds
Light: Bright to moderate sunlight
Grow these plants in a rich, loamy soil with good drainage. Rather easy to grow. Delicate plants with purple to pink flowers.

THERMOPSIS CAROLINIANA
Height: To four feet
Use: Background
Light: Sun
These plants produce yellow flowers. They need good sun and loamy soil.

TRADESANTIA Spiderwort
Height: Eighteen inches
Use: General
Light: Shade
Usually grown indoors, these make an interesting addition to a garden. Decorative leaves and blue flowers that last a long time. Will thrive in virtually any soil.

TROLLIUS Globeflower
Height: Twenty inches
Use: Borders
Light: Sun
These plants bloom from May to July, producing orange or yellow blossoms and palm-shaped leaves. Interesting in gardens because they are unusual. Need lots of water, sun, and a good, loamy soil.

VALERIANA OFFICINALIS
Height: To four feet
Use: General
Light: Sun
This is the perfect plant for beginners. It will grow in any kind of soil, provided it gets lots of water. Bears pretty pink flowers.

VERBASCUM
Height: To four feet
Use: Background
Light: Sun
These plants need good drainage. Characterized by furry leaves and lavender flowers. Easy to grow.

VERONICA Speedwell
Height: Eighteen inches
Use: Bedding, edging, boxes
Light: Sun
Requires a loamy soil and lots of sun. Flowers will persist all summer if old blooms are removed.

VIOLA Violet, Pansy
Height: One foot
Use: Borders, edging
Light: Sun
Violets bear blue flowers; pansies bear in many colors. Both do well in rich, moist soil. In hot climates, some shade should be provided.

4 *Primula veris flore geminato.*
Cowslips two in a hose.

ANNUALS

Annuals are flowers grown from seed that flower, set seed, and die in a few months. The usual life cycle is one year or less, but some can be started in mid- or late-summer and flourish the next year. *Biennials* take two years to complete their life cycle. The roots remain alive at the end of the first season allowing the plant to bloom the following year, after which time it dies.

Because annuals have but one season to live, they are active in producing and distributing seeds to continue the breed. They have no reserves, no means of storage, so all the plant's energy is concentrated in the blossoms. Consequently, annuals produce the most spectacular garden flowers. Varieties are classed as either hardy or half-hardy. Hardy plants are those that can be sown outside in spring right into the soil in which they will grow. Half-hardy seeds need some protection and warmth and must be germinated indoors or in a greenhouse. When buying seeds, check directions on how they should be germinated.

Annuals make good borders or edging at the front of a border. They can be used in hanging baskets or in window boxes. With annuals you have a choice of height, size of blossoms, color, even the scent of your garden. Add to this versatility that annuals require almost no care and they become a requisite part of every garden.

The soil should be dug up and turned over the autumn before you plant. At this time, work in some manure or compost and some slow-acting bonemeal or bloodmeal. Just prior to planting, level the ground and rake out all substantial stones. When hardy seedlings appear, thin them out, as overcrowding stunts all the plants. See also Propagating from Seeds.

Just about all annuals should be pruned when a few inches tall by pinching off the first terminal buds. This procedure encourages branching and will improve both the general appearance and the bloom of your plant. (Annuals that should not be pinched include balsam, cockscomb, and poppy.)

Removal of old flower heads keeps your garden neat and in most cases promotes additional blooming. Be sure to do this with ageratum, calendula, pansy, snapdragon, and zinnia.

The best method of watering is to wait until the soil is dry. Do not sprinkle your plants. Thoroughly soak the soil until the water has reached its roots (7 to 10 inches down). This will usually take two to three hours. Do not pour again until the soil is dry. Mulching prevents water from evaporating and will all but eliminate weeds.

Be careful not to overfertilize. Too much feeding can stop plants from blooming. If the soil is good, not much feeding is necessary. Most plants require a 10-10-5 food formula once a month, but to expedite blooming, use a plant food with high phosphorus content, like 5-10-5. There are special formulas designed for specific plants, such as roses, azaleas, and camellias.

AGERATUM Flossflower
Height: Six inches to two feet
Use: Edging, borders, beds
Light: Sun

Can be depended on for a lovely blue flower in summer and fall. They like loamy soil and a moderate amount of water.

AGROSTEMMA GITHAGO Corn Cockle
Height: Three feet
Use: Beds, landscapes
Light: Sun

This pink wildflower will grow in any soil and is tolerant of extremes.

ALONSOA WARSCEWICZII
Mask-Flower
Height: Two feet
Use: Beds
Light: Sun

This plant does not enjoy hot weather, but is excellent in a cooler climate when a dramatic burst of red is needed. It thrives in light, sandy soil.

ALTHAEA Hollyhock
Height: To six feet
Use: Ornamental individuals, cuttings
Light: Sun

Colors include pink, red, yellow, and white. These will grow in almost any soil and are hardy.

AMARANTHUS Tassel Flower
Height: To four feet
Use: Background
Light: Sun

These yellow-leaved, crimson-blossomed plants will grow in just about any soil.

ANAGALLIS Pimpernel
Height: To four feet
Use: In groups to provide masses of color
Light: Sun

Though slow to germinate, these are spectacular; flowers are usually orange. Amagallis will grow in most soils. Also grown as a perennial.

ANTIRRHINUM Snapdragon
Height: To five feet
Use: Background, beds, cuttings, borders
Light: Sun

These versatile plants come in small, medium and large sizes and in various colors. Stems and tips should be pinched when the plant reaches about four inches in height to increase the production of blooms. Grow in a loamy, well-drained soil.

ARCTOTIS GRANDIS African Daisy
Height: To two feet
Use: Ground cover
Light: Sun

These are spectacular plants with a long blooming period. The violet flowers close in the evening.

BRACHYCOME IBERIDIFOLIA
Swan River Daisy
Height: One foot
Use: Filler, ground cover
Light: Sun

This large-leafed plant likes rich soil. It has small blue or white flowers.

BROWALLIA
Height: To two feet
Use: Groups
Light: Sun/shade

Tolerates most soils and produces pretty blue flowers.

CALANDRINA UMBRELLATA
Rock Purslane
Height: Three feet
Use: Rock gardens, borders
Light: Sun

These plants require a warm climate. They grow well in dry soils and produce red flowers. They should not be fed.

CALENDULA
Height: One to two feet
Use: Border, groups
Light: Sun

Very easy to grow. They will grow in virtually any soil and produce yellow or orange flowers. Good for any garden as long as they get lots of water and sun.

CALLISTEPHUS CHINENSIS
China Aster
Height: To two feet
Use: Individual
Light: Sun
This is a difficult plant to grow and is subject to fungus infestation, so use fungicides. Flowers are spectacular, in violet, brilliant red, and bright yellow. Plant these in a rich, well-drained soil.

EARLY FLOWERING COSMOS.

CATANACHE CAERULA Cupid's Dart
Height: To two feet
Use: General
Light: Sun
Easy to grow, even in dry soil. They require a well-drained soil. The blue flowers are often used in dried flower arrangements.

CELOSIA Cockscomb
Height: One to three feet
Use: Borders
Light: Sun
Thrives in hot, fairly dry conditions. This is a good-looking plant with long, slender leaves and clusters of white blossoms.

CENTAUREA Basket Flower
Height: Three feet
Use: Anywhere
Light: Sun
Some of this species are grown as perennials (*dealbata* and *macrocephala*). Grow in a sunny, well-drained spot. They are so versatile they are virtually indispensable. Colors of flowers vary.

CLARKIA ELEGANS Rocky Mountain Garland
Height: Two feet
Use: Cuttings, borders
Light: Sun
These plants like cool summers and a sandy soil. They produce a profusion of purple or red flowers.

CLEOME SPINOSA Spiderflower
Height: To four feet
Use: Background
Light: Sun
These grow best in hot, dry locales, but will grow in any type of soil. Strong scent. Flowers are white or red.

COIX LACRYMA-JOBI Job's Tears
Height: To four feet
Use: Ground cover, background
Light: Sun
Unusual, easy-to-grow, ornamental grass with beautiful decorative seeds. Will grow in ordinary soil.

COSMOS
Height: To five feet
Use: Background, cuttings
Light: Sun
Long-lasting and durable, these lovely plants are available in a variety of colors. They are rapid growers. Can be grown in dry soil. Do not feed.

CROTALARIA RETUSA
Height: Two feet
Use: Edgings, cut flowers
Light: Sun
Flashy plants that require warm climate. Grow in a loamy soil. Bears small yellow flowers.

CYNOGLOSSUM AMABILE Chinese Forget-Me-Not
Height: To two feet
Use: Filler, border
Light: Sun
These are good plants for the beginner. They produce bell-shaped blue, pink or white flowers.

DIANTHUS Pinks, Sweetwilliam
Height: To four feet
Use: Various
Light: Sun
A must for skillful gardeners, these plants create a colorful area anywhere in the garden. Grow in loamy soil and water evenly. Available in numerous varieties, including perennials. Long blooming season.

DIMORPHOTHECA Cape Marigold
Height: To two feet
Use: Accent, cutting, edging
Light: Sun
Beautiful plants with red or yellow flowers, contrasting with dull-green leaves. Grow in plenty of light and well-drained soil. Easy to grow.

Broad leaued Sweet-Williams.

EMILIA FLAMMEA Tassel Flower
Height: Two feet
Use: Cut flowers, accent
Light: Sun
Can be grown in dry soil. Red flowers.

ESCHSCHOLZIA CALIFORNICA California Poppy
Height: Two feet
Use: Individual display
Light: Sun
Relatively easy to grow, offering a nice display of golden flowers. Transplantation is not recommended.

GAILLARDIA ARISTATA Blanket Flower
Height: Two feet
Use: Ornamental gardens
Light: Sun
Some varieties are grown as perennials. Yellow or red flowers are beautiful. Require work and patience. Will not grow in heavy soils, and need good drainage and loamy soil.

GAZANIA LONGISCAPA Gazania
Height: To eighteen inches
Use: Edging, pots, ground cover
Light: Sun
These perennials are usually grown as annuals and must be sown early. They bear yellow or orange flowers. Grow in any soil.

GODETIA Satinflower
Height: To thirty inches
Use: Edging, boxes
Light: Sun
These flourish in cool conditions and a sandy-loamy soil. Flashy, with flowers in a variety of bright colors.

HELICHRYSUM Strawflower
Height: To thirty inches
Use: Cuttings
Light: Sun
You can get this plant in varieties that produce red, yellow, or white blossoms. They grow in most kinds of soil. Make sure they get enough water.

IBERIS Candytuft
Height: One foot
Use: Edging
Light: Sun
These evergreens are available in both annual and perennial varieties. These are dark-green with contrasting light-colored flowers, and can add to any garden. Cut old flower stems as they fade to spur growth of new stems. Annual varieties include *amara coronaria* and *umbrellata*. Well-drained soil is a must.

IMPATIENS Patience Plant
Height: To three feet
Use: Bedding, borders, background
Light: Sun/shade
Various sizes. Pink or red flowers. Grow in sandy soil, in either sun or shade.

IRESINE HERBSTII Bloodleaf
Height: Two feet
Use: Varied
Light: Sun
These plants will put up with bad soil if they are given plenty of water and lots of sun. They are grown for their unusual vari-colored leaves.

LANTANA
Height: Three feet
Use: Ground covers, baskets
Light: Sun
Need loamy soil and heavy watering. Some varieties will grow as perennials in warm winter climates (*L. camara*).

LAVATERA Mallow
Height: Four to six feet
Use: Background, cutting
Light: Sun
Easy to grow. Watch for hollyhock rust. Pretty red and white flowers.

LOBELIA
Height: To one foot
Use: Edges, borders, beds
Light: Sun/shade
These plants like cool summers and prefer shade. Grow in loamy garden soil.

LOBULARIA MARITIMA Sweet Alyssum
Height: Six inches
Use: Edging, rock gardens
Light: Sun
Will bloom virtually all summer and will grow in almost any soil. Pleasant to the olfactories.

LUPINUS
Height: One to four feet
Use: Background
Light: Sun
Plant in loamy soil. Often a bit temperamental about starting to grow, but worth the effort for their beautiful blue flowers. Varieties also have red and pink blooms.

—MIMULUS.
MIMULUS LUTEUS.

MALOPE TRIFIDA Mallow-Wort
Height: To three feet
Use: Borders, bedding, cuttings
Light: Sun
These bushy plants require very good drainage. They produce cupped purple or white flowers. Plant in good sunlight.

MATTHIOLA Stock
Height: One to three feet
Use: Vertical accents, cuttings
Light: Sun
Many varieties with many colors. Great fragrance toward dusk.

MIMULUS Monkey Flower
Height: Six inches to one foot
Use: Rock gardens
Light: Sun/shade
Require very little care. Bright-green leaves are complemented by bright flowers of several colors. Easy flowering.

MIRABILIS JALAPA Four-O'clock
Height: To two feet
Use: Borders
Light: Sun

Fragrant blossoms of white, yellow, red-striped, or blotched with color. Flowers open from afternoon to dawn. Requires well-drained soil and good sun.

NEMESIA
Height: Twelve to eighteen inches
Use: Box, edging
Light: Sun

These are difficult plants to grow. They need a cool climate and a very rich soil in order to bloom. Showy white, yellow, or rose flowers.

NEMOPHILIA MENZIESII Baby Blue-Eyes
Height: To twelve inches
Use: Bedding, borders
Light: Sun

These aren't outstanding, but very good if you need a small blue plant for a filler. Well-drained soil is necessary. Easy to grow.

NIGELLA DAMASCENA Love-In-A-Mist
Height: To eighteen inches
Use: Various
Light: Sun/shade

This pretty plant with blue flowers and feathery foliage grows almost anywhere.

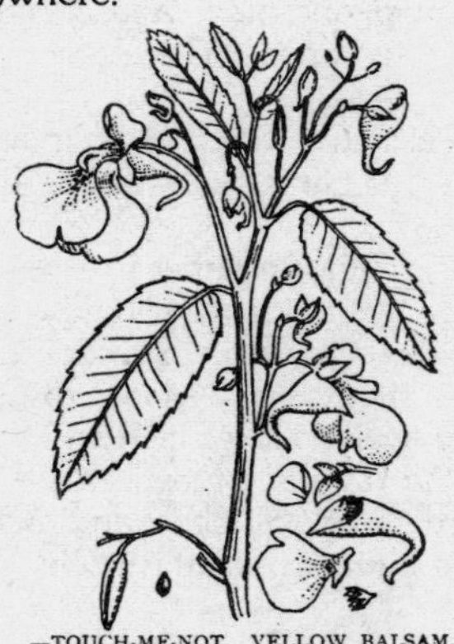

—TOUCH-ME-NOT. YELLOW BALSAM. IMPATIENS NOLI-ME-TANGERE.

SINGLE AND DOUBLE TUBEROUS BEGONIAS.

PELARGONIUM Geranium
Height: To thirty inches
Use: Bedding, borders, individual
Light: Sun

Do not need much attention. In warm areas, they become shrublike. Many colors and many varieties are available. Popular annual varieties are *P. domesticum*, *P. hortorum*, and *P. peltatum*.

PETUNIA
Height: One foot
Use: Border, container
Light: Sun

Showy plants that come in a great variety of colors, endless sizes and shapes, and seem to bloom endlessly. Prune fading flowers to produce a second bloom. They like a great deal of water and sun.

—SINGLE HOLLY-HOCK. ALTHÆA ROSEA.

—"ENGLISH TOBACCO."

PHACELIA CAMPANULARIA
Height: To one foot
Use: Edging
Light: Sun

These easy-to-grow flowers are good-looking and will grow in any soil.

PORTULACA GRANDIFLORA
Rose Moss
Height: To one foot
Use: Ground cover, filler, border
Light: Sun

These thrive in hot, dry places and produce red, yellow, or purple flowers. Flowers open in full sun, but close in shade.

RUDBECKIA
Height: Eighteen inches to three feet
Use: Background, cuttings
Light: Sun

Showy plants with large flowers. Easy to grow in loamy soil. They flower profusely in season, July to October.

SCABIOSA Pincushion Flower
Height: To three feet
Use: Beds, groups
Light: Sun

Good accent for any garden. Grow these in a loamy soil with good drainage. Crimson or blue flowers.

SENECIO Cineraria
Height: To three feet
Use: Individuals, borders
Light: Shade/sun

These are very difficult to grow successfully, but worth the effort. They must have a cool climate and a loamy, rich soil. Bright-red or purple flowers.

SILENE Catchfly
Height: To eighteen inches
Use: Borders
Light: Sun

These pink- or lavender-flowered plants are easy to grow in a sunny spot and in soil that is well-drained.

TAGETES Marigold
Height: To thirty inches
Use: General
Light: Sun

Several varieties are all very useful and pretty. Blooms are either double or single yellow or orange flowers. Marigolds grow easily in any soil if given enough sun and water.

TEN-WEEKS STOCK.

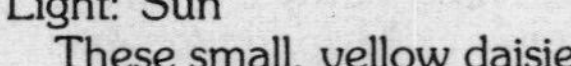

—CORN COCKLE.

THYMOPHYLLA TENUILOBA
Goldenfleece
Height: One foot
Use: Accents
Light: Sun

These small, yellow daisies grow well in a warm climate and need well-drained soil with a good deal of water.

THUNBERGIA Black-Eyed-Susan
Height: To ten feet (Vine)
Use: Trellises, arbors
Light: Sun

White, yellow, or orange flowers. Susans should not be exposed to excessive heat and need a good deal of water.

TITHONIA ROTUNDIFOLIA
Mexican Sunflower
Height: To three feet
Use: Background, individual
Light: Sun

Very lovely plant with bright orange-red flowers. Plants grow well in any soil, but yearn for sunlight.

TORENIA FOURNIERII Wishbone Flower
Height: To two feet
Use: Borders, pots
Light: Sun/shade

These small, attractive plants need loamy soil and should have some shade.

TRACHELIUM CAERULEUM
Height: Three feet
Use: Beds
Light: Sun/shade

This plant produces a blue flower and grows vigorously, almost without human intervention, in any soil. Keep soil moist.

TRACHYMEME CAERULEA
Height: Three feet
Use: Cuttings
Light: Sun

Pretty plant with clusters of blue flowers. Requires a cool spot and sandy soil.

Flos Aphricanus maior Polyanthos.
The great African double Marigold.

—GREAT SNAPDRAGON. ANTIRRHINUM MAJUS.

VENIDIUM FASTUOSUM
Height: To two feet
Use: Beds, borders
Light: Sun

Showy plant. Needs a well-drained spot in sandy soil. Large orange blossoms.

VERBENA
Height: To one foot
Use: Ground cover, edging, accents
Light: Sun

This good-looking plant spreads out and produces masses of red or purple flowers. Grow in a loamy soil with good drainage.

VINCA ROSEA Periwinkle
Height: To one foot
Use: Ground cover, edging
Light: Bright sun/shade

These are nice, small, easy-to-grow flowers. They have lavender-blue flowers.

VIOLA Violet/Pansy
Height: To one foot
Use: Border, edging, bulb gardens
Light: Sun

Both violets and pansies are perennials although often treated as annuals. Violets are blue and pansies come in many colors. While some shade is necessary, these plants should be grown in rich, loamy soil in the sun.

ZINNIA
Height: To three feet
Use: Borders, beds, edging
Light: Sun

These are the backbone of many a garden. Ridiculously easy to grow, the zinnia is a bright flower that comes in many sizes and shades. They will grow in any soil and their bloom lasts and lasts. Pretty in late autumn when most other flowers have passed on.

DOUBLE ZINNIA.

Centaurium magnum.
Great Centorie.

Ageratum floribus albis.
White floured Maudlein.

—VIPER'S BUGLOSS.

ROSES

Roses in all their forms—bushes and climbers—are extremely hardy and can be grown in varying climates. Many varieties offer bloom from mid-spring to near Christmas; some, if brought inside and well tended during winter months, bloom all year-round. Often they offer bonuses of distinctive leaf coloring and, at the end of the flowering season, a magnificent display of hips, or seed pods. If properly tended, roses will continue to bloom for up to fifteen or twenty years.

Though more than 5,000 cultivars currently exist, new varieties are introduced by plant breeders each year with improved cutting qualities, color, fragrance, or other qualities. The American Rose Society, a nonprofit organization founded in 1899 to serve enthusiasts, boasts the largest membership of any specialized plant society on the continent. Among other useful literature, the society publishes a handbook for selecting roses on the basis of color and other characteristics best suited to particular climates.

The thousands of varieties can be grouped into two main classes. *Bush* roses grow into bushes one- to six-feet-high and require no support. Included among these are the hybrid tea, floribunda, grandiflora, polyantha, hybrid perpetual, shrub, old-fashioned, tree or standard, and miniature. *Climbing* roses include rambler and trailers as well as climbing varieties of hybrid teas, polyanthas, and floribundas. The climbing roses produce long canes that require staking or other means of support. Often they are trained on fences or trellises or used as ground covers. Climbing roses are not as easy to categorize as bush roses, so their types may overlap and be listed differently in plant catalogs.

Bush Roses

Hybrid teas are by far the most popular of all roses. In existance for little more than one hundred years, they are the result of extensive crossbreeding that ensures long, strong stems, and elegant blossoms. Colors include yellow (not found in many other rose types), pure-white, orange, pink, red, lavender, maroon, and many blends and multicolors. All varieties are good for cutting.

Hybrid tas grow on bushes two to six feet high. Flowers may be single and have five to seven petals; or be doubles with as many as seventy velvety or satiny petals; and are borne one to a stem or in clusters of three to five. Buds are long and pointed. Most are fragrant; the scent is strongest in the morning before the oils evaporate. Where winter temperatures range from 10° to 40°F, some bloom all year. Most hybrid teas are winter-hardy where the temperature doesn't often drop below 0°F.

Foliage is usually dark- or medium-green, and a few varieties produce young red leaves that later turn green. Most hybrid teas have fairly large thorns, though thornless varieties are available. Examples range from the Peace Rose—its five-inch, double flowers a golden-yellow tinged with rose-pink—to the deep-red and strongly scented Mister Lincoln. Both are hardy, show-quality plants.

Floribundas combine the virtues of their parents—the hardy polyantha, with its clusters of small blossoms, and the showy hybrid tea, with its large blossoms on long stems—to produce their own clusters of moderately large blooms on fairly long stems. Floribundas are relatively hardy; most varieties survive without winter protection in regions where temperatures reach as low as −10°F. They blossom almost continuously from spring until the first frost, and may produce blooms all year-round in temperatures between 10 and 40°F.

Floribundas are good neighbors for hedges and can be grouped in beds of their own or in front of taller roses. They provide constant color and good flowers for cutting. They are also one of the easiest roses to grow, being tolerant of neglect. Examples include Garnette, which will thrive as a potted house plant and produces small flowers suitable for corsages. The orange-red Floradora is excellent for cutting.

Grandifloras have single blooms on long stems like hybrid teas and are hardy. Though the blossoms are smaller than those of hybrid teas, they are more profuse. These make excellent cutting flowers.

Polyanthas have blossoms even smaller than grandifloras', but the flowers are borne in large clusters. The blossoms resemble those of climbing roses, to which polyanthas are closely related. These are so hardy they will grow even in areas where hybrid teas are difficult to manage. They are good for bed plantings, in borders, and for mass plantings, but since they tend to flower only once a year (usually early for summer) they are less popular than other types.

Hybrid perpetuals are very hardy and withstand low winter temperatures without protection. Unlike hybrid teas, though, they do not bloom continuously throughout the growing season. Less popular today than in former years, they nevertheless offer some fine flowers, such as the stunning white Frau Karl Druschki.

Shrub roses is a term applied to a wide variety of wild species and hybrids that have a dense growth pattern useful for hedges, screening, and other landscaping. Though their flowers are small, they develop attractive seed pods. These are especially hardy.

Old-fashioned roses are hardy, neglect-tolerant species that were once popular in Colonial gardens. The flowers, though small and not as attractive as those of newer types, are noted for their fragrance.

Tree rose (or *standard rose*) is distinguished by the plant form rather than by the blossoms. These are created by grafting any of the bush-type roses onto upright trunks. Used as specimens and for garden accent, they tend to be delicate and need winter protection. Many popular bush roses are available as tree roses.

Miniature roses grow to a maximum of about six to twelve inches high and have tiny leaves and flowers, but are available in all the various colors, forms, and fragrances found in their larger cousins. Used for borders, edging beds, and rock gardens, they are excellent choices for containers and for indoor light gardens. They need only a six-inch-square area of soil.

Climbing Roses

Rambler roses grow so quickly some may develop twenty-foot canes in a single growing season. These have small flowers—generally less than two inches across—borne in dense clusters. They bloom only once a season, on wood produced the previous year. Though these have attractive glossy foliage and are very hardy, their popularity is being usurped by roses less susceptible to mildew and other diseases.

Large-flowered climbers, though they grow far less rapidly than ramblers, need heavy annual pruning to keep them in bounds. They may be trained against walls, fences, or trellises. The flowers are large and good for cutting.

Everblooming climbers produce profuse flowers in early summer, scattered flowers until fall, and under the proper conditions may deliver a heavy autumn display. Many new types—bred for hardiness and continuous bloom—are being developed.

Climbing hybrid teas combine the everblooming virtue of bush roses, such as hybrid teas, with climbing characteristics. Though flowers and foliage resemble those of the parent plant, and hardiness is about the same, flowers are not produced as continuously.

Climbing polyanthas and floribundas are identical to bush forms and bloom fairly continuously. Hardier than climbing hybrid teas, they nevertheless need winter protection in severe climates.

Trailing roses are hardy types that do not have flowers as attractive as many other roses. But they make excellent ground cover and are adaptable to banks or for training on walls.

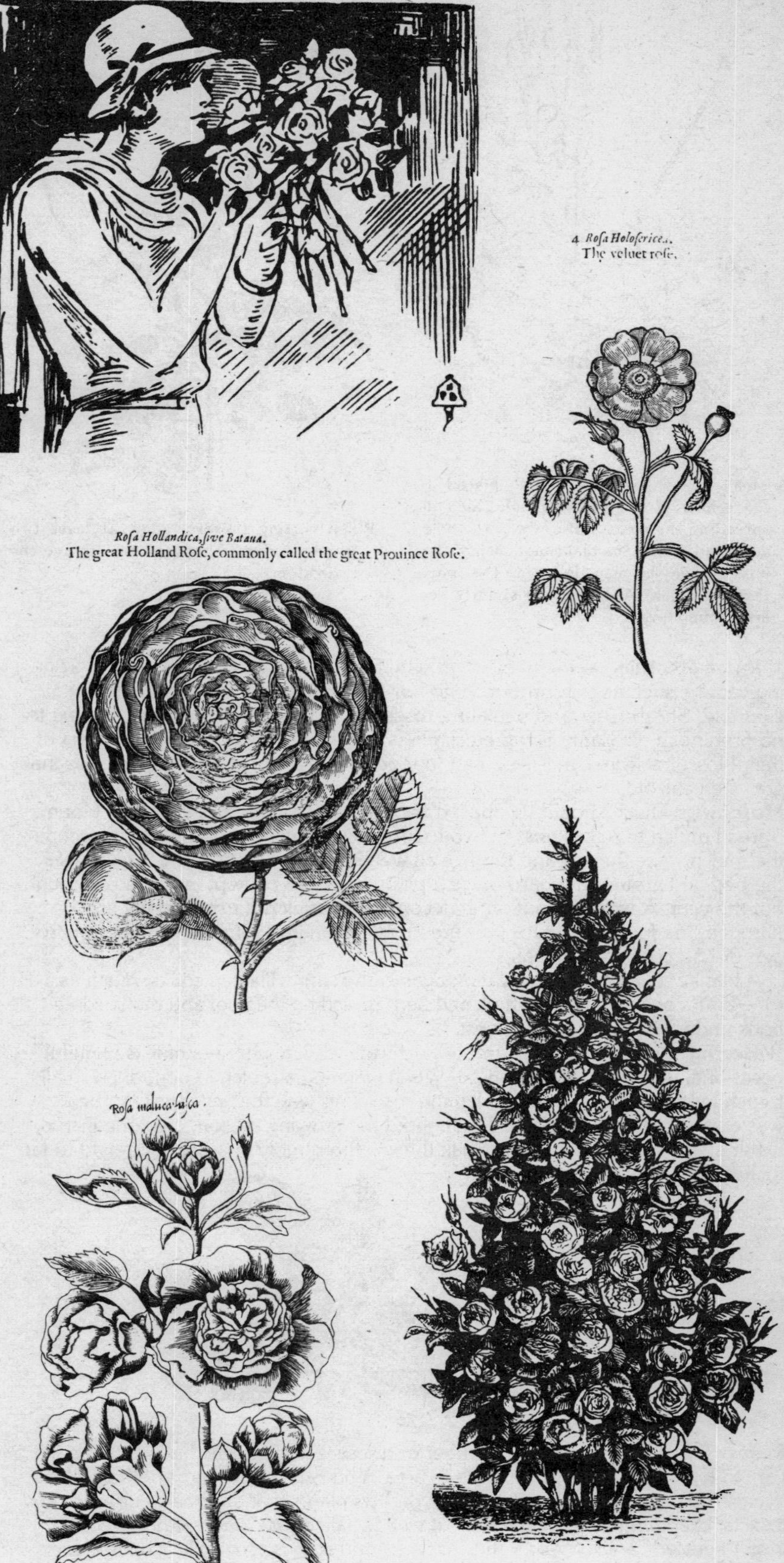

4 Rosa Holosericea.
The velvet rose.
Rosa Hollandica, sive Batava.
The great Holland Rose, commonly called the great Prouince Rose.

Planting

When to Plant: If winter temperatures in your area do not go below 10°F, plant your roses at any time they are fully dormant. If winter temperatures do not go below −10°F, plant in fall or spring. If winter temperatures regularly go below −10°F, plant in spring only. Exceptions are container-grown roses that are sold by some nurseries; these can be transplanted at any time from spring to fall.
Spacing Plants: Hybrid teas, grandifloras, polyanthas, and floribundas should be spaced two feet apart where winter temperatures fall to −10°F or below; two and one-half feet apart where temperatures fall to 10°F to −10°F; and at least three feet apart where temperatures never fall below 10°F. Hybrid perpetuals should be spaced three to five feet apart (or more) along fences in any area.
Preparation for Planting: Prepare the soil and dig holes before the plants arrive so that you can plant your roses immediately on receipt. If the plants dry out before they are planted, blossoming will be delayed. Never expose the roots to sun or drying winds. Move your plants to the garden in a bucket of water or coat the roots with mud or wet burlap until planted.

You may receive your plants frozen, in which case you should let them thaw gradually and completely before unpacking and planting them. If your plants are not frozen, unpack the roses at once and inspect the roots to see if they are dry. If they are dry, soak them in warm water (100°F) for an hour or two before planting. Otherwise plant immediately.

If you can't plant your roses immediately, you must keep them moist. Saturating the packing material with water and rewrapping the plants will keep them safe for two or three days. If you must delay planting longer than this, put the plants in a trench in a protected area of the garden and cover the roots with moist soil. If the canes are also dry, cover them with soil as well.

Examine the roots. Remove any dead or injured growth, and if necessary cut the canes back to a foot in length. (Your nursery may already have cut the canes back to a foot, in which case you should not recut.) Do not cut back to ten inches or less, or flowering will be delayed.
Setting Roses: You will usually dig a hole a foot deep in which to set your rose bush. Then place a small, cone-shaped pile of soil in the center of the hole. Set the plant on the peak of the cone and spread the roots down the slope.

The depth of planting depends on climate. If you've bought a plant from a local nursery you can use the soil mark on the bush as a guide. Otherwise, set the bud union of your plant two inches below ground level if your winter temperatures regularly go below −10°F; one inch below ground level if the temperature goes below 10°F but not under −10°F; and at ground level or slightly below it if the temperature is warmer than 10°F. If your rose bush is potted, dig a hole large enough to hold the roots and soil ball and so the bud union is at ground surface.

Work the soil around the roots so that all roots are in contact with earth. Avoid air pockets and the possibility that wind will uproot the bush, yet don't compact the soil. As you fill the hole with soil, pat the soil snug but not too hard; add water after the hole is about three-quarters full. Fill the remainder of the hole and add extra earth to create a mound. Bush and climbing roses should be surrounded by mounds eight- to ten-inches-high; for miniature roses a three- to four-inch mound is sufficient. Keep the mound in place until the danger of frost is past. Tree roses will also need to be tied to a sturdy pole or other support to prevent uprooting from the wind.

Culture

Sun: Roses grow best if they have sun all day. Most will grow satisfactorily, however, if they get at least six hours of sun daily. If you have a choice, plant them where they get morning rather than afternoon sun, as morning sun will dry the dew from their leaves and discourage the leaf diseases.
Soil: Because roses are hardy, any good garden soil will usually produce good roses. If you grow healthy grass, shrubs, and other plants, it is unlikely that your soil needs special preparation for roses.

While you needn't buy special soil for rose plants, it is important that your soil have a pH balance that is slightly acidic, somewhere between 5.5 and 6.5. Soil with a pH under 5.5 may lack calcium—a deficiency detected by dying rose leaflets or brown spots on flower petals. Add three or four pounds of agricultural loam per every one hundred square feet. Soil with a very high pH level may lack iron and cause the foliage to turn white. For every one hundred square feet use one pound of sulfur if the pH is 7.0 to 7.5; two pounds if it is 8.0; and three pounds if it is 8.5. Allow to stand at least a week before planting the roses, check acidity at monthly intervals to see if new applications are needed.

Roses need well-drained soil. Growers disagree on the exact nature of ingredients to assure the best blooms, and you'll find strong adherents of peat moss, leafmold, sawdust, human hair (for nitrogen), banana skins (for potash), or dehydrated cow manure. Whatever your preference, the usual mixture is two parts organic matter, one part coarse sand or sawdust, to two parts loam. Spread a layer of organic matter about two to four inches thick over a spaded bed, and then work it into the soil to spade depth. Do this at least four weeks before planting—but prefereably the fall before planting.
Fertilizing: Except for newly-planted roses, rose plants need a balanced feeding at the beginning of the growing season. Depending on your soil, a 10-6-4, 5-10-5, 4-8-4, or 4-8-6 formula may be satisfactory.

Although this application must be made at the beginning of the growing season (and after the danger of freezing is past), it can be made again and again if plants begin to show mineral deficiencies: yellowing of leaves from lack of nitrogen, leaves turning green-gray from lack of phosphorus, or the browning of leaf margins from lack of potassium. To avoid these problems, some growers feed the plants small amounts of fertilizer every month of the growing season, regardless of signs of deficiencies. In any case, do not fertilize beyond mid-August in warm climates or mid-July in cold climates, because fertilizer may stimulate fresh growth and delay hardening of the wood before winter sets in.
Pruning: Pruning is essential. Unpruned roses grow into a briar patch and produce small, poor-quality blooms. As the new rose buds begin to swell, beginning in January in very warm climates and late April in cold northern zones, remove growth that is hazardous to the plants' health—winter-killed branches, infected stems and canes, and canes that have grown inward to the center of the bush and nub other canes. In warmer climates, you may want to severely cut back your bushes. Often shoots with small, dark-green leaves grow from the understock; remove these as soon as they appear or they may dominate the plant.

The length of wood that must be cut varies with each type of plant. A general rule is to cut down to good live wood. Always cut just above the bud. (If there are no live buds, remove the entire stem or cane.) Examine the pith in the center of the cane to determine whether or not you have reached live wood. The pith inside healthy growth is creamy white. If you see brownish pith, the wood is dead, so continue cutting back.

Pruning cuts should be clean, firm, and at a 45-degree angle to the stem axis. This insures that rain and dew will slide off the stem end rather than collect and cause rot. Cuts made in this direction will force roses to bloom away from the stem and have more room to spread. To discourage stem borers, coat large pruning cuts with rose-cane dressing or tree-wood paint.

While the basic rule in pruning is to cut back all dead wood, bush roses can be pruned either "high" (cutting away only dead wood) or "moderate" (up to one half the length of all canes). The moderate method produces fewer but larger blooms prized for exhibition and cutting purposes. Single-stem and exhibition flowers also require disbudding (removal of all but the terminal bud on each stem), which allows the terminal bud to develop into a larger flower. Removing some of the buds of clustered roses such as polyanthas improves the remaining blooms.

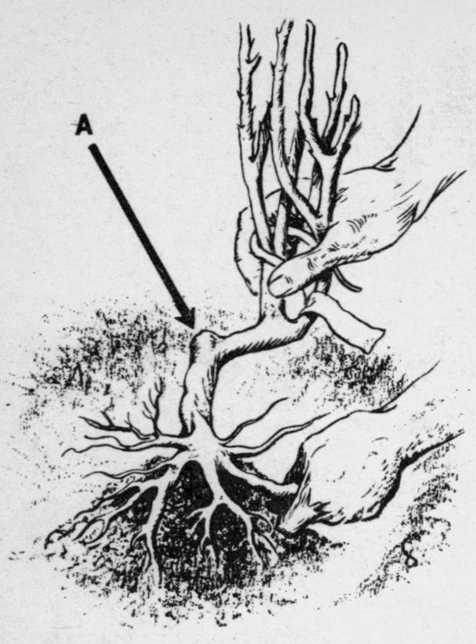

A small cone-shaped pile of soil, placed in the center of the planting hole, aids in spreading the roots uniformly in the hole and in adjusting the planting depth of the bush. When the plant is set on the cone, the bud union (*A*) should be slightly below ground level.

When cutting flowers, allow at least two leaves to remain between the cut and the main stem.

Prune according to the habit of growth. Do not cut back a naturally tall-growing variety, such as the shrub rose, to match the height of the hybrid tea, for example. Shrub roses and miniature roses are so hardy that they require next to no pruning at all. Large-flowered climbers, on the other hand, produce most of their blossoms from canes less than four years old, and ramblers from canes that are one year old.

Mulching: Mulch should be applied about one month before the roses bloom. Spread mulch to a thickness of two to four inches over the bed. Before spreading the mulch, rake the soil and remove all weeds. Then distribute the mulch over the bed and around the base of each plant. It should be kept on the soil throughout the year. A word of caution: If decomposing mulch is using up the soil's nitrogen, the foliage will turn pale green; use a fertilizer formula with more nitrogen or add cottonseed meal.

A blanket of mulch, as insulation against the sun, will keep soil as much as 10° to −20°F cooler than an unmulched bed, providing the cool and moist conditions under which roses grow best.

Watering: Roses need large amounts of water. Even where rainfall is plentiful, occasional waterings are beneficial. When watering a mulched bed, dig a small trench in the mulch in which to lay the rose. This way the water will not be wasted saturating the surface. Throughout the growing season, give one inch of water every seven to ten days. Soak the soil thoroughly to a depth of eight to ten inches at each watering.

Pests: The distressingly large number of diseases and insects that attack roses vary in type and severity from area to area. You can control most of them effectively—no matter where you live—if you buy plants that are free of diseases and insects; keep the rose garden clean of weeds, fallen rose leaves, and disease or insect-infested canes; apply a mulch. Dusts and sprays especially prepared for roses are available commercialy. You can make your own by mixing one-half cup of boiled cloves and garlic husks, and one tablespoon of biodegradable detergent, with one gallon of water.

Of the many diseases attacking roses, black spot, powdery mildew, rust, crown gall, and cankers are the most serious. Several species of wasplike insects called *rose galls* lay their eggs in the stems of roses. Their larvae cause large swelling of galls. One species makes a gall that resembles fibrous moss. Another causes a large warty gall near the ground surface. These galls may be confused with crown galls, which are caused by bacteria. However, if insect galls are cut open, numerous larvae—or the cells in which they develop—will be visible. No insecticides known can control these insects. The best control is to prune the infested stems and to bury them promptly to destroy the larvae before they emerge.

Winter Protection: If rose plants have been healthy and properly nourished during the full growing season, they are more likely to escape winter injury than plants that have lost their leaves because of diseases or nutrient deficiencies. Still the extent of winter protection depends on both the kind of plant and the climate zone.

Roses must be protected against fluctuating temperatures. Often roses that are hardy in the North, where winter temperatures are constantly low, are injured during the winter in areas farther south, where the temperatures fluctuate considerably. In these warmer climates, roses can be subject to repeated freezing, melting, and refreezing, as well as to drying winds. This can do far more damage to plant tissue than a single, long-lasting freeze.

In warm or moderate climates, where temperatures seldom go below 10°F, it is unnecessary to protect any roses, except for possibly the most tender hybrid teas. Bind them with evergreen branches, cornstalks, or burlap, and mound six to eight inches of soil around their bases.

In moderate climates, where temperatures occasionally drop to 0°F or below, some protection is needed for most hybrids, climbers, and other roses, as well as bush types. For bush roses, the same protection used in warmer climates for hybrid teas should be used. If the temperature leans closer to subzero than it does to above, tie the canes of the hybrid tea together and mound a foot or more of soil around the base of each plant. Wrap the canes of a climbing rose in the fall with burlap, hay, straw, or evergreen branches. If the plant is trained to a post, first tie its canes close to the post with twine. Once the plant is tied and wrapped, add a soil mound of eight to twelve inches around the base. For a tree rose, trim its top to a ten- to fifteen-inch crown. Wrap the trunk and its stake in stem-wrapping paper overlapped from the bottom up, until only the cane tips are exposed.

In harsh winter climates, where subzero temperatures are common, even the hardiest roses require heavy protection. Tie the canes together and enclose them in a tarpaper cylinder filled with peat moss or bark. A burlap cover can be tied to the top and a soil mound packed around the base.

To guard climbing roses from severe winters, shed the entire plant with earth. Detach the climber from its support and tie its canes together. Bend the canes to the ground, arching them near the plant's base to avoid breakage. Then pin the canes down with crossed stakes. Finally cover the entire plant with a mound of soil, and drive a stake into the ground at each corner of the mound so the plant will be marked and not trampled.

In subzero climates, protect tree roses by burying them in the surrounding soil. Loosen the soil a foot away from the tree base on the side that is opposite from the direction you plan to lay the tree in. Dig a spade into the ground the depth of its blade and rock the tree gently to free the roots without exposing them. Remove the tree's stake and bend the roots into a hole dug in the ground. Peg the trunk to the ground with crossed stakes, cover the tree with soil, and mark the location with stakes. Remove straw, soil, or other covering materials in spring after the last frost.

Miniature roses, aside from being extremely hardy, can be taken indoors for the winter. With at least three hours of sunshine daily, some humidity, and moderate room temperature, miniature roses produce blooms all winter long. When spring comes they can be transplanted outside.

Propagation: Most roses can be propagated from cuttings taken in summer (after flowers have fallen) or fall (after the wood has ripened).

Cut summer stems of six or eight inches. Remove all leaves except one or two at the top. Then plant the cutting with half its length beneath the soil. Water it and invert a fruit jar over it. Remove the jar the following spring.

Fall cuttings should be eight or ten inches long. Remove all leaves and plant the stem in a sunny spot so only the top bud is above the soil. When freezing weather approaches, cover with several inches of mulch to keep the ground from freezing.

SUPPLIERS

Jackson & Perkins
Medford, Or. 97501

Joseph J. Kern Rose Nursery
Box 33
Mentor, Oh. 44060

The Miniature Rose Company
200 Rose Ridge
Greenwood, S.C. 29647

Mini-roses
P.O. Box 4255, Sta. A
Dallas, Tx. 75208

Rosehill Farm
Gregg Neck Rd., Box 406
Galena, Md. 21635

Spring Hill Nurseries
110 W. Elm St.
Tipp City, Oh. 45371

Stocking Rose Nursery
785 North Capital Ave.
San Jose, Ca. 95133

Tate Nursery
Rt. 3
Tyler, Tx. 75705

Thomasville Nurseries Inc.
P.O. Box 7
Thomasville, Ga. 31792

10
Outdoor Plant Lore

Thinking About Soil.

Soil has two functions, to support and nourish plants. How well it performs is less a matter of luck than know-how. The type of soil in your garden is not so important as how well it is managed. Fortunately, garden plants will grow in a variety of soil types. Poor-quality soil can almost always be made into a better, more fertile version of itself.

Some soils, however, are superior growth mediums because they are more fertile and more workable. Good soil permits root growth to support the plant and must supply water and oxygen. It is free of toxic elements, nearly level or gently sloping, and has favorable air and water movement. It is medium acid to neutral (pH 5.5 to 7.0) and contains a good supply of organic matter in the surface layer.

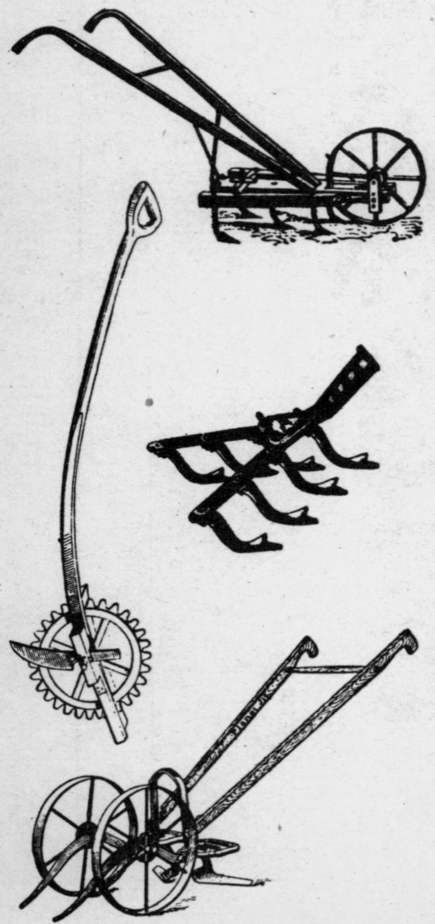

How would you describe your soil? If the question stumps you, learning more about the following categories of soil characteristics, you can think more effectively about the productivity of your garden—which begins and ends with high-grade soil.

Criteria of Garden Soil

Texture. Texture refers to the size of the particles of sand, silt, and clay that make up the soil. The best texture soils are loams and sandy loams, which have a desirable mixture of particles. An example of a loam is a soil mixture containing about 20% clay (the smallest particles), 40% silt (medium-size particles), and 40% sand (largest particles).

Loams are workable, have good drainage and water-holding capacity, and are well aerated. Loams and sandy loams do not stick to shoes or tools.

Structure. This refers to the arrangement of soil particles. A sandy soil usually has a "single-grain" structure, whereas clay is described as "compact." The preferred garden soil falls somewhere between the two extremes, and has a "crumb" structure that affords good drainage and aeration.

Profile. Although very important, a 6-inch layer of topsoil does not a good garden make. A favorable soil profile consists of several layers, or horizons, optimally with a layer of gravel or coarse sand at a depth of three to five feet that aids aeration and drainage. Most natural soil profiles divide into three horizons: topsoil (horizon A), subsoil (horizon B), and substratum (horizon C). The texture of most soils changes from horizon to horizon—commonly, the subsoil contains more clay than horizon A or horizon C.

In towns and cities, the soil profile has been disturbed when land was cleared and again during construction. In addition, grading operations around homesites result in a greater degree of soil compaction than that in natural soils, and water and root penetration may be restricted.

Drainage. A saturated soil prevents not only aeration but also the conditions favoring desirable soil microorganisms. A well-draining soil absorbs rain rapidly and is unlikely to be washed away. It has good surface drainage and good internal drainage. Important factors in good drainage are soil texture, structure, and profile.

To check the drainage of a prospective garden plot, dig holes two to three feet deep and fill them with water. Allow the water to drain away and fill them again. After the second filling, the water level should fall at least one inch every 45 minutes and disappear within about 24 hours. If it takes longer than this, the soil has slow permeability, and you can expect only shallow-rooted crops to do well.

Soil chemistry. What is the mineral composition of your soil? This is an important question because plants live on dissolved mineral salts and cannot thrive when certain minerals are either absent or present in excessive concentrations. Good soil contains perhaps a hundred separate mineral compounds especially the so-called major plant foods—nitrogen, phosphorus, potassium or potash, calcium, and magnesium. Gardeners learn about the mineral content of soil by making a soil test.

Organic matter. Fertile garden soil contains a high amount of organic matter, especially in the upper five or six inches. Formed in the biological decomposition of plant and animal residues, beneficial fungi and bacteria live on or in the organic matter and break it down to produce humus and release nutrients used by plants. Organic matter also conditions soil. For example, decay bacteria secrete a mucous that glues together the soil particles that would otherwise erode very easily following a rainfall. Organic content also increases the capacity of sandy soil to hold water and promotes a granular texture in clay soils.

Stoniness. A certain amount of stones in a garden does not impair its productivity. Too many stones, however, add to the difficulty of gardening.

Topography. Topography refers to the overall terrain, not to the soil, but it greatly affects the soil. For instance, a slight slope aids aeration and drainage. A sloping surface also receives increased or lessened radiation from the sun and therefore more or less heat, depending on the direction of the slope.

Color. The direct effect of the color of the soil is not very significant even though very dark soils may absorb more heat than light soil. Soil color can serve as an indication of other important characteristics. Blackish and dark brown soil is usually rich in humus, the stable product of decomposed organic matter. Red soil can be good if the color is not just the result of the underlying rock; in tropical areas, red soil is desirable although it requires much improvement by the gardener. Properly improved, yellow soil in temperate zones can make a good garden, whereas it has low fertility and poor drainage in tropical areas. White soil? Not very fertile at all.

Acidity. This is measured by pH, which is an indication of the relative acidity (or alkalinity). It is an important concept for gardeners to understand because the majority of plants grow best in neutral to slightly acid. A pH rating of 6.5 is neutral, anything higher is alkaline, and a

Conn. Ag. Exp. Station—New Haven Conn.
Aug 18th 1877

Analysis of "Composition for Grass" sold by Pollard Bros. Manufacturers and Dealers in Improved Fertilizers. 3 Custom House Square New Haven Ct.

Analysis on Barrels { "Organic and soluble Plant Food 86" / Inorganic Matter. 54

Station Analysis + Valuation.

	Pounds per 100.	Pounds per Ton	Value per lb	Value per ton.
Water	16.72	637.5		
Vegetable Matter	13.92	227.7		
(Nitrogen of Veg. M.)	(.19)	(3.1)	18 cts	56 cts
Sand + Earth	65.27	1067.8		
Potash	.15	2.5	6 cts	32 cts
Soda	.23	2.8		
Lime	1.38	22.6		
Magnesia	.96	15.7		
Phosphoric acid	.37	6.1	5 cts	15 ct

lower rating is acid. A complete assessment of the soil's suitability for growing particular crops must include a pH rating of the subsoil as well as topsoil, for the two are not necessarily the same. In the Southeast, some subsoils are leached to the point that subsoil acidity actually reduces the rooting depth of certain plants.

Contamination. Soils in vacant, rubble-strewn lots may be high in poisonous heavy metals such as lead and cadmium. Sometimes such soil contains five times the average concentration of these metals and has three times more lead than the threshold level of toxicity. Lead hazards are said to depend on whether the person consuming high-lead produce also absorbs lead from other sources such as exhaust from vehicles using leaded gasoline or particles of peeling lead-based paints.

A garden need not be in an inner city to be contaminated. In housing developments and wherever the soil has been disturbed, look for buried trash left by the builders.

Certain elements such as aluminum and manganese found in large quantities in soils with a pH below 5.5 become soluble in levels that stop plant growth.

Soil Improvement

Soil quality is the most vital factor in seed germination and growth. A good soil has aeration, a light, crumby texture, and contains organic matter. If your garden soil lacks some of those characteristics, it is less productive than it could be. Soil productivity can be enhanced by adding other materials to the soil and by using certain cultural practices. These methods can be used together.

Soil supplements fall into two categories, inorganic and organic. These supplements affect the structure of the soil, the texture, or only the chemical composition. All may affect its biological condition.

Inorganic supplements include sand, clay, ashes, lime, and inorganic, or chemical, fertilizers.

Organic supplements include leafmold, sawdust, manure, peat moss, sphagnum moss, compost, cover crops such as alfalfa, and organic fertilizers.

Clay soil: A 3-year program. The trouble with clay soil is that it is airless and hardpacked. But it can be improved at any time of the year by spreading gypsum (from a garden supply store) over the surface of the area to be planted. Use fifty pounds of gypsum for every one thousand square feet. The gypsum will penetrate about 6 inches of the clay per year, and three annual additions of gypsum should result in a decent planting medium.

Of course, few gardeners want to wait until the process is completed to begin growing things. No problem. Just mix up gypsum with clay in planting holes for the first two years.

Sandy soil. The difficulties gardeners experience with sandy soil are due largely to its low water-holding capacity and generally low nutrient content. Organic matter has an enhancing effect on the water-holding capacity, and certain types add substantially to the nutrient supply.

One way to improve sandy soil is to dig a two-foot trench the size of the garden-to-be and set the sandy soil to one side. After lining the trench bottom with roofing paper, lay a one-foot layer of organic material (compost if you have it) and cover the rest with sand. You now have a garden ready for planting. It is preferable to do this preparation in autumn.

Overfertilized soil. Soil with too many soluble mineral salts as the result of overfertilization is as useless as pure sand. The problem is to leach out or wash away the accumulated salts without washing away topsoil. To do so, *slowly* flood the garden area with water so that the moisture seeps down a couple of feet. Apply enough water to flood the area so that the excess water that does not seep downward will wash away. Then incorporate a thick layer of compost or peat moss into the upper 6 inches of soil.

Alkaline soil. A pH above the neutral 6.5 can be brought down by adding peat moss, rotted pine needles, or oak leafmold to the soil. Sulfur or ferrous sulfate also neutralize highly alkaline soil or create the properly acid medium for ericaceous plants such as rhododendrons and blueberries. The usual proportions for applications of these supplements are one to three pounds for every hundred square feet. First, however, measure the pH and contact your local extension for advice on what proportions to apply to your soil. Lime, which raises the pH, should not be used unless indicated by a soil test.

Acid soil. Apply ground limestone or agricultural lime at the rate of three to eight pounds for every hundred square feet of ground area, depending on the degree of acidity. If you let your local USDA extension office know the pH rating of your soil and the kinds of crops you want to grow, they will advise you on the exact proportions.

Soil Testing

Soil testing is a practical way to learn more about the makeup of your garden soil. But is it really necessary? Soils vary tremendously, and so do the nutrient requirements of plants. It is therefore virtually impossible to guess with complete accuracy whether your garden soil is what your crops need to thrive. Testing removes from the realm of chance the kind, rate, and method of fertilizer and supplement application.

Remember, soils constantly undergo change. From season to season, plant nutrient elements in the soil change as the result of removal by the growing of harvested crop, leaching, or erosion, or they become more plentiful when fertilizer, compost, or manure is added, or nitrogen-fixing crops are grown. A soil test reveals current fertility status and provides the information you need to maintain (or attain) optimal growing conditions for your plants.

Measuring pH. The acid-alkaline balance in soil rarely stays static. As a general rule, cultivation tends to increase acidity, and a corrective measure such as adding lime is called for. Although labs can do this test for you, it is one of the soil tests that home gardeners can perform easily. To keep tabs on your soil pH, you need a pH testing kit or soil test tape, which ordinarily costs under five dollars and can perform several tests, or a pH computer, a meter to insert into moist soil that costs slightly over twenty dollars.

What makes pH so important? The availability of most nutrient elements is greatest at a pH of about 6.5. When the pH rises above the "normal" range of 6.0 to 6.9 (experts differ slightly on this), trace elements such as iron, manganese, copper,

and zinc become less available to plants, and too-acid soil releases toxic levels of other minerals.

Some plants, however, thrive in relatively acid soils (5.0-5.5), and are actually damaged by alkaline or pH neutral soil. Some of the acid-loving plants are:

andromeda	heath
azalea	heather
blueberry	mountain laurel
calla	orchid
camellia	rhododendron
galaz	trailing arbutis

Measuring soil nutrients. To grow properly, plants need 16 elements in the form of dissolved mineral salts. They are: carbon (C), oxygen (O), hydrogen (H), nitrogen (N), phosphorus (P), potassium or potash (K), calcium (Ca), magnesium (Mg), sulfur (S), boron (B), chlorine (Cl), copper (Cu), iron (Fe), manganese (Mn), molybdenum (Mo), and zinc (Zn). Carbon, oxygen, and hydrogen are supplied by carbon dioxide (CO_2) and water (H_2O). The remaining thirteen elements come from the soil—or ought to.

Of these thirteen, nitrogen, phosphorus, and potassium or potash are the major plant nutrients. They are needed in the greatest amounts and are removed from the soil in greater quantities.

Some experts suggest retesting one-third through the growing season to determine whether more or different kinds of fertilizer should be added. Fertilizing too late in the season has adverse effects.

How to take a soil sample. A soil sample is best taken with a soil probe or an auger, but you can also use a spade, trowel, garden dibble, or a narrow shovel with straight sides. To gather the soil, you will need coffee cans, small cardboard boxes, yogurt containers—anything with a top that holds about a pint of soil. Be certain that tools and containers are scrupulously clean and free of foreign matter, especially fertilizers or other chemical products, that could distort the test results.

If you use a laboratory, put the sample in a container for shipping. Label the sample, indicate where and when you took it, what crop or crops grew on the land last year, and what you intend to plant in the coming year. If you garden with organic methods, say so in your note to the lab, and they will provide their suggestions in those terms.

Soil testing kit or lab test? Should you invest in a soil testing kit? At most, an analysis by your state cooperation extension or by a commercial laboratory costs about as much as the least expensive soil testing kit. So unless you intend to use a kit frequently and analyze many samples, a kit is not a particularly practical investment. Also, home tests are as good as the person using them. Inexperienced growers often have difficulty understanding their test results and determining the proper corrective measures.

Generally, laboratory and extension tests reports express nitrogen, potassium, and phosphorus content as "excessive," "high," "medium," and "low," and express nutrient content as "deficient," if that be the case. Most of these analyses also recommend ways in which to improve less than satisfactory conditions. If you use a state lab, you can also contact them for further help on what to do with your garden.

To get the most from soil tests, plan to work with your garden soil for a balance among nutrients. You have balanced soil when enough of each nutrient is available to the roots of the plants growing in it. If you have a kitchen garden, this is of particular importance because fertile soil produces higher quality crops.

Sources

Soil tests:
Prescription Soil Analysis
Box 80631
Lincoln, NB 68406

Soil testing equipment:
W. Atlee Burpee Co.
Warminster, PA 18974

Comstock, Ferre & Co.
263 Main St.
Wethersfield, CT 06109

Joseph Harris Co., Inc.
Moreton Farm
Rochester, NY 14624

Herbst Seedsmen, Inc.
1000 North Main St.
Brewster, NY 10509

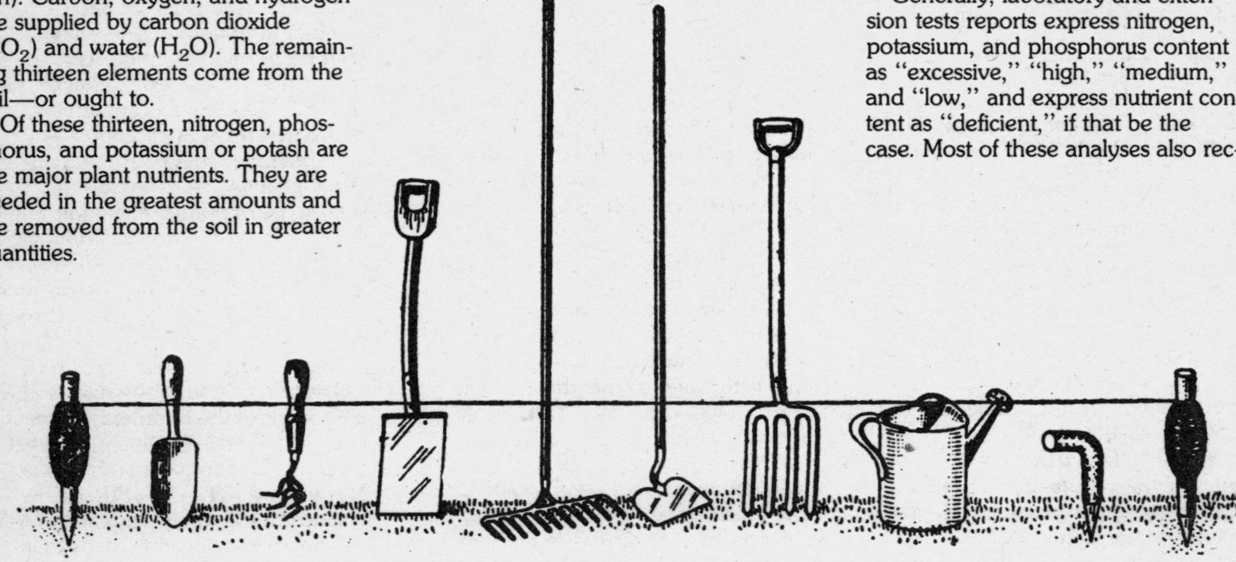

—Tools most commonly needed in a small garden. From left to right, between the balls of cord, they are: Trowel, weeder, spade, steel toothed rake, hoe, garden fork, watering pot and dibble.

When soil tests are made, the nutrients most often determined are potassium, phosphorus, calcium, and magnesium. Tests also can be run for nitrate and ammonium nitrate, and in areas where they are a problem, aluminum, sodium, lead, cadmium, sulfate sulfur, and boron can be determined. In western states, the levels of chlorides and carbonates ought to be determined.

If you or the previous gardener have been adding organic material to the soil all along, a test for its humus content will indicate how successful these additivies have been. An *Organic Gardening and Farming* magazine survey found that the average organic gardener has about 2.5% organic matter in his or her garden soil. That's a full percentage point higher than the average U.S. soil, although only a little more than half as much virgin soil, which contained 4% organic matter.

When to test soil. Soil samples should be taken in the fall for two practical reasons. First, if your pH rating is high (i.e., you have a fairly alkaline soil), it will take six months for the lime or sulfur you must add to bring the reading down to where you want it. Second, if you wait until the beginning of planting time, because of the spring rush the lab can take up to a month to return the results.

Begin by assembling your tools, a pen, and some small containers. If you smoke, leave your cigarettes or pipe in the house because tobacco ash in soil can significantly alter test results.

Next, if you have an auger, remove surface litter and about a half-inch of topsoil before inserting the tool to its full depth. If you are using a trowel or spade, make a six-inch vertical cut in the soil and remove this soil. Then make a second slice along the face of the first cut to a thickness of at least ½ inch. Put this sample of the upper soil into a container and label it to identify the source.

It is not hard to decide how many samples to take. The idea is to obtain a highly representative sampling, so take several random samples from points spaced about two yards apart until you have covered the entire garden plot. If an area of your property is obviously different, you will want to sample it separately and run a separate test. In a large yard or field that will be planted, increase the distance between sampling points.

When you have finished sampling, mix all the soil together, remove about a half pint, and set it out to dry on a clean tray. When it is completely dry, remove lumps, stones, and debris.

Building Soil with Compost

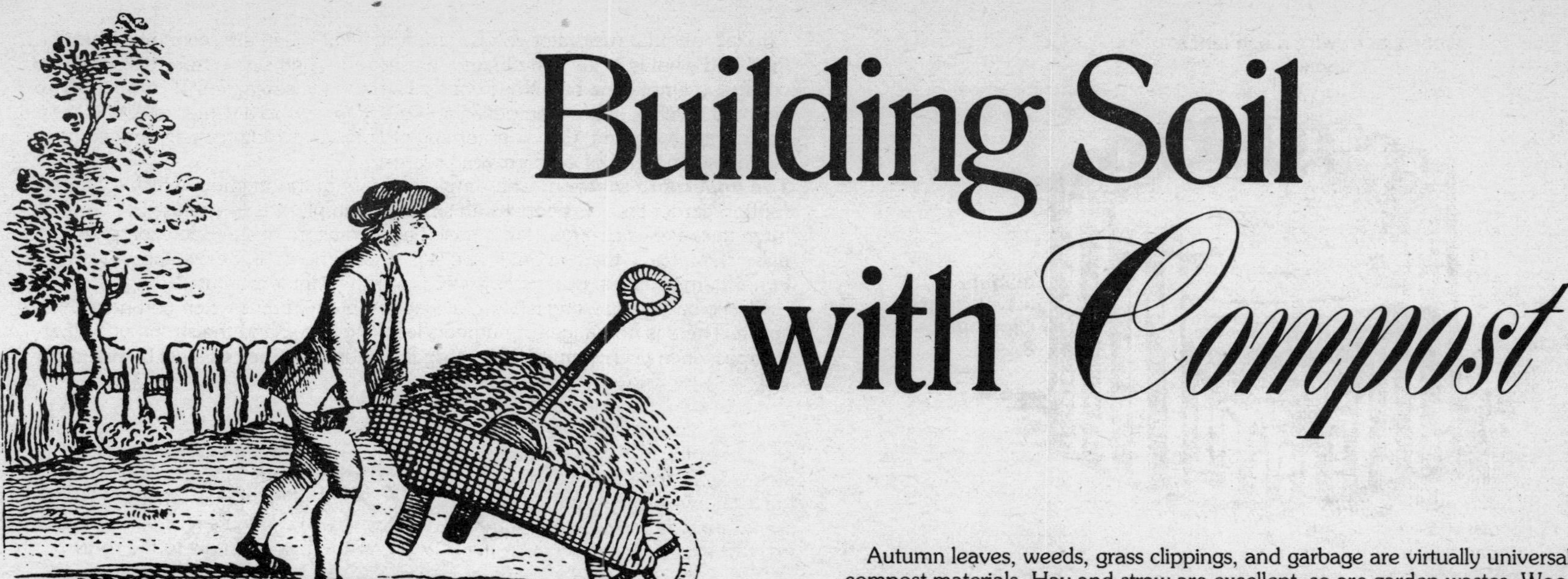

A method of recycling waste into dark, rich humus, composting lies at the heart of organic gardening. A compost heap transforms dead organic matter into new humus, paralleling the process of adding decaying organic material to soil that takes place everywhere in nature.

Before agriculture, natural processes took care of soil fertility. When people began growing food on the land, however, soil fertility started (and continued) to decrease because nature's way of maintaining soil had been disrupted. Composting is a way of returning to the soil what you have received in the form of crops and of making the garden richer than it was when you first began growing things there.

A compost heap is always a compost heap, but what is in it is not always compost. To be considered compost, the material must be decomposed. When vegetable material breaks down into compost, it is ready to be returned to the soil.

There are two types of compost, unfinished and finished. Finished compost still contains organic matter that can continue to decay and release nutrients into the soil; unfinished compost has a way to go yet before it becomes humus.

Compost can be kept in a free-standing pile; in corrals you construct of snow fencing or cinder block; in bins sold by garden suppliers; or, for city dwellers, even in a trash can perforated on sides and bottom and set into the ground.

How Composting Works

A good compost heap is sheer heaven for decay-causing bacteria. They thrive, reproduce at a high rate, and work hard to decompose plant residues. Two types of bacterial activity occur in composting: aerobic decay, which requires air, and anaerobic decay, which takes place without air. Because it is difficult for many home gardeners to make a lot of compost in an airless environment (such as in polyethelene bags), aerobic decomposition predominates in most home compost heaps.

Aerobic bacterial activity results in what is known as the "cooking," or heating up, that takes place inside compost heaps. Heat is generated as countless microbes convert into energy the carbon in the organic matter in the compost heap. When compost is really cooking, its internal temperature reaches 150 to 160°F.

To compost rapidly, a heap needs a generous supply of nitrogen. When only low-nitrogen materials have gone into a heap, it may not heat up and decay. On the other hand, heaps to which manure or dried blood have been added compost very rapidly.

No two alike. Because compost heaps are in part a convenient place to toss garden and table scraps, every compost heap is unique. And content is only one factor affecting the activity of decay-causing aerobic bacteria. Another is the amount of air that reaches the microorganisms. In general, compost heaps need to be turned regularly to provide the bacteria with a supply of air. Another way to aerate compost heaps is to add preshredded material that does not compact as easily.

Moisture is also important to compost, which ripens best in a well-moistened, but not soggy, condition. Too much water keeps out needed air. Gardeners in dry climates often drape a plastic sheet over their compost piles to keep moisture levels constant. If you leave your heap exposed, a concave top may catch and hold moisture.

Getting Started

Where to do it. Choose a site for a compost pile with care. The ground under it ought to be flat so the nutrients do not wash away. Try to find a spot near the garden, within reach of a hose, and close to the driveway, yet away from trees whose roots may turn upward to take advantage of all the nourishment in the compost heap. And, unless your neighbors are also compost buffs, put the compost heap where it will not invite attention. Convincing the unenlightened that compost heaps are not open garbage piles that attract rodents can be exhausting.

Ingredients. The only organic matter *not* to use in compost are plant residues treated with herbicides or pesticides, human feces, grease, and diseased animal or vegetable corpses. Otherwise, just about anything goes, although common sense dictates leaving out slow-to-decompose materials like big pieces of wood.

Autumn leaves, weeds, grass clippings, and garbage are virtually universal compost materials. Hay and straw are excellent, so are garden wastes. Wood chips, sawdust, and unprinted paper can be added, too. If you live near the ocean, gather salt marsh hay as well as seaweed and kelp, which are high in potassium. Fish scraps, eggshells, animal manures, phosphate rock, bonemeal, and dried blood also supply many desirable nutrients to compost. Hair (available in abundance from dog groomers and barbers) is extremely rich in nitrogen; wood ashes, as long as they have not been wetted down, are high in potassium.

Collected material in a heap does not start to be compost until a source of nitrogen is added and decomposition begins to take place. In most instances, for a compost pile to heat up properly, you need a height of three to five feet, usually of layered materials. For this reason, begin with a fairly sizable basic heap.

To obtain enough compost material should not present a problem, even for a city gardener with no lawn. Fruit stands and grocery stores are sources of spoiled produce, riding stables have strawy manure, and the local parks department certainly can spare grass clippings and leaves. But do go beyond the obvious sources. Look up lumber companies (sawdust, wood chips), dairies (manure, spoiled hay), printers (paper), breweries (spent hops), and other local industries whose waste products are organic.

Additives. To ensure a high nutrient value in compost, many organic gardeners add natural fertilizers to the compost heap. Lime in sparing amounts helps prevent an overacid compost from forming. It should be counterbalanced, however, with lots of nitrogen-rich material.

Several natural substances can be added to feed the decay-causing bacteria and fungi the nitrogen they need to carry on their work. If you have already a lot of high-nitrogen materials like manure and grass clippings, very little of these additives are needed, but if your compost is low on nitrogen-rich ingredients, add about two pounds per 100 pounds of compost of one of the following materials: dried blood or bloodmeal; manure, bonemeal, tankage, or cottonseed meal. Commercial composting aids are unnecessary if you follow organic methods strictly.

Composting Methods

The Indore method. The Indore method of composting can be done in bins or heaps. Indore compost piles consist of several layers of material and usually measure three to five feet in height, six feet in width, and are at least ten feet long.

Begin by laying down a six-inch-deep layer of green matter such as shredded plant residues or weeds. Mix in some leaves, table scraps, straw, or spoiled hay. The second layer is two inches of manure on top of which is spread a *thin* covering of topsoil. (The soil provides the microorganisms that decompose the raw materials of compost.) Next comes a light sprinkling of a mineral additive, such as phosphate rock, granite dust, wood ashes, or lime (avoid lime if you are making an acid compost for blueberries or other acid-loving plants). Then water the heap and continue layering and watering until the pile grows from three to five feet high. (A compost heap needs about as much moisture as in packaged potting soil. To keep it from drying out, cover it with a sheet of plastic.)

To be sure the pile is well aerated, it pays to lay three or four poles across every few layers.

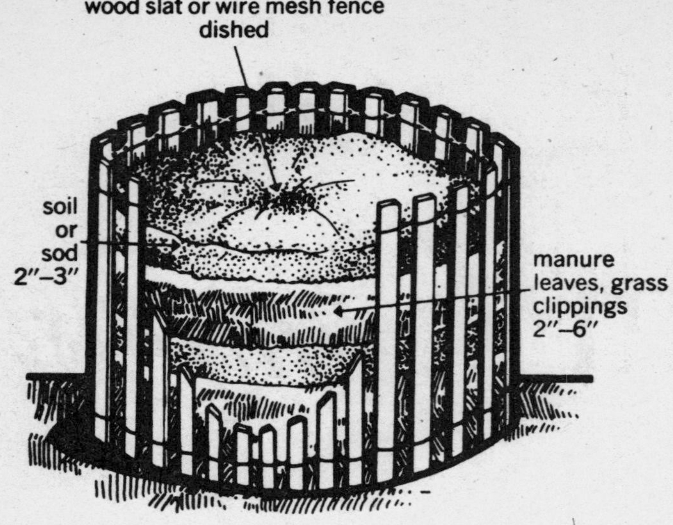

Soon, the heap will heat up, indicating the start of microbial activity. As the microorganisms consume carbon contained in the compost materials, the heap also shrinks in size.

After six weeks, turn the heap with a pitchfork so that what was on the outside goes near the center of the heap. Turn every six weeks thereafter until three months have passed and the compost is finished.

The 14-day method. Speed is the great appeal of this method, which is good for gardeners with small plots and/or limited space. Shredding improves aeration and increases the surface area of the contents. Consequently, the compost materials heat up quickly. So start by shredding everything shreddable. Running a power mower back and forth over the ingredients usually does the job. A small garden shredder, which costs about $100 (from seed companies and well-stocked garden centers) is a labor-saving luxury item.

Toss all the ingredients into a bin or pile up to five feet high and turn the whole thing over every three days for two weeks. The compost is then ready to be incorporated into soil.

Sheet composting. Sheet composting is used by farmers and gardeners who have a good-sized piece of land in need of soil enrichment. Natural fertilizers such as fresh manure and other organic material, naturally occurring minerals, and sawdust are spread evenly over a patch of land and worked into the top few inches of the soil with a rototiller or plow. Then, the land is left alone for one or two months while the organic material decays and the minerals release nutrients into the soil.

Earthworm composting. This easy, neat way of acquiring compost with little work can be done indoors in the cellar as well as outside. Use wooden boxes two or three feet deep (or dig a trench three feet deep) and fill them to a height of two feet with a mixture of 70% green organic material, 12% topsoil, and 15% manure or kitchen scraps. Water the containers thoroughly and put earthworms in right away. Turn off the light if you are working in the cellar or cover the containers with a dark cloth or wooden covers to create the dark environment earthworms like.

Like regular compost heaps, earthworm compost heats up, but a lot of heat is not so essential to this method and too much will kill the earthworms, whose nitrogen laced castings contribute richness to the end product. Their castings actually are more desirable soil additives than animal manures. Keep the compost material moist but not soggy and turn the compost every once in a while to keep the temperature at a bearable level for the earthworms.

The three-bin method. This is useful when you need a supply of both finished and unfinished compost because you use compost both as part of a mulch and as a soil conditioner and fertilizer. The container needed is really a three-compartment bin. To start the first batch of compost, fill to overflowing one bin with dead plants from the garden, autumn leaves, grass clippings, and kitchen scraps, and let the whole heap alone over the winter. By spring, decomposition will have taken place and the compost will have shrunk. Turn the heap by moving all the semidecomposed matter into the empty bin next to the first bin. Then start a second pile in the original bin.

In fall, about a year after you began, turn what it is in the second bin into the third and what is in the first bin into the second. Then start a new third compost pile in the empty first bin. Now, you will have three containers of compost. The year-old batch is half-decomposed and ready for use as a winter mulch. It should be finished by spring. Continue turning old bins and adding a new one at the beginning and end of each growing season.

The anaerobic method. The simplest variant of this method, which is handy for rooftop gardeners and people with small garden plots, is to enclose in two or three thicknesses of large plastic trash bags a mixture of shredded compost materials. Then, leave the bag out in the sun to decompose if the weather is warm, or, in northern climates, put the bag aside over the winter months.

Plastic-bag composting is a useful way to obtain humus when you have little space. There is no danger of nutrients leaching away, and the strong odor that escapes when you open the bag dissipates soon after the compost is spread on soil.

Applying Compost

There is no difference between humus and finished compost except that "humus" is the dark, rich soil on a forest floor, while "compost" designates the same sort of decayed organic matter made in compost heaps. Unfinished compost is still in the process of decaying and generates heat, whereas compost and humus are cool.

Because it might burn roots of plants, unfinished compost should be worked into the garden soil in autumn. As it winters over, it will finish decomposing and release nutrients into the soil before the spring planting.

Finished compost should be spread on the garden and rototilled or spaded into the top four inches of soil about a month before spring planting. Whether to apply compost twice in a year depends on the fertility of the particular soil.

For a first garden on poor soil, use unfinished compost during your fall soil conditioning and fertilizing. Rototill or spade in a thick layer to a depth of twelve to eighteen inches. After incorporating the compost, leave the soil surface rough through the winter, and apply three inches of finished compost a month before spring planting.

Vegetables appreciate one to three inches of compost per year along with natural mineral fertilizers and other soil amendments. A third part of finely sifted homemade compost mixed with a third each of potting soil and sand makes a fertile seed-starting medium for flats and coldframes.

Compost water. Compost water, or compost tea, is an easy-to-make liquid fertilizer and plant revitalizer. It can be used safely on houseplants, in greenhouses, and on vegetables, flowers, and lawns.

To "brew," fill a bucket or watering can half full with finished compost and add water to an inch below the brim. Stir a dozen times or more, allow the compost to settle, and pour. The same compost can be reused two or three times. Use the spent compost outdoors as a mulch.

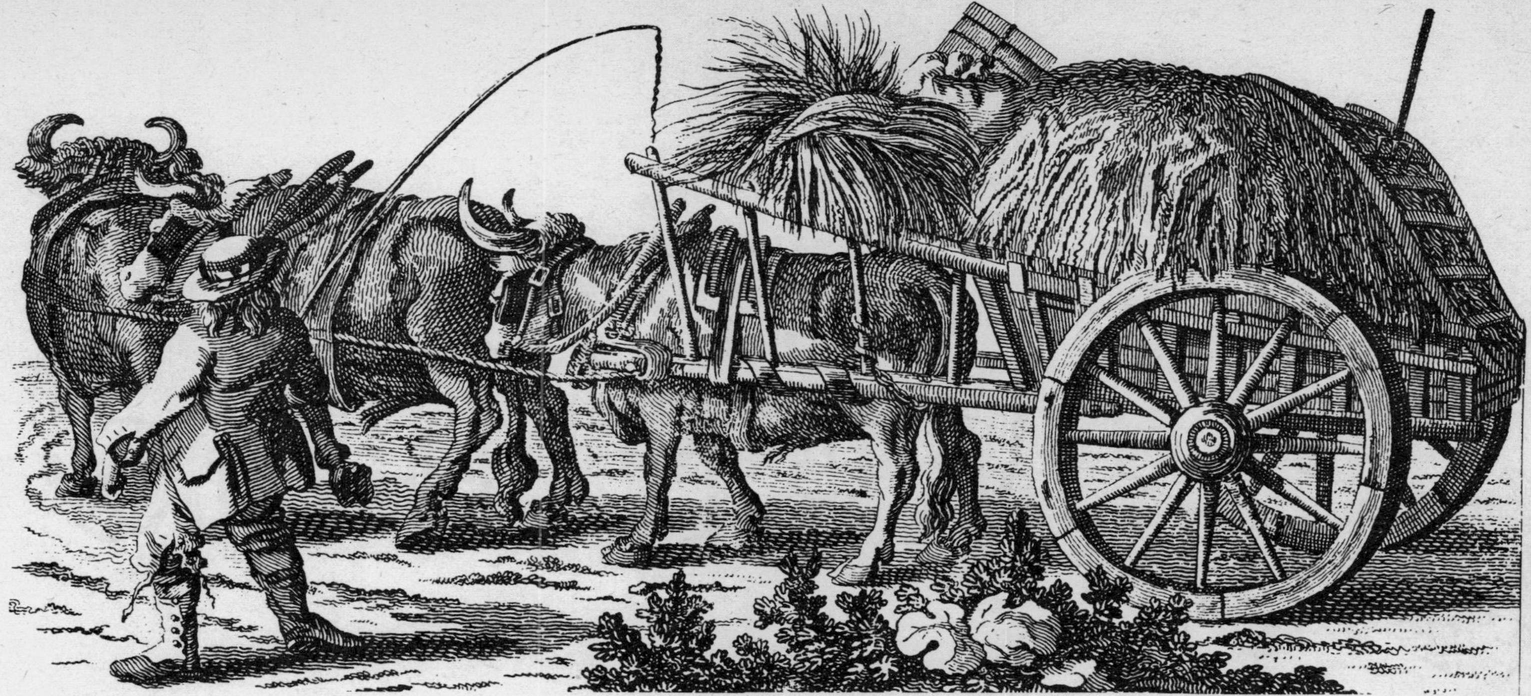

Natural Fertilizers

Organic gardening is a way of growing crops without the use of chemical fertilizers or pesticides. The key ingredient is healthy, fertile soil. Organic gardening duplicates nature's way of replenishing the soil as closely as possible.

Nowadays, most farmers and gardeners use inorganic chemical fertilizers without a second thought. Compared to organic fertilizers, such as manure or compost, chemical fertilizers are clean and relatively inexpensive (the cost, however, is rising along with the price of energy because these are energy-intensive products). Their nutrients are immediately available to plants, whereas organic fertilizers take time to break down to the ionic form usable by plants. For example, chemical fertilizers can be applied to a garden at the same time or shortly before seeds are sown and seedlings transplanted. Fresh manure, a common organic fertilizer, needs time to "cool down" and should be worked into the ground at least two weeks before you begin planting. Chemical fertilizers can be found at any farm or garden supply center, whereas some natural fertilizers are hard to obtain.

In the short run, chemical fertilizers are definitely better. But they do nothing to replenish and recondition the soil. Without an ample amount of organic matter in soil, its overall fertility drops. As the soil loses humus, it also becomes less workable. It compacts, does not absorb or hold water as well, and the damaged structure restricts plant growth. Eventually, what once was fertile topsoil becomes little more than pieces of stone. Nothing grows unless increasing quantities of fertilizer are applied.

Nitrogen and Nitrates: Nitrogen is an essential nutrient in healthy soil, but a surplus of nitrogen can be dangerous to the environment. Overuse of chemical fertilizer or fresh manure adds too much soluble nitrogen to the soil. This causes weak, succulent growth that is subject to disease. Eventually, too, health-threatening nitrates leach away to pollute the local water supply.

Fertilizers containing nitrogen are not an ecological threat per se. They become dangerous only in the hands of a person who thinks, "If a little is good, more must be better." Ideally, the way to feed crops balanced amounts of all the major and minor nutrients, including nitrogen, is to add compost to the soil. Another safe, rewarding method of restoring nitrogen to soil is to plant inoculated, nitrogen-fixing legume crops this year where nitrogen-consuming crops grew the previous year. These crops can add 50 to 200 pounds per acre of nitrogen each year. Other sources of nitrogen are soil animals and insects. Earthworm castings and the excrement and dead bodies of the millions of soil insects also contribute nitrogen to the earth.

Fertilizing the Organic Way

In the home garden, organic methods can be followed successfully without significantly more work than in conventional gardening. Organiculturists all agree on basics—no pesticides and no chemical fertilizers—but they sometimes part company when it comes to the details of raising crops. There are at least two factions in the organic movement. Both emphasize building humus-rich soil, but with somewhat different methods. Adherents of one school believe in keeping their gardens under a permanent mulch, exposing the soil only when planting. By this method, gardeners need only add a little cottonseed meal to the mulch, and keep the mulch thick and plush. Otherwise, after the soil is sufficiently enriched (at least three years of permanent mulching are needed), not even manure is necessary to keep the garden fertile. This mulch method also does away with spading and plowing.

Organic gardeners in the other faction use mulch as one component of a gardening program that also includes composting, cover cropping, and fertilizing.

Where to obtain natural fertilizer. When starting an organic garden, having decided to put off the permanent-mulch method for another season, you may encounter difficulties when you look for natural fertilizers. First, try your garden supply store or a farmer's supply center. If they come up short, you may have to make some phone calls to locate the substance you need. Organic fertilizers are also available through the mail. To locate suppliers, check out the Classified Ad section of *Organic Gardening* magazine (Emmaus, PA 18049).

In the following list, you will notice that not all natural fertilizers are organic, that is, derived from plant or animal sources. Some substances, such as greensand and granite dust, are naturally occurring mineral materials.

Bonemeal. The type and age of bones from which bonemeal is made determine the mineral content. *Raw* bonemeal, which does not break down readily, contains 2 to 4% nitrogen. Most of the phosphorus content is insoluble. *Steamed* bonemeal is a good source of phosphorus that is available fairly quickly. Apply both bonemeals 5 lbs per 100 sq ft.

Cottonseed meal. A fine nitrogen supplement and general fertilizer, cottonseed meal contains 7% nitrogen, 2 to 3% phosphorus, and 1.5% potassium. It has a low pH and is good for acid-loving plants. Apply 1½ lbs per 100 sq ft.

Dried blood. The high nitrogen content of dried blood and bloodmeal dictate sparing use. Rapidly available for use by plants, they should be sprinkled lightly over the garden or on the compost pile to stimulate the activity of soil microorganisms. Apply 3 lbs per 100 sq ft.

Fish emulsion. Available in concentrated form, its average analysis is 5-2-2. Fish emlusion can be applied directly to soil or sprayed on foliage. Buy a deodorized variety or be prepared for feline visitations. Apply according to directions.

Granite dust. A good source of potassium. Apply 2 lbs per 100 sq ft.

Grass clippings. One hundred pounds of grass clippings furnishes one pound of nitrogen and two pounds of potassium. They make a good compost ingredient or a mulch that can be turned under later.

Greensand. Geologists call greensand glauconite. It is a good source of potassium. Apply 2 lbs per 100 sq ft.

Manure. The value of manure depends on its source and whether it is mixed with straw, as is *stable manure*, which is the type preferred by many gardeners. *Chicken manure* contains the highest nutrient levels. *Horse manure* is somewhat better than *cow manure* and is "hotter," that is, it decomposes more rapidly. A layer of manure on the garden adds humus to the soil and increases its water-holding capacity. Manure is low in phosphorus. Work fresh manure into soil at least two weeks before planting. Slow-to-decompose strawy manure decays faster when combined with a high-nitrogen fertilizer.

Oyster shells. Ground oyster shells are a better pH raiser than fertilizer. They are low in nitrogen and phosphorus and contain no potassium. Apply 5 lbs per 100 sq ft.

Peat moss. Peat moss breaks down rapidly but is a better soil conditioner than fertilizer. It should always be moistened before used in the garden.

Phosphate rock. An excellent, inexpensive source of phosphorus sold at most farm supply stores. Apply ¾ lb per 100 sq ft.

Sludge. Available from municipal sewage treatment plants, *air-dried, digested sewage sludge* has an average analysis of 2-2-0.5 and can be used safely on home gardens. It is safest when applied in autumn and allowed to decompose thoroughly. Odor can be a problem. *Dried activated sludge* contains no pathogenic organisms. Its average analysis is 6-4-0.5. *Raw sewage* stinks and contains a multitude of disease organisms.

Tobacco stems. High in potassium but alkaline, these are available only in tobacco-growing areas. Apply 1½ lbs per 100 sq ft.

Weeds. Weeds often contain high concentrations of minerals and are excellent additions to compost. Avoid using weeds from along highways where herbicides have been sprayed.

Wood ashes. These are a good source of potassium and some trace elements are quite alkaline. Apply 14 oz per 100 sq ft.

GREEN MANURES

"Green manure" is a special crop planted to be turned into the soil before it is ready to be harvested. When turned under, it adds an enormous amount of organic matter to the soil, but the green manure crop—frequently legumes such as alfalfa or nonlegumes such as buckwheat—has several other benefits:

Green manures cut down on work. Green manures and compost both add organic matter to soil. But making compost takes a lot of time and work. Growing a green manure involves broadcasting seed over a prepared seed bed, covering the seed, and applying water. When the crop is grown, it is turned under with a rototiller with *rear-mounted tines.* (Green manure can also be turned under by hand. Cut the crop with a scythe or power mower, then use a shovel or spading fork to mix the material with topsoil.)

Green manure improves soil structure. Added to *clay soil*, green manure opens up the soil and makes it more permeable, whereas a green manure turned into quick-draining, quick-drying *sandy soil* improves the soil's water-holding capacity.

Green manure makes soil more fertile. Green manuring accelerates the natural system of making fertile soil, reducing the need for chemical or organic fertilizers. Chopping up and tilling under crops so that they decompose is a faster version of nature's process of making soil from decomposed vegetable matter. And that is not quite all—green manure incorporated into the soil also increases the activity of soil microorganisms. The weak acids that these microbes produce work away at insoluble minerals that are present in soil in the form of little rock particles. When dissolved by microbic action, these minerals are transformed into water-soluble nutrients that plants can absorb. For example, when a crop of buckwheat, sweet clover, or rye is planted in poor soil, it releases into the soil a form of the mineral phosphorus that can be utilized by a crop of vegetables planted later in the same area.

Green manures can add nitrogen to soil. Legumes are called "nitrogen-fixers." When their seeds are treated with a special inoculant containing a strain of nitrogen-fixing bacteria, their root hairs form nodules that enable the plants to take nitrogen from the air and enrich the soil. (This inexpensive inoculant is available at garden centers or from seed companies.) An acre of ground planted with alfalfa that is chopped up and turned under receives an amount of nitrogen more or less equivalent to a ton of 10-10-10 chemical fertilizer spread over the area.

Green manure also can add nitrogen to soil in an indirect way. Tilled under, chopped-up crops give earthworms huge quantities of food and provides the worms with insulation against cold and frost and against the heat of the sun in summer. Earthworm populations increase—and earthworms add nitrogen-rich castings to the soil. Compared to topsoil, earthworm castings contain five times the nitrates, seven times the phosphorus, eleven times the potassium, or potash, two-and-a-half times the magnesium, and two times the calcium.

Two other legumes, yellow and white sweet clover—in addition to fixing nitrogen in the soil—have strong taproots that grow down into the subsoil and bring up minerals unreached by more shallow-rooted plants. When sweet clover is tilled into the soil, its roots decay quickly into usable organic material. By loosening up the subsoil, these green manures also improve drainage.

Green manures fight weeds. Green manures crowd out the unwanted plants. After a season of a few successive green manure crops, all signs of weeds will be gone. Annual ryegrass and buckwheat are especially good; beans and peas, broadcast over an area or sown in wide rows, are edible weedkillers.

Green manures protect the soil. Aside from improving the appearance of your property, a winter *cover crop* prevents soil nutrients from being leached away and topsoil from being eroded. Cover crops are especially useful in the rainy Pacific Coast and in the South where the soil microorganisms remain active all year. Where winter crops are mild and often rainy, cover crops are called *catch crops*—they literally catch and store the good topsoil nutrients, and re-enrich the earth when they are plowed under.

How to Grow Green Manures

Begin with a pH test to discover whether the soil is too acid. Also, whatever is growing in the area should be turned under and allowed ten days to decompose, at which point the soil needs to be rototilled to a fine texture. If fertilizer, compost, or lime are needed, now is the time to add them.

Sow the seeds by broadcasting them over the area by hand. Rake the seeds in to a depth of about a half inch or set a rear-mounted rototiller at a shallow depth and go over the area. (Beans and peas should be sown one-and-a-half inches deep and two inches apart in wide rows. They can be harvested before being chopped up and turned under.) Pat down the seedbed by walking on it or rolling it. Keep the seeds moist to permit germination. It won't be necessary to thin out the crop because part of the reason for green manuring is to crowd out weeds.

Green manures need to be watched. They should be chopped up and tilled into the soil before they go to seed, unless you want the crop to reappear in short order. Apart from that general principle, when you turn the crop into the soil depends on your reason for growing it.

Usually, vegetable crops should be planted about fourteen days after the green manure is turned under. Wait any longer and the newly added soil nutrients begin to leach away. If the purpose in green manuring is to raise the mineral content of the garden soil, for example, turn the crop under while it is still green and tender—be-

fore it turns woody. If you are increasing the organic content of the garden, the crop should be allowed to mature. The chopped-up manure crop being more fibrous, takes longer to start decomposing than a young crop so the ground needs a rest of six to eight weeks before a crop of vegetables ought to be planted there.

Green Manures for Every Garden
Most green manures can be grown throughout North America, although some crops do best in the North and others prefer a southern climate. Legumes for spring and summer seeding include alfalfa, white clover, snapbeans, soybeans, and sweet white or yellow clover. Nonlegumes include buckwheat, pearl millet, and Sudan grass. For late summer and fall planting, hairy vetch is a good legume; nonlegumes are barley, kale, oats, rye, annual ryegrass, and wheat.

Alsike and red clover are two spring and summer legumes that grow well in the North. Red clover needs a full season to grow plus a pH above 6.0. Alsike clover makes a good green manure where the soil is too acid or too wet for red clover. Smooth bromegrass is a fine northern winter cover crop, with an abundant, fibrous root system and good top growth. When turned under in spring, it decomposes quickly, improving the soil structure and fertility. Annual ryegrass, hairy vetch, kale, and winter rye also make excellent winter cover crops.

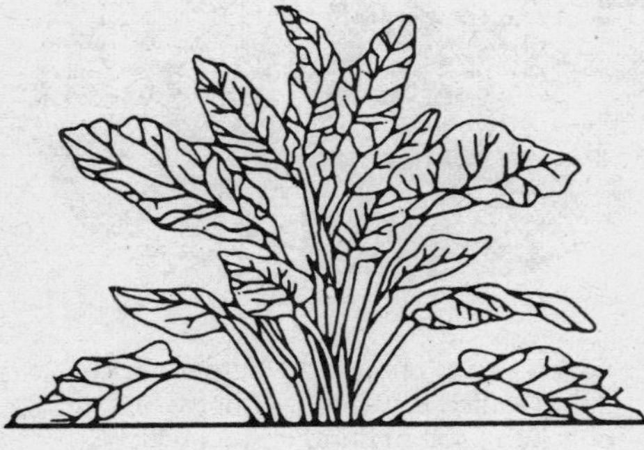

In the Northwest, where the climate is cool and moist, crimson clover and purple vetch are good cover crops. Planted after the autumn harvest, these crops should be allowed to grow about one-and-one-half years and turned under in the second spring four to six weeks before planting vegetables again.

Several green manure, spring and summer legume crops for the South include cowpeas, lespedeza, and hairy indigo. Lespediza restores eroded, poor, acid soil, and hairy indigo adapts well to conditions in the southernmost parts of the U.S. and is highly resistant to root-knot nematodes. Crops suited to late summer and fall planting are bur and crimson clover, field peas, sweet clover, common and Hungarian vetch. These all make good cover crops in winter. Kale can be planted most of the year. Blue lupine and purple vetch grow well on the Gulf Coast, white lupine is a Deep South crop. Yellow lupine does well in fertile, moderately acid Florida soil.

Crop Rotation
Switching where you plant certain related vegetables is a fundamental principle of good gardening. Crop rotation is possible even in a small garden where every inch counts. By dividing your vegetable plot into thirds, you can adopt a three-year rotation plan in which you plant green manure in one section each year. During the first growing season, choose an edible legume (beans or peas). In autumn, two weeks after the first crop is turned under, plant a cover crop in the entire garden.

When the second spring arrives, because the former green manure section is weed-free, plant it with crops like carrots and onions, which have small seeds. For the third year, large-seeded crops (seed potatoes, melons, and corn) go in the original green manure section and the small-seeded crops move on to the area where a green manure was most recently grown. This rotation schedule continues each year.

A fairly large garden can be divided into two segments, with one devoted to vegetables and the other used for a green manure during alternate years.

ESSAYS
UPON
FIELD-HUSBANDRY.

Jared Eliot.

PART I.

IT is not an Hundred and Thirty Years ſince the firſt Settlement of *New-England*, and much leſs than that ſince the greater Part hath been Planted.

When we conſider the ſmall Number of the firſt Settlers, and coming from an old Cultivated Country, to thick Woods, rough unimproved Lands; where all their former Experience and Knowledge was now of very little Service to them: They were deſtitute of Beaſts of Burthen or Carriage; Unſkill'd in every Part of Service to be done: It may be ſaid, That in a Sort, *they began the World a New*.

Their unacquaintedneſs with the Country, led them to make choice of the worſt Land for their Improvement, and the moſt expenſive and chargeable Methods of Cultivation: They tho't themſelves obliged to ſtubb all Staddle, and cut down or lop all great Trees; in which they expended much Coſt and Time, to the prejudice of the Crop and impoveriſhing the Land.

When

Facsimile page of Jared Eliot's "Essays upon Field-Husbandry."

Essays upon Field-Husbandy was the first major American work on agriculture. It was written by Jared Eliot (1685–1763), a minister who had graduated from Yale College and then taught school for a time. From 1709 until his death, he was pastor at Killingworth, Connecticut, where he had developed numerous interests that included medicine and botany. His essays on agriculture, first separatedly published over a twelve-year period beginning in 1747, were finally collected into one volume in 1760. As the above excerpt shows, his concern for the land was remarkably in advance of his era.

A Soil-improvement Plan
In spring, before the naturally occurring weeds go to seed, look upon them as a winter cover crop and turn them under. Give them two weeks to begin to decompose and sow buckwheat in the area. Grow this crop until it is seven to ten inches high, turn it under, and, after ten to fourteen days, resow the buckwheat. Repeat this process as often as the length of your local growing season allows. Complete the improvement process by sowing a cover crop of winter rye at least ten days after turning the last buckwheat crop. Rye can survive extreme cold, and its growth will pick up during the following spring.

When the rye is eight to ten inches tall, turn it under and wait two weeks. At this point, all the green manuring should have enriched the humus content of the soil and sufficiently improved the soil structure that, with the addition of fertilizer and soil amendments, the ground is ready to handle a vegetable crop.

Sometimes, a year of green manuring is not enough. People who live on land where the soil structure has been disturbed by bulldozing and construction may need to repeat the process for a second year.

Sources
Seeds for green manures are sold at farm supply centers. Or you can write to the following concerns for their catalogs and order through the mail. Of the seven companies mentioned, the three gardener's seed companies (Harris, Herbst, and Park) offer the smallest selections.

Henry Field Seed & Nursery Co.
5564 Oak St.
Shenandoah, IA 51601

Joseph Harris Co., Inc.
Moreton Farm
Rochester, NY 14624

Herbst Seedsmen, Inc.
1000 North Main St.
Brewster, NY 10509

Early May Seed & Nursery Co.
Elm St.
Shenandoah, IA 51601

Geo. W. Park Seed Co., Inc.
S.C. Hwy 254 N.
Greenwood, SC 29647

R. H. Shumway Seedsman
628 Cedar St.
Rockford, IL 61101

Wyatt Quaries Seed Co.
P.O. Box 2131
Raleigh, NC 27602

The Magic of Mulch

Nature has a wonderful system of building and maintaining healthy, fertile soil. Dead plants, leaves, twigs, stalks, and bits of bark fall to the ground to form a soft layer of material that eventually decomposes and becomes part of the soil. While it is decomposing, this layer of organic waste serves as a natural mulch. It eventually becomes humus, the rich, black organic material that gives plants a healthy environment to live in.

Wise gardeners follow nature's lead and cover the soil around vegetables, flowers, shrubs, and some trees with a mulch. Putting down several inches of mulch has many benefits:

1. Suppresses weeds.
2. Protects plant roots from sudden changes in temperature as well as from temperature extremes.
3. Preserves soil moisture by slowing evaporation and inhibiting the drying-out effects of sun and wind.
4. Provides ideal conditions for earthworms.
5. Protects soil against compaction.
6. Protects against erosion by preventing runoff after sudden rain.
7. Adds nutrients to the soil.
8. Improves soil structure.

Mulch Materials

Materials for mulch are everywhere. Anything that decomposes cleanly and safely will do for an organic, soil-building mulch. Organic mulches put back into the soil the nutrients that have been removed by plants as they grew. Some inorganic materials, such as stones or black plastic sheeting, also are employed as mulches. The main criterion for inorganic mulches is that they work without harming soil or vegetation.

Bark. Shredded bark is a neat-looking, long-lasting mulch that adds humus to the soil. A finely shredded bark can be turned under. It does not compact after rain or watering.

Coffee grounds. Being slightly acid, recycled coffee grounds need to be balanced with a sprinkling of lime when used as mulch. Good soil conditioners, they are rich in nitrogen.

Compost. Partially decomposed compost (not so decomposed that weeds can grow in it) is a valuable mulch. A layer of finished compost under other mulches adds to soil fertility.

Field hay. If you are near a farm or stable, try to arrange for a supply of hay, which is a very good mulch. Use hay before it has gone to seed. Spoiled hay, which is just hay that is not good enough for livestock to eat, is as good as regular hay and is cheaper.

Garden wastes. When put through a shredder (sold through seed catalogues and at well-stocked garden centers), garden wastes can be treated as a mulch, as long as they have not been treated with insecticide, fungicide, or herbicide. Weeds that have gone to seed could take root. Ground or chopped corncobs and cornstalks need a sprinkling of bloodmeal, cottonseed meal, or nitrogen fertilizer mixed in.

Grass clippings. Except in arid areas where lawns are scarce, this mulch is available free to most gardeners. To obtain enough for a fairly large garden, though, you may have to ask neighbors for contributions. To prevent grass clippings from compacting and overheating the soil, wait a couple of days until they are dry before spreading them among plants. You can also mix them with other mulch material. Do not use grass from lawns treated with chemical weedkiller. Mix in a generous handful of bloodmeal to each bushel of clippings.

Leaves. Leaves are almost universally available in fall. Soft leaves like maple leaves get soggy when wet and may further the growth of disease spores unless they are shredded first (run a power mower back and forth over the leaves). Oak leaves are an excellent mulch that acidify slightly when turned under. Apply a two-inch layer of leaves.

Newspaper. Several sheets of newspaper placed between rows does the same job as a mulch. To make the garden more attractive, cover the paper with peat moss, weeds, wood chips, or other organic material that will also encourage the paper to decompose. Like sawdust, newspaper may deplete soil nitrogen and supplementation may be needed.

Peat moss. Easy to obtain and use, peat is best when mixed with wood chips or sawdust because it dries out, gets crusty, and becomes impermeable to water. Always moisten peat moss before using it in the garden. Peat moss mulch may compact and become crusty after watering or rain, and needs light cultivation. Use three or four inches.

Pine needles. Pine needles stay down in wind and form a uniform mulch. They are good where an acidifying mulch is wanted. Otherwise, check the soil pH and correct with lime, if necessary.

Plastic. Not very pretty to look at, black or green polyethelene mulch warms up the soil during spring and serves as a reliable weed-suppressing barrier between plants and soil. Clear plastic sheeting allows weeds to grow. Plastic prevents rain from reaching the soil; you must slit it to transplant seedlings, and it can't be plowed under.

Sawdust. A two-inch layer of sawdust is an inexpensive, soil-conditioning mulch, but it can rob the soil of nitrogen. Replace the nitrogen each spring by applying bloodmeal or a nitrogen fertilizer. Sawdust mixes nicely with peat moss. After rain or watering, sawdust tends to compact and needs some cultivation. A three-inch sawdust mulch benefits evergreens, shrubs, and fruit trees.

Seaweed. When seaweed decomposes, it releases nutrients, amino acids, and hormones that aid plant growth. For best results, shred the seaweed.

Snow. Snow is a good winter mulch in areas where snow falls predictably and stays.

Spanish moss. This light, airy mulch is available only in the South.

Stones. Decorative stones and pebbles around trees and among shrubbery are more than fine touches. They reduce weeds, protect soil from temperature extremes, retain moisture, and (ever so slowly) release minerals into the soil.

Straw. Flammability is the main drawback of straw, which may also contain weed seeds. Use buckwheat, oat, and wheat straw five or six inches deep.

Wood chips. Wood chips often are chips of hardwood barks. They do everything a good mulch should do, and they are attractive. A mulch around a newly planted tree protects the roots and conserves soil moisture.

How to Mulch

If you covered your garden with a mulch during the winter, all you need to do at planting time is pull back the old mulch and sow seeds or plant seedlings in the exposed areas. If you are just starting a garden, wait until seedlings are several inches high and then spread mulch material close to plants. Mulch can go between rows right away.

When laying down an organic mulch around garden plants, be certain it is six to eight inches thick. Before long, what may seem like a terribly deep mulch ought to settle down to a thickness of only two or three inches. The reason for a thick mulch in summer is to keep weeds down.

As the season progresses, you may notice that the mulch you've chosen decomposes rapidly. Whenever you see a bald spot developing, toss some more mulch on it to maintain desirable thickness.

Organic mulches ought to remain plush and loose, but some materials such as peat moss and grass clippings tend to compact. If that happens to your mulch, cultivate it lightly to let some air in again. Since mulching is supposed to be a labor-saving gardening method, however, once you find that a material compacts, mix in a mulch material that stays loose and use something else next time.

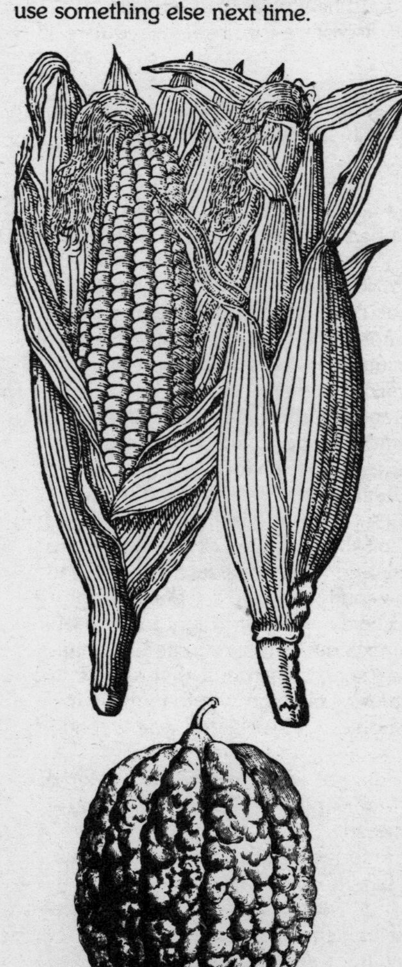

PLASTIC MULCH FOR FLOWER BEDS

STEPS IN PLANTING

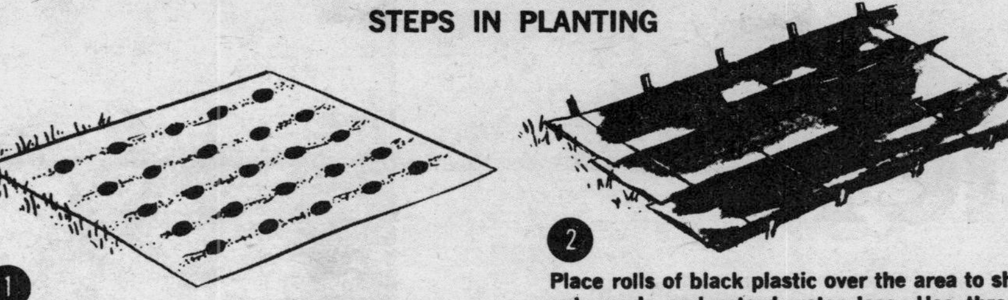

1 Prepare the planting site in the fall. Dig planting holes 4 to 6 inches wider and deeper than the plant root ball. Mix peat moss and organic matter in the planting holes. Space plants evenly over the site.

2 Place rolls of black plastic over the area to shade out weeds and retard water loss. Use three or four wide strips slightly overlapping. Tie down the plastic with rocks, wires, or stakes. You may cover the area with a mulch of organic matter instead of using plastic if you wish. Keep the mulch moist to keep it in place.

3 Cut an X slit in the plastic over each planting hole. Enlarge the slits to the proper size hole and set the plants through them.

4 Set the plants at the same level they were growing before they were transplanted. Fill the hole with good soil and pack the soil firmly around the roots. Leave a slight basin at the top to hold water. Water thoroughly after planting.

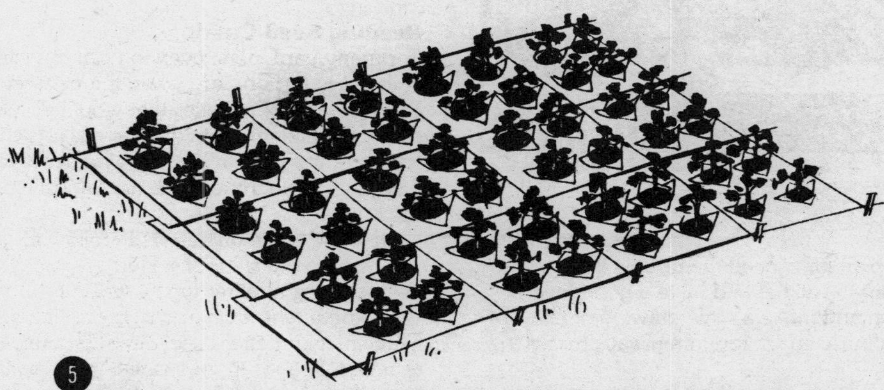

5 Keep the plants in place with an organic mulch over the plastic until the plants are established. Use a mulch of pine bark, wood chips, or hulls. Pull weeds by hand if they grow.

In autumn, after crops are harvested, turn an organic mulch into the soil where it will break down much the same way as in composting. Soil bacteria immediately start to work decomposing the mulch and transforming it into humus. To keep decomposition going at a fast pace, you must feed nitrogen to the soil microorganisms. Before turning the mulch under, spread a complete fertilizer, bloodmeal, or cottonseed meal on the plot.

When a summer mulch has been incorporated into the topsoil, the garden is bare and once again exposed to the elements. Overwintering without protecting can be harmful to soil. You can cover the garden with a green manure crop or a mulch. If your gardening program does not include sowing a green manure or cover crop, a good thick mulch is the answer. In northern climates, a sufficiently thick mulch keeps the ground frozen and prevents root heave. This is especially important for perennial flowers and vegetable crops like asparagus and rhubarb. If you have compost, spread a layer of finished and/or half-decomposed compost where your vegetables once grew. Cover that with, say, a thick layer of shredded leaves mixed with grass clippings, hay, or other mulch material. When spring planting time approaches, pull back the winter mulch (and hold it in place with boards or a sheet of plastic). The cold soil will need a couple of weeks to warm up before sowing and transplanting can take place.

"No-Work Gardening"

To many home gardeners, mulching is an essential part of an on-going soil-building program which also includes, among other things, composting, cultivating, cover cropping, and fertilizing. According to the late Ruth Stout, however, mulching is *everything*. The inventor of a year-round mulch method, she suggests an approach that imitates nature's way of creating rich soil through yearly accumulation of rotted vegetable matter. Basically, Stout's books, *How to Have a Green Thumb without an Aching Back* and *The Ruth Stout No-Work Garden Book* (Rodale Press), assert that a permanent mulch of hay, grass, or other material builds incredibly rich, healthy soil. With this system, weeding and composting soon become unnecessary, and the only fertilizer Stout recommends is cottonseed meal (to replenish nitrogen). Before using the mulch method, Stout gardened organically with compost, manure fertilizer, and other soil amendments.

The author gardened a forty-by-sixty foot plot into her eighties without exerting herself. She had figured out how to do away with the work of weeding, cultivating, and maintaining a compost pile and then carting compost to the garden where it must be spread.

No compost? No, because kitchen and garden wastes that more conventional gardeners consign to the compost heap are added directly to the mulch (Stout used hay as a basis) to decompose *in situ*, as would occur in nature.

Permanent mulch needs no hoeing or rototilling. It simply decomposes naturally. At planting time, the gardener draws the mulch back and sows the seed or plants transplants. That's all! When a thin spot appears in the mulch, the mulcher adds more hay or grass clippings and walks away.

After three years of permanent mulching, the soil becomes so fertile that compost, manure, and fertilizer are no longer necessary. Only a nitrogen supplement need be added periodically. Ruth Stout also writes that her garden suffered little from harmful insects and soil-borne disease, sparing her the problems and expense of pesticides. And, needless to say, no weeds can sprout through a thick mulch.

A Garden Plan

The benefits of a well-thought-out garden plan far exceed the trouble it takes to make one. Once you know where your garden will be, and have a good idea of what you want to plant, it's time to sit down and make a scale drawing or chart of the prospective plot (or plots). Simply planting seeds at random always results in waste and disappointment.

Before you begin to make a plan, however, ask yourself:

• Is the garden in one or more units? With two plots, you may want to have lettuce, radishes, beets, spinach, and other vegetables that take up little space in a small kitchen garden, and plant elsewhere vegetables requiring lots of room, i.e., corn, potatoes, melons.

• Is the soil composition of the plot uniform? If part of the land is low and moist, crops such as celery, onions, and late cucumbers, or moisture-loving decorative plants, should be placed there. If part of the plot is high, warm, and dry, put in early crops or other plants needing a soil that warms up quickly.

• Are you planting perennial flowers, permanent shrubs, strawberries, and/or rhubarb? These and other permanent plants should be planted where they do not interfere with the annual plowing and cultivation.

• Will you plant tall-growing species? Keep in mind the angle of sun. Rows of tall plants should be placed where they will not shade or interfere with the growth of smaller plants.

What a garden plan is *not* is a surefire route to complete success. Particularly if you are new at it, the art of gardening is learned by doing, not by armchair planning. As the season progresses, there may be some change in the plan. These should be recorded along with the dates flowers bloomed or crops were harvested and replanted. You then have a record of what turned out well and what didn't.

To make the plan, refer to your list of what you want to plant. Figure out when they can be sown or transplanted into the garden, how long until bloom or harvest. Keep in mind that there are two general types of plants: those that are planted once and remain in place throughout the season and those that are replanted successively or replaced with another quick-growing variety.

If you ordered your seeds early, you can find much of the information you need on the seed packages. They tell you when to plant and how to plant.

As you decide what goes where, give a thought to separating vegetables that belong to the same family. Crowding cabbage family crops together, for example, invites insect infestation as well as disease. If you are replanting a garden where vegetables grew the previous year, try to relocate, or rotate, crops that belong to the same family.

Efficient gardening. Garden plans are the best tool you have to use all the garden space you have throughout the growing season. With a plan, you can group all early-maturing flowers and crops together so that as soon as one is finished blooming or has been harvested another can take its place. In fact, it is not always necessary to wait until the early food crop is entirely removed. A later crop can be planted between rows of the early one—corn planted between rows of potatoes, for example.

By knowing when your crops mature, if your local growing seasons lasts from spring to autumn, you can be ready midseason for late-season plantings of new crops as well as for second and third plantings of the same crop. In the South, where gardens are active year round, or nearly, it's virtually impossible to utilize garden space without a plan.

A computerized plan. If all this seems too arduous for vegetable gardeners, Northrup King Co., the seed people, offer a unique service. By filling out a questionnaire, you can receive a detailed computer printout garden plan. The questionnaire asks for the garden location according to Zip Code, dimensions and shape of the plot, a description of the soil and weeding method (hand, rototiller, or tractor), and what vegetables you want to grow for how many adults.

The Northrup King plan tells how much seed to plant, how and when to plant each vegetable, and when to make successive plantings. The printout also includes a row-by-row diagram utilizing the entire garden space while reducing plant competition. Write to:

Northrup King Co.
Consumer Products Division
Box 1615
Minneapolis, MN 55440

Reading Seed Catalogs

For many gardeners, even in northern climates, the new growing season begins in January or February when the new seed catalogs arrive. As you go through the catalogs, list the varieties that would do well in your area. Many seed catalogs contain useful information, such as lists of quick crops and easy-to-grow varieties; length of the growth season; whether a vegetable is suited for canning or freezing; earliness of bloom; disease resistance; and adaptability, if any, to a particular region.

Here are some guidelines to follow to get the most from your seed catalogs.

• *Stick to old standbys.* Don't replace a variety that you know produces well before giving another type a trial run.

• *Experiment.* Every year, horticulturists introduce new hybrids developed for heavier yield, better taste, larger blooms, and other desirable characteristics such as heat tolerance in greens, earliness, tightly wrapped ears in corn, or new shades in flowers. And sometimes, seed companies come out with surprises, like the new Explorer potato that can be grown from seed.

• *Buy in large amounts.* Seed is cheap even when bought by small-size packet, which is usually enough for a home garden. Yet it is far more economical to buy in larger quantities. Splitting large orders with a neighbor or two is a good way to take advantages of such savings.

• *Look for disease-resistant varieties.* With good healthy soil, which keeps down the incidence of soil-borne disease, plus disease-resistant strains, your chances of failure are significantly lower.

• *Order early.*

• *Notice whether late-crop foods can be frozen or canned, or stored.* Certain vegetable varieties have been bred especially for these purposes.

Choosing a Site

Choosing a good location for the garden is the first practical step. It is also one of the most important decisions because you will be stuck with your choice for an entire season.

With luck, you decided to establish a garden some months before the actual growing season and have plenty of time to look carefully at your property, pick a site, and begin preparing the soil. With even more luck, you have found the ideal spot near a source of water and away from established trees where your garden receives full sun and slopes slightly down toward the south.

More likely, however, your survey for a potential garden site will be an exercise in compromise. After all, most flowers and vegetables need sun. Full sun is best, except in desert locations where shade from the afternoon sun can improve growth and prolong the harvest season. Although most vegetables and many flowers can tolerate some shade, plant growth improves the farther the garden is from a shade-casting source. This is because soil shaded much of the day warms and dries out slowly, and both bacterial activity and nutrient release are retarded.

If you must garden near a structure, pick the south side or a spot far enough away on the north or west side so as not to receive a shadow. (Eight to ten feet for a one-story building.) Eastern and western exposure are adequate but not as good as south-facing locations. Gardens, or segments of gardens, that receive two to four hours of shade daily produce slower rates of plant growth than those in full sun. Fruit and early-maturing vegetables should not be planted where shade hits them.

Locating a garden at the south side of a building or fence has the advantage of being protected from chilly winds blowing or high winds. In windy areas, windbreakers can add significantly to the growing season.

Winter gardens in the South and Southwest merit special consideration. Full sun is essential for satisfactory winter growth; heat absorbed during the day promotes root activity and slows the cooling at night. These gardens should be away from any fence, structures, or trees that throw long shadows.

The nearness of trees means more than unwanted shade. The roots of shallow-rooted trees turn upward to absorb moisture and fertilizer from the garden plot.

Size

Size is a particularly important question for a new gardener. Overdoing it during the first season will probably turn you off, even if you last it out.

To grow a substantial part of the food for a four-person vegetable-loving family, a 50′ × 50′ (2500 square feet) garden plot is sufficient. Unless you have experience and/or help and you intend to can and freeze a goodly portion of your yield, this is too much for a beginner.

A small plot measuring about 100 square feet (10′ × 10′ or 12′ × 9′) can grow lots of salad greens, tomatoes, carrots, onions, beans, and beets as well as a few herbs and some insect-inhibiting flowers like marigolds and zinnias.

A garden measuring 300 square feet or slightly more, with good luck and careful planning, can supply four voracious vegetarians with a large proportion of their food over the growing season.

Budgeting space. To make the most of a small garden, plant flowers or crops that produce a copious yield over an extended period; for example, among vegetables, brush and pole snapbeans, lima beans, onions, peppers, summer squash, and tomatoes.

If you are limited to a small garden, container gardening is one way to add room for more. New potatoes, summer squash, and tomatoes do quite well in containers, as do begonias and dozens of other flowers. Another strategy for maximizing the size of your crop is to plant vegetables elsewhere in the yard. Vining varieties of flowers, or vegetables such as beans, squash, cucumber, and watermelon, grow nicely along fences or the side of a house; and the crops look good too because of their lovely flowers.

Not all plants are inveterate sun-lovers, however, and if you are cramped for space in the sunniest locations, perhaps you can find a strip of land that receives indirect light for part of the day. If so, these vegetables and herbs can be grown there: scarlet runner beans, spinach, Swiss chard, parsley, peas, chicory, collards, kale, lettuce, and mint. Shade-loving flowers are indicated in our sections on annuals, perennials, and other plants.

Raised Beds and Wide Rows. When space is limited, raising the growing beds maximizes planting space, and prepares garden soil so that it is porous and loose. You have wider rows and can plant more flowers or vegetables on the same amount of land. To make a raised bed, you "double dig" the soil in rows up to four-feet wide and as long as you like. The principle of double digging involves digging the top soil one way and the subsoil another, keeping both layers separate and intact during the process. To do this, you need a flat-bottom spade for the topsoil and a digging fork for the subsoil. The result will be more productive soil.

Step 1. Using the spade, dig a trench across the prospective bed. It should be as wide and as deep as the spade. Put all the topsoil to one side.

Step 2. Using the digging fork, loosen up the subsoil in the bottom of the trench. Do not remove any of the subsoil.

Step 3. Take the spade again, and dig a second trench next to the first. Put all the topsoil into the first trench. Loosen the subsoil with the fork, and go from one end of the garden to the other.

Once your raised beds are double dry, condition the soil by blending in compost, rotted manure, and/or peat moss and cover with a mulch just like a single-row garden. Shape the bed so that it forms a mound with slightly curved edges. Wooden strips along the edges of the bed keeps them separate from the paths.

Future care of the raised beds entails working in the mulch and adding new compost—and turning under cover crops, a "green manure." It is important to keep the soil rich in humus, well-aerated, and well-draining.

Intercropping. Wide beds enable you to grow more food crops or flowers closer together because their root systems are at different levels and do not compete. For example, you can plant a line of carrots and a line of lettuce right next to each other. A raised bed is also a good place to grow beans amid corn stalks or lettuce and radishes in the partial shade of trellised peas. To obtain maximum benefits from wide beds, all vining plants should be staked or trellised to take up less ground space.

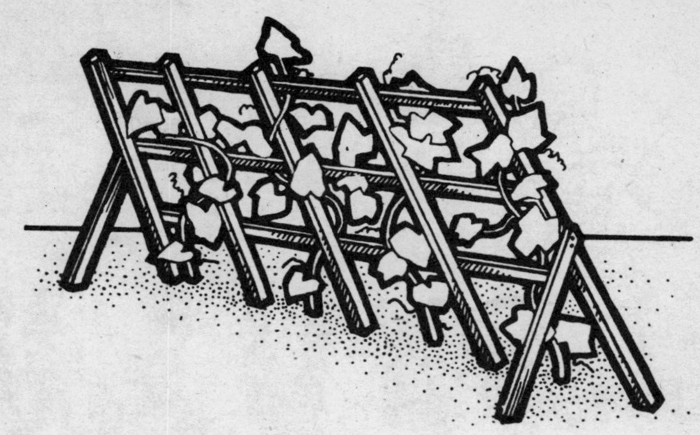

Food Garden Pointers

Smart gardeners plant to get the highest possible yield from their plot. That means planting (1) vegetables that mature early in the season and can be replanted once or several times or replaced with another quick-growing crop for a fall garden, and (2) vegetables that take the whole summer to grow. Fast-maturing crops include bush and pole beans, which can be planted several times during a season, and cabbage, lettuce, beets, broccoli, and carrots, which can be planted twice in a single season. If well cared for, tomatoes, peppers, and eggplant will continue to bear until killed by frost. Although mainstays like lettuce and spinach thrive in cool weather, other vegetables that require a lot of space and yield a small return, relatively speaking, include muskmelons, corn, watermelon, and winter squash. These crops are best suited to a large garden.

Successive Cropping: Vegetables vary greatly in their response to heat and cold. Some, like lettuce and spinach, grow in spring and fall in the North or in winter in the South. They need cool weather. Other vegetables typically thrive only during warm weather. In recent years, the distinction has blurred between cool-weather and hot-weather crops. Now there are varieties of lettuce, spinach, collards, cabbage, mustard kale, and turnips that are more tolerant of heat.

Knowledge of both the climate requirements of your vegetables and how long they take to mature (bear fruit) enables you to use successive cropping. This conserves space and enables you to grow a variety of crops. Examples are: spinach, lettuce, endive, followed by beans, tomatoes, peppers, or eggplant; cabbages, cauliflower, carrots, beets, or peas, followed by snap beans or corn; beans followed by late cabbage, cauliflower, or corn; or corn followed by beans, beets, lettuce, turnips, carrots, or spinach.

Which Varieties? When you know what vegetables you want to grow, you must decide what varieties. If you've ordered several seed catalogs with a couple of dozen confusing types of corn or tomatoes from which to choose, be aware that varieties differ in their (1) adaptation to areas of the country and soil types; (2) resistance to diseases and nematodes; (3) quality for fresh use, canning, or for freezing; (4) and days from planting to maturity. To learn which varieties grow best in your area, consult experienced gardeners in your town, or contact local agricultural agents.

Growing a variety resistant to diseases and nematodes can make a crucial difference, especially with plant diseases that cannot be controlled by spraying or dusting. Examples of such diseases include fusarium and verticullum wilt of tomatoes, Stewart's wilt of sweet corn, and mosaic virus of peppers, cucumber, and muskmelons. Although downy and powdery mildew of cucumbers and gray leaf spot and late blight of tomatoes can be curtailed with chemical sprays, why spray when you can plant a resistant variety? Not all diseases occur in all parts of North America. Because nematodes are a problem mainly in warm climates, Michigan gardeners, for example, have no particular need to grow a nematode-resistant tomato variety.

If you garden primarily to have a supply of fresh vegetables, avoid varieties developed for machine harvest, such as determinate tomatoes, which ripen all at once. If you plan to can or freeze some of your vegetables, however, machine-harvest varieties may be desirable. Greens that do well in full summer heat can keep family salad bowls piled high with garden green. Among such second-phase crops are Malabar spinach and New Zealand spinach. Swiss chard is a full-season crop that can be planted early but does not come into its own until summer.

Crop Rotation: In addition to acting as *aide-memoire* throughout the season, a chart of your garden comes in handy in successive years when you need to recall where you planted what to achieve when you need to recall where you planted what to achieve as much crop rotation as possible. Shifting crops each year keeps insect activity and diseases at a low.

Crop rotation may not be practical in a small backyard plot. In that case, shift only those vegetables that would tend to become diseased after more than one season in the same location. First choices to be moved every year are members of the cabbage family.

Another advantage to crop rotation is that vegetables such as peas and beans are nitrogen-fixing legumes—cabbage, radishes, tomatoes, and lettuce do well in a space previously occupied by any of the legumes. Corn also likes soil where beans have grown.

Perennials: Rhubarb, strawberries, and asparagus are difficult to incorporate in a small vegetable plot. Apart from being too large, rhubarb must not be disturbed at the end of summer, which puts it in the way of fall soil preparation. The solution is to exclude rhubarb or, better, plant it elsewhere in your yard, such as in a flowerbed. Asparagus and strawberries take up a lot of space and require two seasons before yielding a decent harvest. If you have a sunny growing area away from the main garden and a couple of years worth of patience, strawberry and asparagus beds will be rewarding (especially the asaparagus, which lasts from ten to twenty years).

Preparing a Garden

Preparing for a summer garden ought to begin the previous autumn with soil conditioning and fertilizing.

First make a soil test to determine whether the pH balance of your soil is right for your plants,, and make any adjustments necessary. To raise the pH one point, add about 5 pounds of limestone for every 100 square feet; to lower the pH, apply gypsum at the same rate.

Conditioning the soil means improving both its organic content and overall structure. The best way to condition soil is to use compost (see "Building Soil with Compost"). If you have no compost, you can gather a supply of autumn leaves, grass clippings, and/or seaweed and shred these with a shredder or by running an electric rotary lawnmower back and forth over them. Then spread the shredded material over the bare dirt and dig or rototill it into the topsoil along with any amendments indicated by your soil test. Over the winter, the shredded material will enrich the earth by decomposing and becoming part of the topsoil. If you have leaves left over, spread a thick layer over the garden as a mulch (see "The Magic of Mulch").

If you are worried about a sloppy-looking garden, you can use peat moss as a soil conditioner. Peat moss is decayed vegetable matter that has been partially carbonized and decomposed over a long period of time in bogs or marshes. Not all peats are alike. Most peat is imported from Ireland, Germany, or Sweden and is highly acidic, light brown, and has a coarse texture. Worked into heavy soil, peat improves aeration; added to clay soils, it enhances drainage. It can also be used as a mulch to preserve soil moisture and inhibit weed growth. Michigan peat is a domestic type of darker color and finer texture; it holds three to six times its weight in water.

When you buy peat moss, it is dry and powdery. If you work it into garden soil in this form, it will absorb moisture, and if you try to use it as a mulch, it will simply blow away. To prepare peat moss, tear several holes in the bag it comes in and pour water into the peat. Let the wet peat stand overnight before using.

Some people confuse sphagnum moss with peat moss. Sphagnum moss is a rough, fibrous moss belonging to the genus Sphagnum found in bogs. It absorbs twenty times its weight in water, enhances aeration, and possesses antibiotic properties that ward off damping-off fungi and root rot. Sphagnum moss is available commercially in long-strand form, ground, or chopped, and is an excellent medium for sowing seeds and rooting cuttings. Chopped moss is the most useful kind (chop long-strand moss into ¾-inch pieces for best results). Like peat, sphagnum moss needs to be moistened before use.

Clay soil can be opened up for better aeration by adding sawdust, compost, peat moss, leaves, grass clippings, or wood chips. This kind of soil, more than sandy soil, needs to be conditioned in the fall. Working clay soil in spring with either a shovel or rototiller may damage the soil structure. Working clay soil when it is wet breaks down the soil structure and compacts it.

Not long after the last frost of winter, the ground is ready for preliminary work that must precede planting. You can discern soil readiness by grasping a handful of dirt and squeezing it. If the soil compresses because it is too wet, a few more days remain before the plot should be prepared. When the soil breaks into large clumps as you open your hand, the moment is at hand.

A completely new plot or a reconverted bed being put to a new use needs fertilizer, either organic or chemical. Fertilizer applied in the fall or early winter should be high in phosphorus and potash, but nitrogen-rich fertilizer will leach away nitrogen before the planting season. Spring fertilizers should be rich in nitrogen. If you choose a chemical fertilizer, follow the package directions as to proportions, rake it into the topsoil (along with lime or other additives), and give the plot a good daily soaking for at least a week before planting. Freshly applied chemical fertilizer, especially in combination with lime, can destroy the fine roots of seedlings. If you are using organic fertilizer, such as chicken manure, you can plant right away. Organic fertilizer releases its nutrients more slowly and should not burn the roots of new plants.

How to Apply Fertilizers

Broadcast application. Apply dry fertilizer evenly to the entire surface of the plot, and rake into the top three inches of topsoil. This method raises the general fertility of the earth, but some of the nutrients are lost because they are leached out of the soil or just do not reach the roots of the vegetables or flowers.

Band application. Sow fertilizer at planting time in a narrow band or furrow to the side or directly under the seed. This method does not increase the overall soil fertility but is the most effecient way of fertilizing a particular plant. Open a deep furrow, sprinkle in some organic or commercial fertilizer (the latter at the rate of one pound per fifty feet or row), cover it with dirt, and then sow the seed, which is covered with soil. If you use a dry fertilizer, take care not to let it touch the seeds.

Hill application. A variation on band application, hill application is used for preraised plants that are widely spaced, such as tomatoes and peppers. Instead of a furrow, dig a planting hole about one foot deep. Put all the soil to one side. Fill the hole mostly with compost or well-rotted manure, cover with soil, and plant the seedlings as usual. Bean seeds can be planted in similarly prepared planting holes.

Side-dressing. This is the way of giving young plants a boost when they exhibit signs of doing poorly and a soil test indicates a nutrient deficiency. Open a furrow that is about three inches deep and four to five inches to the side of the plant or plants. Add dry fertilizer in the recommended amount, cover the soil, and water; or, in an organic garden, add bloodmeal or bonemeal mixed with compost to the furrow, cover with soil, and water.

Compost water. Half fill a bucket with compost and fill it to the brim with water. Stir and allow the mixture to settle. Pour the water off into another container and use it to water plants around flowering time. Return the compost to the compost heap.

Manure tea. A combination of water and manure, this is prepared by percolating water through a container filled with manure. *Method 1.* Fill ¾ full with rotted manure a container with many holes in it. Place it in the garden among the plants. Watering and rainfall will make a "tea" that automatically seeps out and reaches nearby plants. *Method 2.* Fill a bucket half full with rotted manure. Add water to the brim and allow the sediment to settle. The "tea" from the upper part of the bucket can be applied around garden plants. You can use the same manure a couple of times before adding it to the compost heap.

Liquid fertilizer. There are three ways to apply liquid fertilizer: (1) pour it into the ground around the plant; (2) apply it via the watering or irrigation system (you can buy the attachments at a garden center or when you install a drip irrigation system); (3) spray the fertilizer on the leaves of plants with a hand or compressed-air sprayer.

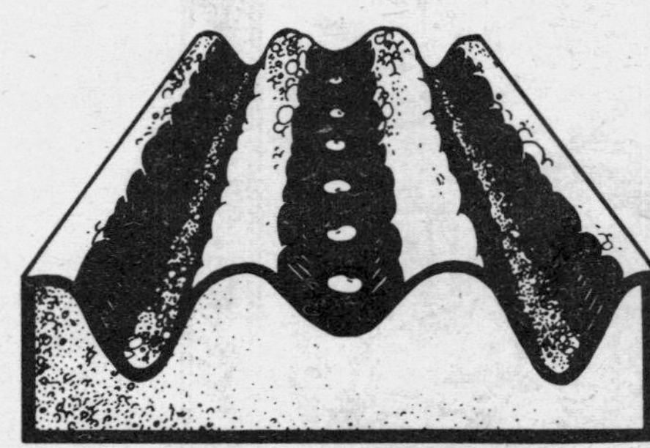

Banding fertilizer. Place band 2 or 3 inches to each side of seed and about 1 or 2 inches deeper.

Your Own *Vegetables*

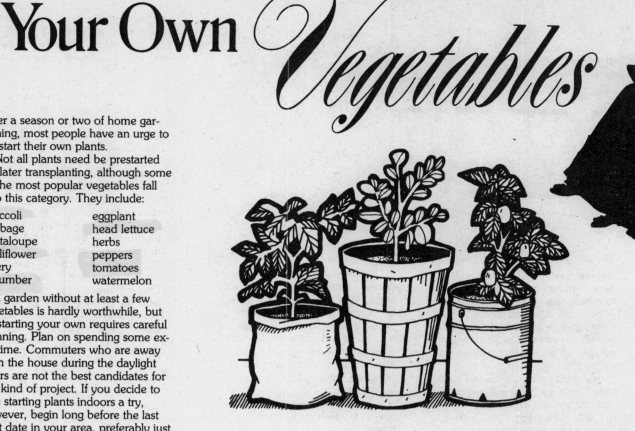

After a season or two of home gardening, most people have an urge to prestart their own plants.

Not all plants need be prestarted for later transplanting, although some of the most popular vegetables fall into this category. They include:

broccoli	eggplant
cabbage	head lettuce
cantaloupe	herbs
cauliflower	peppers
celery	tomatoes
cucumber	watermelon

A garden without at least a few vegetables is hardly worthwhile, but prestarting your own requires careful planning. Plan on spending some extra time. Commuters who are away from the house during the daylight hours are not the best candidates for this kind of project. If you decide to give starting plants indoors a try, however, begin long before the last frost date in your area, preferably just after New Year when seed catalogs come out (unless, of course, you live in the South where you can have both a winter and summer garden).

When you have your seeds, calculate the germination time for each kind of plant and count backward from the last frost date in your part of the country. Remember that *average* dates come slightly earlier or slightly later in any given year.

Sowing seeds for preraised plants is not a one-shot deal: Each variety has its own germination requirements. One way to avoid timing errors is to prepare a schedule that indicates (1) when to start the germination for each vegetable and (2) the date each can be transplanted into the garden. Although seed packets provide much of this information, if it's your first time check with a more experienced gardener who knows how to fine-tune theoretical planting dates to the actual local weather.

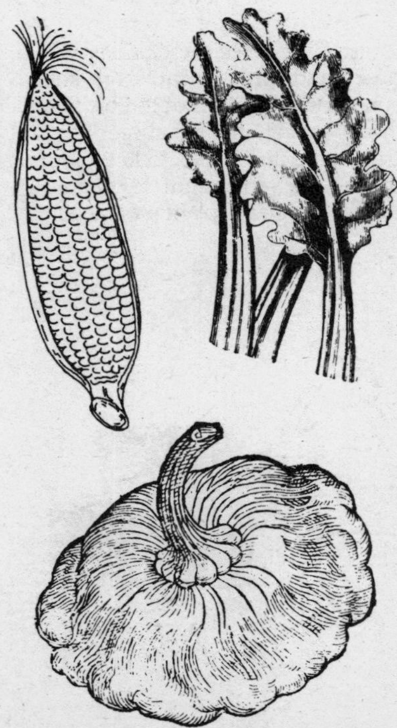

The major seed companies and large garden supply centers market many types of containers designed for prestarting garden plants. Some even offer inexpensive kits complete with seeds, trays divided into individual growing compartments filled with a special growing medium, and a plastic cover for the tray. Ranging from basic to fancy, you can send for or buy in a local store peat pots and strips; Jiffy-7 pellets, and bedding trays designed to hold them; Nodampoff, which is a germinating medium that prevents damping off; and even portable hot houses.

If you don't want the expense of seed-starting supplies, you can use all sorts of containers for germinating your seedlings. Milk and juice cartons cut lengthwise make excellent seed beds, as do aluminum trays used to take-out foods. Plastic tubes of all types are fine, as are paper and styrofoam cups and egg cartons. An advantage to buying biodegradable peat pots, though, is that they go directly into the ground without your having to disturb the seedlings' root systems. Damage to the roots of young plants markedly retards their growth.

Your best bet for sure germination is one of the commercially available growing mediums available at garden supply centers or from large seed companies. Geo. W. Park Seed Company, for example, markets one of the Cornell University soilless mixtures composed of shredded peat moss, perlite, vermiculite, and nutrients. Like similar commercial products, it is free of insects, weeds, and soil-borne diseases.

For instructions on germinating seed, see "Propagation."

An easy way to harden off seedlings is to use a cold frame that opens to the south. (Cold frames are fairly easy to construct if you are at all handy, or they can be purchased prefabricated or in kit form from the large seed companies.) After you relocate a group of seedlings in the cold frame, you gradually expose seedlings to the elements. This is done by opening the frame for increasing periods until the seedlings can live through entire days and nights without injury from the cold. Spring weather can be tricky, and you cannot count on every day being warmer than the preceding one. At times, you may need to hurry out to the cold frame, close the top, and, at nightfall, cover it with a tarpaulin to retain the heat.

In areas where winter is long and summer short, a safer way to introduce preraised plants to the elements is a hot bed, which is merely a heated cold frame with its northern end set flush against a building or fence. Insulated along the sides and warmed from the bottom with waterproof heating coils connected to an outdoor electrical outlet, in cold climates hot beds are in use when there is still a possibility of snow, thereby extending the gardening season comfortably.

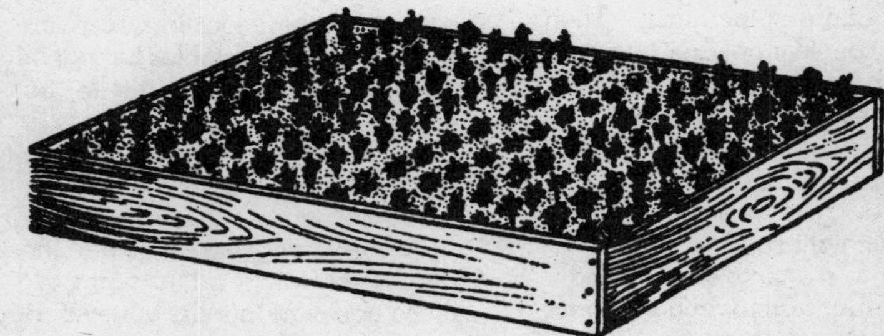

Seed box for starting plants indoors.

Sowing Seeds Outdoors

Preparing the Soil: Seeds can begin to go into the ground as soon as danger of frost is past and the ground is dry enough to work in the spring. The precise date to start planting depends on your location and the weather, but in general some very hardy crops—broccoli, lettuce, peas, spinach—can be planted about four weeks before the last freeze. Above all, the soil must not be wet or the structure will be seriously damaged.

Prepare the garden soil by plowing, spading, or rototilling the area to a minimal depth of six to eight inches, mixing in whatever organic matter you have—cover crops, mulch, compost, moistened peat moss. Remove rocks, stones, twigs, and other debris, and break down clods with a hoe. This is also the time to incorporate fertilizer and lime. After digging in the organic matter and loosening and aerating the soil, rake the seed bed lightly to create a level surface.

How to Sow: Here is where your planting plan comes in handy, but you must go out to the garden equipped with several stakes and a ball of heavy twine to make it work. Following the planting plan, stretch the twine tautly between stakes to mark the row of seed you want to plant. Let each row run north to south to keep the plants from casting shadows on each other. Then draw the corner or handle of a hoe, pressing lightly, along the full length of the twine to create a furrow of a depth equal to about two to four times the diameter of the seed you are planting. Beets, Swiss chard, and New Zealand spinach are exceptions and should be planted in shallow furrows.

Sow the seed according to the directions on the seed packet—not more, or you will waste time and work later on when the extra seedlings will need thinning. The old-fashioned way to seed a small home garden is to take a small amount of seed in your hand, bend over, and plop down individual seeds at the indicated uniform intervals. For gadget-loving gardeners, modern technology, via American seed companies and garden centers, offers several de-

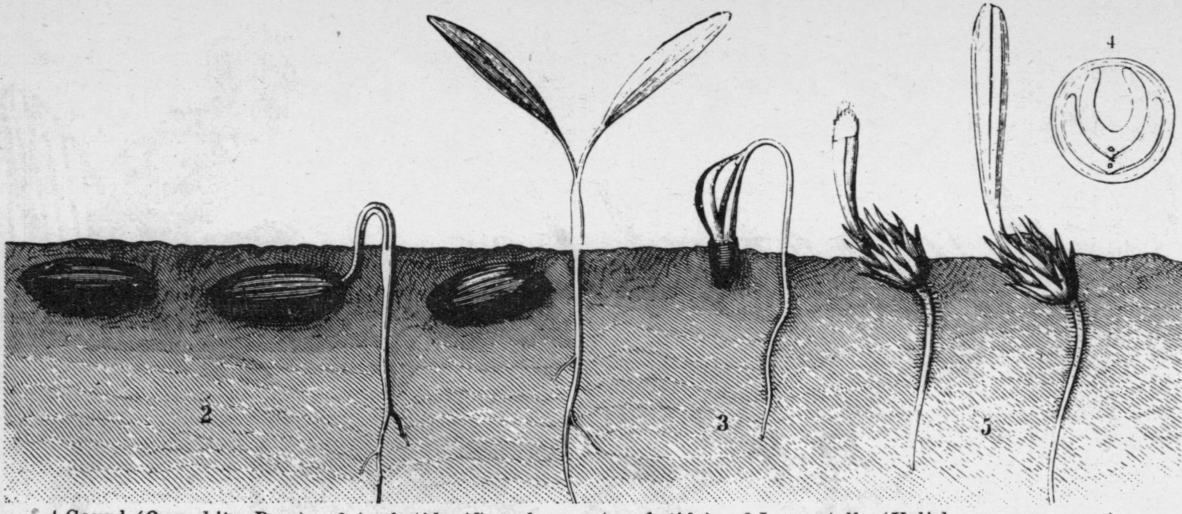

[1] Gourd (*Cucurbita Pepo*). [2] Asafœtida (*Scorodosma Asa fœtida*). [3] Immortelle (*Helichrysum annuum*).
[4] Cross-section through the cotyledons, showing them curled up in the pericarp of the Immortelle.
[5] *Cardopatium corymbosum* **Fig. 1–3, natural size; fig. 4–5, somewhat enlarged.**

vices at various prices and levels of sophistication that make the job easier. Some eliminate the necessity of opening a furrow or most of the bending and stooping. In large gardens, where you may expect to make an initial investment in labor-saving equipment, using a seeder is an efficient way of planting.

When the seed is in the ground, it can be recovered with soil, but compost or sieved leafmold are better covers. They are richer in nutrients and their darker color retains heat better than does soil. To give the seeds the darkness they require for germination, firm down the covering over the seed furrow, but do not pack it down. Use your hand or a hoe. Beets, which produce a rather weak little sprout at first, should be covered with a mixture of sand and moistened peat moss.

If you do not fill the furrows with soil, a ridge of soil will mark each row. You may also want to assist your memory with little white plastic markets that one can write on with indelible ink. Many gardeners like to sprinkle quick-growing radish seeds next to slow-germinating crops like parsley, carrots, and parsnips. Of all the methods of marking rows, seed packages on sticks are the least useful: one or two good rainfalls and they are finished.

Seed tapes with several yards of seed spaced at equal intervals take some of the work out of planting. To use these water-soluble tapes, open a furrow to the correct depth for the particular crop and unroll the tape along the bottom of the furrow. Then cover with soil, leafmold, or compost.

Slow-germinating seeds can benefit by some extra help from the gardener. Celery and parsley, which have hard seed shells and take forever to sprout, can be speeded up with an overnight soaking in tepid water prior to planting. Carrots and parsnips sprout faster when you pour boiling water on them just before covering them in their furrow.

When the seeds are in the ground, water the soil with the fine spray from the garden hose. While the seeds are germinating, keep the soil evenly moist—delicate sprouts cannot survive a drought. During the germination period, weeds will start to pop up along with your crop. Taking care not to confuse vegetable seedlings with baby weeds, remove the interlopers because they sap nutrients from the soil and threaten to overwhelm the vegetables.

Raised Beds. In clay soil and in gardens in moist climates and damp locations, raised beds for crops such as beets, turnips, and carrots aid germination. In spring, raising a planting bed six to eight inches also makes the soil dry out and warm up faster for earlier planting.

In a small garden, beds can be raised by digging the soil as deeply as you can and adding soil and compost to a strip measuring from fifteen inches to five feet (if you are tall), depending on how far you can reach and what you are planting. In a larger area, a rototiller can till the raised seed bed easily. If the machine has a special hilling attachment, it can make raised beds with soil already in the garden.

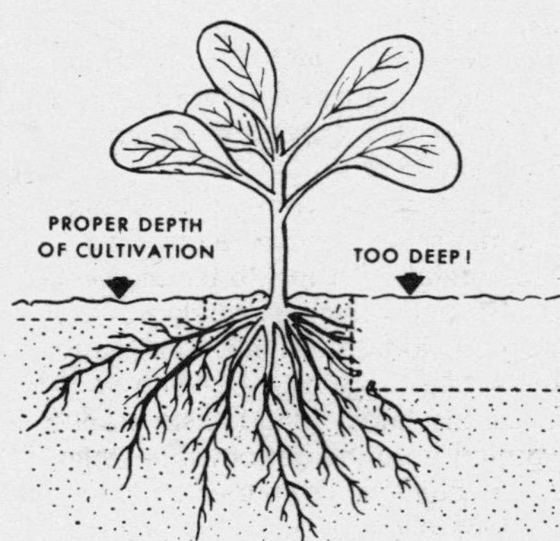

Transplanting

Home gardeners in areas where the growing season spans between spring and autumn frosts find prestarted plants a way to get a headstart on the season. In some locations, certain slow-growing vegetables cannot be sown outside until after the last frost and would not mature before fall frost, while others take a long time to reach their peaks if they are sown outdoors.

Preraised vegetables include those purchased from local nurseries or those you start indoors yourself. Buying tomato, pepper, and eggplant seedlings is an easy way to begin a new garden, especially if it is a last-minute plot.

When you buy seedlings from a nursery, look for specimens that were started in an individual container—little square peat-moss pots, peat pellets fitted into flats, or flats with dividers between seedlings. Grown individually, seedlings in these containers do not get their root systems intertwined, so that you need not take a knife to them in order to separate and plant them.

Whatever the variety, nursery-started plants should be short and sturdy. Tall, leggy seedlings have been underfed and may not have received sufficient light. Optimal care at the crucial early stage of development ensures a healthier mature plant. Other warning signs when choosing seedling for transplant include:

—dried-out roots

—dead, yellowed, or mottled foliage

—foliage perforated with tiny holes

—insect infestation on the underside of leaves

Reputable nurseries sell plants that have already been conditioned to go into the ground, and the sooner seedings are placed into the earth the better. But that does not mean immediately. A couple of hours before seeding, set them in a bright, protected spot and give them a thorough watering. When it comes time for planting, they will be slightly on the dry side.

To avoid seedling casualties, wait until after the last frost in your area. If you don't mind a slightly later harvest, put off transplanting until a full week after the frost. A few vegetables and herbs, including lettuce, dill, parsley, peas, and spinach, can tolerate a few degrees of frost.

Begin by making the row where you are going to plant by staking a piece of string tautly. Then push aside the mulch on top of the soil. For each plant, dig a hole substantially larger than the root ball. (The proper distance between planting holes can be found on the original seed packages.) Don't miss the chance to examine the holes and the soil you have removed for cutworms or Japanese beetle larvae. Any suspicious creatures should meet a prompt doom, lest they live to chomp away at your garden.

Unless you have started your own seedlings, you could be dealing with young plants grown in a soil mixture lighter than your garden earth. Seedlings that suddenly find themselves in heavy soil go through extra trauma getting established unless the soil surrounding their root balls is lightened.

If you have no compost, purchase some commercial houseplant soil and mix it with the backfill. This improved soil provides a lighter growth medium while adding organic matter to the garden. For sandy soil, which may drain too well for thirsty seedlings, line the bottom of each little hole with some dampened peat moss to retain moisture.

Next, prepare each hole for its occupant by filling it three-quarters full with your improved garden soil or with compost. Press the fill down firmly but not so tightly that it will resist the expansion of plant roots.

Now the planting holes are ready for their new residents. Place the root ball in the hole just as if you were potting up a plant and fill in the hole with soil, putting it down tightly enough so that it supports the plant. Transplants stand sturdier when a bit of the stem is below the soil level. Once in the ground, newly set out plants should be watered with warm water containing a water-soluble fertilizer.

There is a slight variation to observe when transplanting seedlings raised in peat pots. Just before they and their occupants go into the garden, place them in a tray with an inch or so of warm water and let the pots absorb enough liquid to become nice and soft. Plants in Jiffy pots are bound by a nonbiodegradable plastic netting that could imprison the roots of seedlings, and this should be clipped loose in order not to inhibit growth. All types of peat pots should be set about a half-inch below the soil surface.

Plants grown in flats and not individual containers also merit special attention. Often these specimens come four or five to a container. Inevitably, their roots are entangled, but this is okay as long as the roots have not been allowed to grow through the drainage holes in the bottom of the flat and dried out. To separate the individual plants, remove from the flat the whole block of soil, taking care not to damage the roots. Then place the block on a board and, with a clean sharp knife, cut across the width of the block and then between individual seedlings. Cut with a firm stroke to keep root damage to a minimum. Even if a seedling is weak, plant it anyway.

Once separated, these transplants go into the ground in the same gentle manner as other transplants, but their roots should receive about half the concentration of fertilizer during the first watering.

Careful watering is important. Keep the earth around the plants moist without dislodging their roots. When the weather report predicts a hot day, take the time in the morning to mist the foliage as a prevention against wilting. Shade is another protection against the ravages of the sun's heat; stick some branches in the ground so that the afternoon sun is filtered.

Tender young plants are a favorite item on the diet of cutworms who emerge from the soil at night to eat their way through stems. Don't wait to see whether your plot contains a colony of cutworms. Prepare for the worst by making a little collar for each seedling out of waxed cardboard from juice or milk cartons or from a paper cup with the bottom cut out.

A bout of cold, damp weather can be as injurious to transplants as hot weather or lack of water. Little tents of clear plastic spread over bent wire frames protect transplants from chilly air while retaining the moist atmosphere they need. Of course, this measure necessitates watchfulness. As soon as the weather warms up, the tents must come off.

Plant Early for Fall Harvest:
Broccoli
Cabbage
Cauliflower

Late Summer Planting for Fall Harvest:

Beets	Leeks
Carrots	Lettuce
Chard	Mustard
Collards	Spinach
Kale	Parsnips
Kohlrabi	Turnips

Midseason Gardening

Keeping the garden going from the beginning of the season to the end is the mark of a good gardener. If you water your crops regularly and thoroughly, your garden will continue to grow when you cope with watering and weeding, diseases and pests, and the tendency of some plants to go to seed. On-going care also includes harvesting early crops and sowing midseason and late crops; harvesting late crops; protecting late crops from the frost; and, in some instances, applying fertilizer.

Watering: Vegetables, some of which are 90% water, need an average of one to two inches of water per week. An inch of rain is the equivalent of about 28,000 gallons on an acre or nine hundred gallons on a 30 × 50 foot garden. On a small scale, one inch of rainfall equals about two-thirds of a gallon of water for every square foot.

You can overwater plants. In clay soils, too much water results in poor soil aeration, which suffocates plants; in sandy soils, heavy waterings may wash away nitrogen. Overwatering tomato plants causes cracking of tomato skins. A thorough watering means giving enough water so that moisture reaches the plant roots. In most cases, that means wetting the upper twelve inches of garden soil. Sprinkling is not the best watering method. Sprinklers splash water onto the foliage and tend to increase leaf

Rapum majus.
Great Turnep.

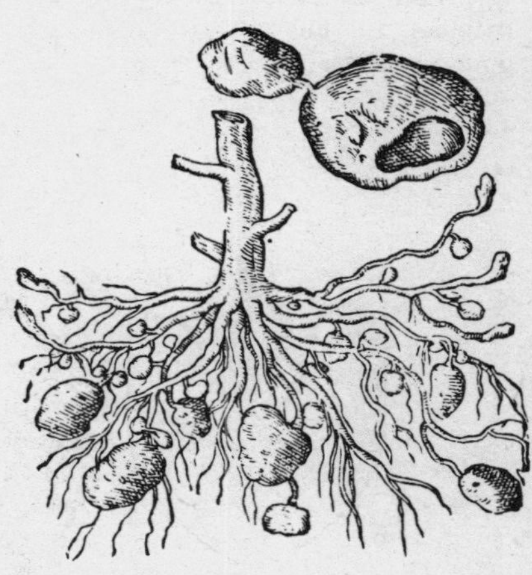

spot and other diseases. Perforated hoses are the best before the water soaks right into the ground. In areas like the Southwest where water is scarce, the most efficient means of watering may be drip irrigation.

In hot weather, save moisture by trapping it in the soil. Hoeing deeply between rows is just plain wrong because it causes precious moisture to evaporate. On the other hand, if the soil surface has formed a hard crust, when you irrigate the water will not be able to seep into the ground. In that case, a very shallow cultivation is called for. To keep the soil moist when daytime temperatures are in the 90's, apply a mulch to conserve moisture, prevent blossom-end rot, leaf curl, and control weeds.

Between the rough waterings, let most plants dry out a bit. How dry depends on the climate, the soil, and the weather. Don't let the garden get so dry that your plants begin to wilt or that the soil does not absorb water. A drought in spring or autumn is not as serious as a dry spell during midsummer when plants require the most water.

Once you have a feel for your garden, if you conclude that the soil is drying out too quickly, consider adding more organic matter to incrase its water-holding capacity. Remember, though, that a greater water-holding capacity means that more water will be needed.

Dealing with Weeds: What is wrong with weeds? Nothing when they aren't in your garden soaking up nutrients needed by food plants. Among vegetables, weeds can compete for water and soil nutrients and, sometimes, sunlight. Some weeds harbor diseases, insects, and nematodes that reinfest garden crops in succeeding years. Unless you garden under mulch, regular weeding should be part of the gardening routine.

Hand weeding is the most accurate method. That means crawling amid your vegetable rows on your knees during the warmest hours of the day. Weeds uprooted in the evening are liable to reroot, whereas those put under the sun's full rays dry up. Morning weeding should be done prior to watering the garden. Touching wet vegetable foliage is a good way to spread plant diseases, and walking on wet soil between furrors compacts the soil.

Heavy mulch of grass clippings or straw spread between rows of vegetables help retain soil moisture while suppressing weeds. Unmulched gardens where the rows of vegetables are widely spaced attract crabgrass and prolific weeds like purslane. (If you are an organic gardener, however, you know that some weeds, including purslane, can serve as a ground cover to retain moisture around particular crops, such as corn. The idea is not to allow weeds to overwhelm the vegetables.)

Fertilizing: If garden soil has been prepared properly, no fertilizing, or very little, is needed during the growing season. Overfeeding leads to big vegetables with very little taste—and why grow them when you can buy them in any supermarket? The use of fertilizer also adds to the cost of your garden.

If your plants are doing poorly and you have not tested the nutrient content of the soil, fertilizer may be called for. Once you have overruled other causes of poor plants, such as irregular watering, disease, and insufficient light, have the soil tested before adding extra stimulants.

Second Crops: When summer weather arrives and early season crops like lettuce, spinach, turnips, and peas are finished, your garden is ready for a second planting of hot-weather vegetables. The work of sowing new crops is made easier if you clean up each row of early vegetables right after harvesting. Toss what's left of the old plants onto your compost heap and remove nuisance weeds. You do not have to wait for an entire crop to be finished before getting ready for the next one if you pick the vegetables by section rather than from different points along a row. (It is a temptation to go for the biggest plants first, but keep in mind that you are eventually going to harvest the entire row.)

This is the time to improve soil structure and nutrient content by laying down a couple of inches of compost or raking in a couple of inches of moistened peat moss. Supplement the compost of peat moss with an application of a balanced fertilizer, organic or chemical, according to your preference. As usual, when you use organic fertilizer, you need about twice as much as a chemical product, but you can replant right away. After using a chemical fertilizer on cleared-away areas of your plot, water the ground and cover with mulch or several layers of newspaper to keep the moisture in. After a week, you can safely reseed.

How long in the season to continue reseeding depends on when the first so-called killing frost is due in your area. To keep the garden going right up to the wire, choose varieties with short growing seasons like beans, beets, carrots, or lettuce, and count far enough backward from the expected frost date to give late-sown vegetables the time to mature.

Vegetables like cabbage, broccoli, and cauliflower, which are popular foods in autumn, take a long time to mature. Late-sown broccoli and cauliflower continue to produce until the daytime temperature goes below freezing.

The first killing frost is generally preceded by several light frosts, often separated with long spells of beautiful Indian summer weather. While early frosts do not harm cabbage, broccoli, and the green vegetables like Swiss chard and spinach, a sudden drop in temperature can finish tender crops (squash, lettuce, bush and pole beans, and tomatoes). Root vegetables like turnips and parsnips like some cold weather to make them sweet.

End of Season: When it's too late for another round of succession planting, your garden will begin to have more and more open space as you continue to harvest the fruits of your labor. What then? If you leave the ground uncovered, nature will step in with its own agenda, a late crop of weeds. To save work next year, when you have cleared away the dead plants from your garden (and added them to your compost heap), rake a couple of inches of compost into the topsoil, spread on a good thick mulch of dead leaves or grass clippings over the now-unused portions of the garden. Whatever you do to avoid carrying over insects and diseases into the following gardening season, remove old plants or add them in shredded form to the mulch.

The alternative to mulch is a cover crop or constant weeding until past the first killing frost.

Cucumis vulgaris.
Common Cucumber.

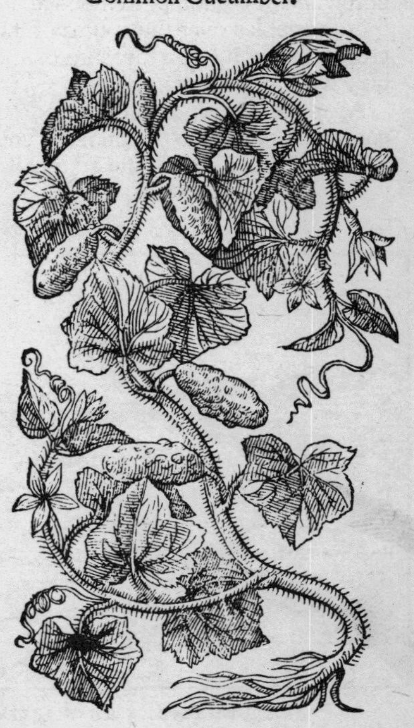

Water-Saving Drip Irrigation

A property developed under irrigation.

To live, plants need an adequate supply of water. Everyone knows that. Yet there is an art to watering *correctly*. Even though you are getting out there with the hose and your plants are growing, you could be either wasting water and spending more money than necessary on your garden or not applying water so that moisture reaches down to the root system of your plants in the correct amounts for optimal absorption. In short, you might not be getting the most out of your time, money, effort, and garden.

What is effective watering? Ideally, it is the maintenance of an optimal level of soil moisture. Irrigation should not be too shallow, thereby wasting water by direct evaporation from the soil. Nor should you apply too much water and keep the soil saturated. The intervals at which you water are also important. For millennia, humans have been imitating nature and saturating their gardens, as does rainfall, and allowing the earth to dry up, which naturally occurs during periods of sunny weather. From the point of view of a plant that needs water every day this is an extreme regime.

Several other factors, besides what the gardener does, go into effective watering. The rates at which plants absorb water and at which soil moisture evaporates depend on the soil texture, or tilth, the climate, the sun, the amount of wind and humidity, and the temperature.

Balancing all the elements to create the perfect watering conditions for your garden is next to impossible. Yet how close you come to perfection when you attempt to manage all these variables over the course of the growing season is the measure of how well your garden will do.

Apart from hosing down your garden or even using a sprinkler, you may not be applying water so that it seeps down below the soil surface to the roots of plants. Nature is bound to give you a hard time by remaining its inconsistent, unpredictable self.

A Better Way?

How to improve on nature? How to have a successful garden without spending every waking hour keeping one step ahead of the elements? One answer is drip irrigation, a watering technique that supplies water to plant roots at a constant, measured rate so that the optimal soil moisture is maintained. While making the job of watering flowers, shrubs, trees, and vegetables almost worry-free, this system also pays off by increasing yields and saving water (and money). And it is relatively inexpensive and easy to install.

How does drip irrigation work? In its most primitive form, it consists of porous garden hoses through which water oozes at a constant rate. Usually, however, drip irrigation is somewhat more sophisticated and consists of flexible or rigid plastic tubing set into the garden, or amid trees and shrubs, on the soil surface or about 3 inches below the surface. Near the roots of each plant, an emitter is inserted into the hose or tubing. Through the emitter water passes at a regulated pressure. When the system is turned on and fills with water, water comes out of the emitters and moistens only the areas near the roots of plants. Because the soil moisture level is kept constant and below the saturation point, the soil is always well aerated. Also, since the entire soil surface is not irrigated, fewer weeds take hold.

Less soil surface receives water, too, thereby saving money and water, yet water is distributed to a larger percentage of the root area than by conventional watering and the result is improved growth. Unlike ordinary watering methods, drip irrigation loses virtually no water to evaporation because the water goes down into the soil to the roots instead of spreading along the top few inches of soil surface. This is a good feature when you want to irrigate, say, a flower garden or ground cover planted on sloping land: the water does not run off before it reaches the roots. Gardeners in parts of the country where water is scarce also appreciate the efficiency of drip irrigation.

Drip irrigation is also an excellent method of watering seed beds where consistent moisture is crucial to germination and the growth of sturdy young plants.

The initial price of a drip irrigation system is more than the cost of standard watering equipment, but considering the lower water bills and higher crop yields that result, you may find the extra expense worthwhile. The conservation of water, and the savings that go along with it, appeals to many gardeners in arid areas of the Southwest.

A useful primer on making your own system or picking and using a commercial product is Jack Kramer's *Drip-System Watering* (Norton). Drip irrigation systems are increasingly available at local garden supply centers. If none is sold in your area, the following suppliers will send you information on their products.

Reward of irrigation. Sweet-potato, weight 42½ pounds, grown on irrigated land in Yuma, Arizona.

What Kind of System Is Best?

Drip irrigation systems now come in many variations on the original theme. You can buy anything from simple tubing with above- or below-ground emitters (there are several dozen types of emitters, some more subject to clogging than others) to a nearly carefree automatic moisture-sensitive system with fittings for fertilizer applications and a timer. Most systems are fairly simple to put in to the garden, although some home owners look to their landscape architect for advice or help with the actual layout of the tubing.

Sources

Bosco Farms Drip Irrigation, Inc.
E. Weymouth Rd.
Vineland, NJ 08360

Care-Free Irrigation Suppliers, Inc.
Box 151
San Juan Capistrano, CA 92675

Chapin Watermatics
Box 298
Watertown, NY 13601

Gro-Mor
3156 East Palma
Anaheim, CA 92806

Reed Irrigation Systems
Box X
El Cajon, CA 91766

Sub Terrain Irrigation Co.
1534 East Ediger
Santa Ana, CA 92705

Write to Borg-Warner Co. (200 S. Michigan Ave., Chicago, IL 60604) for the nearest supplier of Micro-Por Hose, a porous tubing, and to Du Pont Co. (Wilmington, DE 19898) for suppliers of Viaflow Irrigation Tubing.

Appearanee of an irrigation ditch when first completed.

An irrigation ditch ten years after completion.

11 Food Gardening

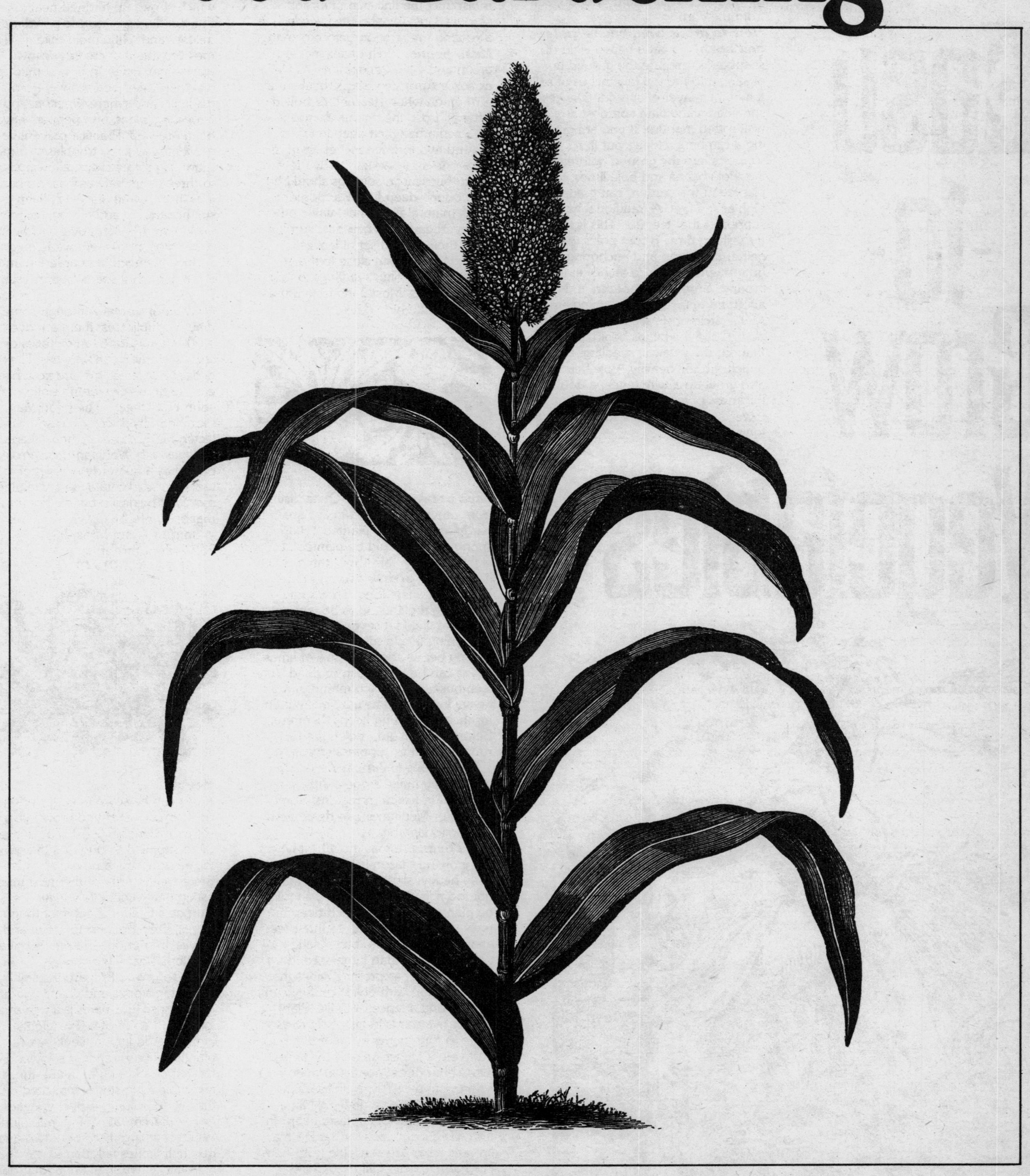

Easy -to- Grow Vegetables

Beans

Beans are fun to grow because they can be sown directly in the garden and they mature quickly, for the most part. With proper care, they produce heavy yields over a long harvest season. Climbing beans are also great space-savers. Their lovely flowering vines can grow up a fence or along the sunny side of the garage or house. Many gardeners interplant pole beans with corn as soon as little corn stalks appear. In return for the favor of being allowed to climb up the cornstalks, beans add nitrogen to the soil to benefit the corn crop.

Their yield will be somewhat less than if planted alone, but they take up no space at all and do not detract from the corn.

How to grow: Snapbeans (pole and bush) To get a heavy yield of snapbeans, prepare the ground by digging into the top few inches of soil a two-inch layer of shredded leaves sprinkled with some compost and well-rotted manure. If you are growing a climbing variety, put the supports into the ground before sowing. Pole beans and pole limes, too, if planted in the garden, can go up as high as ten feet. A traditional type of support is the "teepee." This is rigged by sashing three 8-foot poles together at the top and anchoring their bottom ends six or so inches in the ground. Spread the bottom ends about thirty inches. At planting time, sow a circle of six seeds around each pole. Once the beans begin to climb, thin out the weakest seedlings and mulch the soil heavily. Pole beans also grow up a wire fence, a double thickness of twine, or up a "bean tower" such as Burpee markets in their catalog.

Pole beans: Pole beans are really climbing bush beans. They include Kentucky Wonders, a popular greenbean, Romano or "Italian" beans, which are flat and broad, climbing yellow snapbeans, and the ornamental, yet edible, Scarlet Runners. They take about 65 days to mature and bear more heavily than bush beans as long as they are harvested frequently. Pole bean seeds take eight to fourteen days to germinate. To hasten the process, soak seeds overnight in water. Drain the water out (pour it into the garden—it's full of good things) and keep the seeds moist until the first sign of a root sprouts. Dust the sprouted seeds with a rooting preparation before planting.

Bush beans: Bush beans include green and yellow snapbeans as well as some surprising purple beans that turn green when steamed or boiled. After all frost, the first bean crop can be sown a half-inch deep in warm ground two to three inches apart in rows one-and-one-half to two feet apart. Midseason sowings should be in two-inch-deep furrows. Some types mature all at once, while others are everbearing. When new sprouts grow their second set of leaves, spread your mulch close to the young plants. Thin seedlings to four-inch intervals. Most varieties mature in fifty to fifty-nine days.

Fava or broad beans: Quite distinct from other beans, fava beans are hardy and must be planted in early spring. They should be planted at eight-inch intervals about three inches deep in rows two-and-one-half to three feet long. They grow into upright plants 30 to 36 inches high that yield fat seven-inch pods containing five to nine large, flat, oblong beans about the size of limas. Favas can be used fresh or dried. As fava bushes approach maturity, their heavy load of beans may make them top-heavy. Staking keeps them erect. Before they fill out, mulch the surrounding soil to suppress weeds.

Fava beans mature in 70 to 100 days. They make a good substitute for limas in northern regions. Some people of Mediterranean descent are allergic to fava beans.

Lima beans: Limas grow best where the growing season is long. They like fairly heavy, slightly acidic soil that is not too rich. In general, they should be planted about one-inch deep in rows two-and-one-half- to three-feet apart. Bary limas are better suited to warm climates than large-seeded types. Pole limas produce vines that need support with poles, or they can climb along a fence or trellis. Plant four or five seeds in hills or in rows three to four inches apart and thin to six to eight inches apart. Pole limas take about three months to mature.

In the mid-1970s, a Philadelphia dentist developed a new pole lima bean that bears lots of tasty beans in a small space. Seeds for the Dr. Martin pole limas are available from Fern Hill Farm, Jersey Mill Rd., Clarksboro, NJ 08020.

Diseases/pests: The major pests are Mexican bean beetles, aphids, leafhoppers, and the bean weevil, which shows up in dried beans. Fungus diseases include powdery mildew and white mold mildew. The mosaic virus that creates yellow leaves may occur in hot, humid weather. Keep beans away from gladiolas and where tomatoes, potatoes, eggplant, and peppers have been growing. Practice preventive gardening to keep troubles to a minimum: (1) rotate crops, allowing two to three years between bean plantings in the same place; (2) keep the soil healthy by adding organic matter each year; (3) don't overfeed beans with nitrogen; (4) remove leftover bean straw from the garden in autumn; (5) plant seeds from resistant strains.

Heirloom beans Although some may be duplicates, there are over 1,000 names for bean varieties or strains. Some bean varieties, like varieties of other plants, are no longer easy to find—or weren't until John E. Withee, "The Bean Man," searched for, discovered, and collected many "lost" or home-kept varieties. His Wanigan Bean Project publishes a quarterly newsletter as well as a seed catalogue containing scores of heirloom beans. For information, write to
Wanigan Associates, Inc.
262 Salem Street
Lynnfield, MA 01940

Beets

Beets can be sown in early spring in northern climates and grown year round in zones 9 & 10. To keep your table supplied throughout the growing season, sow a new crop every three weeks. One of the most interesting new vegetable varieties is Burpee's Golden Beet. Not found in stores, they are easy to grow, and the leaves are not only nutritious but also delicious steamed or boiled.

How to grow: Prepare the soil by removing stones and clumps of dirt. The best soil for beets is a rich sandy loam with a pH of 6.0 or slightly higher. (Add lime a week before planting if your reading is lower. Better yet, check the pH in autumn.) How thickly to sow is indicated on the seed packages—beet varieties have different rates of germination. When seedlings are about two-and-one-half inches tall, thin to one-inch intervals; when they are about four inches tall, thin to three or four

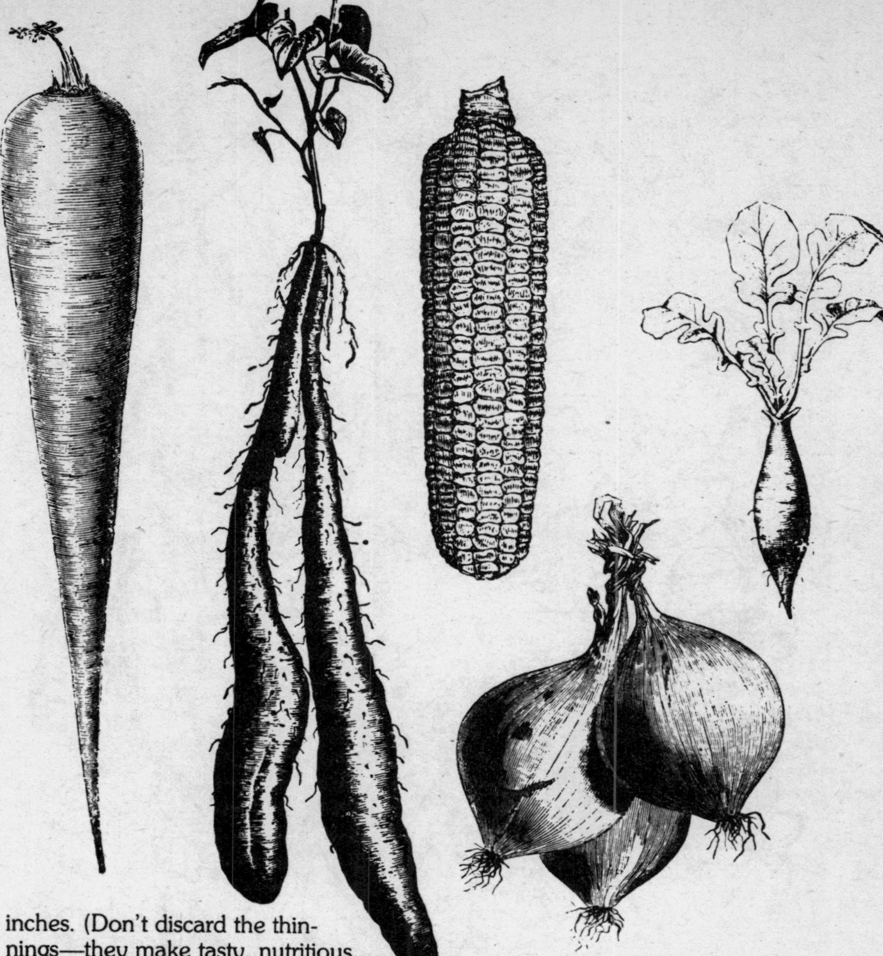

inches. (Don't discard the thinnings—they make tasty, nutritious salad greens.) Some beets become fibrous in hot weather. Choose varieties that remain succulent all season long, or match varieties developed for late or early crops to the appropriate part of the growing season. Most beets take 55 to 60 days to mature.
Diseases/pests: Leaf miners, webworm.

Broccoli
A member of the brassica or cabbage family, broccoli is a good cool-weather and fall crop, and different varieties are available for spring and fall harvest. Matching local climate and weather with the right varieties is the best way to have good results. Hardened-off seedlings can go into the garden when the earth becomes workable.
How to grow: Spring crops must be sown indoors five to seven weeks before setting out, which can be as early as two weeks before the last frost date. Before transplanting, test the pH rating and apply lime if necessary because broccoli does not do well in acid soil. Plant seedlings two feet apart in rows two feet apart. Broccoli takes 55 to 60 days to mature. Don't plant broccoli where other brassicas (cabbage, cauliflower, Brussels sprouts) have been growing. For later crops, begin new seedlings in a short row and transplant thinnings gradually until plants stand two feet apart. Broccoli heads begin to appear when night temperatures start to cool down. Well-developed side shoots provide a continued harvest for several weeks after the main crop is picked.
Diseases/pests: Aphids, green worms, cabbage worms. All brassicas are susceptible to severe soil-borne diseases, which is why crop rotation is important.

Brussels sprouts
A member of the brassica family, Brussels sprouts are grown as a fall crop in northern regions and as a fall and winter crop in zones 8, 9, 10. Light frost actually improves their flavor.
How to grow: Seeds can be sown indoors or in the garden in late spring. Transplant or thin so that plants are two feet apart in rows two-and-one-half to three feet apart. Brussels sprouts take about three months to mature, during which time these shallow-rooted plants need moist soil, which can be ensured by regular watering and growing the Brussels sprouts under a mulch. As heads begin to crowd, leave the top leaves but break off the lower leaves from the stem to make more room.
Diseases/pests: Same as broccoli.

Cabbage
Cabbage is the king of the brassica family, easy to grow, and comes in many sizes, shapes, colors, and textures. Where winters are cold, cabbage seedlings can be set out as soon as the ground is workable, and fall crops last until cold weather takes over again. With the help of plant protectors, such as a "tent" of clear plastic or hotkaps, cabbage can grow until winter weather. In zones 9 and 10, you can grow a winter crop from seeds sown in late fall and a spring crop from seeds planted in early winter.
How to grow: Early crops begin with seeds raised indoors or in a hot bed six to ten weeks before the final killing frost and set out early. Most seed companies offer several varieties with widely different time requirements to reach maturity. It is possible, therefore, to sow successive crops outdoors at the same time and expect new harvests every fortnight.

Like other brassicas, cabbage has a shallow root system and does best under mulch. It needs soil with a pH rating between 6.0 and 7.5 as well as containing a lot of organic matter.

Plant early cabbage one to one-and-one-half feet apart in rows two-and-one-half feet apart and varieties for midsummer and late harvest one-and-one-half to two feet apart in rows with two-and-one-half to three feet between them. Avoid planting cabbage where other brassicas have grown in the last year.

Fig. 73. Loading cars on a sidetrack with tomatoes. Texas.

Diseases/pests: Clubroot, a fungus that lasts for six or seven years in acid soil, is the worst enemy. To prevent, keep the soil pH to about 7, avoid setting out seedlings with swellings on the roots, and rotate crops in the brassica family. Black leaf spot disease can be contained with dustings by Captan, a safe, organic fungicide. Insect pests include cutworms, cabbage loopers (green caterpillars), aphids, and cabbage maggots. For more information, order "Control of Caterpillars on Cabbage and Other Cole Crops," Farmers' Bulletin number 2271, from the Superintendent of Documents, U.S. Government Printing Office, Washington, D.C. 20402.

Carrots
For home gardeners who also really love the flavor of vegetables, a crop of carrots, especially of the Nantes variety, promises gustatory pleasures that the usual run of woody-flavored store-bought carrots barely suggest. As long as they are not planted too early, carrots are good early crops in northern areas. They also make great late crops. They grow until the ground grows cold and can be stored right in the earth until winter weather takes over. They can be eaten at any stage of their development, but they are most delicious, tender, and sweet when small.
How to grow: Most varieties of carrot like well-drained, loose-textured soil, but the short kinds adapt to heavy soil. Long, thin varieties need deep topsoil (up to nine inches). In general, the topsoil should not be too acid—add lime if needed to obtain a pH of about 6.5 (this is best done in autumn).

Allow thawed ground to dry before sowing spring crops. If the soil is overly heavy or sticky, mix up equal parts peat moss and sand or just gather some compost and lay down a strip of the material to a depth of four inches. Then, rototill the soil supplement to a depth of one foot. Plant seeds a half-inch deep and thin to two-inch intervals. Rows should stand one-and-one-half feet apart. Covering the carrot bed with a mulch keeps away weeds and retains moisture, thereby improving the quality of the crop.

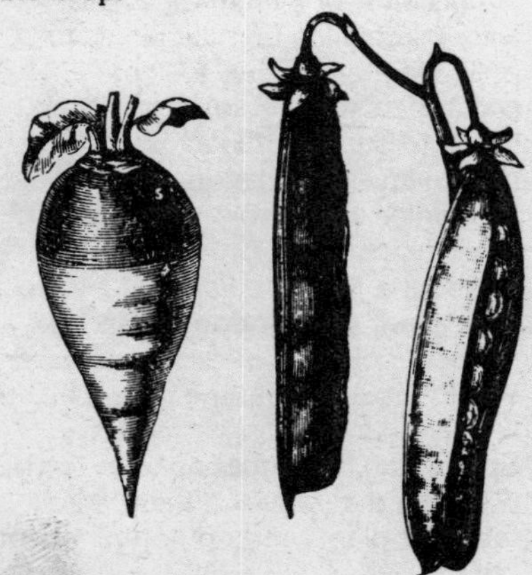

Diseases/pests: Damping-off fungus and cutworms get young plants. Older plants are sometimes prey to the larvae of the carrot rust fly, which looks like an ordinary fly but is more delicate and long-legged.

Cauliflower
Cauliflower is a hardy fall crop belonging to the brassica family. A few early varieties are also available. Purple Head cauliflower, which is hard to find in stores, is an interesting vegetable with a taste and appearance somewhere between regular cauliflower and its near relative, broccoli.
How to grow: Early varieties should be sown indoors five to seven weeks before the garden soil will be workable, at which time seedlings should be set out in the same rich, loamy soil that cabbages like. Fall crops can be planted between June and August. Most varieties take about 50 to 57 days to mature; Purple Head cauliflower takes about 85 days. In zones 9 and 10, cauliflower grows as a fall and winter crop because it needs cool soil. Cauliflower takes up a good deal of space: plants should be one-and-one-half to two feet apart in rows separated by at least two-and-one-half feet.

To keep cauliflower heads white, tie the leaves together when the heads begin to form.
Diseases/pests: Like other brassicas, cauliflower is vulnerable to disease and pests when planted where any member of its family have grown during the past year. Maggots may infest cauliflower heads.

Chard
The great thing about chard, or Swiss chard, is that it can endure all but the coldest weather yet last through a hot season without bolting. A highly productive vegetable in the beet family, it can be sown only once and continue to provide nutritious, tender greens all season.
How to grow: As soon as the earth is workable in spring, sow chard seeds in rows about one-and-one-half feet apart. Thin sprouts to six-inch intervals (the thinned tops are highly edible), and wherever two plants begin to compete, pull the weaker one. Allow two months until plants reach maturity. To keep production up, *cut* (do not pull) the outer leaves. Mulch thickly to retain soil moisture. When chard plants loose their flavor or stop growing, the surrounding soil may need a dusting of dried bloodmeal or cottonseed meal to restore nitrogen to the soil.

Well-protected, chard can often winter over if the winter is not too severe. Second-year crops will flower, though, which ruins the plants as table vegetables. To maintain food production, cut off flowering heads as they appear.
Diseases/pests: Leafminers.

PLANTING GUIDE FOR BEANS AND PEAS

Type	Pounds of seed per 50-ft row	Depth of planting, inches	Spacing between rows, inches	Spacing in rows, inches		Days to harvest
				Seeds	Plants	
Snap beans, bush	¼–½	1–1½	18–30	1–2	2–4	50–60
Snap beans, pole	¼–½	1–1½	24–48	3–6	4–8	60–70
Lima beans, bush	¼–½	1–1½	18–30	2–4	4–8	65–75
Lima beans, pole	¼–½	1–1½	36	3–6	6–8	70–90
Peas, garden	¼	1–2	6 (double rows) 36–48	1–1½	1–1½	55–70
Peas, southern	¼–½	1–1½	30–54	2–4	2–4	55–80

Chinese Cabbage
One need not be a connoisseur of Oriental cooking to appreciate a home-grown crop of this delicate-tasting yet satisfying vegetable. Chinese cabbage can be eaten raw in salads, steamed or stir-fried as a side dish, or substituted for ordinary cabbage in cole slaw. It makes an interesting late-season crop in northern climates and a good winter crop in the South.
How to grow: Chinese cabbage grows in well-drained soil. For a spring harvest, obtain seeds of an early variety especially developed to resist bolting (going to seed). Set out preraised seedlings as soon as the ground can be worked or sow seeds directly in rich, well-drained, yet moist, soil after the last frost. Thin to 18-inch intervals in rows two-and-one-half feet apart. Plants for a fall harvest, which have a better chance of making it, can be sown about three months before the first expected killing frost.
Diseases/pests: Same as broccoli; also fleabeetles and leaf hoppers.

Corn
Freshly picked corn is one of the finest foods in the world. It is also one of the rarest—available only to farmers, gardeners, and their friends and neighbors. Corn that is a day or two old loses the sweetness and special flavor and the kernals become tough, transforming into the truly inferior version of corn that markets pass off as fresh.
How to grow: With few exceptions, most corn varieties like good warm soil. All should be sown after danger of frost is past. Seeds treated with Captan, a mild organic fungicide, are the most reliable. (You can treat seeds yourself by shaking seeds in a glass jar to which Captan has been added.)

The numerous varieties of corn have growth periods ranging from just under 70 days for early types to over 90 days for some of the late-summer and fall corn. By planning ahead, therefore, you can have high-quality corn throughout most of the growing season by planting several varieties at the same time and re-planting early-harvest rows with midseason corn for fall harvest.

Corn takes up a good deal of space. To facilitate pollination, plant corn in blocks of at least four side-by-side-rows for each variety. The rows should be two-and-one-half to three feet apart, with seeds spaced four to six inches. Early corn should be thinned to ten- and twelve-inch intervals and later corn to fifteen and eighteen inches.

Cornstalks make good beanstalks. Plant pole beans next to two-foot-high corn plants, which the beans will climb when they send out shoots. Beans repay their companions by adding nitrogen to the soil.

When replanting a row where corn has grown, enrich the soil by digging or rototilling in about eight or nine inches of compost and applying a 5-10-10 fertilizer, chemical or organic.
Diseases/pests: The corn borer and corn earworm are serious pests. Corn also attracts raccoons and crows. The latter can be discouraged by covering corn ears with plastic bags.

Cucumbers
Cucumbers are a vine fruit that grow along the ground as well as up a trellis or fence. Garden-grown cucumbers put mass-marketed kinds to shame. They have a more distinct taste and skins that are hardly bitter at all. The only drawback to the presence of cucumbers in a vegetable garden is their natural vulnerability to lots of diseases and pests. To increase chances of a healthy crop, plant disease-resistant hybrids.
How to grow: Most packages of the seeds you can buy contain gynoecious, or all-female, plants, with a sprinkling of male plants to pollinate them. Other all-female cucumbers require no nearby male plants to bear and, to avoid detrimental cross-pollination, they should be planted away from male plants of other types.

About a month before the last frost date, plant seeds indoors in individual peat pots. About two weeks *after* the last frost, set out the young plants in well-drained, composted soil. Space plants one foot apart in rows with four feet between them. Mark the male plants and do not thin them out.

Cucumbers are sensitive to cold and young plants may need extra protection during cold springs—i.e., little clear plastic "tents" or Hotkaps to keep them warm. With a well-developed, yet smaller, root system that requires constantly moist soil, cucumbers grow best under mulch.
Diseases/pests: Scab and cucumber mosaic are apt to be troublesome in cool weather, but several types of cucumber are bred to resist these problems. The striped cucumber beetle transmits bacterial wild and other diseases. Other problems include downy and powdery mildew, aphids, and anthronose.

Garlic
Garlic is a good friend to cook and gardener, and especially to cook-gardeners who count on healthy vegetables from a kitchen garden. Why? Because, planted at random among vegetables, garlic repells all manner of insects and does much to increase overall yield. For gardeners who avoid garlic in their food lest they repell other people, there is now a milder form with a pleasing aroma called Elephant garlic. Not sold in stores, this unusual French import is characterized by huge four- or five-ounce cloves that produce five-clove garlics when planted.
How to grow: When the soil is warm, plant cloves with the tip up about two inches under the surface. Garlic bulbs ordered from seed companies or bought at the garden center may be fresher than store-bought bulbs, but the kind you have in your kitchen usually do okay. Like other members of the onion family, garlic sends up green stems. When these cease to stand up tall, you can dig up the new bulb. If you leave garlic bulbs in mulch-covered ground over the winter and do not disturb them during spring cultivation, they will continue to grow larger during the second year.
Diseases/pests: None.

Kale
An excellent alternative to spinach, kale can be harvested in spring and again in fall—and winter, too, as far north as northern Maryland and where similarly mild winter conditions prevail. It may also continue into a second year if protected from cold with a good mulch.
How to grow: Sow the spring crop in rich loamy soil as soon as the garden can be worked. Plant seeds every couple of inches in rows two feet apart and thin bit by bit to allow mature plants breathing space of about two feet on all sides. Kale takes about two months to mature and can be planted for a harvest that is timed for after the first snow is expected. To harvest kale, cut off the larger leaves while the plant is young or cut the entire plant. Old kale is not very palatable.
Diseases/pests: Same as other brassicas.

Lettuce
Lettuce is a cool-weather vegetable, traditionally sown in early spring and late summer in the North. In the South, it is grown during late autumn, winter, and spring, although in colder parts of the South lettuce may not survive the winter. When hot weather comes, most lettuce types bolt to seed. Practically speaking, that means that succulent lettuce heads rapidly transform into small-leaved stalks no longer worth eating. Recently, scientists have developed head and bibb lettuce that tolerate midsummer heat, making it possible to enjoy home-grown lettuce in the same salad with home-grown tomatoes.

How to grow: Begin lettuce seeds indoors in flats about four weeks before you expect your garden soil to be workable, or when the soil reaches 52°F. Sow seeds directly in the soil, which should be prepared in advance with the addition of a couple of inches of compost or moistened peat moss. Space looseleaf transplants five inches apart, cos and Boston lettuce eight to ten inches, and head lettuce twelve inches. Thin so that leaves touch but do not overlap. For plantings destined to last into warm weather (over 70°F), sow a lot of seeds so that you will have a certain proportion that does not bolt.

Fall plantings begin in late August in northern areas and commensurately later to the south. Now, seeds can be sown directly in the ground. Little plants are likely to want some shade during the hottest part of the day, especially when the weather is extra warm.

A straw or peat moss mulch in the lettuce bed keeps soil moist and prevents leaves from becoming mud-spattered from watering.

Diseases/pests: Slugs and snails in some gardens, the local rabbit population in others.

Onions

If your garden is short on space, onions are not likely to fit into the overall garden plan. Yet, if you have ample room after accommodating "important" vegetables, they are easy to grow and many varieties can be stored and enjoyed for a long time after harvest. Also, if you care about eating organic onions, which are a staple of vegetarian cooking, you can produce your own under conditions you can control. Gardeners who are attracted to unusual plants may want to try the odd-looking but yummy Egyptian onions that are now available through seed companies.

How to grow: Gardeners sow onions in two forms, seeds and sets. Seeds come in regular packages and can be planted indoors in flats in midwinter if you have the patience to wait until midspring (when seedlings are at least five inches tall) to transplant them. These young plants can be placed in well-drained soil at three-inch intervals as well as in bunches (bunched seedlings produce scallions). Full-size onions need six inches of growing space, so as the season progresses, the delicious little green onions should be thinned to make room for big ones. Depending on the variety, onions from seed take about 100 to 140 days to mature from the date seedlings are set out.

Onion sets are tiny, closely planted seedlings that a grower or seed company has grown from seed and kept over the cold months. Sets become available when winter weather starts to moderate. When you receive your order, open the package immediately and spread out the sets in a cool, dry place until you can plant them. Sets do well if put in one-inch-deep furrows spaced at one-inch intervals for green onions and two to three inches for mature bulbs. You can enjoy both kinds of onions by doing a close planting and systematically thinning every other onion. Sets become mature in about 85 days after planting.

How does one tell when an onion bulb is ready for harvest if it's underground? when the green tops yellow and fall over, the time has come. When tops dry out entirely, dig the bulbs up and spread them out to dry for two to three weeks before storage.

Diseases/pests: Onion maggots and onion thrips can plague all types of onions. Downy mildew and blast, both fungus diseases, can be curbed with the application of Captan.

SPACING DISTANCES, PLANTING DEPTHS FOR CUCURBIT CROPS
Measurements are in Inches

Crop	Spacing Between plants in row	Spacing Between rows	Planting Depth
Cucumber	12[1] 24–36[2]	48–72	1
Muskmelon	12[1] 24–36[2]	60–84	1–1½
Pumpkin	36–40	72–96	2–3
Squash (bush)	24–30	36	2–3
Squash (vining)	36–40	72–96	2–3
Gourd	36–40	72–96	2–3
Watermelon	24–36[1] 72[2]	72–84	1–2

[1] Single plants.
[2] Hills.

Peas

Like freshly picked corn, peas taste best when brought from the garden right to the table. Also like corn, peas come in numerous varieties that take different periods to reach maturity. By planting several kinds together, you can have a steady supply of peas over a fairly long period. If you have space for peas, include a row of edible-podded peas, which are delicious raw in salads. They also make a fine winter crop in southern gardens (zones 9 and 10).

How to grow: Most peas like cool weather and can go in the ground as soon as the soil is workable. In hot climates, peas grow best during fall, winter, and early spring. In areas where summers are extremely hot, they do well only in spring and autumn. Because they are nitrogen fixers, they do not appreciate too much organic content or fertilizers with a high nitrogen content. For the same reason, peas do not do their best in soil where beans grew the previous year.

Pea seeds are smooth and wrinkled, the latter producing a sweeter-tasting harvest.

An awareness of your soil's pH rating is essential when you are growing peas, which react poorly to overacid soil. An adequate pH range is between 5.5 and 6.7

Select a seed bed for peas that is level and well drained. Never plant them in the same location in succession. Sow pea seeds in a flat-bottomed, three-inch-deep furrow at two-inch intervals. Leave two-and-one-half feet between rows, and, if possible, give tall-growing peas something to cimb, such as a trellis, chicken wire stretched between poles, or Burpee's wire "pea fence" (which folds up for storage at the end of the season). Of the edible-podded peas, Early Snap needs no staking, while Sugar Snap pea vines ascend five or six feet and require string or a trellis to climb. Put supports in place when the pea plants are about twelve inches tall.

Extend your pea harvest by sowing succession crops every ten days for a month. Keep the soil moist with sufficient watering and a mulch. When the vines are about three inches tall, make little mounds of earth around each one to support them until they reach the support fence. When they are about a foot high, tie the vines to the wire with soft twine.

Harvest peas from the bottom of the vine first. Ordinary peas yield maximum food value if picked when seeds are full size. Edible-podded peas (Sugar Snap peas, snow peas) should be harvested before the peas develop fully.

Diseases/pests: Aphids, powdery mildew.

Peppers

Despite their unique appearance, peppers belong to the nightshade family along with eggplant, potatoes, tomatoes, and tobacco. This group has in common star-shaped flowers and a fondness for long, hot summers. Peppers should not be grown near their relatives, nor should they grow where fellow nightshades grew the year before. Like tomatoes and eggplant, pepper plants are preraised indoors or in hotbeds.

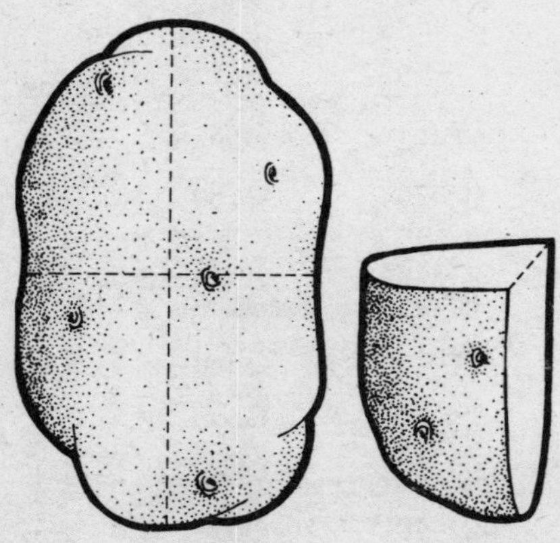

Potatoes are grown from "seed pieces" or "seed eyes" that are a quarter cut of the potato and include a couple of "eyes."

How to grow: Sow seeds in individual containers and keep in a warm, bright place or under artificial lights. The tricky part of growing peppers comes when making the transition outdoors, and gardeners who lack the necessary combination of confidence, self-discipline, and experience (or luck) ought to start with preraised plants from the garden center. Pepper plants go into the ground when the soil is warm. Space them 18 to 24 inches apart in composted soil and leave two or three feet between rows. If the weather gets chilly, keep young peppers warm with plastic "tents" ot Hotkaps.

There are two kinds of peppers: sweet and hot. Green peppers of either group are simply less mature than red ones. Red peppers are richer in vitamins A and C. Peppers can be cut from the plant at any time. Mature sweet peppers take about 60 to 78 days; hot peppers need about 65 to 77 days.

Diseases/pests: Cutworms threaten seedlings, which should be protected when transplanted with rings of paper cups of waxed-cardboard. Peppers also attract aphids and whiteflies.

Potatoes

In 1982, the first "true" potato seeds became available to American gardeners. Until that year, potatoes had been grown from "seed pieces," slices of mature potatoes containing a so-called eye. The new, aptly dubbed Explorer potato is a light russet potato that can be harvested as a small potato or when mature. Seeds can be ordered from seed companies.

Whether to grow potatoes depends on how much space you have. Because the tubers spread out laterally, they are usually not for small plots, but sometimes early-crop potatoes (which are the most delicious!) can fit in a fairly small garden by alternating rows of potatoes with vine crops like cucumbers, melons, and squash. Once the early potatoes are harvested, the vine crops are free to spread and produce their fruit.

How to grow: Explorer potatoes: Much like peppers and tomatoes, explorer potatoes can be sown indoors four to six weeks before the last expected frost date, which is planting time. Start seeds in individual Jiffy-7 peat pots or spread the seeds over a premoistened soil mixture containing organic matter as well as sand to enhance drainage. Cover the seed with a light sprinkling of vermiculite or soil. The highest rate of seed germination can be expected in a location where the temperature remains between 64 and 72°F. Until roots have developed, water seeds gently (with a plant mister). Grow seedlings in a southern exposure or under artificial lights. Move them to individual pots when they are a half-inch tall.

After the last frost, in a spot away from peppers, tomatoes, and eggplant, dig a flat-bottomed furrow ten inches wide and six to eight inches deep, depending on the size of your seedlings. Pile the soil along one side of the trench. Plant three seedlings together in the middle of the trench, leaving a 12- to 18-inch space between each group or hill. Each hill will make a single plant that should yield two to three pounds of potatoes. Cover the plants with soil but let three or four inches of the topmost leaves stick out above the ground. Draw soil up around the bottom of each potato vine as it grows to create "hills" or mounds. Should you run out of earth for the hilling, continue with a mulch of leaves, half-decayed compost, or straw (good aeration is important) until the mound is about eight inches high. New potatoes can be harvested 90 days after the transplant date; mature potatoes are ready at 120 days.

Water potatoes thoroughly each week as needed, to keep soil moist. Dry periods alternating with wet periods can cause abnormalities.

From seed potatoes: Eyes from supermarket potatoes are treated with a chemical to prevent sprouting. Instead of using these poor prospects in your garden, order a bag of "certified" (by the USDA) seed potatoes from a seed house. This stock is developed for its heavy yield and blight and disease resistance. Plant the potatoes deep enough in moist soil so the new tubers develop sufficiently to prevent their contact with sunlight (some gardeners grow potatoes under black plastic mulch).

Diseases/pests: Potatoes are vulnerable to foliage diseases such as blight, scab, and verticulum. Troublesome insects include soil pests like white grubs, wireworms, and cutworms; leaf-feeders like the Colorado potato beetle; and leaf-suckers like leaf hoppers and aphids. Intercropping potatoes with garlic repells many insects. Crop rotation of disease-resistant seed potatoes also keeps the rate of disease low.

Seed companies with several varieties of seed potatoes:

Farmer Seed & Nursery
818 N.W. 4th St.
Faribault, MN 55021

Henry Field Seed & Nursery Co.
Dept. 87, Box 277
Shenandoah, IA 51602

Gurney Seed & Nursery Co.
Yankton, SD 57079

L. L. Olds Seed Co.
Box 7790
Madison, WI 53707

Earl May Seed & Nursery Co.
205 Elm St.
Shenandoah, IA 51603

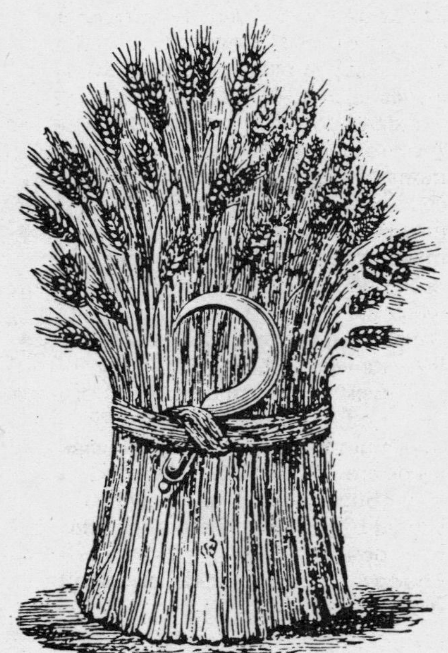

Radishes

Radishes come as close as a vegetable can come to being failure-proof. They like decent, well-drained soil but will develop anyway under most conditions. A cool-weather crop with a growth period of only three or four weeks (except for special hybrids), radishes are often the first harvest of the season. When they are ready, though, they must be harvested quickly. In the North, radishes are spring and fall crops; in the South, they are grown from fall through spring.

How to grow: In the North, plant radishes as soon as the soil can be worked and continue plantings at ten-day intervals until a month before hot weather is expected. Fall crops can be sown a month before the first frost date. In zones 9 and 10, radishes grow from autumn through spring. Gardeners sprinkle a few radish seeds along rows of slow-growing crops like beets, carrots, and parsley to serve as markers.

Scientists have developed new hybrids that extend the growing season and also add new meaning to the word "radish." Seed companies now offer all-season types, including a long white Oriental variety, and late-harvest radishes that need cool to cold weather to cap off their growing season.

Diseases/pests: Cabbageworms, flea beetles, root maggots.

Shallots

The shallot is a tiny onion. Traditionally an indispensable ingredient in French cooking, little by little the delicately flavored shallot is becoming popular with Americans who stray from straight-and-narrow meat-and-potato fare. Seed companies offer both sets and bulbs for planting.

How to grow: Shallots like the same growing conditions as other onions. They are perennials that can safely winter over in the garden. Best results are obtained by taking up the clusters of bulbs at the end of the growing season and replanting the smallest bulbs.

Diseases/pests: Same as onions.

Spinach

Spinach s a cool-weather crop that dislikes the combination of long days and daytime temperatures over 70°F. Where winters are cold, spinach grows in spring and early fall, and in mild climates it grows from autumn through early spring. During summer, substitute Malabar spinach and/or New Zealand spinach, hot-weather vegetables that, along with Swiss chard, pinch-hit for real spinach in salads and other dishes.

How to grow: Sow spinach in early spring in pH neutral soil (6.5). Plant a seed every half-inch in rows spaced one-and-one-half to two feet apart and thin the young plants to six-inch intervals. Taking into consideration the length of the growing season (40 to 50 days), time succession plantings to finish before hot weather. For the final spring planting, select an extra-long-standing variety; for autumn plantings in cold climates, choose a hardy type and protect the spinach bed with a hay and straw mulch into winter. Properly cared for, spinach can endure frost and even snow.

ROOT CROP CHARACTERISTICS

	Optimum monthly average growing temperature (Fahrenheit)		Optimum soil temperatures range for germination (Fahrenheit)	Frost tolerance	Spacing suggested in inches		Days to maturity	Time and frequency of planting	Harvest duration for each planting
	Min.	*Max.*			*In row*	*Between rows*			
Beets	40°	65°	50°–85°	Moderate	2–4	16–24	55–80	Early spring and early summer	2–3 months
Celeriac	45°	70°	60°–70°	Good	4–6	23–30	100–110 (56–84 for transplants)	Early spring only	3–6 weeks
Carrots	45°	70°	45°–85°	Moderate	1–3	16–24	60–85	Early spring and early summer	2–4 months
Parsnips	40°	75°	50°–70°	Good	3–6	18–30	100–130	Early spring only	3–4 months
Salsify	45°	85°	50°–90°	Good	2–4	18–30	150–155	Early spring only	1–2 months
Radishes (spring)	40°	75°	45°–90°	Good	½–1	9–18	25–30	Early spring and weekly	1 week
(winter)	40°	75°	45°–90°	Good	½–1	9–18	52–56	Early fall	3–5 weeks
Turnips	40°	75°	60°–95°	Good	2–6	12–30	45–75	Early spring and late summer	2–3 weeks
Rutabagas	40°	75°	50°–90°	Good	5–8	18–36	90–95	Early spring and midsummer	1–2 months

New Zealand spinach: To get an early start, a month before the last frost date, even before the early spinach is sown, New Zealand spinach seeds can be planted in individual peat pots. The seed germinates slowly and should be soaked in water for 24 hours prior to planting to speed things up. With about a week to go before the last frost, remove whatever mulch you've spread on the garden and let the soil warm up for a few days before transplanting seedlings. Leave two feet between seedlings—New Zealand spinach is a large, spreading plant. If you don't want to bother with indoor seedlings, sow the seed directly in the garden after the last frost. In about 70 days, harvest the tender tips of the branches. To keep production up, continue cutting back the plant when tips become the same approximate size as spinach leaves.

Malabar spinach: On a plate, Malabar spinach looks and tastes like a smooth spinach; in the garden it looks like a vine, or should, because it is a climbing vegetable that does best growing up a fence or trellis. This heat-resistant vegetable takes about 10 weeks to mature and can be sown directly in garden soil after the last frost.

Diseases/pests: Spinach crops should have a two-year break before occupying the same bed to control mildew. Insect pests include leaf miners and aphids.

Squash

All varieties of squash, along with melons, pumpkins, and gourds, are called cucurbit crops. Except for some bush-type squash, cucurbits grow on vines. Although tropical and semitropical in origin, this plant family adapts well to a wide range of climates and soil conditions, making them staples in vegetable gardens in the north temperate zone. Some baking squash, pumpkins, and gourds actually improve in quality if the harvest is delayed until after the vines have stopped growing or have been killed by frost.

How to grow: Squash comes in two classes: summer and winter. Both kinds grow well in well-drained, aerated, and composted soil. The best way to supply their roots with the constant moisture they need is to grow squash under a thick mulch. Because moisture on the leaves encourages several foliar diseases, sprinkler irrigation is the least desirable way to water cucurbits. Another way to prevent the spread of disease in the garden is to clear away dead squash (and other) vines right away.

Summer squash: This highly productive group includes zucchini and yellow squash as well as the round, flattened Patty Pan type squash, all of which grow on bushes. Achieving success with these plants is not hard and they are ready for picking within 50 to 54 days.

After the last frost, sow six seeds two to three inches apart in a "hill," or group, to be thinned to the strongest two or three plants. Or plant seeds at six-inch intervals in rows spaced three feet apart. After seedlings appear, thin row crops to 18 inches. The long squash taste best when picked young and relatively small in size. A regular harvest keeps production up. Time successive plantings to be certain you have squash until the first frost.

Winter squash: Like summer squash, Hubbard and Butternut varieties can be picked young. Winter squash, or baking squash, is normally harvested when mature. The fruit is mature when the skin is hard and resists scratching with your thumbnail.

Sow winter squash after the last killing frost. Plant six seeds two to three inches apart in "hills" spaced at three-foot intervals for bush types and six to eight feet apart for vine types. Thin hills to the healthiest three or four plants. The growing season for winter squash ranges from about 60 days for Burpee's new Jersey Golden Acorn, an acorn squash harvested young, to over 100 days for Hubbard and Vegetable Spaghetti squash. Stored in a dry, moderately warm place, some winter squash keep until midwinter.

Diseases/pests: Squash borers and cucumber beetles spread bacterial wild. Other troubles include aphids, downy mildew and powdery mildew, squash mosaic, nematodes. Garden sanitation and fall tillage keeps down many problems. You can trap bugs by placing a shingle or board at the base of plants. At night, insects will gather underneath the flat hiding places and can be destroyed the following morning.

PLANTING CHART FOR VEGETABLES

Crop	Depth to plant (inches)	Planting distances: Between rows (inches)	Planting distances: In the row (inches)
Cool Season Crops			
Asparagus (crowns)	6–8	36–60	12–18
Beets	¼–½	15–24	2–3
Broccoli	¼–½	24–36	12–18
Brussels sprouts	¼–½	24–36	18–24
Cabbage	¼–½	24–36	12–18
Cabbage, Chinese	¼–½	18–30	8–12
Carrots	¼–½	15–30	2–3
Cauliflower	¼–½	24–36	18–24
Celery	⅛	18–36	4–6
Chard, Swiss	¼–½	18–36	6–8
Chives	½	15–24	6–8
Collards	¼–½	24–36	18–24
Cress, upland	¼–½	15–30	2–3
Endive	¼–½	18–36	12
Garlic (cloves)	1½	18–24	3
Kale	¼–½	18–36	8–12
Kohlrabi	¼–½	18–36	4–6
Leeks	½	12–30	2–3
Lettuce, heading	¼	18–30	12
Lettuce, leaf	¼	12–18	4–6
Mustard	¼–½	18–24	3–4
Onions, plants		15–24	3–4
Onions, seed	½	15–24	3–4
Onions, sets	1–2	15–24	3–4
Parsley	¼	15–24	6–8
Parsnips	½	18–30	3–4
Peas	1–2	8–24	1
Potatoes	4	30–36	12
Radishes	½	12–24	1
Rhubarb, crowns		36–48	36–48
Rutabagas	¼–½	18–30	3–4
Spinach	½	12–24	2–4
Turnips	¼–½	18–30	2–3
Warm Season Crops			
Beans, lima	1–1½	24–36	3–4
Beans, snap	1–1½	24–36	1–2
Cantaloupes	1	48–72	24–30
Cucumbers	1	48–60	12–18
Eggplant	¼	30–42	18–24
Okra	1	36–48	12–18
Peas, southern	1	24–36	4
Peppers	¼	30–42	18–24
Pumpkins	1	60–96	36–48
Spinach, New Zealand	½–1	30–42	15–18
Squash, summer	1–1½	48–60	18–24
Squash, winter	1–1½	60–96	36–48
Sweet corn	1–2	30–36	10–12
Sweet potatoes		30–36	12–15
Tomatoes	¼	36–60	18–24
Watermelons	1–1½	60–96	36–60

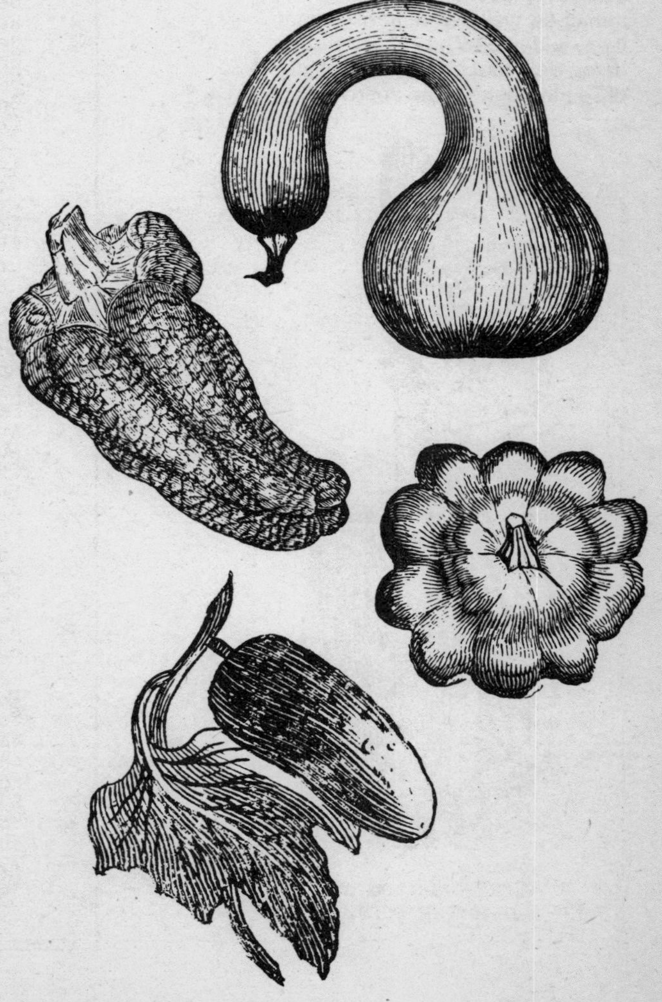

Tomatoes

Everybody wants to grow tomatoes, and there are a bewildering variety from which to choose. When seed catalogs arrive or when you go to the nursery to buy seedlings, look for varieties possessing resistance to as many of the commonly occurring diseases as possible as well as resistance to growth cracks and bursting caused by alternating dry and wet weather. For best results, the tomatoes you select should also be adapted to your local environment and soil, produce a good flower, and have a high nutritional value.

Plant *indeterminate* types if you want tomato plants that set fruit over a long period and *determinate* types if you want plants with fruit that ripen all at once. About a fourth of the tomato varieties on the market are determinate bushy plants. These have smaller fruit, such as the cherry tomato, and their flavor is thinner than that of most indeterminate tomatoes. They are popular, however, because they bear about two-and-one-half months after being set out.

How to grow: A beautiful tomato starts with good soil. Lots of organic matter is important both to nourish the crop and to keep down a buildup of disease organisms and nematodes. This can be provided by growing a cover crop over the winter and spading it into the soil well in advance of planting time. Clay topsoils in northern areas improve when two inches of compost or two inches of damp peat moss is worked into the upper six inches of the garden and covered with a thick mulch throughout the cold months. Gardens in dry climates should also be tilled in fall and left rough so the ground will absorb and retain moisture that falls during winter.

If you did not prepare the soil in autumn, there is still time to create the right conditions for tomato plants. In the section of your vegetable plot that you expect to devote to tomatoes, well before transplanting time, add two inches of compost or damp peat moss to the top six inches of soil throughout the entire bed.

Crude method of mashing corn.

Then, count the number of seedlings for transplanting and, allowing 18 inches on all sides for staked tomatoes and three feet for unstaked, sprawling plants, put a stake or marker to designate their eventual locations. Next to each marker, dig a six-inch-deep hole and line it with compost or damp peat moss mixed with one of the tomato-growing formula fertilizers. Fill the holes up again and water the soil thoroughly 24 hours before transplanting.

Planting: Tomatoes can be set out when the soil warms to about 50°F. For gardens in the North, where the growing season is short, this means that tomato seeds start indoors five to seven weeks before the last frost date. To raise as many seedlings as possible, transplant them into individual peat pots when the second set of leaves appear. Bury the stem a little deeper in the new soil than it stood before, and hold seedlings by the leaves because even gentle handling can damage the stem.

If seedlings in a plant store or supermarket catch your fancy, before transplanting time, repot them right away in individual containers to give their roots room to spread out.

Tomatoes are sensitive to cold, but they also do not care much for the hot, dry weather of southern midsummers. For this reason, fruit does not set well when daytime temperatures rise about 90°F or nighttime temperatures stay above 70°F. If you live in the South, grow tomato varieties developed for your region. In the extreme South, where summers are extra sultry, grow tomatoes as a winter crop.

Sowing seeds: Where the growing season is long, tomatoes can be planted directly into garden soil. Sow the seeds in rows four to five feet apart. Keep the soil moist until seeds germinate. Begin to thin seedlings to one every one-and-one-half to three feet when the young plants have three leaves.

Care: 1. *Watering* Tomatoes need about an inch of rainfall per week or extra watering courtesy of the gardener. Plants should be watered *thoroughly* once a week and more often if the soil is sandy or during very hot weather. (Water must reach the tomato plants' deep, extensive root systems.) A deep grass mulch

VEGETABLE PLANTING

Vegetables	Plants or seed per 100 feet	Spacing (Inches) Rows	Spacing (Inches) Plants	Number days ready for use
Asparagus	66 plants or 1 oz.	36–48	18	(2 years)
Beans, snap bush	½ lb.	24–36	3–4	45–60
Beans, snap pole	½ lb.	36–48	4–6	60–70
Beans, Lima bush	½ lb.	30–36	3–4	65–80
Beans, Lima pole	¼ lb.	36–48	12–18	75–85
Beets	1 oz.	15–24	2	50–60
Broccoli	*40-50 pl. or ¼ oz.	24–36	14–24	60–80
Brussels sprouts	*50–60 pl. or ¼ oz.	24–36	14–24	90–100
Cabbage	*50–60 pl. or ¼ oz.	24–36	14–24	60–90
Cabbage, Chinese	*60–70 pl. or ¼ oz.	18–30	8–12	65–70
Carrots	½ oz.	15–24	2	70–80
Cauliflower	*50–60 pl. or ¼ oz.	24–36	14–24	70–90
Celeriac	200 pl.	18–24	4–8	120
Celery	200 pl.	30–36		125
Chard, Swiss	2 oz.	18–30	6	45–55
Collards and kale	¼ oz.	18–36	8–16	50–80
Corn, sweet	3–4 oz.	24–36	12–18	70–90
Cucumbers	½ oz.	48–72	24–48	50–70
Eggplant	⅛ oz.	24–36	18–24	80–90
Garlic (cloves)	1 lb.	15–24	2–4	140–150
Kohlrabi	½ oz.	15–24	4–6	55–75
Lettuce, head	¼ oz.	18–24	6–10	70–75
Lettuce, leaf	¼ oz.	15–18	2–3	40–50
Muskmelon (cantaloupe)	*50 pl. or ½ oz.	60–96	24–36	85–100
Mustard	¼ oz.	15–24	6–12	30–40
Okra	2 oz.	36–42	12–24	55–65
Onions	400–600 plants or sets	15–24	3–4	80–120
Onions (seed)	1 oz.	15–24	3–4	90–120
Parsley	¼ oz.	15–24	6–8	70–90
Parsnips	½ oz.	18–30	3–4	120–170
Peas, English	1 lb.	18–36	1	55–90
Peas, southern	½ lb.	24–36	4–6	60–70
Peppers	⅛ oz.	24–36	18–24	60–90
Potatoes, Irish	6–10 lb. of seed tubers	30–36	10–15	75–100
Potatoes, sweet	75–100 pl.	36–48	12–16	100–130
Pumpkins	½ oz.	60–96	36–48	75–100
Radishes	1 oz.	14–24	1	25–40
Salsify	½ oz.	15–18	3–4	150
Soybeans	1 lb.	24–30	2	120
Spinach	1 oz.	14–24	3–4	40–60
Squash, summer	1 oz.	36–60	18–36	50–60
Squash, winter	½ oz.	60–96	24–48	85–100
Tomatoes	50 pl. or ⅛ oz.	24–48	18–36	70–90
Turnip greens	½ oz.	14–24	2–3	30
Turnip, roots	½ oz.	14–24	2–3	30–60
Watermelon	1 oz.	72–96	36–72	80–100

*Transplants

VEGETABLE YIELDS

Vegetables	Average crop expected per 100 feet	Approximate planting per person: Fresh	Approximate planting per person: Storage, canning or freezing
Asparagus	30 lb.	10–15 plants	10–15 plants
Beans, snap bush	120 lb.	15–16 feet	10–15 feet
Beans, snap pole	150 lb.	5–6 feet	8–10 feet
Beans, Lima bush	25 lb. shelled	10–15 feet	15–20 feet
Beans, Lima pole	50 lb. shelled	5–6 feet	8–10 feet
Beets	150 lb.	5–10 feet	10–20 feet
Broccoli	100 lb.	3–5 plants	5–6 plants
Brussels sprouts	75 lb.	2–5 plants	5–8 plants
Cabbage	150 lb.	3–4 plants	5–10 plants
Cabbage, Chinese	80 heads	3–10 feet	——
Carrots	100 lb.	5–10 feet	10–15 feet
Cauliflower	100 lb.	3–5 plants	8–12 plants
Celeriac	60 lb.	5 feet	5 feet
Celery	180 stalks	10 stalks	——
Chard, Swiss	75 lb.	3–5 plants	8–12 plants
Collards and kale	100 lb.	5–10 feet	5–10 feet
Corn, sweet	10 dozen	10–15 feet	30–50 feet
Cucumbers	120 lb.	1–2 hills	3–5 hills
Eggplant	100 lb.	2–3 plants	2–3 plants
Garlic	40 lb.	——	1–5 feet
Kohlrabi	75 lb.	3–5 feet	5–10 feet
Lettuce, head	100 heads	10 feet	——
Lettuce, leaf	50 lb.	10 feet	——
Muskmelon (cantaloupe)	100 fruits	3–5 hills	——
Mustard	100 lb.	5–10 feet	10–15 feet
Okra	100 lb.	4–6 feet	6–10 feet
Onions (plants or sets)	100 lb.	3–5 feet	30–50 feet
Onions (seed)	100 lb.	3–5 feet	30–50 feet
Parsley	30 lb.	1–3 feet	1–3 feet
Parsnips	100 lb.	10 feet	10 feet
Peas, English	20 lb.	15–20 feet	40–60 feet
Peas, southern	40 lb.	10–15 feet	20–50 feet
Peppers	60 lb.	3–5 plants	3–5 plants
Potatoes, Irish	100 lb.	50–100 feet	——
Potatoes, sweet	100 lb.	5–10 plants	10–20 plants
Pumpkins	100 lb.	1–2 hills	1–2 hills
Radishes	100 bunches	3–5 feet	——
Salsify	100 lb.	5 feet	5 feet
Soybeans	20 lb.	50 feet	50 feet
Spinach	40–50 lb.	5–10 feet	10–15 feet
Squash, summer	150 lb.	2–3 hills	2–3 hills
Squash, winter	100 lb.	1–3 hills	1–3 hills
Tomatoes	100 lb.	3–5 plants	5–10 plants
Turnip greens	50–100 lb.	5–10 feet	——
Turnip, roots	50–100 lb.	5–10 feet	5–10 feet
Watermelon	40 fruits	2–4 hills	——

around the plants controls weeds and conserves moisture. An occasional watering with manure tea will supply the tomato plot with nitrogen.

2. Staking If you have lots of space, you may want to consider the advantages of unstaked tomato plants:

—less work
—less blossom-end rot
—twice as much per-plant fruit production
—less sunscald and splitting

When space is limited and you have time to prune, staking individual plants or growing them within tomato cages keeps fruit clean and enables fruit to mature about a week earlier because plants receive more sunlight. In addition, even though sprawling plants are individually more productive, staked plants can be spaced more closely together, enabling the gardener to grow more plants in equivalent space and thereby increase overall production.

If you cannot decide whether you prefer staked to sprawling tomatoes, experiment with both methods to see which works better. The late-season varieties, which grow very tall, are good candidates for staking.

Put stakes in place soon after transplanting (before you actually need them) so as not to disturb the roots. Use wooden stakes eight feet long and one-and-one-half inches wide. Push them two feet into the soil. Tie plants to the stakes with soft twine, strips of nylon stocking or cloth, or plant ties.

3. Pruning The purpose of pruning is to keep staked plants from sprawling, to keep tomatoes off the ground while encouraging larger and quicker ripening fruit. It is accomplished by removing the small shoots (called "suckers") that appear at the point where the leaf stem joins the main stem. Grasp the sucker between thumb and forefinger and bend it to one side until it snaps; then pull it off in the opposite direction.

4. Troubles Two common problems are early blight and blossom-end rot. Early blight, a yellowing of the lower leaves that spreads to the entire plant, can be controlled by applications of fungicide. Blossom-end rot is recognizable by dark marks at the bases of tomatoes. It is caused by irregular watering and calcium-deficient soil. Watering practices can be improved, and the soil can be improved with some ground eggshells or horticultural limestone worked into it. (During the following year, add bonemeal or ground eggshells to tomato planting holes.) Use a fertilizer with a high middle number.

5. End-of-season care About six weeks before a killing frost is due, begin removing new flowers as they appear. Fruit needs 35 to 45 days to mature, and anything that starts this late will not make it. Continue pruning and remove the terminal buds on the major vines. This practice directs all the plant energy to the fruit that will reach maturity before the frost.

To extend the growing season somewhat, mulch around the base of each plant with stones, rocks, or bricks. Make a chicken-wire cage that almost encircles each plant. Leave an open gap for picking. Wrap the structure with clear plastic sheeting to protect the occupants from wind. During the day, leave the top of the cool-weather "greenhouse" open, but cover it at night. On cold nights, put a plastic bottle filled with hot water inside the cages.

Diseases/pests: The two common diseases afflicting tomatoes are verticillium wilt and fusarium wilt. Seed catalog listings state the inbred resistance to these of each variety, and garden centers often provide this information about their seedlings. In the South, nematodes can be a problem. Several insects damage tomatoes: aphids, leaf miners, spider mites, flea beetles, tomato fruitworm, and hornworms. Cut down infestation by practicing crop rotation of tomatoes and other nightshade family members.

Tomato Varieties for Your Area

Variety	*Region*
Ace	West, Southwest
Atkinson	South
Better Boy	All
Big Girl	All
Burpee Early Pick Hybrid	West
California 145	Southwest
Early Pack No. 7	Southwest
Floramerica	South, Southwest
Jet Star	East
Pearson	Southwest
Ramapo	East, North
Springset	East, North
Supersonic	East, Midwest
Tropi-Gro	South

GROWING Asparagus

Asparagus is a perennial crop that yields little or nothing the first year but keeps coming back with good harvests for ten or even twenty-five years. Since an asparagus bed is to be a permanent feature of the garden, it ought to be located where it will not be disturbed by attentions paid to other crops. One solution is to plant these vegetables along a fence. Their green, fernlike foliage grows to five or six feet in height, making them an attractive ornamental summer screen.

How to Grow

Asparagus is usually planted in the form of one-year-old roots purchased from nurseries or seed companies. To estimate how large to make the asparagus bed, allow about fifteen feet per person. Thirty to fifty plants feed a four-person family. Asparagus plants require lots of sun and well-drained soil with a neutral or slightly alkaline pH. They also grow best in soil enriched with lots of humus. Although springtime is planting time, it helps to prepare the asparagus bed in autumn.

In spring, rake in some 5-10-5 or 5-10-10 fertilizer (1.2 pounds per one hundred square feet) and a generous amount of well-rotted manure, green manure, compost, or leafmold before planting. When you have the roots, plant them in the bottom of a six-inch-deep V-shape furrow and cover with one to two inches of soil. Spacing between shoots is from twelve to eighteen inches apart within rows and three to five feet between rows. If you are planting a single row along the side of the vegetable plot, keep a yard between the asparagus and the other vegetables.

As the asparagus plants grow, fill in the soil of the furrow without covering any of the foliage that has appeared. By the end of the first summer, the furrows should be filled. In midsummer, side-dress the plants with 1.2 pounds of 5-10-10 fertilizer or the equivalent for every twenty feet. Spread the fertilizer to the side of the plants, and cultivate it lightly into the soil.

Organic gardeners often make a one-foot-deep trench and fill in the first six inches with compost or a mixture of soil and well-rotted manure. When the plants reach the surface, they can be fertilized with a mixture of two parts bloodmeal, one part wood ash, and two parts rock phosphate as a side-dressing.

During the first year, water the asparagus thoroughly at regular intervals and take care during dry spells that the bed does not dry out. From the second year onward, two inches of water every two weeks is usually sufficient because asparagus plants develop deep and extensive root systems.

Early in the second spring, remove old asparagus stalks and weeds, recheck the soil pH, and add lime, if necessary. At the same time, apply manure and fertilizer. A midseason side-dressing of commercial fertilizer or the organic mixture may also be needed.

To thwart weeds, you can weed by hand or, when the shoots are six to eight inches tall, mulch the bed with a four-inch layer of salt marsh hay, seaweed, or another nonacidic material. If you apply a mulch, draw it back in late winter to allow the ground to warm up for earlier growth. To extend your asparagus harvest, leave part of the bed mulched and it will develop a little later. Asparagus stalks are ready for harvest when they are four to eight inches tall. Snap the stalks off at their most tender point. Be careful not to hurt nearby stalks that may be pushing their way up. After about a month, stop picking and add a two-inch layer of compost to the bed. (Established beds can be harvested for about two months.)

The first harvest will not be as copious as succeeding ones. Look upon it as a test of your cultivation methods: If the asparagus spears are tough and pithy, the soil is not fertile enough.

An easy way to keep the asparagus bed rich in humus yet virtually weed-free is to plant annual ryegrass after the final harvest. During the summer, the thick growth of ryegrass crowds out weeds; in winter, because you have planted the annual variety, the cover crop dries and makes way for new asparagus shoots in spring.

In autumn, many gardeners cut back their asparagus plants to prevent seeds from scattering, but this procedure is a matter of choice and taste. If you do cut the plants back, leave six to eight inches above the ground to hold the mulch and hold snow, which is also a mulch.

Diseases/pests: Rust disease can be prevented by planting resistant varieties. Chewed tips or black spots indicate an invasion by the spotted asparagus beetle or the common asparagus beetle. Both pests spend the winter in garden litter—a good reason to keep the garden clear of debris.

GROWING RHUBARB

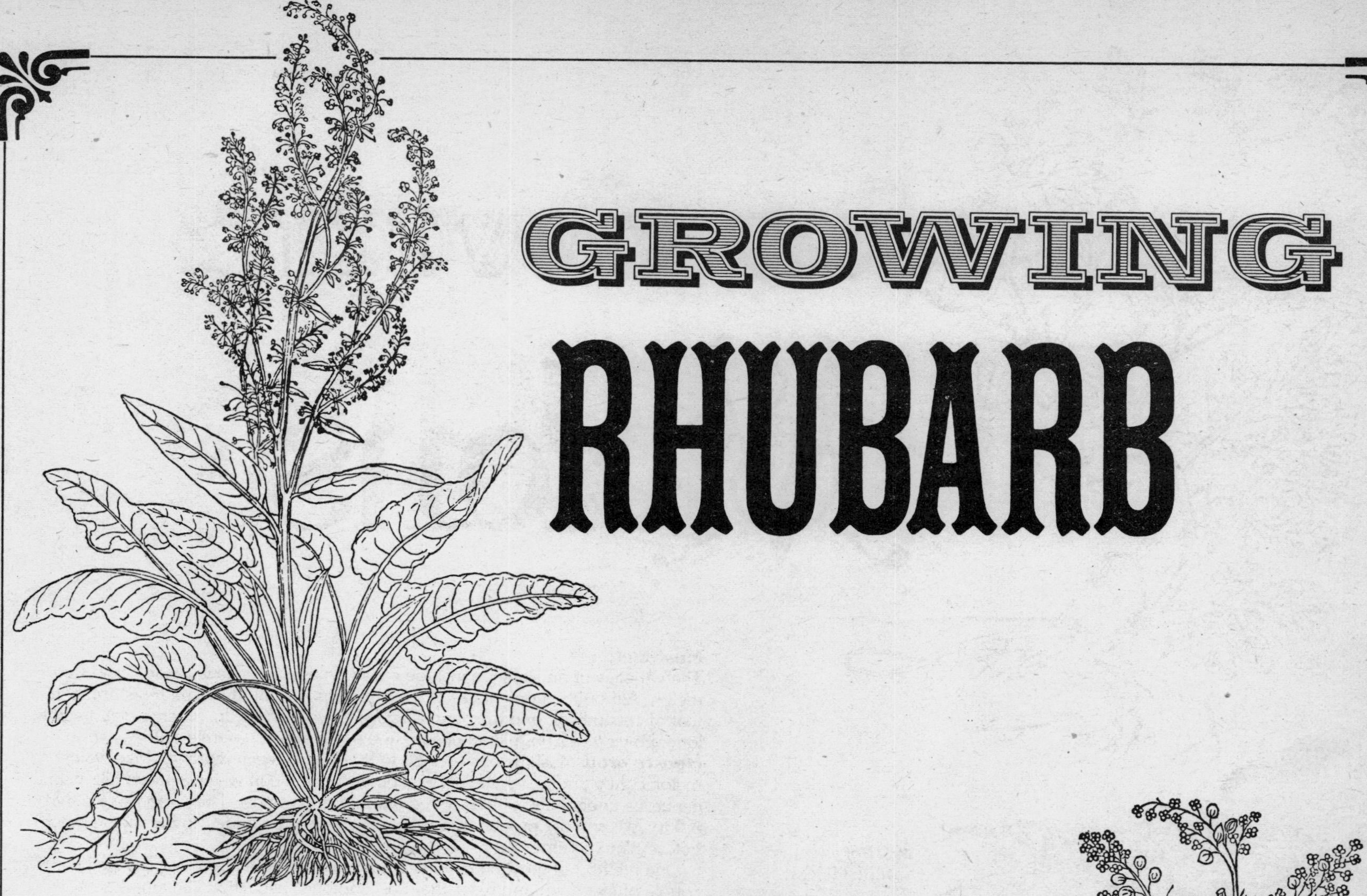

Rhubarb makes you wait three years for the first harvest, but thereafter it continues producing heavily for decades. Although this fruitlike vegetable can be started from seed, the usual way to begin a rhubarb patch is to plant well-established roots purchased from a local nursery or, better, obtained from a friend's garden. Rhubarb likes cold winters and cool, humid summers so it is not well adapted to most parts of the South. It prefers full sun; if grown in the shade, rhubarb stalks turn green.

How to Plant

Rhubarb does well in deeply cultivated soil containing a generous amount of manure, compost, or partially rotted mulch material (three to six bushels per one hundred square feet). Dig planting holes to a depth of twelve to sixteen inches, fill them with five inches of organic material, then plant the roots at three- to five-foot intervals. The crowns should be level with the soil surface to prevent rotting, but cover the rest of the roots with soil, and water the patch lightly. Spread a layer of well-rotted manure over the bed and then lay down a deep, loose mulch of straw or hay to suppress weeds.

As flower stalks appear, remove them because they weaken the plant. Otherwise, don't touch the rhubarb: the root system needs time to develop. In fall, spread another layer of manure among the rhubarb plants.

To harvest, when the third spring finally comes, pull up the rhubarb stalks from the garden with a slight side twist, taking care not to injure the primary buds. Never eat the leaves because they contain the poison oxalic acid. Stop picking after four to six weeks.

Diseases/pests: Afflicted with few diseases or insects, rhubarb nevertheless has a couple of troubles. In the East, *phytophthora* crown rot, or foot rot, which is uncontrollable at present, and the rhubarb curculio, a beetle, can destroy crops. The rhubarb wilt disease that sometimes occurs is a fungus.

Rha verum antiquorum.
The true Rubarbe of the Antients.

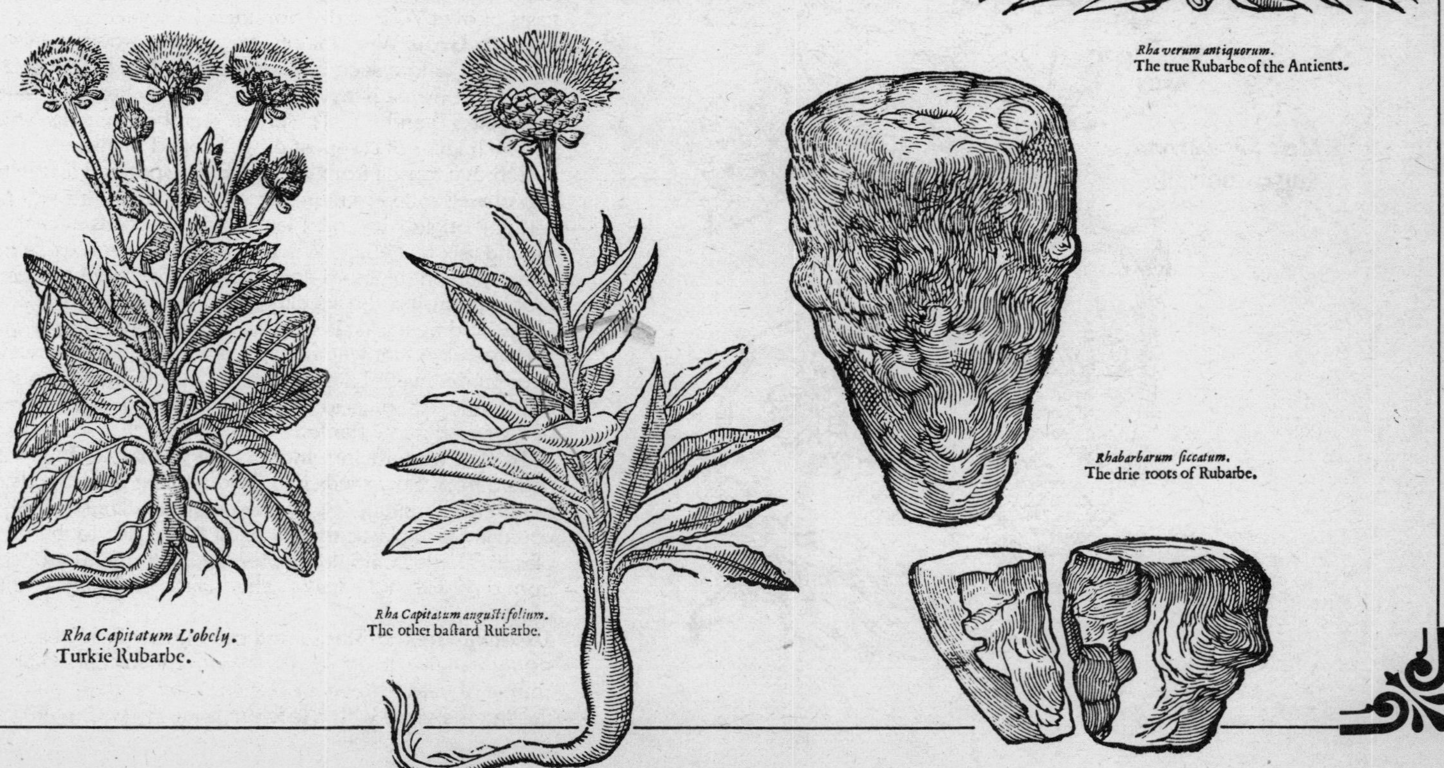

Rha Capitatum L'obely.
Turkie Rubarbe.

Rha Capitatum angustifolium.
The other baſtard Rubarbe.

Rhabarbarum ſiccatum.
The drie roots of Rubarbe.

GROWING Melons

Melo Hispanicus.
Spanish Melons.

Melo Saccharinus.
Sugar melon.

Muskmelon
The varieties of muskmelon include cantaloupes, honeydew, casaba, and Persian melon. Although people think of these melons as fruit, their culture is similar to that of cucumbers, and they are classified as vegetables. In general, they need a long growing season, plenty of sun, and a well-drained, fertile soil.

How to grow Muskmelons take 82 to 90 days to reach maturity. Like watermelons, they are heavy feeders and do well planted in widely spaced hills with a generous underlining of well-rotted manure or compost. They also like a pH from 6.0 to 7.0, and the proper amount of lime should be added to the melon patch before planting time.

One method of growing melons is, for each hill, to dig a wide planting hole a couple of feet deep and place the topsoil to one side. After filling the hole with organic matter, form a mound with a flat top and rounded sides above the ground, using the original topsoil. Space hills five to seven feet apart. Sow six to eight seeds in each mound and thin to the strongest two plants.

Protect tender seedlings from cold and chill wind with hot caps or other "greenhouse" devices. Mulch hills to suppress weeds and keep fruit clean and out of direct contact with the ground. Black plastic mulch is especially effective.

If you live in an area with a fairly short growing season, muskmelons can be started indoors in individual peat pots three to four weeks before the last expected frost. Growers living in cool climates sometimes accelerate melon growth by placing squares of black plastic mulch or black tar paper or a square piece of board under each fruit.

Diseases/pests: Bacterial wilt, downy mildew, blossom-end rot. Seeds treated with Captain resist damping-off fungus. Plant wilt-resistant varieties and spray or dust new seedlings with Captan and continue application weekly as long as needed. Striped cucumber beetles and aphids, which may bother all melon varieties, spread a wilt organism. Keep melons away from flowers such as gladiolus, hollyhock, petunia, and phlox.

Watermelon
Watermelons grow wherever tomato transplants thrive. That is a rule of thumb to follow when deciding whether to plant watermelon, assuming, of course, that you have the requisite space in your garden. But there's a slight catch—watermelons need a growing season that is both long and hot. They need nighttime temperatures of over 70°F to develop their full sweetness.

How to Grow Watermelons are usually grown in hills spaced six to ten feet apart, but before seed is sown, the planting holes need some careful preparation. Watermelons are heavy feeders. They do best in a sandy-loam soil with a pH between 5.0 and 6.5. The entire seed bed benefits when you turn into the soil a two-inch layer of compost or well-rotted manure.

Remove topsoil from each planting spot and fill the hole with a good bushel or two of well-rotted manure or compost. Then form a mound on top of the filling with the original topsoil. Plant five or six seeds in each mound, and space mounds six feet apart. When seedlings appear, use a mulch to keep the plants clean, prevent blossom-end rot, and conserve moisture. If you have a cutworm problem, protect the seedlings with little collars. A black plastic mulch, despite its aesthetic drawbacks, is very serviceable underneath spreading watermelon vines.

Remember that watermelons are about 93% water, and irrigate their section of your garden well. Thin each hill to the strongest two seedlings. They will take from 70 to 100 days to mature, depending on the weather and the characteristics of the variety you planted.

To start watermelons indoors, begin three to four weeks before the last expected frost. Sow seeds in individual peat pots. Seeds need at least 70°F (85°F is better) to germinate. Put watermelon seedlings out before they start to vine. If you use black plastic mulch, plant them, two to three to a hill, in slits in the plastic. The hills should be prepared with manure or compost. Protect seedlings from cold with hot caps or other plastic coverings and temporary wind barriers, if necessary.

Diseases/pests: The striped cucumber beetle likes watermelons. Plant wilt-resistant varieties to stave off fusarium fungus and rotate watermelon patches every couple of years. Prevent downy mildew and anthranose and other troubles by dusting the vines with a safe fungicide (e.g., Captan).

GROWING Berries

Food prices are skyrocketing these days, and the cost of our favorite fruits, like the seasonal berries—straw, blue, black, goose—is no exception.

More gardeners would grow their own berries if they realized how easy it is. Berries do require a lot of attention, but they are nevertheless mangeable and worth the care. Literally, eating the fruits of your labor is a delectable experience. What you can do with these fruits once picked will keep you as busy as growing them.

Raspberries, strawberries, blackberries, etc., while providing an excellent source of vitamin C, also can be made into jams or preserves. These fruits can also be served fresh, canned, frozen, or they can make tasty pie filling.

Before planting your berry plants, a plethora of questions must first be answered: What variety is best suited to your region? What type of soil should be used? A general discussion about preparing, buying, and caring for your berries that follows should help the gardener get a handle on his task.

Most berries come from the Rose family. Blackberries and raspberries are bramble plants and belong to the genus Rubus. Strawberries belong to a different genus. Different varieties of berries bear fruits at different times of the year depending on where they are grown.

Preparing the Soil

For most berries, the important factors are drainage, subsoil, moisture and acidity. Berries must be properly drained. Raspberries, especially, because they will suffer badly from root rot if the ground retains too much moisture. Strawberries, as well, will have a difficult time if not well-drained. Though berries do well in most types of soil, certain types, like strawberry, do best in a sandy loam with a slightly acidic balance of 5.5 to 6.8. Raspberries also favor this combination. Blueberries do better in a more acidic soil (pH 4.5) but blackberries do much worse. The subsoil must be deep; the cane fruits have a highly developed root system and any restriction in its growth will damage the plant. When selecting a site for the berries all perennial weeds must be completely eliminated. Tomatoes, peppers, eggplants, and potatoes should not be grown in that spot for at least two years before planting the berries. These plants build up a fungus disease called verticillium wilt. The disease is especially harmful to cane fruits, killing many who contract it. Another consideration is not to plant in soil that contains recent additions of lime.

Except for strawberries, the brambles do best on a sloping site rather than in a valley. This protects them in winter, and reduces root problems. The slope, if possible, should be facing north. Such exposure helps retain needed moisture, and also promotes more humus in the soil. Strawberries, on the other hand, are more susceptible to uprooting by heavy rains, and should be planted on a flatter surface. All plant sites must have excellent exposure to strong sun to promote flower bud development.

Suggested Berry Crops and Regions of Adaptation

Hardiness Zone*	Approx. Range of ave. minimum temperature (°F)	Suggested Berry Crops	
10	30 to 40	Strawberries	(Winter producing varieties developed in Calif., Fla.)
9	20 to 30	Strawberries	(Early Spring vars. developed in Fla., La., Calif.)
		Blueberries	(Short Chilling Rabbiteye in upper half, low chilling highbush throughout zone)
		Blackberries	(low chilling trailing types)
8	10 to 20	Strawberries	(Mid Spring vars. developed in N. C., Ore., Wash.)
		Blueberries	(Rabbiteye vars., canker-resistant highbush in Carolinas and Va., and Northern highbush in Pacific Coast States)
		Blackberries	(Erect and trailing, but different varieties are adapted to eastern and western U.S.)
		Raspberries	(Certain reds and blacks in cooler areas of zone)
7	0 to 10	Strawberries	(Late Spring vars. developed in Md., Ark., N.J., Wash., Ore.)
		Blueberries	(Highbush types)
		Blackberries	(Thorny and thornless erect and trailing types)
		Raspberries	(Reds and blacks in cooler areas of zone)
6	−10 to 0	Strawberries	(Late Spring vars. developed in Md., N.J., N.Y., Ill., Ark., Canada)
		Blueberries	(Highbush)
		Blackberries	(Erect types and some thornless vars. if protected)
		Raspberries	(Reds and blacks developed from Minn. to the East and in British Col.)
5	−20 to −10	Strawberries	(Late Spring vars. developed in N.Y., Mich., Wisc., Minn., Canada)
		Blueberries	(Highbush in warmer areas)
		Blackberries	(Hardiest erect types)
		Raspberries	(Most of the hardy red and black fruited types)
4	−30 to −20	Strawberries	(Early Summer vars. devel. in Minn., Wyo., Alaska)
		Raspberries	(Hardiest reds)

Preparation for Planting

When you have picked your plant site and bought the correct variety of berry for your area, the next step is to begin planting. To prepare the soil, plow in early spring to a depth of eight inches. It's possible to plant as early as late winter in the South; the earlier, the better. Before planting and plowing, it is recommended that you seed and plow under one or two green-manure crops of oat or barley with vetch. This thorough going over gets the soil in good condition for planting. It also provides the bed with organic matter and nitrogen, which will help to produce an early crop. Disk and harrow after you have plowed and just before you set the plants. The soil should be as well prepared as your flower garden soil.

Setting and Spacing the Plants

Berry plants should be bought in early spring and planted as soon as possible. The most important factor involved in setting the plants is not to let the stock dry out. If the plants are well wrapped when you purchase them, simply keep them in a cool place. If they aren't wrapped, a method to keep them from drying out called "heeling" is employed. To heel the plants, dig a trench deep enough to hold the roots. Spread the plants along the trench with the roots facing down. Cover the roots with moist soil. If the plants you bought are dry, the best thing is to soak the roots in water for several hours before planting or heeling.

When you are ready to set the plants in the soil, take some thin mud clay and rub it on the roots of the plants. This will keep the roots from drying out while the plants are being set. The tops of the plants ought to be cut back as well. Make the cuts about six inches long. These cuttings also can serve as handles while setting the plant. Handles are used to help align the plants while setting.

To make the planting hole, take a shovel, and with the blade, make a slit in the soil. Then press the handle of the shovel or mattock forward to open the slit. Take the plant and set it in the hole. Blackberry, strawberry, black and purple raspberry are planted at the same depth they were in the nursery. Red raspberries should be set two to three inches deeper than they were in the nursery. When this is done, remove the shovel and pack the soil around the plant firmly.

—GOOSEBERRIES.
Ribes Grossularia.

Planting and Planning Guide for Strawberries, Blueberries and Brambles

Type	Planting distances		Planting stock	Years from planting to economic return	No. of bearing years	Average mature yield (lbs)
	Between rows (ft)	In the rows (ft)				
Strawberries						
matted rows	3.5-4	1.5-2	1-yr runners (virus free)	1	2-3	1/row foot
hill	4-5	0.5-1	1-yr runners (virus free)	1	2-3	1.5/plant
Blueberries						
Highbush	8-10	4-5	2-yr plants	3	25+	6-8/plant
Rabbiteye	10-12	6-8	2-yr plants	4	30+	12-15/plant
Brambles						
Blackberries						
Erect	8-12	2-6	root pieces	3	10-12	1.5/row foot
Trailing	8-12	6-8	rooted cane tips	2	5-10	9/plant
Raspberries						
Red	8-10	2-4	1-yr suckers (virus free)	3	10-12	1.5/row foot
Black	8-10	3-4	rooted cane tips (virus free)	3	3-4	1.5/plant

Spacing of the plants vary according to the type of berry you are planting and the variety that you use. Raspberries, strawberries, and blackberries will be spaced approximately five feet from each other. If you plan to cultivate with a tractor, ten feet between the plants is suggested so that there will be enough room to pass.

Training Your Plants

Though many cane fruits such as blackberries or purple raspberries are erect plants and don't need trellises, we recommend their use anyway. They will pay for themselves in time saved tending your crops, and the increased yield their use will bring.

The simplest way to construct a trellis is by stretching a wire between posts that are set twenty feet apart from each other in a straight row. There should be two wires in all, one three feet from the ground and the other approximately five feet from the ground. Tie the canes of the plants with a soft string. Tie the erect canes where they cross the wires, the horizontal growing (trailing) canes should be tied where they cross the wires. Let the trailing canes cross in the natural pattern of their growth.

Red raspberries, which grow in a hedgerow, can be trellised. This helps them grow taller and hold the fruit while protecting them from certain fungal diseases. Boysenberry, dewberry, thornless blackberry and youngberry all are trellised. For the first year of their growth, let the new canes grow along the ground, then tie them to the wire. Remove all old canes after fruiting.

Pruning

Each berry has different pruning needs. For instance, black and purple raspberries require pruning in May and June, while blueberries don't need to be pruned at all. Instructions for pruning berries are simple to follow and can be performed with a pair of shears.

Black and purple raspberry canes should be tipped in early spring. This allows the buds near the tip to grow. At the end of summer these buds will have grown, if all goes well, approximately five feet in length. At the end of winter, or if you live in a snow belt at the end of November, prune back these laterals to about one foot each.

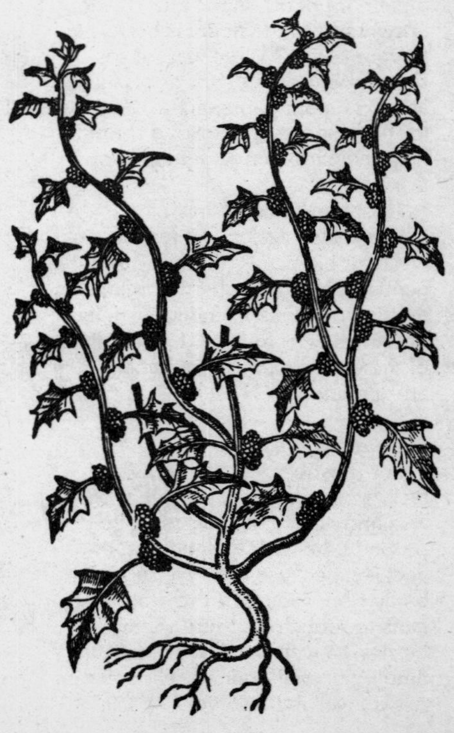

This procedure allows the berries to produce healthy fruit-bearing buds.

Red raspberries should not be pruned in their first year. Pruning begins at the end of the following winter when all the old canes and any decayed or damaged ones are cut off to prepare the plant for its new season. There should be at least three strong canes left on the plant that will grow.

Currants and gooseberries are perennials and therefore don't need to be pruned. Nevertheless, it is suggested that canes and branches be cut back every four years in the early spring.

Blackberries do need to be cut back and spring is the best time for this job. Most commercial growers do not prune their laterals, but home gardeners who do will be pleasantly surprised to find out how much tastier the blackberries will be. After harvest, blackberries need to be cut back. They are prone to diseases like anthracnose and rosette and preventive measures must be taken. Cut off all the canes on the bush both old and new.

Blueberries do not need pruning. Nevertheless, a cutting is suggested during dormant seasons to help promote good health.

Cultivating

Many gardeners grow their berries under a permanent mulch or sod. This reduces the need to culture. Unfortunately, mulching is expensive and not necessarily the best way to help your plants. If you have time, cultivating the plot once every two weeks will relieve the need to mulch or sod. Cultivate by cleaning all the weeds approximately two inches into the ground. Any farther and you will risk harming shallow roots. You should cultivate right through summer until fall.

Sometimes gardeners have a strong desire to grow berries but cannot find a suitable patch of land in which to plant. One way around this problem is to grow other crops along with the berry trees, thereby creating nutrients in the soil that will be of benefit. Good crops for this purpose are cabbage, cauliflower, beans, peas and squash.

Shapes of strawberries.

Characteristics of leading strawberry varieties when grown in favorable areas

	Plant disease resistance					Fruit characteristics					
Variety	Leaf spot	Leaf scorch	Red stele	Verticillium wilt	Virus tolerance	Ripening season: days after Midland	Size	Flesh firmness	Skin firmness	Dessert quality	Processing quality for freezing
Aiko[1]	Intermediate	Unknown	Susceptible	Susceptible	Tolerant	10	Medium-large	Firm	Firm	Fair	Unknown
Albritton	Resistant	Very resistant	Susceptible	Susceptible	Susceptible	12	Large	Very firm	Firm	Excellent	Good
Aliso	Unknown	Unknown	Susceptible	Susceptible	Unknown	7	Large	Medium	Medium	Good	Good
Apollo	Resistant	Very resistant	Susceptible	Intermediate	Unknown	7	Large	Very firm	Firm	Good	Good
Atlas	Resistant	Very resistant	Susceptible	Intermediate	Unknown	3	Very large	Firm	Firm	Good	Poor
Badgerbelle	Resistant	Susceptible	Susceptible	Unknown	Unknown	14	Large	Soft	Soft	Fair	Fair
Badgerglo	Unknown	Susceptible	Susceptible	Susceptible	Unknown	14	Large	Medium	Medium	Good	Unknown
Benton	Unknown	Unknown	Resistant	Unknown	Tolerant	16	Large	Soft	Tender	Very good	Good
Blakemore	Susceptible	Very susceptible	Susceptible	Resistant	Tolerant	3	Small	Firm	Tender	Fair	Good
Cardinal	Resistant	Resistant	Susceptible	Susceptible	Unknown	7	Large	Firm	Firm	Fair	Good
Catskill	Susceptible	Resistant	Susceptible	Very resistant	Very susceptible	7	Very large	Soft	Soft	Good	Fair to good
Comet	Resistant	Resistant	Susceptible	Unknown	Unknown	3	Medium-large	Very firm	Firm	Good	Good
Cruz[1]	Unknown	Unknown	Susceptible	Susceptible	Tolerant	7	Large	Firm	Firm	Very good	Unknown
Cyclone	Resistant	Unknown	Susceptible	Unknown	Tolerant	3	Large	Soft	Soft	Very good	Good
Darrow	Intermediate	Intermediate	Resistant	Intermediate	Unknown	3	Large	Firm	Firm	Good	Very good
Dabreak	Very resistant	Resistant	Susceptible	Susceptible	Tolerant	0	Medium	Medium	Medium	Good	Good
Delite	Resistant	Resistant	Resistant	Resistant	Unknown	12	Large	Medium-soft	Firm	Fair	Unknown
Earlibelle	Very resistant	Very resistant	Susceptible	Susceptible	Tolerant	3	Large	Very firm	Very firm	Good	Very good
Earlidawn	Susceptible	Intermediate	Susceptible	Susceptible	Susceptible	0	Large	Medium	Medium	Fair	Very good
Earliglow	Resistant	Resistant	Resistant	Resistant	Unknown	3	Medium-large	Firm	Firm	Very good	Very good
EarliMiss	Resistant	Resistant	Susceptible	Unknown	Unknown	5	Medium-large	Medium	Medium	Good	Unknown
Fairfax	Resistant	Resistant	Susceptible	Unknown	Susceptible	7	Medium	Firm	Soft	Excellent	Fair
Fletcher	Resistant	Very resistant	Susceptible	Susceptible	Unknown	7	Medium	Medium	Soft	Very good	Good
Florida Belle	Unknown	Unknown	Susceptible	Unknown	Unknown	5	Large	Medium	Tender	Good	Unknown
Florida Ninety	Very susceptible	Very susceptible	Susceptible	Susceptible	Unknown	5	Very large	Soft	Soft	Very good	Fair
Fort Laramie	Intermediate	Intermediate	Susceptible	Unknown	Unknown	7	Medium	Medium	Medium	Good	Unknown
Fresno	Intermediate	Unknown	Susceptible	Susceptible	Intermediate	7	Very large	Firm	Firm	Fair	Fair
Gem	Susceptible	Resistant	Susceptible	Unknown	Unknown	7	Small	Soft	Soft	Fair	Fair
Guardian	Resistant	Resistant	Resistant	Very resistant	Unknown	7	Very large	Firm	Firm	Good	Fair
Headliner	Resistant	Unknown	Susceptible	Unknown	Unknown	7	Large	Medium	Medium	Good	Good
Heidi[1]	Unknown	Unknown	Susceptible	Unknown	Tolerant	7	Large	Firm	Firm	Good	Unknown
Holiday	Resistant	Resistant	Susceptible	Intermediate	Unknown	5	Large	Very firm	Very firm	Good	Good
Hood	Resistant	Resistant	Resistant	Resistant	Susceptible	10	Large	Medium	Medium	Very good	Good
Jerseybelle	Very susceptible	Susceptible	Susceptible	Susceptible	Susceptible	14	Very large	Soft	Firm	Fair	Poor
Linn	Unknown	Unknown	Resistant	Unknown	Intermediate	17	Large	Very firm	Very firm	Fair	Good
Marlate	Resistant	Resistant	Susceptible	Susceptible	Unknown	14	Medium-large	Firm	Firm	Good	Unknown
Midland	Resistant	Resistant	Susceptible	Susceptible	Susceptible	0	Large	Firm	Soft	Excellent	Very good

[1] Patented.

Characteristics of leading strawberry varieties when grown in favorable areas—Continued

Variety	Plant disease resistance					Fruit characteristics					
	Leaf spot	Leaf scorch	Red stele	Verticillium wilt	Virus tolerance	Ripening season: days after Midland	Size	Flesh firmness	Skin firmness	Dessert quality	Processing quality for freezing
Midway	Very susceptible	Susceptible	Resistant	Intermediate	Unknown	10	Large	Firm	Firm	Good	Very good
Northwest	Resistant	Unknown	Susceptible	Intermediate	Tolerant	14	Medium	Medium	Medium	Good	Very good
Ogallala	Unknown	Unknown	Susceptible	Unknown	Unknown	7	Medium	Soft	Soft	Good	Good
Olympus	Unknown	Unknown	Resistant	Unknown	Tolerant	14	Medium	Medium	Soft	Good	Very good
Ozark Beauty	Resistant	Resistant	Susceptible	Susceptible	Unknown	14	Medium	Medium	Medium	Very good	Good
Pocohontas	Resistant	Intermediate	Susceptible	Susceptible	Unknown	7	Large	Medium	Medium	Good	Very good
Puget Beauty	Resistant	Resistant	Susceptible	Unknown	Susceptible	7	Large	Medium	Soft	Very good	Good
Quinault	Resistant	Resistant	Resistant	Unknown	Susceptible	7	Medium	Soft	Soft	Good	Fair
Rainier	Unknown	Unknown	Resistant	Resistant	Tolerant	16	Large	Medium	Medium	Very good	Excellent
Raritan	Susceptible	Susceptible	Susceptible	Susceptible	Unknown	7	Large	Firm	Medium	Fair	Fair
Redchief	Resistant	Resistant	Resistant	Intermediate	Unknown	7	Large	Firm	Firm	Good	Very good
Redcoat	Unknown	Unknown	Susceptible	Unknown	Unknown	10	Medium-large	Medium	Medium	Good	Unknown
Redglow	Susceptible	Intermediate	Resistant	Susceptible	Unknown	3	Large	Firm	Firm	Good	Very good
Redstar	Susceptible	Resistant	Susceptible	Intermediate	Tolerant	18	Large	Firm	Firm	Good	Good
Robinson	Intermediate	Susceptible	Susceptible	Resistant	Tolerant	10	Large	Soft	Soft	Fair	Poor
Rockhill	Intermediate	Unknown	Susceptible	Unknown	Unknown	7	Medium	Soft	Soft	Very good	Good
Salinas	Unknown	Unknown	Susceptible	Resistant	Tolerant	0	Large	Medium	Medium	Good	Unknown
Sequoia	Unknown	Unknown	Susceptible	Susceptible	Tolerant	0	Very large	Soft	Soft	Very good	Unknown
Shasta	Susceptible	Unknown	Susceptible	Susceptible	Tolerant	7	Large	Medium	Medium	Good	Good
Shuksan	Unknown	Unknown	Resistant	Resistant	Tolerant	16	Large	Medium	Medium	Good	Excellent
Sparkle	Susceptible	Intermediate	Resistant	Susceptible	Susceptible	12	Small	Soft	Soft	Very good	Very good
Stoplight	Intermediate	Intermediate	Susceptible	Unknown	Unknown	7	Medium	Soft	Medium	Good	Very good
	Very susceptible	Resistant	Resistant	Resistant	Unknown	0	Large	Firm	Firm	Good	Fair
Surecrop	Resistant	Resistant	Resistant	Very resistant	Tolerant	5	Large	Firm	Medium	Good	Good
Tangi	Resistant	Resistant	Susceptible	Unknown	Unknown	5	Medium	Medium	Medium	Good	Unknown
Tenn. Beauty	Resistant	Resistant	Susceptible	Unknown	Tolerant	12	Small	Firm	Firm	Good	Good
Tioga	Susceptible	Unknown	Susceptible	Susceptible	Tolerant	10	Very large	Firm	Firm	Good	Good
Titan	Resistant	Resistant	Susceptible	Susceptible	Unknown	3	Large	Firm	Firm	Good	Good
Toro[1]	Unknown	Unknown	Susceptible	Susceptible	Tolerant	7	Large	Medium	Medium	Fair	Unknown
Torrey	Unknown	Unknown	Susceptible	Susceptible	Intermediate	14	Large	Medium	Medium	Fair	Fair
Totem	Unknown	Unknown	Resistant	Unknown	Tolerant	14	Large	Medium	Medium	Good	Good
Trumpeter	Very susceptible	Unknown	Susceptible	Unknown	Tolerant	10	Medium	Soft	Soft	Good	Very good
Tufts[1]	Intermediate	Unknown	Susceptible	Susceptible	Tolerant	7	Large	Firm	Firm	Good	Unknown

[1] Patented.

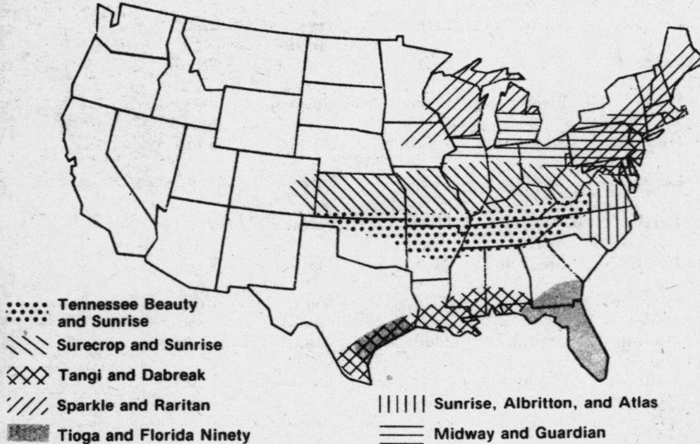

Map shows the regions in which Tennessee Beauty, Sunrise, Surecrop, Tangi, Dabreak, Sparkle, Rariatan, Tioga, Florida Ninety, Albritton, Atlas, Midway, and Guardian are grown profitable.

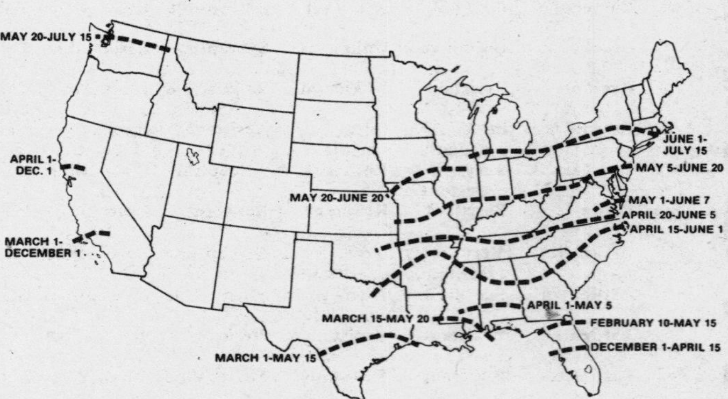

Map shows the location of the principal commercial strawberry-producing regions, the approximate ripening time in each region, and northward progression of the strawberry season.

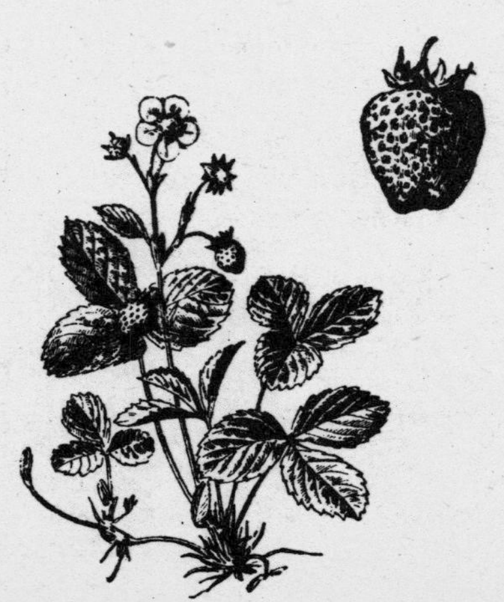

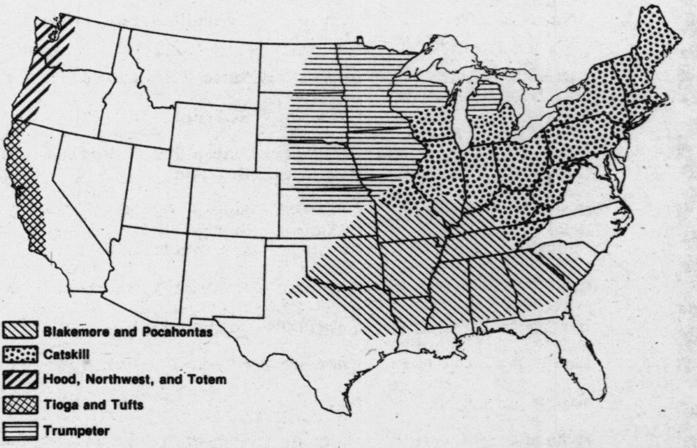

Map shows the regions in which Blakemore, Pocahontas, Catskill, Hood, Northwest, Totem, Tioga, Tufts, and Trumpeter are grown extensively.

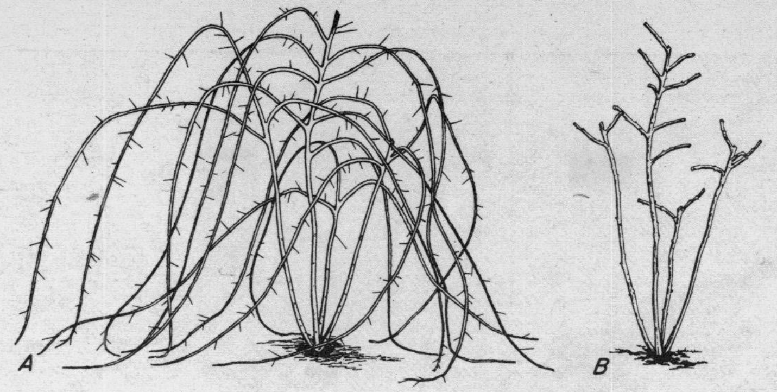

BN-35909
Left: Black raspberry plant before pruning. Right: The same plant after pruning.

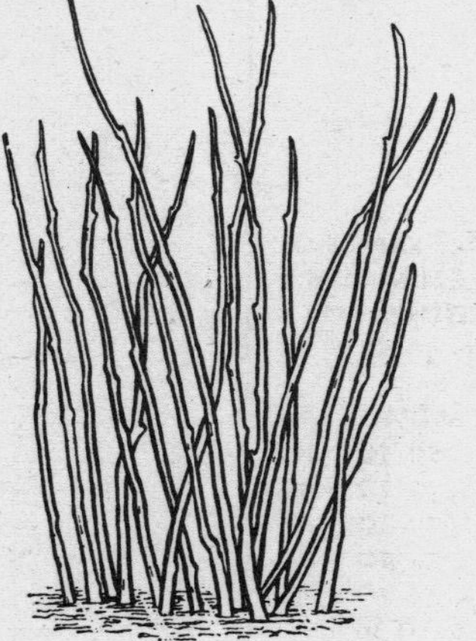

BN-35910
Left: Red raspberry plant before thinning and pruning. Right. The same plant after thinning and pruning.

Fertilizing

Depending on the berry, the use of fertilizer is either a welcomed touch or a sad event. Most berry patches are fertilized in early spring but even then, for some berries like strawberries, the fertilizer can cause more harm than good.

Strawberries should never be fertilized during the growing season. The only time it might be necessary to apply a nitrogen fertilizer during the growing season is when the leaf color appears unhealthy and the plants don't seem to be coming in well. The fertilizer, in this case, should be applied sparingly. Leaves should be wiped after applying the fertilizer. The best type of day to pick is a dry one to prevent the fertilizer from doing too much damage. Too much nitrogen will cause excessive growth in the strawberry plants and thus reduce the yield of berries, which is why other means of care are recommended. Do not spray the patches in early spring as you do with other berries, this might cause soft fruit and a reduced yield.

In the case of raspberries and blackberries, fertilizing is a welcomed activity. Before applying, a soil test should be performed to get a good analysis of what type of nutrients are most needed. The fertilizer should be applied every year in spring just as the new growth becomes visible for blackberries, and around blossoming time for blackberries. For blackberries, a 5-10-5 fertilizer should be used for the first application. In the case of raspberries, a stable manure (if available) is best. If not, a 5-10-5 should be used. The fertilizer should be applied at the rate of five hundred to a thousand pounds per acre. Blackberries also need a nitrate of soda or an ammonium nitrate applied after fruiting at the rate of two hundred to three hundred pounds per acre.

For blueberries, a good rule of thumb is one ounce of fertilizer per year of plant age, up to a maximum of eight ounces per plant per year for mature plants. The purpose of fertilizing blueberries is to establish a few well-spaced, stocky canes with branches containing about six to ten flower buds each. Blueberries should be fertilized four to six weeks after planting with an ammonium nitrate fertilizer such as an 8-8-8 or a 5-10-5. If leaves are quite yellow after the harvest an application of nitrogen is advised but be careful, blueberries are extremely sensitive to fertilizer and more harm than good can be done.

Harvesting

Again, varying forms of brambles should be treated differently during harvest time. Each fruit should be handled delicately to insure the best quality and least damage possible.

The prize berry on the market is the blackberry. They should be picked as soon as the fruit becomes ripe; the berry will still feel firm. Blackberries should be picked every other day, early in the day. Try to finish before noon, the berries picked in the morning will not spoil as quickly as those in the afternoon.

Raspberries should be picked twice a week, and during harvest as often as three times a week. During a heat wave, picking often will be necessary as well.

The blueberry is ready to be picked approximately seven days after it has turned colors. A weekly harvest of the fully colored and plumpest ones is suggested for maximum quality.

Strawberries ripen approximately thirty days after the first blossom appears. Harvesting should occur twice a week until the first frost.

All berries must be handled with extreme care. Use the thumb, index and middle finger to pick the berries. After picking, immediately place them gently in a cup of basket. Do not drop or handle them excessively.

Take all the overripe, injured, or decaying berries you find while picking, and discard them. The ripened berries should be kept in a shaded or cool area.

Varieties of Strawberry

Albritton
Description: large, uniform conic, very firm
Harvest: late
Growing regions: Eastern Virginia, North and South Carolina, northern Georgia, Alabama, Mississippi
Special qualities: excellent variety, good for freezing

Atlas
Description: large, globose conic, firm glossy skin, medium-red color
Harvest: midseason
Growing region: Virginia to Gulf Coast
Special qualities: resistant to leaf scorch, large and productive

Blakemore
Description: small, blunt conic, firm
Harvest: early
Growing region: Virginia to Georgia, Oklahoma to Southern Missouri
Special qualities: leading variety in the U.S., resistant to verticillium wilt, leaf scorch and leaf spots.

Catskill
Description: very large, long conic, irregular, not firm
Harvest: midseason
Growing region: New England, New Jersey, Southern Minnesota
Special qualities: good dessert variety, good for freezing, sensitive to viruses and leaf spots

Dabreak
Description: large and attractive, medium red color
Harvest: early
Growing region: most popular in Louisiana
Qualities: resistant to leaf spot, good dessert, preserving

Earlidawn
Description: large, conic, irregular shaped, medium firm, bright red flesh
Harvest: early
Growing region: Maryland to New England, west to Missouri
Qualities: good dessert quality, moderately resistant to leaf spots and leaf scorch

Fairfax
Description: medium sized, wedge shaped, deep red flesh
Harvest: medium early
Growing region: southern New England to Maryland, westward to Kansas
Qualities: excellent dessert quality, resistant to leaf spots and scorches, sensitive to virus diseases.

Fletcher
Description: medium sized, soft, conic shaped, medium red color
Harvest: midseason
Growing region: New York, New England
Qualities: freezing, excellent flavor

Florida Ninety
Description: soft, irregular, long conic, medium redcolor
Harvest: early
Growing region: Florida
Qualities: productive, sensitive to leaf spots and scorch

Fresno
Description: large, long conic, firm fleshed, bright-red skin
Harvest: midsummer
Growing region: southern California
Qualities: resistant to virus, summer planting only

Gem
Description: soft, small, irregular short wedge
Harvest: everbearer
Growing region: New Jersey westward to Great Plain States and northward, high elevation
Qualities: leading everbearer, dessert, susceptible to leaf spots, resistant to leaf scorch

Guardian
Description: large conic, firm flesh, first fruits irregular, light-red color
Growing region: central East coast to Missouri
Qualities: resistant to red stele, verticillium wilt leaf scorch and powdery mildew

Headliner
Description: large, blunt conic, medium firm
Harvest: midseason
Growing region: not good for Central or Northern States
Qualities: good dessert, productive, resistant to leaf spots

Holiday
Description: medium large, very firm, bright red color
Harvest: early/midseason
Growing region: northeastern United States
Qualities: moderately productive, resistant to leaf scorch and spot

Midland
Description: large, round conic, deep-red color, medium firm
Harvest: very early
Growing region: southern New England to Virginia, westward to Iowa and Kansas
Qualities: excellent dessert, freezing, productive, resistant to leaf spot and scorch

Midway
Description: long conic, firm flesh, large sized, glossy-red color
Harvest: midseason
Growing region: leading variety in Michigan, northeastern United States
Qualities: freezing, good dessert, sensitive to leaf scorch and spot, verticillium wilt

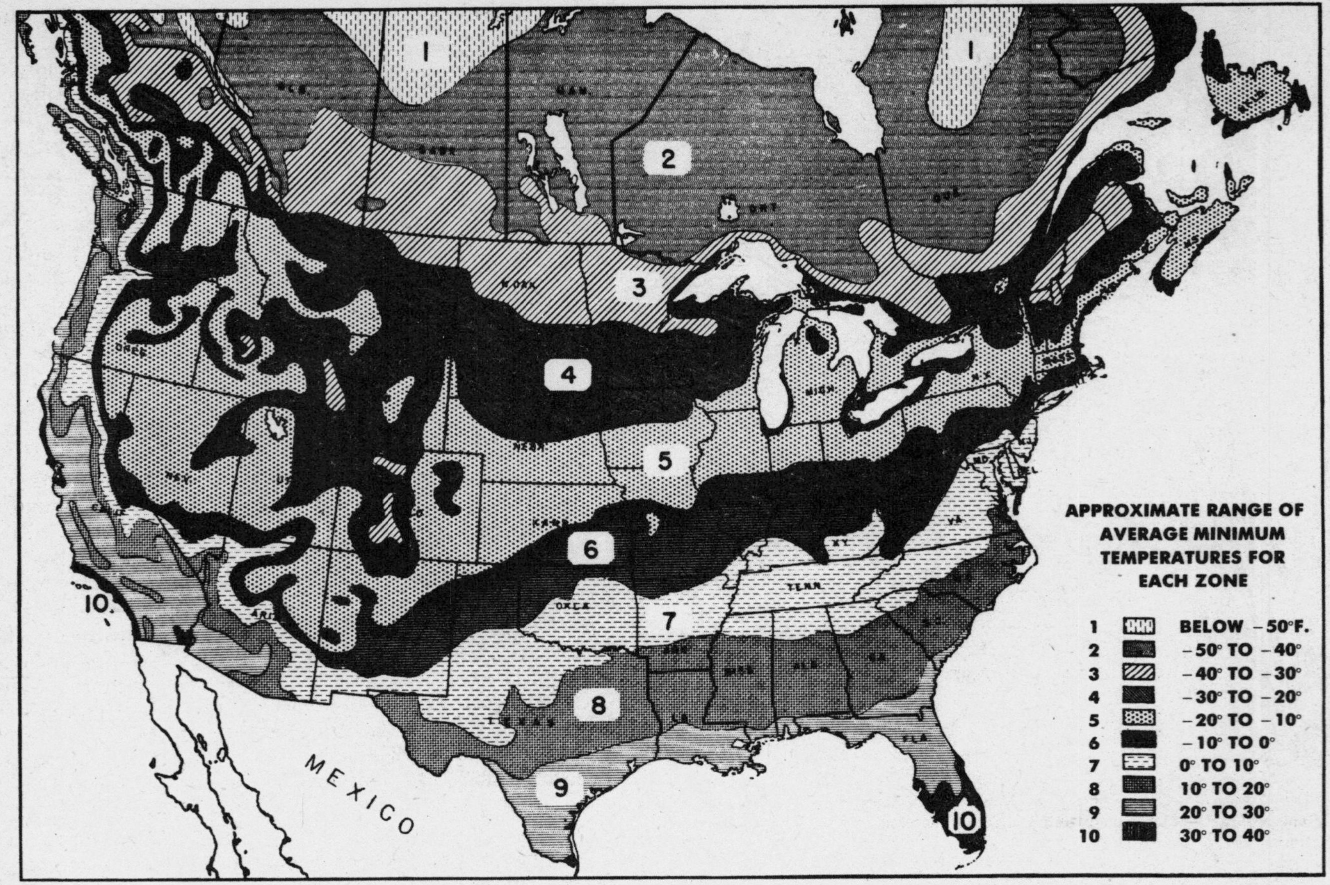

HARDINESS OF BLACKBERRY VARIETIES BY TEMPERATURE ZONES

Variety	*Zone*	*Variety*	*Zone*
Austin Thornless	7,[a] 8	Flint	7, 8
Black Satin	6, 7, 8	Flordagrand	9
Boysen	7, 8	Georgia Thornless	9
Brainerd	6,[a] 7, 8	Jerseyblack	6, 7
Brazos	8, 9	Logan	7,[a] 8 [c]
Cascade [b]	7,[a] 8 [c]	Lucretia	7, 8 [c]
Chehalem [b]	7,[a] 8 [c]	Marion [b]	8 [c]
Cherokee	6, 7, 8	Mayes	7,[a] 8
Comanche	6, 7, 8	Oklawaha	9
Cory Thornless [b]	7,[a] 8	Olallie [b]	8 [c]
Dallas	6,[a] 7, 8 [c]	Ranger	6,[a] 7
Darrow	5, 6, 7	Raven	6,[a] 7
Dewblack	6,[a] 7, 8 [c]	Smoothstem	7, 8 [c]
Early Harvest	6,[a] 7, 8 [c]	Thornfree	6,[a] 7, 8 [c]
Ebony King	5,[a] 6, 7	Young	6,[a] 7, 8
Eldorado	5, 6, 7		
Evergreen [b]	8 [c]		

[a] Subject to winter injury in some years if not protected.
[b] Not adapted to States east of Arizona.
[c] Adapted to northern part of zone or higher elevations.

Northwest
Description: medium sized, long, blunt conic, medium firm
Harvest: late
Growing region: western United States
Qualities: very good dessert, freezing, resistant to viruses, susceptible to leaf spots

Pocohontas
Description: large, attractive, blunt conic medium firm, red color
Harvest: early
Growing region: southern New England south to Virginia, westward to Missouri
Qualities: good dessert, very good freezing, productive, resistant to leaf scorch, partially resistant to leaf spot

Raritan
Description: large, firm, glossy, bright-red color
Harvest: midseason
Growing region: northeastern United States
Qualities: good flavor, sensitive to drought, susceptible to red stele and verticillium wilt

Redstar
Description: large, irregular, medium firm, medium red color
Harvest: late
Growing region: southern New England southward to Maryland, westward to Missouri and Iowa
Qualities: very good dessert, good late variety

Sparkle
Description: short blunt conic, glossy rich red
Harvest: late
Growing region: northeastern States, westward to Wisconsin
Qualities: very good dessert, good freezing, productive, susceptible to virus diseases

Sunrise
Description: medium sized, conic, light red color
Harvest: early
Growing region: south central States
Qualities: good flavor, productive, resistant to red stele, verticillium, leaf scorch

Surecrop
Description: large, round conic, medium-red color
Harvest: early
Growing region: Maryland
Qualities: resistant to everything except virus diseases, good dessert, freezing

Tennessee Beauty
Description: long conic, medium sized, uniform, attractive
Harvest: late midseason
Growing region: leading variety from Kentucky to Missouri
Qualities: great flavor, good firmness, productive, good freezing, resistant to everything except drought

Tioga
Description: long conic, firm flesh, light-red color, attractive
Harvest: March and April
Growing region: leading variety in California, Florida
Qualities: good for shipping, productive, good dessert

Trumpeter
Description: medium sized, short conic, soft
Harvest: late
Growing region: Mississippi valley, Plains states
Qualities: good flavor, freezing, winter hardy, susceptible to leaf spot

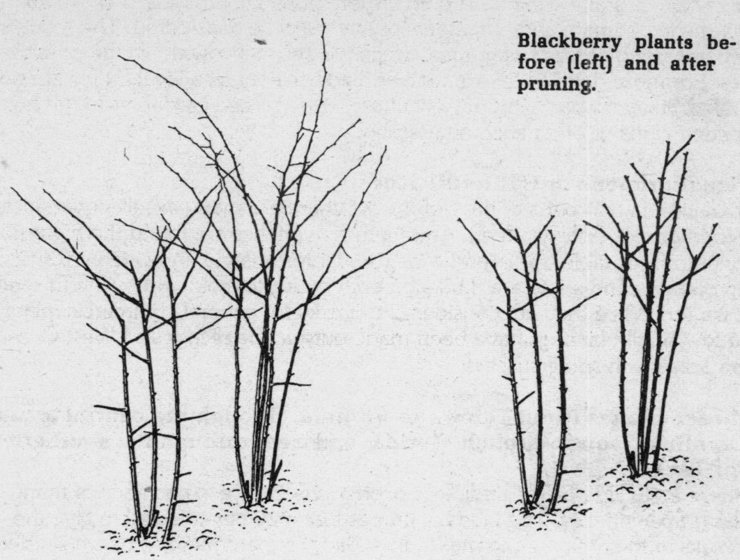

Blackberry plants before (left) and after pruning.

Sumner
Description: medium sized, medium red color, firm
Harvest: late
Growing region: Pacific Northwest
Qualities: resistant to root rot and yellow rust, productive

Taylor
Description: very large
Harvest: late
Growing region: leading variety in New York and New England, northeastern States
Qualities: susceptible to mosaic viruses, good for freezing

Williamette
Description: very large, nearly round, medium red, very firm
Harvest: midseason
Growing region: Pacific Northwest
Qualities: good freezing and canning

Bristol
Description: large, firm
Harvest: midseason
Growing region: eastern United States
Qualities: susceptible to anthracnose, highly flavored, hardy, productive

Cumberland
Description: large, firm
Harvest: midseason
Growing region: eastern United States
Qualities: susceptible to anthracnose and mosaic viruses

Dundee
Description: large, firm, glossy color
Harvest: midseason
Growing region: New York
Qualities: productive, hardy, susceptible to mildew

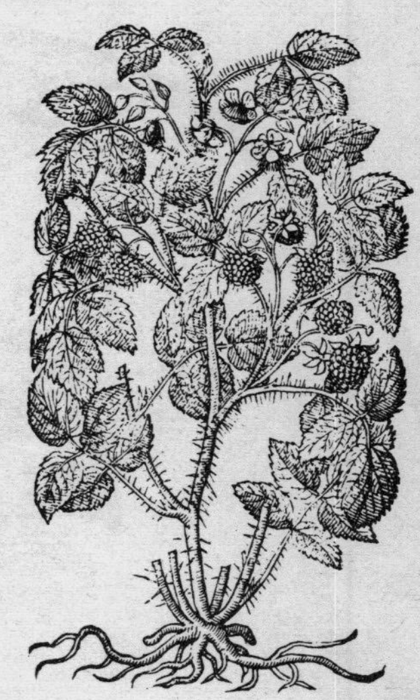

Varieties of Raspberry

RED RASPBERRIES

August Red
Description: medium soft, medium sunlight, bright red
Harvest: fall
Growing region: northeastern United States

Canby
Description: large, firm, light bright red, hardy
Harvest: midseason
Growing region: Pacific Northwest
Qualities: freezing

Fairview
Description: large, bright red, firm, productive
Harvest: midseason
Growing region: Oregon, Washington
Qualities: resistant to root rot, good flavor

Fallred
Description: medium sized, firm, everbearing
Harvest: late summer
Growing region: northeastern United States
Qualities: productive, hardy, grow only in mosaic-free soil

Haida
Description: medium sized, light bright red, medium firm
Harvest: midseason
Growing region: northwestern United States, British Columbia
Qualities: hardy

Heritage
Description: medium sized, medium firm, bright red color
Harvest: fall
Growing region: northeastern United States
Qualities: hardy, vigorous

Hilton
Description: very large, firm, medium red color
Harvest: midseason
Growing region: northeastern United States
Qualities: erect canes, productive

Meeker
Description: large size, firm, bright red color
Harvest: midseason
Growing region: northwestern United States
Qualities: resistant to mildew, long fruiting laterals

Newburgh
Description: very large, bright red color, firm
Harvest: midseason
Growing region: Pacific Northwest, northeastern United States
Qualities: resistant to root rot

Puyallup
Description: large, bright red color, soft
Harvest: late
Growing region: Pacific Northwest
Qualities: very good flavor, freezing, canning, productive

Sentinel
Description: medium to large sized, bright red colors
Harvest: midseason/late
Growing region: mid-Atlantic States
Qualities: resistant to fluctuating winter temperatures, productive

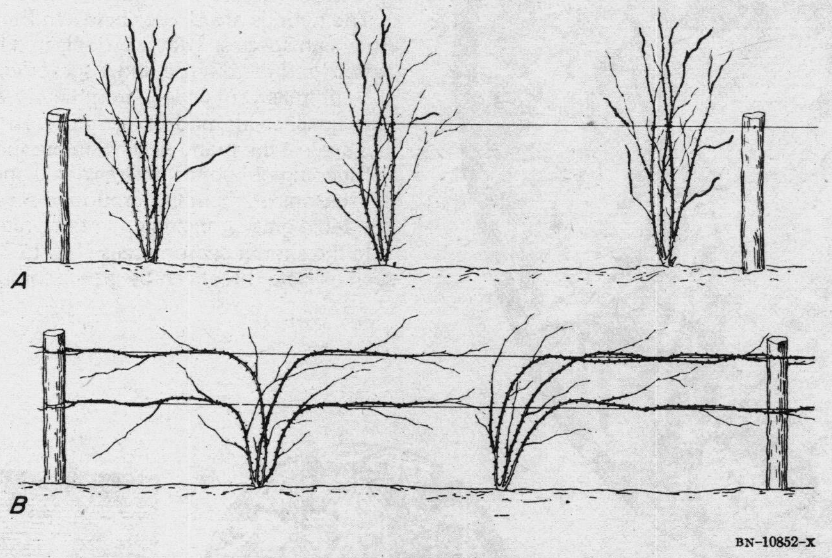

Trellises for blackberries: A, train erect plants to a one-wire trellis; B, train trailing plants to a two-wire trellis.

Scepter
Description: large, bright red color
Harvest: fall
Growing region: mid-Atlantic states
Qualities: resistant to fluctuating winter temperatures, vigorous

September
Description: medium sized, bright red color
Harvest: early summer/fall
Growing region: eastern United States
Qualities: generally escapes mosaics

Southland
Description: medium sized, light red color, medium firm
Harvest: early
Growing region: North Carolina to Maryland and westward to Illinois, southward to Arkansas
Qualities: resistant to leaf spot, anthracnose, mildew

PURPLE RASPBERRIES

Brandywine
Description: very large, firm
Harvest: midseason
Growing region: northeastern United States
Qualities: productive, susceptible to mosaic viruses

Clyde
Description: large, firm
Harvest: late
Growing region: northeastern United States
Qualities: resistant to anthracnose, tart, very productive, hardy

BLACK RASPBERRIES

Allegheny
Description: medium to large, firm
Harvest: midseason
Growing region: mid-Atlantic
Qualities: resistant to mildew, productive, hardy, good flavor

Allen
Description: large, firm
Harvest: midseason
Growing region: north central and northeastern United States
Qualities: productive, vigorous

Black Hawk
Description: large, firm, glossy color
Harvest: late
Growing region: eastern United States
Qualities: productive, good flavor, very hardy

Huron
Description: large, firm, glossy color
Harvest: late midseason
Growing region: western New York and worthy of trial anywhere
Qualities: good flavor, productive, partially resistant to anthracnose

New Logan
Description: medium sized
Harvest: early
Growing region: Michigan and eastern United States
Qualities: good quality

Munger
Description: large, firm
Harvest: midseason
Growing region: leading variety in Oregon
Qualities: susceptible to mildew, good flavor

Plum Farmer
Description: large, firm
Harvest: early
Growing region: Oregon
Qualities: resistant to drought, and curl virus, susceptible to anthracnose and mosaic viruses.

BLUEBERRIES

Blueberries comprise two types of groups—the rabbiteye and the highbush. Highbush blueberries need one hundred sixty or more days or frost-free weather with at least eight hundred hours below 45° F. The rabbiteye needs at least four hundred hours below 45° F. The rabbiteye ripens four to six weeks later than the highbush.

All highbush varieties are susceptible to root rot. A particularly pernicious strand of fungus that grows in the south called Phytophtora cinnamomi wreaks havoc on the highbush. A new fungus-resistant variety called Patriot has just been tested by the U.S.D.A. and it performs well. It's a good idea to plant more than one variety of blueberry in each location, which will increase productivity.

Growing Grapes

The grape is a versatile fruit. It may be used as fresh or stored table fruit, made into jellies or juice, or fermented into wine. There is a wide range of flavors among the many varieties. Grapes can be one of the easiest home-garden fruits to grow and one of the most rewarding.

Grape growing has been tried at some time during the last 400 years in almost every area of this country. There are several types, each suited to particular climates, areas, and use. One should select varieties best suited to the area rather than attempting to grow the "premium" varieties because trying to grow types not adapted to particular regions can be a frustrating experience.

The following basic requirements are essential for successful grape growing regardless of the variety:

- A growing season of at least 140 frost-free days.
- A site with full sunshine and good air drainage (not frosty).
- Soils that are neither waterlogged nor shallow, at least 3 feet deep.
- Willingness to spray at least three times a year to control insects and diseases.
- Patience to wait three to four years for vines to reach maturity before cropping.
- Annual pruning of vines.
- Readiness to defend the fruit against birds by netting the vines or bagging clusters.

The choice of grape varieties is both important and complicated. There are many varieties, climate and judgments of quality to be considered. The following is a general listing of types of grapes, which will help narrow down the possible choices. For more detailed information and advice contact a local Extension office the United States Department of Agriculture, experienced gardeners in the area, and garden clubs or other such organizations.

Vinifera (European or California types)

For California and parts of the Southwest, there are many excellent varieties of Old World grapes (Vitis vinifera). Among these varieties are found the highest quality grapes for table, raisin and wine use. Unfortunately, they are very susceptible to diseases and some are damaged both by winter cold and by warm spells in the winter. While they are considered too risky for general commercial plantings, a few small plantings have been made outside the recognized West Coast vinifera areas with some success.

Southeast Grapes (from Tidewater Virginia, through the central areas of the Carolinas, south through Florida, and west through the southern part of Texas)

In these areas, Pierce's disease kills or shortens the life expectancy of many popular grape varieties. The kinds of grapes that may be expected to give the best results in the area are the muscadines, like Scupernong or modern self-fertile varieties, and a few tolerant varieties introduced from Florida, Stover, and Lake Emerald, and a few of the older varieties such as Champanel, Herbemont and Lukfata. Other varieties may survive to produce a crop or two, but have not proven successful over a longer period.

For the rest of the country, where the climate is humid enough to permit wild grapes to survive, the problem of variety selection is complicated by several diseases and insects that attack cultivated grapes. The American and French-American varieties are somewhat tolerant of these problems and therefore less risky to grow.

American

These are the hardy, disease-tolerant varieties. Most are derived in some degree from the wild American fox grape (Vitis labrusca). Well known varieties are Concord, Delaware and Niagara. Several modern varieties in this group are seedless and well suited for table use.

Hybrids

The hybrids include the so-called "French hybrids" developed in France over the past 80 years primarily for wine. They are more neutral in flavor than most American varieties and a few are well adapted for table use.

The hybrids are crosses between European grape varieties and various native American species. They were selected for the fruit quality of their European ancestors and the disease and insect tolerance of their American ancestors.

Both traits vary widely, from nearly wild with excellent resistance to pests, to high quality with modest resistance. As a group, hybrids are much easier to protect against the many pests than are the vinifera varieties.

Ripening of hybrids differs widely and there are varieties suited to most growing seasons. Also, in this group are several of the most recently introduced wine and table grapes originated in the United States.

In the shorter season areas (140 to 160 frost-free days), early ripening varieties such as Beta (blue) can be grown for juice and jelly, Foch (blue), Cascada (blue),

and in better sites, Aurore (white) can be grown for wine. Light cropping of vines may be useful in short-season areas because it can advance ripening of the fruit by about two weeks.

In the medium season areas (160 to 200 frost-free days), Concord (blue) and Niagara (white) are two of the most popular and easily grown varieties for table use and for juice and jelly. There are several semi-seedless varieties, like Himrod (white) and Suffolk Red, table grapes such as Seneca (white), Alden (blue) and Steuben (blue), and many French-American wine grapes that are satisfactory. Chardonnay and White Reisling, representatives of vinifera wine grapes, may survive if sprayed carefully and frequently.

For growing seasons longer than 200 days, late ripening varieties are preferred. Concord and Niagara are suitable for juice or jelly. White wine varieties include Villard blanc and Vidal 256, red wines include Chambourcin and Villard noir. A muscat flavored grape of interest is Golden Muscat.

Once a variety has been decided on that satisfies the grower's taste and intended use, there are a few other factors to consider before purchasing grapevines.

The purchase of rooted vines from a nursery or garden store saves a year over propagating vines from cuttings. If muscadines or grafted vines are to be grown, the purchase of plants is preferable.

Whether rootstocks are necessary and if so, which one to use, is especially confusing to the beginner. For most purposes only the vinifera varieties may need to be grafted. A rootstock enables the plant to grow under conditions where the own-rooted (non-grafted) vine might fall. Reasons for failure include phyllo-xera root-louse damage (on heavy soils) and nematode damage (on lighter soils, especially when the area is being replanted with new vines).

Certain rootstock varieties may increase vigor, permit good growth on lime soils, reduce damage from drought or wet soils, or tolerate certain soil-borne diseases. Rootstocks are advisable only when one of these particular situations has been found repeatedly in the area. The rootstock variety chosen is of the group that best corrects the situation.

Culture

Planting. Site selection is an important consideration when planning to put in grapevines. To be productive, grapevines require full sunlight. Nearby trees, even when they do not shade vines, compete for moisture and provide birds with a perch from which to attack the vines. Wet soils are not good for grapes.

At least three feet of medium to heavy soil or five feet of sand should be available. Shallower soils reduce vigor and size of crop. Grapes are adapted to a wide variety of soil types. The low fertility of light or poor soils can be corrected with fertilizers. Deep, rich soils can result in overly vigorous vines that have poor clusters, mature later, and are of lower quality for wine.

In most areas of this country, nearly level to rolling ground is most practical for grapes. Moderate slopes may be practical in areas where air drainage gives protection against frosts after the tender vine shoots have begun to grow. Avoid frost pockets, those areas where cold air tends to collect at the bottom of slopes.

A few vines may be planted along an existing fence, or a fence or arbor may be built in an aesthetically pleasant place. Vines form an excellent summer privacy screen, but after leaf fall and pruning there is little left.

Planting will be easier if the soil is spaded or tilled beforehand. Grapevine roots rapidly grow out several feet in the first two years, so working compost or fertilizer into the planting hole will be of little value.

Vines should be planted at about the same depth they were grown in the nursery. If vines are grafted, the graft union should be about two inches above ground level.

Roots should be spread out in all directions in the planting hole. They may be trimmed to about two inches if the vines are planted in a narrow hole made with a post-hole digger.

The top should be cut back to leave two or three buds. When the new shoots begin to grow, remove all except the one or two shoots that are the most vigorous and straight. Tie these loosely to a light stake. Several times during the first season remove lateral shoots that develop at the point of attachment of each leaf. This allows the main shoot to grow more rapidly and a full year may be gained in establishing the vine.

Failure to remove these lateral shoots and the sprouts that appear from the base of the vine throughout the season will result in a bushy vine that seldom has any shoots long enough to reach the trellis.

Leave about four lateral shoots just below any horizontal wires along which the vine will grow. When the shoot or shoots reach the highest point of the trellis or arbor, tie them there, pinch off the tip and allow several of the lateral shoots to grow.

If for any reason a vine fails to make good growth during the first growing season, cut the top back to two buds and treat it as a newly planted vine. It will generally grow more vigorously during the second season.

Training places the crop in a convenient location for care and harvest. Pruning controls the size of the crop to a level that can be ripened successfully.

For at least the first two years, an area one or two feet around each vine should be kept free of weeds by hoeing, or with a heavy mulch of grass clippings or black plastic. Fertilize young plants only on very poor soils.

Spacing

Spacing of vines is not critical. Six to ten feet between vines gives room for each vine, makes pruning easier, and is an economical use of the space. A closer spacing is possible but the actual yield for the area does not increase in proportion to the number of vines. In humid areas where diseases are prevalent, close spacing of rows slows the drying of leaves and fruit and makes disease control more difficult.

Spacing between vines is often most determined by the vigor of the variety. For vigorous vines nine to ten feet will usually fill the trellis with foliage. For some less vigorous hybrids, a spacing of six feet between vines is preferred.

Fruit yield is based on foliage exposed to the sun, so as long as the trellis is filled, optimum yield can be expected. Vine foliage should at least meet between the vines so that maximum use is made of sunlight. Some overlap of foliage is usual and expected.

Structures

Structures on which the vines may be trained range from two or more posts set in the ground and strung with two or three horizontal wires (a trellis) to decorative arbors. Bracing should be sufficient to carry the weight of vines and crop under the sort of wind conditions experienced in the area. Trellis posts should not be more than twenty feet apart and arbor posts not more than ten feet apart.

Wires (11- or 12-gauge smooth galvanized) should be spaced about two feet apart up the posts or along the top of an arbor. Closer spacing causes excessive shading. To permit weed control under the vine and to keep the fruit up, the lowest wire should be 30 to 36 inches above the ground.

Train a permanent trunk to the top wire of a trellis or to the top edge of an arbor.

During the dormant season when vines are pruned, fruiting canes should be trained outward along each fire on the trellis or along an arbor's top edges.

Each bud on the fruiting canes grows into a shoot from four to twenty feet long. These are tied along trellis wires as they grow, or on an arbor where they are spaced out across the top wires to give even exposure to sunlight.

Pest Control

It is possible to get an occasional crop without spraying for diseases and insects of grapes, but both diseases tend to become progressively more severe from year to year. It is customary to spray about three times a year. Schedules and recommendations for types of sprays for a particular area are usually available at a local Extension office of the Agricultural Research Service of the US Department of Agriculture.

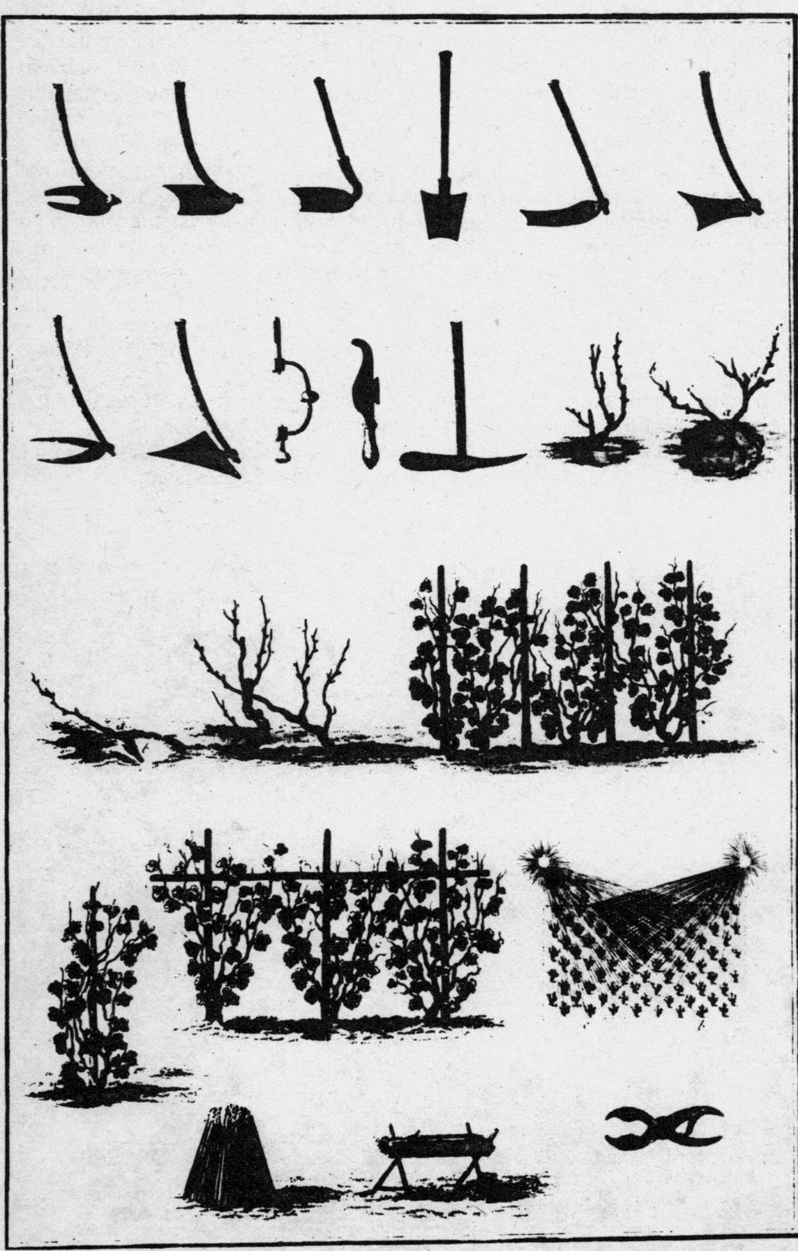

Control of weeds for a foot or two around young vines is worth the effort in the improvement of growth of the vines. Once established, the vine will shade out some weed growth. Some types of weedkiller should not be used near grapes as they are extremely sensitive. Do not use the combination of fertilizer plus weedkiller on lawn areas within 15 feet of a grapevine. The weedkiller may be picked up by the grape roots that extend out this far and the vine can be damaged.

In many areas birds can be a major problem. Netting, which can be used earlier in the season for strawberries and blueberries, is available and if placed carefully over the vines will protect the fruit.

Hornets and wasps on ripe fruit are a common complaint. They are able to attack the fruit only if it has been damaged by insects, diseases or birds, or if it is overripe.

Maintenance and Harvesting

Fruiting canes can be readily identified by looking at the vine in the spring before growth begins. They are the one-year-old shoots (wood of the previous season), with bark that is smooth and brown. At each place where a leaf grew the previous season, there is a conical swelling, or bud.

During the growing season, each bud grows into a shoot that bears leaves and generally three clusters of grapes. The more buds that are left after pruning, the more clusters will appear on the vine.

An unpruned grapevine will set far more fruit than it can ripen successfully. Fruit from overcropped vines is low in sugar, sour, and has poor color. Excessive over-cropping can severely damage the vine.

Obviously the cluster size must be considered in calculating the size of a crop. With very large clustered varieties, such as Thompson Seedless, as few as ten clusters per vine (8-foot spacing) should be left. Perhaps 50 clusters of Concord can ripen and as many as 100 of small clustered varieties such as Beta or Foch.

The commercial grower controls crop size by leaving exactly the right number of buds. The home gardener can achieve a far more accurate control of crop size, and do it despite variations in weather or fruitset, by leaving an excess number of buds, two or three times as many as needed, and removing clusters until the right number remain. Removal of excess clusters can be done any time from before bloom until mid-season.

An acceptable taste is the main criterion for table use of grapes. On a vine that is not overcropped, the berries of blue varieties will lose their red color and white varieties will change from green to golden yellow as they ripen. Ripe berries will soften and seeds become brown.

As the berries ripen, sugar content rises while the acid level decreases. Both these changes are reflected in improved taste.

Determining the harvest of wine grapes requires either experience or a means of measuring both sugar and acid levels.

The yields of a grapevine greatly affect fruit quality. If vines spaced at eight feet are permitted to produce over 30 pounds of fruit each, the quality will almost surely be low. Only under ideal circumstances and climate can this size crop be ripened successfully.

It is better, especially on young vines, to leave a smaller crop than optimum, about five to 10 pounds of fruit, until it is determined how much fruit can be ripened successfully in the particular situation.

Varieties and the number of vines to plant for home use are best determined by the grower's goals. For juice, ten Concord vines set at eight to ten feet apart will usually provide 50 quarts of grape juice each year.

For table use, each vine will produce five to 15 pounds of fruit. One or two vines of ten varieties chosen to ripen over a period of one and one half to two months will usually produce enough for lavish home consumption and gift baskets for friends.

For wine, a quarter acre is the maximum size for a home winemaker operating under the Federal permit (BATF 1541) limit of 200 gallons per year. The size can be scaled down to suit the grower's own goals.

Growing Dwarf Fruit Trees

Dwarf fruit trees are ideal for a small, backyard orchard. They use sunshine more efficiently and produce better fruit than standard trees. They are easier to spray, prune, and harvest. Their fruit ripes earlier than standard-size trees, and they require less space per tree. Production per acre is higher with dwarf trees, even though they produce less fruit than larger trees. In general, although dwarf trees requires more care, they repay the extra attention with earlier and higher production.

Dwarf trees grow from about 6 to 8 feet tall. Semidwarf trees are usually 10 to 12 feet tall, and standard trees may grow as high as 20 feet.

Dwarf apple and pear trees are widely available. Dwarf peach, plum, cherry, apricot, and nectarine trees are not as hardly in the Northeast, but tree breeders are experimenting with genetic dwarfing techniques that may soon result in a full selection of fruit trees.

In general, the size of the tree is determined by the rootstock, the richness of the soil, the size of its fruit, pruning technique, and by controlled hybridization and induced mutations.

All apple trees are grafted. Standard trees are produced by planting seeds, growing the seedlings for two years, and grafting the desired variety on them. Dwarfing rootstocks must be propagated vegetatively by rooting the shoots of specific rootstocks in stoolbeds. The East Malling Research Station, East Malling, Kent, England, played a leading role in selecting dwarfing rootstocks from wild small-growing apple species. Therefore, most of the common dwarfing rootstocks carry the designation M (Malling) and a number.

A common rootstock with the greatest dwarfing effect is M9. Trees on this rootstock rarely grow larger than 8 feet. However, M9 has a poor root system that requires good soil and frequent irrigation. These trees also must be staked or grown beside a trellis. Free-standing trees grown on M9 rootstock without support often are toppled over by the heavy weight of fruit or by high winds.

The next most successful dwarfing rootstock is M26. These trees are somewhat larger than the M9. Their root system is stronger than that of M9, but the trees still require staking.

M7 and M106 both produce semidwarf trees. Although these rootstocks do not require staking, M7 trees have poor anchorage and may be pushed over by heavy winds. M2 and M11 rootstocks produce more vigorous semidwarf trees than M7 and M106, and their root systems are less sensitive to diseases. Trees on M106, M2, and M11 are relatively large and require a more laborious training method during their early years.

Trees dwarfed by the interstem method are usually grafted twice. First, a piece of dwarfing rootstock (equivalent to M9) is grafted on a larger root system of a semidwarf rootstock. This variety is then grafted back on to the top of a stempiece, which becomes an interstem.

The length of the interstem determines the degree of dwarfing. Such trees are produced to take advantage of the larger root and the dwarfing effect of the interstem. However, it takes one year longer to produce double-grafted trees than to produce single-grafted trees. M9, M26, and M9 interstem are considered to be the only rootstocks that produce truly dwarf trees.

Pear trees are dwarfed by using quince root. Some varieties, including Bartlett, do not unite well with quince. In these cases, a compatible variety is first grafted on quince. The desired variety is then grafted on the stem. In fact, most dwarf pear trees are interstem-type trees. However, in this interstem combination the root is dwarfing and the interstem is used only to overcome incompatibility.

The quince is a shallow-rooted tree and requires very good soil with even soil moisture. On poor soils or with inadequate soil moisture, pears and quince do not produce well.

Factors Affecting Dwarfing

Size of the Variety. Apple trees vary in size regardless of their rootstock. For example, Golden Delicious and Jonathan are small trees whereas McIntosh and Delicious are large trees. This means that if Golden Delicious and McIntosh are grafted on the same rootstock the McIntosh tree will be much larger than the Golden Delicious trees.

Fruit growers of the Northwest were the first to notice that some Delicious trees are less vigorous than others. The stems on such trees elongate less and the leaves are closer together. Such trees produce spurs on which the fruit blooms. They are called spur-type trees. Various agricultural research stations have produced spur types of other varieties by artificially-induced mutations.

Today there are spur types of Delicious, Golden Delicious, Rome, McIntosh, and some other varieties. The spur-type tree of a given variety is much smaller than the non-spur type of the same variety.

Pear trees also differ in size. Magness is the largest of the pear varieties. Bartlett, Moonglow, and many other varieties are considerably smaller. There are no spur-type pears.

Soil Types. Trees grow better on rich than on poor soil. On good soil use a dwarfing rootstock in combination with a small variety. It may even be necessary to use the spur type of a small variety to get a truly dwarf tree.

A Golden Delicious / M9 or Jonathan / M9 combination is considered to produce a good dwarf tree. In contrast, a McIntosh / M9 or Delicious / M9 combination may be too large on good soils and may require the spur type of these varieties or additional pruning. On poor soils, M9 may produce too small a tree even with Delicious grafted on it. Therefore, M26 or M106 with a spur-type variety should be chosen if the soil is poor.

Early Fruit Production. Early fruiting is the most powerful dwarfing agent known to date. Some people believe that the dwarfing rootstock produces a dwarf tree because it forces early fruit production, not because it somehow interferes with the growth of the trees. Before fruiting begins, trees on dwarfing rootstock grow about as much as trees on standard roots. Only after the third year when the dwarfs begin to produce fruit do they slow down in growth.

On rich soils, or on semidwarf roots, the additional effect of forced early production is needed to produce dwarf trees. Flower buds develop during June and July in the year previous to flowering. Therefore, all manipulation needed to enhance flowering should be done during early summer in order to successfully influence fruiting the next year.

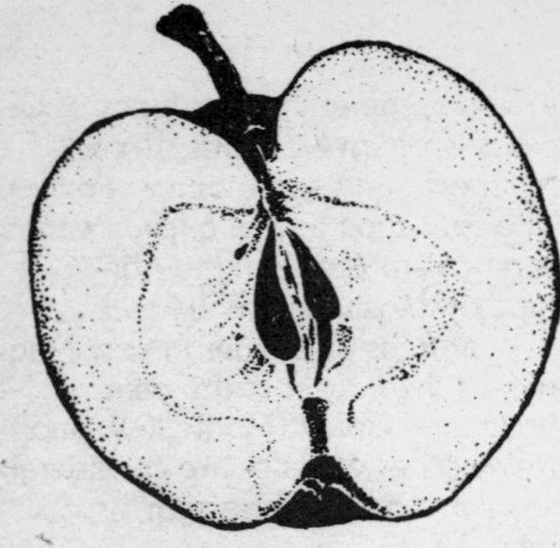

Pruning Techniques. For the development of flowerbuds the tree needs carbohydrates. Severe pruning early in the life of the tree will restrict the leaf area and consequently reduce carbohydrate production. Fruiting will be delayed and tree size will increase. However, occasional pruning is still needed to shape the tree and insure good light penetration to the inside branches and leaves.

The terminal bud of a shoot produces a hormone that keeps the lateral buds from growing. When this terminal bud is removed, the four to six buds below the cut will grow and produce shoots. Every such heading can produce four to six shoots. Often this is desirable; other times it is not.

During the first two years of the life of the tree, heading cuts are desirable. During the later years, thinning cuts are more needed. These thinning cuts remove the entire shoot at its base where a visible ring is located. If thinning cuts are made in August they have a strong dwarfing effect on the tree. In contrast, heading cuts, especially when applied during the winter, strongly promote growth.

Pulling or bending the branches down to near horizontal position strongly promotes the formation of flowerbuds. Pulling the branches down can be done in various ways. Tie a string to the end of the shoot and to the base of the tree. Then place a styrofoam block in the crotch angle between the main stem and the side shoot, forcing the shoot into the right position. A clothespin can be used to attach a weight to the end of the shoot, pulling it into the right position.

Any of the above methods will work. If the side shoot was pulled down or bent below the horizontal level it should be released from this position about three weeks later. This shoot will not go back to its original position, but if left too long in the bent position it will produce strong shoots at the top of the bow, which is undesirable. If the trees are grown along a trellis, bending the shoots to the wire and tying them there serves the same purpose.

Genetic Manipulation. Genetic dwarf fruit trees are produced by controlled hybridization or by inducing mutations in the budwood of standard types. This budwood is grafted onto standard fruit tree rootstocks, not dwarfing rootstocks discussed above. The genetic dwarf trees tend to put out less vegetative growth and more fruiting wood, but their standard rootstocks are more adaptable to a variety of soil conditions and do not require support.

The genetic dwarf fruit trees are somewhat less hardy than their standard counterparts. When planted in the ground, not in tubs, these trees can survive zero degrees in the winter. However, dwarf fruit trees are often planted in tubs as they are small enough and decorative enough for patios and yards. Tubbed trees should be set on castors so they can be easily wheeled to protective shelter if winter temperatures go below 25°F.

Development of a dwarf tree. First year: A, after planting is pruned back at the mark; B, the side shoots are developed; C, side shoots pulled down. Second year: D, leader is cut back; E, second tier of branches developed; F, side shoots of second tier pulled down.

Dwarf Fruit Tree Culture

Planting and Training. When purchased, dwarf trees may have only a single stem or perhaps two or three branches along the main stem. Plant them in early spring in areas where the winters are severe; in late fall or early spring in areas where the climate is milder.

Place trees six to eight feet apart depending on soil type, variety, and rootstock.

Trees must be planted in soils that are well drained. In poorly drained soils, dwarf trees soon die. If you are uncertain about the soil's drainage capacity, dig the hole for a tree and fill it with water. If the water drains within 24 hours the soil is drained well enough for dwarf trees. If the water remains in the hole after 24 hours, dwarf trees should not be planted at that location.

Plant the trees at the depth at which they stood in the nursery. There will be a change in the color of the bark of the tree near the root below the graft union. This color change is usually visible at the soil line. Be sure that the graft union is above the ground when the tree is planted. It is better to plant the tree too high than too deep.

When planting a dwarf tree, place a metal stake (fence stake) or a 2- to 3-inch-diameter redwood or treated wood post into the hole about 6 inches from the stem. The pole should extend 5 feet above the ground. Pack good topsoil firmly around the roots, and water the plant well. Do not apply fertilizer at the time of planting.

After planting, prune the stem or "head back" the tree about 30 inches above the ground. If the tree has strong side branches, head back the stem leader about 12 inches above the side branches. The buds below the heading will grow. (See illustration.)

When the side shoots are about 12 inches long pull them into horizontal position. If the tree has side branches at the time of planting, pull these down. In the latter case, styrofoam blocks or clothespins are easier to apply than strings.

The following spring, head back the leader about 12 inches above the first tier of branches. Develop the second tier of branches the same way as the first tier the year before. The first-tier branches should produce a few apples during this year.

From then on no further heading cuts should be needed. If the tree is too full, use thinning cuts in July or August. If the tree is too high and cutting it back is necessary, make sure the heading cut is made in such a way that a pencil-size shoot remains on the top. The terminal bud of this small shoot will produce enough hormone to keep the other buds from growing.

Fertilizing. Dwarf trees require a well-limed soil. Liming can be done successfully only at the time of planting. Mix about 10 pounds of dolomitic limestone into the soil dug out from the hole. Make sure that the lime is thoroughly mixed with the soil.

Do not apply fertilizer in the year of planting. From the second year on, apply fertilizer only when shoots grow less than 12 to 18 inches and the leaves are light green. The only exception is Golden Delicious, which normally has pale green leaves.

When fertilizer is needed the ideal choice is 10-4-10 at a rate of ½ pound per year of age of the tree. If this fertilizer is not available, apply the available mixture at the same calculated rate for nitrogen. For example, if only a 20-6-4 fertilizer is available, use half the recommended rate. (The first number is the one that indicates the percentage of nitrogen in the mixture.)

Mulching. Mulching is an excellent practice for growing dwarf trees. Mulch provides a better uptake of nutrients, insures a more even supply of moisture, and prevents the overheating of soil around the roots.

Keep mulch away from the trunk: this keeps mice away from the tree. Sharp bluestone chips can be put around the trunk if they are available. This prevents rodents from damaging the bark during winter.

Rabbits may also damage the bark. To protect against rabbits a chicken wire mesh should be placed around the trunk of each tree.

Pest Control. Control of insects and fungus diseases is an important part of successful fruit production. Information on recommended practices for pest control is readily available from the Department of Agriculture in Washington, D.C. and from local Agricultural Research Service stations.

Two new apple varieties, Prima and Priscilla, are resistant to apple scab, a common fungus disease of apples. These varieties do not require sprays against apple scab, but they still need protection against insects.

Dawn, Moonglow, Magness, Mac, Maxine, and Seckel pears are resistant to fireblight, a bacterial disease. Eastern climates (with the exception of cool areas in Michigan and New York) are not generally suitable for pear production because of fireblight, therefore it is best to plant only these resistant varieties when planting pears in these areas.

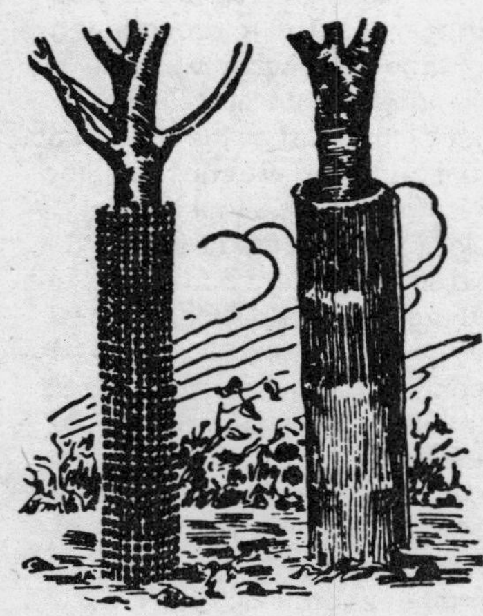

Wire or other rabbit guards must be fastened loosely to permit expansion

Container Planting. When planting genetic dwarf trees for a very small crop, or primarily for ornamentation, containers may be used. Choose a tub at least 20 inches wide and 18 inches deep. A thick-walled pot will minimize evaporation. To insure good drainage drill at least four one-inch holes in the bottom of the tub or pot and cover it with screening or potsherds. A 2-inch layer of rock or gravel should be added. A suggested soil mix would be one-third loam, one-third peat moss, and one-third sand. Vermiculite or perlite can substitute for sand to reduce the weight.

Genetic Dwarf Fruit Tree Varieties

Apples. Garden Delicious, the first genetic dwarf apple to be developed, produces sweet, crisp fruit on a 6- to 8-foot tree. In warm areas the apples are yellow-green with a slight pink blush and in coldern climates they turn dark red.

Starkspur Compact Mac and Starkspur Compact Red Delicious, introduced in 1980, are natural mutations or "sports" and bear fruits identical to those of standard trees. Bright 'n Early Apple, a new spur type, is a limb sport that produces a crop in 124 days after flowering. Nugget, a spur-type Yellow Delicious, is a hardy semidwarf.

Cherries. Garden Bing is the only fully dwarf, sweet cherry, reaching 6 feet at maturity. Compact Stella, Compact Lambert, and Starkrimson are hardy sweet cherries, all less than half the size of a standard 30-foot sweet cherry.

North Star is a compact, self-pollinating pie cherry that produces tart, deep red fruit in northern areas where other genetic dwarfs will not survive. Meteor is a slightly larger pie cherry that produces clear, light red fruit.

Nectarines. Garden King, Garden Delight, and Garden Beauty, all developed by hybridizer Chris Zaiger of California, are self-pollinating nectarine genetic dwarfs that do well in mild winter growing areas.

Stark HoneyGlo Nectarine and Stark Sweet Melody Nectarine grow only 6- to 8-feet tall.

Peaches. Stark Starlet Peach is shrub-like in growth and produces large, flavorful fruit. Pratt's Compact Red Haven is a new genetic dwarf peach that grows to about 8 feet and has a fruit almost identical to its standard-sized parent.

Apricots. The apricot genetic dwarfs are the most decorative of these trees, displaying brilliant green leaves and bright golden fruit. Aprigold was the first genetic dwarf apricot to be developed. More recently the mildly sweet Stark GoldenGlo and semi-freestone Garden Annie have been introduced. Both bear fruit the second or third year and are less than half the size of a standard apricot tree.

New home orchardists are advised to consider the climate, particularly winter temperatures, when selecting dwarf fruit varieties; to follow nursery instructions when planting whether in the ground or in containers; and to remember that good culture practices are the key to successful fruit production whether the new tree is genetic or rootstock dwarf.

Growing Subtropical Fruits

Subtropical fruits such as avocados, citrus fruits, figs, and guava are not difficult to grow in most parts of the south and southwestern United States. Single trees also can be grown indoors or in containers for areas where there is winter freezing.

Over a hundred subtropical fruits are available to home horticulturists, and detailed information on all of them can be easily obtained from any local Extension office of the Agricultural Research Service of the United States Department of Agriculture. Other valuable sources of information include nurserymen, experienced gardeners, garden clubs, and specialized groups such as the rare fruit organizations active in Florida and California.

The horticultural requirements for most subtropical fruits do not differ from those of other shrubs, trees or vines grown for fruit, ornament, shade or other specialized use. In fact the outstanding ornamental value of most fruit crops permits them a dual role.

Because they come from many parts of the world, subtropical fruit crops differ in the degree of cold they can withstand and in soil and moisture requirements. Some are adapted to warm-temperate conditions, others will tolerate brief cold spells and survive winters in the warmest parts of the continental United States.

When selecting fruits to plant around the home, choose those known to grow well in the area or the best of efforts may prove disappointing. Personal preferences should be tempered by what you know will work.

The Maull and Jones pneumatic sizer. A device used in grading citrus fruits.

Culture

Planting. Most tree fruits should be planted 12 to 20 feet apart and away from the house, walks, drives, and power lines. Those tropical fruits listed as small trees or shrubs in the descriptions below can be planted somewhat closer. Where there is significant danger of cold damage, plant subtropical fruits in the warmest part of the yard, which generally is the south side of the house.

Most failures in growing fruit trees at home result from poor transplanting or poor care. Yet commercial fruit growers routinely transplant fruit trees with almost no failures.

Good preparation of the planting hole is essential. Dig the hole only as deep as—and about a foot wider than—needed to accomodate the root system. Regardless of the soil type, add liberal amounts of organic matter such as rotted manure, compost or peat.

For bare-root plants, prune off dead or damaged roots. Make a cone of soil in the center of the hole and set the plant on it, carefully spreading the roots out in the hole. For container-grown plants, remove the container and set the plant in the hole.

In either case, set the plant at the same depth it grew in the nursery or container.

Fill the hole three-fourths full of soil. Add water to settle soil around the roots and eliminate air pockets. After the water drains through, finish filling the hole with soil, then add water again. A ring of soil a few inches high around the planting hole can be used to form a water basin during the first year.

At planting, bare-root fruit trees should be pruned to balance the top with the reduced root system, which requires removing about a third of the top. Most people are reluctant to prune this heavily, but it's for the good of the tree. The nursery where the tree is purchased will usually do this pruning, if asked. Container-grown plants are not usually pruned since they have an intact root system.

Training. Initial training of the fruit tree is done at planting to assure that the tree takes the desired shape. For example, the growing tips of branches are pruned off to force branching.

Pruning cuts should be clean and close to the trunk to avoid leaving stubs which enable wood-rooting organisms to enter the tree. Protection with pruning paint is recommended if the cut is larger than an inch or so in diameter.

Mature trees are pruned to remove dead or damaged wood, or to eliminate limbs that may interfere with traffic in the yard. Such pruning can be done at any time of year.

Fertilizing. Specialized fertilizers for subtropical fruit trees are not commercially available. However, the trees will grow just as well on a complete, balanced garden fertilizer such as 6-8-8, 10-10-10, or 12-12-12. If the area has alkaline soils or soils known to lack specific micronutrients such as iron, manganese or zinc, these may be supplied.

Newly planted trees should not be fertilized until they resume active growth after transplanting. Then, fertilize sparingly and frequently until they mature and begin to produce fruit. Using 10-10-10 as an example, young trees should receive about a pound of fertilizer per year of tree age, that is, 1 pound in the first year, 2 in the second, and so on. Simply spread the fertilizer on the ground under the tree and then water it in. Total fertilizer for the year should be divided into several applications so young trees receive some fertilizer every 2 to 3 months.

Mature, bearing trees can be fertilized at double that rate, or 2 pounds per year of tree age. A 10-year-old tree would receive 20 pounds per year, split into three applications: early spring, early summer, and early fall.

Lime may be needed in some cases to raise the soil pH for optimum tree growth. However, liming should be based on a soil test and recommendations for the local area.

Occasionally, some fruit trees may need certain micro-elements, particularly in very sandy soils or alkaline soils. Micro-elements such as iron, manganese or zinc are included in some fertilizers and are also available in nutritional sprays, which are applied separately as foliar (leaf) sprays. The addition of micro-elements is also dependent on local soil conditions. Local soil analyses and recommendations concerning additives can be obtained from any local Extension service of the Department of Agriculture.

Mulches. Mulches around fruit trees help in weed control and water conservation. They also reduce lawn mower damage to tree trunks since there is no need to mow close to the trees.

In some cases, organic mulches can lead to fertilizer deficiencies as the micro-organisms that decompose them rob the tree of nutrients. They also contribute to increased cold damage by inhibiting radiation of ground heat to the tree. In other cases, organic mulches increase the incidence of diseases such as foot rot and root rot. For these reasons clean cultivation instead of mulches is recommended for citrus, avocado, lychee and some other fruits.

Mulches from the yard could include leaves and grass clippings. Sawdust, wood chips, pine bark, gravel or other mulches can be obtained from local nurseries.

Watering. Watering plants is the most misunderstood part of plant culture. It's one reason why so many fruit trees die shortly after transplanting. Too little water causes the tiny root hairs to die, and the leaves then wilt for lack of water. Too much water forces air from the soil, again causing the root hairs to die for lack of oxygen, and the leaves will wilt. For best results, water fruit trees infrequently but thoroughly.

Frequent shallow waterings cause shallow rooting. A shallow-rooted fruit tree is subject to drought and poor growth, so when watering, water long and water well. Apply water only as fast as the soil can absorb it and keep watering until the soil is wet at least a foot down.

Newly transplanted trees need a good soaking every 2 to 4 days until they are well established. Mature trees need water every 7 to 12 days, depending on the climate and soil type. Since sandy soils don't hold much water, they require watering about once a week, while clay soils will go several days longer before drying out.

Fruit trees growing on a lawn will compete with the lawn for fertilizer and water. In such situations pay particular attention to the specific needs of both tree and lawn. The tree will compete more aggressively than the grass. The grass will soon begin to thin out and may disappear completely once the tree begins to create heavy shade.

Winter Care. Cold protection is required for many subtropical fruits. Young trees are more susceptible to cold than large, mature trees, but also easier to protect. Banking a mound of soil around the trunk of a young fruit tree will keep the rootstock and trunk alive even if the top should freeze. Pull the bank down in spring after cold danger is past.

Small trees can be covered with blankets, paper or plastic to prevent freezing. Lawn sprinklers have been turned on trees, but too much water can cause problems for the root system and ice can cause limb breakage. In some cases, a frame covered with clear polyethylene built around the tree forms a mini-greenhouse. Some slow-burning heating materials are available and work quite well.

Container Growing. Many subtropical fruits can be grown in containers in areas where freezes occur each year. The size and mobility of the containers allows the plants to be moved indoors during winter months. Here the plants are treated pretty much as houseplants with regard to water, fertilizer, humidity, light, and pest control.

As with houseplants, water container plants infrequently but thoroughly. Take care to acclimate the plants to the different conditions when they are moved outdoors in spring or indoors in fall. Plants going outdoors should be moved to a shady spot for a couple of weeks before being exposed to full sunlight. Reverse this process when moving them indoors in fall.

When plants are indoors, put them in areas receiving the most natural light. Keep them away from heaters, doors and heating ducts. Because of lower humidity indoors, increase the humidity around the plants by misting or other means.

Growing plants in containers or patio tubs limits the volume of soil in which they're growing. Even so, the plant may soon grow too large to bring indoors. When this happens, prune back the plant severely.

Description

Here is some specific information about fruits that can be grown in many parts of the Southern and Southwestern States. The letters WT (Warm-temperate), ST (Subtropical) and T (Tropical) give an approximation of temperature requirements for each species. However, other factors, such as amount of rainfall and the time of year that rain comes, also will determine whether a particular fruit can be grown in specific areas.

Avocado (Persea americana). ST, T. Shade tree with rough dark bark suitable for growing bromeliads and orchids. More than one variety should be planted together for cross-pollination. Plant locally adapted varieties. Will not tolerate heavy, poorly drained soils.

Banana (Musa acuminata, Musa hybrids). T. Rootstock may survive light freezes. Giant, treelike herb, planted for ornament where cold precludes fruiting. Many varieties are available but the most widely grown are Cavendish (as commercial crops), Apple (sometimes called Ladyfinger), and Orinoco (also called Horse banana, and good for cooking). The starchy cooking banana called Plantain is very susceptible to cold.

Carambola (Averrhoa carambola). T. Tree varying from small to large. Characteristic five-angled fruit of yellow or deep orange color varies from sour to sweet and is pleasantly aromatic. Plant grafted varieties (Golden Star, Mih Tao). Cross-pollination helps fruit set.

Carob (Ceratonia siliqua). WT. Small tree with attractive dark green leaves that prefers a Mediterranean climate, very dry in summer with rains during winter. Trees may be male or female, so more than one should be planted to ensure fruiting. The brown, leathery pods are rich in sugar and furnish a chocolate substitute.

Cattley guava (Psidium cattleianum). ST. Shrub or small tree with beautiful mottled trunk and glossy dark green leaves. The small, round fruit, bright red or yellow-colored, has a tart flavor and may be eaten fresh or made into jellies or jams. Plants grow readily from seed and are propagated accordingly.

Feijoa (Feijoa sellowiana). WT. Shrub. Compact cold-resistant and most attractive, selected varieties such as Coolidge fruit well without cross-pollination, but seedlings may not. Flowers are edible. Fruit can be eaten fresh, and makes a firm jelly.

Fig (Ficus carica). WT. Small tree. Adapted to a wide range of climates, fig will not tolerate nematodes. Where these are a problem, heavy mulching and occasional application of an approved nematicide, according to prescribed rules, will help. Lemon, Brown Turkey, and Celeste varieties are recommended.

Guava (Psidium quajava). T. Small tree. Somewhat weedy unless pruned to shape it, the guava can be attractive, particularly when in bloom. Certain seedlings make excellent jelly, while varieties such as Ruby-X Supreme and Indian Red are good to eat out-of-hand. Fruit flies are a problem where abundant.

Jaboticaba (Myrciaria cauliflora). ST. Shrubbery tree. Grows slowly but produces abundant crops of black, grapelike fruit excellent to eat fresh or use in jellies or wines.

Kiwi, Yangtao (Actinidia chinensis). WT. Vine. Not successful in warmer parts of Florida, this deciduous species is sensitive to nematode damage. Flowers of named varieties (Hayward females, for example) must be pollinated in order to fruit, so a pollinator should grow nearby. Because of its excellent quality this fruit should be planted wherever it can be grown well.

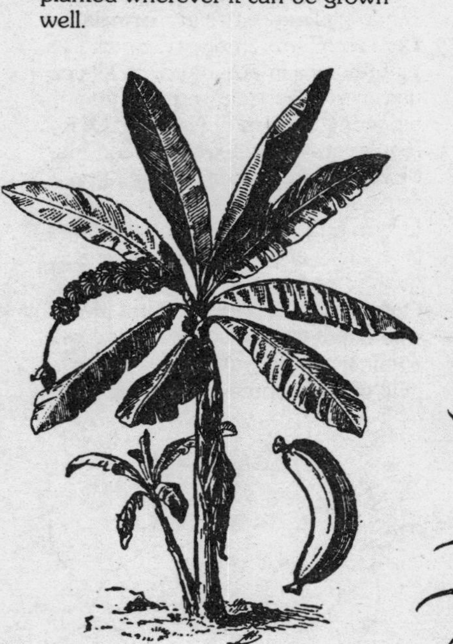

Longan (Dimocarpus longan). T. This tree is a lychee relative that bears clusters of attractive, smooth, golden brown, sweet-flavored fruit that is less tart than lychee fruit. The tree demands less soil and moisture than lychee, and makes a shade tree of stately proportions. Kohala, from Hawaii, bears large fruit of good quality.

Loquat (Eriobotrya japonica). WT. Small tree. The dark green, deeply ribbed leaves of this tree combined with its tendency to produce fragrant creamy-white flowers over a period of months make the loquat a universally valued ornamental. The excellent fruit quality of grated varieties such as Wolfe, Gold Nugget (Thales), and Champagne make these worth the effort needed to find them. Fruit is excellent eaten fresh, but may also be made into pie, jam, and jelly.

Lychee (Litchi chinensis). T. Tree. Somewhat finicky, demanding, slightly acid, well-drained soil with abundant moisture and no salts in soil or water, this tree covered with bright red fruit is a sight to remember where it grows well. Long popular in Southeast Asia, the fruit has many American devotees. It may be eaten fresh or dried like raisins. The most dependably productive varieties are Sweetcliff and Mauritius.

Mango (Mangifera indica). T. Tree. Of the many existing varieties, take the time to select one that is especially appealing: Carrie, Irwin, Glenn, Keitt and Tommy Atkins are outstanding. Blooming trees can cause allergic reactions; do not plant near bedroom windows or air conditioner intake. Mango is one of the world's most popular fruits.

Passion fruits (Passiflora edulis, purple and P. flavicarpa, yellow). ST., T. Vines are ornamental. The purple-fruited form is sensitive to nematodes and soil-borne fungus disease, but withstands more cold than the yellow-fruited form, which is disease-resistant. Self-pollinating types should be planted where possible, otherwise fruit production may be sparse.

Pineapple (Ananas comosus). T. Perennial herb. This bromeliad makes an attractive house plant where outdoor temperatures are too low for it. The plant can be moved to a porch or patio during warm weather. Given enough light it will eventually flower, then produce a fruit of fine quality provided conditions are warm enough.

Pomegranate (Punica granatum). WT. Small tree that tolerates extremes of heat and alkaline soils, but thrives under a wide range of conditions. Needs full sun for best performance. Wonderful and Sweet are the varieties best known for their fruit quality. Other varieties are grown primarily as ornamentals.

Tamarind (Tamarindus indica). T. Large tree related to the carob, with very acid fruit in pods. Pulp of the tamarind, an essential ingredient of many chutney recipes, also is used to make a refreshing ade-like drink. Where the climate is warm enough, this tree is easily grown.

Annonaceous Fruits

Atemoya (Annona cherimola x A. squamosa). T. Moderate-sized tree, a hybrid of the cherimoya and the sugar-apple, that combines the excellent fruit quality of the cherimoya with the fitness for low elevations of the sugar-apple. Flowers abundantly in warm weather, but may need to be hand-pollinated to assure fruit set. Desirable varieties are Kaller (African Pride) and Bradley. Others are being tested.

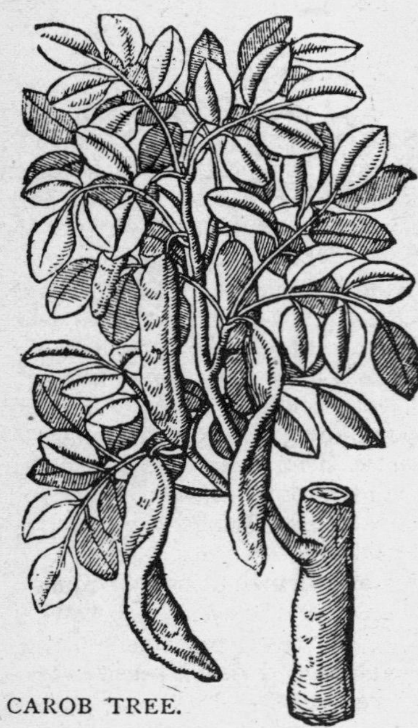

CAROB TREE.

Cherimoya (A. cherimola). ST. Small tree adapted to high elevations in tropical South America, producing a large green fruit with a sweet, delicately aromatic pulp that surrounds many smooth dark seeds. Does not grow well in southern Florida but is more successful in California where it withstands temperatures as low as 25°F.

Soursop or guanabana (A. muricata). T. Small tree, very sensitive to sudden cold spells, that bears a large rough fruit with a refreshing acid flavor that is excellent in drinks and sherbets. Should be planted in a sheltered location.

Sugar-apple (A. squamosa). T. Small tree that bears a soft-pulped, many-seeded fruit similar to the cherimoya but without that fruit's fine aroma. Grows well at sea level in southern Florida and other areas of similar climate.

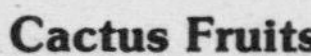

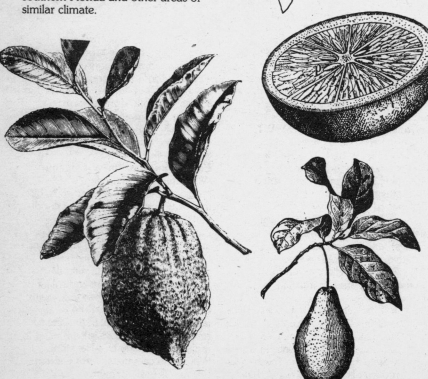

Cactus Fruits

Indian fig (Opuntia ficus-indica). WT. Large treelike cactus with smooth flat joints and few spines. Yellow flowers in spring are followed by large red and yellow fruit. Bristles can be irritating; handle fruit with care. Prefers a dry climate and does not thrive in humid situations.

Citrus

Calamodin (Citrus blancoi). WT., ST. Small tree of great ornamental value that grows and fruits well in small containers. The fruits resemble small oranges but have an acid taste and should not be eaten out-of-hand. Flavor is excellent for drinks and marmalades.

Grapefruit (Citrus paradisi). ST. Medium to large-size tree, excellent for shade and for growing orchids and hanging plants, providing up to 300 pounds of excellent breakfast or juice fruit per year. Varieties include Duncan (white, seedy pulp, excellent flavor), Marsh (white, seedless) and Ruby (pink pulp, seedless).

Kumquat (Fortunella japonica). WT. Shrub or small tree, very cold-tolerant, extremely attractive when in fruit. Nagami is the most common variety, with oblong fruit, deep orange in color having a thick edible skin and an acid pulp. Adapted to candy making or use in marmalades.

Lemon (Citrus limon). T. Small tree that remains in active growth all year and thus is less cold-resistant than the tangerine or even the orange. Of irregular growth habit, the lemon must be pruned from time to time to promote an attractive shape. Eureka, Lisbon and Villa Franca all bear similar fruit, of acceptable commercial quality; Eureka makes a smaller tree than the others. Novelties are Meyer with a less acid fruit, and Ponderosa, which bears very large, mild-flavored lemons.

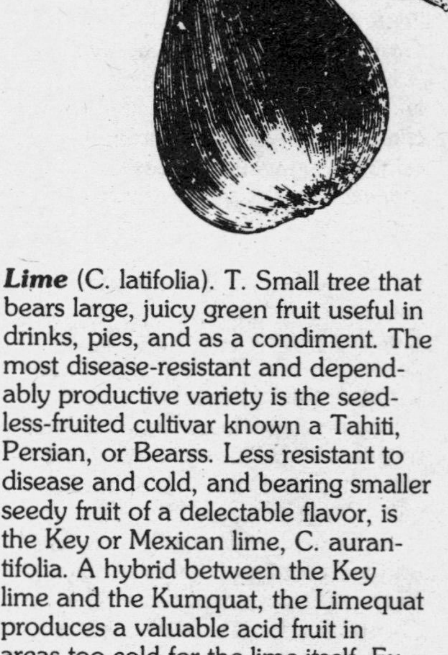

Lime (C. latifolia). T. Small tree that bears large, juicy green fruit useful in drinks, pies, and as a condiment. The most disease-resistant and dependably productive variety is the seedless-fruited cultivar known a Tahiti, Persian, or Bearss. Less resistant to disease and cold, and bearing smaller seedy fruit of a delectable flavor, is the Key or Mexican lime, C. aurantifolia. A hybrid between the Key lime and the Kumquat, the Limequat produces a valuable acid fruit in areas too cold for the lime itself. Eustis fruits well in the open as well as in containers.

Orange (C. sinense). ST. Tree of moderate size, probably the most popular of all citrus fruits, available in a number of varieties that ripen at various seasons. Hamlin is one of the earliest, ripening in November, followed by Pineapple and Washington Navel, which ripen from December to February, and then by Valencia, which ripens in April or later and can be "stored on the tree" into the summer months.

Tangelo (C. reticulata x C. paradisi). ST. Tree, hybrid between tangerine and grapefruit, bearing fruit that combines characters from both parents. Vigorous and cold-resistant. Several varieties are available. Minneola and Orlando need to be planted near other citrus trees for cross-pollination. The Templer tangor (C. sinensis x C. paradisi) bears a sweet, juicy fruit similar to tangelos.

Tangerine (C. reticulata). ST. Tree of attractive growth habit, fairly resistant to cold, whose beauty is enhanced by the waxy, deep orange-colored fruit in season. Dancy ripens before Christmas, as does Clementine, which can be "stored on the tree" in good condition for months. Closely related are the cold-hardy and early dwarf Owari Satsuma, which ripen from October to Christmas, and the Kara, Honey and Kimow mandarins.

Persimmons

Black-sapote (Diospyros digyna). T. A tropical Mexican and Central American persimmon that grows well in southern Florida. The dark brown pulp is rich in vitamin C, and also a source of calcium and protein. It was important in the diet of Central America before Columbus.

Japanese persimmon (Diospyros kaki). WT. Small tree, attractive even when out of fruit with its large, hairy leaves; highly ornamental when the bright orange-colored fruit is ripening. Trees grafted on D. lotus or the native American D. virginiana are available. Fuya bears fruit that is non-astringent even before fully ripe. Fruit of Hachiya and Tane Nashi is astringent until fully ripe, but then delectable. In dry climates, fruit may be sun-dried to make a fine-flavored product.

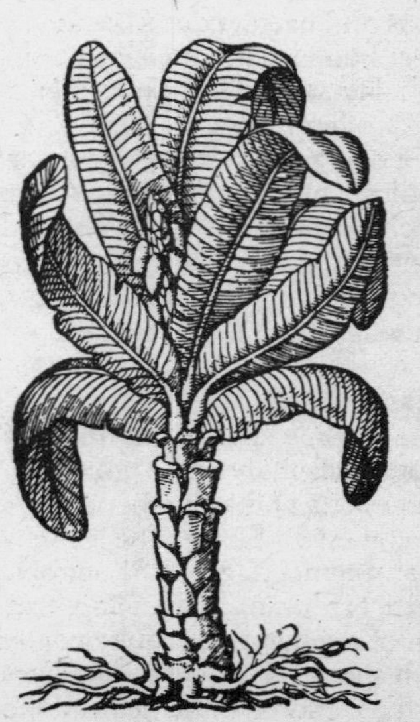

GROWING

Nut Trees

Trees bearing nuts are often not considered by home gardeners. Possibly this is because many of these trees have limited growing ranges, they are slow to bear, some are subject to disease, and for people choosing trees purely for ornamental purposes the fruit may even be a nuisance. Nevertheless, many nut trees are handsome and make excellent shade trees. And the nutritious and delicious nuts are not only a cost-savings for family consumption but can also encourage animals and birds onto your grounds.

You have to be of a patient temperament to enjoy nut trees, because it may take between five and ten years from the time of planting until your trees bear fruit. For this reason, you should take extra care in establishing and maintaining these trees. While a mistake in a vegetable or flower garden can be rectified the following year, it can take you a number of years to realize you've bought the wrong nut tree. Many nut fanciers, however, find this more of a challenge than a deterrent.

In buying a nut tree, you are best off bypassing seedlings and buying a grafted tree. Grafting and budding are skills you may want to learn at some point in your gardening career, but if you are starting out with a nut tree you will want to give yourself the benefits of all the odds by selecting one suitable to your area and of proven selection.

By far the most popular species is pecan, and English walnut comes in second. But you might also consider chestnut, filbert, black walnut, butternut, hickory, pistachio, and macadamia.

If you are buying a single nut tree for a garden, beware of walnut. This tree produces a toxic substance (juglone) that inhibits growth of many other plants (such as azaleas and rhododendrons) that you might try to grow near it.

Pecans, black walnuts, and hickories are tall trees, growing to ninety feet and beyond. Spreading trees include Chinese chestnut, butternut, Japanese walnut, and heartnut—all dainty-foliaged and branching species that look something like old-fashioned apple trees. Almond trees are also spreaders, even smaller, and have lovely blossoms. Filberts and chinkapin chestnuts are hardly more than shrubs. If you want an evergreen, try a large seeded nut pine.

Except for pecans and walnuts, which are extensively grown commercially, you may have trouble finding suitable trees in your area. You may find it profitable to exchange information with other amateur growers in your neighborhood.

Pecan

Pecan trees grow throughout the southern states from the Carolinas to California and extend north along river bottoms—especially in the Mississippi River valleys—as far as Illinois.

Pecans like rich, deep, well-drained soil and a long and warm growing season. Though they prefer a frost-free season of 190 to 220 days, you can buy varieties adapted to only 150 frost-free days. If you want a pecan tree for decoration, you can grow one for this purpose in colder regions of the Northeast and Northwest; cool temperatures, though, do not allow the development of full kernels. In the Midwest, choose a variety that matures early. In the humid Southeast, look for disease-resistant types.

Hickory

Related to both pecans and walnuts, hickories are hardier than pecans and produce sweet-tasting nuts that are easy to shell. Shellbark and shagbark, both native species have slightly different requirements. Shellbark flourishes in lowland and river-bottom soil, while shagbark survives in thinner, more acid, upland soils.

Walnut

Eastern black walnuts are native to the East Coast and grow from southern Vermont to Texas. It does best on limestone-derived soil, and the flavor of the nut is prized because it does not diminish even during baking.

More popular for cultivation, however, is the English walnut or Persian walnut, a variety that probably originated in Persia but was brought to the New World on English ships. Singly these trees can grow to ninety feet and have sixty-foot spreads, but grown in orchards they attain only half this size. They need well-drained and deep soil, because their roots can develop extensively at fifteen-foot depths. They thrive especially on the West Coast. They do best in an area with 200 or more frost-free days, but will thrive and produce nuts with only 150 frost-free days. In winter they need about 1,000 hours or temperatures below 45°F to complete the chilling necessary for nut production, yet they can be damaged by temperatures as low as 14°F. If you live in a cold area, get one of the Carpathian strains that can withstand temperatures of 20°F below zero.

Consult local nurserymen for walnut trees appropriate to your conditions. Butternut is a hardy species of walnut valued in colder regions of the Northwest and Northeast. Japanese walnut, heartnut, and many hybrids are available for a number of climate conditions.

Walnuts generally prefer a soil acidity of about 6.5 pH.

Chestnuts

American chestnut trees were destroyed by a bark parasite in the early twentieth century. Though some are regrowing, they have been replaced by Far East varieties, especially the Chinese chestnut that grows about forty feet tall. These are hardy, can survive wherever peach trees thrive, and can produce fruit as early as three to four years after planting. They like well-drained, acid (pH 5.5 to 6.0) soil. They may bear within three years of transplanting, and unlike other nut trees that are prone to a biennial cycle, are regular bearers.

Other Nuts

Filberts, almonds, and pistachios originated in arid, mild climates of Europe, Asia, and the Middle East and thrive in the similar habitats of California (especially the Sacramento and the San Joaquin valleys), Oregon (especially the Willamette Valley), and Washington.

Filberts, also called hazelnuts, are restricted by blight and cold, but some of the hybrids are adaptable to colder conditions and can be grown even in the Northeast. Almonds and pistachios react adversely to early frost and high humidity, and they also like plentiful rainfall so are less widely adaptable.

Chinkapin nuts, native to the Southeast, are small trees or shrubs whose fruit is favored by wildlife.

Macadamia, originally a tree of tropical Australia, is widely cultivated in Hawaii. In warmer areas of Florida and California it might be a feasible choice.

Persian Walnut Varieties for West Coast

Old varieties	Danger of spring frost damage	Relative production	Kernel quality	best adapted to
Eureka	moderate	good	excellent	cool
Franquette	none	poor	good	cool
Hartley	slight	good	good	hot
Payne	great	excellent	excellent	cool
New varieties				
Amigo*	slight	good	fair	cool
Chico*	moderate	good	good	hot
Gustine	moderate	excellent	excellent	hot
Lompoc	moderate	good	good	cool
Midland	slight	good	good	cool
Pioneer	slight	good	fair	hot
Pedro*	slight to none	good	good	cool
Serr	moderate	good	excellent	hot
Tehema	slight to none	excellent	good	hot
Viva	moderate	excellent	excellent	hot

* Good pollen producers for cross pollination with other varieties.

Pecan Varieties

Variety	State of origin	Pollination type*	Relative production	Kernel quality	Disease resistance
		Southeast			
Chickasaw	Tex.	II	excellent	fair	good
Desirable	Fla.	I	good	good	fair
Elliott	Fla.	II	good	fair	good
Farley	—	I	fair	excellent	fair
Kernodle	Fla.	II	fair	good	fair
Mahan	Miss.	II	fair	poor	poor
Schley	Miss.	II	good	excellent	poor
Stuart	Miss.	II	good	good	good
		Southwest			
Ideal	—	II	good	good	poor
San Saba Imp.	Tex.	I	good	good	poor
Sioux	Tex.	II	good	excellent	poor
Western	Tex.	I	excellent	good	poor
Wichita	Tex.	II	excellent	excellen	poor

Midwest

Variety	State of origin	Pollination type*	Kernel quality	Remarks
Colby	Ill.	II	poor	Retains foliage late in fall
Fritz	Ill.	II	—	Hardy tree for extreme north
Greenriver	Ky.	II	good	Susceptible to spring frost
Major	Ky.	I	good	Good producer; susceptible to aphids
Perque	Mo.	I	good	Susceptible to aphids, squirrels and birds

* I. Pollen shed before females are receptive. II. Pollen shed after females are receptive. Interplant at least one tree from each group for best pollination.

—WALNUT.

Among the nut pines, pinyon is native to the arid Southwest, Korean is hardy in the Northeast, and Italian stone pine does well in the Deep South.

Pollination

Pecans, hickories, walnuts, filberts and chestnuts have male and female parts on the same shoot but in different flowers. Flowers are not showy because they are usually wind-pollinated, though chestnuts are also insect-pollinated. Often these trees will not be fruitful unless they receive pollen from another tree of the same species, because the male and female organs may not mature simultaneously. To insure cross pollination, plant two or more varieties. Walnuts, pecans, and hickories shed pollen about a month after the buds break out in spring; chestnuts about two months after shoot growth begins in spring; and filberts flower in the winter or early spring before new growth begins.

In pistachios, the male and female flowers are borne on separate trees, and with almonds you must also plant two or more varieties to insure pollination. Macadamia, which like almond has showy blossoms pollinated by bees, is self-fertile.

Planting

Pecans and large walnut trees should be spaced at least forty to fifty feet from each other, other trees, buildings, or other obstacles. If the soil is poor, they may attain only half of their normal height. To avoid frost pockets, plant on the upper portions of slopes; and if you have early frost, plant on the north side of buildings to delay bud break in spring.

Filberts and almonds may be planted 25 feet apart. Almonds are tolerant of drought and poor soil but must not be exposed to late spring frosts. Filberts can be grown in shallow soil due to shallow root systems.

Plant Chinese chestnuts about forty feet apart.

All nut trees should be planted when dormant after leaf fall and before reviving in spring. The pecan has a deep tap root requiring a deep hole, but other nut trees have spreading roots. Make the planting hole large enough so that the roots will not be twisted or folded back during planting. After you have filled the hole with soil, lift the tree gently so the roots point down. Settle the soil with water, and don't let the roots dry out.

Maintenance

During the first year, adequate water is vital. An inch of water or rain a week is adequate, and overwatering can kill the tree. Keep the area around the tree free of weeds—a mulch will help, as well as conserve moisture.

Pruning can begin the winter after the first summer of growth. Large trees—such as pecan and Persian walnut—should be trained to a modified main trunk rather than to an

open vase. This makes the branches stronger and less breakable. After the tree is shaped, in about five years, little pruning is required. Just remove dead branches or eliminate crowded ones. Chinese chestnut should be pruned only enough to develop a single trunk and basic scaffold; over-pruning will delay the onset of bearing.

As trees mature, prune out crowded branches. On pecans, however, don't cut back the terminal portion of twigs, because these bear the fruit. For walnuts, terminals can be pruned because nuts are borne on lateral twigs.

On older pecans and walnut trees with slow growth, you may have to make many small cuts to thin the fruiting wood and open up crowded areas of the tree to rejuvenate fruiting.

Filberts commonly form suckers at the base and grow in bush form. In the Northwest, suckers are removed to maintain single-stemmed trees. In the East, filberts grow best as multi-stemmed shrubs, but you should thin suckers constantly to maintain tree vigor.

Fertilizing

Shortly after planting, throw a handful of 10-10-10 fertilizer around the tree (but not in the tree hole, as excessive feeding can be damaging).

In the second and successive years, add one to four pounds of 10-10-10 per square inch of trunk diameter. This should be done in winter in the south and in early spring in the north.

Nitrogen is the most common deficiency—evidenced by weak growth, pale foliage, and small leaves.

Diseases and Pests

Each species is usually susceptible to a limited number of pests and diseases.

Pecans and hickories may develop scab in humid areas; crown gall (a tumor at the base of the trunk); or be attacked by aphids, mites, leaf casebearers, shuckworm, pecan weevil, or spittlebug.

Persian walnuts, especially in the West, may be attacked by the navel orange worm larvae that eat the kernel while the nut is still on the tree. Harvest the nuts early, and clean up husks, leaves, and dead limbs to reduce damage. Husk fly maggots or codling moth larvae may attack kernels, while the walnut weevil and butternut curculio mostly damage stems and branches. Persian walnut is the most susceptible to walnut blight, though other species may also be infected (though rarely fatally). Since the bacteria overwinters in dead twigs, good sanitation is the key. Walnut anthrachose or leaf blotch, another bacterium, defoliates trees and leads to deformed nuts.

All walnuts and some pecans are susceptible to bunch disease, resulting in stunted growth, which has no known cure.

The chestnut blight fungus may attack Chinese chestnut unless the trees are kept healthy and vigorous with pruning of weak and shaded branches and suckers. The chestnut weevil is more of a problem; adults lay eggs in the nuts and then feed as the fruit ripens.

With almonds, watch for brown rot and shot hole fungus; a bacterial canker can also affect blossoms and young shoots in rainy spring weather.

Filberts are generally pest- and disease-free in the Northwest but are susceptible to eastern Filbert blight and Filbert lava mite in the East.

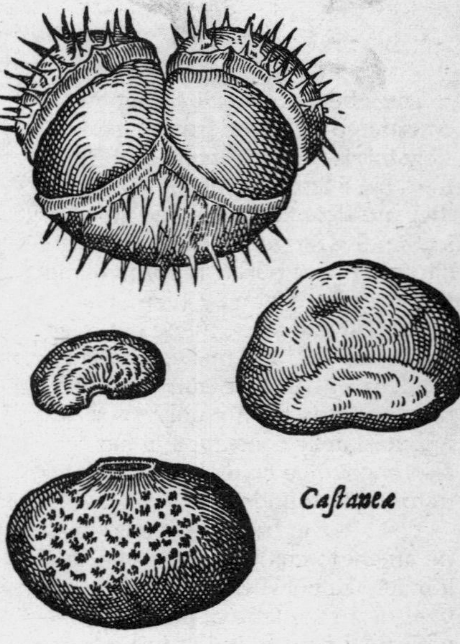

Harvest

Nuts generally ripen from August to November and should be harvested as soon as they fall to prevent damage from rain, high humidity, hot weather, or predation. Ripe nuts remaining on the tree can be knocked off with a long pole.

All nuts should be air-dried before storage. (Commercially, they are treated with forced hot air at 109°F for 24 to 36 hours.)

Except the chestnuts, most nuts have a high oil content and long shelf life. They keep longer if left in the shell and refrigerated at 35°F. Shelled nuts should be kept well frozen.

Because of their low oil content, chestnuts should be refrigerated at 35° to 40° and kept under high humidity. Wrapping them in damp peat moss, enclosing them in a plastic bag, and putting them in the refrigerator should do the trick.

THE PECAN-TREES AT VILLERE'S, NEW ORLEANS.

Gardening in the Dark–
Mushrooms

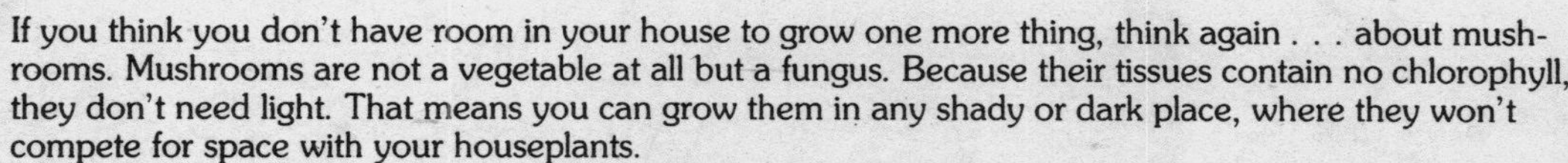

If you think you don't have room in your house to grow one more thing, think again . . . about mushrooms. Mushrooms are not a vegetable at all but a fungus. Because their tissues contain no chlorophyll, they don't need light. That means you can grow them in any shady or dark place, where they won't compete for space with your houseplants.

The main requirements for a home mushroom farm are mushroom compost, which you can make or buy, a temperature between 60° and 70°F, and steady humidity of about 80 percent. Basements are the usual setting for an indoor mushroom garden, but wherever you decide to keep the mushrooms, don't bother trying to grow them in direct sunlight. It won't work.

The easiest way to start mushrooming is to buy a preplanted kit at a garden center or from a supplier. To produce a crop, all you have to do is water the tray. Between October and April is the time to look for these kits. They come complete with special mushroom compost and mushroom spawn. Full directions are furnished, and if you follow them carefully you should have a harvest in about sixty days.

Making Compost

If you have some gardening experience, you may prefer to make your own mushroom soil the old-fashioned way. Allow 15 to 20 days for the process.

You will need a supply of fresh strawy horse manure—enough to fill the boxes or trays in which you plan to plant the mushroom spawn. Make a little pile of the manure and leave it in the sunlight for five days. Then turn it so that the entire batch is remixed. Water thoroughly. After four more turnings and waterings at five-day intervals, the compost is nearly ready. You can tell because the manure smell has dissipated.

Now fill the trays you are going to use with the compost. (Old desk and dresser drawers are excellent containers.) After another seven or eight days, when the compost has heated to 140°F, it will be ready for planting.

Caring for Spawn

There are two kinds of mushroom spawn: "grain" spawn, which you sprinkle over the compost, and "manure" spawn, which is the more reliable kind for home growing. Some seed companies offer it in their catalogs.

To start, break the manure spawn into pieces about the size of a walnut and plant them eight to ten inches apart at a depth of two inches. In the beginning, the mushroom garden should receive no light, if possible. Keep the temperature at 70°F (for sure, don't let it exceed 90°F). At the end of three weeks, you should see fine white threads called mycelium growing out of the compost.

The room temperature should now cool down to about 60°F and "casing" should be applied. Casing is a one-inch layer of sterilized loam mixed with some moistened peat moss.

How does one lower the room temperature? If you've set up your farm in the basement, you can probably find a far corner away from the furnace. Otherwise, move the whole operation to another dark place in the house.

After the mushroom trays are cased, spray them gently with a plant mister to water them. Mushroom soil should be moist but not wetter than a damp sponge. You'll know that the trays are getting too dry when the top of the soil begins to be powdery. Tiny mushrooms usually appear in three weeks after casing. Give them a little water and continue watching the room temperature.

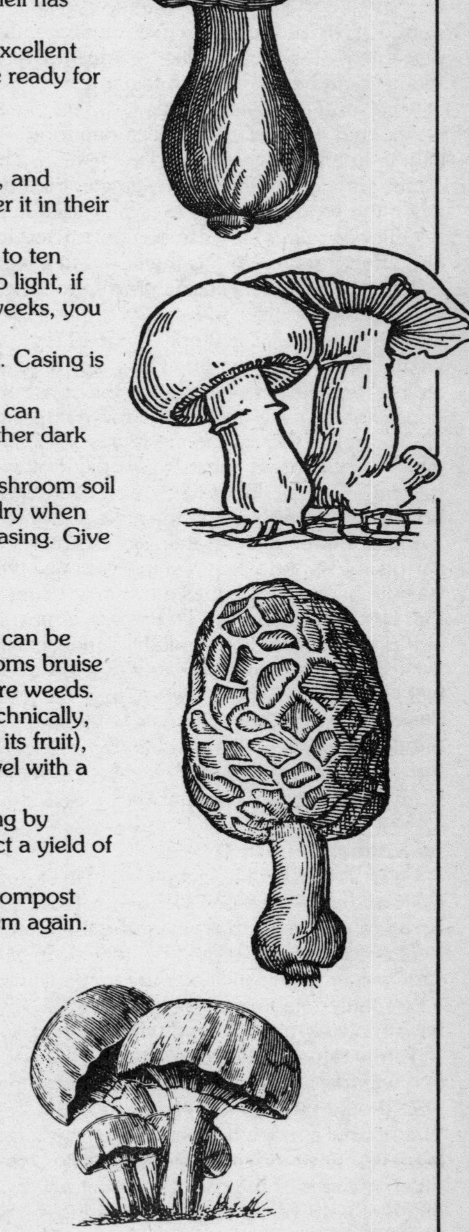

Harvesting

Harvesting the mushroom trays selectively keeps crops coming for several months. Mushrooms can be picked as tiny buttons or you can wait until they are full-sized. At all stages of maturity, mushrooms bruise easily, so handle them with care. Above all, don't pull them roughly out of the soil as if they were weeds. Although you may never have seen them, in a certain sense, mushrooms have root systems (technically, the mycelium, which seems like roots, is the body of the mushroom fungus and the buttons are its fruit), and yanking one mushroom out will hurt others. To harvest, cut the mushroom stems at soil level with a knife.

As your trays seem to be reaching the end of their run, try to coax them to continue producing by watering the mushroom soil with a dilute salt solution. With practice and luck, you should expect a yield of a half pound to a pound of mushrooms per square foot.

When the trays stop yielding for good, don't throw away the mushroom soil. Add it to your compost heap. Scrub the trays well and leave them outside in the sun for a month or so before using them again.

For More Information

Mushroom Growing, by Arthur J. Simons. Garden Way Publishing, Charlotte, VT 05445.

Mushroom Growing Today, by Fred C. Atkins. Macmillan.

Sources

Edmund Scientific Co., 555 Edscorp Bldg., Barrington, NJ 08007.

W. Atlee Burpee Co., Philadelphia, PA 19132.

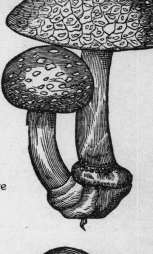

Storing Fruits and Vegetables

Proper storage keeps your fruits and vegetables exactly the way you picked them. Your ability to store food, in general, is dependent on the weather in your area. Temperatures must average less than 30°F during the winter months, otherwise the proper storing temperature for most fruits and vegetables cannot be achieved.

One of the most common indoor storage rooms is the converted basement. Basements are usually too dry and warm to accommodate food, but it is possible to build a room within your basement space that will be suitable. Portion off an area, preferably in the north or east corner of your basement, and close it off with insulation and construction board. Make sure there are no heating pipes or air ducts running through the partitioned room. At least one but preferably two windows will be needed to help ventilate and cool the room. The windows should be well shaded to keep up unwanted sunlight. The floor should be covered with slats. This helps the air circulate underneath the food as well as allowing for the placement of wet matter like sawdust to help raise the humidity of the room. The food should be stored in crates or boxes.

A cellar underneath a house with no central heating has traditionally been considered the best place for storing food. Again, it should have a window to help with temperature control and ventilation. The room, if properly cooled, should be about 35°F. A good way to maintain the humidity is to sprinkle water on the floor when the produce seems to wilt. A reliable thermometer is a must.

Outdoor cellars can also be constructed to store your fruit. There is much time and effort invested in this method, but it works well. The walls and roof of the cellar must be strong enough to support the weight of the earth around it. Stone and masonry block can be used to reinforce the roof and walls, but the best underground cellar is simply made of reinforced concrete. The entire structure should be covered by dirt. This helps regulate the temperature of the room. An air intake should be included in the construction to allow for ventilation. It is also important to make the storage room impervious to birds and animals.

Outdoor buildings, expressly designed for storage, are recommended only when the climate is consistently cold, but with an average temperature not below freezing. This is a lot of work, and you might want to consult a carpenter about how to go about building the storage hut to insure correct construction.

Pits are often used to help store certain vegetables and fruits like potatoes, carrots, beets, turnips, parsnips, cabbage, winter apples, and pears. The pit can be built on the ground, as a mounded construction, or in a hole eight inches deep that has good drainage. To prepare a pit spread a layer of straw on the ground, and place the fruits or vegetables (never both together) on the bedding. Cover the food with yet another layer of straw and then cover this with a mound of soil eight inches thick. Firm the soil to make it waterproof, and dig a shallow drainage ditch next to the pile. The pit's contents should be entirely removed when opened. Once a pit is opened, any remaining food will rot, as well as contaminate the ground it was stored in. It is best to make several small pits so that you can store your fruits and vegetables over a longer period of time.

Maintenance

Once your food has been placed in storage, the next task is to insure that the fruits and vegetables are well protected. Plenty of moisture, a fairly constant temperature, and a clean area are the three most important factors to be considered.

The storage area should be kept clean at all times. Any fruit or vegetable that shows signs of decay should be immediately thrown out. At least once every year a thorough going over is recommended. All containers, walls, and shelves should be completely cleaned and whitewashed.

Temperature will be regulated by the opening and closing of the cellar doors and windows. Two thermometers are needed to regulate temperatures properly. One should be placed in the coldest part of the cellar, and the other one outside. The normal storage temperature is about 32°F. Particular fruits and vegetables, however, have different optimal storage temperatures. They can be placed in different areas of the cellar since there will be a natural variation in temperature at different parts of the room. Regulating the temperature is a daily routine. Cool the room to 32°F. When outside temperatures rise above the storage room temperature, close off the windows and ventilation ducts tightly.

Moisture must be maintained at all times. If the storage room dries out the food will shrivel and rot. Good ways of controlling humidity are through the use of water and ventilated polyethylene bags. By sprinkling the floor frequently, placing large pans of water underneath the windows, and covering the floors with wet sawdust and straw, enough moisture can be generated to retard the decaying process. If you put all the food that you are storing in polyethylene bags, this will help it retain moisture.

Cabbages are placed head down in a long pit.

Different varieties of fruit and vegetables have different storing requirements. How moist or dry, hot or cold, and where best stored, are all factors to be considered with each individual item. The accompanying chart gives a general overview of these requirements.

To prepare vegetables and fruits for storage, discard all badly bruised ones and decayed pieces. Produce should have as little field heat in it as possible, so you should either pick early in the day or let the food sit overnight before storing.

Peas and beans

Beans, including lima beans, peas, and soybeans, may be stored provided you process them one of two ways.

1. Pick the pods as soon as they are mature and spread them in a warm, dry place until they are thoroughly dry; or

Home Storage Chart

	Where to store	Storage conditions Temperature (F)	Humidity	Storage period
Vegetables:				
Beans and peas, dried	Any cool, dry place	32–40	Dry	Many Years
Beets	Storage cellar or pit	32–40	Moist	Fall-winter
Cabbage	Storage cellar or pit	32–35	Moist	Fall-winter
Carrots	Storage cellar or pit	32–40	Moist	Fall-winter
Celery	Roots in soil in storage cellar	32–40	Moist	Fall-winter
Onions	Any cool, dry place	As near 32 as possible	Dry	Fall-winter
Parsnips	Leave in ground or put in storage cellar	32–40	Moist	Fall-winter
Potatoes	Storage cellar or pit	45–48	Moist	Fall-winter
Pumpkin, winter squash	Unheated room or basement	55–60	Dry	Fall-winter
Rutabagas	Storage cellar or pit	32–40	Moist	Fall-winter
Sweet Potatoes	Unheated room or basement	55–60	Dry	Fall-winter
Tomatoes (green or white)	Unheated room or basement	55–60	Dry	1-6 weeks
Turnips	Storage cellar or pit	32–40	Moist	Fall-winter
Fruits:				
Most apples	Fruit storage cellar	30–32	Moist	Fall-winter
McIntosh, Yellow Newton & Rhode Island Greening	Fruit storage cellar	35–38	Moist	Fall-winter
Grapes	Fruit storage cellar	31–32	Moist	4-6 weeks
Pears	Fruit storage cellar	30–31	Moist	Fall-winter
Peaches	Fruit storage cellar	32	Moist	2 weeks
Apricots	Fruit storage cellar	32	Moist	2 weeks

2. Pull and dry the entire bean plants like hay after most of the pods are ripe.

After drying, shell them. Then, to protect them from moths and weevils, treat them in one of the following ways:

1. Refrigerate them at 0°F or below for three or four days.
2. Heat them in the oven at 180°F for fifteen minutes. Turn off the heat and leave the beans in the oven an hour or more.

Late cabbage

Cabbage may be stored in outdoor storage cellars, cone-shaped pits, or in long pits. Long pits are a bit handier, as you can remove a few heads of cabbage without disturbing the rest of the pit. To store cabbage in a long pit, pull the plants out by the roots, place them head down in the pit, and cover them with soil.

If you prefer, you may store cabbage in a shallow trench framed with stakes or poles and covered with straw. Again, pull the plants out by the roots. Set the plants side by side, with their roots in the trench. Pack soil around the roots. Then build a frame about two feet high around the trench. This can be done easily by driving poles or stakes into the ground, and then banking soil around them. Then place poles across the top of the frame to hold a covering of straw, hay, or corn fodder.

Cabbage should not be stored in a celler, because its odor is apt to permeate the house. You can, however, store it on shelves in an outdoor storage cellar.

Late celery

Celery can be stored a month or two right in the garden if you bank a few inches of soil around the base of the plants at the end of the growing season. Build the bank up to the top of the plants before severe freezing occurs. As the weather becomes colder, cover the banking with straw or corn fodder held in place with boards.

You can also store celery in a trench. Dig the trench as long as you like, and about a foot wide and two feet deep. When the celery plants are fully grown, dig them up, taking a clump of soil with the roots, and pack them into the trench. Water the plants as you put them in. Leave the trench open until the plant tops dry off, then roof the trench over. You can do this by setting a twelve-inch board on edge beside the trench and banking soil against it. Then place boards or poles across the trench so that one end rests on the upright board and the other end on the ground. Cover lightly with straw, more of which should be added as the weather becomes colder. Celery stored in this way will keep until late winter.

Endive

Endive may be stored the same way celery is, in a storage cellar, and will keep for two or three months. Before storing, tie the leaves together to help blanching.

Onions

To keep well in storage, onions must be mature and thoroughly dry. Damaged onions or those with thick heads will not keep. Store them in dry, well-ventilated places such as an attic or unheated room, or in well-ventilated containers such as slatted crates of open-mesh bags. Fill the bags only half full, and suspend them from overhead hooks. Fill the crates half full and stack them on crossbars.

Do not store onions in cellars. Slight freezing will not affect onions, provided you do not handle them while they are frozen.

Parsnips, Salsify, and Horseradish

These crops can be stored by being left undug in the garden because they withstand freezing. Alternate freezing and thawing, however, damages them. If you store them in the ground, mulch them lightly at the end of the growing season. Keep them covered until outdoor temperatures are consistently low. Then remove the mulch to permit thorough freezing. After they have frozen, mulch them deeply enough to keep them frozen.

These vegetables may also be stored like other root crops.

Peppers

Choose firm, dark green, mature green bell peppers that have been picked just before frost. Wash them and sort them according to their maturity and firmness.

Close control of moisture and temperature conditions is needed for successful storage of peppers. A polyethylene liner with twelve to fifteen ¼-inch holes placed in a container such as a lug box is a good way to maintain high humidity. The temperature should be between 45° and 50°F. Serious decay can occur at 40° or lower in three weeks.

Hot varieties of peppers are easiest to store after they are dry.

You can dry them in two ways:

1. Pull the plants and hang them up; or—
2. Pick the peppers from the plants and string the peppers up on a line.

Store dry peppers in a cool, dry place such as an attic or unheated room. Do not store them in cellars.

Potatoes

Potatoes to be stored require careful attention at harvest. The skin condition of the potato and its optimal storing temperature and humidity are the most important factors, and are directly related to the length of time the potato will keep in storage.

Harvest only mature potatoes, since immature ones tend to have a weak, flaky skin that allows easy decay. Dig potatoes carefully to prevent bruising and scarring. Let freshly dug potatoes dry out overnight at a temperature of 45° to 50°F before transferring them to their final drying containers, such as wood crates or burlap sacks.

Temperature and humidity are the main considerations once potatoes are ready for storage. Humidity of storage room should remain about 95 percent. The optimal temperature for medium range potato storage is between 45° and 48°F. For long term storage, reduce to between 38° and 40°F.

Tomatoes

Fresh tomatoes can be stored from four to seven weeks if carefully handled and properly stored. If you are growing tomatoes with the intension of storing them, plant them late in the season, since the optimal picking period is when the vines are still vigorous and hardy.

You can pick tomatoes any time after they have become mature. Maturity depends not on the color but on the setting of the seed gel. For a test, cut open a green tomato that seems of a mature size. If the substance around the seeds is a soft gel which can be easily pulled out, then the tomato is mature. If the substance is still hard and cannot be easily pulled out, then the tomato is not mature.

Pick only the best tomatoes for storing. Wash them carefully and let them dry. Then separate into boxes or trays the tomatoes which are at approximately similar stages of development—same color. The humidity of the storage room should be kept around 65 percent. A well-ventilated cellar or outbuilding where temperatures between 55° and 59°F can be maintained is best for tomato storage.

Ripening time can be fairly accurately controlled by the storing tempearture. At temperatures between 65° and 70°F, mature green tomatoes require about fourteen days to ripen. Ripening time of the same tomatoes can be slowed to twenty-eight days by reducing the temperature to 55°F. Less mature tomatoes will take longer to ripen. Storage of tomatoes at temperatures of 50°F or less for more than a few days will result in damage.

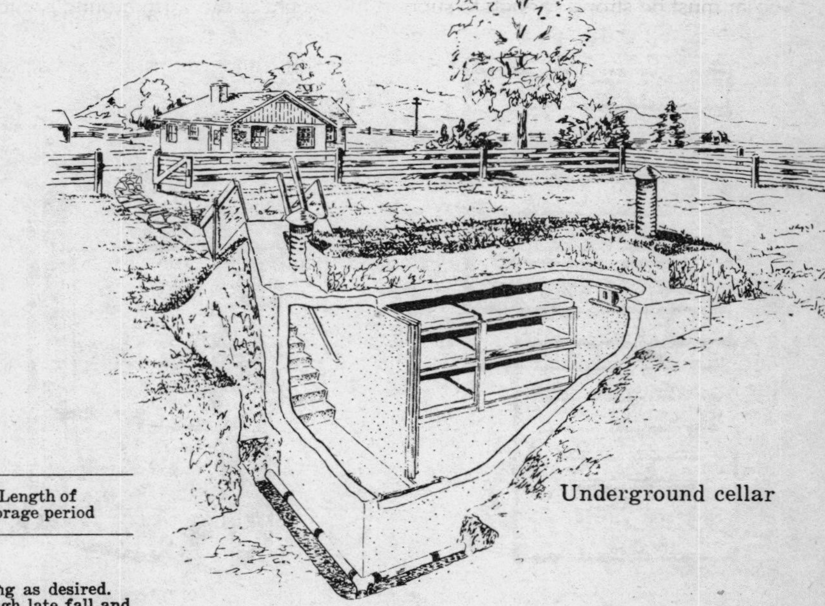

Underground cellar

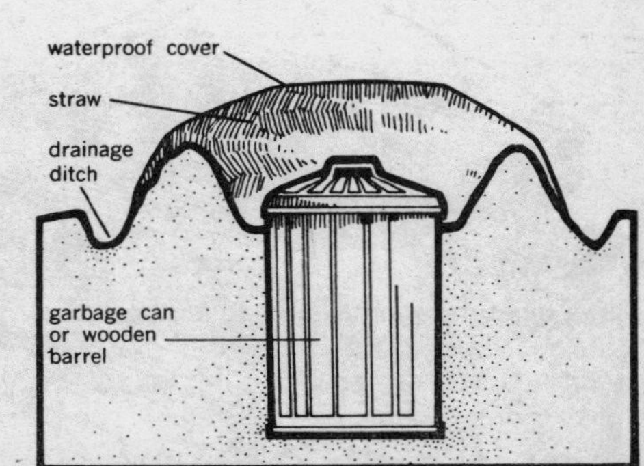

Freezing points, recommended storage conditions, and length of storage period of vegetables and fruits.

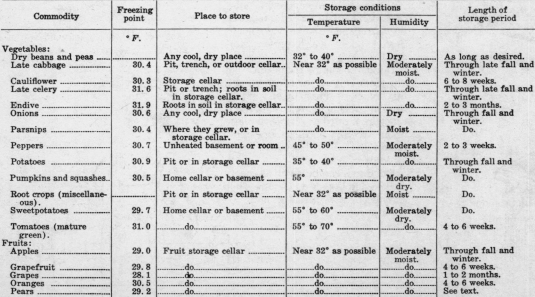

Commodity	Freezing point	Place to store	Storage conditions		Length of storage period
			Temperature	Humidity	
	°F.		°F.		
Vegetables:					
Dry beans and peas		Any cool, dry place	32° to 40°	Dry	As long as desired.
Late cabbage	30.4	Pit, trench, or outdoor cellar	Near 32° as possible	Moderately moist.	Through late fall and winter.
Cauliflower	30.3	Storage cellar	do	do	6 to 8 weeks.
Late celery	31.6	Pit or trench; roots in soil in storage cellar.	do	do	Through late fall and winter.
Endive	31.9	Roots in soil in storage cellar	do	do	2 to 3 months.
Onions	30.6	Any cool, dry place	do	Dry	Through fall and winter.
Parsnips	30.4	Where they grew, or in storage cellar.	do	Moist	Do.
Peppers	30.7	Unheated basement or room	45° to 50°	Moderately moist.	2 to 3 weeks.
Potatoes	30.9	Pit or in storage cellar	35° to 40°	do	Through fall and winter.
Pumpkins and squashes	30.5	Home cellar or basement	55°	Moderately dry.	Do.
Root crops (miscellaneous).		Pit or in storage cellar	Near 32° as possible	Moist	Do.
Sweetpotatoes	29.7	Home cellar or basement	55° to 60°	Moderately dry.	Do.
Tomatoes (mature green).	31.0	do	55° to 70°	do	4 to 6 weeks.
Fruits:					
Apples	29.0	Fruit storage cellar	Near 32° as possible	Moderately moist.	Through fall and winter.
Grapefruit	29.8	do	do	do	4 to 6 weeks.
Grapes	28.1	do	do	do	1 to 2 months.
Oranges	30.5	do	do	do	4 to 6 weeks.
Pears	29.2	do	do	do	See text.

Drying Fruits and Vegetables

Vegetable and fruit slicer.

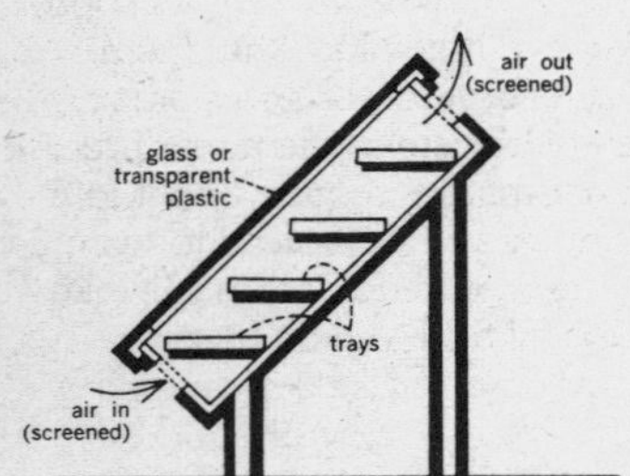

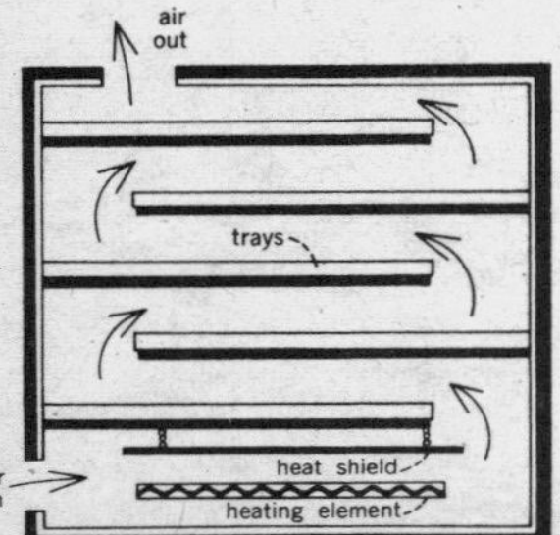

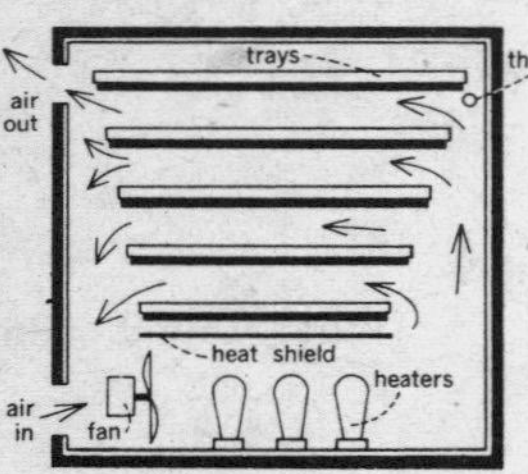

One of the oldest and simplest forms of food preservation is drying. The ancients routinely extended the life of their food by "baking" it in the sun. Sundried foods are still eaten today. There are more modern methods available today for drying your food.

In general, drying needs very little preparation. The purchase of a wooden slat tray or aluminum screen and a fan for air circulation is all that is needed.

Set your oven to 150 degrees. Leave the door partially open to let air circulate while you dry the food. Put the fruits or vegetables on the baking tray and dry for about thirty minutes. To accelerate the drying process, a fan will help circulate the air, allowing the food to absorb larger amounts of heat which allows for quicker evaporation.

Drying your fruits and vegetables will not make them taste any better, so pick the best quality food possible to start with. To insure maximum flavor, start drying as soon as you pick your fruit. To prepare, wash, clean and cut into strips. Discard all damaged food.

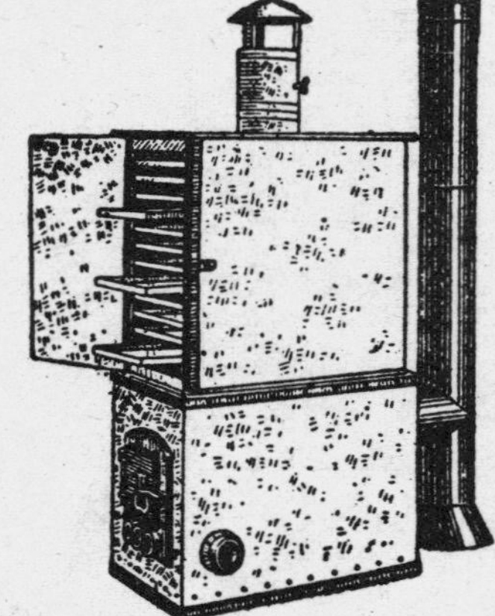

Commercial drier with furnace.

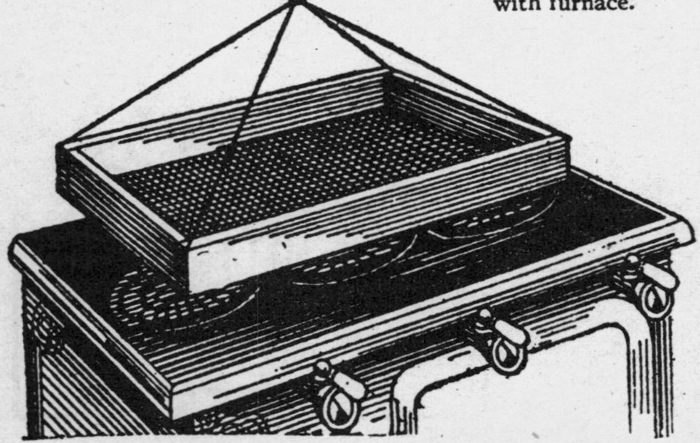

Simple tray drier made at home.

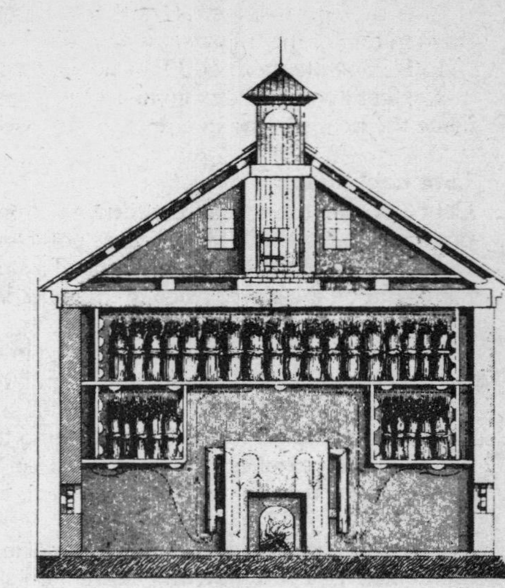

Apples peeled and sliced for drying.

Blanching is a treatment that helps preserve vegetable color and vitamins, and also hastens drying. Fruits can be blanched as well but they run the risk of becoming soft and hard to handle. Fruits such as plums, prunes, and grapes, can be water blanched.

The drying should be a simple process. Temperature best suited for drying is 135 to 140° F. If the temperature is too low the food will not dry adequately and if it is too high, the food will harden and not allow moisture to escape. Each fruit has a different drying time and further varies according to size of piece and load that is drying. Food should be cooled before testing to see if it is done. Dried vegetables will be hard and brittle, fruits will be leathery and pliable.

To store the dried foods, conditioning needs to take place first. The food needs to "sweat" for about a week before putting the food into long-term storage. "Sweating" equalizes the moisture among the pieces. Sun-dried foods need to be treated before storage as well. Place them in the oven for about thirty minutes at 150 degrees to prevent any chance of contamination. Stored dried foods do lose vitamins, flavor and color. Store in cool places to prolong storage life.

Dried fruit can be reconstituted at any time. This can be accomplished by cooking or simply by soaking. If used in cooking the rule of thumb is, one cup of dried vegetables equals about two cups normally; one cup of dried fruit is about 1½ cups of regular fruit.

Dried fruit can be eaten as snacks or baked in breads and soups. They can also be used in sauces and compotes.

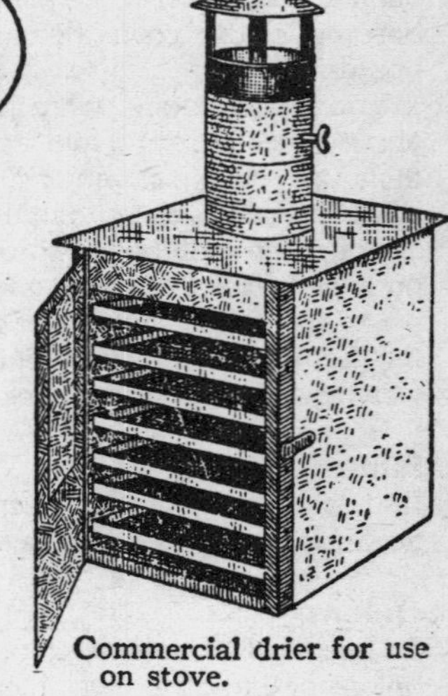

Commercial drier for use on stove.

Home-made drier of galvanized iron, for use on stove.

One of the most convenient and economical ways to preserve fresh fruits and vegetables is by freezing. Freezing is considered by many to be the best form of preservation because it keeps the foods' natural color, flavor and nutritive values intact. Freezing is not beyond the scope of most people to learn, nor is it prohibitive because of cost or time. Freezing is easily mastered and can become both an extremely lucrative as well as fun gardening experience.

Since freezing doesn't improve the quality of the fruits or vegetables you freeze, it is important to pay attention to all the points along the way in the process of making frozen foods. Any error can lessen the quality of the final product.

Picking the correct container is as important as any other step in the process. To retain the best quality possible the materials should be moisture-vapor-proof such as glass, metal or rigid plastic. Unfortunately, most packaging bought for freezing is moisture-vapor-resistant. Though these packages are good, they do not totally prevent evaporation. If necessary they can be used without too much quality loss. What should never be used is ordinary wax paper or paper cartons, like the ones used for ice cream and milk.

The types of containers that are good for freezing break down into rigid and nonrigid. Rigid containers made of aluminum, glass, plastic, tin or heavily waxed cardboard are suitable for all types of vegetables and fruits. C-enamel containers have sulfur in their lining and are especially good for corn, lima beans, and carrots. The R-enamel containers prove best for foods like beets, berries, red cherries, fruit juices, plums. In short, all highly colored foods. Nonrigid containers like cellophane, heavy aluminum foil, pliofilm, polyethylene, and laminated paper are good for dry-packed vegetables and fruits.

The size and shape of the containers should also be considered. The correctly sized container is the one that will serve enough food for one meal for your family. The shape of rigid containers should be flat on both top and bottom. This conserves freezer space. The flared containers save space when stacking them in the cupboard, but they do waste a certain amount of freezer space. Nonrigid containers that bulge because of their construction waste freezer space as well.

Sealing the containers is something to be considered in purchasing, as well as the actual process. Tin cans need special utensils, cardboard cartons need special freezer tape, and glass jars are screwed on and sealed with the use of a rubber ring. Most nonrigid containers can be either heat-sealed or sealed by twisting and folding back the top of the bag. There are special sealing devices on the market that can be purchased but a home iron is also sufficient.

Containers such as slip-top tin cans, glass jars, and rigid plastic can be reused. Nonrigid containers are in general not reuseable. This should be taken into account when you purchase your freezing equipment.

Preparing for Packaging

Both fruits and vegetables need to be prepared for freezing. Fruit is essentially prepared as if you were going to serve it fresh; the preparation for vegetables is a little more elaborate.

All fruits need to be washed in cold water. Be careful not to bruise the fruit, use a colander if possible to minimize handling. Carefully pick through the fruit to make sure there are no damaged pieces; discard all damaged pieces. Do not let the fruit soak in the water, this will catalyze food value and flavor loss. Large pieces of fruit can be cut to better retain flavor and nutrients. Peel, trim, slice, and pit the fruit according to instructions for that particular fruit. Prepare two to three quarts at a time. It is a manageable quantity and can be handled quickly.

Some directions call for fruit to be crushed. The best method for soft fruit is by using a wire potato masher, pastry fork or slotted spoon. For hard fruit, a food chopper is recommended. Never use galvanized ware in direct contact with the fruit. There is a chance that the acid in the fruit will interact with the zinc content and produce a poisonous substance.

Vegetables on the other hand must be blanched before freezing. Blanching is simply the heating of the vegetable in boiling water. It is also possible to steam blanch vegetables as well. Blanching is important because it slows the action of the enzymes that are present in the vegetables. Enzymes are active agents that, if left unchecked in freezing, will turn the food bad. Bad taste, discoloring, toughening of the fibrous are all results of enzyme interaction. Blanching also softens the vegetables, which makes them easier to pack.

Take all the vegetables that are to be boiled, and place them in a blancher, or wire basket. Place this in a large kettle with boiling water. For every pound of vegetables use about one gallon of water. As soon as you put the blancher in the water and close the lid, start timing. Keep the heat high for the time prescribed.

To blanch by steaming, put a basket at least three inches above the bottom of the kettle. Put an inch or two of water into the pot and bring it to a boil. Lay the vegetables out so that they are not on top of each other. Cover the kettle and keep the heat high. Start counting as soon as the lid is put on. Broccoli, pumpkin, sweetpotatoes and winter squash should all be steam blanched.

As soon as the vegetables have cooked for the proper amount of time, they should be cooled by placing them in a large bucket of cool water. Use ice or cold running water to keep the temperature below 60 degrees.

Approximate yield of frozen fruits from fresh

FRUIT	FRESH, AS PURCHASED OR PICKED	FROZEN
Apples	1 bu. (48 lb.) 1 box (44 lb.) 1 ¼ to 1½ lb.	32 to 40 pt. 29 to 35 pt. 1 pt.
Apricots	1 bu. (48 lb.) 1 crate (22 lb.) ⅔ to 4/5 lb.	60 to 72 pt. 28 to 33 pt. 1 pt.
Berries [1]	1 crate (24 qt.) 1⅓ to 1½ pt.	32 to 36 pt. 1 pt.
Cantaloups	1 dozen (28 lb.) 1 to 1¼ lb.	22 pt. 1 pt.
Cherries, sweet or sour	1 bu. (56 lb.) 1¼ to 1½ lb.	36 to 44 pt. 1 pt.
Cranberries	1 box (25 lb.) 1 peck (8 lb.) ½ lb.	50 pt. 16 pt. 1 pt.
Currants	2 qt. (3 lb.) ¾ lb.	4 pt. 1 pt.
Peaches	1 bu. (48 lb.) 1 lug box (20 lb.) 1 to 1½ lb.	32 to 48 pt. 13 to 20 pt. 1 pt.
Pears	1 bu. (50 lb.) 1 western box (46 lb.) 1 to 1¼ lb.	40 to 50 pt. 37 to 46 pt. 1 pt.
Pineapple	5 lb.	4 pt.
Plums and prunes	1 bu. (56 lb.) 1 crate (20 lb.) 1 to 1½ lb.	38 to 56 pt. 13 to 20 pt. 1 pt.
Raspberries	1 crate (24 pt.) 1 pt.	24 pt. 1 pt.
Rhubarb	15 lb. ⅔ to 1 lb.	15 to 22 pt. 1 pt.
Strawberries	1 crate (24 qt.) ⅔ qt.	38 pt. 1 pt.

[1] Includes blackberries, blueberries, boysenberries, dewberries, elderberries, gooseberries, huckleberries, loganberries, and youngberries.

1 *Armeniaca malus maior.*
The greater Aprecocke tree.

2 *Prunus Mirobalana.*
The Mirobalane Plum tree.

Packing Fruits and Vegetables

The most important thing to keep in mind while freezing is that the quicker and better you pack, the better the food will taste. The most amount of time that it should take from picking the fruit or vegetable to freezing it, should be no more than two hours. This will insure maximum taste and quality.

Fruits in general need to be packed in a syrup or some form of sugar. It seems that the quality and taste of fruit is better when it is frozen with some form of sugar. Fruits that are intended to be used as a dessert should be packed in syrup. Fruits that are intended for use in cooking should be packed in sugar. In general, except for fruits such as gooseberries, currants, cranberries, rhubarb, and figs, all fruits taste better and are of better quality when packed in sugar.

The syrup that will be most often used when packing is a 40-percent syrup. Milder fruits take a lighter syrup and sour fruits take a heavier one. To make 40-percent syrup take three cups of sugar, four cups of water and dissolve the sugar in hot or cold water. The syrup should be made the day before using and kept cold in the refrigerator overnight. When packing the fruit make sure the syrup covers the fruit entirely for best results.

The sugar should be put on the fruit and then mixed until the sugar is entirely dissolved. This will draw out the juice of the fruit. Take the juice and the fruit and place them in a container and freeze them.

Vegetables should be packed dry. It is easier to pack and serve if this method is followed.

One of the bigger problems facing those who try to freeze fruit is darkening. Fruits naturally darken and this is not good for the fruit. Ascorbic acid is good as an antidarkening agent. When using syrup the acid should be dissolved just before use. When packing with sugar, the ascorbic acid should be sprinkled on the fruit just before adding the sugar. In unsweetened packs, dissolve over the fruit and mix it thoroughly. Other less effective methods are the use of lemon juice, citric, and ascorbic acid mixtures. Steaming also can serve as an antidarkening agent.

Freezing Fruits

Apples

Syrup pack: Use a 40-percent syrup, one-half teaspoon of ascorbic acid

Sugar pack: To prevent darkening, slice and place apples into a gallon of water with two tablespoons of salt. Leave it to soak for fifteen to twenty minutes. Over each quart of apples sprinkle one-half cup sugar.

Unsweetened pack: Follow directions for sugar pack but don't use the sugar.

Applesauce

Wash, peel, core and slice apples. To each quart of apple slices add a third of a cup of water; cook until tender. Cool and strain; sweeten to taste with approximately one-half cup of sugar for each quart (two pounds).

Apricots

Use syrup pack for uncooked usage; use sugar pack for pies or other cooked dishes. Use firm, ripe, yellow apricots. Sort, wash, halve and pit.

Syrup pack: Use 40-percent syrup, ¾ teaspoon ascorbic acid, pack directly into the container, cover with syrup, seal.

Sugar pack: Dissolve ¼ teaspoon of ascorbic acid in quarter cup cold water and sprinkle over one quart of fruit. Mix quarter cup sugar with each quart of fruit. Stir until sugar is dissolved. Pack into containers and squeeze fruit until covered with juice. Seal and freeze.

Crushed: Dip in boiling water for one-half minute and cool in cold water. Peel, pit and crush. For every quart use one cup sugar, dissolve and seal.

Puree: Pit and quarter. Press through sieve. For every quart of fruit add one cup sugar. Dissolve and seal.

Avocados

Avocados do not freeze well whole or sliced. The best way to prepare them for freezing is by pureeing them.

Puree: Select soft ripe avocados without blemishes. Peel, halve, pit, and mash pulp. For sugar pack, one cup sugar for every quart of puree. Pack, leave headspace, seal and freeze.

Blackberries, boysenberries, dewberries, loganberries

Syrup packing is preferred for uncooked; sugar packing is preferred for use in pies and jams.

Syrup pack: Use 40- or 50-percent syrup depending on sweetness of fruit. Leave head space and seal.

Sugar pack: For every quart of berries, ¾ cup sugar. Stir until dissolved, fill containers, leave headspace.

Puree: Prepare as you would for whole berries. To every quart add one cup sugar. Mash berries first. Dissolve and pack.

Blueberries, elderberries, huckleberries

Pick ripe berries about the same size with tender skins. Sort, wash, drain and steam if desired. Steaming tenderizes the skin and makes the berry taste better. Use syrup packing for use when serving uncooked, sugar pack or unsweetened for cooking.

Syrup pack: use 40-percent syrup. Cover with syrup, seal and freeze.

Unsweetened: Pack berries into containers leaving head space.

Puree: Sort, wash, drain and press berries through fine sieve. For every quart add one cup sugar. Stir until dissolved.

Cherries, sour

Use syrup pack for cherries to be used uncooked, sugar pack for cooking. Select bright-red cherries that are ripe. Stem, sort, wash, drain and pit.

Syrup pack: Use 60- or 65-percent syrup depending on tartness. Cover cherries leaving head space, seal and freeze.

Sugar pack: For every quart add ¾ cup sugar.

Puree: Almost same as sugar, just crush cherries, heat to boiling, cool and press through sieve.

Cherries, sweet

Prepare quickly to avoid color and flavor changes. Red varieties are best for freezing. Pick ripe berries, sort, stem, wash, drain and pit.

Syrup pack: Use 40-percent syrup, add one-half teaspoon of ascorbic acid. Pack into containers, leave head space, seal and freeze.

Coconut
Shred coconut. Pack into containers and cover with coconut milk.

Cranberries
Choose firm red berries with glossy skins. Stem, sort, wash and drain.
Syrup pack: Use 50-percent syrup. Pack, leave head space and freeze.
Unsweetened: Pack into containers without sugar. Leave head space. Seal and freeze.

Currants
Pick plump, fully ripe bright-red currants. Wash in cold water and remove the stems.
Syrup pack: Use cold 50-percent syrup. Cover currants leaving head space. Seal and freeze.
Sugar pack: For every quart add ¾ cup sugar. Stir until sugar is dissolved.

Dates
Pick dates with good flavor and tender texture. Wash, slit, pit and press through sieve. Pack into containers leaving head room.

Figs
Take ripened figs and sort, wash, cut off the stems and peel and slice if desired. Make sure figs are not sour-tasting in the middle.
Syrup pack: Use 35 percent syrup, ¾ teaspoon ascorbic acid. Cover figs with cold syrup, leave head space, seal.
Unsweetened: Pack into containers leaving head space. If you cover with water use ¾ teaspoons of ascorbic acid to every quart of water.

Gooseberries
Choose fully ripe berries, sort, remove ends, and wash.
Syrup pack: Use 50-percent syrup. Leave head space.
Unsweetened: Pack into containers using head space.

Grapefruit, Oranges
Select ripe fruits. Wash and peel. Remove all seeds and slice.
Syrup pack: Pack into container. Use 40-percent syrup leaving head space but covering fruit. Add one-half teaspoon of ascorbic acid.

Grapes
Pick ripe grapes with full color. Wash and stem. Remove seeds from grapes. Leave seedless grapes whole.
Syrup pack: Use 40-percent syrup, cover leaving head space.
Unsweetened: Pack, leaving head space. Seal and freeze.

Melons
Take firm, ripe melons. Cut in half, remove seeds and peel. Cut the melon into slices, cubes or balls. Leave head space, and cover with 30-percent syrup.

Nectarines
Pick fully ripe fruit. Sort, wash and pit fruits. Peel and slice. Put directly into a 40-percent syrup, one-half cup for each pint container. Press fruit down and cover with sirup.

Peaches
Select firm, ripe peaches with no blemishes. Sort, wash, pit and peel. Slice and pack.
Syrup pack: Use 40-percent syrup, add one-half teaspoon ascorbic acid. Put fruit directly into container like nectarines.
Sugar pack: For every quart add ⅔ cups sugar. Mix until dissolved.

Pears
Select firm, ripe pears. Wash, peel, and cut in quarters. Remove cores. Heat pears in boiling 40-percent syrup for one to two minutes. Drain and cool. Pack pears into a 40-percent syrup, add ¾ cup ascorbic acid.

The fruit and floures of the Date tree.

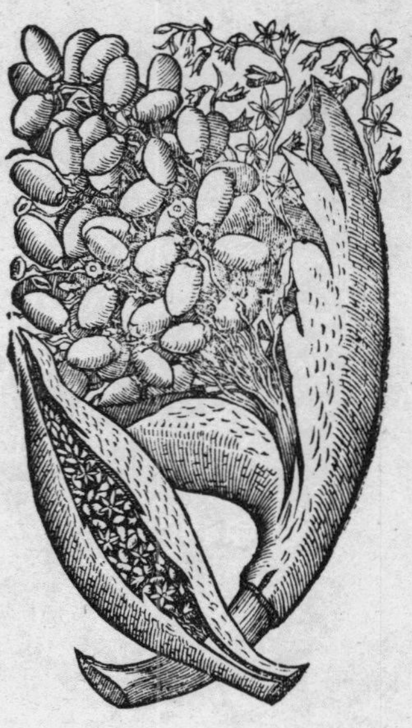

—PUMPKIN.

Plums and prunes
Plums and prunes are especially good for pies and jams. Freeze them in unsweetened packs. Pick ripe, deep colored fruit. Sort and wash. Cut in half.
Unsweetened pack: Pack whole fruit into containers. Seal and freeze.
Syrup pack: Place cut fruit into containers. Cover fruit with 40-percent syrup, add one-half teaspoon ascorbic acid. Leave head space and seal.

Raspberries
Select fully ripe berries. Sort, wash and drain.
Unsweetened: Pack in containers, leave head space. Seal.
Syrup pack: Put berries in container cover with 40-percent syrup. Seal and freeze.
Sugar pack: For every quart, add ¾ cup sugar. Mix carefully to avoid crushing.

Strawberries
Select firm, ripe, red ones. Sort, wash, drain and remove hulls. Pack in syrup or sugar for best results.
Syrup pack: Put berries in container, cover with 50-percent syrup. Leave head space.
Sugar pack: For every quart add ¾ cup sugar. Mix thoroughly until dissolved. Leave head space when packing.

Approximate yield of frozen vegetables from fresh

VEGETABLE	FRESH, AS PURCHASED OR PICKED	FROZEN
Asparagus	1 crate (12 2-lb. bunches) 1 to 1½ lb.	15 to 22 pt. 1 pt.
Beans, lima (in pods)	1 bu. (32 lb.) 2 to 2½ lb.	12 to 16 pt. 1 pt.
Beans, snap, green, and wax	1 bu. (30 lb.) ⅔ to 1 lb.	30 to 45 pt. 1 pt.
Beet greens	15 lb. 1 to 1½ lb.	10 to 15 pt. 1 pt.
Beets (without tops)	1 bu. (52 lb.) 1¼ to 1½ lb.	35 to 42 pt. 1 pt.
Broccoli	1 crate (25 lb.) 1 lb.	24 pt. 1 pt.
Brussels sprouts	4 quart boxes 1 lb.	6 pt. 1 pt.
Carrots (without tops)	1 bu. (50 lb.) 1¼ to 1½ lb.	32 to 40 pt. 1 pt.
Cauliflower	2 medium heads 1⅓ lb.	3 pt. 1 pt.
Chard	1 bu. (12 lb.) 1 to 1½ lb.	8 to 12 pt. 1 pt.
Collards	1 bu. (12 lb.) 1 to 1½ lb.	8 to 12 pt. 1 pt.
Corn, sweet (in husks)	1 bu. (35 lb.) 2 to 2½ lb.	14 to 17 pt. 1 pt.
Kale	1 bu. (18 lb.) 1 to 1½ lb.	12 to 18 pt. 1 pt.
Mustard greens	1 bu. (12 lb.) 1 to 1½ lb.	8 to 12 pt. 1 pt.
Peas	1 bu. (30 lb.) 2 to 2½ lb.	12 to 15 pt. 1 pt.
Peppers, sweet	⅔ lb. (3 peppers)	1 pt.
Pumpkin	3 lb.	2 pt.
Spinach	1 bu. (18 lb.) 1 to 1½ lb.	12 to 18 pt. 1 pt.
Squash, summer	1 bu. (40 lb.) 1 to 1¼ lb.	32 to 40 pt. 1 pt.
Squash, winter	3 lb.	2 pt.
Sweetpotatoes	⅔ lb.	1 pt.

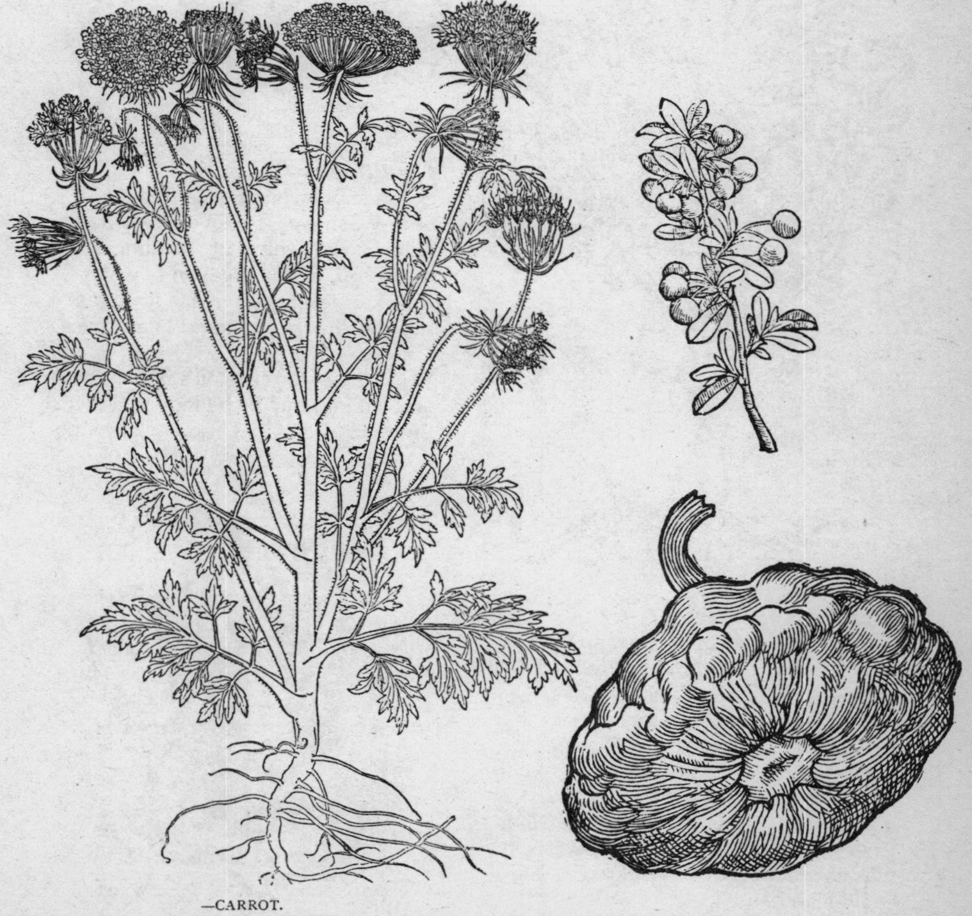

—CARROT.

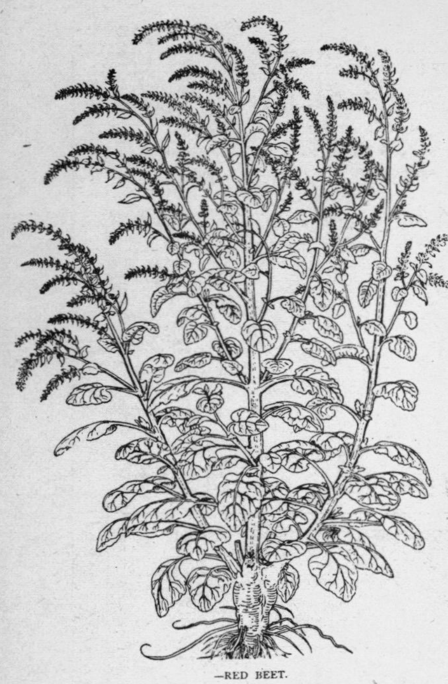

—RED BEET.

Freezing Vegetables

Asparagus
Select young tender stalks. Wash asparagus thoroughly. Cut or break off the hard parts of the stalks. Heat stalks in boiling water. Time should be judged according to thickness of stalks. One minute for small, two minutes for medium, three minutes for thick. Cool immediately and drain. Pack into containers leaving no head space.

Beans, lima
Select well-filled beans. Shell and sort, then heat in boiling water. Two minutes for small beans, three for medium, four for large. Cool and drain. Pack leaving one-half-inch head space.

Beans, green
Select plump pods. Shell and boil in water for one minute. Pack leaving one-half-inch head space.

Beans, snap
Select tender beans that snap when broken. Wash thoroughly, removing ends. Boil for three minutes, after cutting them into two-inch strips, drain and cool. Pack leaving one-half-inch head room.

Beans, soybeans
Select firm bright green pods. Boil for five minutes, cool, and squeeze soybeans out of pods. Pack leaving one-half-inch head space.

Beets
Select mature beets not longer than three inches. Wash, sort and trim tops. Boil until tender—small beets thirty minutes, medium forty-five minutes. Cool, peel and cut immediately. Pack with one-half-inch head space.

Broccoli
Select dark-green heads. Wash, peel, and trim. Boil for five minutes or steam for three. Cool, and pack immediately leaving no head space.

Brussels Sprouts
Select green, firm ones. Make sure they are insect free. Wash and sort into small, medium, large. Boil in water three minutes for small, four for medium, five for large. Cool and pack leaving no head space.

Cabbage
Only good for cooking. Cannot freeze and then eat fresh. Trim outside leaves. Boil in water 1½ minutes. Pack leaving one-half-inch head space.

Carrots
Select tender, mild-flavored carrots. Remove tops, wash and peel. Cut into strips or one-quarter-inch cubes. Boil for two minutes. Pack with one-half inch head room.

Cauliflower
Select snow white heads that are firm. Wash well, remove insects carefully. Soak in salt water solution if necessary. Boil in a gallon of water with four teaspoons of salt for three minutes. Pack leaving no head space.

Celery
Select crisp, tender stalks. Wash, trim and cut into one inch lengths. Boil for three minutes. Cool and pack leaving no head space.

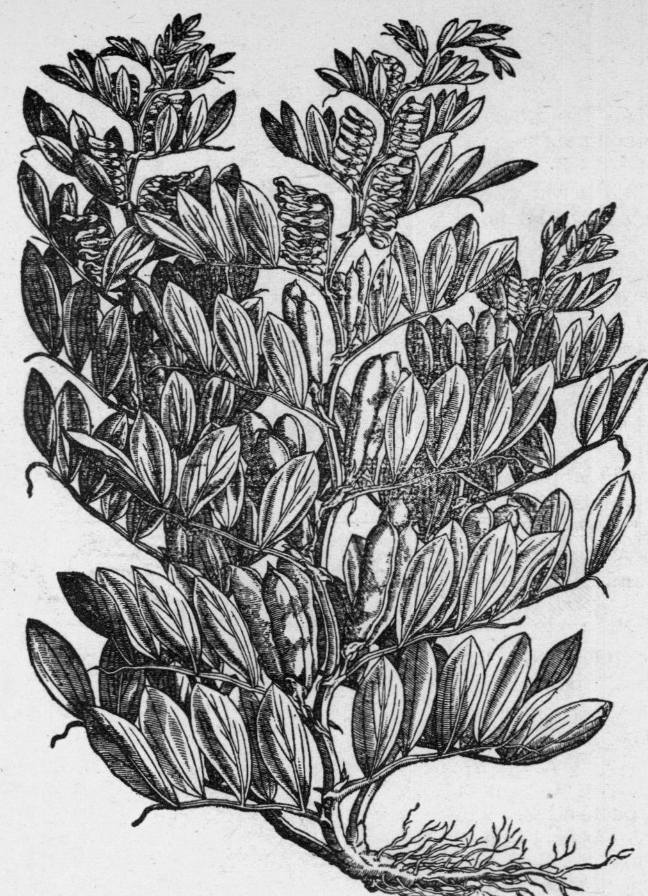

—BROAD BEAN.

Corn
Select ears that are plump with tender kernels. Husk and wash. Boil ears for four minutes and cool promptly. Cut kernels from corn. Pack leaving one-half inch head space.
For on-the-cob: Boil ears for seven minutes. Cool and pack.

Greens
Select young tender leaves. Wash and sort. Remove imperfect leaves. Boil for two minutes. Pack leaving one-half inch head space.

Kohlrabi
Select young tender, mild flavored pieces. Cut off tops and roots. Wash and peel and dice into one-half inch cubes. Boil for one minute. Pack leaving one-half inch head space.

Mushrooms
Choose healthy ones. Wash, sort and trim stems. Dip in a solution containing one teaspoon of lemon juice for about five minutes. Steam for about five minutes. Cool and pack leaving one-half inch head space.

Okra
Select tender, green pods. Wash, cut off stems and heat in boiling water for three minutes. Cool and pack, leaving one-half inch head space.

Parsnips
Choose small ones. Remove tops, wash, peel and cut into one-half inch cubes. Boil for two minutes. Cool. Pack leaving one-half inch head space.

Peas
Choose bright green, plump, pods. Shell peas. Boil for 1½ minutes. Cool, and pack leaving one-half inch head space.

Peppers
Select firm, crisp thick-walled peppers. Wash, cut stems, and remove seeds. Boil in water for two minutes. Cool and pack leaving one-half inch head space. These are best for cooking.

Pimientos
Select firm, crisp, thick-walled pimientos. Peel by roasting at 400 degrees for four minutes. Remove skins in cold water. Pack leaving one-half inch head space.

Pumpkin
Select full-colored, mature pumpkins. Wash, cut into quarters and seed. Boil until soft. Mash through sieve after removing rind. Cool by placing pan containing crushed pumpkin under cold water. Pack leaving one-half inch head space.

Rutabagas
Select tender ones. Cut off tops, wash and peel. Cut into one-half inch cubes and boil for two minutes. Cool, drain and pack leaving one-half inch head space.

Squash
Select young summer squash. Wash and cut into one-half inch slices. Boil for three minutes. Cool, drain, and pack leaving one-half inch head space.

Sweet Potatoes
Choose medium to large sized potatoes that have been cured. Cook until almost tender, let stand at room temperature until cooled. Peel and cut or mash. Add lemon juice to prevent darkening. Pack leaving one-half inch head space.

Tomatoes, stewed
Remove stem ends, peel and quarter. Cover and cook until tender (twenty minutes). Place pan containing tomatoes in cold water to cool. Pack leaving head space.

Turnips
Select small, firm turnips. Wash, peel and cut into one-half inch cubes. Boil for two minutes. Cool, drain, and pack leaving one-half inch head space.

12 Landscaping

FLORILEGIVM
EMANVELIS SWEERTI SEPTIMON,
TI BATAVI AMSTELEDAMI COMORANTIS, TRA,
CTANS DE VARIIS FLORIB, ET ALIIS INDICIS PLA,
TIS AD VIVVM DELINEATVM IN DVABVS
PARTIB, ET QVATVOR LINGVIS
CONCINNATVM.

Do-It-Yourself LANDSCAPING

Landscaping your own grounds—whether you are starting with a barren plot, improving on a previous owner's good taste, or contending with a haphazard arrangement of plantings put in by previous occupants without taste—can be a joy.

But it also entails a good deal of work and can be costly. The only sensible way to be sure to get what you really want and to avoid the frustration and waste of money of having to replant, or of discovering errors, is to plan the landscape on paper first.

This initial paperwork may seem a bother, but it enables you to clarify concepts in your own mind in advance. And chances are that, as you go along, you'll find yourself changing your mind about a lot of particulars—and perhaps even about major goals.

Many people, quite naturally, think of landscaping in terms of the particular trees or flowers they'd like to have around them. But in fact, plants should be the last consideration. First consider your family and its needs and pleasures; how your grounds can enhance your home life; whether you want your plantings to help save on fuel bills; how much time you want to put into mowing lawn or other garden maintenance; how many of your desires your plot can acommodate; how much time and money you want to put into landscaping now and in the future—in short, an entire list of practicalities should be established before you consider the plants themselves.

To do all this you will need lots of scrap paper for making preliminary notes. When you are ready to begin planning, you will need large sheets of graph paper—the larger the better. And, you will need a pad of tracing paper large enough in size to fit over the graph paper (you'll be redoing lots of the tracking paper sketches). In addition to a pencil, it is also handy to have felt pens, pencils, or crayons of various colors. As your planning becomes more complex, you'll find it less confusing if you can note parts of the whole in different colors; for example, walks in blue, buildings in red, and plants in green.

Whether or not you plan to consult a landscape architect, preliminary thought and planning is essential. A professional landscape architect can help you design and implement your plan, but is not in a position to evaluate your personal needs. Even if you do plan landscaping consultation, you can save time and fees by making an analysis in advance. For limited work on a small lot, you may not need consultation. For larger investments of time and money, and complexities such as grade changes, consultation fees for a professional landscape architect could be money well spent.

If you do not get help from a landscape architect, try to check the appropriateness of proposed plantings with the landscape department of the garden center or retail nursery through which you buy.

Step 1: Setting Priorities

On your scrap paper, note your basic priorities. Only you can draw up a complete list of what will make your family most happy and comfortable, but here are some examples of the types of things you might consider:

1. Do you want one or more outdoor living areas? If so, will this be primarily for the family or for entertaining? Will the groups using this outdoor area be large or small? Will you cook outdoors, how often, and do you want to include a barbecue or other dining equipment as part of your permanent design; and will you store all this between use? Do you want an outdoor nook for breakfasts, picnic tables for lunch, or some other special feature?
2. Are there family hobbies, like tennis or horseshoes, that should be considered?
3. Are some needs temporary—a playground that might be converted to other uses as the children grow older?—a lawn where you eventually hope to install a swimming pool?
4. Instead of active use, does your family prefer quiet areas for swimming and reading, or conversational groupings?
5. Do you have a view you want to preserve and/or enhance or do you see sights you'd rather have screened? Do you want more privacy from your neighbors?
6. Do you enjoy gardening and want to raise your own food, tend flowers, or fuss over pruning? Or do you want only low-maintenance plantings?
7. Do you want windscreens, shading, or other vegetation to help save on energy bills?
8. Do you have special interests you want to pursue, such as attracting birds, or an area for making pottery and a shed for storing equipment?
9. Are there things you hate about your property, such as a too-small driveway, moth-eaten lawn, or inconvenient path from the garage to the house?
10. Are there little extras that might be nice—such as a way to hide garbage cans or a little area for growing kitchen herbs?

Obviously, in drawing up such a list, you will find contradictions, not to mention that your property might not be large enough to accommodate everything you'd like. But that's the reason for thinking about your needs in the first place—it allows you to sort out those things that are truly most important.

Step 2: Plotting Your Land

On graph paper, you should now record the basics with which you have to work. If your land is long and narrow, you will find graph paper two or three feet long handy, and if your plot is square you will want paper that is shorter and wider. Make a plan of your land on a scale of at least a quarter-inch to the foot—or larger, if you can manage it.

To plot accurately, examine your deed map showing the exact dimensions of your property. If you do not have one, you can obtain information through the local government office that handles taxes or real estate through your mortgage-holder. This will enable you to transfer to the graph paper the exact boundaries of your land as well as orientations.

If your land is on a hilly site, you may also need a contour map to show the grades on your property—and to mark drainage or other aspects of neighboring land that could affect yours. If your land presents unusual problems in grade, you may have to obtain a topographical survey.

Then, through architects' drawings or your own measurements, transfer to the graph paper the exact outline of your home and any other buildings on your property, garage, walks, and driveways.

When completed, your graph-paper replica should show everything of importance. On your house, you should mark the exact location and size of windows and doors, roof extensions, and any other details (such as downspouts) that could influence your landscaping. Note traffic patterns, and whether they are convenient or should be rerouted. Anything that cannot be changed, such as the sidewalk or huge rocks, should also be indicated. Include location and depth of underground telephone lines and other utilities—also occasional problems such as septic tank cleanouts that could disturb plantings. If you intend to add any outbuildings or fences, gather information on local building codes.

Also, mark any large trees or other features of your property that you'd like to keep. Don't, however, be intimidated by the existing plantings. Most landscaping is the result of slapdash efforts by a series of owners that is neither practical nor beautiful. Don't hesitate to eliminate trees that are blocking light or to rip out shrubs that are out-of-scale or poorly placed.

Now, jot down data on such things as the prevailing winds, duration and angles of sun, unattractive sights you'd like to block or beautiful views you want to keep, and anything else not actually on your property but that will influence your landscape plans.

Note: If you prefer to work with modules, pick the size of your modular unit. The module can be square (say, four by four feet) or rectangular (say, four by five feet) and is most useful if it is based on a realistic measurement. For example, if your house is thirty feet long, your module could be based on three or five feet because thirty can be divided evenly in six or ten modules; four-foot modules would be awkward, because four doesn't divide evenly into thirty. In addition, if you will be using extensive construction materials—such as paving, bricks, concrete blocks, or tile—you should take into account their dimensions when creating your module. If your paving blocks are one-and-one-half feet square, then a three-by-three-foot or three-by-six-foot module makes sense.

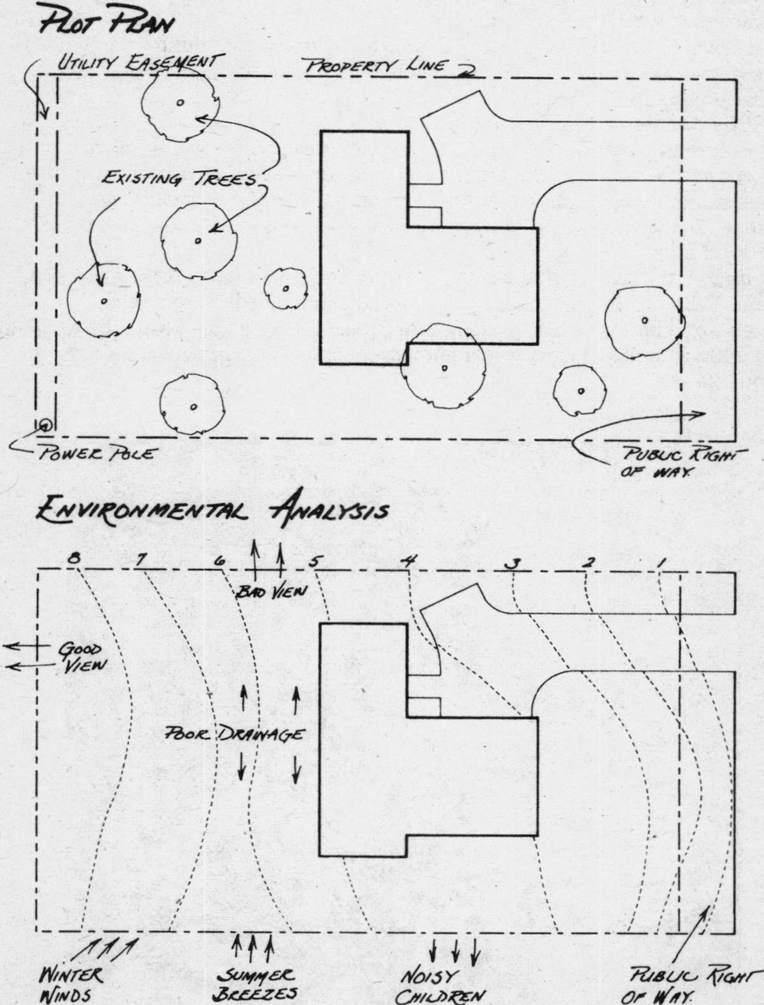

The module has several advantages. If your property is eighty feet wide and you have chosen a four-by-four foot module, you would be calculating with only twenty modules rather than with eighty feet. This makes it easy to budget your time and money—you can improve only two or three modules at a time. You get a feeling of satisfaction at having completed a module, whereas if you are working with feet there may be a tendency to become discouraged that another seventy-six to ninety feet remain. More important, though, is the aesthetic value. If you have not had much training in the arts, creating pleasing proportions and appropriate scale can be difficult. Modules will give your scheme more unity, because you will be using multiples of the same dimensions over and over again, which will enable you to keep a firmer grasp on scale.

Whether you use feet or modules, the graph-paper replica you create should be kept clean and unwrinkled. It will be your basic working tool. If you have a simple landscaping problem for a small area, it may be the only reference you need. More likely, you will be using it as a basis for making more detailed graph-paper plots for various aspects of your property.

Step 3: Big Ideas

Once you have completed the nitty-gritty, boring details, you are ready for the fun. Still forgetting about the plants themselves, place a piece of tracing paper over the graph paper and begin to draw designs of how you'd like your property to look—ideally.

Here you will be combining the ideal priorities you set out in Step 1 with the realities you have just measured in Step 2. Your ideas may, in fact, be too big for your lot. On the other hand, creative design and grading may enable you to include more than you think. So, the object now is to think big, playing around on the tracing paper with possible designs, and using as many pieces of tracing paper as possible to clarify ideas.

At this stage, the types of questions you should be asking yourself fall into an organized pattern, and you will want to give consideration to:

1. Your site—its limitations and advantages.
2. The public face of your house. This probably includes the driveway and front entrance and may also include a garage and other elements.
3. A service area. This is where deliveries are made, meters are read, and where you put out your garbage.
4. Depending on your property and house placement, you may have a private side area, on the opposite side of the house from the service area.
5. The private area. This is usually the area behind the house and the most complicated to design.

At first, think in practical terms about realities such as traffic patterns; tips on particular problems are given below in discussions of each major area. Gradually you should also begin to think about aesthetics—how the practical problems can be solved in the most attractive ways. Still don't focus on specific plants, but rather figure the general height, breadth, form, texture, and perhaps color of general planting groups. Tips on styling and principles of aesthetics are given below. After reading these sections, you may find yourself redoing your original tracing paper plans, but that is okay. The idea is to have all your needs and desires firmly in mind and in the proper order of priority before you touch spade to soil.

By this point you have probably found the original graph-paper replica too small. Work out the public area, service area, and private area to scale on separate sheets of graph paper that allow you to show more detail and insert smaller measurements. These will become more useful as you get down to the even smaller details of choosing plants. For the private area, which is usually the largest and most important, you may even want to make one to-scale overall plan and then break this down into easy-to-use smaller segments.

One factor that could make you alter original plans is that you have been working in two dimensions. As you move closer to a consideration of plantings, you have to visualize increasingly in three-dimensional form. You may want to supplement your ground plan with sketches that will show your home and the projected height and breadth of plantings and open areas in three dimensions. Even if you don't draw very well, rude sketches will help you with scale, balance, and other aesthetic elements hard to visualize from a grand plan.

Step 4: Down to Earth

Your plan may look very good to you practically as well as aesthetically, but now is the time to look it over for possible miscalculations.

Here you should consider the cost of any grading changes and construction involved, and begin to set up a time schedule and a budget. You will not complete the schedule and budget until you have chosen the plants, but you can't fully decide on the plants until you have a preliminary idea of how much you want to spend and how patient you are about awaiting results.

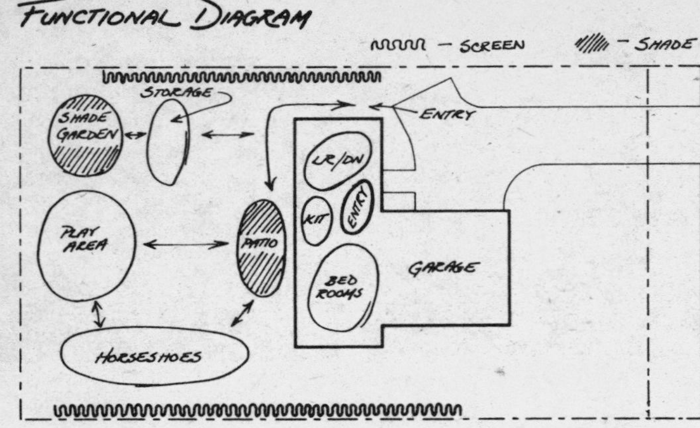

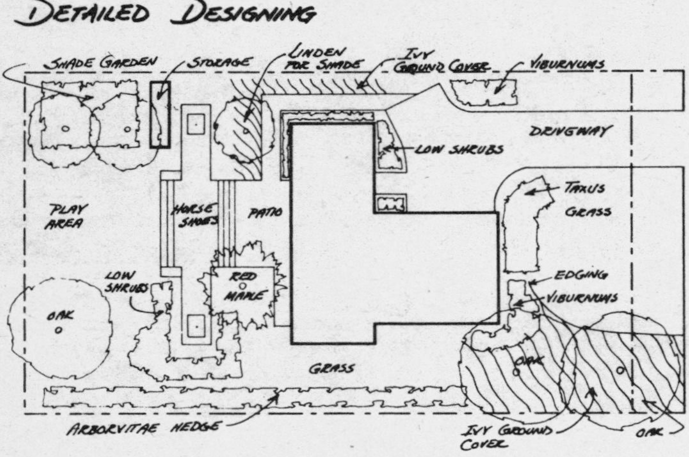

For instance, for your plan to spring full-blown into reality, you would have to buy mature trees and other plantings. Few people can afford that. The larger the full-grown plant, the more you save by buying it young. A good-sized tree, for example one over twelve feet tall, is not only expensive but will probably entail professional transportation and installation. For a fraction of the price you can buy the same species three to six feet tall and plant it yourself. The cost differential is so enormous that, even in the case of energy-saving plantings, it can take years to recoup. Most people therefore opt for smaller and cheaper plants even though this means a longer wait before the landscape reaches planned maturity.

On many properties this is less of a problem than it seems. The norm today is a small lot with a low house. Large trees are usually out-of-scale on such properties, and several trees that remain small at mature height probably will look better than one huge one.

In addition, since you are unlikely to be implementing your entire landscape scheme the first year, schedule planting of the largest and slowest-growing species first. This will give them a head start while you concentrate on faster growing, lower plantings. This is a sensible way to proceed, since the larger plantings have the most impact on energy bills, enclose your private area to provide screening, and give your landscape its basic mass and structure.

Step 5: At Last—The Plants

On your tracing paper plan, or perhaps on a new piece of tracing paper you impose over the original tracing paper plan, you can now begin to work out the specific plantings. Start with the largest elements first—trees, massive shrub plantings for screening, and the like—and work gradually down to the smallest plants.

Even if your tracing paper model is fairly large, you will probably not find room to write in all the plant names. Mark on the tracing paper the amount and shape of space the plant needs—with, say a circle for a tree and a rectangle for a flower bed or hedge—and give it a number. Then list plants on a separate sheet of paper that also serves as a shopping list and on which you can record the prices you'll have to pay. (On the shopping list, enumerate plants of each species you intend to buy and the height at which you intend to buy them. For example, you might be buying a maple tree eight feet tall, twenty azalea bushes each a foot high, and 200 three-inch pachysandra plants. This list will help you figure costs, so that you can budget time and money for any given area of your grounds.)

On the tracing paper, however, it is vital to mark the total area to be covered by these plants *once they reach their mature height.* This will keep you from planting another large tree too close to the maple or from planning to underplant the maple with shrubs that require sun. It will also keep you from buying too many young plants and planting them too closely together, with the result that you'll later have to transplant or discard some.

A temptation, once you have figured the total cost of your landscaping scheme and found it high, is to buy a few large plants and to scatter them here and there to fill space. This is not a good solution, because no section of your grounds will look good. It is best—after having planted major elements such as trees—to proceed to one small section and do it well and completely before going on to the next.

Of course, when you buy plants well under their mature height, it will take them time—perhaps years in the case of trees—to look as you envisioned them on your grand scheme. There will be gaps between shrubs, and the scale will be off. Few newly planted landscapes look cohesive for the first two or three years.

The solution used by professional landscape architects is to buy what they call "fillers." Fillers are whatever plants are cheapest and fastest growing for your area—ligustrum, viburnum, and so forth. Use these to fill in gaps between permanent plantings and to cover any bare areas before you get around to planting them. But, be ruthless about tearing the fillers out and discarding them before they have a chance to damage your permanent plants. Fast-growing plants have fast-growing root systems that can entangle your permanent plantings. Container plants are a second solution to filling gaps. These can be moved about to cover bare areas without the nuisance of planting and digging up. With careful planning, the container plants might be permanent parts of your landscaping plan. They can eventually be used on a terrace or elsewhere. In this case, they represent no additional cost.

Money Saving Landscape Tips

1. The cost, rarity, or uniqueness of any particular plant has nothing to do with whether it's right for your landscape. What matters is whether its height, form, texture, and cultural requirements are right for your grounds. An inexpensive and common plant in first-rate condition looks worlds better than a dying exotic.
2. Buy small. Start from seeds and cuttings when feasible.
3. Buy only as many plants as you need, and calculate planting spaces based on *mature* heights. Planting too many young shrubs too close together will result in a jungle once they take root and flourish. You will have to periodically thin and discard plants.
4. Before buying trees, learn what they will look like when grown. Young nursery trees frequently appear quite different from their mature counterparts four or six years later. Most pines, some firs, spruces, and other trees lose their lower branches as they grow. Cedars, pines, eucalyptus can lose their early symmetrical forms; in strong wind they may assume fantastic shapes—which may or may not fit into your garden. Unless you plan for mature heights, some fast-growing species may soon grow out of scale.
5. Whenever possible, visit the nursery to select plants yourself.
6. Buy from a good nursery or landscape center that will guarantee plants through at least one growing season.
7. If trees are to be planted for you, try to visit the nursery to select your trees and tag the best side so it will be planted to look its best. Be sure you have a firm agreement about where the trees are to be planted, how they are to be planted, and exactly what the costs will be.
8. Design your landscape so many plants can do double duty—serve as enclosure *and* screen wind; provide shade *and* encourage birds; add color *and* discourage pests; produce flowers *and* usable fruit or herbs.
9. Buy disease-resistant varieties.
10. Before buying, investigate the root systems of your proposed plants so your trees will not damage underground utilities and lawns, or so your shrubs and creepers will not invade other plantings. Privet and other plants with invasive roots may have to be kept in bounds by sheet metal inserted as deep as three feet around them.
11. If money is tight, figure out the most inexpensive way to solve a landscape problem. Let's say you want a sun screen and can't afford a large tree. Cheaper—and far faster than waiting for a small tree to grow—would be to make a do-it-yourself trellis of less costly materials that can be covered with a fast-growing vine.

Design Elements

Few people want either the exaggerated formality or informality that characterized European landscaping in the previous century. A more moderate course is usually steered. Philosophically, the difference between the two styles is that formality stresses man's domination over nature, while informality stresses nature over man.

In practice, this means that in formal style the overall plan is geometric. The garden paths and beds are carved into geometric shapes, and balance and other design effects are achieved by greater use of identical companion plants, measured spacing, and greater precision. The informal style depends on more irregular shapes, flowing lines, gently curved paths and beds, and greater freedom in attaining balance and other effects.

Since most residential plots are small and dominated by the house, your home's architecture will have a great bearing on the degree of formality or informality. A Georgian-style home—or any design like it, in which the windows and other elements of facade are formally balanced on either side of the door—calls for formal plantings. Even if your house design is not so evenly balanced but is rectangular in form, you will have to use some amount of formality.

If your house is curved or irregular in shape, then the curving forms of an informal style are suitable. Rustic cabins and some picturesque styles also lend themselves to informal landscaping.

These are broad categories, however, and either style can be modified to be appropriate to the design of your home. Examine the length, breadth, placement of windows and doors, roof lines, and other elements to establish the proper landscape formula.

The shape, contours, and size of your plot are a second major consideration. Even if you yearn for a formal landscape design, it will be almost impossible to implement on a hilly site, especially where rocks and other such features naturally create irregularity. On slopes that have gentle grades and few natural obstructions to neat order you have a better chance. On level properties, in contrast, introducing grade changes and other irregularities for a highly informal design could be costly and impractical, and you'd do better to lean toward some formality. Informality would be the key on a lot surrounded by natural landscape such as forest, meadows, or dunes. On a lot that is neatly squared off, a more formal design is easier, while on oddly shaped grounds informal designs are easier.

Where you have room to maneuver, the style of planting dictated by the house can be contained close to the house. As you move away from the house, the plantings can become transitional, so that at a distance from the house the landscape design can be quite different. Many of the showplace plantation homes of

the South, for instance, have formal plantings in the vicinity of the house that are in keeping with the classical lines of the buildings. Rosedown, Afton Villa, and others include geometric parterres, clipped hedges, and formal balance. But moving away from the house, the gardens gradually become less formal, until at the edges of the estate they blend into the natural landscape.

Often people shy away from formality, thinking it is stiff and pretentious. This is a holdover from the excesses of the nineteenth century, and many of the most beautiful gardens on our continent use a great deal of formality—often so subtly employed that it seems informal to the unwary observer. Formal designs have an advantage, too, in being easier to implement successfully. Good informal schemes run the hazard of degenerating into a hodgepodge unless you are trained in the arts or have a good natural feeling for the third dimension.

Before designing your own landscape, visit botanical gardens and great homes where you can see the top-notch creations of professionals. Middleton Place, in South Carolina, is the oldest landscaped garden in America; its beautiful reflective pools and lush, overhanging live oaks cure any notion that formality has to be stiff. If you despair of your hopeless site with a sterile soil, a trip to the Royal Botanical Gardens in Hamilton, Ontario, should cheer you up. Constructed in an old gravel pit, here is stately grandeur combined with charm. The Arizona-Sonora Desert Museum in Tucson has a demonstration area for home landscaping. At the Garden Center of Greater Cleveland the herb garden is elegantly formal. Branches of the University of California maintain outstanding displays in several locations, and Florida maintains numerous gardens of native tropical species, including the Fairchild Tropical Garden in Miami.

Unity

A beautiful landscape theme, like any work of art, has to be unifed. All the elements you use should fit together to create a harmonious whole. Nothing should look out-of-place. The best methods for assuring unity are:

1. *Enclosure.* If you design your garden on a plan that opens to neighboring lots or landscapes, you will have to include these influences in your overall design. Obviously this will make your job much bigger. If you have a beautiful distant view, naturally you will want to include it. Or, your neighbors may have such beautifully landscaped grounds that it would be foolish not to give yourself the benefit of enjoying them too. But in most cases, you will make your own enclave more serene and enjoyable by blocking out neighboring distractions.

Where climate and other factors make it possible, screen the private area of your home completely with high, thick plantings of trees and shrubs around the perimeters. If space is at a premium, fences and thinner plantings will serve the purpose. On small properties where sun or breeze would be blocked by high vegetation, thinner screens of low, spreading trees, open-work trellises covered with vines, and low-growing plantings are good choices. In a few types of homes—those built around patios or atriums—some enclosure is provided by the architecture, but often an additional garden outside the house needs screening.

Blocking off the outside world makes it easier to cope with design problems. No exterior factors will detract from the climax you are trying to create or intrude on the unity you are trying to establish. In a self-contained unit, you can retain control over line—whether it is vertical height, or the horizontal pattern of garden paths, lawn and bed edges, or paving—and regulate it to conform with the lot and house lines.

2. *Similar form.* A design will have more unity if you don't try to mix together too many trees or shrubs of vertical, horizontal, or globular form. The larger your property, the more room you will have for varying effects, but even then, plant forms in any one area should be restricted. An alternate plant form may be used for accent, and a series of an alternate form may be used for rhythmic effect, but neither of these devices will succeed if the basic forms of your plant mass are too varied.

3. *Similar texture.* A planting of glossy-leaved holly, needled trees or bushes, elms, and other textures is going to create a restless, chaotic feeling. Your major plantings will look better if they are all similar types such as needled species, fleshy foliage, or closely related intermediate textures. Again, the smaller your property the more important it is to restrict the number of textures you use; alternate textures should be saved for special effects.

4. *Restricted color.* A single color can be used to tie together a garden scheme and/or to create rhythm, leaving another color choice for accent. The more colors you use, the harder the garden is to unify. A riotous display of colors should be saved for special purposes, such as a flower bed as a climax to the garden. Plants with foliage of purple, bluish, or reddish hues offer subtler color variations than do flowers.

5. *Similar ecological species.* In general, plants that grow together naturally look best together, and you will achieve better unity by basing your design on plantings from similar ecological zones. This does not mean you are restricted to native species, because plants from around the world make interesting additions to native gardens—provided they come from similar climates. But planting a cactus beside a pine tree will simply look bizarre. Also, the number of plants involved in landscaping can mean onerous maintenance, unless plantings in any one area require the same type of soil, moisture, and other conditions.

The test for a successful design is to cover successive parts of your graph-paper plan with a piece of plain paper. If all of your design elements are truly integrated, the design will lose force, look lopsided, and seem unfinished when any segment is not included. If removing a section makes no visual or aesthetic difference, then that section is extraneous and not properly integrated into the total scheme.

Balance

Balance in a landscape is a feeling of equilibrium. Balance gives your garden a serene, peaceful feeling.

Balance is, quite literally, weight. The gateposts to imposing estates were always massive blocks, of identical design and height, on either side of the driveway. They create a feeling of stability, permanence, and confidence. One gatepost half the size of the other would be lopsided and ludicrous, because uneven weight distribution is measured by the mind's eye.

The easiest way to achieve balance is to contrast two identical forms, like the gateposts. You can't go wrong if you flank a rectangular doorway with identical bushes or trees. In many of the great gardens of Europe the designers took no chances, and the gardens were designed so that right and left sides of the entire layout, even if it covered acres, were mirror images. With identical plantings on either side, balanced weight was a certainty. This type of balance is called *symmetrical*, because the balance is true.

A more subtle form of balance is where the weight is not true, but only *appears* to be true. One tall, massive tree, for instance, could be balanced by plantings that appear to the mind's eye to have equal weight—perhaps because two shorter but broader trees were placed side-by-side or because one drooping tree draped over high bushes. The weight of the large tree appears to equal the sum of the weight of the smaller plantings. This type of balance is called *asymmetrical*. It is also called occult balance, because it is so subtle you are not immediately aware that you are looking at identical weights.

Asymmetrical balance, harder to achieve, offers more interesting options. A grove of trees can be balanced with an open expanse of meadow, provided proportions to the height and width are finely attuned. A storage shed on one side of your garden can be balanced by a massive planting on the other side, again provided their apparent weights are attuned. Even in a formal garden, where you have a good deal of symmetrical balance, some asymmetrical plantings can soften the rigidity.

But there are two dangers in asymmetrical balance. First, when you plant two identical trees or shrubs or groups, you can be fairly certain they will grow at roughly the same rate and remain in balance for years. With asymmetrical groupings, varying growth rates may set the balance off. When you are balancing nongrowing material such as a shed with plantings, the danger of imbalance will be worse. You will have to choose slow-growing species, or plantings already at mature height, to assure the balance remains.

The second disadvantage of asymmetrical balance is that, since it is apparent rather than actual, it may appear stable only from selected points of view. Identical forms will be balanced from no matter what direction you view them. Many asymmetrical arrangements, in contrast, are easy to create only if placed against walls or other places where they are viewed chiefly from one direction. Trying to create an asymmetrical arrangement that looks balanced from four points of view is extremely difficult.

Usually you achieve asymmetrical balance with mass, but the apparent mass can depend on form, height, and texture of the plants you are using. A densely formed shrub with dark, glossy leaves will appear equal in weight to a larger shrub with loose branching and light-colored leaves. You can also balance with color—such as placing four pots of similarly colored flowers at the four corners of a square or rectangular pool.

As with other design elements, the choice of which type of balance to use is not always yours. If the facade of your home has formal architectural balance, then you would have to use formal planting balance. If you have a modern-style home with asymmetrical balance and sweeping curves, then asymmetrical plantings are appropriate. As with other design elements, balance should be evident not only in the overall garden scheme but also in its smaller components.

Rhythm

Rhythm is achieved by repetition, and the object is to introduce a sense of movement into the design. Rhythm keeps your design from being dull.

Rhythm can be created in the overall basic ground pattern and related to any architectural forms on the grounds. In the large gardens of Europe, for instance, where the homes were rectangular, the gardens were also laid out in rectangular shapes. The entire garden was enclosed with a wall or tall trees to emphasize the rectangular form. Within the garden, the same form would be repeated in rectangular panels of grass, flowerbeds, pools, and perhaps in stone benches, as well as in straight, parallel garden paths. This type of repetition helps give a garden balance and unity.

You can achieve similar effects by surrounding your oval swimming pool with oval plantings or by repeating the angularities of your home, garage, and storage shed with similarly shaped plantings. A problem on many properties today, however, is that the lot may be rectangular, the swimming pool round, and the house lines free-flowing. When you have such disparately shaped elements, unity is difficult to achieve. If you have space between the elements, you can spread the plants out to create transitions between the architectural forms. You can also use forms of semi-enclosure—for example, cradling part of the round pool with an arc of low-growing juniper bushes that would then extend beyond the pool area to gentler curves similar to those of the house. Because the grand gardens of Europe are usually planted on flat land and conceived to be viewed from a height, any irregularities are immediately evident. On your property, you can create transitions between the disparate elements with changes in grade, with small, spreading trees, and with other plantings that help to disguise the actual ground-plan problems.

In most small gardens, rhythm is achieved through a repetition of the same plantings made at intervals. Depending on the size of your garden, you can do this with a group of several plants that you plant at evenly spaced intervals; or you can do it with a single plant, say a recurring holly or dwarf fruit tree. You can also repeat flowers at intervals; but once they fade you lose the rhythm unless you keep replacing the dead flowers with new species on a year-round basis. Evergreens are therefore best; if you want color, use a species with foliage color that contrasts with most of the background plantings.

You can lose unity by attempting rhythm in too many ways—especially if your garden is small. It is best to achieve rhythm through only *one* plant characteristic—use plants of the same form in recurrent patterns, but choose those with similar color and texture or foliage; or use plants of the same distinctively green foliage that vary in shape.

Unity will be strongest if you carry out rhythm with elements other than plants. A round swimming pool or goldfish pool can be complemented by a round table, a bench girdling a tree, a round lawn area, and rounded steppingstones for pathways.

Though repeating basic forms and plants is an aid to balance and unity, repetition alone as a device can become boring. In ornate European gardens, variety was introduced with small details. For example, when the garden was laid out in square flower beds lined up in a row, small indentations might be made at the edge of each bed in the center. Into these recesses, benches or sculptures were placed. The solid rhythm of the flower beds was thereby supplemented with the lighter rhythm of these smaller objects. Where the sculpture and benches alternated, three rhythms were possible. Similar effects are easily created in smaller gardens with small container plants, pieces of pottery, or bedding plants.

Finally, while rhythm is satisfying in itself, it is even more effective if, in addition to repetition, it gives a feeling of progression. Let's say you have a curving garden path punctuated by little pine trees that increase slightly in size; then, as you round the curve, you find the same tree, but this one is especially large. You have introduced a feeling of suspense along the path and built it to a satisfying climax.

Accent

While balance and rhythm are used to create a feeling of harmony, accent is used to avoid monotony and to give the whole a feeling of moving toward a climax or finishing point.

One of the most effective accents is a change in grade. Ascending or descending only a step or two to the swimming pool, a fern glade, or a flower path creates a feeling of anticipation. You are forced to change pace, preparing you for a slightly different area from the one you are leaving. For this reason, grade change is handy when you have disparate forms on your property—such as the pool, house, and lot forms mentioned above—that you are trying to tie together into a harmonious whole.

Changes in grade may be emphasized with plantings or with a combination of an architectural element and plantings. A pair of balanced trees or shrubs against a low wall, or a pair of containers with flowers flanking steps, warn of the change in grade as well as make a decorative focal point. An archway or trellis is also effective.

Another effective accent is a change in line—a garden path that angles or curves, or planting beds that do the same—provided such changes are in harmony with their surroundings. To design an angle in a path leading from a circular flower bed would be awkward. To introduce curves into a rectangular ground plan is also difficult.

Paving for a terrace, curbings and borders of plants or man-made materials; birdhouses, fountains, even garden furniture can all be called into double duty for function as well as for accent.

Above all, accent is important among the plants themselves. An area of light green foliage can be accented with a purple plum or a deep green myrtle, and an area of dark foliage can be accented with a tree or shrub with silvery leaves. Even more subtle accent is possible if you contrast texture—a glossy holly against a background of plantings with softer leaves. Accent can also be created through using height and form—a columnar tree to create a skyline silhouette, or a drooping tree to moderate the sharp angles of stiff-branched conifers.

It is easy to overdo accent, however. To work, it must be subtle. Too much accent loses effectiveness and gives a restless, disjointed feeling.

Climax

Though a landscape may be well balanced, have rhythm and handsome accent, it is not complete until it terminates in a climax. The climax is the area or feature around which the entire scheme revolves. To fashion the climax, call into play all the forces you have been employing elsewhere in the garden—balance, rhythm, and accent—but make them strongest here.

The Front of Belton House extending 150 feet —

The North or Garden front of Belton House extending 150 feet.

How prominent and elaborate your climax is depends to a large extent on the size of your garden. As you must build toward a climax, creating suspense and movement toward it with other parts of the garden, a large expanse of ground allows room for lesser focal points along the way. These focal points are simpler and subordinate, and heighten the anticipation. At Villa d'Este, near Rome, for example, the gardens are on a slope; you descend, through planted terraces with fountains that form smaller focal points, to a mammoth and elaborate statue at the base. Great gardens built on flat land generally lead you through series of parterres and other low-lying plantings to a climax that is taller, often set on a height, and that may be an architectural construction surrounded by stately and massive vegetation.

In a small garden, the climax can be simple and geared to your interests. An art lover's garden might culminate with a large piece of sculpture. A bird lover's garden might culminate in a birdbath surrounded by bird feeders. A particularly beautiful tree, a mass of boulders, or any other natural feature of your property can serve as the climax. In some cases you may not have much choice. If you have a small lot with a large, prominent feature such as a swimming pool, it will call such attention to itself that you cannot avoid using it as the climax for your scheme. While plantings can enhance certain aspects of your grounds and play down others, they cannot dictate the landscape in opposition to existing elements on the site.

What you use as a climax is less important than how you unify the landscape around it. In a landscape that terminates at a stream overhung with willows, you might employ descending grade changes along a path that incorporates small, drooping plant forms. Where your climax is on a hilltop, you might point the way with spired or triangular forms of vegetation. Rhythm and accent should create movement toward the climax. On flat land, a change in grade is effective. If you have a goldfish pond as your climax, a recessed basin would be functional and serve to draw attention. If your flower bed is the climax, raising the planting bed a foot or so would work well.

Strongly delineating the focal point with paving, edging, flower borders, or other ground-level devices will also draw and hold attention. Plants around the focal point should be chosen to enhance it. A tall tree might be flanked with contrasting or complementary forms that are shorter the farther they are from the tree. If your principal feature is horizontal, such as a wide-basined fountain or birdbath, you might flank it with trees that branch horizontally. An upright form such as a sundial on a pedestal might be nestled beneath draping foliage or be set against a trellis of thick vines.

Whether your principal focal point is large and prominent or more subtle, it should be strong enough to draw your attention, and balanced enough to make you want to linger over the view. The object is not only to construct a point that adds polish and finish to your scheme, but also to direct your sight back into the garden.

Your Site

Whether your site is a small city lot or expansive grounds in a suburban or rural setting, the success of your landscape design will depend largely on how well you evaluate the site. Tiny, jewellike gardens have been created under the most adverse conditions, but such transformations require a thorough knowledge of the site's characteristics.

In addition to climate and site data noted in Step 2 of Do-It-Yourself Landscaping, temperature range, frost-free period, and annual rainfall will influence your choice of plantings. Though it is possible to culture water-loving plants in an arid area and to protect delicate plants from northern cold and wind, such plants will create maintenance problems and, in the latter case, unsightly seasonal problems too.

Soil is another major consideration. Most landscaping plants thrive on a variety of soils and are adaptable to pH ranges between 6.0 and 8.0. Greater acidity or alkalinity will influence your choice of plants. You can, of course, construct any type of soil you want by buying the proper ingredients and additives—but while this is feasible for container specimens, it is impractical on a large scale such as landscaping. Preconceived notions of growing particular plants can run into a lot of work and money. For any type of soil you will find a variety of handsome plants that are adaptable and will thrive with little maintenance. Look over the existing plants on your property to see which are doing well and which are doing poorly. They can tell you quite a lot about your soil and growing conditions. Trees such as red maple and sour gum, or shrubs such as arrowwood viburnum, can indicate wet soil that drains poorly.

Is your soil wet? Dig a hole twelve to eighteen inches deep and fill it with water. If your water flushes away between five and ten hours, you will have a fairly porous soil, and can grow a variety of plants. If the water does not drain away within about ten hours, you have soil best for ferns, mosses, and other water-tolerant plants.

Drainage is a major problem on many properties and is often related not only to soil composition but to grading as well. To save money, many developers grade only the front of the property, and occasionally the side. In addition, if the original grading was not well done, pockets and sinkages could have occurred over the years; you may have depressions and runoffs, especially in the area behind the house where you intend to do the most landscaping. Some regrading would therefore be advantageous. Though regrading is expensive, even a minimal amount is often worth the investment.

If your property, or part of it, is on a steep slope, consider installing planting terraces held in place with retaining walls. Slopes severely limit what you can plant and frequently are accompanied by soil erosion.

Though lawns need a slight degree of slope for drainage, and look best when not absolutely level, those with steep slopes are difficult to mow and maintain. If you intend to install a lawn area, regrading may therefore be necessary to provide proper drainage and a moderate degree of slope, and to avoid depressions where water will pool. Providing proper drainage for a terrace may also involve regrading.

If your property is totally flat, you might want to regrade it a bit to create changes in level. Gardens where you climb or descend, even if only a step or two, are almost always more interesting than those that are absolutely flat. Level changes are excellent ways to delineate the activities associated with different areas of your garden. Even on a small property a raised corner surrounded with trellises can create a private, quiet bower for reading. On a very tiny lot, grade changes can increase apparent size; a minuscule dining terrace four or five feet above a small lawn and flower bed can appear double its size.

Grade changes of this sort, if planned into the overall landscaping costs, need not add significantly to the expense. If you are building a terrace anyway, the cost, depending on the materials and construction, will often be the same whether you set it level with the garden or raise it.

Grade is often inseparable from drainage, but drainage problems can occur on flat land with little grade change. In many areas, though the rainfall is not significantly high when calculated on an annual average, the rain tends to come in spurts. A couple of inches falling in one day quickly displays any drainage problems, and a rainy period of a week can wreak havoc in a garden or on a lawn. You should note any drainage problems and correct them in your landscaping scheme. If you require underground drains and dry wells, these can be installed at the same time any regrading is done. If you are going to use surface drains, incorporate these inconspicuously into your overall scheme so they seem a natural part of the landscape. A garden walk can be both a walk and a drain if it has raised borders or a central depression—an arrangement you can make with concrete, tile, brick, or other materials. Shallow ditches between flower beds, covered with water-loving creepers, can seem a natural part of the garden. Even surface catch basins can do double duty if they are made in the form of pools or fountains.

If you are regrading, here are a few tips:

1. Try to create your design to equalize the cuts and fills. That is, if you are going to move earth from one area, try to find another area that could benefit from added height. That way you won't have to incur extra cost by having excess earth removed from your property or new earth brought in.

2. Before grading, consider whether you want to install underground irrigation systems (for watering your plants and for supplying water to any pools, birdbaths, or fountains); underground drainage systems, lighting cables, or other amenities. At one time, underground irrigation systems were expensive. Today, however, plastic tubing is inexpensive and pumps for circulating water are moderately priced. Virtually any public garden you visit today is now watered this way—with revolving sprinkler heads placed so that their spray covers all the vegetation—and there is no reason your own garden cannot be watered the same easy way. These systems come with automatic timers as well as with soil moisture sensors that will keep them off after rainfall. These systems should be installed before topsoil is put in.

Fig. 53. Correcting a torrent in the Sihlwald. The German method of preventing erosion.

3. If you are doing extensive regrading, the water movement and moisture levels in the soil may be affected. Existing trees, even if they are at a distance from the excavation, may be suddenly flooded or drought-stricken. Discuss this possibility in advance with whoever is doing your grading and take measures to protect your trees.

4. If you are doing considerable regrading with heavy, earth-moving equipment, the weight of the equipment may compact the soil. Even if you will be spreading ample topsoil, the roots of many large plants will still reach into the subsoil. Before the topsoil is spread, therefore, be sure the subsoil is thoroughly loosened so that water and air can reach the deeper plant roots.

5. Even if you are regrading for purely practical purposes, make the regrading serve double duty by making it an effective part of your landscape theme so that it will add beauty as well as efficiency.

The Public Area

Landscaping the public approach to your property is usually easier than the private area. One reason is that most homes are placed closer to the street side of the lot than to the back. This leaves you far less land to design in the front. More important, though, your choices are frequently limited. Sometimes there are legal restrictions against fences or high plantings. In any case, the public area, though a setting for your individual home, cannot be properly designed without some consideration of the harmony of the entire street.

In some places, community efforts have resulted in harmonious plantings. The Japanese plantings of Yoshino cherries in Tokyo are world-famous. In Virginia, many towns feature flowering dogwood, and in many Midwestern cities flowering crabapples have been adopted. Millville, New Jersey, specializes in American holly, and in Victoria, British Columbia, hanging baskets of annual flowers is a tradition. If your street has not organized for similar plantings, you might start a committee for this purpose, as it would do much to enhance the part of the landscape you cannot personally control.

Whatever the practice on your street, for your own entrance you want plantings that will seem to welcome guests. As you will want this effect all year, this is not an area for deciduous plantings. The object of public side plantings is to call attention to the house, and especially the door, not to distract visitors. A restrained planting in good taste with low-maintenance plants makes more sense. For color, azaleas, rhododendrons, or other flowering shrubs, or plants such as hollies that develop berries—but that also look good year-round—are wise choices.

At one time, homes were built with cellars of stone or other durable material topped with the house proper—constructed of wood, brick, or other contrasting material. This unattractive division was quite sensibly concealed with plantings along the foundations. Unfortunately, foundation plantings became a tradition. Many people still use them today when modern building methods bring the facing material right down to the ground. No longer is there any ugliness to hide, so planting flowers, bushes, and small trees (some of which have the nasty habit of growing into large trees) all around the perimeter of the building is unnecessary and usually detrimental to the look of the property.

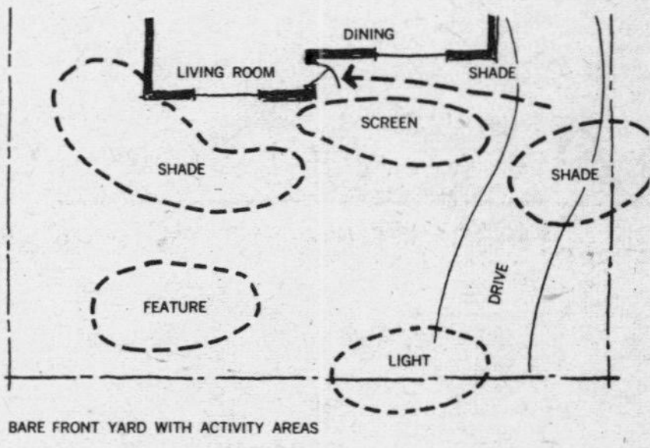

BARE FRONT YARD WITH ACTIVITY AREAS

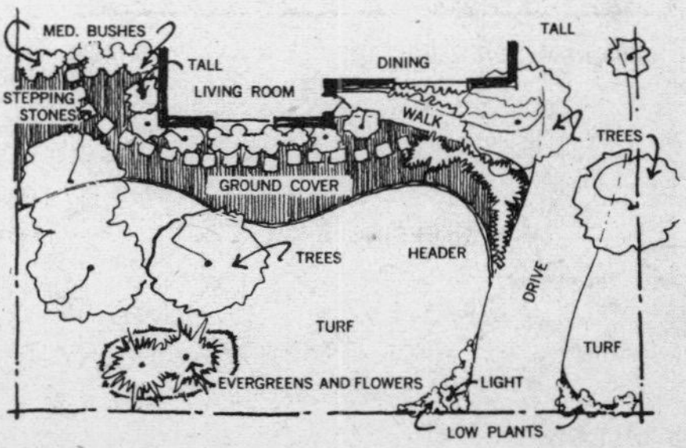

COMPLETED FRONT YARD

Usually, if your house is close to the street, you will want to give an open effect in good proportion to the height of the house—so you will want widely spaced plantings. You can do this with a stretch of lawn, with ground covers, or with a minimal piece of irregularly or formally shaped lawn that blends into ground cover and is then carried higher into shrubs. Ground covers need less maintenance than lawn. Pachysandra and others will also grow on slopes too steep for lawn and where the house or shade trees do not allow much sun to penetrate.

The plantings near the house will be somewhat dictated by the style of the building. A formal house should have balanced plantings on either side—a pair of shade trees, for example, placed far enough away so that they don't overshadow the house—while an informal house might have balanced groupings of trees if the door is centered, or a single tree arching over the doorway if the door is to a side or corner. Trees should *frame* the house, not obscure it—unless, of course, the house is unattractive. In that case, trees and vines can be used to hide architectural defects.

This planting design emphasizes a more functional and important entry approach.

The height of your house also influences plant choice. A tall house needs to be brought down to human scale, and a tall shade tree fronted by low-spreading varieties such as crabapple could work here. Low-lying houses need only heavy foliage at the corners, to soften the angles and extend the apparent width. These can be plantings that combine trees and shrubs. You might place a tree around a corner of the house, too, or even one that pokes up from behind the house to accent a flat or low roof. Star magnolia, dogwoods, fringe-trees, crabapples, Japanese pagoda trees, and other spreading forms are good choices for the fronts of most homes.

Between the trees you will not need many shrubs, and—except for a very formal house—you certainly don't want these lined up in military precision. A tree at the corner of the house may need edging down with some shrubs. If you are not using trees at the corners, a mixture of tall shrubs edged down with smaller ones will soften edges on a low house. If part of the facade is recessed, you might want to emphasize this line with a low line of shrubs or hedge.

For these purposes, dwarf or prostrate forms of plants are best; they do not overgrow or require too much pruning. Hollies, spreading yews and junipers, laurel, firethorn, evergreen barberries, spireas, and euonymus are good selections, as are the already mentioned azaleas and rhododendrons.

If your door is not prominent, you might want to emphasize it with a pair of upright junipers, arborvitae, hollies, a colorful vine, or with container plants in handsome holders.

Shrubs placed elsewhere—to outline a boxy lawn or placed at its corners—usually look lonely and isolated, out of scale with the house, and add nothing to the overall effect. Scattering shrubs on a lawn simply cuts down the apparent size of your front yard.

A complication is created when the entry to the house must be reached by climbing stairs. Instead of a stoop, a more gracious welcome is usually extended by lower risers, wider steps, and fewer steps. Where there is room, an attractive solution is to arrange low risers, widely spaced, which allow platforms between steps. Trees or planters with shrubs can be recessed into the paving, or container

Typical planting in front of a 1900 period house, planned to overcome the architectural styles of that era and hide the foundation.

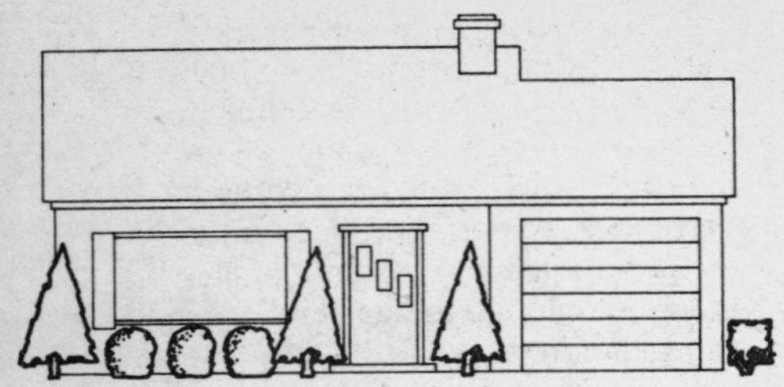

Typical foundation planting of a modern house but no longer needed to hide the foundation.

plants can be used. For a house close to the street, an attractive paving of this sort can eliminate the need for lawn or ground cover.

Where, for lack of room, the steps must remain steep, it is more attractive to eliminate the frontal arrangement that leads directly to the front door. Install instead stairs that curve to one side. This allows you a greater stretch of planting area and a more enticing entry. Where the stairs are high, as on a steep-sloped site, a danger is that any trees framing the house will appear overpowering and forbidding from below. Spreading trees with light colored, delicate foliage are a solution. Prostrate forms of plants such as junipers, or pots of container plants on the risers, can be used to make the stairs welcoming or to deliniate their form.

The Service Area

The approach to most nonurban homes and to many city plots is complicated by a driveway and one or more foot paths to the house. In addition, there is usually a garage.

In relandscaping your grounds, consider eliminating excess walks. Walks tend to chop up the design of the front of your house, making a handsome entrance difficult. A walkway directly from the street to the front door is unnecessary, because most visitors today arrive by car and park in the drive. So, remove this type of entrance walk and cover the area with the same lawn or groundcover you are using elsewhere. Replace it with a path leading from the driveway, across the front of the house, to the door.

Usually the driveway is at the side of the house. A short drive should be straight on a small property, and either long enough or wide enough to park at least two cars. A circular drive on a small lot seldom makes sense, as it consumes a lot of space and breaks up whatever area you might otherwise landscape. If you need more off-the-street parking space, a solution might be to pave the entire area in front of your house. You can turn this into an attractive terrace-style area with handsome paving; spreading trees to screen it from the street, perhaps with a bit of select underplanting; and pretty plants (perhaps in containers) near the house.

If you have room for a circular drive—and parking in front of the door—you can altogether eliminate a pathway to the entry. Most of your plantings in this case should be placed on the opposite side of the driveway, where you can make them high enough to screen the house from the street.

In improving your driveway, here are some tips:

1. Protective curbs are a good idea to keep lawns or plants from being bumped. In fact, lawns with mowing strips help in mowing corners and hard-to-reach areas as well as giving clear definition to the lawn.

2. For safety, trees overhanging the lawn should have branches that do not start until the six- or seven-foot level.

3. Also for safety, the grade of your drive should be fairly level so cars will not roll when parked.

4. To avoid messy tires, avoid trees and shrubs that drop fruit on or near the driveway.

5. If you want to screen cars from view when parked in the driveway, use hedges of buckthorn or cuban laurel or other plants with dense foliage, or light but leafy trees like pin oak, white ash, or American linden.

The so-called service area was once beside the house, often near a kitchen entrance, and sometimes reached from a path different from that to the front door. Today, the service area is often through the garage or somewhere around the juncture of the garage and the house. Depending on where your service area is—and whether it is in one more unit—can present a myriad of problems in keeping your premises attractive. This area is boring to consider, but it pays to analyze your problems and try to incorporate solutions in your overall landscape theme.

Consider such services as heating oil intakes that bring service people onto your property, and arrange your driveway so that such matters can be attended to there. If you can create a unified area of this sort, you can also keep your garbage cans and miscellaneous equipment (barbecue units, gardening tools, some children's toys) there. Your compost heap could go here too. The entire area can be screened with plantings of whatever height are necessary. If space is limited, vines trained to lattices or poles can provide protection.

Frequently the garage is not large enough to hold all the gardening, sports, hobby, or other equipment you can't store in the house. You might consider including a gazebo or toolshed as part of your landscape. If you are installing raised decks, retaining walls, stairs, raised planters, benches, or making similar constructions, these too can be used to hide storage units for garden hoses, rakes, shovels, and other equipment.

wall fountain, or a paved area for sitting or other activities.

The side yard has disappeared in most plots where the house and garage now consume almost the full width of the plot. If you have narrow space here, you could plant a dense hedge of honeysuckle, or other fragrant or flowering plant, which grows profusely. A side yard large enough to be planted is usually best incorporated as part of the private area

Cream Hill School, from an early print.

If your garage is attached to the house, it will not need landscaping different from that you are providing for the house. A detached garage, though, can pose a problem. You can attach it to the house, if it is close enough, with arbors; or plant a couple of low-spreading trees combined with shrubs, which will serve to connect it to the house. Otherwise, like a garden shed, a detached garage can be treated as a separate entity and tied to your overall scheme with such devices as trellises, espalier trees, a

behind the house, providing a trellis or tall plantings to screen it from the front of the house. Trying to treat it as a separate area is time-consuming and can be costly as well.

The Private Area

The private area on most properties is behind the house, and it may include land on one or both sides as well. Only once in a while is it totally in front of the house.

This is the most difficult to design because it also functions as the family's outdoor recreational space, so here a number of family activities must be reconciled. For example, it may include a swimming pool; terrace (near the kitchen door, if you intend to eat there; near the living room, if you intend to entertain); an additional terrace for quiet sitting; food or flower garden; access to the terrace, garden, and recreation areas from the house and from one area to another.

You must decide how much screening you want—from the outside world, from sun and wind, and to segregate the areas of activity from each other. Is the screening to be year-round or seasonal? The food garden, for instance, might be screened with evergreens because it will be otherwise unattractive in winter, whereas screening for a quiet sitting area that won't be used in cold weather could be deciduous. How high will the vegetation be? To block out the outside world and create a truly private enclave you may want screening *above eye* level around the perimeter of your property; unless you have extensive grounds you will probably not want any other high vegetation except for shade trees. For screening a planned seating area, plants growing about chest-high are usually sufficient. Screening may be

SOLID SCREENING—TALL PLANTS

PARTIAL SCREENING—MEDIUM PLANTS

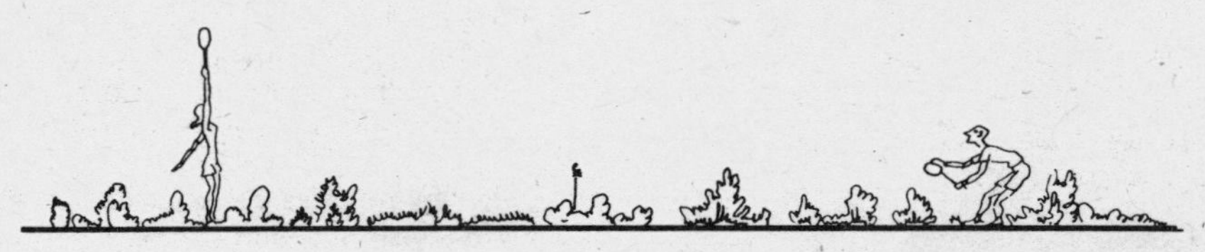

GROUND COVER DEMARCATION—LOW PLANTS

PLAN VIEW PATH, WALK OR STEPPING STONES

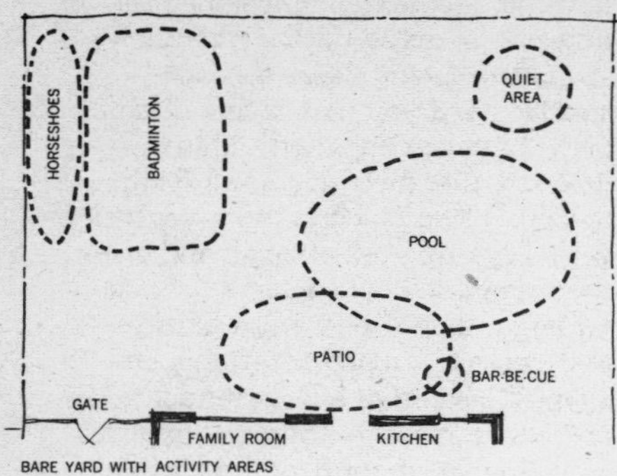

BARE YARD WITH ACTIVITY AREAS

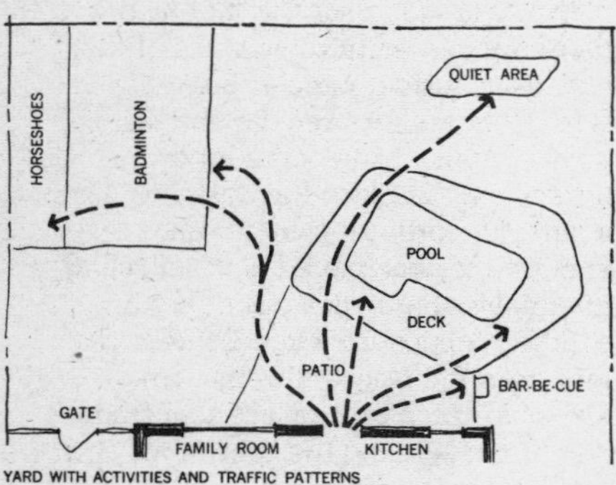

YARD WITH ACTIVITIES AND TRAFFIC PATTERNS

more psychological than actual. Plants about three feet high are tall enough to give you a feeling of enclosure around an outdoor dining area and yet will not obstruct views. Those at ankle or knee level are tall enough to deliniate traffic paths. The lower your plantings within your garden, the more spacious it will seem.

Finally, as this is your private retreat, you will be designing for beauty and serenity too. While an activity-centered private area can be busy, views and open space should be stressed for contemplative needs.

On tracing paper laid over your graph-paper plot, roughly block out the activity areas and circulation patterns, as well as any outbuildings and trees. This will give you an idea of whether you have a good proportion of open area to dense plantings, and the trees and building heights will help you set the scale for lower plantings. On an average lot, which runs about 150 feet long and perhaps only half that width, the house takes up about half your land, and you will have room for only one shade tree and two or three small shade trees. If space is a problem, vine-covered trellises and fences take up less lateral space. Small flowering trees with spreading branches can also be planted in groups, to create a shady grove, or in rows, to form a shady allee. Arbors also give shade and take up little space. And clipped hedges don't take up much space and can be grown under shade trees. If you have a space problem, don't fall into the trap of planting an even row of vegetation around the perimeter of your property. Stagger the plants so they make a thin screen at one point and are five or ten feet deep at other points, creating a far better effect in both the foreground and background. Create interesting silhouettes by thinking also of height variation and treetop form. Silhouettes are important in maintaining balance and can carry your eye to the climax area.

Toolsheds and other outbuildings are generally best situated on the perimeter of small lots, where they can do double-duty as screening devices.

In roughing out the major elements of your garden, calculate the amount of shade and sun that will be available after trees and other high, screening devices are in place. Food and most flower gardens need lots of sun, so you can't shunt them off to corners where they will be overly shaded. With trees, you also have to consider the root systems and what will grow under them. Conifers will restrict the type of underplantings you can use; many of the faster-growing trees such as poplars have fibrous root systems close to the surface and cannot be grown near lawn areas. Lawns need trees with deep tap roots such as oaks.

The transition between your house and garden will be solved if you include a terrace at the house. If you have glass doors, the transition can be made more effective by placing plants inside the doors to soften the path between the geometric interior and the more flowing lines of vegetation outside. If you do not plan a terrace, then some widely spaced paving blocks or perhaps a low wall, or neatly clipped hedge, outside the door will help create a transition. Or, an enclosed area with formal plantings might serve as an outdoor anteroom to the informality of the rest of the grounds.

On small lots, where most of the space is used for family activities, think in terms of pocket gardens. A tiny area framed with ivy-covered lattice, with only an archway left open for entry, can be a cosy retreat for one or two people and uses very little space. Tiny gardens made up of rocks, dwarf ferns, or alpines—any miniature plant—can be made into secluded enclaves behind low screening plants and need not take up more than four or five square feet of space. It is also possible to screen off the area of major activity, leaving a long thin strip of lawn surrounded by high vegetation to tie a vertical view from a vantage point planned for relaxing.

Or, the pool and other activity area could be put close to the house, so that long views are possible to peaceful greenery beyond them from a raised terrace.

If you have an exceptionally tiny garden area, as you might with a city apartment or a suburban garden apartment, a relatively formal design can work wonders. Let's say you have only a ten-foot square area. You could pave it attractively and enclose it with a pierced or solid fence. A couple of small spreading dogwoods, or several tall palms, could be grouped in one corner as background for a fountain or statue, and you could run planters or separate containers with shrubs along the walls at either side. At the corner opposite the trees you could place a table and chairs for dining, flanked by two large container plants and partially embraced by a pair of several sets of low planters with trim hedges, compact foliage, or flowering

plants. Perfect symmetry, neat line, and tidyness give such an area a more spacious and restful feel than if it is crowded with exuberant, junglelike plantings.

When you have a distant view to be incorporated into your landscape plans, frame the view with careful plantings that will enhance it. Usually you would want a clear expanse over

which your eye would pass to the view, so a lawn or low plantings are preferable. A flower garden in the foreground would be distracting, while trees and shrubs massed at either end of the view will enhance it and visually tie it to your grounds. Often, too, framing the terrace or other vantage points with low plantings is a good idea. This gives a cosier feeling when looking out into vast space. Boxwoods or dwarf myrtles are good for this type of enclosure.

Once you have your basic needs and major garden elements settled, you can begin on the design. Decide where your climax is going to be. As you must build up to a climax with vegetation, the climax is generally at the farthest point from where you enter the garden. On a rectangular plot, you would put it in the middle or at one corner of the end farthest from the house. On a square or oddly-shaped plot, it would do best in a distant corner. The climax, however, could also be placed in the center of the plot, as is often the case in homes in the Southwest that are built around patios.

It is easier to create a garden design if you think in terms of axial lines along which you create balance and visual interest. Highly formal gardens are framed along axes that are laid out on the ground and usually act as the walking paths. Your axial lines need not physically exist, but drawing them in on your tracing paper will help you create a unified and pleasing scheme.

Long Layouts: The most formal arrangement is a main axis that is laid out perpendicular to the house. It starts at the terrace or other entry point to the garden and extends to the far end of the property, the climax. In the great gardens of Europe, the main axis is a perfectly straight and flat lane along which you walk toward an elaborate climax that is usually raised—via several grade changes—to create a greater dramatic impression. At this terminal there might be a fancy templelike structure such as a colossal sculpture or other awesome feature surrounded by massive plantings. This frequently includes a pair of particularly stunning specimen trees that flank the main feature of the climax. Plantings just before the climax are low, stressing the importance of the climax. As you walk down this long axial walk toward its termination you pass planting beds in geometric shapes, panels of lawn, fountains and pools, statuary, and other accoutrements—usually identical on either side. Balance is therefore symmetrical and perfect.

The long, main axis is intersected at right angles by crosswalks, each of which also leads straight to a focal point. These focal points are smaller and less impressive than the climax terminating the main axis. Here, the statue might be smaller or the fountain less elaborate; the plantings lower and less important-looking. Nevertheless, the function of the terminal feature is to attract your attention, hold it, and then force your attention back to the garden.

While your scheme is unlikely to be this formal, the basic precepts are crucial to formulating a restful design. Your main axis need not be perpendicular to the house—it may go off at an angle. Your main axis need not be a path—it could be a line of sight across a lawn or across flower beds or a paved area. However, the main axis should terminate at something that is visually pleasing and that concentrates your attention on the sheltered world of the garden rather than moving restlessly onto traffic or other annoying distractions.

The climax might be a beautifully landscaped pool or garden shed seen across a stretch of lawn. Or, you might look across the pool to an arbor with flowering vines or to a distant landscape. The climax could be a single, beautiful tree or a playing fountain, or a grouping of your most beautiful plants. Plantings on either side of the axis need not be identical, but they should be balanced. A low, spreading, flowering tree on the right might be balanced by flower beds on the left. Or, if your plot is long and narrow, pleasing masses of shrubs and trees could be designed from the perimeters inward, providing complementary forms, heights, and color in smooth, curving configurations.

Your main axis need not run all the way to the far end of your property. You might want a shorter vista—say a path that runs from your terrace halfway down your property, where the view is terminated by hedges hiding a food garden. At this point the path might turn left or right, to take you to an activity area or a flower garden or perhaps in back to the food garden. At the point where the straightforward vista ends and the path makes the turn, it is nice to place a birdbath, small statue, a bench flanked with interesting plants, or container plant to satisfy the eye. You might even create a little circular garden at this point to serve as a modest focus.

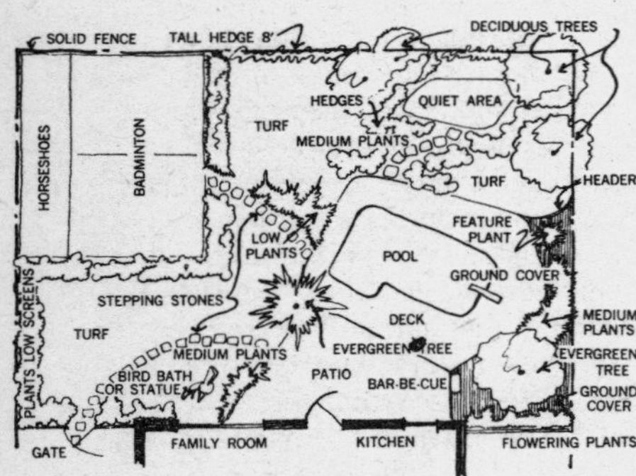

SKETCH OF BACK YARD LANDSCAPING

Any paths you might have off the main axial path need not cross it completely as in truly formal layouts and need not be identical on either side—but again they should be balanced and have something to stop your vision as you walk or sight along them. Something simple like a specimen plant will do.

If your lot is wide, you may prefer several axial lines radiating outward from your terrace—in the form of, say, one or two paths and/or sighting lines—rather than a single main axis. This is a little harder to achieve, as it can become busy and complex, especially in smaller spaces, but with restraint it does offer another attractive possibility. Though the various axes need terminating, your most elaborate plantings should be on the terrace, which is the climax from elsewhere in the garden.

The more formal the garden plan, the more prominent the axial lines and the more obvious the terminations. In an informal scheme, the axials are almost imperceptible—you *feel* them rather than see them—and the terminations are subtle.

Central Layouts: When your lot dimensions are square or oddly sized, or when you are designing an interior courtyard, a scheme in which the climax is at the center is usually the most appropriate. Here the climax might be a fountain, an elegantly composed grouping of especially interesting plants, a garden house, a rock garden, or even a piece of sculpture. Since this type of climax will be viewed from all sides, it requires more careful composition than a focal point at the end of an axis.

Any paths that radiate from this center should be terminated with a specimen plant, a colorful ceramic, or another simple device, but your most elaborate design should be at the center. Elevating the central display a foot or so above ground level is effective. You could also use a recessed pool, a garden of dwarf ferns or other small species, or a high-spouting fountain set below ground level. In this case, you will need to terminate any views past the central motif more severely than otherwise—severely enough to halt vision but not so powerfully to detract from the central motif. You could also draw attention to the flatness of the central motif by planting high, upright plants in the beds surrounding the center one.

Placing the macadam foundation.

Surfacing a macadam road.

Central layouts lend themselves to pretty designs at ground level. You can make the central motif round, and then round off the corners of the surrounding beds so that they form arcs repeating the lines of the central motif. Or, you can make the central motif square, indenting its corners or the corners of the surrounding beds.

With most central layouts on small properties, you would probably have, at most, four paths radiating from a central motif. In extensive gardens, eight or ten planting beds radiating outward are possible. Whatever the number, they look best if they have well-defined edges at the point of departure from the center. In formal gardens, low, clipped hedges are often used to define the bed edges, and often turf or low ground cover is planted within to stress line over vegetation. Only as the beds extend outward are higher plantings used. As the beds extend away from the central motif, they can become more informal, with highly varied plantings and less line definition.

Although the central motif is usually a highly elaborate area, it is also possible to construct a garden design in which the center is a lawn or is planted in ground cover, soft and low ferns, or a mound of tiny flowers. Paths might circle rather than cross the center, but they eye will always be drawn across the expanse to views on the other side.

Terraces and Decks

Terraces, patios, and decks should be properly installed (with a good foundation and subsurface) to insure a long life. Within a few years, temperature change, frost, and water can destroy poorly planned areas. Use expansion joints where needed. Provide a drain or a slope away from the house. Consider the sun and prevailing wind, so that you can locate the terrace where conditions are best. (Prevailing wind is especially important if you intend to construct a permanent barbecue.) In placing a terrace, consider seasonal conditions—one placed where it will be sheltered from spring wind may prove too hot in summer. If your terrace doesn't have a natural view, create one for it with your landscape.

Terraces and decks, particularly in warmer climates, can more than double your living area. If you entertain a good deal, a terrace flush with the lawn area will enable guests to overflow into the garden. On sloped sites, however, a raised deck is often better. Overhanging decks can be spectacular if you have a fine distant view, but even enclosed within a wooded area they give a satisfying feeling of living high in the trees. Incidentally, terraces that angle and give more than one view invariably look far larger than similar-sized terraces and decks in square or rectangular shapes. Instead of a wide terrace, consider a narrower one that angles. Though placement near the kitchen is handy for food service, not all of the terrace need hug the walls of the house—consider circular areas, forms that arc, or irregular shapes. If you don't intend to serve food, the terrace can be placed almost anywhere. In northern climates an enclosed terrace paved with reflecting material is sometimes put facing a southern exposure, even if this is distant from the house; this placement serves to catch and reflect heat from the sun, extending the season for outdoor enjoyment.

Flooring for a terrace can be any waterproof or semi-waterproof material—flagstone, brick, tile, concrete, even grass, or a combination of two of these—and raised decks can be of wood. Flagstone, concrete block, or brick can be set in sand with spaces between the units or can be set with mortar. With brick and concrete block you can create a variety of patterns—herringbone, basketweave, concentric squares, and flowing curves—and colors. You can pour concrete blocks yourself in whatever shapes you desire; and you can add aggregates for interesting texture and color. Wood can be used either in boards or in blocks. In hot and arid climates, dark and nonreflective surfaces will be cooler.

Paving need not be solid or of only one material. Attractive flooring can be designed with large areas of brick or tile separated into patterns by railroad ties or other wood. Turf can be interspersed with concrete or flagstones. Or, wood can be used to frame gravel patterns.

Trees can be incorporated on terraces or decks level with the ground, provided the paving is one laid without mortar. Raised decks or terraces with mortar require container plants. Low walls around trees and edges of large planters can be designed with broad tops set at seating height. Then they can be used as benches and can even be furnished with waterproof cushions. At this height plants are also easier to tend.

Since trees must usually grow to one side of a terrace, those with spreading branches that extend onto the terrace are best. Finge trees and dogwoods arch gracefully. Japanese maple, mosquitoes, and the golden

rain tree give heavier shade and branch low to the ground, with branches that grow to the sides. If your terrace is not attached to the house, enclosing it with climbing vines and high shrubs makes it cosier, provided you are not blocking the sun or breeze. Growing fragrant species of plants near the terrace is also a nice touch. In very hot climates, overhead lattice made with lathe, arbors, or other devices may be necessary; and in areas with high rainfall, lathe that can be covered with plastic panels or plastic film may be more convenient.

Walls and Fences

Garden walls fail more often than any other garden feature because they are so frequently installed improperly. Before installing a wall, check your property line and local building codes.

Retaining walls must have an especially solid foundation, but even freestanding walls require an adequate foundation below the frost line as well as good footing. If soil is placed against one side of a wall, then "weep holes" or tile drains are necessary. Otherwise, after a heavy rain or spring thaw, water pressure can cause the wall to explode. Concrete block and other thin materials with earth piled behind them are soon overturned or thrown out of plumb even by light water pressure and frost action.

Retaining walls need either steel reinforcing rods or very thick bases (almost half the thickness of the height) below the frost line. On a steep slope, one wall may be insufficient, and you may need a series. Such walls also require a dip in the grade away from the wall. It is wise to get professional advice.

If stone is easily obtainable, quarried limestone is a good choice for formal effects, less polished native stones for informal gardens. Native fieldstone can be laid without mortar. Brick walls are more versatile, because bricks are available in a number of colors and can be laid in patterns—with some bricks projecting or with openings for wrought-iron grilles or insets of tile or other decorative material. More versatile yet is concrete. It can be tinted with vibrant or pastel colors; textured with additives such as grits or pebbles or tooled with a rake or trowel; laid in blocks to alternate with other materials. Walls can also be built of cast concrete tiles—either solid or with pierced designs allowing for the same types of insets and openings possible with brick. In most areas, a concrete wall faced with a brick or stone veneer is less expensive than a wall of solid brick or stone. Veneer walls, however, must be carefully coped; otherwise, water falling (and especially freezing) between the veneer and the concrete can force the veneer off its backing.

Wooden walls made from cedar, juniper, osage, orange, catalpa, black locust, and redwood contain natural preservatives. Other woods must be treated with commercial preservatives.

Other fencing materials include plastic, glass, wire, and fiberglass. A fence of inexpensive materials can screen a garden until permanent plantings grow high enough to provide screening. If you use unattractive fencing, cover it with fast-growing vines, sheared privet or bay laurel, or espalier trees. If your fence or trellis material will need repair or painting, cover it with an annual, such as morning glory, that will die in winter.

Fences are an option when space is limited. To provide a screen six feet high with plantings would require a ground width of at least four to six feet, while a fence consumes minimal space.

Walks and Paving

Walks should be carefully laid out when you first outline your plan, not only to accommodate ordinary family traffic but also with plant maintenance and enjoyment in mind. It's a shame to plan a flower garden and then forget to include paths that allow you in among the flowers. By opening vistas, paths make small gardens seem larger.

Don't design paths that lead nowhere. Put at least a bench, a garden ornament, or a rare or especially beautiful plant at the end of the walk. If possible, incorporate color or fragrance or other surprises—even a few feet of footbridge over a tiny pond—along the route. Tight curves and sharp angles are uncomfortable, so slow curves and diagonals are more desirable.

The nature of the path should reflect its purpose. One leading to a signal feature, such as a swimming pool, can be boldly outlined with colorful flowers, rigidly defined, and straight and direct. A path leading to a secluded sanctuary should have softer lines and less definition.

No path, though, is pleasant unless it is built on a well-drained foundation of sand or concrete so that neither soft mud nor upheaving frost destroys your creation. Don't design your walk through a bottom that will collect water. Material should stand up under your plot's temperature, moisture, and freezing stresses. In very hot climates, avoid a glaring surface.

A rather durable material is best for the surface of your path. Ground covers do not tolerate foot traffic; turf will disintegrate under heavy traffic.

Bricks can be used on end, on the edge, or on the side, or in combinations of these, to create parallel, perpendicular, or angled walk designs. Be sure to leave room around each unit, to allow for expansion. Mortar can be used to set the surface permanently and to eliminate water from beneath the walk.

Flagstones should be large enough—a foot or more wide—not to create a hazard. These and other types of steppingstones are easy to install and easy to remove if you want to change the direction of a path later. You can make your own steppingstones by digging round, oval, rectangular, or irregularly shaped holes in the ground and pouring in concrete. Dig the holes four inches deep and a foot or more across. Pour or shovel in the concrete to soil level and smooth it over with a trowel. You can mix color and texture additives to the concrete before pouring.

In wooded areas, soft pine needles or pine bark make for a comfortable walking surface. You can also buy tanbark as a covering. Wood decking is another possibility, and like soft coverings it will not inhibit root systems of surrounding vegetation. Crushed stone or gravel may also be used, though in northerly climates these can present a problem with snow removal. If you use a loose aggregate, select a rounded rock of one-fourth- to three-fourth-inch screen size. Pea gravel sticks to shoes and makes footing difficult. Finally, in arid areas, especially, raked ground can be sufficient.

Where you are incorporating steps, stones should be large and flat. If you are using fieldstone, choose a type that has a flat surface at least a foot long. With either stone or brick, steps need not be straight—you can use circular forms too. If you are using logs, they should be durable wood and stripped of bark. Unless the wood contains a natural preservative, you will have to apply a commercial one. Cut the logs a foot or so wider than the steps and bury the ends in the soil on either side to prevent erosion.

Make the risers a comfortable height—say, six to eight inches. The tread should be wide enough for you to place your foot comfortably on it—a foot at the minimum but longer if possible. Give the tread some slope for drainage—and the longer the tread the more important the slope.

Because it is disconcerting to walkers to encounter steps of varying heights and widths, try to make steps uniform. On steep slopes, where this is impossible, make three or four steps alike, and then incorporate an extra-wide tread as a landing. Then continue with three or four more steps, then another landing, and so forth. On steep slopes, enclosure is comforting. This may take the form of railings or solid enclosures; or you can make psychological enclosures with plantings, which create a feeling of safety.

Tips on Paths

1. A three-foot path is the minimum width, but a walk four feet wide is necessary if you want two people to be able to walk side-by-side—five feet is even more comfortable and more proportionately pleasing.

2. On spacious grounds, a walk eight or ten feet, or even wider, can be a handsome feature. In this case it can be overhung with trees on either side, or shaded on one side and open to low flower beds or other plantings on the other.

3. Walks can be used to enhance a particular feature of the garden. A beautiful old tree or a pond can assume new importance with an encircling path that gives perspective from all sides.

4. If you are incorporating steps in a walk, start at the bottom and build up.

Gazebos and Toolsheds

In Elizabethan times, gardens became an important part of outdoor living. Although earlier the "privy garden" had offered screened solitude among fragrant and colorful flowers, the lifestyle of the Elizabethan period created new ways to live out-of-doors. The leisurely paths in gardens, often a mile or more long, were screened with overhead vined arches or vaults that rose twelve feet or more above the paths. Some plants were trained onto metal supports for this purpose and others were simply pruned and trained to intertwine. Among the plants used were willows, limes, hornbeam, privet, maples, sycamores, and elms. At the same time, outdoor eating became a fad, so "banqueting houses" were constructed. Some of these were made of cut boughs of plants such as ivy and evergreen, erected temporarily for a revel. One banquet hall was forty feet long; another, constructed at Whitehall in 1581, was 332 feet in circumference. Poorer folk had less elaborate and more permanent bowers under which to eat.

In the seventeenth century, a roofed summer house with a dining table and benches was common. Called gazebos, probably because they were slightly elevated to provide a view—or gaze—these became standardized with little peaked roofs and open sides. In informal gardens they were made of rustic logs, while in more formal gardens they were often more refined and made of painted wood. Though they proliferated in Victorian times, they gradually went out of style.

Today, however, gazebos are back in style. They come in modern versions with flat roofs, even in the form of geodesic domes, to serve as children's playhouses, cocktail and barbecue centers, bathhouses, and hot tub enclosures. The base of a raised gazebo can serve as a storage area for garden tools and other equipment, and it can have its own terrace. Storage units of seat-level height can be built inside the gazebo. Covered with glass or plastic panels in winter a gazebo can be converted into a greenhouse.

Many of the less expensive prefabricated tool sheds are ugly, but these can be covered and screened with vines or espaliers or serve as background for a specimen plant. A few nicely designed tool sheds, that need not be hidden, are also available. Even prefabricated Japanese

tea houses, made of plywood and plastic panels, and moderately priced, can serve as tool sheds, bathhouses, and dining pavillions in certain climates.

If you live in a dry region, you can do as the Elizabethans did: Construct your bathhouse, tool shed, or dining alcove entirely of vegetation. Arbors and breezeways are ideal in humid climates. You can easily construct a slated structure of two-by-fours and two-by-sixes of the proper scale for your garden. Evenly-spaced slats for the roof will keep out the sun except when it is almost directly overhead; and if you intend to use the structure at midday, vines can be trained above to provide screening. If you add slatted panels to form off-and-on wall areas, these will definitely require sun shading by means of vines or other plants. Variations include using bamboo, adjustable wood louvers, or, for rainy areas, removable fiberglass panels for the roof.

Ornaments

In choosing ornaments for the garden, scale is a major consideration. Small units often need a plain but complementary base to elevate them high enough to be appreciated. Give thought to the size of ornament in proportion to the entire garden before investing in sculpture, weathervanes, or other decorative pieces.

A second factor is the background. Usually ornaments, such as sculpture, look better against a building, wall, or fence, or carefully set off against foliage, than they do when placed against a busy background. Yet on a busy area such as a terrace, a row of identical or almost identical ornaments—such as urns or container plants—can lend a sense of order and serenity.

The third factor in choosing ornaments is that they should look as though they fit. A huge boulder placed on a flat lawn will look like it dropped out of the sky. Corners, ends of pathways, wall parapets, pool aprons, and awkward angles in your ground plan or in its three-dimensional form are all areas that frequently benefit from garden ornaments. Ornaments are also handy for filling shaded spots where plants are hard to cultivate; for adding accent to a boring area, such as a line of hedge; for adding color when seasonal flowers have faded.

Decorative pieces need not be ornate or expensive. Plants in clay containers often do nicely. If you are going to use something more intricate, such as sculpture, don't go overboard and try to crowd in too many or too varied pieces. If you are going to incorporate several dissimilar pieces, choose one for prominence and make the others subsidiary.

To avoid overdoing things in a small garden, your decorative pieces might be chosen so that they perform dual function—a birdbath encourages birds; windchimes add sound; a pool or fountain gives you water play.

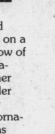

Outdoor Lighting

Creative use of outdoor lighting can greatly enhance the beauty of your garden or landscape. There are three major techniques to outdoor lighting—floodlighting, spotlighting, and underlighting—each with its specific range of purposes.

Floodlighting is used mainly to light large areas such as broad lawns, or dark paths and driveways, often for reason of security. It is perhaps the least creative but most practical kind of lighting. A general rule for better, more effective floodlighting is to use six or eight smaller lamps as opposed to two or three large ones. Large bright lights are harsh, while smaller lamps give a softer, more inviting appearance.

Spotlighting, if used cleverly, can be practical and aesthetically pleasing. It consists of a more subtle illumination, usually from above, of specific garden features such as low-path hedges, statues, particular shrubs, address and family nameplates, and pool borders. Spotlights can also be mounted under eaves to achieve interesting angular, shadowed effects. Probably the central concern is to make sure the source of light is not visible. That is, the light one sees should be indirect, not the light element itself. If you cannot hide the fixture, buy a fixture that attractively hides the light element. Otherwise, couch spotlighting fixtures amid bushes or behind low walls. Spotlights are also an effective means of bug control. Situate them along the borders of the patio to attract insects away from patio activity.

Underlighting is the most artful kind of outdoor lighting, usually decorative in purpose, but also effective as a security measure. It consists of soft, indirect illumination from below, offering the same sort of beneficial features as does spotlighting. The main difference, besides underlighting being from below and spotlighting from above, is that spotlighting has a single focused light source, while underlighting has a broader, softer source, which consists of many small incandescent lights or a few long fluorescent tubes. Underlighting is particularly effective as a means of emphasizing structure, form, or foliage. Underlighting a specimen tree or shrub can create beautiful shadowplay among the limbs and foliage. Underlighting is better with fluorescent tubes than incandescent bulbs.

13
Special Gardens

The Privy Garden

In England during the Middle Ages, pleasure gardens were unknown. Only food crops, herbs, and medicinal plants were grown. Flowers—such as lilies, violets, peonies, and poppies—were possible only because they had medicinal qualities or because they could be used to decorate churches or crown priests.

By the fourteenth and fifteenth centuries, gardens incorporated a "privy playing place"—that is, an enclosure screened by hedges or trees where flowers were planted for color and fragrance. Garlands were no longer exclusively for religous purposes; poets described women bedecking themselves or their lovers with wreaths of flowers. Wildflowers (such as iris, foxglove, columbines and peonies) began to be cultivated, and finally the first flower garden emerged—the "railed bed"—enclosed by low fences made of trellises.

By the sixteenth century, another new type of flower bed was introduced—the "knotted bed" or "knot." These were elaborate designs held in rigid geometric shapes by borders or bricks or tiles. Gardeners who could create knots in gardens were much in demand, and the designs were so valued that when flowers were unavailable the beds were filled in with colored soil. (Flowers were always laid out in the open because people feared they would otherwise rob trees of nourishment.) A century later flowers had become so important that they took up half the garden.

Some concept of design also emerged, and gardeners, who had previously planted low flower beds geared to knotted geometric designs, were now urged to consider height. The center of flower beds were planted with taller species such as peonies, while smaller lilies and other varieties were planted at the edges. Concern over seasonal plants, and the need for year-round attractiveness, also developed. "Bulb fever" reached its height as gardeners discovered tulips and other imports that provided color long before native annuals and perennials. Hothouses and conservatories proliferated to provide early bloom and cultivation of tropical species. Knots (now called parterres) became so elaborate that rebellion set in, and soon the old geometric shapes were deplored.

Advocates of the new style complained that the traditional, tiny, walled gardens were too crimped, clipped, and cramped. "Is there anything more shocking than a stiff, regular garden?", asked one of the new school of gardeners. Now fast-growing fragrant flowers like honeysuckle and jasmine were encouraged to overflow in exuberant heaps around cheerful plantings of pinks and candytuft. Borders and scrollwork were replaced with clumps and sweeping, irregular beds. In describing Paradise, Milton wrote that the flowers ". . . poured forth profuse on hill, and dale, and plain . . ." —but critics called the new look "neglected."

In time this attempt at "natural wildness" was seen as equally inappropriate, and in our own time gardeners take the more sensible course of choosing from among the historic styles those best suited to their own conditions. Though more urban and suburban crowding has meant a return to the concept of a "privy" garden, its design can be as formal or as informal as individual taste dictates.

KNOT FROM THE GARDENER'S LABYRINTH.

Arid-Area Gardens

In the arid and semiarid regions of the Great Plains west of the 100th meridian, the intermountain region between the Rockies and the west coastal ranges, and the desert Southwest, growing ornamentals successfully depends on intelligent selection of adaptable species. Low rainfall is a major problem, often intensified by low humidity, temperature over 100°F, winds as high as 100 mph, or medium to high altitude.

The higher the altitude, the lower the atmospheric pressure. Low atmospheric pressure coupled with strong winds and low humidity allows moisture to evaporate quickly, thus contributing to drought conditions. Where strong winds and low humidity prevail, plants dessicate (dry out) unless you choose species with special mechanisms such as sunken breathing pores, an ability to store water, or small bark pores to prevent evaporation of moisture. You can also sometimes erect windbreaks to modify the force of the wind.

Another factor causing problems in arid areas is alkaline soil. Soils in these areas are classified as saline alkali, saline nonalkali, and nonsaline alkali. All have a high pH, accentuated where irrigation water accumulates or where good drainage is lacking. Installing drainage canals, or breaking up the subsoil to insure drainage and to leach out the alkali with water during the off-season, may help; but more important is selecting plants tolerant of highly saline or alkaline soils. Many of these are plants native to the area.

In regions of low annual rainfall, wind erosion of soil is more severe than water erosion. Water erosion sometimes occurs, however, during the spring runoff of melted snow and during flash floods after thunderstorms. Though these problems are more serious in cultivated fields than in areas around homes where ornamentals are grown, thick plant cover is a solution.

Prepare soil for ornamental planting by deep spading or plowing. Incorporate organic materials (well-rotted barnyard fertilizer, leafmold, compost, peat moss, or vermiculite) to improve texture and water-holding capacity. If you have especially thin soil, consider buying fertile topsoil. Fertilizer needs vary from area to area, but iron deficiency in soil is a common problem. Though plenty of iron compounds exist in Western soils, these are often unavailable to plants—you can tell when the leaves yellow but the veins remain green. Use chelated iron compounds and iron salts to eliminate the problem.

Transplant all dormant woody and herbaceous ornamentals during the first month or six weeks after the soil thaws in the late winter or early spring. Iris, peonies, and oriental poppies are the few perennials planted in early fall. Container-grown and balled-and-burlapped ornamentals may be planted throughout the summer months, but the earlier the better. They should be established before frost and cold weather return in the fall.

Until newly-set woody plants become established, usually two to five years, put up wind barriers in dry, windy winters; thoroughly water at monthly intervals; and eliminate weeds. Mulching is not a common practice except for winter protection of perennials that are not hardy. In areas of heavy wind or rain, a few ornamentals require staking or trellises. These include dahlias, climbing or trailing plants, and tall perennials such as peonies.

The zones referred to on the accompanying charts are those shown in the map in "Living with Plants."

Common name	Annual rainfall: Less than 10″	Annual rainfall: 10″–20″	Zones: III	Zones: IV	Zones: V	Zones: VI	Zones: VII	Salt or alkaline soils: pH–8.0+	Altitude requirement: ft.+	Shade
Adaptability to:										
Trees (Evergreen)										
Arborvitae, Eastern		x			x	x	x			x
Arborvitae, Oriental		x		x	x	x				x
Cypress, Arizona		x				x	x	x		x
Fir, White		x		x	x				3,000	x
Juniper, Alligator		x				x	x			
Juniper, Oneseed	x	x		x	x	x	x	x		
Juniper, Redberry		x				x	x			
Juniper, Redcedar (many cultivars)		x	x	x	x	x	x			x
Juniper, Rocky Mountain (many cultivars)	x	x	x	x	x	x	x			x
Larch, Siberian		x	x							
Pine, Aleppo		x				x	x			
Pine, Austrian		x		x	x	x	x			
Pine, Bristlecone		x		x	x			x	4,000	
Pine, Colorado Pinyon		x		x	x	x	x	x		
Pine, Limber		x		x						
Pine, Ponderosa		x	x	x	x	x	x	x		x
Pine, Scotch		x	x	x	x	x	x			
Pine, Swiss Mountain (mugo)		x		x	x	x	x			
Spruce, Black Hills		x		x	x					x
Spruce, Colorado		x	x	x	x	x			3,000	x
Spruce, Engelmann		x	x	x	x				3,000	x
Shrubs (Evergreen)										
Juniper, Common		x		x	x	x	x			x
Juniper, Creeping		x		x	x	x	x			x
Juniper, Meyer Singleseed		x		x	x					
Juniper, Pfitzer Chinese		x	x	x	x	x	x			
Juniper, Savin 'Tamarix'		x	x	x	x	x	x			
Pine, Mugho Swiss Mountain		x		x	x	x				x
Trees (Broadleaf)										
Albizzia, Silktree (Mimosa)		x				x	x			
Ash, Green		x	x	x	x					
Ash, European Mountain		x		x	x					
Birch, Cutleaf Weeping		x		x	x				4,000	
Buckeye		x		x	x	x	x			
Cottonwood		x+	x	x	x	x	x			
Crabapple, Flowering		x	x	x	x	x	x			
Elm, Lacebark Chinese		x				x	x			
Elm, Siberian		x	x	x	x	x	x	x		
Hackberry, Common		x	x	x	x	x	x			
Honeylocust (thornless)		x		x	x	x	x			
Jujube, Common		x			x	x	x			
Linden, American		x		x	x	x				
Linden, Littleleaf		x		x	x	x				
Locust, Black		x			x	x	x			
Maple, Amur		x	x	x	x	x	x			
Maple, Manchurian		x		x	x	x				
Maple, Norway		x		x	x	x	x			
Maple, Silver		x	x	x	x	x	x			
Maple, Sugar		x		x	x	x	x			
Maple, Tatarian		x		x	x	x				
Mulberry, Russian		x			x	x	x			
Oak, Bur		x	x	x	x	x	x			
Oak, Live (sometimes evergreen)		x				x	x			
Oak, Northern Red		x			x	x	x			
Oak, Pin		x			x	x	x			
Pecan		x				x	x			
Redbud, Eastern		x				x	x			
Russian-Olive		x	x	x	x	x	x	x		
Sweetgum, American		x				x	x			
Sycamore		x				x	x			
Walnut, Black		x			x	x	x			
Shrubs (Broadleaf)										
Adina (*Adina rubella*)		x				x	x			
Almond, Flowering		x			x	x	x			
Almond, Prairie (*Prunus triloba* x *P. pedunculata*)		x	x	x	x					
Almond, Russian		x	x	x	x	x				
Amorpha, Indigobush		x		x	x	x	x			
Apacheplume	x	x		x	x	x	x	x		
Beautybush		x			x	x	x			
Bitterbrush, Antelope	x	x		x	x	x	x	x	4,000	
Bluebeard (*Caryopteris* sp.)		x		x	x	x	x			
Buckthorn, Common		x	x	x	x	x				
Buckthorn, Dahurian		x	x	x	x	x				
Buckthorn, Rock		x	x	x	x	x				
Buffaloberry		x	x	x						
Butterflybush		x			x	x	x			
Ceanothus, Inland	x	x			x	x	x			
Chaste-tree		x			x	x				
Cherry, Manchu		x	x	x	x	x	x			
Chokecherry, Western 'Schubert'		x	x	x	x	x			4,000	
Cinquefoil, Bush		x		x	x			x		
Cliffrose, Stansbury		x		x	x	x			4,000	
Coralberry		x		x	x	x	x			
Cotoneaster, European		x		x	x	x				
Cotoneaster, Hedge		x	x	x	x					
Cotoneaster, Multiflora		x			x	x	x			
Cotoneaster, Peking		x	x	x	x	x	x			
Cotoneaster, Sungari Redbead		x		x	x	x		x		
Crapemyrtle		x				x	x			
Desertwillow	x	x				x	x	x		
Dogwood, Colorado Redosier		x		x	x					
Dogwood, Siberian		x		x	x					
Elderberry, Blueberry		x		x	x	x	x			
Elderberry, European Red 'Redman'		x		x	x	x	x			
Euonymus, European		x		x	x	x	x			x
Euonymus, Winterberry		x		x	x	x	x			x
Firethorn, Laland		x			x	x	x			
Fontanesia, Fortune	x	x				x	x	x		
Forestiera, New Mexican	x	x		x	x	x	x	x		
Forsythia, Border		x			x	x	x			
Forsythia, Fortune Weeping		x			x	x	x			

Common name	Annual rainfall: Less than 10"	Annual rainfall: 10"–20"	Zones: III	Zones: IV	Zones: V	Zones: VI	Zones: VII	Salt or alkaline soils: pH–8.0+	Altitude requirement: ft.+	Shade
Adaptability to:										
Goldraintree		x				x	x			
Greasewood	x	x		x	x	x	x	x		
Hawthorn, Cockspur		x	x	x						
Hawthorn, Downy		x		x	x	x				
Hawthorn, English		x			x	x				
Hawthorn, Russian		x		x	x	x				
Honeysuckle, Amur		x			x	x	x			
Honeysuckle, 'Arnold Red', 'Cardinal', 'Carlton', 'Valentia'		x	x	x	x	x				
Honeysuckle, Winter		x			x	x	x			
Honeysuckle, Zabel Blueleaf		x		x	x	x	x			
Leadplant	x	x		x	x	x	x	x		
Lilac, Early		x	x	x	x					
Lilac, French Hybrids		x		x	x	x	x			
Lilac, Hungarian		x		x	x	x				
Lilac, Japanese Tree		x	x	x	x	x	x			
Lilac, Late		x		x	x					
Lilac, Persian		x	x	x	x	x	x			
Mockorange, Lewis		x		x	x					
Mockorange, Sweet		x			x	x	x			
Mockorange, Virginalis		x			x	x	x			
Mountainmahogany, Douglas	x	x		x	x				4,000	
Nandina		x				x	x			x
Peach, Flowering		x			x	x	x			
Peashrub, Globe Russian		x	x	x	x					
Peashrub, Pygmy		x	x	x	x					
Peashrub, Siberian		x	x	x	x					
Perovskia, Russiansage		x		x	x	x				
Plum, Cistena		x	x	x	x					
Plum, Flowering		x	x	x	x					
Plum, Newport		x		x	x	x				
Privet, European		x		x	x	x	x			x
Quince, Flowering		x			x	x	x			
Quince, Japanese Flowering		x			x	x	x			
Rabbitbrush	x	x	x	x	x	x		x		
Rose, Austrian Copper		x	x	x	x					
Rose, 'Harison's Yellow'		x	x	x	x					
Rose, Hybrid Tea		x		x	x	x	x			
Rosewood, Arizona	x	x				x	x			x
Sagebrush	x	x		x	x	x	x	x		
Saltbush	x	x		x	x	x	x	x		
Serviceberry, Allegany		x		x	x					
Serviceberry, Saskatoon		x	x	x	x					
Serviceberry, Shadblow		x	x	x	x	x				
Shrubalthea		x			x	x	x			
Sibirea, Smooth		x		x	x					
Smoketree, Common		x				x	x			
Snowberry	x	x	x	x	x	x				
Spirea, Mongolian		x		x	x	x	x			
Spirea, Nippon		x		x	x	x	x			
Spirea, Sargent		x	x	x	x	x				
Spirea, Threelobe		x	x	x	x	x	x			
Spirea, Vanhoutte		x	x	x	x	x	x			
Sumac, Skunkbush		x	x	x	x	x	x			
Sumac, Staghorn		x		x	x	x	x			
Tamarix, Amur		x	x	x	x	x	x	x		
Tamarix, Kashgar		x			x	x	x	x		
Viburnum, Common Snowball		x		x	x	x				
Viburnum, European Cranberrybush		x		x	x	x				
Viburnum, Koreanspice		x		x	x					
Viburnum, Manchurian		x	x	x	x					
Viburnum, Nannyberry		x	x	x						
Viburnum, Wayfaring Tree		x	x	x	x					
Plants for the Desert Southwest										
Agave	x	x					x	x		
Boojam Tree	x	x					x	x		
Brittlebush	x	x					x	x		
Broom Baccharis	x	x					x	x		
Cacti (many types)	x	x				x	x	x		
Catclaw	x	x					x	x		
Creosotebush	x	x					x	x		
Hackberry, Spiny	x	x				x	x	x		
Jojoba	x	x					x	x		
Mesquite	x	x				x	x	x		
Ocotillo	x	x					x	x		
Paloverde	x	x					x	x		
Sotol	x	x					x	x		
Tesota	x	x					x	x		
Yucca (many types)	x	x				x	x	x		
Vines										
Clematis, Drummond		x				x	x			
Clematis, Jackman		x		x	x					
Grape (use the native species in each zone)		x	x	x	x	x	x			x
Honeysuckle, Dropmore Scarlet Trumpet		x	x	x	x					
Honeysuckle, Everblooming		x				x	x			
Ivy, Engelmann		x		x	x	x				x
Monkshoodvine		x				x	x			
Moonseed, Asiatic		x	x	x	x					x
Rose, Climbing		x	x	x	x	x				
Silkvine (Grecian and Chinese)		x				x	x			
Silverlacevine		x		x	x	x				
Trumpetcreeper, Common 'Mme. Galen'		x			x	x	x			
Virginia Creeper		x	x	x	x	x	x			x

Ornamental Plants for Problem Areas of the West—Continued

Common name	Annual rainfall (Adaptability to:)		Zones					Salt or alkaline soils	Altitude requirement	Shade
	Less than 10"	10"–20"	III	IV	V	VI	VII	pH–8.0+	ft.+	
Perennial Flowers										
Althea, Perennial		x	x	x	x	x				
Aster, Perennial		x		x	x					
Babysbreath 'Pink Star'		x	x	x	x	x				
Bellflower, Top		x		x	x	x				
Bugloss, Italian		x	x	x	x					x
Campion, Maltesecross		x		x	x	x				x
Centaurea, Globe		x		x	x	x				
Centaurea, Persian		x		x	x	x				
Chrysanthemum (hardy garden forms)		x	x	x	x	x	x			
Cinquefoil, Northwest		x		x	x	x				x
Cinquefoil, Small Nepal		x		x	x					x
Cinquefoil, Sulfur		x		x	x	x				x
Clematis, Caripensis		x		x	x	x				
Clematis, Douglas		x		x	x					
Clematis, Solitary		x		x	x					
Columbine, Colorado		x		x	x	x	x			
Coneflower, Cutleaf		x		x	x					
Coreopsis, Bigflower		x		x	x					
Daylily (many cultivars). Some daylilies are subject to chlorosis		x	x	x	x	x	x			
Delphinium		x	x	x	x	x				
Dianthus (Carnation, Pinks, Sweet-william)		x		x	x	x				
Dittany, Gasplant		x		x	x					
Euphorbia, Cushion		x		x	x	x				
Euphorbia, Cypress		x		x	x	x				
Euphorbia, Myrtle		x		x	x	x				x
Flax, Perennial		x		x	x					x
Four-o'clock, Colorado		x		x	x	x				x
Gaillardia, Perennial		x		x	x	x				
Geranium, Meadow		x		x	x				4,000	
Globethistle, Small		x		x	x					
Goutweed, Bishops		x		x	x					x
Hen-and-chickens		x		x	x					
Iris (many cultivars)		x	x	x	x	x	x			
Larkspur, Slender Siberian		x		x	x					
Lily, Henry		x	x	x	x	x				
Lily, Madonna		x		x	x					
Lily, Tiger		x	x	x	x	x				
Lily, Turkscap		x		x	x	x				
Lily, Western Orangecup		x	x	x	x					
Nepeta, Persian		x		x	x	x				x
Peavine, Perennial		x	x	x	x	x	x		2,000	
Penstemon, Beardlip		x		x	x	x			3,000	
Penstemon, Oneside		x		x	x	x			3,000	
Penstemon, Sawsepal		x		x	x	x			3,000	
Peony (many cultivars)		x	x	x	x	x	x			
Periwinkle		x				x	x			x
Phlox, Summer		x	x	x	x	x	x			
Prairieconeflower, Upright		x		x	x	x	x			
Sage, Perennial (*Salvia* sp.)		x		x	x	x				
Speedwell, Bastard		x		x	x					
Speedwell, Wooly		x		x	x					
Stonecrop (Liveforever, Showy, Tworow)		x		x	x					
Tansy		x		x	x	x	x	x		x
Thermopsis, Carolina		x		x	x					
Wormwood, Common		x		x	x	x	x			
Yarrow, Sneezewort		x	x	x	x	x	x	x		
Annual Flowers										
Most of the common kinds are satisfactory. Set as bedding plants in all zones. The large seeded kinds may be planted directly in the garden in all zones.										
Hardy Bulbs										
Daffodil		x	x	x	x	x				
Grape Hyacinth		x		x	x					
Tulip		x	x	x	x	x				
Tender Bulbs (harvest and store over winter)										
Canna		x	x	x	x	x	x			
Dahlia		x	x	x	x	x	x			
Gladioli		x	x	x	x	x	x		3,000 (in zones VI & VII)	
Lawn Grasses (irrigated)										
Bermudagrass (and its cultivars)		x				x	x			
Centipedegrass		x				x	x			x
Fescue (the fine bladed species and cultivars)		x	x	x	x					x
Kentucky Bluegrass (and its cultivars)		x	x	x	x	x				
Lawn Grasses (dryland)										
Buffalograss		x	x	x	x	x	x			
Crested Wheat, Fairway		x	x	x	x					
Grama, Blue		x	x	x	x	x	x			

Cutting Gardens

Before selecting plants for your cutting garden, consider the types of floral arrangements that you enjoy most.

When do you want cut flowers? Most outdoor flowers bloom in spring and summer, and if seasonal arrangements are satisfactory you may be content to bring indoors whatever flowers you are growing outdoors, or to buy seasonal varieties when they are least expensive at the florists. But if you want flowers out of season, then your cutting garden should include indoor varieties and plants such as bulbs that provide year-round blooms.

Color is another factor. For a traditional living room in muted tones, flowers of soft pastel shades might be appropriate, while a contemporary interior might call for blossoms in vivid colors. Form is important, too. For drama you might want to grow bird-of-paradise (strelitzia). If you enjoy arranging flowers, you might want to grow bells-of-Ireland, which have tall stalks covered with blossoms, asters that grow singly at medium levels, and low-growing alyssum, so that you have a full choice of heights and forms with which to create complex effects. If, in contrast, you simply want a vase of bold color, easy-to-grow zinnias may be all you need; and if you like tumbling, informal bouquets, perhaps your cutting garden should be a wildflower garden.

What do you want from your flowers? Pentas are especially long-lasting in cut form, but if beauty of flower construction matters, you might prefer passiflora, which is exceedingly handsome but won't last long after cutting. Even with a family, such as orchids, you have a choice of varieties good for cutting; oncidiums are excellent for elegance, while cypripediums are better if you want informality. If fragrance is important, choose an aromatic plant.

How will you arrange your flowers? For tall vases you will want long-stemmed plants for the center, lower stemmed plants for edging down the grouping, and perhaps some blossoms to trail over the edge of the container. To create space between larger blossoms, the tiny, stiff, separated flowers of baby's breath (gysophilia) are handy. A bud vase, tiny bottle, or cup can hold a single blossom effectively. You can buy "frogs"—holders of wire or glass used by florists to tilt flowers at attractive angles—or use wire to hold flowers into handsome display positions.

You may want to grow a few plants especially suited to unusual arrangements. Cortaderia (pampas grass), stipa (feather grass), and carex (sedges), especially *C. pendula*, are nice for contrasting texture. Echinops (thistle) is another plant good for contrast, but an arrangement of thistle alone can be handsome. You might also look around your local nursery for plants of dramatic shapes and colors, such as Kniphofia, poker plants that are hardy in the North; eremurus, desert candles, with stately scapes; or dierama, South African corms that can be grown under glass or in warm climates.

For flowers that bloom in winter, see page 17. For information on making your flowers last longer, see pages 171 and 172.

Virtually any plant you grow can be considered part of your cutting garden. Ferns and grasses can be used to complement arrangements. Holly, bayberry, and other berry-bearing plants, as well as small trees with unusual branching such as dogwood, are dramatic either alone or in combination with selected flowers. Bushes such as forsythia can be effective additions to flower arrangements. Even the flowers of tulip trees can contribute to indoor enjoyment.

Flowers that are long-lasting after being cut include roses and bulbs, as well as the following: ***Achillea:*** Ageratum (*A. houstonianum* is best); *Alyssum saxatile*; *Anchusa azurea*; anemones; aquilegia; asters, especially dwarfs; *Begonia semperflorens*; browallia; calendula; campanula; centaurea; China aster; Clarkia; coreopsis; delphinium; dianthus; gaillardia; gerbera; *Gypsophila paniculata*; helianthus; helichrysum; heliopsis; impatiens; lathyrus; limonium; *Lobularia maritima*; *Mirabilis jalapa*; *Myosotis sylvatica*; *Nigella damascena*; oenothera; papaver; petunias; phlox; primula; *Reseda odorata*; rudbeckia; salpiglossis; tagetes; tithonia; *Tropaeolum majus*; veronica; *Viola cornuta*; zinnias. Perhaps the most versatile of all, however, are the chrysanthemums, whose flowers are especially long-lasting.

Chrysanthemums

Originally imported from the Far East, where they have been cultivated for centuries, mums are popular not only for their bold color but also because they bloom from mid-July until fall after other flowers have died. Flowers may be yellow, orange, red, purple, bronze, pink, or white, and they range in size from little pompons to four-inch decoratives. Provided you buy the proper variety, they are easy to grow indoors or out.

Hardy varieties are perennials that produce underground shoots (stolons) and persist from year to year. These are best for home gardens because their small flowers bloom before killing frost. Nonhardy varieties produce few or no stolons, are winter-killed, or bloom so late that the flowers are killed by frost. These can be grown outdoors only with winter protection. They are, however, popular with greenhouse gardeners, who encourage the plants to bloom at any season by manipulating the amount of light exposure. These mums have larger blooms, sometimes more than three inches in diameter.

Mums are classified according to the shape and arrangement of their petals. *Single* mums look like daisies, with one to five rows of long petals radiating from a central "eye"; nearly all varieties are hardy. *Pompon* have globular flowers with so many tiny petals they look stiff; some varieties are hardy. *Cushion*, also called azalea mums, grow on low, bush plants and flower early; nearly all are hardy. *Decorative* mums have large, splendid blossoms that may be incurred, incurring, or reflexed; many varieties are hardy. *Spoon* have spoon-shaped petals; some of these are hardy. *Spider* mums have long, tubular petals with hooked ends; few of these are hardy. *Quill* have petals that are straight, long, and tubular; few of these are hardy.

You can buy packaged plants with burlap-wrapped roots and well-developed buds in spring (plant them after frost danger is past) and fall (plant these at least six weeks before the first frost). In spring you can also buy rooted cuttings that will bloom later in the year. Potted chrysanthemums can be bought year-round. You can propagate them by dividing or taking cuttings in spring.

Mums require full sunshine all day, and well-drained soil rich in organic matter (at least one-fourth well-decayed manure or peat moss). In most areas, you need not water because mums will get sufficient moisture from rain; never let them wilt, however. From the time buds begin until they develop full color, fertilize every ten days to two weeks with a 5-10-5 and 7-6-5 formula. The taller varieties, especially those with large blossoms, need to be staked, and if you are in an area subject to hail or pounding rain, you may need to protect the flowers with frames covered with cheesecloth or soft plastic sheeting.

When small-flowered varieties are six to eight inches high, pinch off the tips to encourage branching; otherwise you'll get tall, weak stems and few flowers. Continue to pinch all new shoots that develop every two weeks until June 10 for early varieties and July 1 for late varieties. Don't pinch after these dates or flowers will fail to develop.

With large-flowered varieties, pinch out tips when the plants are five to six inches high. As new shoots develop along the stem, break off all but two or three of these new shoots. Let the remaining shoots grow into branches, but every two weeks remove any side shoots that grow on these branches. When flower buds show, remove all except those on the top three inches of the branch; later, if the topmost bud looks healthy and is developing well, remove all the other buds on the branch (snap off the stems with a downward motion at their juncture with the branch).

Mums are subject to mildew, rust, bud rot, verticillium wilt, nematode infection, and other problems. Most of these problems can be prevented if plants are planted in sun, in well-drained soil, are not crowded, and are watered early in the day. Also stake them so leaves do not drag on the ground, and remove and destroy any diseased parts. When plants are well-established but before buds show color, you can also spray (especially leaf undersides) with zineb.

Chrysanthemum Suppliers

Bristol Nurseries, Inc.
73 Pinehurst Rd.
Bristol, CT 06010

Dooley Gardens
Hutchinson, MN 55350

Huff's Garden Mums
710 Juniatta, Box 187
Burlington, KS 66839

King's Mums
P.O. Box 368
Clement, CA 95227

The Lehman Gardens
Faribault, MN 55021

Sunnyslope Gardens
8638 Huntington Drive
San Gabriel, CA 91775

Thon's Garden Mums
4815 Oak St.
Crystal Lake, IL 60014

Yoder Brothers, Inc.
P.O. Box 230
Barberton, OH 44203

The Lazy Gardener's Special

If you want easy-to-grow flowers to cut and bring indoors for long-lasting bloom, your best bets are probably the following:

Zinnias grow quickly and are reliable bloomers even if you do nothing for them except keep them well watered. Pot marigolds (calendulas) are easily grown from seed. Blanketflowers like sun but are otherwise undemanding. Hollyhock grows almost like a weed. Snapdragons are stately and intricate.

Dooryard Gardens

One of the traditions that the colonists brought with them to America was the dooryard garden. Rigidly defined, a dooryard garden is simply one in which the plants grown are those cultivated by American colonists. It is largely a practical kind of garden, including many herbs, spices, and fruits. However, a dooryard garden also includes ornamentals such as dahlias, chrysanthemums, and lilac.

The essential character of the dooryard garden is defined by the part it played in the lives of American colonists. These people developed their own styles of dooryard gardens, staying within the traditional bounds of plants grown in the British Isles, but also adding a few specimens better suited to their new climate. They exchanged plant information and materials among themselves and with those in the motherland. This trade of ideas makes the dooryard garden tradition at once an interesting social phenomenon and a quaint trademark of our cultural heritage.

The following list includes most of the original members of the traditional dooryard garden. The dooryard garden layout, or plan, was never a major concern. So, simply pick the plants you wish to include in your garden, and arrange them how you will.

Achillea
Ajuga
American holly
Anchusa
Angelica
Anthemis
Aquilegia
Artemisia
Basil
Blue agerantum
Bugle
Calendula
Carnation
Catmint
Chamomile
Chives
Cordon apple
Cordon pear
Dianthus
Dogwood
Dwarf apple
Dwarf boxwood
English daisy
English ivy
English walnut
Espalier plum
Fig
Flame azalea
Gentiana
Gerbera
Germander
Goat's beard
Heliotrope
Hollywood
Iris
Johnny-jump-ups
Lavender
Lemon balm
Lilies
Lily-of-the-valley
Live oak
Loosestrife
Lythrum
Marjoram
Mertensia
Mint
Myrtle
Nectarine
Nicotiana
Old roses
Oregano
Parsley
Peach
Peony
Periwinkle
Persimmon
Pink
Pomegranate
Poppy
Poppy anemone
Potentilla
Primrose
Pyrethrum
Red salvia
Rosemary
Rose
Sage
Santolina
Savory
Saxifraga
Scuppernong grape
Simplex tonquil
Solitary brodiaea
Spearmint
Spanish quill
Stock
Sunflower
Tarragon
Thyme
Verbena
Yaupon holly

FLOWERING DOGWOOD.

—MARSH GENTIAN.

—HELIOTROPE.

—MUGWORT.

SWEET BASIL.

ROSEMARY.

Fragrance Gardens

A fragrance garden can be one of the most pleasant and satisfying gardens you will ever grow. The common act of walking down your garden path, or through a room in your house, can be a delightful experience of added dimension when the natural, sweet aroma of fragrant flowers exists. And cultivating a fragrance garden does not mean sacrificing visual beauty, because most fragrant plants are noted for beautiful flowers and foliage.

Trees suited to a fragrance garden include citrus varieties, black locust, apple, magnolia, and eucalyptus. Vine-like flowers include sweet pea, clematis, honeysuckle, and morning glory.

Best bets for ground covers are sweet alyssum and lily-of-the-valley, both of which flower all summer and produce tiny white or pink blossoms. Lily-of-the-valley survives in shade. Either one can also be used as a border. Creeping thyme and Roman chamomile are among herbs and spices that are low-growing: woodruff, lemon verbena, and most other herbs are also favorites for the fragrance gardens.

Among succulents, wax plant (*Hoya carnosa*) produces waxy white flowers (sometimes called "porcelain flowers") that give off an extremely strong, sweet scent; it can be grown indoors or outdoors. Orchids such as bifrenaria and coelogyne are fragrant. Iris, narcissus, and other bulbs are perfumed, with hyacinths and lilies producing especially strong scents. Day lilies (*Hemeroeallis*) bloom at night and smell like honeysuckle. *Exacum affine*, the German violet, has a subtle fragrance. Several geraniums smell like lemons, apples, roses, mint, and other plants. A few aquatic plants such as water lilies also produce perfume.

Popular garden flowers and shrubs include heliotrope, lavender, petunias (especially *Petunia axillaris*), pinks and carnations, nasturtiums, sweet william, violets, and, of course, roses. Easy to grow, so long as it has sun and well-drained soil, is *Silene noctiflora*, which smells like raspberries when it blooms at night. The four o'clock (*Mirabilis jalapa*), true to its name, opens its red, lemon-scented flowers in early evening; tubers must be stored in winter and replanted in May; it grows to heights of three feet and can be trimmed into a hedge.

Flowering tobacco (*Nicotiana alata*) grows to five feet. Its white, rose, or red flowers bloom from early spring to late fall and have a spicy scent akin to that of nasturtiums or carnations. It needs full sun and lots of water.

The moonflower (*Ipomoea bonanox*) has sweetly scented flowers six inches across that you can watch opening with jerking movements about 8 P.M. Evening primrose (*Oenothera*) has sweet-smelling yellow and orange flowers that first appear as little balloons and then actually pop as they open. It can be grown in any well-drained soil so long as it gets full sun and lots of water. Sweet olive (*Osmanthus fragrans*) has shiny foliage attractive year-round and emits a sweet fragrance in or out of bloom.

Glory bower (*Clerodendrum fragrans*), a hardy shrub, can be kept to 18 inches indoors but grows to ten feet outdoors. In addition to handsome foliage, it has large, fragrant, red flowers tinged with white. It needs full sun and liberal water. Move potted indoor specimens to a cool (58°F) spot such as the garage in winter, when it rests.

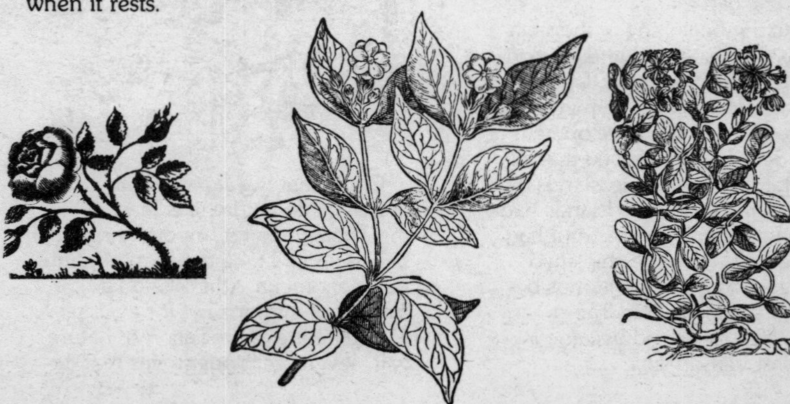

Jasmine (*Jasminum*) is an all-time favorite, and varieties grow from one foot to over six feet tall. All are attractive even when not in bloom. *J. nudiform* blooms in December; "Gold Coast" during June and July nights; "Poet's Jasmine" throughout the summer. *J. parkeri* is the best variety for indoors. Jasmine loves full sun, high humidity, and a fairly rich soil kept evenly moist. Night jasmine (*Cestrum nocturnum*) blooms most of the year with fragrant, star-shaped white flowers that open evenings.

Gardenia: These evergreens with glossly dark-green leaves are attractive for their foliage alone but are generally grown for their exceptionally large (three-inch) and fragrant blossoms. Gardenias are somewhat temperamental, though, demanding a temperature change. With pampering they can be grown indoors, but they do best if taken outdoors for the summer.

Plant them in an acid soil mix of equal parts loam, peat moss, and well-decayed manure, with either sand or perlite for drainage. Keep soil evenly moist. Use an acid fertilizer during vigorous growth, but gardenias rest in winter and should not be fed then. Humidity should be at least 50%. Gardenias need strong light, but as noontime sun burns the foliage, put them under trees where they will get only early morning and late afternoon sun. Indoors, give them sun in winter but only bright light in summer, and they may bloom any time of year. Outdoors, they bloom in winter in the South and in summer in the North. Gardenias, which grow about four feet tall, can be pruned (even cut back to a third of new growth), and shoots can be pinched, after flowering. Propagate by cuttings taken January through March. Bud drop (or failure of buds to open) and blackening of the leaves and new growth are due to insufficient light, insufficient humidity, or change in temperature.

Those easiest to grow and most commonly available are *G. radicans floraplena* (a low shrub with small double blossoms) and *G. jasminoides 'Florida'* (three-inch double blossoms in summer, best for indoor culture).

Japanese Gardens

As a part of Japanese culture, the garden had its origin in the religious and philosophical life of the country. The goal of the garden is the creation of an image that appears to be natural, but is, at the same time, a work of art. Nature is shaped in order to suggest elements of the larger order, the cosmos, and so lead the viewer to contemplation and reflection.

The Japanese garden grew out of a complex tangle of cultural and religious influences, some from China and Korea, that stressed man as a part of nature. And conversely, nature is a part of man. When man shapes nature he shapes himself. He does not seek to control the natural world, but to understand it and express himself through it.

Two religious concepts in particular are important. In the Shinto (the way of the gods) religion, nature is both generated and preserved by *Kami*, spirits that inhabit natural phenomena such as hills, trees, and waterfalls. *Tei* or *niwa* developed as pure places created for man to revere these divine beings. Shintoism also asserts that a higher divinity manifests itself on earth. The early Japanese created rock seats—sacred places to which the gods could descend. These seats took several forms, one of which was called an *iwasaka*, or a consecrated area surrounded on all sides by rocks. In both the *niwa* and the *iwasaka* the groundwork was laid for the first garden.

About the beginning of the sixth century, Taoist legend and religion began to make its way to Japan from China. One aspect of the mythology strongly affected the development of the garden. It was believed that all immortals lived on three islands. It was rumored that these islands had even been seen by sailors, but had disappeared when the ships had drawn too close. These islands became very important in Taoist legend, and the island became a symbol of immortality.

Another significant import was Buddhism, which brought to Japan the concept of *Shumisen*. This is the concept of the world mountain that rises from the center of the earth. At the peak resides the prevailing deity, Shukra, while the four kings of heaven live on the sides of the mountain. At the base of the mountain are nine hills with eight seas. At the outer edges of these seas are islands. Beneath the mountain are the circles of the earth, consisting of the elements of which the world is made: metal, water, and wind. Above and around the mountain revolve the sun and moon. This schematic representation of the way in which the world is organized was given formal expression in the seventh-century garden of the Empress Suiko-Tenno in the form of a *shumisen-seki stone*. Described variously as a fountain supplying water, an object used to inspire religious awe, and a token of hospitality, the *shumisens-seki stone* is made up of three small boulders, positioned one atop the other, and covered with sculptured motifs. Some form of the *shumisen-seki stone* is found in most gardens, even today, in Japan.

Given that the Japanese, perceive the divine in nature, it is reasonable that metaphors for important spiritual beliefs should take the form of natural phenomena—the island as a symbol of immortality, for example. Combine the appreciation of nature with several religious strains that define the world in pastoral terms, and the garden becomes the perfect expression of the spiritual cosmos.

Over a period of about two hundred years, beginning in the eleventh century, several other factors helped to develop the garden as an integral part of Japanese life. One was the appearance and growth of *Kakkai-Shuho* rites—ceremonies that rewarded and encouraged piety. The rites were performed in places remote from the secular world, in gardens around which earth had been piled, and through which paths had been laid. This helped to establish the garden as a sacred place, away from the hectic world.

Simultaneously and as a result of both political and religious forces, a mood of melancholy and societal decadence descended upon Japan. Those alive during this particular period believed their age to be the last. Earthly objects retained little of their former significance, and reflection on life and preparation for death became much more important. Religious teachings began to describe the Pure Land to which one ascends as a paradise garden. As a result, paradise gardens were constructed as places in which to contemplate one's self and one's spiritual state. A great number of these gardens were attached to temples, establishing the garden as a direct outgrowth of religious belief. The development of the tea-garden in the sixteenth century—part of the larger tradition of the tea ceremony—gave gardens even greater prestige.

So the garden is an artistic expression of wonder and of deep-rooted belief. It is unique in that the materials used in the composition of this art are those provided by nature. Nature is shaped by man to reflect the whole of which they are both a part.

To more fully understand the nature of the Japanese garden, compare it to the gardens of Europe. While the Japanese garden attempts to preserve the integrity of a setting, mirroring the belief that man is simply part of nature and nature part of man, the European garden is an example of man's mastery over nature. The biblical dictum to "replenish the earth, and subdue it" was taken to heart by European designers. The first gardens were usually attached to monasteries and had the practical purpose of cultivating medicinal herbs. Even when pleasure gardens developed, man's mastery over natural materials was stressed by formal design, including exaggerated demonstrations of control such as topiary and espalier. In literature and in fact, these gardens were the stages on which man played out his drama and his life. The garden reflected not the cosmos, but man and his accomplishments. The garden was not an expression of man's place within nature, but of his dominance over nature. Gardens, even when extensions of a home, were clearly subordinate to the architecture they complemented. And while the garden was regarded as a work of art, the physical artistry was more important than the materials from which it was created.

The Japanese garden, on the other hand, is not used as a means of self-expression, not as a stage for man's actions, but as a means to the contemplation of nature and the universe. Nature—though shaped by man—is predominant. The garden is a work of art, but one of such subtlety and respect for the materials from which it is formed, that the artistry is hardly evident. And, through its philosophical content, it should affect the spirit in the same way as a work of art.

The Japanese garden reveres nature and expresses that reverence in respect for the integrity of the natural. The gardener is as much a part of nature as the trees, shrubs, and rocks with which he works. Man is as much a part of the garden as are the elements from which the garden is composed.

Rock Gardening and Alpines

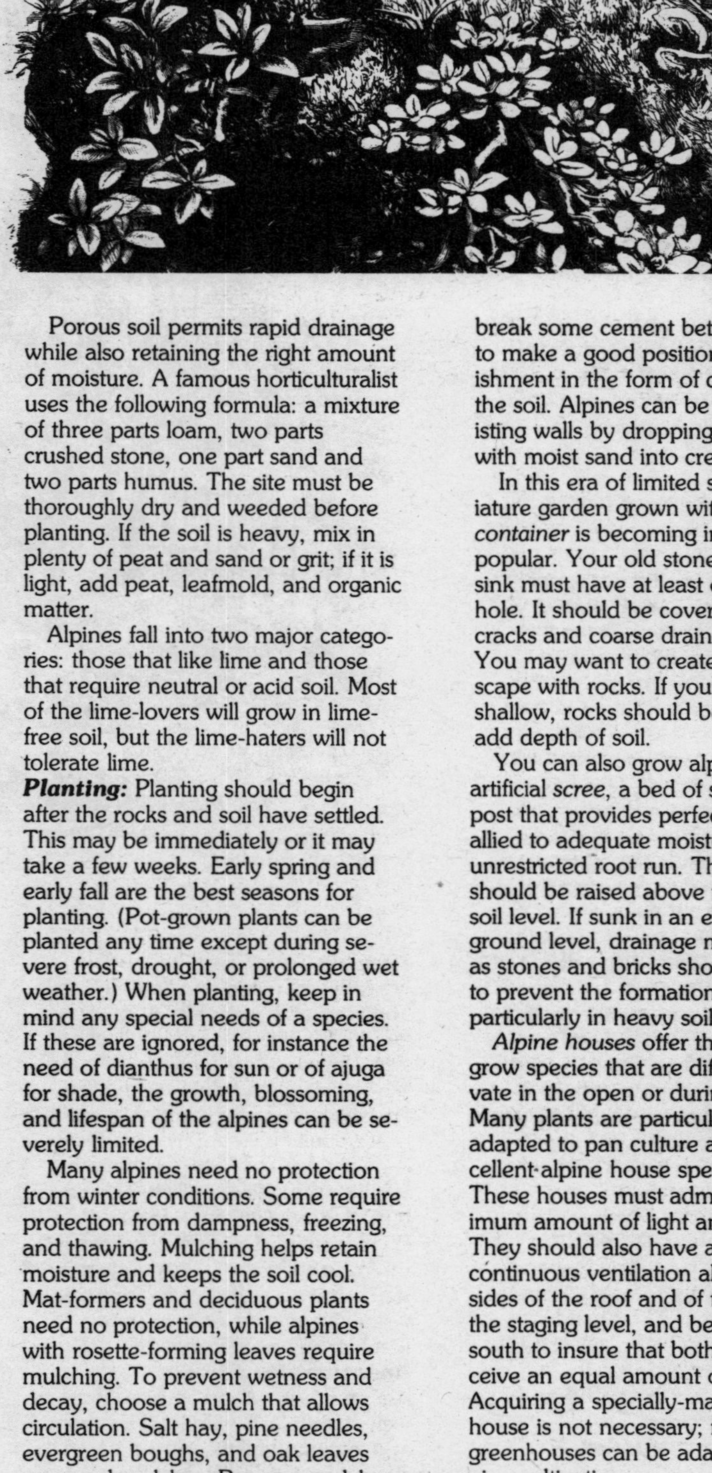

A successful rock garden should remind you of the landscape on a mountaintop, the natural habitat of most alpine vegetation. Rock gardening is laborious, but the delicate beauty and wide range of textures and forms alpines offer make it worthwhile. Although the rock garden is the ideal manmade environment for certain plants, they can also be grown in greenhouses, sinks, and between the cracks of walls and stone pavings. Their relatively small size makes them a good choice for gardeners with limited space.

The delicate appearance of alpines belie their hardiness. They are well adapted to the cold, wind, and snow that is characteristic of mountain climates. Provide them with plenty of moisture, sun, and coolness. The soil must always be damp beneath the surface—which means planting in soil where water is constantly running off and draining through, rather than settling. The rocks should be selected and arranged with this in mind. Place them firmly into the ground to prevent air pockets. Air pockets are undesirable because they cause the soil to dry out so that plant roots wither and die.

Careful planning is required to make a rock garden look natural. Before acquiring any plants, prepare a planting plan, designing attractive arrangements according to cultural requirements and flowering schedules. Know the flowering season, size, growth pattern, color, form, and texture of each species you plant. To capture the charm of a mountain environment, everything must look as though "it just grew that way." Therefore, do not grow alpines in geometric patterns or uniform rows. Irregularity adds to the natural look.

Ideally, a rock garden should be situated in an open area. Keep it removed from buildings, tall trees, or other structures that can cause dripping, shade, and drafts. A slightly south or southeastern slope is preferable. However, problems can be minimized by choosing plants carefully if these conditions are wanting.

Stones: Local stone is cheaper and preferable to imported stone, which may look incongruous or be unsuited to the conditions in your ara. Porousness is an important consideration because during dry spells the plants extract water from the moisture the stones store. Good porous stones include limestone, sandstone, tufa, and shale. Granite, although hard, can also be used successfully.

However small the garden, select rocks that are not too small. Using numerous small stones will create an artificial effect. Do not situate them far from each other or in isolation. Place them firmly into the ground so their bases will not show. Tilting the rocks slightly backward will allow them to hold rainfall and conduct it into the soil.

Drainage and Soil: Good drainage is vital to alpines. These plants will not withstand soggy soil. Give them abundant water, but make sure it flows quickly through the soil and does not accumulate at the roots. If they are planted on level ground it will be necessary to dig holes and fill them with cinder, pieces of clay, or broken stone, through which excess moisture can pass.

Porous soil permits rapid drainage while also retaining the right amount of moisture. A famous horticulturalist uses the following formula: a mixture of three parts loam, two parts crushed stone, one part sand and two parts humus. The site must be thoroughly dry and weeded before planting. If the soil is heavy, mix in plenty of peat and sand or grit; if it is light, add peat, leafmold, and organic matter.

Alpines fall into two major categories: those that like lime and those that require neutral or acid soil. Most of the lime-lovers will grow in lime-free soil, but the lime-haters will not tolerate lime.

Planting: Planting should begin after the rocks and soil have settled. This may be immediately or it may take a few weeks. Early spring and early fall are the best seasons for planting. (Pot-grown plants can be planted any time except during severe frost, drought, or prolonged wet weather.) When planting, keep in mind any special needs of a species. If these are ignored, for instance the need of dianthus for sun or of ajuga for shade, the growth, blossoming, and lifespan of the alpines can be severely limited.

Many alpines need no protection from winter conditions. Some require protection from dampness, freezing, and thawing. Mulching helps retain moisture and keeps the soil cool. Mat-formers and deciduous plants need no protection, while alpines with rosette-forming leaves require mulching. To prevent wetness and decay, choose a mulch that allows circulation. Salt hay, pine needles, evergreen boughs, and oak leaves are good mulches. Remove mulches in the spring when frost has disappeared.

Alternative Methods of Alpine Gardening

The *cracks and crannies* between stone pavement or between the bricks and stones of walls are excellent places for alpine growth. The soil beneath paving stones is cool and moist. Alpine stems will be protected from excessive water accumulation, and the flowers and leaves will receive light. It may be necessary to break some cement between stones to make a good position. Add nourishment in the form of compost to the soil. Alpines can be planted in existing walls by dropping seeds mixed with moist sand into crevices.

In this era of limited space the miniature garden grown within a *container* is becoming increasingly popular. Your old stone trough or sink must have at least one drainage hole. It should be covered with cracks and coarse drainage material. You may want to create a little landscape with rocks. If your container is shallow, rocks should be built up to add depth of soil.

You can also grow alpines on an artificial *scree*, a bed of special compost that provides perfect drainage allied to adequate moisture and an unrestricted root run. This bed should be raised above the general soil level. If sunk in an excavation at ground level, drainage material such as stones and bricks should be used to prevent the formation of a pond, particularly in heavy soil.

Alpine houses offer the chance to grow species that are difficult to cultivate in the open or during winter. Many plants are particularly well adapted to pan culture and make excellent alpine house specimens. These houses must admit the maximum amount of light and fresh air. They should also have a low span, continuous ventilation along both sides of the roof and of the sides at the staging level, and be set north-south to insure that both sides receive an equal amount of light. Acquiring a specially-made alpine house is not necessary; regular greenhouses can be adapted to alpine cultivation.

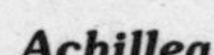

Achillea

Achilleas range in size from tallish border plants to small, mat-forming flora. They are suited to rock gardens, cracks in paving and crannies in walls. *A. argentea* (Eastern Alps) is an easy and charming plant for sunny conditions. It forms close mats of silvery leaves. In the summer it blooms a long succession of white flowers on six-inch stems. *A. tomentosa*—This frequently encountered species, commonly called wooly yar-

—ROCK CRESS.

row, grows very hairy leaves, forming dense mats. Its short stems carry tight clusters of beautiful, bright-yellow flowers.

Actaea
These are rather tall perennials with coarse leaves and small, spikey white flowers in the spring: *A. spicata alba*—(North America), called baneberry, has short, spikey white flowers in the spring, and by late summer, white berries.

Aethionema (cruciferae)
These somewhat shrubby, dwarf plants like long days of warm sunshine. They flower abundantly from summer onward: *A. grandiflora*—(Lebanon) Very decorative, blossoms with dark-pink flowers in early summer. This sun-lover grows well from a dry wall.

Ajuga
This group of ground covers appreciates occasional shade: *A. reptans Delightful*—Vigorous plants that require little work to grow successfully. They have six-inch blue flowers but are grown primarily for their foliage, which is gold and bronze, washed over with pink. *A. reptans metallica*—As its name suggests, this has shiny, almost metallic leaves of red. *A. reptans Rainbow*—This metallic purple ground cover has foliage that is mottled with green, pink, and gold at different times of the year.

Alchemilla (roseceae)
A. mollis (Asia Minor) At twelve to fifteen inches, mollis serves as a good ground cover. Its beautiful grayish-green leaves are rounded and scalloped. Flower arrangers often select this plant, which blooms soft, lime-green flowers in summer. Mollis can grow in almost any soil, whether sunny or moderately shady.

COMMON ROCK-ROSE.

Allium
A varied genus of plants possessed of an onionlike odor when crushed: *A. beesianum*—A sun worshipper with straight and narrow foliage and charming blue flowers on top of six-inch stems. Easy care. *A. cernuum*—(East USA) A charming, easy to grow form with rosy purple bells growing over flat rush-like leaves. *A. flavum*—This pretty plant has eight- to ten-inch stems that support bell-shaped flowers of primrose yellow. *A. narcissiflora*—Possibly the most beautiful of alliums, with one-inch-long bells of rosy red atop six-inch stems. Thrives in sunny conditions and well-drained soil, but can take one or two years to reach its growth potential. *A. pulchellum*—(Mediterranean) Easily grown, vigorous, and handsome, this has deep red-to-maroon flowers on wiry eighteen-inch stems. Blooms mid- to late summer. *A. neapoltanium*—Indigenous to mediterranean regions, its decorative white flowers have a subtle fragrance.

Alyssum (cruciferae)
Alyssums love sun and lime-rich soil. They are ideal for walls: *A. montanum*—(Central Europe) Its woody stems support small, hairy ash-gray leaves. Fragrant, bright-yellow flowers bloom in early spring. *A. saxatile*—A popular alyssum that blooms in early spring. The "Dudley Neville" form is an especially pretty orange buff. *A. serpyllifolium*—(Spain) Very small, neat and attractive, its leaves resemble thyme, and its thin woody stems spread horizontally. Tiny yellow flowers blossom in spring. Ideal for sinks or troughs.

Anacylus (compositae)
A. depressus—(North Africa) It grows well in gritty soil with good drainage and intense sunlight. Horizontal stems carry finely shaped gray-green leaves. Its daisy flowers are bright-white on the upper side and deep-crimson beneath. Strikingly beautiful.

Anchusa (boraginaceae)
These tall border plants include only one species that qualifies as an alpine: *A. caespitosa*—(Crete) This form has brilliant blue flowers nestling among a cluster of narrow leathery leaves. Plant in a deep bed of gritty, humus-filled soil and in an open, sunny site.

Androsace (primulaceae) primrose family:
This genus includes some of the choiciest and handsomest alpines from Europe, Asia, and North America: *A. arachoidea superba*—A tiny plant with half-inch leaves forming rosettes and a cluster of showy flowers—each with a little yellow spot that turns crimson a few days after blooming. Needs plenty of sun and excellent drainage. *A. jacquemontii*—(Himalayas) Gray, woolly leaf-rosettes, and gorgeous lavender-pink flowers. Very hardy; grows two to three inches high. *A. lanuginosa*—(Himalayas) A popular rock jasmine, easy to grow. Trailing stems with brilliantly silver leaves and clusters of pretty pink flowers. *A. sarmentosa*—Green leaves with silvery hairs in neat rosettes. From the center spring six- to eight-inch stems that carry sweet-looking, rose-colored flowers. *A. sempervivoides*—(Himalayas) An easy outdoor species. Small, smooth leaf rosettes and compact pink flowers bloom in early summer. Attractive and accomodating in scree or trough garden. Grows to two to three inches high. *A. villosa*—(Alps of Europe and Asia) Loose tufts of soft leaves carried at the ends of red stolons. The fragrant flowers are usually white but can be soft-pink with a darker eye. Suitable for a sunny scree, trough, or alpine house.

Anemone
A. magellanica major—(South America) The tufts of the basal leaves are hairy and divided. From them rise six- to nine-inch stems with cream-colored flowers. Good in almost any soil. Needs good sun. *A. narcissiflora*—(Europe, Asia, and North America) From the basal clump of lobed leaves arise fifteen-inch stems, each bearing a cluster of white, pink-flushed blossoms. Likes well-drained loam in abundant sunlight. *A. obtusiloba*—Looks like a buttercup. Its lobed, hairy leaves form tufts from which grow soft blue flowers.

Antennaria
A useful group of ground covers, usually with silver leaves and tufty heads of white, red, or pink flowers: *A. droica rubra*—A neat, unimposing carpet of small silver leaves. The tight heads of red flowers bloom in late spring on three- to four-inch stems.

Anthemis
A. rudolphiana—Attractive, hardy plants with bright silver, finely-shaped leaves and one-inch wide golden flowers. They grow to a height of six to eight inches. *A. einseliana*—(Italy, France) Distinctive-looking, with dark-grayish leaves that contrast with the dusky flowers. Plant in sunny soil and they will grow to a height of eight inches.

Aquilegia
These are widely used and decorative plants from the Northern Hemisphere: *A. bertolonii*—(European Alps) A four-inch pygmy with a sapphire flower on its three-inch stem. For a sunny pocket in the rock garden or lovely in a trough garden.

Arabis
A. albida variegata—A lovely plant with light-green leaves splashed with gold. Good as a border or on a dry wall to add brightness.

Arenaria
A. purpurascens—(Pyrenees) Mats of green leaves studded with purple flowers.

Armeria
A. caespitosa—(Spain) Dwarfed, with mounds of narrow, dark-green leaves and bearing soft pink flowers on short stems. Well-suited to a sunny scree or trough, or in the alpine house. Grows to two to three inches.

Artemisia
A group of fragrant, sun-loving plants: *A. lanata*—Planted for its fine foliage, which forms a one-inch high carpet of bright silver. Quite outstanding if provided with abundant sunlight and good drainage. It can spread to a few feet wide.

Arum
A. italicum pictum—Loved by flower arrangers, this has arrow-shaped, shiny leaves splashed with yellowish-white. Active growth throughout winter and spring; slows down in the summer. Tolerant of shade.

—STEEPLE BELLS.

Astilbe
Many from this group are used as borders, but a few are dainty: *A. glaberrima*—A little Japanese treasure with neat tufts of fine, deep-green, sometimes-bronzed leaves and graceful pink flowers. Well suited for a cool position in a rock or peat garden.

Berberis
B. corollina compacta—A charming miniature that reaches a height of no more than one foot. Glossy evergreen foliage; in summer, manes of bright-orange flowers; often produces another, smaller crop of blooms in autumn.

Brachycome
B. rigidula—(Australia) Forms a short, foot-wide mat of shiny, light-green, divided leaves. During the summer and autumn a succession of small, lavender, daisylike flowers bloom on three- to four-inch stems. Grows hardily in the U.S.

Calceolaria
C. darwinii—(Straight of Magellan) Tufts of smooth, dark-green leaves form an inch-high mat. Surprisingly large flowers of yellowish-brown with a curious white stripe across the mouth. A plant with character. Grow in moist, humus-rich soil and intense sun.

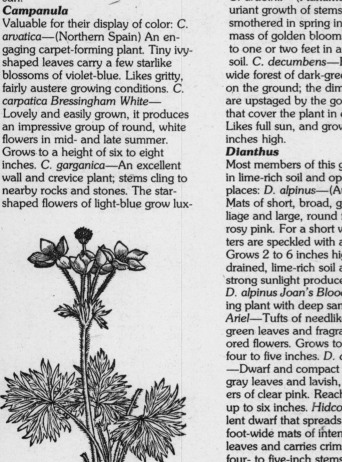

Campanula
Valuable for their display of color: *C. arvatica*—(Northern Spain) An engaging carpet-forming plant. Tiny ivy-shaped leaves carry a few starlike blossoms of violet-blue. Likes gritty, fairly austere growing conditions. *C. carpatica Bressingham White*—Lovely and easily grown, it produces an impressive group of round, white flowers in mid- and late summer. Grows to a height of six to eight inches. *C. garganica*—An excellent wall and crevice plant; stems cling to nearby rocks and stones. The star-shaped flowers of light-blue grow luxuriantly in June and July. *Mist Maiden*—A plant with exquisite, bell-shaped blossoms of pure white. Cheerful and vigorous. The stems grow to eight or ten inches. Place in sunny spot. *Molly Pinset*—A rounded plant six- to eight-inches-high with bronzed leaves and open, bell-shaped flowers of lavender. *C. morettiana*—Another producer of flower bells, of violet-blue. The small, ivy-shaped foliage forms tufts from which emerge one-inch stems. This alpine should be planted between small stones in pots or pans. *C. muralis major*—More violet bell-shaped flowers, lasting all summer. An accomodating plant that grows six to eight inches high. *C. nitida alba*—An alpine of singular appearance. The leaves are deep, glossy green, and crimped at the edges; they grow in flat, two-inch rosettes. During June and July six-inch spikes bear round, brilliant white flowers. *C. pilosa superba*—(Japan) Two-inch rosettes of glossy foliage, and straight, funnel-shaped flowers of violet-blue form from June. Good in scree, trough or alpine house. Grows to a height of two inches.

Cytisus
C. ardoinii—(Maritime Alps) A luxuriant growth of stems and leaves, smothered in spring in a glowing mass of golden blooms. Will spread to one or two feet in any light, sunny soil. *C. decumbens*—Forms a foot-wide forest of dark-green stems flat on the ground; the diminutive leaves are upstaged by the golden flowers that cover the plant in early summer. Likes full sun, and grows to 1 to 2 inches high.

Dianthus
Most members of this genus flourish in lime-rich soil and open, sunny places: *D. alpinus*—(Australian Alps) Mats of short, broad, grassy-green foliage and large, round flat flowers of rosy pink. For a short while the centers are speckled with a crimson ring. Grows 2 to 6 inches high. A well-drained, lime-rich soil and fairly strong sunlight produce best results. *D. alpinus Joan's Blood*—A surprising plant with deep sanguine floors. *Ariel*—Tufts of needlike, grayish-green leaves and fragrant, cherry-colored flowers. Grows to a height of four to five inches. *D. caesius plenus*—Dwarf and compact mats of silver-gray leaves and lavish, aromatic flowers of clear pink. Reaches heights of up to six inches. *Hidcote*—An excellent dwarf that spreads into thick, foot-wide mats of intense silver-gray leaves and carries crimson florets on four- to five-inch stems.

Dionysia
Plants of this genus come from the Middle East and the Southern USSR: *D. aretiodes*—Forms compact rosettes of wee, hairy, gray-green leaves. In the spring stemless, primrose-scented yellow flowers cover the foliage. Used to dry period, so water carefully.

Douglasia
D. laevigata—(North America) Neat green tufts, rosetted leaves, and heads of rose-red flowers characterize this growth. Heights reach to 2 to 3 inches. Prefers lime-free soil. *D. vitaliana praetutiana*—A free-flowering alpine with silvery leaves and luxuriant, diminutive flowers of gold during the spring.

Draba
D. aizoides—(European Alps) A nice, common plant with deep-green, bristly leaves and golden flowers that bloom in April. Very adaptable in any sunny soil in the rock garden or trough. *D. bryoides*—An "aristocratic" plant with tiny emerald rosettes during early spring. The miniscule gold blossoms grow atop threadlike, one-inch stems.

Dryas
D. octopetala—Its woody stems spread at ground-level, clad with small, leathery, oak-like leaves. The eight-petalled flowers are followed by attractive fluffy seed-herbs. Plant in a sunny position almost anywhere and they will grow to four to five inches high.

Epilobium
Broadway Hybrid—The six- to seven-inch stems grow a succession of funnel-shaped flowers flushed with pink. The shiny leaves turn bronze with age. Easy culture and long-lasting. *E. globellum*—(New Zealand) Straight one-foot-high stems sprouting glossy green to bronze leaves. Pretty, milky blossoms grow all summer. Easy culture.

Erinus
E. alpinus—Delightfully pretty alpine with neat, tiny leaves that it shrouds with short-stemmed clusters of white or dark-pink flowers. Grows to a few inches high. A free-seeder, but doesn't get out of hand. Inhabits chinks and crannies.

Eriophyllum
E. lanatum—A vigorous plant with silver leaves that form a low patch. The deep-gold, daisy flowers last for several weeks in the spring.

Erodium
A sun-loving genus of low, bushy, mat-forming plants: *E. chamaedrioides*—Now called *E. reichardii*, this plant spreads into tiny prostrate mats of deep-colored leaves. White flowers crossed with thin pink lines sprout in the spring. In the form "*Roseum*," flowers are totally pink.

Erysium
E. alpinum—(Northern Europe) Carries aromatic yellow leaves on six-inch stems.

Festuca
A genus of alpine grasses good for tucking into chinks and corners in the garden: *F. glauca*—A decorative, noninvasive grass, formed by slender, nine-inch leaves of intense blue-gray.

Gentiana
An important alpine group: *G. acaulis*—(Alps and Pyrenees) One of the most familiar alpines. Great sapphire trumpets, splattered and lined with green. A rich, moist soil on a north slope and abundant sunlight pleases this mat-former. *G. bellidifolia*—(New Zealand) Carries ivory blossoms on its dark stems. *G. farreri*—(Northwest China) An exquisite plant with prostrate mats of crowded stems adorned by intense Cambridge-blue flowers. It needs a lot of moisture during the growing season, and good drainage. Allow about a

year for it to get acclimated and established. Its maximum height is three to four inches. *G. septemfida*—Owes its popularity to the fact it grows well in almost any soil or situation. Forms healthy clumps of foot-high leafy stems, ending in rosettes of blue, trumpet-shaped flowers.

Geranium

Dwarf hardy geraniums are well-suited for rock gardens with good soil and ample sunlight: *G. argentum*—(Mountains of Central and Eastern Europe) Its soft, hairy leaves are silvery and divided. It supports nice pink flowers with deeper pink veins on four-inch stems. *G. cinereum*—(Pyrenees) A beautiful and unusual species. Segmented tufts of gray-green leaves and cup-shaped, deep-pink flowers. The petals are usually veined with a deeper pink hue. *G. dalmatucum*—(Eastern Europe) A friendly and pretty form with tufts of round, glossy leaves of autumn colors. In late spring a succession of lovely deep-pink flowers bloom. Will thrive in most sunny, open situations. Grows to a height of four to five inches.

Globularia

A genus of dwarf, woody plants from dry situations in the Alps. They flower in the summer. *G. cordifolia*—Forms its woody stems into prostrate mats. The globelike, blue flowers are supported by two-inch stems. The leaves are long and spoon-shaped.

Haberlea

A small genus whose members require cool, northfacing or shaded crevices between rocks or in walls: *H. rhodopensis*—Makes rosettes of deep-green, leather leaves. The profusion of lavender florets are carried in pendant umbels. Grows to a height of five to six inches.

Helianthemum

H. alpestre serpyllifulium—(Southern Europe) A tiny, prostrate shrub of neat habit with golden flowers that grows to a height of one inch. *H. lunalatum*—Forms a neat, gray-leafed bush six to eight inches in height. Covers itself all summer with myriads of yellow flowers and enjoys a sunny position.

Helichrysum

H. bellidioides—A useful carpet-former, often used as ground cover in the rock garden. Grows well when tucked into cracks between paving stones. Mats of gray leaves with white flowers on short stems. *H. coralloides*—(New Zealand) Curious, very hardy plants of shrubby habit. Has scale-like leaves pressed close to the stems. *H. virgineum*—One of the finest alpine plants. Its wide silvery leaves form loose rosettes and on the nine-inch stems. Pretty global buds, covered by shell-pink bracts, open into large white flowers.

Hypericum

H. coris—(Southern Europe) A small shrub about six inches high, enveloped in heath-like leaves and covered for most of the summer with one-inch-wide gold flowers. Give it a sunny position. *H. olympicum*—(Southeast Europe) Very attractive and useful; blooms in summer. This shrubby form has rich golden flowers, filled with masses of stamens. Easy and long flowering. Suitable for walls and all sunny positions. Reaches heights of six to eight inches.

Iberis

Little Gem—A neat, dwarf candytuft. Its white flowers and narrow evergreen leaves look lovely growing in a rock wall.

Iris

I. pumila—(Central Europe and Asia Minor) Ranges in color from white to yellow and lavender. About 8 inches high. Provide excellent drainage for best results.

Juniperus

J. communis compressa—Commonly called the Noah's Ark Tree, this species grows an inch or less each year, but forms a beautifully upright column of evergreen leaves.

Lavandula

Baby Blue—Pleasantly scented gray-green bushes adorned with three-inch spikey flowers. Plant in sunny position.

Lewisia

Pinkie—A pretty hybrid with three- to four-inch rosettes of narrow, fleshy leaves and an almost continuous succession of pink florets, enhanced by deep-red anthers. Plant in gritty soil in the alpine house or shady crevice.

Mertensia

M. pterocarpa—(Japan) An elegant growth with glaucous leaves and a succession of curving, foot-high stems bearing many pendant bells of blue. Provide moist, leafy or peaty soil in semi-shade.

Oenothera

O. glober—A striking plant with erect, foot-high stems enveloped in round, blackish-red leaves. The summer-blossoming yellow flowers grow in clusters. Before opening they are enclosed in scarlet buds.

Phlox

P. ad surgens—Prostrate stems spread into tangled mats and support rounded flowers of different shades of pink. Prefers a cool, shaded position. Good in peat gardens. *P. douglasii*—A desireable cushion plant with flowers that range from white to dark-pink. *Kelseyi Rosette*—Prostrate, mat-forming leaves bear interesting flowers of lilac. Grows to two to three inches.

Prunella

Loveliness—Its longlasting lavender flowers are large. Used as a ground cover to border a rock garden. Has thick mat of leaves that weeds find hard to penetrate.

Thymus

T. citridorus—Useful, sun-loving, and smells like lemon. Grows into a neat, low bush.

Viola

V. cornuta alba—(Pyrenees) Mint-like leaves and five-petaled flowers of pure white. A wonderful garden plant.

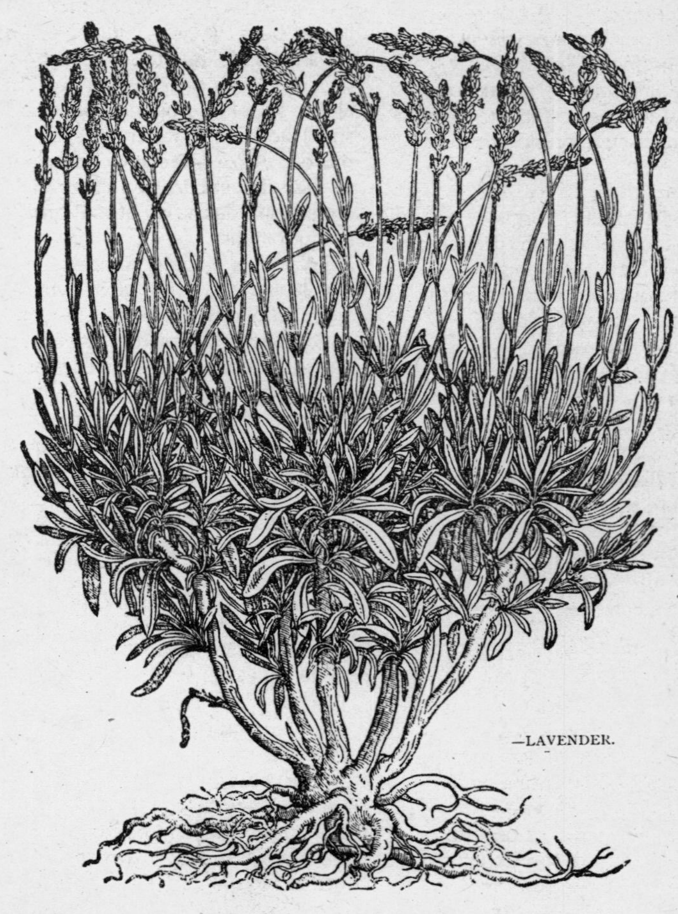

—LAVENDER.

Pusatilla

P. vulgaris—(Europe) Large, goblet-shaped flowers are purple inside, with golden stamens. The outside is paler, with a downy cover. Blooms in early spring, after which grow fine, fernlike leaves.

Raymonda

R. myconii—A flat rosette, six to eight inches across, of leaves that are spoon-shaped, hairy, and crinkly. The four-inch group of lavender flowers is reflexed and clear.

Salix

S. repens argentea—A dwarf willow carrying attractive yellow catkins. Excellent little garden shrub.

Sedum

S. cauticolum—(Japan) The large leaves are blue-gray, ending in big crimson flowers. Turns a lovely color in late summer and autumn. Happy in crevices.

ARRANGEMENT OF ROCKS.

Suppliers

Alpenglow Gardens
13328 King George Hwy.
Surrey, B.C., Canada V3T2T6

Far North Gardens
15621 Auburndale Ave.
Livonia, MI 48154

Lamb Nurseries
E. 101 Sharp Ave.
Spokane, WA 99202

Oliver Nurseries
1159 Bronson Rd.
Fairfield, CT 06430

Palette Gardens
Rare Plant Nursery
26 West Zion Hill Road
Quakertown, PA 18951

Powell's Gardens
Rt. 2, Hwy 70
Princeton, NC 27569

Rainer Mt. Alpine Gardens
2007 South 126th St.
Seattle, WA 98168

The Rock Garden
Hallowell Rd., RFD 2
Litchfield, ME 04350

Rocknoll Nursery
2210 U.S. 50
Hillsboro, OH 45133

Savory's Greenhouses
5300 Whiting Ave.
Edina, MN 55435

Siskiyou Rare Plant Nursery
522 Franquette St.
Medford, OR 97501

Alex J. Summers
14 I.U. Willetts Rd. W.
Roslyn, NY 11576

Sylvan Nursery
1028 Horseneck Rd.
South Westport, MA 02790

Thurman's Gardens
Route 2, Box 259
Spokane, WA 99207

Washfield Nurseries
Hawkhurst, Kent

The Wild Garden
Box 487
Bothell, WA 98011

Seashore Gardens

For gardens by the sea, you need plants that are tolerant of salt, sandy soil, and usually also of wind. *Pinus thunbergii*, Japanese black pine, is a good choice for a tree; an alternate is Russian olive (*Elaeagnus*).

Shrubs that thrive in oceanside environments are the lovely beach plum (*Prunus maritima*), *Rosa rugosa*, bayberry, and some holly—all with long-lasting fruit for color. Other choices include some of the heathers, cotoneasters (especially rockspray), and black chokeberry. But few shore gardens can do without junipers—common, Andorra, Sargent, Parson, or shore—which provide thick mats of evergreen as a background to other plantings and as a transition to wild dune grasses. Other choices are Mugho pine, some privets (such as California), blue spirea, fragrant sumac, and the beach primrose (*Oenothera humifusa*).

For ground cover and vines, the beautiful, light lavender Chinese wisteria (*Wisteria sinensis*) is hard to beat when it's in bloom, but bearberry, some honeysuckles, celastrus, and *Phlox subulata* are other possibilities.

Bulbs, especially iris, do well by the sea, as does sweet flag (*Acorus calamus*). Take advantage, too, of cat-tails, seaside goldenrod, Carolina sea-lavender, and other wild plants that grow nearby and that can provide a transition between your property and its surroundings. Sea oats and beadgrass (*Ammophila arenaria*) can be exceedingly attractive additions to your garden.

Shade Gardens

Plants that are shade-tolerant need varying amounts of shade. Many will survive with as much as three or four hours of sun a day, especially if they get early morning or late afternoon sun. Most grow with only an hour or two of direct sunlight, and some tolerate complete shade, such as indirect light received under overhangs or filtered through tree branches and other foliage above them.

For deep shade you are safest with plants that grow naturally in indirect light—ferns; orchids; bromeliads; evergreen ground covers such as periwinkle, Japanese spurge, wintercreeper, and galax; and low, flowering perennials such as leadwort and fragrant lily-of-the-valley. Climbers used to filtered light include several ivies, honeysuckle, Dutchman's pipe (*Aristolochia durier*), and Carolina yellow jessamine (*Gelsemium sempervirens*).

A surprisingly large number of flowering annuals and perennials tolerate shade or semi-shade—bulbs such as iris; fragrant plants such as star jasmine, flowering tobacco, violets, and primrose; aconitum, ajuga, alyssum, anemone, astilbe, begonia, browallia, calla, campanula, centaurea, coleus, cyclamen, digitalis, helleborus, hypericum, impatiens, lobelia, mignonette, mimulus, myosotis, paeonia, torenia, and tradescantia.

Deciduous shrubs that tolerate shade include glossy abelia, dogwood, privet, viburnum, redbud (*Cercis canadensis*), and Japanese barberry.

Among evergreen shrubs you have an even wider choice that includes boxwood, holly, mountain laurel, yellowroot, yew, *Fatsia japonica*, *Nandina domestica*, and *Aucuba japonica*. But the favorites remain azaleas, rhododendrons, and camellias.

Azaleas and Rhododendrons

Technically, azaleas belong to the genus *Rhododendron*; but this versatile genus is so adaptable to indoor and outdoor culture, so handy for landscaping, and so easy to grow, that a proliferation of hybrids have blurred distinctions. Well over 10,000 varieties of rhododendrons now exist, both deciduous and evergreen, with new ones named annually and older types bred to extend their ranges. You can find a rhododendron for almost any purpose, from dwarfs to spreading varieties to those that grow over ten feet tall. Flowers may be red, white, pink, lavender, yellow, or blue, and vary from delicate starlike blossoms to well-defined, robust formations. A few have brilliantly colored fall foliage or aromatic leaves.

Rhododendrons appreciate coolness (50 to 60°F or less), and while most varieties will not thrive or bloom well in warm climates, these plants are a boon to northern gardeners—*R. rupicola* and others tolerate temperatures to minus 15°. Most important is an acid soil (4.0 to 5.5 pH) with good drainage—most gardeners use peat moss. Generally, roots are so shallow that the root-ball top should be set at the soil surface to avoid smothering new growth when planting. Fertilizer once a month may be sufficient, but eliminate feedings during dormancy periods after blooming. Many need to be cut back. While in vigorous growth, rhododendrons tend to soak up large quantities of water, and they appreciate mulch. Good sun encourages flowering especially on the small-leaved varieties, but those native to ravines and other shaded locations tolerate dappled sites or places where shadow falls for several hours daily.

Camellias

Native to the Indochina mainland and islands offshore, camellias are unusually satisfying plants because their glossy dark-green foliage is beautiful year-round and their blooming periods are long—five to eight months, depending on the variety. Moreover they require very little care and can be grown outdoors, or in cool greenhouess or home interiors.

Plant them in a mix of two parts loam, one part peat moss, and one part sand, with a pH of 5.0 to 5.5 Be sure the soil drains well, because camellias like plenty of water—you may have to soak the soil as frequently as every other day during the active growing period to keep the earth from drying out. Mist daily in summer and every other day in cool weather; they like a humidity of 50 to 60%. Bud drop is usually due to too-dry air or insufficient watering. Outdoors, camellias like dappled shade and do well under trees; indoors, they need good light with about three hours of sun daily.

Vital to camellias is that they be grown cool. Preferably, temperatures should be between 42 and 45°F at night (though they will bloom at up to 55°) and no more than 60°F in the day. Good air circulation is also vital and will discourage attacks by scale, mealybugs, or other pests. With coolness and circulating air, you should have no problems with camellias. These are slow-growers that require little or no pruning unless you want to control size—most varieties eventually grow three to four feet. Unless you wish extra-large flowers, you need not debud. You can propagate from seed (though it takes five years or more to produce a flowering plant), cuttings taken in fall from new growth, or by layering or grafting.

Most nurseries carry *C. japonica* (the most hardy, with white, pink, or red blooms) and *C. sasanqua* (almost as hardy, with pink or red flowers, some fragrant). Depending on the variety, they bloom from October through spring. Some nurseries carry *C. reticulata*, which can be grown outdoors in warm climates (such as Southern California) but otherwise requires winter protection.

Water Gardens

For centuries water has been incorporated into gardens in a variety of means and forms. Large and small ponds, fountains surrounded by statues, streams with waterfalls, tiled pools in strict symmetry, birdbaths, and outdoor baths for humans are just a few of the innumerable variations. The sight and sound of water is one of the most aesthetically pleasing things to be found in nature. So it is not surprising that builders of the world's best gardens have commonly gone to great expense and effort to include water, if not make it their garden's central feature.

During medieval times, monasteries usually had cisterns for fresh water in their gardens, frequently decorated with ornamental fountains, and often fishponds (though sometimes fish were cultivated in a moat surrounding the grounds). Until the sixteenth century, ponds were usually decorated, if at all, with either animal statues or sundials. England's King Henry VIII had ponds at Hampton Court, for instance, which were surrounded by statues of dragons, tigers, greyhounds, and badgers. Henry employed laborers to work during the night to ladle water from the Thames into his ponds so they would be full for his enjoyment during the day.

—Water-Poppy (*Lymnocharis Humboldtii*)

By Elizabethan times, a fountain in the garden was almost mandatory. Underground pipes were installed to supply the fountain when a convenient source of water existed. Otherwise, the water was transported in large jars and stored near the fountain so it could be replenished as needed. Francis Bacon considered fountains superior to ponds. He wrote that ponds marred a garden because they were "unwholesome and full of flies and frogs." He liked fountains that sprayed or spouted water, and especially if they were ornamented with gilt or marble statues. He merely tolerated pools, and only if they were free of "fish, slime, or mud." Despite Bacon's liking for ponds paved with colorful tile, most ponds of his day were simply cut into the soil and surrounded only by turf—used to raise fish for food rather than as a form of decoration.

The fountains of the rich were quite another matter. These were a luxury for enjoyment and playfulness, and were occasionally large enough for bathing. The sixteenth-century fountain at Hampton Court was prized not only for its massive size, but also for hidden devices that allowed those "in the know" to spray unwary visitors with water. Queen Elizabeth had a fountain built in 1590 for just that purpose. Fountains of this period were also used to create a spray over garden sculpture, such as statues of Diana and other Greek figures. Sometimes, however, water displays were combined with statues in the center of the pond in an effort to create an aquatic theme. The shape of these ponds was, without variation, rigidly geometric, having clearly delineated perimeters.

By the seventeenth century, the waterworks mania had reached its zenith. Spraying unsuspecting spectators was still popular, but now even exotic entertainment was expected. In one garden, water was piped throughout a willow tree so that it could be made to rain at will "from each leaf." Other fountains moved clocks and struck the hours, or played tunes on chimes.

Later, during the naturalistic period, marble basins, decorated fountains, and straight canals were abandoned. Instead, miniature waterfalls tumbled over rocks, natural looking lakes were created, and streams were made to wind and eddy. One nobleman who visited an early example of the new style in gardening could not believe his eyes. As he looked over the meandering stream he did not for a moment consider that it had been purposefully constructed, and attributed the design to its owner's frugality. For only a little more money, he lamented, the owner could have had a nice straight brook!

Today we benefit from our ancestors' experiments with water gardens, as well as from advances of modern technology. We are not only free to choose from the many styles and forms that have evolved over the centuries; we are able to include water in our gardens at far less expense and with far greater ease than gardeners in past times.

The first decision is whether the water will be still or running. Both have advantages, but your central concern should be to create a harmony between the style of your garden and the water element you intend to use.

Still-water pools and ponds provide a variety of pleasing effects—the reflective quality being foremost. Reflections created by standing water are very relaxing, and lend a contemplative aspect to the garden. If this is your aim, you will want the water to be as still as possible. Since small pools are less subject to water turbulence than large ponds, having limited space is not a disadvantage. The Japanese have mastered many beautiful techniques to create small ponds. An effective pool need be only two or three inches deep and can be any dimension you please—a small basin or pot, surrounded with attractive plantings to scale, will do.

Goldfish are an attractive addition, and they usually compound the contemplative quality of a still pool. Depending on the light and the angle at which it hits the surface, you will sometimes see the fish, and sometimes they disappear into reflecting light.

A foot or two below eye-level is the best location for achieving the greatest reflective effect in a still pool. Also, consider the possibility of tiling your pool. Nowadays many beautiful tile patterns and colors are available at relatively low cost.

In a still-water pond you can control the amount of reflection by the color you paint the water receptacle. The greatest reflective effect is achieved by painting the receptacle black. This duplicates the conditions you find in southern swamps, where the water is almost mirrorlike. Plantings surrounding this type of pond will seem doubly large. For less reflective quality, use paint of decreasingly light shades of blue or green. You might even want to experiment by changing the color of your receptacle once a year. With enough space you can have a large pond, even one for fishing or swimming or drifting in a small boat. Ponds outfitted with pumps and filters can also be reservoirs for water to be used for the garden and the house. The USDA will help you engineer your pond, and will stock it with fish for you—free of charge.

—East India Lotus

It is virtually impossible to name all the possible variations of form and style possible when you introduce running water into your garden. Perhaps you will want only a simple wall fountain with a single dribbling spigot, to break up a long stretch of wall. Or, if you have a larger area to fill, a more elaborate fountain could be just the thing.

What kind of sound do you want to create? Apparatus can be bought that will trickle, rush, spray, or sprinkle water with just about any degree of force. Of course, space will, to

some degree, determine the possible variations you can employ. But with a little ingenuity, a surprising amount of variation can be achieved. For example, you might have a spot at the end of your garden path that is three feet square. Here you could conceivably recreate the sound of a quietly babbling brook, a small but audible waterfall, or the trickle of a mountain spring.

If you have a formal or semi-formal garden, you can use a traditional spigot—such as a fish with water flowing from its mouth, or a cherub with a tilted urn—and a scallop-shelled basin. In a naturalistic setting, you would want the spigot to be hidden among rocks and ferns or mosses, and the basin formed of rough, hollowed-out rocks.

Give advance thought to the direction of the prevailing wind and the plantings situated around the fountain. You may want to grow particularly thirsty plants on the downwind side of the fountain, where drier plants could drown.

If you are lucky enough to have a natural brook or stream on your property, the possibilities for variation of water usage are almost endless. Of course, it may suit you to simply leave the stream as it is. But you can usually divert part of the water closer to where you would like it without adversely affecting the natural balance. You can design a fountain that uses only gravity to force the flow of water. Or, you might want a waterfall, perhaps several small ones.

No matter what size or form of water garden you are contemplating, visit one of America's great water gardens, such as Longue Vue Gardens in New Orleans, to examine an array of water-garden styles and techniques. The professionally designed arrangements not only give you an idea of how to use water itself, but also of how to use plants as complements. If for convenience in construction you end up with a square or round pool, for instance, you can use plants along the perimeters and in the water to soften the severe outlines of the pool.

Most popular of all aquatic plants are water lilies, which grow best where the water is two to four feet deep. (They can, however, be grown in containers if the soil is kept sufficiently moist.) Most bloom from early summer until the first frost if given plenty of sun. Flowers of tropical varieties (many of which are fragrant) open in the evening; flowers of hardy varieties open during strong daylight. The underwater root systems spread quickly, so if you want to contain these plants, confine them in containers of wood or plastic.

American lotus (*Nelumbo lutea*) has leaves up to two feet across and flowers up to six inches across, so it is suitable only for large ponds. It occurs in the wild in southern states. Almost as large is the yellow pond-lily (*Nuphar advena*), a hardy type that thrives almost to the Canadian border. *Nymphaea* are smaller, suitable for tiny pools with water only a foot deep, and *N. odorata* is fragrant; these are hardy, thriving into Ontario and Manitoba.

Plant water lilies in a box about a foot square and a foot deep filled with a mix of three parts loam and one part well-decayed manure plus a handful or two of general purpose fertilizer. Plant the lily root one to three inches deep, depending on its size—you may have to place a rock on it to hold it in place—and lower the box into the water so that the root is three inches below the water surface. (As large lilies grow, you may have to lower the box later, an inch or so at a time.) Large lilies should be placed about three feet apart.

In northern climates, put a log into the pool in winter to absorb the impact as ice expands and contracts. Also, lower the planting box to the pool so that the root crowns will be below the ice line. If you have a shallow pool, remove the lily box to a cool place, such as a cellar, and keep the soil moist. Beware of rodents—muskrat eat lily roots in ponds and mice eat roots of lilies brought indoors.

White Water Lillie.

Small Pondweed.

The arum family also offers aquatic plants. Golden club (*Orontium aquaticum*), named for golden flower clusters, is a small, dark-foliaged species adapted from Florida to temperate zones. Arrow arum (*Peltandra*) has arrow-shaped leaves, grows from Florida to Michigan, and is one of the few water plants not given to spreading. Hardier still, found into Alberta, is the calla lily (*Calla*), with white flowers followed by bright red fruit. The pickleweed (*Pontederia*), growing from Florida well into Canada, is another possibility. Other water plants you might consider are bladderworts (*Utricularia*), water lobelia, and floating marsh marigolds.

Along the edges of your pond, or in any boggy area of your property, you have a wide choice of plants that love marsh or bog. Included are isis, forget-me-not, some asters, swamp buttercup, many lilies, sundew, violets, many ferns, many carniverous plants, a number of orchids, some gentians, *Lobelia cardinalis*, several mints, many figworts, and jack-in-the-pulpit and other arums.

Yellow Water Lillie.

Small Frogs-Lettuce.

Suppliers

Beefork Water Gardens
Rt 1, Bon 115
Bunker, MO 63629

Lilypons Water Gardens
1612 Hort Rd.
Lilypons, MD 21717
also in: Brookeshire, TX 77423

Paradise Gardens
14 Mary St.
Whitman, MA 02382

William Tricker, Inc.
74 Allendale Ave., P.O. Box 398
Saddle River, NJ 07548

William Tricker, Inc.
7125 Tanglewood Drive
P.O. Box 7843
Independence, OH 44131

Van Ness Water Gardens
2460 North Euclid Ave.
Upland, CA 91786

Ranunculus aquatilis.
Water Crow-foot.

Viola Palustris tenuifolia.
The smaller leaued water violet.

Water Caltrops.

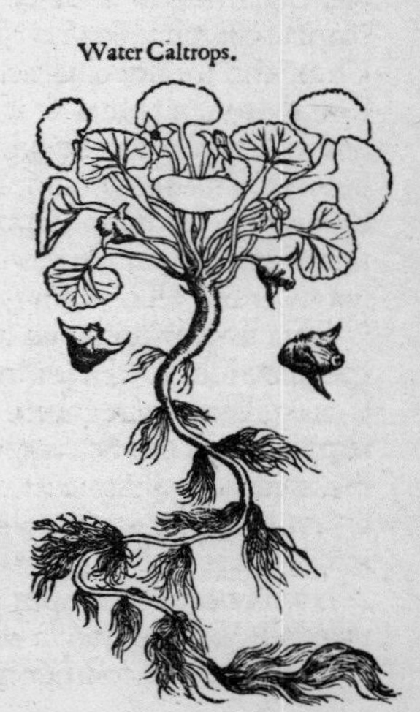

Wildflower Gardens

Because wildflowers are just that—wild—and thrive without the assistance of a gardener's careful hand, it would seem that nothing could be easier to cultivate than a wildflower garden. However, this is far from the truth. Actually, wildflowers are very sensitive, surviving on a delicate balance of several complex factors. If a particular wildflower abundantly inhabits a specific area along a country road or mountain trail, it is because all the cultural factors necessary to that flower's growth exist in ideal proportions. Because of this prerequisite for ideal environmental conditions, growing wildflowers is entirely different from growing more common, hybridized garden plants. You must be alert to a variety of minute details such as the amount of moisture present during the flowering period as opposed to moisture present at other times. But if the wildflower garden requires more attention than ordinary gardens, it also affords more satisfaction to the true nature-loving gardener. Indeed, few gardens are more aesthetically pleasing than a well-planned wildflower garden.

Of the two different approaches to growing a wildflower garden, one is called the *artificial approach*. An artificial wildflower garden is comprised of species that are not native to the area, but that are adaptable to your area's conditions. For example, an artificial wildflower garden in southern California may be comprised of plants native to Texas, New Mexico, Utah, and Idaho. The advantage to this approach is that you can choose among many varying types of wildflowers. The second approach is called the *restoration approach*. In this case you attempt to restore in your garden all of many of the wildflowers originally native to your specific area. Although this approach is more limiting in choice of types of plants, it has the advantage that once these native wildflowers are established they will require very little maintenance.

No matter which approach you use, start by accurately determining the general environmental conditions of your area, as well as the specific variations peculiar to your garden. In addition to assessing temperature range, average amounts of sunlight and rainfall, and the pH level of your soil, consider details like whether the trees on your property are deciduous, coniferous, or a combination of both. Success will ultimately depend on your ability to evaluate all the various factors necessary to your plants' growth.

The easiest and best way to determine the kinds of wildflowers that will grow easily in your area is to examine the existing native vegetation. Native plants will provide you with clues about general conditions that prevail, so you can apply these to non-native species with similar requirements. Also, native plants may help you to discover species that are environmentally capable of thriving in your region but that for some reason do not grow there naturally.

Soil: It is vital to know what kind of trees are naturally associated with your specific wildflowers, because different tree leaves have different pH levels. The soil in your wildflower garden must have the proper pH level for the particular varieties of flowers you choose. The level of organic matter is also important, since most wildflowers are used to naturally rich soil. You can mock this natural organic process accurately enough to ensure a successful garden by starting a leafmold pile and a compost heap, and by making regular applications of the mold and compost to your soil. Most wildflowers grow better with an occasional sprinkling of bone meal, and with mulching.

If yours is a restoration garden, you will, of course, not have to worry about watering. But an artificial garden will probably require watering during the summer, especially if it includes woodland wildflowers, the most common kind. Heavy watering will be necessary if you grow woodland plants on a slope, where fast drainage keeps the ground dry. In this case, consider an underground watering system as part of your plan.

Because most wildflowers are native to heavily wooded areas, they need full or partial shade either year-round or during specific seasonal periods. For example, hepaticas require dappled sunlight during their flowering period, but otherwise prefer full shade. If the appropriate shade trees are not on your property, you can improvise a simple shading structure of crosshatched wood laths.

Seed is the most common method of propagation. But certain wildflowers are easier to start by cuttings, division, layering, or spores.

Should you buy your plants or collect them from the wild? Buying is perhaps safest, both for the natural landscape and for succeeding with wildflowers in your garden. Most nurseries carry a variety of wildflower seeds from which to choose. But collecting wildflowers to transplant to your garden can be rewarding, as long as you are conscientious about not taking species that are scarce and about not upsetting the ecological balance. Also, learn in advance which wildflowers are impossible to successfully transplant, for many fall into that category. A book to get you started is *Handbook of Wild Flower Cultivation* by Kathryn S. Taylor and Stephen F. Hamblin (New York: Macmillan, 1963).

The following list includes common wildflowers that are easy-to-grow and widely available at local nurseries or through mail order.

Aster
American bugbane
Black-eyed Susan
Bluebeard lily
Blue flax
Butterfly flower
California poppy
Canada lily
Chicory
Clarkia
Columbine
Coreopsis
Daisy
Dutchman's breeches
False spikenard
Fireweed
Forget-me-not
Foxglove
Godetia
Goldfields
Indian paintbrush
Linaria
Lupine
Mallow
Merrybells
Moneywort
Mullein
Nodding trillium
Ox-eye daisy
Ozark trillium
Painted trillium
Penstemon
Quaking grass
Queen-Anne's lace
Saint John's wort
Siberian wallflower
Silverweed
Starflower
Teasel
Tidytips
Violet
Wood anemone
Yarrow
Yellow stargrass

Wildflower and Hardy Perennial Suppliers

Abundant Life Seed Foundation
P.O. Box 772
Port Townsend, WA 98368

Arthur Eames Allgrove
North Wilmington, MA 01887

Alpenglow Gardens
13328 King George Hwy
North Surrey, B.C.
Canada V3T 2T6

Applewood Seed Company
P.O. Box 4000
Golden, CO 80401

Fern Hill Farm
Rt. 3, Box 191
Greenville, AL 36307

Gardens of the Blue Ridge
P.O. Box 10
Rt. 221
Pineola, NC 28862

Henderson's Botanical Gardens
Rt. 6
Greensburg, IN

Illini Gardens
P.O. Box 125
Oakford, IL 62673

Mellinger's, Inc.
2310 W. South Range Rd.
North Lima, OH 61072

Midwest Flowers
Box 64
Rockton, IL 61072

The Naturalists
P.O. Box 435
Yorktown Heights, NY 10598

Plants of the Southwest
Building E15, Plaza de Comercio
1570 Pacheco St.
Sante Fe, NM 87501

Putney Nursery, Inc.
Putney, VT 05346

Clyde Robin
P.O. Box 2855
Castro Valley, CA 94546

The Rock Garden
R.F.D. No. 2
Litchville, ME 04350

The Shop in the Sierra
Box 1
Midpines, CA 95345

Francis M. Sinclair
RFD 1, New Fields Rd.
Exeter, NH 03833

Siskiyou Rare Plant Nursery
522 Franquette St.
Medford, OR 97501

Sperka's Woodland Acres Nursery
R 2
Crivitiz, WI 54114

Sunny Borde Nurseries Inc.
Kinsington, CT 06037

Vick's Wild Gardens
Gladwyne, PA 19035

The Wild Garden
Box 489
Bothell, WA 98011

14

The Gardener's World

Attracting Birds and Animals

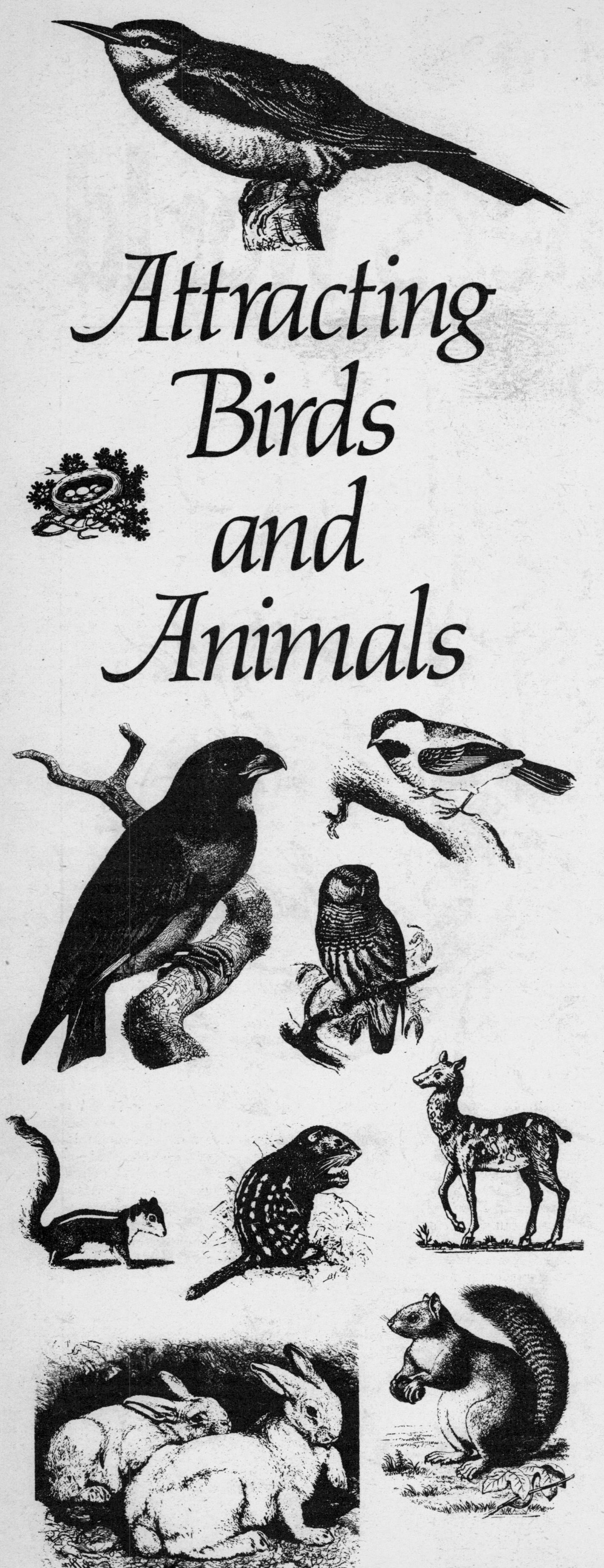

Your garden can be a miniature wildlife sanctuary if you plan it to serve birds and animals as well as family needs. The size or location doesn't matter. What matters is how well you fulfill the needs of wildlife in your particular area for food, water, and shelter (not any one, but all three needs).

Food is the easiest. By landscaping with plants that provide food for animals and birds, you encourage wildlife without having to work at it. With forethought, you can supply year-round provisions by selecting plants that overlap in fruiting times. You can also supplement vegetation with store-bought food placed at a feeding station. Before embarking on a food-supplement feeding program, though, consider whether you will be able to continue it on a regular and permanent basis. Bird and animal feeders extend the range of species and the numbers that would normally be in your locality. Birds, especially in winter, will become dependent on you for food—they are apt to starve to death if you are away or otherwise unable to supply the feeder.

Water is also easy to provide—a saucer on a windowsill, or a basin, birdbath, or fountain in a small garden. You'll get the widest variety of wildlife, though, if you have space for a pool.

Shelter is the trickiest. For some creatures, it's easy to set up proper conditions. A toad may be happy in an inverted clay pot, with a little door broken into the side, hidden under evergreen shrubs, plus a pan of water in which to sit (toads drink through their skins). For many birds and larger animals, dense growth (hedges, thorny tangles) spells security. For winter you will need a species such as red cedar (*Juniperus virginiana*) that has dense foliage and fruit from September to May, or any one of the junipers, cedars, yews, and other evergreens with similar characteristics.

Although feeding and watering areas should be backed by dense vegetation to provide refuse, a stretch of lawn gives you a view of the wildlife from your terrace and windows, and encourages species that hunt for grubs or other food in open areas. Edges or borders—that is, open areas surrounded by shrubs and trees—attract the greatest numbers and varieties of wildlife to the smallest amount of land. On a small property, design at least one open area; on large wooded properties, consider creating several clearings.

The National Wildlife Federation (1412 16th Street, NW, Washington, DC 20036) has a Backyard Wildlife Habitat Program that will advise you on plantings and designs for attracting a maximum variety of wildlife. So will your local Audubon Society chapter (to get the address, write National Audubon Society, 950 Third Avenue, New York, NY 10022).

For identifying birds, Roger Tory Peterson's *A Field Guide to the Birds* (Boston: Houghton Mifflin; 1980) is tops. *Watching Birds, An Introduction to Ornithology* by Roger F. Pasquier (Boston: Houghton Mifflin; 1977) will give you an understanding of bird behavior. *A Complete Guide to Bird Feeding* by John V. Dennis (New York: Knopf; 1975), *The New Handbook of Attracting Birds* by Thomas P. McElroy (New York: Knopf; 1960), and *Hummingbirds and Their Flowers* by Karen A. and Verne Grant (New York: Columbia University Press; 1968) are standard works. For animals, butterflies, and other garden visitors, the Peterson Field Guide series (Houghton Mifflin) or the Audubon Society field guides (Knopf) are excellent.

Plantings

Try to landscape with plants that supply not only cover and reproductive areas but also food. Examples of large trees that produce nuts, acorns, or seeds are beech, oak (loved by warblers), maples, pine, pecan; smaller trees include dogwood, olive, cherry, crabapple, serviceberry, palmetto, mesquite. Though deciduous trees are in leaf during the nesting season of most birds, evergreens are necessary for early-nesting owls, for winter birds and nonhibernating animals, and for attracting species (such as some warblers) that simply prefer evergreens. Even dead trees will attract woodpeckers, and old tree cavities serve as dens for animals.

For most wildlife, shrubs are more important than trees. Choose shrubs that serve more than one purpose and that fruit in succession. Crabapple, some dogwood, mulberries, honeysuckle, and hawthorn flower and fruit for nestlings by June. For summer feeding of fledgeling birds and young animals, try grapes, wild plum, blueberries, blackberries, and other berries; and for late summer into fall, crabapple, autumn olive, pokeberries (thrushes love these), cherries (vireos and warblers like black cherry). In late fall, hawthorn, firethorn, viburnum, rhododendron are good choices. Look especially for plants with long-lasting fall fruit such as holly, Japanese barberry, bayberry, and Russian olive; in the Southwest, algerita, manzanita, madrone, lote bush, and prickly pear are suitable; in the Northwest, madrone and bitterbrush are excellent. Sumacs are fine in almost any region.

Flowers that produce seed—such as black-eyed susans and chrysanthemums—provide winter food for seed-eating birds and small mammals. Even grasses, groundcovers, and food crops (millet, corn, grain sorghum) can help your wildlife habitat—lupines (attract Western bluebirds), ferns, panicgrass, sunflower, and timothy are examples.

Bird Feeders

Since some birds are ground-feeders, and others feed at a height, installing several types of feeders and providing several types of bird food will encourage the greatest number of birds.

The simplest feeder is a tray set on a pole five to six feet off the ground or placed on a windowsill. A square or rectangle three or four feet long is a good size, and it should have rims to keep the food from blowing away. (A break in the corners of the rim will make the tray easier to clean.) If at all possible, the feeder should have a sloping roof to keep off rain and snow and to provide shelter.

Where squirrels are a problem, the feeder should be on a metal pole and have an inverted cone or sleeve at least 18 inches off the ground; the feeder should also not be placed under trees where squirrels can leap to it.

The disadvantage of a tray is that it may be used by pigeons and other large birds. Try inserting upright dowels at regular intervals to keep out the larger species. You can also buy hanging feeders made especially for small clinging and perching birds.

Feeders should be placed in the open where they will be sheltered from wind and from too much direct sun. They should be near bushes for refuge and should have holes in the bottom or some other form of drainage to keep the food supply dry. If you are constructing your own, avoid thread or light string in which birds can become entangled, sharp edges, and metal projections.

For ground-feeding birds, select an open, windless spot several feet from shrubbery—close enough for shelter but not so close as to provide cover for cats. You can scatter the food on the ground or keep it in a shallow basket or a tray with holes punched in the bottom for drainage.

Wild bird seed, a commercially prepackaged mixture, is widely available in supermarkets, hardware stores, garden centers, and through the Audubon Society and some conservation groups. These convenient mixes are usually based on sunflower seeds and cracked corn but may contain a number of other ingredients. The contents are often calculated to attract a large variety of species. For large-scale feeding, you may find it cheaper to mix your own or to buy only those ingredients best suited to the particular birds you want to attract.

Sunflower seeds are popular with a wide variety of seed-eating birds, including sparrows, finches, titmice, grosbeaks, nuthatches, pine siskin, jays, and cardinals. Sometimes insect-eating birds are tempted too. Since these seeds are cheapest in large sacks (say, 50 lbs or more), share a sack with other bird lovers in your neighborhood. *Thistle seed* also attracts seed-eaters.

Cracked corn, excellent for ground-feeding birds such as quails, pheasants, and towhees, will also be eaten by other birds. Cracked corn is often cheaper at feed stores in large sacks (25 lbs or more); but check the ingredients, because some chickenfeed contains seeds that wild birds will not eat. A paste of ground cornmeal and peanut butter—with or without cracked corn, sunflower seeds, raisins, suet, or other additions—is good for attracting winter birds.

Nutmeats are enjoyed by many birds but only those with strong bills—jays, nutcrackers—are able to hammer shells open. Shell and chop the nuts to entice a wider variety of birds.

Suet, or beef fat, hung in a string bag, is a sure way to attract woodpeckers, chickadees, titmice, nuthatches, brown creepers, jays, orioles, kinglets, yellow-rumped warblers, and other wintering birds. In cool weather, suet substitutes for the insects birds eat at other times of year. Bacon and other fats can also be used, but they do not remain as firm as suet in the sun or at mild temperatures. To make suet even firmer, melt it to a liquid, cool it, and then melt it again; let it harden in the refrigerator in small dishes or cupcake tins that will yield small cakes. You can add cornmeal, flour, peanut butter, sugar, nutmeats, raisins, or a combination; but don't bother adding seeds—suet eaters are generally not seed-eating birds.

Some butchers sell suet already packaged in string bags or baskets. If you make your own, use heavy cord to enable birds to get a firm grip with their feet. Hang the suet basket from a tree limb, clothesline, or an overhang so that animals cannot raid it.

Syrup is a specialty for hummingbirds; and since these hover rather than perch to eat, you must supply the syrup in a feeding tube. In the East, only the ruby-throated hummingbird occurs, but the Southwest has more than a dozen species.

Hummingbirds favor red, tubular flowers, and the best way to get their attention is to plant red or orange trumpet-shaped flowers (petunias, morning glories, scarlet sage, etc.) in your garden or in containers. If you hang your feeding tube among such flowers at first, you can later move the tube elsewhere on your grounds and the birds will continue to visit it. Without flowers, attract hummingbirds by using anything red—tape an artificial red flower to the feeding tube; paint the tube red; color the syrup red; or tie a red ribbon around the mouth of the tube. You can buy hummingbird feeders, but any plastic or glass pill vial, or a test tube, will do. Twist thin wire around the lip and hang the tube—at a tilt—from a tree limb, shrub, trellis, pole, house post, or any other support.

To make hummingbird syrup, boil one part sugar and two parts water, or one part honey and three parts water, for about two minutes. Allow the mix to cool, and then fill the feeding tube. Keep the extra syrup in the refrigerator. Hummingbirds eat twice their weight in nectar daily, so you may have to refill the tube rather quickly—their bills generally penetrate less than an inch into the tube. To keep the syrup clean, rub salad oil on the tube to prevent insects from getting a foothold.

Incidentally, although adult hummingbirds drink nectar, they feed insects to their young, and are therefore effective in ridding your garden of pests.

Other foods that will attract birds are:

1. Peanut butter—but birds, like people, can choke on it. Always mix it with suet, cornmeal, or something else.
2. Fresh fruits such as a cut-up apple, orange, or banana will attract a few birds, especially tropical varieties; bluebirds and many others enjoy berries.
3. Dried raisins, currants, figs, and dates—especially if softened.
4. Grains will bring not only grain-eaters but many insect-eaters as well. Crumple stale bread, cookies, or doughnuts, or scatter dry cereals.
5. Leftovers are always worth a try. Birds have been known to feast on meat scraps, cheese, even dog food.
6. Many birds obtain minerals from ground egg shells, crushed oyyster or clam shells, or sand. And since birds have no teeth, they frequently swallow fine gravel or sand to help them grind up hard and bulky foods. Offer grit in hanging feeders or on the ground; grind up your own shells or buy packaged grit in pet shops and in farm stores that supply poultry farmers.

Water

Birds not attracted to feeding stations may be enticed by a birdbath. Most species bathe in late afternoon, but in hot weather birds may bathe frequently and at any hour. Because birds cannot fly with wet wings, they prefer a bath in the sun; and because they do a lot of grooming after bathing, an ideal bath is close to trees and shrubs for perching. One under trees that is reached by late-afternoon sun is perfect. A birdbath raised on a pedestal or post will attract some species (and is a good idea where cats are a problem), but a pool at ground level will attract the greatest variety of birds as well as animals.

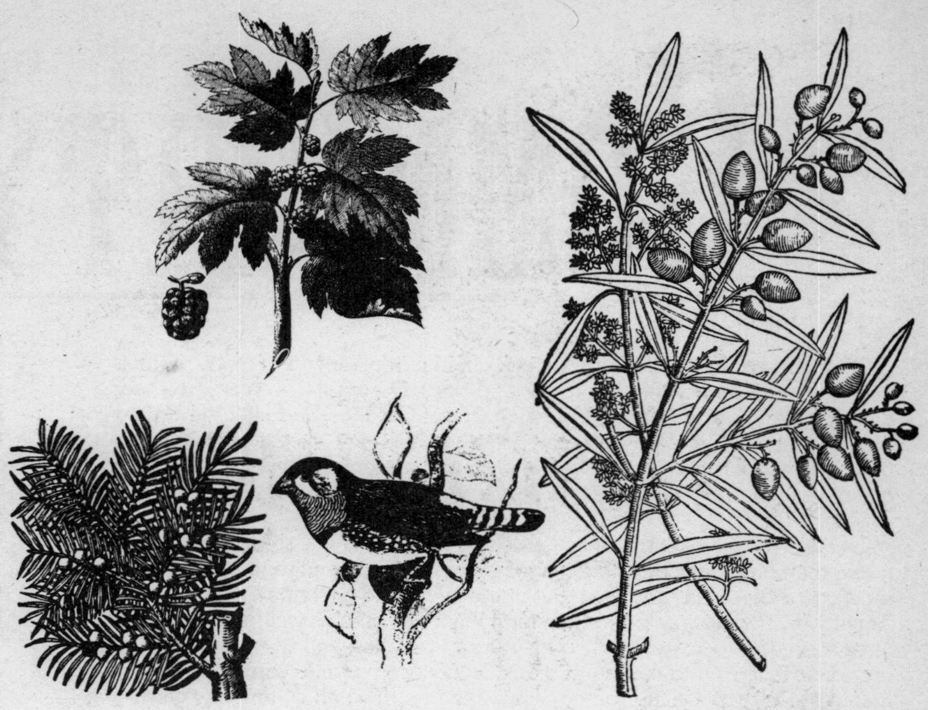

Birds like the sound of water, so let water drip slowly into the bath from a fountain; from a garden hose supported on a frame; or from a suspended pail with a hole punched in the bottom. Some birds—including hummingbirds, warblers, orioles, grosbeaks, tanagers, and thrushes—prefer to bathe in spray. For these, hook up a spraying fountain or use a lawn sprinkler or a garden hose with a spray nozzle.

The bath should be about three inches deep in the center for large species and taper at the rims or at one end to be no more than an inch deep for small birds. Birds like a firm footing, so the surface of the basin should be rough to keep them from slipping. If you are making your own basin, concrete with aggregates is ideal. Even if you cannot provide ideal conditions, any shallow dish or other container will attract some birds; a layer of gravel or small stones will help them get a footing.

Try to keep your pool open year-round. A drop of glycerine will keep water from freezing in a small birdbath, and antifreeze devices and livestock trough warmers are available for larger pools. Putting a mirror in the bottom will help draw heat from the sun.

Some birds bathe in dust. Scatter ash, sand, or powdery soil a few inches deep and a yard or so across in the sun for these.

Birdhouses

Many species will use a birdhouse for roosting or shelter against rain but disdain artificial housing and have their own ideas about what constitues a proper nest. Some birds demand woven nests at particular heights and in particular shapes; others nest in open ground, in underground tunnels, or in other places of their choosing. For these, try providing the raw materials for a nest at the proper season. By creating a mud pile, you can watch barn swallows cart off the mud for their nests; a pile of twigs, yarn and string (neither more than six inches long), dog hair, or soft chicken feathers may be accepted by some birds in nesting season. A few species, such as the Eastern phoebe, nest in garages or under eaves with no encouragement at all.

Candidates for your birdhouse are birds that nest in holes. Normally, hole-nesters use tree cavities or holes bored by woodpeckers; but with the decline of natural forest and woodpeckers, good holes are scarce. Many species will accept your birdhouse provided it is of proper design.

The usual design is deeper than wide, with an entry hole near the top, and with a roof that is hinged for cleaning and sloped to keep out rain and snow. But the floor area should vary from 10 × 10 inches for a wood duck to 4 × 4 inches for a house wren; and an osprey platform should be six feet in diameter and raised on a pole thirty feet tall. A hole 1⅛ inch in diameter usually excludes starlings and house sparrows, yet these will also be discouraged if you build a bluebird box with a 1½-inch hole on a post three to four feet off the ground at the edge of an open field. Purple martins—terrific insect-eaters—demand apartment-style dwellings, but might inspect a perfectly constructed house for several years before occupying it. So, before buying or building a birdhouse, learn the nesting requirements of species in your area—depth of birdhouse interior, height from ground, nesting shelves, and other needs.

COMMUNITY GARDENS

Since the turn of the century, several different forms of community gardens have sprouted up in American towns and cities. During World War I, we had Liberty Gardens, during the Depression, Relief Gardens, and after the United States entered World War II, Victory Gardens. With few exceptions, once the patriotic need for them ended, the community gardens of the 1940s vanished, and it was not until the 1970s that people again began to cooperate by making gardens.

The latest wave of community gardening began as a grassroots movement, rather than a patriotic one encouraged by national authorities. It developed mostly in urban areas and grew out of the increasing environmental awareness of Americans. People wanted to humanize the inner cities as well as once again to have fresh, unprocessed food on their tables. Inflation and unemployment added economic incentive to the raison d'être of most community-gardening programs that exist today. A Gallup survey during the 1970s, when community gardening began to spread on a wide scale, showed that the main reason for starting a garden is economic—to save money. Although the potential yield of a garden plot varies according to many factors, Gardens for All, Inc., estimates that a careful gardener can produce $250 worth of vegetables with about ten dollars worth of seed. Put another way, the typical 25 × 30 plot can grow about three hundred dollars worth of produce.

For urban dwellers living in a forest of concrete with very little greenery to relieve the monotony, the practice of gardening—preparing the soil, tending vegetables and flowers, and harvesting a crop—offers extra satisfaction because it reconnects the city gardener with nature in his or her daily life. In addition, working with neighbors on a garden plot provides a relaxing recreation that draws upon one's creative abilities while also being a social pastime. And, of course, farm fresh vegetables on the table bring improved nutrition.

Besides brightening up neighborhoods, community gardens lift people's spirits. This is especially true for neighborhoods that have begun to deteriorate and whose residents have become despondent about their environments. Such environments can be turned around when unsightly, rubble-filled vacant lots are revitalized with vegetables, flowers, and the presence of people of all ages enjoying themselves. Not only do these urban gardens produce food, they can reunify a community by giving neighbors a renewed "sense of place."

Depending on the aspirations of their organizers, community gardens take many sizes, shapes, and types. They can be informal, that is, in a nearby vacant lot and governed by the participants; or they can be administered in a more formal way, for instance, by a civic agency, apartment complex, or company committee. When an outside "authority" is involved, individual gardeners often exercise less control over the group policy on methods of soil preparations, weed and pest management, and the use of fertilizers, and so on, but they may spend less time fund-raising, doing heavy work, and tending to administrative matters.

Getting Started

Successful community gardening groups have two characteristics in common: They are well organized and well planned. Enthusiasm alone isn't enough to carry people through when it comes to nitty gritty work like negotiating a lease, buying tools and preparing soil, teaching novices, or raising money. If a group gets too organized in the beginning and plans who is to do what when and how, that group, regardless of its size or administrative setup, has a good chance of weathering inevitable problems, be they financial, interpersonal, legal, or horticultural.

Initial planning and organizing, which must begin long before anyone puts a seed in the earth, can be broken down into general steps, although every new group has needs particular to its situation that must also be met.

1. Get a sponsor. Typical sponsors are churches, block associations, tenant groups, senior citizen organizations, and businesses.
2. Get the land. Land is usually donated, loaned, or leased by private owners, city park departments, schools, churches, housing developments, companies. What kind of garden does the group want: on a vacant lot, on the grounds of an apartment complex or park, on land adjacent to a business? Will the garden be supported by individuals or will funds be raised outside the gardening group?
3. Discuss the aspirations of each garden member.
4. Establish the scope and purpose of the garden. Write down what group members decide to serve as the guiding principles.
5. Work with resource people and organizations. Several kinds of organizations may be willing to help with gardening advice, equipment and seeds, or financial support—out of sheer generosity or for community-relations purposes.

Local garden supply centers, retailers, banks, greenhouses and nurseries, country agricultural extension agents, and horticultural societies are among the resources to cultivate.

6. Decide how much time members should put into the project. Talk over the adjustments each person will need to make in his or her schedule to meet gardening committments.

7. Determine how many people will work on which plots during the first season.

8. Set geographical residency requirements for participants.

9. Make a tentative, yet detailed, gardening calendar, from when tools will be purchased and soil prepared, to when crops will be harvested.

10. Break down the various gardening tasks on the gardening calendar into one-time chores and long-term responsibilities. Decide what work must be done immediately as opposed to what will crop up later in the season.

11. Match people with chores in a frank discussion of the interests, talents, and capabilities needed for each job, e.g, really heavy work should go to people physically capable of exertion; the job of treasurer ought to go to someone interested, if not experienced, in keeping detailed records and handling accounts.

12. Pick a name for the garden.

13. Determine the kind of leadership the group wants/needs, and choose people to fill these roles. Many successful gardens have a horticultural coordinator who is an experienced gardener. He or she handles the technical aspects of planning the garden: laying out the plots, advising other gardeners, and so on. If the gardening group is large enough to elect a governing committee and have several volunteers for specific posts, written job descriptions are a good idea. They ensure that elected leaders remain accountable to the group.

14. Be realistic. Nothing succeeds like success. During the first year, the group should plant crops they can count on at a harvest time.

Some Issues to Discuss

During the organization and planning phase, it is wise to allow time to exchange opinions about some emotionally charged subjects that could disrupt the group's cooperative spirit during the growing season.

Chemicals. One of the most common divisive questions is whether to use or avoid chemical fertilizers, fungicides, and weedkillers and how (or whether) to accommodate people with opposing approaches to horticulture. Organic gardeners choose their approach to avoid the dangers they perceive to be inherent in the use of petrochemical products in gardens. If a community garden encompasses people who want to use chemicals and those who do not, there may be acrimony between the two factions. It is a fact that chemicals pose a threat to the health of children and pets who visit the garden. Also, once *persistent* chemicals have been used on a plot of land, that plot cannot be used in following years by organic gardeners. If a group attempts to incorporate users of pesticides and other toxic chemicals, these gardeners will need to have a separate section with wind barriers. When plots treated with chemicals are interspersed with "organic" plots, gardeners not favoring chemical methods can be exposed to toxic fumes. Some of the chemicals used may reach beyond the land where they have been sprayed or spread.

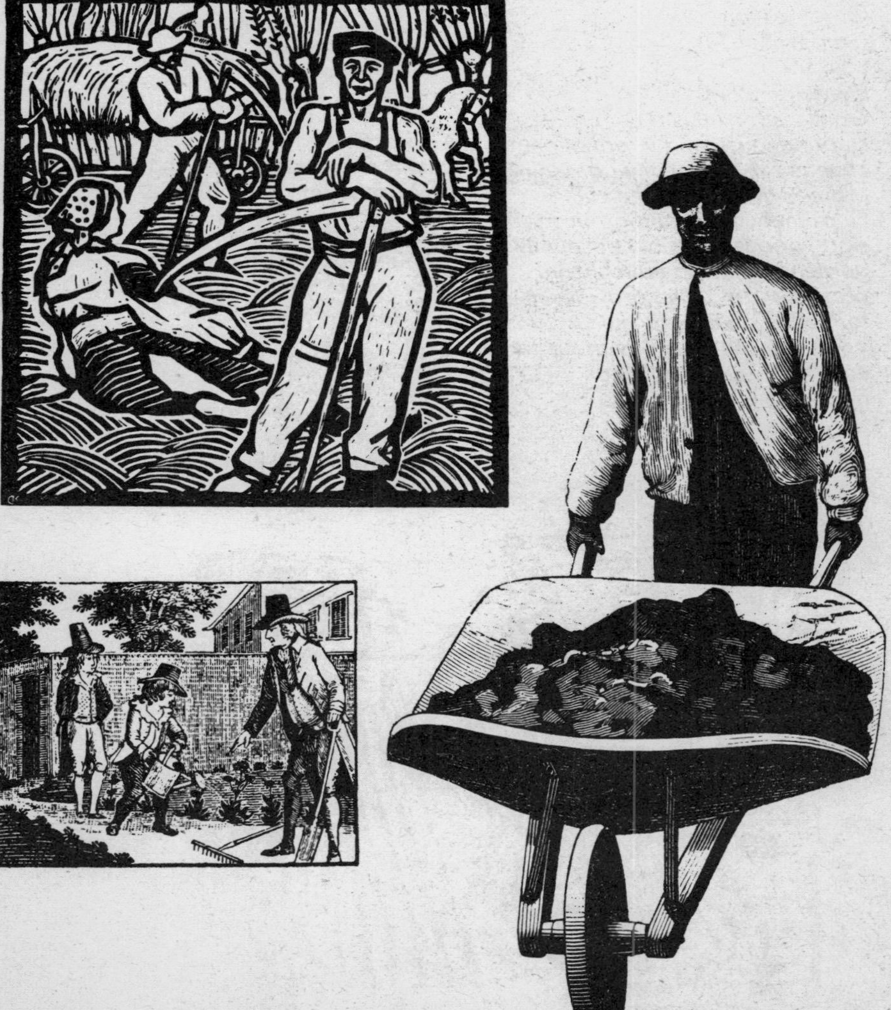

Even if no one brings up this issue because no one has an opinion, the topic merits consideration. Gardeners with little experience to begin with are bound to adopt opinions on the subject of chemicals by the time the soil is ready for preparation.

Smokers vs. nonsmokers. What could be wrong with smoking in the open air? If people must smoke, isn't that the best place to do it? The answer is usually yes . . . except around gardens. Cigarette smoke transmits a virus called tobacco mosaic that damages broad-leafed plants, particularly those belonging to the nightshade family—peppers, tomatoes, eggplant, etc. Because smoke is actually a menace to healthy plants, it is a good idea to settle this question long before the garden gets going.

Guidelines and regulations. The use of chemicals and smoking in the garden are not the only problems that can divide group members. People can get all charged up on how to deter vandals and poachers, whether to order seeds in bulk, or whether to keep bees in the garden. Besides ironing out differences on these issues, project members ought to reach agreement before the first growing season on such matters as:

- When gardeners shall have access to their plots
- What financial obligation the garden shall entail
- A policy for reclaiming neglected plots
- Planting excessively tall plants that could shade adjacent plots
- Bringing unleashed pets and untended children into the garden
- Driving cars onto the garden property
- Who may enter the garden besides members (an attorney's advice might help)
- Playing radios and musical instruments
- Consuming alcoholic beverages and smoking marijuana on garden property

The Money Side

Saving money on food bills is one of the main reasons for starting a community garden. Yet to save money, it is necessary first to invest some. Unless the garden is being run under the auspices of an institution, i.e., as part of an employee recreation program, a school or parks department project, or as a recreational facility in an apartment complex, the people who do the actual gardening will need to put their heads together on exactly how much money will be needed, how the money would be budgeted, and where the money ought to be raised. Whether the group votes to rely on contributions from individual members, raise funds among local businesses and civic groups, or seek grants from governmental sources, an itemized budget should be the foundation of every group's financial strategy.

Some Possible Startup Costs

Preplanting
lease
site clearance or cleanup (held and/or materials)
fence
gate, lock, keys
water (pipe, faucet, hose, labor)
sign
buckets
stakes
tools
construction materials
trash receptacles

Soil preparation
wheelbarrow
tools
soil improvement materials (compost, peat moss, mulches)
plowing or tilling expenses

Planting
seeds and plants
fertilizer
additional hand tools
wire fencing
tomato stakes
bean poles

Administration and outreach
answering machine
telephone
postage, paper, etc.
photocopying
Luxuries
benches, chairs, umbrellas, tables
toolshed
time-saving equipment
trees, shrubs

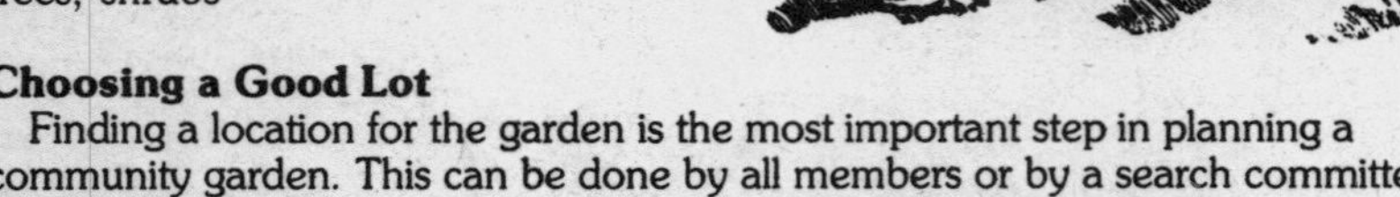

Choosing a Good Lot

Finding a location for the garden is the most important step in planning a community garden. This can be done by all members or by a search committee that has studied what features constitute potentially arable land in an urban environment.

The first step is to make a neighborhood survey assessing vacant lots, idle land around civic and business buildings, apartment houses and churches. Help is available in most communities from the city parks department, the county Cooperative Extension agent, the Cooperative Extension Office at a nearby state university or land grant college, and/or the local garden supply store.

Once a likely piece of land is discovered, it can then be evaluated for the suitability of its soil, location, and size.

Soil. Is the drainage good? Poor drainage in an area with heavy rainfall in springtime can spell disaster for an entire garden. Is there enough organic content to support growth? Abundant weeds are a good sign. Does the soil contain toxic chemicals? Was the land once a site of a structure painted with lead-based paint? When a potential location for a community garden has been found, the soil needs to be tested for pH levels. At that time, particularly if the lot is in the inner city, soil ought to be tested for traces of lead and cadmium.

Location. Does the lot have good exposure to the sun? Is it away from smokestacks, busy roads, microwave installations, large TV antennas, and radar? Is there a source of water? Is access easy? Is the lot protected from wind and storm damage? Is natural shade available in some areas?

Size. Is the lot large enough to accommodate group members' plots plus walkways, storage areas, flower gardens, picnic areas? Plots for adult gardeners range from 200 to 1000 square feet and not over 100 square feet for child gardeners. In most community gardens, plots average 25 × 30 feet.

Making It Final

Once a potential location for the garden has been found and laboratory results confirm that the soil can support edible crops, the next step is to get in touch with the landowner(s) and negotiate a contract for use. Because so much labor and love go into starting a garden, the negotiators should try to get the longest term lease possible, with the minimum being 5 years. If the group is affiliated with a nonprofit organization, the landowner might be enticed to offer favorable terms given the possibility of a tax deduction.

With the lease signed, the next thing to do is to prepare the site by building wind barriers and fences, readying the water source, and laying out plots, walkways, and common areas (for example, flowerbeds, picnic space, parking places, a place for a cold frame, compost heap, and storage hut, a plot for plants, such as corn, that require extra space).

Potential Problems

Even though a community gardening group is well organized, able to carry out plans, and is in complete agreement about horticultural methods, other problems are likely to arise that the group must face with a more or less united front. Here are a few of the most common ones:

Weather. Spring weather determines how early plowing and planting can begin, and all members of the group need to understand this. If plowing is done when the ground is too wet, compact masses of soil will result, and these will be almost impossible to break apart. In a wet spring, plowing and planting must be delayed.

Poor soil. This becomes a problem only if it is left until planting time. Soil conditions can be improved through the addition of compost, sewage sludge, manure, peat moss, and other soil builders. The local Soil Conservation Service and the U.S.D.A. Extension staff often assist in evaluating sites and recommending cover crops and other remedies.

Lack of water. Not all community gardens do have an on-site source of water yet manage to function by bringing in 50-gallon drums (filled regularly by the local fire department), using fire hydrants, or arranging with local homeowners to run hoses into the garden. Obviously, access to water is a key factor in the success of most gardening projects.

Vandalism and poaching. Although most community gardens are located in inner city neighborhoods, vandalism and poaching are seldom major problems. Lest a project prove to be an exception to the rule, however, care should be taken during site selection and the group should consider using fences. One of the best ways to prevent vandalism is to maintain good relationships with neighborhood people, such as by having a garden area open for their children or inviting nonmembers to attend house-plant clinics.

Abandoned gardens. Midseason and end-of-summer abandonment sometimes happens. What to do if somebody cannot tend their plot ought to be decided well in advance. An individual's circumstances can affect their committment but so can seemingly insoluble problems. Information-sharing networks help prevent novice gardeners from giving up out of frustration.

Surplus produce. Much food is wasted at community gardens, yet there are many ways to distribute the harvest to, say, senior citizens or halfway houses. Produce can also be sold to raise funds for charitable causes and/or to buy equipment for the garden.

Fall cleanup. Group members who readied the site in spring often are somewhat less enthusiastic come autumn. An agreed-upon policy requiring everyone to commit a specific amount of time to cleaning up the site prior to fall plowing spreads responsibilities equitably.

RESOURCES

"Organizing Community Gardens: An Annotated Bibliography"
National Center for Appropriate Technology
Box 3838
Butte, MT 59701

"Community Gardens" and "Guide to Community Garden Organization"
Gardens for All, Inc.
Box 371
Shelburne, VT 05482
Gardens for All is a nonprofit clearinghouse and information exchange for community gardening projects throughout the U.S. It helps individuals and groups to start various types of community gardens, to set up educational programs, and also provides information on the community gardening policies of various federal, state, and municipal agencies.

"Organizing a Community Garden Project"
prepared by the Community Nutrition Institute
Community Food and Nutrition Program
Community Services Administration
Washington, D.C. 20006

Soil test for heavy metals, pH, and major and minor nutrients. Write to Soil and Health Society
33 East Minor St.
Emmaus, PA 18049

Recreational Community Gardening
U.S. Government Printing Office
Washington, D.C. 20402

Community Gardening: A Handbook
Brooklyn Botanic Garden
1000 Washington Ave.
Brooklyn, NY 11225
$1.75

The Complete Book of Community Gardening, by Jamie Jobb.
Morrow Quill Paperbacks $7.95

PUBLIC GARDENS AND ARBORETA

Alabama
Bellingrath Gardens
Theodore, AL 36582

Special collections: azalea; camellia; African violet; lily; rose; hibiscus; hydrangea; dogwood; mountain laurel; gardenia; oleandar

Birmingham Botanical Gardens
2612 Lane Park Road
Birmingham, AL 35223

Special collections: Japanese garden; bonsai exhibit; rhododendron garden; wildflower garden; fern glade, cacti and other succulents ; one of the largest conservatories in the Southeast

University of Alabama Arboretum
Box 1927
University, AL 35486

Special collections: native plants of Alabama

Arizona
Arizona-Sonora Desert Museum
Route 9, Box 900
Tuxson, AZ 85702

Special collections: species of the Sonora Desert region

Desert Botanical Garden
Galvin Parkway, Papago Park
Phoenix, AZ 85010

Special collections: plants of all arid parts of the world, particularly cacti and other succulents

Boyce Thompson Southwestern Arboretum
Box AB
Superior, AZ 85273

Special collections: arid-land plants including cacti and other succulents, Eucalyptus and native plants of the Southwest

California
Descanso Gardens
1418 Descanso Drive
La Canada, CA 91011

Special collections: rose; Japanese and Chinese gardens; lilac; iris; annuals; native plants; lily

Los Angeles State and County Arboretum
301 North Baldwin Avenue
Arcadia, CA 91006

Special collections: eucalyptus; bottlebrush; acacia; palm; passia; magnolia; juniper; bamboo; herbs; ground covers; Orchidaceae

William Joseph McInnes Botanic Garden and the Campus Arboretum of Mills College
Box 9949
Oakland, CA 94613

Special collections: South African bulbous plants; conifer and broad-leafed trees

Regional Parks Garden
Tilden Regional Park
Berkeley, CA 94708

Special collections: Santa Lucia fir; red fir; California nutmeg; dune; sea bluff; alpine and mountain meadow; wildflowers; giant sequoia

Strybing Arboretum and Botanical Gardens
Ninth Avenue at Lincoln Way
San Francisco, CA 94122

Special collections: succulents; magnolia; rhododendron; native plants of California, Australia, and New Zealand

UCLA Botanical Garden
Hilgard and LeConte Avenue
University of California
Los Angeles, CA 90024

Special collections: acacia; melaleuca; aloe; camellia; eucalyptus

University of California Arboretum
Department of Biology
University of California
Davis, CA 95616

Special collections: eucalyptus; acacea; woody plants of California, Australia, South America, and the Mediterranean; melaleuca; iris

Colorado
Denver Botanic Gardens, Inc.
909 York Street
Denver, CO 80206

Special collections: herb; vegetable; rose; annual; perennial; rock garden plants

Connecticut
Audubon Fairchild Garden of the National Audubon Society
North Porchuck Road
Greenwich, CT 06830

Special collections: native plants of Connecticut; medicinal plants; plants from Appalachia and the Blue Ridge Mountains

Connecticut Arboretum
Connecticut College
New London, CT 06320

Special collections: 375 woody species native to Northeast; hawthorn; holly

Delaware
Winterthur Gardens
Route 52
Winterthur, DE 19735

Special collections: azalea; dogwood; tulip tree; heather garden

District of Columbia
Dumbarton Oaks
1703 32nd Street, NW
Washington, DC 20007

Special collections: fern; rose garden; forsythia dell; fountain terrace; beach terrace; herbaceous border

Kenilworth Aquatic Gardens
National Capital Parks-East
National Park Service
Anacostia Avenue and Douglas Street, NE
Washington, DC 20019

Special collections: native aquatic plant species; tropical lotus; waterlily

Smithsonian Institution Pleasure Gardens
Washington, DC 20560

Special collections: Victorian garden; annuals; bulbs; orchid

U.S. National Arboretum
24th and R Streets, NE
Washington, DC 20002

Special collections: azalea; rhododendron; flowering quince; crabapple; bonsai collection; Japanese garden; native wildflowers

Florida
Cypress Gardens
Box 1
Cypress Gardens, FL 33880

Special collections: palm; plumaria; bamboo; ornamental fig trees

Fairchild Tropical Garden
10901 Old Cutler Road
Miami, FL 33156

Special collections: fern; tropical flowering trees; native trees of South Florida and the Bahamas

Florida's Sunken Gardens
1825 Fourth Street, North
St. Petersburg, FL 33704

Special collections: more than 5,000 species and cultivars of tropical and subtropical plants

Marie Selby Botanical Gardens
800 South Palm Avenue
Sarasota, FL 33577

Special collections: orchid; gesneriad; aroid; bromeliad; hybrid hibiscus; fern; epiphytic plants

Wilmot Memorial Garden
Dept. of Ornamental Horticulture
105 Rolfs Hall
University of Florida
Gainesville, FL 32611

Special collections: orchid; bromeliad; aroid; azalea; juniper

Georgia
Callaway Gardens
Pine Mountain, GA 31822

Special collections: wildflowers; holly; rhododendron; vegetable gardens; azalea; southeastern natives

University of Georgia Botanical Garden
Box 164B
Rt. 4, Whitehall Road
Athens, GA 30602

Special collections: dogwood, azalea, camellia, southeastern native

Hawaii
Harold L. Lyon Arboretum
3860 Manoa Road
Honolulu, HI 96822

Special collections: economic tropical plants; Hawaiian natives, gesneriads

Olu Pua Gardens
Box 518
Kalaheo, Kauai, HI 96741

Special collections: edible tropical plants; succulents; bromeliad; palm

Waimea Arboretum and Botanical Garden
59-865 Kamehameha Highway
Haleiwa, HI 96712

Special collections: lily; palm; hibiscus; plants of the Canary Islands, Malesia, Mascarene Islands; Hawaiian natives

Idaho
Charles Huston Shattuck Arboretum
College of Forestry
University of Idaho
Moscow, ID 83893

Special collections: trees of temperate areas

Illinois
Chicago Horticultural Society Botanic Garden
Lake Cook Road
Glencoe, IL 60022

Special collections: home landscape center; regional ornamentals

Garfield Park Conservatory
300 North Central Park Boulevard
Chicago, IL 60624

Special collections: palm; fern; economic plants; aroid; cacti and other succulents

The Morton Arboretum
Route 53
Lisle, IL 60532

Special collections: hedge and street trees; conifer; groundcover

Indiana
The Holcomb Garden
Department of Botany
Butler University
4600 Sunset Avenue
Indianapolis, IN 46208

Special collections: many flowering shrubs; bulbs; annuals; 600 trees

International Friendship Gardens
Michigan City, IN 46360

Special collections: tulip; rose; phlox; hibiscus; delphinium

Iowa
H. G. Kobes Rock and Flower Garden
403 Frankfort Avenue, NE
Orange City, IA 51041

Special collections: tulip; lilac; honeysuckle; annuals; rock garden plants

Kentucky
Bernheim Forest
Route 245
Clermont, KY 40110

Special collections: dogwood; holly; azalea; redbud; nut trees; crabapple

Louisiana
Hodges Gardens
Box 921
Many, LA 71448

Special collections: Louisian iris; waterlily gardens; wildflowers; azalea; rose; camellia

Jungle Gardens
Avery Island, LA 70513

Special collections: bamboo; camellia; palm; tropical and subtropical plants; native plants

Maine
Thuya Garden
Asticou Terraces
Northeast Harbor, ME 04662

Special collections: rhododendrons; exotic evergreens; formal English garden; Japanese garden

Maryland
Brookside Gardens
1500 Glenallan Avenue
Wheaton, MD 20902

Special collections: azalea; fragrance and aquatic gardens; Japanese-style garden

Clyburn Wild Flower Preserve and Garden Center
Clyburn Park
4915 Greenspring Avenue
Baltimore, MD 21209

Special collections: native trees; shrubs; formal garden; herb garden; flowering and nonflowering plants

Massachusetts
The Arnold Arboretum of Harvard University
The Arbor Way
Jamaica Plain, MA 02130

Special collections: extensive collection of shrubs, vines, and trees from temperate areas throughout the world; hardy plants of Massachusetts

Garden in the Woods
Hemenway Road
Framingham, MA 01701

Special collections: largest landscaped collection of native plants in the Northeast

Michigan
The Gardens of Cranbrook
380 Lone Pine Road
Bloomfield, MI 48103

Special collections: herb, rock, rose, bog; wildflower, and Oriental gardens

Hidden Lake Gardens
Route 50
Tipton, MI 49287

Special collections: juniper; maple; crabapple; cherry; lilac; ornamental evergreen

Matthaei Botanical Gardens
The University of Michigan
1800 North Dixboro Road
Ann Arbor, MI 48105

Special collections: native plants; tropical, temperate, and desert plants

Minnesota
Como Park Conservatory
Midway Parkway and Kaufman Drive
St. Paul, MN 55103

Special collections: bromeliad; cacti; palm; fern

University of Minnesota Landscape Arboretum
3675 Arboretum Drive
Chaska, MN 55318

Special collections: groundcovers; vine; hedges; lilac; azalea; peony; rose; crabapple

Mississippi
Gloster Arboretum
Gloster Aboretum Road
Gloster, MS 39638

Special collections: azalea; wildflower; magnolia; iris

Missouri
Missouri Botanical Garden
2101 Tower Grove Avenue
St. Louis, MO 63163

Special collections: over 1,00 plants from the subtropical forests of Africa and South America; Japanese garden; waterlily pools; camellia; old-fashioned rose garden; scented garden for the blind; formal Italian garden; English woodland garden

Nebraska
Nebraska Statewide Arboretum
111 Forestry Science Laboratory
University of Nebraska at Lincoln
Lincoln, NE 68508

New Hampshire
Fuller Gardens
10 Willow Avenue
North Hampton, NH 03862

Special collections: formal flower gardens; perennials; rose garden

New Jersey
Duke Gardens Foundation, Inc.
Box 2030, Route 206 South
Somerville, NJ 08876

Special collections: Japanese, Chinese, Italian, English, French, Colonial, Edwardian, Indo-Persian, tropical and subtropical gardens; gardens under glass; reservations required

New York
Bailey Arboretum
Nassau County Recreation and Parks
194 Bayville Road
Locust Valley, NY 11560

Special collections: unusual trees and shrubs; perennial borders; tree peony; dwarf conifer

Brooklyn Botanic Garden
1000 Washington Avenue
Brooklyn, NY 11225

Special collections: bonsai; ferns; cacti and other succulents; lily pools; wisteria arbors; rock gardens; herb gardens; fragrance gardens; monocot bed; Shakespeare garden

Cornell Plantations
100 Judd Falls Road
Ithaca, NY 14853

Special collections: azalea, wildflowers, hedges, others; elsewhere on campus are an herb garden and poisonous plant garden.

New York Botanical Garden
Bronx, NY 10458

Special collections: alpines; bog plants; ferns; succulents; carnivorous plants; native; bromeliad

Planting Fields Arboretum
Planting Fields Road
Oyster Bay, NY 11771

Special collections: more than 600 species of rhododendron and azalea; wildflowers; greenhouse collections of cacti and other succulents; bromeliad; dwarf conifer

Root Glen
College Hill Road
Clinton, NY 13323

Special collections: ferns of New York State; specimen trees; azalea; hemlocks; narcissus; iris

North Carolina
Sarah P. Duke Gardens
Duke University
Durham, NC 27706

Special collections: rose; iris; chrysanthemum; native plants; bulbs; perennials; formal terraced gardens

North Carolina Botanical Gardens
University of North Carolina
Totten Center 457-A
Chapel Hill, NC 27514

Special collections: shrubs and herbs of the Southeast

Orton Plantation
Route 133
Box 3625
Wilmington, NC 28401

Special collections: sun, white, water gardens; azalea, camellia

Reynolda Gardens at Wake Forest University
100 Reynolda Village
Winston-Salem, NC 27106

Special collections: native plants of North Carolina

Tryon Palace Restoration Comples
1618 Pollock Street
New Bern, NC 28560

Special collections: 18th-century formal gardens with espaliers, parterres; laurel; magnolia; myrtle

Ohio
Cincinnati Nature Center
4949 Tealtown Road
Perintown, OH 45161

Special collections: vast plantings of daffodils, beech trees, wildflowers, and herbs

The Garden Center of Greater Cleveland
Western Reserve Herb Garden
110 East Boulevard
Cleveland, OH 44106

Special collections: rose garden; Japanese garden; unusual perennials; vines; groundcovers; one of the country's outstanding herb gardens

Holden Arboretum
9500 Sperry Road
Mentor, OH 44060

Special collections: over 6,000 plants from worldwide sources; acres of azalea, rhododendron, and lilac; wildflowers; nut and ornamental fruit trees

Stan Hyet Hall and Gardens
714 North Portage Path
Akron, OH 44303

Special collections: English, Japanese, rose gardens; specimen trees

Irwin M. Krohn Conservatory
Eden Park Drive
Cincinnati, OH 45202

Special collections: cactus; tropicals; Hinkle bulb garden; magnolia

Oklahoma
Will Rogers Park and Horticulture Garden
Oklahoma City Municipal Park
3500 NW 36th Street
Oklahoma City, OK 73112

Special collections: rose; cacti and other succulents

Oregon
Crystal Springs Rhododendron Garden
Box 8408 SE 28th Avenue
Portland, OR 97207

Special collections: over 300 rhododendron species, 400 cultivars

International Rose Test Gardens
Washington Park
400 SW Kingston Street
Portland, OR 97201

Special collections: 10,000 roses, over 500 varieties

The Japanese Garden Society of Oregon
Box 3847
Portland, OR 97208

Special collections: authentic Japanese garden is one of the finest in the country; plants indigenous to U.S.

Pennsylvania
Longwood Gardens, Inc.
Kennett Square, PA 19348

Special collections: tropical ferns; orchid; rare shrub; herb; rose, rock, and heather gardens; Italian water garden; arboretum from 1800

Morris Arboretum of the University of Pennsylvania
9414 Meadowbrook Avenue
Philadelphia, PA 19118

Special collections: native and exotic trees; tropical fern house; natural woodlands; medicinal garden

Swiss Pines
Charleston Road
Malvern, PA 19355

Special collections: outstanding Japanese garden; rose, herb, heather, and heath gardens; nature trails; rare conifers

Rhode Island
Green Animals
Cory's Lane, off Route 14
Portsmouth, RI 02871

Special collections: 7-acre topiary garden with 80 sculptured trees and shrubs; vegetables and perennials

South Carolina
Brookgreen Gardens
Box 3, Route 1
Murrells Inlet, SC 29576

Special collections: boxwood; indigenous plants; holly; statuary gardens

Edisto Memorial Gardens
Box 863
Route 301 South
Orangeburg, SC 29115

Special collections: roses; azalea; camellia; daylily

The Horticultural Gardens of Clemson University
Clemson, SC 29631

Special collections: bog garden; fern; wildflowers; colonial kitchen garden; azalea; camellia

Magnolia Gardens
Route 4
Charleston, SC 29407

Special collections: camellia; azalea; magnolia; live oak; baldcypress

Middleton Place Route
Route 4
Charleston, SC 29407

Special collections: oldest garden in North America; camellia; azalea; secret, octagonal, moon, and other gardens; baldcypress lake; magnolia

Tennessee
Memphis Botanic Garden
750 Cherry Road
Memphis, TN 38117

Special collections: dahlia garden; wildflower garden; azalea and dogwood trail; rose garden; Iris garden

Tennessee Botanical Gardens and Fine Arts Center
Cheekwood
Nashville, TN 37205

Special collections: bromeliad; camellia; magnolia; orchid

Texas
Bayou Bend Collection and Gardens
1 Westcott
Houston, TX 77007

Special collections: formal and wooded 14-acre gardens featuring camellia, azalea, native trees, and shrubs

Fort Worth Botanic Garden
3220 Botanic Garden Drive
Fort Worth, TX 76107

Special collections: Japanese garden; rose gardens; exhibition greenhouses; fragrance garden for the blind

The Garden Center
Forest and First Avenue
State Fair Grounds
Dallas, TX 75201

Special collections: perennials; herb and scent garden; daylily; iris, rose, and water gardens; Shakespeare garden

Utah
State Arboretum of Utah
University of Utah
Salt Lake City, UT 84112

Special collections: rose and cactus gardens; rare and endangered species; specimen trees

Vermont
Vermont Institute of Natural Science
Church Hill Road
Woodstock, VT 05091

Special collections: nature trails; ferns; wildflowers

Virginia
Norfolk Botanical Gardens
Airport Road
Norfolk, VA 23518

Special collections: holly; rhododendron; azalea; camellia

Note: Virginia's best gardens are scattered at Colonial Williamsburg, the James River Plantations, Woodlawn Plantation, Gunston Hall, River Farm, O. E. Whaite Arboretum, and elsewhere.

Washington
The Bloedal Reserve
7571 NE Dolphin Drive
Bainbridge Island, WA 98110

Special collections: Pacific Northwest native plants

University of Washington Arboretum
Madison and 31st Avenue East
Seattle, WA 98112

Special collections: rare trees; broadleaf evergreens; flowering trees and shrubs; Japanese tea garden

Core Arboretum
Department of Biology
West Virginia University
Morgantown, WV 26506

Wisconsin
Boerner Botanical Gardens
Milwaukee County Department of Parks, Recreation, and Culture
5879 South 92nd Street
Hales Corner, WI 53130

Special collections: conifers; shrub roses; shade trees

University of Wisconsin Arboretum
1207 Seminole Highway
Madison, WI 53711

Special collections: woodlands; marshes; lakes and prairies; display gardens.

CANADA

Ontario
Royal Botanical Gardens
680 Plains Road, West
Burlington, ON
Box 399
Hamilton, ON L8N 3H8

Special collections: perennials; rose; iris; Syringa

Humber Arboretum
205 Humber College Boulevard
Rexdale, ON M9W 5L7

Special collections: native trees and wildflowers of Ontario

The Niagara Park Commission School of Horticulture
Box 150
Niagara Falls, ON L2E 6T2

Special collections: native and exotic trees

Quebec
Montreal Botanical Garden
4101 est, rue Sherbrooke
Montreal, PQ B1X 2B2

Special collections: alpine flowers; cacti and succulents; begonia; orchid; fern; rose

British Columbia
The Botanical Garden
6501 NW Marine Drive
University of British Columbia
Vancouver, BC V6T 1W5

Special collections: native flora of British Columbia; alpines; woody asian plants

SOCIETIES

African Violet Society of America
Box 1326
Knoxville, TN 37901 (615)524-8949

State and local chapters. Benefits: *African Violet Magazine*, five issues per year for members only. Free publications; annual conventions; plant exchange; horticultural library; horticultural slide collection

American Begonia Society, Inc.
369 Ridge Vista Avenue
San Jose, CA 95127 (408)258-4670

52 branches throughout U.S. Benefits: free publications; invitation to annual convention; seed fund; bookstore; round robins. Horticultural library: books and various color slide shows may be borrowed by mail. Publication: *The Begonian*, monthly magazine, $1 per issue nonmembers

American Bonsai Society, Inc.
Box 358
Kenne, NH 03431

Benefits: free publications; annual symposium; book discounts. Publications: *Bonsai Journal*, quarterly magazine, $15 per year nonmembers; *Abstracts*, bimonthly newsletter. Educational program: annual symposium on college campuses; workshops and demonstration lectures

American Boxwood Society
Box 85
Boyce, VA 22620 (703)837-1758

Benefits: free publications; invitation to annual meeting. Publication: *American Boxwood Bulletin*, quarterly, $1.50 per issue nonmembers

American Daffodil Society
Tyner, NC 27980 (919)221-8388

Regional chapters. Benefits: free publications; special publications; invitation to annual convention; membership roster; opportunity to become accredited judge; technical advice on culture and hybridizing. Publication: *Daffodil Journal*, quarterly magazine, $1.50 per issue nonmembers. Educational programs: slide programs, $5.00

American Dahlia Society
2044 Great Falls Street
Falls Church, VA 22043

62 local societies. Benefits: free publications; invitation to annual meetings; root exchanges through local services. Publications: *Bulletin of the American Dahlia Society*, quarterly; classification of dahlia distributed annually

American Fern Society, Inc.
Department of Botany
University of Tennessee
Knoxville, TN 37916 (615)974-2256

Benefits: annual meeting; several field trips; spore exchange 25¢ per packet. Publications: *Fiddlehead Forum*, quarterly newsletter; *American Fern Journal*, quarterly magazine.

American Gloxinia and Gesneriad Society, Inc.
Box 312
Ayer, MA 01432 (617)772-4482

Benefits: free publications; invitation to annual convention; seed fund 75¢; judges' training school. Publications: *The Gloxinian*, bimonthly magazine, $1.50 per issue nonmembers; *How to Know and Grow Gesneriads*, booklet, $2 nonmbers; *Plant Registers*, $2 nonmembers

American Gourd Society
Box 274
Mount Gilead, OH 43338 (419)946-3302
State chapters: NC, OH. Benefits: free publications; invitation to annual July meeting and to annual show in Mount Gilead, OH, first week in October. Publications: *The Gourd*, newsletter, three issues per year, $1 nonmembers; bulletins on gourds, irregularly issued, 10¢ per issue nonmembers. Horticultural library: horticultural slide collection; 120-slide set on culture of gourds and gourd craft; rental fee $7.50, script included

American Hemerocallis Society
Route 2, Box 360
De Queen, AR 71832 (501)642-3778

Regional, state, and local chapters. Benefits: free publications; invitations to regional meetings; lectures on local and regional basis. Publications: *The Hemerocallis Journal*, quarterly, $2 per issue nonmembers; *Beginner's Handbook*, $2.50 nonmembers; membership roster; regional newsletters; checklist. Horticultural library: 2,500 slides of new and old cultivars and gardens featuring *Hemerocallis*

American Hibiscus Society
Drawer 5430
Pompano Beach, FL 33064 (305)943-8625

Benefits: free quarterly publications; seed bank; garden service. Publications: *The Seed Pod*, quarterly magazine, $1 per issue nonmembers; call or write for list of other books about Hibiscus and its nomenclature. Educational programs: talks, slide shows, and educational material free of charge. Horticultural library: horticultural slide collection.

American Hosta Society
5605 11th Avenue, South
Birmingham, AL 35222 (205)592-7054

Benefits: free publications; invitations to conventions; garden tours and auctions; seed list; seed exchanges. Publications: *American Hosta Society Bulletin*, annual magazine, $3 per issue nonmembers; newsletter, three issues per year. Educational program: lectures, workshops, and slide programs

American Iris Society
5618 Beachy Avenue
Wichita, KS 67206 (316)686-8734

Benefits: free quarterly publication; automatic membership in one of 24 regions, which also issue publications; invitations to local, regional, and annual meetings; option of joining a section. Publications: *Bulletin of the American Iris Society*, quarterly magazine, $3 per issue nonmembers; *Registrations & Introductions*, annual booklet, $3.50; other books. Educational programs: extensive judges' training and accreditation; seminars during national conventions

American Ivy Society
c/o Cox Arboretum
6733 Springboro Pike
Dayton, OH 45449 (513)434-9005

Benefits: free publications; invitation to annual meeting; free identification service for Hedera; garden service; plant exchange. Publications: *The Ivy Bulletin*, quarterly magazine, $5 nonmembers; plant checklist; standards for judging; other publications

American Magnolia Society
Box 129
Nanuet, NY 10954 (914)354-3981

Benefits: free publications; invitation to annual convention; pollen and seed exchange, $1 per seed packet. Publication: *The Magnolia, Journal of the American Magnolia society*, semiannual magazine, $6 per issue nonmembers

American Orchid Society, Inc.
84 Sherman Street
Cambridge, MA 02140 (617)868-8416

Benefits: free publications; invitation to meeting; question box (experts answer questions on raising orchids); free 80-page book on orchid culture to new members. Publications: *A.O.S. Bulletin*, monthly magazine, $2.50 per issue nonmembers; *Awards Quarterly*, magazine, $3 per issue nonmembers; write for list of other publications

American Penstemon Society
Box 450
Briarcliff Manor, NY 10510

Benefits: free publications; invitations to semiannual conventions; round robins. Publication: *ASP Bulletin*, semiannual, members only

American Peony Society
250 Interlachen Road
Hopkins, MN 55343 (612)938-4706

Benefits: free publications; invitation to annual convention and exhibitions; free peony seed (postage charge). Publications: *American Peony Society Bulletin*, quarterly, $2 issue nonmembers; *Paeonian*, quarterly hybridizers' newsletter, $2.50 per year members and nonmembers in the U.S. and Canada, $4 in Europe and Australia

American Primrose Society
2568 Jackson Highway
Chenalis, WA 98532 (206)748-7627

Benefits: free publications; invitation to annual meeting; seed exchange, 10¢ per packet. Publications: *American Primrose Society Quarterly*; *Dictionary of Cultivated Species of Primula*. Educational programs: Speakers and slide lectures. Horticultural library: horticultural slide collection

American Rhododendron Society
14635 SW Bull Mountain Road
Tigard, OR 97223 (503)639-5922

Benefits: free publications; invitation to conference; seed exchange; pollen bank. Publication: *Quarterly Bulletin: American Rhododendron Society*, magazine, members only. Horticultural library: horticultural slide collection

American Rock Garden Society
Box 282, Route 1
Mena, AR 71953 (501)394-6584

Benefits: free publications; invitation to local, regional, and national meetings; annual seed exchange. Publication: *Bulletin of the American Rock Garden Society*, quarterly magazine, members only

American Rose Society
Box 30,000
Shreveport, LA 71130 (318)938-5402

Benefits: free publications; invitations to National Rose Meetings (two annually) and rose shows; judges' training schools; group and special insurance plans; mail-lending library of books. Publications: *American Rose Magazine*, monthly, $1.25 per issue nonmembers; *American Rose Annual*, $8.50 nonmembers; *American Rose Handbook*, annual booklet, 35¢ per issue nonmembers; other publications

Bonsai Clubs International
Box 2098
Sunnyvale, CA 94087 (213)288-2506

Benefits: free publications. Publications: *Bonsai Clubs International*, magazine, ten issues per year, $2 per issue nonmembers; other publications

Bromeliad Society, Inc.
Box 41261
Los Angeles, CA 90041 (213)257-0170

Benefits: free publications; purchase of bromeliad seed through the *Society Seed Fund*. Publications: *Journal of the Bromeliad Society*, bimonthly magazine, $2.50 per issue nonmembers; glossary; cultural handbook; plant checklist.

Cactus and Succulent Society of America, Inc.
2631 Fairgreen Avenue
Arcadia, CA 91006 (213)447-6180

Benefits: free publications; invitation to annual plant show at Los Angeles State and County Arboretum and to biennial conventions. Publication: *Cactus and Succulent Journal*, bimonthly magazine, members only

Cymbidium Society of America, Inc.
469 West Norman Avenue
Arcadia, CA 91006

Benefits: Free publications; participation in orchid show; judges' accreditation program. Publication: *Orchid Advocate*, bimonthly magazine, $2 nonmembers

Epiphyllum Society of America
Box 1395
Monrovia, CA 91016 (805)259-4637

Benefits: free publications including membership directory; invitations to monthly meetings. Publication: *ESA Bulletin*, bimonthly newsletter, members only

Herb Society of America
300 Massachusetts Avenue
Boston, MA 02115 (617)536-7136

Benefits: free publications; lectures; workshops; plant exchanges; herb sales. Publication: *The Herbalist*, annual magazine, $2 plus postage per issue nonmembers. Horticultural library: 600 books and pamphlets

Holly Society of America
407 Fountain Green Road
Bel Air, MD 21014 (301)879-0976

Benefits: free publications; invitations to national and local meetings. Publications: *Proceedings of the Holly Society of America*, annual newsletter; *Holly Letter*, newsletter, three issues per year. Horticultural library: ten sets of slides depicting holly usage and culture.

International Geranium Society
6501 (AHS) Yosemite Drive
Buena Park, CA 90620 (213)222-6809

Benefits: free publications; invitations to meetings; seed bank. Publication: *Geraniums around the World*, quarterly magazine, members only

Los Angeles International Fern Society
14895 Gardenhill Drive
La Mirada, CA 90638 (213)941-5384

Benefits: free publications; round robins on various topics; spore store; annual fern and exotic plant show; fern cultivation lessons by mail; library of fern literature available for purchase. Publication: *LAIFS Journal*, ten issues per year; membership roster; biennial; fern classification and fern cultures

National Chrysanthemum Society, Inc. USA
2612 Beverly Boulevard
Roanoke, VA 24105

Benefits: free publications; invitation to annual meeting and show. Publications: *The Chrysanthemum*, quarterly magazine, members only; *Beginners Handbook*, free to new members

National Fuschia Society
South Coast Botanic Garden
26300 Crenshaw Boulevard
Palos Verdes, CA 90274 (213)377-0468

Benefits: free publications; invitations to meetings; plant shows; tours. Publications: *The Fuchsia Fan*, monthly magazine, $1 per issue nonmembers. Educational programs: Culture classes and workshops; demonstrations at gardens and shows

National Oleander Society
Box 3431
Galveston, TX 77552 (713)762-9334

Benefits: free publications; Nerium cultivation information service; seed distribution; cuttings shipped for $4. Publication: *National Oleander Society Newsletter*, quarterly, free to members

North American Gladiolus Council
30 Highland Place
Peru, IN 46970 (317)473-7478

Benefits: free publications. Publication: *Quarterly Bulletin of the North American Gladiolus Council*, free

North American Lily Society
Box 476
Waukee, IA 50263

Benefits: free publications; annual show; seed exchange; round robins; slide exchange; gardening and advice. Publications: *North American Lily Society Quarterly Bulletin*, magazine, $2 per issue nonmembers; *Yearbook*, $12 nonmembers

Palm Society, Inc.
Box 368
Lawrence, KS 66044

Benefits: free publications; invitation to biennial meetings; participation in seed bank. Publication: *Principes*, quarterly

Saintpaulia International
1800 Grand
Box 549
Knoxville, TN 37901 (615)524-9881

Benefits: free publications. Publications: *Gesneriad-Sauntpaulia News* (*GNS*), bimonthly magazine (also official publication of Gesneriad Society International)

Society for Louisiana Irises
Box 40175 USL
Lafayette, LA 70504 (318)264-6203

Benefits: free publications; invitation to annual meeting and show. Publications: *Newsletter of the Society for Louisiana Irises*, quarterly, members only; booklet, published every four years

CONSERVATION ORGANIZATIONS

American Foresty Association
1319 18th Street, NW
Washington, DC 20005 (202)467-5810

Center for Natural Areas
1525 New Hampshire Avenue, NW
Washington, DC 20036 (202)265-0066

Friends of the Earth
530 Seventh Street, SE
Washington, DC 20003 (202)543-4312, Ext. 3

Garden Club of America
598 Madison Avenue
NY, NY 10022 (212)753-8287

National Audubon Society
950 Third Avenue
NY, NY 10022 (212)832-3200

The National Parks and Conservation Association
1701 18th Street, NW
Washington, DC 20009 (202)265-2717

National Wildlife Federation
1412 16th Street, NW
Washington, DC 20036 (202)797-6800

The Nature Conservancy
1800 North Kent Street, Suite 800
Arlington, VA 22209 (703)841-5300

Sierra Club
530 Bush Street
San Francisco, CA 94108

The Wilderness Society
1901 Pennsylvania Avenue, NW
Washington, DC 20006 (202)293-2732

Izaak Walton League of America
1800 North Kent Street, Suite 806
Arlington, VA 22209 (703)528-1818

PROFESSIONAL AND TRADE ASSOCIATIONS

All-American Rose Selections (AARS)
Box 218
Shenandoah, IA 51601 (712)246-2884

Publications: *Roses Are for You*, booklet; periodic news releases advising the public of new rose cultivars proven superior in AARS's two-year testing program

All-America Selections (AAS)
204 South Main Street
Sycamore, IL 60178 (815)895-2073

Publication: *Proving Grounds for New Flowers and Vegetables*, brochure, updated annually, lists names and addresses of trial grounds and display gardens featuring All-American award winners in the U.S. and Canada, 50¢

American Association of Botanical Gardens and Arboreta, Inc.
Box 206
Swarthmore, PA 19081 (215)328-9145

Benefits: free publications; invitation to annual meeting; regional meetings; placement service. Publications: *AABGA Bulletin*, quarterly journal; *AABGA Newsletter*, monthly; technical papers and handbooks, irregularly issued

American Association of Nurserymen
230 Southern Building
Washington, DC 20005 (202)737-4060

Benefits: free publications; regional and national meetings; legislative clout; legal service; marketing assistance; reference and management aids; consulting services; insurance programs. Publications: *UPDATE*, biweekly newsletter; *ALT*, quarterly; *Membership Directory*, annual; *Sources of Plants and Related Supples*, annual; marketing and management publications; special research-project reports

American Promological Society
103 Tyson Building
University Park, PA 16802 (814)863-2198

Benefits: free quarterly publication; invitation to annual meeting. Publication: *Fruit Varieties Journal*, quarterly magazine, $3 per issue nonmembers

American Seed Trade Association
1030 15th Street, NW, Suite 964
Washington, DC 20005 (202)223-4080

Benefits: Legislative services and information exchange through meetings, $5 per nonmember

American Society of Consulting Arborists
12 Lakeview Avenue
Milltown, NJ 08850 (201)821-8948

Benefits: free publications; annual 4-day educational meeting and a one-day meeting; tree consultation files. Publication: *Arborcultural Consultant*, bimonthly, members only

American Society of Landscape Architects, Inc.
1733 Connecticut Avenue, NW
Washington, DC 20009 (202)466-7730

Benefits: free publications; reduced rates to ASLA-sponsored seminars; annual meetings; government liaison service; professional placement service

American Association of Plant Physiologists
Box 1688
Rockville, MD 20850 (301)251-0560

Benefits: publications; annual meetings; opportunity to present research papers at meetings and public information in the society's publications. Publication: *Plant Physiology*, monthly magazine

American Society of Plant Taxonomists
770 Van Vleet Oval
Norman, OK 73019 (405)325-6443

Benefits: opportunity to present papers at annual meeting; free publications. Publications: *Systematic Botany*, quarterly journal; *Systematic Botany, Monographs*, journal, irregularly published

Associated Landscape Contractors of America
1750 Old Meadow Road
McLean, VA 22102 (703)821-8611

Benefits: free publications; annual convention and trade show; educational seminars. Publications: *Action Letter*, monthly newsletter, members only; *ACLA Membership Directory*; miscellaneous reports and manuals

Botanical Society of America, Inc.
School of Biological Sciences
University of Kentucky
Lexington, KY 40506 (606)258-8770

Benefits: free publications; opportunities to present papers at annual meeting. Publications: *American Journal of Botany*, 10 issues per year, $34 per year nonmembers; *Plant Science Bulletin*, bimonthly, $10 per year nonmembers

Garden Centers of America
230 Southern Building
Washington, D.C. 20005 (202)737-4060

Publication: *GCA Newsletter*, monthly

Garden Writers Association of America
Box 10221
Fort Wayne, IN 46851 (219)486-3972

Benefits: Free publications; invitation to annual meeting. Publication: *Garden Writers Bulletin*, bimonthly newsletter, $3 per year nonmembers

Horticultural Research Institute
230 Southern Building
Washington, DC 20005 (202)737-4060

Benefits: numerous scientific and business-management-related publications; annual conventions. Publications: *Research Letter*, quarterly: *New Horizons*, annual journal; *Minute Memos*, information releases on current research; manuals; handbooks; glossaries

International Plant Propagators' Society
Department of Horticulture
Purdue University
West Lafayette, IN 47907 (317)749-2261

Benefits: free publications and meetings. Publications: quarterly newsletter, annual proceedings

Mailorder Association of Nurserymen, Inc.
210 Cartwright Boulevard
Massapequa Park, NY
11762 (516)541-6902

Benefits: two meetings and trade show annually; legislative liaison services through the American Association of Nurserymen. Publications: *MAN Annual Bulletin*, members only; *MAN Membership Bulletin*, quarterly newsletter, members only

National Arborist Association, Inc.
3537 Stratford Road
Wantagh, NY 11793 (516)221-3082

Benefits: free publications; annual meetings. Publication: monthly newsletter, members only

National Association of Plant Patent Owners
230 Southern Building
Washington, DC 20005 (202)737-4060

Publications: annual membership roster and occasional bulletins

National Christmas Tree Association, Inc.
611 East Wells Street
Milwaukee, WI 53202 (414)276-6410

Publications: *American Christmas Tree Journal*, quarterly magazine; and *Christmas Merchandiser*, annual magazine, members only; *National Action*, irregularly issued newsletter

National Garden Bureau, Inc.
204 South Main Street
Sycamore, IL 60178 (815)895-2073

Benefits: semiannual meetings. Publications: *Press Service Sheets*, quarterly

National Landscape Association, Inc.
230 Southern Building
Washington, DC 20005 (202)737-4060

Benefits: free publication on subjects such as landscape design, estimating, competitive bidding, and landscape maintenance contracts; annual meetings. Publications: *NLA New Notes*, monthly; *Tech Notes*, bimonthly; other publications

Professional Grounds Management Society
7 Church Lane, Suite 13
Pikesville, MD 21208 (301)653-2742

Benefits: publications; annual conference and trade show; employment referral service. Publications: *Grounds Management Forum*, monthly newsletter; *PGMS Membership Directory*, annual; other publications

Society of American Florists
901 North Washington Street
Alexandria, VA 22134 (703)836-8700

Publications: *American Florist Dateline*, monthly tabloid, nonmembers $25 per year; *Who's Who in Floriculture*, annual book; *U.S. Retailer* and *U.S. Grower*, monthly newsletters.

Society of American Forests
5400 Grosvenor Lane
Washington, DC 20014 (301)897-8720

Benefits: free publications; meetings and seminars; employment referral service; life insurance. Publication: *Journal of American Forestry*, monthly magazine, $27 per year nonmembers

Soil Society of America
677 South Segoe Road
Madison, WI 53711 (608)274-1212

Benefits: free publications; annual meeting; publishing program; public relations program; placement service; career information. Publications: *SSA Journal, Agronomy News, Agronomy Abstracts*, write for list of other publications

Weed Science Society of America, Inc.
309 West Clark Street
Champaign, IL 61820 (217)356-3182

Wholesale Nursery Growers of America
230 Southern Building
Washington, DC 20005 (202)737-4060

Benefits: free publications; many public and private meetings for information exchange. Publications: *The Grower*, bimonthly newsletter; special publications

PERIODICALS

African Violet Magazine
Box 1326
Knoxville, TN 37901

American Horticulturalist
American Horticulture Society
Box 0105
Mount Vernon, VA 22121

American Orchid Society Bulletin
84 Sherman Street
Cambridge, MA 02140

American Rose Magazine
Box 30,000
Shreveport, LA 71130

The Avant Gardener
Box 489
New York, NY 10028

The Begonian
369 Ridge Vista Avenue
San Jose, CA 95127

Better Homes and Gardens
Locust at 17th
Des Moines, IA 50336

Better Living!
1480 Great Plain Avenue
Needham, MA 02192

Blair and Ketchum's Country Journal
205 Main Street
Brattleboro, VT 05301

Bonsai Club International Magazine
Box 2098
Sunnyvale, CA 94087

Brooklyn Botanic Garden Garden Record, Plants and Gardens
Brooklyn Botanic Garden
1000 Washington Avenue
Brooklyn, NY 11225

The Family Food Garden
693 Commonwealth Avenue
Newton, MA 02159

Flower and Garden
4251 Pennsylvania
Kansas City, MO 64111

Garden
The New York Botanical Garden
Bronx, NY 10458

Gesneriad-Saintpaulia News (GSN)
1800 Grand
Box 549
Knoxville, TN 37901

The Green Scene
The Pennsylvania Horticultural Society
325 Walnut Street
Philadelphia, PA 19106

The Herb Quarterly
West Street
Box 275
New Fare, VT 05345

Horticulture
300 Massachusetts Avenue
Boston, MA 02115

House and Garden
350 Madison Avenue
NY, NY 10017

The IPM Practitioner
The Newsletter of Integrated Pest Management
Box 7242
Berkeley, CA 94707

Journal of the Bromeliad Society
Box 41261
Los Angeles, CA 90041

Landscaping Homes & Gardens
Box 99
Amawalk, NY 10501

Living Off the Land
A Subtropic Newsletter
Box 2131
398 Dayton Blvd.
Melbourne, FL 32901

Organic Gardening
33 East Minor Street
Emmaus, PA 18049

Pacific Horticulture
Box 22609
San Francisco, CA 94112

Southern Living
820 Shades Creek Parkway
Birmingham, AL 35209

Sunset Magazine
Lane Publishing Company
Menlo Park, CA 94025

Texas Gardener
2509 Washington,
Box 9005
Waco, TX 76714

CANADA
Early Canadian Life
591 Argus Road
Aoakville, ON

Trellis
Civic Garden Center
777 Lawrence Avenue East
Don Mills, ON M3C 1P2

Western Living
2930 Arbutus Street
Vancouver, BC V61 3Y9

HORTICULTURAL LIBRARIES

Alabama
Horace Hammond Memorial Library
Birmingham Botanical Gardens
2612 Lane Park Road
Birmingham, AL 35223

Arizona
Richter Memorial Library
Desert Botanical Garden
Galvin Parkway
Papago Park
Phoenix, AZ 85010

California
California Academy of Sciences Library
Golden Gate Park
San Francisco, CA 94118

Los Angeles State and County Arboretum
Plant Science Library
301 North Baldwin Avenue
Arcadia, CA 91006

Forest History Society
Box 1581
Santa Cruz, CA 95061

Helen Crocker Russell Library
Strybing Arboretum and Botanical Gardens
Ninth Avenue at Lincoln Way
San Francisco, CA 94112

Rancho Santa Ana Botanic Garden Library
1500 North College Avenue
Claremont, CA 91711

Colorado
Helen Fowler Library
Denver Botanic Gardens
909 York Street
Denver, CO 80206

Connecticut
The Greenwich Garden Center Library
Bible Street
Cos Cob, CT 06807

District of Columbia
Dumbarton Oaks Garden Library
1703 32nd Street, NW
Washington, DC 20007

Smithsonian Institution Libraries
National Museum of Natural History
Smithsonian Institution
Washington, DC 20560

Florida
Hume Library
University of Florida Institute of Food and Agricultural Services
Gainesville, FL 32611

Montgomery Library
Fairchild Tropical Garden
10901 Old Cutler Road
Miami, FL 33156

Georgia
Cherokee Garden Library
Atlanta Historical Society
McElreath Hall
3101 Andrews Drive, NW
Atlanta, GA 30305

Fernbank Science Center Library
156 Heaton Park Drive, NE
Atlanta, GA 30307

American Camellia Society Library
Box 1217
Fort Valley, GA 31030

Hawaii
Rock Library
Honolulu Botanic Gardens
50 North Vineyard Boulevard
Honolulu, HI 96817

Illinois
Chicago Botanic Garden Library
Lake Cook Road
Box 400
Glencoe, IL 60022

Field Museum of Natural History
Roosevelt Road and Lake Shore Drive
Chicago, IL 60605

Indiana
Hayes Regional Arboretum Library
801 Elks Road
Richmond, IN 47374

Iowa
Men's Garden Clubs of America Lending Library
5560 Merle Hay Road
Des Moines, IA 50323

Kentucky
University of Kentucky Agriculture Library
Agricultural Science Center North
Lexington, KY 40506

Louisiana
American Rose Society Lending Library
Box 30,000
Shreveport, LA 71130

Maine
Thuya Lodge Library
Asticou Terraces
Northeast Harbor, ME 04662

Maryland
The Cylburn Horticultural Library
Cylburn Park Mansion
4915 Greenspring Avenue
Baltimore, MD 21209

National Agricultural Library
Technical Information Systems
USDA, Science and Educational Administration
Beltsville, MD 20705

Massachusetts
Morrill Library
University of Massachusetts, Amherst
Amherst, MA 01002

Massachusetts Horticultural Society Library
300 Massachusetts Avenue
Boston, MA 02115

The Arnold Arboretum Library
Harvard University Herbaria Building
22 Divinity Avenue
Cambridge, MA 02138

Michigan
The Detroit Garden Center Library
1460 East Jefferson Avenue
Detroit, MI 48207

Fernwood Library
Fernwood, Inc.
1720 Range Line Road
Niles, MI 49120

Minnesota
Andersen Horticultural Library
Minnesota Landscape Arboretum
3675 Arboretum Drive
Chaska, MN 55318

St. Paul Campus Library
University of Minnesota
St. Paul, MN 55101

Missouri
National Council of State Garden Clubs, Inc.
4401 Magnolia Avenue
St. Louis, MO 63110

Missouri Botanical Garden Library
Box 299
St. Louis, MO 63166

New Jersey
Elizabeth Donnell Kay Botanical Library
Julia Appleton Cross Horticultural Library
The George Griswold Frelinghuysen Arboretum
Box 1295R
East Hanover Avenue
Morristown, NJ 07960

Rutgers University
Cook College
Box 231
New Brunswick, NJ 08903

New York
Library of the New York Botanical Garden
Bronx, NY 10458

Brooklyn Botanic Garden Library
1000 Washington Avenue
Brooklyn, NY 11225

Liberty Hyde Bailey Hortorium
467 Mann Library
Cornell University
Ithaca, NY 14853

Horticultural Society of New York Library
128 West 58th Street
New York, NY 10019

Monroe County Park Department Herbarium Library
County Park Office
375 Westfall Road
Rochester, NY 14620

North Carolina
Totten Library
North Carolina Botanical Garden
University of North Carolina at Chapel Hill
Totten Center 457A
Chapel Hill, NC 27541

Ohio
Lloyd Library and Museum
917 Plum Street
Cincinnati, OH 45202

Eleanor Squire Library
The Garden Center of Greater Cleveland
11030 East Boulevard
Cleveland, OH 44106

The Corning Library
The Holden Arboretum
9500 Sperry Road
Mentor, OH 44060

Environmental Library
George P. Crosby Gardens
5403 Elmer Drive
Toledo, OH 43651

Ohio Agricultural Research and Development Center Library
Wooster, OH 44691

Oklahoma
Tulsa Garden Center Library
2435 South Peoria
Tulsa, OK 74114

Pennsylvania
Longwood Library
Longwood Gardens, Inc.
Kennett Square, PA 19348

Pennsylvania Horticultural Society Library
325 Walnut Street
Philadelphia, PA 19106

Hunt Institute for Botanical Documentation
Carnegie-Mellon University
Pittsburgh, PA 15213

Tennessee
Tennessee Botanical Gardens and Fine Arts Center
Cheekwod
Cheek Road
Nashville, TN 37205

Texas
Fort Worth Garden Center Library
3220 Botanic Garden Drive
Fort Worth, TX 76107

Virginia
Harold B. Tukey Memorial Library
American Horticultural Society
7931 East Boulevard Drive
Alexandria, VA 22308

Norfolk Botanical Gardens Library
Airport Road
Norfolk, VA 23518

Washington
University of Washington Arboretum Library
University of Washington Arboretum
XD-10
East Madison and Lake Washington Boulevard East
Seattle, WA 98195

West Virginia
Wheeling Garden Center Library
Oglebay Park
Wheeling, WV 26003

Wisconsin
Reference Library of the Boerner Botanical Gardens
5879 South 92nd Street
Hales Corner, WI 53130

CANADA
Manitoba
Morden Research Station Library
Box 3001
Morden, MB ROG 1J0

British Columbia
University of British Columbia Botanical Garden Library
6501 NW Marine Drive
Vancouver, BC V6T 1W5

Ontario
Royal Botanical Gardens Library
Box 399
Hamilton, ON L8N 3H8

The Niagra Parks Commission School of Horticulture Library
Box 150
Niagra Falls, ON L2E 6T2

Quebec
Library of the Montreal Botanical Gardens
4101 est, rue Sherbrooke
Montreal, PQ H1X 2B2

MAIL-ORDER RETAIL NURSERIES

Adams Nursery, Box 606, Route 20, Westfield, Massachusetts 01085. (413) 562-3644, 736-0443. Retail and wholesale. General nursery stock. Catalog.

J. Herbert Alexander, 1224 Wareham Street, Middleboro, Massachusetts 02346. (617) 947-3397. Lilacs, flowering quince, blueberries, phlox. Descriptive mail-order list.

Armstrong Nurseries, 830 West Phillips, Ontario, California 91761 (714) 984-1211. Retail and wholesale. Hybrid tea and other roses. Mail-order catalog.

Arrowhead Gardens, 115 Boston Post Road, Wayland, Massachusetts 01778. (617) 235-9520. Retail and wholesale. General nursery stock.

Avalon Mountain Gardens, Dana, North Carolina 38724. (704) 692-9898. Retail. Azalea, heather, and perennials. List. Ships.

Bachman's, Inc., 6010 Lyndale Ave. South, Minneapolis, Minnesota 55423. (612) 861-7600. Retail and wholesale. Garden centers. General nursery stock. Retail catalog. Ships.

Warren Baldsiefen, Box 88, Bellvale, New York 10912. Retail. Rhododendrons. Mail-order catalog, refundable on first purchase. Nursery not open to visitors.

Bountiful Ridge Nurseries, Princess Anne, Maryland 21853. (301) 651-0400. Fruit and nut trees, berry plants and ornamentals. Retail and wholesale. Garden center. Mail-order catalog.

The Bovees, 1737 SW Coronado, Portland, Oregon 97219. (503) 244-9341. Retail only. Uncommon rhododendron species and hybrids. Exbury azalea. Visitors by appointment. Mail-order catalog. 25¢.

Bunting's Nurseries, Selbyville, Delaware 19975. (302) 436-8231. Separate retail and wholesale catalogs. Strawberries, fruit and nut trees, ornamentals. Mail-order catalog.

Burgess Seed and Plant Co., Box 3000, Galesburg, Michigan 49053. (616) 665-7079. Retail. Fruit and nut trees, berry plants, ornamentals. Vegetable and flower seed. House plants, garden supplies. Mail-order catalog.

W. Atlee Burpee Co., 300 Park Avenue, Warminster, Pa. 18974 (215) 674-4900. Branches in Clinton, Iowa, and Riverside, California. Vegetable and flower seeds, general nursery stock. Trees and shrubs sold retail. Mail-order catalog.

Carroll Gardens, East Main Street, Extension, Westminster, Maryland 21157. (301) 848-5422. Retail and wholesale. Dwarf evergreens, trees and shrubs, roses, perennials, herbs and groundcovers. Mail-order catalog.

Corliss Bros. Garden Center, Ipswich, Massachusetts 01938. See No. 6 in wholesale list.

Dauber's Nurseries, 1705 North George Street, Box 1746, York, Pennsylvania 17405. (717) 764-4553. Retail and wholesale. Uncommon trees and shrubs, often of landscape size. Hollies. Retail catalog.

Dilatush Nursery, RR 4, Robbinsville, New Jersey 08691. (609) 585-5387. Dwarf evergreens, uncommon trees and shrubs. Closed July and August. No shipping.

Eastern Shore Nurseries, Box 743, Route 331, Easton, Maryland 21601. (301) 822-1320. Retail and wholesale. General nursery stock, often of landscape size. Catalog. Ships.

Eisler Nurseries, Box 70, 219 East Pearl Street, Butler, Pennsylvania 16001. (412) 287-3703. General nursery stock with emphasis on landscape sizes. Retail catalog, with price adjustment for trade customers.

Emlong Nurseries, Stevensville, Michigan 49127. (616) 429-3431. Retail and wholesale. Garden centers in Stevensville and Niles, Mich. General nursery stock. Fruit trees. Mail-order catalog.

Farmer Seed and Nursery Co., Route 60, Faribault, Minnesota 55021. (507) 334-6421. Seven Minn. stores. General nursery stock, vegetable and flower seeds, and garden supplies. Mail-order catalog.

Earl Ferris Nursery, 811 Fourth Street NE, Hampton, Iowa 50441. (515) 456-2563. Retail. Wholesale mainly for evergreens and shrubs. Garden Center. General nursery stock. Mail-order catalog.

Henry Field Seed and Nursery Co., 407 Sycamore Street, Shenandoah, Iowa 51601. (712) 246-2110. Retail and wholesale. General nursery stock. Mail-order catalog.

Fiore Enterprises, Route 22, Prairie View, Illinois 60069. (312) 634-3400. Trees and shrubs, mainly of landscape size. Separate retail and wholesale catalogs. Ships.

Flickingers' Nursery, Sagamore, Pennsylvania 16250. (412) 783-6528. Retail and wholesale. Evergreen seedlings for Christmas trees and reforestation. Mail-order price list.

Game Food Nurseries, Box V, Omro, Wisconsin 54963. (414) 685-2929. Wild rice; other marsh and upland plants for gamebirds. Seeds. Catalog. Ships.

Gardens of the Blue Ridge, P.O. Box 10 Route 221, Pineola, North Carolina 28662. (704) 756-4339. Nursery on Route 221 in Pineola. Retail, limited wholesale. Native trees and shrubs, wide selection of wildflowers. Mail-order catalog.

D.S. George Nurseries, 2491 Penfield Road, Fairport, New York 14450. (716) 377-0731. Retail and wholesale. Clematis. Ships.

Girard Nurseries, Box 428, Geneva, Ohio 44041. (216) 466-2881. Retail and wholesale. Dwarf and unusual evergreens, azaleas, uncommon trees. Prebonsai conifers. Conifer seeds. Mail-order catalog.

Gossler Farms Nursery, 1200 Weaver Road, Springfield, Oregon 97477. (503) 746-3922. Retail. Rare magnolias. Flowering cherries. Trees chosen for bar character. Eucryphia. Unusually refined selection. Price list. Ships.

Greer Gardens, 1280 Goodpasture Island Road, Eugene, Oregon 97401. (503) 686-8226. Rhododendron, azalea, Japanese and other maples. Catalog.

Gurney Seed & Nursery Co., Yankton, South Dakota 57078. (605) 665-7481. Retail. Vegetable and flower seeds. Trees and shrubs for the Plains. Garden supplies. Mail-order catalog.

H.G. Hastings Co., Box 4214, Atlanta, Georgia 30302. (404) 522-9464. Three garden centers in Atlanta, one each in Birmingham and Charlotte. Retail and wholesale. Camellia, azalea, and other broadleaf evergreens for the South. Roses, vegetable and flower seed. Fruit trees. Ornamental trees and shrubs. Mail-order catalog.

Heard Gardens, 5355 Merle Hay Rd. (Route No. a, Box 134), Des Moines, Iowa 50323. (515) 276-4533. Retail and wholesale. Trees and shrubs of landscape size. Large selection of lilacs and crab apples. No catalog, but willing to ship particular items retail.

Thomas Henny Nursery, 7811 Stratford Drive, NE, Brooks, Oregon 97305. (503) 792-3376. Retail, with quantity discount. Gable and Glenn Dale azalea, also a good selection of rhododendrons. Pieris. Mail-order catalog.

C. M. Hobbs & Sons, 9300 West Washington Street, Bridgeport, Indiana 46231. (317) 241-9253. Retail and wholesale. Trees and shrubs, often of landscape size. Limited retail shipment.

Holly Heath Nursery, Route 25A, Wading River, New York (mailing address: Box 55A, Calverton, New York 11933). (516) 727-0859. Retail. Holly, heather, Glenn Dale and other azalea, dwarf plants. Does not ship.

Indian Run Nursery, Allentown Road, Robbinsville, New Jersey 08691. (609) 259-2600. Retail. Rhododendron. Catalog. Does not ship. Closed Monday.

Island Gardens, 701 Goodpasture Road, Eugene, Oregon 97401. (503) 343-4711. Retail and wholesale. Exbury azalea, rhododendron. Mail-order catalog.

Jackson & Perkins Co., Box 1028, Medford, Oregon 97501. (503) 779-4521. Retail and wholesale. Roses, spring bulbs. Mail-order catalog.

Kelly Bros. Nurseries, 23 Maple Street, Dansville, New York 14437. (716) 987-2211. Retail and wholesale. General nursery stock, fruit and nut trees, bulbs. Mail-order catalog.

Rudolph Kluis Nursery, Box 116, Ryan Road, Marlboro, New Jersey 07746. (201) 462-4694. Retail. Dwarf conifers, hard-to-find shrubs. Catalog 25¢. Does not ship. No deliveries. Visitors by appointment only. Closed Sunday.

Joseph J. Kern Rose Nursery, Box 33, Jackson Street & Heisley Road, Mentor, Ohio 44060. (216) 255-8627. Retail and wholesale. Old and new roses. Rare kinds. Custom budding. Visitors June–October by appointment only. Mail-order catalog.

Kimberly Barn Floral & Garden Center, 1221 E. Kimberly Rd., Davenport, Iowa 52807. (319) 386-1309. Local retail. General nursery stock.

Krider Nurseries, Middlebury, Indiana 46540. (219) 825-5714. Retail and wholesale. Fruit trees, ornamental trees and shrubs. Mail-order catalog.

Kroh Nurseries, Box 536, Rte. 287, Loveland, Colorado 80537. (303) 667-2443. Retail and wholesale. Ornamental trees and shrubs for the Rocky Mountains. Fruit trees. Large specimens at nursery. Mail-order catalog.

LaBars' Rhododendron Nursery, Box 111, Bryant St., Stroudsburg, Pennsylvania 18360. (717) 5880. Retail and wholesale. Landscape-size trees and shrubs available at the nursery. Mail-order catalog for rhododendron and other ericaceous plants.

LaFayette Home Nursery, Box 1A, RR #1, Route 17, LaFayette, Illinois 61449. (309) 995-3311. Retail and wholesale. Extensive selection of trees and shrubs, many in large specimen size. Lengthy retail price list. Nursery ships wholesale to other firms; also ships retail if customer so desires.

Lamb Nurseries, East 101 Sharp Avenue, Spokane, Washington 99202. (509) 328-7956. Dwarf shrubs, rock garden plants, perennials, groundcovers, herbs, hardy succulents. Mail-order catalog.

H. L. Larson, 3656 Bridgeport Way, Tacoma, Washington 98466. (206) 564-1488. Seeds of uncommon rhododendron species. No plants shipped. List.

A. M. Leonard, Inc., Box 816, Piqua, Ohio 45356. (513) 773-2694. Gardening and pruning tools. Extensive catalog.

Henry Leuthardt Nurseries, Montauk Highway, East Moriches, New York 11940. (516) 878-1387. Dwarf and espaliered fruit trees. Mail-order list.

Light's Landscape Nurserymen, 9153 East D Ave., Richland, Michigan 49083. (616) 629-9761. Retail and limited wholesale. Unusually wide range of trees and shrubs. Large specimens at nursery. Delivery arranged to various points. Catalog. Ships.

Littlefield-Wyman Nurseries, 227 Centre Ave. (Route 123), Abington, Massachusetts 02351. (617) 878-1800 (from Boston area call 472-1195.) General nursery and garden center. Landscape-size trees and shrubs, evergreens. Delivery within 20 miles of Abington, beyond by special arrangement. Catalog.

May Nursery Co., Box 1312, 2115 Lincoln Avenue, Yakima, Washington 98907. (509) 453-8219. Retail and wholesale. Fruit trees, berry plants and other nursery stock. Mail-order catalog.

Earl May Seed & Nursery Co., 100 North Elm Street, Shenandoah, Iowa 51601. (712) 246-1020. Primarily retail. 42 garden centers in Iowa, Nebraska, Missouri, and South Dakota. General nursery stock, fruit trees, flower and vegetable seed. Mail-order catalog.

McKay Nursery Co., 254 Jefferson Street, Waterloo, Wisconsin 53594. (414) 478-2121. (Sales offices in Milwaukee and Madison). Retail and wholesale. General nursery stock, specimen-size trees and shrubs. Landscape catalog.

Mellinger's, Inc., 2310 West South Range Road, North Lima, Ohio 44452. (216) 549-2027. Retail. Extensive variety of trees and shrubs in small sizes. Prebonsai. Tree seeds. Unusually large list of garden supplies, grafting tools, pruning shears, etc. Reference books. Mail-order catalog.

Musser Forests, Inc., Box 340, Route 119, Indiana, Pennsylvania 15701. (412) 456-5686. Conifers in quantity units for Christmas tree planting and reforestation. Deciduous trees, flowering shrubs. Mail-order catalog.

Neosho Nurseries, Box 550, Neosho, Missouri 64850. (417) 451-1212. Retail and wholesale. General nursery stock, fruit trees, roses and perennials. Gardening supplies. The firm issues a mail-order catalog.

Nuccio's Nurseries, 3555 Chaney Trail, Altadena, California 91001. (213) 794-3383. Retail. Extensive camellia listing. Azaleas. Nursery closed Wednesday. Mail-order catalog.

Oliver Nurseries, 1159 Bronson Road, Fairfield, Connecticut 06430. (203) 259-5609. Retail. Dwarf conifers and rock garden evergreens. Dwarf rhododendrons. Uncommon trees. Prebonsai plants. Catalog. Does not ship.

Palette Gardens, 26 West Zion Hill Road, Quakertown, Pennsylvania 18951. (215) 536-4027. Dwarf conifers (no catalog), uncommon rock garden perennials (price lists). Will ship conifers and perennials. Best call for appointment, since hours vary.

Panfield Nurseries, 322 Southdown Road, Huntington, New York 11743. (516) 427-0112. Retail and wholesale. Extensive selection of trees and shrubs, many in specimen size. Heathers, conifers, broadleaf evergreens. Separate retail and wholesale lists.

George W. Park Seed Co., Greenwood, South Carolina 29647. (803) 374-3341. Retail and wholesale for vegetable and flower seed, exclusively retail for nursery stock. Small sizes. Mail-order catalog.

Pellett Gardens, Atlantic, Iowa 50022. (712) 243-1917. Honey plants. Mail-order list.

Peters & Wilson Nursery, East Millbrae Ave. & Rollins Road, Millbrae, California 94030. (415) 697-5373. Retail and wholesale. Garden center. Closed Wednesday. Wide selection of ornamental trees and shrubs for southern California. Fruit trees. Catalog $1.

Plumfield Nurseries, Box 410, 2105 North Nye Avenue, Fremont, Nebraska 68025. (402) 721-3622. Garden center, 735 West 23rd Street (Route 30). (403) 721-3520. Retail orders handled through garden center, wholesale orders through the nursery. General nursery stock. Separate retail and trade lists.

Orlando S. Pride, PO Box 1865, Butler, Pennsylvania 16001. (412) 283-0962. Retail and wholesale. Azalea, holly, rhododendron, others. Catalog. Ships.

Putney Nursery, Putney, Vermont 05346. (802) 387-5577. Retail. Wildflowers, ferns, perennials, ornamental trees and shrubs. Woody plants available only at the nursery. Mail-order catalog.

Rainer Mt. Alpine Gardens, 2007 South 126th, Seattle, Washington 98168. (206) 242-4090. Retail (wholesale only at nursery). Dwarf conifers, uncommon rhododendrons, rock garden shrubs. Mail-order catalog.

Rayner Bros., Salisbury, Maryland 21801. (301) 742-1594. Retail. Fruit and nut trees, strawberries, other berry plants. Mail-order catalog.

Clyde Robin, Box 2091, Castro Valley, California 94546. (415) 581-3467. Retail. Unusual conifers, ornamental trees and shrubs in small sizes. Pre-bonsai. California native plants. Tree and wildflower seeds. Mail-order catalog 50¢.

Rosedale Nurseries, Saw Mill River Parkway, Hawthorne, New York 10532. (914) 769-1300. Also, Rosedale-in-Dutchess, Route 44, Millbrook, New York 12545. (914) 677-3938. Retail. Large selection of general nursery stock. Shade trees of landscape size. Many plants not in catalog are stocked. Does not ship.

Rose Hill Nursery, 2380 West Larpenteur Avenue, St. Paul, Minnesota 55113. (612) 646-7541. Also at E. Hennepin & Fulham, Minneapolis. Retail. General stock, fruit trees, berry plants. Catalog. Ships.

Scarff's Nursery, Route 1, New Carlisle, Ohio 45344. (513) 845-2551. Retail and wholesale. General nursery stock.

Seven Dees Nursery, 6025 SE Powell, Portland, Oregon 97206. (503) 777-1412. Retail outlet of Sherwood Nursery Co.

A. Shammarello & Son Nursery, 4508 Monticello Boulevard, South Euclid, Ohio 44143. (216) 381-2510. Retail and wholesale. Rhododendrons and other broadleaf evergreens. Mail-order catalog.

The Shop in the Sierra, Carl Stephens, Box 1, Midpines, California 95345. Western native trees and shrubs. Mail-order catalog.

Silver Falls Nursery & Christmas Tree Farm, Silver Falls Highway, Star Route, Box 84, Silverton, Oregon 97381. (503) 873-4945. Retail. Large selection of unusual conifers, shrubs and trees, western native plants. Small sizes, many plants suited for bonsai initiation. Mail-order catalog.

Francis M. Sinclair, RFD 1, Newmarket Rd., Exeter, New Hampshire 03833. (603) 772-2362. Quantity dealer in wildflowers, native trees and shrubs. Material collected from the wild. Price list. Ships.

Siskiyou Rare Plant Nursery, 522 Franquette St., Medford, Oregon 97501. Retail. Dwarf shrubs, rare alpine plants. Mail order catalog 50¢.

Joel W. Spingarn, 1535 Forest Avenue, Baldwin, New York 11510. (516) 623-7810. Retail. Extensive collection of dwarf conifers, Japanese maples, rock garden rhododendron. Ships. Visitors by appointment only.

Spring Hill Nurseries, Elm Street, Tipp City, Ohio 45371. (513) 667-2491. Retail and wholesale. General stock, perennials, groundcovers, vines. Mail-order catalog.

Star Roses (Conrad-Pyle Co.), West Grove, Pennsylvania 19390. (215) 869-2426. Retail mail order catalog limited to roses. Garden centers in West Grove and Lancaster offer a wide range of shrubs and trees, besides roses. Wholesale catalog for roses and general stock.

Stark Bros. Nurseries & Orchards Co., Louisiana, Missouri 63353. (314) 754-5511. Retail. Large selection of fruit trees. Ornamental shrubs and trees. Mail-order catalog.

Stern's Nurseries, Geneva, New York 14456. General nursery stock, including fruit plants, roses and perennials. Mail-order catalog.

Sylvan Nursery, 1028 Horseneck Road, South Westport, Massachusetts 02790. (617) 636-4573. Retail. Heaths, heathers, seashore plants. List. Ships.

Thomasville Nurseries, Box 7, 1842 Smith Avenue, Thomasville, Georgia 31792. (912) 226-5568. Retail. Camellia, roses, daylily, liriope. Mail-order catalog.

Tillotson's Roses, 992 Brown's Valley Rd., Watsonville, California 95076. (408) 724-3537. Retail, with discount for quantity purchase. Extensive selection of old-fashioned and modern roses. Catalog.

William Tricker, Inc., 74 Allendale Avenue, Saddle River, New Jersey 07458. (201) 327-0721. Also, 7125 Tanglewood Drive, Independence, Ohio 44131, (216) 524-2430. Waterlilies and bog plants. Mail-order catalog.

Valley Nursery, Box 4845, 2801 North Montana, Helena, Montana 59601. (406) 442-8460. Retail and wholesale. Uncommon trees and shrubs for cold climates. Seedlings in quantity units. Price list. Ships.

Martin Viette Nurseries, Route 25A (Northern Boulevard), Muttontown, New York 11732. (516) 922-5530. Retail and wholesale. Extensive nursery stock, including an unusually wide range of perennials and wildflowers. Catalog. Does not ship.

Watnong Nursery, The Don Smiths, Morris Plains, New Jersey 07950. (201) 539-0312. Retail. Extensive selection of dwarf evergreens, rare shrubs and trees. Container-grown. Availability lists. Does not ship. Open by appointment only.

Waynesboro Nurseries, Box 987, Lyndhurst-Sherando Lake Rd., Waynesboro, Virginia 22980. (703) 942-4141. Retail and wholesale. General nursery stock, fruit trees, berry plants. Smaller trees and shrubs shipped, larger ones at the nursery. Mail-order catalog.

Additional Suppliers

Bamboo

J. Herbert Alexander
Route 28, Cranberry Highway
Middleboro, MA 02346

Bamboo Jungle Nursery
29100 SW 16th Avenue
Homestead, FL

Brimfield Gardens Nursery
245 Brimfield Road
Wethersfield, CT 06109

Robert Lester
280 West 4th Street
NY, NY 10014

Mellinger's
2310 West South Range
North Lima, OH 44452

Paletter Gardens
26 West Zion Hill Road
Quakerstown, PA 18951

Bromeliads

Bromeliads
639 Bend Drive
Sunnyvale, CA 94087

Cornelison's Bromeliad Nursery
225 San Bernardino Street
North Fort Myers, FL 33903

Edelweiss Gardens
Box 66
Robinsville, NJ 08691

Lakeview Gardens
Route 3
Box 447
Escondis, CA 92025

North Jersey Bromeliads
Box 181
Alpine, NJ 07620

Broadleaf Evergreens

Adams Nursery, Inc.
Box 606
Westfield, MA 01086

The Bovees
1636 SW Coronado Street
Portland, OR 97219

Warren and Susan Baldsiefen
Box 88
Bellvale, NY 10912

Eccles Nurseries
Rimersburg, PA 16248

Greer Gardens
1280 Goodpasture Island Road
Eugene, OR 97401

Ingleside Plantation & Nurseries
Box 1038
Oak Grove, VA 22443

Island Gardens
701 Goodpasture Island Road
Eugene, OR 97401

Kelly Brothers Nurseries
Dansville, NY 11437

H. L. Larson
3656 Bridgeport Way
Tacoma, WA 98466

Monrovia Nursery Co.
Box Q
Azusa, CA 91702

Musser Forests
Box 340
Indiana, PA 15701

Nuccio's Nurseries
3555 Chaney Trail
Altadena, CA 91001

Oliver Nurseries
1159 Bronson Road
Fairfield, CT 06430

Pikes Peak Nurseries
RD 1
Penn Run, PA 15765

Savage Farm Nursery
Box 125
McMinnville, TN 37110

Shessin Nurseries
1081 King Street
Box 64
Glenville Station
Greenwich, CT 06830

Sprainbrook Nursery, Inc.
448 Underhill Road
Scarsdale, NY 10583

Vans Pines, Inc.
West Olive, MI 49460

Van Veen Nursery
4201 SE Franklin
Portland, OR 97026

Western Maine Forest Nursery Co.
Fyreburg, ME 04037

Weston Nurseries, Inc.
East Main Street
Route 135
Hopkinton, MA 01748

Dahlias

Bateman's Dahlias
6911 SE Drew Street
Portland, OR 97222

Legg Dahlia Gardens
RD 2, Hastings Road
Geneva, NY 11456

S & K Gardens
401 Quick Road
Castle Rock, WA 98611

Swan Island Dahlias
Box 800
Canby, OR 97013

Daylilies

Howard J. Hite
Lake Angelus Gardens
370 Gallogly Road
Pontiac, MI 48055

Klehn Nursery
2 East Algonquine Road
Arlington Heights, IL 60005

Lenington Gardens
7007 Manchester Ave.
Kansas City, MO 64133

Louisiana Nursery
Route 7
Box 43
Opleousas, LA 70570

Putney Nursery, Inc.
Putney, VT 05346

The Saxton Gardens
1 First Street
Saratoga Springs, NY 12866

Fruit Trees

Baums Nursery
RD 4
New Fairfield, CT 06815

Bountiful Ridge Nurseries, Inc.
Princess Anne, MD 21853

Brittingham Plant Farms
Ocean City Boulevard
Salisbury, MD 21801

Buntings' Berries
Buntings' Nurseries, Inc.
Selbyville, DE 19975

Common Fields Nurseries
Ipswich, MA 01938

Fruit Haven Nursery, Inc.
Route 1
Kaleva, MI 49645

Henry Leuthardt Nurseries, Inc.
East Moriches, NY 11940

Mayo Nurseries
Route 14, North
Lyons, NY 14489

J. E. Miller Nurseries, Inc.
Canadaigua, NY 14424

Ozark Nursery Garden Center
Route No. 2
Tahlequah, OK 74464

Rayner Bros., Inc.
Salisbury, MD 21801

Rider Nurseries
Farmington, IA 52626

Southmeadow Fruit Gardens
2363 Tilbury Place
Birmingham, MI 48009

Stark Bros. Nurseries
Louisiana, MO 63353

Stribling's Nurseries Inc.
Box 793
1620 West 16th
Merced, CA 95340

Talbott Nursery
Route 3
Linton, IN 47441

Waynesboro Nurseries
Waynesboro, VA 22980

Gardening Equipment

Charley's Greenhouse Supply
12815 WE 124th Street
Kirkland, WA 98033

Cheyenne Corp.
30961 Agoura Road
Westlake Village, CA 91360

Clairmont Products Co.
Box 364
Hamburg, NJ 07419

Farnam Companies
Box 12068
Omaha, NB 68112

Garden Systems, Inc.
Box 117006
Gordon, WI 54838

Garden Tech Ltd.
Box 612
Needham, MA 02192

Hardware & Industrial Tool Co.
2607 River Road
Cinnaminson, NJ 08077

The House of Pots
Box 1274
Gainesville, FL 32601

Walter F. Nicke
Box 667
Hudson, NY 12534

Earl May Seed Co. and Nursery
Shenandoah, IA 51602

The National Development Co.
Bainbridge, PA 17502

L. L. Olds Seeds
Box 1069
Madison, WI 53701

PBI-Gordon Corp.
300 South 3rd Street
Kansas City, KS 66118

Planter' Equipment Corp.
Route 2
Box 439
Johns Island, SC 29455

Reforestation Suppliers
Box 5547
Eugene, OR 97405

Smith & Hawken Tool Co.
68 Homer
Palo Alto, CA 94301

Wimberly
4000 Clark Drive
Kelseyville, CA 95451

Gladiolus

Bevington Greenaces
RR 1
Galveston, IN 46932

Flad's Glads
2109 Cliff Court
Madison, WI 53713

Gladside Gardens
61 Main Street
Northfield, MA 01360

Gurney Seed and Nursery Co.
2nd and Capitol
Yankton, SD 57078

Idaho Ruffled Gladiolus Garden
612 East Main Street
Jerome, ID 83338

J. W. Jung Seed Co.
335 South High Street
Randolph, WI 53956

Kingfish Glads
11345 Moreno Avenue
Lakeside, CA 92040

Lake Angelus Gardens
370 Gallaghy Road
Pontiac, MI 48055

Mountainview Glads
Route 2
Box 353A6
Coeur-D'Alene, ID 83814

Noweta Gardens
949 Saint Charles Avenue
Saint Charles, MN 55972

Pleasant Valley Glads
163 Senator Avenue
Agawan, MA 01001

Squires Bulb Farm
3419 Eccles Avenue
Ogden, UT 84403

Alex Summerville
Route 1
Box 449
Glassboro, NJ 08028

Van Bourgondien and Sons, Inc.
Box A
Babylon, NY 11702

Walnut Grove Glad Gardens
6572 West Smith Road
Medina, OH 44256
(send stamped envelope)

The Wanshara Gardens
Plainfield, NJ 54966

Groundcovers

The Alestake
Elkwood, VA 22718

Burgess Seed & Plant
Galesburg, MI 49053

Edelweiss Gardens
Robbinsville, NJ 08691

Gardens of the Blue Ridge
Box 16
Route 221
Pineola, NC 28662

Gilson Gardens, Inc.
Box 277
Perry, OH 44081

Hemlock Hill Herb Farm
Litchfield, CT 06109

Kelly Bros. Nurseries, Inc.
Dansville, NY 14437

Lamb Nurseries
East 101 Sharp Avenue
Spokane, WA 99207

Monrovia Nursery Co.
East Foothill Boulevard
Azusa, CA 91702

Musser Forests
Box 340
Indiana, PA 15701

Rakestraw's Gardens
G-3094 South Term Street
Burton, MI 48507

Spring Hill Nurseries
311 Elm Street
Tipp City, OH 45371

Sunnybrook Farm
9448 Mayfield Road
Chesterland, OH 44026

Vans Pines Inc.
West Olive, MI 49460

Wayside Gardens
Hodges, NC 29695

Weston Nurseries
East Main Street
Hopinkton, MA 01748

White Flower Farm
Litchfield, CT 06759

The Wild Garden
Box 487
Bothall, WA 98011

Indoor Lighting

Burgess Seed & Plant Co.
Box 218
67 East Brattle Street
Galesburg, MI 49053

Floralite Company
4124 East Oakwood Road
Oak Creek, WI 53154

Greenhouse Specialties
9849 Kimkar Lane
St. Louis, MO 63127

House Plant Corner
Box 810
Oxford, MD 21654

Lord & Burnham
CSB 3181
Melville, NY 11747

Rosetta Electric Company
21 West 46th Street
NY, NY 10036

Shoplite Co.
650 Franklin Avenue
Nutley, NJ 07110

Tube Craft, Inc.
1311 West 80th Street
Cleveland, OH 44102

Irises

Bay View Gardens
1201 Bay Street
Santa Cruz, CA 95060

Bushey's Gardens
6731 Akrich Street
Redding, CA 96001

Ralph B. Coleman
Mount Olive Iris Garden
10349 Empire Grade
Santa Cruz, CA 95060

Cooley's Iris Gardens
Box 12
Silverton, OR 97381

Eden Road Iris Garden
Box 117
Wenatchee, WA 98801

Doris Foster
321 East Montecito Avenue
Sierra Madre, CA 91024

Hildenbrandt's Iris Garden
Star Route
Box 4
Lexington, NB 68850

Iris Test Gardens
1010 Highland Park Drive
College Place, WA 99324

Melrose Gardens
309 Best Road South
Stockton, CA 95206

Mid-America Iris Garden
Box 425
Wheatland, OK 73097

Mission Bell Gardens
2778 West 5600 South
Roy, UT 84067

Pacific Coast Hybridizers
Box 972
Cambell, CA 95008

Richland Iris Productions Ltd.
Box 268
Route 3
Richland Center, WI 53581

Riverdale Iris Gardens
7124 Riverdale Road
Minneapolis, MN 55430

Schliefert Iris Gardens
RFD
Murdock, NB 68407

Schreiner's
3625 Quinaby Road NE
Salem, OR 97303

Seaways Gardens
Dr. and Mrs. Currier McEwan
South Harpswell, ME 04079

Smith's Iris Gardens
614 Bryden Avenue
Box 483
Lewiston, ID 83501

Southern Meadows Garden
1424 South Perrine
Walnut Hill Road
Box 230
Centralia, IL 72801

Species Specialties
5809 Rahke Road
Indianapolis, IN 46217

Summerlong Iris Gardens
Route 2
Box 163
Perrysville, OH 44864

Tell's Gardens
Box 331
Orem, UT 84057

Mrs. Wilma Vallette
Delco, ID 83323

Valley's End Iris Gardens
32375 Dunlap Road
Yucalpa, CA 92399

D. Steve Varner
North State Street Road
Illini Iris
Monticello, IL 61856

Whisperwood Gardens
Box 357
Canton, TX 75103

Peonies

Brand Peony Farms & Nursery
Box 842
St. Cloud, MN 56301

Louis Smirnow
85 Linden Lane
Glen Head Post Office
Brookville, NY 11545

David Reath
Vulcan, MI 49892

Sarcoxie Nurseries, Inc.
Peony Fields
Box 306
Sarxocie, MO 64862

Top O' the Ridge
100 NE 81st Street
Kansas City, MO 64118

Gilbert H. Wild & Son, Inc.
Sarcoxie, MO 64862

Rare Houseplants

Edelweiss Gardens
Robinsville, NJ 08691
Unusual houseplants

Fischer Greenhouses
Linwood, NJ 08221
African violets

Greenland Flower Shop
Route 1, Stormstown
Port Mathilda, PA 16871
Rare houseplants

Margaret Ilgenfritz
Box 1114
Monroe, MI 48161
Orchids

Kartuz Greenhouses
92 Chestnut Street
Wilmington, MA 01887
Gesneriads, begonias, geraniums

Robert Lester
280 West 4th Street
NY, NY 10014
Orchids

Lilypons Water Gardens
1612 Hort Road
Lilypons, MD 21717
Hardy waterlilies, aquatic plants

Logee's Greenhouses
Danielson, CT 06239
Begonias, rare plants, geraniums

Rod McLellan Co.
1450 El Camino Real
South San Francisco, CA 94080
Bonsai

Merry Gardens
Camden, ME 04843
Flowering and foliage houseplants, geraniums, begonias

Paradise Gardens
14 Mary Street
Whitman, MA 02382
Aquatic plants, goldfish, pools

Julius Roehrs Co.
Box 144
Route 33
Rutherford, NJ 07073
Rare houseplants

William Tricker, Inc.
74 Allendale Avenue Box 398
Saddle River, NJ 07548
Waterlilies

Van Ness Water Gardens
2460 North Euclid Avenue
Upland, CA 91786
Waterlilies

John Vermeulen & Sons
Heshanic Station, NJ 08553

Seeds and Plants

Abbey Garden
176 Toro Canyon
Carpinteria, CA 93103
Succulents

Antonelli Bros.
2545 Capitola Road
Santa Cruz, CA 95060
Tuberous begonias

Armacost & Royston
2005 Armacost Avenue
West Los Angeles, CA 90025
Orchids

Burgess Seed & Plant Co.
Box 218
67 East Brattle Street
Galesburg, MI 49053
Seeds of annuals, biennials, and perennials

W. Atlee Burpee Co.
Philadelphia, PA 19132
Seeds of annuals, biennials, and perennials

Edelweiss Gardens
Robbinsville, NJ 08691
General plants

Fennell Orchid Co.
26715 SW 157th Avenue
Homestead, FL 33031
Orchids

Fischer Greenhouse
Linwood, NJ 08221
African violets

Joseph Harris Co., Inc.
Moreton Farm, Buffalo Road
Rochester, NY 14624
Vegetable seeds

Logee's Greenhouses
Danielson, CT 06239
General plants

Lyndon Lyon
Dolgeville, NY 13329
African violets

Merry Gardens
Camden, ME 04843
General plants

George W. Park Seed Co.
Greenwood, SC 29646
Seeds of annuals, biennials, and perennials

J. A. Peterson
3132 McHenry Avenue
Cincinnati, OH 45211
African violets

John Scheepers, Inc.
63 Wall Street
NY, NY 10005
Bulbs

Strawberries

The Connor Company
Box 534
Augusta, AR 72006

Jackson & Perkins
Medford, OR 97501

Lewis Strawberry Nursery, Inc.
Box 24
Rocky Point, NC 28457

W. F. Allen Co.
Salisbury, MD 21801

CANADIAN NURSERIES

Alberta Nurseries & Seeds, Ltd., Bowden, MA. (403) 224-3362. Mostly retail. Ornamental and fruit trees. Vegetable and flower seed. Mail-order catalog.

Alpenglow Gardens, 13328 King George Highway, North Surrey, BC V3T 2T6. (604) 581-8733. Specializes in rare alpines, dwarf slow-growing conifers and flowering shrubs. Mail-order catalog. Exports.

Beaverlodge Nursery Ltd., Box 127, Beaverlodge, AL T0H 0C0. (403) 354-2195. Hardy plants for nothern gardens, including many fruit varieties. Exports.

John Connon Nurseries, Waterdown, ON L0R 2H0. (416) 689-4631. Retail and wholesale. General nursery stock. Mail-order catalog.

William Dam Seeds, Highway 8, West Flamboro, ON L0R. (416) 628-6641. Untreated vegetable and flower seeds; European and Canadian varieties, some for short growing seasons. Exports.

H. M. Eddie & Sons, 4100 SW Marine Drive, Vancouver, BC. (604) 261-3188. Retail and wholesale. General nursery stock, roses. Mail-order catalog.

Patmore Nurseries, Brandon, MA R7A 5Z7. (204) 728-1321. Retail nursery stock for the Northern Plains. Mail-order catalog.

Richters, Goodwood, ON L0C 1A0 (416) 640-6677. Specializes in herb seeds, including several types of basil; gingseng seed; books on herbs and medicinal plants. Catalog $1. Exports.

Sheridan Nurseries, 700 Evans Avenue, Etobicoke, ON. (416) 621-9111. Sales stations also at Greenhedges, 650 Montée de Lièsse, Montreal, PQ (514) 744-2451; Glenpark, 2827 Yonge Street, Toronto, ON (416) 481-6429. Others in Clarkson and Unionville, ON. Retail and wholesale. Wide selection of general nursery stock, perennials, roses. Deliveries in Toronto-Hamilton and Metropolitan Montreal. Mail-order catalog. Ships.

IMPORTING PLANTS

You may not bring plants into the continental United States without a special permit from the U.S. Department of Agriculture. The procedure for importing plants legally is simple, however. The first step is to write for a permit application to: Permit Unit, Plant Protection and Quarantine, Animal Plant Health Inspection Station, U.S.D.A., Room 638, Federal Bldg., Hyattsville, MD 20782.

The application will ask you to state specifically what plant you wish to import. For each type of plant, you need a separate application. You may import a single plant or a hundred or more. U.S.D.A. import permits, issued at no charge and valid for five years, are numbered. The numbers are recorded at the Permit Unit in a central file, as well as at each port of entry.

Next, obtain shipping labels from the Hyattsville office of the U.S.D.A. These will bear your permit number and will entitle you to the services of the U.S.D.A. laboratory that will inspect, and fumigate if necessary, any plants sent from abroad or that you bring into the country yourself. Ask for labels for a specific port of entry. If you are ordering plants through the mail, the dealer will tell you to which port of entry your plants will be sent.

Mail-order plants must bear your label on the outside of the package and, on the inside, contain your name and address, an invoice stating value, and a phytosanitary certificate obtained from the ministry of agriculture from the country of origin.

When dealing with a plant exporter, you must decide how your plants will be shipped. Air parcel post is the fastest way. It is also convenient because the Postal Service mail carrier will collect all duties on your plant at the time of delivery. If a plant is small, ordinary air mail may be fine.

Slower methods of shipment have obvious disadvantages. The container used must have holes for ventilation. You may also have to obtain the services of a broker who handles matters at the port of entry. Brokers' fees, for the most part, are higher than the cost of air parcel post.

If you expect to bring plants home from a trip abroad, take along your shipping labels. It is also a good idea to speak to a Customs official at the airport to learn about the procedure from that angle. Before starting for home, pack the plants in a cardboard box. Include in the package your name and address, a receipt for the cost of the plants, and a phytosanitary certificate from the minister of agriculture.

Some plants, such as orchids, can be harmed by a heavy dose of fumigation at the inspection station at the port of entry. If you are worried about losing your plants at the hands of the U.S.D.A., include instructions about their care. As long as your plants are healthy, however, nothing will be done to them; only infested plants are fumigated.

The following mail-order concerns are experienced plant exporters. Since there is no way your dealings with them can be predicted, you might request the name of an American customer as a reference if you have any doubts.

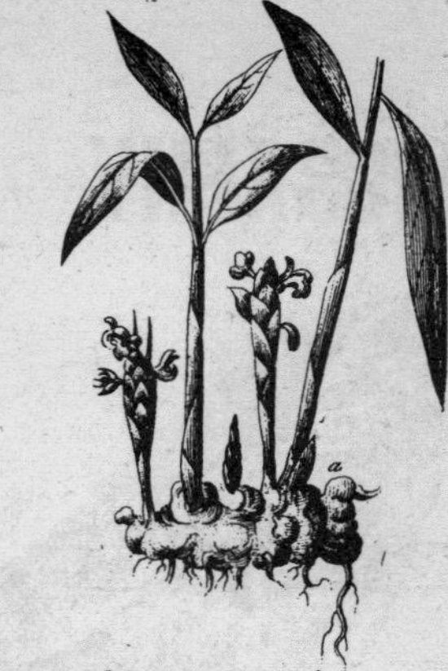

Bermuda

Aberfeldy Nurseries Ltd., Box 1538, Hamilton. Assortment of trees, shrubs, and plants, including wind- and/or salt-hardy tropical varieties.

England

Bees Unlimited, Sealand, Chester CH1 6BA. Roses, ornamental trees and shrubs, hardy border plants, bulbs, fruit, and culinary herbs.

Bressinham Gardens, Diss, Norfolk IP22 2AB. Large assortment of hardy perennials and shrubs; heaths and heathers; alpine species.

Thomas Butcher Ltd., 60 Wickham Rd., Shirley, Croydon CR9 8AG. Annuals and perennials, trees, seeds and plants for greenhouses; vegetable seeds.

France

Marcel Lecoufle Orchidées, 5 rue de Paris, 94470 Boissy Saint Léger. Large assortment of orchids.

Germany

Blossfeld, Postfach 1550, D-2400 Lübeck. Exotic plants, cyclamen, begonia.

Herman A. Hesse Baumschulen, 2952 Weener 1, Postfach 240. 200-page catalog offering huge variety of trees, shrubs, vines, and plants.

G. Köhres, Bahnstrasse 101, D-6106 Erzhausen/Darmstadt. Seed list comprising seeds of hundreds of cactus and succulents, e.g., 30 kinds of opuntia.

Hawaii

Exotics Hawaii, Ltd., 1344 Hoaka Place, Honolulu, HA 98621.

Jim Fobel, 598 Kipuka Pl., Kailua, HA 96734.

Lehua Anthurium Nursery, 80 Kokea St., Hilo, HA 96720.

Maile's Anthurium, Ltd., 41-1019 Kakaina St., Wainmanalo, Oahu HA 96795. Anthuriums and other tropical plants.

India

J. N. Enterprises, Box 1642, Kathmandu, Nepal. Flowering bulbs, tubers, and rhyzomes, including new hybrid gerberas; wholesale orchids.

P. Kohli & Co., Park Rd., Srinagar, Kashmir. Rare Himalayan flower bulbs; trees, shrubs, vines, perennials.

Japan

T. Sakata & Co., C.P.O. Box Yokohama No. 11, Yokohama 220-91. Flower seeds, many types developed for mild climates.

The Netherlands

Dutch Gardens, Inc., Box 30, Lisse. U.S. address: Box 168, Montvale, NJ 07645. Assortment of tulips, hyacinths, daffodils, narcissi, and other bulbs.

Royalsluis, Box 22, 1600 AA Enkhuizen. Vegetable seeds, including many new varieties and hybrids.

New Zealand

Peter B. Dow & Co., Box 696, Gisborne. U.S. subsidiary: Dow Seeds Hawaii, Ltd., Box 30144, Honolulu, HA 96820. Exotic and tropical plants, ferns, cactus, and succulents.

Thailand

T. Orchids, 30/71 Suthisanvinichai Rd., Bangkok. Large assortment of orchids, including many new hybrids. Catalog $2.

Spain

La Horticola Aragonesa, Morés, Zaragoza. Fruit trees and root stock, conifers, vineyard plants, shrubs, palms, cactus, vegetable and flower seeds.

BIBLIOGRAPHY

Bees

Berto, Hazel. *Cooking with Honey.* New York: Crown, 1972. Novel and exciting ways to use honey to make dishes more exciting.
Dandant, C. P. *First Lessons in Beekeeping.* New York: Charles Scribner's Sons, 1976. Reliable guide to bees, hives, producing honey.
Eckert, J. E. *Beekeeping.* New York: Macmillan, 1960. All phases of bees and beekeeping.
Elkton, Juliette. *Honey Cookbook.* New York: Knopf, 1955. Excellent; with 250 recipes.
Ellison, Virginia. *The Pooh Cookbook.* New York: Dell, 1975. Delightful honey recipes for children with quotations from Pooh Bear stories.
Free, J. B. *Insect Pollination of Crops.* New York: Academic Press, 1971. A masterful presentation of the honeybee's role in world pollination needs.
Laidlaw, H. H., and J. E. Eckert. *Queen Rearing.* Berkeley: University of California Press, 1962. Thorough explanation of modern queen-rearing methods.
Lovell, Harvey B. *Honey Plants Manual.* Medina, Oh. A. E. I. Root, 1977. Field manual for identifying honey flora.
Morse, Roger. *The Complete Guide to Beekeeping.* New York: Dutton, 1980. Practical and complete guide to beekeeping.

Cacti and Succulents
Benson, Lyman. *Cacti of Arizona,* 3rd edition. Tucson: University of Arizona Press, 1969.
Britton, N. L., and J. N. Rose. *The Cactacea: Descriptions and Illustrations of Plants of the Cactus Family.* 2 vols. New York: Dover, 1963.
Cutak, Ladislaus. *Cactus Guide.* New York: Van Nostrand Reinhold, 1956.
Higgins, Verna. *Succulents in Cultivation.* New York: St. Martin's Press, 1960.
Jacobsen, H. *A Handbook of Succulent Plants.* Reseda, Ca.: Abbey Garden Press, 1960.
Teuscher, Henry, ed. *A Handbook of Succulent Plants.* New York: Brooklyn Botanic Gardens, 1963.

Carnivorous Plants
Schwartz, Randall. *Carnivorous Plants.* New York: Avon, 1975. Probably the best book available on carnivorous plants.

Community Gardening
Jobb, Jamie. *The Complete Book of Community Gardening.* New York: William Morrow, 1979.
Wearne, Robert A., ed. *Community Gardening: A Handbook.* New York: Brooklyn Botanic Garden, 1979.

Flowers
Crockett, James Underwood. *Crockett's Flower Garden.* Boston: Little, Brown, 1981. A month-by-month approach to growing 100 different kinds of annuals, biennials, perennials (including roses), and bulbs.

Kramer, Jack. *1000 Beautiful Garden Plants and How to Grow Them.* New York: Morrow Quill Paperbacks, 1976.
Wilson, Helen Van Pelt. *Successful Gardening with Perennials.* New York: Doubleday, 1976. Illustrated, readable guide by one of America's most famous gardeners.

Horticultural Structures
Blake, Claire. *Greenhouse Gardening for Fun.* New York: William Morrow, 1967.
Boodey, James W. *Commercial Greenhouse.* Albany: Delmar, 1981.
Crockett, James U. *Greenhouse Gardening.* Alexandria, Va.: Time-Life, 1977.
Crockett, James Underwood, ed. *Greenhouse Handbook for the Amateur,* New York: Brooklyn Botanic Gardens, 1976.
Ellwood, Charles C. *How to Build and Operate Your Greenhouse.* Tucson: HP Books, 1977.
Kramer, Jack. *Your Homemade Greenhouse and How to Build It.* New York: Walker & Co., 1980.
Laurie, Alex, and D. C. Kiplinger. *Commercial Flower Forcing,* 8th edition. New York: McGraw-Hill, 1979.
McDonald, Elvin. *Greenhouse Gardens.* New York: New American Library, 1976.
Menager, Ronald H. *Greenhouse Gardening.* New York: Penguin, 1977.
Minar, William M. *Greenhouse Gardening in the South.* Houston: Pacesetter Press, 1976.
Nelson, K. S. *Flower and Plant Production in the Greenhouse,* 3rd edition. Danville, Il.: Interstate Printers & Publishers, 1978.
Nelson, K. S. *Greenhouse Management for Flower and Plant Production,* 4th edition. Danville, Il.: Interstate Printers & Publishers, 1980.
Oldale, Adrienne. *Growing Food Under Glass, 1001 Questions Answered.* North Pomfret, Vt.: David & Charles, 1978.
Pierce, John H. *Greenhouse Grow-How.* New York: Charles Scriber's Sons, 1978.
Walls, Ian G. *Complete Book of Greenhouse Gardening.* New York: Times Books, 1975.
Wolfe, Dolores. *Growing Food in Solar Greenhouses: A Month-by-Month Guide to Raising Vegetables, Fruits and Herbs Under Glass.* New York: Dolphin, 1981.

Indoor and Terrace Gardening
Abraham, George. *The Green Thumb Book of Indoor Gardening.* Englewood Cliffs, N.J.: Prentice-Hall, 1967.
Cruso, Thalassa. *Making Things Grow.* New York: Knopf, 1973.
Geiger, Maggy. *The Window Box Primer.* New York: Popular Library, 1979.
Halpin, Anne M., ed. *Rodale's Encyclopedia of Indoor Gardening.* Emmaus, Pa: Rodale Press, 1980. 874-page how-to compendium covering every aspect of indoor gardening; illustrated.
Yang, Linda. *The Terrace Gardener's Handbook.* New York: Doubleday, 1975.

Landscape and Garden Design
Crockett, J. V. *Landscape Gardening.* Alexandria, Va.: Time-Life Books, 1971.
Eckbo, Garret. *Art of Home Landscaping.* New York: F. W. Dodge Corp., 1956.
Lewis, Clarence E., ed. *Trees and Shrub Forms: Their Landscape Use.* Brooklyn Botanic Gardens, 1980.
McClenon, C., and G. O. Robinette. *Landscape Planning for Energy Conservation.* Newtonville, Ma.: Environmental Design Press, 1977.
Moffat, Ann Simon, and Marc Schiller. *Landscape Design that Saves Energy.* New York: William Morrow, 1981.
Ortloff, H. Stuart, and Henry B. Raymore. *The Book of Landscape Design.* New York: William Morrow, 1975.
Zion, Robert. *Trees for Architecture & and the Landscape.* New York: Van Nostrand, 1979.

Outdoor Gardening in General
Alth, Max. *How to Farm Your Backyard the Mulch-Organic Way.* New York: McGraw-Hill, 1975.
Cruso, Thalassa. *Making Things Grow Outdoors.* New York: Knopf, 1971. A highly readable guide for beginners and experienced gardeners on all aspects of gardening.
Jankowiak, James. *The Prosperous Gardener: A Guide to Gardening the Organic Way.* Emmaus, Pa.: Rodale Press, 1978.
Foster, H. Lincoln. *Rock Gardening: A Guide to Growing Alpines and Other Wildflowers in the American Garden.* Boston: Houghton Mifflin, 1968.
Minnion, Jerry, et al. *The Rodale Guide to Composting.* Emmaus, Pa.: Rodale Press, 1979. Techniques, tools, and materials for making composts.
Organic Gardening Magazine. *The Encyclopedia of Organic Gardening.* Emmaus, Pa.: Rodale Press, 1978. Everything about outdoor vegetable gardening without pesticides or chemicals; a good basic reference.

Propagation
Adriance, Guy W., and Fred R. Brison. *Propagation of Horticultural Plants.* Melbourne, Fl.: R. E. Kreiger, 1979.
James, Wilma R. *Propagate Your Own Plants.* Happy Camp, Ca.: Naturegraph, 1978.

Roses
Anderson, Frank. *An Illustrated History of Redoubté Roses.* New York: Abbeville Press, 1979.
Krussman, G. *The Complete Book of Roses.* Portland: Timber Press, 1982. A lavish book on every aspect of roses, with fine drawings and full-color plates.

Terrariums
Elbert, George A. *The Indoor Light Gardening Book.* New York: Crown, 1975.
Weisman, Brenda, ed. *Terrariums: A Handbook,* 2nd edition. New York: Brooklyn Botanic Gardens, 1975.

Trees and Shrubs
Behne, Robert Lee. *Bonsai, Saikei and Bonkei.* New York: William Morrow, 1969.
Crockett, James. *Trees.* Alexandria, Va.: Time-Life Books, 1972.
Harris, Cyril. *Trees and Shrubs in the Modern Garden.* New York: Merrimack Book Service, 1975.
Grounds, Roger, ed. *The Complete Book of Pruning.* New York: Macmillan, 1973. When, where, and how to prune.
Kraft, Ken, and Pat Kraft. *Grow Your Own Dwarf Fruit Trees.* New York: Walker and Company, 1974.
Muenscher, W. C. *Aquatic Plants.* Sausalito: Comstock Editions, 1944.
Taylor, Norman. *The Guide to Garden Shrubs and Trees.* Boston: Houghton Mifflin, 1965. Gardening know-how on 500 species of trees and shrubs, including culture and hardiness.
Wyman, Donald. *Trees for American Gardens.* New York: Macmillan, 1965.

Wildflowers
Aiken, George D. *Pioneering with Wildflowers.* Rochester, N.Y.: Genessee Press, 1978.
Angier, Bradford. *A Field Guide to Edible Wild Plants.* Harrisburg, Pa.: Stackpole, 1974.
Busch, Phyllis S., and Anne O. Dowden. *Wildflowers and the Stories Behind Their Names.* New York: Charles Scribner's Sons, 1979.
Miles, Bebe. *Wildflower Perennials for Your Garden.* New York: Hawthorn, 1979.
Niehaus, Theodore F., and Charles L. Ripper. *A Field Guide to Pacific States' Wildflowers.* Boston: Houghton Mifflin, 1976.
Peterson, Roger Tory, and Margaret McKenny. *A Field Guide to Wildflowers of Northeastern and North Central America.* Boston: Houghton Mifflin, 1968.
Rickett, Harold W. *Wildflowers of the United States, Vols. 1–6.* New York: McGraw-Hill, 1966–1970.
Taylor & Douglas. *Mountain Wild Flowers of the Pacific Northwest.* Portland, Or.: Binford & Mort, 1975.

Index

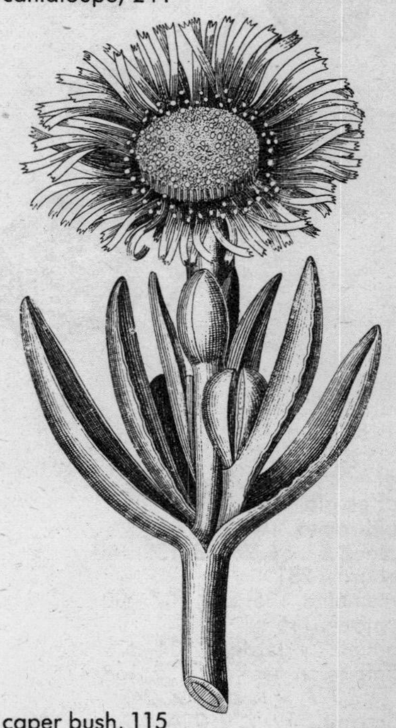

I

J

K

L

M

N

O

P

Q

R

S

T

V

W

Y

Z